THE OXFORD HANDBOOK OF

WITTGENSTEIN

Since the middle of the twentieth century Ludwig Wittgenstein has been an exceptionally influential and controversial figure wherever philosophy is studied. This is the most comprehensive volume ever published on Wittgenstein: thirty-five leading scholars explore the whole range of his thought, offering critical engagement and original interpretation, and tracing his philosophical development. Topics discussed include logic and mathematics, language and mind, epistemology, philosophical methodology, religion, ethics, and aesthetics. Wittgenstein's relation to other founders of analytic philosophy such as Gottlob Frege, Bertrand Russell, and G. E. Moore is explored. This Handbook is the place to look for a full understanding of Wittgenstein's special importance to modern philosophy.

Oskari Kuusela is Senior Lecturer in Philosophy at the University of East Anglia.

Marie McGinn is Professor Emerita of the University of York.

THE OXFORD HANDBOOK OF

WITTGENSTEIN

Edited by

OSKARI KUUSELA

and

MARIE McGINN

OXFORD
UNIVERSITY PRESS

OXFORD

UNIVERSITY PRESS

Great Clarendon Street, Oxford, OX2 6DP,
United Kingdom

Oxford University Press is a department of the University of Oxford.
It furthers the University's objective of excellence in research, scholarship,
and education by publishing worldwide. Oxford is a registered trade mark of
Oxford University Press in the UK and in certain other countries

First published 2011
First published in paperback 2014

Impression: 1

Published in the United States of America by Oxford University Press
198 Madison Avenue, New York, NY 10016, United States of America

British Library Cataloguing in Publication Data
Data available

ISBN 978–0–19–928750–5 (Hbk.)
ISBN 978–0–19–870899–5 (Pbk.)

Printed and bound by
CPI Group (UK) Ltd, Croydon, CR0 4YY

CONTENTS

PART III PHILOSOPHY OF LANGUAGE

PART IV PHILOSOPHY OF MIND

PART V EPISTEMOLOGY

PART VI METHOD

PART VII RELIGION, AESTHETICS, ETHICS

LIST OF CONTRIBUTORS

Joel Backström, Åbo Akademi University and University of Helsinki

Thomas Baldwin, University of York

Avner Baz, Tufts University

Malcolm Budd, University College London

David R. Cerbone, West Virginia University

William Child, University of Oxford

Anne-Marie S. Christensen, University of Southern Denmark

James Conant, University of Chicago

Cora Diamond, University of Virginia, Charlottesville

Kim van Gennip, University of Utrecht

Michel ter Hark, University of Groningen

Lars Hertzberg, Åbo Akademi University

John Hyman, University of Oxford

Colin Johnston, University of Stirling

Wolfgang Kienzler, University of Jena

Oskari Kuusela, University of East Anglia

Gregory Landini, University of Iowa

Mathieu Marion, University of Quebec at Montreal

Marie McGinn, University of York and University of East Anglia

Brian McGuinness, University of Siena

Edward Minar, University of Arkansas

A. W. Moore, University of Oxford

Stephen Mulhall, University of Oxford

Marjorie Perloff, Stanford University

Michael Potter, University of Cambridge

Duncan Pritchard, University of Edinburgh

Ian Proops, University of Texas, Austin

Simo Säätelä, University of Bergen

Beth Savickey, University of Winnipeg

Joachim Schulte, University of Zürich

Paul Snowdon, University College London

David Stern, University of Iowa

Barry Stroud, University of California, Berkeley

Charles Travis, King's College London

Edward Witherspoon, Colgate University

ABBREVIATIONS OF
WITTGENSTEIN'S WORKS

··

BIBLIOGRAPHICAL information regarding the edition used is given in the list of references attached to the relevant chapter. When a reference is to a numbered remark, this is indicated by a '§'; otherwise reference is to a page. Abbreviations used to refer to works of other philosophers are given in the individual lists of references.

BB	*The Blue and Brown Books*
BT	*The Big Typescript* (TS 213)
CE	'Cause and Effect: Intuitive Awareness'
CV	*Culture and Value*
DB	*Denkbewegungen: Tagebücher 1930–1932, 1936–1937*
EPB	*Eine Philosophische Betrachtung* (Revision of parts of *The Brown Book*)
GT	*Geheime Tagebücher*
LC	*Lectures and Conversations on Aesthetics, Psychology and Religious Belief*
LE	'(Wittgenstein's) Lecture on Ethics'
LWPP I	*Last Writings on the Philosophy of Psychology*, Vol. 1
LWPP II	*Last Writings on the Philosophy of Psychology*, Vol. 2
NB	*Notebooks 1914–1916*
NFL	'Notes for Lectures on "Private Experience" and "Sense Data"'
OC	*On Certainty*
P	'Philosophy' (in BT/TS 213)
PG	*Philosophical Grammar*
PI	*Philosophical Investigations* (Part two is referred to as PI II, pg. nr.)
PO	*Philosophical Occasions*
PPO	*Private and Public Occasions*
PR	*Philosophical Remarks*
PTLP	*Prototractatus: An Early Version of Tractatus Logico-Philosophicus*

RC   *Remarks on Colour*

RFGB   'Remarks on Frazer's Golden Bough'

RFM   *Remarks on the Foundations of Mathematics*

RPP I   *Remarks on the Philosophy of Psychology*, Vol. 1

RPP II   *Remarks on the Philosophy of Psychology*, Vol. 2

TLP   *Tractatus Logico-Philosophicus*

WLPP   *Wittgenstein's Lectures on the Philosophy of Psychology 1946–1947*

Z   *Zettel*

References to Wittgenstein's manuscripts and typescripts are by MS and TS number following the G. H. von Wright catalogue (in *Wittgenstein*, Oxford: Basil Blackwell, 1982; reprinted with an addendum in PO).

Letters

CL   *Ludwig Wittgenstein: Cambridge Letters*, ed. Brian McGuinness and G. H. von Wright.

EL   *Letters from Ludwig Wittgenstein–With a Memoir*, by Paul Engelmann, trans. L. Furtmüller, ed. Brian McGuinness.

FB   *Familienbriefe*, ed. M. Ascher, B. McGuinness, and O. Pfersmann.

GB   *Gesamtbriefwechsel*, ed. B. McGuinness, M. Seekircher, and A. Unterkircher.

LO   *Letters to Ogden*, ed. Charles K. Ogden and G. H. von Wright.

LRKM   *Letters to Russell, Keynes and Moore*, ed. G. H. von Wright.

WC   *Wittgenstein in Cambridge: Letters and Documents 1911–1951*, ed. Brian McGuinness.

WE   *Wittgenstein–Engelmann: Briefe, Begegnungen, Erinnerungen*

Notes taken by others

AWL   *Wittgenstein's Lectures, Cambridge 1932–3*, ed. Alice Ambrose.

LC   *Lectures and Conversations on Aesthetics, Psychology and Religious Belief*

LFM   *Wittgenstein's Lectures on the Foundations of Mathematics, Cambridge 1939*, ed. Cora Diamond.

LSD   'The Language of Sense Data and Private Experience'

MA Unpublished: Wittgenstein's lectures 1932–3 from the notes of G. E. Moore, Cambridge University Library G. E. Moore Archive, ref: ADD 8875, 10/7/7

MWL 'Wittgenstein's Lectures 1930–33', G. E. Moore's notes from Wittgenstein's lectures

NTW 'Notes on Talks with Wittgenstein'

VW *The Voices of Wittgenstein: The Vienna Circle*, Gordon Baker ed.

WL *Wittgenstein's Lectures, Cambridge 1930–32*, ed. Desmond Lee.

WLPP *Wittgenstein's Lectures on the Philosophy of Psychology 1946–47*, ed. Peter Geach.

WVC *Wittgenstein and the Vienna Circle: Conversations recorded by Friedrich Waismann*, ed. Brian McGuinness.

PART I

INTRODUCTION

EDITORS' INTRODUCTION

OSKARI KUUSELA AND MARIE McGINN

WITTGENSTEIN is a contested figure on the philosophical scene. Having played an important role in the rise and development of not just one but two schools of analytic philosophy – one that emphasizes the use of formal logical tools in philosophical analysis, originating with Bertrand Russell, and one that sticks, more or less, to the use of everyday language in philosophy, connected also with the name of G. E. Moore – he is for good reasons associated with the analytic tradition.[1] Nevertheless, Wittgenstein's relation to (what we now call) analytic philosophy tended to be somewhat uneasy. While both Russell and Moore describe the young Wittgenstein as a genius in philosophy and logic, Wittgenstein himself thought they failed to understand his work in certain crucial respects. About the value of Wittgenstein's later philosophy (from the early 1930s onwards), Russell's and Moore's judgements differed greatly. On the one hand, as far as Russell is concerned (judging the matter retrospectively in 1959), these developments testified to Wittgenstein having given up serious philosophy altogether, whereas Moore took the trouble of attending Wittgenstein's lectures in Cambridge over several years, maintaining that 'he was really succeeding giving what he called a "synoptic" view of things we all know' (PO, 51; Russell 1959, 161).[2] On the other hand, while the later Wittgenstein took great interest in some of Moore's philosophical observations and

---

[1] For discussion of these developments and trends in analytic philosophy, see Rorty ed. 1967 and Beaney ed. 2007. How analytic philosophy should be characterized, and whether it is possible to give an overarching definition of its essential features that captures it in all its forms, is a complicated question that we will not discuss here. Wittgenstein has also been read in the light of and in comparison with the so-called continental philosophy, especially Heidegger, Merleau-Ponty, and Derrida. (See, for example, Glendinning 1998, Staten 1986 and Morris 2007.) This is indicative of the difficulty of placing Wittgenstein within contemporary philosophical traditions, some aspects of which are discussed in this introduction.

[2] By a synoptic view Moore is referring to what Wittgenstein also calls 'perspicuous (re)presentation', and characterizes as fundamental to his philosophy (see PI §122). Moore says he took very detailed notes of these lectures, filling almost six notebook volumes (PO, 50). Only Moore's summary of the lectures has been published, while the rest of the material remains in his archives.

arguments, subjecting them to sustained discussion in his own writings, at the same time he regarded them as deeply confused. Russell figures almost exclusively as an object of criticism in Wittgenstein's later writings, being discussed especially in connection with the philosophy of mathematics. Wittgenstein also blames Russell for having given rise to a trend of pseudo-exactness in philosophy which, according to Wittgenstein, is the 'worst enemy of real exactness' (MS 112, 101v, 102r; MS 153a, 144v, 145r; TS 213/BT, 540; for discussion of Wittgenstein and Moore, see Baldwin's contribution to this volume; for Russell and Wittgenstein, see the chapters by van Gennip, Johnston, Landini, and Proops).

In contemporary analytic philosophy, by contrast to its earlier phases, Wittgenstein tends to play a less central role. There are, of course, figures deeply influenced by Wittgenstein – such as Robert Brandom, Stanley Cavell, Cora Diamond, John McDowell, Barry Stroud, Charles Travis, and Crispin Wright. Wittgenstein scholarship is also actively pursued in many philosophy departments, resulting in several new books every year.[3] Nevertheless, the philosophical climate has clearly changed since the heyday of Wittgenstein's influence. Metaphysics – which Wittgenstein argued to involve a conflation of factual and logical statements – is again regarded as a respectable undertaking among analytic philosophers, and generally current trends favour the idea that philosophy should be understood and pursued as a science – an idea Wittgenstein was highly critical of throughout his career.[4] Interestingly, these developments seem describable by reference to the different philosophical approaches just characterized. For it is the Russellian line, which associates philosophy with formal logic and science, that has come to dominate analytic philosophy, in the wake of philosophers such as Rudolf Carnap (himself also heavily influenced by the early Wittgenstein; see Carnap 1963, 25) and W. V. O. Quine. Perhaps this development also reflects more general cultural trends, including the valuation of natural science over humanistic research in academic institutions and by their funders, it being characteristic of the Russellian brand of analytic philosophy to align itself with science and promote what are regarded as scientific ways of thinking. The later Wittgensteinian line, by contrast, as developed, for example, by the so-called ordinary language philosophers, such as Gilbert Ryle, J. L. Austin, and P. F. Strawson, has receded somewhat into the background. Nevertheless, Wittgensteinian philosophy does continue to be practised in this manner, sometimes in direct confrontation with scientifically oriented philosophy, by philosophers such as Peter Hacker, who seek to engage and challenge scientific philosophy through an investigation of its use of con-

---

[3] A number of Wittgenstein societies also exist that organize conferences and in other ways promote academic work on Wittgenstein, including the Austrian, British, Nordic (Scandinavian), and North American societies.

[4] To conceive of philosophy as a science means, among other things, seeing philosophy as a research programme whose goal is to answer questions, rather than to critically examine them, and in this way dissolve philosophical problems. Another feature is that philosophical questions are not understood in any important sense to be questions that involve the investigator herself in the sense of requiring self-examination. Accordingly, from this perspective the way in which philosophy is written should not be expressive of the person and the character behind it, but neutral and anonymous like scientific prose. See below for discussion of these themes.

cepts in relation to their everyday uses (see Hacker and Bennett 2003). Another recent attempt to challenge mainstream analytic philosophy along the lines of ordinary language philosophy is Baz's discussion of analytic epistemology (see Baz 2012). Wittgensteinian approaches are a live force also at that end of the spectrum where philosophy meets literary theory and film studies, and contemporary moral philosophy has an important strand inspired by the later Wittgenstein (represented by, for example, McDowell, Cavell, Diamond, Alice Crary, Raimond Gaita, Sabina Lovibond, the late Peter Winch, and to an extent by Philippa Foot). Notably, in areas such as the philosophy of mind, and language and epistemology, often regarded as analytic philosophy's core areas, Wittgensteinian approaches continue to be practised in others forms too, besides those connected closely with ordinary language philosophy. Here Wittgensteinian influences are often found blended with others, such as Kantianism, Hegelianism, and pragmatism, and Wittgensteinianism assumes a form that is more sympathetic to systematic philosophical theorizing than Wittgenstein himself, who emphasized the complexities of language and concepts that make them resistant to theoretical generalization and simplification. Despite the domination of the Russellian line, therefore, Wittgensteinian approaches are alive and well, and developed in a variety of ways in contemporary analytic philosophy.

Importantly, the diverse ways in which Wittgenstein influences contemporary philosophy, for example how ordinary language philosophy and Kantian, Hegelian, or pragmatist forms of Wittgensteinianism relate to Wittgenstein's own thought, and the issue of the relation between Wittgensteinian and Russellian approaches, also raise questions about the identity of philosophy and its methods. Can philosophy be practised on the model of science or as a scientific research programme? What forms should philosophical explanations take? What is the role of systematization in philosophy and how well does it serve philosophical clarity? What is the role and relevance of considerations regarding language in philosophy? Do they have general methodological significance for philosophy, and if so, in what way, or should analytic philosophy be regarded as having moved past the so-called linguistic turn of which Wittgenstein was an essential part? Such questions are partly kept alive in contemporary analytic philosophy by the existence of the divide between Russellian and Wittgensteinian approaches, which in this way creates a space for an ongoing debate about fundamental issues in philosophy. Thus the importance of the divide is far greater than any questions about which views dominate discussions on this or that topic, or which school has the upper hand. Relating to this debate, Wittgenstein's position in analytic philosophy also remains open to debate and reassessment.

As regards Wittgenstein's early philosophy, it has generated an extensive secondary literature, and continues to be a topic of immense philosophical interest among Wittgenstein-interpreters, also with respect to the issue of the nature of philosophy. As fate has it, for mainstream analytic philosophy Wittgenstein's early philosophy of logic has come to seem overshadowed by the emergence of the contemporary (or Hilbertian) model theoretical conception of logic in the 1930s, in the development of which, for example, Carnap enthusiastically took part. Among Carnap's reasons for trying to find an alternative to the then influential Wittgensteinian conception of logic was that the Hilbertian account made possible the formulation of statements about logic or syntax in an exact – and therefore in appearance scientific – manner which the *Tractatus'* conception of logic seemed to exclude (Carnap 1937, 283). About Wittgenstein's apparent denial of statements regarding logic Russell had expressed doubts in his introduction to the *Tractatus*. The early Wittgenstein was also committed to the idea of there being something like *the* logic which allows for no alternatives, as if – so it seemed to Carnap and others – we were urged to stick with Euclidean geometry and not consider any non-Euclidean ones. From this 'Wittgensteinian prison' Carnap among others wanted to escape, and so he did, whereby the *Tractatus'* conception of logic came to be seen as essentially superseded.

But arguably matters are more complicated than the received wisdom allows. Firstly, it is far from clear that the account of the *Tractatus'* philosophy of logic that has become part of the lore of analytic philosophy, related in essentially Carnapian terms, is accurrate. Wittgenstein, for one, disputed it, blaming Carnap, on the one hand, for plagiarism and not having said anything new in his own work, and on the other, for having missed the central point of the *Tractatus* (GB, letters to Schlick on 6 May 1932 and 8 August 1932; see Kienzler 2008 and Kuusela 2012 for discussion). Secondly, at the time when Carnap and others were developing the model theoretic conception, Wittgenstein came to critique the *Tractatus'* conception of logic himself, developing a novel conception of the status of logical calculi as a means of philosophical clarification and more generally of the status of philosophical statements (definitions, examples, and so on). Interestingly, this novel – although to date largely ignored – conception makes it possible for Wittgenstein to continue to regard formal logic as a useful tool in philosophical clarification (more precisely, a potentially useful tool, depending on the clarificatory task at hand), while maintaining that it is not the only possible, or a privileged method of, clarification. According to his later view, no calculus or philosophical account can be claimed to capture *the* logic of language. This view, as Wittgenstein develops it, resolves the problem of dogmatism in the *Tractatus* to which Wittgenstein had succumbed, and helps to resolve important difficulties relating to the notion of logical analysis. Now formal logical methods can also be complemented with other methods of conceptual, grammatical, or logical clarification that take into account other aspects of language besides its rule-governedness, and don't presuppose a conception of language as a calculus according to precise rules. Consequently, from this point of view, the Russellian and ordinary language approaches no longer appear to be in conflict or competition with each other, a perception that the representatives of these approaches have had difficulty avoiding, despite a certain willingness to do so. (See Carnap 1963a; Strawson 1956 and 1963.) Hence, surprisingly enough, the later Wittgenstein, who often is perceived as a partisan of ordinary language philosophy, might in fact be able to help analytic philosophy to discover its underlying unity.[5] In so doing he might also enable analytic philosophy to make more self-conscious use of both formal and non-formal methodological resources, avoiding the appearance

---

[5] It is, of course, not difficult to see why the ordinary language philosophers wanted to claim a powerful mind such as the later Wittgenstein to be on their side – despite the fact that Wittgenstein himself rejected the idea of parties and taking sides in philosophy. (See TS 213/BT, 420.)

of the latter as suspicious, due to a perception of their being in conflict with the scientific aspirations of analytic philosophy and as committed to common sense. But regardless of these speculations about how analytic philosophy might further develop and perhaps again learn from Wittgenstein, it seems clear that just as the value of the work of the later Wittgenstein is in continuing need of reassessment, so also is his early work, or the work of Wittgenstein-the-logician in general. (For discussion of the *Tractatus'* logic and/or the further methodological developments in Wittgenstein's thought, see Conant, Diamond, Johnston, Kienzler, Kuusela, McGinn, and Travis in this volume.)

Besides his contributions to the philosophy of logic and philosophical methodology or 'metaphilosophy', Wittgenstein is best known for his work in the philosophy of language, mind, and mathematics.[6] Discussions of these topics constitute the bulk of this volume, with separate parts of the book devoted to logic and mathematics (II; including contributions by Moore, Potter, Marion, and Säätelä on Wittgenstein's philosophy of mathematics), the philosophy of language (III; with contributions not already mentioned by Minar, Stroud, Cerbone, Stern, and Hertzberg), and the philosophy of mind (IV; including chapters by Child, Hyman, and Witherspoon). The volume also contains a part devoted to epistemology (V), where Wittgenstein's treatment of certainty, causal knowledge, the notion of intuition, and scepticism is discussed (of those not already mentioned is Pritchard). Part VI is devoted to issues relating to methodology or 'metaphilosophy' (including a chapter on Wittgenstein's use of examples by Savickey), and VII to religion, aesthetics, and ethics (including contributions by Mulhall and Budd). As this shows, the range of issues Wittgenstein worked on is very broad. We have tried to collect in this volume a representative sample of discussions of such topics by some of the leading scholars in the field. By their nature the chapters are original contributions to relevant discussions and, indeed, several of them seek in different ways to contest existing interpretational orthodoxies and so to break new ground. (Examples of this, not mentioned elsewhere in this introduction, are the chapters by Baz and ter Hark.)

It is notable, however, that from the point of view of the later Wittgenstein any attempts to divide philosophical discussions into separate areas of philosophy, or to regard discussions with different foci as constituting independent philosophical topics, are at best artificial. This is to be understood in light of his resistance to specialization and compartmentalization in philosophy, the main reason for which seems to be his perception of the interconnectedness of philosophical problems. In order to solve one problem one must solve many connected problems that together constitute a highly deceptive and powerful web of confusion. This then also explains the difficulty of philosophy. (See MS 116, 216–18; MS 120, 39v.) But if

---

[6] Asked in 1944 if he wanted to make any amendments to a biographical sketch by John Wisdom, Wittgenstein added this sentence: 'Wittgenstein's chief contribution has been in the philosophy of mathematics' (Monk 2007, 273). Originally he also envisaged the *Philosophical Investigations* as continuing, after the rule-following discussion, with a discussion of this topic. As is evident, he ultimately decided otherwise, addressing instead issues in the philosophy of mind and language. Mostly mainstream analytic philosophy still seems too scandalized by Wittgenstein's philosophy of mathematics to consider it very seriously, for example by his view that set theory involves conceptual confusions (see PR, 209, 211; PG, 460ff.), and his non-standard views of the philosophical significance of Gödel's incompleteness proof (RFM, 385ff.).

Wittgenstein is right about this characteristic of philosophical problems, we cannot assume that all such further issues and problems lie conveniently in some particular area of specialization. And even if they do, to reliably establish this seems to require being able to find one's way about in those other areas too. An especially noteworthy 'area of philosophy' in this regard is ethics, which one might, from Wittgenstein's point of view, characterize as a dimension of philosophy rather than a separate segment. This view is connected with his conception that philosophical work necessarily involves the examination of one's own preconceptions and any prejudices that might stand in the way of being able to understand whatever one is trying to understand. Even more broadly, philosophy requires one to examine one's inclinations to think about matters in particular ways. This includes the scrutiny of one's philosophical motives (fears, desires, and so on), and the attraction one may feel towards particular views, with the purpose of avoiding blindly following one's philosophical instincts. For we may be quite unclear about the constitution and origin of such instincts; they may well have been acquired through a process more akin to enculturation than rational examination. Hence an important part of philosophy for Wittgenstein is a pursuit of self-knowledge, and from his point of view philosophy emerges as a deeply reflective undertaking. (For discussion of these themes, see the chapters by Backström and Christensen.)

Again the differences between Wittgenstein's views and those common in mainstream analytic philosophy that embraces specialization might be helpfully considered in the light of certain historical developments. For the earliest period of the development of analytic philosophy (at the turn of the nineteenth and twentieth centuries) is also the time of the secularization of the teaching of philosophy in the universities, philosophy's disassociation from theology, as well as its consequent professionalization and allying with science. This is a period when professional journals of philosophy (such as *Mind* and *The Proceedings of the Aristotelian Society*) emerged. In other words, it is a time when philosophy largely assumed its current form as a discipline for specialists, whereby a key form of philosophy's dissemination became a relatively short article in scientific style, focused on some specific topic or some aspect of it, and assuming in-depth knowledge of relevant discussions as its background. (See Ryle 1957 for a description of these developments.) But although we may currently be inclined to take this mode of philosophizing for granted (and certainly contemporary academic institutions do), this clearly is a form of philosophy far removed from the discussions of Socrates with his fellow citizens, i.e. his trying to contest their self-understanding, including their conceptual and moral commitments. Given that Wittgenstein's philosophy, with its concern with self-knowledge, may naturally be classified together with the Socratic approach, his thought might then be seen as an important reminder of other possible ways of doing philosophy besides the currently dominating ones, and as pointing to potential resources for philosophical success that the mainstream of analytic philosophy has by and large neglected. (This is not to say that other features of Wittgenstein's approach could not justifiably suggest other classifications, besides the Socratic one.) In particular, provided that the scientific results that everyone can agree upon, promised by the founders of the scientifically oriented analytic philosophy (Russell and, in his wake, Carnap), let us wait for them, and there seems not to be much more agreement on the conceptual mappings of ordinary language philosophers and how they contribute to the solution of philosophical problems, perhaps this Socratic side of the practice of philosophy should be seriously reconsidered for its significance. Notably, Wittgenstein too was keen on the idea of progress in philosophy, and getting matters done and settled (see PO, 185, 195; BT/TS 213, 424, 432). But he thought that progress could only be achieved by means of an approach different from Russell's. Consequently, dropping the assumption that either the scientific approach or the Socratic approach alone should represent *the* true essence of philosophy, we might do well to keep an open mind about what our methodological commitments should be, and about the possibility that something methodologically important might be found in the Socratic approach. In this manner too we might then come to see Wittgenstein as enriching analytic philosophy, and as challenging us to think harder about our philosophical practice, not as a threat to be quickly argued out of the way, as sometimes has been the case.[7]

A factor that has undoubtedly contributed to the perception of Wittgenstein's thought as alien to analytic philosophy is his style of writing. His style does not conform to the standard academic style (with the possible exception of two short pieces from 1929, 'Some Remarks on Logical Form' and 'A Lecture on Ethics'; see PO). Rather, it is more readily associated with authors such as Nietzsche who see their writing as an expression of a cultivated philosophical self (again following the footsteps of Socrates), not the presentation of scientific results. Accordingly, although Wittgenstein has, of course, often been read as an academic philosopher and discussed in professional articles (as indeed in this volume), he himself was very suspicious of such prospects and expressed dislike of professional academic philosophy. As he writes in a note (from 1948) for the preface of the *Philosophical Investigations*: 'It is not without reluctance that I offer the book to the public. The hands into which it will fall are for the most part not those in which I like to imagine it. May it soon – this is what I wish for it – be completely forgotten by the philosophical journalists & thus perhaps be kept for a more upright kind of reader' (CV, 75; cf. 69). The point is that rather than dismissing such remarks as mere idiosyncrasies, we might do well to seriously consider them in order to understand Wittgenstein's uneasy relation to analytic philosophy. For what is at stake here is the nature of his philosophical approach, whereby we should not forget that mostly his philosophical inquiries do concern topics discussed by academic philosophers. This means that, unless we are facing here a tension or a conflict in Wittgenstein's thinking that he was unaware of, he really regards it as necessary to approach such philosophical issues in a way that does not conform to the format of professional articles and the mindset of academic philosophizing. (Cf. also CV, 28: 'I believe I summed up where I stand in relation to philosophy when

[7] A classic example of such a quick argument to make room for one's own philosophical project is Fodor's discussion of Wittgenstein's private language argument in *The Language of Thought* (1975). On a very different note, when in troubled economic times fingers point at university philosophy as not in any way obviously good science, a solid understanding of the Socratic inheritance unique to philosophy could help philosophers also to defend their discipline.

I said: really one should write philosophy only as one *writes a poem*.' For discussion of Wittgenstein' style, see Perloff's chapter.)

More concretely, although there would certainly seem to be grounds for aligning Wittgenstein with analytic philosophy in the sense that we could with apparent natural- ness count, for example, his so-called private language argument or his conception of meaning as use among the celebrated results of analytic philosophy, along with, for instance, Russell's theory of definite descriptions and Moore's open question argument, it may also be asked whether the characterization of them as results aptly captures Wittgenstein's achievements and intentions. Perhaps it is not results and conclusions that we are intended to learn from the *Investigations,* but something different. This could be, for example, methods of philosophical investigation to be made our own in some deeper sense than just learning to imitate the moves of, for instance, the private language argu- ment in order to apply those moves in discussions with fellow analytic philosophers, thus achieving some kind of an analogous extension of the argument. If so, Wittgenstein's goals would indeed seem to differ from those of science and from those of analytic philosophy, insofar as the latter aspires to produce results comparable to scientific ones (as Russell certainly hoped; see Russell 1914/1926). Thus understood, philosophy's goal for Wittgenstein would not be to impart knowledge or true beliefs, i.e. make us believe some- thing, but to teach us how to deal with the philosophical issues we confront ourselves, to teach us to do something (see AWL, 97; LFM, 22, 103). (For discussions of privacy and private language, see Stern, Schulte, and Snowdon in this volume.)

Then again, however, it is perhaps not obvious how the mentioned achievements of Russell and Moore would be best understood, and whether they should not be seen as methodological at their core. Interpreted in this way, Russell's theory, for example, would really give us a particular conception or a picture of logical analysis which we might adopt, though his example of an analysis still leaves it undecided whether this should be understood as anything like *the* method of philosophical analysis – not to even go into the issue of whether it necessarily commits us to an epistemology of objects of acquaint- ance. Such interpretational possibilities illustrate difficulties connected with under- standing Wittgenstein's relation to or his place in analytic philosophy, but also urge us to address the still unsettled question of how philosophy in the analytic mode would be best pursued.

In this connection it is noteworthy that several contributions to this volume are com- missioned from philosophers who do not regard themselves as Wittgenstein specialists or Wittgensteinians, but whose main interests lie within mainstream analytic philosophy. It is on such topics that they write here. The purpose of this is to try to understand the percep- tion of Wittgenstein's work from the point of view of contemporary analytic philosophy, how he might be understood as contributing to discussions in its context, and simply to engage in discussion over dividing lines. Input from Wittgenstein to such discussions may, of course, take various forms, besides being based on painstaking scholarship. Examples are Wittgenstein being an inspiration for views to be developed in a non-Wittgensteinian manner, being the designer of philosophical concepts to be employed in such conversa- tions (for instance, language-game and family-resemblance), or being the originator of certain debates which then take on a life of their own within analytic philosophy. (The last form of his influence is exemplified by the debates on rule-following in the wake of Saul Kripke's interpretation of Wittgenstein.) It would seem narrow-minded to deny the value of such ways of using Wittgenstein merely because on the basis of some interpretation we might consider that some Wittgenstein-inspired view does not conform with the Master's own view. Presumably all agree that the method of arguing by reference to some authority does not belong to philosophy. Yet it also remains a question how patiently we should try to understand Wittgenstein before trying to make use of his ideas, in order to maximally benefit from them – or before launching arguments against them. Ironically enough from the point of view of Wittgenstein's resistance to specialization, Wittgenstein scholars might here also come to the aid of the mainstream analytic philosopher when she is wondering about what he might have thought about a particular topic. Perhaps such collaborations are not as unimaginable as they may seem when Wittgenstein is seen in opposition to discussions in the mainstream. In any case, we presumably have already had enough of Wittgensteinians trying to beat non-Wittgensteinians over the head with the *Investigations* from their allegedly superior position, which to the mainstreamer seems anything but. For while the mainstream may be inclined to see Wittgenstein as having been superseded by subsequent developments in analytic philosophy, similarly the Wittgensteinians tend to think the mainstream still has to catch up with Wittgenstein. But who is right (if anyone) can only be settled by calm discussion (and not at this level of generality). Perhaps the time is now ripe for this, about sixty years after Wittgenstein's death.

As already suggested, the differences between mainstream analytic philosophy and Wittgenstein could be used by representatives on each side to pose questions to themselves about their own philosophical practice and views. The point is: why not see the difference between Wittgensteinian and mainstream analytic approaches as an opportunity for reflection on how we should proceed, rather than trying to convince the others that they are – obviously – wrong? Indeed, since when, one might ask, did matters in philosophy become so obvious? And if obviousness means the death of (the urge to) philosophical thinking, should we not make sure that matters do not become so obvious to us; that we really ask questions from ourselves rather than merely acting as if we did?

References

Baz, Avner (2012). *When Words are Called For: In Defense of Ordinary Language Philosophy*. Cambridge, MA: Harvard University Press.

Beaney, Michael ed. (2007). *The Analytic Turn: Analysis in Early Analytic Philosophy and Phenomenology*. London: Routledge.

Carnap, Rudolf (1937). *The Logical Syntax of Language*. London: Routledge & Kegan Paul.

—— (1963). 'Intellectual Autobiography', in P. A. Schilpp ed., *The Philosophy of Rudolf Carnap*. La Salle, IL: Open Court.

—— (1963a). 'P. F. Strawson on Linguistic Naturalism', in P. A. Schilpp ed., *The Philosophy of Rudolf Carnap*. La Salle, IL: Open Court.

Fodor, Jerry (1975). *The Language of Thought*. Cambridge, MA: Harvard University Press.

GLENDINNING, SIMON (1998). *On Being With Others: Heidegger – Derrida – Wittgenstein*. London: Routledge.

HACKER, P. M. S. and BENNETT, M. R. (2003). *Philosophical Foundations of Neuroscience*. Oxford: Blackwell.

KIENZLER, WOLFGANG (2008). 'Wittgenstein und Carnap: Klarheit oder Deutlichkeit als Ideal der Philosophie', in C. Schildknecht, D. Teichert, and T. van Zantwijk eds., *Genese und Geltung*. Paderborn: Mentis.

KUUSELA, OSKARI (2012). 'Carnap and the *Tractatus*' Philosophy of Logic', *Journal for the History of Analytic Philosophy*, 1:3: 1–26.

MONK, RAY (2007). 'Bourgeois, Bolshevist or Anarchist? The Reception of Wittgenstein's Philosophy of Mathematics', in G. Kahane, E. Kanterian, and O. Kuusela eds., *Wittgenstein's Interpreters: Essays in Memory of Gordon Baker*. Oxford: Blackwell.

MORRIS, KATHERINE (2007). 'Wittgenstein's Method: Ridding People of Philosophical Prejudices', in G. Kahane, E. Kanterian, and O. Kuusela eds., *Wittgenstein's Interpreters: Essays in Memory of Gordon Baker*. Oxford: Blackwell.

RORTY, RICHARD ed. (1967). *The Linguistic Turn*. Chicago: University of Chicago Press.

RUSSELL, BERTRAND (1914/1926). *Our Knowledge of the External World*. La Salle, IL: Open Court.

—— (1959). *My Philosophical Development*. London: Unwin.

RYLE, GILBERT (1957). 'Introduction', in A. J. Ayer *et al.*, *The Revolution in Philosophy*. London: Macmillan.

STATEN, HENRY (1986). *Wittgenstein and Derrida*. Lincoln: University of Nebraska Press.

STRAWSON, P. F. (1956). 'Construction and Analysis', in A. J. Ayer *et al.*, *The Revolution in Philosophy*. London: Macmillan.

—— (1963). 'Carnap's Views on Constructed Systems versus Natural Languages in Analytic Philosophy', in P. A. Schilpp ed., *The Philosophy of Rudolf Carnap*. La Salle, IL: Open Court.

WITTGENSTEIN, LUDWIG (1976). *Lectures on the Foundations of Mathematics, Cambridge 1939*, ed. Cora Diamond. Hassocks, Sussex: Harvester Press.

—— (1979). *Wittgenstein's Lectures, Cambridge 1932–35*, ed. Alice Ambrose. Oxford: Basil Blackwell.

—— (1993). *Philosophical Occasions 1912–1951*, ed. J. Klagge and A. Nordmann. Indianapolis: Hackett Publishing Company.

—— (1998). *Culture and Value*, revised edition. Oxford: Blackwell.

—— (2004). *Ludwig Wittgenstein: Gesamtbriefwechsel/Complete Correspondence*. Innsbrucker Electronic Edition, ed. Monika Seekircher, Brian McGuinness, Anton Unterkircher. InteLex.

CHAPTER 1

....

WITTGENSTEIN AND BIOGRAPHY

....

BRIAN McGUINNESS

THERE are obvious ways in which the study of Wittgenstein's thought must have recourse to the facts of his life. The innocent reader, *der Unbefangene*, who reads 'The world is all that is the case' or the description of St Augustine's account of a child's learning (or rather coming) to talk may be swept along by the author's art like someone caught up in a conversation on a Russian train, and this is in part the aim. But when reflection sets in he is bound to ask who the author is and what cultural assumptions he is making. There are literary and other allusions that the reader needs to catch and this cannot be done without some knowledge of the background and even education of the author. This becomes more necessary as these, from being alien in language and geography, become also remote in time.[1] There are further difficulties arising from the fact that Wittgenstein's 'works' are by far the most part the product of posthumous selection and editing, in the first place by trusted friends and then by those whom these in turn trusted. Such works are incomplete if left without some account of their genesis and genre – for the author is not there to define them.[2] Such an account will necessarily explain what Wittgenstein was engaged on at various times of his life and any hindrances that prevented him for all the second half of his life from producing a finished work – *die wohlgeratne Butterwälze*, the well-turned-out slab of butter, to which Wilhelm Busch, deliberately down to earth, likens the final product of the poet.[3]

---

[1] Paul Engelmann's *Letters from Ludwig Wittgenstein – With A Memoir* was perhaps the first essay in this direction. An influential general survey was given by Janik and Toulmin 1973, and the problems are now generally appreciated.

[2] Much work remains to be done on the history of Wittgenstein's manuscripts and typescripts: for some of the problems see Schulte 2001 and some of the pieces in my 2001.

[3] This aspect is of course not neglected in G. H. von Wright's 'Biographical Sketch', my own partial biography 2005 (1988), or Monk's full biography 1991.

But apart from the facts that 'a shilling life will give you', what help in understanding his philosophy does the detail, whether core or husk, of his life give us, fascinating though it may be in itself? Isn't biography in the end a distraction from our aim of understanding his thought? Do we need to ask 'what porridge had John Keats'? When Paul Engelmann was planning the publication of the first memoir describing Wittgenstein's early life, Elizabeth Anscombe told him that if by pressing a button she could have destroyed all biographical material, she would have done so. Margaret Stonborough (Wittgenstein's sister) told Hayek, who had similar plans, that Ludwig would have disdainfully rejected any idea of a 'life' that went into his education, family, and feelings. We owe to the dead respectful silence: his work would speak for him.

Yet Wittgenstein himself could almost be said to have lived his life in order to recount it (to borrow García Márquez's title *Vivir para contarla*). At the end of his life, full of change and incident, certainly, but also of much sadness, he said it had been a wonderful life. We shall see later why it was only at this moment that it could be seen as such. From all the accidents there had been something to be gained or learnt. Everything was lived at a high level of interiorization. Every element: war, love, rejection, the death of loved ones, exile, racial persecution, concern for his sins and salvation, was wrestled with in search of the perfect – usually the most difficult – solution and this was usually a search for the right spontaneous reaction (a typical Wittgensteinian paradox or 'double bind'). And this wrestling was not so much recorded as conducted in diaries or *Tagebücher*. Reading of books so entitled – by Tolstoy, Kierkegaard, Dostoevsky, and Gottfried Keller – was part of the culture of his generation of the family. They tended to model and guide their lives by literature such as this. It was perhaps their nearest approach to religion. Much of the most intimate part of Wittgenstein's own diaries was written in a simple code understood in his family, as if it were addressed to them, like one of the 'confessions' (*Geständnisse*) he often talked about and more than once made. The most confessional volume of his diary passed after his death to his most trusted sister until she confided it to his best friend in Austria. Much time passed before it came to light.[4]

In Keller we find the idea that keeping a diary was the only road to integrity and constancy: a man should always be reflecting on his own character. (We are not far from Socrates' 'the unexamined life is not one a man should live' [*ho anexetastos bios ou biôtos anthrôpôi*].) Wittgenstein in general had more need of this kind of writing than Keller. There were intervals – in a note of 1929 (just returned to Cambridge and philosophy) he comments that ('strangely enough', as he significantly says) he had for some years not felt this need, and indeed we have no *Tagebücher* between the wartime notebooks and precisely this remark. The only writings that remain from that period are reports of dreams (W. W. Bartley III must have seen some of these[5]) and a brief sketch of an autobiography covering his earlier years. Since these were preserved it is unlikely that much else was

---

[4] *Denkbewegungen: Tagebücher 1930–1932, 1936–1937.*

[5] Dreams not otherwise documented are recounted in his partial biography *Wittgenstein*. Bartley had been assisted by the best friend just mentioned, who dissociated himself from the resulting book.

destroyed. He was trying to collect his thoughts, as he told Keynes, and clearly some of these ran towards 'biography' (autobiography was meant), but he did not get far. In these years he tried everything but philosophy to occupy himself – architecture, music, physical labour, sculpture. It is natural to think that he, like the comrades from whom he received letters, was recovering from the war, which marked so many of his generation. F. R. Leavis noted this as late as 1930. It is a plausible speculation that his reluctance to return to philosophy was a part of this crisis. He gave that up, just as, at the same juncture, he freed himself of his fortune.

When he returned to philosophy (we are drawn to conclude), the writing of diary-like notes also again seemed called for. In the notebooks in which he recorded his thoughts for future reflection or use, personal reflections abound. He interrupts his philosophical writing to exclaim, sometimes but not always in code, on his weaknesses, his vanity, his sins, or his aspirations – all of which of course might infect his philosophical writing as much as any other aspect of his life. He constantly felt that he could easily relapse into vanity, in philosophy as elsewhere. In the case of autobiography itself (he said, reflecting on his current activity), this would compound his faults, make him yet *schmutziger* (sully him yet further). One mustn't minimize, embellish, or pretend but, like Pepys (whom he added to the list of models), write at the level of the life one lived, neither exploring what lay beneath the surface nor looking down from a height.[6] One may say that his real life was there in such writing. He once wrote:

> Something in me speaks in favour of writing my biography. The fact is I want for once to spread my life out clearly, so as to have it clear in front of me and also for others. (MS 108, 47)[7]

His first aim was, as he often said, *mit sich selbst ins reine zu kommen*, to come to terms with himself, to see and accept, and by so doing change, as far as was possible, his nature – as a poor sinner.

The particular form of his own life Wittgenstein saw as a function of his unhappy family, from which each member tried to escape in his own way. Looking back in 1934 he says, 'If everything in a household is in order, then the members of the family sit down to breakfast together and have similar habits and so on. But if there's a terrible illness in the house, then everybody is in search of help and thinks of a different way out and totally contrasting tendencies can easily make their appearance. Paul and I, for example.'[8] It is natural to suppose that he was thinking also of his other brothers, of whom all three had

---

[6] To be sure, he (like Keller) included dream reports, but these are treated (almost biblically) as moral insights.

[7] 'Etwas in mir spricht dafür meine Biographie zu schreiben und zwar möchte ich mein Leben einmal klar ausbreiten um es klar vor mir zu haben und auch für andere' (28 December 1929).

[8] 'Wenn in einem Haushalt alles in Ordnung ist, so sitzen die Familienmitglieder alle zugleich beim Frühstück, haben ähnliche Gepflogenheiten etc. Herrscht aber eine furchtbare Krankheit im Haus, dann denkt jeder auf einem andern Ausweg um Hilfe zu schaffen und es zeigen sich leicht ganz entgegengesetzte Bestrebungen. Paul und ich' (MS 157a, 25r; notes written during a stay in Norway). The remark is, perhaps consciously, reminiscent of the opening of *Anna Karenina*. Further on the theme of the family see my 2006.

committed suicide. There were failings too on the female side: he speaks later of making a confession on behalf of his mother, which her withdrawn nature would not have allowed her to make for herself. Perhaps her withdrawal was what she had to confess: there was so much she had failed to do. At the same time he found her love stifling and indeed thought that the whole female family erred by excess of *Liebenswürdigkeit*. This is of a piece with his fiercely holding himself aloof from his sister Hermine in the 1920s. His relation with the active sister, Margaret, was the nearest to a relation of equals, but note that she defined herself by, wanted to be known for, the achievements of her father, brothers, and sons. The male element was the defining one, typified by the father, the great industrialist who carried all before him. Wittgenstein hardly ever speaks of his attitude towards his father (who died when he himself was 24): in notes for a biography (mentioned above)[9] he juxtaposes 'Latin exercises for Papa' with 'Thoughts of suicide,' and we know that his father (not the most patient of men) became dissatisfied with the poor results of home education. At the end Wittgenstein wrote movingly to Russell of his father's 'most beautiful death....I think that this death was worth a whole life'.[10] Perhaps through all his life the philosopher was hoping for such a death himself, the *totum simul* (the unique chance to see one's life as whole), the acceptance.[11] The figure of his father perhaps also appears in the constant struggle within him between male and female elements (Weininger's classification actually fitted this family situation). A degree of violence and intolerance was expected of the brothers, following the model of the father.[12] Commenting on how difficult it was to share a house with Paul, one sister says, 'But suppose it had been Kurt!' The Wittgenstein we are concerned with was, it seems, the easiest of these three. He indeed favoured in theory the driven and practical side of his father, so he started life as an engineering student with the design of being an aviator, and later he wanted to do philosophy in a businesslike way.[13] Two of his brothers tried to escape from the father's model through music: one seems to have been driven to suicide; the other (Paul) succeeded in living a musician's life, but (since he had to overcome the loss of his right arm) only by supreme efforts of will. Ludwig, for his part, said that music was half of his life, but a half he had written nothing about: compare his remark that his mother had never brought a thought to completion except at the piano. In this and many ways the female side of him was obvious to others – his sisters thought of him as the Alyosha of the family, and he was probably thinking of this identification when he exclaimed, 'I am Smerdyakov, I am Dr Mabuse!'[14]

---

[9] See my 2001, 48.

[10] Letter to Russell, 22 January 1913, in WC.

[11] His attitude is uncannily reflected by Tolstoy's *The Death of Ivan Illich*, where the dying man is finally redeemed by his acceptance of what is happening.

[12] Hermine describes Paul's playing with his one arm as a *Vergewaltigung* (here not quite 'rape'): as if he were doing violence to the music, the piano, or himself. In this it reminded her of something in their father.

[13] See his remarks to Drury in Drury 1984, 110; and to Isaiah Berlin in WC, 322.

[14] It is relevant that Alyosha in fact understands and shares the impulses of the others: he too is a Karamazov. In another remark to Drury (1984, 108) Wittgenstein said he would have liked to see how Smerdyakov might have been saved rather than Alyosha.

He made a different (but compatible) exclamation to Fania pascal, 'Of course I want to be perfect!', but deep rifts within him made this bewildering for others – perhaps an inevitable consequence of the overweening ambition it represented.[15] He could be the kindest and most inspiring of friends and companions. But this was partly in virtue of a character and a concentration upon the other so forceful that his fierceness, if and when it broke out, issued in breaks with friends and denunciations. He could be a charming companion when met by chance but also, when he had not established a relationship, timid, tongue-tied, and awkward. He accused himself of cowardice, though his almost foolhardy courage in the First World War is well attested. It is impossible not to be reminded of Freud's well-known analysis of Dostoevsky:[16] a man of the greatest need and capacity for love possessed by destructive tendencies directed chiefly (but not only) against himself, full of feelings of guilt, writing about great sinners and presenting himself as one of them, given to attacks of illness, constantly speculating on the possibility of an early death, his greatest wish to die in an inspired moment, such as often preceded his epileptic attacks. Freud saw here a need to be punished, stemming from Dostoevsky's relation with his father, and thought that the neurosis so generated finally led to a misapplication of great affective and intellectual gifts. Still Freud himself thinks *The Brothers Karamazov* one of the four great works of Western civilization (all Oedipal, of course), and the neurosis was perhaps necessary for its production. If analysis had counterfactually changed Dostoevsky into a progressive liberal and Westernizer, he could never have written that book.

A Freudian account of his own life would have had little interest for Wittgenstein either. The only advantage he saw in a nephew's entering analysis was the shame bound to be engendered by all the things he had to admit to his analyst. Confession was of the first importance. When Wittgenstein said, in 1931, that it (*eine Beichte*) must be part of the new life (i.e. the new life that he meant to lead), he was not saying that confession without a new life was pointless but that no change was possible without confession. A true life meant the acknowledgement of all the meanness of the past and not just, as in Goethe's ideal vision, confession to a wise adviser who will enable one to bear the burden of guilt and order one's life better,[17] but precisely confession to those on whom or in relation to whom past meannesses or deceptions have been practised. Thus in 1931 and again in 1936–7 he went round (or when necessary wrote) forcing on former pupils now peasants, or on relations, friends, colleagues, or patrons, recitations and requests for forgiveness that they often misunderstood and whose purpose baffled them – 'eccentric' Keynes called it, and Moore thought him 'impatient'. Others wrote saying that they thought even

---

[15] See Drury 1984, 37. Hers is perhaps the best account of one of Wittgenstein's 'confessions'. She does not comment on the echo of the Gospel precept, 'Be perfect therefore as your heavenly Father is perfect', *Matthew* 5:48. Remarks of this kind by Wittgenstein make one wonder why Ray Monk chose 'The Duty of Genius' as the sub-title of his biography.

[16] Freud 1962, 98–111. Joseph Frank, who is justly critical of Freud's limited biographical knowledge and lack of scruple in enhancing it, nonetheless says, 'Freud's article contains some shrewd and penetrating remarks about Dostoevsky's masochistic and guilt-ridden personality' (Frank 1979, 28).

[17] In Goethe 1998, II, 7 ('Fiction and Truth').

better of him, so George Thomson and Ludwig Hänsel. 'What a booby-trap!' Wittgenstein exclaimed, though his mentor Wilhelm Busch could have told him what would happen.[18] The aim had been to destroy a whole edifice of lies (as he thought it) that made him seem better than he really was, but by another Wittgensteinian double bind the effect was, not to establish the truth, but to make him seem better or worse than it. Part of what he had hoped, to judge by a later passage, was that persons who both loved and valued him would make this humbling of himself easier for him.

For the confessions were not merely something owed to them, but were principally parts of his effort to reach a true life for himself, precisely by recognizing (not just writing) that he was an *armer Sünder*, a miserable sinner. This is what Spinoza had failed to do, so that his remarks about himself left Wittgenstein uneasy.[19] The admission of guilt (*Geständnis* is the word he uses in these passages) is the recognition of one's own worthlessness. Unable to be good, he muses (tentative as always in religious matters), this recognition of worthlessness may enable a man to have faith in and identify with a Redeemer who will take the guilt from him. In another place he speaks of one who opens his heart to God in a contrite confession and thereby also comes, to others too, as a child, laying aside all dignity or position.[20] The word *Bekenntnis* used here has more of a religious implication than his usual *Geständnis*: it is a term Faust uses in his evasive reply to Gretchen's question (how he stands in relation to God), a reply which Wittgenstein misquotes as *Wer darf ihn nennen, wer ihn bekennen?*[21] (Who dares name him, / Who proclaim him?). The plural *Bekenntnisse* is the usual German title of the *Confessions* of St Augustine, where the confessions attest equally the sins of the writer and the glory of God, as so often in the Psalms, from which Augustine drew his inspiration.[22] The word indicates a commitment as well as an admission, and the former element at least can be found in Wittgenstein's philosophy.

For it is time to ask how much of what we have discussed enters into his philosophy and how much we need to know of his life or at any rate of his 'life' (his musing on it), in order to understand or profit from that philosophy? It must be said that it is not always so easy to distinguish the two objects of comparison. Remarks of a general or personal nature are cheek by jowl with others. This is not to advocate printing them as part of edited philosophical work. Many considerations tell against that, but we might think of

[18] Paul Engelmann copied out, as a warning to himself, Busch's 'Die Selbstkritik': one who castigates himself gets credit for modesty and for honesty, silences other critics, is contradicted and found to be, in the end, *ein ganz famoses Haus* – a real brick.

[19] In *Denkbewegungen*; MS 183, 96 (12 October 1931).

[20] 'Wer das Herz so öffnet im reuigen Bekenntnis zu Gott öffnet es auch für die Anderen. Er verliert damit seine Würde als besonderer/ausgezeichneter Mensch und wird daher wie ein Kind' (MS 128, 51; a notebook of 1943).

[21] Really 'Wer darf ihn nennen? / Und wer bekennen, / Ich glaub ihn?' (Who dares say God's name / Who dares to claim / That he believes in God?) In Wittgenstein's form: 'Who dares to name him? / Who proclaim him?' The quotation is in a notebook of 1950 (hence very late), from which part of *On Certainty* is taken.

[22] Compare the prayers at the end of the Day of Atonement, 'besides Thee we have no King who pardoneth and forgiveth.'

the remarks in his notebooks (often selected from many written on loose sheets) as the real record of his thought-world,[23] while the works he extracted or began to extract from them are parallel to the *Geständnisse* that we have described. At all events it is not perfectly clear what the category of the non-philosophical is.[24] His struggle for honesty in life was not distinct in nature from the struggle against the temptation to cheat oneself or others in dealing with an intellectual problem. He himself thought that the train of his thought (his *Denkbewegung*) when philosophizing must be retraceable in the story of his mind and its moral concepts and in an understanding of his situation (in life).

Perhaps in fact our question is put the wrong way round: it is not that his life enters into his philosophy but rather that his philosophy is part of his life and since that was, as we have said, essentially a recounted life, his philosophical thoughts are simply part, to be sure the major part, of his journals. Philosophizing was an activity (on which he also reflects) which imposed itself on him and it was an intellectual work on himself just as the rest was a moral work on himself. He sometimes thought this philosophical work was comparatively unimportant. It dealt with one form of the illusions of grandeur or profundity that beset us – but only those of us who are thinkers.[25] Its methods, though, the same in essence as those required in the moral sphere. A man has to realize that he is just a man ('Er ist, wie die Menschen sind,' – perhaps 'He's no more than human' – was a characteristic dismissive judgement), so he has to be aware of the temptations and idols that mislead him. Again and again in philosophy it is a problem of the will, not of the understanding, that is attacked. We must not insist on a justification or ground for everything. The a priori is something to which we adhere (precisely *bekennen*) and a theorem in algebra or any mathematical proof is a *Bekenntnis*, which we, as part of our mathematical community, make or accept.[26] This accounts for the passion that sometimes invested Wittgenstein's criticism of the mathematicians, for example. They insisted on the reality of a system that was in fact a set of decisions.

We may compare G. E. Moore's, normally a kindly man, going red at the neck in discussion. For him, as for Wittgenstein, philosophy was not a game. Truth had to be sought seriously. But that brings us near to another temptation: vanity and the wish to win at all costs. There was vanity too in the composition of the *Tagebücher* and the invention of similes – another Wittgensteinian 'bind': the more he hit the nail on the head, the more he damaged himself. I think it is arguable, however, that his method in philosophy was Wittgenstein's nearest approach to the insight he wanted to win through to (and if possible convey), a help to see the world aright. Wittgenstein's own example was that of the 'hero' at the end of Wilhelm Busch's *Eduards Traum*. Only a man with a heart can see that he is worth nothing, and then everything will turn out right. *Alles andere findet sich* (an

---

[23] The late Denis Paul did this in his 2007, a book inevitably difficult to follow but invaluable for scholars.

[24] *Vermischte Bemerkungen* was von Wright's cautious title for the selection he made. *Culture and Value* for the English edition is hardly an improvement – as if these were two departments in a bookshop!

[25] He told Hugh Sykes Davies, 'You haven't got the sort of stomach ache that I cure.'

[26] Passages drawn from MSS 107, 94 (1929) and 122, 76 (1940).

echo of this phrase of Busch's) is what Wittgenstein himself says at the end of one of his most fervent *Bekenntnisse*[27] and perhaps this was the kind of tranquillity he hoped his philosophy would lead to. He frequently quoted Heinrich Hertz's ideal: *der nicht mehr gequälte Geist*, the mind no longer plagued – by confusions – as being the goal of philosophizing. Several times he thought that he had achieved this (or come as near it as was in his power) and so could turn to other things, but circumstances, combined with the itch for clarity, always brought him back.

Guided as it has been by confessional passages in his journals, our pen has been constrained to dwell on guilt and misery. 'An autobiography', Wittgenstein said in his criticism of Spinoza mentioned above, 'could be said to be written from Hell by one of the damned', rather as the psycho-analyst W. R. Bion called one of his memoirs *All My Sins Remembered*.[28] It is obvious, however, that Wittgenstein's life did not consist entirely of episodes painful to recall. His philosophy itself was, generally, redemptive rather than a burden on his conscience. To be sure, he was serious and severe beyond the norm. Conversations with friends tended to become intellectually testing explorations of the profundity of some question not necessarily philosophical – the idea of national character, vivisection, the progress of the war.[29] On holidays with Drury and his family they would read aloud to one another and discuss what they had read.[30] Music was an important means of escape, though it had to be performed in an appropriate, not a frivolous, manner. In this, and in other ways, he knew how to relax. He would go away after his Cambridge seminars to immerse himself in Westerns at the cheaper and less intellectually respectable cinema (the Kinema, in fact, not the Arts Cinema): inevitably there was an element of theory even there. Engelmann spells it out in his memoir: the need for the Happy End, the lack of pretentiousness. Ryle was almost banished for maintaining that a good English film was not a priori impossible.

We can see Wittgenstein fully relaxed in photographs taken when he was on one of his holidays. (Normally he insisted on a stiff portrait pose.) He would go off with a friend, Drury or Pattisson, say, sometimes just short visits to the seaside to escape Cambridge, to recover his health or his ability to work. His nature went to extremes. He could laugh, even laugh too heartily. Engelmann describes an occasion when Peter Eng read them a satire on 'An evening at the Stonboroughs', which represented Tolstoy (then Wittgenstein's model) as a chained bear. Wittgenstein slipped from the sofa and rolled on the carpet, overcome by laughter. 'It must have been the eruption of long pent-up psychological resistances,' says Engelmann, solemnly but perhaps rightly. It was also a way of neutralizing the implied criticism. His preferred relaxation (he said, forgetting, perhaps, the Kinema) was to talk nonsense by the hour, as with his friend Roy Fouracre from the pharmacy where he worked in the war – *blödeln* he called it when writing to his sister

---

[27] In *Denkbewegungen*, MS 183, 233 (6 April 1937).

[28] A syncopation of Hamlet's prayer, it has been used as a book-title by others also.

[29] See Drury's accounts of conversations in Drury 1984, and the recently reconstructed exchanges with Sraffa in WC.

[30] See Drury 1996. Books could be a strain: 'I am not reading much, thank God,' he told Malcolm in 1948 (McGuinness ed. 2008, 422).

Helene. These were two favourite partners.[31] His correspondence, too, with his great friends, David Pinsent before the First War and Gilbert Pattisson in the 1930s, was conducted in a hilarious manner with comic abbreviations and (in the latter case) constant imitation of the language of advertising. Simple jokes, jokes without a barb, were what he liked and, as we have seen, he would laugh uproariously. One of his own jokes, not exactly nonsense but verses written in a deliberately high-flown manner not appropriate to their subject, has been printed as a *Gedicht* (poem) at the end of the revised editions of *Vermischte Bemerkungen* and *Culture and Value*. It is in fact a mock-poetic form of thanks for a pair of socks knitted for him by a family friend, the singer Marie Fillunger, at a time when he was working as a gardener.[32] There are jokes in his philosophical writings – one remembers the French politician who said that French was the only language in which the words came in the order in which one thought them and the (imagined) man who buys a second copy of the newspaper to assure himself of the truth of its reports (PI §336). Wittgenstein indeed says that it would be possible to write a philosophical book consisting entirely of jokes. Nonsense might be called unconscious humour and jokes the conscious form of nonsense, so that Freud found 'den Sinn im Unsinn' ('the sense in nonsense') a useful tool in analysing them.[33]

The explicit awareness that one of the main tasks of philosophy was to distinguish between sense and nonsense came about only in the twenties of the last century. No doubt Frege was at its origin[34] and Ryle perhaps got it from Husserl (himself influenced by Frege),[35] but the most evident and influential proponent of the view was Wittgenstein in his *Tractatus* and then in conversations or informal discussions. His thought went in tandem with his hobby of collecting Nonsense (or *Stiefel*) (see my 2006a), for the absurdities he found could be regarded with a weeping or with a laughing eye. It was merely amusing when a newspaper reader asked, 'How do we know the names of the stars?' but it was infuriating when Jeans or Eddington sought to explain creation and religion by an astrophysics which their readers in any case could not understand.

At first Wittgenstein thought that language itself would protect us from nonsense – in the sense that we got bumps on the head as a result of running against the limits of language. Later (under Sraffa's influence and having read Spengler – see my 2008) he abandoned this too concrete, or as he says too pneumatic (in English ethereal), view of language. Language was simply the family of practices that we are embedded in, not an independent court of appeal. Limits remain – they are those of possible human practice. Certain uses would of themselves or, rightly considered, be recognized as nonsense (this

---

[31] 'What I miss most is someone I can talk nonsense to by the yard,' Letter to Roy Fouracre, 22 November 1946 (GB). For Helene, see FB, 188, 192.

[32] *Vermischte Bemerkungen*, 165; CV, 100. The *Gedicht* as printed there omits the last line, cancelled in the original manuscript: 'Und der Gärtner nickt: 's ist Filus Treue' ('And the gardener nods: 'tis Filu's troth'), supporting the interpretation in the text.

[33] See Freud 1973 (*Der Witz und seine Beziehung zum Unbewussten*).

[34] See Dummett 1993, Chapter 2, 'The Linguistic Turn.'

[35] See the autobiographical remarks in Ryle 1970. Some indications of an earlier stage when Ryle was influenced by Lotze and Windelband have come to light: see my (with Charlotte Vrijen) 2006.

too is a practice) just as certain human actions manifestly lie outside the acceptable. As in the *Tractatus* (6.422) he had said that any punishment must be an ethical punishment residing in the action itself (the sin becomes its own punishment), so later he included in his collection of Nonsense an (of course poisonous) issue of the anti-Semitic *Der Stürmer*. Words fail one here, as they did at the end of his first work. It remains that philosophy is one way of approaching the right view of the world and enables us to see where words are needed and where they can do no more. A typical expression of this, coming of course after a long discussion, is, 'The chain of reasons has an end.'[36]

REFERENCES

BARTLEY, W. W. III. (1973). *Wittgenstein*. Philadelphia: J. B. Lippincott.

DRURY, M. O'C. (1984). 'Conversations with Wittgenstein', in Rush Rhees ed., *Recollections of Wittgenstein*. Oxford: Oxford University Press.

—— (1996). *The Danger of Words: And Writings on Wittgenstein*. Bristol: Thoemmes Press.

DUMMETT, MICHAEL (1993). *Origins of Analytic Philosophy*. London: Duckworth.

ENGELMANN, PAUL (1967). *Letters from Ludwig Wittgenstein - With A Memoir*. Oxford: Blackwell.

FRANK, JOSEPH (1979). *Dostoevsky: The Seeds of Revolt*. Princeton: Princeton University Press.

FREUD, SIGMUND (1962). 'Dostoevsky and Parricide', in René Wellek ed., *Dostoevsky: A Collection of Critical Essays*. Englewood Cliffs, NJ: Prentice-Hall.

—— (1973). *Jokes and Their Relation to the Unconscious*. London: Hogarth Press.

GOETHE, J. W. (1998). *Dichtung und Wahrheit*. Stuttgart: Reclam.

JANIK, ALLAN and TOULMIN, STEPHEN (1973). *Wittgenstein's Vienna*. London: Weidenfeld & Nicolson.

McGUINNESS, BRIAN (2001). *Approaches to Wittgenstein*. London: Routledge.

—— (2005). *Young Ludwig: Wittgenstein's Life 1889–1921*. Oxford: Clarendon Press. (First published as *Wittgenstein: A Life, Young Ludwig 1889–1921*. London: Duckworth, 1988.)

—— (2006). 'The Brothers Wittgenstein', in Irene Suchy, Allan Janik, and Georg Predota eds., *Empty Sleeve, Der Musiker und Mäzen Paul Wittgenstein*. Innsbruck: Studienverlag.

—— (2006a). 'In Praise of Nonsense', in Rosa M. Calcaterra ed., *Le Ragioni del Conoscere e dell'Agire: Scritti in onore di Rosaria Egidi*. Milan: Franco Angeli.

—— (2008). 'What Wittgenstein owed to Sraffa', in G. Chiodi and L. Ditta eds., *Sraffa or an Alternative Economics*. Basingstoke: Palgrave Macmillan.

—— ed. (2008). *Wittgenstein in Cambridge: Letters and Documents 1911–1951*. Oxford: Blackwell.

—— and VRIJEN, CHARLOTTE (2006). 'First Thoughts: An Unpublished Letter from Gilbert Ryle to H. J. Paton', *British Journal for the History of Philosophy*, 14.4: 747–56.

MONK, RAY (1991). *Ludwig Wittgenstein: The Duty of Genius*. London: Vintage.

PAUL, DENIS (2007). *Wittgenstein's Progress 1929–1951*. Bergen: Publications from the Wittgenstein Archives.

---

[36] BB, 143; cf. WC, 229. For other contexts see PI §§29, 326.

RYLE, GILBERT (1970). *Ryle: A Collection of Critical Essays*, ed. O. P. Wood and G. Pitcher. London: Macmillan.

SCHULTE, JOACHIM ed. (2001). *Ludwig Wittgenstein: Philosophische Untersuchungen. Kritisch-genetische Edition*. Frankfurt: Suhrkamp.

WITTGENSTEIN, LUDWIG (1953). *Philosophical Investigations*, ed. G. E. M Anscombe and R. Rhees, trans. G. E. M. Anscombe. Oxford: Basil Blackwell.

—— (1958). *Preliminary Studies for the 'Philosophical Investigations', Generally Known as the Blue and Brown Books*. Oxford: Basil Blackwell

—— (1994). *Vermischte Bemerkungen*, rev. edn by Alois Pichler, Frankfurt: Suhrkamp.

—— (1996). *Familienbriefe*, ed. M. Ascher, B. McGuinness, O. Pfersmann. Vienna: Hölder–Pichler–Tempsky.

—— (1997). *Denkbewegungen: Tagebücher 1930–1932, 1936–1937*, ed. Ilse Somavilla. Innsbruck: Haymon.

—— (1998). *Culture and Value*, rev. edn, ed. G. H. von Wright in collaboration with H. Nyman, rev. edn by A. Pichler, trans. P. Winch. Oxford: Blackwell.

—— (2002). *Gesamtbriefwechsel*, ed. B. McGuinness, M. Seekircher, A. Unterkircher. InteLex Past Masters. [GB]

VON WRIGHT, G. H. (1958). 'Biographical Sketch', in Norman Malcolm, *Ludwig Wittgenstein: A Memoir*. Oxford: Oxford University Press.

PART II

LOGIC AND THE PHILOSOPHY OF MATHEMATICS

CHAPTER 2

....

WITTGENSTEIN READS RUSSELL

....

GREGORY LANDINI

THE portraits of Wittgenstein given to us by Russell tell a colorful and engaging story which, over the years, has been greatly expanded into a legend of a genius who shook the world of philosophy. Of course, Russell's life and philosophical achievements are no less the substance of genius and legend. Russell and Wittgenstein both left voluminous work notes and letters and they knew a great many people—statesmen, poets, academicians, lovers, and friends—who themselves wrote memoirs. The wealth of material naturally lends itself to a variety of interpretations. The two have become popular subjects for philosophers, biographers, and even film makers.[1]

Russell regarded Wittgenstein as a protégé and did much to establish a career for him. He secured the publications of Wittgenstein's oracular and unorthodox *Tractatus Logico-Philosophicus*. He presided over the *Viva* which accepted the *Tractatus* as a dissertation for Wittgenstein's Ph.D. degree (1929). He was instrumental in Wittgenstein's Fellowship at Trinity College (1930) and in evaluating his *Philosophische Bemerkungen* on behalf of his research funding. A good story must, however, have an antagonist, and the legends have produced one. Wittgenstein is often presented as both temperamentally and philosophically opposed to Russell—Wittgenstein was earnest, inspired, and emotional, and Russell methodical, rational, and detached. Their relationship was certainly complicated. Russell describes Wittgenstein as "perhaps the most perfect example I have ever known of genius as traditionally conceived, passionate, profound, intense, and dominating. He had a kind of purity which I have never known equaled except by G. E. Moore" (Russell 1968, 137). Russell relates the story of taking Wittgenstein to a meeting of the Aristotelian Society, at which there were various people whom Russell treated with polite interest but privately dismissed as fools. Russell says that Wittgenstein

---

[1] For example, *Tom and Viv* (directed by Brian Gilbert, 1994). See also *Wittgenstein* (directed by Derek Jarman, 1993).

"raged and stormed against my moral degradation in not telling these men what fools they were" (ibid.). Is this purity or insensitivity? What sort of men were Russell and Wittgenstein?

In 1914, when his notes on logic (some of which were dictated to Moore in Norway) were to be submitted for fulfillment of the requirements of a B.A. degree, Wittgenstein wrote a letter to Moore containing the following tirade (McGuinness 1988, 200):

> I think my examiners will easily see how much I have cribbed from Bosanquet.—If I'm not worth your making an exception for me even in some STUPID details then I may as well go to Hell directly; and if I am worth it and you don't do it then—by God—you might go there.

In the process of dismissing the Cambridge regulations on citations, he insulted Moore. Such episodes harmed their relationship. Moore's sensibilities were jolted again in 1931 when Wittgenstein was recommending Weininger's *Sex and Gender* to some undergraduate students (Lee and Drury) and to Moore. Wittgenstein wrote this explanation to Moore (Monk 1990, 313):

> It isn't necessary or rather not possible to agree with him [Weininger] but the greatness lies in that with which we disagree. It is his enormous mistake which is great, i.e., roughly speaking if you add a ~ to the whole book it says an important truth.

It is hard to imagine what this "great truth" could have been. Did Wittgenstein embrace Weininger's thesis that it is the nature of women to accept dependence and subservience because of the biological–psychological foundation of sex? Did he embrace Weininger's ultimate solution to the female/Jewish question—namely, that men should end the human race by siring no new children and embracing Platonic love and Christianity's promise of the union of their immortal souls with God? Did Wittgenstein identify with the self-opprobrium Weininger derived from his disgust at his own Jewishness and homosexuality? Did he accept Weininger's thesis that 'Jew' is a corrupt personality type that all men must oppose in themselves and the irony of Weininger's thesis that Aryan anti-Semites have particularly Jewish characters? It is difficult to gauge the extent to which Wittgenstein identified with Weininger. Wittgenstein wrote that his own accomplishments are typical of Jewish parasitism and reproductiveness and not original or creative (CV, 18). But we also find Wittgenstein telling Drury: "How wrong he [Weininger] was, my God he was wrong" (Rhees 1984, 91).

Passages like these present very inconclusive evidence. It is all too easy to be seduced by them into presenting disparaging portraits of character. When the Americans entered the war, Wittgenstein wrote: "Things will be terrible when the war is over, whoever wins. Of course, terrible if the Nazis won, but terribly slimy if the Allies won" (McGuinness 2002, 51). One would certainly have hoped he would say that it is terribly important that the Allies win, given that by this time he couldn't have been unaware of the atrocities of Nazism. But if we knew the details of the actual context of the remark we might think differently. Monk's recent biographies of Wittgenstein and Russell give in to such seductions. Monk presents Russell's work after *Principia* as self-indulgent and philosophically shallow. Consider the following passage from *On Marriage and Morals*, which Russell would soon redact in later editions. Writing on eugenics and its relation to the *scientific* question of whether there are intellectual differences among races, Russell wrote (Russell 1929, 267):

> It seems on the whole fair to regard negros as on the average inferior to white men, although for their work in the tropics they are indispensable, so that their extermination (apart from questions of humanity) should be highly undesirable. But when it comes to discriminating among the races of Europe, a mass of bad science has to be brought in to support political prejudice. Nor do I see any valid ground for regarding the yellow races as in any degree inferior to our noble selves. In all such cases, racial eugenics is merely an excuse for chauvinism.

Is this racism, as Monk suggests, or is it that Russell hadn't fully broken through the mass of pseudo-scientific data that abounded in 1921? These are among the many episodes that serve as Rorschach inkblots for interpretations of Russell and Wittgenstein.

Looking back from the vantage point of the 1950s, Russell recounts the history in black and white. There were two Wittgensteins: the young writer of the *Tractatus* who was "passionately addicted to intense thinking, profoundly aware of difficult problems of which I, like him, felt the importance, and possessed (or at least so I thought) of true philosophical genius"; and the later writer of work notes such as the *Philosophical Investigations* who "seems to have grown tired of serious thinking and to have invented a doctrine which would make such activity unnecessary . . .", making philosophy ". . . at best, a slight help to lexicographers, and at worst an idle tea-table amusement" (Russell 1959, 217). Wittgenstein got in a few barbs at Russell's popular writings, reportedly calling Russell's *Conquest of Happiness* a "vomitive" and his *What I Believe*? "harmful" (Monk 1990, 294). Drury recounts him saying that "Russell's books should be bound in two colours: those dealing with mathematical logic in red, and all students of philosophy should read them; those dealing with ethics and politics in blue, and no one should be allowed to read them" (Drury 1981, 127). Neither philosopher could resist hyperbole. Most everyone has followed suit. A more balanced account is long overdue. In the short context of this chapter, we cannot hope to provide the truth, the whole truth and nothing but the truth. By focusing on correcting some of the mistakes, we hope to bring the two together as allies.

REREADING RUSSELL

Two theses have dominated the understanding of Russell's philosophy. The two are so widely held that it is rare to find challenges to either in the vast literature on Russell. They have become dogmas of Russellian interpretation. They are:

1) In *Principia Mathematica*, Russell advanced a ramified type-theory of *entities*.
2) Russell's logical atomism is a form of reductive empiricistic epistemology.

With the help of the volumes of manuscripts that Russell left, it now appears that both are false. Rejecting them has very important consequences for rereading Russell and Wittgenstein. To borrow a colorful phrase from Kant, the manuscripts awaken us from a dogmatic slumber.

Broad once remarked that Russell published a new system of philosophy every few years (Weitz 1944, 57). There are indeed a great many twists and turns in Russell's views on ontology. But the correct way to understand this is not by attributing to Russell the ability to change his mind in light of new philosophical discoveries—laudable though it is. The correct way to understand it is by recognizing that Russell's many changes are directed by what Kuhn would call a "research paradigm" or "research program." The research paradigm he belonged to, and himself helped to refine, is one of logical analysis, elimination, and reconstruction. There are many examples Russell offers of theories within the research program. Here are a few:

> Frege on natural numbers as concepts of equinumerosity.
> Cantor on infinity and continuity.
> Weierstrass's construction of the notion of the limit in analysis without
>   infinitesimals.
> Analytic geometry, non-Euclidean geometry, and the elimination of motion
>   and superposition from the metrical notion of congruence.
> Hertz's construction of Newtonian force without action at a distance.
> Material continuants (in time) as series (four-dimensionalism).
> Russell's elimination of reals in favor of relations on rationals defined by lower
>   sections of Dedekind cuts.
> Einstein's recovery of Maxwell's equations for the propagation of light without
>   the ontology of the aether.
> Russell's theory of propositions and "substitutional" reconstruction of math-
>   ematics without comprehension principles for classes or attributes.
> *Principia*'s reconstruction of mathematics without comprehension principles
>   for classes.
> *Principia*'s "no-propositions" theory and its recursive definition of "truth" and
>   "falsehood" based on a multiple-relation theory of judgment.
> Neutral monism and the reconstruction of matter (physical continuants) and
>   mind (selves) in terms of orderings of space-time phases.

These are not regarded by Russell as reductive identifications. In a reductive identity one argues, for example, that water is H_2O, that a gene is a sequence of DNA, that a pain is a neural sequence of a sort, etc. Russell has in mind a reductive elimination, where one theory replaces another, abandoning the former ontology but recovering (where possible) its structure. These are each "no entity" theories. There are no classes, but the structure of such a theory is recovered. There are no triangles, but the structure of a given geometric space is recovered as relations on numbers. There are no real numbers, but the structure is recovered by sequences of rationals (which in turn are relations on natural numbers). There are no infinitesimals, but the notion of a "limit" is recovered by relational order. There is no matter, but the physics of continuants is recovered by orderings of phases in space-time. The unity of Russell's philosophy is to be found in the distinctive research program he distilled from his work on the philosophy of mathematics. He called this program "logical atomism." The program maintains that the only necessity is logical necessity. All other purported necessities—mathematical, geometric, causal, metaphysical, and the like—are ultimately either logical or are will o' the wisp. The task of philosophical logical analysis is to separate the logical components from the hybrid concepts of ordinary and technical theories, recovering (where possible) the *structure* of the given theory without the ontology conjured by the reveries of speculative metaphysics.

Russell's logical atomism is a research program in philosophy. The sub-theories within the program may come and go. Indeed, even some of what one would have hoped were Russell's cherished theories seem to be rejected by him in later years. But we must not confuse Russell's research program of logical atomism with any particular sub-theory within it. For example, identifying logical atomism as an empiricist epistemological program based on a theory that the mind is *acquainted* with sense-data and with universals hopelessly distorts logical atomism as a research program. Matters become even worse when the sense-data are interpreted, in spite of Russell's explicit comments that they are physical, as mental entities of a phenomenalism in the spirit of C. I. Lewis's *Mind and World Order*. If we identify Russell's program of logical atomism with this or that among its sub-theories, we lose sight of Russell's philosophy. And if we lose sight of Russell, we also lose sight of Wittgenstein. We present Wittgenstein chasing windmills—criticizing Russell for holding positions that he abandoned years earlier or never held at all. If we misunderstand Russell's eliminativism, we cannot hope to understand the work of his apprentice and protégé.

Wittgenstein began as Russell's student in October of 1911. Russell tells the story of an Austrian arriving in Cambridge and demanding to be told whether he has a gift for philosophy or is better suited for aeronautics (Russell 1968, 137):

> At the end of his first term at Trinity, he came to me and said: "Do you think I am an absolute idiot?" I said: "Why do you want to know?" He replied: "Because if I am I shall become an aeronaut, but if I am not I shall become a philosopher". I said: "My dear fellow, I don't know whether you are an absolute idiot or not, but if you will write me an essay during the vacation upon any philosophical topic that interests you, I will read it and tell you." He did so, and brought it to me at the beginning of the next term. As soon as I read the first sentence, I became persuaded that he was a man of genius, and assured him that he should on no account become an aeronaut.

Ray Monk's engaging biographies observe that Wittgenstein pursued his studies in mathematical logic which such vigor that, by the end of one term of study, Russell was to say that he had learnt all he had to teach, and indeed gone further (Monk 1990, 72). Monk comes to believe, however, that by January 1913 the cooperation between the two had come to an end. "In the field of logic, Wittgenstein, far from being Russell's student, had become Russell's teacher" (ibid.).

This makes a good story line, but it is historical fiction. The proper understanding of the relationship between Russell and Wittgenstein requires a careful understanding of Russell's research program, and not a little understanding of the technical details of some of the theories he advocated within it. Much has been made, for instance, of Wittgenstein's criticisms of Russell's multiple-relation theory of judgment, a theory first espoused in *Principia*, and later worked out in Russell's 1913 manuscript for a book on the theory of knowledge. Russell abandoned his book project in the wake of what he describes as a storm of protest from Wittgenstein. In one letter to Russell from the period, Wittgenstein writes that "all theory of types must be done away with by a theory of symbolism" (*NB*, 105). One can find Russell writing Ottoline that Wittgenstein's criticisms "were an event of first-rate importance in my life, and affected everything I have done since. I saw he was right, and I saw that I could not hope ever again to do fundamental work in philosophy" (Russell 1968, 66). When Russell writes Ottoline of despair of ever again doing fundamental work in philosophy, of suicidal depression over failed work—feelings which, he says, were caused by exasperating exchanges with the sometimes turbulent temper of Wittgenstein—Monk imagines evidence of Wittgenstein's philosophical and *intellectual* superiority. Russell's pupil becomes Russell's "master."

The truth is much more complicated. On Monk's view, Wittgenstein was dismissing the multiple-relation theory because it cannot rule out nonsensical judgments without relying on *Principia*'s theory of types of *entities*—a theory Wittgenstein vehemently rejected with the remark that all theories of types must be done away with by a theory of symbolism (LRKM, 19). Monk writes (Monk 1990, 71):

> In the face of such a sweeping dismissal of his theory, Russell might have been expected to present a spirited defense of his position or at least some tough question as to how his logicist foundations of mathematics might avoid contradiction without a theory of types. But he had by this time abandoned logic almost entirely.

Russell's unpublished manuscripts reveal that the very idea of doing away with types (of classes and attributes) by a theory of symbolism is something Wittgenstein *learned* from Russell. Ramified type distinctions *are* done away with (built into the significance conditions of the use of predicate variables) in *Principia*. In light of this history, an entirely different perspective emerges with Wittgenstein as Russell's ally. Wittgenstein's objection was that Russell's constructions in *Principia* had not gone far enough. The predicable nature of a universal, as opposed to a particular, is *another* "type" distinction that must *also* be done away with. It is not at all odd or perplexing, then, that Monk cannot find Russell bridling at Wittgenstein's alleged "sweeping dismissal" of a type-theory of *entities*. There was no such theory and no such dismissal.

Russell did not conceive of the advance that the new logic had made over categorical syllogisms to be confined merely to quantification theory. He thought that logic contains comprehension principles and that this makes it every bit as genuine a science as mathematics. The comprehension of new numeric functions in mathematics is to be captured by means of comprehension principles of logic. Frege had seen this even in his *Begriffsschrift* (1879). Logic contains the comprehension of functions, and functions (as Frege sees it) are not objects.

Similarly, logic embraces comprehension principles for an ontology of attributes, where attributes have a predicable nature only. Such a theory is perfectly consistent and makes logic a genuine informative science. But Russell could not accept a meta-physics which embraced Frege's distinction between *entities* (such as attributes or functions) and *objects*. For Russell, whatever is, is an individual. Moreover, Russell dis-covered paradoxes of classes and attributes (where attributes can occur predicatively as well as occur as subjects of predication). The lesson he drew from the paradoxes is that mathematics must be emulated by means of a "no-classes" and "no-attributes" theory. More exactly, he concluded that general comprehension principles for classes or attributes must be avoided by a logical re-conceptualization and reconstruction of mathematics.

Russell hoped to achieve this re-conceptualization of mathematics by couching it within a general theory of structure—reifying structures as propositions.[2] On the heels of his 1905 theory of definite descriptions, Russell was successful in emulating arithmetic in terms of his logic of propositional structure. He called this his "substitu-tional theory." Russell explains (Russell 1973, 205):

> the range of significance must somehow be given with the variable; this can only be done by employing variables having some internal structure for such as are to be of some definite logical type other than individuals...But then we have to assume that a single letter, such as *x*, can only stand for an individual; and that can only be the case if individuals are really all entities, and classes, etc., are merely *façon de parler*.

The founding idea of the theory is that the only genuine variables are individual vari-ables and that, by logical ingenuity, one must emulate a theory of classes (or attributes) by employing structured variables.

To see how a type-stratified theory of classes is emulated in the substitutional theory, observe that a type-theory of classes introduces classes (of individuals) of lowest type (0) by the following comprehension principle:

$$(\exists y^{(0)})(\forall z^0)(z^0 \in y^{(0)} \leftrightarrow A),$$

where $y^{(0)}$ is not free in the formula A. The uniqueness of such a class is assured by exten-sionality axioms, so that classes with the same members are identical. Thus, for instance, we assure that every individual of type 0 is a member of the class of individuals of type 0 that are self-identical as follows:

$$(\forall x^0)(x^0 \in (\imath y^{(0)})[z^0 \in y^{(0)} \leftrightarrow_{z0} z^0 = z^0]).$$

---

[2] In this period, Russell held that propositions are mind- and language-independent entities. They are akin to states of affairs. Some obtain (are true) and others are non-obtaining (are false).

This is emulated in Russell's type-free substitutional theory using only individual variables. Comprehension is given with:

$$(\exists y, w)(\forall z)(\exists v)(y/w;z!v. \bullet .v \equiv A),$$

where y and w are not free in A. The expression

$$y/w;z \ !v$$

means that structurally v is exactly like y except for containing entity z wherever y contains w. For example, if y is the proposition $\{w = w\}$, then v is the proposition $\{z = z\}$. Russell calls y/w a "matrix" and he calls y the "prototype" of the matrix. To emulate the statement that every individual of type o is a member of the class of type (o) of all individuals of type o that are self-identical, substitution has

$$(\forall x^0)(x^0 \in \iota \ (y/w)[z \in y/w \equiv {}_{z0}z=z]),$$

where

$$z \in y/w = df \ (\exists v)(y/w;z!v. \bullet .v).$$

$$x^0 \in \iota(y/w)[z \in y/w \equiv {}_{z0}z = z] = df$$

$$(\exists y)(\exists w)(z \in y/w \equiv {}_{z0}z = z. \bullet .x \in y/w).^3$$

These definitions are only possible because the logical particles of the substitutional theory are relation signs.

The "if...then ..." sign $\to$, the biconditional sign $\leftrightarrow$, the conjunction sign $\wedge$, and so forth of modern logic are statement connectives. They are flanked by formulas to form formulas. While he embraced an ontology of propositions, Russell used the horseshoe sign $\supset$ and the signs $\equiv$, $\bullet$ as relation signs. They are flanked by terms (variables and nominalized formulas) to form formulas. It is convenient to adopt brackets to mark the nominalization of a formula. Thus, where A is a formula, $\{A\}$ is a term. In order to prevent the incoherence of having a singular term occurring on a line of proof, the inference rule *Modus Ponens* in the theory of propositions is this:

From A and $\{A\}\supset\{B\}$ infer B.

The formula $x \supset y$ is read "x implies y." The term $\{x \supset y\}$ is read "x's implying y". Thus the expression "$x \supset \{y \supset z\}$" is read "$x$ implies y's implying z." For convenience we can use dots for punctuation to mark the transformation from a formula to a term, writing "$x \supset . y \supset z$". But this must not be confused with the modern "$A . \to . B \to C$", which is read "If A

---

3 For a detailed account of Russell's substitutional theory, see Landini 1998.

then if B then C." Confusion on this point is, unfortunately, all too common. It derives in part from Russell's use of the letters p, q, r as individual variables (alternatives of x, y, z, etc.). These are easily confused with P, Q, R used as letters for formulas. But Russell's $p \supset q$ ("p implies q") should not be conflated with P $\rightarrow$ Q ("If P then Q"). Similarly, the expression $x \cdot y$ would be incoherent if $\cdot$ were the modern conjunction sign which must be flanked by well-formed formulas, not terms. Russell defines as follows:

$$x \cdot y = df(z)(x \mathbin{.}\supset\mathbin{.} y \supset z :\supset: z)$$

This is clearly not ordinary conjunction.

In Russell's substitutional theory, it is possible to emulate classes of type ((o)) of classes of individuals of type o. Classes of this type are emulated by using three individual variables.

Thus the notion of type is tracked in the substitutional theory, in part, by the number of individual variables used. The expression "$y/w;y,w!\ v$" which would be required to emulate "$y \in y$" (or analogously "$\varphi(\varphi)$") is grammatically ill formed. Thus it is impossible to formulate Russell's paradox of the class C of all classes y that are not members of themselves. (Similarly, it is impossible to formulate Russell's paradox concerning the attribute F that an attribute G exemplifies if and only if G does not exemplify itself.) In this way, the structure of types of classes (or attributes) is built into the grammar of the type-free substitutional theory.

The substitutional theory is a marvel. Had it succeeded, I venture to say that the notion of a set (or class) in mathematics would have gone the way of such entities as caloric fluid, phlogiston, and the aether in physics. Unfortunately, Russell came to believe that the emulation of arithmetic couched in his metaphysics of propositions requires comprehension principles (unique to the substitutional theory) that generate a new paradox. Russell revealed this paradox only to a few friends. In 1907 he wrote Hawtrey a letter explaining things. I have called this new paradox Russell's "p_0/a_0 paradox" (see Landini 1998). Though it is the focus of many lengthy manuscripts in 1906, the new paradox never appeared in Russell's publications. Because of the paradox, Russell withdrew from publication an early paper in which he had planned to herald the substitutional theory as the solution of the paradoxes plaguing logicism.[4] In 1906, however, he published a paper in French replying to Poincaré's criticism of logicism. The English title wonderfully reveals Russell's enthusiasm for the substitutional theory. It is called "On 'Insolubilia' and Their Solution by Symbolic Logic."[5] Russell thought that he had avoided the needling p_0/a_0 paradox and went boldly forth with a new substitutional theory purged of the ontology of general propositions.

Russell was chagrined to discover, however, that in spite of his great efforts to work without an ontology of general propositions, he had again adopted substitutional comprehension principles for propositions that revive the p_0/a_0 paradox.[6] In "Mathematical

[4] The paper was called "On the Substitutional Theory of Classes and Relations."
[5] The French title is "Les Paradoxes de la Logique" and it was published in *Revue de Métaphysique et de Morale*, 14 (1906). The English manuscript is published in *Essays in Analysis By Bertrand Russell* (1973).
[6] I think I have discovered a way to avoid this. See Landini 2004.

Logic as Based on the Theory of Types" (1908), Russell advocates the substitutional theory, but reluctantly concludes that its language must introduce order indices on its variables. This order regimentation, he thinks, cannot be the last word. Some new theory of structured variables couched within a non-assumption of an ontology of propositions must be found. In his efforts to find it, Russell now gives his thesis about variables a semantic twist which sets the stage for the account of predicate variables in *Principia*. We find (Russell 1908, 73):

> The difficulty which besets attempts to restrict the variable is that restrictions naturally express themselves as hypotheses that the variable is of such or such a kind, and that, when so expressed, the resulting hypothesis is free from the intended restriction…Thus a variable can never be restricted within a certain range if the propositional function in which the variable occurs remains significant when the variable is outside that range. But if the function ceases to be significant when the variable goes outside a certain range, then the variable *is ipso facto* confined to that range, without the need of any explicit statement. This principle is to be born in mind in the development of logical types… [The variable *is internally limited* by its range of significance.]

In *Principia*, Russell abandoned his theory of propositions. The logical particles of the theory are now statement connectives, not signs for relations between propositions. The language of the theory introduces order\type-regimented predicate variables, but these variables are semantically interpreted nominalistically, not objectually.

The semantic interpretation adopts a fixed hierarchy of languages, L_1, L_2, etc. The lowest in the hierarchy contains formulas involving free predicate variables of order\ type regimentation 1, formulas with no bound variables and formulas containing bound individual variables only. Next the formulas of L_2 include bound predicate variables of order\type regimentation 1, the formulas of L_3 include bound variables of order\type regimentation 2, and so on as we ascend the languages. The truth-conditions for formulas in which predicate variables with order\type regimentation 1 occur are semantically given in terms of whether their replacement by formulas of L_1 make them come out true. Similarly, the truth-conditions for formulas in which predicate variables with order\type regimentation 2 occur are semantically given in terms of whether their replacement by formulas of L_2 make them come out true. The basis of this recursively defined hierarchy of senses of "truth" and "falsehood" rests on Russell's multiple-relation theory of judgment. In this way, Russell hopes to have established that the order\type regimentation is given "internally" by the significance conditions of the predicate variable in question. The limits of the variable are supposed to be given by the structure of the variables and not made by statements of the formal language of the theory. Their limitations are "internal" to the signs of the language itself. The definition of "truth" and "falsehood" in *Principia* is recursive. This is the seed of what would come to be the Tractarian thesis of the logical independence of facts. The facts that are the truth-makers of *Principia*'s recursive definition are logically independent. This is at the center of Russell's recursive definition, for it is precisely what builds the structure of orders into *Principia*'s predicate variables.

Rereading Wittgenstein

Wittgenstein accepted ramified type-"theory." More exactly, he accepted the challenge posed by Russell of finding a symbolism that builds the structure (not the ontology) of ramified types into structured variables. But Wittgenstein could not accept *Principia*'s semantic approach toward building structure into variables. Russell's approach introduces predicates such as "... is true," "... is a universal," "... is a fact." Wittgenstein regarded these as pseudo-predicates. A different technique is needed. Wittgenstein writes (TLP 3.333):

> The reason why a function cannot be its own argument is that the sign for a function already contains the prototype of its argument, and it cannot contain itself.
>
> For let us suppose that the function $F(fx)$ could be its own argument: in that case there would be a proposition '$F(F(fx))$' in which the outer function F and the inner function F must have different meanings, since the inner one has the form $\varphi(fx)$ and the outer one has the form $\psi(\varphi(fx))$. Only letter 'F' is common to the two functions, but the letter by itself signifies nothing.
>
> This immediately becomes clear if instead of '$F(F(fu))$' we write '$(\exists\varphi): F(\varphi(u)) . \varphi(u) = Fu$'.
>
> That disposes of Russell's paradox.

Wittgenstein's plan is that a variable contains a prototype—a picture of the structure of its values. By means of the prototype and picturing, no semantic theory is needed. The syntactic complexity of the structured variable pictures the structure that all of its admissible values are to have. Like Russell before him, Wittgenstein advocates finding a notation in which the structure, not the ontology, of types and orders is *shown* by the syntax of the variables.[7]

In the *Tractatus*, Wittgenstein does not even attempt to offer a notation which realizes the goal. Borrowing from Frege, however, we can imagine a notation of structured variables that does justice to type structures.[8] Frege's *Begriffsschrift* introduced different *levels* of functions. The notations for the levels have important similarities to Russell's simple type structures. A brief chart of one-place expressions helps to see the relationships (see table).

Russellian types	Fregean levels
x^0	X
$\varphi^{(o)}$	φ
$\varphi^{((o))}$	$M_\beta f_\beta$
$\varphi^{(((o)))}$	$\Sigma_\beta[M_\beta \psi_\beta]$

---

[7] Sackur notices the connection between Wittgenstein's idea of structured variables (as prototypes) and Russell's use, during the era of his substitutional theory of propositions, of the "prototype of a matrix." See Sackur 2005, 89, 121.

[8] I do not mean to suggest that Frege himself embraced such variables in his *Grundgesetze*.

Fregean levels are captured by using structured variables which display higher-level concepts as quantifier-concepts. Such structured variables are not exploited in the notation of *Principia*'s ramified type structure. But type structures are *shown* in the Fregean notation. By keeping function symbols in function position, the structured variables provide prototypes of the structure of their values. On Frege's view, a first-level function *f* yields a value for an object *x* taken as its *argument*. As Frege puts it, the argument "falls under" the first-level function. A first-level function, on the other hand, can "fall within" a second-level function when it "mutually saturates" it. Second-level functions (and higher-level functions) are quantifier concepts for Frege. For example, Frege takes the quantifier concept: $(\forall x)fx$ to be a second-level function under which first-level functions may fall. (To distinguish the Fregean language, we use the symbol $\forall$ for the universal quantifier.[9]) For example, the first-level function of self-identity *falls within* this second-level function, because every object *x* is self-identical. To introduce a structured variable that ranges over second-level quantifier concepts, put: $M_\beta f_\beta$. The lower-case Greek β appears as a subscript in $M_\beta f_\beta$ to remind us of the bound individual variable β in expressions of second-level quantifier concepts. Then we can quantify over second-level quantifier concepts with the notation $(\forall M)M_\beta f_\beta$. For example we have:

$$(\forall M)M_\beta f_\beta \supset (\forall x)fx.$$

Since function signs can only appear in predicate (function) positions, quantifier concepts are extensional, and so we have:

$$(\forall M)(\varphi x \equiv_x \psi x . \supset_{\varphi\psi} . M_\beta \varphi_\beta \equiv_M M_\beta \psi_\beta).$$

Next we have third-level quantifier-concepts. For instance, we can represent $(\forall x)(\varphi x \supset (\exists x)\psi x)$ as a context resulting from the mutual saturation of the quantifier-concept $(\forall x)fx$ with the concept $\Omega_\beta \varphi_\beta \supset_\varphi (\exists x)\psi x$. Accordingly, we represent a notation perspicuous of the quantificational structures of third-level concepts as follows: $\Sigma_\psi[M_\beta \psi_\beta]$. The occurrence of the subscripted Greek ψ indicates that a first-level function variable ψ is bound in the quantifier concept. The pattern continues as we ascend the levels.

Wittgenstein hopes that a similar technique of prototypes (structured variables) is possible so that both type and order are pictured by structured variables. It is unclear how this would be done for ramification. All the same, once we understand the historical evolution of Russell's ramified types, we see how Wittgenstein's ideas are related to those of Russell. Indeed, the very "fundamental idea" or *Grundgedanke* of the *Tractatus* (4.0312), the idea that the logical constants are not representatives, is itself an extension of Russell's own technique of solving philosophical problems by building structure into variables. By "logical constants," Wittgenstein means much more than just the logical particles. With the abandonment of propositions, *Principia* had already adopted the view that the logical particles ("or", "not", etc.) are not relation signs. Wittgenstein meant to include among "logical constants" all "formal concepts." He includes all concepts with

---

[9] Accordingly, $\varphi x \equiv_x \psi x$ abbreviates $(\forall x)(\varphi x \equiv \psi x)$.

logical or semantic content—notions such as "object," "property," "truth," "fact," "existence," "identity," and so on. In the *Tractatus* we find the following:

> TLP 4.126
> We can now talk about formal concepts, in the same sense that we speak of formal properties. (I introduce this expression in order to exhibit the source of the confusion between formal concepts and concepts proper, which pervades the whole of traditional logic.) When something falls under a formal concept as one of its objects, this cannot be expressed by means of a proposition. Instead it is shown in the very sign for this object. (A name shows that it signifies an object, a sign for a number that it signifies a number, etc.)...So the expression for a formal concept is a propositional variable in which this distinctive feature alone is constant.

> TLP 4.1271
> Thus, the variable name "x" is the proper sign of the pseudo-concept *object*. Whenever the word "object" ("thing," "entity," etc.) is rightly used, it is expressed in logical symbolism by the variable name....The same holds for the words "complex," "fact," "function," "number," etc. They all signify formal concepts and are presented in logical symbolism by variables....

Wittgenstein accepts Russell's idea of building structure into variables. It is part of his notion that "formal concepts" are properly expressed by variables. The plan in the *Tractatus* is to extend Russell's method of solving philosophical problems by eliminating certain questionable ontological commitments and employing structured variables.

The fundamental idea of the *Tractatus* should be identified with Wittgenstein's *Doctrine of Showing*. In a letter to Russell of August 1919, Wittgenstein corroborates this view. Explaining the *Tractatus* he wrote (LRKM, 71):

> Now I'm afraid you haven't really got hold of my main contention, to which the whole business of logical propositions is only corollary. The main point is the theory of what can be expressed (*gesagt*) by prop[osition]s—i.e., by language (and, what comes to the same, what can be thought) and what can not be expressed by prop[osition]s, but only shown (*gezeigt*); which, I believe, is the cardinal problem of philosophy.

The central point of the *Tractatus* is to suggest new ontologically eliminativistic reconstructions which realize the following:

> *All and only logical (and semantic) notions are pseudo-concepts that are shown by structured variables.*

In Wittgenstein's view, Russell's eliminativistic reconstructions do not go far enough.

Tractarian Logic

Accounts of Russell's intellectual relationship with Wittgenstein must change in light of the improved understanding of *Principia* that Russell's unpublished manuscripts provide. One very significant change concerns Wittgenstein's views on *Principia*. Russell once remarked to Ottoline that "Wittgenstein has persuaded me that the early parts of *Principia Mathematica* are very inexact, but fortunately it is his business to put them right, not mine" (Griffin 1992, 448).[10] August 1913 dates the following entry in Pinsent's Diary: "It is probable that the first volume of *Principia* will have to be re-written, and Wittgenstein may write himself the first eleven chapters. That is a splendid triumph for him!" (McGuinness 1988, 180). Monk makes the following conclusion (Monk 1999, 290):

> These remarks are revealing. They show how Russell was still inclined to look upon Wittgenstein's work as a kind of 'fine tuning' of his own. He talks as if the inexactitude of the early parts of *Principia* is a mere detail, but those early parts contain the very foundation upon which the whole of the rest was built. And Wittgenstein was not repairing it, as Russell continued to think; he was demolishing it altogether.

Monk's account accepts the folklore of Wittgenstein as pupil turned master, but this cannot withstand scrutiny. The history is much more interesting.

Norway provided Wittgenstein the focus he thought necessary for work on logic. He had vacationed with his close friend Pinsent at Øystese, a tiny village with majestic hills rising behind in a little bay at Hardangerfjord. When he returned to Cambridge on 2 October, he told Russell of his firm intention to leave Cambridge and live in Norway. Russell wrote to Lucy Donnelly in October of 1913 ('Letter to Lucy Donelly', quoted in McGuinness 1988, 184):

> Then my Austrian, Wittgenstein, burst in like a whirlwind, just back from Norway, and determined to return there at once to live in compete solitude until he has solved *all* the problems of logic. I said it would be dark, and he said he hated daylight. I said it would be lonely, and he said he prostituted his mind talking to intelligent people. I said he was mad, and he said God preserve him from sanity. (God certainly will.)

The catalyst for this sudden focused determination is likely to have been the fact that Russell came to know of Sheffer's result that all the quantifier-free formulas of *Principia*'s sentential calculus can be expressed via one logical connective—the Sheffer stroke.[11] Russell received a copy of a paper from Sheffer on 15 April 1913 and surely shared it with Wittgenstein. Russell read a paper to the Cambridge Moral Sciences Club in April 1912 entitled "On Matter." On the back page of a later draft of Russell's paper entitled "On Matter—The Problem Stated," there are jottings in Russell's and Wittgenstein's hands which reveal that they were discussing truth-tables and Sheffer's stroke (McGuinness 1988, 160). In the verso,[12] the Sheffer stroke appears as $p \times q$ and is said to be equal (equivalent) to $\sim p \vee \sim q$. Close scrutiny suggests Russell's hand writing $\sim p$ on the left, with Wittgenstein's hand writing W (*Wahrheit*) for true and F (*Falsch*) for false. This offers an explanation of the comments concerning Wittgenstein's "rewriting" of *Principia*. Russell may well have

---

[10] Letter to Ottoline Morrell, 23 February 1913.

[11] Sheffer (1913). Peirce's unpublished papers show that he had discovered this result earlier.

[12] Verso turned upside down of folio 1, "Matter: The Problem Stated" (Bertrand Russell Archives, McMaster University, Hamilton, Ontario).

discussed whether Wittgenstein might make it part of his B.A. dissertation (which was required of a research student) to work out a new reduction of the propositional part of *Principia*'s *1–*5 based on Sheffer's single connective (McGuinness 1988, 199).

There is ample evidence in letters to Russell that Wittgenstein was working to find a reduction based on Sheffer's ideas. In a letter to Russell from Norway dated 30 October 1913, Wittgenstein claims to have found such a reduction: "One of the consequences of my new ideas will—I think—be that the whole of Logic follows from one Pp only!" (NB, 123). Wittgenstein's famous self-imposed isolation in Norway failed to produce the reduction that Nicod found in 1916. (See Nicod 1917.) Nicod showed that the whole propositional system of *Principia*'s *1–*5 can proceed from one axiom and one inference rule. In the 1925 introduction to the second edition of *Principia*, Russell even recommends that Sheffer "rewrite" the propositional theory of *Principia* using the stroke (Whitehead and Russell 1925, xv).

There is no question that Wittgenstein had ideas for improving the philosophical foundation of *Principia* and that Russell was enticed by them. The first "eleven chapters" of *Principia* alluded to by Pinsent are likely to be *1–*5 and *9–*14.[13] In the course of his investigations, Wittgenstein came to hope that a proper elimination of the identity symbol (introduced at *13) would obviate *Principia*'s need to add statements of the infinity of individuals as antecedents of central theorems concerning inductive cardinals. He also advocated an extensionalist position that "a function can appear only through its values" and suggested that this would avoid the need for *Principia*'s Reducibility Principle (introduced at *12). The theory of definite descriptions is introduced at *14 and Wittgenstein's new treatment of identity would require modifications of its notation. Wittgenstein wrote to Russell that "your theory of descriptions is *quite undoubtedly* right, even if the individual primitive signs in it are quite different from what you believe."[14] In *Principia* Russell held that the theory of classes may not yet have found its final formulation and, though convinced that some formulation embodying type structures must be correct, he expressed a hope that with further work in the area, the axiom of reducibility might yet be supplanted. He acknowledged that there remained philosophical difficulties with *Principia*'s reliance on reducibility and invited *all* his readers to work on them.[15]

The fact that Russell was interested in Wittgenstein's ideas for solving philosophical problems remaining in the *Principia* provides no basis for concluding that Russell had become his "pupil" or that Wittgenstein was demolishing the *Principia*. Quite the contrary, the evidence represents Wittgenstein as very much under Russell's tutelage. It presents Wittgenstein as an apprentice working *within* a research program set forth by Russell.

Wittgenstein's logical investigations in Norway brought him to believe something far more sweeping than a reduction to one proposition and one inference rule. He came to

---

[13] There are no sections *6–*8 in the first edition of *Principia*.

[14] Letter of November 1913 in NB, 129. Wittgenstein objected to Russell's use of the identity sign in his theory of definite descriptions.

[15] Whitehead and Russell 1925, vii, xiv, 60.

hold that the mark of a logical proposition is tautologyhood—something that can be shown immediately if the proposition is represented in a proper notation. One of Wittgenstein's early attempts at finding such a principle is embedded in an amusing story of the odd events of Wittgenstein's first meeting with the Whiteheads. Russell explains (Russell 1968, 139):

> Whitehead described to me the first time that Wittgenstein came to see him. He was shown into the drawing room during afternoon tea. He appeared scarcely aware of the presence of Mrs. Whitehead, but marched up and down the room for some time in silence, and at last said explosively: "A proposition has two poles. It is *apb*." Whitehead, in telling me, said: "I naturally asked what are *a* and *b*, but I found I had said the wrong thing. '*a* and *b* are indefinable,' Wittgenstein answered in voice of thunder."

The *ab*-notation remained obscure for many years. Happily we now know what Wittgenstein was up to. Martin Gardner independently rediscovered the technique in 1951, calling such diagrams "shuttles" (Gardner 1982, 60–79). Wittgenstein hoped that the *ab*-notation would offer a notation which represents all and only logical equivalents in one and the same way. In this way, Wittgenstein endeavored to use his *ab*-notation to obviate a *theory* of deduction. A genuine theory of deduction would require that logical concepts have a genuine content—as if logic were itself a science. In Wittgenstein's view, logical notions are to be shown by structured variables; logic has no content. Hence deduction must be supplanted by a notation in which the status of a formula as belonging to logic is immediately given in its syntactic representation.

The *ab*-notation offers a decision procedure for propositional tautologies. Wittgenstein was after much more than just this, however. Consider the following letter to Russell from Norway. Wittgenstein speaks as if he has found a way to extend the *ab*-notation to quantification theory. He writes (NB, 96):

> The application of the *ab*-notation to apparent variable propositions becomes clear if we consider that, for instance, the proposition "for all x, φx" is to be true when φx is true for all x's and false when φx is false for some x's. We see that *some* and *all* occur simultaneously in the proper apparent variable notation. The notation is:
>
> for $(x)\varphi x : a-(x)-a\varphi xb-(\exists x)-b$ and
> for $(\exists x)\varphi x : a-(\exists x)-a\varphi xb-(x)-b$
>
> Old definitions now become tautologous.

One can only guess how this proposal was supposed to proceed. But Wittgenstein's intent is crystal clear. He hopes to convince Russell that the *ab*-notation (or something like it) can, in principle, be found for quantification theory with identity. He writes (NB, 126):

> Of course the rule I have given applies first of all only for what you call elementary propositions. But it is easy to see that it must also apply to all others. For consider two Pps in the theory of apparent variables *9.1 and *9.11. Put then instead of φx, $(\exists y).\varphi y.\ y = x$ and it becomes obvious that the special cases of these two Pps like those of all the previous ones become tautologous if you apply the *ab*-Notation.

The *ab-Notation* for Identity is not yet clear enough to show this clearly but it is obvious that such a Notation can be made up. I can sum up by saying that a logical proposition is one the special cases of which are either tautologous—and then the proposition is true—or self-contradictory (as I shall call it) and then it is false. And the *ab-Notation* simply shows directly which of these two it is (if any).

The reference to *Principia*'s *9 is important. Wittgenstein claims that if one examines *9.1 and *9.11 (the two axioms for quantification theory in *9 of *Principia*) one can see that it is "obvious" that the logical truths of quantification theory are tautologies.

What explains Russell's complacency and Wittgenstein's hubris in proclaiming that the logical truths of quantification theory are "tautologies"? The answer lies in the fact that *Principia*'s *9 succeeds in revealing that every logical truth of quantification theory can be reached by starting from some propositional tautology, generalizing (existentially or universally) and distributing the quantifiers by means of the definitions of *9 (Landini 2000). This does not provide a decision procedure because we cannot know, for a given formula, what tautology is the starting point of its would-be derivation. But it does explain why Wittgenstein and later Ramsey came later to regard *all* the fundamental principles of *Principia*, excepting its comprehension axiom of reducibility, as "tautologies" (Ramsey 1931, 11).

Of course, the success of *9 does not reveal that there is a decision procedure for the logical truths of quantification theory. Wittgenstein's view that quantification theory is decidable was a brash guess due to his being caught up in a philosophical theory according to which logic has no content. Wittgenstein cannot be expected to have known better in 1913. The result that quantification theory is undecidable awaited Church's result of 1936. Hopeful and unaware, Wittgenstein forged ahead, focusing his efforts on identity. He writes (NB, 126):

> I can't myself say quite clearly yet what tautologies are, but I'll try to give a rough account. It is the peculiar (and most important) characteristic of non-logical propositions, that their truth cannot be seen in the propositional sign itself....But the propositions of logic—and they alone—have the property of expressing their truth or falsehood in the very sign itself. I haven't yet succeeded in getting a notation for identity which satisfies this condition; but I *don't doubt* that such a notation must be discoverable. For compounded propositions (elementary propositions) the *ab*-Notation is adequate.

Wittgenstein is after a notation which would display all logical equivalents of quantification theory with identity in one and the same way—a way in which their status as tautologies is shown in the notation itself. This was to form a decision procedure for logical truth. Once a formula is expressed in the notation, one could discern from the notation itself whether or not it has the status of a logical truth.

The *ab*-notation is presented in the *Tractatus* as a *t–f* notation. This gives way to a notation that represents propositional formulas in terms of their truth-table. Wittgenstein certainly did not invent truth-tables. There are clear examples in Huntington's independence proofs of 1905 which were known to Russell (and cited in *Principia*'s 1910 first edition), and a truth-table (with 0 and 1 in place of *t* and *f*) occurs in Müller's 1909 *Abriss* of Schröder's *Algebra of Logic*. Adopting a fixed order of rows of a truth-table, Wittgenstein pictures the truth-conditions of a propositional formula involving $p_1,...,p_n$ as

$$(\gamma_1,...,\gamma_{2^n})(p_1,...,p_n).$$

Obviously, all and only logical equivalents have the name expression and tautologies have each of $\gamma_1,..., \gamma_{2^n}$ filled by a *t*. This technique parallels Venn's propositional diagrams which picture propositional formulas by shading areas to represent truth-conditions. A Venn diagram pictures the truth-conditions of $p \supset q$, and all logical equivalents such as $\sim q \supset \sim p, \sim p \vee q .\&. r \supset r$, and so on (see Figure 1). Tautologies have no areas shaded. As we noted, Wittgenstein was on a quest to find a notation in which all and only logical equivalents of quantification theory with identity have one and the same representation. This led him to the Tractarian N-operator.

The N-operator remained mystifying for many years and was often wrongly confused with Sheffer's dagger (the 'nor' logical connective $p \downarrow q$). Interestingly, the techniques of the N-operator were independently rediscovered by George Spencer Brown and set out in his book *Laws of Form* (1970). The N-operator succeeds at the propositional level in *picturing* all and only logical equivalents in one and the same way and hopes to extend this idea to quantification theory with identity. There are rules implicit in the *Tractatus* for calculating by means of the N-operation whether a given expression is a tautology. All and only tautologies have their truth conditions pictured in N-notation by the form $NN(...Np...p...)$. The rules are these:

(1) $N(...\xi_i,...,\xi_j...) = N(...\xi_j,...,\xi_i...).$
(2) $N(...\xi,...,\xi...) = N(...\xi...).$
(3) $N(...NN(\xi_1,...,\xi_n)...) = N(...\xi_1,...,\xi_n...).$
(4) $N(...N(...\xi,...,N\xi,...)...) = N(...).$
(5) $NN(\gamma, N(\xi_1,...,\xi_n)) = N(N(\gamma, N\xi_1),...,N(\gamma, N\xi_n)).$

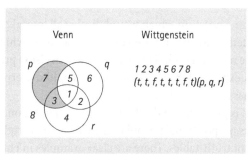

FIGURE 1.

The addition of an N to both sides of any among (2)–(5) is allowed as well. These rules assert the sameness of certain *practices* of operation. They are not, therefore, identity statements.

We can readily transform an expression from the dagger notation into Wittgenstein N-notation by relacing each tilde by N and replacing each dagger by N as well. The result, however, is not a formula, but a picture of truth-conditions (like a Venn diagram). To illustrate, consider p .⊃. q ⊃ p. In the notation of the Sheffer dagger, this is ~(~p ↓ ~(~q ↓ p)). In Wittgenstein's notation we have:

$$NN(Np, NN(Nq, p))$$

By simple rules of transformation, we get

$$NN(Np, Nq, p).$$

Thus Wittgenstein writes the transition as follows:

$$NN(Np, NN(Nq, p)) = NN(Np, Nq, p).$$

The tautologous nature of the formula is *shown* in the picture of its truth conditions. This is a central thesis of the *Tractatus*. Logic is not a body of truths about logical entities. There are no logical entities. Logic consists in a practice of calculating with the N-operation whether a symbolism expresses a tautology.

With respect to quantifier-free formulas, the N-operation notation forms no significant advance over the truth-tabular representation $(y_1,..., y_{2^n})(p_1, ..., p_n)$. But the truth-tabular representation cannot work in general for quantificational formulas. Changes of the number of entities in the range of the bound variables would alter the positions of the *t*'s and *f*'s in the truth-tabular form. Wittgenstein imagined the N-operator notation to be an advance over the truth-tabular representation. To express $(x)Fx$ in N-notation, we have:

$$N(NFx_1,...,NFx_n),$$

where the free variables $x_1,..., x_n$ are pair-wise exclusive. The idea is that n is used schematically and can therefore be any arbitrarily large (finite) number. To express $(\exists x)Fx$, note that over an n-element domain this is equivalent to $(x_1),..., (x_n)(Fx_1. v.,..., .v. Fx_n)$. Thus, in N-notation, and with $x_1,..., x_n$ pair-wise exclusive, this is:

$$NN(Fx_1,...,Fx_n).$$

Wittgenstein hoped that all logical equivalents of quantification theory have one and the same expression in N-notation. For example, $(x)(Fx \& Gx)$ would be expressed as

$$N(NFx_1, NGx_1,...,NFx_n, NGx_n).$$

The logically equivalent $(x)(Fx)$ & $(x)Gx$ would be expressed as:

$$N(NFx_1,\ldots,NFx_n, NGx_1,\ldots, NGx_n).$$

Given the rules of permutation governing N, these are taken to be the same. The expression $(x)Fx \vee (\exists x)\neg Fx$ is expressed in N-notation as:

$$NN(N(NFx_1,\ldots,NFx_n), NN(NFx_1,\ldots,NFx_n)).$$

In N-notation this has a tautologous form and so is immediately recognizable as a truth of logic.

By using n schematically Wittgenstein hoped to recover quantification theory with identity in N-notation.[16]

According to the *Tractatus*, logic consists in the calculation by the N-operation of whether a given formula is a tautology. The decidability of logic was embraced by Wittgenstein because of his commitment to the doctrine of showing. If there were a substantive *theory* of logic, logic would have a subject matter and be about a realm of purely logical objects. In Wittgenstein's view, logic is not a theory of special logical objects. Logic is not known. It is *shown* by the impossibility of illogical thought—*shown* in the practice of calculating with the N-operator. The N-operator fails because its expressive adequacy entails that quantification theory is decidable. The expression of a formula in N-notation would *show* (by picturing truth-conditions) whether or not it is a tautology. The result is a significant blow to the Tractarian doctrine of showing.

Tractarian Logicism

As we have seen, Wittgenstein held that logic consists in a practice of calculating with respect to the N-operation. Arithmetic is said to consist in a practice of calculation on operations too. But these calculations involve *equations*, not tautologies. Russell had a tendency to ignore Wittgenstein's view that arithmetic involves equations and seems to consider the difference as trifling. It is not mentioned in Russell's *Introduction to Mathematical Philosophy* (1919). In the first printing of the second edition of *The Principles of Mathematics* (1937) Russell continued to ignore it. He admitted that *Principia*'s multiplicative axiom and axiom of infinity are fully general and explained that in the context of ramified type structure, he must abandon his former view that truth and full generality (in the calculus for pure logic) are sufficient for logical truth. What then, he wonders, is sufficient for a statement to belong to logic (mathematics)? Russell answers as follows: "In order that a proposition may belong to mathematics, it

---

[16] For a detailed account of the N-operator, see Landini 2007.

must have a further property: according to Wittgenstein it must be 'tautological', and according to Carnap it must be 'analytic'" (Russell 1937, ix). Wittgenstein soon became vociferous in his objection to Russell's repeated mischaracterization. When G. H. Hardy read a paper at the Moral Sciences Club in Cambridge in 1940, he attributed to Wittgenstein the view that mathematics consists of tautologies. Reportedly, Wittgenstein attended and denied having ever held the view, pointing to himself and saying in an incredulous tone of voice: "Who, I?" (Wolfe 1967, 82). At last, in a letter to Stanley Unwin of 17 July 1947, Russell instructed that the word "some" replace "Wittgenstein" in the passage, altering subsequent printings of the second edition of *Principles* (Blackwell 1981, fn 3, p. 27).

Why did Wittgenstein reject the view that arithmetic consists of tautologies? The answer is not that Wittgenstein rejected logicism. Wittgenstein accepted logicism. The appearance that he rejected it is due largely to a misunderstanding of logicism itself. Fregean logicism is the thesis that all mathematical truths except geometry are among the truths of logic. Russellian logicism is the broader thesis that all mathematical truths are among the truths of logic. Observe that these characterizations, on behalf of Frege and Russell, omit any mention of a "reduction" in the sense of a derivation of arithmetic (or mathematics) from a consistent axiomatization of logic. Unbeknown to Frege and Russell, logical truths of higher-order logic cannot be consistently axiomatized. A "reduction" in the sense of a derivation of even the logical truths is not possible. But this is no ground for rejecting logicism (though it might lend itself to a rejection of the thesis that logicism provides an *epistemic* foundation for knowledge of arithmetic or mathematics). Logicism is not committed to the axiomatization of logic. Neither is it committed to classes or other logical *objects*—though Frege certainly was committed to logical objects in both his *Grundlagen* (1884) and *Grundgesetze* (1893). Wittgenstein's doctrine of showing rejects logical objects, and this certainly distances him from Frege's logicism. The doctrine of showing also distances him from the constructions of Russell's logicism. But this is *not* because Russell's logicism takes logic to be a theory of logical objects such as classes, numbers, propositions, propositional functions, etc. Russell's work on the philosophy of mathematics from 1901 to 1940 is not committed to such objects. We must not lose sight of the fact that *Principia* is *very* eliminativistic in its approach to the foundations of mathematics. *Principia* is a "no comprehension of classes," "no-numbers," "no-propositions" and "no-comprehension of attributes" theory of structure.

Why did Wittgenstein reject Russell's logical reconstruction of arithmetic? The answer is hinted at in the following rather cryptic passage (*Tractatus* 6.031):

> The theory of classes is completely superfluous in mathematics. This is connected with the fact that the generality required in mathematics is not accidental generality.

This passage is exceedingly odd if intended as criticizing *Principia* for embracing a theory of classes. Russell toiled for many years to make classes superfluous in mathematics. *Principia emulates* a theory of classes without the ontology of classes by employing structured variables whose ranges are "internally limited" by their significance conditions.

Surely Wittgenstein meant something new in emphasizing Russell's *own thesis* that "classes are superfluous in mathematics."[17] What Wittgenstein meant is this: Don't emulate classes. Russell's attempt to emulate classes in *Principia* creates an impasse—the comprehension axioms of Reducibility. The logical validity of this axiom is questionable because the conception of logic in *Principia* espouses can only validate comprehension principles weaker than Reducibility. But nothing weaker seems able to emulate classes in a way that would recover arithmetic (and mathematics). Wittgenstein concluded that a radically new and even more extremely eliminativistic method must be found to recover arithmetic.

In *Principia*, certain basic arithmetic results (such as $2 \neq 3$) are consequents of a conditional with an antecedent clause saying that no natural number numbers the property of self-identity. The problem is independent of the structure of ramification and occurs in simple Russellian type-theory even if one assumes an ontology of attributes that are intentional (not extensional) entities. *Principia* called this antecedent clause an "axiom of infinity." Some early passages of Wittgenstein's *Notes on Logic* (and the *Tractatus* itself on exclusive quantifiers) suggest that at one time Wittgenstein entertained a construction according to which numbers are built into early Fregean type-structured variables in a way that would emulate classes and construe arithmetic truths as tautologies. Exclusive quantifiers, together with this approach to number, seems at first to be an attractive way to avoid the problem that an infinity of objects is needed in *Principia* to recover ordinary results about natural numbers. Wittgenstein's exclusive quantifiers builds infinity into the use of variables. Each distinct variable has a distinct referent. In an early entry from October 1914 in his *Notebooks*, Wittgenstein wrote (NB, 10):

> The question about the possibility of existence propositions does not come in the middle but at the very first beginning of logic.
> All the problems that go with the Axiom of Infinity have already to be solved in the proposition '$(\exists x)(x = x)$'.

Wittgenstein may well have originally thought that his treatment of identity "solves" the problem of the infinity axiom in *Principia* by building infinity into logical scaffolding.

To be sure, both Wittgenstein and Russell (at the time of *Principia*) considered it to be contingent whether there are finitely or infinitely ($\aleph_0$) many *individuals*.[18] Russell's anecdote on the matter is illuminating (Russell 1959, 116):

> Wittgenstein will not permit any statement about all the things in the world. In *Principia Mathematica*, the totality of things is defined as the class of all those x's which are such that $x = x$, and we can assign a number to this class just as to any other class, although of course we do not know what is the right number to assign. Wittgenstein will not admit this. He says that such a proposition as 'there are more than three things in the world' is meaningless. When I was discussing the *Tractatus* with him at The Hague in 1919, I had before me a sheet of white paper and I made on

---

[17] Russell said this several times in his quest for the solution of the paradoxes plaguing logicism.

[18] Indeed, by the time of the Logical Atomism Lectures, Russell had changed his mind and come to hold that universals are not logical entities but causal structures posited as a part of empirical science.

it three blobs of ink. I besought him to admit that, since there were these three blobs, there must be at least three things in the world; but he refused, resolutely. He would admit that there were three blobs on the page, because that was a finite assertion, but he would not admit that anything at all could be said about the world as a whole. This was connected with his mysticism, but was justified by his refusal to admit identity.

Wittgenstein holds that a statement of the number of self-identicals is a pseudo-proposition since "identity" is a pseudo-predicate. Nonetheless, like the *Notebooks*, the *Tractatus* proclaims that the "solution" of the problem of *Principia*'s axiom of infinity is found in the proper theory of identity. We find:

> And now we see that in a correct conceptual notation pseudo-propositions like '$a = a$,' '$a = b \ \& \ b = c \ . \supset. \ a = c$,' '$(x)(x = x)$,' '$(\exists x)(x = a)$,' etc. cannot even be written down. (TLP 5.534)
> This also disposes of all the problems that were connected with such pseudo-propositions. The solution of all the problems that Russell's 'axiom of infinity' brings with it can be given at this point. What the axiom of infinity is intended to say would express itself in language through the existence of infinitely many names with different meanings. (TLP 5.535)

Infinity is *shown* by the distinct free variables of logic. (The value of each free variable in a given formula must exclude the value of every distinct free variable in the formula.)

Identity is a logical notion and as such Wittgenstein demands that it be built into the use of structured variables. This is done by means of exclusive quantifiers and Wittgenstein regarded this construction as a most important achievement of the *Tractatus*. Wittgenstein soon came to see, however, that the approach fails to recover arithmetic. The trouble is that when exclusive quantifiers are paired with the doctrine that all *genuine* properties and relations (i.e., "material" properties and relations) are logically independent from one another, empirical *applications* of the Frege/Russell notion of one–one correspondence (at the heart of their conceptions of *number* and *counting*) collapse. This interpretation is corroborated by Ambrose's lecture notes. We find (AWL, 117):

> The criterion for sameness of number, namely that the classes concerned are 1–1 correlated, is, however, peculiar. For no correlation seems to be made. Russell had a way of getting around this difficulty. No correlation need actually be made, since two things are always correlated with two others by identity. For there are two functions, the one satisfied by only a, b and the other only by c, d, namely $x = a . v . x = b$ and $y = c . v . y = d$. ... We can then construct a function satisfied only by the pairs ac and bd, that is, a function correlating one term of one group with one term of the other, namely, $x = a . y = c . v . x = b . y = d$, or the function $x = a . v . y = d : x = b . v . y = c$. These correlate a with c and b with d by mere identity when there is no correlation by strings or other material correlation. But if "=" makes no sense, then it is no correlation.[19]

---

[19] This matter concerned Wittgenstein as well. Hints can be found in his 1914 notes dictated to Moore from Norway. See NB, 117.

Wittgenstein objects to the use of identity in the notion of one–one correspondence. His objection does not arise with the uses of the identity sign in the normal laws of arithmetic (Landini 2007). These uses vanish in the logical reconstructions of *Principia*. No illicit uses of the identity sign arise in pure arithmetic. But illicit uses do arise in the application of arithmetic. Wittgenstein's thesis of the logical independence of facts, however, entails that there might well be cases where distinct entities share all properties and relations. Hence, if F and G are material properties and relations, there may be no material relation R that correlates F's one–one with G's. When paired with the elimination of identity in terms of exclusive quantifiers, the Frege/Russell approach to number undermines the *application* of arithmetic.

This is a serious *impasse*. Wittgenstein felt its sting. Writing to Russell from Norway in 1913, he says that "identity is the very Devil and *immensely important*; very much more so than I thought…I have all sorts of ideas for a solution of the problem but could not yet arrive at anything definite. However, I don't lose courage and go on thinking" (NB, 123). Wittgenstein felt that he had to reject an analysis of arithmetic that makes it consist of tautologies. But we must not conclude from this that he rejected logicism. Quite the contrary, Wittgenstein came to hold a more radically eliminativistic form of logicism than in *Principia*.

Wittgenstein's view of arithmetic tracks his view of logic. Genuine comprehension principles for logical *objects* are vehemently rejected. There are no logical objects. Wittgenstein thought quantification "theory" is a legitimate part of logic because he thought that Russell had demonstrated in *Principia*'s section *9 that its theorems are generalized tautologies. Wittgenstein can even allow the weak comprehension principles of a predicative "type-theory" as long as they are interpreted nominalistically (as Russell had in *Principia*). By means of a nominalistic semantics, any instance of a predicative comprehension principle can be construed by Wittgenstein as a tautology. Instances of the comprehension principle (axiom) Reducibility, on the other hand, must be rejected. They certainly are not generalized tautologies. In Wittgenstein's view, neither logic nor mathematics is a genuine science of objects. Logic has no subject matter that is a proper object of knowledge. The *Tractatus* attempts to offer a similar approach to arithmetic. Arithmetic is not a body of truths about arithmetic objects. There are no numbers. Arithmetic is not known as a body of truths; it is *shown* in the practice of calculating using operations with exponents.

According to the *Tractatus*, arithmetic consists in a *practice of calculating* with respect to operations transforming numeric expressions. For example, consider the following operation:

$$\Omega`m = m + /$$

The operation Ω transforms the sign m into the sign $m +/$. Wittgenstein uses numeral exponents to mark repeated applications of the operation. At *Tractatus* 6.01 and 6.02 we find:

$$\Omega^{0`}x = x$$

$$\Omega^{v+/\,\prime}x = \Omega^{\prime}\Omega^{v\prime}x$$

$$(\Omega^{v\mathbf{X}u})^{\prime}x = (\Omega^{v})^{u\,\prime}x$$

Now adopt the numerals

$$1 = 0+/\text{Def.},$$

$$2 = (0+/)+/\text{Def.},$$

$$3 = ((0+/)+/)+/\text{Def.}$$

Wittgenstein can then put:

$$\Omega^{2\,\prime}0 = \Omega^{\prime}\Omega^{\prime}\Omega^{0\,\prime}0$$
$$= 0+/+/$$

$$(\Omega^{2\mathbf{X}2})^{\prime}0 = (\Omega^{2})^{2\,\prime}0$$
$$= (\Omega^{2})^{0+/+/\,\prime}0$$
$$= \Omega^{2\,\prime}\Omega^{2\,\prime}\Omega^{0\,\prime}0$$
$$= \Omega^{\prime}\Omega^{\prime}\Omega^{\prime}\Omega^{\prime}\Omega^{0\,\prime}0$$
$$= 0+/+/+/+/$$
$$= (\Omega^{4})^{\,\prime}0$$

In this way, Wittgenstein proclaims that "a number is an exponent of an operation." More exactly, in arithmetic, one calculates equational identities by means of repeated applications of a given operation—with the repetitions consecutively discharged by a counter.

The notion of repetition does not depend on an ontology of numbers and truths about such entities. This is rigorously demonstrated in *Principia* itself and Wittgenstein could hardly have failed to notice. In Wittgenstein's view, however, *Principia* errs in attempting to transform arithmetic expressions into expressions of the language of logic. The right view, according to the *Tractatus*, is that the foundation of both logic and arithmetic is the practice of calculation with operators. Logic involves calculation of whether a formula is a tautology by means of identifications made by the rules of the N-operator. Arithmetic involves calculating identities of equations generated by repeated applications of operations. Both arithmetic and logic find their foundation in the *practice* of calculating with respect to operations on *signs*. Wittgenstein writes in *Tractatus* (TLP 6.22):

> The logic of the world, which is shown in tautologies by the propositions of logic, is shown in equations by mathematics.

"Mathematics," he continued, "is a method of logic" (TLP 6.234). The logical method is that of the *calculation* of the internal properties of operations that are *shown* in their signs. Such calculations occur with the N-operator of logic and with the numeral operators of arithmetic. Waismann reports that Wittgenstein gave the following explanation of what it is that mathematics and logic have in common (WVC, 218):

What is right about Russell's idea is that in mathematics as well as in logic, we are dealing with *systems*. Both systems are due to operations. What is wrong about it is the attempt at construing mathematics as a part of logic. The true analogy between mathematics and logic is completely different. In mathematics, too, there is an operation that corresponds to the operation which generates a new sense from the sense of a given proposition, namely the operation which generates a new number from given numbers. That is, *a number corresponds to a truth-function*. Logical operations are performed with propositions, arithmetical ones with numbers. The result of a logical operation is a proposition, the result of an arithmetical one is a *number*.

Wittgenstein's logicism does not "reduce" arithmetic to logic. But on Wittgenstein's view, both logic and arithmetic form practices of calculation involving operations (with numeric powers) that generate transitions among signs (not logical or arithmetic objects).

Wittgenstein took his elimination of identity to be a central achievement of the *Tractatus*, and it was precisely because of the elimination of identity that he maintained that logical analysis *must* re-conceptualize arithmetic truths in terms of equations rather than tautologies. The rejection of identity would thoroughly alter the constructions of the first edition of *Principia*. In a letter of 1923 to his mother, Ramsey wrote that he had reported his knowledge of Russell's work notes for the second edition of *Principia* to Wittgenstein. He characterized Wittgenstein's response vividly: "He [Wittgenstein] is, I can see, a little annoyed that Russell is doing a new edit[ion] of *Principia* because he thought he had shown Russell that it was so wrong that a new edition would be futile. It must be done altogether afresh" (Ramsey 1973, 78). Russell planned to discuss Wittgenstein's *Tractarian* ideas in the 1925 second edition, evaluating their strengths and weaknesses. But he certainly had no intention to alter the work to accommodate the Tractarian rejection of identity (and restructure arithmetic in terms of equations). Wittgenstein was markedly disappointed. Ramsey corroborates this in the following letter to Wittgenstein (Ramsey 1973, 84):

> I went to see Russell a few weeks ago, and am reading the manuscript of the new stuff he is putting in to the *Principia*. You are right that it is of no importance; all that it really *amounts to is a clever proof of mathematical induction without using the axiom of reducibility*. There are no fundamental changes; identity is just as it used to be.

In the second edition, Russell concludes that Wittgenstein's ideas lead to a dead end. Analysis is lost. Ramsey was more sanguine. His review of *Principia*'s second edition offers hope of finding a different interpretation and development of the oracular Tractarian ideas (Ramsey 1925).

Russell was enticed by Wittgenstein's views on identity but soon came to the conclusion that it made mathematical logic impossible and, in fact, that Wittgenstein's criticisms of *Principia*'s use of identity are invalid.[20] Though Ramsey's initial letters and his

---

[20] See Russell 1959, 115. Russell seems to endorse Wittgenstein against identity in *Our Knowledge of the External World* (1969, 212). A footnote to "unpublished work of Wittgenstein" in the first edition was altered in subsequent editions to reference the *Tractatus*.

review of the second edition are in sympathy with Wittgenstein on identity, it wasn't long until he also had a change of heart. Ramsey's diary entry of February 1924 reports that in his meeting with Russell to discuss the second edition, Russell was "rather good against W's [Wittgenstein's] identity . . ." Ramsey died tragically in 1930 and so remained unaware that logic is not decidable. He did not realize the failure of Wittgenstein's N-operator. But soon after his initial enthusiasm for Wittgenstein's exclusive quantifiers, he came to see that Wittgenstein's account of arithmetic in terms of equations is inadequate. "I have spent a lot of time developing such a theory," he wrote, "and found that it was faced with what seemed to me to be insuperable difficulties" (Ramsey 1931, 17). Ramsey rightly concluded that Wittgenstein's strictures against the identity sign were too austere to recover even elementary arithmetic. Ramsey offers his "propositional functions in extension" as a compromise. "By using these variables [functions in extension]," he wrote, "we obtain the system of *Principia Mathematica*, simplified by the omission of the Axiom of Reducibility, and a few corresponding alterations. Formally it is almost unaltered; but its meaning has been considerably changed" (Ramsey 1931, 56). Ramsey rejects Wittgenstein's demand that arithmetic consist of equations, not tautologies. The notations of *Principia* remain unaltered, though the semantics has changed their meanings. *Principia* wouldn't have to be "done afresh" after all.

It is well known that Ramsey was enamored of Wittgenstein's Tractarian ideas. It is less well reported that it wasn't long until he abandoned them. Ramsey came to reject Wittgenstein's most prized thesis concerning identity and its corollary that arithmetic (and pure mathematics) consists of equations, and worked instead toward a demonstration that it consists of tautologies. Russell's second edition and Ramsey's subsequent work fail to vindicate Wittgenstein's ideas. In light of their early support, how disappointing it must have been for Wittgenstein to find both Russell and Ramsey abandoning him (Ramsey 1991).

RUSSELL AND WITTGENSTEIN AS ALLIES

Research on Russell's voluminous work notes has shed a flood of new light on his views. Without carefully considering this evidence, one cannot be in a position to assess Wittgenstein's points of agreement or disagreement with Russell. The new evidence shows that Russell and Wittgenstein were allies in a research program in philosophy. Wittgenstein's doctrine of showing is but a radical extension of the foundational ideas of Russell's research program of logical atomism. The research program seeks eliminativistic reconstructions in its efforts to dissolve philosophical conundrums.

The solutions of the paradoxes and puzzles of the philosophy of mathematics, physics, and mind are to be found in eliminativistic reconstruction. The paradoxes and conundrums of philosophy are not analogous to the Barber—the paradox of a person of a town who shaves all and only those of the town who do not shave themselves. The solution of the Barber is simple—there is no such barber. Metaphysical problems arise because ordinary (and quasi-scientific) notions such as "space," "time," "matter," "motion," "limit," "continuity," "change," and the like, are hybrid notions whose logico-semantic components have not been separated from their empirical/physical components. Logical atomism aims at a separation of these components, accomplished by means of a *logical* analysis running side by side with advancements and empirical discoveries in mathematical and empirical sciences. In the process, a new, more exacting account of the world emerges. Abandoning the ontological speculations of philosophers working in darkness, the new theory offers a re-conceptualization of the issues involved and a solution of philosophical problems.

Consider the sentence: (P) "The temperature of x is 98 degrees and rising." We all know what this means—in some sense of "knowing meaning." But we may well be equally unclear as to what ontology its truth commits us. The naïve philosopher might conclude that numbers can rise, that there are quantitative properties such as '98 degrees of temperature.' Logical atomism enjoins philosophers to sort out the interplay of physical, logical, and mathematical notions involved. Of course, ordinary acts of communication using expressions of temperature can be perfectly successful and blissfully independent of ontological concern. It only is the metaphysician who does philosophical ontology and (unscrupulously in the present case) generates entities which are temperatures, rising numbers, quantitative properties, and the like. Logical analysis asks "What is temperature in the physical sense, and how are numeric measures to be applied to it?" Logical analysis certainly does not neglect facts about communication in ordinary language. But it is interested in getting the ontology right. Once the proper "logical form" is given—i.e., once we write the technically accurate sentence that makes perspicuous the interplay of operational definitions which link physical and mathematical notions—the inclination our naïve philosopher may have toward the adoption of an ontology of temperatures, rising numbers, or quantitative properties is dismantled.

The research tradition of logical atomism was inaugurated by the success Russell felt that mathematicians and scientists of a philosophical orientation had in dissolving the metaphysical muddles (produced by Hegel, Kant, and others) that had engulfed geometry and notions such as *infinity, continuity, limits*, and the like in the calculus. Russell and his apprentice Wittgenstein are working within this research tradition. Indeed, the criticism in the *Tractatus* (TLP 6.36111) of Kant's argument from incongruent counterparts—i.e., Kant's argument that Euclidean space is necessary because motion and superposition cannot make a left hand congruent with a right hand—is simply a paraphrase of the logical analysis it receives in Russell's *Principles of Mathematics* (see Russell 1903, 417ff.). The ordinary notion of "congruence" was informed by empirical sensory experience and certainly connoted the motion of figures in space and superposition, but its metrical reconstruction in analytic geometry purges it of all such connections. A metaphysician adhering to the thesis that triangles are special sorts of non-physical *objects* may well develop the intuition that the Pythagorean theorem is a necessary truth of right triangles. Similarly, his synthetic experiences of physical objects colors his belief that it is a necessary truth of these abstract *objects* he calls triangles that the sum of their internal angles equals the sum of two right angles. If an account is offered that professes to capture geometry, such a metaphysician will evaluate it by its ability to capture the properties of triangles he takes to be necessary. If it is proposed that his cherished truths about triangles are consequents of a conditional whose antecedent is the Parallel Postulate, which may well *not* be necessary, this metaphysician will scoff. The failure of the theory to produce the essential truth of triangles demonstrates to the satisfaction of this metaphysician that the new theory of geometry is false. Contrast the situation with one who accepts the new analytic geometry, in which triangles are relations on ordered pairs of real numbers. There are no *objects* which are triangles. It is this theory of relations that now drives intuitions as to what is or is not necessary in geometry. The failure of analytic geometry to capture the metaphysician's necessities is no basis for its rejection. Once geometry is reconstructed without the ontological objects of the metaphysician's reverie, arguments for necessities of Euclidean geometry (such as Kant's incongruent counterparts) are undermined.

Russell and Wittgenstein presented one and the same conception of philosophy as logical analysis. But differing conceptions of the nature of logic and how it is "known" generate different conceptions of what is to be analyzed and what is to be the primitive foundation from which analysis is to begin. What is analyzed? Which concepts are those whose structure is to be analyzed? Which analyses should be reductive identifications as opposed to eliminativistic reconstructions? Reductive identifications afford a preservation of truth of ordinary statements. Eliminations seem to make ordinary statements false (or meaningless). But this does not do justice to the differences. An eliminativistic analysis does not have to proclaim that ordinary language statements are false. Neither reductivists nor eliminativists need be construed as analyzing or preserving what ordinary people mean (or intend to mean) when they speak. In fact, both reductive and eliminativistic methodologies may embrace the thesis that ordinary language is perfectly right in itself since it is blithely free of *any* commitment to a philosophical ontology.

How, then, does one assess the success of a given eliminativistic or reductive analysis? If analysis is not endeavoring to recover the (or any of the) connotations of the ordinary language sentence, what is it recovering? Russell and Wittgenstein (TLP 6.375) shared a straightforward and bold answer: Analysis is warranted *wherever* there appear to be necessities that are not logical. Misunderstanding of the hybrid nature of notions such as "exists," "number," "class," "matter," "continuity," "space," "time," "motion," and the like gives rise to the philosophical postulation of metaphysical forms of necessity and essentialism that are not of a logical nature. Analysis and reconstruction aim at separating the logico-semantic components of these notions from the physical components. Once separated, non-logical necessities and essences vanish. The only necessity is logical necessity; and logical necessity is fundamentally a matter of form or ontological structure, not something grounded in the inner metaphysical essence of a special realm of objects.

Any purportedly necessary connection that is non-logical requires a logical analysis that separates the logico-semantic components of the concepts involved from the empirical (material) components. Wittgenstein criticized Russell for offering some constructions that fall short of the goal. Belief contexts, relations between universals, and all semantic contexts call for much deeper reconstructions than Russell had hitherto found.

Wittgenstein held that no genuinely atomic statement has a logical contrary. At the limit of analysis and reconstruction all facts are atomic ("elementary"), and all contexts are extensional. Wittgenstein suggests that even ordinary predicate expressions would disappear at the limit of philosophical reconstruction. At *Tractatus* (TLP 2.0272) we find him saying that an elementary state of affairs is a configuration of objects (Griffin 1964, 78). It is unclear to what extent Wittgenstein's passage alludes to Russell's four-dimensional theory of time according to which matter (continuants persisting in time) is reconstructed out of configurations of events. On such a view, exemplification of a physical property is itself a series of events in space-time. Whatever was Wittgenstein's conception of universals as properties of matter, it is clear that he regards the universals (material properties and relations) that inhere in atomic facts to be logically independent of one another. If there are universal words for material properties and relations, they must occur in predicate positions only. All material contexts are extensional. The exemplification of one universal never excludes the exemplification of any other. There are no non-logical necessary relations among material properties and relations. The appearance of such relationships raises the red flag; they require further analysis—the only necessity being logical necessity.

Wittgenstein inherited Russell's program of logical analysis and reconstruction and extended it broadly. In the *Tractatus* he maintained that *all and only* those concepts that have logical or semantic content must be analyzed. All and only logical and semantic components ("formal concepts") are to be built into structured variables. The material concepts that remain are part of empirical science. We have argued that this is the doctrine of showing and is also the *Grundgedanke* of the *Tractatus*. Understood in this way, *showing* is an extreme form of Russellian eliminativism. It proclaims that all (and only) logical and semantic notions ("formal notions") are pseudo-concepts that in an ideal language for empirical science are shown with structured variables. At the eliminativistic ideal there are no ontological predicates; ontology is scaffolding.

In Wittgenstein's view, logic (and knowledge of logic) is the shared scaffolding of the world and of thought. But this means that if we attempt to answer questions as to the nature of logic and our knowledge of logic we will travel in a loop. Knowledge of logic is presupposed in any such account. Russell's original logical atomism avoids the loop by accepting logic and knowledge of logic as a genuine science and exempting it from eliminativistic reconstruction. The *Tractatus* proclaims that logic is not a science, that it has no subject matter, and that there cannot be a genuine knowledge of logic. Wittgenstein unabashedly embraced the loop. The consequences are dramatic. At *Tractatus* (TLP 7) we find the now infamous last entry:

> *Wovon man nicht sprechen kann, darüber muß man schweigen.*[21]

Pure adherence to Wittgenstein's extension of Russell's research program of logical atomism requires that we be content with speaking in the new framework and otherwise be silent, letting the structured variables of its syntax do the work of *showing* logical

---

[21] "Whereof one cannot speak, thereof one must be silent."

and semantic relations. But this silence jeopardizes justification of the eliminativistic reconstructions themselves. This silence collapses the philosophy of logical atomism into the ineffable pronouncements of an oracle.

Russell's logical atomism began modestly. Russell did not extend his eliminativistic analyses to logic itself. But his resolve weakened over the years as his philosophy edged toward the naturalization of mind and knowledge. In *Philosophy* we find (Russell 1927, 86):

> To "understand" even the simplest formula in algebra, say $(x + y)^2 = x^2 + 2xy + y^2$, is to be able to react to two sets of symbols in virtue of the form which they express, and to perceive that the form is the same in both cases.... We may sum up this discussion by saying that mathematical inference consists in attaching the same reactions to two different groups of signs, whose meanings are fixed by convention in relation to their constituent parts, whereas induction consists, first in taking something as a sign of something else, and later, when we have learned to take A as a sign of B, in taking A also as a sign of C.... both kinds of inferences are concerned with the relation of a sign to what it signifies, and therefore come within the scope of the law of association.

This holds logic hostage to empirical psychology. In later years, Russell described his thoughts on the philosophy of logic and mathematics as a reluctant "retreat from Pythagoras" (Russell 1959, 208). Wittgenstein's *Tractatus* certainly did not intend to surrender logic to psychology, conventionalism, naturalism, or any empirical science. But his Tractarian metaphor of a ladder to be climbed and kicked away and his notion of an elucidation that is (literally) meaningless offers little help for the perplexed. Ramsey nicely summed up the situation: "But what we can't say we can't say, and we can't whistle it either" (Ramsey 1931a, 238). The Russell–Wittgenstein program of logical atomism is worth reviving. Its revival, however, requires that a concession be made to Pythagoras. The research program of logical atomism seeks ontologically eliminativistic re-conceptualizations and reconstructions that reveal that all necessity is logical necessity. As Russell put it: (Russell 1914, 42):

> every philosophical problem, when it is subjected to the necessary analysis and purification, is found either to be not really philosophical at all, or else to be, in the sense in which we are using the word, logical.

This manifesto, if you will, fits both Russell and Wittgenstein. But we now see that the program depends on the view that logic is a genuine science of structure and that knowledge of logic cannot be submitted to a philosophical analysis of *any* kind. Logic is the *essence* of philosophy and, therefore, must transcend it.

REFERENCES

AMBROSE, ALICE ed. (2001). *Wittgenstein's Lectures 1932–1935*. Amherst, NY: Prometheus Books.

BLACKWELL, KENNETH (1981). "The Early Wittgenstein and the Middle Russell," in Irving Block ed., *Perspectives on the Philosophy of Wittgenstein*. Cambridge, MA: MIT Press.

BROWN, GEORGE SPENCER (1970). *Laws of Form*. New York: The Julian Press.

DRURY, M. O'C. (1981). "Some Notes on Conversations with Wittgenstein" and "Conversations with Wittgenstein," in *Ludwig Wittgenstein: Personal Recollections*, ed. Rush Rhees. Totowa, NJ: Rowman and Littlefield.

FREGE, G. (1879) *Begriffsschrift*. Halle: L. Nebert.

—— (1884). *Grundlagen der Arithmetik*. Breslau: W. Koebner.

—— (1893). *Grundgesetze der Arithmetik*, vol. 1. Jena: Hermann Pohle.

GARDNER, MARTIN (1982). *Logic Machines and Diagrams*. Chicago: University of Chicago Press.

GRIFFIN, JAMES (1964). *Wittgenstein's Logical Atomism*. Seattle: University of Washington Press.

GRIFFIN, NICHOLAS (1992). *The Selected Letters of Bertrand Russell 1884–1913*. New York: Houghton Mifflin Co.

LANDINI, GREGORY (1998). *Russell's Hidden Substitutional Theory*. New York: Oxford University Press.

—— (2000). "Quantification Theory in *9 of *Principia Mathematica*," *History and Philosophy of Logic*, 21: 57–78.

—— (2004). "On 'Insolubilia' and Their Solution By Russell's Substitutional Theory," in Godehard Link ed., *One Hundred Years of Russell's Paradox*. Berlin: de Gruyter.

—— (2007). *Wittgenstein's Apprenticeship with Russell*. Cambridge: Cambridge University Press.

McGUINNESS, BRIAN (1988). *Wittgenstein: A Life*. Berkeley: University of California Press.

—— (2002). *Approaches to Wittgenstein*. London: Routledge.

MONK, RAY (1990). *Wittgenstein: The Duty of a Genius*. New York: The Free Press.

—— (1999). *Bertrand Russell: The Spirit of Solitude 1872–1921*. New York: The Free Press.

NICOD, JEAN (1917). "A Reduction in the Number of the Primitive Propositions of Logic," *Proceedings of the Cambridge Philosophical Society*, 19: 32–41. [The paper was read before the Society 30 October 1916.]

RAMSEY, FRANK (1925). "Review of the Second Edition of *Principia Mathematica*," *Nature*, 116: 127–8.

—— (1931). "The Foundations of Mathematics," in R. B. Braithwaite ed., *The Foundations of Mathematics and Other Essays by Frank Plumpton Ramsey*. New York: Harcourt, Brace and Co.

—— (1931a). "General Propositions and Causality," in R. B. Braithwaite ed., *The Foundations of Mathematics and Other Essays by Frank Plumpton Ramsey*. New York: Harcourt, Brace and Co.

—— (1973). "Letter to Wittgenstein of 20 September 1923," in G. H. von Wright ed., *Ludwig Wittgenstein: Letters to C. K. Ogden*. Oxford: Basil Blackwell.

—— (1991). *Notes on Philosophy, Probability and Mathematics*, ed. Maria Carla Galavotti. Naples: Bibliopolis.

RHEES, RUSH (1984). *Recollections of Wittgenstein*. Oxford: Oxford University Press.

RUSSELL, BERTRAND (1903). *Principles of Mathematics*, 1st edn. Cambridge: Cambridge University Press.

—— (1907). "Letter to Hawtrey of 1907." Bertrand Russell Archives, McMaster University, Hamilton, Ontario, Canada.

—— (1908). "Mathematical Logic as Based on the Theory of Types," *American Journal of Mathematics*, 30: 222–62.

—— (1914). *Our Knowledge of the External World*. London: Allen & Unwin.

—— (1919). *Introduction to Mathematical Philosophy*. London: Allen & Unwin.

—— (1927). *Philosophy*. New York: W. W. Norton & Co.

—— (1929). *Marriage and Morals*. London: Allen & Unwin.

—— (1937). *The Principles of Mathematics*, 2nd edn. New York: Norton & Norton.

—— (1959). *My Philosophical Development*. New York: Simon & Schuster.

—— (1968). *Autobiography*, Vol. II. Boston: Little, Brown and Co.

—— (1969). *Our Knowledge of the External World*. London: Allen & Unwin.

—— (1973). "On 'Insolubilia' and Their Solution by Symbolic Logic," in Douglas Lackey ed., *Essays in Analysis By Bertrand Russell*. London: Allen & Unwin. [Originally published as "Les Paradoxes de la Logique," *Revue de Métaphysique et de Morale*, 14 (1906): 627–50.]

SACKUR, JÉRÔME (2005). *Formes et faits*. Paris: Librairie Philospohique J. Vrin.

SHEFFER, H. (1913). "A Set of Five Independent Postulates for Boolean Algebras, with Application to Logical Constants," *Transactions of the American Mathematical Society*, 14: 481–8.

WAISMANN, FRIEDRICH (1979). *Wittgenstein and the Vienna Circle*, ed. Brian McGuinness, trans. Joachim Schute and Brian McGuinness. Oxford: Blackwell.

WEITZ, MORRIS (1944). "The Unity of Russell's Philosophy," in Paul Schilpp ed., *The Philosophy of Bertrand Russell*. Evanston, IL Northwestern University Press, 57–121.

WHITEHEAD, ALFRED and RUSSELL, BERTRAND (1925). *Principia Mathematica to *56*. Cambridge: Cambridge University Press. (Reprinted 1970.)

WITTGENSTEIN, LUDWIG. *Notebooks 1914–1916*, ed. G. H. von Wright and G. E. M. Anscombe. Chicago: University of Chicago Press.

—— (1961). *Tractatus Logico-Philosophicus*, trans. D. F. Pears and B. F. McGuinness. London: Routledge.

—— (1974). *Letters to Russell, Keynes and Moore*, ed. G. H. von Wright. Oxford: Basil Blackwell.

—— (1980). *Culture and Value*, ed. G. H. von Wright in collaboration with Heikki Nyman. Oxford: Blackwell.

WOLFE, MAYS (1967). "Recollections of Wittgenstein," in K. T. Fann ed., *Ludwig Wittgenstein: The Man and His Philosophy*. New Jersey: Humanities Press.

CHAPTER 3

··

ASSERTION, SAYING, AND PROPOSITIONAL COMPLEXITY IN WITTGENSTEIN'S *TRACTATUS*

··

COLIN JOHNSTON

WITTGENSTEIN responds in his *Notes on Logic* to a discussion of Russell's *Principles of Mathematics* concerning assertion. Where Russell writes:

> It is plain that, if I may be allowed to use the word assertion in a non-psychological sense, the proposition '*p* implies *q*' *asserts* an implication, though it does not *assert* *p* or *q*. The *p* and the *q* which enter into this proposition are not strictly the same as the *p* or the *q* which are separate propositions. (Russell 1992, 35)

Wittgenstein replies:

> Assertion is merely psychological. In *not-p*, *p* is exactly the same as if it stands alone; this point is absolutely fundamental. (NB, 95)

Wittgenstein's response is intriguing, not least because of the centrality to his *Tractatus* of the idea that a proposition says something. This chapter will examine that idea, distinguishing it from 'merely psychological' assertion, and explore in this context how we should understand the occurrence of a Tractarian proposition within another.

1.

··

In his 1903 *Principles of Mathematics* Russell makes a distinction between asserted and unasserted propositions. Whilst this distinction is not given a fully worked-out account, Russell sees it as a point of considerable theoretical importance. It is introduced in the context of a separation by Russell of *modus ponens* from the proposition that 'if p and q be propositions then p together with "p implies q" implies q' (Russell 1992, 35). An instance of inferring with *modus ponens* has the form 'p; p implies q; therefore q', and is distinct, Russell insists, from any proposition of the form '$(p$ and $(p$ implies $q))$ implies q'.[1] Spelling this distinction out, Russell writes that 'the notion of *therefore* ...is quite different from the notion of *implies*', and indeed that these different notions 'hold between different entities' (ibid., 35):

> When we say *therefore*, we state a relation which can only hold between asserted propositions, and which thus differs from implication. (Russell 1992, 35)

While the 'p', 'p implies q', and 'q' that figure in 'p; p implies q; therefore q' are asserted propositions, the 'p', 'p implies q', and 'q' that figure in '$(p$ and $(p$ implies $q))$ implies q' are unasserted propositions.

Over the course of introducing in this way the idea of asserted and unasserted propositions, Russell makes a number of further points. Most firmly, Russell insists that for a proposition to be asserted is not for it to be the object of an external act of assertion. On the contrary, 'assertion ... is, in some sense, contained in an asserted proposition. ... [A]ssertion is not a term to which p, when asserted, has an external relation' (Russell 1992, 504). This may sound a little odd; indeed, the idea that assertion is 'contained in' an asserted proposition sounds very much like the idea that an asserted proposition is a proposition that asserts something, that an assert*ed* proposition is an assert*ing* proposition. Russell, however, appears to endorse this move: the asserted proposition 'p', he implies, asserts that p:

> It is plain that, if I may be allowed to use the word assertion in a non-psychological sense, the proposition 'p implies q' *asserts* an implication, though it does not *assert* p or q. The p and the q which enter into this proposition are not strictly the same as the p or the q which are separate propositions. (Russell 1992, 35)

These two sentences offer important further insight into Russell's thinking. First, Russell is eager to emphasize here as elsewhere that 'the difference which [he] desires to express is genuinely logical' (Russell 1992, 35) as opposed to psychological. This is reasonable given on the one hand that mental acts of judgement are certainly not what he wants to discuss, and on the other that he takes the notion of assertion, connecting as it does with his notion of *therefore*, to be centrally involved in the notion of proof.[2] More, Russell appears to commit in the above passage to 'separate propositions', that is – it would seem – to propositions that are not a part of another proposition, being asserted propositions. This, together with the claim that 'p' is unasserted in 'p implies

---

[1] Russell refers here to Lewis Carroll's 'What the Tortoise Said to Achilles' (Carroll 1895), arguing that if *modus ponens* is not distinguished, it will be supposed that '$(p$ and $(p$ implies $q))$ implies q' is necessary for asserting 'q' on the basis of 'p' and 'p implies q', and then on reflection that '$(p$ and $(p$ implies $q)$ and $((p$ and $(p$ implies $q))$ implies $q))$ implies q' is also necessary for asserting 'q', and so on. One will 'be led into an endless regress of more and more complicated implications, without ever arriving at the assertion of q' (Russell 1992, 34).

[2] Russell writes that his principle of *modus ponens* 'is employed whenever a proposition is said to be *proved*' (Russell 1992, 34).

q', suggests also its converse, namely that a proposition which is a part of another proposition is unasserted. Thus 'p' is unasserted as it occurs in 'p or q' and 'not-p' just as it is in 'p implies q'. Finally, in reasoning from the fact that 'p implies q' does not assert that p to the claim that the 'p' that occurs in 'p implies q' is not asserted/asserting, Russell tacitly assumes that if the 'p' which enters into 'p implies q' were to assert that p, then so too would 'p implies q'. This is a substantial assumption, suggesting – for one thing – that Russell thinks of assertion as quite different from reference: it is normal to suppose with Frege that a referring expression may occur within another without the latter thereby referring to the referent of the former.

A further line in Russell's thinking about assertedness connects assertedness to truth, but this line leads immediately, as Russell recognizes, to 'grave difficulties' (Russell 1992, 35), and is in any case of no interest to Wittgenstein. We shall therefore restrict our attention to the above remarks. And idiosyncratic and inexplicit as they may be, it might be thought that Russell is picking up here on something we shall want to endorse. There is a sense of assertion such that whilst the first premise of the argument 'p; p implies q; therefore q' asserts that p, the 'p' of the second premise does not assert anything. More, it seems correct that assertion in this sense is quite unlike reference. We should, however, be careful in our endorsement. For Russellian propositions are not sentences: they are rather what sentences express.[3] And if in the argument 'p; p implies q; therefore q' the propositions 'p' and 'q' that are (expressed by) the first premise and conclusion are not strictly the same as the propositions 'p' and 'q' that appear in (what is expressed by) the second premise, then how is the proof to be valid? For the proof to be valid, the propositions 'p' and 'q' must surely be the same throughout. How, one might well wonder, does Russell's distinction of assertedness not in fact undermine *modus ponens*?

2.

Russell adds as a footnote to his discussion that Frege 'has a special symbol to denote assertion' (Russell 1992, 35). Frege's ideas came to Russell too late to influence his main text, but they do significantly inform Wittgenstein's thinking. Before turning to Wittgenstein, then, let's take a look also at Frege.

When introducing the formal script of his *Grundgesetze*, Frege writes:

> We have already said that nothing at all is asserted in a mere equation; '2+3 = 5' sim-
> ply designates a truth value, without saying which of the two it is. . . . We therefore
> need a special sign to be able to assert something as true. For this purpose I place
> before the name of the truth-value the sign '⊢', so that, for example, in
> ⊢ $2^2 = 4$
> it is asserted that the square of 2 is 4. (Frege 1893 §5)

---

[3] Russell talks of 'the sentence expressing the proposition' (Russell 1992, 42) and writes that '[a] proposition, unless it happens to be linguistic, does not itself contain words: it contains the entities indicated by words' (ibid., 47).

This sign '⊢' may be placed at the beginning of a formula only, never within a formula – '⊢ Δ implies ⊢ Γ' is not well formed.

More, the sign has a central role in Frege's conduct of proof. In particular, it is involved in Frege's principle of *modus ponens*:

From the sentences '⊢ Δ implies Γ' and '⊢ Δ' one can infer: '⊢ Γ'. (Frege 1893 §14)

As Russell's footnote suggests, this all looks very much like his own discussion in the *Principles*, with Frege's distinction in his script between '⊢ p' and 'p' corresponding to Russell's distinction between asserted and unasserted propositions. Frege goes beyond anything Russell says, however, when he explains his *Urteilsstrich* – the vertical component of his sign '⊢' – as 'conveying assertoric force' (PW, 195).[4] A short account of what Frege means by this will be useful.

Frege makes a distinction between assertoric force and assertoric form. Assertoric form is what conveys assertoric force, and is what is constituted in Frege's script by his sign '⊢'. '⊢ p' is a sentence of assertoric form; it is an assertoric sentence of Frege's script. Assertoric form conveys assertoric force in that a token sentence's being of assertoric form is *ceteris paribus* sufficient for its having assertoric force. (So Frege speaks of assertoric force as 'arising from' and 'lying in' assertoric form.) Assertoric form is not, however, sufficient *simpliciter* for assertoric force: a sentence of assertoric form may on occasion 'lose its assertoric force', as, for example, when spoken by an actor on a stage:

> [B]y *judgment* I understand the acknowledgement of the truth of a *thought*. The representation of a judgment in *Begriffsschrift* by means of the sign '⊢' I call a *Begriffsschrift proposition*. (Frege 1893 §5)

> We express acknowledgement of truth in the form of an assertoric sentence. We do not need the word 'true' for this. And even when we do use it the properly assertoric force does not lie in it, but in the assertoric sentence-form; and where this form loses its assertoric force, the word 'true' cannot put it back again. (Frege 1918, 330)

> The truth claim arises in each case from the form of the assertoric sentence, and when the latter lacks its usual force, e.g., in the mouth of an actor upon the stage, even the sentence 'The thought that 5 is a prime number is true' contains only a thought. (Frege 1892, 158)

But what is assertoric force, and why does Frege hold that an actor's utterances on the stage do not have it? Well, for a token sentence to have assertoric force is for its production to constitute a conventional act by its author of representing himself as judging. This is the linguistic act of *assertion*: in introducing his sign '⊢', Frege is laying down a convention for his script such that 'by writing "⊢ 2+3 = 5" we assert that 2+3 equals 5'

---

[4] That Frege's sign '⊢' is composite, and that it is only its vertical component that 'conveys assertoric force', will not be of concern in this chapter. (The principal role of the horizontal component as such is to prevent the appearance of assertoric force belonging to a token of what does not express a thought, e.g. the symbol '2^2'. '—p' expresses a thought even if 'p' does not.)

(Frege 1891, 142). This linguistic act of assertion, Frege further suggests, is to be contrasted with that of *asking*:

> An interrogative sentence and an assertoric one contain the same thought; but the assertoric sentence contains something else as well, namely assertion. The interrogative sentence contains something more too, namely a request. (Frege 1918, 329)

The Fregean (style) formula '⊢ The door is shut' would, it seems, be Frege's writing of the English sentence 'The door is shut.' as this contrasts with the sentences 'Is the door shut?' and 'Shut the door!'. As for the actor on the stage, the actor's utterances do not have assertoric or interrogative etc. force because the context of the stage is such that assertoric or interrogative form makes there only for the pretence of assertion or asking and not for assertion or asking proper:

> When we utter an assertoric sentence, we do not always utter it with assertoric force. An actor on the stage and poet reading from his works will both give frequent utterance to assertoric sentences, but the circumstances show that their utterances do not have assertoric force. They only act as if they were making assertions. (PW, 233)

It would take us too far astray significantly to expand upon or defend this interpretation of Fregean force. We can, however, quickly fit the account given back with certain key features seen above of Frege's use of his sign '⊢', and also provide a Fregean diagnosis of the difficulty arising for Russell at the end of the last section. First, here, we can see why the sign is to appear at the beginning of sentences only. The author of a sentence 'p implies q' asserts, if anything, only that p implies q. In particular, she asserts neither that p nor that q:

> Even if the whole compound [conditional] sentence is uttered with assertoric force, one is still asserting neither the truth of the thought in the antecedent nor that of the thought in the consequent. The recognition of truth extends rather over a thought that is expressed in the whole compound sentence. (PW, 185–6)

Secondly, sense is made of Frege's use of the sign in formulating *modus ponens*. The author of a proof does not merely put the proof's premises and conclusion forward for inspection: she asserts them. A rule of inference is thus a rule permitting transitions between sentences of assertoric form. And thirdly, the claim that assertoric form is sufficient by default for assertoric force provides for thinking of the sentence '⊢ $2+3 = 5$' as itself asserting, or 'containing the assertion', that 2+3 equals 5. So we find Frege's claim that 'in "⊢ $2^2 = 4$" it is asserted that the square of 2 is 4' (Frege 1893 §5).

Looking again at Russell's discussion, a Fregean response will begin with the thought that in distinguishing asserted and unasserted propositions in the way he did – that is, in the context of his distinction between *implies* and *therefore*, and with the idea that a proposition occurring within another is unasserted – Russell takes hold of the distinction found in Frege's script between the non-assertoric symbol 'p' contained in '⊢ p implies q' and the assertoric sentence '⊢ p'. This proposal is reinforced by the sense it makes of Russell's implicit assumption that if 'p' as it appears in 'p implies q' were to assert that p, then so too would 'p implies q'. What contains a sentence 'p' of assertoric form (an argument perhaps, or a paragraph) will thereby assert that p: an author of such a piece will *ceteris paribus* assert that p. From here, the Fregean suggestion will however be, Russell stumbles. Centrally, he *mislocates* force. To see how, note that the bearers of Fregean force are linguistic entities: they are sentences. Russellian propositions, on the other hand, are not sentences: they are, as we have seen, what sentences express. From Frege's perspective, then, Russell mistakenly supposes that the distinction he would have in view belongs not (only) to language but (also) to the world.[5] This mistake shows its head in Russell's awkward picture of a proposition's being at once asserting and asserted. For Frege the sentence asserts; what it expresses is asserted. And once the mistake is corrected – once it is recognized that assertion is a linguistic phenomenon belonging to sentences only and not to the thoughts/propositions they express – the apparent threat to the validity of *modus ponens* disappears. Whilst the sentence '⊢ p' is no part of the sentence '⊢ p implies q', and so whilst the thought that is asserted by '⊢ p' is not asserted by '⊢ p implies q', this same thought is nonetheless expressed by the symbol 'p' as it appears in both sentences.

3.

Wittgenstein was familiar with Russell's *Principles of Mathematics* from before his arrival in Cambridge, and in 1913 he reacts directly to Russell's discussion there of assertion. To Russell's claim that the logically unasserted 'p' which occurs in 'p implies q' is 'not strictly the same' as the logically asserted 'p' which is a 'separate proposition', Wittgenstein replies:

> Assertion is merely psychological. In *not-p, p* is exactly the same as if it stands alone; this point is absolutely fundamental. (NB, 95)

Following this up, we find:

> Judgment, question and command are all on the same level. What interests logic in them is only the unasserted proposition. (NB, 96)

Let's begin with the claim against Russell that assertion is merely psychological; the claim that 'in *not-p, p* is exactly the same as if it stands alone' will occupy us later on in the chapter. What phenomenon of assertion is Wittgenstein speaking of here? And what is it for something to be psychological as opposed to logical?

The key historical context for Wittgenstein's psychological–logical distinction is the fundamental principle of Frege's *Grundlagen* that there must be 'a sharp separation of the psychological from the logical' (Frege 1884, x). In short, this Fregean separation is of

---

[5] Russell is, in his own terms, too easily taking 'a grammatical distinction…to correspond to a genuine philosophical difference' (Russell 1992, 42).

what is mental and subjective on the one hand from what concerns truth on the other. As we have seen, Russell's *Principles of Mathematics* also uses the terms 'psychological' and 'logical' as a contrasting pair. The distinction here, at least in the context of assertion, appears to be between mental acts and states directed on propositions and what belongs to the propositions themselves. Russell's distinction looks similar, then, to Frege's. Wittgenstein's distinction, on the other hand, can seem importantly different. Whilst Wittgenstein's notion of logic is, as Frege's, tied to that of truth – the domain of logic is, roughly, those aspects of the world and our representation of it to which the concept of truth is bound – his use of the term 'psychological' is very different from Frege's. Most noticeably, as Wittgenstein uses the word it does not carry connotations of mentality or subjectivity. So for example Wittgenstein says in the *Notes on Logic* that 'the correlation of name and meaning' – the constitution of reference – is psychological (NB, 104), but he does not thereby mean that reference is subjective, or is constituted in a mental act.[6] Indeed, one has the strong impression that by 'psychological' Wittgenstein means nothing more than 'of no concern to logic'.

Moving on to the question of what phenomenon of assertion Wittgenstein takes Russell to have mischaracterized as logical, recall our Fregean diagnosis above of Russell's distinction as pertaining to force. Wittgenstein, it seems, takes this same view. What interests logic in judgement, question, and command, he says, is the unasserted proposition they have in common. The saying something that belongs to an assertoric sentence but not to an interrogative or imperatival sentence – the saying something that is the having of assertoric form (or perhaps assertoric force: Wittgenstein is not clear on the detail of the assertion he has in view) – is a psychological phenomenon of no interest to logic.[7] This position is neatly expressible if one adopts Ramsey's understanding of a Wittgensteinian proposition as 'a type whose instances consist of all propositional sign tokens which have in common, not a certain appearance, but a certain *sense*'

---

[6] On the contrary, the *Tractatus* makes clear that the correlation of name and meaning is a matter of public convention (see TLP 5.526). I agree here with Potter:

> It is clear that Wittgenstein did not, as Frege did, intend the word 'psychology' to demarcate the mental as a private sphere in contrast to the public sphere of language. For, as we have just noted, he was explicit that the correlation of name and meaning is psychological, and that is a matter of linguistic convention if anything is. For this reason we can, I think, agree with Wittgenstein's claim that 'assertion is psychological', by which he meant only that it is not a matter for logic, without disagreeing with the conclusion we reached earlier that assertion is not in Frege's sense psychological, since it is not private. (Potter 2009, 100)

Dummett, by contrast, misinterprets Wittgenstein's use of the word 'psychological', assimilating it to Frege's:

> Wittgenstein goes even further, and says that 'assertion is merely psychological'...This supposed 'psychological' kind of assertion which appears in Russell and Wittgenstein is a phantasm produced by the mistake of interpreting assertion as the manifestation of an internal mental attitude adopted towards the proposition. (Dummett 1981, 312)

[7] Wittgenstein is not here, I think, distinguishing judgement from assertion.

(Ramsey 1923, 469). Assertion, Wittgenstein's claim will be, is an achievement belonging to certain tokens of a proposition, but is not an achievement belonging to the proposition itself. Tokens of the sentences 'The door is shut' and 'Is the door shut?' are tokens of the same proposition: they have the same sense. Certainly, where tokens of the former will typically be of assertoric force, those of the latter will typically be of interrogative force, but what concerns logic in the sentences 'The door is shut', 'Is the door shut?' and 'Shut the door!' is the unasserted (unquestioned, uncommanded) proposition – the *proposition*, that is – of which their tokens are all instances.

It may be emphasized again that Wittgenstein's taking force to be a merely psychological phenomenon does not mean he takes it to be a mental phenomenon. On the contrary, Wittgenstein would, I take it, hold the form and force of a token proposition to be as conventionally determined and public a matter as the correlation of a name and its referent. If the author of 'Is the door shut?' asks something, his doing so does not for Wittgenstein any more than for Frege depend upon the existence of some interrogative mental act, but rather on the context of his utterance and the conventions of the language he is speaking. What *is* meant by the claim that force is psychological, however, is that all force is equally psychological: 'judgment, question and command are all on the same [psychological] level' (NB, 96). For Wittgenstein's purposes, assertoric force does not occupy a privileged theoretical position.

4.

This position of Wittgenstein's 1913 *Notes on Logic* that assertoric force is psychological may give us pause for two reasons. The first reason concerns the connection both Frege and Russell make between assertoric force and inference. The premises and conclusion of an argument are assertoric sentences/propositions, and it is accordingly in terms of such sentences/propositions that rules of inference are framed. Does this not bring assertion into the logical fold? The short, Wittgensteinian response here is that it does not: logic's concern is not with proof but with truth. Wittgenstein is concerned not with inference (Russell's *therefore*) but with entailment (Russell's *implies*). The specification of an inferential calculus would, for Wittgenstein, be a merely psychological matter. The second reason to pause on Wittgenstein's 1913 claim that assertoric force is psychological will hold us for rather longer.

In the *Tractatus* Wittgenstein declares:

> A proposition *shows* how things stand if it is true. And it *says that* they do so stand. (TLP 4.022)[8]

---

[8] I have mainly used Pears and McGuinness's 1961 translation of *Tractatus Logico-Philosophicus*, but where I found that unsatisfactory I have used Ogden's earlier translation or my own translation, as indicated in the text.

How is this 1918 Tractarian position that a proposition says something – a central and familiar Tractarian doctrine – to be squared with the 1913 position on force? There are three options for us here. If we assume that the Tractarian propositional saying talked of in section 4.022 and elsewhere is the having of assertoric form or force, we can either try to reconcile such sections with the claim that such phenomena are psychological, or we can suggest that between 1913 and 1918 Wittgenstein changed his mind as to assertion's logical status. Alternatively we can suggest that Tractarian propositional saying is something quite different from assertion. Let's take these options in turn.

Wittgenstein holds in 1913 that assertoric force is a non-logical phenomenon belonging not to the proposition itself but only to certain of its tokens. If Wittgenstein is to maintain this position in the *Tractatus* and also be speaking in section 4.022 of assertoric force, then more fully spelled out the section would read: 'A proposition shows how things stand if it is true. And when it occurs with assertoric force it says that they do so stand.' But this reading is unacceptable. To see why, we need to be clear that Wittgenstein's claim in the *Notes* is not (merely) that the constitution of a proposition's having assertoric force – what makes it the case that it occurs with that force – is psychological. It is rather that assertoric force is itself a psychological phenomenon. This is apparent in the fact that it does not follow from the claim that the constitution of assertion is psychological that logic is interested only in the unasserted (/unasserting) proposition. The constitution of reference is psychological, but this does not mean that logic is interested only in the unreferring name! Indeed, if Wittgenstein's position were that assertion is a logical phenomenon, and that it is only the constitution of assertion that is psychological, then logic would not be interested only in the unasserted proposition: it would be interested in the asserted proposition too. Taking this clarification back to *Tractatus* 4.022, the mooted reading becomes: 'when it occurs with assertoric force, what it says, psychologically, is that they do so stand.' And with this the reading's unacceptability becomes transparent. The saying of which Wittgenstein speaks in *Tractatus* 4.022 is not a psychological saying. It is, as that section implies and as we shall explore below, a logical phenomenon intimately connected with truth. For a proposition to be true is for things to be as that proposition says.

An alternative way to square *Tractatus* 4.022 with the 1913 claim that assertion is merely psychological is to hold as before that *Tractatus* 4.022 speaks of assertoric force but, admitting that what is spoken of there is not a psychological phenomenon, propose that Wittgenstein changed his mind on the nature of assertion. At some point between the 1913 *Notes* and the 1918 *Tractatus* Wittgenstein decides that assertoric force is not psychological after all and brings it back into the realm of logic. This suggestion, straightforward as it may be, is seriously undermined by the fact that Wittgenstein speaks not only in the *Tractatus* but also in the *Notes* of a proposition's saying something. Indeed, in the *Notes* Wittgenstein both types propositions by the kind of thing that they say (NB, 96, 107), and also explicitly offers an account of propositional saying (NB, 96). Whatever it is that Wittgenstein is offering an account of here, it is certainly not the assertion he dismisses elsewhere in the same text as psychological. We have to recognize, then, that Wittgenstein is involved in the *Notes* with two notions of assertion/saying, one to be explained, the other to be ignored as psychological. And once this is recognized, there is no reason to attribute to Wittgenstein a radical change of mind on assertoric force: the clear option is rather to identify Tractarian propositional saying with the non-psychological propositional saying of which Wittgenstein offers an account in the *Notes*. The position to which we are led, then, is the third option from above, namely that Wittgenstein is operating both in the *Notes* and in the *Tractatus* with two distinct notions of assertion. The saying something that is the having of assertoric force (or form) is a psychological phenomenon. This does not belong to the proposition itself but is rather a feature of certain of its occurrences. There is, however, another propositional saying of which Wittgenstein speaks in both the *Tractatus* and the *Notes*. This is a logical phenomenon belonging to a token proposition merely as such, and it is a phenomenon of which Wittgenstein is in both texts interested to give an account. 'Is the door shut?' says something in the logical sense of *Tractatus* 4.022 exactly as does 'The door is shut'.

5.

What, then, is this Tractarian logical saying that is not the having of assertoric force? We may take our lead in responding to this question from Wittgenstein's claim that a proposition is a picture (TLP 4.01). With this in mind, consider Figure 2. Does this diagram say anything? We might hesitate to use the word 'say' here. It certainly *represents* something, however: it represents that Millie, Fido, and Chocky are Jack's pets. Alternatively we might speak of *situation representation*: the diagram represents the situation of Millie, Fido, and Chocky being Jack's pets. These modes of expression are of course equivalent – to represent that Millie, Fido, and Chocky are Jack's pets is to represent the situation of Millie, Fido, and Chocky being Jack's pets. And the equivalence here is quite general. A situation is *that p*: it is something that may be the case – it may be that *p* – and something that may be represented – it may be represented that *p*. The situation of Millie being

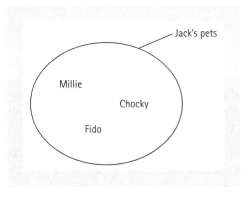

FIGURE 2.

Jack's pet is the situation that Millie is Jack's pet, and to represent the situation that Millie is Jack's pet is to represent that Millie is Jack's pet.

Now the *Tractatus* is full of remarks involving the idea that a picture, and more particularly a proposition, 'represents a possible situation' (TLP 2.202). It also speaks of 'representation that' (TLP 2.15). And with these remarks my straightforward suggestion for propositional saying is that Wittgenstein means by this nothing other than situation representation – the representation, that is, that something is the case. The above diagram says, in this sense, that Millie, Chocky, and Fido are Jack's pets.

The purpose of introducing a diagrammatic example here is to make it plausible – even obvious – that this notion of 'saying that' is distinct from the notion of assertoric force. Diagrams can occur with a variety of forces. The above diagram might occur with interrogative force through a convention of placing a question mark underneath it; on another occasion it might have assertoric force through a convention of placing a square underneath it, or if drawn as a response to the question: which animals are Jack's pets? Alternatively, the diagram might have no force at all: it might be used merely to 'arouse in the reader the idea' (Frege 1879 §2) of Millie, Chocky, and Fido being Jack's pets. Even with the question mark underneath it, however, and even when it is without force, the picture would still represent Millie, Chocky, and Fido as Jack's pets. We would still have a representation of the situation of Millie, Chocky, and Fido being Jack's pets, a representation that Millie, Chocky, and Fido are Jack's pets.

Wittgenstein's position on sentences, the suggestion therefore is, parallels this take on diagrams. An interrogative utterance of 'Is Millie Jack's pet?' represents the situation of Millie being Jack's pet exactly as does an assertoric utterance of 'Millie is Jack's pet.' They both say that Millie is Jack's pet.

This suggestion, we can quickly further note, is precisely the suggestion made above that utterances of 'The door is shut' and 'Is the door shut?' have the same sense. A Tractarian sense is a Tractarian situation, and 'what a picture represents is its sense' (TLP 2.221, cf. TLP 2.202: 'A picture represents a possible situation'). Indeed, a proposition's having a certain sense *is* its representing that situation:

> Instead of, 'This proposition has such and such a sense', we can simply say, 'This proposition represents such and such a situation'. (TLP 4.031)

6.

We have made much of the idea that the saying something that is the having of a sense is a logical phenomenon, that it has to do with truth. Let's be explicit now as to what the connection to truth is. Wittgenstein wrote in 1914:

> '[T]rue' and 'false' are not accidental properties of a proposition such that, when it has meaning, we can say it is also true or false: on the contrary, to have meaning means to be true or false: the being true or false actually constitutes the relation of the proposition to reality, which we mean by saying that it has meaning (*Sinn* [sense]). (NB, 113)

To have a sense is to be true or false: it is to have a truth condition. A sense – a situation – is a truth condition. This identification should come as no surprise: the proposition '*p*' has as its truth condition *that p*. Before moving forward with it, however, we should note that it is not uncontroversial.

It has been an orthodoxy that the *Tractatus* offers a correspondence theory of truth: the *Tractatus* holds, it has been supposed, that the obtaining of a truth condition consists, at least in the basic case, in the existence of a situation. The identification of a situation with a truth condition clearly stands against this orthodoxy – indeed it stands against any theory in which the obtaining of a truth condition is explained by reference to some further fact-item. Now there are certainly passages in the *Tractatus* that *suggest* a correspondence theory. Wittgenstein writes, for example:

> If an elementary proposition is true, the state of affairs exists: if an elementary proposition is false, the state of affairs does not exist. (TLP 4.25)

Whilst suggestive, however, such passages are far from decisive against an identification of Tractarian situations and truth conditions. For one, whenever Wittgenstein wants to emphasize that something is a fact, he invariably deploys the idiom of 'that *p*'. So for instance we find:

> A propositional sign is a fact. (TLP 3.14) . . .
>
> Instead of, 'The complex sign "*aRb*" says that *a* stands to *b* in the relation *R*', we ought to put, 'That "*a*" stands to "*b*" in a certain relation says *that aRb*'. (TLP 3.1432)

More, Wittgenstein's talk of fact existence can readily be given a deflationary reading. A truth condition – that *p* – is a way things may be: it may be that *p*. Given an identification of truth conditions with facts, then, to say that a certain fact exists will be to say that a certain way things may be exists, and this will mean nothing more than that things are indeed that way. As Ramsey wrote: '"The fact that a has R to b exists" is no different from "a has R to b"' (Ramsey 1990, 39). The relevant point here is that more substantial support is required for attributing a correspondence theory to the *Tractatus* than merely pointing to sections in which Wittgenstein talks of the existence of a situation. I want now to defend my identification of fact and truth condition by suggesting that such support simply isn't there. Attending more closely to, thinking harder about, Wittgenstein's theorizing reveals that the Tractarian system doesn't provide for thinking of the obtaining of a truth condition in terms of distinct fact-items.

There are, I take it, two places where one might look to substantiate a conception of situations other than as truth conditions: one might look either at how situations interrelate or at how they are represented. Russell's work over the period 1910–1913 provides an illustration of the first of these two possibilities. Russell holds at this time that the obtaining of a truth condition consists in the existence of a corresponding fact, and this Russellian claim draws for its substance on a theoretical context in which facts are themselves constituents as objects of further facts. For example, the fact 'knife-to-the-left-of-book' – the fact in whose existence is constituted the knife's being to the left of the book – is for Russell a constituent, along with Jack and the relation of perceiving, of the further fact 'Jack-perceiving-(knife-to-the-left-of-book)', this latter complex again existing just in case Jack enjoys the relevant perception. Wittgenstein, we can however straightaway note, emphatically rules out thinking in this way of facts as objects, and so not as truth conditions. He both vigorously disassociates facts from objects and insists that objects are simple. A fact is not a constituent, as an object, of further facts. One might still wonder, of course, whether Wittgenstein doesn't hold there to be a different system of relations amongst Tractarian situations which could substantiate distinguishing them from truth conditions. Looking around for such relations, however, what one finds is Wittgenstein speaking of a relation between senses of *opposition*: 'the propositions "*p*" and "*~p*",' Wittgenstein writes, 'have opposite sense' (TLP 4.0621). And far from distinguishing senses and truth conditions, this strongly supports their identification. (Someone who wants to maintain that situations are not truth conditions will, I take it, have to respond here with an improbable distinction between situations and senses.)

Putting this last comment to one side, let's consider Wittgenstein's account of situation representation. If one wanted to distinguish facts from truth conditions, a second place to do this would be within one's theory of representation. In particular, the likely suggestion to make would be that a token proposition has a truth condition by virtue of picking out a fact. A proposition first picks out a fact; subsequently it does something like 'affirm the fact', coming thereby to have the relevant truth condition. On such a theory, a fact would be the object of a 'picking out' relation, and – depending on how the affirmation part of the theory is understood – the door would be open for explaining the obtaining of a truth condition in terms of the existence (or something similar) of such an object. Certain commentators have, I think, understood the *Tractatus* as proposing just such a two-step theory of the proposition. First, a proposition picks out a fact – it *depicts* or *images* a fact in a way which does not presume that fact's existence. Subsequently, the proposition affirms the picked out fact. This two-step picture of judgement is, however, wholly and conspicuously absent from Wittgenstein's central statement of his account:

> In a picture the elements of the picture are the representatives of objects. (TLP 2.131)

> The picture is a fact.
>   That the elements of the picture are combined with one another in a definite way, represents that the things are so combined with one another. (TLP [Ogden] 2.141–2.15)

A proposition's having a certain truth condition – its representing *that something is the case* – is explained *directly* in terms of its elements referring to objects; it is not explained via the proposition as a whole imaging some non-truth-condition fact-item.

Nothing in Wittgenstein's theorizing, I would therefore press, provides for interpreting those points at which he talks of fact existence as the expression of a correspondence theory, or indeed of any theory in which facts are distinguished from truth conditions.

Nothing in the *Tractatus* provides for thinking of the sentence 'The fact "aRb" exists' as anything other than a periphrasis of the sentence 'aRb'.[9]

7.

We can move on now from Wittgenstein's claim that assertion is psychological and look towards his second claim against Russell, that 'in *not-p, p* is exactly the same as if it stands alone'. This remark targets Russell's assertion that 'the *p* and the *q* which enter into [the proposition "*p* implies *q*"] are not strictly the same as the *p* or the *q* which are separate propositions' (Russell 1992, 35). But what exactly is its content?

An obvious suggestion is that Wittgenstein means, straightforwardly, that there is only one proposition '*p*' and this proposition does indeed occur in the propositions 'not-*p*', '*p* implies *q*', etc. So where Russell argues (more or less):

(1) '*p*' asserts that *p*.
(2) What occurs strictly within a proposition does not assert anything. Therefore,
(C) '*p*' does not occur within '*p* implies *q*', 'not-*p*', etc.

Wittgenstein responds by denying (C), agreeing with (2), and so denying (1). Assertion does not belong to the proposition: it is merely psychological. We need to be careful here, however. In particular, it may be unclear what notion of a proposition Wittgenstein is deploying, and so how we should be looking for his remarks to engage Russell.

Let's continue for now thinking of a proposition as a type whose tokens have in common a certain sense. For such a proposition to occur within another is for a sense to occur within another. So, do Tractarian senses occur within each other? We mentioned above that a sense is not a possible constituent as an object of another sense. Senses are not complex objects; they do not stand to each other in part–whole relations. This does not entail, however, that there is *no* structuring of containment amongst senses. Indeed, the surface of the *Tractatus* would seem to hold that there is. On its surface, the *Tractatus* divides situations into simple and complex, a simple situation being that certain objects are combined in a certain way and a complex situation being composed of such simple situations. If that *p* is simple, then that not-*p* is an essentially negative possibility involving the possibility that *p*: it is the possibility that the basic possibility that *p* does not obtain. The possibility that *p* or *q* is a disjunctive possibility composed of the possibilities that *p* and that *q*: it is, essentially and exhaustively, the possibility that one or other of these basic, logically simple possibilities obtains.

It will be correct to think of Tractarian senses as occurring within each other in this way if, and only if, Wittgenstein holds there to be essentially simple, and so essentially negative, disjunctive, etc. situations. And whilst the opening remarks of the *Tractatus* appear to commit Wittgenstein to such a categorization of situations, certain other remarks by Wittgenstein may appear to find him rejecting it. For instance, Wittgenstein writes in the *Notes on Logic*:

> In 'not-not-*p*', 'not-*p*' does not occur; for 'not-not-*p*' is the same as '*p*', and therefore, if 'not-*p*' occurred in 'not-not-*p*', it would occur in '*p*'. (NB, 99)

On closer inspection, however, this passage can be seen to be inconclusive on the point in question. The obvious argument to find within it is that if we both allow that propositions occur within each other, and accept at face value the suggestions for such occurrences of token propositions, then we will arrive at the absurd conclusion that every proposition occurs in its negation. It is not obvious, however, whether Wittgenstein takes the lesson to be that propositions do not occur within each other, or that we should be wary of naively reading such occurrences from the surface of token propositions. A very similar remark in the *Tractatus* is similarly inconclusive:

> That negation occurs in a proposition, is not enough to characterize its sense. ($\sim\sim p = p$). (TLP 4.0621; author's translation)[10]

One can agree with Wittgenstein that '$\sim\sim p$' and 'p' ('p or q' and '$\sim(\sim p$ and $\sim q)$' etc.) express the same sense, endorse the lesson that the occurrence of a logical sign such as '$\sim$', 'and', or 'or' in a proposition is insufficient to characterize its sense, but maintain nonetheless that there are elementary, negative, and disjunctive senses.

What, though, of the claim against Russell that '[i]n *not-p*, *p* is exactly the same as if it stands alone' (NB, 95)? Does this not commit Wittgenstein to the occurrence of senses within each other? Where Russell had held that the proposition (/sense) '*p*' occurring in the proposition 'not-*p*' is distinct from the separate proposition '*p*', Wittgenstein insists that they are identical. What occurs in the situation that not-*p* is not some unasserted or otherwise distinct version of the situation that *p*: it is precisely the situation that *p*. Again, though, this reading is not compulsory – not even if we agree that Wittgenstein is talking here of senses. For there is the option of understanding Wittgenstein's remark as nothing more than a pressing of a version of the concern that Russell has undermined *modus ponens*. Russell's claim that in the argument '*p*; *p* implies *q*; therefore *q*' the '*p*' that is the first premise is a different entity from the '*p*' that appears within the second premise threatens to be the claim that what the sentence '*p* implies *q*' says implies *q* is not what the sentence '*p*' says, and so threatens to entail that the argument is invalid. Similarly, Wittgenstein may be understanding the Russellian claim that '*p*' is a different entity as it stands by itself from when it appears in 'not-*p*' as the claim that what the sentence 'not-*p*' says is not the case is not what the sentence '*p*' says (that these two senses are not opposites), and his response may simply be a forthright rejection of this error.

---

[10] Ogden translates TLP 4.0621 as 'That negation occurs in a proposition, is no characteristic of its sense. ($\sim\sim p = p$).' This simply ignores, however, the 'noch' in Wittgenstein's 'ist noch kein Merkmal seines Sinnes'. Pears and McGuinness more closely follow Wittgenstein's German.

We can consider what is at issue in the question of whether or not senses occur within each other by imagining a language in which there are two types of names {A, B, C, ...} and {a, b, c, ...}, elementary propositions consisting of one name of each type. Suppose someone were to criticize this language saying that the symbol 'A' is not in fact a name; 'aA', 'bA', etc. are not in fact elementary. Rather, 'aA', 'bA', etc. express negative senses and 'A' should be replaced by a real name 'X' rewriting 'aA', 'bA', etc. as '~aX', '~bX', etc. Would Wittgenstein see it as a substantial issue whether 'X' or 'A' is the real name? If one answers 'no' to this question, one will hold that being elementary, negative, disjunctive, etc are characteristics of token propositions only and not of senses. A positive answer will endorse the *Tractatus*' surface claim that these are characteristics also of senses. Which answer one should give is not, it however seems clear, decidable by looking in the way we have tried at a few isolated passages of Wittgenstein's writings.[11] Rather, the answer one gives will depend largely on the kind of reading one is inclined to give to the *Tractatus* as a whole. Speaking very broadly, someone who sees the book as offering a realist metaphysic of language-independent objects will likely insist that there are indeed essentially elementary, negative, etc. senses, whilst someone who does not find such a metaphysic may rather take it that senses are not essentially characterized in such ways. This being so, there is not space to pursue the question further in this chapter.

To move on towards the chapter's end I want rather to consider a third option for interpreting Wittgenstein's claim that '[i]n *not-p, p* is exactly the same as if it stands alone' (NB, 95). Perhaps Wittgenstein is concerned here not with senses but with *linguistic symbols*. Even if Wittgenstein denies that senses are built out of each other, he might nonetheless hold that propositional symbols (roughly, sentences) are built out of each other. Indeed, this is something Wittgenstein would seem to accept (see, e.g., TLP 5.5151). So perhaps Wittgenstein is reading Russell as claiming that the propositional symbol '*p*' does not occur within the propositional symbol '~*p*', and reacting with a rejection of that claim.

8.

Wittgenstein writes in the *Tractatus*:

> In the general propositional form propositions occur in other propositions only as bases of truth-operations. (TLP 5.54)

Earlier, he introduces the idea of a (truth-) operation as follows:

> The structures of propositions stand to one another in internal relations.
> We can bring out these internal relations in our manner of expression, by presenting a proposition as the result of an operation which produces it from other propositions (the bases of the operation). (TLP [Ogden] 5.2–5.21)

> Negation, logical addition, logical multiplication, etc. etc. are operations.
> (Negation reverses the sense of a proposition). (TLP 5.2341)

---

[11] Geach (2006) appears to think otherwise; in particular he appears to take TLP 4.0621 as straightforwardly decisive against essentially negative senses.

What the bases of an operation and its result have in common is just the bases themselves. (TLP 5.24)

Truth conditions stand in internal relations to each other. Two truth conditions may for
example be opposites – for things to be the one way may be for them not to be the other.
Such relations between senses can be brought out in our manner of expression. If 'p' and 'q'
are propositions of opposite sense, we can 'bring this out' by writing 'q' as 'not-p'. Again, if 'r',
's', and 't' are propositions such that for things to be as 't' says is for them to be either as 'r' says
or as 's' says, this can be brought out by writing 't' as 'r or s'. And in doing this, Wittgenstein
says, we present 't' as the result of an operation which produces it from 'r' and 's'.

One might on reading these remarks take an operation to be a function of a certain
kind from n-tuples of senses to senses. Negation maps a sense to its opposite; logical
addition (disjunction) takes two argument senses and delivers the sense such that for
things to be that way is for them to be either the way of the first argument or the way of
the second argument. In writing 't' as 'r or s', the thought would then be, we present the
sense of 't' as the result of an operation of disjunction on the senses of 'r' and 's', much as
the Fregean expression '2+3' represents the number 5 as the result of combining addition
and the numbers 2 and 3 as function and arguments. This understanding of an operation
is, however, inconsistent with the idea, apparently endorsed by Wittgenstein in both
section 5.24 and section 5.54, that the result of an operation *contains* its bases. On the
current interpretation, an operation's bases will be its arguments, but even if one holds
that certain senses are contained in certain others, not every way of representing a
situation as the result of an operation could reflect structuring of containment in the
realm of sense. (In particular, not every sense can contain its opposite: if that p is contained in that not-p, then that not-p is not contained in that p.)

The alternative to thinking of operations as functions on senses is to see them as a part
of the symbolism. At various points in the *Tractatus* Wittgenstein appears to speak of propositions not as Ramsey defines them, namely as a type whose tokens have in common a
certain sense, but more narrowly as a propositional symbol of a particular language – as,
more or less, a sentence. (Similarly he speaks of a name not as a type whose tokens have in
common a certain meaning, but as a type whose tokens belong to the same language and
have in common not only a certain meaning but also a certain sign. Thus there might be
two names for the same object.) If we take the bases and results of operations to be
propositions in this sense, then we can think of an operation '( ) or ( )' of disjunction as a
linguistic rule for the construction of propositions of a certain language which takes propositional symbols 'p' and 'q' and produces from them a propositional symbol 'p or q' whose
sense obtains just in case either of the senses of the two bases obtains. There might in the
same language be a rule of proposition construction which, given a propositional symbol
'p', provides for the construction of the symbol '~p' with a sense opposed to that of 'p'.

No problem arises on such an understanding of an operation that every proposition
contains its negation. The propositional symbol '~p' is the result of applying the
operation of negation to the basis symbol 'p', and so '~p' contains 'p'. '~~p' similarly

contains '~p'. But 'p' does not contain '~p', for '~~p' and 'p' are different propositional symbols despite having the same sense, and so being the same proposition in Ramsey's sense. In the same vein, whilst the truth values of 'p or q' and '~(~p and ~q)' are determined in the same way by those of 'p' and 'q', they are not the result of the same operations on 'p' and 'q'. Indeed, there is no single operation '~(~( ) and ~( ))' – the propositional symbol '~(~p and ~q)' is the result not of one operation on the bases 'p' and 'q' but of successive operations on those propositions first separately and then together.

This said, it remains to be clarified what it would be for one propositional symbol to occur within another. To close the chapter we may say something very brief to this point. Consider again the Fregean symbol '2+3'. This is a name of the number 5 in which the names '2', '3', and '( )+( )' occur. It is a distinct name from the name '5', and the occurrence within it of '2', '3', and '( )+( )' finds no reflection at the level of what is referred to: the numbers 2 and 3 and the addition function do not in any sense occur within the number 5. As to the precise way in which the name '2' occurs in '2+3', this is a question for Frege scholarship. It is both necessary and sufficient for there to be *some* way in which '2' occurs within '2+3', however, that wherever '2+3' is tokened there too is tokened '2', and so there too the number 2 is referred to. In the same way, it is necessary and sufficient for the symbol 'p' to be said to occur within the symbol '~p', that where '~p' is tokened, there too is tokened 'p', and so there too it is said that p. And in this way, I would suggest, Wittgenstein does indeed hold – without implying relations of containment at the level of sense – that 'p' occurs within '~p'. One might react to this suggestion by saying that nothing occurring strictly within a proposition says anything. Such a reaction, Wittgenstein would however hold, confuses saying with assertion. Whilst it is true that assertoric force does not belong to propositions as they are tokened strictly within other propositions, Tractarian saying is not assertoric force. Rather, such saying is the representation of a situation, and whilst this is absolutely no kind of reference, there is no more problem for Wittgenstein with the idea that what occurs strictly within the representation of a situation might itself represent a situation than there is for Frege with the idea that what occurs strictly within a referring expression might itself refer. The diagram concerning Jack's pets says something when it occurs with interrogative force; it would equally well say something if were to occur with a '~' sign in front of it, the wider diagram there occurring having the opposite sense to the diagram occurring within it.

REFERENCES

CARROLL, L. (1895). 'What the Tortoise Said to Achilles', *Mind*, 4: 278–80.

DUMMETT, M. (1981). *Frege: Philosophy of Language*. Melksham: Redwood Press.

FREGE, G. (1879). *Begriffsschrift*. Halle: L. Nebert. [Translated by T. W. Bynum (1972) as *Conceptual Notation*. Oxford: Oxford University Press.]

—— (1884). *Die Grundlagen der Arithmetik*. Breslau: W. Koebner. [Translated by J. L. Austin (1974) as *The Foundations of Arithmetic*. Oxford: Blackwell.]

—— (1891). *Funktion und Begriff*. Jena: Hermann Pohle. [Translated as 'Function and Concept' in Frege (1997): 130–48.]

FREGE, G. (1892). 'Über Sinn und Bedeutung', *Zeitschrift für Philosophie und Philosophische Kritik*, 100: 25–50. [Translated as 'On *Sinn* and *Bedeutung*' in Frege (1997): 151–71.]

—— (1893). *Grundgesetze der Arithmetik*, Vol. I. Jena: Hermann Pohle. [Preface, Introduction and §§1–51 translated by Furth in Frege (1964).]

—— (1918). 'Der Gedanke', *Beiträge zur Philosophie des deutschen Idealismus*, 1: 58–77. [Translated as 'Thought' in Frege (1997): 325–45.]

—— (1964). *The Basic Laws of Arithmetic*, ed. M. Furth. Berkeley: University of California Press.

—— (1979). *Posthumous Writings*, ed. H. Hermes, F. Kambartel, and F. Kaulbach, trans. P. Long and R. White. Oxford: Blackwell. [PW]

—— (1997). *The Frege Reader*, ed. M. Beaney. Oxford: Blackwell.

GEACH, P. T. (2006). 'The *Tractatus* is not all Rubbish', *Analysis*, 66: 172.

POTTER, M. (2009). *Wittgenstein's Notes on Logic*. Oxford: Oxford University Press.

RAMSEY, F. (1923). 'Critical Notice of *Tractatus Logico-Philosophicus*', *Mind*, 32: 465–78.

—— (1990). *Philosophical Papers*, ed. D. H. Mellor. Cambridge: Cambridge University Press.

RUSSELL, B. (1992). *The Principles of Mathematics*. London: Routledge.

WITTGENSTEIN, L. (1922). *Tractatus Logico-Philosophicus*, trans. Ogden. London: Routledge.

—— (1961). *Tractatus Logico-Philosophicus*, trans. Pears and McGuinness. London: Routledge.

—— (1979). *Notebooks 1914–1916*. Oxford: Blackwell.

....

CHAPTER 4

WITTGENSTEIN AND FREGE

....

WOLFGANG KIENZLER

THROUGHOUT his philosophical career, Wittgenstein considered Frege to be of first-rank importance to him.[1] In the Preface to the *Tractatus*, Wittgenstein acknowledges his debt to 'the great works of Frege'; and even during the years in which he resigned from doing philosophy Wittgenstein directed others to read Frege, even when he himself did not continue to do so; Frege was one of the very few philosophers Wittgenstein recommended to anyone.[2] Wittgenstein claimed that his own style of writing (Z §712), as well as his entire way of thinking, was influenced by Frege (CV, 19). Frege is most probably also the only philosopher Wittgenstein ever called 'a great thinker' (LFM, 144), and shortly before his death Wittgenstein confessed that he wished he could have written like Frege (Geach 1977, viii).

All this makes it difficult to describe adequately the importance that Frege held for Wittgenstein; to do it justice would require writing Wittgenstein's philosophical biography. This chapter will focus on describing Wittgenstein and Frege's personal relationship (section I) and on investigating how much we know about the extent to which Wittgenstein studied Frege's work (section II). I will give a brief genetic account of Frege's influence on the pre-*Tractatus* manuscripts and will introduce some of the approaches that have been taken to the Frege–Wittgenstein question in the literature (sections III and IV). My main focus will be on the way Frege is discussed in the *Tractatus*. First, the passages which refer to Frege will be presented (section V), then a systematic account of Frege's most basic approach is given (section VI) and compared to some suggestions by Cora Diamond (section VII). Finally, I will again look at the *Tractatus* passages discussing Frege in order to bring out some connections more clearly (section VIII).

---

[1] Frege's writings are referred to by paragraphs or original pages. These are given in the margin of the Geach and Black edition. Translations have sometimes been modified. Letters are referred to by date; often they will be found also in other editions than the one indicated here. Abbreviations of Frege's works are given in the list of references.

[2] Examples include F. P. Ramsey (1923), members of the Vienna Circle (1930/31), W. H. Watson (1932), P. Geach (1949/50).

I

There is some evidence that it was the paradox which Russell communicated to Frege that first awoke Wittgenstein's active interest in philosophy. In 1909, Wittgenstein appears to have sent a proposal for a solution to the paradox (now lost) to Jourdain (McGuinness 1988, 74). The most likely source of Wittgenstein's knowledge of the paradox is Russell's book *Principles of Mathematics*, Chapter X, 'The Contradiction', and especially its appendix on the doctrines of Frege.

Wittgenstein met Frege several times between 1911 and 1914 at Jena and Brunshaupten,[3] Frege's long-time summer resort on the Baltic Sea in his home state Mecklenburg, for extended discussions of logic and philosophy which left a lasting impression on both participants (FW 12/9/18).[4] During World War I they exchanged postcards and letters rather frequently, in which Frege repeatedly expressed his hope that they might be able to continue their 'scientific (*wissenschaftliche*) conversations' (FW 24/6/15). Wittgenstein in turn valued the possibility of having philosophical conversations with Frege so highly that he twice invited him to come to Vienna in order to explain and discuss his new ideas with him in person (FW 21/4/16 and 30/6/17). Frege, however, declined on both occasions; he felt that his by then frail health left him unable to make such a long and strenuous trip, especially under wartime conditions.

In April 1918, as work on the *Tractatus* manuscript was drawing to a close, Wittgenstein presented Frege with an unknown sum of money in order to express his gratitude for the help and stimulation he had received. Frege disclaimed that there existed any such debt and stressed that they had both gained from their mutual intellectual exchange (FW 9/4/18). Later, in 1918 or 1919, Wittgenstein sent Frege a copy of the *Tractatus* typescript, which Frege commented on in several letters. However, he found reading Wittgenstein's work so difficult that he later felt unable to recommend the book for publication.[5] When

---

[3] Today Brunshaupten is part of Kühlungsborn.

[4] In a letter to W. H. Watson (WC 8/4/32) Wittgenstein relates: 'What kind of information do you want about Frege? His views? That would be a tall order. And about his life I know very little indeed. He was when I first met him in 1911 about 60 and Professor at Jena and died about 1922.' Actually Frege was 63 in 1911 and he died in 1925. Whether their last meeting was in 1913 or in 1914 remains uncertain, 1913 being the more likely year. For an extensive and fairly complete account of the details of their personal relationship see Reck 2002.

[5] In reaction to Frege's first letter of reaction Wittgenstein wrote to his sister Hermine: 'The day before yesterday I received Frege's letter.... It is true that I always thought that he would not understand my work at all. Still I was somewhat depressed by his letter' (GB 1/8/19). To Russell he was more explicit: 'I also sent my M.S. to Frege. He wrote me a week ago and I gather that he doesn't understand a word of it all. So my only hope is to see you soon and explain all to you, for it is very hard not to be understood by a single soul!' (WC 19/8/19) The letter indicates that Wittgenstein was certain that Russell would only have a chance of understanding the book if he helped along with very detailed oral explanations. Earlier that year Wittgenstein had written to Russell on receiving his book *Introduction to Mathematical Philosophy*: 'I should never have thought that the stuff I dictated to Moore in Norway would have passed over you so completely without any trace' (WC 12/6/19). This indicates how far Wittgenstein had moved beyond the two people that had taught him most.

Frege did try to help Wittgenstein to get his work published, he advised him to divide it into a series of separate papers.[6]

Wittgenstein's plans for a visit to Frege after 1919 apparently never materialized (Frege 1976, 268). The last exchange of letters, from 1920, indicates that Wittgenstein severely criticized Frege's article 'Thoughts' ('Der Gedanke'), expressing the conviction that Frege had not understood 'the deeper grounds of idealism' (FW 3/4/20). Frege's last letter tries to specify how the word 'is' is to be understood in its two occurrences in the opening sentence of the *Tractatus*: 'The world is everything that is the case.' In the end, the two thinkers did not reach any mutual understanding.

How seriously Frege took his exchanges with Wittgenstein is emphasized by the fact that among his papers there was (no longer extant) 'a package of drafts towards answers to Wittgenstein', as well as '4 pages of notes about Wittgenstein's standpoint as it was expressed in personal conversation' (Frege 1976, 265).

II

Although Wittgenstein acknowledges the importance of 'the great works of Frege' for his own work, it is not easy to decide which of Frege's works he actually owned, read, or studied in detail. There is little reliable information about Wittgenstein's books, but at the time of his death he seems to have owned just *Grundlagen* in the 1950 edition by J. L. Austin (Hallett 1977, 765).[7] He is also reported to have known where to find several of Frege's papers in the Cambridge Library (Geach 1977, viii).[8] This strongly indicates that later Wittgenstein *did not own any* of Frege's works other than *Grundlagen*: Russell and Ryle were able to lend some of Frege's writings (Geach and Black 1970, v), but not Wittgenstein.

We know that before 1914 Wittgenstein did own Frege's *Begriffsschrift* and *Grundlagen*, as well as Russell's *Principles*, because his copies are preserved in the Russell Archives.

---

[6] Wittgenstein wrote to von Ficker that he would be able to have his work published 'if I would mutilate it from beginning to end, and – in a word – turn it into a different work' (GB mid-10/19). To his friend Hänsel he wrote that he had received an '*extremely* strange' letter from Frege (GB before 13/10/19).

[7] Ben Richards relates that on a 1950 trip to Norway 'I had brought Austin's recently published translation of Frege's *Foundations of Arithmetic* (*Grundlagen*) with German text, and we used to read and discuss this' (Richards, unpublished).

[8] The relevant papers are the Husserl review showing much of Frege's sarcasm so esteemed by Wittgenstein (similar to his favourite passages from the preface of *Grundgesetze*, from Frege's criticism of the formalists in *Grundgesetze* II, and his pamphlet against Schubert), published in the same journal where 'On Sense and Reference' had appeared two years earlier; 'What is a Function?' from the Festschrift for Boltzmann, one of the people who influenced Wittgenstein according to his famous 1931 list; and 'Negation', the article published while Frege and Wittgenstein were corresponding, and which Wittgenstein favoured over 'Thoughts.'

Wittgenstein had abandoned a number of books in Cambridge in 1914 and Russell had bought them, in a sale of Wittgenstein's possessions, in 1919.[9] It is remarkable that all three books lack any kind of annotation. In a way this fits with the fact that we have little evidence that Wittgenstein did much reading in any of these books. Frege's *Grundgesetze der Arithmetik* is the only one of Frege's books Wittgenstein repeatedly refers to and quotes from.

There is, however, no positive evidence that Wittgenstein had *Grundgesetze* with him on any specific occasion. There is no trace of his personal copy and we have positive evidence that he did not own the book after World War I. In 1919, and again in 1920, he asks for both volumes to be sent to him, first to Monte Cassino, and then to Puchberg (GB 24/5/19 and 31/10/20). On both occasions, he does not write for his own copy (which would have been much more accessible in Vienna), but asks for Engelmann's copy to be sent from Olmütz, although, as it turned out, not even Engelmann owned a copy of the book.[10]

There also is no positive evidence that he had copies of any of Frege's writings with him during his time in Cambridge after 1929, as none are mentioned in any reports.[11]

In 1923, Wittgenstein recommended the heavily satirical pamphlet *On Mr Schubert's Numbers* to Ramsey, but again he had no copy he could show him (WC 11/11/23). In particular, there is no positive evidence that he ever actually studied 'On Sense and Reference' (before 1949) or *Function and Concept*, also published as a pamphlet, or 'On Concept and Object'.[12]

There are only scant indications that Wittgenstein read or appreciated Frege's earlier writings, such as *Begriffsschrift*.[13] His references are consistently to Frege's mature views, as expressed in *Grundgesetze*, and he shows no signs of awareness whatsoever that there existed a Frege who did *not* hold the views about truth-values, courses-of-values, or the

---

[9] The copies of *Begriffsschrift* and *Grundlagen* are expensively rebound in Wiener Werkstätte style (personal communication from Kenneth Blackwell, August 2009) but without any signatures or markings. They seem not to have been working copies (Hide 2004, 83). In addition, a letter from Russell to Ogden mentions a copy of the first volume of *Principia Mathematica* with 'decorations by Wittgenstein' (23/6/1922; quoted in Potter 2009, 47).

[10] See WE 20/4/21, where Engelmann relates that he sent only volume 2 and that Heini Groag, a friend from Olmütz, was the owner of that copy.

[11] Reports mention books by Plato and Novalis in Wittgenstein's rooms, but not by Frege.

[12] Both pamphlets are reprinted in the original in Frege 1999.

[13] There is one reference in TLP 4.431 about 'the expression of the agreement and disagreement with the truth-possibilities of the elementary propositions' and that Frege 'quite rightly put them at the beginning, as explaining the signs of his Begriffsschrift'. This remark fits with Frege's exposition in *Begriffsschrift*, §5 and §7, while in *Grundgesetze* he proceeds differently. The remark in TLP 4.063 about Frege believing that 'is true' might be the verb of every true sentence also sounds like an allusion to *Begriffsschrift*, §2. *Grundlagen* is explicitly mentioned just once in passing in a 1929 manuscript (MS 109, 162) and there are a few more allusions, most famously to the context principle (TLP 3.3), which is mentioned nowhere else in Frege's writings. AWL, 225 mentions *Grundlagen*, chapter 2 but this is a slip for *Grundgesetze*, vol. 2.

distinction between sense and reference, that he held in his later work.[14] This may seem surprising since in many respects Frege's earlier views appear much more attractive from Wittgenstein's point of view. In any case, Wittgenstein does not show any appreciation of the *development* of Frege's views. This, however, does not mean that he held mistaken views about Frege's development, but rather that he was simply not interested in it.[15] This does, however, agree with Frege's view of his own development: that it did not consist in the discovery of new ideas, but was more or less included or contained in the earlier view, being a natural, almost necessary explication of them.

Given this scanty evidence, the story of Frege's importance for Wittgenstein cannot be told step by step from the written sources available. This may seem to support the idea that Wittgenstein had at best a superficial understanding of Frege's thought, and that the well-documented exchanges with Russell are more important. However, Wittgenstein's own testimony, as well as Frege's letters, very strongly support the view that Frege's work was of the greatest importance when Wittgenstein was framing his early thought.

The perspective from which to assess Frege's significance for Wittgenstein can therefore only be the systematic comparison of their respective approaches. And this is especially difficult because a considered answer to the question depends upon a sound judgement on the nature and value of their respective works in logic and philosophy. An overview of the existing interpretations may provide some clues as to the nature of this difficulty.

III

The topic of Frege's significance for Wittgenstein can be approached in a number of ways. We can ask: did Wittgenstein follow Frege in important respects? Or we can ask: did Wittgenstein understand Frege? Or we can ask: did Wittgenstein criticize Frege in important ways? Or: did Wittgenstein continue Frege's work?

In her classical *Introduction to Wittgenstein's Tractatus*, G. E. M. Anscombe stressed the fact that many passages in the *Tractatus* are almost impossible to understand without a thorough knowledge of Frege's work, especially his notion of sense and his distinction between concept and object.[16] Wittgenstein's account of formal concepts, operations,

---

[14] One somewhat curious textual detail supports this view: in his handwritten version of TLP in TS 202 as well as TS 204 4.442 Wittgenstein spells Frege's 'Urteilstrich' (judgement stroke) as Frege does in *Grundgesetze*, vol. 1, only, whereas in all of his other writings Frege uses the more natural spelling 'Urteilsstrich' (or, taking into account the rules for spelling before 1900, 'Urtheilsstrich'), so in *Begriffsschrift* and *Function and Concept* and even in *Grundgesetze*, vol. 2 (Frege 1903, 256). The particular reference seems to be to *Grundgesetze* §5, where the sign '⊢' is introduced (although Frege then explains how it is composed of *two* primitive signs); incidentally the *Prototractatus* version of this remark has 'Frege's sign "⊢"' (PTLP 4.431) and this is only later changed to 'Urteilstrich'.

[15] Curiously, Wittgenstein seems to have been quite unaware of any such substantial development. Maybe (if we take him to have been aware at all) he found that even Frege's early conception was *already on the wrong track*. The criticism in TLP 4.063 would support this idea, and also the way earlier and later Frege are fused in TLP 4.431.

[16] This central notion is discussed in more detail in section VI below.

and hence his account of the nature of logic are presented as radical further developments of these Fregean distinctions.[17]

Michael Dummett has also discussed Wittgenstein's reactions to Frege, in a paper 'Frege and Wittgenstein', where, obviously (and justly) impressed by the coherence and vigour of Frege's thought, he expresses the opinion that 'whenever Wittgenstein diverges from Frege on any essential point, he gets on to the wrong track' (Dummett 1991, 241).

The opposite view was taken by Baker and Hacker in their book *Frege: Logical Excavations*, which is written as a direct reply to Dummett. Baker and Hacker are highly critical of Frege's philosophical views, arguing that he is mainly a mathematician who held rather naive philosophical views of a Pythagorean kind. This view, focussing mainly on questions of doctrine, makes it difficult to understand why Wittgenstein should have held Frege in such high esteem.

Baker and Hacker's estimation of Frege's significance for Wittgenstein is made possible by their largely skipping over the *Tractatus*, which Baker and Hacker believe to be a comparatively weak book, perhaps because it is too much influenced by Fregean ways of thinking. However, this is also to ignore Wittgenstein's numerous later expressions of admiration for Frege.[18]

In spite of their fundamental disagreement, the approaches of both Dummett and Baker/Hacker have the effect of making the relation between Wittgenstein and Frege seem rather uninteresting. For Dummett, it suffices to read Frege; for Baker and Hacker, we can forget about Frege and just read (later) Wittgenstein. We get a more interesting approach to the comparison between Wittgenstein and Frege if we ask: How did Wittgenstein transform things he found in Frege?

In recent years, Cora Diamond and Thomas Ricketts have developed readings of Frege and Wittgenstein that stress the important continuities between them, arguing that the *Tractatus* is a book written very much in a Fregean spirit (if not letter). Seen from their angle, the most basic features of the *Tractatus* can be seen as developing naturally from a starting-point in Frege. One obvious objection to their view is that it reads too much *Tractatus* back into Frege; from the point of view of historical scholarship this charge is partly justified and will be discussed below.

IV

Recently there has been some debate about whether Frege or Russell was more influential on Wittgenstein's early thought.[19] The period in which Wittgenstein develops his early views can be divided into four parts: (1) his studies with Russell, beginning in late

---

[17] Cora Diamond's work, and also the perspective developed in this chapter, are in many ways inspired by Anscombe's great little book, especially by Anscombe's lack of appreciation for the saying–showing distinction.

[18] On the other hand they claim quite correctly that Frege held 'on almost every major point... demonstrably a view antithetical to the one presented in the *Tractatus*' (Baker and Hacker 1984, 380), but they are little interested in explaining just how this is and comes about.

[19] Following Anscombe and Geach, Diamond (1991 and 2010), Ricketts (1986 and 2002), and Conant (2002) have emphasized Frege's importance, which in turn has been doubted by Goldfarb (2002). A more balanced view is developed in McGinn (2006). For a different approach, paying more attention to Frege's work at the time, see Künne (2009).

1911 and documented in some letters to Russell, (2) the 'Notes on Logic', written in mid-1913, (3) the 'Notes Dictated to Moore', written in 1914, and (4) the wartime notebooks from 1914 to 1916. Although the earliest letters to Russell show some signs of collaboration on what Wittgenstein calls 'our theory', by October 1912 Russell has abandoned his own attempt to answer the question 'What is logic?', and handed the task over to Wittgenstein. Almost from the beginning, Wittgenstein is trying, not merely to study and understand Russell's, or Frege's, ideas, but to engage in systematic work of his own. He is not *reading* logic and philosophy, but is rather trying to *write* almost from the start.[20]

The 1913 'Notes on Logic' first present Wittgenstein's new conception of logic and of the nature of the proposition. While his own conception is not fully developed in the notes, his criticism of Frege and Russell is firm and concise:

> Frege said 'propositions are names'; Russell 'propositions correspond to complexes'. Both are false; and especially false is the statement 'propositions are names of complexes'.[21]

This manuscript addresses Russell only in a few places, but it engages deeply with Frege's ideas.[22] The notes dictated to Moore in 1914 already develop the distinction between saying and showing, something Russell never quite accepted (or understood). The distinction has its roots in ideas of Frege, but Wittgenstein develops it in a radical way, going beyond anything Frege could accept. By 1914, Wittgenstein had passed a long way beyond anything either Russell or Frege had ever done in their own work.[23] This, too, explains why in many of Wittgenstein's critical remarks both Frege and Russell are mentioned: from the radically new perspective Wittgenstein was developing, their approaches shared some important mistakes about logic, which have to do with truth, and about the nature of philosophy, which have to do with its relation to science.

V

The *Tractatus* explicitly refers to Frege in seventeen different remarks. The majority of these already occur in the 'Notes on Logic', indicating that Frege was especially important in developing the most basic outlook of the *Tractatus*, rather than in working out the details later. This outlook, however, already marks a radical break away from Fregean

---

[20] Even the first extant letter to Russell has a postscript relating not to Russell's but to his own logic: 'My (!) logic is all in the melting-pot' (WC 11/6/12).

[21] NB 97. Potter (2009, 276–89) introduces a convenient numbering system to the individual remarks of the *Notes on Logic*. This remark is B4 in Potter's numbering.

[22] Michael Potter justly emphasizes the importance of Frege for the 'Notes on Logic'. He also sketches Wittgenstein's move away from Russell's agenda: 'These guiding principles Wittgenstein owed to Frege, not to Russell' (Potter 2009, 262). Putting it more accurately, we might say: Wittgenstein did not follow any guiding principles from Frege but rather he tried to develop his own guiding principles for logic, taking up some leads from Frege.

[23] Ricketts puts it this way: 'From the perspective Wittgenstein acquires in 1913, Frege's and Russell's philosophies of logic alike look hopeless' (Ricketts 2002, 245).

(and even more from Russellian) lines of thought. Most importantly, Wittgenstein rejects any notion of philosophy being 'scientific' or in any way similar to the natural sciences. Thus Wittgenstein also rejects the idea that philosophical questions could be answered by technical means or formal derivations. His aim was not to give any kind of proof for anything but rather to clarify the most basic notions of logic and language. In this way, Wittgenstein from the start mainly criticizes Russell's, as well as Frege's, outlook, and in many cases he mentions both in one breath. Nine of the seventeen places where Frege is mentioned also refer to Russell. The seventeen passages are as follows (in order of appearance):

(1) TLP 3.143 (cf. NB 97/B2 and B4): Wittgenstein claims that Frege was led astray by the fact that there is no essential difference between a propositional sign and a word into calling a proposition a 'compounded name'. Although the reference to Frege occurs in parentheses, the remark introduces one of Wittgenstein's main points of criticism against Frege.

(2) TLP 3.318: Wittgenstein remarks that, '[l]ike Frege and Russell', he takes a proposition to be a function of the expressions contained in it. The agreement expressed here is very general, since the term 'function' is not used in any technical sense.[24]

(3) TLP 3.325: Wittgenstein introduces the idea of an ideal or perfect Begriffsschrift (Frege's term) and remarks, again in parentheses, that the symbolic notation of Russell and Frege tries to obey the rules of logical syntax, but that it still does not exclude all errors.

(4) TLP 4.063 (cf. NB 99/B10): Wittgenstein argues that there is something wrong with Frege's conception of truth. He uses an analogy to illustrate the concept of truth: If we take a black spot on white paper we can signify (point to) any point on the paper and it will be either black or white. This move can be called an 'assumption' and likened to a Fregean truth-value (which would be either the true or the false). However, we can only say that a point is black or white if we know when to *call* a point 'black' or 'white', and likewise we have to know when to call a proposition 'true' or 'false' if we want to be able to say that it is true. According to Wittgenstein, Frege leaves out this crucial step of first determining the sense of both 'not p' and 'p' before giving a truth-value in order to determine the reference of 'p'. Therefore, even if we do not know what 'white' or 'black' *means*, we can still point to the surface; while nothing corresponds to a proposition without a determined sense, because it would not signify anything, it would not

---

[24] In TLP 3.3 Wittgenstein also refers to Frege even if he does not mention the name: 'only in the context of a sentence has a name meaning'. This is almost verbatim from the introduction to *Grundlagen* (Frege 1884, x). However, for one thing this refers to Frege's earlier conception before he developed the distinction between sense and reference; and also it is critical of Frege because it *separates* the notions of sense (which Wittgenstein applies to sentences only) and reference (which he applies to names only), so that he uses something from (earlier) Frege in order to criticize (later) Frege. In this spirit the first part of the remark reads: 'Only the sentence has sense'. Thus 3.3 is a remark taking up an idea from Frege which is not (or no longer) any part of Frege's mature system.

specify any truth-value. Wittgenstein claims that Frege's conception amounts to believing that 'is true' or 'is false' must function like the verb in a proposition and he objects that anything which could be called true or false must *already* have a verb, and thus be a complete proposition. According to Frege's theory of truth-values, the (linguistic) meaning of a proposition is only completely given if we include its truth-value – and Wittgenstein compares this to completing a sentence by writing 'such-and-such'...'is true' (or 'is false').

(5) TLP 4.1272: Wittgenstein claims that Frege and Russell failed to recognize the nature of formal concepts, which is shown by the fact that in any adequate notation formal concepts are represented by types of variables, not by functions or classes (which can only be used to express 'genuine' concepts).

(6) TLP 4.1273: Wittgenstein considers an important example of a formal concept: the ancestral. The fact that this is a formal concept was overlooked by Frege and Russell. Their definition of the ancestral is therefore circular,[25] insofar as it seeks to derive something which really is part of the most basic vocabulary.

(7) TLP 4.431: Wittgenstein acknowledges that Frege rightly uses the idea that a proposition is the expression of its truth-conditions as his starting point for explaining the notation of his Begriffsschrift. However, his explanation of the concept of truth (his introduction of the True and the False as objects) is wrong, because it would be unable to determine the sense of a negative proposition 'not p'.

(8) TLP 4.442 (cf. NB 103, 95/B32, C40): Wittgenstein argues that Frege's assertion sign (judgement stroke) has no logical relevance.[26] It just indicates that Frege and Russell believe the respective propositions to be true.

(9) TLP 5.02: Wittgenstein suspects that Frege confused the notions of argument and index and thus arrived at his conception that propositions are names. To him they are names of truth-values and their arguments he took to be indices of these names. In the end, complex names are taken to be logically unstructured wholes (like names with an index indicating which one of all the bearers of the same name is being referred to), while the signs of propositions really should be logically compounded in such a way that each component has a sense, contributing it to the whole.

(10) TLP 5.132 (cf. NB 100/B12): Wittgenstein claims that Frege and Russell believed that laws of inference are needed to justify logical inferences, and argues that this is wrong: the justification for any inference rests with the propositions in question themselves and their internal relations. In logic there can be no justification from outside the propositions in question.

(11) TLP 5.4 (cf. NB 107/B74): Wittgenstein claims that it is now clear that there are and can be no 'logical objects' or 'logical constants' in the sense of Frege and Russell.

---

[25] Wittgenstein writes that it contains a 'circulus vitiosus' and this is sometimes taken to refer to the Russell paradox. However, what is vicious about the ancestral is just that it needs to be presupposed in order to be introduced, not that it leads to paradox.

[26] Wittgenstein is not concerned about the judgement stroke having no reference (*Bedeutung*) according to Frege's distinction of sense and reference. Frege himself had pointed out that the job of the judgement stroke was not to signify anything, but to express an act of assertion (Frege 1891, 22).

(12) TLP 5.42 (cf. NB 100/B14): Wittgenstein argues that, because Frege's and Russell's primitive logical signs can be mutually defined, this shows that these logical signs are not fundamental, and also that they do not represent relations. Nothing expressed or signified by the logical signs or constants makes up the 'subject matter' of logic; these signs show only the formal or internal relations between the propositions themselves.

(13) TLP 5.451 (cf. NB 105/B52): Wittgenstein expresses agreement with Frege: the introduction of primitive signs should be guided by the principles laid down for definitions in *Grundgesetze*.

(14) TLP 5.4733: Wittgenstein claims that Frege postulated that every well-formed proposition must have a sense; and argues that this is an empty postulate, insofar as we cannot give a sign a wrong meaning. This is the first of Wittgenstein's remarks which starts with the word 'Frege'.

(15) TLP 5.521: Wittgenstein objects to the fact that Frege and Russell introduce generality in connection with logical sum and product. He argues that this is insufficient, insofar as the expression of generality contains *two* basic notions, generality *and* logical product or sum, not just *one*, as a downright assimilation to the notion of logical sum or product might suggest.

(16) TLP 6.1271: Wittgenstein argues that the number of primitive propositions of logic is quite arbitrary, insofar as one could derive logic from a single primitive proposition simply by forming the logical product of, say, Frege's primitive propositions. He remarks that Frege's idea that the primitive propositions of logic could be 'self-evident' to different degrees is strange for somebody who otherwise is such an 'exact thinker'; the notion of some proposition being more or less 'self-evident' than another one belongs not to logic but to psychology.[27] In logic, there are no *degrees*, as there are in perception.

(17) TLP 6.232: Wittgenstein observes that Frege held that the expressions on each side of an equation, such as 5+7=12, have *different sense* but the *same Bedeutung*. He argues that the identity of the *Bedeutung* of the two expressions can be seen from the expressions themselves. It follows that we cannot *assert* the identity of the *Bedeutung* of two expressions (TLP 6.2322), because in order to *use* the two expressions I must already know whether they have, or have not, the same *Bedeutung*. If therefore identity cannot be asserted, it follows that Frege's theory of the nature of mathematics must be wrong.

Looking over the remarks, it is striking that most of them are written as asides to Wittgenstein's main line of thought, which is organized strictly systematically. Frege's name occurs most frequently in remarks made within parentheses or within dashes (as

---

[27] In his appendix to *Grundgesetze*, vol. 2, Frege writes about his basic law (V), leading to the contradiction: 'I have never disguised from myself that it is not as self-evident (*einleuchtend*) as the others, and as it really ought to be demanded from a logical law' (Frege 1903 253). The translation by Geach has 'its lack of evidence'(Geach and Black 1970, 234), which obscures the point.

in 3.318, 4.063, 5.132), or his name is used as a qualifying adjective (as in 4.063, 5.42, 6.1271). The only exceptions are the preface, and remarks 5.02, 5.4733, 5.521, and 6.232.

Most of the references to Frege occur in remarks that are highly critical; the only remarks expressing a degree of agreement are those numbered (2), (3), (7), and (13) above. The points of agreement are that propositions are built up in a meaningful way out of components and that we judge propositions by paying attention to the specific way in which they are built from specific components in a specific way; that in order to make things clear we need a good symbolic notation like those developed by Frege and Russell; that a proposition is an expression of its truth-conditions; and that there are principles which should govern the introduction of primitive signs in logic.

Although Wittgenstein endorses the idea of a Begriffsschrift, he suggests that the notation of both Frege and Russell is imperfect. In the remarks numbered (8) and (16) above, Wittgenstein makes clear one source of imperfection, namely that everything merely psychological ought to be removed from logical notation. This criticism applies especially to the assertion sign introduced by Frege, which is also used by Russell, and also to their appeal to 'the degree of self-evidence'.[28] Fundamental to logic is the possibility of doing mechanical proofs which serve merely to facilitate the recognition of tautologies (TLP 6.1262); the difference between primitive and derived propositions is relative to the setup of a particular symbolic system, but this has nothing to do with *degrees* of any kind, and thus there is especially no role for the notion of degees of self-evidence. The remaining points will be discussed later.

VI

In this section, I want to look more closely at the principal divergences between Frege and Wittgenstein. Frege's mature logical system is organized around the basic distinction between function and object. Frege explains *everything* in terms of these two basic notions, thus giving his outlook a very strong unity. He first consistently introduces this in his lecture and pamphlet *Function and Concept* (1891), where he explains all the fundamental parts of his system, in terms of functions and objects alone. Thus Frege introduces propositional logic only after he has established his 'functional logic'.[29] It is the notion of a function that really carries the weight while objects have no logical distinctions,[30] and if asked what an object is, Frege simply explains: 'an object is anything

---

[28] It may seem curious that Wittgenstein does not distinguish between Frege's judgement stroke and Russell's assertion sign. The sign he reproduces looks like Russell's assertion sign, which, according to Frege, is composed of the vertical judgement stroke and the 'horizontal' or content stroke. These fine distinctions, however, are unimportant to the point Wittgenstein is making here.

[29] This diverges markedly from the exposition in *Begriffsschrift*.

[30] This amorphous character of objects is closely connected to the Russell paradox about classes of classes. Frege takes classes to be objects, but then he cannot introduce logical distinctions between types of classes.

that is not a function, so that an expression for it does not contain any empty space' (Frege 1891, 18).

This basic conception leads Frege to the idea that concepts can best be regarded as 'truth-functions', i.e. functions which, when completed, have truth-values as their reference. This means that Frege takes sentences to be constructed from concept-words, completed by proper names to form complex names (logically treated as unstructured wholes) which stand either for the True or the False. Since Frege regards the values of functions, other than the functions themselves, as objects because they are saturated and have no empty place, sentences, being names of truth-values, must be taken to stand for special kinds of objects.

In order to make this conception plausible in the case of ordinary sentences, Frege needs to explain how we are to think about the content, or thought, expressed by a sentence – that which usually would be taken to be the *Bedeutung* of a sentence. Frege famously solved this problem by introducing his distinction between sense and reference: The *reference* of a sentence is its truth-value, and the *sense* of a sentence is the thought expressed by it.[31]

Frege's account assimilates ordinary functions and propositional functions, as it also assimilates logical sentences and mathematical equations to empirical statements. They all are seen as names of truth-values (not taking into account whatever that truth may be *about*). Every regular expression consists of a sign which has a sense and a reference.[32] The difference between ordinary proper names, denotational phrases, and sentences is reduced to a difference in the *objects signified*, not in the *ways of symbolizing*, as Wittgenstein will later point out (TLP 3.322).

But how could Frege find his own account convincing? Why would he *want* to assimilate sentences to the case of names? Wittgenstein offers an answer that makes it seem a mistake, or an oversight, on Frege's part. In TLP 3.143, he writes that because a written sentence does not look very much different from a written word (or a written complex denoting phrase, one might like to add) it was 'possible for Frege to call the sentence a compound name'. In TLP 5.02, he writes more specifically: 'The confusion of argument and index is, if I am not mistaken, at the root of Frege's theory of the meaning [*Bedeutung*] of sentences and functions.' Thus Wittgenstein seems to believe that certain features of the expressions of language misled Frege into believing that the *Bedeutung* of a sentence must be an object, and that he then decided that the object in question could only be a truth-value.

---

[31] There has been much discussion about the best translation of *Bedeutung* into English. This very fact shows that Frege is doing something peculiar here. He is conscious that he is doing something unusual with the (German) word and his main argument in favour of his use is that in 'scientific discourse' we are interested mainly in truth. Therefore, he argues, the *Bedeutung* of a sentence must be something closely tied to truth – and what could be more closely tied to truth than a truth-value? In this way Frege quite strategically moves *away* from the way we *use* sentences (and the task to explain how sentences work) to questions about truth (Frege's strategy is defended in Burge 2005).

[32] Cases of fictional or indirect speech are seen as defective or borderline cases, not as something altogether different. According to Frege, fictional discourse can only be a kind of discourse where something is *lacking*, not where something entirely *different* comes into play.

We should, however, be careful in reading these remarks. For one thing, Wittgenstein himself expresses some hesitation ('if I am not mistaken', TLP 5.02) about his guess as to the source of Frege's theory of the meaning of propositions and functions, something very rare in the *Tractatus*.[33] Wittgenstein presupposes that Frege wanted to develop an account of language and that he slipped along the way, but this is contradicted by Frege's own proceedings and reports. Most importantly, Frege was interested in his own logicist project and thus in deriving arithmetic from logic.

In carrying out his project, Frege used only two very specialized types of 'sentences'. First, simple sentences indefinitely indicated by letters, namely sentences that could be substituted *at liberty* for the letters in his Begriffsschrift sentences such as 'if *a*, then (if *b*, then *a*)'. The content as well as the truth-value of these sentences simply does not matter, because it cancels out in the way Frege constructs his more complex Begriffsschrift sentences. Secondly, Frege uses complex Begriffsschrift sentences which he himself constructs, and which he designs in such a way that they are (necessarily) true; that is, they 'cannot be false'. Today we would call them tautologies.[34]

Ordinary empirical sentences play no role in Frege's logical project and he has little interest in explaining how they work. His professed aim is *maximum generality* and in the light of this aim he is interested in being able to treat sentences and singular terms as much alike as possible, and in treating all kinds of sentences uniformly.[35] In this way, Frege's very aim is the opposite of Wittgenstein's. He seeks out ways to *minimize* the conceptual difference between sentences and names, and he is very outspoken about this.

In the preface to *Grundgesetze* he gives two arguments for, or rather he says two things about, his introduction of truth-values. The first thing sounds very curious: 'only thus can indirect discourse be correctly construed'. This is curious because indirect discourse plays no role whatsoever in *Grundgesetze* and Frege uses this argument (taken from the

---

[33] Wittgenstein seems to sense that exegesis is *not* his strong point. Much later, around 1933, we find him articulating another guess about Frege which seems equally off target: 'And if I may dare to guess at Frege's fundamental thought in his theory of sense and reference, then I would continue: the *Bedeutung* of a sentence is its use/application (*Verwendung/Anwendung*)' (BT267v).

[34] A third type of sentences Frege is interested in are mathematical equations and mainly for these he develops his theory of sense and reference in order to explain how a third possibility between trivial equations (like $a=a$) and false ones (like $a=b$) could be conceived. However, in his logical work the notion of sense plays no substantial role, as Simons (1992) has pointed out.

[35] In doing this, Frege combines several confusions (or non-distinctions). First, he treats all sentences as names of truth-values that also express a thought, on the side, so to speak. Secondly, according to his principle of maximum generality he postulates that *all* types of sentences must express a thought, because they all must have sense in addition to having reference. Mathematical equations must express a thought, and logical sentences or formulae must do so, too. This is the reason for Frege's fierce opposition to any kind of formalism in mathematics and for his insistence that there are to be objects in logic. Otherwise logical sentences would lack reference. On top of this, his logicist idea forces Frege to find something which can serve as objects for both logic and arithmetic. From Wittgenstein's point of view the function – object approach wrecks not only Frege's philosophy of language but also his philosophy of mathematics and of logic. However, in insisting on his ideas as he did and drawing the consequences, Frege helped Wittgenstein reach clarity about how things are *not*, which is the first and most important step in clarifying how they *are*.

second part, 'On Sense and Reference') to (somewhat spuriously) legitimate his move.[36] The second thing he says is much closer to his motivation: 'How much simpler and sharper everything becomes through the introduction of truth-values only a detailed study of this book can show' (Frege 1893, x).[37] Frege modified his logical system in order to improve his work in formal logic and he was not misled by modes of expression in language, but rather he modified his system with the purpose of making 'everything simpler and sharper'. It is for this reason that he felt that the difference between words and sentences (and what they stand for) could be made more slight.[38]

Wittgenstein's remarks about Frege's motivation are, therefore, quite mistaken. The question about genesis or motivation, however, is not the main point here.[39] We first of all need a better appreciation of the background to Frege's approach. This can help to achieve a better understanding of the Frege–Wittgenstein controversy. It also makes clear that they disagree nearly always on philosophical, and only rarely on technical, matters.[40] Thus disagreements over apparent details will prove to be grounded in a more fundamental opposition of perspective. This can also, in turn, show how the various points of criticism that Wittgenstein levels against Frege (and Russell) interconnect and serve to highlight what Wittgenstein calls 'the single great problem': this could be termed the problem of 'explaining the nature of the proposition' (NB, 39) but also the problem of 'saying and showing'. For Wittgenstein these phrasings are just different aspects of the same fundamental problem.

The upshot of Frege's reasoning, from Wittgenstein's view, is that Frege's systematic approach is unable to explain the difference between a sentential and a non-sentential sign, that is, between a name and a sentence. Seen in this light, Frege's theory of sense and reference is part of the strategy of assimilation, and, contrary to the received view, not Frege's main contribution to a theory of language. This should be explained in more detail.

The fundamental notion for Frege's distinction between sense and reference is the notion of *substitution*.[41] This notion is closely tied to the notion of a function, in which we can fill the empty space by different arguments. Frege introduces the notion of

---

[36] Frege really has no intrinsic interest in indirect discourse – his interest wakes up only if he can use it to draw an argument for something else from it.

[37] There is a certain amount of ambiguity in Frege about his mature conception as he is aware that it will seem paradoxical, and not free from difficulties. The most obvious point is the introduction of courses-of-values as a special type of objects. Frege undertook this step already with a bad conscience, but as he wrote to Russell, 'what other way do we have?' On the whole, however, Frege was convinced that his new developments amounted to a substantial progress in logic (and in the philosophy of language, too, but this he took to be a mere side-effect) – and even after the contradiction he stayed convinced that the distinctions of sense and reference as well as of concept and object were sound and important (see the Darmstaedter notes from 1919, in Frege 1979).

[38] See the next section for more on this point.

[39] One might put Frege's motivation this way: Frege wanted to *substitute* a principle of coordination between sentence-type names and truth-values for a description of how sentences actually work in order to make things around sentences more sharply and easily manageable. Systematically, Frege probably conceived of this move as part of his campaign against psychologism (language use being in the end something merely psychological for him).

[40] Wittgenstein shows no interest at all in making proofs more secure, or in guarding logic against paradox.

[41] This was first pointed out in Carnap 1947, §21.

reference in such a way that he states that the truth-value of a sentence remains unchanged if any expression in it is replaced by an expression having the same reference. Frege does not give an independent explanation of his notion of reference, but ties his explanation to the idea of the substitution of expressions.[42] For Frege, *truth-preservation* is the standard by which to judge sameness of reference. Also, the examples Frege uses to introduce the notion are statements where (good or bad) substitution is the main issue.

From Wittgenstein's point of view, Frege's examples are far from being ordinary sentences; they simply do not belong to the philosophy of language, but rather to the philosophy of mathematics. In TLP 6.23 he writes: 'If two expressions are connected by the sign of equality, this means that they can be substituted for one another. But whether this is the case must show itself in the two expressions themselves.'[43] Wittgenstein then mentions Frege: 'Frege says, both expressions have the same reference, but different sense' (TLP 6.232). This, however, is something we need to know before we can say anything, i.e. before we make any kind of assertion. Therefore, he states calmly: 'The identity of the reference of two expressions cannot be *asserted*'[44] (TLP 6.2322). This intended act of assertion is plainly impossible (as well as unnecessary) because this identity must be *presupposed* the moment we write down the respective expressions; we can use only vocabulary we are familiar with, where we already know the meanings of the words.

These considerations show that Wittgenstein does not consider Frege's theory of sense and reference to be of any importance to his own project of clarifying the logic of our language. He therefore cannot be seen as 'refashioning' Frege's conception – rather he points out that (and how) Frege's distinction really has a lot to do with function – object analysis, but very little with philosophy of language as he approaches it.

---

[42] Thomas Ricketts has emphasized the idea that for Frege everything is about logic and not about ontology, and that for him ontology follows from logic but has no independent source. See Ricketts 2004, 184–5.

[43] Frege, of course, explained equations as asserting that on both sides of the sign there is a name of the same object. This explanation works both for words (or number-words) and for entire sentences (if we take sentences to be names of truth-values) – and thus equations offer a paradigm case of how everything becomes much simpler by the introduction of his mature theory of the reference of sentences. Earlier he would have had to distinguish between the case of numbers and regular objects on one hand and the case of sentences on the other – with all the known difficulties around the question: What are the precise conditions for connecting two sentences by the equality sign? The usual answer would have been that sentences cannot be joined by the equality sign unless it is the *same* sentence twice, but then we could never have non-trivial equations between sentences. Now Frege can extend his principle that we should be allowed to substitute *anything* in any place (as long as it is a complete expression).

[44] In this passage, 'meaning' would be a more natural rendering for *Bedeutung*. This, however, is really part of the problem with Frege's conception. Wittgenstein insists that we know the (linguistic) meaning of the words or more generally of the signs we use according to specified rules, and concludes that in many cases (such as mathematics) to know that meaning is all we need to do our work in formal logic or mathematics. We need no spatial or other intuition but we simply need to know the way the words or signs are *used* in our language or calculus (to see how our calculus works, see TLP 6.2331). Somewhat sarcastically he states that 'language itself supplies the necessary intuition' (TLP 6.233). Frege introduces something of an empirical or causal ring when he ties *Bedeutung* to the objects referred to – something beyond the reach of language itself. If there is *Bedeutung* in logic, then logic cannot 'take care of itself' (TLP 5.473).

Frege's famous distinction of sense and reference is actually an important, if subservient,[45] part in his project to get *as far away as possible* from ordinary language and to subject everything to the function-object model.[46] Remember that Frege is convinced that ordinary language is quite useless for logical investigations and should, if at all possible, be replaced by something more precise.

Wittgenstein's fundamental insight that the language of logic and mathematics works in a totally different way from the language of empirical statements organizes his *Tractatus* and the main task of the book is to bring this point across. Frege, on the other hand, develops a model where all statements, whether they be empirical, logical, or mathematical, are fashioned on *one and the same* basic pattern, namely that of function and argument, supplemented by sense and reference. In the light of these considerations, the remarks mentioning Frege can be seen as a series of particular points where the train of thought of the *Tractatus* touches upon questions where the contrast between the respective conceptions becomes especially *striking*.

VII

Recently, Cora Diamond and Thomas Ricketts have offered some highly interesting contributions toward a better understanding of the general nature of the Frege–Wittgenstein relation. To highlight some of these points, I will discuss some aspects of Diamond's remarkable paper, 'Inheriting from Frege'.

Diamond's strategy is just about the opposite to the one employed here. After briefly discussing some preliminary issues, she develops the Frege–Wittgenstein difference by investigating the details of the notoriously obscure remark TLP 5.02, advancing from some very intricate questions of exegesis to the basic issue underlying the disagreement.[47] This basic issue is then explained in an admirably clear way. This strategy of going from the obscure and intricate to the clear and simple goes with presenting the problems in a way that can easily be misunderstood, as will be seen.[48]

Diamond's first example is intended to provide a specimen of something Wittgenstein 'learned from Frege' (Diamond 2010, 559). Section 2 is titled: 'On distinguishing sharply

[45] Remember that 'On Sense and Reference' is written in order to expand on a footnote in *Function and Concept* (Frege 1891, 14). In his introduction to *Grundgesetze* Frege states that 'concept and relation are the foundation stones upon which I raise my structure' (Frege 1893, 3); sense and reference are only very briefly mentioned in §2.

[46] In addition, on Wittgenstein's view the distinction between sense and reference furthermore gives a wrong picture of philosophy of mathematics. It introduces *objects* into mathematics and thus in turn assimilates mathematics to ordinary sentences dealing with and describing objects and states of affairs. Thus it obscures the formal nature of mathematics.

[47] Remark TLP 5.02 is quite generally regarded as 'obscure' and hard to make sense of, let alone defend (McGinn 2006, 207–8).

[48] It is quite possible that some of the more critical remarks about Diamond's reasoning may be misunderstandings on my part. Yet even then they may serve to illustrate the kind of questions that suggest themselves when reading her fine paper.

enough'. Just as Frege shows that others do not distinguish 'proper names and concept-words sharply enough' (ibid., 555), Wittgenstein in turn observes that it is a source of philosophical confusion to make a 'difference too slight' (ibid., 559). He also uses this method to criticize Frege, who made the difference 'between physical and mathematical facts' (ibid., 558) or 'between numerals and numbers' too slight (ibid., 555; the reference is to PI §339). While this makes it sound as if Wittgenstein used an idea from Frege to criticize Frege, the issue actually runs much deeper.

Wittgenstein's basic methodological outlook is quite different from Frege's, and Frege's importance for Wittgenstein has very little to do with similarity of opinion but a lot to do with the fact that this very contrast enabled Wittgenstein to bring out his view of the matter more clearly. Wittgenstein used Frege's work as a tool, not as a source of doctrine. Whereas Frege insists on sharp distinctions from the beginning, and insists that we stick to the sharp distinctions we make in order to frame one consistent system, Wittgenstein's main idea is to clarify essential differences. Thus Frege goes for a systematic science as a system of truths, while Wittgenstein first of all wants to clarify the most basic notions, something that can essentially 'be said in three words' (see the motto to the *Tractatus*). Thus Wittgenstein is not interested in introducing a sharp distinction between numbers and numerals, but rather he wants to convey a sense of the huge conceptual difference between the two notions, so that once we have grasped it, we will no longer be in need of any sharp distinction. Thus, while Frege's favourite word is 'sharp' (see above the way he advocates truth-values!), Wittgenstein's preferred term is 'clear'.[49] In this way, Wittgenstein is doing something which is only superficially similar to what Frege is doing, and he is doing it in such a different way that it is somewhat misleading to call what he is doing something 'he learned from Frege'.[50]

This difference is closely related to the second way in which Diamond claims Wittgenstein learned from Frege. This is the idea of 'overcoming by taking seriously' (section 3). One favourite method of both Frege and Wittgenstein is to take some conception at its word and then have a close look at what it leads to. This will usually lead to an outright rejection of the examined theory. Frege's main example is his critique of the formalist conception of arithmetic (Diamond 2010, 559–60) and Wittgenstein picks up 'Frege's awareness of the tension within the philosophically confused view' (ibid., 563), which usually depends 'on a kind of failure to mean fully what we say' (ibid., 564).

Diamond notices, however, one difference between 'Frege's ridicule and Wittgenstein's patient unravellings' (ibid., 654): Frege thinks that he is uncovering 'stupid prejudices', while

[49] The key word to the *Tractatus* is 'clear', and neither 'sharp' nor 'exact', nor for that matter 'nonsense' or 'elucidation'. Frege as well as Wittgenstein seems to have sensed this difference in philosophical outlook. Wittgenstein once calls Frege an 'exact thinker' (TLP 6.1271), not a clear one, while Frege seemed startled at Wittgenstein's philosophical aims, calling them 'artistic rather than scientific' and stating that to him 'greatest distinctness (*Deutlichkeit*) would always be greatest beauty' (FW 16/9/19). Using some more traditional vocabulary, this difference could be expressed by saying that Wittgenstein aims at clarity while Frege tries to outrun clarity by going for distinctness. For more on this see Kienzler 2009.

[50] Maybe it is difficult to do justice to both aspects when stressing both the issue of 'learning form Frege' and 'fundamentally disagreeing with Frege'.

Wittgenstein speaks of 'an urge to misunderstand the workings of our language' (ibid., 563). This difference has to do with another fundamental contrast between Frege and Wittgenstein. Whereas Frege always aims at truth *behind* the different modes of expression, and thus tries to *refute* false opinions, Wittgenstein is aware that the main philosophical problem is always one of expression, of the way we put things. In Wittgenstein's view, the most eminent danger for philosophy is not that somebody holds a *false theory*, but rather that people are stuck in *unclear ways of expression*.[51] The main problem is not that we do not begin with sharp distinctions, but rather that we are unclear about where the distinctions are to be drawn in the first place. In this way both thinkers use a similar tool but in pursuit of quite different goals.[52]

Consider Frege's criticism of formalist arithmetic. It is remarkable that in the end Wittgenstein used this very example, upon which Frege had spent more anger and analytical power than on any other theory, in order to show that Frege had certainly distinguished both conceptions of arithmetic sharply enough, but that he still had not reached clarity about the real issue. Some of the most important seeds of Wittgenstein's later philosophy of mathematics, as well as of language, come exactly from taking up the formalist's comparison between mathematics and a game according to rules.[53] Actually Wittgenstein can be taken to start from the point of maximum ridicule Frege ever reached, in his satirical pamphlet *On Mr Schubert's Numbers*, about the 'principle of not distinguishing what is different', namely the sign and the thing signified (Diamond 2010, 565). According to later Wittgenstein, we only get off the ground once we *stop* trying to 'sharply distinguish' the 'sign from that which is signified' (*Zeichen und Bezeichnetes*) and start thinking about rules (use of expressions) rather than meanings or references.[54, 55]

[51] One might be tempted to say: the basic aim of the *Tractatus* is to show where and how precise, exact, and sharp (mainly technical) work can in the end still be philosophically very unclear. Another aspect of this kind of difference is that it is very difficult to express it in the right way, because one has to use different modes of expression for distinguishing sharply and for making elementary points clear. To use a certain language means already having taken a side.

[52] In Frege's case the situation is somewhat more complicated because quite a few of his examples can be understood along Wittgensteinian lines – i.e. in contrast to Frege's own official view about philosophy. Sometimes he simply 'makes things clear' – and this is the inspiration of much of Diamond's work.

[53] One of the first remarks about this problem is particularly striking: 'It would then turn out that what Frege called the "ginger-snap viewpoint" in arithmetic could in the end yet be justified' (PR §103; MS 107, 21). To Frege, this *Pfeffernussstandpunkt*, identifying numbers with physical objects, was the top of stupidity one could possibly reach (see *Grundgesetze*, §149; in this case the derision is directed against Weierstrass).

[54] Wittgenstein knew and liked the pamphlet, recommending it to Ramsey in 1923. See Frege 1899, 4 and 17 about 'the power of stupidity' and about the principle mentioned, respectively, and also the afterword in Frege 1999. This is not to say that Wittgenstein found Frege's satirical attack worthless – quite to the contrary, he found it extremely useful, and the following motto could be seen as directed at Frege: 'Much is gained once a false thought is only boldly and clearly expressed' (CV, 75). This is definitely not something Frege could have written. In Wittgenstein's view Frege had become clearer through treating the issue in a very heavy-handed way. There is some irony in the fact that Carnap, who also liked the pamphlet, used the remark about the principle to distinguish sharply enough between the sign and what is signified and made it something like the motto of his *Logical Syntax of Language* (Carnap 1937, §42 about this 'witty but fundamentally serious satire').

[55] Especially the *Blue Book* can be regarded as a series of reactions to Frege, taking a start from the question 'what is the meaning of a word?' and then discussing Frege's anti-formalist answer that the sign

The main part of Diamond's paper officially deals with 'sense and reference' (sections 4 to 7). We are promised a clarification of 'Wittgenstein's rethinking of the distinction between sense and reference' (Diamond 2010, 566). However, not only is this not what we get, but it is not what Wittgenstein did.[56] What we do get is an exegesis of TLP 5.02 as a starting point. The discussion then quickly moves to the more central topic of negation and to the point that, 'counter to his intentions', Frege's account 'makes the sense of "~p" *not* depend on the sense of "p"' (ibid., 572). Diamond explains this by distinguishing 'sentential' and 'non-sentential' sense: 'only when a sentence is actually used as a sentence' can negation be properly understood. According to Frege's conception, the reference of a sentence is its truth-value and a sentence and its negation simply have two different objects as their reference, just as the function $f(x) = 2x$ will give two different values if we insert two different numbers in the argument-place. It will then come as a coincidence, so to speak, without any essential connection, that the reference of a sentence with added double negation is the same as that of that sentence without any negation.[57]

cannot be the important part, and that therefore the object the word stands for must be the meaning of a word (BB, 4). It is noteworthy that several of Wittgenstein's book-projects from this period take their lead from Frege and the formalism issue: compare the beginning of the *Big Typescript* (BT, 1–4), the *Philosophical Grammar*, also the 'Dictation for Schlick' (TS 302) and the beginning of the obscure Yellow Book (in AWL, 43). (See Kienzler 1997, 215–17.)

[56] Diamond compares Wittgenstein's rethinking of Frege to Frege's relation to Kant (Diamond 2010, 550, also 566). This is misleading in several respects: Kant is in no way as closely tied to Frege's enterprise as Frege is to Wittgenstein's. From Wittgenstein we can learn a lot about Frege but from Frege we can learn very little about Kant, as there is only a very slight connection between Frege's and Kant's work. The most that can be said is that Frege lived in a Kantian, or rather Neokantian, intellectual climate, which made it convenient to express certain basic differences in Kantian terms, even if one had rather little interest in (and maybe understanding of) Kant's philosophy. In particular, Frege professedly could not come to terms with the notion of 'pure intuition' without which Kant's theory of arithmetic cannot be made sense of. In many respects Wittgenstein is closer to Kant than Frege is.

[57] To be sure, Wittgenstein is not accusing Frege of getting any *false results* from his stipulations; his point is merely philosophical: Frege will get the correct results but his conception cannot explain to us *how a sentence works*. He is, so to speak, *simulating* the behaviour of sentences through certain functions. In a sense it is very *easy* to accommodate negation on a function–argument basis in such a way that 'everything comes out correctly'. The remark that according to Frege's own standards the sense of '~p' would 'by no means be determinate' if the True and the False were really objects (TLP 4.431) means that Frege's conception cannot adequately *express* the relation between a sentence and its negation. It is of course always possible to *stipulate* the results in a convenient way. Frege can easily stipulate the values for expressions carrying negation in such a way as to picture 'the reversed use of the sentence and its negation' (Diamond 2010, 582), say by arbitrarily defining some function oscillating between the two truth-values. Diamond makes it very clear that Wittgenstein's objection basically turns on the idea of 'the *essential* role of the argument in the recognition of what the Bedeutung of the whole sign is' (ibid., 598); this relation must not be *arbitrary*. Frege's logic, however, does not systematically distinguish between an arbitrary and an essential connection, as becomes clear from his notion of quantification: he has no notational device for the difference between cases where something is by coincidence true of all objects and those where the truth is grounded in some essential, or conceptual, relation. If he had such a distinction, he would see 'that the theory of classes is entirely superfluous in mathematics' because 'the generality we need in mathematics is not one of contingency' (TLP 6.031). This is a second philosophical objection against Frege's way of expressing generality (or quantification) – although Wittgenstein feels free to use that notation himself on many occasions.

Thus Wittgenstein is criticizing Frege's basic model, and his use of the terms 'index' and 'argument' is not intended to be logically precise (and 'distinguishing sharply enough'), but rather to explain one very basic, and in a way very simple, point.[58] That point was already present in the early 'Notes on Logic': the p in ~p is exactly the same as when it stands alone (Diamond 2010, 577), and conspicuously the *Tractatus* repeatedly discusses the basically very simple operation of negation (e.g. in passages beginning at 4.061, 4.431, 5.44, and 5.512), which does not have any technically interesting aspects. The reason for this is that negation is the operation that most easily and clearly brings out the conceptual difference between sentences and the role they play in language, as opposed to Frege's function–object account, which deliberately assimilates the cases.[59]

It is, therefore, quite misleading to speak of 'Wittgenstein's move away from Frege on sense and reference' (Diamond 2010, 580), because Wittgenstein never started from Frege's idea of sense and reference at all. The way negation works can be explained quite independently of the sense–reference distinction. Wittgenstein really is above all interested in what might be called the 'name–sentence distinction'.[60] *This* is what he stresses again and again, while his rather few remarks on sense and reference are very much spoken aside. Diamond writes that Wittgenstein shares 'with Frege an understanding of what talk of sense and reference is responsible to' (ibid., 584).[61] This presupposes that it is Frege's aim to achieve 'a cer-

---

[58] In this connection Diamond convincingly answers exegetical moves and objections by Black (Diamond 2010, 570) and Dummett (ibid., 571), as well as Goldfarb (ibid., 597–8).

[59] It is tempting to think that Frege originally had the right idea about negation and that Wittgenstein 'alleges that this healthy insight is throttled by Frege's post-1891 grammar that…takes sentential connectives to mean functions that map truth-values to truth-values' (Ricketts 2002, 229). While this is an important difference, the fact remains that Wittgenstein nowhere singles out the 1879 account as correct. It is true that for Frege it is just natural that double negation cancels out: two negation strokes immediately following one another are as good as none, but this is something he also explicitly, if in passing, states in the exposition of *Grundgesetze*: 'Obviously in this case two negation strokes cancel out (Frege 1893, §13). Wittgenstein therefore has no reason to object to Frege's *practical use* of negation. What he does object to is Frege's *understanding*, or one could say *philosophical interpretation*, of negation. In this respect he criticizes later Frege for interpreting negation as a type of function (having a function-sign that needs to have sense as well as reference; see Frege 1891, 22), and he points out how the theory of truth-values destroys the essential (and one might say 'natural') relation between sentences and their negation (or double or triple etc. negation). But he would also criticize very late Frege for concluding his essay 'Negation' with the statement: 'Double negation covering a thought does not alter the truth-value of the thought' (Frege 1919, 157) – even though technically there is nothing wrong with Frege's view – except for the fact that Frege's illustration of a thought being dressed in one or two negations simply breaks down in the case of double negation: the double garment would have to disappear. But to return to *Begriffsschrift*: Wittgenstein would also object to the way Frege treats negation here, introducing negation not in the scope of his 'exposition of the signs' but by giving special 'basic laws' (*Grundgesetze*) for the introduction as well as the removal of double negation. (And then he found a trick to collapse both cases into one, as he notes in the Preface.) According to Wittgenstein, the fact that double negation cancels out is not a (true) basic law *about* negation, but simply already part of its meaning, an essential feature of the way we use that particular sign.

[60] This parallel way of expression must, again, be taken with caution: it is not just that Wittgenstein builds a system out of two different blocks, but his entire way of proceeding is quite different.

[61] Frege might answer: Talk of sense and reference is responsible for explaining how equations can be informative, yet analytic.

tain *redescription* of certain features of our linguistic practices' (ibid., 585), and that he failed to achieve this aim.[62] If the account given above of Frege's way of proceeding is correct, then this was definitely *not* Frege's aim, but he rather intended to forge a more powerful tool for formal logic than the one that he had available before. Frege was happy to move away from any kind of description of our linguistic practices and he tried to build a system of logic which could eventually, that much is true, serve as a standard for our linguistic practices, too.

Frege's priorities were with a logical system giving an account of truth, and he believed that our linguistic practices would have to conform to that standard, not the other way around. It is therefore wrong to suggest that 'Frege is unwittingly equivocating, and can do so because his notation fails to mark clearly the logical features which belong to the use of sentences' (ibid., 590).[63] It is wrong because Frege is quite consciously organizing his notation in such a way that the fundamental difference between names and sentences is 'overcome', so that they can be treated as uniformly as possible within his logical system. It is also fairly certain that Frege would have been unimpressed by Wittgenstein's criticism. There is no place in Frege's logical system where anything wrong would follow from this assimilation of names and sentences; this is not a problem similar to the Russell paradox; there is no problem of deriving something false such as a contradiction. In this way, it is striking that Wittgenstein is in turn very little impressed by the fact that the paradox leads to an inconsistency, but very much concerned about the logical role of names and sentences. For Frege, quite the opposite is true and he would be unimpressed by any charge of 'conceptual distortion', simply because he did not feel obliged to faithfully reconstruct any concepts, but he would be very worried if not everything would come out having the correct truth-value.[64]

---

[62] This idea that Frege was mainly interested in our linguistic practices was stressed by Thomas Ricketts (see Diamond 2010, 592). This notion fits better with early Frege, who had the idea that we ought to replace our use of word-language by some more precise use of *Begriffsschrift* notation, viewing his logical system much like an improved *tool*. In a certain sense (different from the sense Ricketts seems to intend) the mature Frege offers such a *redescription*, too: he develops a logical system that is to contain all the truths we could strive to attain using our linguistic practices, without having to refer to any of these practices. He tries to offer the (system of) results only. (In some respects Frege's approach is similar to theoretical reconstructions of language use through set theory.)

[63] Frege would be happy to accept the charge that his 'notation encourages what one might think of as a kind of blindness to use, blindness to logical differences dependent on use' (ibid., 590). He might answer: I am not interested in *use* but in *truth* only and in logical differences only insofar as they touch on questions of truth. In this sense he was more of a Platonist than Diamond and Ricketts would like him to be.

There is, however, right at the end of Diamond's paper a hint that Wittgenstein's criticism has little to do with a slip in Frege and this very much agrees with the way things have been presented here: 'So I read the strong claim made by Wittgenstein, that the index-argument confusion lies at the root of Frege's account of the meaning of propositions and functions, to be an abbreviated way of saying that Frege's conception of propositions as complete signs and his conception of functions on the model of arithmetical functions, taken together, *give him no options*' (ibid., 600–1; emphasis added).

[64] In this sense Warren Goldfarb's suggestion that there 'is no hint of influence from Frege's judgement-based approach to analysis' (Diamond 2010, 596) is quite correct: Wittgenstein's agenda was from the start very much different from Frege in subject-matter as well as in kind and method – so that there can be no talk of Wittgenstein working through 'Frege's approach and uncovering the tensions from inside. Frege himself is very little concerned with the problem 'of what is involved in a proposition's having sense' (ibid., 596).

VIII

Now a second brief look at the seventeen points where Frege is mentioned in the *Tractatus* may bring out some of these connections more clearly:

(1) It is the fact that a word does not look essentially different from a sentence – that they are both expressions made up from letters – that enables Frege to treat a proposition as a compound name. However, it seems likely that Frege would be quite undisturbed by Wittgenstein's criticism of his unified function–argument conception.

(2) It is agreed that sentences are functions of the expressions contained in them, but not in the technical way Frege declared them to be (see also TLP 5.02).

(3) In particular, Frege's and Russell's notations do not keep them from treating names and sentences alike, or prevent them from believing that the Russell Paradox could be written down (which it cannot, according to TLP 3.333), or from misinterpreting sentences written in their own notation (most notably 'identity statements'; see TLP 5.5301).

(4) 'Being true' or 'is true' is not the verb that transforms a sentence from a name to a judgement,[65] nor can Truth be an object and the reference of all true sentences. Frege's system leads to wrong ways to think about truth (TLP 4.063).

(5) It is because Frege (and Russell) have a material conception of logic as a system of truths that they are unable to see the nature of formal concepts correctly. Following his uniform function–object approach, Frege could not distinguish formal from material concepts, nor logical and mathematical from empirical statements.

(6) One of the most striking examples of the confusion about the nature of formal concepts within the scope of Frege's logicism concerns the notion of the ancestral. Frege's attempt to define it by purely logical means is circular because as a formal concept it is presupposed in all formal derivations. A formal notion equivalent to the ancestral is already included in the notion of logic. This dissolves one of the central ideas of logicism.[66]

(7) Frege is right in listing truth-conditions before introducing his logical connectives; he is, however (to repeat the point of TLP 4.063), wrong in taking the True to be an object, as this makes negation incomprehensible.

---

[65] This could be a reference to *Begriffsschrift* stating that 'the symbol ⊢ is the common predicate for all judgements' (Frege 1879, §2).

[66] Wittgenstein objects that Frege's way of framing the notion of the ancestral and thus of logic in relation to arithmetic is 'not a priori enough'. The a priori does not come in instalments but everything a priori is there from the very beginning, before we can start making assertions, because the a priori is what makes assertions possible. Therefore logicism cannot be asserted; it would have to be obvious from the beginning – through a comparison of the most basic forms of logical and mathematical notation. And in this regard Wittgenstein perceives much similarity and therefore he speaks of mathematics as 'a logical method' (TLP 6.2) but then he also emphasizes the *essential difference* between tautologies in logic and equations in mathematics. He would, however, see no point at all in either reducing tautologies to equations nor the other way around.

(8) The assertion sign has no logical, but only psychological relevance. In a way this is yet another aspect of Frege's misunderstanding of the notion of truth, trying to express what cannot be expressed.[67]

(9) Negation cannot be understood on Frege's function–object model.

(10) Frege's conception not only postulated that every sign has a meaning, but also that every move in logic must be *justified*. This led him to believe that logical inferences have to be justified by logical laws of inference. This again misunderstands the purely formal nature of logic: logical inference consists in a certain (formal) relation between several sentences; making an inference means nothing above our perceiving that internal relation. There are especially no new logical sentences (no truths) generated under any law of justification.

(11) Because of the formal nature of logic, there cannot be anything material – no material relation – expressed or designated by the logical connectives. They are rather to be compared to mere brackets (see TLP 5.461).This becomes especially clear when we consider that they can be mutually cross-defined: what is seemingly 'fundamental' in one way of defining comes out as 'derived' in another way of doing it.

(12) There are therefore also no 'logical objects'. The idea that there are logical objects also follows from Frege's function–object analysis. According to this conception, every singular, as well as every functional, term 'must have some meaning' and thus must stand for an object.

(13) When we define primitive signs in logic, they must each be defined independently of one another. This agrees with Frege's principles for defining in *Grundgesetze*.

(14) Frege's function–object analysis requires that every sign must be given some meaning. However, the meaning of a sign simply consists in the rules we stipulate for it. Frege's idea that there might be signs without meaning misunderstands the relation of sign and meaning as an external, accidental relation.[68]

(15) Frege (and Russell) do not separate the notion 'every' from the logical sum or product. This makes it difficult to understand sentences using expressions of generality.[69] (Wittgenstein here turns against attempts to express modalities, 'certainty, possibility, impossibility' (TLP 5.525) by using quantifier notation.) We do not get wrong results this way; it is only that we *misunderstand* what we say and thus also the results we get.

(16) The notion that there are *degrees* of 'self-evidence' again brings something psychological into logic. Even a thinker as exact as Frege believed this.

---

[67] Curiously, later Wittgenstein came to see that the judgement stroke could also be seen to highlight the difference between a (complete) sentence as opposed to what is not a complete sentence; just as we use a period or full stop to mark the end of a sentence (PI §22).

[68] Here *Bedeutung* is rendered as 'meaning' – Wittgenstein's point may also be put like this: signs do not necessarily have to have some *reference*; it suffices if they have some *meaning* – and they get this meaning through the rules we stipulate for their use.

[69] Wittgenstein does not object to the close connection between quantifiers and logical sum or product; in fact he endorses this view (compare his self-critique in PG, 268–9). He objects that the notions of logical sum and product and the notion of 'every', respectively, are not introduced *separately*. This difficult remark is carefully untangled in Ricketts (unpublished).

(17) Equations are not meaningful sentences but express possibilities of substitution among the expressions involved. This solely depends on the meaning of the expressions and this must be known (or stipulated) to begin with. Frege's theory of mathematics is therefore wrong, and his theory of sense and reference is also mistaken, and in particular all of this has nothing to do with explaining language.

Finally, where should we look in order to find the real Frege–Wittgenstein difference? We would have to look at the structure of the whole book. When Frege tried to read the *Tractatus* he stumbled over the very first page. This has partly to do with the style it is written in. Frege could, however, have sensed that the very beginning – 'The world is the totality of facts, not things' (TLP 1.1) – presents a view in which the difference between names (corresponding to things) and sentences (which correspond to facts) is fundamental – and not the difference between functions and objects as Frege would have it.[70] Not only this, Wittgenstein is developing an account of language and expression *without* any unifying formal notion of 'sentence': he is interested in the different forms in language, and especially those that *cannot* be reduced to the logical form of a 'sentence with sense' of the form *fa*. Thus he sorts out different types of linguistic practices without postulating that there be a *summum genus* to all of them. Thus everything in the book is designed to elucidate a view that was developed in contrast to Frege's. This is one more reason why it is almost impossible to understand that book without understanding Frege.[71]

---

[70] Wittgenstein even writes simple function terms just like fx – that is, he omits the brackets indicating the empty space. He uses brackets as organizing devices only, as in f(x,y), but not to indicate anything ontological (see LO, 19–20).

[71] In later years Wittgenstein repeatedly attributed the invention of truth-tables to Frege: 'Incidentally, this kind of schema is not my invention; Frege used it. The only part of it which is my invention—not that it matters in the least—was to use this as a symbol for the proposition, not as an explanation of it (like Frege).' (LFM, 177; 1939)

He points out that, strictly speaking, a truth-table is not an *explanation* of, say, negation or disjunction, but simply one perspicuous way of writing it down: 'This schema does not say anything about ~p; it is another way of writing it.' (AWL, 135; 1935) Therefore the truth-table in 4.442 already is a propositional sign, and needs no extra sign, like Frege's judgement stroke, to turn it into one. (4.431 still sensed agreement about 'Frege's explanations of the signs of his Begriffsschrift'.)

Wittgenstein used this device against Frege (and Russell) and their idea that logic was *about* something: 'Then one day I made up the T-F symbolism [i.e. his, truth-tables', W.K.]. This symbolism was a means of transforming Russell's [and Frege's, W.K.] propositions into a form where they all looked similar. If you have any of Russell's propositions—either primitive propositions or propositions which follow from these—you always get the same in T-F notation: you get a column of T's' (LFM, 280).

Frege lists the different cases when he introduces his main connectives, but he nowhere presents an actual table. The earliest remark about this suggests that it was Wittgenstein, after all, who 'made up the T-F symbolism': 'Frege's explanation of the truth-functions, *organized into a schema*, results in a new notation of the truth-functions.' (MS 109, 94; 1930, emphasis added) Systematically speaking, of course, Frege's introduction of a truth-functional approach is a more important step than organizing his explanations into a truth-table.

References

ANSCOMBE, G. E. M. (1971). *An Introduction to Wittgenstein's Tractatus*. London: Hutchinson.

BAKER, GORDON and HACKER, P. M. S. (1984). *Frege: Logical Excavations*. New York: Oxford University Press and Oxford: Blackwell.

BURGE, TYLER (2005). 'Frege on Truth', in Burge, *Truth, Thought, Reason: Essays on Frege*. Oxford: Clarendon, pp. 83–152.

CARNAP, RUDOLF (1937). *Logical Syntax of Language*. London: Routledge & Kegan Paul.

—— (1947). *Meaning and Necessity*. Chicago: Chicago University Press.

CONANT, JAMES (2002). 'The Method of the Tractatus', in Reck ed. (2002), pp. 374–462.

DIAMOND, CORA (1991). *The Realistic Spirit*. Cambridge, MA: MIT Press.

—— (2010). 'Inheriting from Frege: the work of reception, as Wittgenstein did it', in M. Potter and T. Ricketts eds., *The Cambridge Companion to Frege*. Cambridge: Cambridge University Press, pp. 550–601.

DUMMETT, MICHAEL (1991). 'Frege and Wittgenstein', in Dummett, *Frege and other Philosophers*. Blackwell: Oxford.

FREGE, GOTTLOB (1879). *Begriffsschrift*. Halle: L. Nebert. [Extracts trans. Geach and Black (1970), pp. 1–20.]

—— (1884). *Die Grundlagen der Arithmetik*. Breslau: W. Koebner. [*The Foundations of Arithmetic* (1974), ed. and trans. J. L. Austin. Oxford: Blackwell.]

—— (1891). *Function and Concept*, trans. Geach and Black (1970), 21–41.

—— (1892). 'On Sense and Reference', trans. Geach and Black (1970), 56–78.

—— (1892a). 'Concept and Object', trans. Geach and Black (1970), 42–55.

—— (1893). *Grundgesetze der Arithmetik*, I. Jena: Hermann Pohle. [Extracts trans. Geach and Black (1970), 137–244.]

—— (1894) 'Husserl review', trans. Geach and Black (1970), 79–85.

—— (1899). *On Mr Schubert's Numbers*, trans. in Frege, *Collected Papers on Mathematics, Logic, and Philosophy* (1984), ed. B. McGuinness. Oxford: Blackwell, pp. 249–72.

—— (1903). *Grundgesetze der Arithmetik*, II. [Extracts trans. Geach and Black (1970), 137–244.]

—— (1904). 'What is a Function?', trans. Geach and Black (1970), 107–16.

—— (1918). 'Thoughts', trans. in *Logical Investigations* (1977), ed. with preface by P. Geach. Oxford: Blackwell, pp. 1–30.

—— (1919). 'Negation', trans. Geach and Black (1970), 117–36.

—— (1976). *Wissenschaftlicher Briefwechsel*, ed. G. Gabriel *et al*. Hamburg: Meiner.

—— (1979). 'Notes to Ludwig Darmstaedter', trans. in *Posthumous Writings*, ed. H. Hermes *et al*. Oxford: Blackwell, pp. 253–7.

—— (1989). 'Briefe an Ludwig Wittgenstein', in *Grazer Philosophische Studien*, 33/34: 5–34.

—— (1999). *Zwei Schriften zur Arithmetik: Funktion und Begriff* and *Ueber die Zahlen des Herrn H. Schubert*, ed. W. Kienzler. Hildesheim: Olms.

GEACH, PETER (1977). Preface to Frege, *Logical Investigations*. Oxford: Blackwell, pp. vii–ix.

GEACH, PETER and BLACK, MAX (1970). *Translations from the Philosophical Writings of Gottlob Frege*. Oxford: Blackwell.

GOLDFARB, WARREN (2002). 'Wittgenstein's understanding of Frege. Pre-Tractarian Evidence', in Reck ed. (2002), pp. 185–200.

HALLETT, GARTH (1977). *A Companion to Wittgenstein's Philosophical Investigations*. Ithaca: Cornell University Press.

HIDE, OYSTEIN (2004). 'Wittgenstein's Books at the Bertrand Russell Archives', *Philosophical Investigations*, 27: 68–91.

KIENZLER, WOLFGANG (1997). *Wittgensteins Wende zu seiner Spätphilosophie 1930–1932*. Frankfurt am Main: Suhrkamp.

—— (2009). 'Die Sprache des Tractatus: klar oder deutlich? Karl Kraus, Wittgenstein und die Frage der Terminologie', in G. Gebauer, F. Goppelsröder, and J. Volbers eds., *Wittgenstein: Philosophie als 'Arbeit an Einem selbst'*. Munich: Fink, pp. 223–47.

KÜNNE, WOLFGANG (2009). 'Wittgenstein and Frege's Logical Investigations', in J. Hyman and H. J. Glock eds., *Wittgenstein and Analytic Philosophy: Essays for P. M. S. Hacker*. Oxford: Oxford University Press, pp. 26–62.

McGINN, MARIE (2006). *Elucidating the Tractatus*. Oxford: Oxford University Press.

McGUINNESS, BRIAN (1988). *Wittgenstein: A Life. Young Ludwig*. London: Duckworth.

POTTER, MICHAEL (2009). *Wittgenstein's Notes on Logic*. Oxford: Oxford University Press.

RECK, ERICH (2002). 'Wittgenstein's "Great Debt to Frege": Biographical Traces and Philosophical Themes', in Reck ed. (2002), 3–38.

—— ed. (2002). *From Frege to Wittgenstein: Perspectives on Early Analytical Philosophy*. Oxford: Oxford University Press.

RICHARDS, BEN (unpublished). 'Letter to G. H. v. Wright', dated 15/8/92.

RICKETTS, THOMAS (1986). 'Objectivity and Objecthood in Frege', in L. Haaparanta and J. Hintikka eds., *Frege Synthesized*. Dordrecht: Reidel, pp. 65–95.

—— (2002). 'Wittgenstein against Frege and Russell', in Reck ed. (2002), 227–51.

—— (2004). 'Frege, Carnap, and Quine', in S. Awodey and C. Klein eds., *Carnap Brought Home*. Chicago and La Salle, IL: Open Court, pp. 181–202.

—— (unpublished). 'Generality and Logical Segmentation in Frege and Wittgenstein'.

RUSSELL, BERTRAND (1903). *Principles of Mathematics*. Cambridge: Cambridge University Press.

SIMONS, PETER (1992). 'Why is there so little sense in Grundgesetze?', in *Mind*, 101: 763–5.

WITTGENSTEIN, LUDWIG (1933). *Tractatus Logico-Philosophicus*. London: Routledge & Kegan Paul.

—— (1953). *Philosophical Investigations*. Oxford: Blackwell.

—— (1958). *The Blue and Brown Books*. Oxford: Blackwell.

—— (1967). *Zettel*. Oxford: Blackwell.

—— (1973). *Letters to C. K. Ogden*. Oxford: Blackwell and London: Routledge.

—— (1974). *Philosophical Grammar*. Oxford: Blackwell.

—— (1975). *Philosophical Remarks*. Oxford: Blackwell.

—— (1979). *Notebooks, 1914–16*. Oxford: Blackwell.

—— (1979a). *Wittgenstein's Lectures. Cambridge, 1932–1935*, ed. A. Ambrose and M. Macdonald. Oxford: Blackwell.

—— (1980). *Culture and Value*. Oxford: Blackwell.

—— (1989). *Lectures on the Foundations of Mathematics*, ed. C. Diamond. Chicago: Chicago University Press.

—— (1996). *Prototractatus: An Early Version of Tractatus Logico-Philosophicus*. London: Routledge.

—— (2000). *Wittgenstein's Nachlass: The Bergen Electronic Edition*. Oxford: Oxford University Press.

—— (2004). *Ludwig Wittgenstein: Gesamtbriefwechsel/Complete Correspondence*, Innsbrucker Electronic Edition, ed. Monika Seekircher, Brian McGuinness, and Anton Unterkircher. InteLex.

—— (2005). *The Big Typescript*, trans. C. G. Luckhardt and M. A. E. Aue. Oxford: Blackwell.

—— (2006). *Wittgenstein-Engelmann, Briefe, Begegnungen, Erinnerungen*, ed. I. Somavilla. Innsbruck: Haymon.

—— (2008). *Wittgenstein in Cambridge: Letters and Documents 1911–1951*, ed. B. McGuinness. Oxford: Blackwell.

CHAPTER 5

....

WITTGENSTEIN AND INFINITY

....

A. W. MOORE

1.

....

DESCARTES, in his Third Meditation, famously argues that the only possible explanation for his having an idea of God, given his own finitude and given God's essential infinitude, is that God actually exists; and that his idea of God is an innate idea placed in him by God, 'as it were, the mark of the craftsman stamped on his work.' (Descartes 1986, 35) The details of Descartes's argument need not detain us now—except to comment that the scholastic elements in it put it more or less beyond the pale of contemporary analytic philosophy. Nevertheless, something strikingly similar, in broad outline, can be found in a book that is very much of our time and squarely within the analytic tradition, namely Nagel's (1997) *The Last Word*.

Nagel reflects on our use of reason—'a local activity of finite creatures' (Nagel 1997, 70)—to arrive at the idea of infinity. And, as against those who think that this both can and must be understood purely in terms of our finite resources, without appeal to infinity itself, he urges:

> To get [the idea of infinity], we need to be operating with the concept of numbers as the sizes of sets, which can have anything whatever as their elements. What we understand, then, is that the numbers we use to count things...are merely the first part of a series that never ends.
>
> ...Though our direct acquaintance with and designation of specific numbers is extremely limited, we cannot make sense of it except by putting them, and ourselves, in the context of something larger, something whose existence is independent of our fragmentary experience of it...When we think about the finite activity of counting, we come to realize that it can only be understood as part of something infinite. (Nagel 1997, 71)

He goes on to say that 'the description of what happens when we count must include the relation of that activity to the infinite series of natural numbers, since that is part of what our operation with the concept of number makes evident' (Nagel 1997, 72), an interesting echo of Descartes's claim that our idea of God is a 'mark' of God, providing us with an image of an infinite reality beyond us.[1]

To be sure, there are crucial differences between Descartes's account and Nagel's, even at this high level of generality. Notice in particular that, where Descartes urges that we need to acknowledge the infinite if we are to explain how we have our idea of the infinite, Nagel urges that we need to acknowledge the infinite if we are so much as to characterize our idea.[2] As regards explaining how we have our idea, Nagel takes seriously the possibility that this is something we cannot do. (Nagel 1997, 76) So it would be procrustean at best to claim to find the same argument in both. But I am in any case less concerned with the argument that either of them gives than with a certain picture of the conclusion that they share.

Having taken a critical step back from our idea of the infinite, and having concluded (rightly or wrongly) that a fully satisfactory account of that idea must involve further implementation of it, both Descartes and Nagel adopt a quasi-perceptual model of the relation between our idea and that which it is an idea of. Both of them take our idea to be the source of beliefs that we have, which are answerable to how things are in an independent reality.[3] The reason why I call this model a quasi-perceptual model—the label 'realist' would be equally appropriate—is that, on one natural way of construing a perception, whenever I perceive an object, my perception is likewise a source of beliefs that I have (about the object) and these beliefs are likewise answerable to how things are in an independent reality (the reality of how the object is); and, we might add, my perception is a 'mark' of the object itself.

2.

Very well; what are we to say about this quasi-perceptual, or realist, model? (There is an issue about how far any such model is adequate even in the case of perception. But let

---

[1] There are other connections too. Nagel, in pondering the understanding of the infinite which we finite creatures can attain, given that we can never fully grasp it, draws a distinction that Descartes draws: the distinction, in roughly Descartes's words in the 'Reply to the first set of objections' (Descartes 1984, AT VII 112), between our understanding clearly *that* the infinite is infinite and our being able to grasp the infinite, *qua* infinite; or, in roughly Nagel's words, between our seeing *that* there is something there that we cannot grasp and our being able to grasp all of it (Nagel 1997, 70).

[2] There is an interesting comparison here with what Stroud argues, in Stroud 2000, with respect to our idea of colour.

[3] Independent? Is it not a primary concern of both Descartes and Nagel to infer from the fact that we have certain beliefs about the infinite that those beliefs are true? Yes; but not because either of them fails to see a logical gap here; rather because they both see a logical gap that they think they have the argumentative means to bridge. They both think that, having taken the critical step back, they can show that things are how, granted our idea, we believe them to be, that is to say there is actually a God (Descartes) or there is actually an infinite series of natural numbers (Nagel). But neither of them would have the least sympathy for the suggestion that, in having these beliefs, we *make* them true. (For a forthright expression of a similar realism see Aristotle 1941a, Bk III, Ch. 8, 15–20.)

that pass.) One thing that we can say about the model is that it would be an utter anathema to Wittgenstein.[4]

What our 'idea' of the infinite comes to, on a Wittgensteinian conception, is our way of handling the concept of the infinite and related concepts: the set of rules that govern our use of the corresponding language. It is what Wittgenstein himself would call our 'grammar' of the infinite. What it leads us to 'believe'—if 'believe' is the right word—are the various associated grammatical propositions, propositions to state which is to enunciate the rules of the grammar: for instance, that an infinitely long object is an object with no end (PG, 455); or, to take an example close to Nagel's concerns, that there are infinitely many natural numbers (PG, 465).

On the realist model, our acceptance of these rules is both explained and justified by the nature of reality. We preclude talk of a biggest natural number, for example, because we are sensitive to the fact that there is no biggest natural number. This fact is quite independent of us. It is something that we have *discerned*, like the fact that there is no planet between Mercury and the sun. It also of course means that we are *right* to preclude talk of a biggest natural number, and right, accordingly, to 'believe' that the series of natural numbers is infinite.

For Wittgenstein, this model is utterly confused. Nothing justifies and explains our accepting whatever grammatical rules we accept, or at least not in the sense intended in the model. We might be justified in the sense that our rules fulfil some important function in our lives, and this too might explain why we have them. But that is not the sense intended in the model, for we have not thereby got anything 'right'. Our rules do not answer correctly to some independent reality. As Wittgenstein memorably says in *Zettel*, after posing the question whether our number system resides in our nature or in the nature of things, 'How are we to put it?—*Not* in the nature of numbers.'[5]

Does this mean that Wittgenstein rejects the realist model in favour of some sort of idealist alternative? For there does seem to be a constitutive link between the rules we accept and the essential features of reality that correspond to them. And if this is not due to the fact that the former answer to the latter, must it not be due to the fact that the latter answer to the former; so that, for example, the reason why there are infinitely many natural numbers is simply that we preclude talk of a biggest one?

The relation between Wittgenstein and idealism is an exegetical quagmire in its own right and I am not going to try to wade through it now.[6] Suffice to say that Wittgenstein is under no obvious pressure to acknowledge an answerability in *either* direction. True, in saying that a biggest natural number is impossible, we are adverting to the fact that talk

---

[4] The early Wittgenstein or the late Wittgenstein? This chapter is more concerned with the latter, though it treats of topics on which there is important convergence between the two. (It is worth noting in this connection that the majority of the material cited below is from transitional work.) Much of what follows, incidentally, derives from A. W. Moore 2001, esp. Ch. 9, §3.

[5] Z §357; his emphasis. For helpful exegesis of Wittgenstein on the 'autonomy' of grammar see Hacker 1986, Ch. VII, §2.

[6] I try to say something about it in A. W. Moore 2007. See also Williams 2006.

of a biggest natural number is disallowed by one of our grammatical rules. And, as with any of our rules, this is a rule that we might not have had. But this is not to say that, but for us, there might have been a biggest natural number; or that, but for us, the series of natural numbers might have been only finite. It is to say rather that we might not have thought and spoken in those terms. We have not *made* the series of natural numbers infinite. That the series of natural numbers is infinite is a mathematical necessity. If it has any explanation, it has a mathematical explanation. The point is simply this. *For it to be* a mathematical necessity *is* for our stating it to be an enunciation of one of the rules of our mathematical grammar. 'Essence', as Wittgenstein puts it in *Philosophical Investigations*, 'is expressed by grammar.' (PI §371; emphasis removed)[7]

3.

Wittgenstein would recoil from a realist model of the relation between our grammar of the infinite and the infinite itself, then. But that is not because of any peculiarity of the infinite. Wittgenstein would recoil from a realist model of the relation between any grammar and that which it is a grammar of.

Even so, there are certain features of our grammar of the infinite that make the realist model especially compelling in this case. This is something that I hope to show in the next section. In this section, as a necessary preliminary, I shall focus on some of the details of our grammar, as Wittgenstein sees them.

Note first that the word 'infinity' has, in Wittgenstein's view, 'many different meanings'. (PR, 304) 'Our grammar' of 'the infinite', to the extent that there *is* such a thing, must therefore consist of—to use a metaphor that Wittgenstein himself uses elsewhere—many overlapping fibres. (PI §67) In what follows I shall only be able to unravel and examine what I take to be the most significant of these.

Wittgenstein's treatment of the infinite is part of a tradition whose roots lie in Aristotle. Aristotle insists that the infinite exists potentially, but not actually. What he means by this is something temporal: the infinite exists *over* time, but never *in* time. The endless ticking of a clock, for example, is potentially infinite, but never actually infinite.[8]

In a similar vein—I shall try to indicate shortly how similar—various medieval thinkers distinguish between a *categorematic* use of the expressions 'infinite number', 'infinitely many', 'infinity', and suchlike and a *syncategorematic* use of them. Roughly: to use

---

[7] PI §371, emphasis removed. Note that, just as Wittgenstein's views prevent us from being said to legislate correctly, so too they prevent us from being said to legislate incorrectly. Thus, suppose there were people whose grammatical rules demanded application of the epithet 'biggest natural number' to 999. This would not show that they took 999 to be the biggest natural number. It would show that they were legislating for a use of the expressions 'biggest' and 'natural number' that was different from that which they have in standard English. There are connections here with Wittgenstein's early work: see e.g. TLP 3.02–3.03, 5.473–5.4732, and 5.5422.

[8] For further discussion, and references, see A. W. Moore 2001, Ch. 2, esp. §3.

one of these expressions categorematically is to say that there is something with a property that surpasses any finite measure; to use one of these expressions syncategorematically is to say that, given any finite measure, there is something with a property that surpasses it. With a little regimentation Aristotle's distinction can be subsumed under this. For—and again this is rough—to use one of these expressions in order to refer to an actual infinite is to say that there is some *time* at which a given magnitude surpasses any finite measure, while to use it in order to refer to a potential infinite is to say that, given any finite measure, there is some time at which a given magnitude surpasses it. Suppose, for example, that I say, 'An infinite number of people will be dead.' If I am using 'infinite number' categorematically, I mean that there will come a time when the number of dead people exceeds any finite number: an actual infinity of people will then be dead. If I am using 'infinite number' syncategorematically, I mean that, given any finite number, there will come a time when the number of dead people exceeds it: a potential infinity of people will, each in his or her own time, be dead. And, just as Aristotle champions the potential infinite and repudiates the actual infinite, so too a number of these medieval thinkers hold that it is legitimate to use 'infinite number' and other such expressions syncategorematically but illegitimate to use them categorematically.[9]

Wittgenstein insists on something very like this. In *Philosophical Remarks* he says:

> You could put it like this: it makes sense to say that there can be infinitely many objects in a direction, but no sense to say that there are infinitely many... The 'infinitely many' is so to speak used adverbially and is to be understood accordingly.
>
> That is to say, the proposition 'Three things can lie in this direction' and 'Infinitely many things can lie in this direction' are only apparently formed in the same way, but are in fact different in structure: the 'infinitely many' of the second proposition doesn't play the same role as the 'three' of the first. (PR §142)

Note, incidentally, the three dots of ellipsis in this quotation. The omitted material deserves special mention. Having insisted that it makes sense to say that there *can be* infinitely many objects in a direction, but no sense to say that there *are*, Wittgenstein comments:

> This conflicts with the way the word 'can' is normally used. For, if it makes sense to say a book can lie on this table, it also makes sense to say it is lying there.

This is a very clear echo of something we find in Aristotle. Aristotle, having insisted that the infinite has a potential existence, but not an actual existence, comments:

> But the phrase 'potential existence' is ambiguous. When we speak of the potential existence of a statue we mean that there will be an actual statue.[10] It is not so with the infinite. There will not be an actual infinite. (Aristotle 1941a, Bk III, Ch. 6, 206a 18–21)

The connections between Aristotle and Wittgenstein intimated here are in my view very deep. I said above that Aristotle's distinction between the actual infinite and the

---

[9] For further discussion, and references, see A. W. Moore 2001, Ch. 3, esp. §3.
[10] Will be? Or only can be? For discussion of this point see below.

potential infinite could be viewed as a result of one particular application of the more overtly grammatical distinction drawn by the medievals. In a way, Wittgenstein too is concerned with one particular application of that more general distinction. At one point he toys sympathetically with the suggestion that 'infinity is an attribute of possibility, not of reality'; that 'the word "infinite" always goes with the word "possible", and the like'. (PR, 313) Linking the language of infinity with the language of possibility in this way, he in effect applies the categorematic/syncategorematic distinction to possible situations— just as Aristotle, in effect, applies the distinction to times. Thus Wittgenstein sanctions uses of expressions such as 'infinitely many' to say that, given any finite measure, there is some *possible situation* in which a given magnitude surpasses it, but not to say that there is some possible situation in which a given magnitude surpasses any finite measure. This is illustrated in the quotation above. It is also illustrated by Wittgenstein's view of a sentence such as 'This stick is infinitely divisible.' We might have thought that this sentence was ambiguous, meaning either that, however many pieces this stick is divided into, it can be divided into more, or that this stick can be divided into infinitely many pieces. For Wittgenstein, as indeed for Aristotle, only the first of these is a legitimate interpretation. (PR §139)

Nor is this connection between Aristotle and Wittgenstein the purely structural affair that these remarks suggest. It is not just that, where Aristotle sanctions syncategorematic uses of the language of infinity (as opposed to categorematic uses of it) to characterize the variation of finite objects across time, Wittgenstein sanctions syncategorematic uses of the language of infinity (as opposed to categorematic uses of it) to characterize the variation of finite objects across the space of possibilities. Both Aristotle and Wittgenstein recognize a fundamental and intimate relation between time and possibility. For Aristotle, the question whether something is possible *is*, at least on one plausible reading, the question whether it has ever been so or will ever be so.[11] And for Wittgenstein, 'infinity lies in the nature of time ... [; it] is an internal quality of the form of time' (PR §143), a remark that can be compared with his claim that 'we all ... know what it means to say that there is an infinite possibility and a finite reality, since we say ... time [is] infinite but we can always only ... live through finite bits of [it].' (PR §138)

For Wittgenstein, then, the language of infinity has paradigmatic application in any situation that has written into it a never-ending series of nested possibilities, each involving an increase in some magnitude. (The case of an infinitely divisible stick is a clear case in point.) Somewhat more precisely, the language of infinity has paradigmatic application in any situation satisfying the two following conditions: first, something in this situation admits of a possibility, in which it admits of a second possibility, in which it admits in turn of a third possibility, *and so on*,[12] where each of these possibilities involves an

---

[11] Aristotle 1941b, Bk I, Ch. 12. Cf. Aristotle 1941a, Bk III, Ch. 6, 207b 10–14. (This addresses the concern raised above in footnote 10.)

[12] For interesting comments by Wittgenstein on the workings of the expression 'and so on', proffered in both his early work and his late work, see: TLP 5.25–5.2523; and PI §§208, 229.

increase in some magnitude over its predecessor; and secondly, something about the very form of the situation determines that these possibilities always arise. The reason for the second condition is that, unless the possibilities arise in some *principled* way, the language cannot get a grip. This relates to Wittgenstein's frequent insistence that 'the word "infinite" is always part of a *rule*'. (PR, 313; his emphasis)

So does Wittgenstein reject entirely any use of the language of infinity to characterize the way things actually are, as opposed to the various interconnected ways they are capable of being? Not quite. Or at least, this is a misleading way to put it, as Wittgenstein himself warns. (Ibid.) After all, if a stick is infinitely divisible, that is a fact about how the stick actually is, just as, if a particular peg can fit into a particular hole, that is a fact about the respective sizes and shapes of the peg and the hole. Wittgenstein is not even unequivocally hostile to a use of the language of infinity to characterize a contingency about how an infinite region of space is filled. For instance, he would not dismiss out of hand, as entirely without sense, the claim that there are, as a matter of contingent fact, infinitely many stars to be observed in some particular direction—despite his apparent insistence to the contrary in the quotation above.[13] What *is* true is that, even in this case, Wittgenstein would demand that the contingency be governed by some kind of rule. To say that there are infinitely many stars to be observed in some direction, where this is an inference from some well corroborated law of nature, would be one thing. To add that these stars differ from one another in some totally unprincipled way, for instance that they are all of different sizes and their sizes vary at random, would be something else entirely. The latter, on Wittgenstein's view, *would* be without sense.[14] The proposition that there are infinitely many stars to be observed in some direction is thus, on Wittgenstein's view, very different in kind from the proposition that there are three.[15] The former proposition still, crucially, has something of the syncategorematic and the modal about it. (What it comes to, in fact, is this: however many stars have been observed in this direction, there is a nomically guaranteed possibility of observing more. The supplementary proposition about the stars varying randomly in size lacks any analogous paraphrase.) We should *not* think of infinity as like a natural number, only much bigger.

4.

Very well; why might there be some special temptation to adopt the realist model in the case of the grammar of the infinite?

---

[13] Here perhaps it is salutary to remind ourselves of Wittgenstein's caution that the word 'infinity' has many different meanings—although, as I hope to show, there is nothing yet that really forces us to revert to that.

[14] See e.g. RFM V, §6; and PR §§145 and 147, and pp. 304–6. This compares with the following combination of doctrines in Kant: (i) that, as a matter of necessity, every event has a prior cause (Kant 1998, A532/B560); and (ii) that there is no such thing as contingent infinite history (ibid., A518–520/B546–548).

[15] Cf. PR, 306–7; and PG, 464. Cf. also Wittgenstein's conviction that an infinite set is very different in kind from a set with three members; 'set', on Wittgenstein's view, is hardly even univocal in the two cases. (This is discussed in Shanker 1987, Ch. 5, §1, with references.)

One of the reasons why there is a temptation to adopt the realist model in the case of *any* grammar is the fact that when we take a critical step back from the grammar and raise questions about how we have arrived at it, why it takes the form it does, what it enables us to do, and suchlike, it is very natural to redeploy the grammar itself. For there is no more obvious toolkit for reflecting on the provenance, character, and power of some set of concepts that we use than that very set of concepts. Nor indeed is there any clear reason why we should *not* redeploy the grammar in this way. There need be no question of circularity (any more than there would be a question of circularity if we explained our facility with the concept of simplicity by appeal to the fact that it is a simple concept).[16] The point, however, is that when we do redeploy the grammar in this way, it is enormously enticing to take that crucial extra step: of using the grammar to explain our possession of it in accord with the realist model; of employing such explanatory schemata as the following:

> We have a rule that disallows talk of Xs because we have discerned that there are no Xs.

This enticement exists in the case of any grammar. The peculiarity of the grammar of the infinite, which gives the enticement a special stimulus in that case, is this. Because the concept of the infinite applies whenever there is a process that admits of principled indefinite extension—because 'the word "infinite"', to quote Wittgenstein again, 'is always part of a rule'—*that* grammar, the grammar of the infinite, is one that we are liable to employ *whatever* critical step back we have taken, whatever other grammar we are investigating. As long as our own rules and their application to ever new possibilities constitute our subject matter, then we are liable to find a use for the language of infinity. (In particular, of course, we are liable to find a use for the expression 'and so on.') And as long as we are tempted to say that we have adopted those rules because they answer to essential features of reality that we have discerned, in other words as long as we are tempted to endorse the realist model, then one such use of the language of infinity will, apparently, be to provide us with the wherewithal to do so, that is to endorse the realist model. Thus if what is at issue is why we have adopted this or that particular rule, we might end up talking in terms that Wittgenstein himself familiarly canvasses and depict ourselves as having erected a signpost that points in the direction of rails that we have glimpsed, invisibly laid to infinity.[17] How much stronger, then, will the temptation to talk in such realist terms be when our very subject matter is the way in which our own signposts give direction, that is to say when our very subject matter is, to that extent, the infinite?

---

[16] Contrast the circularity that Wittgenstein himself bemoans, specifically in connection with infinity, when he says, 'It's no wonder that time and again I can only explain infinity in terms of itself, i.e. *cannot explain* it' (PR §138; his emphasis). There is no critical step back in that case: the object of investigation there is infinity, not the concept of infinity. (Cf. CV, 10, second paragraph.)

[17] This is an allusion to PI §§85 and 218; cf. also §229.

5.

Now if there are no objections (in principle) to redeploying any given grammar in taking a critical step back from it, and if there *are* objections (in principle) to adopting a realist model of that grammar, then, whatever enticement doing the former provides for doing the latter, the enticement must be resistible—even in the case of the grammar of the infinite, where I have just been arguing it is peculiarly strong. Similarly, in order to rebut the realist account of our idea of the infinite which both Descartes and Nagel offer, it is not necessary to rebut their shared lemma: that a fully satisfactory account of our idea must involve further implementation of it. Nevertheless, for all we have seen so far, that shared lemma may be false.[18] Likewise, for all we have seen so far, it may be possible to take a critical step back from our grammar of the infinite and give a good account of it *without* redeploying it. It may be possible, in other words, to say how we have arrived at the grammar, why it takes the form it does, what it enables us to do, and suchlike, in thoroughly finite terms, that is in terms of our finite capacities, our facility with manipulating finite symbols, our skill in both giving and understanding finite instructions, the applications that we make of our grammar in characterizing finite objects, and suchlike. And in so far as it is possible to do all of this, then doing it will provide one particularly effective way of keeping the realist model at bay. It is scarcely surprising, then, that time and again we find Wittgenstein discussing our grammar of the infinite in just this way, with a self-conscious and pointed emphasis on its several *finite* features. Here is a representative sample of quotations.

> We learn an endless technique: that is to say, something is done for us first, and then we do it; we are told rules and we do exercises in following them; perhaps some expression like 'and so on *ad inf.*' is also used, but what is in question here is not some gigantic extension.
> *These* are the facts. (RFM V, §19; his emphasis)

> When one is a child, 'infinite' is explained as something huge... But if you say that a child has learned to multiply, so that there is an infinite number of multiplications he can do—then you no longer have the image of something huge. (LFM, 255)

> Suppose... I say 'By "cardinal number" I mean whatever results from 1 by continued addition of 1'. The word 'continued' doesn't represent a nebulous continuation of 1, $1 + 1, 1 + 1 + 1$; on the contrary the sign '$1, 1 + 1, 1 + 1 + 1 \ldots$' is to be taken as perfectly exact; governed by definite rules which are different from those for '$1, 1 + 1, 1 + 1 + 1$', and not a substitute for a series 'which cannot be written down'. (PG, 284)[19]

---

[18] It is worth noting in this connection that defending the lemma creates a distinctive quandary for both Descartes and Nagel. They need our idea to be clear enough to resist being dismissed as not a genuine idea at all, but not so clear as to be readily defined in simple finite terms, thereby leaving the lemma open to easy attack (cf. Williams 1978, 144–5). This accounts for the distinction that each of them draws, to which I drew attention in footnote 1 above. Cf. Nagel's uneasy claim (Nagel 1997, 70) that 'the infinity of the natural numbers is something we come to grasp through our recognition that in a sense we cannot grasp all of it'.

[19] Cf. Wittgenstein's discussion of the notation for a recurring decimal in PG, 428.

The expression 'and so on' is nothing but the *expression* 'and so on' (nothing, that is, but a sign in a calculus which can't do more than have meaning via the rules that hold of it; which can't say more than it shows).

That is, the expression 'and so on' does not harbour a secret power by which the series is continued without being continued. (PG, 282; his emphasis)

We reflect far too little on the fact that a sign really cannot mean more than it is. (PR §144)[20]

But how do we construct an infinite hypothesis, such as that there are infinitely many fixed stars (it's clear that *in the end* only a finite reality corresponds to it)?... [It] can only be given through a law... It's clear to us that no experience *corresponds* with [such a hypothesis]. It only exists...in language...(PR §139; his emphasis)

'We only know the infinite by description.' Well then, there's just the description and nothing else. (PR §135)

Let us not forget: mathematicians' discussions of the infinite are clearly finite discussions. By which I mean, they come to an end. (PG, 483)[21]

Not that the possibility of giving an account of our grammar of the infinite in these finite terms should occasion any kind of doubt about the grammar. We are at perfect liberty to re-immerse ourselves in it; and, when we do, we will of course talk once again in unashamedly infinitary terms. Wittgenstein himself, in one of his lectures, imagines an interlocutor whose reaction to the idea that we can give an account of our grammar without reference to any 'gigantic extension' is to say, 'We aren't talking of anything you would call *big*, and therefore not of anything infinite.' (LFM, 255; his emphasis) Wittgenstein gives the following telling reply: 'But as long as you try to point out that we are not treating of anything infinite, this means nothing, because why not say that this *is* infinite?' (RFM II, §62; his emphasis)

This reply is just as we would expect. It is a familiar and cardinal precept of Wittgenstein's philosophy that it is not our business, as philosophers, to *challenge* any given grammar. 'Philosophy may in no way interfere with the actual use of language', he says; 'it can in the end only describe it... It leaves everything as it is.—It also leaves mathematics as it is.' (PI §124) The grammar of the infinite is simply there to be reckoned with, neither justified nor unjustified. All that we, as philosophers, need aspire to do is to gain

---

[20] The idea that a sign cannot mean more than it is may seem a curious idea: how, for instance, does it relate to the fact that the word 'big' is not big? But what Wittgenstein is expressing here is his view that 'in mathematics, the signs themselves *do* mathematics, they don't describe it' (PR §157; his emphasis) or again that 'in mathematics *everything* is algorithm and *nothing* is meaning' (PG, 468; his emphasis).

[21] Note: several of these quotations allude to a distinction that Wittgenstein frequently draws, between two kinds of dots of ellipsis: the 'dots of laziness', as he calls them, which occur in the expression 'A, B, C,...', used to represent the alphabet; and the 'dots of infinity', as we could call them, which occur in the expression '1, 2, 3,...', used to represent the series of natural numbers (see e.g. MWL, 298; LFM, 170–1; and PI §208). The former are an abbreviation. The latter are not: they are part of the mathematical symbolism with their own precise, specifiable use.

a sufficiently clear view of it to be able to combat the confusion and perplexity that arise when it is mishandled.[22]

And yet ... So great is Wittgenstein's concern to characterize the grammar of the infinite without redeploying it, in particular without mention of any infinite subject matter, that he does at times visibly struggle to maintain his grip on the grammar. He comes close to saying the very thing that he criticizes his interlocutor for saying, namely that it *lacks* an infinite subject matter.[23] Thus at one point, in order to emphasize that there is nothing more to the impossibility of a biggest natural number than our precluding talk of such a number, he objects to our simply saying (what we do say when we are immersed in the grammar), 'There is no biggest natural number.' He writes:

> A proposition like 'there is no [biggest natural] number' is offensive to naive—and correct—common sense ... The proposition 'There isn't a [biggest] one' should rather be: it makes no sense to speak of a '[biggest natural] number', that expression is ill-formed. (PG, 465)[24]

But there *is* no biggest natural number! We are not obliged to adopt the formal mode.[25] It is revisionist to say that we are.

---

[22] This is perhaps an apt point at which to note that the question whether it *is* possible to give an account of our grammar of the infinite in finite terms, without redeploying it, is quite independent of the question whether Wittgenstein's own quasi-Aristotelian account of that grammar is correct. There is room, at least in epistemic space, for all four combinations of answers to these two questions. In particular, there is room for each of the two following combinations of answers: (i) Wittgenstein's account is correct but it cannot be given in finite terms because it cannot be given without adverting to the endless possibilities that the grammar of infinity affords; and (ii) Wittgenstein's account is incorrect, because we can perfectly well talk about a non-rule-governed infinite contingency, but we can account for such talk in terms of the finite rules that govern the finite processes of extrapolation which make it possible. (This is highly schematic, of course. I am not committing myself one way or the other on whether either of these stances would withstand much scrutiny.)

[23] The fifth and sixth quotations in the list above already testify to this. Of course, if the grammar of the infinite lacks an infinite subject matter, this means that we cannot talk about the infinite; for if we cannot use *the grammar of the infinite* to talk about the infinite, then what *can* we use to talk about it? And this in turn means that the grammar does after all need to be challenged; for if we cannot use the grammar of the infinite *to talk about the infinite*, then what *can* we use it for? To this last question, which is intended rhetorically, somebody might reply, 'We can use the grammar of the infinite to generalize about the possibilities that finite things afford! Is that not the whole point of Wittgenstein's critique?' But 'our talking about the infinite' here is meant to include our generalizing about just such endless possibilities. And 'the grammar's having an infinite subject matter' is meant to be simply its providing us with the wherewithal to do this. (A grammar with an infinite subject matter must therefore, among other things, enable us to invoke the infinite series of natural numbers—as in §3 above, where I talked about an object's admitting of a possibility in which it admits of a *second* possibility, in which it admits of a *third* possibility, *and so on.*)

[24] Wittgenstein himself uses the terminology 'last cardinal number', but this is an inessential difference.

[25] This is an allusion to Carnap's distinction between the material mode and the formal mode: see Carnap 1995, Lecture II, §8. It is clear, of course, what Wittgenstein's concern about the material mode is: to say, 'There is no biggest natural number' is to disguise the fact that one is stating a rule for how to speak, not a fact about how things are. But note that this is by no means a peculiarity of this example. On Wittgenstein's view, to say '3 + 3 = 6' is likewise to state a rule for how to speak: see MWL, 279. What is required is not a wholesale shift within mathematical discourse from the material mode to the formal mode—which would be utterly unworkable—but rather due circumspection vis-à-vis the ways in which the material mode can be philosophically misleading.

Wittgenstein struggles in other ways too. He suggests that it is because there are not infinitely many 'things', by which he means 'elements of knowledge', that it makes no sense to talk as though there were. In the manuscript of *Philosophical Remarks* he writes:

> The only reason why you can't say there are infinitely many things is that there aren't.
> If there were, you could also express the fact! (PR §147, footnote 1)

But that is precisely to adopt the realist model. Had Wittgenstein written, 'The only reason why you can't say there are infinitely many bananas is that there aren't', we could have understood him in a non-realist way: you 'can't say' that because it is false. But the 'can't say' in this context is the 'can't say' of nonsense, not of falsity. (And this implies, incidentally, that there is an additional problem with the quoted remark, namely the self-stultification of *saying* that it makes no sense to *say* this or that.[26]) Still, the remark is a pencilled revision to something that Wittgenstein never submitted for publication.[27] There may even be an issue, as there so often is in Wittgenstein, about how far the remark is intended *in propria persona*. At any rate it is unfair to dwell on it. Suffice to observe (for now) that Wittgenstein does not always find it easy to combine respect for his own philosophical principles, and in particular for his conservatism and his anti-realism, with maintaining a critical distance from our grammar.

Elsewhere we find something more modest. We find Wittgenstein calling into question the ways in which we actually couch our grammar, and more specifically the vocabulary that we use to couch it, rather than the grammar itself.[28] (True, this is still revisionist, and we might think that it still sits ill with his claim that 'philosophy may in no way interfere with the actual use of language'. But at least it respects the 'autonomy' of the grammar.) The point is this. Wittgenstein thinks that there is, in the very language we use to express our grammar—in the metaphors we exploit, in the pictures we conjure up—something to encourage the realist model. This is especially true in mathematical contexts, where he thinks we talk as though we were engaged in some elevated species of geography. Thus, in the thrall of transfinite mathematics, we claim that the set of real

---

[26] Cf. A. W. Moore 2003b, §VIII. One way to avoid this problem, in terms once again of Carnap's distinction (see above, footnote 25), would have been to adopt the formal mode—to mention, not to use, the offending nonsense—which is what Wittgenstein does in PR §144. There he writes, 'If I were to say, "If we were acquainted with an infinite extension, then it would be all right to talk of an actual infinite", that would really be like saying, "If there were a sense of abracadabra, then it would be all right to talk about abracadabraic sense-perception".'

[27] See Rhees 1975, 349.

[28] Cf. the distinction that Wittgenstein draws between the 'prose' and the 'calculus' in mathematical discourse (WVC, 149). Note: calling into question the vocabulary that we use to couch our grammar is more modest even than calling into question the mode (material or formal) that we adopt to express it, which is what we saw Wittgenstein doing above. Even so, they are two variations on a theme, and the response to the latter given in footnote 25 above—that what is required of us is not so much to find new ways of couching our grammar as to be on the lookout for the philosophical dangers inherent in the ways we already have—has some purchase here too. (The response given in the main text below is somewhat different. It fastens on the dangers that revision itself can incur.)

numbers is 'bigger' than the set of natural numbers, just as we might claim that Everest is bigger than Snowdon. Again, we claim that irrational points fill the 'gaps' on a line left by the rational points, just as we might claim that certain sediments fill the gaps in a rock left by the igneous material. Wittgenstein rails against this. 'The dangerous, deceptive thing about the idea: ["the set of real numbers is bigger than the set of natural numbers"]', he writes, '... is that it makes the determination of a concept—concept formation—look like a fact of nature.'(RFM II, §19)[29] And again: 'We are surprised to find that "between the everywhere dense rational points", there is still room for the irrationals. (What balderdash!)' (PG, 460; and see more generally ibid., §§40–1.)

Furthermore, it is Wittgenstein's conviction that, if we only stopped talking in these terms, perhaps in favour of some purpose-specific mathematical jargon, then interest in transfinite mathematics would altogether wane. It would lose what Wittgenstein calls its 'schoolboy charm'. (LFM, 16) Hilbert famously said, referring to the work by Cantor in which transfinite mathematics was founded, 'No one shall be able to drive us from the paradise that Cantor has created for us.' (Hilbert 1967, 376) Wittgenstein replies:

> I wouldn't dream of trying to drive anyone from this paradise...I would do something quite different: I would try to show you that it is not a paradise—so that you'll leave of your own accord. I would say, 'You're welcome to this; just look about you.' (LFM, 103)

These, then, are some of the ways in which Wittgenstein tries to discredit the garb in which transfinite mathematics tends to be paraded. Yet here too he struggles. In challenging the terms in which the relevant mathematical results are couched, he is constantly on the brink of challenging the results themselves, in just the way that drives mathematicians to distraction—and in just the way that he himself claims to abjure. Thus he writes at one point, 'One pretends to compare the "set" of real numbers in magnitude with that of [natural] numbers...I believe, and hope, that a future generation will laugh at this hocus pocus.' (RFM II, §22) But this invites precisely the same impatient retort as he himself would give if the legitimacy of a more homespun measuring technique were at issue: 'One *pretends* no such thing. One does it.' 'Comparing sets in magnitude' may not be the most felicitous description of what mathematicians do, but that *is* what they do, and that *is*, for better or worse, its description.[30] There is something almost paranoiac about his abhorrence of what he finds on the pens and in the mouths of mathematicians; and all too often, in spite of himself, he allows this to become an abhorrence of the mathematics.

---

[29] I have modified Wittgenstein's example, but inessentially: cf. PI, 287.

[30] Likewise when Wittgenstein explicitly denies that the relation $m = 2n$ can be used to correlate the set of natural numbers with one of its own proper subsets (PR §141). Surely it just *can*. Wittgenstein might reply that here too he is challenging, not the result, but how it gets stated. (Later in the same section he talks about 'ambiguous grammar' and claims that 'it all hangs on the syntax of reality and possibility'.) But if that is his reply, then he has not made himself sufficiently clear; and the fact that unclarity comes so easily in such matters is part of my very point.

6.

....

But is this perhaps unfair to Wittgenstein? Does it underestimate how revisionist his own principles allow him to be?

I referred just now to 'the mathematics', as indeed I have been referring to 'the grammar of the infinite', as though these were entities that we had discovered and that now lay preserved in some philosophical analogue of a glass cabinet, rather than products of our own ongoing linguistic activity, which is of course what Wittgenstein takes them to be. But their being products of our ongoing linguistic activity allows for a crucial degree of slack. They cannot be straightforwardly read off from that activity. This is because, even on a Wittgensteinian conception, not all of our day-to-day linguistic activity is immune to philosophical criticism. Not everything that we say is expressive of, or in accord with, any genuine grammar; and not everything that mathematicians say is a contribution to proper unadulterated mathematics. 'What a mathematician is inclined to say about the objectivity and reality of mathematical facts', to quote Wittgenstein himself, '... [is] something for philosophical *treatment*.' (PI §254; his emphasis) Moreover, it is not impossible for mathematicians systematically to mishandle their own grammars and to import conceptual confusion into their own discipline. Many people, Wittgenstein included, would cite the more or less unthinking commitment of mathematicians to the law of the excluded middle as a case in point, another symptom of an unwarranted realism.[31] So is Wittgenstein not at perfect liberty, even by his own lights, to remonstrate not just against the way in which certain mathematical results are presented but against the 'results' themselves? In the particular case of transfinite mathematics, whose subject matter is after all supposed to be the infinite, can he not insist that we have no business trying to use concepts whose proper function is to enable us to generalize about the possibilities that finite things afford to ascribe infinite magnitude to things such as the set of natural numbers (just as we would have no business trying to use expressions whose proper use is syncategorematic categorematically)? As he says in *Philosophical Remarks*, 'when (as in set theory) [mathematics] tries to *express* [the possibility in its signs], i.e. when it confuses them with their reality, we ought to cut it down to size'. (PR §144; his emphasis)[32]

That strikes me as an uneasy defence of Wittgenstein. With the possible exception of this last point about transfinite mathematics trying to express what it has no business trying to express, Wittgenstein's complaint about such mathematics concerns confusion

---

[31] See RFM V, *passim*. Cf. Dummett 1978; cf. also Wright 2001, First Postscript, §IV.

[32] Why does Wittgenstein say, 'when it confuses *them* with their reality' rather than 'when it confuses *their possibility* with their reality'? This may of course be a slip. But I do not think it is. Earlier in the same section, and in the previous section, he contrasts the infinite, inexpressible possibilities contained in things, and in particular contained in signs, with the finite, expressible facts in which they participate—and which constitute their reality.

that it engenders, not confusion that it harbours. The complaint is first and foremost a *philosophical* complaint. It is not a mathematical complaint, a complaint internal to the theory, such as, for instance, the complaint of incoherence which was levelled in the seventeenth and eighteenth centuries at early theories of differentiation and integration. So it *can* only be, it seems to me, a complaint of presentation. (Admittedly, we should include as a feature of the presentation, and therefore as fair game, the use of the very language of infinity; the use, that is, of the same language as is used to characterize the infinitude of, say, time. Indeed Wittgenstein does raise the question whether the word 'infinite' should be avoided in mathematics, and he says that it should—'where it appears to confer a meaning upon the calculus; instead of getting one from it'. (RFM II, §58) Even so, this is still a complaint of presentation.)

A different but related defence of Wittgenstein would be this. Not even when the deliverances of mathematicians are free of all confusion do they count as proper mathematics—in fact, do they count as proper meaningful activity at all—unless they have suitable application. Thus Wittgenstein writes:

> I want to say: it is essential to mathematics that its signs are also employed in *mufti*.
>   It is the use outside mathematics, and so the *meaning* of the signs, that makes the sign-games into mathematics.
>   Just as it is not logical inference either, for me to make a change from one formation to another (say from one arrangement of chairs to another) if these arrangements have not a linguistic function apart from this transformation. (RFM V, §2; his emphasis)

As for transfinite mathematics, if indeed mathematics is what it is, there is a serious question about what use is to be made of it in non-mathematical contexts. We can of course say, unexcitingly enough, that a child who has learned to multiply can now do infinitely many multiplications. But at what point do we need to take the further step, which is the very hallmark of such (so-called) mathematics, of invoking all those distinctions of infinite size? (LFM, 253)

This too, however, strikes me as an uneasy defence of Wittgenstein. Unfortunately, it raises general issues in the philosophy of mathematics which go well beyond the scope of this chapter, so all I can do in this context is to pose some questions (questions that may be targeted as much on Wittgenstein's conception of mathematics as on its application to this case). First, *can* there not be parts of mathematics which do not have any application, but which nevertheless count as proper mathematics because of how they help to systematize other parts which do have application? Secondly, and relatedly, can there not be parts of mathematics which do not have any application *outside mathematics*, but which nevertheless count as proper mathematics because of how they apply elsewhere within it? And thirdly, what about a branch of mathematics that is not applied until well after its development—must we say that only *then* does it count as proper mathematics? All three of these questions, whatever general force they might have, have particular force in the case of transfinite mathematics, which is both vigorous in its relations to other branches of mathematics and relatively young.

But whether or not I am right in my concerns about these two defences of Wittgenstein, which relate to specific issues about a specific grammar, it is worth reflecting in conclusion on a much more general problem to which such issues graphically draw our attention. How do we distinguish between those parts of our linguistic activity that are legitimate and those that are not; between those that implement some genuine grammar and those that do not? There is an apparent circularity: to be sensitive to any such distinction we must have a clear understanding of the grammars involved; to have a clear understanding of the grammars involved we must discern them in our linguistic activity; to discern them in our linguistic activity we must recognize which parts of our linguistic activity implement them; and to recognize which parts of our linguistic activity implement them we must be sensitive to the original distinction. (Cf. A. W. Moore 1997, 162, and 2003a, §7.) I do not say that this apparent circularity is vicious. I am not even certain that it is real. (Each step in this sequence can be disputed.) Perhaps there is a distinctive discomfort and puzzlement occasioned by linguistic activity that is not properly in accord with any genuine grammar. (PI §§54, 123) *Perhaps* there is—though even then, of course, 'distinctive' is the operative word, with its own threat of circularity (for mathematicians engaged in bona fide mathematics feel plenty of discomfort and puzzlement with respect to their mathematical problems). The point, however, is that, whatever the correct verdict on this apparent circularity is, it is a signal feature of the infinite and of Wittgenstein's treatment of it that they put this problem, which I take to be one of the most fundamental problems in philosophy, into particularly sharp focus.[33]

REFERENCES

ARISTOTLE (1941a). *Physics*, trans. R. P. Hardie and R. K. Gaye, in *The Basic Works of Aristotle*, ed. Richard McKeon. New York: Random House.

—— (1941b). *On the Heavens*, trans. J. L. Stocks, in *The Basic Works of Aristotle*, ed. Richard McKeon. New York: Random House.

CARNAP, RUDOLF (1995). *Philosophy and Logical Syntax*. Bristol: Thoemmes Press.

DESCARTES, RENÉ (1984). *The Philosophical Writings of Descartes*, Vol. II, trans. John Cottingham, Robert Stoothoff, and Dugald Murdoch. Cambridge: Cambridge University Press.

—— (1986). *Meditations on First Philosophy*, trans. John Cottingham. Cambridge: Cambridge University Press.

DUMMETT, MICHAEL (1978). 'The Philosophical Basis of Intuitionistic Logic', reprinted in his *Truth and Other Enigmas*. London: Duckworth.

HACKER, P. M. S. (1986). *Insight and Illusion: Themes in the Philosophy of Wittgenstein*, rev. edn. Oxford: Oxford University Press.

HILBERT, DAVID (1967). 'On the Infinite', trans. Stefan Bauer-Mengelberg, in Jean van Heijenoort ed., *From Frege to Gödel: A Source Book in Mathematical Logic, 1879–1931*. Cambridge, MA: Harvard University Press.

[33] I am very grateful to Marie McGinn for some extremely helpful comments on an early draft of this chapter.

KANT, IMMANUEL (1998). *Critique of Pure Reason*, ed. and trans. Paul Guyer and Allen W. Wood. Cambridge: Cambridge University Press.

MOORE, A. (1997). *Points of View*. Oxford: Oxford University Press.

—— (2003a). 'On the Right Track', in *Mind*, 112: 307–22.

—— (2003b). 'Ineffability and Nonsense', *Proceedings of the Aristotelian Society* Supplementary, 77: 169–93.

—— (2007). 'Wittgenstein and Transcendental Idealism', in Guy Kahane, Edward Kanterian, and Oskari Kuusela eds., *Wittgenstein and His Interpreters: Essays in Memory of Gordon Baker*. Oxford: Basil Blackwell.

MOORE, G. E. (1959). 'Wittgenstein's Lectures in 1930–3', in his *Philosophical Papers*. London: Allen & Unwin.

NAGEL, THOMAS (1997). *The Last Word*. Oxford: Oxford University Press.

RHEES, RUSH (1975). 'Editor's Note', in Ludwig Wittgenstein, *Philosophical Remarks*, ed. Rush Rhees and trans. Raymond Hargreaves and Roger White. Oxford: Basil Blackwell.

SHANKER, S. G. (1987). *Wittgenstein and the Turning-Point in the Philosophy of Mathematics*. London: Croom Helm.

STROUD, BARRY (2000). *The Quest for Reality: Subjectivism and the Metaphysics of Colour*. Oxford: Oxford University Press.

WAISMANN, FRIEDRICH (1979). *Wittgenstein and the Vienna Circle*, notes recorded by F. Waismann, ed. B. F. McGuiness, and trans. J. Schulte and B. F. McGuiness. Oxford: Basil Blackwell.

WILLIAMS, BERNARD (1978). *Descartes: The Project of Pure Enquiry*. Harmondsworth: Penguin.

—— (2006). 'Wittgenstein and Idealism', reprinted in his *The Sense of the Past: Essays in the History of Philosophy*, ed. Myles Burnyeat. Princeton: Princeton University Press.

WITTGENSTEIN, LUDWIG (1961). *Tractatus Logico-Philosophicus*, trans. D. F. Pears and B. F. McGuiness. London: Routledge & Kegan Paul.

—— (1967). *Zettel*, ed. G. E. M. Anscombe and G. H. von Wright and trans. G. E. M. Anscombe. Oxford: Basil Blackwell.

—— (1974a). *Philosophical Grammar*, ed. Rush Rhees and trans. Anthony Kenny. Oxford: Basil Blackwell.

—— (1974b). *Philosophical Investigations*, trans. G. E. M. Anscombe, rev. edn. Oxford: Basil Blackwell.

—— (1975). *Philosophical Remarks*, ed. Rush Rhees and trans. Raymond Hargreaves and Roger White. Oxford: Basil Blackwell.

—— (1976). *Lectures on the Foundations of Mathematics, Cambridge, 1939*, from the notes of R. G. Bosanquet, Norman Malcolm, Rush Rhees, and Yorick Smythies, ed. Cora Diamond. Sussex: The Harvester Press.

—— (1978). *Remarks on the Foundations of Mathematics*, ed. G. H. von Wright, Rush Rhees, and G. E. M. Anscombe and trans. G. E. M. Anscombe, 3rd edn. Oxford: Basil Blackwell.

—— (1980). *Culture and Value*, ed. G. H. von Wright and Heikki Nyman and trans. Peter Winch. Oxford: Basil Blackwell.

WRIGHT, CRISPIN (2001). *Rails to Infinity: Essays on Themes from Wittgenstein's Philosophical Investigations*. Cambridge, MA: Harvard University Press.

CHAPTER 6

WITTGENSTEIN ON MATHEMATICS

MICHAEL POTTER

THE philosophy of mathematics was one of Wittgenstein's central concerns from the beginning of his philosophical career until close to the end: it is what he told Russell he wanted to work on when he came to Cambridge in the autumn of 1911; it is one of the issues addressed in the *Tractatus*; it dominates his writings immediately after his return to philosophy, the *Philosophical Remarks* and *Philosophical Grammar*; it was a recurring theme of his Cambridge lecture courses throughout the 1930s; it was to have been the subject of the second half of the *Philosophical Investigations* as he originally conceived them; and it occupied much of his time during the Second World War. Yet Wittgenstein has had nothing like as much influence on contemporary philosophy of mathematics as he has on the philosophy of mind or of language. Although all of Wittgenstein's philosophy no doubt presents difficulties to the interpreter, the secondary literature on his philosophy of mathematics is peculiarly inconclusive even when it is judged by these standards. Why is this? In what follows I shall be describing some of Wittgenstein's views in the hope that this may contribute to answering that question.

After a brief sketch of the central ideas of Wittgenstein's account of mathematics in the *Tractatus*, most of the chapter will be devoted to his middle-period writings in the philosophy of mathematics, focusing on his rejection of the actual infinite and on his suggestion that the meaning of an arithmetical generalization is its proof. One aim will be to show how this led him to some central themes of his later writings, his attitude to formal inconsistency and the rule-following considerations. Then I shall say something about Wittgenstein's later philosophy of mathematics, such as it is. I shall conclude by offering a tentative diagnosis of its evident incompleteness.

1. MATHEMATICS IN THE *TRACTATUS*

Very little is known about the early development of Wittgenstein's views on mathematics, but perhaps an anecdote later reported by Geach gives us a clue.

The last time I saw Frege, as we were waiting at the station for my train, I said to him, 'Don't you ever find *any* difficulty in your theory that numbers are objects?' He replied, 'Sometimes I *seem* to see a difficulty, but then again I *don't* see it.' (Anscombe and Geach 1961, 128)

The last time Wittgenstein saw Frege was probably around Christmas 1913. So it seems that by then Wittgenstein had already rejected Frege's view that numbers are objects. If so, he had pinpointed what is surely a weakness in Frege's *Grundlagen*: the book depends crucially on this view, and yet it contains hardly any argument to show that it is true. Or, to put the point in a more linguistic mode, although Frege notes correctly that there are two kinds of uses to which number-words are put—as nouns and as adjectives—he simply assumes that it is the substantival use that is primary, the adjectival use derivative.

It would be wrong to put too much weight on an anecdote: not everything Wittgenstein's friends from his later life reported him as saying has turned out to be accurate. And the date of this exchange is perhaps a little surprising: Wittgenstein's surviving writings from before the war display no direct engagement with the nature of arithmetic at all. However, many of Wittgenstein's other central philosophical beliefs seem to have come to him very early indeed, so on that ground at least it would not be incredible if by the end of 1913 he had already denied that numbers are objects.

In that case, though, Wittgenstein must have arrived at this view still earlier. For not only do his letters from Norway that autumn show no sign of a concern with the nature of numbers, but this is not a topic that is mentioned in the *Notes on Logic*, the summary of his work that he prepared for Russell in October 1913. If, as I have argued elsewhere (Potter 2009), the *Notes* summarize all that Wittgenstein thought worth preserving of his work from perhaps February of that year onwards, it suggests that the view about numbers was already in place before that.

'The theory of classes', Wittgenstein says in the *Tractatus*, 'is altogether superfluous in mathematics. This is connected with the fact that the generality which we need in mathematics is not the accidental one.' (TLP 6.031) At first sight, it is a little surprising to find Wittgenstein treating it as a strike *against* logicism that the generality of mathematics is not accidental. We might grant readily enough that it is worth distinguishing between generalizations that just happen to be true and those that are true necessarily. But if mathematics belongs on the necessary side of this distinction rather than the contingent one, that surely places it with logic rather than against it.

However, this is to misunderstand the kind of accident that Wittgenstein had in mind. In fact, there is an important argument against Russellian logicism encapsulated in 6.031. That argument is in two stages. First, we note that the notion of class that can be derived from logic is the accidental, not the essential, kind. Russell's idea had been to reduce classes to propositional functions (the so-called 'no-class' theory), and hence to allow us to talk about the 'accidental' class $\{x:\phi(x)\}$ (accidental because it has as its members just those objects that happen to satisfy ϕ). What Russell's reduction could not do was to legitimate talk about 'essential' classes such as $\{a,b\}$ (essential because what their members are does not depend on the properties those members happen to have). Second, Wittgenstein claimed that mathematics is not in this sense accidental and hence cannot be based on the accidental kind of class. Since these are all that Russellian logicism has to offer, it must fail.

It is perhaps worth noting parenthetically, however, that despite its central role in his rejection of logicism, Wittgenstein's claim that 'the generality which we need in mathematics is not the accidental one' receives no more justification in the *Tractatus* than does Frege's claim that numbers are objects in the *Grundlagen*. And although it is no doubt an initially appealing view, it does at any rate stand in need of justification. The contrary idea that mathematics, although in some sense necessary, might nonetheless depend somehow on the world is not confined to the writings of out-and-out empiricists. David Lewis, for instance, chose to define the null set as the fusion of all individuals, a definition which makes mathematics depend on the world. Indeed on his account mathematics would be vulnerable if there were no individuals at all. 'In that case,' he insouciantly noted, 'maybe we can let mathematics fall. Just how much security do we really need?' (Lewis 1991, 13)

Wittgenstein's argument against Russellian logicism is unlikely to date from quite as early as his argument against Frege's conception of numbers as objects. After all, if Wittgenstein had already rejected logicism by 1913, it would surely be a little odd that that summer Russell still thought of him as a suitable person to revise the first two parts of *Principia*. It seems more likely to me that the rejection came about in Norway the following year.

I shall not devote much space here to the positive account of arithmetic in the *Tractatus*, since I have discussed it at length elsewhere (Potter 2000, ch. 6). In essence, Wittgenstein's idea was that numerals are not names of objects but merely indices (labels) used to mark the number of iterations of what he called an operation—a process for deriving one proposition from another. What is important for our purposes about the account in the *Tractatus* is in any case not its exact details but the place it gave to arithmetical equations as attempts to encapsulate in symbolic form the tautologousness of various propositions. Thus the equation 2+2=4 encapsulates such things as the necessity that if there are 2 apples and 2 oranges in the bowl, then there are 4 pieces of fruit. Notice, though, that such necessities as this cannot be said in the language of the *Tractatus* but only shown. Arithmetical equations are therefore according to the *Tractatus* pseudo-propositions—failed attempts to say what cannot be said.

Perhaps it was only when he read the *Tractatus* in 1919 that Russell realized Wittgenstein was not the person to revise the early parts of *Principia*. Russell therefore set about doing the work himself, by writing a new introduction for the second edition. But that introduction does not take much account of the criticisms that Wittgenstein made in the *Tractatus*. To the extent that Russell addressed Wittgenstein's ideas, it was to a large extent the pre-war Wittgenstein that Russell was responding to.

It was left to Ramsey, therefore, to attempt a revision of the philosophical underpinnings of *Principia* in accordance with Tractarian principles. His paper on 'The foundations of mathematics', published in 1926, aims to show that the theorems of *Principia* are not pseudo-propositions at all but rather complicated tautologies. The central step consists in Ramsey's attempt to manufacture identity as a kind of propositional function, with the consequence that the essential class {a,b}, for instance, can then be derived in a no-class theory from the function $x=a \lor x=b$ (see Potter 2005).

It is relevant to note Wittgenstein's reaction to Ramsey's proposals. The part that commentators tend to focus on is Ramsey's argument for the adoption of a simple, rather than a ramified, theory of types. The surviving texts do not show any sign that Wittgenstein objected to this, however: instead Wittgenstein reserved his disapproval for the part of Ramsey's article in which he tried to derive an essential notion of class from logic. Wittgenstein not only objected to this notion in a letter he wrote to Ramsey, but he also returned to the point more than once subsequently, attempting various formulations of his objection in the *Philosophical Remarks* and the *Philosophical Grammar*. This lends further weight to the view that Wittgenstein regarded his objection to Russellian logicism as fundamental. What he evidently objected to in Ramsey was not so much the details of his account as the overall ambition of demonstrating that mathematics consists of tautologies.

2. Finitism

When Wittgenstein returned to philosophy and to Cambridge in 1929, it was the problem of the infinite that he started to consider—first of all in concert with Ramsey. In a sense, this problem was common ground between them since even if Ramsey's manufactured propositional functions were not susceptible to Wittgenstein's objections, there would remain the problem that much of mathematics depends on the assumption that there are infinitely many objects—an assumption which, Ramsey had to grant, is not a tautology even if it is true.

As far as one can judge, Wittgenstein and Ramsey seem to have moved together towards finitism, i.e. a rejection of the extensional view of generalization in the case of infinitely many propositions. Braithwaite, in his introduction to the first posthumous edition of Ramsey's papers (Ramsey 1931, xii), remarks that 'in 1929 [Ramsey] was converted to a finitist view which rejects the existence of any actual infinite aggregate'. This is the context of Ramsey's remark that 'What we can't say we can't say, and we can't whistle it either.' (Ramsey 1990, 146) Around this time Ramsey studied and made notes on several papers on intuitionism, while Wittgenstein also considered Skolem's quantifier-free arithmetic. (PR, 163)

The work in which Wittgenstein's emerging hostility to the infinite first gained expression was the *Philosophical Remarks* of 1930. What confront us there are various remarks intended to cast doubt on the idea that there are actual infinite sets. For instance:

> The infinite number series is only the infinite possibility of finite series of numbers.
> It is senseless to speak of the *whole* infinite number series, as if it, too, were an extension. (PR, 164)

But what was Wittgenstein's objection to infinite sets? Many of his remarks seem to be intended to clarify the distinction between the actual and the potential infinite. For instance:

> A searchlight sends out light into infinite space and so illuminates everything in its direction, but you can't say it illuminates infinity. (PR, 162)

However, the distinction between actual and potential infinities was already a familiar one. (It goes back, after all, to Aristotle.) When we look for an *argument* against the existence of infinite sets, the nearest we find is perhaps the following.

> Let's imagine a man whose life goes back for an infinite time and who says to us: 'I'm just writing down the last digit of π, and it's a 2'. Every day of his life he has written down a digit, without ever having begun; he has just finished.
>
> This seems utter nonsense, and a *reductio ad absurdum* of the concept of an infinite *totality*. (PR, 166)

Yet as an argument against the notion of an infinite totality it is hard to know what to make of this. At any rate, Wittgenstein surely misstated what he meant. Since π is (as was known in the late nineteenth century) irrational, its decimal expansion does not terminate and hence has no 'last digit'. Presumably what Wittgenstein means us to imagine (or fail to imagine) is a man writing down the digits of π *backwards*, in which case the last digit would of course be a 3. But even if we agree with Wittgenstein that *this* is utter nonsense, it is far from clear that what is nonsensical about it is the fault of the infinite totality involved, rather than something inherently directional in our conception of a task performed in time. If so, then the right response might be to reject the kind of appeal to the intuition of time in grounding arithmetic that was advocated by Brouwer; it is not so clear why the coherence of the notion of an infinite set should thereby be threatened.

Nonetheless, in the *Philosophical Remarks* Wittgenstein sees his rejection of the actual infinite as causing a problem for quantification in arithmetic. Evidently if we deny the existence of infinite totalities, we no longer have available the Tractarian account of quantification over an infinite domain as an infinite logical product.

> If no finite product makes a proposition true, that means *no* product makes it true. And so it *isn't* a logical product. (PR, 149)

The difficulty this leads to, according to Wittgenstein, is that

> in that case it seems to me that we can't use generality—all, etc.—in mathematics at all. There's no such thing as 'all numbers', simply because there are infinitely many. (PR, 148)

In fact, the account in the *Tractatus* is probably in trouble even without the extra constraint that finitism brings (as Ramsey had pointed out in his critical notice on the *Tractatus* even before he had met Wittgenstein). What is important in the development of Wittgenstein's views is not so much the link he saw with finitism as his realization of the need to address the problem. In the *Tractatus* he had given the impression that all applications of mathematics could be funnelled through quantifier-free arithmetic. Only in 1929 does he seem to have begun to recognize how implausible this is. This was, of course, just before Gödel proved his incompleteness theorems, which demonstrated dramatically the gulf in complexity between the arithmetic of simple equations and full-blown quantified arithmetic. But if anyone might have had at least a vague sense of this gulf in advance of Gödel's proof, it was surely Ramsey: after all, his work on the decision problem for first-order logic spawned a whole subject in combinatorics now known as Ramsey theory. Perhaps, therefore, it was Ramsey who persuaded Wittgenstein that an account of the meaning of quantified propositions in arithmetic does not follow trivially from what he had said in the *Tractatus* about equations.

3. MEANING AS PROOF

Wittgenstein's route to an account of quantified propositions seems to have started from the verification principle: the meaning of a proposition consists in its means of verification. Wittgenstein certainly espoused this view for several years. It was also, at around the same time, one of the central tenets of the logical positivists. (Whether it was Wittgenstein who initiated its adoption by the members of the Vienna Circle is less clear.) What is distinctive about mathematics, of course, is that its fundamental method is that of proof: the means by which we verify that a mathematical proposition is true is to prove it. And in the case of an arithmetical generalization, in particular, the proof proceeds by the use of mathematical induction. So if we apply the thesis of verificationism to an arithmetical generalization we obtain the conclusion that the meaning of the proposition consists in its inductive proof.

We can trace out this view in the *Philosophical Remarks* of 1930. Wittgenstein first observes that

> *generality* in arithmetic is indicated by an induction.
> An induction is the expression for arithmetical generality. (PR, 150)

He then makes the general remark that

> how a proposition is verified is what it says. The verification is not *one* token of the truth, it is *the* sense of the proposition. (PR, 200)

The moral he draws from this is that

> if we want to see what has been proved, we ought to look at nothing but the proof. (PR, 193)

He then deduces that the sense of an arithmetical generalization is its inductive proof.

> We are not saying that when $f(1)$ holds and when $f(c+1)$ follows from $f(c)$, the proposition $f(x)$ is *therefore* true of all cardinal numbers; but: 'the proposition $f(x)$ holds for all cardinal numbers' *means* 'it holds for $x=1$, and $f(c+1)$ follows from $f(c)$'. (PG II, VI, §32)

Although, as I have suggested, this account flows quite naturally from the verification principle, there is a series of very obvious difficulties with it. One of these is that the account does not explain why we feel entitled to infer from $(x)\phi(x)$ to $\phi(n)$ for any number n: if we try to give an argument for this, we simply find ourselves using induction again, but in a slightly more complicated case.

A related problem is that if we wish to prove $(x)\phi(x)$ by mathematical induction, we must prove two things: first we check that $\phi(0)$ holds; then we prove $(x)(\phi(x)\rightarrow \phi(x+1))$. If the meaning of $(x)\phi(x)$ is an induction, then in the same way we would expect the meaning of $(x)(\phi(x)\rightarrow \phi(x+1))$ to be an induction too. Moreover, the second of these expressions is logically *more* complex than the first. We are therefore in an infinite regress of more and more complex expressions, the meaning of each of which is explained by appeal to the sense of the next in the sequence. We might try to relieve this difficulty by making a distinction between generalizations which have inductive proofs and ones (such as $(x+y)^2=x^2+2xy+y^2$) which have free variable proofs; but the relief is only temporary. The problem is that in most systems these proofs depend in their turn on other inductive proofs.

As Wittgenstein himself noted, another difficulty for his doctrine arises with unsolved problems.

> My explanation mustn't wipe out the existence of mathematical problems. That is to say, it isn't as if it were only certain that a mathematical proposition made sense when it (or its opposite) had been proved. (PR, 170)

The trouble is that Wittgenstein's explanation *does* wipe out mathematical problems. If the meaning of an arithmetical generalization is given by its proof, then none of us understands Goldbach's conjecture, since no proof or refutation of it is currently known. And in that case how could anyone try to find one?

The key distinction for Wittgenstein at this point seems to be whether or not there is a decision procedure for the problem (cf. Säätelä's chapter in this volume). If not, then according to him we do not really understand the problem (despite appearances to the contrary).

> This boils down to saying: If I hear a proposition of, say, number theory, but don't know how to prove it, then I don't understand the proposition either. This sounds extremely paradoxical. It means, that is to say, that I don't understand the proposition that there are infinitely many primes, unless I know its so-called proof: when I learn the proof, I learn something *completely new*, and not just the way leading to a goal with which I'm already familiar. But in that case it's unintelligible that I should admit, when I've got the proof, that it's a proof of precisely *this* proposition, or of the induction meant by this proposition. (PR, 183)

> Only where there's a method of solution is there a problem (of course that doesn't mean 'Only when the solution has been found is there a problem').
> That is, where we can only expect the solution from some sort of revelation, there isn't even a problem. A revelation doesn't correspond to any question. It would be like wanting to ask about experiences belonging to a sense organ we don't yet possess. Our being given a new sense, I would call revelation. (PR, 172)

> Every legitimate mathematical proposition must put a ladder up against the problem it poses, in the way that 12×13=137 does—which I can then climb if I choose.

> This holds for propositions of any degree of generality. (N.B. there is no ladder with 'infinitely many' rungs.) (PR, 179)

Wittgenstein's view leads, then, to the conclusion that we do not really understand Goldbach's conjecture. He has nothing very convincing to say about what mathematicians are doing when they try to prove Goldbach's conjecture.

Moreover, if propositions for which no proof is known constitute a difficulty for Wittgenstein's account, a further difficulty is presented by the opposite case of those for which there is more than one proof. His account renders it unintelligible, that is to say, how two different proofs could be proofs of the same proposition. And yet this is a perfectly common situation in mathematics.

4. CONTRADICTION

Wittgenstein's view concerning arithmetical generalizations applies, via the arithmetization of syntax, to consistency statements. The statement that a formal system is consistent will, when arithmetized, have the form of an arithmetical generalization. Moreover, for any reasonably elaborate formal system there is no decision procedure for finding inconsistencies. Hence on Wittgenstein's view there is no problem of inconsistency until we actually find an inconsistency.

Wittgenstein makes a distinction here between hidden and obvious inconsistencies. He does grant that we should check for obvious inconsistencies. But if there are none, we cannot legitimately worry about hidden inconsistencies because the question whether there are any is devoid of meaning.

> Something tells me that a contradiction in the axioms of a system can't really do any harm until it is revealed. We think of a hidden contradiction as like a hidden illness which does harm even though (and perhaps precisely because) it doesn't show itself in an obvious way. But two rules in a game which in a particular instance contradict each other are perfectly in order until the case turns up, and it's only then that it becomes necessary to make a decision between them by a further rule. (PG, 303)

Wittgenstein attributes the existence of hidden contradictions to ambiguity in the rules.

> If a contradiction is found later on, that means that hitherto the rules have not been clear and unambiguous. So the contradiction doesn't matter, because we can now get rid of it by enunciating a rule.
>
> In a system with a clearly set out grammar there are no hidden contradictions, because such a system must include the rule which makes the contradiction discernible. A contradiction can only be hidden in the sense that it is in the higgledy-piggledy one of the rules, in the unorganized part of the grammar; and there it doesn't matter since it can be removed by organizing the grammar. (PG, 305)

This last remark is very strange indeed. As a matter of fact, there is no decision procedure for settling whether a formal system for arithmetic is consistent. Wittgenstein seems to have imagined that if it is uncertain whether a system is consistent, that can only be because the system has not been set out with sufficient clarity. That is simply false.

Moreover, the first part of the last quotation, in which Wittgenstein ascribes contradictions to lack of clarity in the rules, invites a further question. Why should we be worried by an inconsistency even if we do find it? There is a brief mention of this concern in the *Philosophical Remarks*.

> It seems to me that the idea of the consistency of the axioms of mathematics, by which mathematicians are so haunted these days, rests on a misunderstanding.
> This is tied up with the fact that the axioms of mathematics are not seen for what they are, namely, propositions of syntax. (PR, 189)

This point is taken up again in *Philosophical Grammar*.

> Mathematicians nowadays make so much fuss about proof of the consistency of axioms. I have the feeling that if there were a contradiction in the axioms of a system it wouldn't be such a great misfortune. Nothing easier than to remove it. (RFM, 303)

Lying behind these remarks is a distinction, which Wittgenstein drew in conversation with Schlick and Waismann, between a contradictory sentence and a contradictory rule:

> Axioms have two meanings, as Frege saw:
> 1. The rules *according to* which you play.
> 2. The opening positions of a game.

> If you take the axioms in the second meaning, I can attach no sense to the claim that they contradict each other. It would be very odd to say, This configuration of the pieces ('0≠0', for example, in Hilbert's game with formulas) is a contradiction. Two rules can contradict one another. What do we do in such a case? Very simple—we introduce a new rule and the conflict is resolved. (WVC, 119)

Two rules contradict each other if one says you are allowed to do something and the other says you aren't. This induces puzzlement when you notice the problem, but you can then sort it out with a stipulation, and the stipulation needn't invalidate anything you have done so far. For this sort of contradiction Wittgenstein is quite right that in most precisely formulated formal systems they could not be hidden, i.e. they could have come about only through carelessness. Notice, though, that this is merely a feature of formal systems as we usually formulate them. We could, for example, have a formal system with two rules:

1. You may write down any formula which it would be legitimate to write down in Peano Arithmetic.
2. You may not write down any formula which contradicts what you have already written down.

Does this set of rules lead to contradiction, i.e. to the sort of puzzlement Wittgenstein is referring to, where we simply don't know what to do? That depends entirely on whether Peano Arithmetic is consistent, and we do not have a mechanical means of settling *that* question.

The idea that a contradiction is not harmful per se is one Wittgenstein made repeatedly. In his discussion of Gödel's incompleteness theorems, for instance, he says:

> Is there harm in the contradiction that arises when someone says: 'I am lying.—So I am not lying.—So I am lying.—etc.'? I mean: does it make our language less usable if in this case, according to the ordinary rules, a proposition yields its contradictory, and vice versa?—the proposition itself is unusable, and these inferences equally.... Such a contradiction is of interest only because it has tormented people. (RFM, 120)

Let us compare now what Wittgenstein said in one of his 1939 lectures in Cambridge.

> Is it hidden as long as it hasn't been *noticed*? Then as long as it's hidden, I say that it's as good as gold. And when it comes out in the open it can do no harm. (LFM, 219)

But can't a hidden contradiction do damage without our realizing it? This is a worry that Turing put to Wittgenstein explicitly:

> *Wittgenstein*: You might get $p.{\sim}p$ by means of Frege's system. If you can draw any conclusion you like from it, then that, as far as I can see, is all the trouble you can get into. And I would say, 'Well then, just don't draw any conclusions from a contradiction.'
>   *Turing*: But that would not be enough. For if one made that rule, one could get round it and get any conclusion which one liked without actually going through the contradiction. (LFM, 220)

What, if anything, Wittgenstein had in mind here is quite unclear. Turing's remark is surely correct. Wittgenstein seems to have been labouring under the misconception that we can repair a contradictory system simply by refusing to draw any conclusions from a contradiction. Of course, much work has been done subsequently on formal systems of logic which *can* tolerate contradictions in something like the way Wittgenstein envisaged, but it is hard to see that work as bearing out the insouciance towards contradictions which Wittgenstein recommended. Perhaps, then, one can sympathize with the response Wittgenstein is recorded as having made to Turing's objection: 'Well, we must continue this discussion next time.' (At the next lecture Wittgenstein continued to discuss contradictions, but it is hard to see any of what he said as really answering Turing's objection.)

Perhaps it is significant, given how famous his views on consistency proofs in mathematics have become, that relatively little space in Wittgenstein's published typescripts (which one might regard as his main works, as opposed to lectures and manuscripts) is devoted to the subject. There are a couple of pages on the subject in *Philosophical Remarks*, a couple more in *Philosophical Grammar*, and part of an appendix to the pre-war *Investigations*. Moreover, the remarks Wittgenstein makes in these places are, even by his standards, gnomic in the extreme. Much lengthier remarks on the subject are contained in Wittgenstein's conversations with Schlick and Waismann, in the 1939 lectures, and in the manuscript books for 1939–40 (RFM, part III). But he never really developed this material into a stable account.

5. RULE-FOLLOWING

I have suggested that some of what Wittgenstein thought about contradictions could be seen merely as the application to the 'problem' of consistency of his general view about arithmetical generalizations, that their meaning is given by their proof and they are therefore literally meaningless if we do not yet have proofs of them. I want now to indicate briefly how this general view also leads to Wittgenstein's famous 'rule-following argument', i.e. to the idea that each time we apply a rule there is in some sense—in *some* sense—an indeterminacy to be taken as to what 'applying the rule' amounts to on this occasion.

When I discussed Wittgenstein's views on generalizations, I mentioned the difficulty that he could not account for the validity of the process by which we instantiate a universally quantified proposition. Of course, we want to say that the inductive proof entitles us to deduce any individual instance. The difficulty, though, is that only the complete proof does that. How can we elide the middle steps?

> There's no substitute for stepping on every rung, and whatever is equivalent to doing so must in its turn possess the same multiplicity as doing so. (PR, 171)

If we give a general proof that we can miss the steps out, then this general proof will be another induction, and its application will involve the same problem at one stage removed (at the meta-level, as we—but not Wittgenstein—might naturally be inclined to put it). We seem dangerously close to the conclusion that we must appeal to a form of intuition to license each instantiation. This is what Wittgenstein is gesturing towards when he says:

> Supposing there to be a certain general rule (therefore one containing a variable), I must recognize each time afresh that this rule may be applied *here*. No act of foresight can absolve me from this act of *insight*. (PR, 171)

And elsewhere in the *Philosophical Remarks* Wittgenstein observes:

> Neither can I prove that $a+(b+1)=(a+b)+1$ is a special case of $a+(b+c)=(a+b)+c$; I must see it. (No rule can help me here either, since I would still have to know what would be a special case of this general rule.)
>   This is the unbridgeable gulf between rule and application, or law and special case. (PR, 164)

As early as 1930, therefore, Wittgenstein was explicit about the 'unbridgeable gulf between rule and application', which is the essence of the rule-following argument. However, this is at best a particular case of the general argument. In the case of the rule for instantiating a universal generalization, nothing in the rule forces me to apply it in the 'right' way. Moreover, we have the observation that 'no rule can help me here either, since I would still have to know what would be a special case of this general rule'. What we need now is to generalize that conclusion to any rule whatsoever.

I mentioned earlier that on Wittgenstein's account the sense of a generalization is to be explained by reference to another generalization, namely the one embedded in the inductive proof. For the appeal to the inductive proof as the sense of the generalization not to involve an infinite regress there must be *some* arithmetical statements which have a different justification. These are the recursive definitions of the primitive recursive functions. But calling something a definition does not really solve the problem. Recall what Frege said about definitions:

> The definition of an object does not, as such, really assert anything about the object, but only lays down the meaning of a symbol. After this has been done, the definition transforms itself into a judgement, which does assert about the object; but now it no longer introduces the object, it is exactly on a level with other assertions made about it. (Frege 1953, 78)

If we are to apply this in Wittgenstein's case, we must ignore the talk of judgements as being 'about' objects. For part of what he wanted to deny was that it is helpful to think of arithmetical sentences as being about numbers in the way that 'Blackburn Rovers won the Premiership' is about Blackburn Rovers. But Frege's main point surely stands: once we have adopted a recursive definition it has to be regarded as a generalization like any other. Yet it cannot, since other generalizations have as their sense their inductive proofs, and a definition (being a mere stipulation) is not the kind of thing that can be proved.

The temptation, of course, is to look for another account of the sense of a recursive definition. But if the account of generalizations as logical products is unavailable, and if we retain Wittgenstein's verificationism, it is hard to see what other account there could be. If that is right, then we are driven to the conclusion that there just is no sense to a recursive definition: there is nothing in the rule which compels us to apply it in a particular way. We have thus arrived again at Wittgenstein's rule-following argument, but now in a form that applies to any recursive definition whatever.

6. REJECTION?

Wittgenstein incorporated the rule-following argument into the pre-war version of the *Philosophical Investigations* which he compiled in 1937. He revised and re-arranged this material later, and it is the later re-arrangement that is published as part I of the *Remarks on the Foundations of Mathematics*. The most striking presentational change is that Wittgenstein now goes directly to the rule-following argument, instead of presenting it via the idea that the meaning of an arithmetical generalization is its proof. The case from which the rule-following argument was originally derived is now mentioned only as a special case.

> 'But doesn't e.g. "fa" have to follow from "$(x)fx$" if "$(x)fx$" is meant in the way we mean it?'—And how does *the way* we mean it come out? Doesn't it come out in the constant practice of its use? and perhaps further in certain *gestures*—and similar things.—But it is as if there were also something attached to the word 'all', when *we* say it; something with which a different use could not be combined; namely, the

meaning. ‘“All” surely means: *all!*’ we should like to say, when we have to explain this meaning; and we make a particular gesture and face. (RFM I, §10)

Moreover, what I have presented as the motivating idea of Wittgenstein's middle-period philosophy of mathematics, that the meaning of an arithmetical generalization is its proof, is not explicitly mentioned in the pre-war *Philosophical Investigations* at all. This raises the question whether he eventually gave up the doctrine. Perhaps he did. At any rate, there are various passages in his later writings where we can see him struggling with the doctrine and with its puzzling consequences (cf. again Säätelä's chapter). For instance, he worries about how there can be several different proofs of the same proposition.

> This proof is a mathematical entity that cannot be replaced by any other; one can say that it can convince us of something that nothing else can, and this can be given expression by our assigning to it a proposition that we do not assign to any other proof.
>
> But am I not making a crude mistake? For just this is essential to the propositions of arithmetic and to the propositions of the Russellian logic: various proofs lead to them. Even: infinitely many proofs lead to any one of them.
>
> Is it correct to say that every proof demonstrates something to us which it alone can demonstrate? Would not—so to speak—the proved proposition then be superfluous, and the proof itself also be the thing proved?
>
> Is it only the proved proposition that the proof convinces me of? (RFM III, §§59–60)

Note, though, that this quotation (from late 1939 or early 1940) does not seem to come from someone who has already clearly rejected the doctrine that the meaning of a mathematical proposition should be identified with its proof; instead, it reads as though Wittgenstein was only just beginning to be troubled by the view. He repeats a similar concern a little later (June 1941).

> Now how about this—ought I to say that the same sense can only have *one* proof? Or that when a proof is found the sense alters?
>
> Of course some people would oppose this and say: ‘Then the proof of a proposition cannot ever be found, for, if it has been found, it is no longer the proof of *this* proposition’. (RFM VII, §10)

Wittgenstein's enigmatic response is that ‘to say this is so far to say nothing at all’. He then recalls his earlier view that ‘if you want to know what a mathematical proposition says, look at what its proof proves’, before going as far as to grant that there might be ‘both truth and falsehood’ in this view.

If Wittgenstein began around 1939 to doubt the doctrine that the meaning of an arithmetical generalization is its proof, I think we can come, albeit tentatively, to a diagnosis of the reason why the final version of the *Philosophical Investigations* did not include, as the pre-war version had done, a lengthy section on the philosophy of mathematics. The reason, I believe, is that Wittgenstein's thinking about mathematics had been dominated by this doctrine of meaning as proof. When he came to realize that it is untenable (or at least suspect), the damage done to his account was too great to be easily repaired.

7. A LATE PHILOSOPHY?

Nonetheless, Wittgenstein continued to work on the philosophy of mathematics intermittently until at least 1944. Is there perhaps room, therefore, for the possibility that there might be a distinct view, or cluster of views, that could be described as Wittgenstein's late philosophy of mathematics—a philosophy which he developed after he had rejected the erroneous central doctrine of his middle period?

Since Wittgenstein published nothing after 1929 (except for a letter to the editor of *Mind* complaining that Braithwaite had misrepresented his views), it is a matter for debate which parts of his *Nachlass* we ought to take seriously. It is clear at one extreme that he intended the *Philosophical Investigations* (in their post-war version) for publication. And it is equally clear at the other that some of the material in his pocket notebooks is what one would expect to find in notebooks—ideas that obviously do not work and which he would never have had any temptation to publish.

The point to remember here is that Wittgenstein's working method remained broadly constant throughout his life. He wrote his ideas in journals from day to day, then extracted the best of them to put into further notebooks or typescripts, then cut up the typescripts and re-arranged them (sometimes almost endlessly). We should not regard what we find in the notebooks as having the same status as the worked-over typescripts.

It is therefore worth drawing attention to the status of the *Remarks on the Foundations of Mathematics*, written between 1937 and 1944, on which so much of the secondary literature on Wittgenstein's late philosophy of mathematics relies. As the editors' preface explains, only part I of this book is based on a complete typescript. Of the others, only part VI is a reasonably complete manuscript. The rest are selections (and in some cases arrangements) by the editors from much more extensive notebooks. What this book is not is a complete work by Wittgenstein on the philosophy of mathematics. It must surely be treated with care if it is not to do considerable harm to our understanding of Wittgenstein's later philosophy of mathematics.

Although we find in the *Remarks on the Foundations of Mathematics* explorations (dating from the period up to 1944) of various themes in the philosophy of mathematics that are not to be found in what I have been calling Wittgenstein's middle-period writings, we do not have typescripts from this period that he had worked over for publication (even ones with which he later became dissatisfied), as we do in the case of his middle period. This is part of the reason why it is so hard to state anything that deserves the title of a late-period philosophy of mathematics. The *Remarks on the Foundations of Mathematics* contain many thought-provoking observations and ideas, and anyone interested in the philosophy of mathematics ought to read them, but they are of variable quality and can hardly be said to present something that amounts to a coherent view.

It is often noted that one of the characteristic features of Wittgenstein's later philosophy generally is its lack of *theses*. In his later writings Wittgenstein's technique was neither to make claims nor to present tightly constructed arguments against the view of his opponents. So it is no surprise to find that the *Remarks on the Foundations of Mathematics* conforms to this pattern by refraining from making claims. But the point I am making here goes beyond that general observation. Wittgenstein's late writings on mathematics are fragmentary in a way that his writings on philosophy of mind, for instance, are not. His later writings are no doubt always in a certain sense inconclusive and open-ended—allusive rather than straightforwardly persuasive. But if we put this open-endedness to one side, we usually find that there is a stance we can recognize Wittgenstein as adopting. There are views which we can ascribe to him, even while accepting, perhaps, that by presenting them as views which we can summarize, we inevitably misrepresent them somewhat. In the case of mathematics, though, not even this seems to be true. We know what he was against: Platonism, logicism, intuitionism, and Hilbertian formalism all at various times come in for his criticism. But what, by contrast, was he for? We can be fairly sure, I think, that he never gave up the two views that were central to his early philosophy of mathematics: that numbers are not objects, and that arithmetical equations are not tautologies. But if it is the first task of any philosopher of mathematics who holds these two views to give an account of arithmetical generalizations, and if Wittgenstein eventually gave up his account according to which their meanings are given by their proofs, then it is hard to see what he had to offer instead. Indeed, one struggles to present, even in outline, a positive account of mathematics that can reasonably be called Wittgensteinian. Too often Wittgenstein seems more concerned with offering meta-level advice about how to go about finding a correct account, rather than with developing the account itself.

Perhaps, though, Wittgenstein's failure to make significant progress was inevitable. He was trying to reconcile his radically anti-realist conception of the subject matter of mathematics with an anti-revisionary conception of mathematical practice without collapsing into formalism; and that is surely a very tall order.

Wittgenstein's remarks on Gödel's incompleteness theorems are notoriously controversial: it is a matter of debate whether Wittgenstein succeeds in enunciating a position from which the validity, or the standard interpretation, of Gödel's theorem can coherently be questioned. But he was right to try. For what Gödel's theorem demonstrates, on its standard interpretation, is that conventional mathematics has a richness which the radical anti-realist cannot explain.

REFERENCES

ANSCOMBE, G. E. M. and GEACH, P. T. (1961). *Three Philosophers*. Oxford: Blackwell.

FREGE, GOTTLOB (1953). *The Foundations of Arithmetic*. Oxford: Blackwell.

LEWIS, DAVID (1991). *Parts of Classes*. Oxford: Blackwell.

POTTER, MICHAEL (2000). *Reason's Nearest Kin: Philosophies of Arithmetic from Kant to Carnap*. Oxford: Oxford University Press.

—— (2005). 'Ramsey's transcendental argument', in Hallvard Lillehammer and D. H. Mellor eds., *Ramsey's Legacy*. Oxford: Oxford University Press.

—— (2009). *Wittgenstein's Notes on Logic*. Oxford: Oxford University Press.

RAMSEY, F. P. (1931). *The Foundations of Mathematics and Other Logical Essays*. London: Kegan Paul, Trench & Trubner.

—— (1990). *Philosophical Papers*. Cambridge: Cambridge University Press.

WAISMANN, FRIEDRICH (1979). *Wittgenstein and the Vienna Circle*. Oxford: Blackwell.

WITTGENSTEIN, LUDWIG (1922). *Tractatus Logico-Philosophicus*. London: Kegan Paul & Trubner.

—— (1974). *Philosophical Grammar*. Oxford: Blackwell.

—— (1975). *Philosophical Remarks*. Oxford: Blackwell.

—— (1976). *Lectures on the Foundations of Mathematics, Cambridge, 1939*. Ithaca, NY: Cornell University Press.

—— (1978). *Remarks on the Foundations of Mathematics*. Oxford: Blackwell.

CHAPTER 7

··

WITTGENSTEIN ON SURVEYABILITY OF PROOFS

··

MATHIEU MARION

PHILOSOPHERS of mathematics are often divided between 'mainstream' and 'maverick'.[1] Arising initially from debates surrounding the foundations of mathematics in the early decades of the last century, 'mainstream' philosophy of mathematics has tended, throughout the remainder of that century, to become increasingly detached from issues of concern to mathematicians themselves (for whom foundational debates became increasingly irrelevant), and to address instead issues central to epistemology, metaphysics, and the philosophy of language, within the analytic tradition. Wittgenstein could hardly be classified as 'mainstream', although his writings would be of little use to find out about philosophical issues of his days, other than foundational ones, arising from mathematical practice. He had in common with other 'mavericks', however, a critical stance towards the value of the 'mainstream' philosophy of mathematics of his days, mostly but not only as he knew it from the logicist tradition of Frege, Russell, Ramsey, and Carnap.[2] Nevertheless, his remarks on mathematics were for the most part posthumously read as contributions to it, and this might explain a certain amount of distortion in the presentation of his views, about which commentators and epigones have complained for decades.[3]

Wittgenstein's remarks on the '*Übersichtlichkeit*' or 'surveyability'[4] of proofs are a very good example of this, since they were read as forming part of an argument in support of

---

[1] This distinction was introduced in Aspray and Kitcher 1988, 16–17.

[2] Wittgenstein's knowledge of the foundational debates up to the 1930s is not, of course, limited to the logicist standpoint. On the relation to Brouwer and intuitionism, for example, see Marion 2003 and 2008. I am here simply attracting attention to the centrality for his philosophy of mathematics of his critical stance towards logicism, understood as the *defining* 'mainstream' philosophy of mathematics in his days.

[3] Probably starting with Baker and Hacker 1985, 345.

[4] Elizabeth Anscombe translated Wittgenstein's '*übersichtlich*' with both 'perspicuous' and 'surveyable'. She also used 'can be taken in' for '*übersehbar*' and 'intuitive' for '*anschaulich*'. (There are other cognate terms used by Wittgenstein in his discussion of proofs such as '*durchsichtig*' at RFM I,

a radical 'anti-realist' account of mathematics, which coincides with 'strict finitism' in the foundations of mathematics. In a nutshell, strict finitism arises from a complaint concerning the induction schema of Peano Arithmetic,

$$(F(o) \wedge \forall x (F(x) \to F(Sx))) \to \forall x (F(x))$$

Numerals being of the form:

$$o, So, SSo, SSSo, \ldots,$$

it is usually assumed that within such a series one can reach any natural number, 'in principle' and the common justification of the procedure of proof by induction takes the form of a repeated Modus Ponens:

$$F(o),$$
$$F(o) \to F(So),$$
$$F(So) \to F(SSo),$$
$$\ldots$$

Since each Modus Ponens is true, then for any n, $F(n)$ is also true (Dummett 1978, 251). Strict finitists such as Alexander Esenin-Volpin deny this, arguing that this justification is circular, since induction is itself needed to justify these repeated uses of Modus Ponens. It suffices for one to pick up any number which one would readily recognize as being unreachable by the above procedure, such as 2^{65535}, and to use it as an upper bound to the series of 'feasible numbers', with the following definition, for 'F' now standing for 'feasible':

$$F(o) \qquad \text{(The number o is feasible)}$$
$$F(n) \to n < 2^{65535} \qquad \text{(If } n \text{ is feasible, then } n < 2^{65535})$$
$$F(n) \to F(Sn) \qquad \text{(If } n \text{ is feasible, then } Sn \text{ is also feasible)}$$

App. II, §8). Anscombe's choices are not entirely felicitous, as more than one commentator pointed out. For example, the visual aspect is somehow lost when one translates '*anschaulich*' by 'intuitive'. Commentators have had a tendency, however, to deny that Wittgenstein's remarks were concerned with 'epistemic' aspects of proofs – he was, we are told, focusing exclusively on 'formal' aspects of proofs – and to criticize Anscombe's translation for its bias towards the former. (See Shanker 1987, ch. 4 and Stillwell 1992, 116 and 133, n. 8. A similar claim was made in Mühlhölzer 2005, for different reasons.) This criticism is not without merits but I think, for reasons expressed in this chapter, that it is ultimately wrong to deny the 'epistemic' dimension of Wittgenstein's remarks on 'surveyability'. At all events, I shall, following Mühlhölzer 2005, avert controversies by simply translating both '*übersichtlich*' and '*übersehbar*' with the more neutral 'surveyable'. Anscombe also translated '*einprägsames Bild*' at RFM I, §80 & III, §9 with 'memorable picture', which I translate here as 'significant picture' for reasons that will become clear.

Esenin-Volpin's example was that of 'the number of heartbeats in my childhood' (Esenin-Volpin 1961, 203). Indeed, this series has an upper bound but every heartbeat in my childhood was followed by another heartbeat in my childhood. In his paper 'Wang's Paradox', Dummett characterized numbers series such as this one as being both 'weakly infinite', because there exists a well-ordering of it with no last member, and 'weakly finite', because for a finite ordinal n, there exists a well-ordering with no nth member (Dummett 1978, 258). Dummett then pointed out that the fact that series such as that of the 'feasible' numbers are both weakly infinite and weakly finite renders the predicate 'feasible' susceptible to a variant of the sorites, which he dubbed 'Wang's paradox'. From this, Dummett concluded that concepts such as 'feasible' are vague and thus semantically incoherent; for that reason strict finitism could not be viable as a philosophy of mathematics (Dummett 1978, 265).

This is not the place to evaluate either strict finitism itself or its critique at the hands of Dummett; it suffices that one notices that one could run an analogous argument for the predicate 'surveyable' as it applies to proofs and the number of steps they require. (One should note that 'surveyable' is here defined in terms of length of proofs: a proof is 'unsurveyable' because it has too many steps.) Although there is no equivalent in Wittgenstein of the above line of argument about 'feasible' numbers, he does discuss 'surveyability', and an interpretation of his philosophy of mathematics along those lines was pioneered in a pair of influential papers by Sir Michael Dummett.[5] According to this reading, Wittgenstein required that all mathematical proofs be 'surveyable',[6] and he was, therefore, committed to this unpalatable strict finitist position. Crispin Wright, however, saw that the very possibility of strict finitism meant that the less radical 'anti-realism' that Dummett associated with intuitionism is an inherently unstable position and he developed this reading of Wittgenstein further in the 1970s, in an attempt to argue this point.[7] Saul Kripke's notorious interpretation of the 'rule-following' argument can also be seen as closely related and providing further support.[8]

These readings have come under considerable criticism since the 1980s and they are now generally dismissed, for better or for worse. They were, however, mostly dismissed merely for failing fully to take into account the radical implications of Wittgenstein's

---

[5] Dummett's key paper is 'Wittgenstein's Philosophy of Mathematics', reprinted in Dummett 1978, 166–85. Although ostensibly working out the 'strict finitism' of A. S. Esenin-Volpin on the basis of Esenin-Volpin 1961, Dummett's 'Wang's Paradox' (Dummett 1978, 248–68) can also be seen as working out the foundational stance that he attributed to Wittgenstein (Dummett 1978, 249). The name 'Wang's Paradox' comes from discussions on these issues between Dummett and Hao Wang; one should also note Wang's own discussion of what I call below Wittgenstein's 'circularity argument' in Wang 1961.

[6] That view explains the references to Wittgenstein in the debate in the early 1980s surrounding the computer-assisted proof of the four-colour theorem by Appel, Haken, and Koch. See e.g. Tymoczko 1979, 59, and for discussions of Tymoczko's paper from opposite standpoints, Detlefsen and Luker 1980 and Shanker 1987, 143–58.

[7] See Wright 1980 and some of the papers collected in Wright 2001.

[8] First published in book form as Kripke 1982. Kripke's Alfred North Whitehead Lectures at Harvard University in 1992, 'Logicism, Wittgenstein, and de re Beliefs about Numbers', discuss Wittgenstein's remarks on surveyability, but they remain, alas, unpublished.

claims concerning the nature of philosophy in *Philosophical Investigations* (PI §§89–133), according to which he was not trying to work out an alternative standpoint on the foundations of mathematics or to take sides within the 'mainstream', but without anyone caring to provide an alternative interpretation of the passages concerned.[9] In a more positive fashion, the prima facie case for an alternative reading of Wittgenstein's remarks on 'surveyability' will be developed here, moreover one that does not commit him to strict finitism.

A preliminary account of the argument I am about to discuss, with some scholarly remarks concerning sources and chronology, is in order to fix ideas at the outset. This will be followed by a discussion of 'surveyability' of proofs, as mostly found in Part III of the *Remarks on the Foundations of Mathematics*. The main claim in this central section of the chapter will be that Wittgenstein's 'surveyability argument' is best understood not as an argument concerning the length of proofs but as involving the recognition that formal proofs possess a non-eliminable visual element, neglected by Russell. In a final section, I shall discuss the consequences that Wittgenstein drew from his argument, especially as they relate to the larger issue of the cogency of mathematical 'explicativism'. There will be no attempt at a critical assessment of Wittgenstein's views; to reach a renewed understanding of his remarks is my sole task.

1. Preliminary Account and Sources

Take any ordinary arithmetical equation, say,

(1) $27 + 16 = 43$

which is one of Wittgenstein's examples (RFM III, §11). According to him, this equation must have a counterpart in Russell and Whitehead's *Principia Mathematica*, of the form:

(2) $\exists!27x\,(\phi x) \land \exists!16x\,(\psi x) \land \forall x\,\neg(\phi x \land \psi x) \rightarrow \exists!43x\,(\phi x \lor \psi x),$

or, in plain English:

(3) If the ϕs are 27 in number, and the ψs are 16, and nothing is both a ϕ and a ψ, then the number of things that are either ϕs or ψs is 43.

According to Wittgenstein, Russell wanted *per impossibile* to ground the cogency of (1) on that of (2). Against this, Wittgenstein first noted that (2) must merely be an abbreviation of a longer formula with a total of 43 variables on each side of the sign for the conditional.[10] He then pointed out that this unabbreviated formula is 'unsurveyable' in

---

[9] At times (e.g. Putnam 2001), it just looks as if Wittgenstein's philosophy of mathematics is merely a pretext for a critique of Dummett's 'anti-realism'. This is more like reading one's own agenda in Wittgenstein than earnestly seeking to understand what he is trying to say.

[10] On this point, see footnote [1] to PR §101.

the sense that one cannot tell its precise number of variables unless one starts counting them. Doing this would presuppose the very knowledge of the arithmetical equation (1) which is meant to be ascertained by (2). Therefore, rather than (1) being grounded on (2), it is (2) which requires (1) for its cogency. There appears, therefore, to be a circularity in Russell's attempt to ground arithmetic on logic: in order to understand the logical truth, one must introduce precisely the arithmetical knowledge which is meant to be ascertained by the logical truth. This claim lies at the heart of Wittgenstein's remarks on 'surveyability'.

The latter are known to readers of Part III of the *Remarks on the Foundations of Mathematics*, which is dated from 1939–40, but it would be mistaken to claim that the above 'circularity' argument only forms part of an alleged 'later' philosophy. Wittgenstein discusses it in the first pages of the earliest manuscript that we have from that period, MS 105, which begins in January 1929.[11] The argument occurs also in a conversation recorded by Waismann, at the end of 1929:

> The correctness of an arithmetical proposition is never expressed by a proposition's being a tautology. In the Russellian way of expressing it, the proposition $3 + 4 = 7$ for example can be represented in the following manner:
>
> $(E3x)\phi x.(E4x)\psi x.\sim(Ex)\phi x.\psi x: \rightarrow: (E7x).\phi x \vee \psi x$
>
> Now one might think that the proof of this equation consisted in this: that the proposition written down was a tautology. But in order to be able to write down this proposition, I have to *know* that $3 + 4 = 7$. The whole tautology is an application and not a proof of arithmetic. (WVC, 35)

One noticeable difference is the absence of any consideration about 'surveyability' in this very passage. The verb '*übersehen*' first appears in the *Big Typescript* in 1933,[12] and Wittgenstein's use of '*Übersichtlichkeit*' or cognate expressions in our context does not seem to occur before 1937–8. So it seems that the argument as we know it from Part III of the *Remarks on the Foundations of Mathematics* is merely a 'surveyability' variant of this early version, which merely emphasizes the hidden circularity in Russell (more on this point below). Be this as it may, we have here an indication that claims of an evolution to a 'later philosophy' in the second half of the 1930s, which are invoked in order to by-pass the 'middle period', which is thereby assumed to contain no more than transitory views that are supposedly abandoned, are often simply exaggerated for merely tactical purposes and exegetically unwarranted.[13]

One may wonder where Wittgenstein got (2). The definition of addition in Part II, section B of *Principia Mathematica* is rather complicated because of the need to account for ambiguity of types and, as far as one can tell, there is no formula corresponding to (2).[14] The closest would be:

---

[11] See, for example, footnote 35 for the sources of PR §103, quoted below.

[12] For example at BT, 486f.; PG, 455. See Mühlhölzer 2005, 58n.

[13] Admittedly, this is only one such indication, if the discussion about 'surveyability' is considered to be part of the 'later philosophy', so the claim is not that this conclusively settles the question.

[14] For a brief informal account of the way Russell and Whitehead proceed, see Russell 1919, 117–18.

$$*54.43 \vdash :. \ \alpha, \beta \ \varepsilon \ 1 . \supset : \alpha \cap \beta = \Lambda . \equiv . \alpha \cup \beta \ \varepsilon \ 2$$

This is the *Principia* equivalent of '1 + 1 = 2', a major difference being the replacement of the biconditional in this formula by a conditional in (2). The idea captured in (2) and *54.43 appears to be the same, namely the connection between addition of natural numbers and union of disjoint classes (or sets). One finds, however, the following comment in F. P. Ramsey's 'Mathematical Logic' (1926), in the midst of a critique of Hilbert's formalist philosophy,[15] which could reasonably be seen as providing his own take on *Principia Mathematica*:

> For what are [natural] numbers, that they are about? According to Hilbert marks on paper constructed out of the marks 1 and +. But this account seems to me inadequate, because if I said 'I have two dogs', that would [...] tell you something; you would understand the word 'two', and the whole sentence would be rendered something like 'There are x and y, which are my dogs and are not identical with one another'. This statement appears to involve the idea of existence, and not to be about marks on paper; so that I do not see that it can be seriously held that a cardinal number which answers the question 'How many?' is merely a mark on paper. If then we take one of these individual arithmetical facts, such as 2 + 2 = 4, this seems to me to mean 'If the p's are two in number, and the q's also, and nothing is both a p and a q, then the number of things that are either p's or q's is four'. For this is the meaning in which we must take 2 + 2 = 4 in order to use it, as we do, to infer from I have two dogs and two cats that I have four pets. (Ramsey 1990, 235)

There is a striking parallel between Ramsey's 'If the p's are two in number, and the q's also, and nothing is both a p and a q, then the number of things that are either p's or q's is four' and (2) or (3), which warrants taking this passage as a direct source for Wittgenstein.[16] In this respect, it is worth noting that, in this passage, Ramsey clearly alludes to Russell's idea that logic is needed for numbers to be applicable in daily life, an idea to be presented shortly. As we shall see, Wittgenstein certainly saw this last as a mistaken view and one may assume that it was his negative reaction to this view that prompted him to develop his 'circularity' argument.

Presentations of Russell's logicism usually focus on the following theses (restricted here, for the sake of simplicity, to the arithmetical case):

---

[15] Hilbert's original proof theory was presented in papers such as 'On the Infinite' (Hilbert 1967) by appeal to a form of 'stroke arithmetic', involving strings of the sign '1'. Wittgenstein knew some of Hilbert's papers and it is fitting to notice here that he often framed his argument about 'surveyability' in terms of some sort of 'stroke arithmetic', e.g., at RFM III, §§3 and 11 or, earlier, at PR §103, quoted below.

[16] This is also borne out by the fact that in WVC, 35, quoted above, Wittgenstein is arguing against the idea that arithmetical truths are tautologies, a frequent misunderstanding of the *Tractatus* notoriously put forward by Ramsey. The argument at WVC, 35 also occurs in Wittgenstein's lectures in Cambridge in the spring of 1930, as recorded in G. E. Moore's notebooks (MSS 8875, 10/7/4), at pp. 73–5 of Moore's first notebook, in the midst of a critical discussion of Ramsey's claim that 'equations are tautologies'. (This passage was not selected, however, by Moore for his well-known account of 'Wittgenstein's Lectures in 1930–33'.) Finally, Wittgenstein's earliest remarks on (2) occur first in MS 105, therefore in 1929, at a time when Wittgenstein had weekly conversations with Ramsey. All these point in the same direction: Ramsey.

(4) The concepts of arithmetic can be derived from logical concepts through explicit definitions;

(5) The theorems of arithmetic can be derived from logical axioms through purely logical deduction.[17]

But Russell was concerned with the meaning and justification of arithmetic. In *Mathematical Knowledge*, Mark Steiner captured this side of Russell's logicism by the following pair of theses:

(6) It is sufficient to understand proofs written in the system of *Principia Mathematica* in order to know all the truths of arithmetic that we know;

(7) It is possible for us actually to come to know arithmetical truths by constructing logical proofs of them (Steiner 1975, 25).

In order to get the full picture, however, one needs to supplement (4)–(7) with two seldom-discussed theses. In a well-known passage from *Introduction to Mathematical Philosophy*, Russell pointed out that the primitive concepts contained in the axioms of Peano Arithmetic, '0', 'number', and 'successor', are 'capable of an infinite number of different interpretations, all of which will satisfy the five primitive propositions' (Russell 1919, 7). Given one such interpretation, one obtains a 'progression', which he defined as a series with a beginning but endless and containing no repetition and no terms that cannot be reached from the beginning in a finite number of steps. There is indeed an infinity of such 'progressions' which will, like the series of natural numbers, satisfy the axioms of Peano Arithmetic; it suffices for example to start any given series with a natural number other than 0. So Russell argued that 'there is nothing' in Peano Arithmetic 'to enable us to distinguish between … different interpretations of his primitive ideas', while

> We want our numbers not merely to verify mathematical formulae, but to apply in the right way to common objects. We want to have ten fingers and two eyes and one nose. A system in which '1' meant 100, and '2' meant '101', and so on, might be all right for pure mathematics, but would not suit daily life. We want '0' and 'number' and 'successor' to have meanings which will give us the right allowance of fingers and eyes and nose. We have already some knowledge (though not sufficiently articulate or analytic) of what we mean by '1' and '2' and so on, and our use of numbers in arithmetic must conform to this knowledge. (Russell 1919, 9)

A little further on, this point is reiterated:

> We want our numbers to be such as can be used for counting common objects, and this requires that our numbers should have a *definite* meaning, not merely that they should have certain formal properties. This definite meaning is defined by the logical theory of arithmetic. (Russell 1919, 10)

The claims expressed here may be captured by the following pair of theses:

---

[17] These standard theses can be found, for example, in Carnap's contribution to the Königsberg symposium on the foundations of mathematics in 1931 (Carnap 1983, 41), which was certainly known to Wittgenstein.

(8) Interpretation within a logical system provides a definite meaning to the basic arithmetical concepts;

(9) This interpretation allows for applications of arithmetic.

They indicate clearly the very purpose of the system of *Principia Mathematica*: it was set up as an interpretation of Peano Arithmetic meant to provide a definite meaning to its primitive terms, so that one could recover ordinary applications of arithmetic.[18] As we shall see, these last claims, (6)–(9), form the target of Wittgenstein's criticisms, for which he deployed the above 'circularity argument'. One should note for the moment that it is not really the connection between addition of natural numbers and union of disjoint classes which is at stake here; it is rather the idea that it may serve to explain the applicability of arithmetic to everyday life.

In discussing only elementary cases of the same form as (2), Wittgenstein appears to be preoccupied only with a single aspect of the applicability of mathematics, namely what Mark Steiner called 'canonical empirical applications' of arithmetic (Steiner 2005, 627 and 2009, 23). His remarks are therefore limited in scope and it is worth noticing that they were prompted by Ramsey's remarks in 'Mathematical Logic', above, and by Russell's views in the *Introduction to Mathematical Philosophy*, just quoted. It is thus by focusing on these that one can recover their true meaning.

2. Wittgenstein's 'Surveyability Argument' in *Remarks on the Foundations of Mathematics*

In the posthumous manuscript edited as Part III of the *Remarks on the Foundations of Mathematics*, Wittgenstein is busy trying to reach for himself a proper characterization of 'surveyability'. He distinguishes at least three different meanings of that expression that can be ranked in an ascending order of strength.[19] A first definition occurs in the very first section:

(10) A proof is surveyable if it is reproducible.[20]

---

[18] As is well known, applicability was already an issue for Frege, for whom 'it is applicability alone which elevates arithmetic from a game to the rank of a science' (Frege 1998, II, §91, and Geach and Black 1952, 127). For an interpretation of Frege's views, see Dummett 1991, 48, 59–61, and 257–9). Dummett also discusses (1991, 259–61) an objection by Friedrich Waismann which is said to be inspired by Wittgenstein. Mark Steiner discusses Wittgenstein on applicability in connection with Frege in Steiner 2009, 20f. To my mind, however, the *direct* target of Wittgenstein's 'circularity' and 'surveyability' arguments is Russell's conceptions as just expounded, relayed by Ramsey, not Frege. (One should note indeed that in expounding Frege's view, Steiner appeals (1998, 17) to a theorem which is a generalization of (2), but does not indicate where it is to be found in Frege.) At all events, this does not mean that it would not be profitable to look at their bearing on Frege's views, but this task cannot be undertaken here.

[19] On this, see Wright 1980, 122.

[20] For a refined analysis of this claim, see Mühlhölzer 2005, 59f.

More precisely, after copying a given proof, one must be certain of having reproduced it exactly:

> 'A mathematical proof must be [surveyable].' Only a structure whose reproduction is an easy task is called a 'proof'. It must be possible to decide with certainty whether we really have the same proof or not. The proof must be a configuration whose exact reproduction can be certain. (RFM III, §1)[21]

Wittgenstein's idea seems to be that one should rule out situations in which the mathematician remains unaware that part of the proof has changed under her eyes or that she has made errors in copying it. Indeed, the capacity to duplicate a proof-object exceeds the capacity to recognize that a proof has been exactly duplicated. A visual criterion appears to be implied here; the reasons for this should become clear later on.

Part of the difficulty here is that Wittgenstein does not distinguish clearly between 'informal proofs' that one finds in mathematical books and journals and their 'formal' counterparts, which only occur within mathematical logic (and, now, computer science), e.g., in Russell and Whitehead's *Principia Mathematica*.[22] Let us assume for the moment that he was talking about 'formal proofs'. These are usually defined as finite sequences of well-formed formulas (in a formal language) whose last steps are the theorems, and whose formulas are either an axiom or the result of the application of one of a finitely stated set of rules of inference to previous formulas in the sequence.[23] Given Turing's seminal work on computability,[24] one can say that they are obtained by use of an 'effective' or 'mechanical' method, where the latter is understood in terms of a finite number of (finitely stated) rules, terminating in a finite number of steps, being carried out by a human being with paper and pencil, and as not depending on guesswork on the part of the human being carrying it out.[25] It would thus be easy, albeit tedious, to check one by one every step of such formal proofs; it is also uncontroversial that the capacity to ratify such proofs, by simply checking each step as involving a correct application of one of the given rules, exceeds indeed the capacity to grasp the collective soundness of these steps as proofs of a given result. So one should distinguish the requirement that each of the individual steps be surveyed, or 'local' surveyability:[26]

> (11) A proof is 'surveyable' when one is able to check the steps of the proof one by one, from 'global' surveyability.
>
> (12) A proof is 'surveyable' when one is able to see that the steps are collectively sufficient to prove the theorem.

---

[21] See also (RFM III, §41).

[22] Even today most mathematical theories are not formalized, so most informal proofs in mathematics do not possess a formal counterpart. As a matter of fact, even if mathematical theories can be expressed in a (first-order) set-theoretical language, it is not even clear that all their informal proofs can be formalized. See Rav 1999, 20, n. 20 and Dawson 2006, 270.

[23] See Church 1956, 49–50 for this definition.

[24] See RPP I §§1096–7 for evidence that Wittgenstein had a good understanding of Turing's work.

[25] See Gandy 1980, 124 for this usual definition. One should note, however, that use of 'effective' methods does not rule out the possibility of error in very long computations.

[26] Following Bassler 2006, 100.

This last is ordinarily called 'understanding' the proof, for example by Bourbaki:

> Indeed, every mathematician knows that a proof has not been 'understood' if one has done nothing more than verify step by step the correctness of the deductions of which it is composed and has not tried to gain a clear insight into the ideas which have led to the construction of this particular chain of deductions in preference to every other one. (Bourbaki 1950, 223n.)[27]

There are many reasons why Wittgenstein would have insisted on this last, 'global' surveyability, reasons that link Wittgenstein's remarks on 'surveyability' with some of his more central, not to say 'mainstream', concerns in the philosophy of mathematics. For example, it is essential to his distinction between proof and experiment,[28] since the 'compulsion' to get the result is a missing ingredient in the case of experiment:

> 'Proof must be surveyable': this aims at drawing our attention to the difference between the concepts of 'repeating a proof' and 'repeating an experiment'. To repeat a proof means, not to reproduce the conditions under which a particular result was once obtained, but to repeat every step *and the result*. And although this shews that proof is something that must be capable of being reproduced *in toto* automatically, still every such reproduction must contain the force of proof, which compels the acceptance of the result. (RFM III, §55)

Perhaps more importantly, 'global' surveyability is a necessary condition for the possibility of a proof being able to 'guide' us:

> 'A proof must be [surveyable]' means: we must be prepared to use it as our guideline in judging. (RFM III, §22)

This is a central plank of Wittgenstein's opposition to 'Platonism' or 'realism' in mathematics, i.e. to the thesis that mathematics is composed of statements describing a world of abstract entities whose existence is independent of our own activities, to which he opposed the thesis that the meaning of a theorem is given by its proof or, as he also put it, that proofs 'construct' propositions (RFM III, §28), 'create' or 'alter' concepts (RFM III, §§31, 41, and 49).[29] For example, the various proofs of the infinity of primes surely

---

[27]   One should note here that Bourbaki did not link 'understanding' with 'surveyability', of which there is no mention in this quotation. For a recent discussion of 'understanding' proofs that makes good use of Wittgenstein, see Avigad 2008.

[28]   Some commentators make heavy weather of this distinction. See Shanker 1987, ch. 4 and Stillwell 1992.

[29]   For more passages, RFM V, §§42 and 45, or, from the 'middle period', see e.g. PR §122; AWL, 198–9, 212; PG, 366, 369–70, 373, 375, 455, 462. Wittgenstein realized that in claiming that the meaning of a theorem is given by its proof, he had to deal with a number of counterintuitive consequences. Among these are the fact that two proofs would thus prove two different mathematical propositions, so no theorem could have more than one proof (PR §155), the fact that the proof changes the meaning of the proposition (PG, 371), so that the proof would not prove the originally conjectured mathematical proposition but another one (RFM VII, §10) or that there is no proposition to prove to begin with, perhaps only some images 'in the head' of the mathematician (PR §151). Wittgenstein struggled with these difficulties and proposed some solutions, e.g. at RFM III, §58, that might not appear fully satisfactory at first and deserve a thorough discussion. At all events, this issue falls outside of the scope of the chapter.

convince us that the expression 'the greatest prime' is meaningless, and this is tanta-mount to 'altering' the concept of 'prime number' by eliminating from its definition the concept of 'the greatest prime'. Wittgenstein was predictably explicit about the 'anti-realist' implications of such claims.[30] For example, one reads:

> One would like to say: the proof changes the grammar of our language, changes our concepts. It makes new connexions, and it creates the concept of these con-nexions. (It does not establish that they are there; they do not exist until it makes them.) (RFM III, §31)

Wittgenstein also expressed what is essentially the same thought when he wrote that proofs result in our acceptance of 'rules' (RFM III, §§26 and 28) or of 'paradigms' that are to be placed 'among the paradigms of language' (RFM III, §31) or in the 'archives' (RFM III, §29; LFM, 104 and 111–12). Such 'rules' or 'paradigms' would not just be stored as if obtaining independently from each other, and Wittgenstein also spoke in this connex-ion of a proof as showing where a mathematical proposition stands within a system (RFM III, §§27 and 29) or as a 'decision' in a 'system of decisions' (RFM III, §27). Obviously, it does so through the connexions that it establishes; hence the need, in order to understand the theorem, to understand the proof. And it is the connexions created by the proof that allow us to use it.[31] Again, all this is predictably presented by Wittgenstein as having anti-realist consequences:

> I am trying to say something like this: even if the proved mathematical proposition seems to point out to a reality outside itself, still it is only the expression of accept-ance of a new measure (of reality).
>   Thus we take the constructability (provability) of this symbol (that is, of the math-ematical proposition) as a sign that we are to transform symbols in such and such a way. (RFM III, §27)[32]

The remarks in this last paragraph deserve further elaboration that cannot be under-taken here, my point being simply that, in order for proofs to play the role Wittgenstein

---

[30] My use of the expression 'anti-realist' is meant to be neutral, meaning simply what it means, and not implying any adhesion to the philosophical programme devised by Sir Michael Dummett.

[31] These are all good reasons for finding new proofs of a given theorem.

[32] The remark about 'constructability' (*Konstruktierbarkeit*) also relates to the debate concerning the admissibility of principles of proofs, and it reminds one of the fact that Wittgenstein never subscribed to the universal applicability of the Law of Excluded Middle, and rather tended to think that it is universally inapplicable. It is a pervasive prejudice, based on no serious study of textual evidence, that Wittgenstein did not align himself with critics of the Law of Excluded Middle: if anything he chastised them for not going far enough. Again, on the relationship of Wittgenstein's philosophy with Brouwer's intuitionism, see Marion 2003 and 2008. He always emphasized the need for *constructive* proofs, as opposed to purely existential proofs, as can be seen from the discussion of Euler's proof of the infinity of prime numbers (BT, 434–6; PG, 383–6), to which he appended a new constructive version of it, the only mathematical proof he has ever written down. (For a presentation of this proof, see Mancosu and Marion 2003.) Wittgenstein was of course weary of appeals to philosophical theses, and he would not appeal to some thesis about mathematical existence in order to argue his point. Instead, he emphasized *pragmatic* reasons for the superiority of these proofs; for example, because they establish connexions that are not there when only the existence of a solution is proved by indirect means.

assigned to them without assuming that their results stand in a relation of reference or denotation to a fact in a world of abstract entities, they must indeed 'guide' us to the acceptance of their result, in the particular sense that one who is able to 'understand' the proof must grant that the result obtains, and not as, say, a *pis aller* because of a lack of direct access to that world of abstract entities. Hence the importance of the notion of 'global surveyability' from his standpoint.

Wittgenstein's discussion of 'surveyability' contains a further ambiguity which is in need of clarification at this stage. I have implicitly assumed so far that he linked it with the length of proofs. For example, in (11) lack of surveyability could naturally be associated with the inability to check the steps of the proof one by one, because one could imagine the case of a very, very long proof, with too many steps for this to be feasible, even by a digital computer. The same goes for 'surveyable' in (12): even if the length of the proof does not preclude that one can check the steps of the proof one by one, it is also possible that it is nevertheless too long and complex for any mathematician to see the collective soundness of all these steps. Such worries can be amplified if one thinks of the difference between informal and formal proofs. The latter can be considerably longer than the former to the point that they lose any pretence of surveyability. Adrian Mathias has provided an extreme example of this in his critical study of Bourbaki's half-forgotten *Théorie des ensembles*, showing that their abbreviated definition of 1, when expanded into the primitive symbolism of that theory, consists of 4 trillion, 523 billion, 659 million, 424 thousand and 929 symbols, with 1 trillion 179 billion 618 million 517 thousand and 981 links needing to be disambiguated (Mathias 2002, 76).[33]

There are reasons, however, to believe that this is not exactly what Wittgenstein had in mind. He discusses the case of unsurveyably long proofs only on a few occasions, e.g. at RFM III, §45, in order mainly to entertain the idea that, as Philip Kitcher once put it, 'the increase of length would exacerbate the rational worry that, at some point, one's attention may have lapsed or one may have misremembered some result established earlier' (Kitcher 1984, 42).[34] More to the point, it should be noticed that whenever the 'circularity argument' around variants of (2) occurs, Wittgenstein almost always discusses very simple examples from elementary arithmetic, such as '27 + 16 = 43' or '12 × 12 = 144', where length of computation is not an issue, because there are obvious ways here to circumvent the charge of circularity. At III, §10, before launching into a critical discussion of a variant of (2), he explicitly distinguishes the two cases:

> Suppose a proof were so hugely long that it could not possibly be taken in? Or let us look at a different case: Let there be a long row of strokes engraved in hard rock which is our paradigm for the number that we call 1,000. We call this row the proto-thousand...

---

[33] And not the mere 'tens of thousands of signs' that Bourbaki had nonchalantly estimated (Bourbaki 1956, 55n.). Note that Mathias, who is a set theorist, was not intending to provide a critique of formal proofs in general, but only to shed doubt on the value of Bourbaki's particular system of set theory and criticize some of their more insouciant claims.

[34] See also LFM, 101 and 103. These passages are of great importance for Dummett's and Wright's interpretation of Wittgenstein as a 'strict finitist'. See Marion 1998, 222f. for a discussion.

Now here the sign of the number 1000 has the identity, not of a shape, but of a physical object. We could imagine a 'proto-hundred' similarly, and a proof, which we could not *take in at a glance* [*übersehen*] that 10 × 100 = 1,000.

The figure for 1,000 in the system of 1+1+1+1+...cannot be recognized by its shape [*Gestalt*]. (RFM III, §10)

The use of the word 'Gestalt' shows clearly that Wittgenstein had primarily a *visual* criterion in mind. This is borne out by his early remarks in MS 105, reproduced in the *Philosophical Remarks*, where he wrote:

How can I know that |||||||||| and |||||||||| are the *same* sign? It isn't enough that they look *alike*. For having roughly the same *Gestalt* can't be what constitutes the identity of signs, but just their being the same in number.

If you write (E |||||) etc. (E |||||||) etc. . ⊃ (E ||||||||||||)—A you may be in doubt as to how I obtained the numerical sign in the right-hand bracket if I don't know that it is the result of adding the two left-hand signs. I believe that makes it clear that this expression is only an application of 5 + 7 = 12 but doesn't represent this equation itself. (PR §103)[35]

Of course, Wittgenstein is writing here for himself, therefore sloppily, but one recognizes in the formula A in this quotation a variant of (2). Nevertheless it is an interesting one, as the use of strokes shows what he had in mind. Wittgenstein is relying here on the fact that human beings cannot tell at a glance and without counting that there are, say, fifteen but not sixteen strokes in this figure:

(13) |||||||||||||||

One should note that Wittgenstein is not appealing to vagueness, as one might argue he would have been doing had he considered only the length of proofs, in a manner reminiscent of Esenin-Volpin and Dummett. There is nothing *vague* about the fact that there are fifteen strokes in (13). Arguments that use facts of this kind I shall simply call 'surveyability arguments'. To recognize the truth of the expanded version of (2) without an implicit appeal to the prior truth of the arithmetic equation (1), one would not have the right to count the variables and see that they are equal in number on both sides of the conditional sign. But, as pointed out, no human beings can tell at a glance if there are fifteen or sixteen strokes in the above figure (13); hence this is a 'surveyability argument'.

Wittgenstein appears to have this visual criterion in mind when he speaks in other places of the 'geometrical cogency' of proofs, for example in this passage:

I should like to say that where surveyability is not present, i.e., where there is room for a doubt whether what we have really is the result of this substitution, the *proof* is destroyed. And not in some silly and unimportant way that has nothing to do with the *nature* of proof.

...

---

[35] This passage is composed of two paragraphs written in 1929: the first occurs at MS 106, 21, the second at MS 107, 18. The first paragraph also occurs at BT, 398 and PG, 331, where it is followed instead by this comment: 'The problem of the distinction between 1+1+1+1+1+1+1 and 1+1+1+1+1+1+1+1 is much more fundamental than appears at first sight.'

We incline to the belief that *logical* proof has a peculiar, absolute cogency, deriving from the unconditional certainty in logic of the fundamental laws and the laws of inference. Whereas propositions proved in this way can after all not be more certain than is the correctness of the way those laws of inference are *applied*.

That is to say: logical proof, e.g., of the Russellian kind, is cogent so long as it also possesses geometrical cogency. And an abbreviation of such a logical proof may have this cogency and so be a proof, when the Russellian construction, completely carried out, is not.

The logical certainty of proofs – I want to say – does not extend beyond their geometrical cogency. (RFM III, §43)

Wittgenstein's argument is here that a proof-object in the system of *Principia Mathematica* is not more 'cogent' because of an assumed greater degree of 'cogency' attached to the axioms and rules of inference involved in setting up that system: it is after all just a *proof*, so its 'cogency' as a proof cannot go further than any 'cogency' in the application of these principles. However, such proof-objects quickly lose any form of 'cogency', as one can see by considering the expanded or, as Wittgenstein puts it, 'completely carried out' proof in *Principia Mathematica* of an ordinary arithmetical equation involving numbers *that are on no account big*. Again, the expanded version of (2) would thus lack 'geometrical cogency'. It does not have 'any characteristic visual shape', it does not form an '*einprägsames Bild*' (RFM III, §9) or 'significant picture', in the sense that he does not impress on anyone a visual structure whose reproduction is certain unless one starts counting.

It looks, therefore, as if the remarks in Part III of the *Remarks on the Foundations of Mathematics* contain an argument which results from blending his 'circularity argument' with a 'surveyability argument'. One consequence of this analysis is that proofs of unsurveyable length are not at stake.[36] Furthermore, that there is a circularity in Russell's attempt to ground (1) on (2) is now brought to light by a 'surveyability argument' involving a *visual* element. Thus Wittgenstein's discussion of 'surveyability' involves in an essential way an 'epistemic' element, contrary to what some commentators have claimed.[37]

There has been a lot of recent work spearheaded by an early research programme launched by Jon Barwise in the mid-1990s,[38] which is devoted to the now respectable study of visualization in mathematics. Marcus Giaquinto, who has been one of the main contributors to this field, concluded a recent survey by stating that:

---

[36] As some of the passages quoted suggest, he would simply not consider them as *bona fide* proofs, but even if this is to be rejected, the 'surveyability argument' deployed against Russell would remain untouched.

[37] See e.g. Shanker 1987, ch. 4 or Stillwell 1992, 116. Stillwell, taking her lead from Shanker, goes as far as to claim that 'it is not even clear that [surveyability] need be taken as a Wittgensteinian constraint on proof' (Stillwell 1992, 133 n. 8). The fear of attributing an 'epistemic' element is, I believe, motivated by a rejection of the 'anti-realist' readings of Wittgenstein briefly presented at the beginning of this chapter. One ought, however, to keep one's interpretation free from 'party lines', as they usually blind people to the actual meaning of the text.

[38] See the papers in Allwein and Barwise 1996.

> Visual thinking can occur as a non-superfluous part of thinking through a proof and it can at the same time be irreplaceable, in the sense that one could not think through the same proof by a process of thought in which the visual thinking is replaced by some thinking of a different kind. (Giaquinto 2008, 39–40)

Although Wittgenstein's 'surveyability argument' is never discussed within the literature on visualization, which is often concerned only with the use of diagrams as a tool for discovery, it seems to me that it falls within its purview. Wittgenstein's point here is not only in line with this recognition of the role of visualization in proofs; he is even using something like it against Russell, since his claim amounts here to the fact that *visualization cannot play the role it should play* when we try to *see* the cogency of the expanded version of (2) without an implicit (and circular) appeal to arithmetical knowledge. He is thus accusing Russell of neglecting the role of visualization under the pretence that logical principles have a greater certainty than arithmetical ones. Wittgenstein can thus be seen as relying in his argument against Russell on an implicit recognition of the non-eliminable role of visualization.

This point certainly deserves of itself further critical evaluation, as one would need first to hear what could be said on behalf of Russell, but this task cannot be undertaken here. The claim is merely that it lies at the heart of Wittgenstein's critique of Russell. Implicit here is also the view of proofs as not being fully 'self-sufficient', because they need something outside themselves to carry conviction.[39] In other words, this means that *proofs include an empirical element.* This may come as a surprise, but one should be reminded here that Wittgenstein's worry about the 'limits of empiricism' is not about the presence of an empirical element in proofs,[40] but about the fact that the proved proposition changes its status when 'put in the archives'.

3. CONSEQUENCES OF THE 'SURVEYABILITY ARGUMENT'

Having thus achieved a more appropriate understanding of Wittgenstein's argument, we are now in a position to look at the consequences which he drew from it in his critique of Russell's logicism, i.e., the claims (6)–(9) above. I should, however, say first a few words about some obvious objections. One such objection would consist in simply pointing out that there are also practical limitations to the decimal and positional notation appealed to by Wittgenstein in (1). A moment's consideration is enough, however, to realize the fact that, although this may be true, it would not damage his argument against Russell (and especially the consequences to be drawn below). Another would be to suggest that one does not need to count the variables in the expanded version of (2): one

---

[39] On this point, see Detlefsen and Luker 1980, 810.
[40] On this point, see Steiner 2009.

could, for example, just strike them out and obtain the result by cancelling them out on both sides of the implication sign, or put the variables on both sides in one–one correlation.[41] This may be possible with some 'certainty' with our example, but it suffices that one considers now bigger numbers, e.g. adding 3,000,000 to 4,000,000, to realize that this procedure could not be applied with 'certainty', supposing one would even think about doing it, as the possibility of undetected error would creep in (LFM, 258–9). This point may in fact explain why Wittgenstein discussed the length of proofs on a few occasions (including LFM, 265, to be quoted below).[42]

A careful look at Wittgenstein's remarks allows us to see that he makes in fact three different arguments. The first one might be said to be aimed at what may be called mathematical 'explicativism', another aims at the very idea of 'logical foundations', and the last one concerns Russell's claim that logic is needed for arithmetic to be applicable in daily life. In order to see the point of his first argument, one needs first to recall Aristotle's distinction between demonstrating the 'fact' (οτι) and demonstrating the 'reason why' (διοτι) in *Posterior Analytics*, Book I, section 13. 'Explicativism' may be defined in this context as the claim that we get more from the demonstration of the 'reason why' than from the demonstration of the 'fact', and Aristotle's paragraph stands at the beginning of a long tradition, whose modern era really begins with Bolzano,[43] with his distinction between 'grounds' (*Begründungen*) or explanations of the 'reason why' and 'certificates' (*Gewissmachungen*), whose purpose is merely to convince (Bolzano 1996, 228). According to Bolzano, 'certificates' may be *bona fide* proofs, but they do not provide the 'reason why' and they lack, as in the case of geometrical proofs of the intermediate value theorem, which he discusses, purity: such proofs appeal to geometrical concepts, while they should contain only arithmetical concepts. An analogous distinction was often made in the debates over the foundations of mathematics in the 1920s and 1930s. Closer to Wittgenstein, G. H. Hardy manages to confuse the two notions in 'Mathematical Proof' (Hardy 1929, 18), but Turing introduced a distinction between 'formal proofs' (as 'grounds') and 'proofs designed to convince' during Wittgenstein's 1939 lectures

---

[41] This objection is explicitly envisaged by Wittgenstein at the beginning of PR §104. It is also related to another controversial claim made by Wittgenstein against the use of one-to-one correlation in order to prove numerical equality (PR §118). See Marion 1998, 77–83, for a discussion of the latter.

[42] These are far from exhausting possible rejoinders to Wittgenstein's argument. Another rejoinder would consist in pointing out that the existence of such unabbreviated foundational proofs can be surveyably proved; they are thus theoretically postulated entities and it is enough that one knows how one could *in principle* obtain them. For example, one can provide a surveyable, constructive proof that in a given system of natural deduction one can in principle provide a cut-free proof for every proof that uses the cut rule, although eliminating cut introduces a hyper-exponential increase in the length of the proof, which renders them unsurveyable. An objection of this sort is discussed by Felix Mühlhölzer as the 'theoreticity' rejoinder (Mühlhölzer 2005, 74f.), but in the context of this chapter, it should be noted that this rejoinder deals with the version of the argument which is about length of proofs, and not the more fundamental version concerning the visual element in formal proofs. There is also a further objection by Mark Steiner (1975), based on the fact that numerals can be written as polynomials, which is discussed in Marion 1998, sec. 8.3.

[43] See Mancosu 2000 for a review of this tradition. More specifically, on Bolzano's theory, see Tatzel 2003.

(LFM, 127).[44] If, as I believe, Wittgenstein saw that there is something wrong with 'explicativism', then it is worth unwinding the content of Aristotle's paragraph with care.[45] It is based upon the consideration of two syllogisms of the same form, *Barbara*:

All *A* is *B*
All *B* is *C*
∴ All *A* is *C*

According to one version, one has proved that planets are near by observing that they do not twinkle, and by use of the further independently established claim that what is near does not twinkle:

Planets do not twinkle
Whatever does not twinkle is near
∴ Planets are near

As Aristotle points out, however, this syllogism is merely a demonstration of the 'fact' ($ο\tau\iota$), since it is not because they do not twinkle that the planets are near. It is rather because they are near that they do not twinkle. A demonstration of the 'reason why' ($\delta\iota o\tau\iota$) retains the same syllogistic form, however, as one only changes *B* above so that it means instead 'is near', while *C* is now to mean 'does not twinkle', so that we now have:

Planets are near
Whatever is near does not twinkle
∴ Planets do not twinkle

'Explicativism' thrives on this simple modification, as the demonstration of the 'reason why' shows that the fact that planets do not twinkle is grounded in the fact that they are near, while the demonstration of the 'fact' appears merely to tell us how we ascertained this. One should notice, however, that the two syllogisms really demonstrate two different conclusions, and it remains that the fact that planets are near is not known here from a further 'ground' *but only from its consequence*, i.e., from the fact that planets do not twinkle.[46]

There is, of course, nothing awfully wrong with showing that planets do not twinkle because they are near, as we have other independent ways of ascertaining the objective fact that they are near, but in mathematics matters are different. Of course, Wittgenstein never refers to either Aristotle or Bolzano, but he picks on Turing's distinction between 'formal proofs' and 'proofs designed to convince':

---

[44] This distinction forms later on the topic of the opening of lecture XIV (LFM, 130–33). One should note that the manuscript MS 122 from which Part III of the *Remarks on the Foundations of Mathematics* has been taken, and which contains Wittgenstein's most sustained discussion of the 'surveyability argument', also dates from the year of the *Lectures on the Foundations of Mathematics*: 1939.

[45] In vol. II, §162 of his *Wissenschaftslehre*, Bolzano gives a similar example concerning the fact that the temperature indicated by a thermometer is higher in the summer than in the winter as proof that summer is warmer than winter, while it is because of the latter fact that the temperature indicated by a thermometer is higher in the summer than in the winter. (One should notice that, once more, the example given is an empirical one.)

[46] I owe this point to Dubucs and Lapointe 2006, 232–3.

> This is sometimes considered a most important distinction. I believe that at the basis of this there is a huge confusion. (LFM, 130)

Wittgenstein clearly saw that the confusion in question is a confusion between the empirical case and the foundational mathematical case:

> In this 'convince' talk there is the constant muddle between mathematical and non-mathematical propositions. For the word 'convince' is taken from the case where there is a direct text or criterion for something, and also more or less indirect ways of convincing someone. (LFM, 133)

This is exactly along the lines of the argument just presented. In order to claim that expanded formal proofs *really* are proofs, one would have to claim that, although 'beings with our particular restricted observational and intellectual faculties and spatio-temporal viewpoint' may fail to understand such expanded formal proofs, 'beings with greater powers or a different perspective or scale' will not,[47] so the existence of the latter ensures that the expanded proofs really are *bona fide* proofs, because these beings can take them in. This, however, would just be bad philosophy. As Wittgenstein puts it:

> ...in mathematics it is quite different. What is the criterion that the mathematical proposition is true?...Is it the watertight proof or what?
> Is it like this: God sees it is true. We can get at it in different ways. Some of us are easily persuaded that it is so, others need a long elaborate proof. But it is so.
> But what is the criterion for its being so – if not the proof? The idea seems to be that we get at the truth which was always there apart from the proof. (The proof as a kind of telescope.) (LFM, 131–2)

One ought to note *en passant* how the 'anti-realist' implications of his standpoint are, once more, not lost on Wittgenstein.

What is the role played here by the 'surveyability argument'? Let us recall elementary arithmetical equations such as (1), and their Russellian equivalent, on the model of (2). Now, Russell's claims (6)–(7), taken together, seem to legitimize an 'explicativist' strategy *par excellence*, namely that

(1), (1) because of (2)

Wittgenstein's point is thus that Russell assumes that '(1) because of (2)' while the truth is that we can only know (2) because we already know (1). It is therefore false to claim, as in (7) above, that it is possible for us to come to know arithmetical truths by constructing logical proofs of them.

Wittgenstein also uses his 'surveyability argument' against the idea that the system *Principia Mathematica* is 'foundational' with respect to arithmetic. It is worth quoting at length the following exchange with Turing during the lectures on the foundations of mathematics in 1939:

---

[47] This distinction is taken from Dummett 1993, 61.

> *Turing*: Doesn't this come to saying that counting by making tautologies is more unreliable than counting in the ordinary way?
>
>   *Wittgenstein*: No, it does not come to that. These are two entirely different ways.
>
>   It is not a question of its being unreliable. For all I know it may be perfectly reliable. Whether we can say arithmetic rests on – or is – logic: that's the point. That it might be done that way is a different matter. But the point is that we regard a thing as a tautology by an entirely different method. We introduce new principles. And it is not enough to say that we can make our principles agree with Russell's principles. (LFM, 260)

And, as one can see, he takes a few moments later a shot at the idea that logic stands as the foundation of arithmetic:

> If we take 'Arithmetic is based on logic', we might think this means that *our* arithmetic and no other follows from Russell's logic. You might say, 'this is still inexact. You get any other arithmetic also. Only if you give Russell's definitions, then you get ours only. If you have another arithmetic, you are working with other definitions of "cardinal number", "if-then", "and", etc. You might get, say, 3+4=6, but then the signs just have a different meaning. When we mean by "cardinal number" (for example) what Russell says it means, this arithmetic must follow.'
>
>   This is what I deny. I'd say that not even this arithmetic follows from Russell's calculus – no more than any other – What Russell does is to give a certain calculus for 'if', 'and', 'not', etc.; and as far as these expressions occur in mathematics, this will hold. If Russell's calculus is to be merely an *auxiliary* calculus, dealing with 'if''s and 'then''s etc. – then it is all right. But that it is not what it is meant to be. (LFM, 261)

Wittgenstein's point is that there is no relation of 'grounding', so to speak, between the calculus of *Principia Mathematica* and ordinary arithmetic. This does not imply, however, a wholesale rejection of the elucidatory value of *Principia Mathematica*. On the contrary, Wittgenstein insisted later on in the conversation that *Principia Mathematica* might thus clear out some philosophical problems:

> I do not mean it is valueless. But it does not show the point of anything; it leaves everything as it is. It makes language a *trifle* more explicit ... it makes certain points clearer. (LFM, 265)

His only claim is that there are limits to this, since *Principia Mathematica* is not 'foundational' with respect to arithmetic. This is, after all, in line with his earlier rejection of the theory of classes as 'superfluous' in the *Tractatus* (TLP 6.031).

   With this, one reaches the third and last argument, concerning the application of arithmetic and claims (8)–(9) above. The point is again raised by Turing in the 1939 lectures:

> *Turing*: Russell's definitions show us the *point* of having these ideas of addition and finite cardinals and so on.
>
>   *Wittgenstein*: Yes – and it is just that that I want to deny. (LFM, 262)

Later on, Wittgenstein comes back to this point, alluding again to his 'surveyability argument':

When Turing said that Russell's definitions make clear the *point* of arithmetic, he means: Russell's explanation makes clear, for instance, the connexion between the addition of two numbers and the disjunction of two concepts. '2+3=5' doesn't mean that you put 2 here and 3 there…but that if a concept has 2 and another has 3, the concept which is the disjunction of the two has 5.…So far so good. It shows a relation between addition and 'or'. This clears matters as far as it goes.

What Russell and Frege do is to make connexions between English and German words 'all', 'or', 'and', etc. and numerical statements. This clears up a few points. But that we should actually then say, '3,000,000+4,000,000=7,000,000', does not follow from this. (LFM, 265)

In reading this passage, it is useful to keep in mind the discussion of section 1 above: to repeat, it is not the connection established by Russell (picked up by Ramsey) between addition of natural numbers and union of disjoint classes which is at stake. Wittgenstein is clear about this here, as he remarks that 'so far so good' and that this establishes connections with ordinary words such as 'and' and 'or'. His argument, reverting here to the version of his argument concerning the length of proofs (as put forth earlier on at LFM, 258–9), is that this does not entail that '3,000,000+4,000,000=7,000,000' follows from the corresponding tautology without circularity. And this annuls Russell's suggestion that arithmetic needs *Principia Mathematica* in order to be applicable, i.e. for us to have ten fingers, two eyes, and one nose, etc. In other words, (8) and (9) do not hold, and arithmetic is, to use an earlier expression, 'autonomous' (PR, § 111).[48] This means, as Wittgenstein puts it, that arithmetic 'takes care of its own application', without recourse to a 'mouthpiece' such as *Principia Mathematica*:

> The reduction of arithmetic to symbolic logic is supposed to show the point of application of arithmetic, as it were the attachment by means of which it is plugged in to its application. As if someone were shewn, first a trumpet without a mouthpiece – and then the mouthpiece, which shows how a trumpet is used, brought into contact with the human body.…The calculation takes care of its own application. (RFM III, §4)

'Taking care of its own application' simply means for arithmetic that no intermediary such as *Principia Mathematica* is needed. We can also see this, for example, from an earlier passage:

> If I say: If there are 4 apples on the table, then there are 2 + 2 on it, that only means that the 4 apples already contain the possibility of being grouped into two and two, and I needn't wait for them actually to be grouped by a concept. (PR §102)

Here, 'I needn't wait for them actually to be grouped by a concept' is an obvious allusion to Russell's (8) and (9). Whatever positive story Wittgenstein provides here in order to replace Russell's account,[49] and the potential difficulties it would raise in turn, we need not get into, as that is outside the scope of this chapter, which is merely focusing on the negative argument against Russell.

---

[48] This use of the expression 'autonomy' should not be confused, however, with uses of it in well-known sayings about the 'autonomy of grammar', e.g. at PG, 184–5.

[49] See Steiner 2009 for a discussion.

4. Concluding Remarks

We saw in the last section that Wittgenstein thought that *Principia Mathematica* 'leaves everything as it is' (LFM, 265). This is reminiscent of a well-known passage in the *Philosophical Investigations*, where Wittgenstein says of philosophy that 'it leaves everything as it is' (PI §124). This passage has been used ad nauseam against any reading of Wittgenstein that would attribute to him a hint of 'revisionism'. Independently of this vexed issue, one can see here that the expression 'leaves everything as it is' also means that Wittgenstein drew the conclusions from his argument that not only are logical calculi such as that of *Principia Mathematica* not needed for applicability of arithmetic; they also do not provide it with a 'foundation', so whatever logical calculus one adopts, mathematics is left untouched. Such conclusions also apply to his earlier self, for, by the time he assembled the *Philosophical Remarks*, he had also rejected by the same token his account of arithmetic in terms of 'operations' at 6.02–6.031 and 6.2–6.241 of the *Tractatus*:

> Every mathematical calculation is an application of itself and only as such does it have a sense. *That* is why it isn't necessary to speak about the general form of logical operation when giving a foundation to arithmetic. (PR §109)

It is surprising to note that this move occurs so early in the 'middle period'.

Wittgenstein's philosophy of mathematics has tended to be increasingly alienated from 'mainstream' philosophy of mathematics in the past decades. But the latter is not monolithic, as one can see, e.g., from the current interest in visualization,[50] which would have been almost unthinkable even a decade ago. What is needed today is neither a sharp dismissal of the relevance of Wittgenstein from the 'mainstream' viewpoint, nor disregard of the very idea of a philosophy of mathematics from a radical 'Wittgensteinian' standpoint. Rather, what one needs is more attempts at reading Wittgenstein in ways that allow him still to speak to us, so that his ideas can still play a role in today's debates, as I have tried to do in reading him as providing, through his critique of Russell, arguments that also bear on current discussions concerning applicability, visualization, explicativism, and the relation of foundational systems to informal mathematics, hence the continued relevance of his remarks on surveyability.[51]

---

[50] See Mancosu 2008 for the opening up of new areas, including visualization.

[51] Earlier versions of this chapter were read in 2008 at Keio University, Tokyo, at the University of Helsinki and the University of Tampere in Finland, and at a symposium with Warren Goldfarb and Kai Wehmeier on 'Wittgenstein's Philosophy of Logic and Mathematics' at the Annual Meeting of the Eastern Division of the American Philosophical Association, in Philadelphia in 2009 at the international colloquium on 'Two Streams in the Philosophy of Mathematics' at the University of Hertfordshire, organized by Brendan Larvor and David Corfield, and in 2010 at the Second Middle Wittgenstein Workshop, at the Patrimonio de São Sebastiao da Serra, Brotas S. P., Brazil, organized by João Virgilio Gallerani Cuter and Bento Prado Neto. I would like to thank the participants on these occasions for their comments, in particular Roy Cook, Mauro Engelmann, Warren Goldfarb, Aatu Koskensilta, André Maury, Mitsuhiro Okada, Ludovic Soutif, and, especially, Kai Wehmeier. Thanks are also due to Bento

REFERENCES

ALLWEIN, G. and BARWISE, J. (1996). *Logical Reasoning with Diagrams*. Oxford: Clarendon Press.

AMBROSE, ALICE ed. (1979). *Wittgenstein's Lectures, Cambridge 1932–1935*, from the notes of A. Ambrose and M. McDonald. Oxford: Blackwell.

ASPRAY, W. and KITCHER, P. (1988). 'An Opinionated Introduction', in W. Aspray and P. Kitcher eds., *History and Philosophy of Modern Mathematics: Minnesota Studies in the Philosophy of Science, Volume XI*. Minneapolis: University of Minnesota Press.

AVIGAD, J. (2008). 'Understanding Proofs', in Mancosu 2008.

BAKER, G. and HACKER, P. M. S. (1985). *Wittgenstein: Rules, Grammar and Necessity*. Oxford: Blackwell.

BASSLER, O. B. (2006). 'The Surveyability of Mathematical Proof: A Historical Perspective', *Synthese*, 148: 99–133.

BOLZANO, B. (1996). 'Purely Analytic Proof of the Theorem that Between any Two Values which Give Results of Opposite sign There Lies at Least One Real Root of the Equation', in W. Ewald ed., *From Kant To Hilbert: A Source Book in the Foundations of Mathematics*. Oxford: Clarendon Press.

BOURBAKI, N. (1950). 'The Architecture of Mathematics', *American Mathematical Monthly*, 57: 221–32.

—— (1956). *Éléments de mathématique, XVII, première partie: Les Structures fondamentales de l'analyse. Livre I: Théorie des ensembles*. Paris: Hermann.

CARNAP, R. (1983). 'The Logicist Foundations of Mathematics', in P. Benacerraf and H. Putnam eds., *Philosophy of Mathematics: Selected Readings*, 2nd edn. Cambridge: Cambridge University Press.

CHURCH, A. (1956). *Introduction to Mathematical Logic*. Princeton, NJ: Princeton University Press.

DAWSON, J. W., Jr. (2006). 'Why Do We Re-prove Theorems?', *Philosophia Mathematica (3)*, 14: 269–86.

DETLEFSEN, M. and M. LUKER (1980). 'The Four Color Theorem and Mathematical Proof', *Journal of Philosophy*, 77: 803–20.

DUBUCS, J. and S. LAPOINTE (2006). 'On Bolzano's Alleged Explicativism', *Synthese*, 150: 229–46.

DUMMETT, M. A. E. (1978). *Truth and Other Enigmas*. London: Duckworth.

—— (1991). *Frege: Philosophy of Mathematics*. London: Duckworth.

—— (1993). *The Seas of Language*. Oxford: Clarendon Press.

ESENIN-VOLPIN, A. S. (1961). 'Le programme ultra-intuitionniste des fondements des mathématiques', in *Infinitistic Methods: Proceedings of the Symposium on the Foundations of Mathematics, September 1959, Warsaw*. Warsaw: PWN Warszawa.

FREGE, G. (1998). *Grundgesetze der Arithmetik*. Hildesheim: Georg Olms. (Partial English translation in Geach and Black 1952.)

GANDY, R. (1980). 'Church's Thesis and Principles for Mechanisms', in J. Barwise, H. J. Keisler, and K. Kunen eds., *The Kleene Symposium*. Amsterdam: North-Holland.

Prado Neto in particular for pointing out numerous relevant passages in MS 105. My papers (Marion 2007, 2009) contain early versions of the thoughts expressed in section 3 of this chapter. In Marion 2009, I used Wittgenstein's ideas in the context of a discussion of Dummett's anti-realism, but the argument I attributed to Wittgenstein was concerning length of proofs, therefore not the 'surveyability argument' as presented here in section 2.

GEACH, P. and BLACK, M. eds. (1952). *Translations from the Philosophical Writings of Gottlob Frege*. Oxford: Blackwell.

GIAQUINTO, M. (2008). 'Visualizing in Mathematics', in Mancosu 2008.

HARDY, G. H. (1929). 'Mathematical Proof', *Mind*, 38: 1–25.

HILBERT, D. (1967). 'On the Infinite', in J. van Heijenoort ed., *From Frege to Gödel: A Sourcebook in Mathematical Logic, 1879–1931*. Cambridge, MA: Harvard University Press.

KITCHER, P. (1984). *The Nature of Mathematical Knowledge*. Oxford: Oxford University Press.

KRIPKE, S. (1982). *Wittgenstein on Rules and Private Language: An Elementary Exposition*. Cambridge, MA: Harvard University Press.

MANCOSU, P. (2000). 'Mathematical Explanation', in E. Grosholz and H. Berger eds., *Growth of Mathematical Knowledge*. Dordrecht: Kluwer.

—— ed. (2008). *The Philosophy of Mathematical Practice*. Oxford: Clarendon Press.

—— and Marion, M. (2003). 'Wittgenstein's Constructivization of Euler's Proof of the Infinity of Prime Numbers', in F. Stadler ed., *The Vienna Circle and Logical Empiricism: Vienna Circle Institute Yearbook 10/2002*. Dordrecht: Kluwer.

MARION, M. (1998). *Wittgenstein, Finitism, and the Foundations of Mathematics*. Oxford: Clarendon Press.

—— (2003). 'Wittgenstein and Brouwer', *Synthese*, 137: 103–27.

—— (2007). 'Interpreting Arithmetic: Russell on Applicability and Wittgenstein on Surveyability', in P. Joray (ed.), *Contemporary Perspectives on Logicism and Constructivism, Travaux de Logique*, vol. 18. Neuchâtel.

—— (2008). 'Brouwer on Hypotheses and the Middle Wittgenstein', in M. van Atten, P. Boldini, M. Bourdeau, and G. Heinzmann eds., *One Hundred Years of Intuitionism 1907–2007*. Basel: Birkhäuser.

—— (2009). 'Radical Anti-Realism, Wittgenstein, and the Length of Proofs', *Synthese*, 171: 419–32.

MATHIAS, A. R. D. (2002). 'A Term of Length 4 523 659 424 929', *Synthese*, 133: 75–86.

MÜHLHÖLZER, F. (2005). '"A Mathematical Proof Must be Surveyable": What Wittgenstein Meant by This and What it Implies', *Grazer Philosophische Studien*, 71: 57–86.

PUTNAM, H. (2001). 'Was Wittgenstein *Really* an Anti-realist about Mathematics?', in T. McCarthy and S. C. Stidd eds., *Wittgenstein in America*. Oxford: Clarendon Press.

RAMSEY, F. P. (1990). *Philosophical Papers*, ed. D. H. Mellor. Cambridge: Cambridge University Press.

RAV, Y. (1999). 'Why Do We Prove Theorems?', *Philosophia Mathematica (3)*, 7: 5–41.

RUSSELL, B. (1919). *Introduction to Mathematical Philosophy*. London: Allen and Unwin.

SHANKER, S. G. (1987). *Wittgenstein and the Turning-Point in the Philosophy of Mathematics*. London: Croom Helm.

STEINER, M. (1975). *Mathematical Knowledge*. Ithaca, NY: Cornell University Press.

—— (1998). *The Applicability of Mathematics as a Philosophical Problem*. Cambridge, MA: Harvard University Press.

—— (2005). 'Mathematics – Application, Applicability', in S. Shapiro ed., *The Oxford Handbook of Philosophy of Mathematics and Logic*. Oxford: Oxford University Press.

—— (2009). 'Empirical Regularities in Wittgenstein's Philosophy of Mathematics', *Philosophia Mathematica (3)*, 17: 1–34.

STILLWELL, S. L. (1992). 'Empirical Enquiry and Proof', in M. Detlefsen ed., *Proof and Knowledge in Mathematics*. London: Routledge.

Tatzel, A. (2003). 'Bolzano's Theory of Ground and Consequence', *Notre Dame Journal of Formal Logic*, 43: 1–25.

Tymoczko, T. (1979). 'The Four-Color Problem and its Philosophical Significance', *Journal of Philosophy*, 76: 57–83.

Wang, H. (1961). 'Process and Existence in Mathematics', in Y. Bar-Hillel, E. Poznanski, M. Rabin, and A. Robinson eds., *Essays on the Foundations of Mathematics Dedicated to A. A. Fraenkel on his Seventieth Anniversary*. Jerusalem: Magnes Press.

Wittgenstein, Ludwig (1922). *Tractatus Logico-Philosophicus*, introduction by Bertrand Russell. London: Routledge and Kegan Paul.

—— (1974). *Philosophical Grammar*. Oxford: Blackwell.

—— (1975). *Philosophical Remarks*. Oxford: Blackwell.

—— (1976). *Wittgenstein's Lectures on the Foundations of Mathematics, Cambridge 1939*, from the notes of R. Bosanquet, N. Malcolm, R. Rhees, and Y. Smythies, ed. Cora Diamond. Ithaca, NY: Cornell University Press.

—— (1978). *Remarks on the Foundations of Mathematics*, 3rd edn. Oxford: Blackwell.

—— (1979). *Ludwig Wittgenstein and the Vienna Circle: Conversations recorded by Friedrich Waismann*, ed. Brian McGuinness, trans. Joachim Schulte and Brian McGuinness. Oxford: Basil Blackwell.

—— (1980). *Remarks on the Philosophy of Psychology*, Volume I. Oxford: Blackwell.

—— (2005). *The Big Typescript TS 213*. Oxford: Blackwell.

Wright, C. J. G. (1980). *Wittgenstein on the Foundations of Mathematics*. London: Duckworth.

—— (2001). *Rails to Infinity: Essays on Themes from Wittgenstein's Philosophical Investigations*. Cambridge, MA: Harvard University Press.

CHAPTER 8

....

FROM LOGICAL METHOD TO 'MESSING ABOUT': WITTGENSTEIN ON 'OPEN PROBLEMS' IN MATHEMATICS

....

SIMO SÄÄTELÄ

HILBERT famously claimed that in mathematics 'there is no ignorabimus'; all mathematical problems can be solved. In a certain sense Wittgenstein agrees; however, he also wants (in contrast to Hilbert) to distinguish between different uses of the word 'problem'; we are led into philosophical confusion if we consider mathematical problems to be similar to problems in natural science, or 'open problems' in mathematics to be analogous to elementary mathematical problems. 'Open problems' in mathematics are often understood as being expressed by mathematical propositions that are undecided in the sense that they are not known to be provable or disprovable within currently accepted systems of mathematics. Wittgenstein thinks, controversially, that it is nonsensical to treat such 'propositions' as genuine mathematical propositions. On the other hand, he does not want to claim that it is illegitimate for mathematicians to concern themselves with problems such as Goldbach's conjecture, or Fermat's last theorem. But how, then, does he think we should characterize this kind of mathematical activity?

   In this chapter I will look especially at the way Wittgenstein dealt with these questions in the early 1930s. I will give special attention to his treatment of Fermat's theorem, since the fact that it has since been proved might be thought to undermine his account. I will also say something about how Wittgenstein's treatment of these questions reflects a development towards a less dogmatic view of what is involved in mathematicians' claims to understand such 'propositions', which is an important part of the development of his philosophical views from the 'middle' to the 'late' philosophy.

I

David Hilbert proclaimed in his famous 1930 address in Königsberg (echoing his equally famous 1900 Paris lecture) that all mathematical problems can be solved:

> For the mathematician there is no ignorabimus, and in my opinion none whatever in natural science. In my opinion, the true reason why it was not possible... to find an unsolvable problem is that there are no unsolvable problems. Instead of the foolish ignorabimus our slogan should, on the contrary, be:
> We must know,
> we will know. (Hilbert 1935, 387)

In a certain sense Wittgenstein could be said to share this attitude. However, he also wanted to claim that the very word 'problem' might confuse us when applied to mathematics. A similar risk is present, Wittgenstein suggests, when using words like 'question', 'investigation', 'discovery', 'inference', 'proposition', or 'proof', which are prone to mislead us since they can be used in fundamentally different senses:

> Unfortunately, our language uses each of the words 'question', 'problem', 'investigation', 'discovery', to refer to such fundamentally different things. It's the same with the words 'inference', 'proposition', 'proof'. (TS 213/BT, 616)[1]

This is an example of the kind of confusion or trouble that a philosophical investigation in mathematics must try to address: such an investigation is not a mathematical investigation, but has rather to do with our framework for thinking and speaking about mathematics.

Indeed, Wittgenstein thought that conceiving mathematics in terms of problem-solving can lead to two kinds of misunderstanding about mathematics, which, incidentally, are both illustrated by Hilbert. On the one hand, there is a tendency to treat problems in the natural sciences and problems in mathematics as analogous. This is one main source of philosophical confusion about mathematics. The other source is related, but might be called 'internal' to mathematics: it is the tendency to treat all the things we call 'mathematical problems' as similar, i.e. as problems in precisely the same sense. We can note that Wittgenstein claimed that we can be misled in a very similar way by the use of the word 'problem' in philosophy:

> [I]n their correct and everyday use vagueness is opposed to clearness, flux to stability, inaccuracy to accuracy, and problem to solution.

---

[1] When referring to Wittgenstein's unpublished works I have used, when possible, existing translations, sometimes amending them. Otherwise translations are my own. The dating of the *Nachlass* is a complicated issue. On this point I have received invaluable help from Dr. Josef Rothhaupt. In addition to checking the dating and sources of the quoted passages (and thereby saving me from numerous errors), he has produced a 'transfer profile' of quoted *Nachlass* remarks. This allows the reader not only to locate the remarks, but also to follow the transformation and composition of specific remarks within the *Nachlass*. The particular remark that I quote is referred to in bold.

> The very word 'problem', one might say, is misapplied when used for our philosophi-cal troubles. These difficulties, as long as they are seen as problems, are tantalizing, and appear insoluble. (BB, 46)

But in what sense is the word 'problem' misleading? Well, it is not that Wittgenstein would want to *prohibit* use of the word, but he wants to point out that we must realize that the word is used in fundamentally different senses within mathematics. In the above quotation from the *Blue Book* Wittgenstein implies that in its 'correct and everyday' use a problem is something that can be solved. He also thinks this is the case in mathematics:

> Only where there's a method of solution is there a problem (of course that doesn't mean 'Only when the solution has been found is there a problem').
> (Once again this merely determines the grammar of the word 'problem').[2]

Or:

> We may only put a question in mathematics (or make a conjecture), where the answer runs: 'I must work it out'.... What the 'mathematical question' shares with a genuine question is simply that it can be answered.[3]

Or:

> One could lay down: 'Whatever one can tackle is a problem.—Only where there can be a problem, can something be asserted'.[4]

Thus Wittgenstein seems to want to say that a mathematical problem has sense, i.e. is a real question, only in so far as there is a method for its solution. Indeed, in everyday dis-cussions we do call an elementary question such as 'What does 25 times 25 equal?' a mathematical problem (even if we might prefer to call it a mathematical task of the kind we could give to a child learning multiplication). But what, then, about so-called 'open questions' in mathematical research, i.e., problems for which we lack both a method and a solution?

Is proving, say, Goldbach's conjecture ('every even integer n greater than two is the sum of two primes') a problem in the same sense as '$25 \times 25 = ?$'? If not, then what is the difference? Is the only difference that proving Goldbach's conjecture is much more diffi-cult than solving an elementary equation? Wittgenstein wants to answer 'no'. Mathematical 'open questions' are often characterized as 'problems'—but the word is used here in a sense that is fundamentally different from its 'correct and everyday use', and the trouble is that unless we notice this we tend to see such problems as analogous, and are led into philosophical confusions regarding mathematics and the activity of mathematicians. Multiplication problems are genuine, if trivial, mathematical ques-tions; we have a method or a way of solving them. A 'problem' in this unproblematic(!),

[2] MS 106, 285 (1929) → **TS 208, 50r** (1930) and TS 209, 70 (PR, 172) → MS 113, 104v → TS 211, 676 → TS 212, 1595 → TS 213, 638 (BT, 638).
[3] **MS 107, 115–16** (1929) → TS 208, 87r and TS 209, 72 (PR, 175).
[4] MS 113, 106r (1932) → TS 211, 679 → TS 212, 1606 → TS 213, 641 (**BT, 641**).

everyday sense must be something we know how to tackle (even though we do not, of course, know what the answer will be). However, this is precisely what we do *not* know in the case of Goldbach's conjecture or other similar 'open problems'.

Wittgenstein admits that this way of putting things seems to lead to the paradox that there are no difficult problems in mathematics, since if anything is difficult it isn't a problem. But he does not claim anything like that—'What follows', says Wittgenstein,

> is that the 'difficult mathematical problems', i.e. the problems for mathematical research, aren't in the same relationship to the problem '25 × 25 = ?' as a feat of acrobatics is to a simple somersault. They aren't related, that is, just as very easy to very difficult; they are 'problems' in different senses of the word.[5]

II

Let us, then, take a look at the 'grammar' of such open mathematical problems, and why Wittgenstein wants to claim that we have a tendency to misunderstand it.

It is often thought that 'open questions' in mathematics presuppose the existence of mathematical propositions which are undecided in the sense that they are not known to be provable or disprovable within currently existing systems of mathematics, but are, nonetheless, either true or false. This way of thinking is tempting when one considers the status of many problems of creative research in mathematics—say, the items on Hilbert's famous list of unsolved problems from 1900, or the seven so-called Millennium Prize problems from 2000. Most mathematicians would like to describe this kind of research as trying to answer the question 'Is it the case that p?', where 'p' is a proposition which is considered to express a currently unsolved problem, such as Riemann's hypothesis, or Goldbach's conjecture.

Having returned to philosophy in 1929, Wittgenstein gave much attention to questions pertaining to the philosophy of mathematics, and his remarks contain references to both of these 'propositions'. However, here I want to look especially at what he has to say about Fermat's last theorem.[6] This theorem, which was an 'open problem' when Wittgenstein wrote his remarks, has, as we know, since been proved. Does the fact that the problem has been solved affect what Wittgenstein has to say about 'open' mathematical problems and propositions expressing such problems?

Fermat's last theorem, which states that the Diophantine equation $x^n + y^n = z^n$ has no non-zero integer solutions for x, y, and z when $n > 2$, is probably the most famous solved problem in the history of mathematics. The history of the problem is well known: in 1637

---

[5] MS 113, 106r (1932) → TS 211, 678 → TS 212, 1607 → TS 213, 642 (**BT, 642**).

[6] Wittgenstein's interest in Fermat's theorem goes back at least to 1916, when he evidently wrote to Frege asking him how the problem should be stated. See Frege to Wittgenstein, 6.2.1916 (in Frege 2011, 24). I want to thank Juliet Floyd for calling my attention to this exchange.

Pierre de Fermat wrote this formula in his copy of the *Arithmetica* of Diophantus, add-ing 'I have uncovered a truly marvellous demonstration of this proposition which this margin is too narrow to contain'. (See e.g. Bell 1937, 71) However, in spite of the superficial similarity to the analogous problem for $n = 2$ (for which there are infinitely many solu-tions, so-called Pythagorean triples), Fermat's last theorem turned out to be quite differ-ent and much more difficult to prove. Indeed, for more than 350 years innumerable professional and amateur mathematicians attempted to prove the theorem, no doubt inspired by Fermat's remark and the frustrating fact that the formulation of the problem is seemingly understandable for anybody with even rudimentary mathematical knowl-edge. By the time Andrew Wiles finally published a much discussed proof in 1993 (amended in 1995), Fermat's theorem had already gained almost mythical status. Wiles' proof is very long and exceedingly complex, and it certainly cannot be the proof Fermat himself claimed to have discovered. Not only is it several hundred pages long, but it also builds on mathematics that was not known in Fermat's day (e.g. the theory of elliptic curves). However, now that Fermat's last theorem has become the most famous *solved* problem in the history of mathematics, the status of the most famous open problem is, in the popular imagination, taken over by Goldbach's conjecture, which is also easily stated, and gives the illusion of being provable or disprovable with recourse to no more than high-school-level mathematics.

The question regarding Fermat's theorem is whether, prior to Wiles' proof, we were dealing with a meaningful, well-defined mathematical proposition with a definite truth value, but no way of knowing it. In a remark from 1943 Wittgenstein notes: 'The problem of finding a mathematical decision of a theorem might with some justice be called the prob-lem of giving mathematical sense to a formula'. (MS 127, 161; RFM V, §42) This implies that a mere formula does not, in itself, have mathematical sense. What Wittgenstein seems to be saying, then, is that 'problem' and 'solution' are connected; unless we have a method for solving a problem, we do not have a genuine problem (in the sense of an *Aufgabe* or ques-tion), since the purported proposition does not have mathematical sense.

An open mathematical problem is something that eludes us; it is something that we think of as a proposition having a definite truth value, i.e. a definite solution, but we fail to find it and do not even know where to look for it. A problem of this kind has the character of a puzzle or a riddle; it is something that troubles or irritates us, in precisely the same sense as Wittgenstein claims the philosophical puzzles we tend to call problems irritate or torment us.

How, then, are we to treat such propositions? The problem with these is that they are not really propositions—they do not assert or claim anything, even though they have the appearance of genuine propositions or solvable mathematical equations. Thus they present us with an illusion of sense:

> We cannot *understand* the equation unless we recognize the connection between its two sides.
> Undecidability presupposes that there is, so to speak, a subterranean connection between the two sides; that though the bridge cannot be built in symbols, it does exist, because otherwise the equation would be senseless. Because the equation hints that a bridge *can* be built.

> A connection between symbols which exists but cannot be represented by sym-
> bolic transformations is a thought that cannot be thought. If the connection is there,
> then it must be possible to see it.
>   For it *exists* in the same way as the connection between parts of visual space.
> It isn't a *causal* connection. The transition isn't produced by means of some dark
> speculation different in kind from what it connects. (Like a dark passage between
> two sunlit places.)
>   Of course, if mathematics were the natural science [die Erfahrungswissenschaft]
> of infinite extensions of which we can never have exhaustive knowledge, then a
> question that was in principle undecidable would certainly be conceivable.[7]

To presuppose that there is such a 'hidden connection' that would ascertain the sense of
the equation is, Wittgenstein claims, an illusion—we have been deluded by the form of
the 'proposition'. Here he also notes that the supposition of this kind of undecidability
makes sense only if we think about mathematics as a science of infinite extensions (in
the manner of Cantor and Dedekind). But this would be to understand mathematics as
an empirical science, where we describe and formulate testable hypotheses about a
'mathematical reality'—a view which, Wittgenstein implies, produces a misleading
picture of mathematics.

If we realize that we presuppose something illusory when talking about such
'undecidable propositions' as if they had determinate mathematical sense, we realize that
what we took to be a genuine question in fact builds on speculations about a hidden
'connection' or the idea that we can get the answer through some kind of revelation, or a
'new sense':

> Only where there's a method of solution is there a problem.... Where we can only
> expect the solution from some sort of revelation, there isn't even a problem. To a
> revelation no question corresponds.
>   It would be like wanting to ask about experiences belonging to a sense organ we
> don't yet possess. Our being given a new sense, I would call revelation.
>   Neither can we *search* for a new sense (sense-perception). (Grammar of the word
> 'search'.)[8]

The point here could be expressed as follows: it cannot be that we are *looking for* a revelation; for this would be like looking for a new sense, and since we have no idea what that
would be like, we cannot really be looking for it; the best we can do is hope for it to
appear. So some things we can't search for:

---

    [7] **MS 106, 220-21** (1929) → TS 208, 46r and TS 209, 92 (PR, 212). (Cf. BT, 638-9.) In this passage
Wittgenstein criticizes Brouwer's views on undecidability and the existence of unsolvable mathematical
problems. See Frascolla 1994, 106-7. In addition, it is likely that Wittgenstein here alludes to the same
discussion about 'ignorabimus' as Hilbert (see quote from Hilbert in section I), i.e. the idea that there are
some absolute limits to our knowledge in science, which means that some questions will remain in
principle undecidable. I want to thank Sören Stenlund for calling my attention to this point.
    [8] MS 106, 285 (1929) → **TS 208, 50r+51r** (1930) and TS 209, 70 (PR, 172) → MS 113, 104v → TS 211, 676
→ TS 212, 1595 → TS 213, 638 (BT, 638).

Thus Fermat's proposition makes no *sense* until I can *search* for a solution to the equation in cardinal numbers.

And 'search' must always mean: search systematically. Meandering about in infinite space on the look-out for a gold ring is no kind of search.... You can only *search* within a system: And so there is necessarily something you *can't* search for.[9]

III

Thus Wittgenstein seems to think that Fermat's 'theorem' is senseless, and not a genuine proposition: 'not even a proposition in the sense of "arithmetic proposition"'.[10] Accordingly, viewing it as a well-defined problem, or a meaningful equation, proves to be a misunderstanding; the combination of signs, if understood as expressing a proposition, makes no sense. But just as in the case of philosophical problems, this does not mean we can simply dismiss such 'problems' as 'mere misunderstandings' or nonsense, and thus be done with them. As with philosophical problems, they are 'tantalizing' or 'deeply disquieting'—and they do indeed inspire creative mathematicians.

Thus, the problems such 'propositions' express *are* mathematical problems, not only in the sense that they are irritating and troublesome puzzles for mathematicians, but also in the sense that they stimulate much creative mathematical research. But how does Wittgenstein want to characterize this activity? How are we to understand the mathematician's relation to such problems? Wittgenstein discussed this during a series of lectures entitled 'Philosophy for Mathematicians', in 1932–3. He asked what we should make of a statement such as that of the mathematician G. H. Hardy, who said 'I believe that Goldbach's conjecture is true', or 'Goldbach's conjecture is a proposition, and that is why I can believe it is true'. (Cf. BB, 11) From a philosophical point of view, this is of course nonsense. How could I believe something the sense of which is totally unclear to me? This would indeed be like trying to think 'a thought that cannot be thought'. But Wittgenstein does not want to dismiss this way of talking out of hand:

> When Hardy says he believes Goldbach's theorem, I would ask him what his belief in this theorem led him to. What does he do? It may have led him to attempts to prove it, which shows that *some* meaning attaches to the theorem inasmuch as these activities would not have been caused by another theorem. (AWL, 222; cf. BT, 432)

What we should ask, says Wittgenstein, is what it means to 'believe': what kind of consequences are there in a case like this, i.e. what *use* can mathematicians put the problem to:

[9] MS 105, 18 → TS 208, 38 (1930) and **TS 209, 71–2** (PR, 175) → MS 113, 105v → TS 211, 678 → TS 212, 1596.

[10] 'Ich sage: der sogenannte "Fermatsche Satz" ist kein Satz (auch nicht im Sinne der Arithmetik).' **MS 107, 83** (1929) → TS 208, 82 (1930) and TS 209, 104 (PR, 232).

> In what sense can one say that a question in mathematics makes no sense? It would seem that if it does not make sense, we could never know where the answer lay. Ask yourself, What uses does one make of the question? It does stand for a certain activity by the mathematician, of trying, of messing about. If the question did not stand for something, one would expect *any sort* of activity. The question has then that meaning—as much meaning as that messing about has. The mathematician's activity is carried on in a particular sphere. A question is part of a calculus. What does it prompt you to do? When a question is asked for which there is no method of answering it, we do know certain requirements the answer must fulfill. In one sense it is true to say this, but it is misleading. (AWL, 221–2; cf. PI §578)

The conjecture, then, has a kind of sense or meaning—as much meaning as the mathematical activities it prompts. However, this does not warrant calling it a proposition in any substantial sense—it cannot be used to assert anything. Wittgenstein also compares the mathematician's 'messing about' to an attempt to waggle one's ears: there are two fundamentally different senses in which we can talk about 'trying to move one's ears':

> If you say to someone who has never tried 'Try to move your ears', he will first move some part of his body near his ears that he has moved before, and either his ears will move at once or they won't. Now you could say of this process: He is trying to move his ears. But if that can be called trying, it's trying in a completely different sense from trying to move our ears (or our hands) in a case where we already 'know how to do it' but someone is holding them, so that we can move them only with difficulty or not at all. It is the first sense of trying that corresponds to trying 'to solve a mathematical problem' when there is no method for its solution. One can always strive to solve the apparent problem. If someone says to me 'Try by sheer will power to move that jug at the other end of the room', I will look at it and perhaps make some strange movements with my facial muscles; so that even in that case there seems to be such a thing as trying.[11]

What Wittgenstein wants to say is that in some cases there is trying, and in some cases only an illusion of trying: something that looks or sounds like trying, but is in fact nothing of the sort. But how can we distinguish between genuine trying and mere illusions of trying in mathematics?

IV

Before pursuing this question, I would like to take a brief look at how Wittgenstein's thoughts on this matter developed from the 'middle' to the later philosophy. As we have seen, in the very early 1930s Wittgenstein's view is that we cannot answer a problem unless we can look for a solution, and he seems to think that this means we cannot solve

---

[11] MS 108, 140 (1930) → TS 210, 4 → TS 212, 1638 → TS 213, 657 (**BT, 657**). Cf. PR, 329.

a problem unless we have a *logical method* for solving it. For example, referring to Fermat's theorem, he wrote:

> I said: Where you can't look for an answer, you can't ask either, and that means: Where there's no **logical method** for finding a solution, the question doesn't make sense either.[12]

This remark was originally written in 1929, and still reflects a Tractarian understanding of mathematics as 'logical method'. (TLP 6.2) We can note that in later remarks Wittgenstein put less and less weight on the systematic or 'logical' character of this search for a solution. Just a couple of years later, when he reused this formulation in the *Big Typescript* (1933), he left out the word 'logical'.[13] Instead of stressing a 'logical' rigour in the methods of mathematicians, he seems ready to accept the 'messing about' as a kind of method; as long as it is a *mathematical* messing about, it is all right, even though it cannot be called a 'logical method'. We could say that this indicates a less dogmatic view of 'method' and 'understanding'.

From the late 1930s and onward Wittgenstein accordingly finds other analogies more fruitful than the talk about 'systematic' or 'logical' method. Consider this remark from 1937:

> The odd resemblance between a philosophical investigation (maybe especially in mathematics) and an aesthetic one.
> (E.g. what is bad about this garment, how it should be, etc.)[14]

Here we have a kind of 'methodological' analogy that expresses what is sometimes referred to as Wittgenstein's 'aesthetic conception' of philosophy—which means that he wants to draw our attention to, for instance, the fact that the philosophical or grammatical investigation aims to open our eyes to something that, for one reason or another, we tend not to notice but which can explain our puzzlement when made clear; in other words, he wants to point out that, like philosophical questions, aesthetic problems are not illuminated by theorizing, etc. Although this comparison has a number of interesting aspects, I here want to focus on its relevance for Wittgenstein's views of mathematics. The parenthetic remark '(maybe especially in mathematics)' is often left out when this quotation is adduced. And at first sight it might seem extremely puzzling that Wittgenstein should want to compare 'an aesthetic investigation' to a philosophical investigation *especially in mathematics*. What kind of 'odd resemblance' could he possibly have in mind?

One central aspect of the resemblance is the nature of the problems we are dealing with in these 'investigations', and we already noted that a *philosophical investigation in*

---

[12] **MS 106, 285** (my emphasis) (1929) → TS 208, 50r and TS 209, 70 (PR, 172) → MS 113, 104v → TS 211, 663 → TS 212, 1595. Wittgenstein used the same formulation in 1929–32.

[13] 'Where you can ask you can look for an answer, and where you cannot look for an answer you cannot ask either. Nor can you find an answer. Where there is **no method** of looking for an answer, there the question too cannot have any sense.' BT, 638 (my emphasis).

[14] MS 119, 88v (1937) → **MS 116, 56** (CV, 29).

mathematics is not a mathematical investigation, but deals with (among other things) the nature of mathematical problems. In the above quoted remark Wittgenstein wants to point out how such problems can be clarified by being compared to aesthetic 'problems'—and these problems are, of course, not scientific problems or problems that can be solved by empirical investigation (we are not talking here about aesthetics as a 'science of the beautiful'). Instead, these problems have the character of 'puzzles' or 'difficulties' that must be solved, or dissolved, in a way that differs from our usual methods of resolving substantial scientific or empirical problems. Another remark, from 1947, can illuminate what kind of 'problems' we are dealing with here and how they are related:

> Mathematical questions and answers, mathematical problems and their solutions. Compare a mathematical problem with this: translating a proposition, a poem, a dialog from one language into another. (An interesting and far-reaching comparison). (MS 135, 76)

This also means that it becomes less clear what we should count as *understanding* a proposition, or a theorem or formula. For instance, in the following complex and interesting remark (from about 1941/42; MS 164, 32–5; RFM VI, §13) it seems as if Wittgenstein is reluctant to rule out the possibility of describing the various attempts to prove Fermat's theorem as 'understanding Fermat's theorem', even if they could be characterized as a 'messing about':

> Now isn't it absurd to say that one doesn't understand the sense of Fermat's last theorem?—Well, one might reply: the mathematicians are not *completely* blank and helpless when they are confronted by this proposition. After all, they try certain methods of proving it; and, so far as they try methods, *so far* do they understand the proposition.—But is that correct? Don't they *understand* it just as completely as one can possibly understand it?
> Now let us assume that, quite contrary to mathematicians' expectations, its contrary were proved. So now it is shewn that it *cannot* be so at all.

A proof showing that the theorem was false would, it seems, prove that the supposed 'understanding' was merely illusory. However, it is not at all clear what kind of criterion would allow us to speak of such a 'proposition' being true:

> But, if I am to know what a proposition like Fermat's last theorem says, must I not know what the criterion is, for the proposition to be true? And I am of course acquainted with criteria for the truth of *similar* propositions, but not with any criterion for the truth of this proposition.

All this shows that we get into trouble when thinking about the matter in terms of true or false propositions. Instead we must realize the following:

> 'Understanding' is a vague concept.
> In the first place, there is such a thing as *belief* that one understands a proposition.
> And if understanding is a psychical process—why should it interest us so much? Unless experience connects it with the capacity to make use of the proposition.

'Shew me how' means: shew me the connexions in which you are using this proposition (this machine-part).

Thus 'meaning is use', and 'understanding' should not be thought of as a mental process,
but as connected to a capacity to use such 'propositions'. Again, we can see a move
towards a less dogmatic view of 'understanding', together with a move away from the
question 'What does it mean to understand a mathematical proposition?' (i.e. 'What are
mathematical propositions?'), towards an emphasis on the activities of mathematicians.

V

Let us return to the question of how Wittgenstein wants to understand the mathematician's activities in relation to 'propositions' expressing 'open problems': what does it
mean to try to solve such a problem? In what sense can a mathematician's 'messing
about' be understood as 'trying to do something'?

Wittgenstein's point can be clarified by looking at what he said in a discussion with
Waismann and Schlick in 1931. Here, he does not want to claim that it would be illegitimate to concern oneself with a problem like Fermat's last theorem, even though it is a
mistake to view it as a proposition or a genuine question. The important thing is to clarify how this activity should be characterized, to get clear about what exactly mathematicians are doing when, for example, trying to prove Fermat's theorem. When doing this,
mathematicians let themselves be led 'by certain associations, by analogies to earlier
systems':

> It is just as with ear-waggling. A mathematician is of course guided by associations,
> by certain analogies with the previous system. After all, I do not claim that it is
> wrong or illegitimate if anyone concerns himself with Fermat's Last Theorem. Not
> at all! If e.g. I have a method for looking for integers that satisfy the equation $x^2 + y^2$
> $= z^2$, then the formula $x^n + y^n = z^n$ may stimulate me. I may let a formula stimulate
> me. Thus I shall say, Here there is a *stimulus* [*Anregung*]—but not a *question*.
> Mathematical 'problems' are always such stimuli.
>
> These stimuli are in no way a preliminary to a calculus. (WVC, 144, 1/1/1931)

Such 'propositions', then, are not real questions or propositions; we do not know how to
tackle them, i.e. understand them. But they have some kind of sense, in so far as mathematicians can in some way *use* them. In so far as mathematicians can find a use for
these proposition-like structures, i.e. 'mess about', they have a use—as 'signposts for
mathematical research, stimuli for mathematical constructions'.[15] But as long as they are
undecided they do not have a truth-value and they are not mathematical propositions,
even though they give the illusion of being perfectly meaningful and mathematically well

---

[15] MS 154, 14v (1931/32) → MS 113, 73v (1932) → TS 211,632 → TS 212, 1576 → TS 213, 631 (**BT, 631**).

defined. (Cf. BT, 626; see also PI §520.) A stimulus or a signpost does not have a truth-value. If we insist that Goldbach's conjecture must be true or false, even though we have no way of knowing which it is, we risk lapsing into nonsense.

Looking at the development of Wittgenstein's thought, we could generally say that the later Wittgenstein is less and less interested in a notion of a mathematical proposition as something analogous to the ordinary notion of a proposition. A mathematical 'proposition' does not have a sense prior to its proof. Thus *proof* becomes essential to the meaningfulness of mathematical formulae, or structures, or questions. We could say that mathematical proof and mathematical sense and truth are mutually dependent:

> To *believe* Goldbach's proposition means to believe you have a proof of it, since I can't, as it were, believe it *in extenso*, because that doesn't mean anything, and you cannot imagine an induction corresponding to it until you have one.[16]

What, then, does it mean to ask after the proof for such mathematical 'propositions'? Again, the question is: How are we to distinguish between searching for a proof and the *illusion* of searching for a proof? Wittgenstein was very fond of fairy tales and riddles, and we could clarify his answer to this question by comparing two riddles he discussed. Let's say (this is not Wittgenstein's actual example, but it catches his point) that a high-school kid has got the hang of the Pythagorean equation and its proof. Now we say to him: well, now that you can prove $x^2 + y^2 = z^2$, also prove that $x^n + y^n = z^n$ does not have any solutions for $n > 2$. 'He not merely couldn't answer the question, he couldn't even understand it. (It would be like the task the prince sets the smith in the fairytale: fetch me a "hubbub". Busch, *Volksmärchen*).'[17] Because this task is not only a riddle, but completely nonsensical, it cannot be solved. And, Wittgenstein notes:

> We regard the first as much easier than the second, but we don't see that they are 'tasks' ['Aufgaben'] in different senses. *Of course* the difference isn't a psychological one; for it isn't a matter of whether the pupil can solve the task, but whether the calculus can solve it, or which calculus can solve it.[18]

Thus we do not really have a task here, and not even a genuine riddle. We could say that this order is not merely senseless, but nonsensical. However, sometimes a formerly unsolvable mathematical problem can be solved in a completely unexpected manner. In a lecture in 1935 Wittgenstein referred to another tale involving a riddle and an inventive princess.[19] This is probably from the saga of Ragnar Lodbrok, in which Ragnar's men report seeing a very beautiful woman, Kraka. Ragnar, his interest aroused, sends for her, but in order to test her wits, he commands her to arrive neither dressed nor undressed, neither hungry nor full, and neither alone nor in company. Kraka arrives draped in a net

---

[16] **MS 107, 226** (1929) → TS 208, (110) and TS 209, 87 (PR, 204).

[17] MS 105, 34 (1929) → TS 208, (54) and TS 209, 74 (PR, 178) → MS 113, 113v (1932) → TS 211, 690 → TS 212, 1602 → TS 213, 640 (**BT, 640**).

[18] MS 111, 145 (1931) → TS 211, 88 → TS 212, 1603+1604 → TS 213, 641 (**BT, 641**).

[19] AWL, 185–6. For a further discussion of riddles and mathematical problems, see Diamond 1991, ch. 10. See also Floyd 2000, 250.

and her long hair, biting an onion, and with only her dog as a companion. Impressed, Ragnar marries her.

The difference between these two tasks or riddles and their solutions, i.e. the possibility of making sense of them, might also be used to characterize different kinds of unsolved problems in mathematics. In fact, at one point Wittgenstein says that what we are looking for when trying to solve such a problem is precisely the sense or *Sinn*: 'The mathematical, when it is not proved, is—one could say—the *expression of a problem*. The sense is the *problem*.'[20] (Note that in this remark from 1941 he speaks simply of 'the mathematical', rather than mathematical propositions.) In another notebook (from the same year) he says that in a certain sense the mathematician invents both question and answer when solving such a problem:

> The function of this proposition-like structure can only very remotely be compared to the function of propositions in the ordinary sense.
>   In a certain sense the mathematician discovers both *question and answer*.
>   Russell's idea, that only the fulfilment of a wish shows us what we wished for, truly applies to mathematical wishes. (MS 163, 54v–55r)

Thus some problems can be solved in a surprising manner, e.g. by giving them sense through new mathematical inventions or techniques (cf. the surprising connection between Fermat's theorem and the theory of elliptic curves, which was the first step towards Wiles' proof),[21] while others remain undecided, i.e. lacking any definite mathematical sense (and some are perhaps finally put aside, if they can no longer hold the interest of mathematicians). But this is not something we can know beforehand; we cannot know whether for instance Goldbach's conjecture will be shown to be true or not, or whether future mathematicians will even care about trying to prove it.

VI

This discussion of problems is also connected with what Wittgenstein thought was another major source of confusion in mathematics, namely, our tendency to regard mathematics as a kind of natural science, and the problems and activities of mathematicians as analogous to those of natural scientists. This also has to do with the use of words like 'discovery', 'question', and 'hypothesis' in mathematics. (See e.g. BT, 615–23, 635–6) However, I do not have the opportunity here to delve into this aspect of Wittgenstein's critique.

Let us look instead at the relation of proof to mathematical meaningfulness, and how Wittgenstein's reflections relate to the fact that Fermat's theorem has now been proved. In his 1932–3 lectures he noted:

---

[20] MS 161, 32r (1941) → **MS 123, 65v** (1941).
[21] As with riddles, 'one has no exact way of working out a solution. One can only say: "I shall know a good solution when I see it."' (LFM, 84)

> Each new proof in mathematics widens the meaning of 'proof'. With Fermat's theorem,
> for example, we do not know what it would be like for it to be proved. (AWL, 10)

But, interestingly, he also anticipates the formulation of the proof. Where ordinary mathematical problems are concerned, knowing how to prove a proposition can be called a criterion of understanding it. But, he asks, what about propositions that we do not know how to prove?

> Would one say that someone understood the proposition '563 + 437 = 1,000' if he
> did not know how it can be proved? Can one deny that it is a sign of understanding
> a proposition, if a man knows how it could be proved?
> What, then, about propositions that are not decidable?
> If Fermat's Theorem were proved to me I would understand it better than
> before.
> The problem of finding a mathematical decision of a theorem might with some
> justice be called the problem of giving mathematical sense to a formula.[22]

So until the proof is formulated, the formula is just a structure with no definite mathematical sense. But such proposition-like structures function, as we noted earlier, as 'stimuli' for mathematical research; as 'signposts' for mathematical investigations. 'Problem' and 'solution', or proof, are connected—if we do not have a method for solving a problem, we don't have a genuine problem.

What, then, can the proof tell us about the nature of the problem? We can note that Wittgenstein, especially in his later philosophy, considered the question of proof to be perhaps the most central issue in the philosophy of mathematics. For Wittgenstein, a philosophical investigation in mathematics is concerned with the question of how we talk about and conceive of mathematical activities, i.e. how we understand the nature of mathematical proofs, problems, propositions, etc.—it is here that philosophical ideas and misunderstandings about what mathematics is, or should be, enter the picture. (Cf. PI §254)

As we noted above, the development of Wittgenstein's understanding of mathematics could be characterized as a shift in emphasis, from the question about the nature of mathematical propositions, and what understanding or believing them means, towards an emphasis on the centrality of proof in mathematics. For the later Wittgenstein, a philosophical investigation in mathematics is, to a great extent, an investigation of mathematical proofs, the nature of which we are prone to misunderstand. Indeed, Wittgenstein is often claimed to have stated that mathematics is 'a motley of techniques of proof', and that 'its manifold applicability and importance' is based upon this.[23] But observe that

---

[22] MS 127, 160–1 (1944). Cf. RFM V, §42; the passage about undecidable propositions and Fermat's theorem is, for some reason, not printed in RFM.

[23] 'I should like to say: mathematics is a MOTLEY of techniques of proof.—And upon this is based its manifold applicability and its importance.' (MS 122, 86r; 1940: RFM III, §46) 'Motley' is Anscombe's translation of 'ein buntes Gemisch'; however, as Felix Mühlhölzer (2005, 66) has pointed out, this translation is not altogether felicitous. He suggests 'a multicoloured mix'. See also Mühlhölzer 2010, 311–12, for a discussion of this passage.

Wittgenstein qualifies this statement by preceding it with 'I would like to say'—we should not understand this as a 'conventionalist' definition of mathematics or an attempt to say something about a timeless essence of mathematics; instead, it is a *suggestion to look at* mathematics from a certain perspective, which might show us things we otherwise fail to notice.

Juliet Floyd points out that, in his investigations on the foundations of mathematics, Wittgenstein criticizes the traditional idea that mathematical proof must be regarded as a 'process of step-by-step reasoning from proposition to proposition according to a universally applicable, explicitly specifiable set of logical laws'. (Floyd 2000, 237) Instead he insists on the 'surveyability' or 'Übersichtlichkeit' of a mathematical proof[24]—it shows us something in a convincing way and can thus *persuade* us about something. A mathematical proof *enables one to see something*. A proof should show us, for example, *how* to reach a solution, not simply *that* a problem has a solution:

> Proof, one might say, does not merely shew *that* it is like this, but: *how* it is like this. It shows *how* 13 + 14 yield 27.
>
> 'A proof must be capable of being taken in' [übersehbar] means: we must be prepared to use it as our guide-line in judging....
>
> The proof (the pattern of the proof) shews us the result of a procedure (the construction); and we are convinced that a procedure regulated in *this* way always leads to this configuration.
>
> (The proof exhibits a fact of synthesis to us.) (MS 122,45r–47r (1939); RFM III, §22)

We could say that 'knowing that' a proposition is true does not come before or is not independent of knowing 'how' it is true, i.e. of knowing how to prove it.

In passing, we can observe that this lets us glimpse another aspect of the 'odd resemblance' between an aesthetic investigation and a philosophical investigation *in mathematics*: this observation applies not only to mathematics but also to aesthetic judgements, e.g. 'this picture is balanced' or 'that building is incredibly ugly'. 'Proof' of, or 'reasons' for, such a judgement not only show *that* it is like this but *how* it is like this. Some philosophical confusions concerning mathematics can thus be clarified by taking due note of this 'odd resemblance'—especially in the nature of the problems that function as the starting point for such investigations. One important point here is that the conviction we reach when understanding a mathematical proof is of the same kind as the conviction an 'aesthetic investigation' can produce—here as well the reasons or grounds that are presented have to show not only *that* something is what it is, but also *why* or *how* it is like it is.[25] That is, it is not enough for someone to *tell* me there is a solution; I must also be given reasons to accept the solution. The reasons given, if convincing, can lead to a new

---

[24] See Mühlhölzer 2005 for a further discussion of what this 'surveyability' implies. See also chapter 7 in this volume.

[25] Once again, the same is true for philosophical problems: 'To relieve the mental cramp it is not enough to get rid of it; you must also see why you had it.' (AWL, 90)

way of seeing, to the dawning of a new aspect, i.e. the reasons will induce me to *see* that this is indeed a solution. In this respect, proof is closely connected to the sense of mathematical propositions (which also points to an important *disanalogy* between mathematical problems and problems in the natural sciences):

> We shall first have to ask ourselves: Has the mathematical proposition been proved? And how? For the proof is part of the grammar of the proposition! [A] mathematical proof incorporates the mathematical proposition into a new calculus, and alters its position in mathematics. A proposition with its proof belongs to a different category than a proposition without a proof. (Unproved mathematical propositions—signposts for mathematical research, stimuli for mathematical constructions.)[26]

But how does this kind of idea about the *Übersichtlichkeit* of mathematical proofs relate to the proof of Fermat's theorem? Can we draw any general conclusions on the basis of such a simple example as the one just discussed? Wittgenstein's approach in the philosophy of mathematics, as in his philosophy in general, is to start out from the obvious, that which escapes our attention because of its familiarity. This is why he uses such trivial examples. (Cf. PI §129) But, as Floyd notes, this does not mean that Wittgenstein oversimplifies mathematics or that the relevance of what he is saying is restricted to such elementary cases, or that he would claim that complex and long formal proofs are not proofs. His criticism of lengthy proofs is first and foremost directed at Frege's and Russell's logicistic programme. (See Floyd 2000, 258.)

So how should we relate to the proof of Fermat's theorem? Does this proof help us to 'understand the theorem better than before', and, if it does, in what sense? We just noted that Wittgenstein claims that the proof is 'part of the grammar of the mathematical proposition', and that the proved proposition belongs to another category than the unproved one, which should be counted among the 'signposts for mathematical investigation, stimuli to mathematical constructions'. But what, then, is the relation of the earlier innumerable failed solutions to the problem?

Because it is easily 'understood' by laymen, and of course because Fermat himself claimed to have a proof, Fermat's theorem was a popular target not only for professional mathematicians but also for laymen, who attempted to prove it, or even disprove it, using only high-school-level mathematics. If we are to believe Wittgenstein, these attempts were a kind of 'messing about', which merely 'meandered about the problem'. Wiles' proof would, then, show that these people really did not know what they were looking for.

This does not mean that this kind of 'messing about' has done nothing to inspire mathematical theory, or to help in clarifying the problem. Wiles' proof is of course not 'surveyable' or 'perspicuous' in the same sense as elementary mathematical proofs. This easily leads to a kind of disappointment; what was expected (given the nature of Fermat's claim to have found a proof) was an elegant proof that uses elementary methods. The

---

[26] MS 154, 14v (1931/32) → MS 113, 72v–73v (1932) → TS 211, 631–2 → TS 212, 1575–6 → TS 213, 630–31 (**BT, 630–31**).

current proof is instead exceedingly complicated and builds upon mathematics that goes well beyond the system in which the problem was originally formulated. This leaves us feeling that there is a discrepancy between the statement of the problem and its solution. What made the problem fascinating was precisely the apparent ease with which it could be understood and the illusion it gives of being analogous to well-known Diophantine equations. Not to mention, of course, the legend that has built up around Fermat's supposed 'marvellous demonstration'.

How, then, does the proof relate to what Wittgenstein says about elementary proofs in mathematics? Wittgenstein never claims that all mathematical proofs have to be 'intuitively' convincing in the same sense as his above quoted example (RFM III, §22) of a 'Kantian' synthesis. What he does claim is that a 'perspicuous' proof can be used as a 'guideline in judging', and it is questionable in what sense this is true of Wiles' proof. But of course we now *have* a proof, which shows that we were not dealing with an impossibility, as we are when we search for a method of trisecting an angle using a ruler and compasses. We can perhaps say that our understanding of the nature of the problem has been made clearer, even if we do not understand Wiles' proof. The problem was not what it seemed to be; we have gotten rid of an illusion. The result of this might be that we (the mathematicians) no longer have the same relation to the statement of the problem as before—we stop looking for the solution, we stop 'messing about'. If this is the result, we can say that the problem has lost its fascination, but we have also got rid of the 'mental cramp' and the irritation caused by the original formulation of the problem. Thus the acceptance of the proof leads to a shift in our idea of something, a new way of seeing.[27] (Of course, we might also continue to think that a solution to the problem is not satisfying unless based on some simple idea that gives us a 'perspicuous' and 'elegant' proof, and that unless such a solution can be reached the problem was not really 'a good problem'.)

VII

Does this mean that Wittgenstein is proposing, as some say, a conventionalist theory of mathematics? I would claim not. What he is doing is clearing up philosophical confusions about mathematics; confusions that need not bother mathematicians in their day-to-day activities. Wittgenstein's criticism of certain ways of understanding mathematical problems is not a criticism of mathematics, or an attempt to reform our way of speaking about mathematics, but rather an attempt to answer *philosophical* questions about the nature of mathematical propositions, proofs, and problems that these ways of speaking can give rise to. (Cf. PI §254)

---

[27] For instance, the importance of the proof of the impossibility of trisecting an angle by ruler and compasses lies, according to Wittgenstein, in that it 'changes our idea of trisection', or 'remodels our way of seeing'. See e.g. MWL, 10; LFM, 88; RFM IV, §30. For a further discussion of this see Floyd 2000, 238–9.

Consequently, Wittgenstein in no way attempts to say that creative mathematics is impossible—he does not deny that the mathematical activities inspired or stimulated by 'open problems', even if they can be characterized as a 'messing about', can be mathematically productive, or that they might ultimately lead to a solution of such problems. What he wants to open our eyes to is the misleading classification of these 'open questions' as problems in the same sense as research problems in natural science, or as well-defined questions in mathematics. This confuses us and makes us (i.e. philosophers) suppose things about 'the essence' of mathematics that lead to a mythologization of mathematics and a distorted picture of mathematical practice. We start thinking, for example, that mathematics must consist of propositions dealing with a (Platonic) realm of mathematical objects. What we can realize, through a clearer view of the nature of mathematical problems and the activities of the mathematicians, is that mathematics can indeed be considered 'a motley of techniques of proofs'. This does not, however, amount to a stipulation of what mathematics should be or to a 'conventionalist' theory of mathematics; instead, it means that mathematics, too, is 'left as it is', as Wittgenstein famously puts it in the *Investigations* §124. Indeed, this remark is prefigured already in the *Big Typescript*:

> In mathematics there can only be mathematical troubles, not philosophical ones.[28]
> Really, the philosopher only marks what the mathematician occasionally dashes off about his activities.
> The philosopher easily gets into the position of a clumsy manager, who, instead of doing his *own* work and merely supervising his employees to see they do their work well, takes over their jobs until one day he finds himself overburdened with other people's work while his employees watch and criticize him. He is particularly inclined to saddle himself with the work of the mathematician.[29, 30]

References

AMBROSE, ALICE ed. (1979). *Wittgenstein's Lectures, Cambridge, 1932–1935: From the Notes of Alice Ambrose and Margaret Macdonald*. Oxford: Blackwell.

BELL, E. T. (1937). *Men of Mathematics*. New York: Simon and Schuster.

DIAMOND, CORA (1991). *The Realistic Spirit*. Cambridge, MA: MIT Press.

—— ed. (1976). *Wittgenstein's Lectures on the Foundations of Mathematics, Cambridge 1939*. Ithaca, NY: Cornell University Press.

[28] Here Wittgenstein chose to use the English word 'troubles': 'In der Mathematik kann es nur mathematische troubles ~~Schwierigkeiten~~ geben, nicht philosophische.' MS 112,31v (1931) → TS 211, 438 → TS 212, 1570 → TS 213, 629 (**BT, 629**)

[29] MS 112, 31r (1931) → TS 211, 437 → TS 212, 1571 → TS 213, 629 (**BT, 629**). Cf. PG, 369.

[30] A first version of this chapter was read at the workshop 'Backwards and Forward: Questions of Method', arranged by the Nordic Network for Wittgenstein Research, at the School of Philosophy, University of East Anglia, Norwich, in February 2008. I would like to thank the participants of the workshop for comments and questions. In addition, I want to thank Juliet Floyd and Sören Stenlund for valuable suggestions concerning this chapter.

FLOYD, JULIET (2000). 'Wittgenstein, Mathematics and Philosophy', in A. M. Crary and R. Read eds., *The New Wittgenstein*. London: Routledge.

FRASCOLLA, PASQUALE (1994). *Wittgenstein's Philosophy of Mathematics*. London: Routledge.

FREGE, GOTTLOB (2011). 'Frege–Wittgenstein correspondence', and ed. B. Dreben and trans. J. Floyd in E. De Pellegrin ed., *Interactive Wittgenstein: Essays in Memory of Georg Henrik von Wright*. Dordrecht, Heidelberg, London, New York: Springer.

HILBERT, DAVID (1935). 'Naturerkennen und Logik', in *Gesammelte Abhandlungen*, Vol. 3. Berlin: Springer.

MOORE, G. E. (1955). 'Wittgenstein's Lectures in 1930–33: III', *Mind*, 64 (253): 1–27.

MÜHLHÖLZER, FELIX (2005). ' "A Mathematical Proof Must Be Surveyable": What Wittgenstein Meant by this and what it Implies'. *Grazer Philosophische Studien* 71: 57–86.

—— (2010). *Braucht die Mathematik eine Grundlegung? Ein Kommentar des Teils III von Wittgensteins 'Bemerkungen über die Grundlagen der Mathematik'*. Frankfurt am Main: Vittorio Klostermann.

WAISMANN, FRIEDRICH (1979). *Wittgenstein and the Vienna Circle: Conversations Recorded by Friedrich Waismann*, ed. B. McGuinness, trans. J. Schulte and B. McGuinness. Oxford: Blackwell.

WITTGENSTEIN, LUDWIG (1933). *Tractatus Logico-Philosophicus*, trans. C. K. Ogden and F. Ramsey. London: Routledge.

—— (1958). *Philosophical Investigations*, ed. G. E. M. Anscombe and R. Rhees, trans. G. E. M. Anscombe, 2nd edn. Oxford: Blackwell.

—— (1969). *The Blue and Brown Books*, 2nd edn. Oxford: Blackwell.

—— (1974). *Philosophical Grammar*, ed. R. Rhees, trans. A. Kenny. Blackwell: Oxford.

—— (1975). *Philosophical Remarks*, ed. R. Rhees, trans. R. Hargreaves and R. White. Oxford: Blackwell.

—— (1978). *Remarks on the Foundations of Mathematics*, ed. G. H. von Wright, R. Rhees, and G. E. M. Anscombe, trans. G. E. M. Anscombe, 3rd edn. Oxford: Blackwell.

—— (1998). *Culture and Value*, ed. G. H. von Wright, rev. edn. A. Pichler, trans. P. Winch. Oxford: Blackwell.

—— (2000). *Wittgenstein's Nachlass: The Bergen Electronic Edition*. Oxford: Oxford University Press.

—— (2005). *The Big Typescript: TS 213*, ed. and trans. C. G. Luckhardt and M. A. E. Aue. Oxford: Blackwell.

PART III

PHILOSOPHY OF LANGUAGE

CHAPTER 9

....

THE PROPOSITION'S
PROGRESS

....

CHARLES TRAVIS

I will trace the progress of an idea, *proposition*, in Wittgenstein's thought. *Caveat*: insofar as I discern a finished view, I share it.

What is a proposition? There are three familiar questions here. First, a proposition is the content of a truth-evaluable attitude. It is a way of exposing oneself to risk of error which one escapes or succumbs to *solely* in things being as they are. Which things *are* truth-evaluable? What *can* have its fate decided just in things being as they are? Second, what identifies a given proposition as the one it is? What features identify precisely that form of hostage-giving which it is? Frege's case for *Sinn* (1892a/1979) speaks in one way to this question. Third, how can something which relates to the world as a *proposition* does be formed from what are a proposition's parts? These may not all be *good* questions. They all concern Wittgenstein.

I will explore his views by tracing a path, in steps, from the *Tractatus* to the *Investigations*. I will focus on one intermediate step, found in *Philosophical Grammar*. It is, importantly, *intermediate*; not yet the *Investigations* view. It is beset with problems. But it may make clearer in what way the *Investigations* addresses the same problems as the *Tractatus*, and how its very different answers are just what that fixed problematic requires.

The path I will describe was not, in fact, smooth. Old ideas, which do not fit happily into the emerging new view, still exert their force. They disappear and come back, and only with difficulty are eventually abandoned or transformed. Any story of a *path*, such as the one here, must be selective as to what belongs on it and what does not. I oversimplify, as a *reading* of texts such as the *Grammar* must. Another *caveat*.

Wittgenstein *always* had Frege in mind. One can read the *Investigations* as a reaction *against* Frege. It does depart from his ideas at absolutely crucial points. But it is also important to see how the case for these departures rests on Frege's own ideas. Wittgenstein was deeply Fregean throughout. One can read the *Investigations*—as one might read the *Tractatus*—as simply working out what Frege should have said to be true to his best insights.

This chapter is also published as Chapter 7 of Charles Travis, *Objectivity and the Parochial* (Oxford: Oxford University Press, 2011).

1. A Tractarian View

A path needs a starting point—here the *Tractatus*. My account of that point will be minimalist. It leaves *much* unsaid as to what the *Tractatus* view was.

1.1 The essence of representation

The *Tractatus* contains a view of what is essential to representing something as so. (See 2.12–2.15.) As late as January 1930, Wittgenstein expressed that view this way:

> It is the essential feature of a proposition that it is *a picture* and has compositeness. (WVC, 90)

A proposition is a particular structuring of particular elements. Each of these elements represents an element of reality (that is, that which the proposition represents as a certain way). The proposition as a whole represents precisely those elements as *so* structured, where 'so structured' means: in the very same way as that proposition itself is. A true proposition shares structure with what it represents as so. (I bracket the question what an element might be.)

The structure of a representation is, trivially, representational structure: a structuring of its way of representing something as so. It is a structuring of logical roles: of sub-tasks in the proposition's being true when it would be. What a proposition represents as so— say, that a pig is in the sty—does not represent anything as so (unless we so contrive). So it cannot have representational structure. But, on the view in question, a representational structure is also a structure of a broader sort. To give the broader sort a name, I will call it *conceptual structure*. That a pig is in the sty is (on the *Tractatus* view) also structured in a way instancing conceptual structure. A representation which represents precisely that as so instances the very same conceptual structure as that the pig is in the sty does.

If it is of the essence of representation (as so) to work in this way, then to represent a particular thing—say, that the pig is in the sty—as so, one needs a representation structured in a particular way. Any representation structured otherwise, or out of other elements, necessarily represents something else as so.

1.2 Is the proposition fundamental?

The above story *could* be read as accounting for the unity of the proposition; that is, as answering the third question above. The idea would be: a proposition is composed out of elements, just as a list is. But it is composed by something else which is not an element: a structuring of those elements. This would not represent some further element of reality, but instead would function as described above. Such may or may not have been Wittgenstein's intent. The thought, though, invites comparison with Frege. Frege writes:

> What is distinctive about my conception of logic is that I begin by giving pride of place to the content of the word 'true', and then immediately go on to introduce a thought as that to which the question 'Is it true?' is in principle applicable. So I do not begin with concepts and put them together to form a thought or judgement; I come by the parts of a thought by analysing the thought. (Frege 1919/1979, 253)

It is because of this primacy of the thought that Frege insisted, repeatedly, that, strictly speaking, something can *be* an element of a thought only relative to an analysis. (See e.g. Frege 1892b/1986, 199–200; 1906/1979, 187.) It is not that to be such-and-such thought just *is* to be constructed of such-and-such elements. A thought has a role: to be true just when such-and-such is so. An analysis of a thought divides that role into different sub-tasks. For such sub-tasks to be *elements* of the thought is just for their joint performance to be performance of the thought's role. There need be no unique path to that goal. Thus the relativity of elementhood to an analysis. For a thought to be true just in case Sid grunts, a sub-task might be: being true or not according to how Sid is. An element would then be that in, or by, which the thought was that way: being about Sid. Such a sub-task could be performed only where another was: being true or not according to whether the right thing(s) was/were *thus and so*. There is no being true or not according to how Sid is without a way Sid thus needs to be. Such is Frege's context principle. On this view of what it is to be an element, there is no intelligible call for explanation as to how elements can form a *proposition*. The proposition is that in terms of which elements are to be identified.

If, by contrast, elements of a proposition call for *structuring* into one, then that structuring *is* an answer to an intelligible question how elements can form one. Here elements are conceived as *naming* bits of reality—what *might* also be named in other contexts, say, a list. Now there is a question by virtue of what some given context in which these elements name what they anyway do is a proposition rather than one of the other sorts of contexts in which they may do their work. The *Tractatus appears* to depart here from what Frege rightly regarded as his most important insight.

In the remark of January 1930, cited above, Wittgenstein also says what it is for a thought to have a structure:

> If there were only the proposition 'Φa' but not 'Φb', it would be superfluous to mention 'a'. It would suffice to write just 'Φ'. The proposition would thus not be composite.... But does 'Φa' presuppose 'Ψa'? Decidedly yes. For the same considerations tell us: if there were only a single function 'Φ' for 'a' then it would be superfluous; you could leave it out. (See also TLP 3.328.)

Superfluous symbols (or elements) are meaningless. That is the *Tractatus'* Occam's Razor. An element is *not* superfluous only if it marks the place of a proposition in some range of propositions within a given system; marks a respect in which all these different propositions are *the same*. This is what it is for it to *be* an element.

As the *whole* story of being an element, this, like Frege's story, would leave room for multiple analyses of a proposition. So being an element would still be relative to an analysis. For, for all said so far, a given system of propositions might be decomposable in various competing ways into sets of ranges of propositions, each the same in some respect. A given proposition would find itself at the intersection of different subsets of such ranges under different analyses of the system as a whole. So this cannot be the whole *Tractatus* story. On it, something about the system to which a proposition belongs imposes a unique decomposition of that system into those subsets whose members share a given element. For, in the *Tractatus*, the *same* proposition cannot be analysable both as composed of elements E and as composed of different elements E*. What was composed of E would *ipso facto* represent a different thing as so than would what was composed of E*. If elements need *structuring* into a proposition, and that structure does what the *Tractatus* says it does, then such structure must already be at work in fixing where elements are to be found.

The *Tractatus* thus departs from Frege. In this respect the *Investigations* returns to him. What is most central in Wittgenstein's later philosophy will prove to turn crucially on that return.

2. A First Step Towards the *Investigations*

In the *Tractatus* Wittgenstein tells us that the general form of a proposition is a variable. (TLP 6) This variable is also described as the most general form of truth-function. There is thus a domain over which it ranges: roughly, elementary propositions (whatever they are), and truth-functional combinations of them. The *Grammar* turns on rejecting this idea.

2.1 The indeterminacy of the notion *proposition*

What does the propositional variable range over? The obvious answer would be 'All propositions'. The *Grammar* holds that answer senseless. (See especially PG VI §§79, 80, 82, 122.) For the notion *proposition* leaves it under-determined just which things would count as one. In this respect, one might compare the notion *proposition* with *similar*, or *just like*. Is Tony Blair just like Jacques Chirac? That question makes no sense except in circumstances which fix more as to what is to be understood by being just like. The question 'What propositions are there?' is now cast as in the same boat. Here is a first example of what is to become the rule in later Wittgenstein: a concept does not decide what satisfies it except on some particular way of applying, or deploying, it. There are many ways of thinking of satisfying a given concept, on each of which different things would count as doing so.

In 'Some Remarks on Logical Form' (PO, 29–35; originally published in 1929) Wittgenstein portrayed it as a *project*, yet unachieved, to discover what elementary propositions there are, and thereby what propositions there are *überhaupt*. The project would be philosophical; on the *Tractatus* view it could not be empirical. He quickly abandoned that view. In the *Grammar*, the notion *proposition* does not tell us what to look for to see what propositions there are, nor, therefore, what elementary propositions there are—any more than the notion *alike* tells us what to look for to see whether Chirac and Blair are alike. The *Grammar* also suggests that, in the same way, the notion *elementary*, if coherent, does not on its own tell us what to look for to see which propositions are elementary. (PG, appendix 4) (Wittgenstein was later to call the idea of *discovering* elementary propositions the 'really arrogant' thing about the *Tractatus*.) To see which things count as propositions one needs more of an understanding of what it is to be to count as one—for purposes of the question raised—than the notion *proposition* itself provides.

If I say, 'Blair is just like Chirac', and have said something to be so, it will usually be circumstance that has added the needed content. This is not the *Grammar*'s story. Before telling it, a remark. To lack the content to determine an extension is not to lack content altogether. There is something being the same is, independent of particular understandings of it. There is plenty to say as to what a proposition is, short of saying anything that fixes an extension for that term. Propositions are the contents of truth-evaluable attitudes. This points to the kind of answer later Wittgenstein will give to the first of the three questions with which we began.

2.2 It is a language that gives the notion *proposition* determinacy

That is the *Grammar* story. Each language is a different unfolding of the notion *proposition*. A proposition is, by definition, a way of being hostage to the world: a particular way in which it can be for the world alone to decide whether a certain attitude (judging something) has achieved its aim (truth). In telling us which things in it are propositions, a language tells us that there are such-and-such ways for the world to exercise such authority. In the *Grammar* there is at most one constraint on what a language may thus say: if it is to tell us anything, it must speak coherently. Which *may* mean that it cannot, e.g., give content to *proposition* on which a proposition and its negation can both be true. But if there is such a constraint, it remains to say just what sort of constraint this is.

The grammar of a language says what its propositions are, in saying how each proposition in it works—what rules govern it (though such rules need not be explicit). For a proposition to function as it thus does is for it to have the sense it does.

> The role of a sentence in the calculus is its sense.... It is only in a language that something is a proposition.... A proposition is *one* combination of signs among a number of possible ones, and as opposed to other possible ones. As it were *one* position of an indicator as opposed to other possible ones. (PG VI §84)

The language might, for example, provide an item 'This is red', which occupies a certain position in a system also containing 'This is yellow', 'This is blue'. For it to occupy that position might be, in part, for its correct application to exclude correct applications of those other items. In the *Tractatus* a proposition was not a string of words, but something more abstract: the namings of given things, structured (logically, not spatially) in a given way. *Words* which did such naming, presented as so structured, might themselves be (spatially) ordered however you like. If a language determines what *its* propositions are, then, naturally enough, propositions are much closer to linguistic items. On the other hand, and by the same token, a proposition is no longer under any obligation to be a *picture* of reality in the way a Tractarian proposition must be. Its sense is its role in the language. Being a picture is no longer of the essence of representing as so.

It takes a language to give *proposition* enough determinacy to have an extension. So there are many different specific forms such determinacy might take. There are as many forms as there are possible languages: indefinitely many. As Wittgenstein puts it,

> 'Language' is only languages, plus things I invent by analogy with existing languages. Languages *are* systems. (PG IX §122)

As he later put it, it does not take a logician to tell us what a 'real' proposition looks like. A proposition is just whatever something *we* would call a language makes a proposition. Bracketing coherence, there is nothing beyond this which could decide whether a language is telling us *correctly* what things are propositions. Nor are there any constraints on what the 'logical form' of a proposition might be beyond the constraints on what the grammar of what we recognized as language might be. Perhaps this is a commentary on Frege's idea of 'separating a thought from its trappings' (Frege 1897/1979). There is also here the germ of a need for a step beyond the *Grammar*—the final step to the *Investigations*.

2.3 Unfolding truth

The notions *truth* and *proposition* form a package. One grasps either only in grasping both. Truth is a certain kind of success which it is the world's prerogative to grant or withhold from us. A proposition identifies a specific way for the world to grant or withhold it. One set of core properties of truth is unfolded, Frege tells us, in the laws of truth (logical truths). These fix the most general structure of the commitment one makes in allegiance to a proposition. For example, for each proposition there is another, true just when it is false. Allegiance to the first commits one to rejection of the second.

If *truth* and *proposition* form this sort of packet, and there are indefinitely many unfoldings of the concept *proposition*, then, one would expect, there are also indefinitely many unfoldings of the concept *truth*. The *Grammar* is explicit on that point:

> One can't of course say that a proposition is whatever one can predicate 'true' or 'false' of, as if one could put symbols together with the words 'true' and 'false' by way of experiment to see whether the result makes sense. For something could only be decided by this experiment if 'true' and 'false' already have definite meanings, and they can only have that if the contexts in which they can occur are already settled. (PG VI §79)

Frege tells us that the concept truth is unfolded in the laws of truth (or of logic). Wittgenstein is not here supposing that a language could be an exception to those laws— as if one could think, or operate, correctly according to the grammar of some language, but in violation of them. So he is not envisioning alternative unfoldings to those the laws of logic give. What alternatives *are* envisioned here?

The answer: the laws of logic are no more than half an unfolding of the notion *truth*. The other half emerges if we consider a notion of a way things might be or not—red, say. A *proposition* to the effect that Pia's dress is red would be something over whose success or failure (as a judgement) things being as they are may exercise its unique authority: things being as they are may *be* things being as they are according to that proposition; her dress being as it is may instance a dress being red. Now consider what I might say, viewing the setting sun from my Hackney balcony, in saying the sun to be red. Do I express a proposition? If so, then, again, things being as they are may exercise its authority over that proposition's success or failure. But for purposes of that proposition (if such it be), the colour of the sun could not be independent of the conditions of its viewing—certainly not as the colour of Pia's dress is. The sun's being as I said in calling it red (if there is such a thing) would not suggest, as Pia's dress being red might, that it looks red independent of from where viewed. If Pia's dress is red, you need not be in Hackney to see it so looking. You would be equally placed to do that in Gravelines, if the dress were on view there. Not so the sun. So *could* things being as they are—*inter alia*, the sun's looking all the ways it does on all the ways in which it is on view—add up to things being as they are according to a proposition, such as I would have expressed on my Hackney balcony, to the effect that the sun is red? Would such a proposition really be a way for the world to exercise the authority it must over any proposition? Such is a question about truth—about what may *be* true or false—but not one which logic speaks to. It is an instance of that other half of truth's content. In the *Grammar*, it is a question for a language to speak to. Nothing not part of the language can dictate which way a language *must* decide it.

Frege tells us that the fundamental logical relation is that of an object falling under a concept. All others, he says, reduce to that. (1892a/1979, 118) We can generalize thus: the fundamental relation is between the non-conceptual and the conceptual—between things being as they are (or a thing as it is) and their (or its) being such-and-such way. Logic is silent as to which *are* the instances of being such-and-such way. It says little as to when there *is* a way to instance. It says no more than this: there is such a way only when there is another such that the first is instanced precisely when the second is not. Things being as they are makes for success (truth) in representing things as the first way precisely when it makes for failure (falsehood) in representing them as the second (and vice versa). For there to be something to instance, there must be such a thing as things (being as they are) instancing it, and (or) their not being. *Perhaps* things must often enough do the one thing or the other (though *logic* does not so dictate). But as to how, and when, these conditions may be met—what a way might be of sorting instances from non— logic is silent. The *Grammar* point is: this is a matter for a language to decide for itself: where logic does not dictate to it, nothing else does.

It is a *fact* that the sun, setting over Hackney, is red; but not a fact that white chocolate tastes best. *De gustibus* and all that. So one might be inclined to say. But, the *Grammar* tells us, one *can* say such things only with reference to some given language. A *language* makes the one thing but not the other a proposition—*in it*. The notion *proposition*, as the notion *true*, do not, on their own, decide such things. Thus it is for nothing outside language to settle what engages with truth. As Wittgenstein recognizes, this can be an unsettling idea. The examples Wittgenstein has in mind are not quite like the contrast between taking the sun to be red and holding white chocolate to taste better than dark. They lead more directly to the most fundamental issues.

2.4 The arbitrariness of grammar

As things now stand, a language unfolds the notions *proposition* and *truth*. In one way among indefinitely many it adds enough content to these notions for there to be an extension for 'is a proposition' and for 'is either true or false'. Its grammar provides this content. Still bracketing conflict between grammar and logic, there is no perspective from outside a language from which its grammar is criticizable. With the proviso, grammars are not liable to be *wrong*—in conflict with the notion *proposition*. For, again with the proviso, that notion as such does not have enough content to support any such criticism. Grammars are, in this sense, arbitrary.

Wittgenstein worries about the arbitrariness of grammar. For grammar, so construed, connects with possibility. Bracketing the necessary, a proposition divides ways things might be into two disjoint, non-empty, classes: cases where things are as they are according to the proposition; cases where things are otherwise. So if the proposition is that P, then there is the possibility that P, and the possibility that not. For the necessary true, there is at least one of these possibilities. But a grammar may tell us all sorts of things. If it thus tells us that such-and-such is *possible*—that there is such a thing as things being thus and so—is there really no position from outside it from which it can be decided whether it is right or wrong in this? Is such a grammar really not committed to anything determinately right or wrong independent of what it says? Is there really no such thing as a *proposition*, not referring to a language, that such-and-such is possible?

As Wittgenstein expresses the worry (in the *Grammar* and in the *Investigations*),

> If a proposition is conceived as a picture of the state of affairs it describes and a proposition is said to show just how things stand if it's true, and thus to show the possibility of the asserted state of affairs, still the most that the proposition can do is what a painting or relief does: and so it can at any rate not set forth what is just not the case. (PG VI §82)

A proposition shows the asserted state of affairs as possible, so as a possibility. If the grammar tells us that, possibly, white chocolate really *is* best, then possibly it is. So in telling us what propositions there are (on its understanding of a proposition), a grammar tells us that certain things are possible. But if what a proposition is is up to a grammar, or language, to decide, thus arbitrary, can what is *possible* be arbitrary? Suppose a grammar tells us, in this way, that things may be both red and green in the same place. Is this then possible? Surely what such a grammar told us would be criticizable from without.

If a grammar is thus responsible to something outside it—if it can go right or wrong as to what things are propositions—that is to say that there must be a certain harmony between thought, or language, and the world if thought is to be about the world at all; and that such harmony is a *substantial* requirement, one a would-be proposition might fail. A version of this idea is reported in Lee and King's notes of Wittgenstein's Cambridge lectures in Lent term 1930:

> But in order that propositions may be able to represent at all something further is needed which is the same both in language and reality. For example, a picture can represent a scene rightly or wrongly; but both in picture and scene pictured there will be colour and light and shade. (WL, 10)

But this is not the *Grammar* view. There Wittgenstein says two things. First, if a grammar merely tells us that there are propositions that something is red and green at the same spot, which are contingently either true or false, it has so far told us nothing about how to operate with those propositions—when these things are to count as true, when false, how they are to interact, e.g. inferentially, with others. So far, then, the grammar is not determinate enough to count as having specified, or provided, any propositions at all.

The second thing Wittgenstein tells us is this:

> A construction may have a superficial resemblance to…an empirical proposition and play a somewhat similar role in a calculus without having an analogous application; and if it hasn't we won't be inclined to call it a proposition. (PG VI §82)

A more perspicuous version of the point I want to focus on here is in the *Investigations'* continuation of that passage beginning, 'If a proposition is conceived as a picture…':

> It is not every sentence-like formation that we know how to do something with, not every technique has an application in our life…(PI §520)

So there is, after all, one sort of criticism that can be made of a grammar: what it presents as propositions are not things *we* are able to treat as propositions. A grammar can go wrong in that sense. This is the only sense Wittgenstein provides for the idea that a grammar may go wrong (still bracketing our proviso).

Note the crucial reference to *us*. Who the 'us' is may be somewhat negotiable. But something on the order of we humans; *not*, in any event, we thinkers. For where what a grammar may and may not do is fixed by what it is to be a thinker at all—by, as Frege puts it, 'The Mind, not minds'—there *is* an external standpoint from which grammar is subject to criticism in just the way Wittgenstein says it is not. The grammar proposes such-and-such as a proposition. The question is then whether it is consistent with what thinking is *as such* that this should be allowed as a proposition. 'We cannot treat that something is red and green at the same spot as a proposition', so reading 'we', then becomes, 'it is inconsistent with what thought is *as such* that this should count as a proposition'. So this is inconsistent, full stop, with the notion *proposition*. But this is precisely what was not supposed to be the case. That it is not is *the* main departure, in the *Grammar*, from the *Tractatus*.

So the point needs to be about an entirely parochial form of thought. We are thinkers of a particular kind, equipped by our nature with certain sensitivities, equipped to treat the world, in thought and deed, in certain ways. For thinkers *like us*, the proposition so far on offer, to the effect that something is red and green at the same spot, cannot, perhaps, be treated as a proposition. It is not one for us, by our lights. That, and nothing else, makes it correct, where it *is* correct, for us to say that what is on offer is not a proposition. It is *not* a possibility that something is red and green at the same spot. Insofar as there is something true to be said in saying this, we, a parochial form of thinker, are in some such way the measure of *what* it is true thus to say.

It can easily seem worrying to assign the parochial such work. Much of the *Investigations* is concerned with *why* this should seem worrying, and whether it really is.

2.5 A *caveat*

With Wittgenstein I have spoken of a grammar as telling us that it is possible that something is red and green in one place: it fixes a contingent proposition to that effect. This can seem to be putting things wrongly. Which can introduce another conception of how it is that, in present matters, a grammar cannot be mistaken. I will explore it briefly.

On the alternate conception, my talk of being red and green at one spot was loose talk. What I should have said is this: the grammar provides a contingent proposition to the effect that an object is simultaneously a certain way, and a certain other way, at one spot. By virtue, perhaps, of other things it tells us, I have identified those ways as being red and being green. But perhaps wrongly. For, if the grammar has told us what it has, the thought would go, then for an object to be the first way in question is for it to be a way it might be, at a spot, while also being, there, the second way, and vice versa. To speak of ways for a thing to be of which this was not so would simply be not to speak of the ways the grammar specifies. So if this is not so of being red and being green, then the grammar was not speaking of red and green. A grammar cannot be *wrong* in what it tells us, because anything of which it was wrong would *ipso facto* not be what it was speaking of.

This is an incorrect idea, perhaps flirted with occasionally in the 1930s, but definitely out of the picture in the *Investigations*. One development of a Tractarian idea might tempt one to it. That Tractarian idea is that there is no outer boundary around thought, or propositions:

> We cannot...say in logic: This and this there is in the world, that there is not.
> For that would apparently presuppose that we exclude certain possibilities, and this cannot be the case since otherwise logic must get outside the limits of the world: as if it could consider these limits from the other side also.
> What we cannot think, we cannot think: thus we cannot *say* what it is we cannot think. (TLP 5.61)

To think of thinkables (propositions) as inside a boundary, we would have to think of there being something on the other side of it. So we would have to be able to say what this might be. But this, of course, we cannot do. (If this is a problem, it is also one for our being able to think of ourselves as parochial thinkers, which can also be a way of seeing what is wrong with the idea.)

In the early 1930s, a descendant of this idea returns as follows:

> Can we give a description which will justify the rules of grammar? Can we say why we must use *these* rules? Our justification could only take the form of saying 'As reality is so and so, the rules must be such-and-such'. But this presupposes that I could say 'If reality were otherwise, then the rules of grammar would be otherwise'. But in order to describe a reality in which grammar was otherwise I would have to use the very combinations which grammar forbids. The rules of grammar distinguish sense and non-sense and if I use the forbidden combinations I talk nonsense. (WL, 47: Lent 1931)

So it is not that the notion *proposition* lacks the determinacy that might place a grammar's proposals within or without its extension, but rather that there is no saying a grammar to be wrong without lapsing into nonsense.

This idea meshes with that idea, occasionally floated in the early 1930s, that to change grammar is to change topic. If a grammar provides for the possible truth of 'It's red and green just *there*', then what this could not be true of would not be what *those* words 'red' and 'green' spoke of. So not of red and green if what they are rules out such truth.

The *Investigations* will show why these are bad ideas. Meanwhile, though, there is the following consideration. On the *Grammar* view, what a grammar may do is limited at most only by what logic dictates. It must be consistent; provide *consistently* for propositions. Suppose a grammar tells us that there is a contingent proposition, 'X is both A and B at the same spot', and, further, that 'X is A' is to speak of X being red, 'X is B' of X being green. It thus stipulates that it is *red* and *green* that the relevant propositions speak of. Why can it not do so? Logic does not forbid this. It is no principle of *logic* that something cannot be red and green at the same spot. Something extra-logical must prohibit *ever* taking being red and being green to be what might so behave. But *that* sort of criticism of grammar is just what there cannot be on the *Grammar* view.

So Wittgenstein is right to put the problem, as he does, as one of what goes wrong, or how anything could possibly go wrong, if a grammar tells us that something might be *red* and *green* at the same spot. And the only available answer seems to make reference to thinkers like *us*, and *our* capacities to think of things. We are now almost ready for the last step to the *Investigations*. But we need first to see what forces us out of the *Grammar*.

2.6 Logical form

Wittgenstein's earliest mention of Diderot may be 27 October 1930:

> A French politician once said that French was the most perfect language because in French sentences the words followed exactly the sequence of the thought. The fallacy

here is to think that there are, as it were, two series, a thought series...and a words series, with some relation between them. A further fallacy is to suppose that 'thinking a proposition' means thinking its terms in a certain order. (WL, 16)

Other occasions were *Grammar* V §66 and *Investigations* §336. (See Chomsky 1965 for the relevant bits of Diderot.)

Suppose that in speaking English we express thoughts. Or even that (as the *Grammar* has it) English sentences are expressions of thoughts (or are propositions). Suppose that a *thought* is something essentially structured: built up from given parts in a given way (as per the *Tractatus*). Then an English sentence has three different sorts of structure, each defined by a different goal. There is, first, ordinary English syntactic structure. This is a device for building indefinitely many sentences from a *much* smaller number of parts. Mastering the syntax makes English sentences recognizable to us as such, even if never seen before. That is syntax's goal. A language chooses one means among many possible for achieving this. There is considerable freedom of choice. Second, there is semantic structure: the way in which, in the language, the meaning of a whole expression depends on the meanings of its verbal parts. Syntax shapes what semantic structure must be. Suppose, now, that the sentence 'Sid grunts' expresses the thought that Sid grunts. On the *Tractatus* view, there is a structure (conceptual structure) essential to that thought. So English must assign that sentence that structure too. The structure in question is determined by what is so according to the thought expressed: that such-and-such things are *so* structured. For all of which the *semantic* structure of that sentence might be any of many things, depending on what English syntax is. That semantic structure might be isomorphic with the conceptual structure. Or, so far as the goals of syntax go, might be arbitrarily far from it. Thus Diderot's idea: in French, as it happens, semantic structure mirrors conceptual structure exactly. In other languages, perhaps not. It is this idea that Wittgenstein now mocks. To mock it is to reject his own Tractarian conception of what representing (as so) is.

On the *Tractatus* view, discovering conceptual structure is a project for analysis. Wittgenstein later confessed that he took Russell's method, as applied to definite descriptions, as the model of analysis. (See PG, appendix 4.) Russell deliberately ignored (ordinary) syntax, which he thought could be misleading. His central question was when given words would be *true*. That conception of analysis unfolds, in Wittgenstein, into the above idea, now rejected, of a triple of distinct structures—structurings of different things to meet different goals.

In the *Grammar* a language embodies but two structures: an ordinary syntax; and a grammar. Grammar is here a more general affair than mere semantic structure. It gives rules for use. Such rules may operate entirely within the conceptual ('If it's red, then it isn't green'). Perhaps Wittgenstein also thought of them as connecting the conceptual to the non-conceptual ('*This* (that lawn), e.g., is green.') Grammar makes an expression 'one position of an indicator, among others'. And the now crucial point is: the grammar of a language is as proprietary as its syntax. It represents *one* way, among others, of going about representing things as so, just as a syntax represents one way, among others, of making a large set of sentences recognizable to speakers.

Just here lies a problem. Pia and I are at the *Terminus du Nord*. The waiter announces, 'Les oursins sont arrivés.' Pia speaks no French. Can I tell her what he said? I would be inclined to say, 'The sea urchins have arrived.' *Does* this tell her what he said? The waiter expressed a proposition. That quoted English sentence does too. But, according to the *Grammar*, it is for a language to say what its propositions are. 'Les oursins sont arrivés' is, or expresses, a proposition in French. 'The sea urchins have arrived' expresses what is one in English. The notion *proposition*, aside from its application in a particular language, lacks content that might fix which things are propositions. So this leaves it undefined what it might be for a French proposition to be the *same* as an English one. No such notion of *the same* is yet available. It is undefined, that is, what saying the same thing inter-linguistically might be. Which shows that the *grammar* is not quite the right thing to which to assign that role which the *Grammar* assigns it. Which paves the way for our final step to the *Investigations*.

For Frege, a law of logic is a *thought*, so (since a law) true. It is as general as a thought could be. So it mentions nothing, not even thoughts. It has nothing but structure to make it true. How, then, can such a law speak to thoughts—saying how they are related inferentially? The idea, in brief, is that that structure which identifies the law reflects the most general structure of a system of thoughts to which the law belongs. Thoughts which are related inferentially thereby belong to a system. (And, for Frege, any two thoughts are related inferentially—e.g. from them their conjunction follows.) Their inferential relations are a part of the most general structure of the system they help form. A law identifies those relations in reflecting the structure of that system, to which it, too, belongs.

This conception of logic does not fit with the *Grammar* view. On that view, for a proposition to belong to a system is just for it to belong to a language. Any other proposition which cohabits the system with it, and which, in its structure, reflects the structure of that system, would just be another proposition of that *language*. A law of logic, as Frege conceives it, is not a piece of French or German. There is no such thing as French logic, German logic, etc. A law of logic speaks to all propositions. Conceiving such a law as Frege does, there is, the *Grammar* tells us, no such thing as doing this.

Such need not be a *problem* for the *Grammar*. After all, its starting point was the idea that the notion *proposition* is not well enough defined for there to be such a thing as all propositions. What we do not yet have, though, is any alternative, non-Fregean, conception of what logic might be. This, too, is something the *Investigations* aims to provide.

3. THE FINAL STEP

We begin now on the *Investigations* view. The crucial final step is this: the role the *Grammar* assigns a language is now assigned to a language-game (a notion hinted at in *Grammar* §36). This is not yet to say much. It remains to say what a language-game is.

On the *Grammar* view, the notions *proposition* and *truth* admit of an indefinite variety of different understandings, where what they would apply to varies accordingly. In the *Investigations* the same goes for *any* notion. Language-games will show us how.

The role of the parochial will also now expand, or come into greater prominence. In the *Grammar*, insofar as a language could go wrong in presenting such-and-such as a proposition, its going wrong would consist in the fact that it so presented something which *we* could not treat as a proposition. The problem with which the last section ended was: What would it be for the *same* proposition (or thought) to have been expressed, say, in English and in French? The form this answer will now take is this: there were two expressions of the same proposition—two instances of saying the same thing—where that is what we are prepared to recognize—as we might well be for what the waiter said and my translation at the *Terminus du Nord*. This illustrates and adumbrates the role the parochial will now assume. Such addresses the second of our initial questions. But the same idea operates in the *Investigations'* response to the first: When is something a *proposition*—the content of a judgement, something truth-evaluable? The main locus of this response is §136.

The *Tractatus* gave a picture of the essence of representing. So does the *Investigations*, though it may seem odd to say so. The *Investigations* opens with that picture. Our first task will be to extract it.

3.1 The proposition as fundamental

Frege begins with propositions (thoughts), not with smaller units out of which propositions may be built. So *being* a given proposition is not the same thing as being built, in such-and-such a way, of such-and-such smaller units—just as, now, being a given proposition had better not be the same thing as being such-and-such bit of such-and-such language. In *Investigations* Wittgenstein shares Frege's view of the primacy of the whole (the whole attitude, or, at the opening of the *Investigations*, the whole speech act). But then, by what *is* a given proposition, or whole, identified as the one it is?

A proposition is the content of a judgement. Frege tells us (1918): to judge is to expose oneself to risk of error. Wittgenstein's answer could start from this. We are all, constantly, exposed to risk of error; each of us, at a time, in all the ways he then is. I am in for a comeuppance if today's meeting is not in Stewart House. I will find myself standing in an empty room, counter to my expectations. Your plans, perhaps, will also go awry if there is no meeting there, but perhaps differently—as it may be, the circulars you have left there will be all for nought. Judging that the meeting will be in Stewart House is *a* way to expose *oneself* to error. It is, here, an element in my exposure to risk, and in yours. It is something we share: both our exposures so decompose. Now we can adapt Wittgenstein's 1930 point about elements of a proposition (in its weaker Fregean form): to say that something is an element in an exposure to risk is to say that there is a *range* of exposures to error which are the same in a certain respect. So to say that I think the meeting is in Stewart House is to say that there is an identifiable shape for an exposure to error to have, which is recognizable in my exposure, and would be recognizable in the exposures of a certain range of other thinkers at other times; something for different exposures to share. The proposition is then identified by what would be, recognizably, *someone's* being exposed to risk in this particular way. (This sharability of judgement—a point Frege insists on—already eliminates the possibility of private language.)

One risks error (as Frege also insists) in one's dealings with what there is for *one* to meet with, notably with things in that environment we cohabit. It is in those dealings that the shape of thinking such-and-such is found. What we judge is what can matter to what to do—how to conduct them. Wittgenstein exploits this point.

3.2 'Im Anfang war die Tat'

Faust, translating the Bible's first line, was unimpressed by words. Power would be closer to a beginning. Its exercise—the act—would be closer still. Wittgenstein approved: action is the foundation of representation; representation is, essentially, by, and for, agents. A language-game is a device—an artificial one—which we can use to connect content and action explicitly. For this, we can take such a game to be fixed entirely by how it is to be played, which, further, we can think of as fixed by explicit rules. For a given game there are the moves to be made in playing it. For each of these, there are the rules which govern it. Rules govern *whole* moves. So these are the basic units of the game, just as, for Frege, the proposition is basic for logic.

We can divide the rules governing a move into introduction and elimination rules. Introduction rules say when a move may be made; elimination rules what follows from its correct making—notably, what then is to be, or may be, done. As it may be, if, in the game, I say, 'My glass is empty', the elimination rule for that specifies that you are to fill my glass.

A language-game can thus model particular connections between content and action. The content of given words 'My glass is empty' may consist, in part, in the way my glass is if they are correct; but also in part in what is to be done: you are to fill it. If in this first aspect a proposition is a picture of reality, this second suggests something else for it to be. In the *Grammar* Wittgenstein says,

> The role of a sentence in the calculus is its sense. (PG VI §84)

So a proposition might be identified by its role—by how it is eliminated, how to be acted on—rather than by the picture it provides. A language-game furnishes a reading for this thought.

3.3 The fundamental point: names and content

The *Investigations* begins by using the notion *language-game* to make a specific point as to what representing is. It is as follows.

Suppose a language-game contains a move, 'My glass is empty.' What do that move's parts name? Following Frege, something *is* a part of this move only relative to an analysis. Further, to be a part is to play a logical role: to perform a sub-task which, together with those performed by the move's other elements (on the relevant analysis) adds up to doing what the whole move does. We could say that 'My glass' was an element, and named my glass, if the correctness of the whole depended in some way on how my glass was (or, in the game, was to be treated)—if we then said suitable things as to what the remainder of that move did. Or, again, we could say this if the whole move required, or licensed, certain further moves (verbal or not), and if whether a move was what was thus licensed or required depended on how it related to, or treated, my glass. Similarly we could say that 'is empty' was an element and named being empty—that certain way for a glass to be—if the correctness of the move depended on something or other being empty, or if whether a further (putative) move was licensed or required by it turned on the credentials as a response to the thing(s) in question being empty.

In the opening part of the *Investigations* Wittgenstein takes over this much of Frege's view: there is nothing other than what the whole move does—hence nothing other than how the game is to be played (so, on our present idealization, its rules)—to determine what, in a move, names at all, and what any such thing does name. (PI §10) Saying that such-and-such is a part of a move and names such-and-such is nothing other than another way of saying part of what the rules of the whole game say as to what the move in question does.

Suppose, then, that 'My glass is empty' is a move in a game, such that 'My glass', in it, names a certain glass, and 'is empty' names (speaks of) being empty, *and* that the whole says my glass to be that way. Do these facts determine how that whole is to be treated? Of course not. What said a glass to be that way might require or license any of an indefinite variety of further moves, depending on the game. Do they determine when the move would be *correct* as to what it thus said (as to how my glass was)? Wittgenstein's answer is, 'No. Just as little as they determine how that whole is to be treated.' To see this, consider two games, each containing such a move. In the one, saying 'My glass is empty' licenses you in opening the champagne. The move is correct only if my glass stands ready (or at least is in condition) to receive the bottle's upward welling contents. In the other, the move requires you to refill my glass with pellets of fish food, and is correct only where my glass requires such refilling. Suppose that, in both cases, my glass lies at the bottom of the fish tank, immersed in water. Then the move, as a move in the first game, was incorrect, as a move in the second correct. Yet in both cases parts may be identified as suggested, and in both 'is empty' can be said to name (speak of) being empty. Being devoid of fish food *can* count as being empty for what deems being filled with it, the water it is immersed in notwithstanding. There are just various ways of speaking of a glass being empty, various language-games accordingly. *What parts name, within a given whole, does not, as such, determine when that whole would be correct.* Where correctness would be truth, what parts name determines no unique truth condition. This goes for parts which name such things as my glass and being empty. The moral of the first part of the *Investigations* is that it goes for words which speak of any determinate way things may be or not (or any admitting of novel instances). Language-games are but a convenient device for making this point.

Perhaps Frege is, unusually, a foil here. The culprit is captured in his idea (1891/1962) that a concept is a function from objects to truth values (though this *is* a culprit only on a certain reading of that 'is'). Suppose that in 'Sid snores', 'Sid' names Sid, and 'snores' names being a snorer—thus a function from objects to truth-values. Then the whole names the value of that function for the argument Sid. What these parts name thus does determine just when that whole would be true. The first point in the *Investigations* is that sense does not work like that. One must then explore *why* Frege spoke as if it did.

3.4 Languages

A move in a language-game is made correctly or not. For a part of the move to name such-and-such would be for it to make some specific contribution to when the move would be correct. English is not a game. Nor are its sentences correct or not per se. As we have just seen, 'My glass is empty' may be used to say different things, correct under different conditions, of a given glass. English asserts nothing. So nor do its sentences, unless spoken. When spoken, a sentence may say any of many things. So, on a Fregean account of what it is for something to be named, no bit of English names anything. Nor will a Fregean account of *being* a part apply here. Intuitively, though, English sentences *have* parts, which name, or speak of, things. What sense is to be made of this?

The key is aspect. There is a switch on my wall which operates the dryer. This does not make me worry about what it is up to while I am away. It is *flipping* the switch that does the work. The English 'is on the rug' speaks of being on a rug, in something like the way the switch operates the dryer. There is something 'is on the rug' is *for* in speaking English. Use it speaking English, and so as to say something, and there is something you will thus speak of: being on a then-given rug. What precise contribution this made to what you thus said remains to be negotiated (the *Investigations*' opening point) thus depends on the occasion. In this sense, so in this aspect of 'speak', 'is on the rug' speaks of being on a rug.

There are indefinitely many different language-games with moves in which 'is on the rug' speaks of being on the rug; in each of which, in so doing, it makes a different contribution to the proper treatment of the whole of which it is thus a part. Different such moves would be correct under different conditions, so on a different condition. The English 'is on the rug' is no more bound, by its role in English, to contribute to some one such condition than to contribute to any other. In meaning what it does, it is equally eligible to contribute to any. If this were not so, it would not speak of being on a rug, but rather of, say, being 'on' a rug, on some particular special understanding of 'on'. *It* speaks of being on a rug on a different understanding of *speaking* than that on which Pia is now speaking of this.

3.5 Language-games and what is said

Language-games link content to action. What one may do, or is to do, can be, in them, part of what it is for things to be as said. Propositions carve up exposures to risk of error in a particular way; confer particular understandings on *exposed in the same way*. Language-games carve up such risk by their rules. There is the risk one runs, in taking wine to be on the rug, where wine on the rug would call for salt, and the different risk one runs where wine on the rug would call for a corkscrew. There is something one might think which would be running the one risk and not the other. They thus show how, *pace* Frege, facts as to what parts name do not determine correctness conditions uniquely. This leads to a second departure from Frege.

What is the relation between saying something, in English, in saying, 'My glass is empty'— and playing a language-game? *Not* that to speak of a glass as empty is to play such-and-such game. Wittgenstein stresses that language-games are 'objects of comparison'. (See PI §§81, 130, 131.) Where I say 'My glass is empty', I may have said what would be so just where, or only where, those words would be a correct move in certain language-games. Such games would be one sort of object of comparison. We could use 'play' so as to speak of me as playing them.

Pia says, 'My glass is empty'. Sid, abashed, reaches for the wine. But the glass is in the sink, immersed in soapy water. Are things as Pia said? To say which language-games she was playing, on our present use of 'play', would be to answer that. Things are as she said if they are such as to make so speaking correct in those games—if things being as they are licensed introducing those words there. There *are* games in which such a move *is* correctly introduced. There are others in which it is not. In some it will do for Pia to have finished her wine. In others her glass must await a refill. A glass being empty admits of different understandings. Which games (of either sort) Pia played is a question of for what she is to be held responsible; to what she is hostage for things being as she said— whether, e.g., to her glass being refillable. How is responsibility assigned?

A game's elimination rules say how a move must, or may, be responded to; its introduction rules under what circumstances it is correctly made. If a game has an object, then its elimination rules may show things as to what its introduction rules ought to be—if it is not to be just stupid, or pointless, or senseless. If, say, 'My glass is empty' is eliminated by a refill, then (depending on what the game pretends to be) it may be just stupid or senseless to allow that move unless the relevant glass is, in fact, fillable. It may take a certain sort of introduction rule for given elimination rules to make sense. This models something central to assigning responsibility to those who say things.

Where Pia said to Sid, 'My glass is empty', one would have supposed, in the circumstances, there was a certain point to doing so. *One* would have supposed: such was *to be* supposed. It may be part of what one would have supposed the point to be that reaching for the bottle was, *ceteris paribus*, responding as called for, or at least licensed. (To know what was in fact so, one would have to know Pia, Sid, and the course of the evening, better.) *If* this is so, then (again *ceteris paribus*) it would have been stupid, not sensible, *then* to say 'My glass is empty' unless the glass was then apt for filling. It would be stupid to allow such a move in a game with such elimination rules and with a certain object. Which is to say that a sensible such game would have introduction rules permitting the move only where there was a glass in such condition. In the same way, in real life and real discourse, the stupidity of *then* speaking of a glass as empty when it is in the sink shows or fixes Pia's responsibilities; to what, in *so* speaking, she has made herself hostage for things being as she said—*inter alia*, a refillable glass. (There *may* have been *no* point in Pia saying what she did. There may, by the same token, be no saying whether things as they are is things as she said.) In this way language-games can model the assignment of responsibility, and thus of sense, content, to the things we in fact say.

In the *Grammar*, the parochial—the particular form of thought *we* are endowed with—decides what a *language* may be. This is fixed by what we can treat as one. The parochial now fixes what language-games are played when in our current sense of 'play'. What is stupid, what sensible, in the particular circumstances in which such thinkers as we in fact speak to one another is what would be stupid or sensible for us, by our lights. Which is to say: stupid, or sensible, for those engaging in conversation.

There are two things to be said in saying a glass to be empty: one true of the glass in the soapy water, the other not. Such is no threat to the Fregean idea of a concept as a *function*. It is just—so far—that some words, 'is empty', may name either of two of these. It is another matter when one assigns language-games the role just given them. For now we have a new way of carving up exposure to risk of error. It gives us, for *any* concept—for either of the above supposed two—different things it *could* be to fit *it*, so different things to be said, on different occasions, in saying something to fit it—different language-games one might be playing, on different such occasions, in so speaking. In the language-game of PI §2, the builder calls 'Slab!' and the assistant is to bring a slab. Suppose the assistant brings a broken slab. Is he correct? Nothing said so far decides this. But there *are* games in which it is decided—where it is specified that a slab in halves will do, or that it will not. For any given game, further games may thus refine it. Exposure to risk, carved in this way, is always liable to be carved more finely.

For Frege, there must be a way to identify what words said which finishes the parochial's work: when things would be the way they were *thus* said to be simply cannot depend on more about the circumstances of so saying. With language-games in the role now assigned them there is no such point. For *any* way things may be said to be—a way there is *for* them to be—there are always games one may or may not be playing in speaking of things as that way—differences always liable to matter to when things would be as said in so speaking. We thus arrive at a different picture of representing as so (in saying something). Whether things are as they were said to be on some given occasion is answered by the circumstances of so speaking, and our parochial perceptions of them. Nothing detachable from this, as for Frege a sense *for* words to have is detachable from an occasion of some words having it, answers all questions that could arise as to when things would be as they would thus be said to be.

Representation is *by* a certain sort of thinker *for* that sort. Its content is formed accordingly. Such is the *Investigations*' new conception of what representing is. It can be hard to see how the point could hold so generally. So far we have only discussed language. There is another important case.

3.6 Non-linguistic representing

The other principal case of representing things as so is representing things to oneself as so (taking them to be so, expecting them, noting them, etc.). If I am going to represent something to you as so, I need your attention. So I need something towards which attention can be directed: some perceivable vehicle which *bears* content. I do not need to attract my own attention to think something so. Nor could my representing to myself per vehicle (a note, say) be my thinking something so. Where there is no such vehicle, there is nothing to be *taken* in one way rather than another. It is so far obscure how the above idea of the work of the parochial can have any application in such a case. What is missing from the present story is thus an account of such attitudes as meaning, thinking, and understanding—a topic introduced in *Investigations* §81, and taken up seriously from §138 onwards. I cannot discuss that here.

Here, though, is a hint. Propositions are *one* device for carving up exposure to risk. Language-games are another. Such games are used in the *Investigations* to make a particular point, as above. This is not to banish the notion *proposition*. In suitable circumstances I may say to you, 'Pia said that there is wine on the rug', where this admits the response, 'And is there?' We may then go on to discuss 'the proposition that there is wine on the rug'. What proposition is this? When would it be true? I mentioned it in the words 'there is wine on the rug'. Things would be as they are according to that proposition when they would be as those words speak of things being. When that would be is fixed by the operation of parochial equipment on *my* words in just the way described, above, for Pia's. The above model of representing finds just this application here. Such a proposition, one might say, is what it is to us. Nor does it thereby speak of a way for things to be which admits of no divergent understandings. (Cf. PI §§429–65.)

4. THE LIMITS OF THE PAROCHIAL

The idea of language-games (and equally (PI §81) calculi) as objects of comparison gives the parochial a certain purchase on thought and its objects. Among other things, the parochial gains a role in how logic applies to thought. Which raises questions about Frege's conception of logic's distance from psychology. Here, I think, we encounter an unfinished area in Wittgenstein's thought. I will sketch a few issues.

4.1 Which things are propositions?

(The first of our three initial questions.) In the *Grammar*, it was for a language to tell us which things were propositions *in it*. A language could not tell us the *wrong* thing about this. There is no way it could be purporting that such-and-such were propositions where in fact they were not. With this *caveat*. A language cannot tell *us* that such-and-such is a proposition if we cannot grasp how such a thing could be a proposition (or if for us it just plainly is not one). A language which simply says that there is a contingent proposition that something is red and green at the same spot, Wittgenstein suggests, so far has not told us anything. One might say: what fits *our* notion *proposition* is what we are prepared to recognize as doing so. Here is what this idea has become in the *Investigations*:

> What a proposition is is in one sense determined by the rules of sentence formation (in English, for example), and in another sense by the use of the sign in the language game. And the use of the words 'true' and 'false' may be among the constituent parts of this game; and if so it *belongs* to our concept 'proposition' but does not 'fit' it. As we might also say, check *belongs* to our concept of the king in chess (as so to speak a constituent part of it). To say that check did not *fit* our concept of the pawns would mean that a game in which pawns were checked, in which, say, the players who lost their pawns lost, would be uninteresting or stupid or too complicated or something of the kind. (PI §136)

Here a role of a language, in the *Grammar*, has been taken over by language-games. The rules of English present us with things which *look* like propositions; sentences in some sense apt for stating them. But something *is* a proposition just where it functions as one in the language-games where it occurs.

Language-games, again, are objects of comparison. Pia said, 'My glass is empty.' Did she thus express a proposition? This is a question answered by finding the language-games she counts as thus having played. In those games do her words function as a proposition would? Are they truth-evaluable? Pia's words count as a proposition (or as stating one) just in case the answer to that question is yes. Again, the games she counts as playing are those the right sort of parochial thinker would be prepared to recognize as such. So, in this now-familiar way, the parochial informs the answer to this question.

In the *Grammar*, a *language* fixed an understanding of being a proposition on which it could be true or false to say that such-and-such was a proposition. The language fixed what it was one said in saying so. This function is now assumed by language-games, and, through them, by the parochial. Pia says, 'The room is dark'. There are the games she was thus playing (in our present sense). There are the moves she thus made (in this sense). These moves may be, or not (or express, or not) what we are prepared to recognize as truth-evaluable: in those games, the correctness of 'The room is dark' is to be settled in certain ways; these may or may not be, recognizably for us, ways for the *world* to decide the correctness of a stance as it would in deciding a question of truth. In speaking of a *proposition* that the room is dark, thus expressed by Pia, we say what would be correct or not accordingly. It is on *such* understandings of *proposition* that it may be true or false that such-and-such is one.

The point blocks one reading of PI §136. Imagine people who seriously supposed that it is either true or false that vanilla tastes better than chocolate, or that there is an understanding of a glass being empty on which the matter is decided by an oracle. Some have seen in Wittgenstein the view that, in such a case, all there is to say is, 'Such is the way of their people. For them, there *are* such propositions.' Such is not the present reading. Pia's words may be rightly understood to be purporting to say what is either true or false, and not merely to express sentiment. This may well militate, even heavily, in favour of so taking them. For all of which, if the words tell us that vanilla tastes better than chocolate, it may be wrong so to take them: there is not here a recognizable way for the *world* to speak on correctness. Pia's words cannot be so understood, so they are not to be: they are not, in fact, truth-evaluable. The ways of her people, the language she speaks, are not what is most central to giving *proposition* the understanding on which *we* speak of it. Perhaps the *Grammar* contains a suggestion to the contrary. Such is not the *Investigations* view.

The *Grammar* left us with a problem: if a proposition belongs to a language, how can the same proposition be, or be expressed, in different ones? We now have an answer. The waiter's 'Les oursins sont arrivés' and my 'The sea urchins have arrived' would be one proposition here if (so far as matters) for things to be as the waiter said is for them to be as I said, and vice versa. Which would be so if, so far as mattered, the games the waiter counted as thus playing made the same demands on the correctness of his words (and their treatment) as the ones I counted as playing made on mine. There is indefinite variety in the occasions there may be for raising, and speaking to, the question whether the waiter and I said the same (to be so). On a given one, there is what one who thought parochially as we do would then be prepared to recognize as to when things would be as he said, when as I did, and then as to whether it would be the same thing for things to be as he said and for things to be as I did. What a thinker of our sort would be prepared to recognize (whether this is *realizing* or *acknowledging*) is what one *would* suppose, thus what *is* to be. Propositions are to be counted, as one twice or two once, in different ways on different occasions, and on each according to what those who are to do the counting—thinkers of a particular sort—would (are prepared to) perceive as the same.

An issue remains. Suppose Pia says, 'That sculpture is both red and green just *there*' (pointing to a spot). Could she be counted as expressing a (possibly true) proposition while also counting as using 'red' to speak of red, and 'green' of green? If she expressed (or produced) a proposition, it is recognizable how things, in being as they are, may decide its truth or falsity—may instance the zero-place concept her words expressed. Perhaps that spot does not behave so as to count as red as opposed to green, or vice versa, on any understanding we can muster of it doing so. It may look, sometimes red to an observer, sometimes green, and otherwise behave sometimes as a red thing, sometimes as a green thing, would. But its total behaviour adds up neither to being red rather than green nor to the reverse. Might its behaviour nonetheless add up to its looking red, but not rather than green, and, equally, green, but not rather than red? If so, might this be the behaviour Pia ascribed it? Perhaps (there are sculptures like this) *one* can, by staring for a moment, both see it looking red and see it looking green (though not quite simultaneously). Might this not count as seeing, in one observation, both its being red and its being green? Can we talk this way? Could one so understand being red and being green? Such would supply the right sort of thing *for* Pia to say. The answer now is: there is such an understanding of being red and being green if we (thinkers of our sort) are prepared, in the circumstances, to recognize this as an understanding of that. If so, then, depending on how one would perceive Pia, she may have performed the feat in question. Nothing external to the perceptions we are thus prepared to have can dictate what they here must be.

4.2 The harmony of thought and reality

A proposition makes a demand on the world: to decide, in being as it is, the proposition's fate—true or false. The proposition fixes a way for the world to decide this—if the proposition is that the setting sun is red, then what about the world would make this so or not? Whether deciding things in that way would be deciding *truth* depends on parochial perceptions of what truth might be. But might the way thus fixed not fail to be a way for the world to decide anything at all? The proposition's way, say, supposes that there are such things as colours. Perhaps there just are not? If there is no such failure, we may say that proposition and world are in harmony. Where there is *room* for such failure, harmony is a substantial accomplishment on the part of the proposition. True propositions, of course, are in harmony with the world. But there is then something substantial a proposition must first accomplish to be so much as false. In what ways, if any, might harmony be substantial?

In PI §429 Wittgenstein says,

> The agreement, the harmony, of thought and reality lies in the fact that if I say falsely that something is *red*, still, for all that, it isn't *red*. And when I want to explain the word 'red' to someone, in the sentence 'That is not red', I do it by pointing to something red.

There is such a thing as (something) being red. So if a proposition demands that its truth be decided by something being red or not, there is (*ceteris paribus*) a way for the world to oblige. So there is harmony. Suppose there were no such thing as being red. Then if a proposition demanded that its truth be decided in that way, it would be out of harmony with the world. So if it could do such a thing, then there is the possibility of disharmony, and harmony is a substantial accomplishment. But could it? If there were no such thing as being red, how would a proposition impose such a demand?

If propositions cannot do such things, this is not to say that it is decided, independent of how the world is, which demands are harmonious. It is not yet to say that one can raise questions of truth so formulated that the world *could* do no other than answer them. Frege sometimes speaks as if there were. The *Grammar*'s idea of the arbitrariness of grammar *could* be read so as to suggest this: there is no external standpoint from which a grammar can be held to generate propositions *wrongly* because, whatever it dictates as to how the world is to decide their fate, there is no such thing as the world failing to comply. Modulo logical consistency, one can stipulate just anything.

This sits ill with the *Investigations*' conception of what representing is. Max has knocked over a glass again. Wine spills. Pia says to Sid, 'There is wine on the rug.' But *this* rug is covered with an invisible, removable, film. No molecule of wine reaches any fibre of it. Is there wine on it on the understanding on which Pia said so? Pia raised a question of truth. The world might have been such as to answer it. There might not have been the film. But the world *is* such as to answer it only if Pia's words are one of two ways: such that she is to be held responsible for no more than what is so, or that she is responsible for more (for wine reaching fibres, say). They are the first way just if one (a thinker of a certain sort) would so perceive them. The same goes for their being the second. But a thinker of the right sort *need* not be such as to perceive them either in the one way or the other. Faced with the facts, one may be at a loss. More generally, there need be nothing that one (of the right sort) would find. Correspondingly, it need not be that the world answers the question of truth that Pia raised.

It is one thing for there to be such a thing as something being red. It is another for the world in fact to decide whether such-and-such is red. If there is such a thing as being red, then a *proposition* can, intelligibly, ask the world to decide its fate according to whether such-and-such is red, on some understanding or other of what its being red would be. The world need not oblige. There is that much room at least for disharmony between the way a proposition asks its fate to be decided and the deciding in fact done by things being as they are. That the world does what a proposition asks it to is not achieved by stipulation.

For Wittgenstein, the sense to be made of an explanation *explaining* or failing to is such that some do explain and some do not, and that one is or not 'is no longer a philosophical proposition, but an empirical one'. (PI §85) Similarly, the sense (so far) to be made of disharmony is such that some propositions are in harmony with things and some are not, and that one is or not is an empirical matter. Here is another key idea in later Wittgenstein. Austin had it too, and expressed it thus:

> The feelings of royalty…or fakirs or bushmen or Wykehamists or simple eccentrics—these may be very hard to divine…(Austin 1946/1979, 104)

Can we know the mind of another? Sometimes not. Which supposes there are two kinds of case. A Salopian, perhaps, can never know what *he*, a Wykehamist, was thinking when he said *that*: you would need the Winchester experience. So there is such a thing as knowing. This contrasts with what the philosopher says in saying that one can never know the mind of another. Here there is no such thing as knowing this. On inspection we also lose our grip on what knowing it is meant to be. The philosopher produces something which *looks* like the empirical proposition, but which, Austin suggests, is in fact senseless. The empirical ones capture all the sense there *is* in the idea of knowing, or not, the mind of another. Similarly, for Wittgenstein, that *this* explanation failed to explain, as opposed to *this* one, which succeeded, captures all the sense there is in the idea of an explanation explaining or failing to; that *this* proposition was not in harmony with reality as opposed to *this* one which was captures all the sense there is to the idea of harmony. And so on.

And so on. For some practical ends or other I want, on occasion, to speak as if I knew, or *might* know, what Pia was thinking. For those purposes I accordingly understand knowing to be such-and-such achievable status—an interesting status for the ends in view. For some practical ends or other I speak, and think, as though Pia had spoken truth, or, at worst, falsehood—as though in harmony with how things are. I thus understand harmony as though it were such-and-such achievable condition. To achieve the generality he wants, the philosopher prescinds from practical ends. In this sense he aims for a perspective on the relevant phenomenon. What is it to *know* the mind of another, full stop—independent of any practical use to talk of knowing this or not? Similarly for thought being harmonious. Wittgenstein's point, and Austin's, is that when a philosopher makes this move he stops making sense. From a transcendental standpoint there is nothing to be said.

In the *Investigations* this is a point of principle. It is a corollary to the view there of what representing in words is. Words are to have a point, ends to serve. They are by given thinkers, for thinkers of a given sort. This setting is to give them such point. Point's role is to fix how things are according to the words; *how* the world is to speak to things being as thus said or not. This role is substantial. The world does speak only where it has been played adequately. Such is a substantial requirement on the harmony of words and world. Such is the idea of the essence of representation elaborated in section 3. The abstraction the philosopher aims for precisely blocks the playing of any such role. It thereby blocks making sense. This entirely general point applies in particular to the philosopher who tries to see our ordinary perceptions of truth and falsity as leaving open some further question as to whether our thought is 'really' in harmony with things.

Would-be transcendental propositions, in the present sense, fail to express thoughts in just the way that private language (as per §§243–308) does. What would instance a way for things to be transcendentally, just as what would instance a way for things to be privately, is beyond the reach of the parochial—of what *one*, a thinker of a certain sort, would recognize. On the *Investigations* view, the parochial gives Frege's fundamental logical relation its purchase: allows for facts as which ways for things to be are instanced by the ways things are, and which are the instances of given ways there are for things to be. The parochial's involvement is a condition on the satisfaction of concepts by the non-conceptual, so on representations according to which such-and-such is so—a condition failed equally by would-be private, and by would-be transcendental, thought.

Frege stresses intersubjectivity—availability to *one*—as a condition for being a thought at all. As he notes, this rules out private thought. But it may seem—and may have seemed to him—to leave room for transcendental thought in the present sense: (zero-place) concepts instanced or not full stop, quite apart from any transient point in taking them to be; quite apart from any parochial perception. This last 'one', read widely enough, may even seem to require this. Thinking through, with Wittgenstein, this idea of availability to *one*—of the *same* thought to many—exposes such appearances as mere illusion (if he is right). For, on inspection, it takes the parochial to make good sense of 'same thought'. Such different diagnoses of the incoherence of the idea of private thought mark perhaps the greatest divergence between Frege and later Wittgenstein.

4.3 The hardest thing

A law of logic, Frege tells us, cannot be *explained*, except, perhaps, by other laws of logic. There is nothing (other than more logic) in virtue of which it holds. What brooks no explaining is what *could* not be otherwise—there is no such thing. So it is, on Frege's view, with logic: the *hardest* sort of necessity. What sort is that?

I invite you onto my balcony. You fear it will collapse. I tell you, 'Don't worry. It can't collapse.' Momentarily, you feel relieved. Then I explain: 'Whatever happens, it won't count as my balcony collapsing. It's part of what collapsing is that nothing counts as a *balcony* doing it.' Your relief vanishes. If I am right, the balcony cannot *collapse*. For all of which it might *shmollapse*—like collapsing, except done by a balcony; equally injurious to health. If it really is part of the concept of collapsing that balconies cannot do it, then there is, really, no such thing as a balcony doing it. That my balcony will not holds with that kind of necessity. But such necessity is, as a rule, cold comfort.

Perhaps it is, similarly, part of the concept *proposition* that nothing is one unless governed by Frege's laws of logic. Which leaves open that there might be gropositions, equally useful guides to exposure to error in dealings with the world, equally central to a cognitive economy as rich as ours, but governed by other laws. This is not what Frege had in mind.

Descartes (*Discours*, part 5) pointed to ways our abilities to solve problems, and to communicate, are qualitatively different from those of other animals (as he saw them): a plasticity, and versatility in our dealings with the world which other creatures lack. He called that qualitative difference *intelligence*. Stances in which we risk error at the world's hands are central to such plasticity. If there were a sort of stance which could play this role, while not subject to Frege's laws, intelligence, so thought in any sense that mattered, might be otherwise than those laws prescribe. Logic would not be necessary for thought in the sense Frege had in mind. The *hardest* necessity is not bought on the cheap.

Wittgenstein's view of same-saying does not, anyway, allow *part of the concept* to do the work to which it has just been put. Perhaps, in *some* good sense, it is part of the concept *red* that nothing can be red and green at the same point. Such *can* be put by saying, 'There is no such thing as that.' What we cannot rule out is that, confronted with the unexpected, we will *learn* how to make sense of it—that there will turn out to be something for *this* to be. If someone claims to have discovered such a thing, we (may) need to *look*. Whether he has is a verdict to be given by our *parochial* sensitivities. Such is doubtfully the hardness Frege had in mind.

For Frege, it is part of what judging, so what a proposition, is that for every proposition there is another true just where it is false, and vice versa; for every two propositions there is one true just where both are, and so on. Suppose, confronting the unexpected, we come to speak of 'propositions' which do not always form conjunctions. Would we be speaking of *propositions*? Or of truth? The usual story about speaking of the same thing applies. There are different ways of reading Frege. But his conception of logical necessity *seems* to call for something outside the parochial dictating its verdict on such a point. It would be *wrong* if it allowed propositions which did not form conjunctions: there is *absolutely* no such thing as that.

What logic is, Frege *rightly* held, should not be hostage to chemistry, or geology. Nor should it be hostage to psychology. So, he held, it should not be shaped by anything parochial. *Empirical* psychology does not study what *any* thinker must be. That is not an empirical issue. It only investigates ways we are *different* from what a creature might be. But the parochial is precisely what a thinker need not be. Might psychology not study that—say, what *we* would recognize as a proposition when? Is it not then studying what logic might be?

(Human) psychology studies a particular form of thought. A law of logic should apply to *all* thought—to thought by any thinker. If there are Martians, then if a Martian holds a certain *proposition true*, the same laws of logic apply to him as to us. Nor do laws of logic change. 'From *that A & B, that A* follows up until 2050, but afterwards not always' is shaped wrong to be a law of logic.

For later Wittgenstein, the above conception of hardness misunderstands such truisms. Just as, in the *Grammar*, there is no *independent* standard by which a language might be found to say wrongly what its propositions are, so, in the *Investigations*, there is no external standard by which our parochial equipment might say the wrong things as to how propositions might behave. The misunderstanding makes this seem to threaten the very idea of logic. As Wittgenstein puts it,

> But what becomes of logic now? Its rigour seems to be giving way here.—But in that case doesn't logic altogether disappear?—For how can it lose its rigour? (PI §108)

The objection comes to this. Logic fixes a way *any* proposition must behave, independent of how anyone is parochially equipped. So the parochial equips us to recognize the *right* things only if it equips us to acknowledge just this as the behaviour of any proposition. (One might even—inadvisedly, for Wittgenstein—hold there to be no such thing as acknowledging the *wrong* things.) So for a proposition to behave *thusly* is *not* just for us to be equipped to acknowledge this. There *is* a standard independent of us which decides, so far as logic reaches, what a proposition *really* is.

A way of working towards what the misunderstanding is here is to see just how much of Frege's good motives can be honoured while holding to the *Investigations'* view of the autonomy of the parochial—that development of the *Grammar* idea of the autonomy of language. A preliminary. On a Fregean conception of logic, a law of logic forms a system with all other thoughts; its structure (so its place in it) mirrors the most general structure of that system. That notion of 'all other thoughts' became inadmissible in the *Grammar* and remains inadmissible in the *Investigations*. So we need a new idea of how it is that logic speaks to the things we in fact think. The *Investigations'* new idea is hardly unfamiliar nowadays. It is in §§81, 130, 131. A logical calculus is now an object of comparison in just the way a language-game is. I introduced, above, a notion of playing a language-game: on it, Pia, in saying, 'Wine is on the rug', is playing a language-game in which one says that if, in the circumstances of her speaking, those words (of hers) are subject to the standards of correctness fixed by the rules governing that move in that game.

A (familiar) logical calculus does not have moves in it which consist of words; no moves such as 'Wine is on the rug.' It has formulae, consisting of variables, or placeholders, and proprietary signs for logical constants. Such a formula is a possible move in constructions the calculus designates as 'proof-structures'. As such it is subject to a standard of correctness given by the introduction and elimination rules governing its main connective. Suppose we assign each of some list of thoughts—things said in some 'The room is dark', in some 'There's wine on the rug', etc.—a formula. Then we might say this assignment *models*, jointly, those respective things said just in case they are jointly subject to those standards of correctness fixed by the rules governing those formulae in the calculus.

A familiar calculus is an expression of some laws of logic. By the laws, propositions analysable as of certain forms behave in certain ways. What is analysable as a conjunction, for example, entails each of its conjuncts so analysed. To model an item by a formula with a certain main connective is to analyse it as a conjunction. Where, and insofar as, the item is correctly so modelled, it counts as so behaving. The calculus spells out what that behaviour is. On the *Investigations'* view it is thus that logic speaks through a calculus to thought.

A law of logic is a generalization: *any* conjunction behaves thus and so. That generalization seems about all propositions. We now have a new way of understanding that idea. For now the law need not (and cannot) be understood in terms of some domain over which it extends. Rather, we can think of the law as an instruction, somewhat along these lines. Suppose you are treating some given things as propositions. You must, for any two things you so treat, recognize a third, true precisely when they both are. Suppose you treat some further item as such a third thing. Refer to a calculus which thus models what you are doing (on the above notion of modelling) to see to what you are thus committed.

There is point in this way of thinking of how logic speaks. For a start, it allows us the idea that how a given proposition *is* correctly modelled—so how logic says it must behave—may depend on the occasion for asking what standards of correctness in fact govern it—notably, what standards logic in fact imposes. In particular, it may depend on in the context of which other propositions this one is so to behave or not. Pia says, 'If Sid is already on the motorway, then he will get here on time.' She has expressed a proposition which may be modelled, for some purposes, as a conditional in that proprietary sense of familiar calculi. Logic speaks accordingly. Similarly, if Zoë says, 'If Sid has an accident, he will not be on time.' But this does not mean that it follows from the truth of what each said that if Sid is on the motorway he will not have an accident. Sometimes-correct modellings of each proposition do not jointly form a correct modelling of the pair. Do not model the one in the suggested way in the context of so modelling the other. What is sometimes a good modelling need not always be. We have gained that much.

But, it seems, there must be more than this that logic says to thought, or at least more to say to honour Frege's worthy intuitions. So far, logic, as expressed through a calculus, lays down standards of correctness to which given propositions *may* be subject—if correctly modelled in such-and-such ways. This does not capture the Fregean idea that any proposition (thought) *must* be subject to logic's laws—that one cannot think, because there is no such thing as thinking *illogically*—not that one cannot make logical mistakes, but that one cannot think so as to be governed by standards of correctness at odds with logic's. Nor does it capture for him the absolutely central idea that a law of logic admits of no extra-logical explanation—that, where such a law is concerned, there *cannot* be anything to be explained extra-logically.

We can start from this idea: for what really is a law of logic, no modelling in our present sense which contravened it—which assigned some proposition a standard of correctness inconsistent with it—could be correct. So, since on our present notion of modelling, a proposition, on one, is assigned properties of some formula in a calculus, no calculus which assigned a formula properties inconsistent with the law (e.g. through ill-matched introduction and elimination rules) could model anything. Such things are, literally, inconceivable, as, on Frege's view, they must be.

Which bears on our second question. If it is inconceivable that a law of logic—say, a law capturing conjunction elimination—should not hold, that is one reason, perhaps among several, why the law does not admit of chemical explanation. Nothing explains why things cannot be otherwise where there is no such thing as their being otherwise (except, perhaps, that fact). It is not that if chemistry were different things here might be otherwise. So nor, equally, does its being as it is explain their not. And where otherwise is inconceivable, there is no such thing as being it. If there is anything specially inept about chemistry here, equally so for psychology. For if there were a psychological explanation of a law of logic, there could, in principle, be a chemical one too. As Frege says, whether we *had* the right psychology for the law to be a law *might* turn out to depend on the level of phosphorus in the cerebral cortex. (See 1897/1979, 148.)

We cannot recognize any modelling as correct if it violates what really is a law of logic. We could not correctly model Pia's thoughts, or talk, that way. Nor, equally, a Martian's. If we can ascribe to a Martian the property of thinking such-and-such (so), then what we ascribe to him is thinking one of the things we can recognize there are to think—one of the things, thus, there is for *us* to think—a fortiori, something with the logical features that something there is for us to think would have. As a special case, this is so of the modelling of thought we can ascribe to a Martian—the logical features we can take him to take a thought to have.

We cannot recognize a modelling as correct if it assigns to thoughts features logic says they cannot have. Nor could such a modelling *be* correct. Such is inconceivable. But is it good fortune that what we are prepared to recognize as possible and impossible assignments of logical features to the thoughts we model just happen to be the combinations that really are, respectively, conceivable and inconceivable? Should we give thanks for this? Or is it that what is conceivable, what inconceivable, just *is* what we are prepared to recognize as such? And if the latter—no thanks due, on this score, to a deity—then is this not just our parochial capacities shaping what there is for logic to say?

Wittgenstein says, in a slightly different connection,

> 'There is another solution as well' means: there is something else that I am also prepared to call a 'solution'; to which I am prepared to apply such-and-such a picture...and so on. (PI §140)

For 'there is another solution' one might say, 'there is this combination of logical features', or 'there is this modelling'. So 'logic permits thoughts which behave *thus*, but not ones which behave *so*' means 'I am prepared to recognize thoughts which behave *thus*, but not *so*.' Which, Wittgenstein tells us, 'We might also be inclined to express...like this: we are at most under a psychological, not a logical compulsion.' (PI §140) Logic, that is, places us at most under pyschological compulsion. To which Wittgenstein responds, 'And now it looks quite as if we knew of two kinds of case.' (Ibid.)

These two kinds of case correspond to two notions of recognizing, marked in Dutch and German by different verbs ('herkennen' and 'erkennen'; 'erkennen' and 'anerkennen'). 'Herkennen' (Dutch), or 'erkennen' (German), speaks of a cognitive accomplishment—re-cognition, or identification of something as what it *is*. (Kamagurka: 'Een mooie vrouw herken je aan haar uiterlijk.') 'Erkennen' (Dutch) or 'anerkennen' (German) is being prepared, or committed, to treat something as with a certain status, granting or accepting credentials. 'For me, in my book, she is a leading philosopher' ('She is what *I* call a leading philosopher') versus 'She *is* a leading philosopher', invoking, or presupposing, an agreed standard for being one.

The one sort of recognition is not in general the other. But the two are not *always* to be distinguished. To be prepared as one is to grant credentials—to *call* something a case of such-and-such—may be to be prepared to grant credentials where they are due. Which may be to be able to recognize cases where they are due—cases which do, in fact, count as that such-and-such. It may be to be *equipped* for cognitive *achievements*. A fluent Dutch speaker would *recognize* a certain difference between 'herkennen' and 'erkennen'. On what notion of *recognize*? What would doing the one thing rather than the other come to here? Do we know of two kinds of case—two ways for the fluent speaker to be? A fluent speaker bestows credentials just where they are earned. We accept the sun as it is on the horizon as something its being red might be. What more is needed for there to be this to be *identified* as something its being red might be, and then for us to be equipped to make such identifications? We are prepared to accept (in the end) certain modellings of thoughts as possible, others not. Is there any more question of two kinds of cases here—mere acceptance, short of recognition—than in those others? For Frege, logic, recognizably (by us), dictates such-and-such. Is there really room here for *different* application for our two notions of 'recognize'?

This question begins, rather than ends, a story. The above sketches some of the material Wittgenstein has given us for dealing with it.

References

AUSTIN, J. L. (1946/1979). 'Other Minds', in J. O. Urmson and G. J. Warnock eds., *Philosophical Papers*. Oxford: Clarendon Press.
CHOMSKY, NOAM (1965). *Aspects of the Theory of Syntax*. Cambridge, MA: MIT Press.
FREGE, GOTTLOB (1891/1962). 'Funktion und Begriff', in *Funktion, Begriff, Bedeutung*, ed. G. Patzig. Göttingen: Vandenhoeck und Ruprecht.
—— (1892a/1979). 'Comments on Sense and Meaning', in H. Hermes, F. Kambartel, and F. Kaulbach eds., *Posthumous Writings*. Oxford: Blackwell.
—— (1892b/1986). 'Über Begriff und Gegenstand', in *Funktion, Begriff, Bedeutung*, ed. G. Patzig. Göttingen: Vandenhoeck und Ruprecht.

—— (1897/1979). 'Logic', in H. Hermes, F. Kambartel, and F. Kaulbach eds., *Posthumous Writings*. Oxford: Blackwell.

—— (1906/1979). 'Introduction to Logic', in H. Hermes, F. Kambartel, and F. Kaulbach eds., *Posthumous Writings*. Oxford: Blackwell.

—— (1918). 'Der Gedanke', *Beiträge zur Philosophie des deutschen Idealismus*, 1: 58–77.

—— (1919/1979). 'Notes for Ludwig Darmstaedter', in H. Hermes, F. Kambartel, and F. Kaulbach eds., *Posthumous Writings*. Oxford: Blackwell.

WAISMANN, FRIEDRICH (1979). *Wittgenstein and the Vienna Circle, Conversations recorded by Friedrich Waismann*, ed. B. McGuinness, trans. B. McGuinness and J. Schulte. Oxford: Blackwell.

WITTGENSTEIN, LUDWIG (1951). *Tractatus Logico-Philosophicus*, trans. C. K. Ogden. London: Routledge & Kegan Paul.

—— (1974). *Philosophical Grammar*, ed. R. Rhees, trans. A. Kenny. Oxford: Basil Blackwell.

—— (1980). *Wittgenstein's Lectures 1930–1932: From the notes of John King and Desmond Lee*, ed. D. Lee. Oxford: Blackwell.

—— (1993). *Philosophical Occasions 1912–1951*, ed. J. Klagge and A. Nordmann. Indianapolis: Hackett Publishing Company.

—— (1997). *Philosophical Investigations*, 2nd edn, ed. G. E. M. Anscombe and R. Rhees, trans. G. E. M. Anscombe. Oxford: Blackwell.

CHAPTER 10

....

LOGICAL ATOMISM IN RUSSELL AND WITTGENSTEIN

....

IAN PROOPS

INTRODUCTION

....

RUSSELL and Wittgenstein develop different, though closely related, versions of a position that has come to be known as 'logical atomism'. Wittgenstein's version is presented in the *Tractatus*, and discussed in the various pre-*Tractatus* manuscripts. Russell's is presented most fully in a set of eight lectures given in Gordon Square, London in early 1918. These lectures, which are familiar to us today under the title 'The Philosophy of Logical Atomism' (Russell 1918/1956: 175–281, hereafter 'PLA'), were originally serialized in the *Monist* during the years 1918 and 1919. In them Russell attempts to synthesize his own ideas with those of Wittgenstein's 1913 *Notes on Logic*. Although PLA is often treated as the definitive presentation of Russell's logical atomism, we should not forget that Russell had already arrived at many elements of this doctrine before he encountered Wittgenstein. This earlier, pure Russellian, brand of logical atomism is first set out in Russell's 1911 article 'Analytical Realism'[1]—a text in which the phrase 'logical atomism' appears for the first time. (See Monk 1996, 200.) It is further developed in certain chapters of the *Problems of Philosophy* of 1912.[2]

Analytical realism, Russell explains, is a form of *atomism* because it maintains—in contrast to the British Hegelianism of Bradley, McTaggart, Joachim, and others,[3] first,

---

[1] *Collected Papers* (hereafter 'CP'), vol. 6: 133–46.

[2] This work was composed in the summer of 1911, and so before Russell's first encounter with Wittgenstein.

[3] In PLA too Russell characterizes his position as atomistic in contrast to 'people who more or less follow Hegel' (PLA: 178). There he emphasizes against the Hegelians that analysis does not involve falsification (ibid.).

that the existence of the complex depends on the existence of the simple and not vice versa, and, second, that the atomic entities in its ontology (universals and particulars) have their nature quite independently of the relations they bear to one another.[4] (Notice that this means that the 'atoms' countenanced by analytical realism need not be simple. And, indeed, as we shall see, Russell says things that imply that some of them are complex.) Analytical realism is a *logical* atomism because its atoms need not exist in time or space. In Russell's terminology they are 'purely logical' (*CP*, vol. 6: 135).

Russell advertised PLA as 'very largely concerned with explaining certain ideas which I learnt from my friend and former pupil Ludwig Wittgenstein' (*CP*, vol. 6: 177, cf. 205). And under his influence the term 'logical atomism' became associated with Wittgenstein's early philosophy. In PLA, possibly as a result of Wittgenstein's influence, Russell changes his account of what it is that makes logical atomism *logical*. He now maintains that what makes it appropriate to speak of *logical* atomism is that the atoms in question are to be arrived at by logical rather than physical analysis (PLA: 179). For Wittgenstein, too, the genuine constituents of states of affairs are to be revealed by a process of logical analysis (see section 4 below); so, to that extent, the label may be aptly applied to his Tractarian position. Such a use is not, however, uncontroversial (see Floyd 1998).

The core tenets of Wittgenstein's logical atomism may be summarized as follows: (i) Every proposition has a unique final analysis that reveals it to be a truth-function of elementary propositions (TLP 3.25, 4.221, 4.51, 5); (ii) These elementary propositions assert the existence of atomic states of affairs (4.21); (iii) Elementary propositions are mutually independent—each one can be true or false independently of the truth or falsity of the others (4.211, 5.134); (iv) Elementary propositions are immediate combinations of semantically simple symbols or 'names' (4.221); (v) Names refer to items wholly devoid of complexity, so-called 'objects' (2.02, 3.22); (vi) Atomic states of affairs are combinations of these simple objects (2.01).

1. NAMES AND OBJECTS

The 'names' spoken of in the *Tractatus* are not mere signs (i.e. typographically or phonologically identified inscriptions), but rather signs-together-with-their-meanings—or 'symbols' in Tractarian parlance. Being symbols, names are identified and individuated only in the context of significant sentences. A name is 'semantically simple' in the sense that its meaning does not depend on the meanings of its orthographic parts, even when those parts are, in other contexts, independently meaningful (cf. 4.24). So, for example, it would not count against the semantic simplicity of the symbol 'Battle' as it figures in the sentence 'Battle commenced' that it contains the orthographic part 'Bat', even though this part has a meaning of its own in other sentences. Something else does count against

---

[4] *CP*, vol. 6: 133–4.

this symbol's semantic simplicity, namely, the fact that it is analysable away in favour of talk of the actions of people, etc. This point illustrates the difficulty of finding examples of Tractarian names in natural language. It turns out that even the apparently simple singular terms of everyday language—e.g. 'Plato', 'London', etc.—will not be counted as 'names' by the strict standards of the *Tractatus* since they will disappear on further analysis. (Details of how their 'disappearance' is effected are provided in section 2.1 below.)

For the sake of expository convenience, the capitalized term 'Name' will henceforth be reserved for (a) Tractarian names and (b) what Russell calls 'names in the strict logical sense' (PLA: 201). Because Russell lacks a technical term for the referent of a Name, the capitalized term 'Object' will be used for this purpose. In connection with Wittgenstein the term 'object' will be used for the same purpose, as will 'Tractarian object'. The words that pass for names in ordinary language, such as 'Plato' and 'Socrates', will be referred to as 'ordinary names'.

Whereas Wittgenstein expects not to find Names among the vocabulary of vernacular language,[5] Russell believes that some of the words in everyday use do have this status. In PLA he mentions 'this' and 'that' as examples of 'names in the proper strict logical sense of the word', and he takes them to stand for 'actual object[s] of sense' (i.e. sense-data) (PLA: 201). For Russell there is no more to a sign's being a Name for something than: (a) our being acquainted with the Object[6] it Names; and (b) our knowing that it Names it (PLA: 205). This suggests that at this stage he is committed to counting anything with which we are acquainted as in principle Nameable.[7] What, then, are the objects of acquaintance? In the *Problems of Philosophy* (POP) Russell explains that they include both particulars and universals:

> Among particulars we have acquaintance with sense-data and (probably) with ourselves. Among universals, there seems to be no principle by which we can decide which can be known by acquaintance, but it is clear that among those that can be so known are sensible qualities, relations of space and time, similarily and certain abstract logical universals. (POP: 62)

It seems reasonable to infer that at this stage Russell would have counted both the word 'I' and terms for certain qualities and relations as Names. Evidently, Russell's commitment to the self as an object of acquaintance is only tentatively held. And he expressly repudiates the associated view that 'I' functions as a logically proper name in his 1914 essay 'On the Nature of Acquaintance' (Marsh 1956: 164).

---

[5] The *Notebooks* entry for 23 May 1915 would support this claim. 'It also seems certain that we do not infer the existence of simple objects from the existence of particular simple objects.' If we knew concerning certain words that they were Names, we would be able to do precisely that.

[6] Russell speaks of the particular with which a speaker is acquainted where I have spoken of the Object. But that is just because in this context he is implicitly confining his discussion to *proper* names, which are Names, specifically, of particulars.

[7] It is significant that in PLA when Russell says that the only words one does use as 'names in the strict logical sense' are 'this' and 'that' he does so in the context of a discussion of names 'in the narrow logical sense of a word *whose meaning is a particular*' (PLA: 201). Relaxing the restriction to words for particulars would involve admitting further expressions as names in the strict logical sense.

It is a more controversial matter whether Wittgenstein includes properties and relations among the bearers of Tractarian names. The view that he declines to do so has been defended by Irving Copi (Copi 1958) and Elizabeth Anscombe (Anscombe 1971 [1959]: 108 ff.), among others. Arguably, such a view is supported by *Tractatus* 2.0231, which runs: '[Material properties] are first presented by propositions—first formed by the configuration of objects' (2.0231). If 'material properties' are first formed by the *configuration* of objects (which the *Tractatus* holds to be simple), then they can scarcely *be* objects. Of course, by itself, *Tractatus* 2.0231 does not preclude the possibility that *non-material* properties might count as objects, so it could provide compelling support for the Copi–Anscombe reading only if it were supplemented with a reason to think that non-material properties are not the kind of things that can be the bearers of Tractarian names. Such a reason might be provided by the observation that in the present context the modifier 'material' appears to be intended to establish a contrast with those properties that comprise an object's combinatory possibilities. (Such combinatory possibilities are said to constitute an object's 'form' at 2.0141, and Wittgenstein speaks of 'forms' where we might speak of 'types' at 4.1241. So when he speaks of 'formal properties' of objects at 4.122 it is plausible that he has in mind just their possibilities of combination with other objects.) Since combinatory possibilities are not candidates to be the bearers of *Tractarian* names, the sought-for supplementary ground is arguably available.

The Copi–Anscombe interpretation has been taken to receive further support from *Tractatus* 3.1432: 'We must not say, "The complex sign 'aRb' says 'a stands in relation R to b';" but we must say, "*That* 'a' stands in a certain relation to 'b' says *that aRb*."' This has suggested to some commentators that relations are not, strictly speaking, Nameable (cf. Ricketts 1996: 72–3). But it might rather be taken to indicate just that Names themselves are not confined to particulars, but include relations between certain signs and even properties of those signs. On this picture, a proper Name would be a particular sign that means a particular, a relation between such particular signs would mean (i.e. be a Name of) a relation, and a property of such a sign would mean (i.e. be a Name of) a property. So this second consideration is less compelling than the first.

The opposing view, according to which Names include predicates and relational expressions in addition to symbols for particulars, has been defended by Erik Stenius and Merrill and Jaakko Hintikka, among others (Stenius 1960: 61–9; Hintikka and Hintikka 1986: 30–34). It is supported by a *Notebooks* entry from 1915 in which Tractarian objects are expressly said to include properties and relations (NB: 61), and further buttressed by Wittgenstein's explanation to Desmond Lee (WL) of *Tractatus* 2.01: ' "Objects" also include relations; a proposition is not two things connected by a relation. "Thing" and "relation" are on the same level' (WL: 120). It derives further—if less direct—support from a remark from the *Tractatus*: 'In an atomic state of affairs objects hang one in another, like the links of a chain' (2.03). Wittgenstein was later to explain this remark to C. K. Ogden as meaning that: 'There isn't anything third that connects the links but ... the links themselves make the connection with one another' (LO: 23). The idea is that the reference of every name is, as Frege would say, 'in need of saturation', so that each object plays an equal role in securing the unity of the atomic state of affairs in which it occurs. It is natural to think of this point as being paralleled at the level of language by the idea that every Name is in a related sense 'unsaturated', and plays an equal role in securing the unity of the proposition in which it occurs.

This idea might be developed as follows: In the four-constituent elementary proposition '*ABCD*' we might think of each Name as multiply unsaturated—that is to say, as having a triadic '*n*-adicity'. This model of the elementary proposition is the mirror image of that of Copi and Anscombe, for now *none* of its constituents is taken to name a particular. This model has the merit of exemplifying the Tractarian idea that we cannot conceive of something as a Name outside the context of an elementary proposition (cf. 4.23), for it is only in the context of a given elementary proposition that a Name's *n*-adicity is determinate.

Like the Copi–Anscombe reading, the view just outlined treats the forms of elementary propositions as differing radically from anything we might be familiar with from ordinary—or even Fregean—grammar. Both interpretations thus chime with Wittgenstein's 1929 warning to Waismann that 'The logical structure of elementary propositions need not have the slightest similarly with the logical structure of [non-elementary] propositions' (WVC: 42).

2. LINGUISTIC ATOMISM

By 'linguistic atomism' we shall understand the view that the analysis of every proposition terminates in a proposition all of whose genuine components are Names. Russell believes that the analysis of complexes terminates in simples, though he admits that, for all he can *show*, analysis might go on forever (PLA: 202). If the complexes he has in mind include linguistic complexes, such as sentences, then we may take him to believe in linguistic atomism. But Russell has no argument for this position and he allows that it might well be false (ibid.).

The *Tractatus* is more plainly committed to linguistic atomism (see 3.25 and 4.221), but it offers no explicit argument in its support. This fact has led some commentators—and among them Peter Simons (Simons 1992)—to suppose that Wittgenstein's position here is motivated less by argument than by brute intuition. And indeed, Wittgenstein does present some conclusions in this vicinity as if they needed no argument. At 4.221, for example, he says: '*It is obvious that* in the analysis of propositions we must come to elementary propositions, which consist of names in immediate combination' (emphasis added). Nonetheless, reflection on the *Tractatus*'s conception of analysis makes it easier to understand why Wittgenstein should have thought it obvious that analysis would terminate.

2.1 The *Tractatus*'s conception of analysis

A remark from the *Philosophical Grammar*, written in 1936, illuminates Wittgenstein's earlier conception of analysis:

Formerly, I myself spoke of a 'complete analysis', and I used to believe that philosophy had to give a definitive dissection of propositions so as to set out clearly all their connections and remove all possibilities of misunderstanding. I spoke as if there was a calculus in which such a dissection would be possible. I vaguely had in mind something like the definition that Russell had given for the definite article...(PG: 211)

One of the distinctive features of Russell's definition is that it treats the symbol of *Principia* that we might express in English as 'the *x* such that *Fx*' as an 'incomplete symbol'.[8] Such symbols have no meaning in isolation but are given meaning by the contextual definitions that treat of the sentential contexts in which they occur (cf. PM: 66). Incomplete symbols do, of course, *have* meaning because they make a systematic contribution to the meanings of the sentences in which they occur. This can be seen from the fact that when I utter 'The Queen of Britain had a difficult year', it's not as though I've used a meaningless phrase, as I might in: 'Abracadabra had a difficult year.' What is special about them is that they make this contribution without expressing a propositional constituent.

Russell explains the meaning of definite descriptions by means of the following clauses (for the sake of expository transparency his scope-indicating devices are omitted):

(1) G (the x: Fx) = $(\exists x)((\forall y)\, (Fy \leftrightarrow y=x)\ \&\ Gx)$ Df. (cf. Russell 1905b; PM: 173)
(2)   (the x: Fx) exists = $(\exists x)((\forall y)\, (Fy \leftrightarrow y=x))$ Df. (cf. PM: 174)

Clause (2) brings out the fact that Russell treats the predicate 'exists'—or, in the formal theory, 'E!'—as being itself an incomplete symbol. Note that in the present context when Russell speaks of 'existence' he intends the broad notion he elsewhere terms 'subsistence', rather than the narrow notion of existence as specifically temporal being, which figures in the *Principles of Mathematics*. So Russell is treating predications of being as contextually eliminable in favour of existential quantification.

One can understand why Wittgenstein discerned an affinity between the theory of descriptions and his own envisioned 'calculus', for one can extract from his remarks in the *Tractatus* and elsewhere two somewhat parallel proposals for eliminating what he calls terms for 'complexes':

(3) $F[aRb]$ iff $Fa\ \&\ Fb\ \&\ aRb$
(4) $[aRb]$ exists iff aRb

Proposals (1)–(4) share the feature that any sentence involving a merely apparent reference to something will be regarded as false rather than as neither true nor false in the event that that thing should turn out not to exist.

Wittgenstein's first eliminative proposal—our (3)—occurs in a *Notebooks* entry from 1914 (NB: 4), but it is also alluded to in the *Tractatus*:

---

[8]   Strictly speaking, it is this symbol together with a scope-indicating device that is defined, but for present purposes such details may be suppressed.

> Every statement about complexes can be analysed into a statement about their con-
> stituent parts, and into those propositions which completely describe the complexes.
> (2.0201)

In (3) the statement 'about [the complex's] constituent parts' is '*Fa & Fb*', while the proposition which 'completely describes' the complex is '*aRb*'. If the propositions obtained by
applying (3) and (4) are to be further analysed, a two-stage procedure will be necessary:
first, the apparent names generated by the analysis—in the present case '*a*' and '*b*'—will
need to be replaced[9] by symbols that are overtly terms for complexes, e.g. '[*cSd*]' and
'[*eFg*]'; secondly, clauses (3) and (4) will need to be applied once more to eliminate these
terms. If there is going to be a unique final analysis, each name will have to be *uniquely*
paired with a term for a complex. So Wittgenstein's programme of analysis, in addition
to committing him to something analogous to Russell's theory of descriptions, also commits him to the analogue of Russell's 'description theory of ordinary names' (cf. Russell
1905a). This is the idea that every apparent name not occurring at the end of analysis is
an abbreviation for some definite description.

Wittgenstein's first definition, like Russell's, strictly speaking, stands in need of a
device for indicating scope, for otherwise it would be unclear how to apply the analysis
when we choose say '~*G*' as our instance of '*F*'. In such a case the question would arise
whether the resulting instance of (3) is '~*G*[*aRb*] = ~*Ga* & ~*Gb* & *aRb*', which corresponds to giving the term for a complex wide scope with respect to the negation operator, or whether it is '~*G*[*aRb*] = ~[*Ga* & *Gb* & *aRb*]', which corresponds to giving the term
for a complex narrow scope. One suspects that Wittgenstein's intention would most
likely have been to follow Russell's convention of reading the logical operator as having
narrow scope unless otherwise expressly indicated (cf. PM: 172).

Definition (3) has obvious flaws. While it might work for such predicates as 'ξ is wholly
located in Britain', it obviously fails for certain others, e.g. 'ξ is greater than three feet
long' and 'ξ weighs exactly four pounds'. This problem can hardly have escaped
Wittgenstein, so it seems likely that he would have regarded his proposals as nothing
more than tentative illustrations, open to supplementation and amendment.

Although Wittgenstein's second contextual definition—our (4)—does not occur
in the *Tractatus*, it is implied by a remark from the *Notes on Logic* that anticipates
2.0201:

> Every proposition which seems to be about a complex can be analysed into a propo-
> sition about its constituents and . . . the proposition which describes the complex

---

[9] There are difficulties in stating the appropriate constraints on these replacements. We cannot say
that a given apparent name should be replaced by a *synonymous* term for a complex since Wittgenstein
denies that sub-sentential expressions have sense (3.3). But nor would it be correct to say that an apparent
name should be replaced by a co-referring expression, for, strictly speaking, terms for complexes do not
refer. It seems we can only say that the replacing term should have the same apparent reference as the
term it replaces. In this way we might secure the preservation of modal truth conditions, but whether
that is all that Tractarian analysis is supposed to preserve is a further question.

perfectly; *i.e., that proposition which is equivalent to saying the complex exists.* (NB: 93; emphasis added)[10]

Since the proposition that 'describes the complex', [*aRb*], 'perfectly' is just the proposition that *aRb*, Wittgenstein's clarifying addendum amounts to the claim that the proposition '*aRb*' is equivalent to the proposition '[*aRb*] exists.' And this equivalence is just our (4).

For Wittgenstein, then, 'exists' is defined solely in contexts in which it occurs predicated of complexes. Wittgenstein's proposal thus parallels Russell's insofar as it implies the nonsensicality of statements purporting to ascribe existence to Tractarian objects (cf. PM: 174–5). This is why Wittgenstein was later to refer to such objects as 'that for which there is neither existence nor non-existence' (PR: 72).

One might wonder whether Russell ought to have denied the intelligibility of statements purporting to assert existence (i.e. 'subsistence') of Objects. For one might suppose that he could use the predicate '$\exists x \, (x = \xi)$' for this purpose. Naturally, this predicate, being applicable solely to individuals, cannot be taken to express any imagined conception of trans-categorial subsistence. But there is nothing wrong with it as a predicate of *individuals*—or so the present suggestion would run. However, this proposal must still be regarded as unsatisfactory (from Russell's point of view, at least). For if this predicate were adopted as expressing subsistence, there would be nothing to prevent us from substituting it for '*G*' in (1) above. But then a claim such as 'The round square does not subsist', which strikes us as unequivocally true, would come out as structurally ambiguous between a true claim whose translation into the language of *Principia* would be: '$\sim(\exists x)((\forall y) \, (round \, \& \, square \, y \leftrightarrow y=x) \, \& \, \exists y \, (y = x))$', and a false claim whose translation would be: '$(\exists x)((\forall y) \, (round \, y \, \& \, square \, y \leftrightarrow y=x) \, \& \sim\exists y \, (y = x))$'.

Such considerations might explain Russell's assertion in *Principia* that 'there is no reason, in philosophy, to suppose that a meaning of existence could be found which would be applicable to immediately given subjects' (PM: 175). By 'immediately given subjects' here Russell means objects picked out by demonstration (and known by acquaintance) rather than by description.

Wittgenstein, because he sees sentences involving ineliminable occurrences of the identity sign as 'nonsensical pseudo-propositions' (4.1272), would regard the proposal just discussed as, in any case, a non-starter. He supposes that when '*a*' is a Tractarian name, what we try to say by uttering the nonsense string '*a* exists' will, strictly speaking, be *shown* by the fact that the final analysis of some proposition contains '*a*'.[11] But of course, the *Tractatus* does not always speak strictly. Indeed, what is generally taken to be

[10] In the original the word 'about' occurs ungrammatically in the ellipsis. This seems to be a slip.

[11] This idea is suggested by Wittgenstein's remark that 'What the axiom of infinity is meant to say would be expressed in language by the fact that there is an infinite number of names with different meanings' (5.535). It is even more obviously present in his remark in a letter to Russell of 19 August 1919 that '[w]hat you want to say by the apparent prop[osition] "there are 2 things" is *shown* by there being two names which have different meanings' (CL: 126).

the ultimate conclusion of the *Tractatus*'s so-called 'Argument for Substance' (2.021–2.0211) itself tries to say something that can only be shown, since it asserts the *existence* of objects. The sharpness of the tension here is only partly concealed by the oblique way in which that conclusion is formulated. Instead of arguing for the existence of objects, the *Tractatus* argues for the conclusion that 'the world has substance'. However, because 'objects constitute the substance of the world' (2.021), and because substance is that which *exists* independently of what is the case (2.024), that is tantamount to saying that objects exist. So, in the end, Wittgenstein's argument for substance must be regarded as part of the ladder we are supposed to throw away (6.54). But having acknowledged this important point, we shall set it aside as peripheral to this chapter's main concerns.

Returning to our four analytical proposals, we may observe that the most obvious similarity between the two pairs is that each seeks to provide for the elimination of what purport to be semantically complex referring expressions. The most obvious difference consists in the fact that Wittgenstein's definitions are designed to eliminate not definite descriptions, but expressions such as '[*aRb*]', which, judging by remarks in the *Notebooks*, is intended to be read: '*a in the relation R to b*' (NB: 48). (This gloss seems to derive from Russell's examples of complexes in *Principia Mathematica*, which include, in addition to '*a* in the relation *R* to *b*', '*a* having the quality *q*' and '*a* and *b* and *c* standing in the relation *S*' (PM: 44).) One might wonder why there should be this difference at all. Why not treat the peculiar locution '*a* in the relation *R* to *b*' as a definite description—as, say, 'the complex consisting of *a* and *b*, combined so that *aRb*'? This description could then be eliminated by applying the *Tractatus*'s own version of the theory of descriptions:

The *F* is $G \leftrightarrow \exists x \, (Fx \, \& \, Gx) \, \& \sim (\exists x, y) \, (Fx \, \& \, Fy)$ (cf. 5.5321)

(Here the distinctness of the variables—the fact that they are distinct—replaces the sign of distinctness '≠' (cf. 5.53).)

Since Wittgenstein did not adopt this course, it seems likely that he would have regarded the predicate '. . . is a complex consisting of *a* and *b*, combined so that *aRb*' as illegitimate in virtue of containing ineliminable uses of certain pseudo-concepts such as 'complex' (4.1272)—as well (perhaps) as 'combination' and 'constitution'.

Wittgenstein's analytical proposals differ from Russell's in a further respect. Russell's second definition—our (2)—serves to shift the burden of indicating ontological commitment from the word 'exists' to the existential quantifier. In Wittgenstein's definition, by contrast, no one item of vocabulary has the role of indicating ontological commitment. That commitment is indicated only by the meaningfulness of the Names in the fully analysed proposition—or, more precisely, by the fact that certain symbols are Names (cf. 5.535).[12] The somewhat paradoxical consequence is that one can assert a statement of the form '[*aRb*] exists' without thereby displaying any ontological commitment

---

[12] As Marie McGinn has pointed out to me in correspondence, the present point is subject to the qualification that on Wittgenstein's conception *sentences* might also be thought to carry ontological commitments since, when assertively uttered, they commit the speaker to the existence of the corresponding state of affairs.

to the complex [aRb] (cf. EPB: 121). What this shows is that the two theories serve to relieve the assertor of ontological commitments of quite different kinds. In Russell's case, the analysis—our (2)—removes the appearance of a commitment to an apparent propositional constituent—a 'denoting concept'[13]—expressed by the phrase 'the F', but it does not remove the commitment to the F itself. For Wittgenstein, by contrast, the analysis shows that the assertor never was ontologically committed to such a thing as the complex aRb by an utterance of '[aRb] exists'. It is tempting to say, echoing Berkeley, that when we 'speak with the vulgar', complexes have being—we get along perfectly well treating them as ultimate parts of reality—but when we 'think with the learned'—by grasping sentences in their fully analysed form—they do not have being, for only objects do. But the temptation is better resisted, for the notion of 'being' appealed to here, since it attempts to straddle types, is ultimately unintelligible.

Enough has now been said to make possible a consideration of Wittgenstein's reasons for deeming linguistic atomism 'obvious'. Since the model for Tractarian analysis is the replacement of apparent names with (apparently) co-referring 'terms for complexes', together with eliminative paraphrase of the latter, it follows trivially that the endpoint of analysis, if such there be, will contain no 'terms for complexes'. Nor will it contain any expressions that can be replaced by terms for complexes.

Wittgenstein, moreover, thinks it obvious that the analysis of every proposition *does* terminate. The reason he supposes analysis cannot go on forever is that he conceives an unanalysed proposition as *deriving* its sense from its analysis. As *Tractatus* 3.261 puts it: 'Every defined sign signifies via those signs by which it is defined' (cf. NB: 46; PTLP: 3.20102). It follows that no proposition can have an infinite analysis, on pain of never acquiring a sense. So analysis must terminate in propositions devoid of incomplete symbols.

That much, at least, *is* plausibly obvious. But even allowing (as trivially true) that fully analysed propositions will contain no incomplete symbols (hence no 'terms for complexes' in Wittgenstein's technical sense), it remains possible—for all we have said so far—that they might contain semantically complex symbols. Think, for example, of Russell's denoting phrases on their *Principles of Mathematics* construal, or of Frege's definite descriptions. These are semantically complex symbols that have meaning in their own right. Wittgenstein supposes that fully analysed propositions will contain no such symbols, but it is not altogether clear what justifies that assumption. The merest hint of an answer is suggested by *Tractatus* 3.3, the proposition in which Wittgenstein enunciates his own version of Frege's context principle: 'Only the proposition has sense; only in the context of a proposition has a name meaning' (3.3). The juxtaposition of these two claims may possibly suggest that the context principle is invoked (at this point, ironically,

[13] In the analysis of sentences containing 'the F' espoused by Russell immediately prior to his adoption of the theory of descriptions, the phrase 'the F' is taken to have meaning in isolation. The meaning of 'the F' is a propositional constituent distinct from the F, which bears the special relation of 'denoting' to the F. The phrase 'the F' is considered to both express and designate this 'denoting concept'. The theory of descriptions, because it treats 'the F' as having no meaning in isolation, enables one to recognize sentences in which 'the F' occurs as expressing propositions without being committed to such entities.

against Frege) as the ground for rejecting senses for sub-sentential expressions. But how precisely it would provide such a ground is far from clear. Another, more promising, explanation is that Wittgenstein simply acquiesced in Russell's arguments against sub-sentential senses in 'On Denoting' (and that he also followed Russell in supposing that only 'denoting phrases' were candidates for subsentential expressions with sense). But that can only be a conjecture.

3. METAPHYSICAL ATOMISM

By 'Metaphysical atomism' we shall understand the view that referents of Names are simple. Whereas the *Tractatus* is committed to such a thesis by the claim that 'Objects are simple' (2.02), Russell maintains that some Objects are complex. To see this we need look no further than his characterization of sense-data in his article 'The Relation of Sense-data to Physics'. A sense-datum, he says, is '[not] the whole of what is given in sense at one time... [but] such a part of the whole as might be singled out by attention' (ML: 109). So, since I can single out for attention the colour patch presented in my visual field by the leftmost red leaf on my Poinsettia, it counts as a sense-datum. But I can also single out the leftmost part of that colour patch, so it too counts as a sense-datum. It follows that some sense-data have parts, even parts that are themselves sense-data. But because 'this' and 'that' are Names for sense-data, it follows, further, that some Objects are complex.

For Wittgenstein the simplicity of Tractarian objects is a consequence of their necessary existence, for he takes anything complex to be capable of destruction. Their necessary existence, for its part, is supposed to be established by the so-called 'Argument for Substance':

> 2.0211 If the world had no substance, then whether a proposition had sense would depend on whether another proposition was true.
> 2.0212 It would then be impossible to draw up a picture of the world (true or false).

It may not be immediately obvious that this is an argument for the necessary existence of objects. In order to appreciate that this is indeed so, one needs to pick up on the Kantian resonances of Wittgenstein's invocation of the notion of 'substance'.

3.1 Objects as the substance of the world

The *Tractatus*'s notion of substance is the modal analogue of Kant's temporal notion. Whereas, for Kant, substance is that which 'persists' (i.e. exists at all times), for Wittgenstein it is that which (figuratively speaking) 'persists' through a 'space' of possible worlds. Less metaphorically, Tractarian substance is that which exists with respect to every possible world. Kant maintains (in the 'First Analogy') that there is some stuff—namely substance—such that every existence change (i.e. origination or annihilation)[14] is an alteration or reconfiguration of it. Wittgenstein, analogously, maintains that there are some things—namely, objects—such that every 'existence change' (not in time, but in the metaphorical passage from world to world) is a reconfiguration of them. What undergo these metaphorical 'existence changes' are atomic states of affairs (configurations of objects): a state of affairs exists with respect to one world but fails to exist with respect to another. What remain in existence through these existence changes—and are reconfigured in the 'process'—are Tractarian objects. It follows that the objects that 'constitute the substance of the world' (2.021) are conceived of as necessary existents.

The *Tractatus* compresses this whole metaphorical analogy into one remark: 'The object is the fixed, the existing [*das Bestehende*]; the configuration is the changing [*das Wechselnde*]' (2.0271). ('*Wechsel*,' it should be noted, is the word that Kant expressly reserves for the notion of existence change as opposed to alteration.[15]) Nonetheless, although the analogy is compelling, it is just an analogy: it would be wrong to infer any commitment to Kantian substance from the *Tractatus*'s commitment to 'the substance of the world'. After all, something that exists at some time in every possible world might fail to 'persist' (i.e. exist at every time) in the actual world.

Tractarian objects are what any imagined world has in common with the real world (2.022). Accordingly, they constitute the world's 'fixed form' (2.022-3). The character of any possible world is constrained by the objects because all possible atomic states of affairs are configurations of them. (On Wittgenstein's conception of possibility, the notion of an 'alien' Tractarian object—one which is merely possible—is not even intelligible: whatever is possible is possibly *so*.) Whereas the objects constitute the world's form, the various existing atomic states of affairs constitute its 'content'. So the form-content distinction applies to the world. But it also applies in a different sense to atomic states of affairs. Their content consists of the objects of which they are configurations, while their form is the way in which their constituent objects are configured. It follows that substance—the totality of objects—is both the form of the

---

[14] For example, a fist is being annihilated when a hand is opened and coming into being when it is clenched.

[15] See *Critique*, A187/B230. Wittgenstein may not have read the *Critique* in time for it to have influenced his presentation of this argument, but there is good reason to think that he would have read the *Prolegomena to any Future Metaphysics*—a work in which '*Wechsel*' is similarly expressly reserved for the notion of existence change (see e.g. 'in all that exists the substance persists and only the accidents change [*wechseln*]', Ak 4.368). The main reason to suppose Wittgenstein read the *Prolegomena* is that in his only explicit reference to Kant in the *Tractatus* Wittgenstein mentions a problem discussed in the *Prolegomena* but absent from the first *Critique*, namely the problem of incongruent counterparts. He presents this problem in terms that closely follow Kant's discussion in *Prolegomena* §13 and which differ in major ways from his discussions of incongruent counterparts in other works. (For details see Proops 2004: fn.13.)

world and the content of atomic states of affairs. The fact that the form–content distinction applies in one way to the world and in another to atomic states of affairs fully explains Wittgenstein's otherwise baffling remark that '[Substance] is form and content' (2.024–5). (Further details of this interpretation of substance are provided in Proops 2004.)

3.2 The argument for substance

As we have seen, the immediate goal of the *Tractatus*'s argument for substance is to establish that there are things that exist necessarily. In the context of the Tractarian assumption that anything complex could fail to exist through decomposition, it entails that there are simples (2.021). Although the argument is presented as a two-stage *modus tollens*, it is conveniently reconstructed as a *reductio ad absurdum* (the following discussion of the argument is a compressed version of that provided in Proops 2004):

Suppose, for *reductio*, that:

(1) There is no substance (that is, nothing exists in every possible world).

Then:

(2) Everything exists contingently.

But then:

(3) Whether a proposition has sense depends on whether another proposition is true.

So:

(4) We cannot draw up pictures of the world (true or false)

But:

(5) We *can* draw up such pictures.

Contradiction
So:

(6) There is substance (that is, some things exist in every possible world).

Our (5) is the main suppressed premise. It means, simply, that we can frame senseful propositions. The inference from (2) to (3) may be defended on the following grounds. Given that Wittgenstein equates having truth-poles with having sense in the *Notes on Logic* (NB: 99), it is reasonable to suppose that for a proposition to 'have sense' with respect to a particular world is for a sentence to have a truth value with respect to that world. Now suppose that everything exists contingently. Then, in particular, the referents of the semantically simple symbols in a fully analysed sentence will exist contingently. Suppose, as a background assumption, that there are no contingent simples. (It will be argued below that this assumption plausibly follows from certain Tractarian commitments.) Then the aforementioned referents will be complex. But then any such sentence will contain a semantically simple symbol that fails to refer with respect to some possible world—the world, namely, at which the relevant complex fails to exist. If we assume that a sentence containing a non-referring semantically simple term is neither true nor false—and we do—then any such sentence will depend for its truth valuedness on the truth of some other sentence, viz., the sentence stating that the constituents of the relevant complex are configured in a manner necessary and sufficient for its existence. It follows that if everything exists contingently, then every sentence will depend for its 'sense' (i.e. its truth valuedness) on the truth of some other sentence.

The step from (3) to (4) runs as follows. Suppose that whether any sentence 'has sense' (i.e. on our reading, has a truth value) depends (in the way just explained) on whether another is true. Then every sentence will have an 'indeterminate sense' in the sense that it will lack a truth value with respect to at least one possible world. But an indeterminate sense is no sense at all, for a proposition, by its very nature, 'reaches through the whole logical space' (3.42) (i.e. it is truth valued with respect to every possible world).[16] So if every sentence depended for its 'sense' (i.e. truth valuedness) on the truth of another, no sentence would have a determinate sense, and so no sentence would have a sense. In which case we would be unable to frame senseful propositions (i.e. to 'draw up pictures of the world true or false').

One apparent difficulty for this reconstruction arises from its appearing to contradict *Tractatus* 3.24, which suggests that if the complex entity A were not to exist, the proposition '$F[A]$' would be false, rather than, as the argument requires, without truth value. The difficulty seems to arise because under the *reductio* assumption we are assuming that it is metaphysically possible for a semantically simple name to fail to refer. That suggests that such a failure is something we might discover to obtain. But Wittgenstein seems to be suggesting at 3.24 that it is not discoverable that a simple name should fail to refer: were we to discover that 'A' did not refer, we would thereby discover that 'A' was not after all semantically simple.

But the difficulty is only apparent. It just goes to show that 3.24 belongs to a theory that assumes the world *does* have substance. On that assumption Wittgenstein can say that whenever an apparent name occurs that appears to mention a complex, this is only because it is not, after all, a genuine name—and this is what he does say. But on the assumption that the world has no substance, so that *everything* is complex, Wittgenstein can no longer say this. For now he must allow that even the semantically simple symbols occurring in a proposition's final analysis refer to

---

[16] The claim that having an 'indeterminate sense' is to be understood as failing to be truth valued with respect to some possible world and the claim that Wittgenstein holds it to be essential to a proposition to have a determinate sense are defended in some detail in Proops (2004, § 5).

complexes. So in the context of the assumption that every proposition has a final analysis, the *reductio* assumption of the argument for substance entails the falsity of 3.24. But since 3.24 is assumed to be false only in the context of a *reductio*, it is something that Wittgenstein can consistently endorse. (This solution to the apparent difficulty for the present reconstruction is owed in its essentials to David Pears (Pears 1989 [1987]: 78).)

To complete the argument it only remains to show that Tractarian commitments extrinsic to the argument for substance rule out contingent simples. Suppose *a* is a contingent simple. Then 'a exists' must be a contingent proposition. But it cannot be an elementary proposition because it will be entailed by any elementary proposition containing 'a', and elementary propositions are logically independent (4.211). So 'a exists' must be non-elementary, and so further analysable. And yet there would seem to be no satisfactory analysis of this proposition on the assumption that 'a' names a contingent simple—no analysis, that is to say, that is both intrinsically plausible and compatible with Tractarian principles. Wittgenstein cannot analyse 'a exists' as the proposition '$(\exists x) x = a$' for two reasons. First, he would reject this analysis on the grounds that it makes an ineliminable use of the identity sign (5.534). Secondly, given his analysis of existential quantifications as disjunctions, the proposition '$(\exists x) x = a$' would be further analysed as the *non-contingent* proposition '$a = a \lor a = b \lor a = c \dots$'. Nor can he analyse 'a exists' as '$\sim [\sim Fa \ \& \sim Ga \ \& \sim Ha \dots]$'—that is, as the negation of the conjunction of the negations of every elementary proposition involving 'a'. To suppose that he could is to suppose that the proposition '$\sim Fa \ \& \sim Ga \ \& \sim Ha \dots$' means 'a does not exist', and yet by the lights of the *Tractatus* this proposition would *show* a's existence—or, more correctly, it would show something that one tries to put into words by saying 'a exists' (cf. 5.535; CL: 126). So, pending an unforeseen satisfactory analysis of 'a exists', this proposition will have to be analysed as a complex of propositions not involving a. In other words, 'a' will have to be treated as an incomplete symbol and the fact of a's existence will have to be taken to consist in the fact that objects other than a stand configured thus and so. But this would seem to entail that a is not simple.

The argument for substance may be criticized on several grounds. First, the step leading from (2) to (3) relies on the assumption that a name fails to refer with respect to a possible world at which its actual-world referent does not exist. This amounts to the controversial assumption that names do not function as what Nathan Salmon has called 'obstinately rigid designators' (Salmon 1981: 34). Secondly, the step leading from (3) to (4) relies on the assumption that a sentence that is neither true nor false with respect to some possible world fails to express a sense. As Wittgenstein was later to realize, the case of intuitively senseful, yet vague sentences constitutes a counterexample (cf. PI: § 99). Lastly, one may question the assumption that it makes sense to speak of a 'final analysis', given that the procedure for analysing a sentence of ordinary language has not been made clear (see PI: §§60, 63–4, and 91). (For further discussion of this last point, see the remarks at the close of section 5 below.)

4. The Epistemology of Logical Atomism

We know that a proposition has been completely analysed when its only genuine constituents are Names, but how do we recognize a Name when we see one? It may seem obvious how Russell should answer this question: we will know a word is a Name if we recognize that understanding it requires acquaintance with the Object for which it stands rather than knowledge of a descriptive condition uniquely satisfied by that Object. That answer is correct, as far as it goes, but such recognition may not be easy to come by. Take the case of the first person singular personal pronoun. As we noted earlier, in *The Problems of Philosophy* of 1912 Russell had been inclined to regard it as a Name, but he came to revise his opinion two years later. He defended this change of position with a simple argument:

> Even if by great exertion some rare person could catch a glimpse of himself, this would not suffice; for 'I' is a term which we all know how to use, and which must therefore have some easily accessible meaning. It follows that the word 'I', as commonly employed, must stand for a description; it cannot be a true proper name in the logical sense, since true proper names can only be conferred on objects with which we are acquainted. ('On the Nature of Acquaintance', Marsh 1956: 164)

Russell goes on to suggest that 'I' has the meaning of the description 'the subject of the present experience' (Marsh 1956: 165). It seems, then, that it may not be obvious whether or not a given word is a Name—and, indeed, Russell's position in *The Problems of Philosophy* had only been that 'I' *probably* had this status.

One possible response to these observations might be to say that all the present example shows is that in 1912 Russell had just misapplied his criterion for Namehood. He should have known better than to suppose he was acquainted with himself, and so he should have known that 'I' was not a name, but only a description. Because such a response carries some weight, it is worth mentioning that the present point remains valid even if one sets aside the particular example of 'I'. For even if I know that a word, N, in some suitably broad sense 'stands for' X, I may still be in doubt as to whether X is an object of immediate acquaintance (and so I may not know whether N strictly speaking *Names* X). After all, it took Russell some (dubious) philosophical argumentation to establish to his own satisfaction that tables are not immediate objects of acquaintance (POP: 2–3); so it cannot have been obvious to him from the start that tables cannot be Named.

Whereas it is difficult to know that a certain expression is a Name, it is easier to know that one is *not* a Name. Since I can know that I am not acquainted with the centre of mass of the solar system (since it is a point too small and too remote to see), I can know that no item in my idiolect is a Name for that point. Relatedly, while I may have good reason to think that something is complex, it is far harder to know that it is simple. This last point is one Russell was himself later to concede:

> I believed, originally with Leibniz, that everything complex is composed of simples, and that it is important in considering analysis to regard simples as our goal. I have come to think, however, that, although many things can be known to be complex, nothing can be *known* to be simple, and, moreover, that statements in which complexes are named can be completely accurate, in spite of the fact that the complexes are not recognized as complex…It follows that the whole question whether there are simples to be reached by analysis is unnecessary. (Russell 1959: 123)

This point, Russell supposes, has a bearing on the question of proper names:

> I thought, originally, that, if we were omniscient, we should have a proper name for each simple, but no proper names for complexes, since these could be defined by mentioning their simple constituents and their structure. This view I now reject. (Ibid.: 124)

Turning to Wittgenstein, we find that he has little to say in the *Tractatus* on the topic of how we know that an expression is a Name, and yet it is clear from his retrospective remarks that while composing the *Tractatus* he did think it possible *in principle* to discover the Tractarian objects (see AWL: 11; EPB: 121). So it seems worth asking by what means he thought such a discovery could be made.

At times it can seem as though Wittgenstein just expected to find the simples by reflecting from the armchair on those items that struck him as most plausibly lacking in proper parts. This impression is most strongly suggested by what he says in the *Notebooks*, and, in particular, by a passage from June 1915 in which Wittgenstein expresses confidence that certain objects already within his ken count as Tractarian objects, and that others might well turn out to do so. He says: 'It seems to me perfectly possible that patches in our visual field are simple objects, in that we do not perceive any single point of a patch separately; the visual appearances of stars even seem certainly to be so' (NB: 64). By 'patches in our visual field' in this context Wittgenstein means parts of the visual field with no noticeable parts. In other words, *points* in visual space (cf. WL: 120). Clearly, then, Wittgenstein at one stage believed he could specify some Tractarian objects. However, the balance of the evidence suggests that this idea was short-lived. For one thing, as Anthony Kenny observes, points in the visual field are scarcely the *necessary* objects of the *Tractatus*.[17] For another, Wittgenstein was later to say that he and Russell had pushed the question of examples of simples to one side, as a matter to be settled on a future occasion (AWL: 11). And when Norman Malcolm pressed Wittgenstein to say whether when he wrote the *Tractatus* he had decided on anything as an example of a 'simple object', he had replied—according to Malcolm's report—that 'at the time his thought had been that he was a logician; and that it was not his business as a logician, to try to decide whether this thing or that was a simple thing or a complex thing, that being a purely empirical matter' (Malcolm 1989: 70).

---

[17] Kenny 1973: 74.

Supposing Malcolm's report to be accurate, how are we to understand the claim that the question of simplicity is an 'empirical' question? Not, presumably, as the claim that the correct way to establish that something is a Tractarian object is to gather empirical evidence for the *impossibility* of its decomposition. That reading would only have a chance of being correct if Wittgenstein had taken metaphysical possibility to coincide with physical possibility, and that, evidently, is not the case.[18] His meaning seems more likely to be just that the objects must be discovered rather than postulated or otherwise specified in advance of investigation (cf. AWL: 11). But since Wittgenstein was later to accuse his Tractarian self of having entertained the concept of a distinctive kind of *philosophical* discovery (see WVC: 182, quoted below), we must not leap, as Malcolm may have done, to the conclusion that he conceived the discovery in question as 'empirical' in anything like the contemporary sense of the word.

We know that Wittgenstein had denied categorically that we could *specify* the possible forms of elementary propositions and the simples a priori (4.221, 5.553–5.5541, 5.5571), but he did not deny that these forms would be *revealed* as the result of logical analysis. This idea is not explicit in the *Tractatus*, but it is spelled out in a later self-critical remark, recorded by G. E. Moore in a still unpublished part of Wittgenstein's 1933 lectures at Cambridge:

> I say in [the] *Tractatus* that you can't say anything about [the] structure of atomic prop[osition]s: my idea being the wrong one, that logical analysis would reveal what it would reveal. (MA, 88, entry for 6 February 1933)

Speaking of Tractarian objects in another retrospective remark, this time from a German version of the *Brown Book*, Wittgenstein says: 'What these [fundamental constituents] of reality are it seemed difficult to say. I thought it was the job of further logical analysis to discover them' (EPB: 121). These remarks should be taken at face value: it is logical analysis—the analysis of propositions—that is supposed to facilitate the discovery of the forms of elementary propositions and of the objects. It is supposed to do so by revealing the Tractarian names. The hope is that when propositions have been put into their final, fully analysed forms by applying the 'calculus' spoken of in the *Philosophical Grammar*, we will eventually come to know the objects. Presumably, we will know them by acquaintance in the act of grasping propositions in their final analysed forms. Perhaps we are not *yet* acquainted with any object, but neither, according to Wittgenstein, are we yet in possession of any proposition's final analysis.

Admittedly, Wittgenstein's denial that we can know the objects a priori looks strange given the fact that the analytical procedure described in §2 above seems to presuppose

---

[18] At 3.0321, for example, he says: 'We could present spatially an atomic fact which contradicted the laws of physics…' Although the immediate point of this remark is to draw a contrast with geometrical spatial presentations or pictures which cannot contradict the laws of geometry, it provides clear evidence that Wittgenstein held metaphysical possibility to outstrip physical possibility, for he holds that whatever we can picture—and presumably 'spatial presentations' count as pictures—is possible (cf. TLP 3 together with 3.02).

that we have a priori knowledge both of the correct analyses of ordinary names and of the contextual definitions by means of which terms for complexes are eliminated. This creates a problem concerning how Wittgenstein can be entitled to say that we are not presently acquainted with objects. For to understand a proposition we must understand its analysis, and to understand its final analysis we must understand the names that figure in it, and so be acquainted with the objects that are their meanings. But some tension in Wittgenstein's position on this point is just what we should expect given his later somewhat jaundiced view of his earlier reliance on the idea of philosophical discovery:

> I [used to believe that] the elementary propositions could be specified at a later date. Only in recent years have I broken away from that mistake. At the time I wrote in a manuscript of my book…, 'The answers to philosophical questions must never be surprising. In philosophy you cannot discover anything.' *I myself, however, had not clearly enough understood this and offended against it.* (WVC: 182; emphasis added)

The remark that Wittgenstein quotes here from 'a manuscript of the *Tractatus*' did not survive into the final version, but its sentiment is clearly echoed in the related remark that: 'there can never be surprises in logic' (6.1251). Wittgenstein is clear that despite his better judgement he had unwittingly proceeded in the *Tractatus* as though there could be such a thing as a *philosophical* surprise or discovery. The idea that the true objects would be discovered *through analysis*, but nonetheless not known a priori, is plausibly another illustration of this tendency.

On the conception of the *Tractatus*, the objects are to be discovered by grasping fully analysed propositions—presumably, *with* the awareness that they *are* fully analysed. But since that is so, we shall not have fully explained how we are supposed to be able to discover the objects unless we explain how, in practice, we can know we have arrived at the final analysis of a proposition. But on this point, unfortunately, Wittgenstein has little to say beyond the dark hint of *Tractatus* 3.24:

> That a propositional element signifies [*bezeichnet*] a complex can be seen from an indeterminateness in the propositions in which it occurs. We know that everything is not yet determined by this proposition. (The notation for generality contains a prototype).

An indeterminateness in propositions—whatever it might amount to—is supposed to alert us to the need for further analysis. We therefore possess a positive test for analysability. It by no means follows, however, that the absence of indeterminacy can be used as a positive test for *un*analysability. At the very least, further arguments would need to be given before we could accept this claim. But even then there would be further problems, for it is quite unclear what Wittgenstein means by an 'indeterminateness' in a proposition. The indeterminateness presently at issue is plainly not the one considered earlier: what is in question now is the indeterminateness of propositions, not of senses. But what does that amount to?

According to one line of interpretation, due originally to W. D. Hart (Hart 1971), a proposition is indeterminate when there is more than one way it can be true. Thus if

I say 'G. W. Bush is in the United States,' I leave open where in particular he might be. The source of the indeterminacy is the implied generality of this statement, which is tantamount to: 'Bush is *somewhere* in the United States.' This line of interpretation has the merit that it promises to make sense of the closing parenthetical remark of 3.24. This kind of indeterminacy cannot, however, be what Wittgenstein has in mind at 3.24—viz., a mark by which we could tell that a proposition admits of further analysis—since any disjunction of elementary propositions would be indeterminate in just this sense.

According to a second line of interpretation, a proposition is indeterminate in the relevant sense if the result of embedding it in some context is structurally ambiguous. Consider, for example, the result of embedding '$F[A]$' in the context 'it is not true that…', where 'A' is temporarily treated as a semantically simple term designating a complex. (Keep in place the assumption that a sentence containing a non-referring semantically simple term is neither true nor false.) In this case the question would arise whether the result of this embedding is neither true nor false evaluated with respect to a world in which A does not exist, or simply true. The first option corresponds to giving the apparent name wide scope with respect to the logical operator, the second to giving it narrow scope. Such a scope ambiguity could not exist if 'A' were a genuine Tractarian name, so its presence could reasonably be taken to signal the need for further analysis.

So far, so good, but where does the business about the generality notation 'containing a prototype' come in? Nothing in the present explanation has yet done justice to this remark. Nor does the present explanation really pinpoint what it is that signals the need for further analysis. That, at bottom, is the fact that we can imagine circumstances in which the supposed referent of 'A' fails to exist. So, again, there is reason to be dissatisfied with this gloss on indeterminacy.

It must be concluded that Wittgenstein never really supplied an adequate way of telling when a proposition would be fully analysed, and, consequently, that he failed to indicate a way of recognizing the Tractarian objects.

5. The Dismantling of Logical Atomism

Wittgenstein's turn away from logical atomism may be divided into two main phases. The first (1928–9), documented in his 1929 article 'Some Remarks on Logical Form' (PO, 29–35), exhibits a growing sense of dissatisfaction with certain central details of the *Tractatus*'s logical atomism, and notably with the thesis of the independence of elementary propositions. During this phase, however, Wittgenstein is still working within the broad conception of analysis presupposed in the *Tractatus*. The second phase (1931–2) involves a revolutionary break with this whole conception.

5.1 First phase: The colour-exclusion problem

The so-called 'colour-exclusion' problem is a difficulty that arises for the *Tractatus*'s view that it is metaphysically possible for each elementary proposition to be true or false regardless of the truth or falsity of the others (6.375; cf. 1.21, 4.211). In view of its generality, the problem might more accurately be termed 'the problem of the manifest incompatibility of apparently unanalysable statements'. The problem may be stated as follows: Suppose that *a* is a point in the visual field. Consider the propositions P: '*a* is blue' and Q: '*a* is red' (supposing 'red' and 'blue' to refer to determinate shades). It is clear that P and Q cannot be true together; and yet, on the face of it, it seems that this incompatibility (or 'exclusion' in Wittgenstein's parlance) is not a *logical* impossibility. In the *Tractatus* Wittgenstein's response was to treat the problem as merely apparent. He supposed that in such cases further analysis would always succeed in revealing the incompatibility as logical in nature:

> For two colours, *e.g.*, to be at one place in the visual field is impossible, and indeed logically impossible, for it is excluded by the logical structure of colour.
> Let us consider how this contradiction presents itself in physics. Somewhat as follows: That a particle cannot at the same time have two velocities, that is, that at the same time it cannot be in two places, that is, that particles in different places at the same time cannot be identical. (6.3751)

As Frank Ramsey observes in his review of the *Tractatus* (Ramsey 1923), the analysis described here actually fails to reveal a logical incompatibility between the two statements in question; for, even granting the correctness of the envisaged reduction of the phenomenology of colour perception to facts about the velocities of particles, the fact that one and the same particle cannot be (wholly) in two places at the same time still looks very much like a synthetic a priori truth. It turns out, however, that Wittgenstein was well aware of this point. He knew that he had not taken the analysis far enough to bring out a logical contradiction, but he was confident that he had taken a step in the right direction. In a *Notebooks* entry from August 1916 he remarks that: 'The fact that a particle cannot be in two places at the same time does look *more like* a logical impossibility [than the fact that a point cannot be red and green at the same time]. If we ask why, for example, then straight away comes the thought: Well, we should call particles that were in two places [at the same time] different, and this in its turn all seems to follow from the structure of space and particles' (NB: 81; emphasis added). Here Wittgenstein is *conjecturing* that it will turn out to be a conceptual (hence, for him *logical*) truth about particles and space (and presumably also time) that particles in two distinct places (at the same time) are distinct. He does not yet possess the requisite analyses to demonstrate this conjecture, but he is optimistic that they will be found.

In 'Some Remarks on Logical Form' Wittgenstein finally arrives at the view that some incompatibilities cannot, after all, be reduced to logical impossibilities. His change of heart appears to have been occasioned by a consideration of incompatibilities involving the attribution of qualities that admit of gradation—e.g. the pitch of a tone, the brightness of a shade of colour, etc. Consider, for example, the statements: 'A has exactly one degree of brightness' and 'A has exactly two degrees of brightness.' The challenge is to provide analyses of these statements that make manifest the logical character of the impossibility of their both being true. What Wittgenstein takes to be the most plausible suggestion—or a sympathetic reconstruction of it at least—adapts the standard definitions of the numerically definite quantifiers to the system described in the *Tractatus*. It makes essential use of the idea that the identity or distinctness of the sign does duty for the signs of identity and distinctness. Using 'Bx' to mean 'x is a degree of brightness', the two statements are analysed respectively as: '($\exists x$) (B(x) & A has x) & ~($\exists x,y$) (B(x) & B(y) & A has x and A has y)' and '($\exists x,y$) (B(x) & B(y) & A has x and A has y) & ~($\exists x,y,z$) (B(x) & B(y) & B(z) & A has x & A has y & A has z)'. But the suggestion fails. Wittgenstein diagnoses the problem as follows: the analysis—absurdly—makes it seem as though when something has a degree of brightness there could be a substantive question which of the two—x or y—it was—as though a degree of brightness were some kind of corpuscle whose association with a thing made it bright (cf. PO: 33).

Wittgenstein concludes that the independence of elementary propositions must be abandoned and that terms for real numbers must enter into atomic propositions, so that the impossibility of a thing's having both exactly one and exactly two degrees of brightness is treated as an irreducibly mathematical impossibility. This in turn contradicts the *Tractatus*'s idea that all necessity is logical necessity (6.37).

5.2   Second phase: Generality and analysis

Frege and (arguably) Russell maintain that the quantifiers have meaning in isolation. By contrast, the *Tractatus* treats them as incomplete symbols that are to be eliminated in accordance with the following schemata:

$$\forall x.\Phi x \leftrightarrow \Phi a \ \& \ \Phi b \ \& \ \Phi c \ldots$$
$$\exists x.\Phi x \leftrightarrow \Phi a \ v \ \Phi b \ v \ \Phi c \ldots$$

Universal (existential) quantification is treated as equivalent to a possibly infinite conjunction (disjunction) of propositions. Wittgenstein's dissatisfaction with this view is expressed most clearly in the still unpublished parts of G. E. Moore's notes of Wittgenstein's lectures from Michaelmas term 1932:[19]

> Now there is a temptation to which I yielded in [the] *Tractatus*, to say that
> $(x).fx$ = logical product[20] (of all propositions of the form fx) $fa . fb . fc....$
> $(\exists x).fx$ = [logical] sum, fa v fb v $fc...$
> This is wrong, but not as absurd as it looks. (MA: 34, entry for 25 November 1932)

[19] These remarks from the Moore Archive are further discussed in Proops 2001.
[20] 'Logical product (sum)' is Wittgenstein's terminology—borrowed from Russell—for a conjunction (disjunction).

Explaining why the *Tractatus*'s analysis of generality is not *palpably* absurd, Wittgenstein says:

> Suppose we say that: Everybody in this room has a hat = Ursell has a hat, Richards has a hat etc. This obviously has to be false, because you have to add '& $a, b, c, \ldots$ are the only people in the room.' This I knew and said in [the] *Tractatus*. But now, suppose we talk of 'individuals' in R[ussell]'s sense, e.g. atoms or colours; and give them names, then there would be no prop[osition] analogous to 'And a, b, c are the only people in the room.' (MA: 35, entry for 25 November 1932)

Clearly, in the *Tractatus* Wittgenstein was not making the simple-minded mistake of forgetting that 'Every F is G' cannot be analysed as '$Ga \ \& \ Gb \ \& \ Gc \ldots$' even when a, b, c, etc. are in fact the only Fs. (Unfortunately, his claim that he registered this fact in the *Tractatus* is not borne out by the text.) His idea was rather that the *Tractatus*'s analysis of generality is offered only for the special case in which a, b, c, etc. are individuals in Russell's sense. Wittgenstein had supposed that in this case there is no proposition to express the supplementary clause that is needed in the other cases. Unfortunately, Wittgenstein does not explain why there should be no such proposition, but the answer seems likely to be the following: What we are assumed to be analysing is actually 'Everything is G.' In this case any allegedly necessary competing clause—for example, 'a, b, c, etc. are the only *things*'— would be nonsense produced in the misfired attempt to put into words something that is *shown* by the fact that when analysis bottoms out it yields as names none but those that figure in the conjunction '$Ga \ \& \ Gb \ \& \ Gc \ldots$' (cf. TLP 4.126, 4.1272).

What led Wittgenstein to abandon his analysis of generality was his belief that he had failed to think through the infinite case. He had proceeded as though the finite case could be used as a way of thinking about the infinite case, the details of which could be sorted out at a later date. By 1932 he had come to regard this attitude as mistaken:

> There is a most important mistake in [the] Tract[atus] .... I pretended that [a] proposition was a logical product; but it isn't, because '...' don't give you a logical product. It is [the] fallacy of thinking
> $1 + 1 + 1 \ldots$ is a sum
> It is muddling up a sum with the limit of a sum.
>
> (MA: 37, entry for 25 November 1932)

Wittgenstein came to see his earlier hopeful attitude as, in effect, resting on the mistake of confusing 'dots of infinitude' with 'dots of laziness'. But beyond this: 'There was a deeper mistake—confusing logical analysis with chemical analysis. I thought "$(\exists x).fx$" *is* a definite logical sum, only I can't at the moment tell you which' (MA: 19, 25 November 1932; cf. PG: 210). Wittgenstein had supposed that there was a fact of the matter—unknown, but in principle knowable—about which logical sum '$(\exists x).fx$' is equivalent to. This is but an instance of what Wittgenstein came to see as a more general flaw in his method of proceeding. He had thought that *one* could enumerate the simple objects, although *he* could not do so (MA: 92, entry for 10 February 1933); that analysis would bottom out in truth-functions of elementary propositions, though he could not discover those propositions at the moment (WVC: 182); and that the final analysis would one day display the composition (or 'forms') of elementary propositions (ibid.). He came to regard each of these assumptions as unjustified, and indeed, as symptomatic of an unacceptable 'dogmatism' (WVC: 182). Most sweepingly of all, he came to believe that the very notion of a 'final analysis' of a proposition simply made no sense (MA: 90, entry for 6 February 1933).

We can discern the seeds of Wittgenstein's dissatisfaction with the notion of a 'final analysis' in certain unsatisfactory aspects of Russell's conception of analysis. First, there is the familiar point that there may not be a unique description associated with every ordinary name. Second, even if this were not a problem, in the context of the view, shared by Russell and Wittgenstein, that ordinary names do not have senses, it is unclear what property a description would need to have to qualify as the description associated with a given ordinary name. Russell cannot, for example, say that the description should express the same sense as the ordinary name, since for him neither the ordinary name nor the description has a sense (for that would entail their having meaning in isolation). Russell tries to get around this problem by saying that ordinary names are 'abbreviations' for descriptions (PLA: 200), but that is hardly satisfactory. An abbreviation, after all, is made up of parts of the expression it abbreviates. So whereas 'Homer' might be truly said to abbreviate 'the author of the Homeric poems' (cf. PM: 174–5), 'Scott' can scarcely be thought to abbreviate 'the author of *Waverley*'. Lastly, there is a more general problem with saying what exactly is supposed to be preserved in analysis.

Russell's conception of analysis at the time of the theory of descriptions—*ca*. 1905—is relatively clear: It involves pairing up one sentence with another that expresses, more perspicuously, the very same Russellian proposition. The analysans counts as more perspicuous than the analysandum because the former is free of some of the latter's apparent ontological commitments. By the time of *Principia Mathematica*, however, this relatively transparent conception of analysis is no longer available. Having purged his ontology of propositions in 1910, Russell can no longer appeal to the idea that analysans and analysandum express one and the same proposition. He now adopts 'the multiple relation theory of judgement', according to which the judgement (say) that Othello loves Desdemona instead of being, as Russell had formerly supposed, a dyadic relation between the judging mind and the proposition *Othello loves Desdemona*, is now viewed as a non-dyadic—or, in Russell's terminology, 'multiple'—relation whose terms are the judging mind and those items that were formerly regarded as constituents of the proposition *Othello loves Desdemona* (Russell 1994 [1910]: 155). After 1910 Russell can say that a speaker who sincerely assertively uttered the analysans (in a given context) would be guaranteed to make the same judgement as one who sincerely assertively uttered the analysandum (in the same context), but he can no longer explain this accomplishment by saying that the two sentences express one and the same proposition.

A further departure from the earlier, relatively transparent conception of analysis is occasioned by Russell's resolution of the set-theoretic version of his paradox. The solution involves giving an analysis of a sentence whose utterance could not be taken to express *any* judgement. One argues that the sentence '$\{x: \varphi x\} \notin \{x: \varphi x\}$' is nonsense because the contextual definitions for eliminating class terms yield for this case a sentence that is itself nonsense by the lights of the theory of types (PM: 76). In *Principia*, then, there is no very clear model of what is preserved in analysis. The best we can say is that Russell's contextual definitions have the feature that a (sincere, assertive) utterance of the analysans is guaranteed to express the same judgement as the analysandum, *if* the latter expresses a judgement at all.

Some of the unclarity in the conception of analysis introduced by Russell's rejection of propositions is inherited by Wittgenstein, who similarly rejects any ontology of shadowy entities expressed by sentences. In the *Tractatus* a 'proposition' (*Satz*) is a 'propositional sign in its projective relation to the world' (3.12). This makes it seem as though any difference between propositional signs should suffice for a difference between propositions, in which case analysans and analysandum can at best be distinct propositions with the same truth conditions.

For a variety of reasons, then, one cannot suppose that logical atomism is underlain by any precise or satisfactory conception of analysis. That failing, I would suggest, is precisely what Wittgenstein eventually came to regard as its deepest flaw.[21]

References

AMBROSE, ALICE ed. (1989 [1980]). *Wittgenstein's Lectures, Cambridge 1930–32, From the Notes of Alice Ambrose and Margaret MacDonald.* Midway reprint. Chicago: University of Chicago Press.

ANSCOMBE, G. E. M. (1971 [1959]). *An Introduction to Wittgenstein's Tractatus.* South Bend: St Augustine's Press.

COPI, I. M. (1958). 'Objects, Properties, and Relations in the *Tractatus*', *Mind*, 67.266: 145–65.

FLOYD, J. (1998). 'The Uncaptive Eye: Solipsism in Wittgenstein's *Tractatus*', in L. Rouner ed., *Loneliness.* Boston University Studies in Philosophy and Religion, vol. 19. Notre Dame: University of Notre Dame Press.

HART, W. D. (1971). 'The whole sense of the *Tractatus*', *The Journal of Philosophy*, 68.9: 273–88.

HINTIKKA, M. B., and HINTIKKA, J. (1986). *Investigating Wittgenstein.* Oxford: Blackwell.

KENNY, A. (1973). *Wittgenstein.* London: Allen Lane.

LEE, DESMOND ed. (1980). *Wittgenstein's Lectures, Cambridge 1930–32: From the notes of John King and Desmond Lee.* Midway Reprint. Chicago: University of Chicago Press.

MALCOLM, N. (1989). *Ludwig Wittgenstein: A Memoir* (with a Biographical Sketch by G. H. von Wright), 2nd edn. Oxford: Oxford University Press.

MARSH, R. C. ed. (1956). *Bertrand Russell: Logic and Knowledge, Essays 1901–1950.* London: Unwin Hyman.

MONK, R. (1996). *Bertrand Russell: The Spirit of Solitude, 1872–1921.* New York: The Free Press.

MOORE, G. E. (unpublished). Wittgenstein's lectures 1932–33 from the notes of G. E. Moore. Cambridge University Library G. E. Moore Archive, ref: ADD 8875, 10/7/7. Quoted with the permission of the Syndics of the Cambridge University Library.

PEARS, D. (1989 [1987]). *The False Prison*, vol. 1. Oxford: Oxford University Press.

PROOPS, I. (2001). 'The New Wittgenstein: A Critique', *European Journal of Philosophy*, 9:3: 375–404.

—— (2004). 'Wittgenstein on the Substance of the World', *European Journal of Philosophy*, 12.1: 106–26.

[21] This chapter has benefited from comments by Marie McGinn, Michael Kremer, Michael Potter, and Peter Sullivan. I am grateful, also, to Ivan Mayerhofer for his editorial assistance.

RAMSEY, F. P. (1923). Review of *Tractatus Logico-Philosophicus*, *Mind*, 32/128: 465–74.

RICKETTS, T. (1996). 'Pictures, Logic and the Limits of Sense in Wittgenstein's *Tractatus*', in Sluga and Stern 1996.

RUSSELL, B. (1905a). 'The Existential Import of Propositions', *Mind*, 14: 398–401. (Repr. in Marsh 1956).

—— (1905b). 'On Denoting', *Mind*, 14: 479–93. (Repr. in Marsh 1956.)

—— (1911). 'Le Réalisme analytique', in *Bulletin de la société française de philosophie* 11. English translation in John G. Slater and B. Frohmann eds. (1992), *The Collected Papers of Bertrand Russell*, vol. 6. London: Routledge.

—— (1918/1956). 'Philosophy of Logical Atomism' (PLA), in Marsh 1956. (Originally published in *Monist*, 1918/19.)

—— (1959). *My Philosophical Development*. London: George Allen and Unwin.

—— (1981 [1917]). *Mysticism and Logic* (ML). New Jersey: Barnes and Noble.

—— (1986 [1912]). *The Problems of Philosophy* (POP). Oxford: Oxford University Press.

—— (1990 [1910–1913]). *Principia Mathematica to *56* (PM), with A. N. Whitehead. Cambridge: Cambridge University Press.

—— (1994 [1910]). *Philosophical Essays*. London: Routledge.

SALMON, N. (1981). *Reference and Essence*. Princeton: Princeton University Press.

SIMONS, P. (1992). 'The Old Problem of Complex and Fact', in his *Philosophy and Logic in Central Europe from Bolzano to Tarski*. Dordrecht: Kluwer.

SLUGA, H., and STERN, D. G. eds. (1996). *The Cambridge Companion to Wittgenstein*. Cambridge: Cambridge University Press.

STENIUS, E. (1960). *Wittgenstein's Tractatus: A Critical Exposition of its Main Lines of Thought*. Ithaca, NY: Cornell University Press.

WAISMANN, F. (1979). *Wittgenstein and the Vienna Circle: Conversations recorded by Friedrich Waismann*, ed. B. McGuinness, trans. J. Schulte and B. McGuinness. Barnes and Noble Import Division: Harper and Row.

WITTGENSTEIN, L. (1929). 'Some Remarks on Logical Form'. *Proceedings of the Aristotelian Society*, Supplementary Volume 9: 162–71.

—— (1970 [1969]). *Eine Philosophische Betrachtung* (EPB), in Rush Rhees ed., *Ludwig Wittgenstein: Schriften 5*. Frankfurt am Main.

—— (1973). *Letters to C. K. Ogden*, ed. G. H. von Wright. Oxford: Blackwell.

—— (1974). *Philosophical Grammar*, ed. R. Rhees, trans. A. Kenny. Oxford: Basil Blackwell.

—— (1975 [1964]). *Philosophical Remarks*, ed. R. Rhees, trans. R. Hargreaves and Roger White. Oxford: Blackwell.

—— (1979 [1961]). *Notebooks, 1914–1916*, ed. G. H. von Wright and G. E. M. Anscombe, trans. G. E. M. Anscombe. Oxford: Blackwell.

—— (1981 [1922]). *Tractatus Logico-Philosophicus*, trans. C. K. Ogden. London: Routledge and Kegan Paul.

—— (1993). *Philosophical Occasions 1912–1951*, ed. J. Klagge and A. Nordmann. Indianapolis: Hackett Publishing Company.

—— (1995) *Ludwig Wittgenstein: Cambridge Letters*, ed. Brian McGuinness and G. H. von Wright. Oxford: Blackwell.

—— (1996 [1971]). *Prototractatus: An Early Version of Tractatus Logico-Philosophicus*. London: Routledge & Kegan Paul.

—— (1998 [1953]). *Philosophical Investigations*, 3rd edn., trans. G. E. M. Anscombe. Oxford: Blackwell.

CHAPTER 11

....

THE *TRACTATUS* AND THE LIMITS OF SENSE

....

CORA DIAMOND

> When I say: Here we are at the limits of language, that always sounds as if resignation were necessary at this point, whereas on the contrary complete satisfaction comes about, since **no** question remains.
>
> (BT, 310)

In the quoted remark, Wittgenstein contrasts resignation with satisfaction. If saying 'Here we are at the limits' appears to suggest the need for resignation, that is because it looks as if there is something we cannot do. Why else should we think we need to be resigned? It looks as if whatever question it is that took us to this point, or whatever statement it was that we wished to make, would go beyond what is sayable, and so we are stuck. So long as we have the idea that what we want goes beyond the limit, resignation is in place. If, instead, we were to recognize that the idea that we were trying to ask something, that there was something we wanted to find out, or wanted to say, was confused, and that there was *nothing* that we were asking or wanting to say, there would no longer be anything to be resigned about. Thus 'complete satisfaction' would be possible. We need to look further at that contrast between a conception of the limits of language, or of the limits of sense, which leaves us with resignation and a conception which contrariwise goes with 'complete satisfaction'. Is there at the 'limits of language' genuinely something that we cannot do? Or is that a misunderstanding? I shall examine some of the ways this issue comes up in the *Tractatus*, although I shall start with some slightly later remarks. I want to explore the idea of making limits clear 'von innen', from inside. This is an idea that comes up explicitly at TLP 4.114, and in Wittgenstein's letter to Ludwig von Ficker, explaining his aims in the *Tractatus*. (PTLP, 15) I shall try to show the connection between Wittgenstein's ideas about marking out the limits 'from inside' and his ideas about philosophical method, and the connection between those ideas about method and the contrast between the two ways of understanding the limits of language. The recognition of the limits of language, where such recognition is not a recognition of constraints, can be achieved only through a philosophical approach that works 'from inside'.[1] Although much in this chapter bears on Wittgenstein's conception of logic, a treatment of his understanding of the relation between logic and limits would have doubled its length, and so logic (as a topic in its own right) lies outside its limits. (For a discussion of questions about the relation between logic and limits, see McGinn 2006, especially ch. 11.)

1. A First Look Round

Consider the remarks about ethics from 'Notes on Talks with Wittgenstein'. In December of 1929, Wittgenstein spoke of the astonishment one may feel that anything exists. He said that this astonishment 'cannot be expressed in the form of a question and there is no answer to it'; and he added that whatever we say here must, a priori, be nonsense. Here we are thrusting against the limits of language (NTW, 12–13). But a year later he rejected that description: 'Language', he said, 'is not a cage'. (NTW, 16) Speaking of thrusting against the limits suggests an 'inside' within which we are confined and an 'outside' which we can't get to. He had said that our astonishment that anything exists cannot be expressed in the form of a question. So what happens, then, if we express the astonishment by uttering the words 'Why is there anything?' In an important respect there is no change between 1929 and 1930 in his view about the uttering of such words, the using of the interrogative form in that way. The astonishment 'cannot be expressed in the form of a question': so Wittgenstein's view appears to be that there is on the one hand the astonishment and there are on the other hand the words which grammatically have the form of a 'Why?'-question; and the words and the astonishment do not meet. No question at all has been expressed.

Why not? I shall look briefly at two ways of replying. I am not at this point arguing that either approach is in fact Wittgenstein's; my discussion is meant to use what one might think of as Wittgensteinian material in formulating two related ways of responding to the question. Both approaches begin from the same point, namely that a question anticipates ways of using words in an answer. The first approach goes on this way from that initial point: Any form of words purporting to be an answer to 'Why is there anything?', in which it seemed words were being used to say how things stood, would not be what we want in formulating what purports to be the question 'Why is there anything?' No such 'answer' would tell us why there were things that could be spoken of at all, since it would take for granted the availability of such things to provide explanations, and would not explain the existence of the things themselves. Such an 'answer' would not be

---

[1] There is a contrast between 'limits' and 'limitations' used in discussing Wittgenstein's views, a contrast related to but not identical with the contrast I am using between two ways of understanding limits. See Sullivan (2011), 1–2, for a lucid explanation of the 'limits'/'limitations' contrast.

a genuine answer. Insofar as the 'question' is modelled on questions which look towards the world and what is the case in it for an answer, insofar as we take ourselves to be asking such a question, we are in difficulty: we want to ask a question modelled on those that look to what is the case for answers, but we also want to ask something that would lead us to reject, as an answer, any statement of what is the case. No such answer would satisfy us; and it should become clear that the 'question' fails to anticipate any range of possible answers.

That first account takes for granted that the 'question' is modelled on questions that are answerable by stating something that is the case, that is, by the use of what the *Tractatus* speaks of as senseful propositions. The argument underlying the approach is essentially that we can come to see that no senseful proposition would be what we would find acceptable as an answer to the 'question', and that, if we are able to recognize that we had, without thinking about it very clearly, used a question-form modelled on questions that are answerable by senseful propositions, we can come to give up the 'question' as not asking anything, as a form of words in which the question-form doesn't get so far as genuinely to express a question.

The second approach allows that there are other sorts of question than those that can be answered by saying how things are. Take, for example, 'Why did such-and-such star become a white dwarf?' An answer to such a question will make use of laws of physics, and such laws, on Wittgenstein's view, provide more or less useful ways of describing how things are, but do not themselves say that anything is the case.[2] Words used as they are in laws of physics will not be what we want as an answer to 'Why is there anything?', any more than will words used as they are when we describe how things are. When he wrote the *Tractatus*, and in the years when he first returned to philosophy in 1929–30, Wittgenstein recognized a variety of ways in which words might be used; he did not, as is sometimes suggested, believe that there were only three sorts of case: senseful propositions, the senseless propositions of logic, and nonsense. But if we consider these various ways in which words can be used, we can see that none of them will be what we want as an answer to 'Why is there anything?' It is not just propositions that state how things stand and laws of physics that won't be what we want. Words used as they are in giving logical necessities, words and symbols used as in mathematics, words used as they are in giving useful definitions, or in rules of translation from one language to another, or in presenting, through the use of variables, some or other expressions: all these various ways of using words can be recognized to be *not* what is wanted in reply to 'Why is there anything?' For us to be here at the limits of language is for there to be no way words might be used which would connect with our question-form and provide an answer. If we can see that there is here nothing to be said, it is because we can see that any way of using words would not be what we want. But if we see that that is the case, we

---

[2] Cf. Griffin 1964, ch. 8, §5, esp. pp. 102–3. Griffin says that Wittgenstein held that the function of scientific laws 'is not to make reports, not even very general ones, but to supply representational techniques by which reports can be made'. I discuss Wittgenstein's account of scientific laws in Diamond, forthcoming.

should not be 'resigned' at the impossibility of getting what we want, but should recognize that the question-form only appeared to be asking for something that we might or might not be able to get. It's not that we can't get what we want, not that 'what we want' is on the far side of the limits of language and therefore unobtainable. The second approach, like the first, is not one in which we reach resignation at the limits of language. In both, we see that the recognition of limits is not the idea that something 'beyond the limits' is out of reach.

The two rather similar approaches that I have described are constructed from what one could think of as Wittgensteinian material. The fundamental idea in both approaches is the reverse of what one often sees in discussion of Wittgenstein on 'what can't be said'. The idea, that is, is not that the thing one is trying to say, or such-and-such sort of thing, lies beyond the limits of what can be said, but that nothing that can be said would be what one is seeking, or takes oneself to be seeking. What I want to consider is the role, or possible role, in Wittgenstein's early thought, of coming to recognize that nothing that can be said would be what one is after.

My question, what the role is of the recognition that nothing that could be said would be what one wants, is really part of a larger group of questions concerning what kind of clarity Wittgenstein took himself to be aiming at in the *Tractatus*, how that sort of clarity connects with questions about the limits of language, and whether such limits are constraints of some kind. Consider here 6.5, where Wittgenstein says that, to an answer that cannot be put into words, the question (that seemed to want such an answer) also cannot be put into words. Here the reader whom Wittgenstein has in mind has arrived at the idea that the question that she is asking calls for an answer that must be inexpressible. Can that understanding be transformed? For Wittgenstein appears to want to go on to try to transform it. At 6.52, he invites us to think of a situation in which all possible scientific questions have been answered. If we are able to recognize that none of the gazillion speakable answers to questions will reach to our concern with the problems of life, that none of the speakable answers can be an answer to the questions we take ourselves to be putting, we should see ourselves as rejecting all answers, rejecting anything that would be an answer to any question. If we could have, as it were, *all* answers, we should still not have the answer to the questions we took ourselves to be putting. Here our understanding of ourselves can reach a further point: that the purported questions are not questions at all. (They aren't, that is, questions the answers to which couldn't be spoken; they weren't questions which fail to count as questions because of what is allowed to count as a question, demanding answers which also can't count as answers.) We no longer think of ourselves as having questions which push us beyond where language can reach. There is thus the possibility of a kind of philosophical satisfaction in reaching clarity of this sort, clarity which is not a matter of recognizing and accepting that we cannot do something. Arriving at the 'limits of language' from the inside, i.e. seeing what can be said and seeing that nothing sayable will be what we want, may enable us, not to resign ourselves to saying only what can be said, but to see differently ourselves and our askings, and the relation of our askings to the world.

At 6.53, Wittgenstein says that the correct method in philosophy would really be to say nothing except what can be said, i.e. propositions of natural science. He goes on to say what should be done when someone else wants to say something metaphysical. But let us attend for a moment to the place in this method of saying things that can be said. What would make *that* a 'method of philosophy', or an element in such a method, at all? If philosophy is an activity that aims at making thoughts clear, how can talking about the weather or hydrogen or photosynthesis contribute to philosophical clarification? Because there doesn't seem to be an obvious answer, many people have understood 6.53 as if Wittgenstein meant that we should spend our time talking sense (without suggesting that such talk was part of the 'method of philosophy'), and that the method of philosophy comes into play only when someone wants to say something metaphysical: then we respond to the philosophical provocation. But I think we should take seriously what 6.53 actually seems to say, namely that talking sense is itself a method of philosophy. Sense-making can be directed towards philosophical clarity, can help us to achieve such clarity. If we explore the idea, we can illuminate Wittgenstein's understanding of what kind of limits the 'limits of language' are.

The first thing we should note is that, twice in the *Tractatus* and once again later in the 'Lecture on Ethics', Wittgenstein suggests a philosophical method which is clearly related to that of talking sense. The first such suggestion, at 5.631, I shall discuss below; the second such suggestion we have already seen, namely Wittgenstein's appeal to the imagination, at 6.52. We are to imagine that all possible scientific questions have been answered; we have arrived at the gazillion true scientific propositions. Wittgenstein is asking us, at 6.52, not to utter senseful propositions ourselves, but to imagine a vast body of sayings and writings, the sayings and writings that add up to 'all possible questions' having been answered. Imagining this to have been achieved is what can play a role in the transformation of our understanding of what we had taken to be the questions we wanted to put. We can come to see that nothing in all those *answers* could be what we were seeking. As I have noted, such a realization is not in and of itself the realization that we were not asking a question at all. At this point, I simply want to note that Wittgenstein thinks that we can be helped philosophically by seeing that nothing in the realm of sense is what we are seeking, and that talking only sense, or imagining a huge amount of sense-talking, can itself help us to reach the point at which we can say: I see that nothing that made sense would be what I want; I see that I could reject a priori anything you say in answer to my question if it made sense. Talking sense is a method of philosophy if talking sense is a way of enabling someone to see that anything like *any of this* (all this sense) would not be what she wants. What I am emphasizing here is the difference between thinking of the inexpressibility of something as being a matter of the something lying beyond the expressible and thinking of it as not being anything within the expressible, within what can be said, i.e. thinking of oneself as in a position to reject anything sayable as an expression of the something. How much of a difference this makes may not be obvious, but I shall come back to it. At this point, though, I am concerned to bring out only that *talking sense* can be a method of philosophy if one thinks of it as directed towards helping someone to recognize that no talking of sense would be a solution to the problem with which she is concerned.

Let me turn here to 5.631, where Wittgenstein imagines writing a book called *The World as I Found It*, which includes a report on his body and on which bits are subject to his will, and so on. The book has no mention in it of the philosophical subject. Were he to write such a book, it might not be given any philosophical use, and something similar can be said about imagining such a book: the mere account of such a book need have no particular philosophical use. Wittgenstein does, though, say that, if there were such a book, it would provide a method of showing something philosophically significant. Here again we have the idea of the uttering of senseful propositions (the ones in the book) as a philosophical method. But at 5.631, the actual method Wittgenstein is using is that of imagining the book, just as at 6.52 the method was that of imagining the reaching of answers to all possible scientific questions. In context, in the *Tractatus*, the idea of such a book is taken to be something that can help us to reach philosophical clarity. If we take ourselves to be in search of the philosophical subject, we can see that nothing in the book will be what we are looking for. This of course may only suggest that the philosophical subject belongs in a realm of things not included in the book, the realm of things we can't talk about; and in that case, we are working with the conception of the limits of language, the limits of what can get into the book, as constraints. We take the idea to be that we can't speak of what lies outside, including the philosophical subject. That is how Bernard Williams, for example, takes this section of the *Tractatus*; he takes Wittgenstein's remark that philosophy can in a sense speak of the self in a non-psychological way (5.641) to mean that philosophy can talk about it in the way in which philosophy is able to talk about anything, i.e. not in senseful sentences. (Williams 1981, 146) On this reading, then, the sense in which philosophy is supposed to be able to talk about the self, which does not lie within the limits of senseful talk, is this: it talks about the self by talking nonsense. Insofar as we remain within the limits of senseful talk, there is something we cannot talk about. On this reading, then, those limits are constraints. How else might one see what Wittgenstein is up to? He says that the I enters philosophy through this, that 'the world is my world.' (5.641) What then is the connection between 'the world is my world' and the way in which philosophy can in some sense talk about the self?

Let me pause here. I began by quoting Wittgenstein on two ways in which the notion of the limits of language can be understood. It can be understood as a constraint, and there is supposedly another way in which it can be understood, tied to the achievement of what Wittgenstein referred to as complete satisfaction. Wittgenstein's understanding of the limits of language is tied to his ideas about philosophical method, and I have been trying to explore the connections. One of the most important places in which the idea of limits comes up in the *Tractatus* is the passage in which Wittgenstein says, 'The world is *my* world'. But before considering this enormously puzzling section of the book, we need to enlarge the focus, and to look in somewhat more detail at Wittgenstein's conception of philosophy and what he thought it could accomplish.

2. Enlarging the Focus: More About Philosophy as an Activity of Clarification

Philosophy, according to Wittgenstein, is supposed to be an activity that aims at the clarification of thoughts (4.112). He also thinks that, in the activity of attempting to clarify something that purports to be the expression of a thought, we may come to realize that no thought was expressed. The activity of clarification can be carried on in a variety of ways. The introduction and use of the kind of notation Wittgenstein describes at TLP 3.325 is one such technique of clarification. Analysis, thought of as the rewriting of propositions so that their logical form is more clearly open to view, is a closely related technique. I have suggested that the imagined book at 5.631 and the imagined complete set of 'answers' at 6.52 play a role in a different technique of clarification. (That method of clarification is used also in Wittgenstein's 'Lecture on Ethics', in which we are asked to imagine an omniscient being, who writes everything that he knows in a big book, which thus contains the complete description of the world.[3]) But there is another, more obvious technique in the *Tractatus* itself, namely, the provision of a variable, the values of which are all propositions. We specify a variable, according to the *Tractatus*, by giving its values, and one way in which this can be done is by giving a rule governing the construction of the propositions which will be the values of the variable.[4] So, in the case of that variable, the values of which are supposed to be all propositions, the variable can be specified by a general rule governing the construction of propositions. (The propositions constructed in this way will be capable of having sense, but won't actually have a sense unless meanings have been given to the names in the propositions (cf. TLP 4.5).) Philosophy can provide such a general rule for the construction of propositions; and whatever can be the case can be said to be the case by some such constructed proposition.

How does the method just described fit in with familiar ideas about the kinds of proposition which the *Tractatus* leaves room for, or appears to leave room for? When Wittgenstein says, at TLP 6, that the operation that he has spelled out gives the general form of proposition, does he think that the specification is a piece of nonsense? There are two reasons for answering No.

(a) If we read the *Tractatus* as holding that, besides senseful propositions, there are tautologies and contradictions, which are senseless but not nonsensical, and that, besides those two categories, there are only nonsensical pseudo-propositions, we are imposing a schematism that Wittgenstein does not himself put forward at any point.

---

[3] For a discussion of Wittgenstein's use of imagined 'books', see Friedlander 2001. Friedlander's account of the role of these 'books' in Wittgenstein's method, and in particular of their relation to the aim and character of the *Tractatus*, is very different from mine.

[4] This claim draws on 3.314–3.317 and 5.501.

Among the kinds of proposition-like constructions that he plainly recognizes are definitions and other rules (3.343). A definition of one of the signs in a proposition can be added to the proposition without affecting its sense, and in that respect it resembles a tautology. (One can note the contrast with adding a nonsensical conjunct to a proposition, which makes the whole proposition nonsensical.) In *The Big Typescript*, Wittgenstein says that when one adds a rule to a proposition, it doesn't change the sense of the proposition (BT, 189; also Z §321). I think it is consistent with the general approach of the *Tractatus* to suggest that a rule that helps to clarify any expression or expressions used in a proposition can be added to a proposition without changing its sense.[5]

(b) We need to separate the actual specification of a variable from remarks that may accompany it, and in particular from remarks that appear to say what kind of meaning the values of the variable have, e.g. that they are *propositions*. The specification of the variable, distinguished from the accompanying remarks, is itself an instrument of clarification, something that can help us to look at our own use of language and see underlying commonalities in the expressions we use. The philosophical method of laying out a general rule for the construction of propositions is a kind of approach 'from inside', related to the method of imagining 'all possible' answers to scientific questions, and to imagining (in the 'Lecture on Ethics') the big book written by the omniscient being, containing the whole description of the world. These and other methods enable us more clearly to *see sense*. We may thereby reach a position in which we can see that nothing that made sense would be what we want in connection with the kind of philosophical quest in which we are engaged, or the philosophical difficulty in which we are enmeshed.

I quoted earlier Wittgenstein's remark that the correct method in philosophy would be to say nothing apart from what can be said, and, when someone tries to say something metaphysical, to show the person that he has failed to give a meaning to some or other signs in his propositions. Wittgenstein also says, in the *Tractatus*, that, if we have a proposition like 'Socrates is identical', the reason it is nonsensical is that no adjectival meaning has been given to 'identical'. The implication is that, if we gave an adjectival meaning to 'identical', the proposition would have sense; Wittgenstein explicitly says that we cannot give a sign the wrong sense. (In this case, no adjectival meaning assigned to 'identical', and no resulting sense for 'Socrates is identical', would be wrong.) But let us here ask what the significance is of the fact that we may want *not* to give a meaning to a sign or signs in some proposition, if the result would be that the proposition would then make sense. Think of a proposition

---

[5] For a general discussion of the notion of *senselessness* and of the ways in which a variety of senseless propositions may be used, see Kremer 2002. Philosophy can make extensive use of such senseless propositions in its activity of clarification, distinct from any use it may make of nonsense. Thus e.g. the Russellian analysis of definite descriptions can be treated as a rule for rewriting propositions, and can be added to a proposition containing a definite description without changing its sense.

like 'A is an object.' It may be perfectly consistent with the *Tractatus* that that proposition could be given a sense, if 'object' were given meaning as a word for a kind of thing; but the *Tractatus* can lead us to a further point about such a proposition. If we were to come to see that nothing that could be said to be the case, were we to use 'A is an object' to say that that was the case, would satisfy us, we might want not to give it sense. We might, that is, exclude giving it a sense, not because using 'A is an object' as a senseful proposition would be wrong, but because we do not want that combination of signs to have any sense.

Here I am suggesting we can see a further element in Wittgenstein's understanding of philosophical method. I shall try to make it clear by contrast with the way in which his philosophical method is often understood. Elizabeth Anscombe, for example, discusses the case of 'Red is a colour', and says that it does not express anything that might be false. This is why, on the *Tractatus* view as she is expounding it, the proposition is nonsensical. That red is a colour is something that supposedly is shown in the use of senseful propositions, but which cannot be said. (Anscombe 1963, 82) On the alternative conception that I have just been suggesting, the methods of clarification of sense on offer in the *Tractatus* can help us to recognize that we should not want to give a meaning to the signs in 'Red is a colour' so that it would be a senseful proposition. If we *exclude* 'Red is a colour' from sense, and say that it is nonsensical, we are not recognizing that, because it cannot express something that can be false, it cannot be a senseful proposition. There are good reasons for excluding it, for drawing a boundary here and saying: 'We don't want that combination of signs within senseful language.' But we then really and truly do treat what is 'on the far side' of the limits of language as being nothing but nonsense. The limits of language, construed in this way, don't force us not to do something that we might want to do; rather, we have come to see that there isn't something that we want to do. We have come to understand differently our relation to words which have an attraction for us.

I don't want to suggest that all the cases in which we might exclude giving a sense to a form of words are like the case of 'Red is a colour.' Anscombe describes a case in which she came to see a kind of unthinkingness in something that she herself had said, 'It looks as if the sun goes round the earth.' (Anscombe 1963, 151) If, seeing that her words had meant nothing, she did not want to go on to give them some sense, this would not have been like the case of 'Red is a colour.' But what is the difference? It looks as if the difference is that what we want to mean by 'Red is a colour' is something that is a necessary truth; and that *that* is the reason why we won't be satisfied by assigning meanings to the signs in 'Red is a colour' that would make the whole proposition come out as what the *Tractatus* would count as a senseful proposition. And here the attempt to spell out what is going on in the case of 'Red is a colour' calls on the idea that there is something that we cannot do: the limits of language *constrain* us; what is necessarily the case but not tautologously so *cannot* be put into words. It looks as if my attempt in the paragraph before this one to spell out a difference between Anscombe's approach and the approach that I have been sketching has collapsed.

3. A Serious Objection to the Idea that the Limits of Language, as Understood in the *Tractatus*, are not Constraints: Two Parts of a Response

Does Wittgenstein or does he not exclude from sense propositions that express substantial necessary truths, propositions that are not false in any circumstances? The idea that the limits of language are not constraints may seem to run up against the idea that the *Tractatus* precisely excludes any such substantial necessary truths. For if indeed it does so, then whenever we wanted to say something that was such a necessary truth, we might be persuaded by the *Tractatus* to give it up, but if we did so, this would be a case of resignation, not satisfaction.

My response to that argument has four parts. I should first note that some of the propositional constructions that we might be inclined to characterize as substantial necessary truths are, when looked at with a more critical eye, anything but. Readers of the *Tractatus* sometimes take Wittgenstein's own propositions to express claims that are meant to be both substantial and necessary, and that then count as nonsensical because, supposedly, no such claims can count as sense. A good example to consider here is one of the propositions in 5.3: 'Every proposition is the result of truth-operations on elementary propositions.' If that is supposed to be necessary and yet not empty, then the word 'proposition' as it occurs there cannot be taken to mean the same as 'the result of truth-operations on elementary propositions'. Further, if 5.3 is supposed to be even plausible and not obviously untenable, the word 'proposition' in it cannot mean just any combination of signs that looks like a proposition, or that could be used as a proposition. The idea that the word means *anything at all* in that context (as opposed e.g. to being a sort of blur that we read past without raising questions) should be regarded as at least questionable. (It is indeed arguable that the aims of the *Tractatus* preclude the giving of any clear meaning to 'proposition' in all the talk leading up to the specification of the general form of proposition.) So, in at least some cases, a careful examination of a proposition that we had taken to be both substantial and necessary may show that we may indeed have, instead, a proposition with a blur in it where we had taken there to be meaningful words.

The case of propositions like 'A is an object', 'Red is a colour', and so on is different. In these cases an argument that there is in the proposition a word that lacks any meaning in the context can be made through appeal to the kind of notation that Wittgenstein describes at 3.325. Such a notation will sharpen our eyes to different kinds of use of terms like 'object' or 'colour'. The point of such an argument would be to call into question an idea like Anscombe's about 'Red is a colour', that it cannot express anything that might be false. The argument would be that it does not express anything, simpliciter, because 'is a colour' hasn't been given any appropriate meaning; nor has 'red' as a substantive in such contexts. But such an approach does not in fact take us very far, if our concern is with the character of the limits of language, and with the decided impression that the *Tractatus* gives that the limits of language *rule out* substantial necessary truths. For it might be asked, on the supposition that we had not given to 'is an object' or 'is a colour' any meaning in contexts like 'A is an object' and 'Red is a colour', why we should not give a meaning to the supposedly as-yet-meaningless terms in such a way as to make these propositions come out to be necessary truths.

4. TWO FURTHER PARTS OF A RESPONSE TO THE OBJECTION

Let us turn directly to the supposed ruling out of such truths. This ruling out, it might be said, is done in two ways by the *Tractatus*: in its explicit remarks, and in the general form of proposition itself, as given by the *Tractatus*. The explicit remarks that might be appealed to include 'Whatever we can describe at all could be other than it is' (5.634) and also the remark about logical propositions (i.e. tautologies), that they alone can be recognized to be true from the propositions alone. No propositions other than tautologies can be recognized to be true or false from the propositions themselves; and the fact that tautologies can be seen to be true from the proposition alone is inseparable from their not actually saying anything (6.1–6.113). Mathematical propositions can also be proved to be correct without any comparison with the facts, and that is why Wittgenstein speaks of mathematics as a 'logical method'; mathematics, like logic, is not a sphere in which we express thoughts (6.2–6.2321). Philosophy does not result in 'philosophical propositions' (which is what propositions like 'Red is a colour' or 'Propositions are truth-functions of elementary propositions' might be thought to be). 'The totality of true propositions is the whole of natural science (or the whole corpus of the natural sciences).' (4.11–4.112) Every possible sense can be expressed by a symbol satisfying the description given in the general propositional form (4.5). The significance of these remarks cannot be seen, though, unless we turn to Wittgenstein's specification of the general form of proposition, at TLP 6; and my discussion of what TLP 6 does is the third part of my response to the objection. In the fourth part, I shall get back to explicit remarks like those just mentioned.

There is an important kind of problem concerning the way I treat TLP 6, but a problem which is too complex to get more than just a mention here. Peter Sullivan has argued that Wittgenstein does not succeed in specifying a variable at TLP 6, and that, even if he had succeeded, there would still be a question what the use might be of the variable. I have tried elsewhere to sketch an alternative approach to the difficulties raised by Sullivan. (Sullivan 2004; Diamond 2012) There are certainly fundamental difficulties with Wittgenstein's ideas about the general form of proposition, difficulties which he he explores in *Philosophical Investigations*, especially in the sections beginning at §89. In what follows, I touch on those difficulties but I don't go into them; my aim is to make clear the role that the specification of the general form of proposition has in the *Tractatus*.

At TLP 6, Wittgenstein provides a variable, and says about it that it is the general form of a truth-function, and that it is the general form of proposition. A variable like the one provided gives us (or is meant to give us) what is common to some group of symbols. Which ones? The specification of the variable itself gives us the answer to that question. We can say that the variable provided at TLP 6 specifies a way of using signs. The specified use could be called 'the use as picture-proposition', where what picture-use is is given by the variable, although we have been helped to see what this amounts to in large part through such metaphors as that of sense as 'reversible'. What reversibility comes to in the specified kind of use of signs is the role given, in the specification, to truth-functional construction.[6] What I am suggesting is that Wittgenstein, in specifying the general form of proposition, is (in intention) specifying language 'from the inside'. This means that we cannot assume that his various remarks about symbols of the form described are to be read as his taking up a position outside the specification and telling us, from that position, what the specification does. After the specification of the variable, we should recognize that *that* is what we have: the specification itself, a general rule for the construction of signs. We should, when we read the *Tractatus*, take seriously the question what our situation is, once we have been given this specification of a variable. If we have a rule for churning out a whole bunch of signs of a certain construction, why should we take it to be anything to do with *language*, with saying things that we can understand? If the word 'proposition' is attached to this variable, and we are told that it is 'the general form of proposition', it is something more than a mere label, and can be seen to be something more than a mere label for a calculus of signs, only in the speaking-use of the signs. I can put the point here another way. There are three ways to look at TLP 6.

(1) We can take proposition 6 to provide a method of construction, and use 'senseful proposition' as a label for what it tells us how to construct.

(2) We can see our own talk and talk that we understand as the use of signs of the form given in proposition 6; we can see 'into' language as we ourselves use it, and see in it the general form that has been specified.

(3) We can take the *Tractatus* to convey a view about senseful propositions: that all such propositions have the form specified in proposition 6.

I am suggesting that (1) and (2) are available to us, if we read the *Tractatus* as I think Wittgenstein meant it to be read. That is, the specification of the general form of proposition can be thought of as a rule for constructing signs labelled 'propositions',

---

[6] For the connection between picture-use and reversibility, and between reversibility and a truth-functional understanding of logic, see Ricketts 1996.

but, for it to be anything more than that, we have to see speaking, making sense, our own talk, as the use of signs of the specified form; we have to see Wittgenstein as having, through a variable, presented language, the language we understand, 'from the inside'. I am suggesting that we not read the *Tractatus* in the third way; and I shall come back to this. In *Philosophical Investigations* §103, Wittgenstein spoke of how the ideal conception of what a proposition is had been for him like a pair of glasses on his nose. The 'strict and clear rules' of propositional structure appeared to him to be present in ordinary propositions, but only because the idea of such a structure was being read into them. We can take Wittgenstein's remarks in §§102–3 to indicate also how he had wanted the *Tractatus* to be read. If he himself could see the 'strict and clear rules' of propositional structure in ordinary propositions, his book (I am suggesting) invited its readers to see their own ordinary propositions as the use of signs whose essence they had been given in the general form of proposition. Wittgenstein doesn't want to assert that ordinary senseful propositions are all of the form that he has specified, but rather to lead us to see *in* our ordinary propositions exactly the formal structure laid out in the *Tractatus*. We are being led (that is) to put onto our own noses the glasses that Wittgenstein speaks of at §103, and to see our own language with those glasses on our noses. We are, in doing so, imposing an order on our use of language; see PI §105. It is not a matter, though, of our first picking out *the propositions*, and seeing in them the structure specified at TLP 6. Rather, the book read as it is meant to be read imposes an order in the sense of both identifying some of our talkings as the projective use of propositional signs, as senseful propositions, determinants of a place in logical space, and persuading us that 'in' such signs-in-use there is the common essence, glimpsable down deep.

It sounds like a *Tractatus* thesis to say that Wittgenstein is not putting forward as a thesis that *senseful propositions are values of the variable given in proposition 6*. We may think he is doing so because we don't see an alternative possible account of what he is doing. I have tried to sketch an alternative view. But we can also ask what exactly Wittgenstein would be doing were he to be asserting that what his variable presented was: all propositions. Denis McManus, for example, describes Wittgenstein as 'in some sense' asserting that his general form of proposition is the general form of proposition. (McManus 2009; cf. the similar claim in McManus 2006, 141.) What then is it that Wittgenstein is supposed to be 'in some sense' asserting? What it seems McManus means is something like this: Wittgenstein is 'in some sense' asserting that the values of the variable that he has produced are *the propositions*, i.e., that *propositions* have in common that they are values of Wittgenstein's variable. But any such attempt to give what Wittgenstein is 'in some sense' asserting requires that some term like 'proposition' be used, and that it not be a stand-in for 'values of the variable presented at TLP 6'. But surely the *Tractatus*, if it is committed to anything in this general region, is committed to the idea that the word 'proposition' is the sign for a formal concept, the expression for which is a variable, the variable presented at TLP 6. The suggestion that Wittgenstein is 'in some sense' asserting that his general form of proposition gives what propositions have in common appears to require that he be giving the word 'proposition' a use other than that which the book as a whole can be taken to have laid out. The word can be given any use one wants to give it; but the idea that Wittgenstein is 'in some sense' asserting something, the assertion of which requires some distinct unspecified use of the word 'proposition', is an idea one should greet with scepticism. The book should teach us that we are all too likely to take ourselves to be using words with some determinate meaning when we are not doing so; and the idea that Wittgenstein is 'in some sense' asserting that what *propositions* have in common is given by his general form of proposition should be regarded as an instance of our fooling ourselves by taking a word with no determinate meaning in the particular context in which it occurs to mean something. The alternative is to say: he himself saw the general form of proposition, as specified in proposition 6, as present in language as he used it, and he wanted to lead his readers to take themselves to be *seeing into* what was before them in their own talk, and to see the general form that he had laid out as present in it. I am not suggesting that the trouble with McManus's suggestion is that the word 'proposition', as we use it (and related expressions, like 'sentence', or 'what she said', etc.) in ordinary talk, has no determinate meaning. Its use (on Wittgenstein's view) is that of a variable (TLP 4.126–4.1272), while its use in any sentence like 'What *propositions* have in common is that they are values of Wittgenstein's variable' treats the word 'propositions' as a term with the logical character of 'apples'; it is as a term apparently with that logical role that the word has no determinate meaning. (A further argument about these issues is presented in Section 6.)

The significance of my argument is that, if what proposition 6 does (or is meant to do) is fundamentally to present the picture-use of signs, it is not in the business of ruling anything out. *Making clear a use of signs does not itself rule out any other use.* This is, indeed, evident in the structure of the *Tractatus*, in which three sets of remarks (the 6.1s, the 6.2s, and the 6.3s) are concerned with three different non-picturing uses of signs, none of which is meaningless.[7] What we can see clearly from these three sets of remarks is that there are sign-constructions that may look as if they are picture-propositions, but that have a quite different use. The same point is indeed evident in Wittgenstein's remarks about expressions of the form 'a = b': that they are aids to representation. I am claiming then that there is no argument in the *Tractatus*, about any use of signs, that because it is not the picture-use it is excluded, and lies beyond the limits of language.

I said that we could not see the significance of the *Tractatus* remarks that explicitly rule out propositions that are substantial and necessarily true except in the light of the specification of the general form of proposition. If we take the general form of

---

[7] I have seen it argued that Wittgenstein takes mathematical equations to be nonsensical pseudo-propositions. He certainly speaks of the equations of mathematics as pseudo-propositions, *Scheinsätze* (6.2). He does not identify them with tautologies, but it hardly follows that he regards them as nonsensical. Calling them *Scheinsätze* or pseudo-propositions certainly implies that they misleadingly appear like propositions, sign-constructions used to say that something or other is the case, picture-propositions, but it does not imply that they have no use or that they are meaningless. See Kremer 2002.

proposition to be the specification of a way of using signs, the picture-proposition way, we can think of the defender of substantial necessary propositions as having to provide some account of how the propositions that he takes to be substantial and necessarily true are being used. This would be a matter of providing an account of a mode of use of signs, different from the picturing use, or of providing an account (different from anything the *Tractatus* takes to be available) of how picture-use in some perhaps considerably modified sense can accommodate necessary truths. Thus, for example, suppose we think, or try to think, of there being, for any necessarily true proposition, circumstances in which it would be false, but which *cannot* conceivably be realized, and we think of the proposition as having truth-conditions which are necessarily fulfilled. So we have a kind of bipolarity of the supposedly necessarily true proposition, but a bipolarity which does not lie 'within' the existence and non-existence of states of affairs: there is no possible situation in which the proposition would be false. At the heart of such an exercise of the logical imagination is the idea of the circumstances which cannot be realized; and at 5.61, Wittgenstein says that what we are in effect trying to do here is to station ourselves, as we set out what can be the case and also the circumstances that cannot be the case, 'outside' the limits of the world. We are, as it were, thinking or trying to think in a language in which we can consider, even if only to rule out, things that we take to be not thinkably the case.

I suggested above that the position in which the defender of substantial necessary truths is put by the *Tractatus* is that of needing to explain in what way the propositions supposedly expressing such truths are being used, on his view, since they are not being used in the picture-proposition way. When Anscombe writes about Wittgenstein's account of propositions as pictures, she says that his theory is powerful and beautiful, and that 'there is surely something right about it if one could dispense with "simples" and draw the limits of its applicability'. (Anscombe 1963, 77) One thing she wanted to exclude from its applicability was statements of what is necessarily the case which are nevertheless not tautologies in the *Tractatus* sense. Suppose we agree with her and say: 'Fine, necessary truths should be excluded from the applicability of what Wittgenstein says about picturing. We shouldn't say that there can't be such things, merely because they aren't picture-propositions.' But what the *Tractatus* is at least implicitly suggesting is that the cases we have in mind of such truths are cases we have not examined, and that there are more problems than we may have suspected in laying out the use of such sentences themselves, or the use of the words within them. Take one of Anscombe's own examples: '"Someone" is not the name of someone.' (Anscombe 1963, 85–6, 162) She shows that such a sentence can have a use. But what is that use? Her sentence is meant to clarify one use of 'someone'. Nothing in the *Tractatus* rules out there being proposition-like constructions, the use of which is to help us to use signs in statements of what is the case; and '"Someone" is not the name of someone' is meant to be helpful in such a way. A sentence which is used as an 'aid to representation' ('Behelfe der Darstellung', see TLP 4.242) may seem itself to be a representation of something that must be the case, and therefore to fall under a supposed *Tractatus* interdiction, but that would be a misunderstanding. The misunderstanding arises from the propositional look that an 'aid to representation' may have, which stops us seeing its quite different sort of use. Anscombe's example is actually quite complex and I cannot go into details. (See Diamond 2004.) Here I want to argue only that the specification of the general form of proposition excludes nothing at all. It specifies a use of signs, the picture-proposition use. The various remarks in the *Tractatus* which do explicitly rule out substantial necessary truths need to be thought about as, in a sense, tasks for us. If Wittgenstein says 'Whatever we describe at all could be other than it is', can this be read as excluding nothing? It can be read (I am suggesting) as a challenge to anyone who takes herself to be *describing* something, something which could not be other than it is, to consider whether the kind of way in which words are supposedly being used to describe in the sentence in question can be clarified. Insofar as there really is a claim made by remarks like 'Whatever we describe at all could be other than it is', it is that whenever we take ourselves to be describing something which could not be other than it is, the impression that that is what we are doing reflects unclarity of mind. The unclarity may involve an implicit appeal to the picture-proposition use of words, an appeal which would break down into incoherence if made fully explicit. Wittgenstein's metaphorical description (TLP 5.61) of our wish to station ourselves 'outside' the world suggests just such a half-meant appeal to a kind of picture use. We might see such an attempt in, for example, Schopenhauer's talk of the thing-in-itself as 'something', something groundless which underlies phenomenal happenings and which withdraws itself from investigation. Speaking of this 'that which', this 'what', this 'something', uses the apparatus of quantifier-and-variable, but Schopenhauer's language doesn't involve our quantifying over anything about which we can talk in any way without quantifiers.[8] He is as it were gesturing towards a language which we ourselves cannot use; he is (with the use of quantifiers) invoking logic, but a logic which is not the logic of the language we speak in describing the world. We may have an extremely vivid conception of ourselves as describing something when we do this sort of thing, e.g. as in the case of Schopenhauer, this talking about the thing-in-itself by using quantifiers. But we should take seriously that there is nothing here but *Luftgebäude*, i.e. that 'Whatever we describe at all could be other than it is' excludes nothing.

Many remarks in the *Tractatus* play a role in the way Wittgenstein leads the reader to proposition 6; and many of these remarks use the word 'proposition'. They have a role that can be compared with that of auxiliary construction lines in a geometrical proof. What we have at the end of the geometrical proof is the construction itself, the lines that form part of it. The auxiliary lines helped us to get there, but they are not part of what we are left with at the end. We can think of much of what we have in the *Tractatus* as auxiliary constructions, combinations of signs, using the word 'proposition', that lead us up to proposition 6, which itself enables us to have in clear view a particular use of the word 'proposition'. Once we have that clear view, we can see also that those earlier remarks, those sign-combinations with the word 'proposition', were blurry, said nothing clear at all. This was not because they were necessary truths, but because they contain a word

---

[8] Schopenhauer 1988, Buch II, §24.

with no determinate meaning in the context,[9] and indeed their function in the book requires that they not have any determinate meaning. (This point bears also on the use of the word 'proposition' in discussions of these remarks, e.g. my statement in section 2 that Wittgenstein takes philosophical method to include the provision of a variable which has all propositions as its values.)

My argument in sections 3 and 4 has been largely negative. I have tried to show that the *Tractatus* does not give us a conception of the limits of language which puts something that we might want to do, namely, express substantial necessary truths, on the far side of the limit. I have also had a positive aim, that of making clear how we can read the provision of a variable that supposedly gives the general form of proposition as giving the limits of language 'von innen'. The positive and negative aims of these two sections hang together, and my claims about 6.1, 6.2, 6.3 and about 'aids to representation' bear on both aims. That no uses of language are excluded is tied to those various uses being clearly not excluded. The recognition of various non-picturing uses helps us to see how to investigate the cases we take to be excluded. (The issue of the supposed exclusion of substantial necessary truths is important and I shall return briefly to it in section 6.) The structure of the remarks in the 6s bring out an extremely important point: that there is a real variety of cases in which proposition-like constructions, although they do not have the use specified in the variable at TLP 6, may appear to us to be representations or reports or descriptions of something that is the case. Propositions of logic may seem as if they are totally general truths; equations of mathematics may appear to be reporting mathematical relations; laws of mechanics may seem to be true propositions; 'Good is simple and unanalysable' looks as if it describes something; the sceptic may seem to be claiming something that is true or false. Whether such sentences have a use other than the picture-proposition use or no use at all needs to be investigated in each sort of case.

Sentences of the form 'P entails Q' can illustrate how easy it is to miss what is at stake. Once one sees that such sentences look as if they are a kind of report but that they are, if true, necessarily true, and yet not tautologies, it is easy to go on to take such sentences to be excluded by the *Tractatus* as nonsensical, and indeed to read them as a kind of incoherent attempt to consider logical space from outside it. Such sentences do, however, have an important kind of use that is different from the picture-proposition use, and which is not in any way ruled out by the *Tractatus*.[10] That they can have, as a kind of 'aspect', the aspect of being a report brings out that the existence of such an aspect doesn't itself settle whether they are nonsensical or not. All the various sorts of proposition-like constructions discussed in the 6s, as well as the aids to representation mentioned elsewhere in the book, can have the aspect of being a report or representation, which can mask what we are doing with words when we utter them. Even if we recognize that the sentences are not doing what they appear to be doing, the report aspect may block our

---

[9] The point about the meaningfulness of 'proposition' does not apply to ordinary uses of the word, like 'Every proposition he utters is false', but only to those uses in which it is treated as a 'proper concept-word'; see TLP 4.1271–4.1272.

[10] James Conant and I discuss the case of sentences of the form 'P entails Q' in Conant and Diamond 2004. We pick up the example from Peter Sullivan's discussion of it in his 2004a in the same volume.

capacity to see the quite different kind of use that such a sentence may have, and we may take the sentence in question to be, on the *Tractatus* view, an incoherent attempt to go beyond the limits of language.[11]

5. VIEWING THE WORLD AS A LIMITED WHOLE

Wittgenstein wrote in the *Tractatus* that the aim of philosophy is the clarification of thoughts, but he also said, in his letter to von Ficker, that the point of his book was an ethical one. His book, he said, had two parts, the one he was presenting to von Ficker plus everything that he had not written. The book drew the limits of the ethical 'from the inside'. But in what sense a drawing of the limits of the ethical 'from the inside', since the ethical was precisely what he had said nothing at all about? The limits are hardly drawn 'from the inside' of ethics. And if the activity of philosophy, including the activity constituted by the *Tractatus*, aims at the clarification of things that we do actually say and think, how does keeping silent about ethics belong to the activity of philosophy? We can get some insight into Wittgenstein's ideas here by looking at the analogies that he saw (I believe) between what a work of art can do and what a philosophical work can do.

A work of art can transform the perspective of the reader or viewer or listener; and so can a philosophical work. A work of art can be thought of as treating of something, even when its concern with the thing is not explicit, and similarly for a philosophical work. The analogies in fact go somewhat further, as we can see by turning to what Wittgenstein says about how a work of art can transform the perspective we have on something. His remarks come from before and after the period of the *Tractatus* itself. In October of 1916, he wrote a number of remarks about the relation between ethics and aesthetics. (NB, 83) The work of art, he said 'is the object seen *sub specie aeternitatis*' and the good life is the world seen 'sub specie aeternitatis'. Instead of seeing things as we usually do, from the midst of them, the work of art lets us see them 'from outside', 'with the whole world as background'. He went on to consider the example of contemplating a stove, first as a thing among things, and then 'as a world': one can see the stove as having the dignity of being what it is, a dignity that is not in view in one's ordinary dealings with the stove.

In a fascinating essay on Wittgenstein's thought about such matters, Michael Fried suggests that we connect these early notes with remarks that Wittgenstein made in 1930, in which he spoke about how a work of art can alter the perspective we have on an ordinary thing. (Fried 2007) Without art, the particular thing is simply a fragment of nature like any other thing; but the work of art can force us to see it entirely differently, to see it in the right perspective, as something worthy of contemplation. In these notes, Wittgenstein went on to say that there was a way of capturing the world *sub specie aeterni* other than through the work of the artist; thought can do this: 'it is as though it flies above the world and leaves it as it is observing it from above, in flight'. (CV, 4–5) I am

---

[11] See Mulhall 2007, 246 on the 'dual aspect' of the *Tractatus* remarks in the 6.4s and 6.5s.

suggesting that a philosophical work, on Wittgenstein's view, can transform our perspective on the world, and that it can do this through the presenting of senseful language 'from the inside'. I mentioned another element of the analogy between a work of art and philosophy: that a work of art can treat of something indirectly, can treat of something without explicitly mentioning it, and that is exactly what he took philosophy to be able to do. Wittgenstein's remarks, at various times, about Tolstoy's *Hadji Murad* reflect his idea that the story has ethical significance despite its not dealing in any direct way with Tolstoy's conception of how we should live. Just as that story is ethically significant in part through keeping silent about ethics, so the *Tractatus* can be ethically significant through keeping silent about ethics. It can treat ethics through presenting nothing ethical; it can treat ethics (this is what I want to suggest) through presenting the general form of senseful proposition.

How then can philosophy be thought capable of transforming our perspective? I can begin to explain by going back to the idea in the *Notebooks* about how we see things prior to the transformation that can be effected by art: we see things 'from their midst'. Prior to the transformation that can be effected by philosophy, we are similarly in the midst of things, immersed in seeings and doings and sayings in the world. We investigate whether things stand this way or that; we do things to bring about this or that effect; we say that things stand thus-and-so. And, while we may well think of philosophical questions as deeply different from ordinary questions, we don't really take the distinction deeply enough.[12] And similarly for ethics: we take questions about the meaning of life, the nature of the good, and how it is to be discovered to be questions which differ in a variety of ways from scientific questions, but we take them nevertheless to be, after all, *questions*. We remain, as we see ourselves in our asking of such questions, 'in the midst of things'; the implicit conception of what it would be to have a solution to the questions we ask is that it would add something to what we know to be the case. What difference, then, can be made by a philosophical approach that presents senseful language, that gets it clearly into focus for us? When we are in the midst of sense, talking sense, asking and answering questions, *sense* is not something that is an object of our awareness; or, rather, insofar as it does become an object of awareness at all, it is as something about which we may ask questions. So we remain within the asking and answering of questions. Wittgenstein's presenting of senseful language makes possible a standing back from the asking and answering of questions.

The standing back from the asking and answering of questions can be thought of as possibly leading to a transformation of our understanding of what it is to engage in philosophy, and can also be thought of as possibly leading to a transformation of our understanding of what ethics is. These are not two separable kinds of transformation. In the background of my discussion is a contrast that I think runs through Wittgenstein's discussions of ethics from the time of the *Tractatus* until at least 1930. He spoke in 1929 of

---

[12] I discuss Wittgenstein's ideas on the importance of distinguishing sharply enough, and the relation of his ideas to those of Frege, in Diamond 2010.

the importance of ending the 'chatter' about ethics, the 'Geschwätz', but this desire to end the chatter co-existed with his deep respect for the tendency to come out with various forms of words expressive of a kind of responsiveness to life. (NTW, 12–16) Some ways of talking about ethics should be stopped, and others not. The contrast is implicitly present at the end of the *Tractatus*, when Wittgenstein says that if one overcomes the propositions of the book, one will see the world rightly. The suggestion appears to be that there are ways of speaking and thinking (tied in some cases to one's not having overcome Wittgenstein's propositions) that reflect seeing the world wrongly. When he spoke later about the importance of ending the chatter about ethics, related ideas are in play: philosophical talk about ethics reflects and encourages a kind of failure to see the world rightly. I believe he had Moore's *Principia Ethica* in view both in the *Tractatus* and in the later remarks, and I shall return to this point.[13]

At 6.4 Wittgenstein says that propositions are of equal value. The first sentence of 6.41 says that the sense of the world lies outside the world; the last sentence says that any genuine value must lie outside the world; and in the middle, we are told that genuine value, if there is any, lies outside all happening and being-so. So the idea of an 'outside' is pretty insistently rubbed in. What is inside is: everything being as it is and everything happening as it happens. Obviously, Wittgenstein's remarks about what can only be 'outside' cannot belong to presenting senseful language from the inside. When he makes similar remarks in his 'Lecture on Ethics', their role is clearer: he speaks there of the tendency he himself has, and that (some) other people have, to 'go beyond significant language'. (LE, 11–12) That tendency has, inchoately within it, two elements which can be brought to awareness; the tendency itself can thereby be changed. The tendency to 'go beyond significant language' is the tendency to reject ordinary propositions, descriptive of how things do stand in the world, as not capable of satisfying one's desire to talk about what genuinely is of value, plus the desire to talk beyond ordinary descriptive language in order to speak of what is genuinely valuable. The tendency is evident in, for example, discussion of whether the Good can be defined, in theorizing about ethics, where ethics is taken as a sphere of discourse. What is noteworthy here is that, at this point, 'In the world, everything is as it is, and everything happens as it happens leads, or seems to lead, *outwards*. There is no finding satisfaction *there in the world* in the attempt to understand what genuinely is of value.

How, then, can philosophy affect the tendency 'to go beyond significant language'? The activity of philosophy clarifies what belongs to ordinary senseful propositions; this can be done while remaining 'within' language, in the sense that there is no taking up of a perspective on language in doing so, no making of claims about language from some philosophical perspective. The lineaments of senseful language are put forcefully in front of us; our attention is drawn to them. The more clearly we see language – that language the propositions of which we understand and can use – the more clearly it will appear to us that, in ethics, no proposition at all can be what we want. This is the recognition reflected

[13] See Donatelli 2005 for a discussion of the relation between Wittgenstein's remarks about value and Moore's ideas in *Principia Ethica*.

at TLP 6.42, and in the first clause of 6.5: the answer we want cannot be put into words. What this recognition involves, in terms of the original inchoate tendency, is the rejection of the idea of a sphere of ethical discourse, of there being a kind of proposition dealing with ethical matters. Wittgenstein is not distinguishing factual from evaluative propositions. (In fact, he has no objection to most evaluative propositions, which, on his view, would not belong to ethics as he understood it.[14]) Clarity of the sort reachable by presenting senseful language 'from inside' can enable us to see that the idea of 'propositions of ethics' is itself confused. Wittgenstein's view here is very different from (for example) what we have in his discussion of the laws of mechanics. Statements of such laws are not propositions but a kind of aid in the construction of descriptive propositions, whereas the very idea of 'ethical propositions' involves a misunderstanding of our own desires. The clarity that Wittgenstein thought could be reached about ethics through presenting senseful language 'from the inside' was essentially clarity about the fact that nothing that could be said would be what we wanted, that the very fact that some proposition was intelligible was enough to show that it was beside the point.

What I have said so far is only part of the story. Having our attention drawn to senseful language may do two things at once. The first is what I mentioned, the recognition that no proposition could be what we had wanted. In order to see what the second thing is, we need to return to 'In the world, everything is as it is, and everything happens as it happens', which, as I mentioned, at first leads our attention 'outwards'. We should note here TLP 5.525: the possibility of a situation is expressed by an expression's being a proposition with sense. The general form of proposition gives us the rule by which all senseful propositions can be constructed. (It also gives us the construction of tautologies and contradictions.) In giving us senseful propositions, it expresses the possibility of each and every possible situation, everything that can happen, everything that can be the case. It gives us (that is) 'the essence of the world'; cf. 5.4711: to give the essence of a proposition means to give the essence of description, i.e. to give whatever can be said to be the case and thus the essence of the world. In giving us at one and the same time *senseful description* and *world*, the general form of proposition puts before us what the will (the will as ethical subject) can attach to.

Take now again 'In the world, everything is as it is, and everything happens as it happens.' If we connect this sentence with what one might think of as two aspects of the general form of proposition, then the general form of proposition gives us at once both language and world: senseful language on the one hand, and all possibilities of being the case and not being the case, of happening and not happening, on the other. Think of 'In the world, everything is as it is, and everything happens as it happens' as emphasizing the second aspect of the general form of proposition, its giving us *world*. I said that initially 'In the world, everything is as it is, and everything happens as it happens' goes with the idea

---

[14] Compare his treatment of evaluations in LE, 5. At the time of that lecture, at any rate, he saw no special problems in including within a general account of factual language a treatment of much evaluation, including, for example, the evaluation of chairs and pianists. A similar account of such evaluation would be compatible with the *Tractatus*. What the *Tractatus* excludes is that the 'value' spoken of in evaluating chairs and so on is relevant to the search for genuine value.

that the desire to find what is genuinely of value must take us beyond all happening and being the case. It seemed as if, if one could not reach value that lay beyond the being-so of this and that within the world, one could not reach value *at all*. Thus 'In the world, everything is as it is, and everything happens as it happens' went with a kind of dissatisfaction with the entire realm of the accidental. But this is an essentially ethical matter; we can re-see 'In the world everything is as it is, and everything happens as it happens.' That the facts of the world are whatever they are can become a changed perspective on the world.

In his 'Lecture on Ethics', Wittgenstein said that he was 'tempted to say that the right expression in language for the miracle of the existence of the world, though it is not any proposition in language, is the existence of language itself'. (LE, 11) The presentation of senseful language may draw our attention to *the* language that is the language we understand, and this drawing attention to language can, as we might say, let us see the world in a different perspective, as being whatever it is, everything standing as it does stand. Speaking of this as a 'perspective on the world' is itself a kind of figurative language, since, insofar as a sense has been given to having a perspective on something, the something in question is an object or event or historical movement, or some other particular thing or things; but 'the world' in the context of talk of a 'perspective on the world' has not been given a use as an expression for such a thing. A perspective is from this or that particular spot, or reflects particular interests and concerns; and no such thing is in question here. To speak, then, about the philosophical activity of achieving clarity about language as 'capable of changing one's perspective on the world' is to use words in an irreducibly figurative way. Let me put the matter here another way. Having our attention drawn to senseful language may lead us to stand back from the asking and answering of questions, as we recognize that no satisfaction is to be had from any *answer*. We are, that is, enabled to contemplate things, but no longer 'from their midst', rather from a point of view that sees what is the case as whatever indeed is the case; *how* things are is not the centre of concern, and *that* they are is, in a sense, open to view. Open to view, I am suggesting, in and with the contemplation of '*the* language'. It is as if by presenting the general form of proposition, Wittgenstein had drawn a circle around the totality of language and made its 'thereness' for us open to view. Its 'thereness' stands for the 'thereness' of the world. The upshot of this account is not that 6.41, with all its talk about value being 'outside' the world, is rejected, but it is understood quite differently from the way in which we may at first try to understand it. For we may at first see Wittgenstein as suggesting that value is something that we cannot reach with words, and that *resignation* is therefore appropriate. A figurative use of the language of 'outside', a figurative use of the idea of seeing as from outside, and of the world as something 'seeable' is part of a perspective that we may come to occupy.[15]

---

[15] Contrast Kremer 2001, 60. Kremer argues that Wittgenstein does not invite us to think in terms of a 'perspective on the world'. He refers to James Conant's criticism of the idea of a philosophical perspective on the logical structure of the world. According to Conant, this is an illusion of a perspective, and not a point of view which we are invited to take up by the *Tractatus*. (See Conant 2002, 422–3.) My reading of Wittgenstein is certainly different from Kremer's, in that I think the figurative use of the idea of a perspective on the world does play a role in Wittgenstein's conception of ethics, but such a figurative use of the idea of a perspective does not involve the conception criticized by Conant.

There is more to be said about 'In the world, everything is as it is, and everything happens as it happens.' I have suggested that, when we first read the sentence in 6.41, it can be taken to express dissatisfaction with the realm of the accidental, dissatisfaction that propels us to look 'outside' for what is genuinely of value. There is, though, a further kind of dissatisfaction with the realm of the accidental, with the fact that things happen in the world as they happen: a dissatisfaction with the independence of the world from what we want or choose or try to bring about. This is the kind of dissatisfaction expressed in a pure form in the Grimm tale of the fisherman and his wife, when the wife, who becomes emperor and pope, is nevertheless dissatisfied because things still happen independently of what she wills; she is not God. This sort of dissatisfaction can be read into suicide, as if, in committing suicide, one were responding to the independence of the way things go by putting to an end the very world that is independent of one's will. If the way things go is not as one wants it to be, one's will is turned against the very existence of the world.

Dissatisfaction with the accidentalness of things takes a variety of forms, and here I want to include the sort of dissatisfaction which can be taken to underlie ethical 'chatter'. I'm suggesting that, just as Wittgenstein was inclined to read a kind of profound ethical dissatisfaction in suicide, he read a kind of ethical dissatisfaction in the spirit in which ethics was discussed. Speaking in the 'Lecture on Ethics' of ethics as he understood it, Wittgenstein said that it doesn't 'add to our knowledge in any sense' (LE,12), a remark that may well be directed against Moore, who quite specifically claims that ethics is a science, and that it is directed towards knowledge. (See e.g. Moore 1922, 20.) The pursuit of ethics, understood Moore's way, can be taken to express the desire that there be a 'being-the-case' that is not accidental, and that is the foundation of Value. The problems of life can thus come to appear as *questions*, to which ethics provides a systematic approach. What might be thought to be wrong with this can be seen if we look at TLP 6.43, where Wittgenstein speaks of the ethical will as expressed in relation to the world as a whole, the world as that in which everything is as it is, and everything happens as it happens. The will can be exercised 'happily' in relation to the world thus understood, or 'unhappily'. Ethical 'chatter', in seeking to turn ethics into a subject-matter, can be read as a kind of 'unhappy' responsiveness. The will to 'go beyond' senseful language, and to treat ethics as questions-with-answers manifests a kind of ethical spirit. How one takes 'the limits of sense' is itself an ethical matter. Wittgenstein isn't suggesting that what ethics demands is that we resign ourselves to remaining within the limits of sense. The point, I think, is rather that the idea that resignation is what is at stake would itself be an expression of unhappiness in relation to 'In the world, everything is as it is, and everything happens as it happens.'

We can now see also what Wittgenstein may have meant in saying that ethics and aesthetics are one (TLP 6.421). I spoke of the way in which having our attention drawn to senseful language may enable us to contemplate the 'thereness' of the world, in which things are however they are, and things happen however they happen. Ethics and aesthetics are one in their relation to the world, the essence of which is given by the general form of proposition. The idea, in Wittgenstein's conception of ethics and aesthetics, is of a transformation in our relation to all that is accidental, all that happens and ordinarily absorbs us and matters to us, all that we usually take ourselves to know, to be aware of. Insofar as 'In the world, everything is as it is, and everything happens as it happens can be for us *satisfaction* or *dissatisfaction*, there is *will*, and thus ethics.[16]

The sentence 'In the world, everything is as it is, and everything happens as it happens' serves, I said, to emphasize the way in which the general form of proposition presents 'the essence of the world', in connection with the idea that the general form of proposition had two aspects. But talk of these two aspects, the presenting of all propositions and of all possible situations, the presenting of language on the one hand (that is) and world on the other, inevitably makes it seem as if we are talking about two matching systems of possibilities. This is a conception that we make use of in working our way through the *Tractatus*; but it is a misleading conception, for there are not here *two* anythings. If we say that something is the case, then what we have said *may be the case*. That last remark looks as if it relates language and world, *saying* and *being the case*, although it is quite empty. Here I want to make a connection with the sentence that is focal for much of section 7, 'The world is my world.' That sentence and 'In the world, everything is as it is, and everything happens as it happens' are what one might call propositional misrepresentations of the general form of proposition. They are sentence-constructions that help us to see what significance Wittgenstein took there to be in his presenting of sense 'from the inside'. Although propositional in form, in look, they are essentially figurative in their appeal to the idea of 'the world' as an object of thought. Such ineliminable figures are characteristic of what Wittgenstein spoke of, in 1929, as the 'thrust against the limits of language' that he identified with ethics. And it is worth pointing out here too that I have relied in my discussion of Wittgenstein on a figurative use of the terms *satisfaction* and *dissatisfaction*. The meaning these terms have been given is tied to contexts in which the object of satisfaction or dissatisfaction is some particular thing or something that is the case, whereas, in my talk here about Wittgenstein on ethics, I have repeatedly used the terms as if the object of satisfaction or dissatisfaction were the limits of language (in the case of Moore) or the world in its essential nature. And insofar as my talk of *will* has been tied to such figurative talk of satisfaction and dissatisfaction, it too is a kind of figurative use.

It is not in general a good idea to use remarks from before or after the *Tractatus* to explain what is going on in the book itself. I have, however, done just that; I have taken the continuities noted by Michael Fried between the *Notebooks* and Wittgenstein's remarks in 1930 on seeing the world *sub specie aeterni* to be present also in the *Tractatus*; and I have made use of Wittgenstein's remarks from 1929 about our inclinations, in thinking about ethics, to use words and expressions taken over from contexts in which they have a determinate meaning, but to give them no meaning in the new context. I have been looking at the significance for ethics of Wittgenstein's presenting the limits of language 'from inside', but those words should be brought into question too. For no sense has been given to 'inside' and 'outside' in speaking about language.

---

[16] Compare Floyd 1998, 103, on attachment to life and the refusal of attachment to life.

6. Philosophy and the Limits of Sense: Method and Essence

When he wrote the *Tractatus*, Wittgenstein accepted the philosophical idea that philosophy is concerned with what is essential, but he transforms that concern. He provides a new understanding of what it is for philosophy to treat of the essence of something through his conception of what it is for philosophy to treat of what is essential in a symbol. What is essential in a symbol is what all symbols that can serve the same purpose have in common (TLP 3.341). What they have in common is presented by the general form of the propositions which contain the symbols (3.312). Thus it is presented by a variable, the values of which are all those propositions (3.313). The stipulation of the values of the variable gives us the variable itself. The stipulation is a description of the propositions which are the value of the variable; and Wittgenstein adds that the only thing that is essential to such a stipulation is that it is merely such a description and 'states nothing about what is signified' (3.317). These remarks provide an outline of a philosophical method for presenting essence, in which what is essential to the method is that it *does nothing but present symbols that have something in common*. The method does not involve saying anything about them; it remains within language in simply laying out (in whatever way) the symbols that have something in common through which they serve the purpose that they do serve. If, for example, it is presenting names, the method does not involve saying 'and these are names'. That the symbols presented are 'names' (if that is the label you attach) is nothing but what you see in the symbols themselves.

The presenting of the general form of proposition is thus an application of a general idea about philosophical method. My argument in section 4 about the presenting of the general form of proposition, that it merely presents a use and does not rule out any use, is meant to apply also to Wittgenstein's method understood more generally. The method could be described as a method through which philosophy presents what is essential, but at the same time it is meant to reshape our conception of what 'treating of the essential' is. It is meant to allow us to see a kind of philosophical activity entirely different from *the putting forward of propositions about what is essential* as philosophy treating the essential. You treat of something essential through laying out signs with the way they are used. What you have accomplished in what you have done has to be clear in what you have done. There is not going to be any matter of *adding*: 'and this is what *propositions*' (or *names* or *two-termed relations* or whatever) 'have in common'.

The philosophical error that Wittgenstein is combatting is that of thinking of the contrast between essential and accidental too superficially, an error that is reflected in the use of what we take to be substantially necessary propositions in talking about what is essential. To say (for example) 'propositions are pictures' is to use the word 'proposition' as if we were talking about a class of things that had a certain property; but 'proposition' hasn't been given that sort of meaning, and (if we achieve philosophical clarity) we shall not want to give it that sort of meaning. Thinking of the statement 'propositions are pictures' as if it were a necessary truth (or as if it were something that would be a neces-sary truth if *per impossibile* the *Tractatus* allowed for such truths) makes the difference between essence and accident *too slight*. Essence is, for Wittgenstein, a matter of the gen-erality of a variable. The propositions of the *Tractatus* are not attempts to say something that we need to be resigned about our inability to say. Resignation is not in place. Essence, we might say, cannot be spoken about, but does show itself.

What I have argued here puts in another way the argument given by Michael Kremer, that the difference between saying and showing is the main *problem* of philosophy. That is, it is a problem in that we misunderstand the character of the difference, and make it too slight. (Kremer 2001, 61–5) Insofar as the specification of the values of a propositional variable is the form that the presentation of what is essential takes, on the *Tractatus* view, there is a sense in which what we do in presenting an essence can fail to be what we were trying to do, but such a failure would not be a matter of our getting the essence in question wrong, but rather of our giving something else than what we meant to give.[17] If, when you stipulate the values of a variable, there is no going on to say e.g. 'and this is the general form that all *propositions* have', you aren't making a philosophical claim about what the values of the variable that you have presented all are. The idea that the activity of philoso-phy doesn't result in such claims is inseparable from Wittgenstein's view that his book was not a textbook, a book which presented a doctrine. The presentation of a kind of symbol, of a mode of use of signs, including the presentation of picture-proposition use, is not capable of truth or falsity, and this is part of what is involved in Wittgenstein's claim that the result of philosophy is not 'philosophical propositions' but clarification of proposi-tions. There is, in intention anyway, a profound commitment in the *Tractatus* to absten-tion from the putting forward of theses, and I have tried to show how that commitment is connected with the idea of philosophical method as proceeding from 'within' language, and to the idea that the limits of sense are not constraints on what we can say.[18]

---

[17] Compare Z §320: 'If we follow grammatical rules other than such-and-such ones, that does not mean we speak falsely but rather that we are speaking of something else.' I am arguing that the *Tractatus* conception of the method of philosophy implies that if we give a variable other than such-and-such one, we have not given a false account of propositionhood (say), but have given something else instead.

[18] My argument in section 6 draws on TLP 4.126 in a way that I haven't made explicit. It is often claimed that the *Tractatus* does not take propositions to have a *Bedeutung*; but Kremer (in 2002) has made clear the broad sense of the word as Wittgenstein uses it, and its tie to an expression's having a use. At TLP 4.126, Wittgenstein says that the sign for the marks of a formal concept is a distinctive feature of the symbols whose meanings (*Bedeutungen*) fall under the concept. This applies to the formal concept *being a proposition* as much as to any other formal concept, i.e. it applies to symbols the meaning of which is propositional meaning. When Wittgenstein says in 3.317 that the stipulation of the values of a propositional variable is not concerned with the *Bedeutung* of the symbols in question, this applies to propositions as well as to other symbols. The presenting of a variable like the one at TLP 6 has to be separated from the philosophical 'gas' that accompanies it. The essential thing about the giving of the variable is: 'it states nothing about what is signified'. So far as Wittgenstein does actually say, at TLP 6, that what he is giving is the general form of propositions, the words giving what the general form is *of* drop out; they are no part of the philosophical activity of presenting the variable. It is essential to that activity that it doesn't include saying that the values of the variable have such-and-such sort of meaning.

The philosophical practice of the *Tractatus* itself involves a kind of reflexiveness: the presentation of the general form of proposition, insofar as that succeeds as philosophical clarification, makes plain that the concern of philosophy with what is essential is not a matter of its having a subject matter, truths about which it comes up with; insofar as the method succeeds we shall not take philosophy, in its concern with what is essential, to be different from science only in the questions it asks and in the methods through which it arrives at answers, but not different from science in *asking questions* and *arriving at answers*. That (as I have suggested) would not make the distinction deep enough. But the method of presenting the general form of proposition, insofar as it is a case of presenting an essence through description of symbols, uses the method the point of which can be seen only through the achievement, through the method, of clarity about language and logic. The achieving of philosophical clarity is possible through the directing of attention to what is in some sense before us (though Wittgenstein's idea of what was 'before us' depended on those spectacles on his nose); and the propositions of the *Tractatus*, though they certainly are meant to have a role in the re-directing of attention, are not themselves failed attempts to say what we have to resign ourselves to being unable to say. I have tried here to emphasize that Wittgenstein's intention was to make clear the difference between the scientific asking and answering of questions and the philosophical task of clarification: to make that distinction go deep enough. He later thought that he had failed to do so, and that in various ways the conception of philosophy in the *Tractatus* was still in the grip of the idea of the method of science.

7. Philosophy and the Limits of Sense: The Philosophical I and the Challenge of Solipsism

A general principle of my discussion is that it is a mistake to argue that, of the various forms of philosophical solipsism, Wittgenstein is concerned only with solipsism of some particular type. Very different modes of treatment of the self and subjectivity, including those of Schopenhauer, Lichtenberg, Weininger, and Russell, raise issues all of which are present in Wittgenstein's very condensed treatment of solipsism.

I shall look briefly at three subtle discussions of Wittgenstein on solipsism, which I think will help us understand the issues. In discussing the *Tractatus* view of solipsism, Anscombe summarizes some remarks of Wittgenstein's from 1929–30 about the language we use in describing experience.[19] We could have a language in which someone, A, is

[19] Anscombe 1963, 166–7. Anscombe wrote before the publication of *Philosophical Remarks*, but the remarks which she quotes can be found in PR, 88–9; cf. also WVC, 49–50. The material in the latter dates from late 1929.

treated as a kind of centre for talk of experience. People using this language say 'There is pain' when A is in pain; and they say 'X is behaving as A behaves when there is pain' when, as we might say, X is in pain. Similarly, with 'It is thinking', said when A is thinking (where the 'it' is analogous to that of 'It is snowing') and 'X is behaving as A does when it thinks'. It was G. C. Lichtenberg from whom Wittgenstein picked up the idea of this way of speaking, and I shall refer to such a language as a Lichtenberg-language, and to the centre of such a language as an L-centre.[20] Anyone can be taken as L-centre of such a language; but, Wittgenstein notes, the language in which I am the L-centre 'has a peculiar but quite inexpressible advantage' over the language with anyone else as centre. The various languages are all capable of representing the same situations: they are translatable into each other, and the same reality 'corresponds to them all and to the "physical language"'. Anscombe comments that this passage is quite close to Wittgenstein's thought about solipsism in the *Tractatus*. Her point is that the language with me as L-centre does have an 'absolute' advantage, on Wittgenstein's view: 'I *am* the centre, but this is inexpressible.' On Anscombe's reading of the *Tractatus* remarks about solipsism, the I has a unique position in relation to language and world, but this is not expressible. Marie McGinn, in her discussion of the same group of *Tractatus* remarks, ascribes to Wittgenstein the idea that we need a distinction between the empirical subject and the subject who represents the world to himself. She argues that, although Wittgenstein uses the first-person pronoun in giving his view, his notion of the subject 'is not essentially first-personal'; I can recognize others as subjects. Thus, on this reading, there is a multiplicity of non-empirical subjects allowed for by the *Tractatus* remarks on the self; there isn't one unique subject with an inexpressible position. (McGinn 2006, esp. 275–6) B. F. McGuinness, discussing the same passage, says that Wittgenstein holds that language has to have a centre and, when I speak or think, I am that centre; but this is equally true of whoever speaks. He goes on: 'When I speak or think, it is the World-soul, *die Weltseele*, speaking', and this is equally true of anybody else. The World-soul is something in which we can all participate, and in which we should all participate. (McGuinness 2001, 10)

Anscombe, then, thinks that the *Tractatus* view is that there is, inexpressibly, a unique non-empirical self; McGinn ascribes to Wittgenstein the idea that the notion of the non-empirical subject allows for many such subjects, each of which can represent how things are, can judge what is the case. And McGuinness allows for a multiplicity that is in some sense not a genuine multiplicity but a multiple participation in the World-soul. Reading these discussions, we may take them to treat two inseparable questions about what the non-empirical subject is and whether there is one such subject or many or many-but-in-some-sense-one. It looks as if these questions call for answers that lie beyond what counts as sayable. It may seem, then, that Wittgenstein's remarks on solipsism and the

---

[20] 'It thinks' or 'It is thinking' is a translation of 'Es denkt'. '*Es denkt*, sollte man sagen, so wie man sagt: *es blitzt*. Zu sagen *cogito*, ist schon zu viel, sobald man es durch *Ich denke* übersetzt.' The remark is on p. 74 of the Reclam edition of Lichtenberg's selected writings that Wittgenstein gave Russell in 1913; the remark is also quoted by Weininger in *Geschlecht und Charakter*.

philosophical I constitute a particularly difficult case for anyone who wants to argue that Wittgenstein's conception of the limits of language doesn't demand a kind of resignation to there being things that supposedly cannot be expressed.

Anscombe gives us a place to start: with the idea of an experiential language in which I express what *I* experience, not through the use of 'I' but through taking myself as L-centre in the way she describes. I think she is right in suggesting that the line of thought which is worked out in some detail in the 1929/30 notes and the related conversation with Waismann can help us to see what is going on in the *Tractatus* discussion of solipsism.[21] It helps us to see *how* the solipsist's view crumples, and an understanding of the way it crumples is essential to a grasp of the remarks in the *Tractatus* about the self. But the line of thought she describes is relevant to the later stages of the crumpling of solipsism (5.64). I shall give one way of imagining how the crumpling might go, starting with the earlier stages. (I use the idea of a Lichtenberg-language in formulating the later stages, but in fact the argument could be re-formulated using a more generic account of an experiential language with myself as centre; the important points would be (a) the absence of any terms for any owners of experience and (b) a radical asymmetry between the treatment of 'my' experience and that of others.)

In the initial phase, the solipsist takes himself to be able to use ordinary language and the word 'I' to express what he wants to say about himself as the sole being who thinks and experiences. The trouble is that the I of which we speak in ordinary language is one among many persons, a being who is thought about by others just as he may think about them. So this attempted mode of expression of his solipsism has to be given up. The next stage is the solipsist's resort to an experiential language, a language which will, he hopes, be suited to bring out his unique situation. He attempts at this stage to use the word 'I' in two different ways: to speak about the empirical self that is part of the world and to speak about the self as centre of experience; but at this stage the self as centre is conceived as part of the world, a part that is given a priori. But, as Wittgenstein notes, there is no a priori element in experience; the experiencing self is not something in the world.

The stage which follows and which responds to that difficulty is one in which the solipsist uses a language which appears to give expression to his unique position, but which does so without using the word 'I' or any equivalent. This is the stage at which a Lichtenberg-language of the sort described by Anscombe would play a role. 'There is pain' or 'It is thinking' is used when I am in pain, or when I am thinking something, etc., and other people are described by formulations like 'A is behaving as CD does when there is pain.' A language for my experience, with a Lichtenberg-structure, at first appears to be the ideally right language to give expression to solipsism, and the ideally right language in which I can write *The World as I Found It*. It is indeed the availability of a form of representation distinct from ordinary 'physical' language, which appears to give the

---

[21] Anscombe says that the passage she quotes 'appears very close to [the *Tractatus*] in thought'. Her impression is certainly supported by Wittgenstein's claim that Carnap had plagiarized the *Tractatus* in his claims about the translatability into each other of physical language and experiential language. For discussion of this accusation, see Diamond 2000, 263, 278–9, 287. See also Stern 2007.

solipsist what he is looking for, that carries the argument forward at this point.[22] But there are two difficulties. One is that the language does not allow the solipsist to represent anything which is not representable in ordinary language, so the advantage it at first appears to have seems questionable; the other is that there is a multiplicity of Lichtenberg-languages, which makes it unclear what the special character is of the language with me as L-centre. Whichever of the difficulties one follows up, the result will ultimately be the same. While the language with me as L-centre appears to enable me to express my unique position, it does not enable me to represent as being the case anything that cannot be represented in other Lichtenberg-languages or indeed in our ordinary 'physical' language.

As Anscombe notes, all the Lichtenberg languages and our ordinary way of speaking are equivalent in terms of what situations they can represent. It is what the languages have in common that enables them to represent those situations; and there corresponds to all of them *the* world. Think here of TLP 3.3411, where Wittgenstein said that one could say that the real name of an object was what all symbols that signified it had in common. One could go on to say that *the* language, or language, is simply what all languages that can represent the world have in common. What is the point then of saying that the I is a 'limit of the world'?

The point of saying 'The I is a limit of the world' can be looked at from two directions. First, there is what is granted to the solipsist, who wants that *everything* that is the case can be put in the language with him as centre, and in which what is described is the world as he experiences it. And, secondly, there is the shrinking down of what is thereby granted to the solipsist. Whatever can be the case can be said in any language that is language in the sense explained in the preceding paragraphs; and in particular it can be said in the language which has me as L-centre, and in which I describe the world as I experience it. In that language, everything that can be the case in the world can be said. Wittgenstein writes at TLP 5.641: 'The I gets into philosophy through this, that "the world is my world".' The clause 'the world is my world' combines, though in a form that can be misleading, the point just mentioned (about the reach of experiential language to everything that can be said to be the case in any language) with the point that all the languages, i.e. *the* language, have corresponding to them *the* world. The world is what language/all the languages speak of; it is 'mine' in that everything about the world, everything that is

---

[22] Many discussions of Wittgenstein's remarks on solipsism leave out the idea that there is any further stage beyond the criticism of the idea of the self as an a priori element in all experience. The idea that Anscombe emphasizes, that Wittgenstein's thought about solipsism takes seriously the possibility of a language which appears to give an ideal kind of expression to solipsism *without mentioning the self at all* is simply not considered. But I believe that this idea is an essential part of what Wittgenstein thinks of as the following through of the implications of solipsism, and that it is at the heart of what is involved in 'the world is my world'. It is at any rate clear that there is no obvious step from the collapse of a version of solipsism that takes the self to be an a priori element within experience to the collapse of solipsism simpliciter. Readers of Wittgenstein may disagree about how far the *Tractatus* remains in the grip of some kind of solipsism, but discussion of the issue will be distorted if it is thought that he took the point about there not being any a priori element in experience to finish off solipsism.

the case, everything that might be thought to be the case, can be said in the language with me as L-centre, in which I describe the world as I experience it. My language encompasses *the* world (and by 'my language' here one can slide between meaning the experiential language with me as L-centre and *the* language/all the languages, including the one with me as L-centre; one can speak of it/them as that language which I alone understand). One could think of 'my' Lichtenberg language, with its translatability into all other languages, as providing a shrunk-down notion of a centre of *the* language, an I that is an extensionless point; one could speak of this I as a limit of the world.[23] But then this talk of 'the limit of the world' is simply a way of putting what, on the *Tractatus* account, is open to view in the presentation of what propositions have in common, including the translatability into each other of different forms of description, including the translatability into each other of the language with me as L-centre and non-Lichtenberg language. Rules for translating one language into another remain 'within' language; Wittgenstein's conception of the intertranslatability of all languages is not thought of by him as a kind of theory about language, but as something that can be seen in the shared features of different languages, through which all of them are capable of representing reality. His discussion of the self and solipsism, then, depends on the idea at 3.343 of intertranslatability of languages, which is itself meant to be a mere expansion of the idea that what is essential can be seen in the laying out of symbols which have a common feature. The general form of operation given at TLP 6.01 is meant to cover all translation rules, all transitions from one form of description to another.

It would, I think, be a mistake to try to explain the *Tractatus* view of solipsism (and the sense in which what it 'means' is correct) without looking at the significance of a language which appears to give special expression to my experience. The equivalence between that language and other languages, including 'physical' language, all of which have corresponding to them the same reality, is what enables us to see why the self of solipsism 'shrinks to a point without extension'.[24] But although the self of solipsism shrinks down to an extensionless point, the solipsist is nevertheless granted something: something more, indeed, than that the world can be represented in language that he understands. At the heart of what is granted by Wittgenstein's argument to the solipsist is the translatability of 'physical' language into the experiential language with me as centre; the possibility of translation in that direction is every bit as important to the argument as is the translatability of my experiential language into 'physical' language. The solipsist is meant to be genuinely satisfied: he is to be genuinely offered the reach of his experiential language to everything that is the case. To follow through the implications of solipsism strictly is to begin by trying to express the uniqueness of the I, and, from

---

[23] The notion of a centre introduced here is different from the notion of an L-centre. There are many L-centres, one for each Lichtenberg language. So far as all the Lichtenberg languages, including the one with me as L-centre, are intertranslatable and translatable into ordinary language, they have one centre in the shrunk-down sense, the 'centre' of *the* language.

[24] The importance of the ideas here for Wittgenstein is reflected also in his accusation of plagiarism against Carnap, an accusation which involved Wittgenstein's claim that what Carnap meant by physicalism was already in the *Tractatus*. See Stern 2007.

that starting place, to reach the stage at which one might say 'My language encompasses *the* world' (where 'my language' simply is language, *the* language, but is also at the same time language-with-me-as-L-centre).[25] The forms of words we call on here, like 'The world is my world', are empty; they nevertheless provide useful images, and represent stages in the collapse of the solipsist's attempt at saying his solipsism. In particular, the language used in putting the different stages of the collapse draws on ordinary ways of using 'the' in contrast with 'my'/'me'/'mine' in identifying something, but the ordinary ways of making such contrasts are lacking, and no other mode of making them has been provided. So the final stage of the collapse of the solipsist's attempt to say his solipsism involves a recognition that no saying of anything would be what he wants, but that what he wants is in a sense open to view, just as much as the translatability of English into German and vice versa would have been taken by Wittgenstein at the time of the *Tractatus* to be open to view, and to be expressible in a rule. In suggesting that the translatability of experiential language into physical language, and of physical language into experiential language, gives the solipsist what he wants, I do want to insist that this is not nothing, though it is nothing that would be the content of any senseful proposition, nor is it some ineffable quasi-content beyond the reach of the sayable, any more than is the translatability of English into German.[26]

To see what the solipsist is granted, consider 'The Earth has existed for more than four billion years.' The picture that may accompany such a sentence is of an existence wholly independent of any thinking or experience, an existence that could perfectly well have been what it was, even if no being with experiences had ever existed, and that is causally related to experiences of things that count as evidence of the age of the Earth. What the solipsist is granted by translatability into his experiential language is that, insofar as the sentence about the Earth says that something is the case, what it says is so is sayable also in sentences in the book *The World as I Found It*, i.e. in experiential terms. The sentence about the Earth has a complex use, and the way in which it is descriptive isn't straightforward: it doesn't state any facts over and above experiential facts.[27] The use of the sentence, that is, is not what the picture of the Earth out there, spinning along in its orbit independently of anybody's experience, suggests. And the solipsist is further granted

---

[25] There is more that could be said about the 'peculiar but inexpressible advantage' that the language with me as centre appears to have, but I cannot get into this question here. See WVC, 50. For a discussion of how the *Tractatus* can accommodate the asymmetry between 'I have a pain' and 'He has a pain', see Diamond 2000.

[26] I have not tried to lay out what exactly is meant by 'experiential language' in the context of discussion of the *Tractatus*. I don't think we can identify what is meant with Wittgenstein's later conception of a 'phenomenological language'. But the questions with which he was concerned later, when he wrote about a 'primary' language, were close to the questions involved in the discussion of solipsism in the *Tractatus*. See also Stern 2007, and Stern 1995, ch. 3, esp. p. 78, where Stern quotes F. P. Ramsey's notes from the 1920s on Wittgenstein's treatment of the significance of experiential language.

[27] Ramsey's notes from the 1920s (see previous note) explicitly ascribe to Wittgenstein a treatment of material objects of the sort described. Talk that purports to be about such things enables us to use simplified general laws in descriptions. A corresponding account is suggested of the ordinary language ascription of sense-data to owners of sense-data.

that the relation between the Earth's existence and experiences of things that may be counted as evidence of its age is not a causal relation but a kind of logical relation.[28] The issue here is that of the 'limits of the world'. Before his line of thinking collapses, the solipsist takes there to be a would-be understanding of the sentence about the age of the Earth that puts it beyond the limits; he says 'There is *only* my experience.' What lies within the limits is only what can be said in experiential language. Realism about the world appears to require going beyond the limits recognized by the solipsist. What is offered by Wittgenstein puts the world, including the four-billion-year-old Earth, as we speak about it in ordinary 'physical' language, within the limits of sense, but its lying within the limits is inseparable from translatability of all sentences about the Earth into experiential language. (In figurative language: 'The subject is a limit of the world.') Thus to get something that looks as if it lies beyond the limits, we have to get something that appears to be outside the reach of such translation. Here the *Tractatus* can be thought of as offering us a distinction between *realism* and a kind of *fantasy of realism*. A fantasy of realism would involve the idea of a language in which things could be said that could not be said in my language, an idea which Russell (for example) did hold.[29] The picture here is of the subject as not a limit of *the* world; it is a picture of the world as extending beyond the reach of the subject. How the contrast should be made between realism and a fantasy of realism is a question which, apparently settled in the *Tractatus*, gets unsettled and rethought later.

The self or subject shouldn't be thought of as a special sort of thing, a non-empirical thing, or an active thing, or an impersonal representing thing. Any such way of thinking makes the difference between it and the self of our ordinary thought and talk too slight. 'It' isn't a thing at all; and the thing-y language we may use for it in philosophy is deeply misleading. Anything *spoken of* isn't it. What we are trying to do in our thing-y language is put into words what can be seen in the translatability between 'my' centred-experiential language and our ordinary ways of representing the world. What then does Wittgenstein mean by saying that there really is a sense in which philosophy can talk about the self in a non-psychological way?

The sketch that I have given of the collapse of the solipsist's attempt to say his solipsism suggests, I think, that if we follow through what is involved in the collapse, we shall take the provision of a variable that presents what all propositions have in common to be the way philosophy does, in a sense, talk about the self in a non-psychological way. The earlier stage of the collapse, in which one might say 'The world is my world', even though it is a way of speaking which is 'overcome' (in the sense in which Wittgenstein's propositions are, as he says, to be overcome), nevertheless enables one to take the variable given at TLP 6 to satisfy the desire that philosophy treat of the self. That one moves through and beyond[30] saying such things as 'The world is my world' or

---

[28] Compare WL, 80–83.

[29] Russell 1932, 216–18; the essay was originally published in 1911. I discuss Russell's view and Wittgenstein's response in Diamond 2000.

[30] 'durch sie–auf ihnen–über sie'; see TLP 6.54.

'The subject is a limit of the world' is what enables the collapse of solipsism as a distinct view to be a satisfaction of the desire to speak solipsism. The figurative sentences through which one progresses mark the progress itself as one in which thus-and-such specific philosophical problem has been resolved. What I am here taking for granted is that a theme of all of Wittgenstein's philosophy is the transformation of philosophical desire, i.e. the idea that such desire can be understood to be satisfied, at the end of the activity of philosophy, by something different from what one had originally taken oneself to want. For the solipsist, then, who thinks through the implications of his view, there isn't something on the far side of the limits of language that he would like to be able to say, if only it were possible to do so.

There is a parallel between the structure of the account that I have given and that given by Thomas Ricketts of the collapse of a far more extensive structure of reasoning about sentences as 'logically interconnected representations of reality'. (Ricketts 1996; see especially 88–94.) The crumpling of what appeared to be a stretch of thought, as we attempt to think it through, is an important element in the method of the *Tractatus*. After the crumpling, we may take ourselves to be left back 'within' senseful language. But that picture of our being 'within' language is itself the after-effect of the crumpling of talk of such things as 'The world is my world', talk that might appear to go beyond what can be said. In his letter to von Ficker, Wittgenstein described the book as drawing limits 'gleichsam von innen', 'as it were from inside' and it's time now to emphasize that 'gleichsam'. To say, without that 'as it were', that Wittgenstein draws the limits from inside carries the strong suggestion of an outside where he did not go, and hence of limits which are constraints. The picture there of inside and outside is misleading. (cf. Minar 1995, 443.) Philosophy carried out 'as it were from inside' is simply philosophy, making clear what we say and think, showing us what we do. That was the intention; and measured against that intention, the book could later be recognized to have failed.

There is much in the *Tractatus* discussion of solipsism and the self that I have not touched on at all, including the connections with ethics. I have tried only to show how Wittgenstein's remarks about solipsism do not require us to think of the solipsist as having to be resigned to the impossibility of saying something that he wants to say, and to bring out the shifting character of a remark like 'The world is *my* world', which shifts from its appearance as a kind of conclusion at one stage in the thinking through of the implications of solipsism to its ultimate appearance as something we move through and beyond in the collapse of solipsism as a distinct view. There is also much in the *Tractatus* use of the notion of a limit or limits that I have not been able to discuss. The most important thing that I have not discussed except tangentially is the *Tractatus* understanding of logic and its relation to giving the limits of language 'from within'.[31]

---

[31] I have been greatly helped by comments and suggestions from Marie McGinn, James Conant, and Alice Crary.

References

ANSCOMBE, G. E. M. (1963). *An Introduction to Wittgenstein's Tractatus*. London: Hutchinson.

CONANT, JAMES (2002). 'The Method of the *Tractatus*', in Erich H. Reck ed., *From Frege to Wittgenstein*. New York: Oxford University Press.

CONANT, JAMES and DIAMOND, CORA (2004). 'On Reading the *Tractatus* Resolutely', in Max Kölbel and Bernhard Weiss eds., *Wittgenstein's Lasting Significance*. London: Routledge.

DIAMOND, CORA (2000). 'Does Bismarck Have a Beetle in His Box?', in Alice Crary and Rupert Read eds., *The New Wittgenstein*. London: Routledge.

—— (2004). 'Saying and Showing, an Example from Anscombe', in Barry Stocker ed., *Post-Analytic Tractatus*. Aldershot: Ashgate.

—— (2010). 'Inheriting from Frege: the Work of Reception, as Wittgenstein Did It', in Thomas Ricketts and Michael Potter eds., *The Cambridge Companion to Frege*. Cambridge: Cambridge University Press.

—— (2012). 'What Can You Do With the General Propositional Form?', in José L. Zalabardo ed., *Wittgenstein's Early Philosophy*. Oxford: Oxford University Press.

—— (2014). 'The Hardness of the Soft', in James Conant and Andrea Kern eds., *Varieties of Skepticism*. Berlin: De Gruyter.

DONATELLI, PIERGIORGIO (2005). 'The Problem of "the Higher" in Wittgenstein's *Tractatus*', in D. Z. Phillips and Mario von der Ruhr eds., *Religion and Wittgenstein's Legacy*. Aldershot: Ashgate.

FLOYD, JULIET (1998). 'The Uncaptive Eye', in Leroy S. Rouner ed., *Loneliness*. Notre Dame, IN: University of Notre Dame Press.

FRIED, MICHAEL (2007). 'Jeff Wall, Wittgenstein, and the Everyday', *Critical Inquiry*. 33.3: 495–526.

FRIEDLANDER, ELI (2001). *Signs of Sense*. Cambridge, MA: Harvard University Press.

GRIFFIN, JAMES (1964). *Wittgenstein's Logical Atomism*. Oxford: Clarendon Press.

KREMER, MICHAEL (2001). 'The Purpose of Tractarian Nonsense', *Noûs*, 35: 39–73.

—— (2002). 'Mathematics and Meaning in the *Tractatus*', *Philosophical Investigations*, 25.3: 272–303.

LEE, DESMOND ed. (1980). *Wittgenstein's Lectures 1930–1932: From the notes of John King and Desmond Lee*. Oxford: Blackwell.

MCGINN, MARIE (2006). *Elucidating the Tractatus*. Oxford: Oxford University Press.

MCGUINNESS, BRIAN (2001). '"Solipsism" in the *Tractatus*', in David Charles and William Child eds., *Wittgensteinian Themes: Essays in Honour of David Pears*. Oxford: Oxford University Press.

MCMANUS, DENIS (2006). *The Enchantment of Words*. Oxford: Oxford University Press.

—— (2009). 'The General Form of the Proposition: The Unity of Language and the Generality of Logic in the Early Wittgenstein', *Philosophical Investigations*, 32.4: 295–318.

MINAR, EDWARD (1995). 'Feeling at Home in Language (What Makes Reading *Philosophical Investigations* Possible?)', *Synthese*, 102: 413–52.

MOORE, G. E. (1922). *Principia Ethica*. Cambridge: Cambridge University Press.

MULHALL, STEPHEN (2007). 'Words, Waxing and Waning: Ethics in/and/of the *Tractatus Logico-Philosophicus*', in Guy Kahane, Edward Kanterian, and Oskari Kuusela eds., *Wittgenstein and His Interpreters*. Oxford: Blackwell.

RICKETTS, THOMAS (1996). 'Pictures, Logic, and the Limits of Sense in Wittgenstein's *Tractatus*', in Hans Sluga and David G. Stern eds., *The Cambridge Companion to Wittgenstein*. Cambridge: Cambridge University Press.

RUSSELL, BERTRAND (1932). 'Knowledge by Acquaintance and Knowledge by Description', in *Mysticism and Logic*. London: George Allen & Unwin.

SCHOPENHAUER, ARTHUR (1988). *Die Welt als Wille und Vorstellung*. Zürich: Haffmans Verlag.

STERN, DAVID (1995). *Wittgenstein on Mind and Language*. New York: Oxford University Press.

—— (2007). 'Wittgenstein, the Vienna Circle, and Physicalism: A Reassessment', in Alan Richardson and Thomas Uebel eds., *The Cambridge Companion to Logical Empiricism*. Cambridge: Cambridge University Press.

SULLIVAN, PETER (2004). '"The General Propositional Form is a Variable" (*Tractatus* 4.53)', *Mind*, 113. 449: 43–56.

—— (2004a). 'What Is the *Tractatus* About?', in Max Kölbel and Bernhard Weiss eds., *Wittgenstein's Lasting Significance*. London: Routledge.

—— (2011). 'Synthesizing without Concepts', in Rupert Read and Matthew A. Lavery eds., *Beyond the Tractatus Wars: The New Wittgenstein Debate*. Abingdon. Routledge.

WAISSMANN, FRIEDRICH (1965). 'Notes on Talks with Wittgenstein', *Philosophical Review*, 74.1: 12–16.

WAISMANN, FRIEDRICH (1979). *Wittgenstein and the Vienna Circle: Conversations recorded by Friedrich Waismann*, ed. B. McGuinness, trans. B. McGuinness and J. Schulte. Oxford: Blackwell.

WILLIAMS, BERNARD (1981). 'Wittgenstein and Idealism', in *Moral Luck*. Cambridge: Cambridge University Press.

WITTGENSTEIN, LUDWIG (1951). *Tractatus Logico-Philosophicus*, trans. C. K. Ogden. London: Routledge & Kegan Paul.

—— (1953). *Philosophical Investigations*, ed. G. E. M. Anscombe and R. Rhees, trans. G. E. M. Anscombe. Oxford: Blackwell.

—— (1961). *Notebooks 1914–1916*. Oxford: Blackwell.

—— (1965). 'A Lecture on Ethics', *Philosophical Review*, 74: 3–12.

—— (1967). *Zettel*, ed. G. E. M. Anscombe and G. H. von Wright, trans. G. E. M. Anscombe. Oxford: Basil Blackwell.

—— (1971). *Prototractatus: An Early Version of Tractatus Logico-Philosophicus*. London: Routledge & Kegan Paul.

—— (1975). *Philosophical Remarks*, ed. R. Rhees, trans. R. Hargreaves and R. White. Oxford: Basil Blackwell.

—— (1980). *Culture and Value*, ed. G. H. von Wright in collaboration with H. Nyman. Oxford: Blackwell.

CHAPTER 12

....

THE LIFE OF THE SIGN

Rule-following, Practice, and Agreement

....

EDWARD MINAR

This is how one calculates. Calculating is *this*. What we learn at school, for example. Forget this transcendent certainty, which is connected with your idea of spirit.

(OC §47)

Instead of the unanalysable, specific, indefinable: the fact that we act in such-and-such ways, e.g. *punish* certain actions, *establish* the state of affair[s] thus and so, *give orders*, render accounts, describe colours, take an interest in others' feelings. What has to be accepted, the given – it might be said – are facts of living. [*Tatsachen des Lebens*]

(RPP I §630)

FOR the Wittgenstein of *Philosophical Investigations*, "a philosophical problem has the form: 'I don't know my way about'." (PI §123) Groping for direction in the midst of his investigation of rule-following in *Philosophical Investigations*, he remarks: "Language is a labyrinth of paths. You approach from one side and know your way about; you approach the same place from another side and no longer know your way about." (PI §203) This chapter will traverse some well-trodden but often tangled paths in hope of finding a way with a number of questions about Wittgenstein's conception of philosophy, about his methods, and about the instructions he provides for our use of his "album" of "sketches". (PI, Preface, v) Such questions, however, cannot be addressed without direct engagement in the particular grammatical investigations that occupy most of Wittgenstein's attention. Separating Wittgenstein's remarks about philosophy and his own approaches to it, on the one hand, and his treatment of specific conceptual confusions, on the other, is artificial and misleading. We must jump *in medias res*. Here I hope to elucidate some features of how *agreement* functions in Wittgenstein's treatment of rule-following by working toward an interpretation of his apparently climactic conclu-sion in *Investigations* §242: "If language is to be a means of communication there must be agreement not only in definition but also (queer as this may sound) in judgments. This seems to abolish logic, but does not do so." What is the apparent threat to logic pre-sented by what Wittgenstein calls "agreement in judgments"? Why is the threat merely apparent, when agreement is seen in the right light?

1. Reminders

In §81 of *Philosophical Investigations*, pondering Ramsey's comment that "logic was a 'normative science'" (PI §81), Wittgenstein takes exception to the notion that logical investigation will uncover an ideal structure comprising "strict rules." According to one natural line of thought, this structure would, in some sense, already be there, although it would remain obscured behind the everyday uses it informs:

> The strict and clear rules of the logical structure of propositions appear to us as something in the background – hidden in the medium of the understanding. I already see them (even though through a medium): for I understand the proposi-tional sign, I use it to say something. (PI §102)

Wittgenstein lampoons the idea that there *must* be such a calculus operating in the back-ground, "as if it took the logician to shew people at last what a proper sentence looked like." (PI §81) It should puzzle us, he thinks, how such a model, which could serve as a perfectly appropriate "object of comparison" (PI §131) for some purposes, would *have to* be related to everyday use. What would it mean to say that in unearthing it we *discover* the norms by which use is governed? We are in no position to judge that the so-called ideal represents what is *really* going on; we remain in the dark about what this would mean.

In the sections leading up to §81, Wittgenstein has argued that to take the rigor in question here as a requirement on the logical workings of language is to impose a pic-ture, not to describe the actual phenomena. He will now go on to urge, in §§82–8, that the meaning of signs is not dependent on their use being fixed or justified by the sort of pre-existing, independent standards that the ideal suggested by Ramsey's slogan is designed to provide. "Logic does not treat of language," Wittgenstein reminds us, "in the sense in which natural science treats of a natural phenomenon, and the most that can be said is that we *construct* ideal languages." (PI §81)[1] Why, under what conditions, are we disposed to think otherwise? Wittgenstein anticipates that:

---

[1] Wittgenstein's train of thought in §81 is complex, suggesting that a kind of "crossing of pictures" (§191) lies behind the idea of logic as a normative *science*. The ideal language is not a phenomenon there to be discovered, nor does it function like an *idealization*, an object of comparison; and to say that logic is "like science, only normative" would be helping oneself to the very notion of normativity that the idea of a hidden, ideal calculus constituting the laws of thought would be intended to elucidate.

All this…can only appear in the right light when one has attained greater clarity about the concepts of understanding, meaning and thinking. For it will then also become clear what can lead us (and did lead me) to think that if anyone utters a sentence and *means* or *understands* it he is operating a calculus according to definite rules. (PI §81)

How then will further inquiry into meaning, understanding, and following a rule contribute to the diagnosis of our susceptibility to the attractive but inchoate picture Wittgenstein wants to resist? His treatment of rule-following is a sustained deconstruction of a model of meaning based on a picture of the "hardness of the logical must" (PI §437). Here, determination by norms, conceived as rule-like structures, becomes a "philosophical superlative." (PI §192)[2] Such determination is *like* causal or mechanical necessitation, in that it determines how things *must* happen; but it is also, in some shadowy sense, *more* definite, *more* rigid. And ironically, this is so precisely because, "empirically" as it were, it is *not* the case that things must actually proceed as so determined. Implicit here is the worry that without the underlying ideal mechanism, what we do would be "arbitrary,"[3] because always subject to *interpretation*. And herein lies an apparent challenge to the putative legitimacy – the very rationality – of our practices. Faced with this threat of arbitrariness, we are prone to overlook the sense that logical determination makes in our day-to-day dealings. We "cross pictures" (PI §191) by supposing that the image of a super-causal mechanism provides a schema for a sort of absolute determination that no actual mechanism could accomplish.[4]

This picture of the hardness of the mechanism is so deeply ingrained that it becomes difficult even to notice, let alone to resist. In his lectures, Wittgenstein uses another, less familiar, metaphor to instill in us the sense that the mythology involved here is very peculiar indeed:

One may say that the law condemns him to death, whether or not the judges do so. And so one says that, even though the judge may be lenient, the law is always inexorable. Thus we have the idea of a kind of super-hardness. I want to show that the inexorability of absolute hardness of logic is of just this kind. It seems as if we had got hold of a hardness which we have never experienced. (LFM, 197–8)

Now, how does Wittgenstein seek to reorient us, in our confusion here? As he says, "the work of the philosopher consists in assembling reminders for a particular purpose." (PI §127) By describing rule-following, Wittgenstein battles our captivation by a picture (PI §115) that has prevented us from recognizing "the ground that lies before us as the

---

[2] See PI §97:

We are under the illusion that what is peculiar, profound, essential in our investigation, resides in its trying to grasp the incomparable essence of language. That is, the order existing between the concepts of proposition, word, proof, truth, experience, and so on. This order is a *super*-order between – so to speak – *super*-concepts.

[3] On the specter of such arbitrariness, articulating Wittgenstein's worry in §242 about "abolishing logic," see RFM VI §49.

[4] See PI §§194–5.

ground." (RFM VI §31) Seeking to base our practices in something independent inclines us, quite systematically, to look everywhere *but* in our lives, to search inside and behind and beneath and upward, for the sort of satisfaction we think we need, something that would address the alleged (but in fact quite unspecified) threat of arbitrariness. The rule-following considerations are a series of reminders that serve, among other things of course, to vindicate Wittgenstein's methods. To confront the picture of "the hardness of the logical must" is to take on "what it is that opposes such an examination of details in philosophy" (PI §51), what makes it difficult to look into "the workings of our language, and that in such a way as to make us recognize those workings: *in despite of* an urge to misunderstand them." (PI §109)

Reminders often serve as instructions or rules, or as explanations thereof. "Don't forget to put the trash out on Monday," you remind me; "remember; that's when they pick it up," you explain. "Wear a coat and tie to meet with the Dean – they pay attention to these things in that office. Anyone familiar with how they operate knows that." Wittgensteinian reminders are clarifications of *meaning* for someone who, for some reason or another, has fallen into confusion, forgotten his or her bearings. Like everyday explanations, a reminder serves the purpose of "remov[ing] or…avert[ing] a [particular] misunderstanding – one, that is, that would occur but for the explanation." (PI §87) Reminders may not succeed. They may be rebuked, ignored, or rejected. They may provide inaccurate descriptions of what we say and do. When they do, we generally *disavow* them: they have failed as expressions of our intentions. Thus they do not (as Wittgenstein hints in §128) come up for debate in the way that philosophical theses about the *correctness* of what we say and do would.

Now, what would it be to remind someone of what following a rule *is, überhaupt*? We should not presume that *anything* would count as doing so:

> To what extent can the function of language be described? If someone is not master of a language, I may bring him to a mastery of it by training. Someone who is master of it, I may remind of the kind of training, or I may describe it; for a particular purpose; thus already using a technique of the language. (RFM VI §31)

Were someone genuinely at a loss about what following a rule is – if amnesia of rule-following were really a possibility – would it avail us to provide further formulations, explanations, and examples of rule-following, as we would do in describing the practice to a "master"? What are we imagining here? However we fill in the details, we end up either returning to the back and forth of teaching and learning, or re-explaining how to go on in the particular case, making a molehill of an apparent mountain. But still our questions assert themselves: "'How can one follow rules?' That is what I should like to ask….How can I follow a rule, when after all whatever I do can be interpreted as following it?" (RFM VI §38)

Our more general, apparently deeper, ostensibly *philosophical* questions seem to take the form of transcendental questions concerning the conditions of the possibility of being guided by rules and of following them correctly. Wittgenstein's responses do not remove them or prevent them from arising as much as lay their puzzling character open to view: Thus, following the question raised above about interpretation, he proceeds: "But how does it come about that I want to ask that, when after all I find no kind of difficulty in following a rule? Here we obviously misunderstand the facts that lie before our eyes. Interpretation comes to an end." (RFM VI §38) Nothing so far *counts* as unearthing a transcendental ground of rule-following in itself. In fact it should be mysterious what we would be doing in *asking* for what amounts to an explanation of what it is to *talk*, to make sense, the yearning for which is satisfied neither by appealing to facts about how we have been turned out by nature and upbringing nor by adverting to particular examples of misunderstanding. "Our disease [then] is one of wanting to explain." (RFM VI §31) Wittgenstein's use of reminders is as much to get us to acknowledge responsibility for the singularity of our demands for explanation at the site of our entry into philosophy as it is to give us specific language lessons in rule-following: as if we had somehow managed to forget how to mean something.

When at the end of the rule-following considerations, in §242, Wittgenstein brings up the centrality to our practices of "agreement in judgments," he may be interpreted as advocating a particular view about what makes rule-following possible.[5] In conjunction with the claims that "to obey a rule, to make a report, to give an order, to play a game of chess, are *customs* (uses, institutions)" (PI §199) and that "it is not possible to obey a rule 'privately'"(PI §202), his appeals to community, to the practices, presumably, of particular groups of individuals, have appeared to advance a substantive thesis which, naturally enough, it has proved possible to debate. Wittgenstein disavows this understanding. (See, for example, PI II, 226–7.) To take what constitutes the correct application of a rule to be *decided* by contingencies of human agreement would be to represent logic as part of the natural history of human beings. It would leave us with at best an ersatz for the logical "must." In fact, the temptation to take agreement as constitutive of rule-following gets absorbed into the dialectic through which Wittgenstein hopes to elicit our dissatisfaction with our ways of voicing the felt need for explanation. Agreement, on his view, is part of the grammar of rule-following, which means that it is a feature of our dealings with rules, an aspect rather than a precondition of our practices. Denying the place of agreement would not be challenging a thesis about how rules really work, but rather changing the subject, shifting away from the lives we live with rules. What, then, is the role of agreement, on Wittgenstein's account? Why are we forgetful of our attunements, why are they difficult to acknowledge?

In her paper, "Rules: Looking in the Right Place," Cora Diamond expands on Rush Rhees's invitation to "show how rules of grammar are rules of the lives in which there is language." (Diamond 1989, 12) In particular, Diamond notes that:

---

[5] See, for example, Malcolm 1986. The view that Saul Kripke labels the "skeptical solution" to the putative skeptical paradox of rule-following advanced in §201, on his interpretation, gives a similarly substantive role to community agreement. See Kripke 1982, Chapter 3. But it is difficult to pinpoint exactly what this role is, in the context of the skepticism about rule-following Kripke's Wittgenstein advocates. For criticism of both the success of the skeptical solution and the need for it, see Goldfarb 1982.

> The kind of publicness that characterizes a concept or rule can be seen in the place of the concept or rule in the life people share. (Diamond 1989, 22)

Looking in the right place, Diamond emphasizes, places the emphasis on *people* sharing *lives*, rather than on shared *reactions*:

> In fact, of course, we are not just trained to go "446, 448, 450", etc. and other similar things; we are brought into a life in which we rest on, depend on, people's following rules of many sorts, and in which people depend on us: rules, and agreement in following them, and reliance on agreement in following them, and criticizing or rounding on people who do not do it right – all this is woven into the texture of life; and it is in the context of its having a place in such a form of human life that a "mistake" is recognizably that. (Diamond 1989, 27–8)

Diamond's remarks prompt us to try to understand the role that agreement plays in Wittgenstein's dialectic both by looking at our lives with language and by asking what, in philosophy, diverts our attention from them. Following this lead, how should we understand the role of agreement in the rule-following considerations?[6]

2. RULE-FOLLOWING AND THE SKEPTICAL DIALECTIC

In *Philosophical Investigations* §185, Wittgenstein asks us to consider the case of a child who cannot get the hang of the rule for adding two past 1000, regardless of the examples, explanations, directives, and cajolings we supply:

> He writes 1000, 1004, 1008, 1012. We say to him 'Look what you've done!' – He doesn't understand. We say: 'You were meant to add *two*: look how you began the series!' – He answers: 'Yes, isn't it right? I thought that was how I was meant to do it.' – Or suppose he pointed to the series and said: 'But I went on in the same way.' (PI §185)

What are we to say of our apparently incorrigible "+2" kid? Whatever we do, he seems to reinterpret our efforts at instruction in a way consistent with his, after all incorrect, way of going on. There is something he seems unable to get. He does not pick up on the pattern, grasp the point of calling just *these* steps the same. In the spirit of the practice of following rules like "+2," we want to say that he is missing something already *there*. Hence we may be inclined to say, "the steps are determined by the way the rule is meant" (PI §190), or "the steps are really already taken." (PI §219)

In §185, Wittgenstein offers a rather half-hearted explanation of our predicament with the child, noting that "we might say, perhaps: It comes natural to this person to

---

[6] My approach to the rule-following considerations is indebted to Warren Goldfarb. See Goldfarb, 2012.

understand our order with our explanations as we should understand the order: 'Add 2 up to 1000, 4 up to 2000, 6 up to 3000 and so on.'" (PI §185) This is pretty much empty as an account of what is actually going on. It adds nothing substantial to "he doesn't go on as we do." In its wake, there is a subtle dramatic shift from concern about the child and our relation to him to some deep-seated concern about *ourselves*, our credentials as rule-followers. This finds expression in the nervous response of Wittgenstein's interlocutor – who quite understandably finds something lacking in this appeal to what comes natural to us – to Wittgenstein's intent in bringing up the case: "'What you are saying, then, comes to this: a new insight – intuition – is needed at every step to carry out the order '+n' correctly.'" (PI §186) The feeling that *something* must guide, indeed justify, our way of going on has gotten a grip on us. And without this something, what we do might appear somehow arbitrary. *Un*grounded, our judgment that the child has not understood would represent nothing more than an insistence on *our* way of going on, an imposition of our authority.[7]

At any rate, we seem to have a problem that goes well beyond this rather singular scenario with the child. From the sequel, we find that some version of some general question about how rules determine their applications proves intractable. Further rules, meanings, interpretations, whatever our insight into what *they* dictate, are themselves subject to further interpretation, and thus do not fulfill the burden of ruling out possible misunderstandings beforehand. What we need as the requisite grounding is something that can support the idea that in what we grasp when we follow the rule correctly, the steps are already taken. Our knowledge of how to go on would be our insight into this structure, already there. But nothing we can actually adduce is capable of tying down the steps in a way that the original rule, with our explanations and examples, could not in principle manage on its own. (See PI §§209–10.) And this comes to seem almost inevitable as we realize that what we are appealing to is, in effect, just more rules. The possibility of interpretation, and hence the threat it appears to present, persists. The ostensible problem presents itself as a need for depth, a demand to dig beneath the superficialities of our actual practices; but our explanations, divested of their particular contexts and purposes, do not serve to get us any deeper.

In this much, something very much akin to the skeptical voice of Saul Kripke's Wittgenstein is struggling to find expression in Wittgenstein's actual dialectic. To justify the correctness of our way of following a rule, to serve as our authoritative interpreter of how we are to go on, a candidate item must put on display the ultimate reasons we have for following the rule as we do. (See Kripke 1982, Chapter 1, especially pp. 21–3.) To refer to the underlying meaning of an expression would only answer our question if my understanding of that meaning itself could somehow be made out to be deeper than, explanatory of, knowing how to go on, mastering the practice. And then that item too – whatever it would amount to – would be subject to interpretation. We find ourselves either back where we started, or embarked on a hopeless regress.

---

[7] The interlocutor's slightly panicky tone at the beginning of §186 prompts Wittgenstein's rather sarcastic response at its end: "It would almost be more correct to say, not that an intuition was needed at every stage, but that a new decision was needed at every stage." (PI §186)

Kripke's influential interpretation serves to bring the figure of skepticism to the fore. At the beginning of §186, Wittgenstein's interlocutor has made a distinctively skeptical move: he has shifted from the singular case of the child in §185 to the presumption that something is needed to justify what *we* do, not in its particulars, but in *all* situations, and against all *possible* doubt: "It may *easily* look" – as it does to this interlocutor, and in the initial stages of Kripke's skeptical progression – "as if every doubt merely revealed an existing gap in the foundations; so that secure understanding is only possible if we first doubt everything that *can* be doubted, and then remove all these doubts." (PI §87; my italics) Now back in §87, Wittgenstein simply brushes off the skeptic, observing: "The sign-post is in order – if, under normal circumstances, it fulfils its purpose." (PI §87) Of course, there is no direct answer for the skeptic in this appeal to "practical" circumstances. The force of Wittgenstein's reminder here, rather, is to elicit from us the sense that the skeptic looks for the signpost's meaning in the wrong place, measuring what really goes on in normal circumstances by a fantastical ideal.

In the skeptical setup, no reliance on the surroundings of rule-following in everyday life is tolerated. Descriptions of the surfaces, the data, must be shorn of any presumptions about the normativity internal to the practices. Insofar as such abstraction is genuinely possible, the resulting descriptions are rendered superficial, allowing as they do reference only to the motions and outcalls, the reactions, of the participants. As Diamond puts it, "the idea of a philosophical account of what I really mean by 'he is always to go on in that way' is of an account addressed to someone on whose uptake, on whose responses, we are not depending." (Diamond 1991, 68–9) Here, in producing a kind of description of what we do that seems to fuel the need for a philosophical account that will show our justification in doing it, we have alienated ourselves from our practices. Hence, Diamond again: "The demands we make for philosophical explanations come, seem to come, from a position in which we are looking down onto the relation between ourselves and some reality, some kind of fact or real possibility." (Ibid., 69) We have maneuvered ourselves into the position of thinking that something must be added to show what makes just *this* course of action what the rule, as we mean it, genuinely requires.

At this juncture, it turns out that whatever is added will not really do, and private, ineffable rules come to present the only alternative – the only candidate items that are immune from the supposed risk of interpretation (PI §202). The thought is that at least *I* must know what I mean is the ostensibly deeper sense we seek, even though I cannot put it into words; I have a special, private rule available to me. The dictates of such special entities, however, prove to be indistinguishable from the ways we are inclined to behave with the sign. (See PI §§202, 231, 237.) Thus, ironically, we have come to a point at which we re-encounter the specter of arbitrariness and willfulness just in the place where – in privileged access to our own intentions – it was imagined that it would be most securely exorcized. Dissatisfaction with "normal circumstances," the desire to dig deeper, has led us into a linguistic wasteland.

Now community agreement, as displayed in our shared inclination to react to the training, explanations, and orders involved in getting us to develop the "+2" series, is pretty obviously not going to yield a constitutive account of rule-following – an account that would address, in terms deemed by the skeptic to be responsive to his requirements, the problems he has brought forth within this skeptical framework. Agreement cannot play the necessary explanatory role; it cannot show the grounds for our ways of going on for which the skeptic looks. For one thing, in some circumstances, we can ask whether how the community itself goes on is in fact correct. Further, we cannot take for granted that an appeal to community agreement is available to be exploited by an account that would satisfy the skeptic, given the limited resources his demand for explanation allows. In identifying what counts as agreement, we use the notion of sameness of response, and in doing so we employ what amounts to a grasp of rules for identifying certain responses as the same. (See Goldfarb 1982.) Our grip on the notion of agreement is inseparable from, and not prior to, our understanding of rules.[8] Nor is it particularly fruitful to hold that agreement constitutes the framework or system of presuppositions that provide necessary conditions for rule-following in general. While perhaps not false, this is at best a misleading expression of the idea that particular rule-following practices get their meaning from their role in our forms of life – an idea which triggers the skeptical itch, rather than scratching it.

How does Wittgenstein's treatment of rule-following diagnose the skeptical descent we have been surveying? Putting it bluntly, the skeptical movement that starts the process is neither obligatory nor fully coherent by its own lights. We find that we cannot quite make sense of the "problem of interpretation" that seemed to originate in the case of the child of §185; and when we try to *give* it a sense, we cannot satisfy ourselves that we are adequately expressing our worries about our *own* grounds for following rules. We either revert to psychology (to explain what is going on with us and the child), or we end up rehearsing the features of our practices (as if we need reminding!).

Consider again the case of the child. His failure or inability to emerge as one of us adders is troubling. In the everyday course of things, the first step toward taking the child seriously would be to acknowledge that he is different from us, that our relationship to him is problematic. Nothing compels him to go on in our way. Or rather, nothing *but* compulsion will get him to do so. We may articulate our discomfort here by wondering whether anything internal to our practices, our examples, our explanations establishes how *really* to go on in following the rule correctly. But the case of the child does not force this peculiarly self-reflexive articulation of our predicament on us. We as much as *decide* to take him seriously as a philosophical problem. We see his predicament as reflecting on *our* authority in following rules as we do. In the current setting, the possibility of divergent interpretations is taken to show the need for an underlying level on which the correct interpretation is settled. But behind this lies our own determination to hold "normal circumstances" hostage to the possibility of their breakdown.

[8] See PI §§224–5:

224. The word "agreement" and the word "same" are related to one another, they are cousins. If I teach anyone the use of the one word, he learns the use of the other with it.
225. The use of the word "rule" and the use of the word "same" are interwoven.

Arguably, then, reading the story of §185 as though it forces a global problem about the grounding of rules on us is an intellectualization of real problems we face in understanding others and in making ourselves understood. Wittgenstein's response to the paradox of §201 brings out that moving into the skeptical framework enacts a fantasy of abdicating our responsibility for that intelligibility. By §198, frustrated by Wittgenstein's attempt in §197 to quell his worries by putting the burden of connecting a rule to its application on "day-to-day [*tägliche*] practice," the interlocutor becomes more insistent: "'But how can a rule shew me what I have to do at *this* point? Whatever I do is, on some interpretation, in accord with the rule.'" (PI §198) Wittgenstein goes on in §§198–9 to reiterate that regular use (*ständigen Gebrauch*) is a matter of coming into practices or customs (*Gepflogenheiten*); these reminders are not supposed to address the interlocutor's insistence but rather to call attention to what lies behind it: namely, the isolation of the rule from what gives it life. Then to open §201, he allows his interlocutor's quandary to re-emerge: "This was our paradox: no course of action could be determined by a rule, because every course of action can be made out to accord with it." (PI §201) Immediately, we are given Wittgenstein's rather elusive response, which from the interlocutor's perspective may well seem only to make matters worse: "The answer was: If everything can be made out to accord with the rule, then it can also be made out to conflict with it. And so there would be neither accord nor conflict here." (PI §201)

Now, of course, the question inevitably arises: how is this supposed to be an *answer*? In the interlocutor's stripped down, skeptical setting, in which interpretations, standing alone, would have to determine this or that way of following rules, interpretations themselves amount to nothing more, nothing deeper, than further formulations of rules. Accordingly they are themselves subject to interpretation, and as a result "every course of action can be made out to accord with" any interpretation whatsoever. In that case, however – and this is the point of Wittgenstein's answer – within the impoverished setting, the problem with rules does not get off the ground. It was supposed to stem, recall, from the fact that there is a conflict between what accords with *this* rule interpreted in *this* way, and with the same rule interpreted in this *other* way. Now, however, we have no place to stand from which to judge that ostensibly competing interpretations (including, for example, ours and the child's) as much as disagree with each other. We have deprived ourselves of the wherewithal to make out the notions of accord and conflict with interpretations. Our conclusion is not a paradox about the ungrounded, and hence arbitrary, status of rule-following. Rather, it is that we should have recognized all along that of course "interpretations *by themselves* [*allein*] do not determine meaning" (PI §198) – not in the way the interlocutor was hoping for – but nor is there a clear-cut demand, mounted through the "paradox," that they must somehow do so if rule-following is to be possible.

That is, only by acquiescing in the skeptical setup would we come to think that something like an interpretation, only privileged, not itself subject to interpretation, had to account for a rule's power to determine its application:

As though an explanation as it were hung in the air unless supported by another one. Whereas an explanation may indeed rest on another one that has been given, but none stands in need of another – unless *we* require it to prevent a misunderstanding. (PI §87)

When we restore the surroundings of our everyday traffic with rules, then the very ground of rule-following is no longer staked to whether the interpreting of a rule leaves room for doubt. Whether in a given case it does so is dependent on the occasion: "The sign-post does after all leave no room for doubt. Or rather: it sometimes leaves room for doubt and sometimes not. And now this is no longer a philosophical proposition, but an empirical one." (PI §85) When opposing interpretations are recognizably in play, we deploy our everyday means for defusing the conflict. Trying to give a definite philosophical shape to our worries about rules has failed. The initiating "problem of interpretation" prompted by the possibility of divergent ways of understanding has shown itself to be an inaccurate register of an inarticulate, elusive anxiety about the grounding of our ways of going on.

Wittgenstein adds in conclusion that what this whole progression "shews is that there is a way of grasping a rule which is *not* an *interpretation*, but which is exhibited in what we call 'obeying the rule' and 'going against it' in actual cases." (PI §201) Again, we have no "solution" to the problem of grounding, but a reminder of both the extent to which agreement is taken as a foregone conclusion and its potential limits, the openness of the question of with whom we can add or otherwise commerce. In context the reminder repeats that when we go back to the rough ground, the "data" presented by actual agreements and disagreements, we find ourselves with no clear grip on a general, justificatory problem about how we follow rules. There remains, I think, a certain thinness in the summary nature of the conclusion of §201 and the corollary rejection of private rules in §202. We need further understanding of how the initiating skeptical move takes us in, of what we are missing in the phenomena of rule-following and why we are prone to overlook it. The next "chapter", as it were, of *Philosophical Investigations*, §§203–42, might be regarded as an *übersichtliche Darstellung* (PI §122) of the face of rule-following, including the role of agreement in our proceedings. These sections present a more compelling picture of what results when we restore rule-following to the milieu of day-to-day practice. Here agreement finds its home.

3. The Life of the Sign

To locate the significance of agreement in the practice of rule-following, it will be useful to look at Wittgenstein's remarks about "the life of the sign." How is it that a sign has a meaning, that there is such a thing as its correct use, that how we go on is *this* kind of thing, subject to normative constraints? The life of the sign is a theme from the outset of the *Investigations*: "Where our language suggests a body and there is none: there, we should like to say, is a spirit." (PI §36) Attributing to a child all kinds of meaning and naming activity preparatory for speaking a language, as on the so-called Augustinian picture of language under scrutiny from §1 on, bespeaks a need to attribute special powers to the subject. In conjunction with this need will arise a tendency to view the mind as a self-contained and self-sufficient place that has the power to connect to the life of language by dint of its own spiritual activity. A similar theme is touched in §§431–2: "'There is a gulf between an order and its execution. It has to be filled by the act of understanding.' 'Only the act of understanding can mean that we are to do THIS. The *order* – why, that is nothing but sounds, ink-marks. –'" (PI §431) Wittgenstein's response to these expressions of temptation is both brusque and open-ended: "Every sign *by itself* [*allein*] seems dead. *What* gives it life? – In use it is alive. Is life breathed into it there? – Or is the *use* its life?" (PI §431)

Several points deserve emphasis. First, we have already encountered this idea of some item working "*by itself* [*allein*]" in §198, where interpretations were expected to work alone, but failed to do so without some further, underlying element. There, the idea of such a thing was the expression of a picture, an abstraction from the role interpretations actually play in rule-following. We took it that interpretations of some kind had to explain what was really going on behind the use of the rule if the rule was to determine a course of action. But not only was the general need for such a thing imposed on the "data," we also had isolated interpretations from the particular circumstances in which they could serve any genuine explanatory purpose.

Second, this image of the sign as dead involves a particular picture of the life of the sign, as a force "breathed into it" from outside its use. Life is imagined as an added ingredient, something distinct and localized and prior that must be brought to the occasion of use. We might call this a kind of vitalism. Again, our skeptical movement has produced this conception, and we begin to realize that it calls for desperate measures. Consider Wittgenstein's very striking comparison in §430, hinting at the nature of our need: "It is as if we had imagined that the essential thing about a living man was its outward form. Then we made a lump of wood in that form, and were abashed to see the stupid block, which hadn't even any similarity to a living being." (PI §430) Now, rather than reflecting critically on the source of our shame, we come to cover it up with meaning, "the intangible *something*, only comparable to consciousness itself." (PI §358) Wittgenstein calls this "a dream of our language" (PI §358); it is an expression of fantasy.

Third, Wittgenstein naturally opposes, and indeed ridicules, this vitalist picture. In §454, talking about an arrow pointing in a particular direction, say as part of a set of written instructions, an interlocutor says, "'No, not the dead line on paper; only the psychical thing, the meaning, can do that.'" (PI §454) Wittgenstein responds, "that is both true and false, the arrow points only in the application that a living being makes of it. This pointing is *not* a hocus-pocus which can be performed only by the soul." (PI §454)[9] Magicking

---

[9] See PI §592 for further ridicule of the life of the sign as infused by "the mental act of meaning"; and also PI II, 184: "'The mind seems able to give a word meaning' – isn't this as if I were to say 'The carbon atoms in benzene seem to lie at the corners of a hexagon'? But this is not something that seems to be so; it is a picture."

meaning into the sign to give it life – a discrete force with unique determinative powers – only seems viable insofar as the initiating picture of the sign as dead is taken for granted. As we work through this picture, it becomes increasingly unclear in its own terms how we are even able to make an *issue* of the use of signs, that is, to ask what makes *these* particular phenomena, these movements and noises, amount to *use*. Similarly:

> If I give anyone an order I feel it to be *quite enough* to give him signs. And I should never say: this is only words, and I have got to get behind the words. Equally, when I have asked someone something, and he gives me an answer (i.e. a sign) I am con-tent – that was what I expected – and I don't raise the objection: but that's a mere answer. (PI §503)

Fourth, Wittgenstein expresses himself ambivalently about the notion of *use*. In §432 he does not straightforwardly affirm some thesis that, contrary to the vitalist picture, use *is* the life of the sign. He asks, "Or is the use its life?", haltingly, as if to say that the answer is clearly that it depends on how you conceive of, on the one hand, the life of the sign, and on the other hand, use itself. Neither use nor anything else serves to mediate between the sign and its application; moreover, use "by itself," conceived in isolation from prac-tice, as mere behaviors undertaken by rule-followers, remains inert. Wittgenstein says in the *Blue Book*: "*If* we had to name anything which is the life of the sign, we should have to say that it was its *use*." (BB, 4) Obviously *he* is not thinking of life as a force that *closes* the gap, relates sign and application; rather, he questions what one has to have done to the sign – as the sign it is, *in* its use – to have killed it, to have come to think that it must be resurrected. In other words, he questions the role that the life-giving *ingredient* would play. In the *Blue Book*, perhaps characteristically blunter than the *Investigations*, he observes: "The sign…gets its significance from the language to which it belongs. Roughly: understanding a sentence means understanding a language. As a part of the system of language…the sentence has life." (BB, 5) Now, to avoid the trap of thinking of this "system" as a calculus of rules, add the thought that "to imagine a language means to imagine a form of life." (PI §19) Taking this remark to heart, we are in a position to recog-nize how Wittgenstein sees use, and how it is intrinsic to the life of the sign: "To obey a rule, to make a report, to give an order…are *customs* (uses, institutions)" (PI §199), aspects of our forms of life.[10] We are not given a *solution* to the problem of the life of the sign. Nothing is secreting life into the sign from outside. We see this as, reflectively, we bring the *situation* of the sign's use into view, enabling us to see the life of the sign in use by putting its role in our lives, in our world, on view.

To call rule-following and so on "practices" is not to say how rules determine what we are to do. In any particular case, we can describe how a practice is shaped, what its norms are, how people are trained in it, what role it plays in our lives. And we may speculate, empirically, about why we have the practice; for example, we may hypothesize about the

---

[10] "What has to be accepted, the given, is – so one could say – *forms of life*." (PI II, 226). Or, as Witt-genstein puts it in *Remarks on the Philosophy of Psychology*, Vol. I, §630, "facts of living."

usefulness of having customs that play this particular role. Neither description nor explanation yields a justification of the norms of the practice or an explanation of the possibility thereof. We do not have an account of normativity, but a reminder of where to look for it.

In summary: Only when we begin by imagining the sign as dead does there seem to be a gap between sign and explanation that must be closed by extraordinary measures. But "the occult character of the mental process which you needed for your purposes" (BB, 5) explains nothing; once we return our gaze to what we do, it is not clear that explanation is called for. The life of the sign lies in our lives in language. If that sounds obvious, that is perhaps as it should be; we have here a reminder that the life of our words does not involve *less* than what constitutes our linguistic being-in-the-world.

That a particular "reaction" comes to life – takes on its meaning, say, counts as a particular, correct or incorrect, way of going on with a rule – "presupposes as a surrounding particular circumstances, particular forms of life and speech." (RFM VII §47) What role does the agreement of the community play in this "important movement of thought"? (Ibid.) And again, why do we need to be reminded?

4. AGREEMENT

Sections 203–39 of *Philosophical Investigations* defamiliarize the requirement for some added thing, some ingredient, needed to bridge the gap between rule and application. They show, that is, how distant the philosophical demand remains from anything that actually goes into the "rags and dust" (PI §52) of rule-following. The rule produces its consequences as a matter of course (PI §238); we follow it blindly (PI §219); there need be neither choice, nor further calculation, nor insight, nor inspiration and intimation (PI §232), nor whisper and nod (PI §223) here. §234 asks:

> Would it not be possible for us…to calculate as we actually do (all agreeing, and so on), and still at every step to have a feeling of being guided by rules as by a spell, feeling astonishment at the fact that we agreed? (We might give thanks to the Deity for our agreement). (PI §234)

We are clearly meant to consider both that the figure of "intimation" suggests something critical about rule-following (that in many cases, "*nothing* stands between the rule and my action," RFM VII §60) *and* that the figure is liable to mislead us about the mysteriousness of rule-following. "One follows the rule *mechanically*" (ibid.); "from this," Wittgenstein comments in *Remarks on the Foundations of Mathematics*, "you can see how much there is to the physiognomy of what we call 'following a rule' in everyday life!" (Ibid.)[11] One implication is that the *way* we agree is of utmost significance. In the process

---

[11] RFM VII §60 embeds the text of PI §234 in a different but closely related context from that of the *Investigations*.

of dealing with determinate rules like "+2," we try to eliminate disagreement, in the first instance by checking for mistakes. This kind of rule and this manner of dealing with disagreement mark such activities as measuring, calculating, and developing a series. In doing these things, we do not simply acquiesce in divergent results; we check our work, we train our pupils to repeat the procedures until they get it right, we try to find an explanation of the problem if they are not managing. This is what the normativity of the rules in play in these activities amounts to. Agreement, exemplified by the fact that "disputes do not break out (among mathematicians, say) over the question whether a rule has been obeyed or not," is "part of the framework [*Gerüst*] on which the working of our language is based." (PI §240) Similarly, in following rules, there lies "this peaceful agreement" that is "the characteristic surrounding of the use of the word 'same'." (RFM VI §21) It is a contingent, but crucial, fact that in learning to calculate, we come to acknowledge *these* responses as the same.

This acknowledgment or recognition is the understanding "exhibited in what we call 'obeying the rule' and 'going against it' from case to case." (PI §201) Here, that is, understanding is manifest in specific judgments about whether a way of proceeding accords with a rule. Such agreement is part of the "agreement in judgments" declared in §242 to be necessary for language to be a means of communication. In *Remarks on the Foundations of Mathematics*, Wittgenstein is very explicit about this point: "We say that, in order to communicate, people must agree with one another *about the meanings of words*. But the criterion for this agreement is not just agreement with reference to definitions, e.g. ostensive definitions – but *also* an agreement in judgments." (RFM VI §39) Definitions "by themselves" settle nothing, "hanging in the air" unless applied, just as nothing counts as measuring a length unless it is settled that sometimes *that* counts as a measurement and that *that* counts as getting the same measurement.[12]

Wittgenstein at one point remarks that "going according to a rule is...founded on an agreement."(RFM VII §26) In context, he means to counter the idea that rules or definitions could be abstracted from their shared applications. Immediately before, he has observed "once you have described the procedure of this teaching and learning, you have said everything that can be said about acting according to a rule." (RFM VII §26) We can neither describe this training nor explain what it is to go on in the same way without referring to the norms of the practice in question. In particular, "agreement in judgments" is not the matching of *bare* behavioral reactions, because what makes judgments (responses, reactions) the same from case to case is determined against the background of the activities into which our judgments are woven. There is no standard isolated from this background by which the same noises or the same movements can be judged to be relevantly the same. As Wittgenstein says, "we all act the same way, walk the same way, count the same way." (LFM, 184) As one comes into the practice, one *of course* does not just learn a bunch of rule-formulations or definitions. One learns to acquiesce in and

---

[12] See the related point with respect to basic arithmetical judgments: "If there were not complete agreement, then neither would human beings be learning the technique which we learn. It would be more or less different from ours up to the point of unrecognizability." (PI II, 226)

reject some of the same things in some of the same ways, one picks up on a host of correct judgments, and thus gathers that *this* is how one judges. Now when Wittgenstein refers to agreement in *action* in connection with agreement in judgment, he is not thinking of "bare" action, a separable explanatory substratum that would play some kind of justificatory role. In activities like measuring, judgment enters in determining procedures, enforcing their proper application, deriving and confirming correct results. The founding materials of rule-following are not discernible from an external vantage point; the mutuality of definitions and judgments implies that the "framework" on which our language is based is our "forms of life," nothing less. And this deprives any *theoretical* talk of the framework of its philosophical force and motivation.

In these considerations, the agreement in judgments that is agreement in form of life (PI §241) seems to play a dual function. First, unless we are trained similarly and respond on the whole in similar ways to the training, we might not have a practice of calculating as we do. That we are adders is a contingent fact about us. We might be interested in a "natural-historical" story about this fact. Our practices presuppose agreements of the type we happen to enjoy, if you like. This kind of thing is not the focus of Wittgenstein's concern. If his interlocutor were willing to settle for this kind of empirical account of the "ground" of our practices, he would be relinquishing whatever justificatory aspirations he had for his desired account of their normativity. He would be left doing essentially nothing to illuminate what it *is* for rules to determine their "whole" applications *as norms do*. Second, as we have seen, agreement characterizes particular practices, in particular the role of norms within them. It might be said to make these practices what they are, to lend them their particular physiognomy. Again, in making basic calculations, we do not tolerate disagreement. This manifests the necessity of our results; "peaceful agreement" can be both the result of a hard-won struggle and an expression of what, as it were, provides the identity for the tribe of adders. "If there were not complete agreement, then neither would human beings be learning the technique which we learn." (PI II, 226) Participation in the practices is allowing the norms to govern what we do. We let them show us how to go on. As Diamond emphasizes, we recognize that *anyone* – anyone who is, say, adding – is subject to the rules:

> In the way in which we enter with others into life-with-rules, you can see the "anyone-ness" we have vis-à-vis any rule. Look at our engaging, as "anyones", in the practices of inventing rules, teaching them, using them, correcting people and so on: there you will see the relation between the proceeding of establishing a rule and anyone. (Diamond 1989, 29)

Who counts as "anyone"? This should strikes us as an odd question. The only available answer on this level of generality is: we, who share in the form of life; we, that is, who have a life in which counting, adding, calculating, measuring, play *these* roles. There is no guarantee that we can expand the reach of our norms, and there is no independent way of identifying those whose activities they govern. Is there reason to be leery of this rather tight circle?

Wittgenstein does evince awareness of a concern here, expressing worry that his reminder about agreement in judgments "seems to abolish logic" by supposedly injecting an element of contingency – the sheer fact of agreement – into the framework that is supposed to constitute the laws of thought. He poses the same worry in different terms in RFM VI §49: If "logic belongs to the natural history of man," what are we to make of the hardness of the logical "must"? In what sense does logic belong to natural history? Doubtless it is a contingency that we have come to share these practices, with these uses and these norms. Imagine us, and the world, as quite different, and "the formation of concepts different from the usual ones will become intelligible." (PI II, 230) Here and now, however, insofar as we are actually engaging in the practice that these norms and uses characterize, these norms, these rules, these concepts are to be applied in *these* ways. This is perhaps a good way of capturing Wittgenstein's response to his worry in RFM VI §49: "But the logical 'must' is a component part of the propositions of logic, and these are not propositions of natural history." The character of the "must" shows up in what we do. Call this the fact of normativity.

Now suppose we were to try to construe the fact of normativity as wholly explicable with reference to the details of the aforementioned contingency, and in this sense reducible to it. Then the logical "must" will seem to disappear. Once more, it appears that in a sense it is mere contingency that we go on as we do, that the practices have this shape, with these so-called norms; now it seems that the child of §185 has been willfully coerced into obedience to us (and not the rules); "*this* is what we do" now represents a declaration of our willingness to force the child, "arbitrarily," to go on in our way. Whereas the point is that we do not need an external justification for our quite proper judgment that whatever the child is doing, it is not adding two. Contingency remains in the background here:

> We say: "If you really follow the rule in multiplying, you *must* all get the same result." Now if this is only the somewhat hysterical way of putting things that you get in university talk, it need not interest us overmuch.
>
> It is however the expression of an attitude towards the technique of calculation, which comes out everywhere in our life. The emphasis of the *must* corresponds only to the inexorableness of this attitude both to the technique of calculating and to a host of related techniques. (RFM VII §67)

Most important, on the construction of the fact of normativity under criticism, we make out necessity as a product of our wills, rather than as a part of what constitutes us as a "we." We have proved ourselves resistant to seeing the fact of normativity as expressing our relation to, our recognition of ourselves in, the practice.

The threat to logic arose from taking the contingency of our practices – of their very existence – to undermine the necessities operative *therein*. (To take this "therein" to impose a *limitation* on the sense in which norms operate as such to provide necessities is clearly to operate within this picture of the "threat"; without it, the image of confinement disappears.) The suggestion has been that in taking the threat seriously, we have been blind to crucial aspects of the roles norms play in establishing the practices in which we share. They inform our sense of what grounds are, and do not as such require support from some ultimate ground. As we have seen, the skeptical construction of the surfaces of our practices as dead, along with the consequent, hopeless demand that *something* breathe life into the sign as it comes to use, express discomfort with the place of agreement in our lives. On this construction, agreement has appeared as at best an accomplishment – as too contingent, too arbitrary, too psychological, to constitute a ground on which minds meet. This discomfort with agreement is reflected in the common refusal to acknowledge Wittgenstein's reminders about what we say as anything more than mere facts about how we happen to talk. We refuse to see *how* essence is expressed by grammar (PI §371) and to see that this is no threat to the power of the world to determine what we are to believe. Why does the fact of agreement, then, remain disquieting? Perhaps because we cannot take the measure of the "we," those with whom our minds will meet, prior to occasions on which our actual encounters with others disclose and test the limits of our own ability to make sense.[13]

References

DIAMOND, CORA (1989). "Rules: Looking in the Right Place," in D. Z. Phillips and P. Winch eds., *Wittgenstein: Attention to Particulars*. New York: St. Martin's.

—— (1991). "Realism and the Realistic Spirit," in *The Realistic Spirit*. Cambridge, MA: MIT.

GOLDFARB, WARREN (1982). "Kripke on Wittgenstein on Rules," *Journal of Philosophy*, 79: 471–88.

—— (2012). "Rule-Following Revisited," in Jonathan Ellis and Daniel Guevara eds., *Wittgenstein and the Philosophy of Mind*. Oxford: Oxford University Press.

KRIPKE, SAUL (1982). *Wittgenstein on Rules and Private Language*. Cambridge, MA: Harvard.

MALCOLM, NORMAN (1986). *Nothing Is Hidden*. Oxford: Blackwell.

WITTGENSTEIN, LUDWIG (1953). *Philosophical Investigations*, trans. G. E. M. Anscombe. Oxford: Blackwell.

—— (1958). *The Blue and Brown Books*. Oxford: Blackwell.

—— (1969). *On Certainty*, ed. G. E. M. Anscombe and G. H. von Wright. Oxford: Blackwell.

—— (1976). *Lectures on the Foundations of Mathematics*, ed. Cora Diamond. Chicago: University of Chicago Press.

—— (1978). *Remarks on the Foundations of Mathematics*, trans. G. E. M. Anscombe, rev. edn. Cambridge, MA: MIT.

—— (1980). *Remarks on the Philosophy of Psychology*, Vol. 1, ed. G. H. von Wright and Heikki Nyman. Oxford: Blackwell.

[13] I am grateful to Oskari Kuusela and Marie McGinn for comments.

CHAPTER 13

....

MEANING AND
UNDERSTANDING

....

BARRY STROUD

THE Preface to Wittgenstein's *Tractatus* says that the aim of the book is 'to set a limit to thought, or rather – not to thought, but to the expression of thoughts'. So 'it will there-fore only be in language that the limit can be set, and what lies on the other side of the limit will simply be nonsense'. (TLP, 3)

> 4.12   Propositions [his word is 'Der Satz'] can represent the whole of reality, but they cannot represent what they must have in common with reality in order to be able to represent it – logical form.
>
> In order to be able to represent logical form, we should have to be able to station ourselves with propositions somewhere outside logic, that is to say outside the world.

> 4.121   Propositions cannot represent logical form: it is mirrored in them.
>   …
> Propositions *show* the logical form of reality.
> They display it.

A sentence cannot represent or say what it has in common with reality in order to rep-resent it because sentences are pictures, and:

> 2.172 A picture cannot…depict its pictorial form: it displays it.
> 2.173 A picture represents its subject from a position outside it.

Wittgenstein describes his distinction between 'what can be expressed by propositions – i.e., by language – …and what can not be expressed by propositions, but only shown' as 'the cardinal problem of philosophy'. (Quoted in Black 1964, 188)

Almost from the beginning of his return to philosophy in Cambridge in 1929 Wittgenstein was concerned not only with the relation of sentences or propositions to reality but also with the idea of someone's thinking or meaning or understanding something in a particular way. He also returned to the idea of a 'limit', this time to 'the limit of language'. In 1931 he wrote in a notebook:

> The limit of language is shown by its being impossible to describe the fact that corresponds to (is the translation of) a sentence, without simply repeating the sentence. (This has to do with the Kantian solution of the problem of philosophy). (CV, 10)

This claim about the limit of language does not say that you simply *cannot* state or describe the fact that corresponds to a given sentence. It does not say that the relation between a sentence and the reality it represents is something that cannot be expressed in language at all. It allows that you *can* say what that relation is, but *only* by repeating that sentence. I take 'describing the fact that corresponds to (is the translation of) a sentence' to be a matter of saying what the sentence says or what it means.

A sentence or proposition that represents reality to be a certain way does not itself say how it manages to represent reality in that way. But that does not mean that *no* propositions or sentences can represent or state the way in which *any* proposition or sentence represents reality. Such a thing could even be stated without simply repeating the sentence in question: a sentence in a different language could be used to state the fact that corresponds to the original sentence. Even in one and the same language we would not have to repeat the sentence if there were another sentence in that language that meant the same as the first. But perhaps no two sentences in the same language ever mean exactly the same.

If we describe the relation between the sentence 'This book is red' and reality by saying that the expression 'this book' refers to a certain demonstrated book, and that the predicate 'is red' is true of a thing if and only if the thing is red, we would have explained that that sentence is true if and only if the book designated by 'this book' is red. If we knew which book that is, we would know and we would have said what is stated by the original sentence. We would have a metalinguistic statement that tells us what is so in reality if and only if the first sentence is true. The metalinguistic sentence that gives the meaning of a given sentence does not mean the same as that original sentence. And it does more than simply repeat that sentence. But it does repeat the original sentence in stating the conditions under which that sentence is true. It thereby does appear to say something about how the original sentence represents reality.

If the semantical sentence does say what the original sentence means, or how it represents reality, this is not to say that it does so by representing 'what the [original] sentence has in common with reality in order to be able to represent it'. But it does seem to state a relation between the sentence 'This book is red' and reality. Of course the semantical sentence does not say anything about the relation in which it itself stands to reality. Another sentence would be needed to do that. But if some such sentence could be found, and we could continue to go higher and higher up a hierarchy of sentences or languages, we could describe the relation to reality of all sentences lower down in the hierarchy. This is what Russell appears to have had in mind in his introduction to the *Tractatus*. For each sentence we encounter we could find a way to describe its relation to reality. We could say what would be so in reality if that sentence were true, and we could say it from a position 'inside' language.

Whether or not the original sentence must be repeated exactly, I take the point to be that in saying what a given sentence means or what fact corresponds to it we must *use* the words of the sentence, or at least some other words that equally serve to give the meaning of the sentence. We use the words with the meanings they actually have in the sentence or language in question. It would not be enough simply to refer to or name or mention a certain sentence and say that it means the same as the original sentence. To say of one sentence that it means the same as another is not to say anything about what either sentence means or what fact corresponds to them. I can know that a sentence in one language means the same as a certain sentence in another language without understanding a word of either language. Knowledge of the synonymy of mentioned expressions (even if there is such a thing) is not sufficient for knowing the meaning of either of those expressions.

Obviously, in saying what a given sentence means, or in describing the fact that corresponds to it, we produce some words, typically a sentence. We produce those words in an effort to say what the original sentence means. But we do not do so by *saying* that the sentence we produce means the same as the sentence in question. To do that would be to mention two sentences, or to mention the same sentence twice, and say that the two mean the same. When we *repeat* the original sentence by way of saying what that sentence means we do not at that point mention the sentence we are repeating. We utter the words we use in saying what the original sentence means, but the words we produce are not *said* to have the same meaning as the original sentence. We *give* the meaning in saying what we say. Wittgenstein observes that to know what a sentence means or what fact corresponds to it is 'to be able to answer the question "what does this sentence say?"'. (PG, 44) And being able to answer that question involves being able to *say* what the sentence says, not simply knowing that it means or says the same as some other sentence.

Wittgenstein says that its being impossible to describe the fact that corresponds to a sentence without simply repeating that sentence 'shows' what he calls the 'limit of language'. If what he says is impossible really *is* impossible, does it 'show' a limit of *language*? It does seem to show a certain limit on *explaining* the meanings of sentences and on *understanding* or coming to understand a particular sentence. If you really have to repeat the sentence in order to say what it means, you could not explain the meaning of a sentence in that way to someone who does not already understand it. The same is true of a sentence different from the original, either in the same language or in a different language. And the same for a semantical metalinguistic sentence that gives a sentence's meaning. Whatever sentence is used in stating the meaning of a given sentence, what is said could not explain the meaning of that sentence to someone who did not understand the sentence used in the explanation.

It is obvious that no one can understand anything he is told unless he understands the words in which he is told it. So no one can understand what he is told about what a certain sentence means or what fact corresponds to it unless he understands the words in which he is told it. But this can still be said to express a certain kind of 'limit':

this means that any kind of explanation of a language presupposes a language already. And in a certain sense, the use of language is something that cannot be taught, i.e., I cannot use language to teach it in the way in which language could be used to teach someone to play the piano. – And that of course is just another way of saying: I cannot use language to get outside language. (PG, 54)

What Wittgenstein says 'cannot be taught' is 'the use of language'. Particular languages can be taught, and a teacher can use one language to teach someone a second language. Of course, a pupil has to understand the language the teacher is using. So that would not be a case of teaching the pupil 'the use of language', but only this or that language. Even if the use of language cannot be taught, it is certainly something that can be learned, or acquired.

Wittgenstein does not say, strictly and without qualification, that the use of language cannot be taught. The 'certain sense' in which he thinks it cannot be taught is that 'I cannot use language to teach it in the way in which language could be used to teach someone to play the piano.' What a piano teacher can use language to get the pupil to do are things the pupil could do without the use of language – e.g. to play a particular chord. The pupil needs to be master of the use of language to understand what the piano teacher has told her, but not in order to do what the teacher tells her how to do. But a language-learner could not be simply told in the same way how to do the things involved in being a master of language. Or rather, she could be 'told', but it would do no good. What was said would make sense and would be understood only by someone who has already to some extent mastered the use of language.

Wittgenstein sums this up by saying 'I cannot use language to get outside language'. The *Tractatus* said that one would have to be 'outside logic, that is to say outside the world' in order to represent what a proposition must have in common with reality in order to represent it. A picture was said to represent its subject 'from a position outside it'.

In the early parts of *Philosophical Grammar* Wittgenstein takes up the question of how one can talk about 'understanding' or 'not understanding' a sentence. (PG, 39) Understanding is what he calls 'a psychological reaction while hearing, reading, uttering, etc. a sentence'; 'the phenomenon that occurs when I hear a sentence in a familiar language and not when I hear a sentence in a strange language'. (PG, 41) As soon as I hear or see a sentence in a language familiar to me, I understand it. What I understand are those sounds I hear or those marks on the page. I understand what they express. He thinks someone could even express something by arranging a clump of trees in a certain way – as a kind of code, say. It would make sense in those circumstances to ask 'Do you understand what this clump of trees says?' (PG, 39) And someone could see the trees and understand what they say.

It could be said that someone who sees those trees and understands what they say knows what proposition they express. The same could be said of someone who sees and understands a sentence. But we cannot say that the person who knows what proposition is expressed by those trees or that sentence also understands that proposition in the way he understands the trees or the sentence. It isn't that he knows what proposition the trees or the sentence expresses and in addition also knows what proposition *that proposition* in turn expresses. Apart from the clump of trees, or the sentence there on the page, there is no further item to mean or express anything. Once the person understands what the clump of trees or the sentence says – once he knows what proposition it expresses – there is nothing else in the situation for the person to understand.

Considered simply as a clump of trees, or as sounds in the air or marks on a page, there is no difference between trees or sounds or marks that express propositions and can be understood in a certain way and those that mean or express nothing. Clumps of trees or sounds or marks can be considered simply as 'a phenomenon or fact', as Wittgenstein puts it. (PG, 41) We do not thereby recognize that the trees were arranged with a certain purpose or that the sounds or marks express anything at all. The meaning-ful or expressive aspect of a clump of trees or of sounds or marks is 'absent from the phe-nomenon as such'. (PG, 143) The same can be said of what a person can be observed to do in expressing an expectation, or a wish, or in carrying out an order, when those utter-ances or movements are considered in that same way – simply as 'a phenomenon or fact'. To recognize that people think or expect or wish certain things, we have to be able to read off from the expression of their thought or expectation or wish that it is the thought or expectation or wish that such-and-such. If we regarded the people around us and the marks on paper and the clumps of trees that we see, and so on, solely as 'phenomena' in the sense Wittgenstein has in mind, we would never recognize anything as expressing anything or anyone as thinking or meaning or understanding anything at all. To see things only as 'phenomena' in that sense would be to see them, in Wittgenstein's phrase, only 'from outside'. (PG, 143)

The expression 'from outside' used in this way obviously does not simply mean from a position outside another person or outside a sentence or outside a clump of trees. The idea is not that you can understand what a clump of trees says only by standing inside it. To see a clump of trees, or marks on paper, or people's making noises or behaving in cer-tain ways 'from outside' in this sense is to see them without recognizing or thinking of them as expressing anything or having any meaning.

> If we consider them 'from outside' we have to understand thoughts as thoughts, intentions as intentions and so on, *without* getting any information about some-thing's meaning. (PG, 144)

Anything looked at only 'from outside' in that way will appear 'lifeless and isolated' (PG, 146); 'it does not point outside itself to a reality beyond'. (PG, 148) Looking at things only in that way would mean that we could not recognize any thoughts or intentions or mean-ings at all. That would leave us in the plight Wittgenstein describes like this:

> Whatever phenomenon we saw, it couldn't ever be intention; for that has to contain the very thing that is intended, and any phenomenon would be something complete in itself and unconcerned with anything outside itself, something merely dead if considered by itself. (PG, 144)

Seeing things only in that way is not a plight we are actually in. As things are, we can see a sentence or a clump of trees and know what it says (if there is something it says). We can see and hear people who think and mean things and recognize what they think and mean. But when we do that:

> If a thought is observed there can be no further question of an understanding; for if the thought is seen it must be recognized as a thought with a certain content; it doesn't need to be interpreted! – That really is how it is; when we are thinking, there isn't any interpretation going on. (PG, 144)

When we observe a person's thinking, 'there can be no further question of an understanding' because there is nothing further to be understood. The person's thought has been recognized. When someone knows what proposition is expressed by a certain clump of trees, there is not something else – what that proposition in turn expresses – that also needs to be understood. So it is not just that the thought that has been recognized 'doesn't *need* to be interpreted'; there is nothing relevant that *could* be interpreted. When we see a person's action or a sentence or a clump of trees and know what it means we do not see it 'from outside' all thought and meaning. It is only because we do *not* see it only in that way that we understand it. In the very understanding or thinking anything at all 'there isn't any interpretation going on'.

If we were restricted in our observations or descriptions to what Wittgenstein calls 'mere phenomena' which give no 'information about something's meaning', we could never recognize or specify what a certain sentence expresses or how a person understands a certain expression. We could never mean or understand something or explain the meaning of something if we had to do so 'from outside' all recognition of what some things mean or what some people mean by them. This is what I take it Wittgenstein has in mind in saying that it is impossible to describe the fact that corresponds to a given sentence or to say what that sentence means without repeating the sentence. In giving the meaning of a sentence we must *use* a sentence and not simply refer to or mention a sentence or some other object. Being restricted to 'mere phenomena' without any 'information about something's meaning' would mean that even if one could somehow identify or refer to a certain item or object associated with or expressed by the sentence, that would be only to know that the sentence stands in a certain relation to some other mentioned thing. It would not be to know what that sentence says or means. To know and to say what the sentence means is to know and be able to say something 'from within' a capacity to recognize and understand and say something about the meanings of expressions.

The implications of these middle-period reflections on the impossibility of understanding language and meaning 'from outside' are illustrated and developed at many points and in many ways throughout *Philosophical Investigations*. In sections 185 and following, for instance, we have a pupil who by all the usual criteria has mastered the instructions he has been given in the continuation of different arithmetical series. On being given the number 2 and the order 'Add 2 each time', he writes down 4, 6, 8, 10, and so on, and when encouraged to continue, eventually goes on to…996, 998, 1,000, 1,004, 1,008. It is clear that this pupil has not followed the order he was given. Or he has not followed it correctly, which comes to the same thing.

If we ask whether he has understood the order he was given, we could say he understood it if we think he just got tired of applying the rule or simply refused to follow it after 1000. But if he responds as Wittgenstein imagines him – by saying 'Yes, isn't that right? I thought that was how I was *meant* to do it', or 'But I went on in the same way after 1000 as before' – we recognize that he did not understand the order he was given. He did not follow that order correctly.

We know this about this pupil because we know that what he did after 1000 is not in accord with the order as it was meant. We understand that order and we know what is and is not in accord with it. If, as the pupil claims, he was following the same order after 1000 as he had been before, then the order he was following was not the order to add two each time. That would mean that even before reaching 1000 he was not following the order to add two each time even though every number he wrote up to that point was in fact two more than the previous number. The sequence he had written up to 1000 was in accord with or in agreement with the rule to add two each time, but that would not have been the rule he was following.

Developments of arithmetical series provide especially striking examples of the fundamental point Wittgenstein wishes to draw attention to in discussing meaning and understanding. What a person continuing a series has written down at any given time never uniquely determines what comes next, and so in itself it does not determine what rule the person is following. The person's understanding of his instructions is shown or expressed in his writing down what he does, but the outcomes of those actions – the numbers he writes down – do not fix or indicate uniquely his understanding of the instructions. That remains so no matter how many numbers the person writes. His having written those numbers is compatible with his having understood the instructions in any one of indefinitely many different ways. With respect to fixing what the person understands, the numbers written on the page up to any given point could still be viewed, in Wittgenstein's phrase, 'from outside' any implication of the pupil's having understood the instructions in some particular way. The series of written numbers alone would be to that extent a 'lifeless and isolated' 'phenomenon or fact' which does not point beyond itself to the pupil's having understood the instructions in one way rather than in countless other ways.

Of course in considering this example we do not view everything the pupil does 'from outside' all thought and meaning. We take the pupil to understand the order he is given in some way or other and to have many other intentional attitudes. But even if we grant that the pupil intentionally writes numerals, and that he means each numeral to stand for a number, and we know which numbers they stand for, we cannot determine what rule he is following as long as we are restricted to describing only the numbers he has written down. We would then be confined to describing what he has done only 'from outside' his having understood the instructions in some particular way.

The same holds for any attempted specification of the meaning of the sound or marks 'Add 2 each time' by which the order was given to the pupil. Considered as a 'phenomenon or fact' complete in itself, that sign or form of words – or the utterance of it – could mean, or could have meant, any number of different things, or nothing at all. Viewed 'from outside' all information about thought and meaning and understanding, the sign or utterance itself obviously imposes no constraints on what someone is supposed to do when he hears or sees it. We know that the pupil violated the constraints imposed by the order as it was meant in the example; he did not follow it correctly. So we obviously do not view that sound or mark only 'from outside' in a way that carries with it no constraints. We understand the English expression 'Add 2 each time'; and the meaning of that expression, or how it was meant, is what determines what step is to be taken at each point. What determines how the order was meant, as Wittgenstein says, is 'the kind of way we always use it, the way we are taught to use it'. (PI §190)

As a general observation about meaning, understanding, and use, this must be right. There can be nothing more to an expression's having a certain meaning than its being used in a certain determinate way. And knowing what an expression means can be nothing other than knowing how it is or has been used. But to appeal to the *use* of an expression in accounting for our understanding of its meaning, the idea of use must be understood in a certain way. It is possible to say something true of all those occasions on which a certain expression was used in the past – and in that sense to describe the past use of an expression – without thereby specifying the meaning of that expression. The same holds even if a similar description is true of all future applications of that expression. Describing the use of an expression only in such ways would not serve to specify its meaning. Even if everyone in the past had in fact always responded to the sound or marks 'Add 2 each time' with a series of numbers each of which is two more than the previous number, it would not follow that those sounds or marks mean that two is to be added each time. Even if that same correlation between utterance and behaviour continued forever into the future, it would not follow that that is what those sounds or marks mean.

This general point about meaning and understanding is illustrated by the simple case of the deviant pupil. Every number the pupil writes down before 1,000 is two more than the previous number, but that does not imply that he is following the rule of adding two each time. If we grant that he could have understood the words he heard differently from the way we do and have been following some other order correctly even before he reached 1000, we thereby acknowledge that the expression 'Add 2 each time' *could* be, or could have been, an order to do something other than add two each time, even though every response to it in the past has involved adding two. The meaning of that expression cannot necessarily be read off a description of all the applications that have been or ever will be made of it. A description made only 'from outside' recognition of the expression's meaning what it does will not serve to specify its meaning.

We *can* describe the use of an expression in a way that suffices to fix its meaning or to specify what we know when we know its meaning. We can say ' "Add 2 each time" means add two each time'; we simply repeat the original sentence exactly as it is. But that is not strictly required. We could say 'The words "Add 2 each time" are used by us to mean that two is to be added each time.' In these remarks we employ the idea of meaning in describing how the expression is used and what it is used to mean. We also make use of (and do not mention) the very words whose meaning we are specifying. The same is true in giving semantical metalinguistic explanations of meaning that state the conditions under which a given sentence is true. In understanding what order is given to the pupil, and so what he must do in order to comply with it, we also recognize that the teacher meant the words he uttered in a certain way.

This can raise the question 'how are we to judge whether someone meant such-and-such?' To this Wittgenstein replies:

> The fact that he has, for example, mastered a particular technique in arithmetic and algebra, and that he taught someone else the expansion of a series in the usual way, is such a criterion. (PI §692)

That someone has such mastery and has taught it to others is not something we could recognize 'from outside' all recognition of intention or of what people mean by the words they utter. In recognizing or stating the meaning of an expression in any of these ways we make use of the words in question. We do not just describe some aspect of their use that is available 'from outside' all meaning or understanding of them.

The idea that it is impossible to describe the fact that corresponds to a given sentence without repeating that very sentence is an expression of the requirement that we must describe the use of an expression in some such engaged way in order to succeed in specifying or explaining its meaning. By 'engaged' I mean 'from within' recognition of certain intentions or meanings or by actually using words with determinate meanings to say what certain words mean or how they are to be understood. It is not enough just to mention words and say something only about a relation between them and certain other mentioned words. Nor is it enough to mention words and say something that is so in the world when and only when the words are uttered or heard. A description of the use of an expression cannot succeed in specifying what it means or how someone understands it if it is given only 'from outside' all recognition of the meaning of expressions or of the intentions with which they are used.

This imposes a certain kind of limit on the possibility of someone's coming to understand an expression in a certain way. And it can seem to present a challenge to the very idea of a person's understanding or meaning something in any way at all. If everything a person does or could do in applying a given expression is in accord with his understanding that expression in any one of many different but incompatible ways, how is the person's understanding the expression in the way he does related to the particular applications he makes of it? In the case of the deviant pupil the challenge is expressed like this:

> 'But how can a rule shew me what I have to do at *this* point? Whatever I do is, on some interpretation, in accord with the rule.' (PI §198)

To this last sentence Wittgenstein replies:

> That is not what we ought to say, but rather: every interpretation, together with what is being interpreted, hangs in the air; the former cannot give the latter any support. Interpretations by themselves do not determine meaning. (PI §198)

Here Wittgenstein takes an 'interpretation' of an expression to be another expression that is to serve as an interpretation of the first. So 'interpretations by themselves do not determine meaning' because producing one expression as an interpretation of another is not enough to specify what the first expression means or how it is understood. Without any understanding or specification of the meaning of the second expression, both expressions would still 'hang in the air' without the meaning of either of them having been explained. Saying of two mentioned expressions that they mean the same or that one is an interpretation of the other is not sufficient to specify what either of those expressions means.

To regard interpreting or understanding or explaining the meaning of an expression as a matter only of substituting one mentioned expression for another would lead to an infinite regress of offered explanations. If explaining or understanding the meaning of any expression *always* required another expression, that expression in turn would have to be understood, which would require another expression, and so on. There would be no saying what any expression means and no understanding of anything. This is the source of the apparent 'paradox' referred to in *Philosophical Investigations* §201:

> no course of action could be determined by a rule, because every course of action can be made out to accord with the rule. The answer was: if everything can be made out to accord with the rule, then it can also be made out to conflict with it. And so there would be neither accord nor conflict here.

There would be no such thing as a person's understanding an expression in one way rather than another. Nothing would have any determinate meaning. This, Wittgenstein says, 'was our paradox' (PI §201), growing out of the 'challenge' expressed in §198.

The sources and implications of this apparent 'paradox' have generated a huge body of commentary, most of it in response to Saul Kripke's *Wittgenstein on Rules and Private Language* in 1982. That book presented in striking form what it argued is an unanswerable challenge: to say what it is about a person that constitutes his meaning or understanding an expression in a certain particular way. No present or past facts involving the person were said to constitute his meaning or understanding an expression in one way rather than another when he uses or responds to it on a particular occasion. The unavoidable conclusion is the 'sceptical paradox' that no one means anything by any expression he uses or responds to. The problem seemed easily generalizable from meaning or understanding words or expressions to any determinate thought or intentional attitudes whatever. Pressed to the limit, there appeared to be no such fact as anyone's meaning or understanding or thinking anything at all in one particular way rather than another.

After mentioning the 'paradox' in *Philosophical Investigations* §201, Wittgenstein does not try to meet the challenge by saying what constitutes a person's meaning or understanding something in a particular way. He says rather that there is a 'misunderstanding' behind the alleged paradox; it rests on a confusion. We know that some thought lying behind the challenge must be confused because we know that it is not true, as the 'paradox' claims, that every course of action can be made out to accord with any given rule. As we have just seen, we know that what the deviant pupil did after 1000 is not in accord with the rule to add two each time. Nor can it be 'made out' to accord with that rule. The rule to add two each time requires that 1002 be put next after 1000;

that is the course of action determined by that rule at that point, and the deviant pupil did not do that.

It is true that what the deviant pupil did can be made out to accord with *some* rule. We can perhaps make sense of him as having understood the words 'Add 2 each time' as giving the order that two is to be added each time up to 1000 and four is to be added after that. That is a possible way to understand what he did, but it is not a way of understanding his actions as being in accord with the rule to add two each time. We know that his actions are not in accord with that rule. Nor does thinking of him as having understood the instructions in that more complicated way show that *any* action can be made out to accord with the rule he would then be following. The rule he would be following on that more complicated understanding is a rule that determines that 1004 is the next step after 1000. No other course of action could be 'made out' to accord with that rule at that point either.

It is a confusion to say that the deviant pupil who follows that more complicated rule understands or interprets *the rule to add two each time* differently from the way we do. He does not *interpret* that rule at all; there is no such thing for him to interpret. We can say that he interprets or understands the *words* he hears as expressing the rule to add two up to 1000 and four thereafter. But to understand or interpret those words 'Add 2 each time' in that way is to understand or interpret an *expression*; it is not to interpret a rule. If the deviant pupil can be said to understand the words 'Add 2 each time' to express a certain rule, he does not in the same way understand that *rule* to express something in turn. We who understand or interpret the words 'Add 2 each time' as they are normally meant in English recognize what rule those words express, but it would be confusion to say that in addition we also understand or recognize what rule that *rule* expresses. Once we know what rule those words express, just as a person knows what proposition a certain clump of trees expresses, 'there can be no further question of an understanding'; there is nothing left to be understood. 'That really is how it is; when we are thinking, there isn't any interpretation going on.' (PG, 144)

What leads to the apparent 'paradox' is the idea that understanding and following a rule imposes an apparently unsatisfiable demand for more and more rules for 'interpreting' whatever rules have been accepted so far. One source of that demand in turn is the thought that someone who understands and follows a rule correctly must be instructed or guided in some way in how to follow it.[1] The question is how his

---

[1] This thought finds expression in Kripke's argument when he observes e.g. 'Ordinarily, I suppose that, in computing "68 + 57" as I do...I follow directions I previously gave myself' (Kripke 1982, 10) or 'When I respond in one way rather than another...I feel confident that there is something in my mind...that *instructs* me what I ought to do in all future cases.' (Kripke 1982, 21–2)

The same idea, along with the threat of regress that it gives rise to, is present in Crispin Wright's summary of the rule-following challenge as he understands it:

> what makes it possible for there to *be* such things as rules...at all?...how do I create something which carries determinate instructions for an open range of situations which I do not contemplate in making it? What gives it this content, when anything I say or do in explaining it will be open to an indefinite variety of conflicting interpretations? And how is the content to be got 'into mind' and so made available to inform the successive responses of practitioners? (Wright 2001, 2–3)

understanding and accepting the rule 'issues in' or 'yields' the particular applications he makes of it. As the challenge of §198 has it: 'But how can a rule shew me what I have to do at *this* point?'

As before, in Wittgenstein's words, 'it can be seen that there is a misunderstanding here'. (PI §201) If something were always needed to instruct or guide or show the rule-follower how to proceed, or if there had to be something in his mind that informed him what to do at each point, the thing that contains the instructions would also have to be understood by the person in some way or other. So that thing itself would stand in need of something further, something that gives instruction or guidance about how that first item of instruction or guidance is to be understood. And so on. If it really were a condition of a person's meaning or understanding something in a certain way that there be something that tells or instructs the person how to mean or understand it in that way, it would be impossible for anyone to mean or understand anything.

Once we see through this 'misunderstanding' or confused demand, there is no such threat of regress or paradox. When we say, from inside language, what rule is being followed or what certain words mean or how they are to be understood, there is nothing else to be understood or interpreted other than the words we utter. By 'inside language' I mean that the words we use (and do not just mention) in saying what rule is followed or what certain words mean are used with determinate meanings and are to be taken or understood in a certain way. Of course, the words we utter on a particular occasion might not be understood, so they might have to be further explained. And we will use words in explaining them. But if what we *say* in giving those explanations is understood, it is not something that in turn stands in need of further understanding or interpretation. There is no such thing to interpret.

Even if the deviant pupil does understand the expression 'Add 2 each time' to mean that two is to be added up to 1000 and four thereafter, when we ask him to *say* how he understands that expression he might well reply by uttering the words 'The expression "Add 2 each time" means add two each time.' He might simply repeat the expression whose meaning he is explaining. That is also what we would do in expressing our own understanding of what that expression means; we would utter those same words. The difference between what we would thereby be saying and what the imagined deviant pupil would be saying about the meaning of that expression obviously does not lie in the words we would both utter in explaining its meaning. We both utter the same words, but the difference lies in what those words mean as uttered by us and as uttered by the deviant pupil. That is a matter of how each of us uses those words, and what we use them to say. And what someone who hears us would understand each of us to say depends on how that person understands the words he hears, or what he thinks we mean by them. This illustrates in another way how saying or understanding or being told something about what an expression means is possible only 'from inside' language – only from an engaged position of understanding what one hears or says as meant or understood in a certain way.

One source of resistance to Wittgenstein's idea that meaning and understanding cannot be accounted for 'from outside' all language is that it can seem to make it impossible for anyone to acquire a language in the first place. No one starts out being able to speak. So there appears to be a question of how anyone could ever get into language or come to understand any words at all, if any statement or explanation of the meaning of expressions can succeed only if the person already understands the words in which that explanation is expressed. This could be said to represent a certain kind of 'limit' on the acquisition of language, but it is a 'limit' only on the possibility of stating or explaining the meaning of something to somebody. The most that follows is that we do not get into language in the first place by having the meanings of all the words we come to understand explained or otherwise described to us.

Nor does the fact that we can explain or describe those meanings only 'from inside' language represent a limit of language in the sense that to try to say what a sentence means or what fact corresponds to it would be to try to say something that 'lies on the other side of the limit [and] will simply be nonsense'. (TLP, 3) This kind of 'limit' on the possibility of explaining the meaning of something does not imply that there are no facts of meaning or of correspondence between sentences and reality, or that we cannot know such facts, or cannot express that knowledge in language. We do know what our expressions mean, or what fact corresponds to a given sentence, and it can be expressed in language. We express it in those sentences in which we say what something means or what fact corresponds to a given sentence. We all have that knowledge in being able to speak. But it is not knowledge of meaning that could be given to someone who cannot speak to instruct or guide him into meaning or understanding something in a particular way. No one could receive the proffered information without already possessing at least some measure of what the instructions were trying to impart.

We all start out with no linguistic competence and are brought to full mastery by training, interaction, and socialization with those who speak and live as we come to do. But we do not do so by being given directions or following instructions. Meaning and understanding things in certain ways is a fundamental fact of human life. Wittgenstein observes that commanding, questioning, recounting, chatting, and so on, which are all linguistic activities, 'are as much a part of our natural history as walking, eating, drinking, playing', which do not depend on language. (PI §25)

Appeal to the very 'naturalness' of these facts, and to their being open to view, can give rise to deeper dissatisfaction with the idea that meaning and understanding cannot be accounted for 'from outside' all language. There is an understandable philosophical aspiration to explain language and meaning and understanding in general – to account for their presence in a world that is not already understood to contain language. This encourages the expectation that meaning and understanding must be explainable or intelligible in terms that do not themselves presuppose the ascription of meaning or understanding to anything or anybody in the world. This has even been held to be a condition of success of any properly philosophical theory of meaning: the theory must explain speakers' possession of concepts and their expressing those concepts in the words of their language without itself attributing a grasp of any of those concepts to the speakers whose meanings it would account for. This is Michael Dummett's idea of a 'full-blooded' theory of meaning for a language. He thinks such a theory is required for 'the purpose for which, philosophically, we require a theory of meaning'. (Dummett 1993, 4)[2]

The idea that meaning and understanding cannot be accounted for 'from outside' all language is in conflict with this aspiration for a 'full-blooded' explanation of language and meaning. It implies that we cannot explain how speakers understand all the words they understand by observing and describing in non-intensional terms the conditions under which they utter or respond to those words. The fact that words have the meanings they do for particular speakers cannot be constructed in that way out of materials available 'from outside' all thought and understanding on the part of those speakers. This does not imply that the meanings of expressions or the understanding speakers have of them is somehow hidden or cannot be described in terms of their overt use. It means only that the use of expressions that gives them their determinate meanings is not something that can be described 'from outside' language in that way either.

One obvious and important route into language is demonstrative or ostensive teaching and learning – coming to understand the meanings of certain words in attending to the presence of the very things the words stand for. At some point before any ostensive teaching has begun, every prospective speaker is 'outside language'. But we do learn words by ostension. It is fundamental to our understanding and meaning anything. It is difficult to see how any words would be connected with any of the things we talk about at all if that were not so. But ostensive learning or definition is no exception to the idea that intention or meaning or understanding is not determined by anything available 'from outside' language in Wittgenstein's sense. The point is illustrated again and again in different ways in the early sections of *Philosophical Investigations*.

A sound's being uttered over and over again in the presence of objects which are all of a certain kind does not alone fix the meaning of that sound or anyone's understanding of it. It does not matter how long the ritual goes on. Taken on its own, as a 'phenomenon or fact', any correlation holding between a sound and a certain kind of object remains as 'outside' the meaning of that sound or how it is to be understood as any other correlation between objects of that kind and anything else. Getting a pupil to repeat the sound or to point to an object of a certain kind whenever he hears the sound might be part of what the pupil learns. That is what Wittgenstein calls 'ostensive teaching'; it is not sufficient to fix the meaning of the sound or how it is to be understood. The sound the pupil hears might be uttered in the presence of objects that are all white, and all rectangular, and all slabs, for instance. How the sound he hears is to be understood, given the correlation involved in that 'teaching', depends on something more. What the pupil is meant to do with the word, or what he comes to do with it, determines what kind of word he takes it to be. That further step involves what Wittgenstein calls 'ostensive training'.

---

[2] Dummett does not further specify what that philosophical purpose is, or why philosophy requires it. In Dummett 1991, 247, he describes the task as 'giving an account of the language as from outside', but he does not draw any connection between his use of that phrase and Wittgenstein's earlier use of it.

With different training the same ostensive teaching…would have brought about a quite different understanding. (PI §6)

An ostensive definition or explanation succeeds in giving the pupil the meaning of the word only 'when the overall role of a word [of that kind] in language is clear' (PI §30) or only 'if the place is already prepared' (PI §31) for words of that kind within whatever linguistic or other capacities the pupil already possesses. A speaker needs at least a rudimentary repertoire in order to mean or understand an expression in a determinate way. In Wittgenstein's memorable phrase, there must be a 'post' at which he can 'station' a new word in order for it to mean anything to him. (PI §29)

It might seem that it would be enough for the pupil simply to see the teacher's finger and recognize what the teacher is pointing at. But he cannot do that if he sees the teacher's finger and the object only 'from outside' all thought and meaning – only as two sorts of things that are present together. And to recognize the intention with which the ostension is carried out he must recognize it as an intention or thought 'with a certain content'. (PG, 44) Contents or thoughts of that kind would have to be intelligible to anyone who could recognize them and learn the meaning of a word in that way. The person must have some idea of what a colour is, for example, or what a shape is, or what a building-stone of a certain kind is, if he is to understand the sound he hears as a word for a colour rather than a shape or a kind of building-stone. That can reveal itself only in the kind of use he is prepared to make of the words he has heard.

Describing the workings of language and what competent speakers mean and understand only 'from within' language in this way is fully in accord with what have been called more 'modest' accounts of meaning and understanding. They make use of the very concepts they attribute to speakers whose linguistic competence they describe. To acknowledge the inevitability of understanding meaning in only that way is to acknowledge the poverty of what would be available 'from outside' language in Wittgenstein's sense.[3]

> To what extent can the function of language be described? If someone is not master of a language, I may bring him to a mastery of it by training. Someone who is master of it, I may remind of the kind of training, or I may describe it; for a particular purpose; thus already using a technique of the language.
>
> The difficult thing here is not, to dig down to the ground; no, it is to recognize the ground that lies before us as the ground.
>
> For the ground keeps on giving us the illusory image of a greater depth, and when we seek to reach this, we keep on finding ourselves on the old level.
>
> Our disease is one of wanting to explain. (RFM VI §31)

These remarks express resistance to the aspiration to 'full-blooded' theories on the grounds that meaning and language can be understood or explained only 'from within'

---

[3] For elaboration and defence of the idea that requiring anything beyond 'modest' accounts of meaning and understanding would leave linguistic behaviour altogether unintelligible, and for the sources of that idea in the writings of Wittgenstein, see McDowell 1998a and 1998b.

language. But this resistance on Wittgenstein's part has been regarded as mere 'mystification' (Dummett 1987, 268) or as defeatist or 'quietist' (e.g. Wright 2001, 169) reluctance to take up a recognizably serious intellectual challenge. It is true that Wittgenstein's philosophical treatment of the human fact of meaning and understanding, and his response to attempts to gain a finally satisfying general understanding of it 'from outside', does not yield a 'constitutive analysis' of a person's meaning or understanding something in a particular way. It does not seek or provide explanatorily revealing necessary and sufficient conditions of meaning or understanding something that would satisfy the demands of a 'full-blooded' theory. But what Wittgenstein says does help explain, or at least exhibit, why he thinks such an 'analysis' or theory is not to be had, and what he thinks is the most that can be said. This can be felt as a distinct philosophical disappointment. That feeling perhaps helps explain the impression of 'quietist' or even complacent evasion.

Wittgenstein's remark that it is impossible to describe the fact that corresponds to a sentence without simply repeating the sentence is immediately followed by the observation that 'this has to do with the Kantian solution of the problem of philosophy'. Not the problem*s* of philosophy (plural); 'the problem of philosophy' (singular). I take this to be the problem of how there can be such a thing as philosophy – how there can be, or what can be the upshot of, *philosophical* reflection on such matters as thought, meaning, and understanding. A 'solution' is 'Kantian', presumably, to the extent to which the facts of human meaning and understanding can be understood and accepted only from *within* whatever meaning and understanding we are already capable of.

Wittgenstein sums up the point of his observations in these words:

> What is spoken can only be explained in language, and so in this sense language cannot be explained. (PG, 40)

What he has in mind might then be transposed into something Kant could well have said about thought: 'what is thought, and our thinking it, can only be explained in thought, and so in *this* sense thought itself cannot be explained'. This Kantian observation could also perhaps be found philosophically disappointing. But presumably not because it is an expression of complacent or defeatist reluctance to engage in constructive philosophical reflection.

References

BLACK, MAX (1964). *A Companion to Wittgenstein's Tractatus*. Cambridge: Cambridge University Press.

DUMMETT, MICHAEL (1987). 'Reply to John McDowell', in B. Taylor ed., *Michael Dummett: Contributions to Philosophy*. Dordrecht: Nijhoff.

—— (1991). 'Frege and Wittgenstein', in *Frege and Other Philosophers*. Oxford: Oxford University Press.

—— (1993). 'What is a Theory of Meaning? (I)', in *The Seas of Language*. Oxford: Oxford University Press.

KRIPKE, SAUL A. (1982). *Wittgenstein on Rules and Private Language*. Oxford: Blackwell.

MCDOWELL, JOHN (1998a). 'In Defence of Modesty', in *Meaning, Knowledge, and Reality*. Cambridge, MA: Harvard University Press.

—— (1998b). 'Another Plea for Modesty', in *Meaning, Knowledge, and Reality*. Cambridge, MA: Harvard University Press.

WITTGENSTEIN, LUDWIG (1953). *Philosophical Investigations*, trans. G. E. M. Anscombe. Oxford: Blackwell.

—— (1961). *Tractatus Logico-Philosophicus*, trans. D. F. Pears and B. F. McGuinness. London: Routledge & Kegan Paul.

—— (1974). *Philosophical Grammar*, trans. A. Kenny. Oxford: Blackwell.

—— (1978). *Remarks on the Foundations of Mathematics*, trans. G. E. M. Anscombe, rev. edn. Oxford: Blackwell.

—— (1980). *Culture and Value*, trans. P. Winch. Oxford: Blackwell.

WRIGHT, CRISPIN (2001). *Rails to Infinity*. Cambridge, MA: Harvard University Press.

CHAPTER 14

···

WITTGENSTEIN AND IDEALISM

···

DAVID R. CERBONE

OF the many sources of interpretive conflict in Wittgenstein's philosophy, one of the most recalcitrant is surely the question of his philosophy's ultimate commitment to *idealism*. Many readers of Wittgenstein (for example G. E. M. Anscombe (1981), David Bloor (1996), Michael Forster (2004), Jonathan Lear (1982), Thomas Nagel (1986), and Bernard Williams (1981)) have detected at least some affiliation with, if not outright endorsement of, some form of idealism, while other readers, such as Cora Diamond (1991), Ilham Dilman (2004), Norman Malcolm (1995), John McDowell (1998), Edward Minar (2007), Stephen Mulhall (2009), Barry Stroud (1984), and Michael Williams (2004), have offered persuasive considerations *against* any such affiliation.

Those who argue that Wittgenstein must in the end be some kind of idealist will cite, among other things, his appeal to "forms of life" (either as diverse or ultimately and emphatically singular), his attention to the (alleged) constitutive role of, variously, our practices, community, or "mindedness" in the formation of concepts, and his apparent dismissal of philosophical problems and questions as instances of speaking "outside" of language-games.[1] That just these features of Wittgenstein's philosophy converge to make for an ultimately idealist philosophy is succinctly summarized in Thomas Nagel's

---

[1] It is worth noting that readers who take Wittgenstein to be committed to some form of *conservatism* likewise tend to focus on these features. Wittgenstein's apparent hostility to the notion of any independent check on our concepts, as well as their "rootedness" in our "form of life," tells against the possibility of any radical critique of "our concepts," as well as the possibility of any genuine conceptual innovation or novelty (or so conservative readings maintain). I have previously argued that these interpretations are misreadings of Wittgenstein; in doing so, I have further argued that attributions of conservatism involve misreadings of Wittgenstein that parallel those found in readings that see him as committed to idealism. See Cerbone 2003. The current discussion is in part an attempt to develop the claims I made there about the parallels between conservative and idealist readings of Wittgenstein, and so may be read as something of a companion piece to my earlier paper.

characterization.[2] Nagel, who labels Wittgenstein "one of the most important sources of contemporary idealism," traces this influence to his views on "the conditions of meaning." (Nagel 1986, 105; henceforth VFN) As Nagel sees it, Wittgenstein's views on meaning "imply that nothing can make sense which purports to reach beyond the outer bounds of human experience and life." (VFN, 105) This implication is a result of Wittgenstein's appeal to the "agreement in judgments" among members of a "community" as constitutive of the possibility of distinguishing between correct and incorrect assertions. Nagel writes:

> [F]or it is only within a community of actual or possible users of language that there can exist that possibility of agreement in its application which is a condition of the existence of rules, and of the distinction between getting it right and getting it wrong. This appears to rule out not only languages which could be understood by only one person, but also the use of language – even the general language of existence and states of affairs – to talk about what we cannot in principle make any judgments about. (VFN, 105)

On Nagel's reading, Wittgenstein's philosophy precludes the possibility that "what there is and what is true may extend beyond what [human beings] or their human successors could ever discover or conceive of or describe in some extension of language." (VFN, 106) Thus, Nagel concludes:

> [Wittgenstein's] view of how thought is possible clearly implies that any thoughts we can have of a mind-independent reality must remain within the boundaries set by our human form of life, and that we can't appeal to a completely general idea of what there is to defend the existence of kinds of facts which are in principle beyond the

---

[2] Another reading that concentrates on these features of Wittgenstein's philosophy is Michael Forster's. Forster, like Nagel, detects idealist commitments in Wittgenstein's later philosophy, and argues for an affinity between Wittgenstein's conclusions and Kant's transcendental idealism. Their views are not equivalent, however, as Wittgenstein introduces a kind of *pluralism* lacking in Kant. Forster writes:

> Whereas Kant appeals simply to *the human mind's* imposition of certain principles, Wittgenstein appeals to *diverse* human minds imposing *diverse* principles. Whereas Kant appeals to *noumenal* human nature constraining the human mind to do this, Wittgenstein appeals to *empirical* human nature as one of the things that does so. Whereas Kant *only* appeals to human nature as such a constraint, Wittgenstein also appeals to social practices and traditions, as well as the usefulness and empirical applicability of the principles in question. (Forster 2004, 15)

As a result, Forster asks, "Does this make Wittgenstein's position, like Kant's, a form of idealism, then? The answer, I think, is that it *does*." The form of idealism is different from Kant's owing to the possibility of diverse "impositions" by different human minds upon the world. The character of these impositions, such that what might have appeared to be features of a mind-independent reality turn out to be features of our minds (or, in apparently more Wittgensteinian terms, our grammar), justifies the attribution of idealism. Because of the divergence from Kant, Forster rejects other kinds of idealist readings of Wittgenstein, in particular the Lear–Williams reading, which sees Wittgenstein as following the Kantian model much more closely. I discuss Lear's reading below. I should note here that in criticizing Lear, I should not thereby be understood as endorsing Forster's pluralistic idealism. I will not, however, be arguing directly against Forster in this chapter. I have raised some criticisms of Forster's reading of Wittgenstein elsewhere (see my brief review, Cerbone 2007), but there is certainly further work to be done to address his claims more adequately.

possibility of human confirmation or agreement. We fall into nonsense, he thinks, if we try to take language too far from these conditions. We can't think of our world as part of a larger universe that also contains things revealed only to forms of life inaccessible to us; we can't apply the concepts of belief or truth to a point of view totally unreachable from our own. (VFN, 106–7)

A more approving reading of Wittgenstein as an idealist that nonetheless follows many of the same contours as Nagel's critical reading is Jonathan Lear's. Lear attributes to Wittgenstein a concern with what he calls our "mindedness," which Lear defines in the following manner:

> Let us say a person is *minded* in a certain way, if he has the perceptions of salience, routes of interest, feelings of naturalness in following a rule, etc. that constitute being part of a certain form of life. (Lear 1982, 385; henceforth LWA; see also Lear 1984)

In attending to our mindedness, one comes to see that, for example, the propositions of arithmetic or the principles of valid reasoning depend upon our being minded in the way we are; they are reflections of our mindedness. If we had been minded in some other way, if some other way of following a rule had seemed natural, if other perceptions had seemed salient, the propositions of arithmetic or the principles of valid reasoning would be other than they are. These considerations would seem to imply a kind of relativism. Lear, however, maintains otherwise.

To see why, Lear asks us to consider the following questions:

> What does 7+5 equal?
> (a) 12
> (b) Anything at all, just as long as everyone is so minded.

> What follows from P and If P, then Q?
> (a) Q
> (b) Anything at all, just as long as everyone is so minded. (LWA, 385)

About these questions and the four possible responses, Lear states that in both cases (a) expresses the correct answer. Anyone who offered answers different from (a) would, in both cases, be in error. (LWA, 385) However, Lear further claims that there is something right about (b) in each case as well:

> After studying the later Wittgenstein, one is tempted to say that (b) also expresses some sort of truth. But it is important to realize that (b) does not express [in each case] an empirical truth. (LWA, 386)

So, to the extent that (b) in each case expresses any truth at all, such a truth cannot be understood as an *empirical* one, since, according to Lear, "if (b) were an empirical truth, then the following counterfactuals ought to express genuine possibilities":

> 7+5 would equal something other than 12, if everyone had been other-minded.

> Q would not follow from P and If P, then Q, if everyone had been other-minded.
> (LWA, 386)

Lear claims that "these counterfactuals cannot for us express real possibilities; for the notion of people being 'other-minded' is not something on which we can get any grasp." (LWA, 386) On the one hand, our mindedness informs claims such as "7+5=12," but, on the other hand, our mindedness exhausts our understanding of what it is to be minded at all, and so Lear avoids the problematic situation of there being different species of mindedness with which we might be tempted to try to compare our own. On Lear's reading, when Wittgenstein speaks of what Nagel referred to as the "conditions of meaning," these are not to be understood as some set of empirical conditions, which may be met by one group of like-minded individuals but not by some other, but instead are the transcendental conditions of what it is to be minded at all: "The possibility of there being persons who are minded in any way at all is the possibility of their being minded as we are." (LWA, 386)

Thus, when Nagel writes that on Wittgenstein's view "we can't apply the concepts of belief or truth to a point of view totally unreachable from our own," Lear's Wittgenstein urges instead an acknowledgment or admission that there is nothing here that we *cannot* do, as there is in the end no sense to be made of "a point of view totally unreachable from our own." For Lear, the dissolution of such an idea plays a key role in defending Wittgenstein from the charge of relativism. According to Lear, relativism is only an *apparent* consequence of acknowledging the dependence of our ways of seeing the world upon our mindedness. The relativist consequence can be drawn only to the extent that the articulation of this dependence is understood as an empirical claim. Lear claims that

> relativism's appeal (threat) stems from taking the claim:
> (*) Only because we are minded as we are do we see the world the way we do.
> to express an empirical truth: as delineating one possibility among others. (LWA, 392)

Lear continues by pointing out that the difficulty facing the would-be relativist's construal of (*) as an empirical claim is that the relativist must then make sense of the following counterfactual:

> If we were other-minded, we would see the world differently. (LWA, 392)

Lear claims further that "from a Wittgensteinian point of view, this counterfactual must be nonsense." (LWA, 392) The counterfactual is nonsensical because our way of seeing the world exhausts our understanding of what it is to see the world at all. Nothing could count for us as both a substantially different way of seeing the world and nonetheless a way of seeing. Lear's rejection of the counterfactual is of a piece with his prior point that the features of *our* mindedness inform our understanding of what it is to be minded at all, and so there can be no coherent notion of other-mindedness. From all of this, Lear draws the following conclusion: "To accept the claim (*), but deny that it delimits one possibility among others is to accept a Wittgensteinian form of *transcendental idealism*." (LWA, 392; my emphasis) By accepting (*), what we accept is idealism because of the aforementioned dependence of any claims about the world upon our way of seeing the world (our mindedness), but it is transcendental insofar as our way of seeing the world (our mindedness) cannot be considered one way among many: our way of being minded exhausts what it is to be minded.

While Lear's sympathetic reading of Wittgenstein is more thorough and subtle, and offers perhaps a level of diagnostic insight not found in Nagel's more dismissive reading, the two nonetheless converge in their view of Wittgenstein's conception of our "mindedness" as ruling out as unintelligible anything that somehow transcends or exceeds the "boundaries" of it. Again, as Nagel puts it, Wittgenstein is committed to the claim that "nothing can make sense which purports to reach beyond the outer bounds of human experience and life," and with this Lear's Wittgenstein would no doubt concur, as those "outer bounds," as the limits of our mindedness, are at the same time the bounds of sense. Both readings thus see Wittgenstein as conceiving of "our human form of life" (or our "mindedness") as having a determinate, or at least determinable, form or shape; the critical thrust of Wittgenstein's philosophy, which Lear seems to approve but which Nagel finds objectionable, is his counsel that we stay "within" the confines of our mindedness, since to stray beyond its borders marks a lapse into nonsense.

Now there is, I believe, a fairly obvious tension in Nagel's complaints, since he reads Wittgenstein as committed to there being "boundaries set by our human form of life" and yet he also interprets Wittgenstein as claiming (or perhaps reminding us) that "we can't think of our world as part of a larger universe that also contains things revealed only to forms of life inaccessible to us." But to say our "human form of life" involves "boundaries" implies that there is something beyond, bounded off from, and so inaccessible to, our human form of life. The imagery of boundaries, in other words, invokes the further image of "our world as part of a larger universe," some of which is, owing to those boundaries, "inaccessible to us," but this is supposed to be what Wittgenstein's philosophy says we cannot so much as conceive or think. But if we cannot think of ourselves as occupying some limited part of "a larger universe," then we also cannot think of our human life as setting "boundaries." Nagel's Wittgenstein appears to want to have it both ways; that this appearance is so obvious suggests that something has gone wrong in Nagel's reading.

Finding an analogous tension in Lear's reading is perhaps a bit trickier: although his Wittgenstein would also claim that "we can't think of our world as part of a larger universe that also contains things revealed only to forms of life inaccessible to us," the claim is underwritten by the "transcendental insight" that the notion of "forms of life inaccessible to us" turns out to be nonsensical. To be a form of life to or for whom things are revealed, i.e. to be minded at all, just is to be minded as we are. Given the status of this insight as "transcendental," it is misleading (at best) to claim (or even think) that there is something here that we *cannot* do. Despite the increased sophistication of Lear's interpretation, there remains as residue the imagery of our mindedness as nonetheless bounded or enclosed, as when Lear writes: "There is no getting a glimpse of what it might be like to be other-minded, for as we move toward the *outer bounds* of our mindedness we verge on incoherence and nonsense." (LWA, 386; my emphasis) We can hear in this passage an echo of Williams' prior reading of Wittgenstein as an idealist, a reading upon which Lear explicitly builds. At one juncture, Williams describes Wittgenstein's method as one of "moving reflectively around *inside* our view of things and sensing when one began to be near the *edge* by the increasing incomprehensibility of things regarded from whatever way-out point of view one had moved into." (Williams 1981, 153) As the empha-sized terms indicate, Williams, and by extension Lear, see Wittgenstein as retaining some commitment to boundaries or limits, while at the same time adducing "transcendental insights" to the effect that no other way of being minded is even possible and thus that there is no other point of view on the world that is somehow bounded off from our own.[3]

This (fairly obvious) tension is symptomatic of the confusions that I think beset Nagel's attribution of idealism to Wittgenstein's philosophy (and, ultimately, Lear's more approving idealist reading). These confusions are most evident in the way Nagel and Lear misplace or mischaracterize the role of what Nagel refers to as "Wittgenstein's occa-sional evocation of possible forms of life incomprehensibly different from our own." (VFN, 106) Although Nagel regards such a "gesture in the direction of admitting the reality of what we cannot conceive" as a rather "desperate" attempt to avoid the verdict of idealism (VFN, 106), I want to suggest instead that the real sense of desperation lies in Nagel's insistence that there must be something that Wittgenstein is ruling out or deny-ing, such that our sense of reality – its independence and even potential inaccessibility – is somehow diminished. On the contrary, I will try to show that there is nothing that Nagel really wants that is in any way ruled out by Wittgenstein's philosophy and so his conception of Wittgenstein as "one of the most important sources of contemporary idealism" is erroneous. At the same time, I will also argue that, as their occasionally less than harmonic convergence would suggest, Lear's reading of Wittgenstein is vulnerable to much the same criticisms as Nagel's.

Consider more closely one of Nagel's principal claims about Wittgenstein's idealism:

> (N) Nothing can make sense which purports to reach beyond the outer bounds of human experience and life

Since Nagel finds (N) to be problematic, he would presumably endorse its negation:

> (S) Something can make sense which purports to reach beyond the outer bounds of human experience and life

When confronted with (S), the natural question to ask is what someone who is tempted to assert or endorse (S) has in mind to be the "something" which can make sense. If the someone is able to specify a definite something, then he has failed to specify a suitable "something" since what he has said makes sense "within" the bounds of human experi-ence. If, on the other hand, no specification is forthcoming, then it is unclear just what is being claimed in (S): it appears to be little more than an empty gesture.[4]

---

[3] For Williams, this marks an unresolved tension in Wittgenstein's philosophy, such that any attempt to *state* his view is bound to be misunderstood. I would suggest instead that we read Wittgenstein as more wholeheartedly exorcizing philosophical talk of boundaries or limits. For especially insightful criticisms of Williams on this point, see Mulhall 2009.

[4] As we will see, the idea that a gesture may prove *empty* will be an important one throughout my discus-sion. The idea that Wittgenstein's philosophy has as one of its central concerns the threat of emptiness in thought and speech has been explored in the work of Steven Affeldt. See especially his 2010.

Suppose someone were instead to say "Nothing beyond the outer bounds of the English language makes sense." What *this* someone appears to be saying is that there is nothing that is both a meaningful sentence and not a sentence of the English language. So put, what this someone says is blatantly false. A quick trip to Europe or even to the corner bookstore for a Berlitz guide should reveal the error of his ways: there are many, indeed countless, meaningful sentences which are "outside" the English language, since they are in *different* languages, such as German or French or Chinese or ... However blatantly false our initial claim appears to be, a significant point might be seen to be lurking beneath it. Our someone might say that he has been misunderstood, since he does not wish to deny the actuality of foreign languages, i.e. languages other than English. However, he may wish to reformulate his claim in the following manner: any of those "foreign" sentences which lie "outside" the bounds of the English language can be matched, via a process of translation, with sentences "inside" the bounds of the English language. Nothing beyond the outer bounds of the English makes sense, our someone maintains, since anything that initially appears to lie outside can be suitably domesticated through the process of translation. Thus, his claim is:

> (M) There are no meaningful sentences that cannot be rendered in the English language

Nothing has been said to show that this claim is true, but if it is false, it is not, I take it, blatantly so. Moreover, (M) may be seen to have a rather respectable philosophical pedigree, since it appears to be one of the claims put forward in Donald Davidson's argument against the idea of a conceptual scheme.[5] Davidson's argument is directed at those who appeal to the possibility of "radically different conceptual schemes," by which is meant systems of concepts that cannot be rendered intelligible in terms of one another. Such "schemes" are radically different insofar as they are incommensurable with one another. Against such an appeal, Davidson levels an argument to the effect that the idea that any handle we get on something's being a system of concepts at all is afforded by the process of *interpreting* the putative system: if the putative system of concepts proves to be

---

[5] See Davidson 1984. I am not concerned in this chapter to defend Davidson from Nagel's criticisms, but I should not for that reason be understood as necessarily agreeing with them. I should note here that the issue of the convergence between Wittgenstein's philosophy and Davidson's anti-relativist arguments (as well as the broader commitments that give rise to those arguments) is a matter of considerable debate. Some readers see tremendous affinity; indeed, Lear goes so far as to say that one can "see Davidson as a type of transcendental idealist." See LWA, note 12. Other readers, such as Michael Forster, see almost complete divergence: for Forster, Davidson's arguments are the principal contemporary target of the kind of "diversity thesis" he sees at work in Wittgenstein's later philosophy. My own sense is that Wittgenstein and Davidson do not ultimately converge, owing to their markedly different conceptions of language, meaning, and understanding. Davidson, armed with a worked-out *theory* of meaning and interpretation, can construct the kind of master-argument he deploys in "On the Very Idea of a Conceptual Scheme," whereas Wittgenstein, as hostile to philosophical theorizing about meaning (or an essence of language), not only lacks such a master-argument but rejects the very idea of one. Instead, I see his philosophy as leading toward a kind of ineliminable indeterminacy, which I sketch out at the conclusion of this chapter.

recalcitrant in the face of attempts to interpret it, that, for Davidson, is good evidence for concluding that what we are confronting is not a system of concepts at all.

In order to encourage the idea that (S) rather than (N) is correct, and so make vivid the idea that there are limitations upon human experience and knowledge, Nagel proposes a thought experiment. (It should be emphasized that the thought experiment is directed at Davidson, though I think it is safe to say that Nagel would regard it as equally applicable to Wittgenstein as well.) What Nagel asks us to imagine is a community of people whose mental powers never develop beyond that of a normal human nine-year-old. Such people are thus constrained by severe limitations in terms of their capacity to know various things about the world around them: the subtler, or perhaps even most of the basic, points of physics and mathematics immediately come to mind. We can thus say of such a group things of the following tenor: "There are facts about the world which they will never learn" or "There are concepts which they will never acquire." Now, what Nagel asks us to do is occupy the standpoint of these nine-year-olds: if such a member of their group were to put forward a claim along the lines of (N), and so claim that there was nothing which made sense beyond the bounds of their experience, *we* can see that this claim is patently false. That is, we can enumerate lots of things which are beyond the reach of this group of people and which do make sense, precisely because they make sense to us. Thus a statement along the lines of (N) is, when uttered by one of these mental nine-year-olds, false, and, likewise, were one of these nine-year-olds to say (S), he would be saying something true, even if he couldn't say what it is that might specify the something. Our endorser of (S), whom Nagel labels "Realist Junior," would no doubt be unable to rattle off anything like complex mathematical theorems or the central claims of the theory of evolution, but for all that, we can, it seems, appreciate that his gestures towards what he cannot understand would be far from empty.

The real point of Nagel's thought experiment comes, however, with the reflective application to ourselves of the lessons gleaned from the case of the perpetual mental nine-year-olds. That is, Nagel argues that since we find the first case intelligible, then we should also find the following case intelligible: we can imagine there being another group of people, compared to whom our mental powers are inferior to the same degree as the mental nine-year-olds' powers are to ours. If this is an intelligible possibility, then any one of us who is tempted to utter (N) is guilty of saying something false to the same extent as when (N) is uttered by one of those mental nine-year-olds: from the standpoint of these imagined superior beings, there are lots of things which both lie outside of human experience and which make sense. Thus, from the standpoint of these superior beings, a human being who claims that his or her conceptual repertoire exhausts what it is to be a conceptual repertoire is guilty of delusions of grandeur. Such a person is guilty of attempting "to cut the universe down to size" in just the way Nagel complains idealism strives to do.

The final move in this thought experiment is to keep the world exactly as it is, only we remove these superior beings. Doing so, Nagel claims, leaves the limitations upon human beings which were made vivid by imagining these superior beings fully in place: we are limited to the same degree, irrespective of whether such superior beings really exist or not. All that is required is that such beings, relative to whom we occupy a subordinate conceptual position, be a coherent possibility, in order to impress upon us the idea that we are constrained by potentially insurmountable limitations, that our perspective on the world is bounded in such a way that there are things which do not, and perhaps even cannot, make sense to us that are nonetheless bona fide features of reality.

It should be clear that the lessons Nagel draws from this series of thought experiments are incompatible with Lear's Wittgenstein (and so, of course, with Nagel's Wittgenstein as well). The very terms in which the thought experiment is posed are ones that Lear's Wittgenstein cannot countenance, since what Nagel is asking us to imagine here is our being flanked, on either side, with two species of other-mindedness, one inferior or impoverished and another that is superior. If Lear's reading of Wittgenstein is correct, then Wittgenstein is indeed vulnerable to Nagel's argument (which is precisely what we should expect, given the convergence of Lear's and Nagel's Wittgenstein). If, however, it can be shown that Wittgenstein can more or less acknowledge Nagel's thought experiment, then neither Nagel's nor Lear's conception of Wittgenstein as an idealist (or at least this particular stripe of idealist) can be sustained.

Though Nagel gives no evidence of familiarity with these stretches of Wittgenstein's writings, there are places where he appears to entertain a scenario much like the one Nagel deploys against Davidson. I have in mind especially the following remark from *Zettel*, the beginning of a series of three remarks which are all well worth considering in relation to Lear and Nagel:

> What would a society of all deaf men be like? Or a society of the 'feeble-minded' ('*Geistesschwachen*')? *An important question*! What then of a society that never played many of our customary language-games? (Z §371)

Wittgenstein does not here say exactly where the import of the question lies.[6] On Lear's reading, the import of Wittgenstein's question is that answering it will lead us to transcendental insights about our "mindedness." Again, a principal claim of Lear's reading is that Wittgenstein is concerned to demonstrate the impossibility of other-mindedness,

---

[6] Nor does he really say much about what he has in mind here in talking of the "feeble-minded." While there are numerous references in the later manuscripts to the "feeble-minded" and "mental defectives," the connotations of the term appear to vary according to the topic Wittgenstein is discussing. In some cases, Wittgenstein has in mind people who are said to be incapable of "inward" thinking (they cannot do sums "in their heads," nor work through problems or questions silently); in others, the "feeble-minded" are people who are incapable of fathoming people's intentions or pondering the *meaning* of what people say (they can never think or say things of the form, "I thought you were going to say...," or "What I took you to mean was..."); while in still others, the term applies to those who can only apply and understand names in the presence of their bearers. See the various remarks in the first volume of *Remarks on the Philosophy of Psychology*. However, Wittgenstein also uses the term in more open-ended contexts, where he does not appear to have a specific phenomenon in mind. The context of the *Zettel* remarks (as well as the manuscripts from which these remarks are culled) is open-ended in this way: the feeble-minded are offered as initially appearing to embody some form of conceptual impoverishment (the proximity of Wittgenstein's question concerning the deaf encourages this appearance). The tenor of his remarks is meant to suggest that "impoverishment" is not the best way to think about the matter and this, I will suggest, has ramifications for Nagel's thought experiment.

to show, that is, that "the possibility of there being persons who are minded in any way at all is the possibility of their being minded as we are." (LWA, 386) Indeed, Lear sees this as the general lesson of Wittgenstein's evocation of what *look* to be imagined cases of other-mindedness:

> Wittgenstein occasionally postulates a tribe whose interests and activities differ from ours. Their function is to help us see how our activities are dependent upon the interests we have. But it is a mistake to think of these tribes as providing concrete examples of other-mindedness. Insofar as we can make sense of their activities and interests, that is, insofar as we can fill out the picture, they do not turn out to be other-minded. We are discovering more about what our form of life is like, not what another would be like. (LWA, 389)

By following through on Wittgenstein's sketches of strange tribes, Lear maintains, we come to see that insofar as we can understand the activities of such tribes, we come to see them as essentially like-minded with us. Such sketches should not be read as providing alternatives to our concepts and practices, or indeed as articulating genuine possibilities at all, since, the transcendental reading maintains, Wittgenstein's aim is to show that what it is to be minded is to be minded as we are, i.e. that there is no such thing as being other-minded.

There is certainly something right about these claims regarding how one should understand Wittgenstein's postulation of strange communities and how to answer the questions he raises about them. For one thing, Wittgenstein is careful to say that he is not offering *hypotheses* concerning the formation of concepts different from our own, and so he should not be understood as engaging in any kind of armchair anthropology or natural science. (See especially PI II, 230.) Thus it would be a mistake to see his appeal to imaginary encounters as placeholders for future fieldwork, as though we could not be sure of the lessons Wittgenstein seeks to impart from reflection on such scenes without first finding real-life correlates. (See Cerbone 1994.) Moreover, Lear is certainly correct that the point of engaging our imaginative capacities by reflecting on sketches of alien tribes is for us to learn more about "what our form of life is like," as opposed to finding out more about some other. (Really finding out would seem to require just the kind of fieldwork Wittgenstein shows no interest in conducting; moreover, it would appear to require consideration of real cases, not just imagined ones.) However, it seems incorrect to move from a disinterest in hypotheses and an interest in the acquisition of a kind of self-knowledge to the conclusion that what we learn about our form of life is that it constitutes the only possible one, at least as far as being minded goes. That is, Lear wants to maintain that Wittgenstein is concerned to establish that being what Lear calls "other-minded" is not a genuine possibility, that there are not, and indeed could not be, beings who are other-minded.

Part of the motivation for this conclusion can be seen in the citation offered above, namely in Lear's claim that "insofar as we can make sense of their activities, that is, insofar as we can fill out the picture, [such tribes] do not turn out to be other-minded." Now, in one sense, this claim is trivial, if "filling out the picture" is understood as capturing the sense of their activities (including their linguistic performances) by means of *our* concepts; if we succeed in filling out the picture in this way, then it follows immediately that what we have imagined are beings who are like-minded with us, whose conceptual repertoire is more or less identical with our own. But what of cases where we cannot fill out the picture, where, that is, we cannot make sense of the tribe's or community's activities? Is there room in Wittgenstein for the possibility of such a case? Lear wants to claim that there is no room, that, in other words, being able to fill out the picture is a test for the possibility of the community being imagined.

The sequel to Wittgenstein's series of questions does not sit well with Lear's general assessment of the role of such imaginary scenarios[7] and the questions we might raise about them:

> One imagines the feeble-minded under the aspect of the degenerate, the essentially incomplete, as it were in tatters. And so under that of disorder instead of a more primitive order (which would be a more fruitful way of looking at them).
>
> We just don't see a *society* of such people. (Z §372)

Wittgenstein is here cautioning against thinking of the "feeble-minded" exclusively in terms of our own way of being minded. The temptation is to see such people as instantiating our way(s) of being minded, but in an incomplete, disorderly, or degenerate sense. Succumbing to this temptation does indeed pull in the direction of concluding that we do not really have here a case of other-mindedness, but instead either no real mindedness at all or a rather dim, incomplete form of our own. An incomplete form of our own mindedness would still count, for Lear's Wittgenstein, as being minded in the way we are, since we could, as Lear requires, succeed in "filling out the picture." Of course, we would not have to avail ourselves of everything at our disposal to do so, but that would not affect Lear's point. Wittgenstein does not exactly say here that this way of proceeding is incorrect, but only that another way would be "more fruitful." This other way would be one of regarding the society of the feeble-minded along the lines of a "more primitive order," rather than disorder. The idea here is that in order to think of these feeble-minded beings as really constituting their own society, which Wittgenstein acknowledges is difficult, we need to think of them in ways that do not cast them in terms dependent on our ways of being minded. As an autonomous, free-standing society, they need to be considered as possessing their own order that is not beholden to the concepts constituting our, perhaps less primitive, order. (Part of the difficulty of avoiding this way of thinking is no doubt owing to the labeling of these people as *feeble*-minded in the first place, since that immediately suggests that the form of mindedness being qualified is precisely our own.)

In other words, the challenge posed by a society of the "feeble-minded" is that we need to see them as having a different *kind* of order, one that does not line up in any clean or easy way with our own. While we might, given Wittgenstein's talk of "primitive," be cor-

---

[7] That Lear's reading founders owing to its inability to accommodate Wittgenstein's many appeals to the possibility of concepts different from our own has been emphasized by Barry Stroud. See his 1984.

rect in thinking of the feeble-minded as lacking certain features of our mindedness, indeed ones that are particularly sophisticated or complex, this should not be taken necessarily to imply that we could get from their mindedness to ours simply by grafting on those missing features (any more than one could get from a dog to a cat simply by adding or subtracting some set of capacities or abilities).[8] The third in this series of remarks underscores this idea, as it emphasizes the ways in which concepts different from our own may fail to line up with, and so be readily comparable to, our own:

> Concepts other than though akin to ours might seem *very* queer to us; deviations from the usual *in an unusual direction*. (Z §373)

The sense of "queerness" Wittgenstein invokes here is very much at odds with the kinds of conclusions about our mindedness Lear sees Wittgenstein as drawing. For Lear's Wittgenstein, there is no room for the idea of concepts other than our own, since that would amount to an acknowledgment of the possibility of being other-minded. That Wittgenstein leaves room for just such an idea, indeed that he encourages us to think about a society of the feeble-minded in just these terms (rather than as "essentially incomplete"), tells against the kind of interpretation Lear offers.

That Wittgenstein leaves room for such an idea also suggests that something is amiss in Nagel's thought experiment, understood as a refutation of anything to which Wittgenstein is obviously committed. This is *not* to say that Wittgenstein would wholly endorse Nagel's thought experiment just as it stands, since the kind of caution he offers in *Zettel* §372 would seem to apply as much to Nagel as to Lear. What I mean here is that Nagel's thought experiment, wherein we are flanked on either side with two other forms of mindedness, the feeble-minded and the super-minded, as it were, thereby arranges these forms of mindedness in the kind of linear way Wittgenstein rejects. Nagel's sequence of ways of being minded is structured very much like three concentric circles, such that each successive circle wholly contains the previous one (our form of mindedness contains that of the mental nine-year-olds, while the super-minded would contain ours). The realist amidst each community (Realist Junior in the case of the feeble-minded, Nagel presumably in ours, and, though he does not mention such a possibility, there could no doubt be a Realist Senior among the more powerfully minded community) conceives of himself as probing the edges of his own "circle" and thereby gesturing toward something lying on the far side. Wittgenstein's "more fruitful" way of looking at the feeble-minded interrupts this way of picturing things, since it invites us to think of the feeble-minded as *alongside* our way of being minded, as another, perhaps "queer," way of being minded rather than an "essentially incomplete" version of our own. When Wittgenstein famously declares that "what has to be accepted, the given, is – so one could say – *forms of life*," his more fruitful way of looking at the feeble-minded may be one form of that acceptance.

At this juncture, I want to follow up on Wittgenstein's first question of *Zettel* §371, immediately prior to his question concerning the feeble-minded. Wittgenstein there

---

[8] For this last point concerning how to understand Wittgenstein's appeal to the feeble-minded, including the allusion to dogs and cats, see Dilman 2004, especially 168–9 and 175.

asks after a society of the deaf. Though he proceeds to ask after a society of the feeble-minded without considering an answer or even the form of an answer to his initial one concerning a society of the deaf, it is not at all clear that the two questions should be taken together such that what Wittgenstein goes on to say in the remainder of the remark applies equally to both questions. (Elsewhere, Wittgenstein draws a rather sharp distinction, though it is not clear that he has the same notion of feeble-mindedness in mind there.)[9] In thinking about such a community, let us first consider it as an isolated, self-contained society, such that every member of the community is congenitally deaf and no member of the community has ever encountered anyone (indeed, any creature) capable of hearing. With respect to this imagined community, it is fairly easy for us to specify just what its members cannot do, namely *hear sounds*. We can thus specify a range of facts (about how things sound) that are unavailable to all the members of this community, as well as an associated range of judgments that are likewise unavailable (that one sound is louder than another, that one sound is higher in pitch, and so on).

Matters are far less clear, however, insofar as we try to take up the perspective of those who live within this community and consider the prospect of making out this kind of unavailability. Let us again try to construct an analogue of Nagel's Realist Junior, who again longs to transcend what he feels to be the limitations imposed upon members of his community, himself included. Realist Junior here might note that there seems to be no principled reason why there are only four sensory modalities (seeing, smelling, tasting, and touching). Indeed, if we imagine that the members of this community have bodies much like our own, we can further imagine Realist Junior speculating about what *ears* are for, and so arguing that just as eyes are for seeing, the nose is for smelling, and so on, perhaps the ears could have been for, well, what might Realist Junior gesture toward here? Certainly not *hearing*, since that is something no member of this community has any knowledge of.

Developing Realist Junior's gesture depends significantly on how we develop our description of the community. If we allow for the possibility of these people being acquainted with any creatures that *can* hear, i.e. various kinds of animals, then it would seem that this community could have at least some idea of what hearing was all about, much as we have a good idea of what bats are up to using echo-location. That is, members of this community such as Realist Junior could say, "Suppose our ears were sensitive like the ears many of the animals around us appear to be," though without being able to elaborate upon what this "sensitivity" really amounted to in terms of the kind of *experience* it afforded. (Here, of course, it might appear that we are providing further grist for Nagel's mill, as the appeal to the ways of bats would suggest.) They might be able, as we are with bats, to develop an elaborate account of the way hearing works in other animals,

<hr/>

[9] For example, at §189 of the first volume of *Remarks on the Philosophy of Psychology*, Wittgenstein writes: "For a blind man just is someone who does not have a *sense*. (The mental defective [*Schwachsinnigen*] – e.g. – can't be compared to the blind man.)" However, the context of this remark is one where Wittgenstein has a much more specific phenomenon in mind, along the lines of the ones enumerated above, than he does in the *Zettel* remarks we are considering.

including an understanding of the relevant aspects of physical reality (vibrations in the air, for example) that play a role in hearing. At the same time, even armed with this kind of insight or understanding, they would still not really be able to comprehend in a full and immediate way the reality of *sounds*.[10]

Suppose, for example, that Realist Junior is a talented animator and so tried, through visual means, to gesture toward what he and the other members of his society are missing. What would such a cartoon look like in this case and how much would it really convey? Sound waves could be depicted visually and much in the way of standard responses to those waves could be shown: if a source is shown emitting large, bold waves, the person depicted might cover his ears, grimace in pain, or rush to place a pillow over the offending source (followed by a sigh of relief). Now, it's not at all clear just how Realist Junior would have thought of even this much: he could be reasoning on analogy with responses to bright lights, hot and cold surfaces, or foul odors, or again, we could allow that scientists in this community have figured out enough about other animals to have some sense of their sensitivity to measurably different vibrations in the air. Still, does this cartoon really convey the ability lacking in the members of this community? If the character in the cartoon were depicted as a superhero, would his followers in this community really understand what his "superpower" was all about?[11] (While I'm not able to leap tall buildings in a single bound, I can at least jump over small obstacles and extrapolate accordingly. In the case of this society, it is not clear what the starting point for extrapolation would be.)

What Realist Junior has in mind becomes far less clear insofar as we try to delete *any* familiarity with creatures that are capable of hearing. Insofar as we do this, the content of Realist Junior's gesture is no longer clear, irrespective of whether we try to ascribe that content from within that community or do so instead from some outside perspective. That is, it is not clear even for those of us imagining the goings-on of this community that we should say that what Realist Junior is gesturing toward are *facts about hearing and sound*. But if there is nothing determinate (or really all that determinable) that

---

[10] Notice that a lot of work is being done here by the qualifier "full and immediate." It would be a mistake, I think, to see the absence of that kind of comprehension as precluding genuine comprehension more generally. As the possibility of the members of this community investigating the workings of other animals suggests, there are other, less direct avenues for comprehending the phenomena of hearing and sound. While less direct, we should not read them as somehow failing to reach their destination. For example, it is conceivable that another creature may have direct perceptual access to magnetic fields (I have been told that some ornithologists have speculated that some species of birds in fact do); though it is difficult to imagine "what it would be like" to have this kind of perceptual capacity, the absence of that capacity in us certainly does not mean that we do not understand magnetic fields! I am grateful to William Blattner and Mark Okrent for providing these examples and prompting these points.

[11] Even if the answer to both of these questions is "No," would they for this reason have to regard themselves as incomplete? Are we entitled to the thought that we are more complete than they are? I cannot sense things via echo-location, but I do not for that reason consider myself incomplete in relation to the bat (I am not able to *fly* either, at least not without a great deal of mechanical assistance). Again, see Dilman 2004 for further discussion.

Realist Junior is gesturing toward, then it is not clear how he has succeeded in delineat-
ing, let along making vivid, any kind of limit or limitation upon him or other members
of his community. (His lack of hearing is manifest *as* a lack, even to us, only to the extent
that he is acquainted with hearing.)

This point becomes clearer when we try to think of ourselves as sandwiched between
two possibilities. While we can fairly readily comprehend the possibility of a society of
the deaf and so, as Nagel insists, even see how their Realist Junior might in some way be
right (whatever limitations there might be on his ability to get very clear on what he is
right about), it is not entirely clear how we are to think of the other end of the thought
experiment. One possibility is to think of the other end simply as a community whose
hearing capacities are far superior to those found in any human being. Spelled out this
way, there is a sense in which our predicament is far better than that of the members of
the society of the deaf. Since we have already a good grip on what the experience of hearing is all about, in thinking about the super-human community, we are just increasing
the power of that capacity. Here we might imagine beings with sensitivities akin to what
we find in some other animals and in some of our higher-end technologies for picking
up and recording sound. We might imagine such beings as able to hear pins drop several
rooms or several miles away, provided there was not too much in the way of intervening
louder sounds to drown out the dropping pins. (I cannot hear a pin drop several rooms
away, but this is not because any other sound is drowning it out; I wouldn't hear it even
in the absence of any louder, more proximate sounds.)

This way of developing the thought experiment, however, does not sufficiently maintain a relation between us and the super-humans analogous to the one that obtains
between us and the society of the deaf, and so does not yet convey the sense of limitations Nagel wants us to appreciate. To preserve the analogy, what we need to consider is
the possibility of beings with an entirely different sensory modality, incomparable to,
and unavailable from the perspective of, our own. Whether or not this need can really be
met is far from clear, given precisely the required incomparability and unavailability in
relation to the ways our various sensory modalities work. While we might say, "Imagine
beings who are perceptually receptive or sensitive to some feature of the world," if this is
said without specifying what feature one has in mind, nor what kind of receptivity or
sensitivity is in question, then it is not at all clear what is being asked of us. It is not as
though we are here unable to imagine a particular possibility but that no particular possibility has (yet) been delineated.

For his part, Wittgenstein *does* try to delineate such possibilities. Immediately prior
to the series of passages where Wittgenstein raises his questions concerning societies of
the deaf and feeble-minded, he asks us to imagine a group of people who are masters of
an unusual technique for discriminating and categorizing colors:

> Let us imagine men who express a colour intermediate between red and yellow, say
> by means of a fraction in a kind of binary notation like this: R, LLRL, and the like,
> where we have (say) yellow on the right, and red on the left. – These people learn
> how to describe shades of colour in this way in the kindergarten, how to use such
> descriptions in picking colours out, in mixing them, etc. They would be related to us

roughly as people with absolute pitch are to those who lack it. *They can do* what we cannot. (Z §368)

Because this community "can do what we cannot," the question then arises as to how far we can go in imagining such beings in terms of imaginatively occupying their point of view on the world. The distinctions Wittgenstein draws with respect to this question are illuminating in thinking about the society of the deaf and their ability to fathom their own limitations (notice that the analogy Wittgenstein uses here also appeals to possibilities with respect to *hearing*, though here he considers a discriminatory capacity within hearing):

And here one would like to say: "But then, is it imaginable? Of course, the *behaviour* is! But is the inner process, the experience of colour?" And it is difficult to see what to say in answer to such a question. Could people without absolute pitch have guessed at the existence of people with absolute pitch? (Z §369)

Notice that Wittgenstein here says only that "it is difficult to see what to say" with respect to questions concerning the imaginability of these unavailable experiences. He does *not* reject such a question, nor does he assert that there is, and can only be, nothing to say. Lear and Nagel's Wittgenstein would not be so indecisive.[12]

Elsewhere, in *Remarks on Colour*, Wittgenstein raises similar concerns about accessibility and imaginability, though here he appeals primarily to the phenomenon of color-blindness:

Imagine a *tribe* of color-blind people, and there could easily be one. They would not have the same color concepts as we do. For even assuming they speak, e.g. English, and thus have all the English color words, they would still use them differently than we do and would *learn* their use differently. (RC I, §13)

He concludes this remark by changing the example so that the imagined tribe does not speak English: "Or if they have a foreign language, it would be difficult for us to translate their color words into ours."

In a later passage, Wittgenstein elaborates on what would pose difficulties for the task of translating the language of the color-blind tribe:

---

[12] I find myself indecisive, however, concerning the question of whether this case really constitutes a case of other-mindedness. After all, the different shades of color these beings categorize with their peculiar notation are ones that we comprehend and even perceive, though perhaps in a less fine-grained manner. There are thus no "features of reality" that are ultimately available only to them, but only another route to the same features. However, given Lear's gloss on the notion of mindedness – as involving "perceptions of salience, routes of interest, feelings of naturalness in following a rule, etc. that constitute being part of a certain form of life" – it would seem that these people do indeed count as other-minded. After all, they find their peculiar binary notation to be "natural," and follow different "routes of interest" with respect to perceiving and categorizing colors. Their appearance in *Zettel* thus counts against Lear's reading of Wittgenstein as a kind of transcendental argument against the possibility of other-mindedness. However, they do not on their own open up room for a sense of reality beyond what is available from our point of view, as Nagel's anti-idealist position requires and which Nagel thinks Wittgenstein is unable to accommodate. I suggest below, starting with the examples of color-blindness, that Wittgenstein provides all the accommodation one could ever intelligibly want.

> There could very easily be a tribe of people who are all color-blind and who none-theless live very well; but would they have developed our color names, and how would their nomenclature correspond to ours? What would their natural language be like?? Do we know? Would they perhaps have three primary colors: blue, yellow, and a third which takes the place of red and green? – What if we were to encounter such a tribe and wanted to learn their language? We would no doubt run into certain difficulties. (RC III, §128)

We can imagine, however, that the members of this tribe may eventually come to understand that they *are* color-blind, if we master enough of their language to explain what we mean when we say that we see a different color when we look at kinds of objects which are typically red or green. We can, that is, explain that we see different colors when we look at these objects just as they see different colors when they look at things which are yellow and things which are blue. This will not be sufficient to explain to them what it's like to see red or to see green, but it might be sufficient to convey the fact of our seeing red and seeing green. As Wittgenstein remarks, "And yet the color-blind person understands the statement 'I am color-blind', and its negation as well." (RC III, §120) He continues by noting that despite this understanding, there is still a gap of the kind I described above:

> A color-blind person not merely can't learn to use our color words, he can't learn to use the word "color-blind" exactly as a normal person does. He cannot for example always determine color-blindness in cases where the normal-sighted can.

The cornerstone of Davidson's argument against the intelligibility of radically different conceptual schemes is the demand that conceptuality, so to speak, be vouchsafed via the process of interpretation: alleged failures of interpretation reveal not recalcitrant, inaccessible concepts, but instead the lack of conceptuality at all. Nagel finds this argument unacceptable: part of the point of the example of mental nine-year-olds is to secure the possibility of something beyond the limits of what can be revealed via any straightforward procedure of interpretation. What we understand includes things that the mental nine-year-olds cannot assimilate to their limited conceptual repertoire, nor can we domesticate many of the things available to the imagined superior beings. We have already seen that Wittgenstein does nothing to foreclose the possibility of such failures of accessibility; as he says, "concepts other than though akin to ours might seem *very* queer to us," and there is no guarantee that translation or interpretation will remove that sense of queerness. As he notes in *Zettel* concerning people who have "quite different concepts" from our own:

> "These people would have nothing human about them." Why? – We could not possibly make ourselves understood to them. Not even as we can to a dog. We could not find our feet with them.
>
> And yet there surely could be such beings, who in other respects were human. (Z §390)

Wittgenstein's confidence in the concluding sentence of this remark cuts against the kind of reading Nagel and Lear offer, since just such a failure of mutual intelligibility would be a sure sign of other-mindedness. This is not to say that Wittgenstein is not *troubled* by the possibility of other-mindedness in terms of wondering how far we can go in envisaging such a possibility. The sense of "queerness" he repeatedly evokes and the difficulties he enumerates attest to this. What troubles Wittgenstein is the idea that our capacity to describe practices involving "quite different concepts" is severely limited owing to the rather straightforward fact that our descriptions and attempts at imagining will naturally be couched in terms of our own. Insofar as we manage to describe the practice (insofar as we "fill out the picture," as Lear puts it), then it is questionable, to say the least, that we have really described it *as* a practice involving the use of an alien concept; where they succeed, our descriptions fail, as it were, to capture its otherness. These difficulties are brought out in the following passage, again from *Remarks on Colour*:

> Can I then only say: "These people call *this* (brown, for example) reddish green"? Wouldn't it then just be another word for something that we have a word for? If they really have a different concept than I do, this must be shown by the fact that I can't quite figure out their use of words. (RC III, §123)

To the extent, then, that we employ our conceptual resources to describe the practice of applying concepts we do not possess, the attempt to give a description that captures the difference fails: the people being imagined simply have different *words*, and not different concepts. Our inability to describe the use of concepts we lack at the same time calls into question our ability to *conceive* of essentially different concepts. In the final section of this cluster of remarks, Wittgenstein does not exactly draw this consequence, but alludes to it as a genuine worry: "But I have kept on saying that it's conceivable for our concepts to be different than they are. Was that all nonsense?" (RC III, §124)

Both Nagel and Lear read Wittgenstein as finally answering this last question in the affirmative, but it is important to appreciate that he does not do so. I think it is also important to recognize that he leaves the question unanswered, to leave room for the idea that what appear to be thoughts about concepts other than our own may not always amount to that (they may just be thoughts about our concepts in disguise or they may turn out not really to be thoughts at all). Nagel's thought experiment runs just such a danger, insofar as it insists upon thinking of forms of mindedness in terms of relative completeness. Thinking this way casts us in the role of the color-blind hankering after being normally sighted: such a distinction only makes sense to the extent that both possibilities are, if not actual, at least given some specific content. The color-blind person can, as Wittgenstein allows, come to understand that he *is* color-blind, but that realization is facilitated by engagement with those who are normally sighted. Without that kind of engagement, it is not at all clear how the thought, "I am color-blind," would have occurred to that person, nor, if it did, what that thought could mean. If, right now, I entertain the thought, "I lack a perceptual capacity," nothing emerges in response to that thought without some further specification. If what I have in mind is the ability to see clearly without the assistance of glasses, then what I have in mind is perfectly intelligible. More radically, if I find myself thinking about bats and echo-location or sharks' ability to detect electrical currents emitted by potential prey, then again my thought makes a kind of sense, even if any further thoughts about what *experiences* I'm missing out on quickly grow dim. But if I am simply casting about for *some* capacity, possessed by *some* being not yet encountered, which makes *some* currently unavailable feature of the world manifest, then my gesture runs the risk of emptiness. This does not mean that radically different perceptual capacities can never be discovered, including ones that we might even find ourselves envying, but that does not show that I really have anything in mind *now*.

Now I suspect that it is precisely here that Nagel will complain that I am illustrating or exemplifying his contention about Wittgenstein, namely that he (Wittgenstein) insists that "what there is and what is true" cannot "extend beyond" what we and our successors "could ever discover or conceive of or describe in some extension of language." (To use Lear's idiom, we have here reached the limits of our "mindedness," and would do well to stay within them.) Here, in other words, is where Nagel and Lear see Wittgenstein as trying to demonstrate that we "lapse into nonsense," and that we do so, moreover, owing to the "conditions of meaning" to which his philosophy is committed. We have reached the point where our "agreement in judgments" gives out, such that nothing intelligible can any longer be said. Notice, however, that in raising worries about the potential emptiness of a Nagel-like gesture toward what lies beyond our comprehension, no theses about meaning have been invoked, nor have we reached a point where nonsense emerges or where we cross over anything like "the bounds of sense." Rather, Wittgenstein should be understood here as simply asking what Nagel means by *his* words here, what he wants to have us acknowledge or commit to when he wants us to acknowledge something beyond what we "could ever discover or conceive of or describe in some extension of language." What is one to *say* here, since anything one says will involve the use of *language*? We should recall here Wittgenstein's remark in the face of his interlocutor's frustrations in conveying what work "S" is supposed to do while remaining somehow private and available only to the user of S: "So in the end when one is doing philosophy one gets to the point where one would like just to emit an inarticulate sound. – But such a sound is an expression only as it occurs in a particular language-game, which should now be described." (PI §261)

Nagel's words do not so much "lapse into nonsense" owing to their violation of some Wittgensteinian "conditions of meaning" (again, no such conditions have been invoked). I would suggest instead that they verge on *emptiness*, insofar as Nagel offers them in a way that refuses any further articulation or clarification (since, again, any further articulation would involve our using some language, while what Nagel insists upon is an acknowledgment of something necessarily or "in principle" beyond *that*). While Nagel might charge here that Wittgenstein's accusations of emptiness are a kind of *verificationism* and so indeed tied to a problematic theory of meaning after all, Wittgenstein's response would be along the lines of what he says at *Investigations* §353: "Asking whether and how a proposition can be verified is only a particular way of asking 'How d'you mean?'" An unwillingness to engage this last question is not so much a violation of the "conditions of meaning" as it is a refusal to speak.

Nothing, certainly nothing about "how meaning is possible," prevents the gesture that Nagel wants to make from being empty. (PI §261) Indeed, that the gesture in the direction of the (currently) inconceivable need not prove empty is something Wittgenstein is perfectly willing to acknowledge. As he says in *Zettel*, in close proximity to his questions concerning the deaf and feeble-minded:

Do I want to say, then, that certain facts are favourable to the formation of certain concepts; or again unfavourable? And does experience teach us this? It is a fact of experience that human beings alter their concepts, exchange them for others when they learn new facts; when in this way what was formerly important to them becomes unimportant, and *vice versa*. (It is discovered e.g. that what formerly counted as a difference in kind, is really *only* a difference of degree.) (Z §352)

Wittgenstein's appeal here to *facts* as motivating the formation of new concepts tells against the kind of confinement Nagel sees him as endorsing. The image Wittgenstein encourages here is a kind of ongoing engagement with the world, where new facts may be learned (not created, stipulated, or "imposed" by the mind) that sometimes push and prod us to alter how we think about the world, even at the basic level of our conceptual repertoire.

In *The View From Nowhere*, Nagel complains that Wittgenstein's philosophy fails to acknowledge, or properly account for, the fact that "language reaches beyond itself." The merits of Nagel's complaint may be measured against the following passage, wherein Wittgenstein endorses just such a notion:

How did I arrive at the concept "sentence" or "language"? Surely only through the languages I have learnt. – But they seem to me in a certain sense to have led beyond themselves, for I am now able to construct new language, e.g. to invent words. – So such construction also belongs to the concept of language. But only because that is how I want to fix the concept. (Z §325)

Despite Wittgenstein's final remark, which suggests that whether or not language can be extended is a matter of how one decides to fix the concept of language, the general tenor of this remark does not sit well with Nagel's characterization of Wittgenstein as restricting what there can intelligibly be said to be to what lies within "the boundaries set by our human form of life." Indeed, what Wittgenstein challenges is the idea that we can impose these kinds of boundaries at all. The remark just cited is followed by Wittgenstein's noting that "the concept of a living being has the same indeterminacy as that of a language." (Z §326) The implications of the indeterminacy Wittgenstein invokes here simply do not square with Nagel's characterization of him as an idealist, nor do they square with Lear's reading of Wittgenstein as adducing a transcendental conception of our mindedness: forms of other-mindedness are, after a fashion, conceivable, as is a world that includes facts, even whole realms of facts, that may well be beyond our reach.[13]

---

[13] A version of this chapter was presented at the Regional Working Conference on Wittgenstein at Virginia Tech in April 2007. I am grateful to the members of the audience for stimulating questions and comments. I would like especially to thank James Klagge for organizing the conference and inviting me to participate. A version was also read at the annual meeting of the International Society for Phenomenological Studies; discussion there again provided many useful comments and criticisms. Finally, I would like to thank Marie McGinn for extensive written comments, at least some of which I have tried to accommodate in preparing the final version of this chapter.

REFERENCES

AFFELDT, STEVEN (2010). "On the Difficulty of Seeing Aspects and the 'Therapeutic' Reading of Wittgenstein," in W. Day and V. Krebs eds., *Seeing Wittgenstein Anew*. Cambridge: Cambridge University Press.

ANSCOMBE, G. E. M. (1981). "The Question of Linguistic Idealism," in *The Collected Philosophical Papers of G. E. M. Anscombe*, Volume 1: *From Parmenides to Wittgenstein*. Minneapolis: University of Minnesota Press.

BLOOR, DAVID (1996). "The Question of Linguistic Idealism Revisited," in H. Sluga and D. Stern eds., *The Cambridge Companion to Wittgenstein*. Cambridge: Cambridge University Press.

CERBONE, DAVID (1994). "Don't Look But Think: Imaginary Scenarios in Wittgenstein's Later Philosophy," *Inquiry*, 37: 159–83.

—— (2003). "'The Limits of Conservatism: Wittgenstein on 'Our Life' and 'Our Concepts'," in C. Heyes ed., *The Grammar of Politics: Wittgenstein and Political Philosophy*. Ithaca: Cornell University Press.

—— (2007). Review of Forster 2004, *Mind*, 116 (461): 165–9.

DAVIDSON, DONALD (1984). "On the Very Idea of a Conceptual Scheme," in *Inquiries into Truth and Interpretation*. Oxford: Oxford University Press.

DIAMOND, CORA (1991). *The Realistic Spirit: Wittgenstein, Philosophy, and the Mind*. Cambridge, MA: The MIT Press.

DILMAN, ILHAM (2004). "Wittgenstein and the Question of Linguistic Idealism," in D. McManus ed., *Wittgenstein and Scepticism*. London: Routledge.

FORSTER, MICHAEL N. (2004). *Wittgenstein on the Arbitrariness of Grammar*. Princeton: Princeton University Press.

LEAR, JONATHAN (1982). "Leaving the World Alone," *Journal of Philosophy*, 79: 382–402.

—— (1984). "The Disappearing 'We', Part I," in *The Proceedings of the Aristotelian Society*, Supplementary Volume 58: 219–42.

MALCOLM, NORMAN (1995). "Wittgenstein and Idealism," in G. H. von Wright ed., *Wittgensteinian Themes: Essays 1978–1989*. Ithaca: Cornell University Press.

McDOWELL, JOHN (1998). "Wittgenstein on Following a Rule," in *Mind, Value, and Reality*. Cambridge, MA: Harvard University Press.

MINAR, EDWARD (2007). "A View from Somewhere: Wittgenstein, Nagel, and Idealism," *The Modern Schoolman*, January, 84 (2–3): 185–204.

MULHALL, STEPHEN (2009). "'Hopelessly Strange': Bernard Williams' Portrait of Wittgenstein as a Transcendental Idealist," *European Journal of Philosophy*, 17 (3): 386–404.

NAGEL, THOMAS (1986). *The View from Nowhere*. Oxford: Oxford University Press.

STROUD, BARRY (1984). "The Allure of Idealism: the Disappearing 'We', Part II," in *Proceedings of the Aristotelian Society*, Supplementary Volume 58: 243–58.

WILLIAMS, BERNARD (1981). "Wittgenstein and Idealism," in *Moral Luck*. Cambridge: Cambridge University Press.

WILLIAMS, MICHAEL (2004). "Wittgenstein's Refutation of Idealism," in D. McManus ed., *Wittgenstein and Scepticism*. London: Routledge.

WITTGENSTEIN, LUDWIG (1967). *Zettel*, ed. G. E. M. Anscombe and G. H. von Wright, trans. G. E. M. Anscombe. Oxford: Basil Blackwell.

Wittgenstein, Ludwig (1978). *Remarks on Colour*, ed. G. E. M. Anscombe, trans. L. McAlister and M. Schättle. Oxford: Blackwell.

——(1980). *Remarks on the Philosophy of Psychology*, vol. 1. Chicago: The University of Chicago Press.

——(1997). *Philosophical Investigations*, 2nd edn, ed. G. E. M. Anscombe and R. Rhees, trans. G. E. M. Anscombe. Oxford: Blackwell.

CHAPTER 15

....

PRIVATE LANGUAGE

....

DAVID STERN

1. INTRODUCTION

....

THE literature on this topic is extraordinarily extensive and wide-ranging; Wittgenstein's treatment of private language has received more attention than any other aspect of his philosophy. Yet, for over fifty years, a remarkably self-contained exegetical tradition has defined the terms of debate and the principal positions that are discussed. Indeed, in the vast majority of the secondary literature devoted to discussion of the 'private language argument', a relatively small number of canonical publications have provided the point of departure for scholarly discussion, and have thus become extremely influential. While the precise boundaries of such a list are, of course, debatable, there is a clear consensus concerning its core. The first, and still frequently cited, members of this group are the early exchange between A. J. Ayer (1954) and Rush Rhees (1954), entitled 'Can There Be a Private Language?', and the reviews of the *Philosophical Investigations* by Norman Malcolm (1954) and Peter Strawson (1954). All four were reprinted in two widely read anthologies (Pitcher 1966; Jones 1971). These anthologies also included a number of other contributions that had a comparable impact on the subsequent literature. Most notable were a pair of papers on the verification principle and the private language argument by Judith Jarvis Thomson (1964, reprinted in Jones 1971) and Anthony Kenny (Jones 1971). All six were reprinted in Canfield (1986), an anthology on private language that collects the most frequently discussed articles on the topic from the 1950s to the 1970s.

There is deep disagreement among these authors about almost every aspect of Wittgenstein's discussion of private language, and the correct conclusions to be drawn from it. Nevertheless, these articles succeeded in focusing attention on themes that provided a point of departure and frame of reference for subsequent writing on the topic. Characteristically, the authors are sharply divided between those who take Wittgenstein to have shown that there cannot be a private language (Rhees, Malcolm, Kenny) and those who argue that the arguments that have been provided for that conclusion are unsuccessful (Ayer, Strawson, Thomson). Nevertheless, there is general agreement about a number of basic points, not only among these authors, but also within the exegetical tradition that they have inspired. As Stewart Candlish has observed, what 'these earlier commentators have in common is significant enough to outweigh their differences' (Candlish 2004; see also Candlish 1980). Following Candlish, I will refer to what these readings have in common as the orthodox approach to private language. However, I will use the term rather more broadly than Candlish, who uses it to refer to mainstream work on private language from the 1950s to the 1970s, and subsequent work within that tradition. Thus he treats Kenny's (1971, 1973) observation that the argument of §258 does not depend on scepticism about memory as a rejection of orthodoxy, and describes Kripke's (1982) contribution, which reoriented the majority of work on private language from the 1980s onward towards broader questions concerning scepticism about rule-following, as largely ending 'the orthodox domination of the secondary literature' (Candlish 2004).

Kripke's extremely influential interpretation (Kripke 1982) sidestepped most previous interpreters' reliance on the claim that a user of a private language cannot check whether a rule had been followed. He contended that the 'rule-following considerations', Wittgenstein's discussion of rule-following in PI §§138–242, prior to the discussion of private language in §§243ff., led Wittgenstein to the communitarian conclusion that language is necessarily social, and so had already ruled out the possibility of a private language. He thus gives a central role to *Philosophical Investigations* §201: 'This was our paradox: no course of action could be determined by a rule, because every course of action can be made out to accord with the rule.' On Kripke's reading, the 'impossibility of private language emerges as a corollary of [Wittgenstein's] sceptical solution of his own paradox' (Kripke 1982, 68), because the conditions for that solution involve reference to a community and so are 'inapplicable to a single person considered in isolation' (Kripke 1982, 79). Consequently, Kripke argues that 'the sections following §243—the sections usually called the "private language argument"—deal with the application of the general conclusions about language drawn in §§138–242 to the problem of sensations' (ibid.). However, even these landmark contributions did not challenge the broader consensus about the overall nature and significance of the argument. Thus they actually served to maintain a lively interest in the broader orthodox programme, even though their immediate effect was to undermine doctrines that had previously been widely accepted.

Orthodox interpreters, as I will be using the term, take for granted that the heart of Wittgenstein's discussion of private language is the private language argument, an argument that is supposed to show that a private language is impossible. In other words, they accept the following points about the nature and significance of the argument:

(1) The argument begins with a premise, or premises, about the nature of a private language.
(2) It leads to the conclusion that such a language is impossible.
(3) The conclusion has far-reaching implications for philosophy as a whole.

(4) While the argument is neither fully nor clearly stated in the *Philosophical Investigations*, it is best understood as a deductive, *reductio ad absurdum* argument.

Furthermore, they presuppose that the argument ultimately rests on a semantic or epistemic theory that sets limits to what we can say or know. In other words, they hold that the proof that a private language is impossible turns on showing it is ruled out by some set of systematic philosophical commitments about logic, meaning, and knowledge. Leading candidates for this ground on which the argument depends have included the analysis of concepts, the grammar of our everyday language, the logic of criteria, or the nature of our rule-following, practical activity, or form of life.

In section 2, I briefly review the main issues raised by the four points listed above, and the principal approaches that orthodox interpreters have taken. I also introduce an alternative interpretive tradition, which not only rejects the orthodox methodology, but also rejects the presupposition that Wittgenstein's principal aim is to provide a deductive proof that the idea of a private language leads to contradiction. In sections 3 and 4, I look more closely at some of the leading readings of *Philosophical Investigations* §258, the passage most frequently discussed by orthodox interpreters.

2. THE ORTHODOX INTERPRETATION AND ITS DISCONTENTS

(1) The orthodox point of departure is the notion of a private language, a language that only one person can understand. In this sense, a private language is not a language that happens to have only one speaker, but one that it is, in principle, impossible for more than one person to speak. However, the precise characterization of the privacy in question is a matter of deep disagreement.

On one leading reading, given an early formulation in Malcolm's and Strawson's reviews of the *Philosophical Investigations*, the privacy in question turns on Wittgenstein's stipulation, in his introduction of the idea of a private language, that 'the words of this language are to refer to what can only be known to the speaker; to his immediate, private sensations. So another cannot understand the language' (PI §243). On this construal, what makes a private language private is that its words refer to private inner objects. The other principal interpretive avenue, first mapped out by Ayer and Rhees, casts the net wider, and includes languages that might be developed by a solitary person, a so-called super-Crusoe—not an adult castaway, like Defoe's Crusoe, but the subject of a thought experiment in which a person isolated from birth comes up with a language of their own. On this reading, what makes a private language private is that it is developed without any assistance from others.

(2) The focus of the orthodox discussion is the private language argument: an argument that aims to show that any such language is impossible. Orthodox interpreters, whether or not they regard the private language argument as successful, usually regard it

as a variety of transcendental argument, broadly understood. For the argument turns on identifying a necessary condition for the possibility of language, a condition that supposedly cannot be satisfied within a private language. Hacker, for instance, maintains that the private language argument

> resembles Kant's employment of transcendental arguments…in attacking the adversary at the seemingly indisputable point, viz. that he understands what *he* means by 'pain', 'sensation', etc. It endeavours to show that a condition of the possibility of his so understanding is that others can share a common understanding with him, and hence that the conception of a private language is incoherent. (Hacker 1986, 265, n. 14)

In general terms, the argument for the necessary condition is taken to turn on claims about the nature of language: that it is a rule-governed activity, or a practical skill, to name two of the leading candidates. On a 'communitarian' construal, following Rhees' lead, the skill in question is necessarily social, and thus rules out not only a language for private inner objects, but also the case of a super-Crusoe. An 'individualist' proponent of the private language argument maintains that it is possible for a person completely isolated from other speakers to speak a language, but that a language for only private inner objects is impossible.

A full taxonomy of the leading private language arguments in the literature is far beyond the scope of this chapter. In section 3, I consider some of the main orthodox readings of *Philosophical Investigations* §258, usually regarded as the principal formulation of the private language argument. In the remainder of this section, I briefly review the broader commitments that inform the orthodox approach, and consider some of the challenges they face.

(3) The stakes are particularly high, in that the private language argument is usually seen as the central, or principal, contribution of Wittgenstein's later philosophy, with far-reaching implications for epistemology, philosophy of mind, and philosophy as a whole. However, there is considerable disagreement about the targets, as relatively few philosophers are explicitly committed to the premises of orthodox reconstructions of the argument. The argument in §§243ff. is between a number of voices that are not explicitly identified, and there are no references to the work of other philosophers. If one looks at current work, contemporary exponents of a representational theory of mind, from Fodor to Chalmers, can easily be read as relying on a private language as a foundation for their accounts of our knowledge of mind and world. Another strategy, especially common in introductory accounts, is to cite various historical figures who, it is argued, were implicitly committed to a private language, such as Descartes, Locke, and Hume. However, if Wittgenstein did have other philosophers' views in mind, the natural candidates would have been contemporaries who gave a crucial role to inner ostensive definition, especially Frege, Russell, James, Ogden and Richards, Carnap, and Schlick. On the other hand, the earliest drafts of Wittgenstein's discussion of private language are more naturally construed as a critique of his own earlier work, and especially his discussion of 'phenomenological language' and 'primary language' in his 1929 manuscripts (Stern 1995, chs. 5–6).

(4) All of these orthodox approaches to identifying the position under attack presuppose that the fragmentary discussion we find in the *Philosophical Investigations* calls for an argumentative reconstruction that identifies the precise premises that are the starting point for a *reductio ad absurdum* argument. Usually, this assumption is simply taken for granted. One exception is David Pears, who has written on the private language argument from the 1960s to the present. That account begins and ends with chapters in two short introductory books on Wittgenstein (1969/1986, ch. 8; 2006, ch. 3), but is worked out in much greater detail in the second volume of *The False Prison* (1988). He begins his discussion there by acknowledging some of the dangers in approaching Wittgenstein's writing as a resource from which promising arguments can be extracted: 'It would be simplistic to suppose that it is possible to take a late text of Wittgenstein's, cut along the dotted lines, and find that it falls into neatly separated arguments.' Nevertheless, he maintains that because the private language argument is a *reductio ad absurdum*, it is 'something of an exception. It is brief, looks self-contained, and after it has been cut out of *Philosophical Investigations*, it proves to be memorable and eminently debatable....it is essential to such arguments that the thesis under attack should be clearly formulated, and that all the premises should be unequivocally identified' (1988, 328–9).[1] In other words, the starting point for any orthodox reading is the assumption that the private language argument can be extracted from the larger context of the discussion of private language in *Philosophical Investigations* §§243–315, and approached as a free-standing argument that can be analysed independently.

However, this method of reading the text has meant that there is a quite extraordinary distance between the orthodox interpretive tradition and what is actually said in *Philosophical Investigations* §§243–315. As Robert Fogelin observed in the mid-1970s, 'discussion is often carried out quite independently of the original Wittgenstein text. At this stage it is not clear whether the private language argument as currently discussed has very much to do with the text that originally generated the discussion' (Fogelin 1976, 153). Not long afterwards, Stewart Candlish replied to Fogelin that he 'would go further than this, and say that the discussion has almost always been carried out *quite* independently of the text, in this sense: that nearly all commentators on the argument have *quarried* the text for remarks which suit their purposes, ignoring those which do not fit their preconceptions' (Candlish 1980, 85.) Several decades later, the interpretive traditions have become more intricate and more varied, but Fogelin and Candlish's provocative generalizations remain remarkably accurate. In other words, the vast majority of work on Wittgenstein on private language still consists of critical responses to a relatively small number of canonical interpreters' readings of a very small number of supposedly key passages. While Kripke (1982) succeeded in changing

---

[1] The quoted passage is followed by a quotation from the last three sentences of §258 (quoted below, p. 341). Pears summarizes the individualist argument he finds there: 'The topic is the reidentification of sensation-types, and the argument is that a case can be described in which there would be no distinction between applying a word to a sensation-type correctly, and applying it incorrectly.' For an excellent critical discussion of Pears' construal and Pears' response, see Stroud 2001 and Pears 2006, ch. 3.

the premises and arguments at the focus of scholarly debate, the vast majority of the post-Kripke literature on private language continues the tradition of the detailed articulation and criticism of leading interpreters' work, often with only glancing attention to the primary text.[2]

Furthermore, few authors clearly distinguish the expository work of stating the competing views under discussion from the interpretive task of evaluating their strengths and weaknesses. Instead, each identifies a strand in the debate that she or he finds most promising, and then supplements it with various assumptions about Wittgenstein's philosophical commitments. Consequently, the standard strategy in previous surveys of work on private language, whether or not they advocate an orthodox reading, has been to compare and contrast the main approaches that have been taken to quarrying Wittgenstein's writing in the *locus classicus, Philosophical Investigations* §§243–315. Attention has usually been concentrated on evaluation of the interpretation of certain sections which are usually taken to set out one version or another of the private language argument, principally §256, §257, §258, §265, §270, and §293.[3]

An alternative, Pyrrhonian, tradition maintains that Wittgenstein's principal contribution, not only in his discussion of private language, but throughout his work, is his criticism of the assumptions lying behind the desire for such arguments. Far from advocating a semantic or epistemic theory that provides the basis for a proof that a private language is impossible, he aims to get us to see that we cannot find words that will do justice to the idea; that it falls apart on closer examination. Wittgenstein conceives of language as open-ended and irreducibly complex, a multifarious pattern of activity that cannot be captured by a theory of this kind. On this reading of Wittgenstein, his discussion of private language is designed to help his reader see that such arguments depend on an overly simple conception of language and experience, and that the very idea of a private language is more like an illusion, or a fantasy, than a plausible premise that leads to a contradiction. (Cf. Floyd 2007, 176.)

In my own work, I have argued that the orthodox reading rests on a systematic misunderstanding of the text of the *Philosophical Investigations*. The private language arguments that are the focus of the orthodox debate are not the author's considered views, but rather one reconstruction of the narrator's voice in the dialogue. I set out two main reasons why one might have serious reservations about identifying the arguments we attribute to the narratorial voice in §§243ff. with the views of the author of the *Philosophical Investigations*. One reason for such reservations is that there are more voices there than the two that are usually identified by most interpreters, commonly called 'Wittgenstein' and 'the interlocutor'. The more distant and diagnostic perspective of some of the remarks toward the end of the discussion of private language (such as §§304–9) strikes me as much closer to the author's considered views than the voice that

[2] For a representative collection of work in this vein, see Miller and Wright 2002.
[3] Perhaps the principal development within this literature in recent years has been the recognition that a number of rather different private language arguments can be extracted from these passages. For previous reviews of the literature, see Castañeda 1967; Ameriks 1975; Stroud 1983; Stern 1994, 426–32; Glock 1996, 309–15; Schroeder 2001; Candlish 2004; Law 2004.

argues against the possibility of a private language in passages such as §258 and §293. A second reason, as we shall see in the final part of this paper, is that the very passages that are at the core of the orthodox reading can also be read along Pyrrhonian lines. On that reading, they are not arguing against the possibility of a private language. Rather, they are trying, and failing, to give meaning to the interlocutor's attempts at formulating that notion. On this reading, Wittgenstein is neither saying that a solution to the sceptical paradoxes or a 'private language' is possible, nor proving that such things are impossible. Rather, the author of the *Philosophical Investigations* holds that such words do no useful work at all.[4]

Not only do most orthodox readers fail to give an account of how these snippets of argument fit into the broader context of §§243–315; they also fail to take into consideration the issues that arise once one recognizes that one cannot simply identify the narratorial position they reconstruct with the author's considered opinions. Stanley Cavell (1979) is the most influential exponent of this approach.[5] He points out that the very passages that orthodox interpreters take to be the central loci for statements of private language arguments can also be read in a very different spirit. We can also read Wittgenstein's narrator, not as providing an argument that shows a private language is impossible, but as asking if there is any way of making sense of talk of a language in which only I can give expression to my inner experiences for my private use that does not amount to a commonplace. Cavell provides a concise statement of these considerations at the beginning of his reading of §258.

> It is a mistake, I believe, to say that there are just two essential tones of voice in the *Investigations*, the interlocutor's and Wittgenstein's proper voice. First there is no reason to think that there is just one interlocutor throughout the book; and second, and obviously, Wittgenstein's own speech ranges from the full-throated and the supercilious to the meditative and the bemused. Section 243, which initiates the most continuous prospect of a private language, and 258, which picks up the idea and tries to exemplify it, seem to me largely in half-voice. (Cavell 1979, 344–5)

I take it that what Cavell is suggesting at the end of this passage is not just that the voices of interlocutor and narrator share the stage roughly equally at these points in the text, but that the author does not fully and unqualifiedly stand behind the narrator's voice here. On Cavell's reading, the point of Wittgenstein's discussion

> is to release the fantasy expressed in the denial that language is something essentially shared. The tone of the sections dealing explicitly with the idea of a private language are peculiarly colored by the tone of someone allowing a fantasy to be voiced. (Cavell 1979, 344)

---

[4] The final two sentences of this paragraph are taken from Stern 2004, 26. For further elaboration of this perspective on the relationship between interlocutory and narratorial voices in the *Philosophical Investigations* and Wittgenstein's overall aims in that book, see Stern 2004, ch. 1 §3.

[5] For work along related lines, see also Stroud 2000, chs. 5, 6, 13; Stern 1994a, 1995, chs. 5–6, 2004, ch. 7; McGinn 1997, chs. 6–7; Canfield 2001; Baker 2004, chs. 5–7; Candlish 2004; Conant 2004, 171–7; Mulhall 2007.

In other words, Wittgenstein's principal aim is not to provide an argument that a quite specific conception of private language leads to a contradiction, but rather to get his reader to see that the very idea of a private language cannot be coherently formulated. Two of the most interesting recent contributions in this vein are *Wittgenstein's Private Language* (Mulhall 2007), a close reading of key passages in the *Philosophical Investigations* that also offers a concise introduction to Cavell's reading of Wittgenstein on private language, and a series of papers by Gordon Baker in which he rejects the orthodox reading he once shared with Peter Hacker (Baker 1990, 1992, 1998; 2004, chs. 5–7). Before looking at these criticisms of orthodoxy in more detail, we first need to consider the orthodox approach to §258, widely regarded as the definitive formulation of the private language argument.

3. ORTHODOX READINGS OF *PHILOSOPHICAL INVESTIGATIONS* §258

The precise nature of the supposed argument for the impossibility of a private language has been the focus of heated disagreement. In the most general terms, the rationale for denying the possibility of a private language is that a private language could not be understood by the supposed user of that language, for it would be impossible to establish meanings for its supposed signs. However, under this rubric we can distinguish at least three main strategies, each of which attacks the idea of a private language at a different point. The traditional orthodox interpreter discusses whether one could ever make use of a privately defined term. A second, more radical, approach asks whether one could ever introduce such a term in the first place. On a Pyrrhonian reading, the point of raising these questions is to get us to see that the very idea of a private language is illusory, and falls apart on closer examination.

The traditional orthodox construal attacks the idea that one could ever make use of a privately defined term. On this approach, we accept, for the sake of argument, that such a term has been introduced by the user of a private language, and then go on to consider if he or she could use it. If so, it must be possible to distinguish between actually following whatever rule governs the use of the term, and merely seeming to do so. In other words, the speaker of the private language needs what Wittgenstein calls a 'criterion of correctness', which is usually construed as some kind of a test, or way of checking, that the words have been used correctly. However, it is then argued that it is impossible to draw this distinction within a private language. Therefore a private language is impossible. Jones, in the editorial introduction to his anthology on the topic, taking for granted the correctness of this approach, summarizes 'the crucial bone of contention between the different sides in the controversy' in the following terms:

> Could there be any possible check on the application of words used to refer to private objects…? Wittgenstein, I think, is suggesting that it would not be possible if the

objects were private…There are some who agree with him and some who do not. This is the basic cleavage in the whole debate. (Jones 1971, 18)

However, a great deal depends on precisely how one specifies this check, and what reasons one gives for requiring a check of that kind.

The usual way of setting out this argument in more detail is to ask the reader to imagine that someone takes the first steps involved in getting a suitably private language going: a language which connects words and sensations, but not with the natural expressions of sensation. In the opening lines of §258, Wittgenstein's interlocutor asks us to imagine that 'I want to keep a diary about the occurrence of a certain sensation. To this end I associate it with the sign "S" and write this sign in a calendar for every day on which I have the sensation.' As the putative user of a private language cannot articulate a definition of 'S' in public language (for then it would no longer be private), establishing a meaning for S calls for an act of inner ostensive definition. We are to imagine the supposed private language speaker attending to the sensation in question, and that sensation's name, under ideal conditions: 'I speak, or write the sign down, and at the same time I concentrate my attention on the sensation—and so, as it were, point to it inwardly.' In this way, S's meaning is supposed to be established 'by the concentrating of my attention; for in this way I impress on myself the connection between the sign and the sensation.' §258 ends with Wittgenstein's narrator presenting the following reply to that train of thought, usually regarded as the core of the private language argument:

> But "I impress it on myself" can only mean: this process brings it about that I remember the connection *right* in the future. But in the present case I have no criterion of correctness. One would like to say: whatever is going to seem right to me is right. And that only means that here we can't talk about 'right'.

On the orthodox reading, the point of this reply is that when the time comes to make use of the name on a later occasion, a necessary condition for use of the name cannot be satisfied. Proponents of this line of argument maintain that one would have no reliable test, or no test at all, as to whether one was using 'S' correctly. That condition turns on the supposed speaker of the private language being in command of a 'criterion of correctness', an objective standard by which to tell whether the word has been used correctly. If 'S' is to be meaningful, there must be a difference between correctly applying it to another sensation that is of the same kind as the first, and mistakenly applying it to a sensation of the wrong type. The correct formulation of this necessary condition, which would have to be satisfied if the putative private language is to qualify as a genuine language, and the strength of the rationale that can be provided for it, are the crux of the debate over the orthodox construal of the private language argument in §258. Indeed, the question of how to state this is often regarded as the principal issue at stake in understanding and evaluating the 'private language argument'.

A surprisingly large number of candidates for that necessary condition, satisfied by our everyday language, but absent in the case of a private language, have been proposed, but they can be grouped into a number of well-worn categories. Most of the earliest formulations of the argument that the user of a private language has no criterion of correctness turn

on the idea that there can be no possibility of knowing that one has used a private definition successfully, or that some other condition, such as being able to tell whether one has
remembered the word correctly, is not satisfied. However, as Thomson (1964) observed,
such arguments depend on a strong version of the principle of verification, a premise that
is not only highly controversial, but also once accepted would allow one to directly rule out
the possibility of a private language. Other versions depend on an equally implausible
scepticism about the private language user's memory, a scepticism that, if accepted, would
also rule out the possibility of any knowledge at all (Kenny 1971).

Orthodox proponents of the private language argument strive to find the correct formulation of this argument, and to defend it against criticism; orthodox opponents argue
that one can draw the distinction between seeming to follow a rule correctly, and actually doing so, within the resources provided by a private language. On this approach, 'the
key to understanding Wittgenstein's later thought is to grasp its centre point, some elusive and obscurely presented refutation of the possibility of a (metaphysically) private
language' (Canfield 2001, 377). The result has been a profusion of competing interpretations, many of them highly complex, resting on a very slender textual basis, and requiring the attribution of contentious and questionable further premises in order to ensure
that the resulting argument is valid.

Wittgenstein's writing, composed of dialogues without clearly identified voices, certainly calls for a reconstructive engagement with the text. As the reader works to identify
the positions being attacked and defended, he or she inevitably finds his or her own concerns being addressed there. As a result, each generation of readers has discovered a
Wittgenstein who seems to have anticipated their own philosophical concerns with
remarkable far-sightedness.[6] This is not to deny the value of the first articulations of the
orthodox reading of the private language argument. While none of them is entirely successful, they have enabled readers to appreciate argumentative strategies that were not
previously apparent.

A natural response to this diverse assortment of interpretations would be to look
more carefully at the text for further clues as to how best to understand the deceptively
simple dialogue we find in those key passages. In addition to those passages that have
been the focus of interpretive debate, one would also look at the *Philosophical
Investigations* as a whole and Wittgenstein's other writings on private language. Instead
of reading our own preconceptions into the gaps we find in Wittgenstein's telling of the
story, we might reread the passage in question with an eye to detail, and look to the
broader context for further clarification. Even the best of the canonical orthodox articles, such as the pioneering contributions by Rhees, Malcolm, Kenny, and others, which
are certainly painstaking and thorough in striving to articulate a coherent train of argumentation, all import assumptions that turn Wittgenstein's brief remarks into a compressed, and potentially question-begging, exposition of a number of systematic
commitments, each requiring further defence in turn.

---

[6] For further discussion of these interpretive issues, see Stern 2004, esp. ch. 2.

However, if we are to make any progress, we need to distinguish the well-established practice of making use of Wittgenstein's writings in pursuit of our own philosophical goals from the question of how best to understand Wittgenstein's discussion of private language in the *Philosophical Investigations*. One approach that naturally presents itself at this point would be to focus narrowly on the text of the key passages, with the aim of making explicit precisely what Wittgenstein is doing there. Another complementary approach would be to place those passages in a broader context, connecting them with our reading of the 'private language argument' as a whole. It is striking that only a very small fraction of the literature on the topic actually undertakes to provide this kind of synoptic reading of the argument of *Philosophical Investigations* §§243–315. However, these complementary approaches are pursued with extraordinary thoroughness by Peter Hacker, in both *Insight and Illusion* and *Wittgenstein: Meaning and Mind*.[7]

Hacker's exposition of the private language argument in §258 construes it as Wittgenstein's providing a 'battery of arguments' which show that 'there is no such thing as pointing at any sensation in the sense in which I point at a sample in giving an ostensive definition' (Hacker 1986, 267). He also characterizes it as Wittgenstein's reply to the 'private linguist''s defence of the 'beguiling fiction' of a private ostensive definition.

> The private linguist may respond that…by concentrating my attention I can impress upon myself the connection between the sign and the sensation which is to function as a sample. Not so, Wittgenstein replies, for this process of impressing upon myself the connection must be conceived to mean that I will remember the connection correctly in the future. But no criterion of correctness has been laid down yet for such a case (*PI*, §258). The point does *not* concern the fallibility of memory, but is rather that the putative mental ostensive definition was intended to provide a rule for the correct use of 'S' and now it transpires that in order to do so it presupposes the concept 'S'. For to remember *correctly* can only be to remember that a certain sensation or mental image *is* an image of S. (Hacker 1986, 267)

On Hacker's construal, in a supposed private ostensive definition 'there is no technique of application, there is no *practice* of applying [the supposed word in question], but only the appearance of a practice' (Hacker 1986, 269). In other words, there is no technique of applying words to private objects 'on the model of applying them to public ones. There is no *method* of comparing a sample with a private object.… nothing has been determined to *count as the same*' (Hacker 1990, 112). This, in turn, is because without the possibility of a public, independent check on the private use of a term, no distinction can be established between what seems right to me, and what is right. Hacker draws the moral that

---

[7] The former was published in 1972, when Gordon Baker was a student of Hacker's, and published in a revised second edition in 1986, toward the end of their collaboration on a series of joint projects. The latter was written soon after they had ceased writing together. The two books are among the principal targets of Baker's critical discussion of previous orthodox work on 'the private language argument'. The material on Hacker and Baker in the next few pages is based on the more extensive discussion in my paper, 'The Uses of Wittgenstein's Beetle: *Philosophical Investigations* §293 and its interpreters' (Stern 2007).

there is no such thing as following 'private' rules, i.e. rules which no one else could in principle understand inasmuch as the rules in question *can have no public expression*. Such putative rules are 'private ostensive definitions', which, since there is no such thing as exhibiting 'private samples', are *essentially* incommunicable. (Hacker 1986, 272).

Furthermore, Hacker claims that idealism and solipsism presuppose the intelligibility of such rule-following, and a further consequence of this train of argument is to cast light on 'the deep and ineradicable flaws of these philosophical pictures' (ibid.).

4. Unorthodox Readings of *Philosophical Investigations* §258

Hacker's interpretation of the private language argument attempts to combine two very different approaches to the idea that each of us only knows what pain is from our own case. On the one hand, he insists that the point of the private language argument is that the interlocutor's conception of pain is nonsensical, more like a delusion, or a misconception, than a straightforward falsehood. While it appears intelligible, it is actually incoherent. On the other hand, Hacker also provides a number of sophisticated and intricate chains of reasoning about the nature of language, concerning the need for public rules and objective standards of application that is designed to underwrite this very conclusion. In so doing, he claims to have identified a condition for the possibility of successful reference, and shown that private inner objects cannot satisfy that condition. However, this elaboration of a detailed argument in order to underwrite the analogy carries with it the almost irresistible suggestion that the interlocutor's conception of sensation *is* intelligible, that we do know what he was talking about.

Baker observes that, on Hacker's approach, 'Wittgenstein offers the hypothesis of a private language as something subtle and important which is worthy of thorough and detailed investigation. Consequently, he is taken not to think that this hypothesis, once it is made explicit, is *manifestly* absurd (without further argument)' (Baker 1998, 328). Baker's response to Hacker amounts to a spirited defence of the latter strategy, and a resolute rejection of the former approach. Baker argues that the traditional 'PLA-interpreter', the reader who attempt to reconstruct the subtle reasoning that supposedly underlies the discussion of a private language in the *Philosophical Investigations*, looking for the definitive 'arguments which are parts of a consistent chain of reasoning and which jointly constitute a definitive demonstration of the absurdity of the hypothesis' (ibid.), misses the point of the story. Wittgenstein's aim, Baker proposes, is not to provide a sophisticated proof that it is impossible to answer the question 'What does the word "pain" *name*?', but rather, to get us to see that the question is pointless (Baker 1998, 340–1). Elaborating the impossibility claim leads us toward the elaborate anti-Cartesian train of argument that Hacker imputes to Wittgenstein, and away from the bolder, and simpler, construal on which the very idea of referring to a private, inner object is incoherent. In other words, we are to reject the idea that the private language argument is a species of transcendental argument, a solution, of sorts, to a traditional problem, and instead approach it as a dissolution, a repudiation of the framework it takes for granted.

In the closing section of his final paper on private language (1998, 346–54; 2004, ch. 7), Baker provides a wealth of detailed advice designed to help us develop a different framework of interpretation, one that will provide an alternative approach to the 'anti-Cartesian' reading that seems almost unavoidable to most readers. He proposes that we take our bearings from the remarks 'which open the *Investigations* and set the stage for everything that follows' (1998, 348). Baker reads those opening remarks as a criticism of 'Augustine's picture of language' (1998, 347), a 'set of very general ideas that affects almost everyone who reflects on the meaning of words' (1998, 348). This, to my mind, is still too Hackerian a way of reading those opening sections, which I believe are better read as taking on a much less monolithic target.[8] But Baker is right to stress the deep continuities between the discussion of misunderstandings about reference to outer objects and ostensive definition in the opening sections, and the discussion of misunderstandings about reference to inner objects and private ostensive definition in the remarks that follow §243, and to propose that we explore these continuities in seeking new bearings in understanding Wittgenstein on private language. The methods introduced in the opening sections of the book—and especially the 'method of §2', with the associated technique of articulating a language-game that seems to give the interlocutor what he says he wants, are also the methods that Wittgenstein employs in the subsequent discussion of private language.[9]

However, while I am in broad sympathy with the overall direction that Baker takes, his sweeping dismissal of all argument about private language is surely too swift, and too radical, and perhaps best understood as a polemical recoil from detailed Hackerian exegesis. For we surely need to be able to say something more about the role of argument in Wittgenstein's discussion of private language in particular, and in his dissolution of philosophical problems in general. In downplaying the role of 'constructing rigorous arguments from secure premises' and highlighting the importance of a change in our way of seeing things, Baker flies in the face of the fact that there is a great deal of argument in the *Philosophical Investigations*. He thus appears to offer us, as Glock has termed it, a purely therapeutic irrationalism, 'propaganda for alternate points of view' (Baker 2004, 219; Glock 2007, 58).

Here, I take as my guiding thread a sentence that Wittgenstein repeats in his first post-*Tractatus* notebooks, the *Philosophical Remarks* (§2), the *Big Typescript* (p. 311), and §452 of the post-*Investigations* collection of cuttings know as *Zettel*:

---

[8] For an alternative approach to reading the opening of the *Philosophical Investigations* as an attack on the 'Augustinian picture', see Stern 2004, ch. 4. Oddly, while Baker became such an acute critic of the idea that the remarks following §243 are directed at a single, overarching set of ideas, he continued to read the remarks that open the book along remarkably similar lines.

[9] See Stroud 2000; Stern 2004, ch. 7, and 2007.

–Philosophy unravels the knots in our thinking; hence its results must be simple, but its activity is as complicated as the knots it unravels. (BT, 311)

Baker, I propose, wants a Gordian solution, to cut through the knot at a single stroke. Hacker and the orthodox tradition, on the other hand, take the philosophical activity involved in undoing those knots—the moves that the narrator makes in arguing against the interlocutor—to amount to a freestanding achievement, a proof of the impossibility of private language. The result is the construction of a mirror image of the original knot, rather than its dissolution. However, neither Hacker nor Baker does full justice to an alternative construal, on which those knots are more like an illusion, or a fantasy, than a piece of fallacious reasoning.

The very expressions *Privatsprachenargument* and 'private language argument' never occur in Wittgenstein's writing; even the term 'private language' only occurs three times in the *Philosophical Investigations*. Indeed, as Cavell was the first to observe, the *Philosophical Investigations* never *says* that there can be no private language. Cavell develops this point by noting that Wittgenstein begins his discussion of the topic

> by *asking*: 'Could we also imagine a language…in which a person could write down or give vocal expression to his inner experiences—his feelings, moods, and the rest—for his private use', where 'private' is to mean that 'another person cannot understand' [*Philosophical Investigations* §243]. The upshot of this question turns out to be that we cannot really imagine this, or rather that there is nothing of the sort to imagine, or rather that when we as it were try to imagine this we are imagining something other than we think. (Cavell 1979, 344)

A recent book by Stephen Mulhall, *Wittgenstein's Private Language* (2007), offers a detailed articulation of this interpretation, a close reading of key passages in the *Philosophical Investigations* that also provides a concise introduction to Cavell's reading of Wittgenstein on private language. Mulhall distinguishes between orthodox and Pyrrhonian readings of Wittgenstein's discussion of private language in the following terms:

> If we follow through with the first (call it the substantial) reading of §243, then the most famous succeeding sections—§§244, 246, 253, and 258—constitute points at which Wittgenstein shows that given the meaning of the words in the interlocutor's penultimate sentence, the idea of a private language that he attempts to construct out of them must be nonsensical or incoherent, a violation of grammar….[On this reading] §258 recalls the grammatical conditions for meaning, and hence for the applicability of the terms 'words' and 'language', thereby showing that the private linguist cannot legitimately appropriate them…
>
> If we follow through with the second (call it the resolute) reading of §243, then those succeeding sections appear as points at which Wittgenstein tries to imagine, and then tries out, ways of giving meaning to the constituent terms of the interlocutor's formulation. Since the conclusion of §243 gives us only a form of words, together with a strenuous rejection of one way of understanding it, the succeeding investigations must determine whether there is any other way of taking them that might give them genuine substance. (Mulhall 2007, 18)

The question of the relationship between these readings is a delicate one, and Mulhall is acutely aware of this. The Pyrrhonian can 'stress that Wittgenstein repeatedly begins his investigation of the interlocutor's formulations by asking what their elements might mean, rather than telling us what they do mean' (2007, 19). In reply, the orthodox reader can 'emphasize the numerous occasions on which Wittgenstein seems not so much to exercise his imagination on his interlocutor's behalf, but rather to lay down the law' (ibid.). Mulhall's subsequent discussion of these readings of specific passages from the *Investigations* sometimes seems to lose sight of the distinction between the author of the text, and the two ways of reading it. The standard approach in the literature, which Mulhall follows, is to identify the two leading voices in the dialogues that make up the *Investigations* as the voices of 'Wittgenstein' and his 'interlocutor'. This can make it difficult to avoid identifying the views of the author with the views of 'Wittgenstein', a danger that becomes stronger once one attributes two very different yet closely related trains of thought to 'Wittgenstein'.

However, the central issue in the disagreement between these readings concerns how we are to read those sections that are regarded by orthodox interpreters as the key statements of a private language argument, especially as few orthodox readers even entertain the possibility of a reading of those passages on which the narrator is arguing that the story of the private language speaker is nonsense. If we look at §258 as a whole, rather than plucking the final sentences out of context, it is striking that it is one of the few remarks in which the interlocutor has more words than the narrator, and that the narrator's words are a series of negative replies to the interlocutor's suggestions. The passage begins with the interlocutor asking us to imagine a private language in which he introduces a familiar sign—the letter 'S'—and a familiar category of object—a sensation. In §261, the narrator will point out that these assumptions are illegitimate, that if 'S' names a sensation, then it is a word intelligible to everyone who speaks our language. But in §258 he contents himself with pointing out that no definition can be formulated—for any such definition would unquestionably make 'S' a publicly teachable word. The interlocutor responds that an inner surrogate for ostensive definition is nevertheless possible, with the concentrating of my attention taking the place of pointing to the object in question. As before, the narrator insists that this is an empty charade, for no sign has thereby been given a definition. The interlocutor asserts that the concentrating of my attention amounts to an inner definition, for that is how I impress the connection on myself. In this context, the narrator's closing words are best read as providing a forceful restatement of the case for thinking that the interlocutor has done nothing that amounts to giving a word a meaning. Whatever is going to seem right to me is right, because no word has been defined, no rules have been set up. Interpreters have often read this passage as if Wittgenstein had arrived at a result concerning the lack of a criterion of correctness as the endpoint of a subtle train of reasoning, summed up in the final two sentences. But Wittgenstein's closing words are better read as a robust rejection of the very idea that I could possibly have such a criterion.[10]

---

[10] I should also mention, although I do not have time to develop the point here, that the sections immediately before and after §258, especially §257 and §261, provide further support for this reading. See Stroud 1983a; Stern 1994a and 1995, 182–6; McGinn 1997, 126–34; and Mulhall 2007, 97–101.

References

AMERIKS, KARL (1975). 'Recent Work on Wittgenstein and the Philosophy of Mind', *New Scholasticism*, 49: 94–115.

AYER, A. J. (1954). 'Can There Be a Private Language?', *Proceedings of the Aristotelian Society*, Supplementary Volume, 28: 63–76. (Reprinted in Pitcher 1966, Jones 1971, and Canfield 1986.)

BAKER, GORDON (1990). 'The Reception of the Private Language Argument'. (Originally published in French in Fernando Gil ed., *Acta du Colloque Wittgenstein (Collège Internationale de Philosophie, 1988)*. Mauvezin, France: TER, 1990.) Translated as chapter 5 of Baker 2004.

—— (1992). 'Wittgenstein's Method and the Private Language Argument'. (Originally published in French in J. Sebestik and A. Soulez eds., *Wittgenstein et la philosophie d'aujourd'hui*. Paris: Méridiens Klinksieck, 1992.) Translated as chapter 6 of Baker 2004.

—— (1998). 'The Private Language Argument', *Language & Communication*, 18: 325–56. (Section 4 (pp. 346–54) is reprinted as chapter 7 of Baker 2004.)

—— (2004). *Wittgenstein's Method: Neglected Aspects*. Oxford: Blackwell.

CANDLISH, STEWART (1980). 'The Real Private Language Argument', *Philosophy*, 55: 85–94.

—— (2004). 'Private Language', *The Stanford Encyclopedia of Philosophy* (Spring 2004 edition), ed. Edward N. Zalta. <http://plato.stanford.edu/archives/spr2004/entries/private-language/>

CANFIELD, J. V. ed. (1986). *The Philosophy of Wittgenstein*, Volume 9: *The Private Language Argument*. New York: Garland.

—— (2001). 'Private Language: The Diary Case', *Australasian Journal of Philosophy*, 79: 377–94.

CASTAÑEDA, H. N. (1967). 'Private Language', in Edwards 1967, vol. 6.

CAVELL, STANLEY (1979). *The Claim of Reason*. Oxford: Oxford University Press.

CHARLES, DAVID and CHILD, WILLIAM (2001). *Wittgensteinian Themes: Essays in Honour of David Pears*. Oxford: Oxford University Press.

CONANT, JAMES (2004). 'Why Worry about the *Tractatus*?', in Stocker 2004.

EDWARDS, PAUL ed. (1967). *The Encyclopedia of Philosophy*. New York: Macmillan.

FLOYD, JULIET (2007). 'Wittgenstein and the Inexpressible', in Alice Crary ed., *Wittgenstein and the Moral Life: Essays in Honor of Cora Diamond*. Cambridge, MA: MIT Press.

FOGELIN, ROBERT (1976). *Wittgenstein*. London: Routledge & Kegan Paul. (Revised 2nd edn, 1987.)

GLOCK, HANS-JOHANN (1996). *A Wittgenstein Dictionary*. Oxford: Blackwell.

—— ed. (2001). *Wittgenstein: A Critical Reader*. Oxford: Blackwell.

—— (2007). 'Perspectives on Wittgenstein: An Intermittently Opinionated Survey', in Kahane et al. 2007.

HACKER, P. M. S. (1986). *Insight and Illusion: Themes in the Philosophy of Wittgenstein*, rev. edn. Oxford: Oxford University Press.

—— (1990). *Wittgenstein: Meaning and Mind, Volume 3 of an Analytical Commentary on the Philosophical Investigations*, Part II: *Exegesis*. Oxford: Blackwell.

JONES, O. R. ed. (1971). *The Private Language Argument*. London: Macmillan.

KAHANE, GUY, KANTERIAN, EDWARD, and KUUSELA, OSKARI eds. (2007). *Wittgenstein and his Interpreters*. Oxford: Blackwell.

KENNY, ANTHONY (1971). 'The Verification Principle and the Private Language Argument', in Jones 1971. (Reprinted in Canfield 1986.)

—— (1973). *Wittgenstein*. Cambridge, MA: Harvard University Press. (Revised 2nd edn, Oxford: Blackwell, 2006.)

KRIPKE, SAUL (1982). *Wittgenstein on Rules and Private Language*. Cambridge, MA: Harvard University Press.

LAW, STEPHEN (2004).'Five Private Language Arguments', *International Journal of Philosophical Studies*, 12(2): 159–76.

MALCOLM, NORMAN (1954). 'Wittgenstein's *Philosophical Investigations*', *The Philosophical Review*, 63: 530–59. (Revised version in Pitcher 1966, Jones 1971, and Canfield 1986.)

McGINN, MARIE (1997). *Routledge Philosophy Guidebook to Wittgenstein and the Philosophical Investigations*. London: Routledge.

MILLER, ALEXANDER and WRIGHT, CRISPIN (2002). *Rule-following and Meaning*. Montreal: McGill-Queen's University Press.

MULHALL, STEPHEN (2007). *Wittgenstein's Private Language: Grammar, Nonsense and Imagination in Philosophical Investigations §§243–315*. Oxford: Oxford University Press.

PEARS, DAVID (1969/1986). *Ludwig Wittgenstein*. (1st edn, 1969: 2nd edn, with a new preface by the author, 1986.) Cambridge, MA: Harvard University Press.

—— (1988). *The False Prison*, vol. 2. Oxford: Clarendon Press.

—— (2006). *Paradox and Platitude in Wittgenstein's Philosophy*. Oxford: Oxford University Press.

PITCHER, GEORGE ed. (1966). *Wittgenstein: the Philosophical Investigations*. Garden City, NY: Doubleday.

RHEES, RUSH (1954).'Can There Be a Private Language?', *Proceedings of the Aristotelian Society*, Supplementary Volume, 28: 77–94. (Reprinted in Pitcher 1966, Jones 1971, and Canfield 1986.)

SCHROEDER, SEVERIN (2001).'Private Language and Private Experience', in Glock 2001.

STERN, DAVID G. (1994).'Recent Work on Wittgenstein, 1980–1990', *Synthese*, 98: 415–58.

—— (1994a).'A New Exposition of the "Private Language Argument": Wittgenstein's Notes for the "Philosophical Lecture"', *Philosophical Investigations*, 17: 552–65.

—— (1995). *Wittgenstein on Mind & Language*. Oxford: Oxford University Press.

—— (2004). *Wittgenstein's Philosophical Investigations: An Introduction*. Cambridge: Cambridge University Press.

—— (2007). 'The Uses of Wittgenstein's Beetle: *Philosophical Investigations* §293 and its Interpreters', in Kahane et al. 2007.

STOCKER, BARRY (2004). *Post-Analytic Tractatus*. Aldershot, England: Ashgate.

STRAWSON, PETER (1954). 'Review of Wittgenstein's *Philosophical Investigations*', *Mind*, 63: 70–99. (Reprinted in Pitcher 1966, Jones 1971, and Canfield 1986.)

STROUD, BARRY (1983). 'Wittgenstein's Philosophy of Mind', in G. Flöistad ed., *Contemporary Philosophy: A New Survey*, volume 4. The Hague: Nijhoff. (Reprinted in Canfield 1986).

—— (1983a). 'Wittgenstein's "Treatment" of the Quest for "a Language which Describes My Inner Experiences and which Only I Myself Can Understand"', in P. Weingartner and J. Czermak eds., *Epistemology and Philosophy of Science*, proceedings of the 7th international Wittgenstein symposium. Vienna: Hölder–Pichler–Tempsky.

—— (2000). *Meaning, Understanding and Practice*. Oxford: Oxford University Press.

—— (2001). 'Private Objects, Physical Objects, and Ostension', in Charles and Child 2001. (First published as Stroud 2000, ch. 13.)

THOMSON, JUDITH JARVIS (1964). 'Private Languages', *American Philosophical Quarterly*, 1: 20–31. (Reprinted in Jones 1971, Canfield 1986.)

WITTGENSTEIN, LUDWIG (1953). *Philosophical Investigations*, ed. G. E. M. Anscombe and R. Rhees, trans. G. E. M. Anscombe. Oxford: Blackwell. (2nd edn 1958; rev. edn 2001.)

——(2005). *The Big Typescript*, ed. C. G. Luckhardt, translation on facing pages. Oxford: Blackwell.

CHAPTER 16

VERY GENERAL FACTS
OF NATURE

LARS HERTZBERG

In *Philosophical Investigations* §415 Wittgenstein gives what appears to be a general characterization of his method in philosophy:

> What we are supplying are really remarks on the natural history of human beings; we are not contributing curiosities however, but observations which no one has doubted, but which have escaped remark only because they are always before our eyes.

The remark has no obvious connection with the surrounding remarks. How is it to be understood? How general is its scope?

In this chapter I wish to argue that this remark points to quite an important dimension of Wittgenstein's later thought, a dimension that has largely been bypassed or underplayed (perhaps even, as I shall suggest, by Wittgenstein himself). It concerns the importance, for our way of thinking about language, of recognizing the ways in which the language we speak is contingent on the circumstances of our lives.

Wittgenstein makes explicit reference to this theme on only a few occasions. In *Philosophical Investigations*, II, xii, there are two remarks that bring to mind the one just quoted, although here Wittgenstein no longer insists that he is *doing* natural history:

> If the formation of concepts can be explained by facts of nature, should we not be interested, not in grammar, but rather in that in nature which is the basis of grammar? – Our interest certainly includes the correspondence between concepts and very general facts of nature. (Such facts as mostly do not strike us because of their generality.) But our interest does not fall back upon these possible causes of the formation of concepts; we are not doing natural science; nor yet natural history – since we can also invent fictitious natural history for our purposes.
>
> I am not saying: if such-and-such facts of nature were different people would have different concepts (in the sense of a hypothesis). But: if anyone believes that certain concepts are absolutely the correct ones, and that having different ones

would mean not realizing something that we realize – then let him imagine certain very general facts of nature to be different from what we are used to, and the formation of concepts different from the usual ones will become intelligible to him.

These remarks are somewhat obscure. Wittgenstein is contrasting two approaches to the dependence of our concepts on facts of nature. One approach would be explanatory in the spirit of natural science: it would concern hypotheses about the causes of our having formed the concepts we have. Wittgenstein does not say whether he thinks that such an investigation would be meaningful, although it is a safe bet that he would consider it problematic. What is less clear is the alternative he has in mind. The central notion is apparently the *correspondence* (*Entsprechung*) between concepts and facts of nature. This, the second remark suggests, is something having to do with the correctness of concepts, with the idea that what concepts we have is an expression of our having realized or failed to realize certain things. Wittgenstein seems to accept the idea that concepts may or may not be correct, although suggesting that their correctness is not absolute, but relative to the circumstances in which they are used.

The implication, then, seems to be that it is not a matter of explaining but of *judging* concepts. The idea would be that philosophers may ask themselves whether such and such a range of concepts (say, of an alien culture) makes sense, and they may then decide that it does or does not. On this reading, Wittgenstein is reminding the philosopher that in passing judgement on concepts she should be sure to take into account the actual circumstances in which the concepts are being used.

However, I would contend that this reading would be hard to square with Wittgenstein's later thought in which there seems to be no room for the idea of philosophers passing judgement on the intelligibility of concepts. Rather, philosophy is a matter of creating a clear picture of the ways language is used in various contexts.

Thus, in *Zettel* §320 Wittgenstein writes:

> Why don't I call cookery rules arbitrary, and why am I tempted to call the rules of grammar arbitrary? Because 'cookery' is defined by its end, whereas 'speaking' is not. That is why the use of language is in a certain sense autonomous, as cooking and washing are not. You cook badly if you are guided in your cooking by rules other than the right ones; but if you follow other rules than those of chess you are *playing another game*; and if you follow grammatical rules other than such-and-such ones, that does not mean that you say something wrong, no, you are speaking of something else.

Here, evidently, Wittgenstein is rejecting the idea of an independent yardstick for checking on the correctness or meaningfulness of a vocabulary and its attendant grammar. The idea of looking for a grounding for the concepts we use in our having come to realize certain things about our environment is misguided. For instance, it is only against the background of a received way of classifying things that there can be an incorrect way of applying those classifications: calling a whale a fish only became an error when a new way of classifying animal species had been adopted. If we attempt to describe the use of a range of concepts and it comes out as unintelligible, that is a failure on the part of the description, not of the speakers.

The suggestion I wish to make is that when Wittgenstein speaks about the correspondence between concepts and facts of nature, about the correctness of concepts,[1] or about their intelligibility, what he has in mind is an *internal* relation between the concepts and the life in which they have a place. The circumstances do not define the standard against which the meaningfulness of the concepts is to be adjudicated; rather it is only by taking note of the circumstances that we can get a clear picture of those concepts: we see them for what they are in the context of life in which they have a use. One way of doing this, as Wittgenstein suggests, may be to imagine that context of life as being radically different from what it is, and trying to see how those differences might bear on the concepts we use.

The idea that we could adjudicate the meaningfulness of a range of concepts by asking whether they correspond to certain facts of nature, it might be said, rests on too simple an idea of what that correspondence might consist in. In fact the relations between the concepts we use and the world in which we live is as varied as life itself, and in order to get a clear view of human concepts we must be open to that variety. We need to get clear about the different things it may *mean* for our concepts to correspond to the facts. What are intelligible ways of speaking about the relation between our words and reality? In this chapter I shall try to throw some light on these issues.

There are, I will argue, two sides to the dependence of concepts on general facts of nature in Wittgenstein's account. On the one hand, the use of words may be dependent on facts concerning the surroundings in which words are being used, and on the other hand it may be dependent on facts concerning those who use them. I shall deal with each of these in turn. The way the use of words depends on facts about our surroundings comes out the most clearly in reflecting on ways in which our use of words might be undermined or become impossible if certain very general facts of nature were radically different from what they are. We might speak about facts pulling the rug from under our practices. I shall discuss this issue in section 1. The dependence of the use of words on those who use them, in turn, is seen most clearly in connection with language learning, and the bulk of this chapter is devoted to this theme. In section 2, I shall discuss a received view of Wittgenstein's account of language learning, arguing that this view fails to give an account of the way language comes to have a place in our lives, by tending to reduce

---

[1] The phrase 'absolutely the correct ones' in the remark quoted above is a translation of '*schlechtweg die richtigen*', which would have been better rendered as '*simply* the correct ones' (or perhaps as 'correct *period*', 'correct *sans phrase*'). This could hint at a somewhat different thought: Wittgenstein might be taken not to be questioning the idea that the correctness of concepts might be independent of the circumstances in which *concepts are used*, but rather that the notion of concepts being correct (or incorrect) might be independent of the circumstances *in which the question is raised*. Still, the second remark as a whole does not seem to be open to this reading. Is Wittgenstein possibly running together two different thoughts here: the problematic idea that the *correctness* of concepts is *situation*-dependent and the more natural notion that the *question* of their correctness is *context*-dependent? I find no obvious answer to this question. – I should point out here that in this section I follow Wittgenstein in using the word 'concept' although this is a rather abstract notion and accordingly is bound up with certain problems. It would be preferable to speak about *words*.

language learning to a matter of learning to recognize the objects to which our words refer. In section 3, I argue that what is needed is some account of how language comes to have a place in our lives. In sections 4–5, I reflect on the role of primitive reactions in connection with learning to speak. In the concluding section, I raise the question whether the emphasis on facts of nature makes Wittgenstein a naturalist. I will argue that he was not attempting to formulate a competing theory about concept formation; rather, for him, appeals to real – or imaginary! – facts of nature were part of an attempt to change our ways of thinking about language. For Wittgenstein, the goal of philosophical activity was to rid our thinking of confusion. This means that he saw no use for the hypothetical reasoning of the naturalists, but neither for the a priori approach of those who regard philosophy as conceptual analysis.

1. RUG-PULLING FACTS

In *Philosophical Investigations* §142, Wittgenstein writes:

> if things were quite different from what they actually are – if there were for instance no characteristic expression of pain, of fear, of joy; if rule became exception and exception rule; or if both became phenomena of roughly equal frequency – this would make our normal language-games lose their point. – The procedure of putting a lump of cheese on the balance and fixing the price by the turn of the scale would lose its point if it frequently happened for such lumps to grow or shrink for no obvious reason.

In a note inserted in the manuscript, obviously connected with this remark, Wittgenstein writes:

> What we have to mention in order to explain the significance, I mean the importance, of a concept, are often extremely general facts of nature: such facts as are hardly ever mentioned because of their great generality.

(We may note that these remarks immediately precede the discussion about learning to continue a number series.)

Precisely how are we to understand these remarks? In fact, the conclusion Wittgenstein draws from these thought experiments is strangely cautious. What would be undermined if certain very general facts of nature were different, he is suggesting, is the *importance*, the *point*, of certain concepts or language-games. He seems to leave open the possibility that the language-games might recede into the background but would still exist. Yet in *many* cases it is not clear what it would mean to distinguish importance from intelligibility. In the case of determining the price of a lump of cheese with the help of a scale, the question of what someone is doing and why he is doing it can hardly be separated. If there were no point to the procedure, there would be no distinction between a correct and an incorrect way of doing it (assuming, of course, that it is not part of some other practice, such as a ritual). So if lumps of cheese were to start growing or shrinking unpredictably and unaccountably, it is not just that we should stop weighing them; there would, in a strict sense, *no longer be such a thing* as weighing a piece of cheese; i.e. whatever someone was doing in placing it on a scale would not be described in those terms. Of course, if the same thing were true of products in general, of people, rocks, heaps of sand, cups of liquid, etc., the concepts of weight and scales would lack application, and thus intelligibility, altogether.

The problem is more obvious in some of the remarks in *On Certainty*. In §§513–14, Wittgenstein wrote:

> What if something *really unheard*-of happened? – If I, say, saw houses gradually turning into steam without any obvious cause; if the cattle in the fields stood on their heads and laughed and spoke comprehensible words; if trees gradually changed into men and men into trees. Now, was I right when I said before all these things happened 'I know that that's a house' etc., or simply 'That's a house' etc.?
>
> This statement appeared to me fundamental; if it is false, what are 'true' or 'false' any more?!

Wittgenstein is trying to describe a situation in which our practice of judging would be plunged into chaos. But what precisely is the situation that we are supposed to imagine? Let us assume that it seems to me that something that looks like a cow is laughing or speaking comprehensible words. In this case, it is not clear *what* my response would be. Would I still call it a cow? Would I conclude that the sounds really came from the cow? How would a laughing cow sound? And in what sense would the sounds made by the cow constitute comprehensible words? Am I to imagine the cow parroting words, or actually speaking and responding in ways that make sense from the cow's point of view (and whatever would that be?)? What language would it speak, and in what tone (anguished, bantering, blasé)?

Rather than 'what are "true" or "false" any more?', should Wittgenstein not have asked 'what are "cows" and "trees" any more?'? He says that what characterizes our ways of judging is that in such a case all our certainty would vanish (just as in the case of the cheese, the point of the practice would dissolve). Yet it would, it seems, be more to the point to say that what characterizes our ways of judging is that we could not now imagine circumstances that would lead us to describe what was happening as a case of talking cows, etc.[2]

It appears as if Wittgenstein were suggesting that, in one case the *importance* of the language-game, in the other case its *certainty*, were external to the sense of the game. If this were so, that would indicate that Wittgenstein is still in the grip of a strand of thought that runs through much of Western philosophy: the notion that, however the world may twist and turn, our ideas or concepts or words can never leave us in the lurch: there will always be a correct way of describing what is happening.[3] Classical cases in point are Descartes, who saw no problem in using the words 'dream' and 'awake' in formulating the

---

[2] For a discussion of this point, see Winch 1987.

[3] I have discussed similar issues in Hertzberg 1994, 58ff. However, I would place some of the emphases differently today.

supposition that we might be dreaming when we take ourselves to be awake, and Hume, who thought we should have no difficulty identifying ordinary objects even if they seemed to behave in what, for them, would be extraordinary ways.

This is connected with the notion that ideas or concepts are in the mind, and that the mind's capacity to picture things to itself can in no way be hampered by whatever changes take place outside it. Also, since the meanings of our words are grounded in our connecting them with ideas, language too is impervious to any contingencies. Our capacity for thought and for putting our thoughts into words is in this sense a priori. Our words, as it were, constitute an immutable measuring stick that can be laid against any possible reality – which, as the saying goes, is applicable in 'all possible worlds'.[4]

This is reminiscent of ideas put forward by Wittgenstein himself in the *Tractatus*, where he argues that the simplest objects that enter into states of affairs must be indestructible if we are to be able to make true or false assertions about states of affairs. If they were not, the sense of our sentences would depend on whether or not the constituents that correspond to them happened to exist, and thus, whether one sentence made sense would depend on whether some other sentence was true. That would mean that language is dependent on the a posteriori. This, he held, is unthinkable. Our linguistic resources for giving an account of events must be independent of any contingencies.[5]

Are we to suppose that Wittgenstein meant to hold on to this idea in his later work?[6] Quite the contrary, I would argue: it seems evident that to assume that he does would be

---

[4] The idea that we could talk about possibilities in such a context-independent way is itself highly problematic.

[5] Of course, in referring to the *Tractatus* one will have to add the proviso that there is no widespread consensus on whether and to what extent what he says there is to be taken at face value.

[6] This view has in fact been argued by John Cook in *Wittgenstein's Metaphysics*. Cook calls the type of description given in *On Certainty* §§513–14 a description of a 'metaphysical nightmare'. He explains Wittgenstein's belief that metaphysical nightmares are intelligible by the claim that he accepted a form of phenomenalist metaphysics, 'neutral monism', according to which objects are constituted by appearances. What we call a cow, for instance, is a collection of cow-type appearances, and hence there is no problem about supposing that a cow might start talking at any moment, just as there is no problem about assuming that a man might turn into a tree or a tree into a man. What occurs at any one moment is logically independent of whatever occurs the next moment. According to Cook, Wittgenstein retained this view, which is closely analogous to that of Hume, basically unchanged throughout his philosophical work.

Whatever the disagreements between readers of Wittgenstein, Cook's interpretation is, of course, at loggerheads with almost everybody else's. It is commonly held that Wittgenstein was critical of metaphysical philosophy in general and of all forms of empiricism in particular. To be sure, that in itself is not an argument against Cook's reading. And Cook is right, of course, in pointing out the type of anomaly that we have noted here; however, his claim that it is due to an underlying metaphysical doctrine seems gratuitous. If he is arguing that Wittgenstein was actively trying to propagate his phenomenalist metaphysics, that raises the question why Wittgenstein was trying so hard to convey the opposite impression. On the other hand, the claim might be that Wittgenstein occasionally expressed himself in conflicted ways because he was still, in part, unconsciously under the influence of the empiricist ontology of which he was openly critical. Such predicaments are not unheard of in philosophy, and the unfinished *On Certainty* seems to be a text in which many of the tensions have still not been resolved. That could, of course, account for the problematic formulations in remarks like §§513–14. But Cook seems to argue for the stronger reading.

to miss one of the main thrusts of that work, even if it is true that he did not always express himself clearly in this regard. In PI §80, for instance, he makes it clear that the application of our concepts would be threatened by strange occurrences:

> I say, 'There is a chair.' What if I go up to it, meaning to fetch it, and it suddenly disappears from sight? – 'So it wasn't a chair, but some kind of illusion.' – But in a few moments we are able to see it again and are able to touch it, and so on. – 'So the chair was there after all and its disappearance was some kind of illusion.' – But suppose that after a time it disappears again – or seems to disappear. What are we to say now? Have you rules ready for such cases – rules saying whether one may use the word 'chair' to include this kind of thing? But do we miss them when we use the word 'chair'; and are we to say that we do not really attach any meaning to this word, because we are not equipped with rules for every possible application of it?

This remark is part of an extended questioning of the claim (attributed to Frege, PI §71) that a concept without sharp boundaries is no concept at all. This discussion goes on from PI §68 through §88, and is evidently of central importance to Wittgenstein. Now, why did Wittgenstein relinquish the ironclad requirement of determinacy of sense that he (apparently) upheld in the *Tractatus*? (Hardly just because he had become more flexible with age!) Clearly, determinacy of sense and the a priori character of language went together. On this view, if the character of our concepts were not such that their application in every possible case was unambiguously given, then the question of how they were to be applied, and whether they had any application at all in particular cases, would depend on something external to language, hence to that extent meaning would be an a posteriori matter. In the *Philosophical Investigations*, however, these are no longer seen to be two separate options. The application of what is said does not depend on the form of words itself, but is a matter of the part they play in a context of human interaction. The fact that what would fit the instruction in one situation would not fit it in another, and that in a third situation it is not clear what would fit it, does not rob the words of their sense. Thus 'Stand roughly here' may be a perfectly good instruction, given that speaker and listener share an understanding of the activity going on, whether it is getting ready for a photo session or getting into position for a softball game. (Cf. PI §88.) There is no line, given in advance, between the contribution made by the utterance and that made by the context to our understanding of the words.

The notion that the meaning of what someone says must uniquely be determined by the form of the sentence uttered seems plausible when questions of meaning and understanding are raised in isolation from various contexts of human intercourse.[7]

---

[7] It is true that Wittgenstein, in the *Tractatus*, argues that we need to attend to the use of a sign (e.g. of a given sequence of words) in order to recognize the *symbol* being expressed in it (3.326). But it would be a mistake to read into this an anticipation of his later thoughts about the way the sense of our words is dependent on their role in a context of human interaction. Rather, the point he seems to be making here is that the same sequence of words can sometimes express several different thoughts (since it may admit of different syntactical parsings or contain homonymous words). (Cf. 3.321–3.323.) In such a case, we need to establish which thought is being expressed before we can recognize the syntax of the sentence;

Thus, Bernard Harrison speaks of 'this feeling, that the signs of a language dictate the interpretation which a speaker of the language places upon them' as central to what it means to be a speaker: 'for him [the signs] bear their meaning and their grammatical structure upon their face'. He refers to the ability of linguistic signs to evoke this feeling as 'the autonomy of language' (Harrison 1979, 5). I should be inclined to argue, on the contrary, that what Harrison is referring to is a psychological fact about our attitude towards words and sentences; a psychological fact that actually gives a misleading picture of how we are related to language in using it, since it ignores the way in which the context influences my reading of a sign whether or not I actively think about it. We may be culturally predisposed to regard language from the perspective Harrison advances by the fact that much of our thought about language is concerned with the situation of learning a second language, as well as with translating from one language to another; both of these are activities which primarily take the form of relating words and sentences to other words and sentences. These contexts incline us to think about discussions on meaning along the lines of grammar book exercises. It is from such a perspective that the idea that we should be able, independently of context, to draw a line between what is internal to language and what is external to it arises.

Of course, even if it is admitted that the idea of such a line is illusory, and that the meaning of what someone is saying is not determined solely by the words she uses, it does not follow that in a particular instance we may not want to distinguish *what* a person said from the *point* of his saying it; what needs to be recognized is simply that the way to make that distinction depends on the details of the particular case and the purpose for which the distinction is being made.

I would contend that something analogous is true of Wittgenstein's discussion in *On Certainty*. One of the central aims of that discussion is to draw into question the possibility of separating, once and for all, (what, in that text, he calls) logic from the actual use of words in making judgements about various states of affairs. In any particular inquiry, there will be matters that could not intelligibly be asserted, but the line between what can and what cannot be asserted (hence, between what does and what does not belong to logic) is shifting and depends on the context.

A classical expression of the thought that our ideas or concepts are impervious to whatever happens in the external world is the traditional view of mathematics. Mathematical knowledge is held to be beyond doubt, since it concerns itself exclusively

---

only then can we tell how the sentence is to be compared with reality in order to determine whether it is true or false. Once we have removed this formal ambiguity, on the other hand, the sense of the sentence is given independently of context.

Similarly, it would appear that when Wittgenstein says in 3.328 that if a sign is useless it is meaningless, he is not speaking about the point of using the sign; rather for a sign to be useless seems to mean that it has no bearing on the truth-grounds of the sentence in which it occurs. Thus – to borrow an example of Michael Dummett's – the sentences 'She was poor but she was honest' and 'She was poor and she was honest' would have the same meaning since they have the same truth-value; and yet the *point* being made by the choice of conjunction is clearly different. (On the other hand, 6.211 seems to be pointing towards a broader conception of use.)

with what are considered to be contents of our minds (or with timeless entities with which our minds are in direct, suprasensible contact). In the *Philosophical Investigations*, however, Wittgenstein points out that even our ability to carry out mathematical operations is, as it were, dependent on contingent facts of nature:

> am I trying to say some such thing as that the certainty of mathematics is based on the reliability of pen and paper? *No.* (That would be a vicious circle.) – I have not said *why* mathematicians do not quarrel, but only *that* they do not.
>
> It is no doubt true that you could not calculate with certain sorts of paper and ink, if, that is, they were subject to certain queer changes – but still the fact that they changed could in turn only be got from memory and comparison with other means of calculation. And how are these tested in their turn?
>
> What has to be accepted, the given, is – so one could say – *forms of life*. (PI II §226)

Here, compare Wittgenstein's *Remarks on the Foundations of Mathematics*:

> I have read a proof – and now I am convinced. – What if I straightway forgot this conviction?
>
> For it is a peculiar procedure: I *go through* the proof and then accept its result. – I mean: this is simply what we *do*. This is use and custom among us, or a fact of our natural history. (RFM I §63)

The suggestion seems to be that we could imagine a culture which did not have anything reminiscent of mathematics simply because members of the culture did not trust their memory in these matters – or, in the other case, ink and paper – the way we do (whether this was just an accidental cultural variation or a matter of biology, say, makes no difference). Whether we are right in trusting our memory, or whether they are wrong in not trusting theirs, is not the issue. The point is that what we consider to be 'the certainty of mathematics' is not something laid down in the nature of mathematical concepts themselves, but is ultimately an expression of the place calculations have in our lives. In this way, what we know as 'mathematics' is also dependent on very general facts of nature.

2. LANGUAGE LEARNING: THE SIMPLE STORY

One common way of reading Wittgenstein's remarks about the acquisition of concepts is succinctly described by Peter Strawson as follows:

> Consider the case of somebody learning the meaning of a particular common word or, simply, coming to know what the word means. The followers of Wittgenstein are apt to speak of a preliminary period of *training* in the use…of the word…The point is that after a time the learner comes to find it *utterly natural* to make a certain application of the expression; he comes to apply it in a certain way *as a matter of course*…Here we may see one of the suspect pictures being, as it were, undermined…: viz. the picture of the learner's application being *governed* by, or

determined by, his acquired acquaintance with the abstract thing, its sense or *mean-ing*...(Strawson 1985, 75f.)

Further along Strawson writes:

> The great point, on this view of the matter, is that there is, philosophically speaking, nothing at all behind this, and no need for anything beyond or behind it all to consti-tute a philosophical explanation of it. This is not to say that there are not biological and anthropological and cultural-historical explanations of how speech-communities agreeing in common linguistic practices came about. Such explanations there may well be. But as far as the philosophical problem is concerned, the suggestion is that we can just rest with, or take as primitive, the great natural fact that we *do* form speech-communities...; that we have, if you will, a natural disposition to develop the disposi-tions which qualify us for...the description...'members of a speech-community, agreeing in a common linguistic practice'. (Strawson 1985, 77f.)

We may note that 'facts of nature' are only given a minimal role here. The only relevant fact of nature is that we *are* beings who are disposed to form speech-communities. Of course, Strawson admits, biological, anthropological, and historical circumstances play a role, presumably affecting what particular conceptual schemes are actually developed, what similarities are accorded importance, etc. However, we can 'divide through' with them: these are just contingent details having no bearing on the *philo-sophical* problem, which, for Strawson, as I read him, is this: what kinds of entities do we need to invoke in order to account for the fact that speakers are able to acquire concepts?[8]

On Strawson's account, then, the only philosophically relevant variation would be between beings who are by nature disposed to form language-communities and beings who are not. However, this does not touch on the question how, given that a commu-nity does have concepts, imagining *different* facts of nature might render wholly dif-ferent concepts intelligible. This seems to me to be connected with another point in Strawson's argument: for him, the problem of concept acquisition seems, roughly, to be the problem of *learning to classify things correctly* (Strawson 1985, 78f., 84). The learner encounters a set of examples of the application of some class, say, 'red' or 'apple', and the question is how she learns to go on in the right way. Wittgenstein remarks that there is nothing about the particular red things or the particular apples that will deter-mine any given way of going on as the correct one, or that will infallibly lead her to go on in some specific way; we cannot, for instance, explain the success of our instruction by saying that the learner understood that the relevant property was that of being red or being an apple, since that would presuppose that she already had command of the

---

[8] Strawson goes on to argue, tentatively at least (1985, 84f.), that concept acquisition cannot be accounted for without invoking the notion of universals, which he takes Wittgenstein to be denying; but this need not concern us here; I quote him for his elegant way of presenting a common way of reading Wittgenstein. We find similar readings, for instance, in von Savigny 1991, 109, as well as in Bloor 1996.

classes that we were trying to convey to her (and, indeed, of what it means to classify things in the first place).

More generally, there is no *ground* for our going on in one specific way rather than another; we simply do. The fact that we may be biologically disposed to respond in one way rather than another, while doubtless true in many cases, of course has no bearing on the present issue. In fact, the notion that there is only one way of going on, I would suggest, comes from our mixing together two different ways of describing the learning process: from confusing what the learner ends up knowing (the criteria of the mastery in question) with the explanation of how she manages to pick it up. The relevant concepts or formulae will be part of the former description but not (in many cases) of the latter.[9] If we fail to keep these apart, we end up with an account in which that which we are trying to explain is invoked in the explanation itself. (This may be what lies behind Strawson's felt need for universals.)

Undeniably, the discussion of how we acquire classifications – what we might call the recognition problem – has an important place in the *Philosophical Investigations*. It is closely connected with some of the central discussions of the early parts of the book. One point (though not the only point) made through the discussion about continuing a series of numbers (PI §§143–55) is that even if we find it natural to apply the examples in one particular way, we could have imagined people applying them in some other way, or in a number of different ways (the suggestion that they might do that is not self-contradictory).

However, from large parts of the *Philosophical Investigations* one may get the impression that the recognition problem is the central issue where language learning is concerned. Sharing a language, it seems to be suggested, is simply applying words in the same way; hence by getting clear about the recognition problem, we become clear about what it means to speak a language. PI §242 is often quoted as an expression of this view: 'If language is to be a means of communication there must be agreement not only in definitions but also (queer as this may sound[10]) in judgments.' However, I would argue this account of language learning does not capture the whole story about the contingency of our concepts on the nature of speakers, and that what is left out is as important as what is included.

---

[9] It is true that, once we have learnt to speak, we often learn things simply by reading or hearing a set of verbal instructions, and in these cases the process of learning and the criteria of mastery may seem to mirror one another. Thus I may learn the highway code or French grammar by reading a set of rules; this set of rules at the same time provides the criteria of my having mastered the highway code or French grammar. The prevalence of this type of instruction may be what tempts us to ignore the distinction between process and mastery. However, the ability to apply a set of verbal instructions is of course dependent on our already having mastered a number of more fundamental skills; the actual process of learning, accordingly, is much more complex than it seems on the surface.

[10] This may appear queer to us if we take it to mean that, whenever people fail to agree on some judgement, that would show that they meant different things. That, of course, would mean that there could be no such thing as disagreement. Wittgenstein's point, rather, is that for there even to be disagreement, there must be some degree of overlap between our judgements.

3. PLACE IN LIFE

One of the commentators who seems to consider the recognition problem central is Marie McGinn. She writes:

> Our concept of language describes…a particular form of life, namely, one that displays the characteristic regularities or patterns that constitute the following of rules. Central to the idea of the form of life that our concept of language picks out is that there exists a pattern or structure in the activity of using words which fixes what counts as applying the words of the language correctly or incorrectly…The agreement or harmony that Wittgenstein suggests is essential to our concept of language is the agreement that constitutes the characteristic form of life that speaking a language…consists in. (McGinn 1997, 110)

Let us ask, however: what is *the nature of the agreement* invoked by McGinn in the above passage? Evidently, to say that two persons agree in what they do or say is not simply to say that they do the same thing or utter the same sounds in the same circumstances. For one thing, such a description is empty unless one can assume some relevant point of view from which their actions or vocalizations (as well as the circumstances) are to be compared; the relevant basis of comparison, however, would obviously be one that is internal to the language in question. This does not necessarily render McGinn's description otiose. She only goes wrong if she means to be invoking a relation between two distinct entities – as if the language were dependent on there being a harmony in reactions that could be identified independently of the language in question. Rather, 'agreement' and 'language' should be understood as two sides of the same coin. Or, differently put, the point to be made is that in *calling* something a language, we imply that *there is room for the use of notions* like 'agreement', 'correct', and 'incorrect', etc.: when I regard something as a language I assume that notions like these enter into the interactions of its speakers.[11]

---

[11] Curiously, Wittgenstein seems to be overlooking this point in PI §207, in which he imagines people who speak what sounds like an articulate language, but where, as he says, there is no regular connection between the sounds they make and their actions. He concludes that the lack of regularity prevents our calling this a language. In an apparent fit of absent-mindedness he seems to assume that the notion of regularity can be given content independently of the activities of the speakers. Curiously, he himself notes this point in PI §206, where he observes that it is 'the common behaviour of mankind' – i.e. the activities we share with the speakers – that provides 'the system of reference by means of which we interpret an unknown language'. It is only through the way the speakers make sense to us that we can begin to see how they make sense to one another. Eike von Savigny, however, argues in the opposite direction, claiming that when Wittgenstein speaks of '[d]ie gemeinsame menschliche Handlungsweise', he is simply referring to behaviour *shared by the members of the alien community* (von Savigny 1991). Now, it seems to me that, apart from the difficulties involved in this position, his reading of Wittgenstein's words is rather strained. It is true that it would render PI §206 more consistent with PI §207. But I find it more plausible to suppose that Wittgenstein is not to be taken at his word in PI §207. In fact (as was pointed out to me by Hugo Strandberg), the opening of PI §208 seems to suggest as much. There he implies that the words 'order' and 'rule' are not to be defined by means of 'regularity', but that they are to be conveyed 'by *examples* and by *practice*'.

Furthermore, even setting aside the question of the basis of comparison, the relevant sense of agreement will not simply be a matter of people saying or doing the same thing in the same circumstances. To say that two individuals agree in something is to attribute a sense to what they are saying or doing. Actually, the fact that you and I agree in what we call red may show itself in you and me doing *different* things: for instance, in your *fetching* the book I have in mind when *I ask* you to bring me the red book.

All the same, among the different ways of using language, colour language is a good instance of one in which recognition is central. In many other cases, however, agreement is not even *primarily* a matter of recognition. This is true, say, of a number of psychological expressions. Consider, for instance, what it means to agree on the use of the word 'intention'. Our agreement may show itself in the measures I undertake after you tell me of your intentions. Teaching a child to express her intentions involves getting her to understand what it means to follow through on the intentions one declares. There is no particular state or process we teach her to recognize: for instance, learning to express one's intentions is a different sort of thing from learning to understand someone else's intentions.

In brief, the type of agreement relevant to language is something that will only show itself in the weave of life: in the ways in which we manage to make ourselves understood to one another. In the story about language learning as the acquiring of uniform reactions there is no room for what it means to become a speaker; to make language one's own. If language learners were simply drilled into uttering the same words in the same circumstances, *they would not learn what it means to have something to say.*[12]

This narrowness of perspective actually characterizes Wittgenstein's own treatment of language learning in the opening part of the *Philosophical Investigations*. For instance, the point of the example of the shopkeeper in PI §1 picking out five red apples is obviously to show the difference in procedure between applying colour words, natural kind terms, and numbers (as it were, the different rituals involved); the concern here is limited to the problem of getting the result right, and does not touch on the question of the different things that getting it right might mean or how getting it right might matter in different contexts. The same is true, for instance, of the builders' game, where it is all about bringing the right type of building block. (I am not suggesting that the broader perspective is excluded at the beginning of the *Philosophical Investigations*; rather it is simply ignored.)

In this part of the *Philosophical Investigations* there is, we might say, a strong emphasis on what we do with *words*, on the differences between the way different types of words are applied, rather than on what we do with the sentences in which the words occur, or

---

[12] This point is forcefully argued by Rush Rhees in 'Can there be a Private Language?' (1970). To my mind this essay, which originally appeared in 1954, has hardly been superseded in the discussion of the private language question. See also, along the same lines, 'Wittgenstein's Builders' in the same collection, where Rhees points out some of the limitations of the language-game metaphor in the *Philosophical Investigations* – although there are aspects of that essay that I would not go along with. For more on Rhees's thinking about language, see Rhees 1998.

how the sentences enter into various forms of human interaction. The emphasis on words, I want to suggest, is closely linked to the emphasis on the recognition problem. This goes with a tendency to attend to general features of language use, rather than to the particular situations in which words are spoken. Wittgenstein hardly raises issues such as why we say things to people, or the bearing the context of speaking has on how utterances will be taken. This is true, for instance, when he compares words to the tools in a tool-box (PI §11) or to the handles in the cabin of a locomotive (PI §12). The oft-quoted PI §43 is also concerned with defining the meanings of words in terms of use. (To be sure, sentences are discussed in PI §§23 and 27, but even here, Wittgenstein is focusing on different *types* of sentence rather than on particular *occasions* of speaking. An exception, perhaps, is found in PI §§19–20, where he discusses the relation between a single word and a one-word sentence.) This is, of course, in keeping with the use of the language-game metaphor, which emphasizes set forms of linguistic interaction rather than particular instances of language use.

What I have here described as a narrow perspective on language learning is primarily characteristic of the introductory part of the *Philosophical Investigations*, roughly §§1–88 (or perhaps §§1–108). The perspective is widened in the later parts of the work. Thus the discussion of rule-following (PI §§185–242) partly moves beyond the recognition problem: on the one hand, Wittgenstein argues, there are no particular features we can point to in order to distinguish following a rule from proceeding without a rule; on the other hand, saying 'Now I can go on!' is not expressive of my recognizing some inner state. Further on, in the discussion about privacy, consciousness, and intentionality, as well as various psychological concepts, the asymmetry between first person and third person utterances is a central theme (PI §§244–693; large parts of Part II). This asymmetry can hardly be squared with a view that takes language learning to revolve around the recognition problem. In fact, the private language discussion seems precisely to be aimed at showing how focusing on recognition may lead us astray.

A large part of this discussion, however, is negative: Wittgenstein is pointing to flaws in various received views of what it means to become a speaker, but he is not providing many suggestions as to how to get around the difficulties. What might be wished for, of course, is not some theory of language learning, simply a coherent way of speaking about what it is to become a speaker. Readers of Wittgenstein have often taken him to be gesturing towards some kind of *tabula rasa* behaviourist account, but that is hardly more coherent than some of the more traditional views. In neither case is there room for the notion of learning to speak as connected with having something to say. There are hints, all the same, of a more positive account, a few of them in the *Philosophical Investigations*, more extensive in some of the unpublished writings. This is the theme that has come to be discussed under the heading 'primitive reactions'. This discussion brings into focus an important aspect of what Wittgenstein might have meant by the significance of very general facts of nature.

4. CAUSALITY AND THE SOLITARY RESPONDER

The theme of primitive or unmediated reactions is brought up by Wittgenstein, primarily, in two different connections: on the one hand, in connection with learning the use of psychological expressions (particularly pain language); and on the other hand, in connection with acquiring an understanding of causality. These two discussions, as I shall try to show, point us in different directions. Let me begin with the latter.

PI §415, which was quoted in the introduction, originates in a manuscript from 1937. There it precedes an extended discussion of the concept of cause. None of these remarks on causality is included in the *Philosophical Investigations*; they have since been published, however, under the title 'Cause and Effect: Intuitive Awareness' (reprinted in PO). Of course, one can only speculate on why they were left out of the *Philosophical Investigations*; it is noteworthy that the concept of cause is hardly touched upon in that work. One possible reason for not including them may have been that Wittgenstein thought they gave a misleading emphasis to the discussion, as I shall try to show.

In the manuscript section on cause and effect, Wittgenstein is (evidently) discussing a suggestion made by Bertrand Russell according to which our understanding of causality must be grounded in an ability to 'see' something like causal connections.[13] As he often did, Wittgenstein was trying to fasten on to what might be of value in that suggestion without accepting it wholesale. In this connection, he drew attention to the importance of our unmediated reactions:

> We react to the cause.
>> Calling something 'the cause' is like pointing and saying: '*He's* to blame!'
>> We instinctively get rid of the cause if we don't want the effect. We instinctively look from what has been hit to what has hit it. (I am assuming that we do this.) (CE, 373)

The importance of these kinds of reaction, he suggested, does not lie in their supplying us with an infallible guide to causal knowledge. Rather, they form the context in which the issue of causality comes to have meaning. Actually, Wittgenstein speaks of two kinds of reactions: immediately responding to the cause; and looking for the cause.

> Don't we recognize immediately that the pain is produced by the blow we have received? Isn't this the cause and can there be any doubt about it? – But isn't it quite possible to suppose that in certain cases we are deceived about this? And later recognize the deception? It seems as though something hits us and at the same time we feel a pain....
>> Certainly there is in such cases a genuine experience which can be called 'experience of the cause'. But not because it infallibly shows us the cause; rather because one root of the cause-effect language-game is to be found here, in our looking out for a cause. (Ibid.)[14]

---

[13] On this, see the editors' comments, CE 370f.

[14] In fact, the example rather seems to fit what could be called the other root of the language-game: immediately responding to the cause.

There is a reaction which can be called 'reacting to the cause'. – We also speak of 'tracing' the cause; a simple case would be, say, following a string to see who is pulling at it. If I then find him – how do I know that he, his pulling, is the cause of the string's moving? Do I establish this by a series of experiments? (CE, 387)

Wittgenstein's thinking here seems to be a response to the Humean (or perhaps we should say 'quasi-Humean'[15]) idea that the concept of a cause must originate in the observation of recurrent temporal links between similar types of events. We start by collecting samples, at random as it were, and then study them in order to detect a pattern. What is assumed here is that if something is to be an experience of causal interaction, it must be an experience that we *can only have* when we are witnessing a genuine case of it, and so if it is always possible to be mistaken in the individual case, there can be no such thing as 'experiencing a cause'. (Cf. CE, 429.)

Wittgenstein's aim is to reverse this view of the matter. The idea of a causal connection does not enter only because we detect a similarity between a sufficient number of observations; rather, we, more or less directly, react *to* something as a cause (as in removing the pebble from our shoe) or react *by* looking for the cause (trying to find the sharp point in our shoe). Doubt, on the other hand, is a later reaction. The point he is making is not epistemological (even if it could be said to aim at removing the epistemological penumbra surrounding empiricist thought about causality); rather, he is describing the context of human activity in which the notion of a causal connection has a place. He writes,

The origin and the primitive form of the language game is a reaction; only from this can more complicated forms grow.

Language – I want to say – is a refinement. 'In the beginning was the deed'. (CE, 395)

The outlook he is combating is articulated as follows:

Reason – I feel like saying – presents itself to us as the gauge *par excellence* against which everything that we do, all our language games, measure and judge themselves. – We may say: we are so exclusively preoccupied by contemplating a yardstick that we can't allow our *gaze* to *rest* on certain phenomena or patterns. We are used, as it were, to 'dismissing' these as irrational, as corresponding to a low state of intelligence, etc. The yardstick rivets our attention and keeps distancing us from these phenomena, as it were making us look beyond. (CE, 389)

The yardstick here is the idea that the notion of a cause can only be constructed on the basis of repeated observations and inductive argument, making us overlook the patterns of reaction that characterize our actual dealings with physical objects.[16]

---

[15] It is not inconceivable that Hume himself would have felt at home with Wittgenstein's suggestion.

[16] Wittgenstein's thinking here has parallels with that of Simone Weil, who wrote: 'The elementary perception of nature is a sort of dance; this dance is the source of our perceiving.' On this, see Winch 1989, ch. 4. The quotation is from p. 41.

This theme is also broached in *On Certainty*:

> I want to regard man here as an animal; as a primitive being to which one grants instinct but not ratiocination. As a creature in a primitive state. Any logic good enough for a primitive means of communication needs no apology from us. Language did not emerge from some kind of ratiocination. (OC §475)

Reasoning and doubt, say, about causality can only enter where there is already a language-game in working order in which causal expressions have a use. Only then is there something for the reasoning and the doubting to be *about*.[17]

5. PAIN AND THE EXPRESSIVE RESPONDER

Here, then, Wittgenstein seems to be suggesting, are some of the ways the concept of a cause could make its entry into the language. It would appear, however, that an important part is missing from this story. In this account there is no speaker or listener, only a solitary individual responding to events. So far, there has been no indication of where communication about causes might enter. What connection is there between removing the pebble from one's shoe on the one hand, and discussing causes, asking about them, pointing to them on the other hand? In fact, the protagonist in this story has a close affinity with the solitary perceiver envisaged by Descartes or the empiricists, the main difference being that while they were passive collectors of impressions, the solitary individual in 'Cause and Effect' is active (so perhaps we should rather think of him as a Kantian solitary). Wittgenstein, it seems, is trying to make a shortcut from the reactions of the individual to the language-game of cause and effect. One might think that the reason this discussion was not included in the *Philosophical Investigations* was that Wittgenstein had come to realize that something was missing from it.

The story about gradually acquiring verbal expressions of pain is different from this, however. In one of the most frequently quoted passages in the *Philosophical Investigations* (§244), Wittgenstein writes, pondering how human beings learn the meaning of the names of sensations:

> Here is one possibility: words are connected with the primitive, the natural, expressions of the sensation and used in their place. A child hurts himself and he cries; and then adults talk to him and teach him exclamations and, later, sentences. They teach the child new pain-behaviour.

The role given to natural pain reactions is entirely different from that of reactions to the cause in the other text. For one thing, many of our pain reactions are themselves expressive in nature. Furthermore, their role in the story depends on the ways others respond

---

[17] Wolgast (1994) seems to miss this point. As she reads Wittgenstein, his point was that concepts do not *need* to be based on reasoning; on my reading, what Wittgenstein is arguing, rather, is that the suggestion that concepts might derive from reasoning is not intelligible.

to them. In fact, elsewhere Wittgenstein speaks about our responding to other people's expressions of pain as itself a form of primitive reaction (Z §§540, 545). So what we get here, and what is missing from the remarks about causality, is the story of a natural pattern of interactions gradually evolving into a verbal interchange. Of course, this story is not intended as a factual account, nor even as a speculative hypothesis about some process that may or may not have taken place during some specific period of time (whether in the development of the individual speaker or in the evolution of language). Rather, it is an account of what might be termed a logical order: an indication of the circumstances in which we would be prepared to say that someone has learnt verbal expressions of pain. What is central to such a story are not the reactions considered in themselves, but the interactivity between individuals.

In the story about reacting to the cause, on the other hand, there are logical gaps. Recognizing this does not mean denying that reacting to the cause is important in coming to have a concept of causality; it simply means that the story is incomplete. Some commentators on Wittgenstein, however, have in fact been misled by the individualist emphasis of 'Cause and Effect'. A case in point is Norman Malcolm's essay 'Wittgenstein: The Relation of Language to Instinctive Behavior'.[18] The problem of accounts such as his is that it is made out as if the concept in question (say, that of a cause) could somehow emerge directly from the primitive reaction: as if my reacting to the cause in itself supplied me with an understanding of causality, rather than a pattern of reactions and interactions providing the room in which we can imagine talk about causality developing.[19] This is how Hugh Knott, providing a lucid overview of the debate, summarizes the point at issue:

> It is not as the prototype of the *concept* of pain that Winch speaks of crying. Rather he describes a sense in which we might speak of the crying as the prototype of the linguistic *expression* of pain. Mastery of pain language does mean having the concept of pain, but that which is thought of as being *refined* or *extended* is the expression of pain from a non-linguistic into a linguistic form. (Knott 2007, 50)[20]

This is one context in which the term 'concept' is likely to contribute to the obscurity of the issue (cf. note 1 above). It tempts us to think that we are trying to explain the formation of concepts in the minds of individual speakers, rather than the development of a use of words in human interchange.

There seem, then, to be two currents in Wittgenstein's account of language learning that never fully meet – except at a few points, such as the remark about learning pain language. On the one hand, there is the account in the early parts of the *Philosophical Investigations*, emphasizing the ways in which a speaker's responses are brought into

---

[18] Malcolm 1982. On a similar note, see his 1980. For discussions of Malcolm on primitive reactions, see Winch 1993, 121–4; Wolgast 1994; Rhees 1997; especially important are Winch 1997 and Knott 1998 as well as the latter's 2007. Further on this theme, see Cockburn 1990, 43ff., and Hertzberg 1992, 24–39.

[19] This seems to be another instance of confusing *what* is being learnt with the process *through which* it is learnt.

[20] The reference is to Winch's critical notice of Malcolm (Winch 1997).

agreement with that of the community, but leaving out of the account what it means for her to make language her own; on the other hand, there are the remarks in 'Cause and Effect' bringing the natural responses of the individual into focus, but leaving out the ways in which those responses come to play a part in a shared language.

6. WAS WITTGENSTEIN, THEN, SOME KIND OF NATURALIST?

As we have seen, attention to the role of general facts of nature is distinctive of Wittgenstein's (post-*Tractatus*) way of doing philosophy. On the one hand, he pointed to the way our use of concepts is contingent on the way things work in practice. On the other hand, he emphasized the ways in which our use of language is logically tied up with the lives we actually live. This, I would argue, sets him apart from the mainstream of analytic philosophy in the twentieth century.

Does this make him a naturalist? The term 'naturalism' has many meanings in philosophy; in contemporary debate, a naturalist has mostly come to mean someone who holds, roughly, that there is no clear-cut divide between the methods of philosophy and those of empirical science. While philosophy has predominantly been thought of as a form of a priori reflection on concepts, naturalists will argue that it is quite legitimate, and maybe even necessary, to test the validity of such reflections against empirical data. This line of thought seems mainly to have been inspired by W. V. O. Quine's criticism of the analytic–synthetic distinction in his classical essay 'Two Dogmas of Empiricism'; to some degree also by Saul Kripke's book *Naming and Necessity*, as well as by Hilary Putnam's essay 'Meaning and Reference'.[21] While Kripke and Putnam were trying to show that certain matters external to my awareness have a bearing on the meanings of my words, Quine claimed that there can be no definitive way of distinguishing between matters of meaning on the one hand, and the contingent circumstances of a particular speech situation (specifically the speaker's beliefs) on the other hand.

A naturalist approach might, in principle, take two different directions: it could involve the study of facts concerning people who use a certain word (or respond to its use), or facts concerning the objects being referred to by people using the word. In practice, the latter course has almost invariably been chosen. For one thing, this means that the focus of the naturalist approach is diametrically opposed to that of Wittgenstein. As Winch puts it, 'one of Wittgenstein's most characteristic argumentative moves [is] a shift of attention away from the object to which a problematic concept is applied towards the person applying the concept'.[22]

---

[21] Quine 1963[1951]. Putnam 1996[1973]; Kripke 1981[1972]. The proponents of naturalist views are numerous. For an explicit formulation of a naturalist standpoint in the study of emotions, see Griffiths 1997.

[22] Winch 1997, 60.

However, the difference between Wittgenstein and the naturalists is even more radical. For Wittgenstein, philosophy is concerned with problems arising out of our lack of clarity about what we mean. From that perspective (as is clearly spelled out in PI §109), the suggestion that empirical data could somehow bear on a philosophical problem, whether by supporting or being in competition with the way in which we are inclined to view the issue, is misguided. If I consider the use of words like 'seeing' or 'consciousness' or 'law of nature' bewildering, then part of what I find bewildering is precisely what bearing empirical data could have on the use of those words. Thus, if I am trying to get clear about a deep ambiguity in the way neurologists talk about consciousness, then reading about neurological 'findings' about consciousness in which that ambiguity remains undetected will do nothing to resolve the issue. (Of course, it would be just as irrelevant to observe what happens in someone's brain when he *hears* or *utters* the word 'consciousness'.) Putting the matter in simple terms, for Wittgenstein philosophy is concerned with clarification whereas empirical science is concerned with truth; hence they can neither be in competition with, nor supplement, one another. This is not to deny, of course, that empirical scientists will continually need to address issues requiring clarification in getting on with their work. However, if they confuse matters that, from the point of view of their inquiry, are in need of clarification with questions that need to be settled experimentally, the research they do will be muddled.

All the same, as I have been suggesting throughout this chapter, Wittgenstein does not sit quite comfortably in the mainstream tradition of a priori conceptual analysis. One characteristic method of that tradition is, on the one hand, to propose general definitions of philosophically important concepts, and on the other hand, to test their tenability by considering whether one can construct counter-examples to them. As a paradigmatic case of arguments of the latter kind we might mention Edmund Gettier's attempt to show, by means of counter-examples, that the common definition of knowledge as justified true belief is not tenable, there being cases in which a belief is justified and true but would not count as knowledge.[23] (Analogous examples are plentiful.) The unspoken assumption underlying many discussions of this type is that the correct answer to the question of what will count, say, as knowledge is given once and for all. It can, it is assumed, be answered in what might be called laboratory conditions by a direct appeal to our 'linguistic intuitions', without taking into consideration *the way in which the question might arise in particular cases.*

However, once it is acknowledged that in order to understand what someone is saying I should have to understand her purpose in speaking and how it relates to the particular occasion, it becomes clear that questions such as 'is knowledge really justified true belief?' cannot be raised on a general level. There is no question about what is to be called knowledge that can usefully be separated from the points people are making in using the word 'know' on particular occasions; on those occasions, on the other hand, the question

---

[23] Gettier 1963. For an incisive discussion of the presuppositions of Gettier's argument, see Levi 1995.

whether something is to be called knowledge usually does not give rise to philosophical problems.[24]

Perhaps it will be thought that in doing philosophy we are forced to choose between the apriorism of someone like Gettier and the aposteriorism of the followers of Quine. Both of these, however, are programmes for the solving of general problems of meaning. When meaning is no longer seen to pose a problem on a general level, on the other hand, the distinction between apriorism and aposteriorism dissolves. Instead Wittgenstein proposes that we should attend to particular cases, in the hope that the philosophical problem will lose its hold on us. If the reading put forward here is correct, then, we may conclude that attending to very general facts of nature, as Wittgenstein suggests, will actually teach us to focus on the particularity of what is taking place when people speak to one another.[25]

REFERENCES

BAZ, AVNER (2008). 'The Reaches of Words', *International Journal of Philosophical Studies*, 16.1: 31–56.

BLOOR, DAVID (1996). 'The Question of Linguistic Idealism Revisited', in H. Sluga and D. G. Stern eds., *The Cambridge Companion to Wittgenstein*. Cambridge: Cambridge University Press.

COCKBURN, DAVID (1990). *Other Human Beings*. Basingstoke and London: Macmillan.

COOK, JOHN (1994). Wittgenstein's Metaphysics. Cambridge: Cambridge University Press.

GETTIER, EDMUND (1963). 'Is Justified True Belief Knowledge?', *Analysis*, 23: 121–3.

GRIFFITHS, PAUL E. (1997). *What Emotions Really Are*. Chicago and London: The University of Chicago Press.

HARRISON, BERNARD (1979). *The Philosophy of Language*. Basingstoke and London: Macmillan.

HERTZBERG, LARS (1992). 'Primitive Reactions – Logic or Anthropology?', in P. A. French, T. E Uehling, Jr., and H. K. Wettstein eds., *The Wittgenstein Legacy*. Midwest Studies in Philosophy, Volume 17. Notre Dame, IN: University of Notre Dame Press.

—— (1994). 'The Factual Dependence of the Language Game', in *The Limits of Experience*. Helsinki: Acta Philosophica Fennica.

KNOTT, HUGH (1998). 'Before Language and After', *Philosophical Investigations*, 21: 44–54.

—— (2007). *Wittgenstein, Concept Possession and Philosophy: A Dialogue*. Basingstoke: Palgrave Macmillan.

KRIPKE, SAUL (1981). *Naming and Necessity*. Oxford: Blackwell. (First published in Donald Davidson and Gilbert Harman eds., *Semantics of Natural Language*. Dordrecht: Reidel, 1972.)

[24] As has been shown by Avner Baz, even contextualists like Charles Travis, who emphasize the degree to which meanings of sentences are 'occasion sensitive', are still inclined to approach questions of meaning in an a priori fashion, simply factoring in contextual circumstances into their general account of meaning, rather than attending to the variety of things speakers do with words on particular occasions. See Baz 2008.

[25] I wish to thank Kim-Erik Berts, Alberto Emiliani, Hugh Knott, and Marie McGinn for helpful comments on earlier versions of this chapter. Particular thanks are due to David Cockburn, Hugo Strandberg, and Göran Torrkulla for their very thorough and incisive comments.

LEVI, DON S. (1995). 'The Gettier Problem and the Parable of the Ten Coins', *Philosophy*, 70: 5–25. (Reprinted in Don S. Levi, *In Defense of Informal Logic*. Dordrecht: Kluwer Academic Publishers, 2000.)

MALCOLM, NORMAN (1980). 'Kripke on Heat and Sensations of Heat', *Philosophical Investigations*, 3: 12–20. (Reprinted in Malcolm 1995.)

—— (1982). 'Wittgenstein: The Relation of Language to Instinctive Behavior', *Philosophical Investigations*, 5: 3–22. (Reprinted in Malcolm 1995.)

—— (1995). *Wittgensteinian Themes: Essays 1978–1989*, ed. G. H. Von Wright. Ithaca and London: Cornell University Press.

McGINN, MARIE (1997). *Wittgenstein and the Philosophical Investigations*. London: Routledge.

PUTNAM, HILARY (1996). 'Meaning and Reference', in A. P. Martinich ed., *The Philosophy of Language*, 3rd edn. New York and Oxford: Oxford University Press. (First published in The *The Journal of Philosophy*, 1973.)

QUINE, W. V. O. (1963). *From a Logical Point of View*. New York: Harper & Row. (First published in *The Philosophical Review*, 1951.)

RHEES, RUSH (1970). 'Can there be a Private Language?', in *Discussions of Wittgenstein*. London: Routledge & Kegan Paul.

—— (1997). 'Language as Emerging from Instinctive Behaviour', *Philosophical Investigations*, 20: 1–14.

—— (1998). *Wittgenstein and the Possibility of Discourse*, ed. D. Z. Phillips. Cambridge: Cambridge University Press.

SAVIGNY, EIKE VON (1991). 'Common Behaviour of Many a Kind', in R. L. Arrington and H.-J. Glock eds., *Wittgenstein's Philosophical Investigations: Text and Context*. London and New York: Routledge.

STRAWSON, PETER F. (1985). *Skepticism and Naturalism: Some Varieties*. London: Methuen.

WINCH, PETER (1987). 'Ceasing to Exist', in *Trying to Make Sense*. Oxford: Blackwell.

—— (1989). *Simone Weil: 'The Just Balance'*. Cambridge: Cambridge University Press.

—— (1993). 'Discussion of Malcolm's Essay', in Norman Malcolm, *Wittgenstein: A Religious Point of View?* London: Routledge.

—— (1997). 'Critical Notice', *Philosophical Investigations*, 20.1: 51–64.

WITTGENSTEIN, LUDWIG (1961). *Tractatus Logico-Philosophicus*, trans. D. F. Pears and B. F. McGuinness. London: Routledge & Kegan Paul.

—— (1967). *Zettel*, ed. G. E. M. Anscombe and G. H. Von Wright, trans. G. E. M. Anscombe. Oxford: Basil Blackwell.

—— (1993). 'Cause and Effect: Intuitive Awareness', in James Klagge and Alfred Nordmann eds., *Ludwig Wittgenstein: Philosophical Occasions 1912–1951*. Indianapolis: Hackett Publishing Company.

—— (1993). *On Certainty*, ed. G. E. M. Anscombe and G. H. Von Wright, trans. G. E. M. Anscombe. Oxford: Basil Blackwell.

—— (1997). *Philosophical Investigations*, 2nd edn, ed. G. E. M. Anscombe and R. Rhees, trans. G. E. M. Anscombe. Oxford: Blackwell.

—— (1998). *Remarks on the Foundations of Mathematics*, ed. G. E. M. Anscombe, R. Rhees, and G. H. von Wright, trans. G. E. M. Anscombe. Oxford: Blackwell.

WOLGAST, ELIZABETH (1994). 'Primitive Reactions', *Philosophical Investigations*, 17: 587–603.

PART IV

PHILOSOPHY OF MIND

CHAPTER 17

WITTGENSTEIN ON THE FIRST PERSON

WILLIAM CHILD

QUESTIONS about the self, the use of 'I', and the first-person point of view arise throughout Wittgenstein's writings. I shall focus here on two interrelated issues. First, what is the function and significance of the first-person pronoun? Second, what is the relation between the first-person point of view – the point of view that each of us has on ourselves, our experiences, and our mental states – and the second- or third-person point of view – the point of view we adopt towards others, their experiences, and their mental states?[1]

WITTGENSTEIN'S TREATMENT OF 'I'

The use of 'I' as subject and the use of 'I' as object

A famous passage from the *Blue Book* provides a good way into Wittgenstein's discussion:

> There are two different cases in the use of the word 'I' (or 'my') which I might call 'the use as object' and 'the use as subject'. Examples of the first kind of use are these: 'My arm is broken', 'I have grown six inches', 'I have a bump on my forehead', 'The wind blows my hair about'. Examples of the second kind are: '*I* see so-and-so', '*I* hear so-and-so', '*I* try to lift my arm', '*I* think it will rain', '*I* have toothache'. One can point to the difference between these two categories by saying: The cases of the first category involve the recognition of a particular person, and there is in these cases the possibility of an error, or as I should rather put it: The possibility of an error has been

---

[1] I shall not discuss any differences between the second-person and third-person points of view. So, throughout, I abbreviate 'second- or third-person' to 'third-person'.

provided for....It is possible that, say in an accident, I should feel a pain in my arm, see a broken arm at my side, and think it is mine, when really it is my neighbour's. And I could, looking into a mirror, mistake a bump on his forehead for one on mine. On the other hand, there is no question of recognizing a person when I say I have toothache. To ask 'are you sure that it's *you* who have pains?' would be nonsensical. Now, when in this case no error is possible, it is because the move which we might be inclined to think of as an error, a 'bad move', is no move of the game at all....And now this way of stating our idea suggests itself: that it is as impossible that in making the statement 'I have toothache' I should have mistaken another person for myself, as it is to moan with pain by mistake, having mistaken someone else for me. To say 'I have pain' is no more a statement *about* a particular person than moaning is. (BB, 66–7)

That passage introduces a number of themes that run through Wittgenstein's discussions of 'I': the question whether the use of 'I' involves the recognition of a person; the observation that there is a class of first-person statements that are immune from certain kinds of error; the claim that someone who utters the sentence 'I have a pain' is not making a statement about a particular person. I shall start with the issue of immunity to error.

When 'I' is used 'as object', Wittgenstein says, 'the possibility of an error has been provided for'; when 'I' is used 'as subject', 'no error is possible'. But it is important to be clear about the kind of error Wittgenstein has in mind. On the face of it, someone who asserts 'I have a bump on my forehead' or 'I have toothache' is doing two things: she is saying which person has a particular property (it is *I* rather than *you* who has a bump or a toothache); and she is saying what property that person has (I have a *bump* rather than a scratch, or a *toothache* rather than a headache). A question about the possibility of error arises in each case: can the subject be wrong about *which person it is* who has a bump or a toothache?; and can she be wrong that what that person has is *a bump* or *a toothache*? Discussions of self-knowledge typically focus on the possibility of errors of the second kind: it is often argued, for example, that while a subject can be wrong about whether she has a bump on her forehead, she cannot be wrong about whether or not she is currently in pain. Wittgenstein is certainly interested in that issue and he discusses it elsewhere. (See, for example, PI §288.) But that is not the topic of the *Blue Book* passage. He is concerned in that passage with the first kind of error: when I assert 'I have a bump on my forehead', is it possible for me to be right that *someone* has a bump on his forehead but wrong that it is *I* who have a bump on my forehead; and when I assert 'I have toothache', is it possible for me to be right that *someone* has toothache but wrong that it is *I* who have toothache? In the case of toothache, Wittgenstein argues, such a mistake is impossible: 'To ask "are you sure that it's *you* who have pains?" would be nonsensical.' Using a piece of contemporary terminology, we can put Wittgenstein's point by saying that the judgement 'I have toothache' is *immune to error through misidentification*.[2] But, he thinks, the judgements 'I have a bump on my forehead' or 'My arm is broken' are not immune to error of this kind.

---

[2] The phrase 'immunity to error through misidentification' was introduced by Sydney Shoemaker in Shoemaker 1994 [1968]. For some important discussions of the phenomenon, see: Evans 1982, ch. 7.2; Cassam 1997, ch. 2.7; Campbell 2002, ch. 5.3.

Suppose I judge that I have a bump on my forehead because I see someone in the mirror with a bump on his forehead and think that that person is me. In that situation, it is possible for me to be right that *someone* (the person I see in the mirror) has a bump on his forehead but wrong that that person is *me*. Similarly for the case in which I judge that my arm is broken because I see a broken arm at my side and think that the arm is mine.

It is clear that Wittgenstein has identified a genuine feature of certain self-ascriptions: immunity to error through misidentification. And it is clear that we can distinguish between self-ascriptions that are immune to this kind of error and self-ascriptions that are not; that is the point of Wittgenstein's distinction between the use of 'I' as subject and the use of 'I' as object. But has he drawn the distinction in the right place? The list of examples he gives might suggest that, in Wittgenstein's view, 'I' is used as subject when it is used in self-ascribing a mental property and as object when it is used in self-ascribing a physical property. Two questions arise: Would such a view be correct? And is it really Wittgenstein's view?

The answer to the first question is 'no': it is wrong to align the as-subject/as-object distinction with the distinction between mental self-ascriptions and physical self-ascriptions.[3] Consider the judgement that my legs are crossed. That judgement self-ascribes a physical property. But whether or not I could be wrong that it is *my* legs that are crossed depends on the basis upon which I make the judgement. In normal circumstances, I know whether or not my legs are crossed on the basis of how they feel 'from the inside'. And when the judgement that my legs are crossed is made on that basis, it is immune to error through misidentification; if I assert that my legs are crossed on the basis of feeling them to be crossed, it would be entirely out of place to ask 'are you sure that it's *you* whose legs are crossed?' But there are abnormal cases where things are different. Suppose I have been anaesthetized. In that case, I cannot feel my legs at all. So if I want to know whether they are crossed, I will need to look and see whether they are crossed – just as, if I want to know whether someone else's legs are crossed, I have to look at her legs and see. And when the judgement that my legs are crossed is made on that basis it will not be immune to error through misidentification; it will be possible for me to be right that someone's legs are crossed but wrong that *my* legs are crossed – because I see some legs, see that they are crossed, and wrongly think that they are my legs.[4]

What of the second question posed above? It is commonly assumed that Wittgenstein thinks that it is only in mental self-ascriptions that 'I' is used as subject – so only mental self-ascriptions that can be immune to error through misidentification.[5] But there is a

---

[3] This point is well made by Evans 1982, 218–20.

[4] The case considered in this paragraph shows that there are self-ascriptions of *physical* properties that are immune to error through misidentification. Evans also offers an example of a *mental* self-ascription that is *not* immune to error through misidentification (see 1982, 219–20).

[5] Hans Sluga, for example, thinks Wittgenstein's examples 'make clear that he means to say that we use "I" (or "my") to refer to an object when we use it to speak of a human body and its physical characteristics….The word "I" is used as subject, on the other hand, when we speak of mental states, mental processes, and sensations' (1996, 335). For the same claim, see David Bakhurst 2001, 232. And Evans suggests that, in pointing out that self-ascriptions of physical properties may be immune to error through misidentification, he is disagreeing with Wittgenstein.

good case for denying that interpretative claim. For the *Blue Book* contains a discussion of our judgements about the position and movement of our own limbs in which Wittgenstein is clear that such judgements are typically made on a distinctively first-person basis, a basis different from that on which we make judgements about the position and movement of other people's limbs.[6] I can know that my finger moves from my tooth to my eye, he notes, on the basis of my tactile and kinaesthetic sensations. But in such a case, there is no possibility of my being right that *someone's* finger moved but wrong that *my* finger moved; when the judgement that my finger moved is made on the basis of tactile and kinaesthetic sensations of movement, there is no room for the question 'are you sure it was *your* finger that moved?' That strongly suggests that the *Blue Book* is not committed to the view that *all* self-ascriptions of physical properties involve 'as object' uses of 'I'.[7]

Some writers have criticized Wittgenstein's discussion of the distinction between as-subject and as-object uses of 'I'. For example, it is sometimes complained that he says too little about the connections between the two kinds of use, and thus makes it hard to understand how the first-person and third-person aspects of mental phenomena fit together.[8] And some have argued that Wittgenstein is wrong about the precise kinds of mistake that are possible in as-object cases.[9] Nonetheless, the idea that there is a distinction between as-subject and as-object uses of 'I', and the observation that self-ascriptions made on a distinctively first-personal basis are immune to error through

---

[6] See BB, 50–53. The *Blue Book* discussion also makes the reverse point – that, though we normally judge the position and movement of our own limbs on a distinctively first-person basis, we may on occasion make such judgements on the same basis that we use in making judgements about others' limbs: by looking and seeing.

[7] In a later, post-*Blue-Book* discussion of our judgements of the position and movement of our limbs, Wittgenstein argues against the idea that we make such judgements on the basis of kinaesthetic *sensations* (see PI II, viii). Such knowledge, he thinks, is *direct* or *immediate*; it is not reached *via* knowledge of a sensation. (He offers a comparison: 'I may be able to tell the direction from which a sound comes only because it affects one ear more strongly than the other, but I don't feel this in my ears', PI II, 185.) This later argument challenges the detail of the *Blue Book* account. But it does not challenge the *Blue Book* idea that we normally make such judgements in a distinctively first-personal way – a way that is unavailable for judgements about other people's limbs.

[8] For a complaint of this sort, see Sluga 1996, 336: 'Wittgenstein admits the existence of connections between statements like "My arm is broken" and "I am in pain" but fails to account for these connections. As a result, he comes close to a "conceptual dualism" on which the two utterances belong to two different language games and are, thus, logically and conceptually independent of each other.'

[9] See Glock and Hacker 1996, 100: 'the suggestion that referential error is possible in the "objective" case is questionable....Wittgenstein is right that I might be mistaken in saying "I have a broken arm" because I have mistaken my arm for yours, for example in a rugby scrum. But even in such cases I do not *misidentify* myself or *mistake* myself for you.' (Bakhurst makes similar points in 2001, 232.) These criticisms are misplaced. In the first place, when Wittgenstein says that 'the possibility of an error has been provided for' in the as-object case, he is not talking about the possibility of *referential* error – the possibility that my use of 'I' may fail to refer, or may refer to someone other than me; he is talking about the possibility that I may be wrong in thinking that it is I who have the property that I am ascribing to myself. In the second place, Wittgenstein's idea about the rugby scrum case is not that I mistake myself for someone else; it is that I mistake someone else for me. And that seems an entirely appropriate description of the case: I see that *that* person has a broken arm and wrongly think that that person is me.

misidentification, have been widely accepted. By contrast, the concluding claim of the quoted *Blue Book* passage – 'To say "I have a pain" is no more a statement *about* a particular person than moaning is' – has attracted much less agreement. There at least two dimensions to Wittgenstein's claim. There is the idea that someone who says 'I have a pain' is not *making a statement*, but doing something else: *expressing* their pain, say, or giving a *cry of complaint*.[10] And there is the idea that, when I say 'I have a pain', my intention is not to say something about *a particular person* but to say something about *myself*.[11] These ideas are part of a strand in Wittgenstein's discussion that many readers find implausible. In discussing these less popular features of Wittgenstein's treatment, I shall not defend all that he says. But I will suggest that, when we look closely at what he says and understand why he says it, his views seem less bizarre and more insightful then they are often taken to be.

The eliminability of 'I'

Wittgenstein holds that 'The word "I" belongs to those words that can be eliminated from language' (WVC, 49). And he writes:

> One of the most misleading representational techniques in our language is the use of the word 'I', particularly when it is used in representing immediate experience, as in 'I can see a red patch'.
>
> It would be instructive to replace this way of speaking with another in which immediate experience would be represented without using the personal pronoun; for then we'd be able to see that the previous representation wasn't essential to the facts. (PR, 88)

The alternative way of speaking that Wittgenstein envisages is one in which 'I have a pain' and 'I think' would be replaced by 'There is a pain' and 'It is thinking'. In advancing these claims about the eliminability and misleadingness of 'I', he is making two main points.

First, there is the claim that the self – the subject of experience – does not and could not show up in the content of experience. Part of Wittgenstein's case for that claim is phenomenological:

> The experience of feeling pain is not that a person 'I' has something. I distinguish an intensity, a location, etc. in the pain, but not an owner. (PR, 94)

That makes the point for the case of bodily sensations. And Wittgenstein makes the same observation about visual experience:

> Visual space has essentially no owner…The essential thing is that the representation of visual space is the representation of an object and contains no suggestion of a subject. (PR, 100)

---

[10] For more on this theme, see PI II, ix.

[11] A similar thought is expressed in PI §405: '"But at any rate when you say 'I am in pain', you want to draw the attention of others to a particular person." – The answer might be: No, I want to draw their attention to *myself*.'

As well as this phenomenological point about the character of experience, there is a logical or conceptual claim: that the subject of my experience *could not* itself occur as an element in that experience. This is a claim that is made in the *Tractatus*:

> If I wrote a book called *The World as I found It*, I should have to include a report on my body, and should have to say which parts were subordinate to my will, and which were not, etc., this being a method of isolating the subject, or rather of showing that in an important sense there is no subject; for it alone could *not* be mentioned in that book. (TLP 5.631)

Wittgenstein's point is not just that I *do not* encounter the subject in experience, but that I *could not* do so.[12] And he continues to press the point in later writings – often in connection with the *Tractatus* analogy between the position of the subject in relation to consciousness and the position of the eye in relation to the visual field: for example, 'it makes no sense to say: "I see the seeing eye"' (BT, 332). So one reason why the use of 'I' is not 'logically essential' (PR, 88) in the representation of immediate experience, Wittgenstein thinks, is that there is, and could be, no element in the experience I have when I am in pain, or when I see an object, that corresponds to the word 'I' in the report of those experiences. That is why we could, without loss, 'replace [the ordinary] way of speaking by another in which immediate experience would be represented without using the personal pronoun' (PR, 88).

There is a second line of thought that leads in a different way to the conclusion that the word 'I' could be eliminated, and which has nothing specially to do with the nature of experience. This line of thought relates to the crucial role of context – specifically, the physical identity of the speaker – in determining what is said by someone who utters a sentence containing 'I'. Wittgenstein writes:

> 'I have a pain' is a sign of a completely different kind when I am using the proposition, from what it is to me on the lips of another; the reason being that it is senseless, as far as I'm concerned, on the lips of another until I know through which mouth it was expressed. The propositional sign in this case doesn't consist in the sound alone, but in the fact that the sound came out of this mouth. Whereas in the case in which I say or think it, the sign is the sound itself. (PR, 93)[13]

What does this have to do with the eliminability of the word 'I'? Wittgenstein's point is that to know what has been said by an utterance of 'I have a pain' it is not enough to know which words were uttered; I must also know which person produced them or, as he puts it, which mouth they came out of. But given the role played by the fact that the words came from a particular mouth, the use of the word 'I' is inessential; the same effect could

---

[12] For discussions of the *Tractatus* passage that stress this point, see Williams 1981, 145–6; and Pears 1987, 159–60 and 167. For critical discussion of the claim itself, see Shoemaker 1994, section 2, and Cassam 1997, *passim*.

[13] See also BT, 367: 'If I say "Now I'm going there", then some things occur in the symbol that aren't contained in the sign alone. If, say, I find the sentence somewhere, written by an unknown hand, then it doesn't mean anything at all; by themselves, in the absence of a speaker, a present situation and an indication of a spatial direction, the word "I", the word "now", and "there" are meaningless.'

be achieved if we used a notation in which there was no first-person pronoun. Thus, suppose we replaced the locution 'I have a pain' with the locution 'There is pain'. To know what had been said by an utterance of 'There is pain' – to know who had been said to be in pain – I would only need to know which mouth those words had come from. So people could ascribe pains to themselves, and be perfectly well understood by others, without using 'I' at all. Perhaps it is melodramatic to say on these grounds that the word 'I' could be eliminated from the language. But the underlying point is a good one.

'I' and reference

It can seem a piece of simple common sense to say that the word 'I' is a referring expression – a word that is guaranteed, on each occasion of its use, to refer to whoever produced it. That is certainly the orthodox view in contemporary philosophy.[14] But Wittgenstein appears flatly to deny this view. 'The word "I"', he writes, 'does not designate a person' (NFL, 228). Why does he say that? And are his views defensible?

Wittgenstein's writings contain a series of negative claims about 'I'. For example:

1. The word 'I' does not mean the same as 'LW', even if I am LW (BB, 67).
2. 'I' is not the name of a person (PI §410).
3. The word 'I'…[does not] mean the same as the expression 'the person who is now speaking' (BB, 67).
4. In 'I have pain', 'I' is not a demonstrative pronoun (BB, 68).

What should we make of these claims? The first three claims turn on fundamentally the same point. When I talk about myself, I can use different words and phrases that pick me out: the first-person pronoun; my name; a description that uniquely applies to me; and so on.[15] But amongst these various ways of picking myself out, 'I' is distinctive in the way it is tied to the first-person point of view. When I pick myself out using my name or a description, my success in referring to myself does not depend on the fact that the person I am picking out is *myself*; other people can use my name or a description to pick me out in the exactly the same way as I do. Accordingly, I can in principle pick myself out in these ways without realizing that the person I am picking out is *me*. Suppose I have forgotten my name. Then I might judge on the basis of media reports that the police are looking for William Child but fail to realize that the police are looking for me. By

---

[14] For expressions of that view see: Barwise and Perry 1981, 670: 'Whenever [the expression "I"] is used by a speaker of English, it stands for, or designates, that person'; Kaplan 1989, 505: '"I" refers to the speaker or writer…of the relevant occurrence of the word "I"'; Strawson 1994, 210: 'the first personal pronoun refers, on each occasion of its use, to whoever then uses it'; Shoemaker 1994, 91: the meaning of 'I' is given by the rule that it refers to the person who uses it'; Campbell 1994, 102: 'Any token of "I" refers to whoever produced it.' For other formulations, and discussion of differences between them, see de Gaynesford 2006, ch. 2.

[15] As we shall see, Wittgenstein argues that I do not use 'I' to *pick myself out* at all. But it is harmless for present purposes to express things in the way I just have done.

contrast, when I pick myself out using 'I', my success in referring to myself *does* essentially depend on the fact that the person picked out is myself. Accordingly, I cannot be in the position of using 'I' to pick myself out but failing to realize that the person I am picking out is *me*. One way of bringing out this difference between 'I' and other expressions is to think about the difference in their implications for action. If I judge 'I am about to be attacked by a bear', my judgement has immediate consequences for my behaviour; I know that I must take avoiding action. But I may judge 'William Child is about to be attacked by a bear' without that judgement's having any tendency at all to affect my behaviour; that will happen, as before, if I have forgotten my name and reach the judgement on the basis of testimony.[16] It is these and similar differences between 'I' on the one hand and names and descriptions on the other that motivate Wittgenstein's claims 1–3 in the list above. Those claims are clearly correct: 'I' is not a proper name and it is not equivalent to any definite description.

If 'I' is not a name or a description, how does it function? Wittgenstein anticipates an obvious suggestion – that 'I' is a demonstrative expression like 'this' or 'that'. But he swiftly rejects it: claim 4 says that (in 'I have pain', at least) 'I' is not a demonstrative pronoun. Why does Wittgenstein say that? The use of an ordinary demonstrative – the expression 'That man', for example – requires a perceptual link with the demonstrated object, on the basis of which one is able to distinguish it from other things. But the use of 'I' requires no perceptual link with oneself at all:

> In the cases in which 'I' is used as subject, we don't use it because we recognize a particular person by his bodily characteristics. (BB, 69)

Or again:

> What does it mean to know *who* is in pain? It means, for example, to know which man in this room is in pain: for instance, that it is the one who is sitting over there, or the one who is standing in that corner, the tall one over there with the fair hair, and so on. – What am I getting at? At the fact that there is a great variety of criteria for personal 'identity'.
>   Now which of them determines my saying that '*I* am in pain? None. (PI §404)

The fact that the use of 'I' does not require us to pick ourselves out on the basis of perceptual information, Wittgenstein thinks, is enough to show that it is not a demonstrative expression that we use to pick out a substantial, embodied person.[17] If we are nonetheless determined to hang on to the idea that 'I' is a demonstrative expression of some kind, we are liable to retreat to the claim that it is an *inner* demonstrative, an expression that each of us uses to pick out an inner ego on the basis of some kind of quasi-perceptual,

---

[16] For this example and further discussion of the issue, see Perry 1977. See also Perry 1979.

[17] G. E. M. Anscombe makes essentially the same point with a famous thought-experiment. Even if one were in a sensory deprivation tank, she says, with no perceptual information about one's body, one could still think about oneself using 'I': 'If the object meant by "I" is this body, this human being, then in these circumstances it won't be present to my senses; and how else can it be "present to" me? But have I lost what I mean by "I"?' (1994 [1975], 152). Obviously not, she thinks.

introspective contact. But, Wittgenstein says, it is an 'illusion that we use [the word 'I'] to refer to something bodiless, which, however has its seat in our body' (BB, 69). There is no inner ego for us to refer to, and no inner perception of such a thing.

Where do Wittgenstein's negative arguments leave us? He is absolutely right to say that 'I' is not a name, that it is not equivalent to any description, that it does not refer to a Cartesian ego, and that it is not a demonstrative that picks out a person on the basis of perceived bodily characteristics. But these good points do not support Wittgenstein's apparent conclusion that 'I' does not refer to a person at all: on the face of it, we could conclude, instead, that 'I' is a referring expression that has the same *reference* as a person's name but a different *sense*; it picks out the same object that can be picked out using various names or descriptions, but picks out that object in a distinctive way. But if we do treat 'I' as a referring expression, what sort of referring expression is it?

One proposal, advanced by Gareth Evans, is that despite what Wittgenstein says, 'I' does function in a way that is broadly analogous to a demonstrative; its use requires an information link with a particular human being, on the basis of which one can distinguish that human being from all other things.[18] But the information on which one's use of 'I' depends is not the kind of perceptual information one may have about oneself 'from the outside'; as Wittgenstein says, the use of 'I' does not involve recognizing oneself by one's bodily characteristics. Rather, Evans thinks, the use of 'I' is based on information about oneself that is acquired in distinctively first-personal ways: the information about one's body that is delivered by 'our proprioceptive sense, our sense of balance, of heat and cold, and of pressure' (Evans 1982, 220); the information about one's 'position, orientation, and relation to other objects in the world [that we get] upon the basis of our perceptions of the world' (Evans 1982, 222); and one's first-person knowledge of one's own mental properties. It is a consequence of Evans's view that, just as there are circumstances in which a demonstrative thought will fail to refer to anything, so there are circumstances in which an 'I' thought will fail to refer to anything. Reference failure is possible for demonstrative thoughts in cases where the perceptual information on which a thought is based is derived from a number of different objects, or is entirely hallucinatory. I may think that I am seeing a single tiger through the bushes, for example, when actually what I am glimpsing are parts of two or three different tigers. In such a situation, the thought 'That tiger is fierce', based on my perception, will fail to pick out a particular tiger; there is no determinate answer to the question, 'Which tiger were you thinking about?' Similarly, we can imagine bizarre but possible situations in which the information on which an 'I' thought is based is derived from a number of different people, or is entirely hallucinatory. In such a situation, Evans thinks, that thought will fail to single

---

[18] This formulation slightly oversimplifies Evans's view. In particular, he sees a more complex relation between one's ways of gaining information about oneself and one's knowledge of which thing one is. (On this, see Evans 1982, ch. 7 appendix 2.) But there is no need to explore those complexities here.

out a particular person. The view that an 'I' thought may fail to refer, however, has seemed to many to be plainly unacceptable.[19]

An alternative proposal is that 'I' is a referring expression whose meaning is given by the rule that any token of 'I' refers to the person who produced it.[20] This view agrees with Wittgenstein that 'I' is not like a demonstrative, whose use requires an information link with the referent. But, in holding that anyone who produces a token of 'I' thereby refers to herself, it certainly seems to disagree with Wittgenstein. This *reference-rule view* is not vulnerable to Wittgenstein's argument that 'I' is not equivalent to any description: for the view is not that 'I' *means the same as* 'the person who produced this token of "I"'; the claim is simply that every token of 'I' refers, and that its reference is determined by the rule. As I have said, an account of the meaning of 'I' of this general sort is widespread in contemporary philosophy. What would Wittgenstein say about such a view?

He would certainly reject the *slogan* 'every token of "I" refers to the person who produced it'. For he says explicitly that 'The word "I" does not *designate* a person' (NFL, 228, my emphasis); and he would surely say the same about the suggestion that 'I' *refers to* a person. Furthermore, at one point in the *Blue Book*, Wittgenstein actually considers a version of the reference-rule view: 'But surely the word "I" in the mouth of a man refers to the man who says it; it points to himself; and very often a man who says it actually points to himself with his finger' (BB, 67). He responds to that suggestion with the following comment:

> But it was quite superfluous to point to himself. He might just as well only have raised his hand. It would be wrong to say that when someone points to the sun with his hand, he is pointing both to the sun and himself because it is *he* who points; on the other hand, he may by pointing attract attention both to the sun and to himself. (BB, 67)

That is not an explicit rejection of the reference-rule view. Indeed, Wittgenstein focuses on the idea that one's use of 'I' *points to* oneself rather than the suggestion that it *refers to*

---

[19] For Evans's discussion of the possibility that an 'I' thought might fail to have an object, see 1982, 249–55. For a rejection of that possibility, see Campbell 1994, 125–7. Evans's view is more subtle than some critics have realized. For he distinguishes what we should say about 'I'-*thoughts* from what we should say about the *word* 'I'. And though he insists that there are circumstances in which a subject's 'I' thoughts can fail to refer, he allows that, in those same circumstances, the person's utterances of the word 'I' will still refer to herself. (For these claims, see 1982, 251–2.) So the relation between Evans's views and the views of those who are concerned exclusively with the reference of the word 'I' is not straightforward. (I am grateful to Daniel Morgan for emphasizing this point.)

[20] See the references in note 14 above for different formulations of this reference rule for 'I'. One could accept that 'I' is governed by such a rule without thinking that its being governed by the rule is the whole truth about its meaning. But many philosophers do make that further claim. For example, Shoemaker says that the meaning of 'I' 'is given by the rule' (1994, 91). And Barwise and Perry think that the reference rule 'is all there is to know about the meaning of *I* in English' (1981, 670).

oneself. On the other hand, Wittgenstein's response is certainly not an endorsement of the reference-rule view, either.

Wittgenstein agrees with the reference-rule view that the meaning of 'I' is given by the rules for its use:

> How does grammar explain the word 'now'? Surely via the rules it gives for its use. The same goes for the word 'I'. (BT, 367)

What is at issue, therefore, is what rules do govern the use of 'I'. Now consider the following passage:

> The mouth which says 'I' or the hand which is raised to indicate that it is I who wish to speak, or I who have toothache, does not thereby point to anything....The man who cries out with pain, or says that he has pain, *doesn't choose the mouth which says it.*
>   All this comes to saying that the person of whom we say 'he has pain' is, by the rules of the game, the person who cries, contorts his face, etc. (BB, 68)

That suggests that it is a rule for the use of 'I' that, when someone sincerely says 'I am in pain', the person of whom we may warrantedly assert '*he* is in pain' is the person who uttered the sentence.[21] And Wittgenstein agrees that the speaker who says 'I am in pain' does something (namely, uttering that sentence) that allows others to identify him as the one who is in pain. What he objects to is the idea that the speaker *refers to* himself. (In the same way, he thinks, someone who puts up his hand does something that allows others to identify him as the person who wants to speak; but he does not *point to* himself.) What seems to drive this objection is the principle that referring requires some actual activity of picking out one thing from a range of possible alternatives. But, Wittgenstein insists, when one uses 'I' one does not have to do anything to distinguish the person one picks out from other people; one simply opens one's mouth and utters the word 'I'. So, given his conception of referring, one is not *referring to oneself* at all.

Wittgenstein says what he does because he thinks of referring in epistemic terms: referring to something involves picking something out from a range of alternatives on the basis of its properties. But the reference-rule view of 'I' conceives of reference in semantic terms: 'I' is a referring expression because it has the semantic role of identifying the person whose condition is relevant to the assessment as true or false of sentences in which it occurs. And, if Wittgenstein and the reference-rule view mean different things by the claim that 'I' is (or is not) a referring expression, do we have to choose between them? Might not both claims be right? Seen from Wittgenstein's point of view, that question divides into two: is there any harm in acknowledging a sense in which 'I' refers to the person who produced it? And is there any positive reason for doing so?

To the first question, Wittgenstein's answer should be 'no'. In the discussion of the 'block', 'pillar', 'slab', 'beam' language-game at the start of *Philosophical Investigations*,

---

[21] The same rule is implicit in Wittgenstein's view that one does not know the sense (or meaning) of the sign 'I am in pain', uttered by another, unless one knows which mouth produced it. See note 13 above, and the associated text.

Wittgenstein considers the suggestion that each word *signifies* something.[22] His response is that there is no harm in saying that the word 'slab' signifies a given kind of object, that the word 'a' signifies a particular number, and so on – provided we allow that what is involved in a word's signifying what it does is very different in different cases:

> assimilating the descriptions of the uses of words in this way cannot make the uses themselves any more like one another. For, as we see, they are absolutely unlike. (PI §10)

It is in the spirit of those remarks to say that there is nothing wrong in the view that any token of 'I' refers to the person who produced it – provided that we recognize the differences between the way that 'I' refers to its producer and the ways that proper names and other terms refer to their referents. And the advocate of the reference-rule view of 'I' certainly does recognize the differences between 'I' and other referring expressions; indeed, it was the differences between 'I', on the one hand, and proper names, descriptions, and demonstratives, on the other, that helped to motivate the view. So Wittgenstein can afford to be permissive: he can allow that we may if we like say that every use of 'I' refers to the person who produced it.

By itself, however, that concession is relatively superficial. There will only be agreement between Wittgenstein and the reference-rule view if the sense in which Wittgenstein is prepared to allow that 'I' refers to the person who produced it is the same as the sense in which the reference-rule view insists that 'I' refers to its producer. And on the face of it, the two are not the same: the thesis which Wittgenstein can afford to concede employs an extremely thin and undemanding concept of reference; the concept of reference employed by the reference-rule view, by contrast, has a specific content and is embedded in an approach to meaning that is different from Wittgenstein's. The contrast emerges clearly when we ask if there is any reason why we *should* say that 'I' refers to the person who produced it – anything we will lose if we do not regard 'I' as a referring expression. Wittgenstein thinks there is not. To achieve a philosophical understanding of the meaning of 'I', he thinks, we need to describe its role in detail: the way in which the subject can use 'I' without needing to select herself from a number of possible objects; the way in which the hearer can move from the fact that X produced the sentence 'I am F' to the fact that it is X who has been said to be F; the way in which the use of 'I' depends on a background of contingent facts that make it natural to treat 'our bodies [as] the principle of individuation' of subjects (PR 90);[23] and so on. Once we have described the use of 'I' in detail, we can if we want say that 'I' refers to the person who produced it; that is the point made in the previous paragraph. But nothing is added to our account by

---

[22] For Wittgenstein's description of the language-game see PI §§2, 8. For the suggestion that each word signifies something, see PI §10.

[23] For reflections on the part played in determining the individuation conditions of subjects by the contingent relations between the bodily causes of experience and their physical expression, see PR, 88–96, especially 90, 95. For imagined cases in which it would be natural to individuate subjects in ways that differ from the ordinary one, see BB, 61–2.

incorporating this talk of reference. There is, in Wittgenstein's account, no important philosophical job to be done by the notion of reference: no philosophical purpose that requires us to organize the diverse uses of different words in terms of the framework of reference and predication.

It is here that there is a real and deep disagreement between Wittgenstein and the reference-rule view of 'I'. The reference-rule view recognizes the differences between the functioning of 'I' and the functioning of other referring expressions. But it insists that we must also recognize the similarities. When I say 'NN is tall', I say something that is capable of being true or false; and the truth or falsity of the sentence turns on whether the person picked out by my use of 'NN' is indeed tall. Similarly, when I say 'I am tall', I say something that is capable of being true or false; and the truth or falsity of the sentence turns on whether the person picked out by my use of 'I' is indeed tall. Whatever the differences between 'I' and 'NN', they are alike in this respect: each serves to identify the person whose condition is relevant to the assessment as true or false of sentences in which it occurs. That is something we have to recognize if we are to achieve a proper reflective understanding of language – to 'command a clear view of the aim and functioning of … words', as Wittgenstein puts it (PI §§5, 122).

I suggested above that we might combine Wittgenstein's insights about the phenomenology and epistemology of 'I' with the reference-rule view of the semantics of 'I'. Wittgenstein is right (I said) that the use of 'I' involves no epistemic activity of picking out one thing from a range of alternatives; but that is consistent with the claim that 'I' plays the semantic role of referring to the person who produces it. I do not, however, pretend that Wittgenstein himself would welcome this suggestion. In the first place, he does not think of his observations as bearing on the epistemology of 'I' *rather than* its meaning; he thinks of his account of the use of 'I', with its emphasis on what I have characterized as epistemic features, as itself being an account of the meaning of 'I'. Similarly, Wittgenstein will not be persuaded by the considerations I offered in favour of the claim that, in 'I am tall', 'I' plays the semantic role of identifying the person who is being said to be tall. I emphasized that someone who says 'I am tall' says something that is true or false, and that the truth or falsity of what she says depends on whether she, the person who uttered the words, is indeed tall. But on Wittgenstein's view, the meaning of a sentence is not to be explained in terms of its truth-conditions. For one thing, the use of words in utterances that are not capable of being true or false (orders, questions, and so on) is just as basic and important as their use in utterances that are. (See e.g. PI §§19–24.) For another thing, even where an utterance *is* susceptible of truth or falsity, that is just one aspect of its use amongst others; it is not the *basic* feature, from which other aspects follow. (See PI §§136–7.) And if meaning is not to be understood in terms of truth-conditions, we cannot support the view that 'I' should be classified as a referring expression by appeal to its role in determining the truth-conditions of utterances in which it occurs.

Someone who wants to defend the suggested accommodation between Wittgenstein's epistemological insights and the referential view of 'I' may respond in at least two ways. She might defend a truth-conditional conception of meaning against Wittgenstein's arguments, and thereby defend the idea that the meaning of 'I' is a matter of its contribution to determining the truth-conditions of utterances. Alternatively, she might accept Wittgenstein's arguments against a truth-conditional approach but argue that whatever alternative view of meaning we adopt, we will still need to recognize a category of singular referring expressions and to classify 'I' as a member of that category.[24] I shall not pursue those responses here. But we should recognize what has emerged: that there is no way of resolving the debate between Wittgenstein and the reference-rule view without reaching a verdict on Wittgenstein's views about meaning in general. For my own part, I see no prospect for understanding the use of 'I' without regarding it as belonging to a theoretically significant category of referring expressions. That is compatible with acknowledging that there is a lot that is right in Wittgenstein's discussion of 'I' – even if it means accommodating some of his insights in ways that differ from those in which he presents them.

THE FIRST-PERSON POINT OF VIEW

How should we understand the asymmetry between our relation to our own experiences and attitudes and our relation to other people's experiences and attitudes? I start by considering Wittgenstein's view of that asymmetry as it appears in *Philosophical Investigations*. Then I discuss the route he took to reach that position.

The first-person point of view in *Philosophical Investigations*

One of Wittgenstein's aims in *Philosophical Investigations* is to offer an account of the 'language-game' of ascribing sensations and attitudes to oneself and others that does justice to both first-person and third-person aspects of the mental, while avoiding the twin extremes of Cartesian introspectionism, on the one hand, and behaviourism, on the other. Thus Wittgenstein rejects the Cartesian metaphysics of sensation, on which sensations are conceived as 'private objects' with purely introspective identity conditions. He rejects the associated semantics, on which sensation words get their meanings in the first-person case by direct attachment to introspected sensations and in the third-person case by some sort of extension from there. And he rejects the Cartesian epistemology, on which each person has infallible knowledge of her own sensations but can only guess at the character of other people's. Similarly, he rejects the behaviourist's metaphysical view and its associated semantics and epistemology. More positively, he thinks there are 'internal', or conceptual, relations between conscious mental phenomena and behaviour. So the sensations that one self-ascribes without reference to one's behaviour are also, by their nature, ascribable by others on the basis of that behaviour.[25]

---

[24] For an approach of this sort, see Brandom 1994.
[25] Wittgenstein tends to deny that someone who utters the sentence 'I have toothache' *self-ascribes* a sensation, preferring to say that she *expresses* her sensation. I comment on that tendency below. For the purposes of the present section, nothing turns on this issue.

Sensation words are univocal in these first-person and third-person uses. And grasping the meanings of sensation words requires grasping both their first-person and third-person aspects. One cannot, Wittgenstein argues, start with a purely introspective concept of sensation – a concept that has no links to external circumstances or behaviour – and extrapolate from the first-person case to an understanding of what it is for other people to have sensations. For one thing, it is impossible to form a purely introspective concept of sensation.[26] For another thing, even if we *could* form such a concept, we could make no sense of applying it to others.[27]

One upshot of these points is that, on Wittgenstein's view, there is an important sense in which the first-person and third-person cases are on a par: each is essential to our concepts of sensations and mental states; and neither is more fundamental than the other. At the same time, Wittgenstein insists on the asymmetry between the first-person and third-person cases: our relation to our own sensations and attitudes, he thinks, is fundamentally different from our relation to others' sensations and attitudes. I shall sketch and comment on his account of these differences.

We can start with the case of sensations. A first element in Wittgenstein's account of the asymmetry is that, whereas I learn about others' sensations from their behaviour, 'I cannot be said to learn of [my own sensations]. I *have* them' (PI §246). The same goes for mental images:

> What is the criterion for the sameness of two images? – What is the criterion for the redness of an image? For me, when it is someone else's image: what he says and does. For myself, when it is my image: nothing. And what goes for 'red' also goes for 'same'.
> (PI §377)

I find out about the character of others' mental images from what they say and do. But there is no question of *finding out about* the character of my own images. The redness of my image, Wittgenstein thinks, is not something I *learn about*: it is immediately manifest to me. Similarly, when I say that someone else has toothache, my identification of her sensation as a toothache has to go via observation of her behaviour. But when I say that I have toothache, I do not identify the sensation on the basis of behavioural or introspective criteria; I simply produce the word 'toothache' immediately.[28] All this seems right: there obviously is an asymmetry between the first-person and third-person cases, and Wittgenstein puts his finger on an important element of that asymmetry.

A second element in Wittgenstein's account of the asymmetry concerns the cognitive status of first-person and third-person judgements. Here, what he says is more contentious.

---

[26] That is the burden of the 'private language argument' of PI §§243ff.

[27] See in particular PI §302 and §§351–2. In much earlier writings Wittgenstein was already rejecting the account of the concept of other minds that is criticized in PI. See, for example, PR, 91: 'In explaining the proposition "He has toothache", we even say something like: "Quite simple, I know what it means for *me* to have toothache, and when I say he has toothache, I mean he now has what I once had."' It is clear in *Philosophical Remarks* that Wittgenstein is already rejecting that explanation.

[28] There is an obvious parallel with Wittgenstein's account, discussed above, of the difference between identifying *someone else* as the subject of a sensation, which involves applying criteria of identity, and identifying *oneself*, which does not.

His target is the view that we have infallible knowledge of our own sensations but can never really know about other people's sensations. He disputes both parts of that view. Concerning the first-person case: 'it can't be said of me at all (except perhaps as a joke) that I *know* I am in pain. What is it supposed to mean – except perhaps that I *am* in pain?' (PI §246). And concerning the third-person case: 'other people very often know when I am in pain' (PI §246); 'I can be as *certain* of someone else's sensations as of any fact' (PI II, 224). Commentators have generally accepted Wittgenstein's second claim: that there is no principled barrier to knowledge of another person's sensations. His first claim, though – that it is illegitimate to talk of knowledge of one's own sensations – has puzzled readers. But even if we disagree with him, we can understand why he says it. On Wittgenstein's view, talk of *knowing* that p is appropriate only in cases where we find out that p on the basis of evidence, where it is possible for one's belief that p to be wrong, and where one can doubt whether p is true. But none of those conditions applies, he thinks, in the case of one's current pains: I do not find out that I am in pain on the basis of evidence; I cannot be wrong in thinking that I am in pain; and I cannot intelligibly doubt whether the sensation I am now having is a pain.[29] Suppose we agree with Wittgenstein that in the case of self-ascriptions of pain, his conditions for the appropriateness of talk about knowledge are not satisfied.[30] We need not agree with his conclusion that 'I know I am in pain' is either meaningless or equivalent to 'I am in pain'. For we need not agree that the concept of knowledge is subject to the conditions he sets out. Suppose we have a more relaxed view of knowledge: for example, the view that one knows that p just in case p is true, one believes that p, and one's belief that p is reached by a reliable method. Then we could accept all that Wittgenstein says about the distinctiveness of our relation to our own pains whilst retaining the common-sense thought that, when one is in pain, one knows that one is in pain. For when I am in pain, I typically satisfy these more relaxed conditions for knowing that I am in pain: it is true that I am in pain; I believe that I am in pain; and my belief is reached by a reliable method – namely, judging that I am in pain on the basis of the feeling.

A third feature of Wittgenstein's account is his claim that, while someone who says 'Mary is in pain' thereby makes a statement about Mary, someone who says 'I am in pain' is not normally *making a statement* about herself. That recalls his claim, discussed above, that someone who says 'I have pain' is not *referring to* herself. And the issues involved are exactly parallel – for Wittgenstein's epistemic conception of reference is matched by an epistemic conception of what it is for something to be a statement:

> To call the expression of a sensation a *statement* is misleading because 'testing', 'justification', 'confirmation', 'reinforcement' of the statement are connected with the word 'statement' in the language-game. (Z §549)

[29] See PI §288: 'if anyone said "I do not know if what I have got is a pain or something else", we should think something like, he does not know what the English word "pain" means.'

[30] It is not clear that we *should* agree this. The sensation of pain is so simple and vivid that there is some plausibility in Wittgenstein's view that if someone is uncertain about whether the word 'pain' applies to her current sensation then she does not understand the word. But the view could certainly be disputed. And for arguments against the claim that we cannot go wrong in judging that a given sensation is a pain, see Churchland 1988, 76–7, and Williamson 2000, 14.

On this view, something counts as a statement only if it is subject to certain kinds of epistemic procedures: testing, confirmation, and so forth. Given this conception of a statement, Wittgenstein is right to say that someone who utters the sentence 'I am in pain' will not normally be making a statement about herself. That is clearly so in cases where an utterance of 'I'm in pain' most closely resembles a moan or a cry of pain – cases where the words are an immediate, involuntary expression of pain. But it seems equally true of most other utterances of the same sentence. If the doctor asks how I am feeling, and I reply that I am still in pain, my utterance is not an *expression* of pain. But nor am I putting forward the claim that I am in pain for testing, confirmation, or reinforcement; its truth is immediately evident to me. Given his conception of a statement, then, Wittgenstein is right to say what he does. But we surely need another concept too, on which someone who utters the sentence 'I am in pain' does count as making a statement about herself, in virtue of producing a sentence that is capable of being true or false and whose truth or falsity depends on whether she herself is in pain. As in the cases of reference and knowledge, Wittgenstein's comments are based on a genuine asymmetry between the first-person and third-person cases. But the concept of a statement that they depend on is needlessly restrictive.[31]

Thus far, we have been considering Wittgenstein's treatment of the asymmetry between first-person and third-person ascriptions of *sensations*. But he applies parallel considerations in the case of attitudes, motives, and so on. Thus, he thinks, I learn about your intentions by observing what you do and say. But I do not normally *learn about* my own intentions; I can simply state them, without needing any grounds at all:

> If someone asks me 'Which of [two friends with the same name] are you writing to?' and I answer him, do I infer the answer from the antecedents? Don't I give it almost as I say 'I have toothache'? (Z §7)

Similarly, Wittgenstein thinks, while I can state my own motives immediately, I can know another's motives only from what he says and does: 'If he is sincere he will tell us [what his motives are]; but I need more than sincerity to guess his motives' (PI II, 224). And he explores the difference between my relation to other people's beliefs and my relation to my own:

> This is how I think of it: Believing is a state of mind. It has duration; and that independently of the duration of its expression in a sentence, for example. So it is a kind of disposition of the believing person. This is shown me in the case of someone else by his behaviour; and by his words. And under this head, by the expression 'I believe...' as well as by the simple assertion. (PI II, 191–2)

What does this picture of belief imply about the first-person case?

---

[31] Of course Wittgenstein would not agree that his conception of a statement is *needlessly* restrictive: his conception is part of a wider project that involves challenging the centrality of truth-conditions and emphasizing other aspects of our use of words. But to the extent that Wittgenstein's conception really does seem counterintuitive and restrictive, that gives us some reason for dissatisfaction with the overall picture of which it is a part.

What about my own case: how do I myself recognize my own disposition? – Here it will have been necessary for me to take notice of myself as others do, to listen to myself talking, to be able to draw conclusions from what I say!

My own relation to my words is wholly different from other people's. (PI II, 192)

But Wittgenstein does not endorse the suggestion that in judging 'I believe that *p*' I must 'take notice of myself as others do'. He formulates the suggestion only in order to reject it; there is, he thinks, no question of my having to *recognize* my own disposition. As he puts it, my relation to my words – and to the beliefs they express – is different from my relation to others' words and beliefs. In particular, my assertion 'He believes that *p*' needs some basis in his behaviour; but I normally need no basis for the assertion 'I believe that *p*'. Of course, as Wittgenstein acknowledges, it is *possible* to stand back and consider oneself as one would consider another person. And when one adopts that point of view, one *does* consider one's behaviour and learn about one's beliefs on the basis of evidence. Thus 'it is possible to think out circumstances in which [the] words ["Judging from what I say, *this* is what I believe"] would make sense' (PI II, 192). But, Wittgenstein insists, such cases are necessarily the exception.[32]

What follows from these observations about the first-person case? The natural view is that, just as 'He believes that *p*' is true in virtue of his possession of a certain kind of disposition, so 'I believe that *p*' is true in virtue of my possession of the same kind of disposition. The difference is that, whereas I have to observe his behaviour in order to know that he has the relevant disposition, I can know that I believe that *p* – and thus that I have the relevant disposition – without observing myself or my behaviour at all. It is clear that Wittgenstein would not put things in that way. In the first place, he regards the claim that I know what I believe as misplaced or illegitimate, for reasons that parallel his reasons for rejecting the claim that I know that I am in pain. (See PI II, 221.) In the second place, he thinks that someone who says 'I believe it's going to rain' is not normally *describing her state of mind* or making a statement *about herself* at all; she is making a statement *about the weather*. 'The statement "I believe it's going to rain"', he writes, 'has a meaning like, that is to say a use like, "It's going to rain"' (PI II, 190). So the difference between 'I believe it's going to rain' and 'It's going to rain' is not (as we might have thought) that the first is a statement about oneself (albeit a statement that brings with it a commitment to a view about the weather) while the second is a statement about the weather. It is, rather, that the first is a *guarded* or *hesitant* statement about the weather, while the second is an unqualified statement. As before, however, we should be careful not to overstate the distance between Wittgenstein and what I just called 'the natural view'. The reason Wittgenstein says what he does is, once more, that he sees *describing*, *stating*, and *asserting* as activities that essentially involve observation, the gathering of evidence, the possibility of error, and so on. But it is not clear that Wittgenstein has con-

---

[32] For an account of the self-ascription of belief that is heavily influenced by Wittgenstein, see Evans 1982, 224–6. For a discussion of self-knowledge that follows Wittgenstein in emphasizing the differences between our normal, engaged perspective on our attitudes and the disengaged or alienated perspective we adopt when we view our attitudes 'from the outside', see Moran 2001.

vincing reasons for objecting to the use of less epistemically loaded notions of describing, stating, and asserting on which someone who sincerely says 'I believe it's raining' not only expresses the belief that it is raining but also, and simultaneously, describes herself as having that belief and states that she has it.

Solipsism and the distinctiveness of the first-person point of view

Suppose I ask, 'How can I characterize what is distinctive about my own sensations and attitudes; how can I capture the essential difference between the case where I am in pain and the case where someone else is in pain?' Wittgenstein will give a two-part answer. First, he will list the differences discussed in the previous section: the differences between a subject's relation to her own sensations and attitudes and her relation to other people's. Second, he will make the platitudinous observation that, in the case where I am in pain, it is *I* who am in pain, and in the case where someone else is in pain, it is *the other person* who is in pain. There is, he thinks, nothing more informative to say about the distinctiveness of one's own case; we cannot go beyond or behind the ordinary way of drawing the distinction and explain in other terms what distinguishes my pain from others' pain.[33] Suppose it is suggested, for example, that we can explain the difference between my pain and others' pain by reference to the fact that, in the case where I am in pain, I *feel* the pain, whereas in the case where someone else is in pain, I cannot feel the pain. Wittgenstein will reply that that explains nothing. To say that I *feel* a pain is to say no more than that I am in pain. So to talk of an asymmetry between pains that I feel and pains that I do not feel is simply to restate the original asymmetry between my pains and others' pains; it does nothing to explain it.[34]

Now Wittgenstein's writings about experience and the first-person point of view display a persistent fascination with solipsism.[35] And the kind of solipsism that interests him arises precisely from the attempt to articulate what is distinctive about one's own sensations and mental states. Consider this passage from *Philosophical Investigations*:

---

[33] Wittgenstein makes similar comments about the distinction between genuine pain behaviour and simulated pain behaviour. The critic complains that Wittgenstein has not given a properly informative account of the difference between the two cases: 'But aren't you neglecting something – the experience or whatever you might call it – ? Almost *the world* behind the mere words?' (NFL, 255). To which Wittgenstein replies that there is no better way to capture the distinction than to use our ordinary way of speaking: '"But it seems as if you were neglecting something." But what more can I do than *distinguish* the case of saying "I have toothache" when I really have toothache, and the case of saying the words without having toothache.... Isn't what you reproach me of as though you said: "In your language you're only *speaking*!"' (NFL, 256).

[34] Compare BB, 68.

[35] For important discussions of solipsism in Wittgenstein's writings and conversations, see: NB, 49–50, 79–89; TLP 5.6–5.641; PR, 85; WVC, 45–50; MWL, 102–3; BT, 351–62; BB, 48–74; NFL, 225, 227, 255, 258, 272–4; PI §§402–3.

If I were to reserve the word 'pain' solely for what I had hitherto called 'my pain', and others 'LW's pain', I should do other people no injustice, so long as a notation were provided in which the loss of the word 'pain' in other connexions were somehow supplied. Other people would still be pitied, treated by doctors and so on. It would, of course, be *no* objection to this mode of expression to say: 'But look here, other people have just the same as you!'

But what should I gain from this new kind of account? Nothing. But after all neither does the solipsist *want* any practical advantage when he advances his view! (PI §403)

The solipsist here is someone who wants to do justice to the distinctive character of his own sensations. He does not deny that other people have sensations. But he feels that the use of the same word, 'pain', to talk about both his own sensations and other people's understates or fails to acknowledge what is distinctive about his own pains; the distinctiveness of his own case would be better represented, he feels, by reserving the use of the word 'pain' for his own pains. In the long *Blue Book* discussion of this kind of solipsism, Wittgenstein works through a series of attempts by the solipsist to formulate his solipsistic claim: 'only my pain is real pain' (BB, 57); 'only I really see (or hear)' (BB, 60); 'whenever anything is seen, it is *this* which is seen' (BB, 64); and so on. He offers the following diagnosis.

The person who comes out with these solipsistic claims starts by noticing the genuine asymmetry between the first-person case and the third-person case. The line of thought that leads to solipsism gets going with the attempt to *explain* the distinctiveness of one's own case – to put it into words in a way that does not collapse into the platitudinous observation that when I am in pain, it is *I* who am in pain. That is the point at which the solipsist finds himself tempted to say that it is only *his* pain that is *real* pain, and so on. In the quoted passage from PI §403, Wittgenstein acknowledges the possibility of adopting this solipsistic way of talking. But he is not endorsing solipsism, or acknowledging that the solipsistic way of talking succeeds in doing justice to something that is neglected in our normal way of speaking. On the contrary, he thinks the ordinary way of talking already fully accommodates the difference between the first-person and third-person points of view. And even if we did adopt the new way of talking, he thinks, it would not allow us to express anything we cannot already express in our existing way of talking: if the new forms of words have exactly the same links to the external circumstances and behavioural expression of pain as the forms of words they replace, then they mean just the same as the old forms of words. The aim of the passage, then, is to make a point about the status of disputes between realists, idealists, and solipsists: the disputants think they are having a substantive debate; but their disagreement, Wittgenstein says, turns out to be merely a dispute about terminology.[36]

The account I have been giving represents the orthodox view of Wittgenstein's *Philosophical Investigations* treatment of the asymmetry between the first-person and third-person cases. But there are, of course, dissenting interpretations. An interesting

---

[36] For parallel comments about the status of disputes between realists, idealists, and solipsists, see BB 56–7.

example comes from David Bell (1996). On the orthodox view, Bell writes, *Philosophical Investigations* represents 'a repudiation of the author's earlier solipsistic sympathies, and a presentation of a radically anti-solipsistic alternative'. Against that, Bell contends that 'the private language argument, far from comprising a rejection and refutation of solipsism, is in a number of crucial respects an endorsement and development of it' (Bell 1996, 168). So he sees PI §403 (quoted above) not as a critique of solipsism but as an expression of agreement with it. On this interpretation, Wittgenstein holds that the solipsistic terminology envisaged in PI §403 is philosophically preferable to our ordinary way of speaking, since it more accurately articulates the relation between oneself and others. And part of the point of *Philosophical Investigations* is to recommend a kind of metaphysical solipsism. But that interpretation is hard to believe. It is clearly true that Wittgenstein is concerned to give a proper account of the asymmetry between first-person and third-person cases and to acknowledge the distinctive character of the first-person case. But to see *Philosophical Investigations* as actually advancing some form of solipsism is to lose sight of an equally important aim of Wittgenstein's: the aim of doing justice to the ways in which my sensations and mental states are on a par with those of other people.[37]

The first-person point of view: the development of Wittgenstein's treatment

Wittgenstein's writings from 1929 to the mid-1930s include a number of discussions of the relation between first-person and third-person ascriptions of sensation, and of the distinctiveness of one's own experiences – often interwoven with discussions of solipsism. How should we understand these discussions? And how do they relate to the position that Wittgenstein reached in *Philosophical Investigations*? A full account of the development of Wittgenstein's views would need to cover the discussions in *Philosophical Remarks* and *Wittgenstein and the Vienna Circle*, the *Big Typescript*, the *Blue Book*, and Wittgenstein's 'Notes for Lectures on "Private Experience" and "Sense Data"'. There is room here to consider only a small selection from that literature. But that is enough to give a sense of the philosophical and interpretative issues involved.[38]

We can start with Wittgenstein's 1929 account of sensation language. We have already discussed the treatment of 'I' in *Philosophical Remarks*. But Wittgenstein's 1929 writings and conversations also deal with the other element in self-ascriptions like 'I am in pain' – our use of words for sensations:

[37] For another dissenting interpretation, see Cook 1994. Cook argues that, on Wittgenstein's view, sensation words 'have different meanings in their first-person and third-person applications' (341): purely behaviourist meanings in third-person applications (ch. 9); and pragmatic meanings (analysable in terms of the speaker's practical purposes) in first-person applications (337–8). (In earlier writings, Cook played an important part in helping to establish the standard interpretation of Wittgenstein that he now repudiates. See especially his 1965 and 1969.)

[38] For comprehensive, illuminating, and very different accounts of the development of Wittgenstein's views of sensation language and solipsism, see Hacker 1986 and Pears 1987, 1988.

We could adopt the following way of representing matters: if I, LW, have toothache, then that is expressed by means of the proposition 'There is toothache'. But if that is so, what we now express by the proposition 'A has toothache', is put as follows: 'A is behaving as LW does when there is toothache'. Similarly we shall say 'It is thinking' and 'A is behaving as LW does when it is thinking'. (You could imagine a despotic oriental state where the language is formed with the despot as its centre and his name instead of LW.) It's evident that this way of speaking is equivalent to ours when it comes to questions of intelligibility and freedom from ambiguity. But it's equally clear that this language could have anyone at all as its centre.

Now, among all the languages with different people as their centres, each of which I can understand, the one with me as its centre has a privileged status. This language is particularly adequate. How am I to express this? That is, how can I rightly represent its special advantage in words? This can't be done. For, if I do it in the language with me as its centre, then the exceptional status of the description of this language in its own terms is nothing very remarkable, and in the terms of another language my language occupies no privileged status whatever. – The privileged status lies in the application ... (PR, 88–9)

This last point is driven home in a 1929 discussion:

One of these languages has a distinctive status, namely the language whose centre I am. The distinctiveness of this language lies in its application. It is not expressed. (WVC, 50)

And a footnote links the difference in *application* to a difference in *verification*:

If A has toothache, he can say, 'Now this tooth is hurting', and this is where verification comes to an end. But B would have to say, 'A has toothache', and this proposition is not the end of a verification. This is the point where the particular status of different languages comes clearly to light. (WVC, 50)[39]

It is natural to read these passages as offering not just a *description* of the asymmetry between ascribing sensations to oneself and ascribing sensations to other people, but an *explanation* of that asymmetry. On this reading, Wittgenstein's 1929 account starts with the idea that sensations are private objects: objects that are accessible only to the subject, with identity conditions that are independent of any links to behaviour or external context. The issue addressed in the 1929 discussion is how, on that assumption, we should account for the meanings of sensation words. And the proposal is in effect that each of us has two sensation languages: a purely introspective, private sensation language for our own use; and a public sensation language with which we can communicate about sensations, our own and other people's. So my word 'toothache', say, has two different meanings. In its communicative use, 'toothache' has a purely behavioural meaning; in this

---

[39] This point survives in the 1933 discussion of sensation language in the *Big Typescript*: '"How a proposition is verified – that's what it says": and now, with this in mind, look at the propositions: "I am in pain", "N is in pain". But now what if I am N? – Then the two propositions still have different senses' (BT, 360).

sense, 'the word "toothache" means the same in "I have toothache" and "He has toothache"' (PR, 91). But my word 'toothache' can also be used with another sense, to pick out 'what is *primary*' in my experience. Used in that sense, my word cannot intelligibly be applied to anyone else; nor can its meaning be understood by anyone else.[40] Thus, when Wittgenstein says that I understand all the different languages with different people as their centres, he is referring only to the public languages centred on different people. If Jones says 'There is toothache' or 'Brown is behaving as Jones does when there is tooth-ache', I understand the public meaning of what he says; but his words also have a private meaning which I cannot understand. On this reading of the 1929 account, the solipsist who tries to capture the distinctiveness of his own pains by saying 'only I feel *real* pain' (see WVC, 50), or 'only I really have *sense data*' has a genuine insight: the words 'real pain' and 'sense data' on his lips really do have meanings on which they are applicable to him and no one else. But, on Wittgenstein's view, that very fact makes the insight inexpressible: if the proposition 'Other people have sense data' is unintelligible, he thinks, then the propositions 'Other people do not have sense data' and 'Only I have sense data' are unintelligible, too.[41] So the solipsist's genuine insight is something that can only be shown, not said. As Wittgenstein puts it, the special status of the language with me as its centre lies in its application and cannot be expressed.

This reading of the 1929 theory is very plausible.[42] But is it correct? David Pears offers a somewhat different interpretation. He agrees that in the language with me as its centre, I make 'direct, context-free references to my own bodily sensations and their types' (Pears 1988, 303). But on Pears's reading, Wittgenstein is not proposing that the intro-spectible nature of people's sensations is simply irrelevant to the communicative use of sensation words. That was the position of Schlick and Carnap in writings of this period.[43] But, Pears thinks, 'it is quite certain that Wittgenstein never went to those lengths' (Pears 1988, 307). He took it for granted that we succeed in communicating about the intro-spectible character of our sensations. And the 1929 account was intended to explain how we do so. Wittgenstein subsequently came to realize that this account would not work.[44] But, Pears thinks, behaviourism about the communicative use of sensation language was an unintended consequence of the 1929 theory; it was not something that Wittgenstein was positively advocating.

---

[40] This is 'the sense of the phrase "sense data" in which', Wittgenstein writes, 'it is inconceivable that anyone else should have them' (PR, 90).

[41] See PR, 90: 'In the sense of the phrase "sense data" in which it is inconceivable that someone else should have them, it cannot, for this very reason, be said that someone else does not have them.'

[42] It can be found, for example, in Hacker 1986, 224–6 and in Kripke 1982, 125–6.

[43] Pears cites Schlick 1949, and Carnap 1995, 76–92. On the Schlick/Carnap view, he writes, 'the content of experience remains necessarily incommunicable, but…this does not matter, because if the content of experience does vary from one person to another, the variation will necessarily remain undetectable' (Pears 1988, 303).

[44] Wittgenstein's later reason for thinking that the 1929 account would not work is summed up in the beetle-in-the-box passage at PI §293: 'if we construe the grammar of the expression of sensation on the model of "object and designation" the object drops out of consideration as irrelevant'.

On both the interpretations just outlined, Wittgenstein's 1929 account starts with the idea that sensations are private objects and that sensation words get their meanings in the first-person case by direct attachment to introspected sensations. So on these readings, the 1929 account stands in sharp contrast to Wittgenstein's view in *Philosophical Investigations*. That is the standard view of the 1929 account, and the standard view of the relation between the 1929 account and *Philosophical Investigations*. But it is worth asking whether it is possible to read these texts in a different way, which sees a greater degree of continuity between Wittgenstein's 1929 account and his mature view of sensation language. As we have seen, both *Philosophical Remarks* and *Philosophical Investigations* discuss the possibility of replacing our ordinary sensation language with a new language, in which 'I'm in pain', say, is replaced by 'There's pain', and 'Jones is in pain' is replaced by 'Jones is behaving as TWC behaves when there is pain'.[45] On the standard view, Wittgenstein uses this thought-experiment to make entirely different points in *Philosophical Remarks* and in *Philosophical Investigations*. In *Philosophical Remarks*, the point of the new terminology is to make explicit a real difference in meaning between the first-person and third-person uses of sensation words. In *Philosophical Investigations*, by contrast, Wittgenstein takes it for granted that sensation words are univocal in their first-person and third-person uses: so his point is not that the new terminology is in any way more perspicuous than the ordinary way of speaking; rather, he is arguing that, since the new terminology preserves all the connections of the old, there is nothing genuinely at issue between them. But how clear is it that the point Wittgenstein is making with the proposed new terminology in *Philosophical Remarks* and the point he is making in *Philosophical Investigations* do differ in this way? Couldn't the passages in *Philosophical Remarks* be read in the same spirit as those in *Philosophical Investigations*?

On the standard view, there is a radical shift in Wittgenstein's view of sensation language between *Philosophical Remarks* and *Philosophical Investigations*. But when did that shift take place?[46] It is notable that most of the discussion of sensation language from *Philosophical Remarks*, 88–96 – including the suggestion that 'W is in pain' and 'N is in pain' might be replaced by 'There is pain present' and 'N is behaving like W when there is pain present' – is preserved in the *Big Typescript*, 356–62, which was composed from earlier typescripts in 1933. So Wittgenstein seems to have continued to accept those parts of his *Philosophical Remarks* position as late as 1933. But less than a year later, in the first half of 1934, he was dictating the discussion of sensations and subjectivity in the *Blue Book*. And the *Blue Book* explicitly rejects the suggestion that is

---

[45] See PR, 88–9 and PI §403, both quoted above; note also PR, 93: 'The two hypotheses that other people have toothache and that they behave just as I do but don't have toothache, possibly have identical senses. That is, if I had, for example, learnt the second form of expression, I would talk in a pitying tone of voice about people who don't have toothache, but are behaving as I do when I have.' For other discussions of the same solipsistic terminology, see BT, 359–62 and BB, 59, 66.

[46] Hacker sees the *Philosophical Remarks* view of sensation language as an element in a 'brief verificationist period' (1986, 134) which characterized Wittgenstein's work in 1929 and 1930, but which was abandoned by the time of the 1932–33 lectures reported by G. E. Moore and the *Big Typescript* (1986, 144). Pears says that 'after formulating [the 1929 theory, Wittgenstein] reacted against it almost immediately' (1987, 43).

advanced in the standard reading of *Philosophical Remarks* – the suggestion that sensation words have different meanings in their first-person and third-person uses:

> What we are talking about is connected with that peculiar temptation to say: 'I never know what the other really means by "brown", or what he really sees when he (truthfully) says that he sees a brown object'. – We could propose to one who says this to use two different words instead of the one word 'brown'; one word *for his particular impression*, the other word with that meaning which other people besides himself can understand as well. If he thinks about this proposal he will see that there is something wrong in his conception of the meaning, function, of the word 'brown' and others. (BB, 72–3)

Similarly, in the *Blue Book*, the idea that we could 'adopt…a symbolism in which a certain person always or temporarily holds an exceptional place' (BB, 66) is plainly deployed in the same spirit as in the parallel passage (§403) in *Philosophical Investigations*; the solipsistic terminology is treated as a mere notational variant of our normal terminology, not as a specially perspicuous way of bringing out a real difference in meaning between first-person and third-person uses of sensation words. So if Wittgenstein did in 1929 hold the views ascribed to him by the standard reading of *Philosophical Remarks*, he had certainly abandoned them by 1934. But if his *Philosophical Remarks* view of sensation language is retained in the *Big Typescript* (and the coincidence between the two is striking) then the abandonment must have come between 1933 and 1934. And is there a story about the development of Wittgenstein's views in that year that makes this a credible interpretation?

In the light of all this, it is certainly worth taking seriously the alternative interpretation, on which Wittgenstein's 1929 account of sensation language, and of the asymmetry between the first-person and third-person cases, is much closer to the views expressed in *Philosophical Investigations*. My own view is that some version of the standard interpretation remains more plausible than this alternative. But it is clear that a satisfactory story about the development of Wittgenstein's views on these topics needs to offer a convincing account, first, of the relation between the discussions of sensation language offered in *Philosophical Remarks* and in the *Big Typescript*, and, second, of the relation of those discussions to the treatment in the *Blue Book* and *Philosophical Investigations*. Such an account, I think, has yet to be given.[47, 48]

REFERENCES

ANSCOMBE, G. E. M. (1994). 'The First Person', in Q. Cassam ed., *Self-Knowledge*. Oxford: Oxford University Press. (Originally printed in S. Guttenplan ed., *Mind and Language*. Oxford: Oxford University Press, 1975.)

[47] In a recent paper (published after the completion of this chapter), David Stern suggests a reading of PR 88–9 that is broadly along the lines of the 'alternative interpretation' briefly discussed here, highlighting the similarities between the strategy of PR 88–9 and the strategy of PT §403 (see Stern 2010). I hope to discuss that paper in future work.

[48] I am grateful to Marie McGinn and Daniel Morgan for very helpful comments on an earlier draft.

BAKHURST, DAVID (2001). 'Wittgenstein and "I"', in H. Glock ed., *Wittgenstein: A Critical Reader*. Oxford: Blackwell.

BARWISE, J. and PERRY, J. (1981). 'Situations and Attitudes', *Journal of Philosophy*, 78: 668–91.

BELL, DAVID (1996). 'Solipsism and Subjectivity', *European Journal of Philosophy*, 4: 155–74.

BRANDOM, ROBERT (1994). *Making It Explicit: Reasoning, Representing, and Discursive Commitment*. Cambridge, MA: Harvard University Press.

CAMPBELL, JOHN (1994). *Past, Space, and Self*. Cambridge, MA: MIT Press.

—— (2002). *Reference and Consciousness*. Oxford: Oxford University Press.

CARNAP, RUDOLF (1995). *The Unity of Science*, trans. M. Black. Bristol: Thoemmes Press.

CASSAM, QUASSIM (1997). *Self and World*. Oxford: Oxford University Press.

CHURCHLAND, PAUL (1988). *Matter and Consciousness*, rev. edn. Cambridge, MA: MIT Press.

COOK, JOHN W. (1965). 'Wittgenstein on Privacy', *Philosophical Review*, 74: 281–314.

—— (1969). 'Human Beings', in P. Winch ed., *Studies in the Philosophy of Wittgenstein*. London: Routledge.

—— (1994). *Wittgenstein's Metaphysics*. Cambridge: Cambridge University Press.

EVANS, GARETH (1982). *The Varieties of Reference*. Oxford: Oxford University Press.

GAYNESFORD, MAXIMILIAN DE (2006). *I: The Meaning of the First Person Term*. Oxford: Oxford University Press.

GLOCK, H. and HACKER, P. M. S. (1996). 'Reference and the First-Person Pronoun', *Language and Communication*, 16: 95–105.

HACKER, P. M. S. (1986). *Insight and Illusion*, 2nd edn. Oxford: Oxford University Press.

KAPLAN, DAVID (1989). 'Demonstratives', in J. Almog, J. Perry, and H. Wettstein eds., *Themes from Kaplan*. Oxford: Oxford University Press.

KRIPKE, SAUL (1982). *Wittgenstein on Rules and Private Language*. Oxford: Blackwell.

MOORE, G. E. (1993). 'Wittgenstein's Lectures in 1930–33', in J. Klagge and A. Nordmann eds., *Philosophical Occasions 1912–1951*. Indianapolis: Hackett.

MORAN, RICHARD (2001). *Authority and Estrangement: An Essay on Self-Knowledge*. Princeton, NJ: Princeton University Press.

PEARS, DAVID (1987). *The False Prison*, vol. I. Oxford: Oxford University Press.

—— (1988). *The False Prison*, vol. II. Oxford: Oxford University Press.

PERRY, JOHN (1977). 'Frege on Demonstratives', *Philosophical Review*, 86: 474–97.

—— (1979). 'The Problem of the Essential Indexical', *Nous*, 13: 3–21.

SCHLICK, MORITZ (1949). 'Meaning and Verification', in H. Feigl and W. Sellars eds., *Readings in Philosophical Analysis*. New York: Appleton-Century-Crofts.

SHOEMAKER, SYDNEY (1994). 'Self-Reference and Self-Awareness', in Q. Cassam ed., *Self-Knowledge*. Oxford: Oxford University Press. (Originally printed in *Journal of Philosophy*, 65 (1968): 555–67.)

SLUGA, HANS (1996). '"Whose house is that?" Wittgenstein on the self', in H. Sluga and D. Stern eds., *The Cambridge Companion to Wittgenstein*. Cambridge: Cambridge University Press.

STERN, DAVID (2010). 'Another Strand in the Private Language Argument', in A. Ahmed ed., *Wittgenstein's* Philosophical investigations: *A Critical Guide*. Cambridge: Cambridge University Press.

STRAWSON, P. F. (1994). 'The First Person – and Others', in Q. Cassam ed., *Self-Knowledge*. Oxford: Oxford University Press.

WAISMANN, FRIEDRICH (1979). *Wittgenstein and the Vienna Circle: Conversations recorded by Friedrich Waismann*, ed. B. McGuinness, trans. B. McGuinness and J. Schulte. Oxford: Blackwell.

WILLIAMS, BERNARD (1981). 'Wittgenstein and Idealism', in *Moral Luck*. Cambridge: Cambridge University Press.

WILLIAMSON, TIMOTHY (2000). *Knowledge and Its Limits*. Oxford: Oxford University Press.

WITTGENSTEIN, LUDWIG (1958). *Philosophical Investigations,* 2nd edn, ed. G. E. M. Anscombe and R. Rhees, trans. G. E. M. Anscombe. Oxford: Blackwell.

—— (1969). *The Blue and Brown Books*, 2nd edn. Oxford: Balckwell.

—— (1971). *Tractatus Logico-Philosophicus*, trans. D. Pears and B. McGuinness, 2nd edn. London: Routledge.

—— (1975). *Philosophical Remarks*, ed. R. Rhees, trans. R. Hargreaves and R. White. Oxford: Basil Blackwell.

—— (1979). *Notebooks 1914–16*, 2nd edn, ed. G. H. von Wright and G. E. M. Anscombe. trans. G. E. M. Anscombe. Oxford: Blackwell.

—— (1981). *Zettel,* 2nd edn, ed. G. E. M. Anscombe and G. H. von Wright, trans. G. E. M. Anscombe. Oxford: Blackwell.

—— (1993). 'Notes for Lectures on "Private Experience" and "Sense Data"', in J. Klagge and A. Nordmann eds., *Philosophical Occasions 1912–1951*. Indianapolis: Hackett.

—— (2005). *The Big Typescript: TS 213*, ed. and trans. G. Luckhardt and M. Aue. Oxford: Blackwell.

CHAPTER 18

....

PRIVATE EXPERIENCE
AND SENSE DATA

....

PAUL SNOWDON

IN the mid 1930s Wittgenstein was immersed in problems about, amongst other things, experience, or perhaps one might say, our thought about experience.[1] One record of his developing thinking are the notes he made, probably between 1934 and 1936, and which have been published, in *Philosophical Occasions*, as the 'Notes for Lectures on "Private Experience" and "Sense Data".[2] A second record is the notes that Rush Rhees himself made of the lectures by Wittgenstein on these topics which Rhees attended in 1936, published under the title 'The Language of Sense Data and Private Experience', also in *Philosophical Occasions*.[3] The ideas that Wittgenstein is developing in these notes and lectures culminated in the discussion of the same topics in the *Philosophical Investigations*, primarily in the intensely studied sections 243 to 315. Of course, as we shall see, Wittgenstein made remarks about, and revealed his thinking about, these topics at other places in the *Philosophical Investigations*. My impression is that practically all the ideas

---

[1] A crucial question about the development of Wittgenstein's thought is how by the mid 1930s he had transformed himself from a pure metaphysician into someone with a strong involvement with the philosophy of mind. My discussion really engages only with the transformed thought, and does not look at the developmental background. A clear, brief, and helpful description of the transformation is given in Sluga 1996.

[2] A shortened version of these notes was published by Rush Rhees in the *Philosophical Review* 1968. The complete notes are in Ludwig Wittgenstein *Philosophical Occasions 1912–1951*. I shall refer to these simply as the 'Notes' or NFL. It is clear from the editor's remarks in *Philosophical Occasions* that there are criticisms of Rhees' 1968 version. It leaves out some of the sections and does not explain which or why. At a general level it is not obvious that either is a serious fault. The remarks do vary in interest, and how could Rhees explain the whys and wherefores of his selection? Anyway, we now have the 'Notes' complete (except for some bits on mathematics).

[3] I shall refer to these as the 'Lectures' or LSD. It has to be conceded that we need to be cautious about putting too much weight on Rhees' lecture notes. On general grounds we know that people listening to lectures invariably miss out elements and also misunderstand elements too. Obviously this will have happened with Rhees. They are, though, valuable, and correspond to the 'Notes' in a significant way.

about these topics contained in the *Philosophical Investigations*, and indeed the general concepts employed in their treatment, such as criterion, language game, use, and grammar, can also be found in some form in the 'Notes' and the 'Lectures'. Indeed, one striking thing is how quickly the general direction of Wittgenstein's views is in place.[4] Moreover, the same considerable difficulties of interpretation arise about all three texts. However, the later presentation is more coherent, consistently deep and more focussed, containing only the absolute essentials. A second obvious development is that in the 'Notes' and the 'Lectures' Wittgenstein devotes explicit attention to the theory of sense data, whereas in *Philosophical Investigations* the focus, at least in the core sections referred to above, is almost exclusively on the language of sensations.[5] A question to be considered in section 6 is why there is the narrowing of focus in the *Investigations*. In the *Investigations* the only extensive discussion of perception comes in Part II, in the 'seeing as' section. There is, as far as I can see, virtually no anticipation of most of those ideas in the 'Notes' or 'Lectures'.

I approach this body of work with the following three questions in mind: What views about sense data and private experience is Wittgenstein proposing? How does he support these views? How convincing is the support he provides? The existence of such a large body of work on these topics is in some ways a difficulty. It means that an essay-length consideration of Wittgenstein's views has to leave most of it undiscussed. The appropriate methodology, at least here, when considering such background work is, I believe, to look at it closely either when it contains arguments or views linking in some way with the related passages in the *Philosophical Investigations* or it seems to present a relatively developed view which seems not to surface in the *Investigations*. When I speak of asking how convincing Wittgenstein's arguments are, I regard this task as requiring both creativity in filling out how the arguments are best read, and also as one to be approached with a degree of sympathy which does not look for a level of completeness, decisiveness, or explicitness which his mode of thought (or expression) will not offer.

1. Background: Wittgenstein as a Negative Philosopher

It is fair, I think, to say that Wittgenstein is fundamentally a negative thinker. His aim is primarily to establish claims of the form Not [P], or, perhaps: 'we should not think that P'.[6] This is not only obvious when we read the later philosophy, but it is also in line with

---

[4] One striking, though not especially important, example is that on the fourth page of the 'Notes', which is to say at the very beginning, there occurs the remark, 'My right hand selling to my left hand'. §268 of the *Investigations* starts: 'Why can't my right hand give my left hand money?' 'Selling' has become 'giving', but it is plainly the same example, with the same point.

[5] This is pointed out by David Pears in Pears 2006, 43. I shall discuss the reason later.

[6] In characterizing the intended conclusion as 'not thinking that P', I hope that leaves it as open that the problem in thinking that P might be, according to Wittgenstein, that the state characterized as thinking that P is deficient in proper content.

what seems to be Wittgenstein's official and dominant conception of the proper task of philosophy. Thus, when he says that his aim in philosophy is 'to show the fly the way out of the fly-bottle', we should, surely, think of being trapped in the fly-bottle as a metaphor for being in the grip of an intellectual illusion to the effect that P, and escaping as coming to realize that Not [P]. The significance of his famous remark that 'the philosopher's treatment of a question is like the treatment of an illness' is that the task of philosophy properly conceived is to clear up, and cure, philosophical errors. This remark also conveys the idea that the error is to be superseded, not by a better theory, but by a return to health and normality, in which state the impulse to ask philosophical questions will have subsided. Good philosophy gets thinkers out of distorted (or pathological) cognitive states.[7] Wittgenstein's approach in relation to the sense datum theory is, I think, in line with this attitude. One can summarize it in the proposition: do not worry about perception, but above all please do not say *that* (i.e. what the sense datum theorist says) about it.[8] He certainly does not offer an alternative *theory* about perception.

Although Wittgenstein's overall goal in his philosophical work is to uproot error about some matter, say, the nature of understanding, or the role of rules, etc., and his conception of philosophy encapsulates this negative goal, it is an exaggeration to describe his practice as totally negative. First, Wittgenstein frequently makes positive proposals as part of his philosophical dialogues. Thus, in the *Investigations* §244, Wittgenstein proposes a positive account of how words refer to sensations. He does not affirm that it is true but certainly invites consideration that it might be. If his method were totally negative, such a proposal would have no role. Again, Wittgenstein suggests that bad philosophy is produced by the 'bewitchment of intelligence by language'. This is a positive explanatory proposal. In fact, since Wittgenstein *argues* people out of the bad convictions (this is what the illness metaphor does not bring out) he has to advance some positive claims (to figure in the persuasive arguments) and there really is no chance that such claims can all be, as one might say, a-theoretical. It seems to follow that within Wittgenstein's philosophy as a whole, even if the overarching ideas are negative, there must be a *non-negative level*. Second, in his description of his practice, he does include the making of positive remarks. Thus, in §415, Wittgenstein says: 'What we are supplying are really remarks on the natural history of human beings; we are not contributing curiosities, however, but observations which no one has doubted, but which have escaped remark only because they are always before our eyes.' This seems to mean that Wittgenstein conceives of himself as saying something positive, albeit of such an untheoretical kind that no one has ever doubted it (though they may not have realized it

[7] There is an element in the illness metaphor which can be queried even if we allow that Wittgenstein is correct about philosophy being negative. To compare engagement in ordinary error-producing philosophy to having an illness requires that such engagement is, in some way, bad or harmful for us. There is, however, no obvious reason to suppose that it is bad for us to engage in it, even if it generates errors in our beliefs. Why is it so bad to do that? Maybe it is a perfectly harmless non-pathological way to spend our time. Maybe it is fun, if nothing else.

[8] In fact, if one wanted to summarize in a slogan the 'seeing as' section, it would also be: do not worry about this talk of seeing as, just accept it, do not resist it, and do not theorize about it in this way (e.g. by postulating sense data).

either).[9] The chief problem with this sentence is which of his own remarks Wittgenstein is thinking of as being about 'the natural history of human beings'. Third, there is something close to self-refutation in Wittgenstein's avowed complete conception of philosophy. It is surely clear that his proposed conception of philosophy is not something that no one has doubted or denied. Wittgenstein therefore seems to go against his own idea of philosophy as leaving everything as it is by himself proposing a conception which does not do that.

Reading Wittgenstein as negative forces us to ask a further and very difficult question. What, if anything, unites the cluster of ideas to which Wittgenstein is opposed? Are we to think of Wittgenstein's philosophy as basically consisting in opposition to a group of philosophical distortions, related only in so far as Wittgenstein singles them out for opposition, or is there something (or a limited range of things) that unites them, so that there is, perhaps, a *super-mistake* they can all be regarded as forms of, and which is the basic mistake that Wittgenstein is trying to reveal? This is too large and difficult a question to pursue here, but it is, I believe, a question to keep in mind when considering Wittgenstein's discussion of privacy of experience because it is sometimes unclear quite why Wittgenstein opposes the things he does oppose.

Despite these reservations, it can be said that Wittgenstein's approach is *primarily* negative. The way to read Wittgenstein's discussion is as a complex dialogue in which consequences of the view under scrutiny are identified, and objected to, and support for it is voiced and itself criticized.[10] Of course, in the dialogue supplementary replies are expressed and criticized. The discussion amounts therefore to a complex tree structure in which different aspects are explored, and so understanding the dialogues involves appreciating how the remarks fit into the tree structure, and why they get into the dialogue at any particular point. Now, the most crucial requirement for understanding this type of complex Wittgensteinian dialogue is to know what the *central idea* under scrutiny is. Without a grasp on that, the whole discussion must seem arbitrary and pointless.

In connection with the part of Wittgenstein's work under analysis here, it can be said that one thing Wittgenstein is attacking is the sense datum theory of perceptual experience. He is also attacking a conception of experience which one might gesture at by describing it as the conception of experience as *deeply or fundamentally private* to the subject. It is not hard to pick out what the target is when Wittgenstein is discussing sense

---

[9] Wittgenstein reveals a remarkably sanguine attitude to suppose that there are things no one has ever doubted! I suspect that some degree of strain within his conception is visible in this characterization of what he is proposing.

[10] It is surely undeniable that Wittgenstein's way of writing is appropriately read as a dialogue. A thought is voiced, and then a response voiced, and then a further response voiced, and so on. One problem is locating what we might call Wittgenstein's *own* voice in the complex dialogue. It is hard not to feel that sometimes views are attributed to Wittgenstein which should more properly be treated as expressions of ideas within the dialogue. This has surely happened both with readers who are sympathetic to Wittgenstein and with those who are not. The second major problem, it seems to me, in reading Wittgenstein is his extremely heavy employment of metaphor. We are very much on our own in working out the point, and dialectical value, of the metaphors.

data, since there is a familiar type of philosophical theory, with its well known elements, associated with talk of sense data. Wittgenstein's understanding of sense data is not, of course, epistemological, but is, rather, ontological. His concern is with the postulation of a sensory entity.[11] The difficulty in considering Wittgenstein's discussion of sense datum theory does not lie in understanding its target. Rather, there is virtually unanimous agreement these days that the sense datum theory is incorrect. In opposing it, therefore, Wittgenstein will naturally seem on the side of the angels. This means, I suggest, that it is hard to consider properly how *good* his actual objections are. How far did he show that the idea is a bad one? It is, though, much harder, in contrast, to say what the conception of experience as deeply private *is* or *amounts to*. The problem is this: in Wittgenstein's philosophical practice, as I have been describing it, consequences are derived from a basic central idea. But in relation to the idea of experience as deeply private, *which* are the *consequences* and which the *central idea*?[12] I shall try to show in different ways how difficult it is to get the issue about private experience in focus. Having posed that issue, I want to leave it and concentrate first upon what are three discernible themes in Wittgenstein's discussion of sense data.

2. WITTGENSTEIN'S CONCEPTION OF SENSE DATA

In the *Investigations'* discussion of privacy Wittgenstein introduces visual experience in §272 (which is quite late on). In the next two sections he points out that if you have a sense datum conception then you face questions about the significance of colour words. Now, this difficulty cannot immediately be turned into a ground for rejecting the model. At least, Wittgenstein gives no serious reason to suppose that. It is a problem to be faced by the approach, and a problem its proponents, ever since the seventeenth century, have been aware of. But he then says:

> Look at the blue of the sky and say to yourself 'How blue the sky is!' – when you do it spontaneously – without philosophical intentions – the idea never crosses your mind that this impression of colour belongs only to *you*. And you have no hesitation in exclaiming that to someone else. And if you point at anything as you say the words you point at the sky. I am saying: you have not the feeling of pointing-into-yourself,

[11] See Snowdon 1992, in which I try to trace an ambiguity in the talk of 'direct perception' and its distorting role in the presentation of philosophical arguments about perception. Wittgenstein sticks with a single interpretation, and does not engage with epistemological issues.

[12] One of the fascinations of the so-called rule-following considerations is that it is very difficult to say what supposed misconceptions about rules (or meaning) Wittgenstein is opposing. In fact, we can divide Wittgenstein's targets into two categories. The first category is where the target is fairly obvious, for example, the ideational model of meaning, or the volitional theory of action, or the theory of sense data. The second category is where the target does not correspond to any fairly compact philosophical doctrine; examples are the discussions of rule following, logical necessity, and private experience.

which often accompanies 'naming the sensation' when one is thinking about 'private language'. (PI §275)

Wittgenstein here brings out a genuine contrast between the status of the idea of the private object account of perception and the idea of private objects as involved in the experience of sensations. It is not the case that perceptual experience as we normally enjoy it announces to us, or gives us a sense that, there is a private object possessing, and presenting to us, the qualities in appearance. Whereas, with experience of sensations our experience itself invites our attention inwards and the idea of an inner object seems more attractive. The contrast that it seems to me Wittgenstein is drawing here certainly exists. It is reflected in philosophical practice. Supporters of sense datum models see it as necessary to show by argument that perceptual experience involves an experience of a similar kind to that which is present in, roughly, sensations. With that assimilation in place, the theoretical treatment that *seems* appropriate for sensations gets applied to perception, including vision. Wittgenstein's remark brings out this contrast brilliantly. Again, it would be a mistake to take this as an objection to the sense datum model. It can hardly count against a view that it is not obvious or part of common sense. Wittgenstein himself rightly does not offer it as an objection.[13]

A second place where Wittgenstein conveys his attitude to talk of sense data is Lecture VII in Rhees' notes (which I am calling the 'Lectures').[14] Wittgenstein says; 'the word "sense datum" means the same as "appearance". But the term introduces a particular way of looking at appearance. We might call it objectification.' (LSD, 312) Wittgenstein's idea seems to be that in English we have a way of speaking of appearance in which the verb 'appears' is used. We might say: 'his suit appeared dirty'. However, we also have the language in which we use 'appearance' as a noun. So we might say; 'the suit's appearance was dirty'. Now it seems to be Wittgenstein's idea that objectification occurs when we treat the noun 'appearance' as standing for an object which itself is dirty in the way the suit is. Objectification occurs if I say: 'If the coat appeared grey, then *something* must have been grey.' (LSD, 312; my italics) A little later Wittgenstein puts it this way: 'there are two opposing tendencies of our language: in one symbolic system we would say this, in another that...and then we use both forgetting that they belong to two different systems'. (LSD, 315) The application of Wittgenstein's remark that I am suggesting is that we have one symbol system in which 'appears' is used in complex predicates applying to objects, and then another system in which the same claims are made employing the noun 'appearance'. But we assume that 'appearance' stands for the same kind of thing that the nouns that can link to the verb 'appears' themselves stand for.

---

[13] When discussing this remark Hacker expands it by saying; 'The thought that colour words signify or refer to something "private" does not cross one's mind when one is using colour-names in the bustle of life, but only in philosophical reflection...i.e. when language is idling' (Hacker 1990, 85). The question raised by this remark is, of course, why we should grant what follows the 'i.e.', namely, that simply in virtue of being philosophical reflection the language is idle.

[14] The editors of *Philosophical Occasions* claim, on the basis of comparing Rhees' notes with those of others, that what he calls Lecture VII was in fact the second one. We should also treat the passage and my discussion of it with the caution I talked of in fn 3.

This way of understanding the source of the postulation of sense data was highly influential. Remarks about confused objectification are echoed in many discussions of perception by philosophers in the period after the Second World War, when there was a volte-face against the idea of sense data, and it is plausible to suggest that they have their origins with Wittgenstein. Despite this influence there is one reservation to voice. It is not, it seems to me, a particularly plausible exercise in cognitive dynamics. Is it really because we talk of appearances being e.g. dirty that there is appeal in the idea that the correct account of appearance in perception is that it involves entities which possess properties (such as colour) and thereby exhibit them to the subject? The appeal of that idea surely lies in its apparent explanatoriness. It would have that appeal, it is plausible to say, even if we did not employ the noun 'appearance'.

Finally, Wittgenstein's conception of sense data frequently focusses on, or homes in on, one fundamental consequence of the model, certainly central to Russell's conception of it (and also to Moore's), that the inner sense data are the entities that the subject is in most direct contact with, and so are what the subject can demonstratively pick out. When perception occurs, the subject is in a position to think, of a sense datum, 'THIS is my (private) sense datum'. In Russell's terminology we are acquainted in experience with sense data, and the closeness of the relation of acquaintance grounds the possibility of demonstrative thought. A central element in Wittgenstein's attempt to undermine the idea is to generate a sense that such purported demonstrative thoughts are really not possible. A central question is whether Wittgenstein succeeds.

3. Sense Data and Experience Differences

Wittgenstein starts the first Lecture with these words:

> I want to talk about the *privacy* of sense data.
>   The suggestion arises from the fact that I and another man may look at something and I may say 'He sees it a different colour from what I do.' (LSD, 290)

In the 'Notes' Wittgenstein mentions that same case.

> We said that there were cases in which we should say that the person sees green when I see red. Now the question suggests itself: if this can be so at all, why should it [not] be always the case? (NFL, 285)

Wittgenstein's response to this line of thought is, in effect, to deny or query that there is any such general possibility. His view is that although there are *certain circumstances* in which it is correct to say that another sees as green what I see as red, it is simply not possible that that is the case for everyone. It is worth noting at this point, though, that when he discusses the issue, Wittgenstein frequently brings in two other suggested possibilities to consider. One is that the people I call blind may in fact be sighted but are, as we say, acting as if they were blind.[15] The second is that others, in general, may be in pain without showing it.[16] What Wittgenstein's tendency to shift between different examples indicates, I believe, is that his attitude to the idea of differences in colour experience is just an instance of a more general attitude to suggested differences in experiences (or the possibility of such differences) between people. One central question is what that general attitude is.

Focussing initially on colour experience and sense data, there are two areas that we need to consider. The first is what the relation is, according to Wittgenstein, and also in fact, between the possibilities of differences in colour experience and the theory of sense data. The second, and much more important, one is what Wittgenstein's case *against* the general possibility is, and whether it is convincing. In relation to the first question, it seems to me that Wittgenstein makes three claims. The first is that colour experience differences are cited by sense datum theorists as evidence for their theory. That is true, although such cases are not what are primarily focussed on. The second thought seems to be that if the sense datum model of visual experience is correct, then it follows that there is what we might call a general possibility of differences in visual experience, and the third claim is that there is no such general possibility. According to this interpretation, Wittgenstein is not denying the claim about divergence in colour experience between subjects that sense datum theorists use in *arguing for* their model of perceptual experience. The flaw in their arguments must, therefore, lie elsewhere. Rather, Wittgenstein seems to think that the model *implies* the existence of a certain possibility which actually does not exist. So the argument ranks as an objection to the theory.

I want now to turn to the linked questions as to what exactly the possibilities are that Wittgenstein is claiming the sense datum model leads to, and whether he successfully undermines the possibility.

Wittgenstein presents a compact summary of his attitude to this issue in the final four pages of the 'Notes'. (NFL, 285–8) He says there that there are cases in which we say, and he clearly means correctly, that 'he sees as dark red whereas I see light red'. One thing to note here is that when Wittgenstein is talking about what someone sees, he often, and certainly here, is using what is called an intentional interpretation of 'see'. He is reporting something that we could equally well report by talking of something looking dark red to him but light red to me. In the 'Notes' at the point we are considering, Wittgenstein does

---

[15] In relation to the 'sighted acting as if they are blind' example, it is, I believe, well worth thinking about the recent example of the opposite case. The example, reported in our newspapers, was of a Chinese lady who was in fact (clinically) blind because of cataracts, but who had organized her life into such a limited routine (for example, never going out) that her blindness did not affect her. She did so well that her husband (and, I think, children) had no idea that she was blind. Her deception only came out because she tripped and hit her head so hard that the cataracts were dislodged and she immediately called out 'I can see'. To which her family's reaction was 'But you have always been able to see.' The moral of this case, a moral not terribly congenial to Wittgenstein, is that differences or deficits in experience need not show themselves in the environment *as it happens to be*. Of course, changing that environment by way of doing an experiment might very well have revealed a difference or a deficit.

[16] See NFL, 285 for the blindness case; and 286 for the pain case.

not give examples where such a judgement is true, or, indeed, any indication about the *sorts* of cases where it is correct. But in the 'Lectures' (Lecture I) he does so. He mentions two cases. The first is where 'one of us has put on coloured glasses'. The second case is more complex, and is as follows. 'Or suppose I teach a person colour names in a certain light. He is then able to bring me red objects in the room when asked. Suppose then I bring him into the light of day, and he calls rose petals green and grass red, and so on. If we then bring him back into the artificial light and he behaves as before, then we might say "He sees red where we see green."' (NFL, 290) It is not entirely clear what Wittgenstein means here. Does he mean that in such a case we should say quite generally that he sees red where we see green, but that somehow the teaching has worked and the person understands colour words correctly, or is Wittgenstein talking about him seeing as green what we see as red in the specific circumstances where he and we are in a 'certain light'? In that case there is a sense that he has been taught the language incorrectly. Indeed, given its description, both hypotheses have something to be said for them. However, Wittgenstein's idea is that in such cases such a description of contrasting experiences is correct or merited.

The question, then, as Wittgenstein roughly puts it, is: once we have admitted that it can happen under limited circumstances, may it not always happen? (NFL, 285) Wittgenstein is of course going to argue that the answer to this question is 'no'. However, before considering his complex argument and some of the issues it raises, it needs to be asked what general possibility Wittgenstein has in mind. The language of the contrast suggests that the difference is between claiming that it is possible that a *few* people see colours differently to me, and that it is not possible that *all others* see them differently. But understood at least one way, this is surely not the contrast. It seems evidently possible that everyone except me should be one of those special cases. Wittgenstein's point is, rather, this: concerning some possible *ways* in which people can be different from me, they are ways in which they can have different colour experiences to me, but unless people are different from me *in those restricted ways* it is not possible that they have different colour experiences. Now, this claim is totally programmatic until some indication is given as to what the *sorts* of differences are that according to Wittgenstein are necessary for it to be correct to postulate colour experience differences. It is hard to be sure, but Wittgenstein, in fact, gives every indication that he seems to think that there has to be a difference in behaviour of some kind. Thus one example he mentions is the case of pain. He says; 'And remember that we admit that the other may have pain without showing it! So if this is conceivable, why not that he never shows that he has pain; and why not that everybody has pain constantly without showing it; or that even things have pain?!' (NFL, 286) The form of this question suggests that the possibility that Wittgenstein is interested in opposing is that of experience differences even where nothing at all *shows* the difference. And it is natural to understand by 'showing' the presence of a behavioural difference. Wittgenstein also says: 'the idea that the other person sees something else than I, is only introduced to account for certain expressions:...'. (NFL, 285) By 'expression' here I take it that Wittgenstein means the revealing or showing of a difference – a difference, that is, in the expression of the experience.

Somewhat characteristically, it remains unclear what Wittgenstein's idea is. The proposition that seems to be meant though is, I am inclined to suggest, not plausible. Let me mention, without developing them, two difficult cases. We agree surely that in certain circumstances when seeing O, the colour-blind have different experiences to the non-colour-blind. What is to prevent us taking two subjects, one colour-blind, the other not, and paralysing them throughout their lives? We let them see O. They will have different visual experiences, without a difference in expression. Less grotesquely, if the experience difference does not affect any task (e.g. they are not asked to pick up the objects that look alike, or to describe them) then it will not show.

Wittgenstein's argument starts with the comment that the very idea of seeing red loses its *use* if we can never know if the other does not see something utterly different. (NFL, 285; the italicization of 'use' is mine.) Now, this is a characteristic comment by Wittgenstein, employing the key notion of use. In this context, however, it is far from clear what the claim about use means or whether it follows. One interpretation of Wittgenstein's point is this: if I have up to now said about others that they see something as red, but now come to accept that I do not know whether they do, then I shall not think or say what I used to. So, summarizing, we might say that my use of 'seeing red' will change. It will lose its *old use*. In response to this interpretation we can allow that the words will lose their previous use. The problem is that this consequence does not seem to be a difficulty.

Wittgenstein probably means that the words 'seeing red' etc. will lose their *meaning* or *significance* if we accept that we cannot know about any other subject's experiences. However, if that is what is meant, then Wittgenstein offers nothing corresponding to an argument to show that it would be a consequence, nor is it obvious at all that it would be. Of course, in engaging with such a remark we should approach the text with sympathy and a preparedness to understand and assess it in the light of general assumptions about meaning and use that Wittgenstein adopts and supports elsewhere. The present focus, alas, has to be narrower and so I want to turn to other elements in Wittgenstein's argument.

Wittgenstein's strategy of trying to block a general possibility claim even though he accepts that the possibility exists in particular cases is clearly an available one. Thus, in a race, concerning each runner it is possible that he or she will not win, but it does not follow that it is possible that all the runners will not win. So the option Wittgenstein is taking is available. There is, however, a puzzle. Why is Wittgenstein focussing on the general possibility claim? This puzzle arises because the rejection of the general possibility thesis has no particularly beneficial epistemological consequences. Consider the winning analogy. If I can rule out in advance the possibility that *no one* will win, I cannot, on that basis, *rule out* for any runner that it is possible that he or she will not win. So, even if I can be sure for Wittgenstein's reasons that it is not possible that everyone sees these colours differently to me, I cannot thereby know that it is not possible, for any subject, that he or she does not. So vast ignorance remains. The answer to this puzzle is, I think, that Wittgenstein views the general possibility as a consequence of the conception under consideration, and so he is criticizing the view by criticizing an implied consequence.

The important question is how Wittgenstein tries to undermine the general possibility thesis. On Wittgenstein's conception, the dialectic at this point goes in a novel direction. His idea is that at least one style of opponent of his argument about the loss of use will reply that the intelligibility of the idea of seeing red, etc. is grounded in what we can *imagine*. Wittgenstein investigates this reaction. In a nutshell, his response is summarized in these words: 'Imagine a man, say W, now blind, now seeing and observe what you do. How do these images give sense to the question? They don't, and you see that the expression stands and falls with its usefulness.' (NFL, 285) Wittgenstein makes the same point in relation to another example. He says; 'We arrive at the conclusion that imagining him to have pain (etc.) does not fix the sense of the sentence "he has pain."' (NFL, 286) Wittgenstein's exposition at this point is very compressed, in at least three respects. It is not clear what sentences are supposed to receive their senses on the basis of imaginings, or what imaginings exactly are supposed to provide it; nor is it clear why Wittgenstein is so sure that the images do not give sense. Wittgenstein does of course argue elsewhere that associating expressions with images does not ground sense. He also makes the famous comment 'If one has to imagine someone else's pain on the model of one's own, that is none too easy a thing to do.' (PI §302) The point of this deep remark is that simply imagining a pain does not contain any indication of who the subject is. In the same way, the image of rain when imagining rain two days ago does not itself contain the indication of when it occurred. To employ the image as an image of rain two days ago presupposes the ability to make sense of the thought in question, and so does not ground it. Wittgenstein might be thinking of these points in denying that images can confer sense on the sentences in question. However, it is difficult to understand why the dialectic moves in the direction that Wittgenstein takes it in. His opponents might appeal to imagination, but the natural role for such an appeal would not be as grounds for sense but rather as support for accepting a possibility. Of course, it is not in fact a convincing demonstration of a possibility, but to appeal to imagination in this role is not to ground senses on it.

My conclusion is that Wittgenstein's discussion does not really undermine acceptance of the general possibility of colour experience inversion.

4. The 'Visual Room'

It is natural to read Wittgenstein's brief discussion of the so-called 'visual room' (in PI §§398–402) as another engagement with the sense datum model of perception. The passage in question occurs immediately after a series of remarks about imagination, and the quotation which starts §398 itself talks of imagination. However, it seems clear that the discussion is not uniquely targeted on imagination but, more generally, on a conception of experience. The initial quotation itself talks of seeing, as well as of imagination, and Wittgenstein's wonderful name, 'visual room', for the hypothesized object clearly relates it to a supposed element in visual experience. My aim is to argue that Wittgenstein produces no very strong evidence of difficulties in this idea.

In his discussion of the 'visual room' Wittgenstein's focus is on the idea expressed in the initial quotation. '"But when I imagine something, or even actually see objects, I have got something which my neighbour has not." – I understand you. You want to look about you and say: "At any rate only I have got THIS".' (PI §398) Wittgenstein is focussing on the idea of a privately owned object, an idea central to the sense datum view and to the idea of deep privacy.

Now, although Wittgenstein says that he understands the remark, his purpose is to persuade us that it would be wrong to say any such thing. This raises two questions. The first is whether Wittgenstein does present a case for thinking that it would be wrong. The second question, though, is this: what significance would Wittgenstein's conclusion have if it were correct? This second question is prompted by the existence of theorists who believe or say that there are sense data but who deny the existence of the self related to them. Strawson calls such theorists 'no-ownership theorists'. On the face of it such a view is not against the existence of 'visual rooms' but it would deny the truth of the claim that each one is uniquely owned or had. This means that even if Wittgenstein does establish that the sentence he is targeting is incorrect, he could not thereby show that there were no such entities as 'visual rooms' without further argument to show that the notion of a visual room is (unobviously) committed to the correctness of the rejected sentence. The first question, though, is the one to pursue.

What is striking is how abrupt Wittgenstein is in the discussion. Immediately he offers three reactions to the quotation. The first is to say this: 'What are these words for? They serve no purpose.' It is clear that anyone moved to endorse the sentence in question will not be prompted by this remark into agreeing that there is something wrong with the claim. His second response is to say: 'There is no question of a "seeing" – and therefore none of a "having" – nor of a subject, nor therefore of "I" either.' These remarks merely prompt further questions. Why does Wittgenstein think that there is no question of seeing? He means presumably that the subject does not see the objected designated by 'THIS'. However, without establishing that there is no 'THIS', that claim is not obvious. It is clear that the subject does not train his or her eyes on the item, but it has not been shown that that is the sole use of 'see'. Wittgenstein himself is rather insistent at other places on how flexible the use of 'see' is. One illuminating passage comes from the 'Notes'. On page 214 Wittgenstein says:

> B is trained to describe his after-image when he has looked into a bright red light. He is made to look into the light, then to shut his eyes and he is then asked 'What do you see?' This question was put to him before only if he looked at physical objects. We suppose that he reacts by a description of what he sees with closed eyes. (NFL, 214, §12)

Now, this seems a sequence of linguistic development which is quite plausible. Further, even if there is no seeing, why does it follow that there is no 'having'? The supposed link there is completely obscure. Finally, why is there no question of a subject or an 'I'? Does Wittgenstein mean that there is never any such question, in which case he must be against anyone ever saying 'I have THIS', designating anything whatsoever? If he means there is no such question *in this case*, why is that so?

The third remark is this: 'Might I not ask: In what sense have you got what you are talking about and saying that only you have got it? Do you possess it? You do not even see it.' But these again are merely questions, the significance of which is not obvious. We have seen already that it is not clearly correct to say that you do not see the item. It is equally not obvious that you are not apprehending it or are aware of it. Further, although it is rather hard to say what 'has' means in general, there is no particular reason to allude to possession. It seems to me fair to conclude that this immediate sequence of responses establishes nothing.

Wittgenstein's final immediate remark appeals to a 'matter of logic', as he calls it. He says: 'If as a matter of logic you exclude other people's having something, it loses its sense to say that you have it.' As a matter of logic, this actually seems incorrect. No one other than you can be you, but it is meaningful and true to say that you are you. There is a second problem with the appeal to this principle. The attitude expressed in the quotation that Wittgenstein is discussing is that only the subject *has* 'THIS', picking out the so-called visual room. Now, strictly, this attitude does not claim that only the subject *could have had* THIS. So, Wittgenstein's principle, even though it is false, is not immediately relevant to the claim.

After some more remarks including the observation that there is no 'master' of the visual room, Wittgenstein adds a short paragraph that is remarkably puzzling.[17] Wittgenstein says: 'think of a picture of a landscape with a house in it. – Someone asks "Whose house is that?" – The answer, by the way, might be "It belongs to the farmer who is sitting on the bench in front of it." But then he cannot for example enter his house.' (PI §398) The puzzle raised by this is two-sided. How is this remark meant to help with the overall debate? Is Wittgenstein's remark itself correct? Wittgenstein makes it clear that the picture is of an imaginary house and farmer. If one asks, 'Whose house is that?', then Wittgenstein says that the correct answer might be – the farmer. This question and answer relate to the things depicted, where it is given that the depicted things are not real. So, as we might say, the question and answer have the status of what is sometimes called 'truth in fiction', or perhaps better here, 'truth in depiction'. Now, it seems that we assign truth in this sort of context to what is explicit in the depiction (or fiction), but also to extensions of that. Thus Sherlock Holmes lived in Baker Street, a truth grounded in what the story says, but he also had two legs, in virtue of being a reasonable extension of what is explicit. And we can do the same with pictures. But approached this way, we would surely say that the man could get into his house.[18] That is the *reasonable* extension here. So Wittgenstein's final remark is, I suggest, wrong. But suppose that it were correct, it would still be a remark about the depicted items. The most, therefore, that this illustrates in relation to the visual room are true claims about what, as one might say, is depicted by the visual room. But no question of that status, or anything like it, is really being raised about the visual room. No one is asking about the cans and cannots relating to the items *depicted* by the visual room. The question

---

[17] It is, I think, well brought out by Professor Kemmerling (1991) just how hard it is to make sense of this paragraph.

[18] This is what Kemmerling points out.

is, rather: who has or owns the visual room itself? In the case of the picture, it itself is the analogue of the visual room and it can have an owner. But Wittgenstein's questions and answers in relation to the picture do not relate to the picture but rather to its depicted contents. These references to the picture seem not to engage with the philosophical argument.

Wittgenstein has one final argument to show that the visual room has no owner. 'Surely the owner of the visual room would have to be of the same kind of thing as it is; but he is not to be found in it, and there is no outside.' (PI §399) This is also puzzling. Why would the owner of the visual room have to be the same kind of thing (as the visual room)? There is no reason to suppose he/she would.[19]

It is illuminating to trace similar worries in Wittgenstein's earlier thought. In Lecture I Wittgenstein is clearly worrying about 'having' a private impression. He says:

> Consider the momentary impression which I have and which I call green. There is a question about the 'I *have*'. There is an inclination to say 'I'll give this impression a name, say the name "alpha", and I know then what the name "alpha" means'. – Here again we have the problem of what it is like to christen an impression. (LSD, 290)

Now, Wittgenstein more or less immediately rejects the claim that such a name as 'alpha' has a meaning. 'We don't know at all what to do with the word, and consequently it can't be said to have a meaning.' (LSD, 292) This is an accelerated (indeed over-accelerated) version of the private language argument. But Wittgenstein also queries the 'I have'. He says: 'the proposition "Only I can see" or "Only I can have this sense datum" is not a statement of a fact of experience, an empirical generalization. It means: to say that he and I have the same sense datum is senseless. *Therefore* I can't use the expression that I *have* it.' (LSD, 292) As it stands, this argument is unpersuasive. First, it seems that Wittgenstein is assuming that if a proposition is not an empirical claim it must be a claim about meaning or sense. This is far from obvious. Second, it assumes that if it is senseless to say 'He and I both have this sense datum', it follows that it is senseless to say 'I have it'. But as it stands this is no better than the argument – it is senseless to say 'It is raining and it is not raining' so it is senseless to say 'it is raining'. Finally, Wittgenstein also anticipates another element in the visual room discussion, which is the idea that the reference to the self is also problematic. He says: 'If asked "What is your sense datum?" I should answer "My sense datum is *this*". The "this" is not merely pointing for his benefit. I am taking together myself and what I see – but not in the sense in which "myself" is "Wittgenstein". I am not identifying myself or recognising myself.' (LSD, 293) This seems to be insinuating that the use of 'I' is problematic, but without offering any substantial reason to think so. What is interesting though is that precisely the same suspicions are being voiced that surface later in the visual room discussion.[20]

---

[19] For an exposition of the visual room discussion which is more sympathetic to Wittgenstein but which sketches the contours of the argument in a similar way, see McGinn 1997, 181–9. Our disagreement is over the persuasiveness of Wittgenstein's points.

[20] There is a general theme in Wittgenstein's thought which surfaces here and which needs a thorough exploration which I cannot manage in this chapter. He links a conception of experience as involving private objects with a conception of the self which is problematic. As he remarks in the 'Notes': 'I am trying to bring the whole problem down to our not understanding the function of the word "I" (and "this j ").' (See NFL, 269.) What is the link?

5. Seeing As: Two Arguments

In Part I of *Investigations* Wittgenstein does not focus much on perception. In contrast, the longest (and most famous) section (section xi) in Part II is (by and large) a discussion of perception. It is usually described as being about 'seeing as', or 'aspect perception', and the foremost problems it raises are what the range of phenomena is that Wittgenstein is concerned with and what the major point about such cases is that he is trying to make. These are not questions that I shall pursue. Rather I want to concentrate on two short passages in which Wittgenstein can be counted as discussing sense data.

The first argument comes on the fourth page, quite early in the overall passage. It starts with an example of the sort that Wittgenstein is investigating. The example is that of looking at a puzzle-picture and suddenly seeing the solution. As we might say, the human shape is now seen, whereas before there were merely 'branches'. Wittgenstein talks of his visual impressions changing and cites its 'organization' as what has changed. Now, in speaking this way he gives no indication at all of scepticism about talk of visual impressions, and, perhaps, organization.[21] He is prepared to use the linguistic devices at hand to describe visual experience. He notes, however, that if he attempts to represent by a picture what is seen, before and after, it would be the same picture or drawing, and so no change would be thereby *shown*. Wittgenstein then says: 'And above all do *not* say "After all my visual impression isn't the drawing; it is *this* – which I can't show to anyone."' (PI II, 196) Wittgenstein is instructing us not to say what, according to him, a sense datum theorist would say.

The question now is what has been revealed by the example which counts against saying this. The second comment that Wittgenstein makes, namely, 'Of course it is not the drawing, but neither is it anything of the same category, which I carry within myself', is simply a restatement of the conclusion. And the next comment, that the concept of the 'inner picture' is misleading, is also more of a conclusion than an argument. Wittgenstein's next remark, it seems to me, really does bring out that the inner picture model of visual experience is in significant difficulties when it comes to the aspect of visual experience that Wittgenstein has called 'organization'. The theory faces a dilemma (or perhaps a trilemma). It might claim that the organization which changes is itself an element of the picture. However, it was pointed out that pictures do not 'show' organization, so how can an inner picture do so? Or it denies that organization is a feature of visual experience, precisely because visual experience has to be modelled on inner pictures. It then denies an obvious change in the visual impression. The third option is to say that the inner object is not strictly a picture, but is something with 'organization' built into it. As Wittgenstein comments: 'Of course, this makes this object into a chimera; a queerly

---

[21] It seems that Wittgenstein is happy to use the term 'visual impression', but it is less clear that he is happy to talk of organization. He puts it in quotation marks. Further, it is not an ordinary way of speaking but comes from Kohler and Gestalt theorists, with whom, it seems, Wittgenstein is engaging in the 'seeing as' section. I surmise that his attitude is that Kohler's talk of organization itself incorporates misconceptions, but that there are certainly genuine aspects of experience which lie behind it and which it can be allowed to indicate.

shifting construction. For the similarity to a picture is now impaired.' (PI II, 196) Wittgenstein points out as well that the phenomenon of organization sometimes has to do with the apparent three-dimensional orientation of items. Thus, with a schematic cube it can appear that a certain corner is pointing towards one and then pointing away.[22] This shift Wittgenstein also calls a change in organization. The three-dimensional nature of the experience means that to show the change by employing two-dimensional pictures will fail, and one needs to employ contrasting three-dimensional models to show the change. Wittgenstein summarizes this by saying that 'it wrecks the comparison of "organization" with colour and shape in visual impressions'. (PI II, 196) Colour changes and shape changes can be pictorially represented, whereas this sort of organization cannot be.

These brief remarks of Wittgenstein do not silence the sense datum theorist, but they bring out that the model has no attractive method to explain such experiences adequately. The theory is, of course, at its most appealing when it attempts to model visual experience as the pure apprehension of an inner picture. The absence of anything corresponding to pictures in other modes of perception means that the model has no clear content with non-visual forms of experience. This no doubt accounts in part for the almost total concentration of philosophers of perception on vision. What Wittgenstein brings out is that it is a complete illusion to suppose that pictorial experience can even provide a model for visual experience.

The second argument in PI II (xi) that I wish to scrutinize is presented on p. 207. The context is that Wittgenstein has pointed out that there are differences between different alternating aspects. He then says:

> (The temptation to say 'I see it like *this*', pointing to the same thing for 'it' and 'this'.) Always get rid of the idea of the private object in this way: assume that it constantly changes, but that you do not notice the change because your memory constantly deceives you. (PI II, 207)

This remark is clearly an attack on the idea of a private object (hence on sense data). What, though, does the remark show? We can relate the remark to the context, which concerns what he calls alternating aspects. Now, an account of alternating aspects in terms of private objects would, presumably, be that a change of aspect consisted in a change of some sort on the private object. Wittgenstein seems to be suggesting that the model can be eliminated because if we assume that the subject's memory changes, then the private object change would not be noticed. We can allow that the postulation of a change in the private object can only account for the experience of a change of aspect if the subject's memory is working properly. The question now is why this dependence is a *problem* for, an *objection* to, the model. It is hard, for at least three reasons, to see why it should count as that. First, if we propose a model of what a certain phenomenon consists of, it will often be the case that one element in the postulated structure can fulfil its role

---

[22] Central to the 'seeing as' section are what we might call visually unstable or ambiguous figures. These are pictures or arrays which tend to be seen one way and then another. The perception of them is prone to what Wittgenstein calls aspect-shifting. Schematic cubes are one obvious case.

only if certain other complementary elements are assumed to be functioning in given ways. It seems not to discredit such a theory to point out that the work of the postulated elements depends on other things working, as one might say, properly. Second, in this particular case, that of changing aspects, it is characteristic of the experience to be noticed, to strike the subject in a certain way.[23] It follows therefore that the full phenomenon is only possible in the context of a working memory. So it seems legitimate for a private object model to embed its postulation within the assumption of a working memory. Finally, any account of the phenomenon at all will suffer from the same problem. Any postulated change will fail to generate the distinctive experience if the subject's memory is assumed to deceive him or her.

I conclude that it is hard to see how this remark (which resembles others that Wittgenstein makes) is a refutation of the idea of a private object.

6. Interim Conclusions and Transitions

I want to pull these various strands together to suggest an overall assessment or reading of Wittgenstein on sense data. Wittgenstein has, it seems to me, at least three main types of objection to sense data. One is that the theory implies the possibility of experience differences between subjects where there is no such possibility. Now, Wittgenstein might be right about both the existence of the implication and also about its falsity, but it is very hard to feel that as Wittgenstein presents it in the 'Notes' he handles the argument for error in a convincing way. He seems, as well, to incline to a thesis committed to no experience difference without it showing, which commonsensical grounds indicate is far too strong. Second, Wittgenstein reflected very deeply on the central commitment of the sense datum model to the idea that a subject's perceptual experience puts him or her in a position to demonstratively pick out an inner private object and to think with truth 'I see/have THAT'. This commitment was registered by Russell, who brought the sense datum model into contact with theories of demonstrative thought. Wittgenstein was clearly convinced that there is something deeply mistaken about this implication. Now the problem for Wittgenstein here is, I want to suggest, that the implication is, as it were, highly abstract and, in a sense, insubstantial or almost purely formal and so it is very difficult to *demonstrate* that it is absurd. Looking at two efforts of Wittgenstein to bring out the absurdity (one in the 'Lectures', the other in the *Investigations*), there is a sense that too little is offered to convince someone that the commitment is absurd. There is evidence too that Wittgenstein is often tempted to, as it were, fast-track the objections by appeal to problematic logical principles. I think that Wittgenstein's difficulty arises partly because he shows no inclination to adduce what might be called general ontological objections to private objects. How do they fit into our picture of the world? Such

---

[23] Wittgenstein stresses the way that one might express a change of aspect by saying 'Now it is a rabbit', where the term 'now' expresses the noticing of a change.

arguments hardly conform to his conception of proper philosophy, but this self-imposed limitation makes things harder for him. Third, Wittgenstein argues that the model does not contain enough to serve as a proper model of experience. In developing this, Wittgenstein brings together far richer considerations and really succeeds in generating a sense of a significant explanatory inadequacy in the model. Interestingly, this richer argument is not anticipated in the 'Lectures' or 'Notes'. I am suggesting that the difference in persuasiveness reflects what I am calling a difference in richness of evidence.

There remains the question as to why Wittgenstein narrows his focus, away from sense data, by the time of *Investigations*. David Pears, having raised this question, suggests his own answer in the following passage.

> The answer must be that the two concepts, *painful* and *blue*, have different struc-
> tures. A painful sensation may have various causes, but it has a fairly uniform behav-
> ioural effect – complaint and avoidance; whereas an impression of blue has a single,
> specific cause and no uniform behavioural effect. This difference provides us with an
> explanation of the fact that we do not call surfaces of physical objects 'painful' in the
> flat unqualified way in which we would call an object 'blue'.... This difference makes
> pain a good example for Wittgenstein to use in the controversy about Private
> Language. For the public character of reports of pain follows from the simplest way
> of teaching a child the meaning of the word; which is to introduce it as a substitute
> for the natural expression of pain. (Pears 2006, 55)

The central suggestion seems to be that Wittgenstein concentrates on pain because it a 'good example' for his purposes. Being a good example presumably means that it is one for which Wittgenstein's treatment is obviously better or more plausible. This, it seems to me, makes Pears' suggestion a bit unsatisfactory in that it credits Wittgenstein with the motive of concentrating on the easier case. There are other worrisome aspects to Pears' suggestion. First, it is not in general assumed that the pain case is the easier case from Wittgenstein's point of view. It is generally rated as the case where his view meets most resistance. Second, Pears' picture is, I assume, that both pain and impressions of blue are effects on us (or in us) of objects around us. He seems to think that pains have various causes but uniform effects, whereas impressions of blue have uniform causes and various (if any) effects. That is the fundamental contrast on his view of things.[24] But it then is not at all clear that what Pears calls the 'public character' of reports of such states should be more obvious in the pain case than in the impression-of-blue case. Why should the public character be less clear when the unifying public feature is the cause rather than the effect? Third, Pears' reason seems to be that the idea of the language replacing the expression applies in the pain case but not in the colour impression case. That of course is true according to Pears' characterization of the case, but Pears does not explain why public character should be linked to expression and response rather than to cause and stimulus.

---

[24] It is, of course, far from obvious that this contrast corresponds to anything that Wittgenstein himself thought. Wittgenstein shows no inclination to regard 'impressions of blue' as effects in us of a similar status to pains, only more regularly correlated with a single sort of cause. He is happy to employ the language of 'impression', but what exactly that talk stands for he says nothing about. Pears' reading embeds Wittgenstein's ideas within a framework that might strike one as alien to Wittgenstein's own approach.

Any answer to the present question must be conjectural. My own conjecture is, first, that Wittgenstein's reading of the sense datum model of perceptual experience is that it involves the postulation of a private mental object (whatever exactly that is) and so an argument that brings out the general problems for that idea will count against the theory. Such a general argument *can* be developed in relation to sensations. Second, I assume that Wittgenstein faced up to that case first and foremost because it is the one where the idea of a private object has its strongest appeal, and so that is where it *should* be developed. Third, it is wrong to exaggerate the extent to which Wittgenstein avoids discussion of perception (although he does not talk of sense data). As we have seen, he does focus on it at different places in the *Investigations*.

7. PRIVATE EXPERIENCES: THE QUESTION AND THE TARGET

I want now to focus on the more general idea of private experience and private objects. Our need is to locate the basic target. What is the central element in the idea of private experience that Wittgenstein is attacking? The second question is: is the dialogue that Wittgenstein is constructing a convincing one? I cannot answer these questions fully, but I am going to argue that it is hard to locate a unified target, and that this generates strains in the dialogue. Furthermore, when they are scrutinized there are elements in Wittgenstein's arguments that are dialectically dubious. In this discussion I do not intend to provide any assessment of the argument that is often thought of as *the* Private Language Argument (running from §256 to either §269 or §271), since that is covered elsewhere, although I shall try to locate its significance within the proposed reading.

It seems reasonable to work towards the core idea of private experience by taking those features that Wittgenstein criticizes in his discussion. The first feature that Wittgenstein opposes seems to be that of an occurrence which involves an object which is apprehended or sensed only by the subject. This involves three elements: first, an object or entity; second, the relation of feeling it or sensing it (or having it) in which the subject stands to it; third, the idea that no one else stands to it in that relation. We might call this the *privately owned entity*. The second feature of private experience is that the relation in which the subject stands to the entity enables the subject to *know* what character the sensed private entity has. Now, this positive epistemological property is not pinned down with any greater precision than this. In particular, it can hardly be said that it has to be part of the picture that the subject cannot make a mistake or cannot fail to take in some aspect of the experience. A third feature with which Wittgenstein engages is that such episodes have the basic cognitive role of enabling the subject to form the concept of experience types, e.g. pain, itch, in terms of which the subject subsequently thinks, both about themselves and others. It seems to be part of the picture that such episodes are necessary to form such concepts. What I am calling concept formation is, of course, in Wittgenstein's discussion equated with acquiring an understanding of our sensation language.

There is, however, a fourth feature that Wittgenstein seems to build into the picture. This is the negative epistemological property that only the subject can know what the character of his or her experience is. The inclusion of this element in Wittgenstein's characterization is clearly revealed at two places that I shall note. First, at the very beginning of the consideration of experience in the *Investigations* when Wittgenstein raises the question about the possibility of someone giving 'vocal expression' to their 'inner experiences' he is clearly asking about private experiences on the bad model. But what is striking is that Wittgenstein immediately assumes that such a language would be one that only the subject could understand, the reason being that the words would refer to 'what can only be known to the person speaking'. Wittgenstein assumes then that the model of private experience involves the impossibility of knowledge by another. Second, there is Wittgenstein's very important remark that 'the essential thing about private experience is really not that each person possesses his own exemplar, but that nobody knows whether other people also have *this* or something else'. (PI §272)

Wittgenstein places great stress on this negative epistemological feature, but, I believe, it raises an important question. The question is whether the negative epistemological property should be regarded as following from the first three features or not. Now, although many people think that it does follow, it is not obvious what the proof of that is. Why does it follow that another cannot know what the subject knows? It is not enough to appeal at this point to the supposed fact that those who accept the basic model also accept the sceptical consequence. This is not enough for two reasons. First, even if they all did, it might be that they are mistaken in deriving the consequence. Second, it is not true that everyone holding the basic model does accept other minds scepticism. Rather, many have tried to construct responses which grounded the possibility of knowledge of other minds, for example developing the argument from analogy. Further, Wittgenstein himself is in a dialectically weak position to argue that scepticism is generated by the model since there is no articulated or defended epistemology of his for him to rely on.

It cannot be decided here whether other minds scepticism does follow, but since there is uncertainty in this matter we need to be aware in considering Wittgenstein's criticisms of the privacy model of the question whether the criticism in question depends on the assumption that there is the bad epistemological consequence. Any criticism which does depend has eo ipso a question mark against it.

8. SOME THESES AND ARGUMENTS

In the *Investigations* Wittgenstein's discussion of privacy can be divided into three overall sections; first, §§243–55, in which Wittgenstein poses the question about the possibility of devising a private language but then turns immediately to attacking elements in the privacy picture and suggesting different accounts of sensation language; second, §§256–69, in which the idea of a private language is criticized; and, third, §§270–315, in which Wittgenstein completes his positive and negative engagement with the private conception.

I want to comment initially but briefly on the middle section, the proper anti-private language argument. The question that arises if the worry raised in the previous section is reasonable is: how would it impinge on that argument if we keep an open mind about the negative epistemological implications? It would have the consequence that if the private linguist could construct his language, it would not necessarily be a language no one else could understand. However, would that matter? It links to one argument that Wittgenstein uses. Wittgenstein remarks that the private linguist cannot confer an interpretation on the terms of his language 'as we ordinarily do' because then the words would be 'tied up' with the natural expression of sensations and so 'someone else might understand it'. (PI §256) It looks here as if Wittgenstein is blocking a certain way of conferring an interpretation on sensation language precisely because it would enable another to understand it. That would be illegitimate if there is no reason to assume that another cannot understand the language. But there are some missing steps in Wittgenstein's argument anyway. First, he does not clarify really what 'tied up with' means. After all, the bad privacy model itself does not deny that such episodes involving private objects have causal properties and so they can naturally produce expressions. So such episodes conceived as involving private objects can themselves be 'tied up' with expression. Second, Wittgenstein does not explain in any detail just why the fact that an interpretation is 'tied up' with expression *does* mean that another can understand. However, Wittgenstein's argument at this point is rather compressed and indirect. One supposes that he would object to the idea of interpreting the terms in the normal way on the grounds that that interpretation would not succeed in assigning a term *to an inner property of a private object*. So the problem is not really that another could understand but that the process of interpretation would not generate the right kind of interpretation. However, if this could be shown then there is no dialectical dependence on the supposed negative epistemological consequence of privacy. Is there any such dependence within the argument itself? There is, I want to suggest, dependence at a certain point. One theme in Wittgenstein's discussion (e.g. in §§257 and 261) is that since 'sensation' and 'pain' are public language terms, they cannot indicate the kind of notion the private linguist is aiming to capture. However, this claim simply assumes that the categories the private linguist is introducing cannot be public categories. But if we do not rely on the negative epistemological assumption, what reason is there for claiming that? Wittgenstein's main argument though does not explicitly depend on privacy of meaning. Rather, he argues this way: (1) since the private linguist cannot confer an interpretation on the terms for his private sensations in virtue of their being 'tied' to expression, the only way is by simply associating names with sensations (see §256); (2) no simple act of association can confer a meaning on such terms. Now, most controversy concerns what I am calling premise (2). Does Wittgenstein show that? That question I shall leave unexplored, beyond remarking that the problem is not grounded in the fact that no one else understands, but rather in that supposed fact that the private association cannot generate meaning. What this means is that the supposed necessary publicity of language that the argument yields is at best a *by-product* of the argument. The implication of the passage is that a certain style of meaning generation fails, and that leaves another style which happens to have the property that it generates meaning another could grasp. This means, I suggest, that there are two possible gaps in Wittgenstein's argument. The first is that, if successful, all that has been shown is that sensations cannot generate a private language, but maybe there might be other possible cases. They would need to be ruled out as well. Second, premise (1) is very strong. By what right is it assumed that if the generation of meaning cannot rest on a 'tie' with expression then it must be simply associative? A certain style of objection to the argument in effect tries to flesh this idea out.

9. Some Elements: §§244–55

Having posed the initial question, Wittgenstein immediately develops a number of positive claims, or at least floats some hypotheses. In §244, the very next section, he asks how, in fact, words refer to sensations. In response he says: 'here is one possibility: words are connected with the primitive, the natural, expressions of the sensation and used in their place. A child has hurt himself and he cries; and then adults talk to him and teach him exclamations and, later, sentences. They teach the child new pain-behaviour.' (PI §244) It is fair to say that the idea of language acquiring its interpretation by replacing the non-verbal expression of a sensation is proposed by Wittgenstein as just 'one possibility'. As a proposal, however, it faces two obvious problems. The first is that it is not enough to confer a meaning role on a verbal expression that it is taught as a replacement for the natural form of expression. An example is the word 'yuk', which replaces a more primitive form of expression of dislike. That word is not a name for dislike but is simply a word to express it. The second, more serious, problem is that the words do not actually replace the pre-existing manner of expression. They are, rather, additional to it. In some cultures, perhaps to some of which Wittgenstein himself belonged, it may be that crying as a response to pain was discouraged, especially in boys, as the new language was taught. But it is obvious that such speech does not replace crying. Children who can speak manifestly cry, as do adults. Further, the primitive or natural expression of an itch is to scratch. Obviously the words 'I have an itch' do not replace scratching, a practice it is virtually impossible to eradicate.

In §245, Wittgenstein asks the following question: 'For how can I go so far as to try to use language to get between pain and its expression?' Now, the natural way to understand the point of this question at this stage is as somehow supporting the replacement model. It is not, though, immediately clear how the question might do that. One interpretation of the question is that it is insinuating that whenever pain occurs it must be expressed, and so the acquisition of language cannot prevent its expression, but that acquisition can alter its expression. Language must therefore be a new way of expressing it. This invites two comments. First, if we do grant that nothing can come between pain and its expression, what follows is that the acquisition of language confers a new mode of expression on the subject. It does not follow at all that the replacement thesis is true; nor does it follow that the replacement thesis explains the interpretation of our language. Second, it is not in general true that pain must be expressed. The occurrence of pain in the context of a strong motive to not express or reveal it can block its expression. It would not be correct to say of such cases that language has got between pain and its expression, but it may well be that the acquisition of language abets our ability to intentionally limit our expression of pain.

In §246 Wittgenstein asks 'In what sense are my sensations *private*?' He cites but rejects a double epistemological elucidation of privacy. The double elucidation is that 'only I can know whether I am really in pain; another person can only surmise it'. The proposal is that I can know whether I am in pain but another cannot know whether I am or not. Wittgenstein claims, in contrast, that 'other people very often know when I am in pain' but 'it cannot be said of me at all (except perhaps as a joke) that I *know* I am in pain'. The dismissal of the claim that others cannot know may well be correct, but it is remarkably abrupt. Much more dubious is Wittgenstein's rejection of the idea that a subject knows whether he or she is in pain. Wittgenstein is right in saying that sometimes when we speak of another, knowing that they are in pain, we are joking. We might say of a cricket player hit in a painful place by a fast ball, 'Yes. I think that he knows that he is in pain.' However, it is obviously false to say that joking is the only context for such ascriptions. Here is one case. If S is given a paralysing drug which suppresses reactions but which is not an anaesthetic and then a minor surgical procedure is carried out on him, we might well say that although we cannot tell S himself will know whether he is in pain or not. This seems, quite simply, a true thing to say. This example undermines Wittgenstein's claim. We can develop a more general account. Human beings do know when they are in pain (at least standardly). It is not in fact something that is difficult to know. Not all creatures capable of experiencing pain do know. For example, there is no reason to say that a cat in pain knows that it is in pain. There is no reason to suppose that it recognizes what is happening to it as pain (or, even, that it recognizes anything as happening to it at all). Such creatures simply have and react to pain. The difference between us and them is that we are capable of recognition and thought and can therefore know what is happening to us.[25] Wittgenstein offers the following remark as a reason for denying that we know 'What is it [i.e. talking of knowing that one is in pain] supposed to mean – except perhaps that I *am* in pain?' In fact the picture I have just sketched has already undermined this remark. Strictly, being in pain is not the same as knowing that one is in pain. Many creatures have pain without the knowledge that it is pain. Even if in normal human adults being in pain never occurs without knowledge that one is in pain, the two states are not the same. It is also quite sensible to regard adult humans with severe dementia as capable of pain without recognition.

Wittgenstein concludes this section with the remark: 'The truth is: it makes sense to say about other people that they doubt whether I am in pain; but not to say it about myself'. (PI

[25] If a Martian were sent down to earth with the task of determining what humans know, it would be remarkably odd if it were to report back that earthlings know, amongst many impressive things, about transfinite numbers, the history of evolution, the nature of the brain, general relativity theory, and the structure of DNA, but, alas, do not know when they feel pain! To explain the possibility of knowing that one is in pain in terms of a capacity to recognize things which happen to us is not to provide a deep explanation, of course, but rather to capture in quite commonsensical categories the difference between us and other creatures who are capable of experiencing pain but not capable of knowing they are.

§246) Now, it is not clear whether Wittgenstein thinks that this contrast or asymmetry answers the question as to what privacy is, but he does affirm there is this contrast. Since it is obvious that Wittgenstein is right about what can be sensibly said about others, the only question is whether he is right as to what cannot be sensibly said about oneself. The kinds of creatures already described that can be in pain without knowledge of it are not counter-examples to Wittgenstein, because in effect they lack the concept of pain, and so cannot be doubtful about it in themselves (or indeed in others). But I do not see that it is obvious that doubt is ruled out. In fact it seems ruled in, given the gradualness of the development of pain. There will be levels of discomfort where the subject can quite reasonably say they do not know. Further, the debate here is surely not about pain, but is about sensation descriptions in general, and are there not sources of doubt for them that are possible?

The final parts that I wish to scrutinize briefly are §§253–4. Wittgenstein asks; 'Which are my pains? What counts as a criterion of identity here?' Wittgenstein is attempting to undermine the notion of the privately had *object*. His suggestion is that we have no understanding of the identity of such an object. This, of course, represents one part of his repeated engagement with the idea of private objects. It cannot be said that the remarks amount to a proof that there is no sense to the model, but they give a jolt to those simply assuming that it makes sense.

By the end of this group of remarks Wittgenstein has tried to sweep away certain key elements in the privacy picture. He has opposed the postulation of private objects, the idea that we know about our sensations, and has suggested an alternative idea of how sensation words refer. With the first element we should surely have sympathy, but, as I have argued, the other moves are not as convincing.

10. Some Elements: §§270–315

One striking element in Wittgenstein's discussion of sensations is introduced in §281. He says that his view comes to this: 'only of a living human being and what resembles (behaves like) a living human being can one say: it has sensations; it sees; is blind; is deaf; is conscious or unconscious'. What are we to make of this? Now, whatever finally we think, it seems that this remark has to be regarded as belonging to that level within Wittgenstein's philosophical argument which I earlier argued has to be acknowledged, of a positive theoretical suggestion. It cannot be supposed that this claim is one that no one can deny. What does this claim mean? It is false to say that we cannot say of something which falls outside the general resembling category that it has pains. We can say that. Further, some tree lovers suspect that trees feel pain. Children ask whether they do. The claim has to be that it is not *possible* to feel pain etc. unless the object falls within the resembling class. It is natural to wonder quite how within Wittgenstein's account this claim emerges. The problem is that most of the discussion so far has concerned what is involved in rejecting mistaken understandings of what is involved in grasping sensation terms. It is mysterious how rejecting that mistaken model gets us to the present claim.

Another aspect of this problem is how the condition of resemblance in behaviour could be a condition for e.g. feeling pain. As far as I can see, it can only be so if it is thought that in some sense our psychological predicates stand for conditions that incorporate behavioural requirements. The problem is that Wittgenstein quite fails to explain or justify this condition. Finally, the thesis is, or appears to be, open to counter-examples. The behavioural expression of psychological conditions must rely on the existence of causal chains leading to changes on the surface, and one problem is that these can be disabled close to the periphery by some paralysing agent. We do not think that this destroys the mental processes themselves. Second, there is an imaginary creature which we might call flubber man. He is like a human, except that his exterior is covered in extremely fat flubber. The flubber is so thick that it damps down behavioural responses on the surface. Thus there is no behavioural difference with flubber man between, say, laughing and crying. The thick external covering allows no such behavioural response. Such a creature could have a mental life without resembling us in behaviour. There is evidence that Wittgenstein overemphasized the salience of behaviour to psychological life.

In §293 there comes the very famous beetle in the box passage. This is a brilliant metaphor-based argument. Wittgenstein's claim is that if the word 'beetle' has a use in the public language, it cannot be as name for a type of thing in the box. The conclusion is that 'pain', which has a use in the public language, cannot be a name for a type of private object. However, on closer inspection it is clear that this conclusion rests on the negative epistemological assumption. As Wittgenstein says: 'Here it would be quite possible for everyone to have something different in his box.' This amounts to assuming that no one knows what is in another's box. But without that assumption the argument would not work. So this is a case where maintaining agnosticism about the negative epistemological consequence affects the significance of one of Wittgenstein's points.

Finally, in §304 Wittgenstein makes the very puzzling remark that the sensation 'is not a *something*, but not a *nothing* either!' How can a sensation not be (a) something but also not be (a) nothing? It seems to me that Wittgenstein's point here, at least in part, is rejection of the idea of a sensation as a private *object*. Sense can be made of this remark if the idea of not being a something is – not being an object. However, when we talk of sensations we are not talking of nothing at all. The remark is a rejection of the act/object analysis (although that is not a way that Wittgenstein would put it). What is harder to understand is Wittgenstein's resolution of what he calls the paradox. The resolution consists in making a 'radical break with the idea that language always functions in one way, always serves the same purpose: to convey thoughts – which may be about houses, pains, good and evil, or anything else you please'; this is hard to understand in at least two ways. First, the conception of language to be rejected is unclear. What is meant by it? Second, how does it resolve the paradox? (One might add – what paradox?) This is an example of what one might think of as overkill. Given that so much else in the privacy model has already been abandoned, why must such a general idea about language, whatever exactly it is, also be discarded?

11. CONCLUSION

Wittgenstein was opposed to a conception of experience as deeply private. I suggest that this model can be viewed as a three-layered structure. At the bottom is the idea of a private object in a special relation to, and only to, the subject of the experience. One version of this idea is the sense datum model of perception, but another and more pervasive version is that of sensations as private objects. Wittgenstein was sceptical about such objects and also the demonstrative-style judgements about such items that such a model generates. I have argued that he locates real difficulties for the sense datum model in that it quite fails to account for appearances, but that some elements in his critique are less persuasive. The second level is that such episodes of encountering private objects ground certain positive first person epistemological features, and have special roles in concept development. The third level is that such episodes also ground the negative epistemological property of unknowability by another. It is clear that Wittgenstein assumed that the levels fitted together, and he relied on the negative epistemological property in certain important arguments against the overall model.

A more cautious view, I think, is that it is not obvious that the third level does follow from the other two. This undermines some central arguments. The other important relation is that one can abandon a belief in private objects and a special relation to them, that is the first level in the model, while maintaining claims about the occurrence of sensations on a revised conception corresponding to those at level two. Wittgenstein's objections to the claims at level two are, I have argued, not totally satisfactory. Further, it remains obscure what alternative model of thought about sensations Wittgenstein is suggesting. Finally, in all his discussions of the model Wittgenstein seems to have felt that one problem for it is that it incorporates a conception of experience which is too independent of behaviour. As we might put it: the privacy model incorporates a strong dualism of experience and behaviour. His own view seemed to be that there is some slack in that relation but we must not think in terms of two separable elements. At various places I have hinted that this is far from obviously correct.

Wittgenstein's discussion of privacy amounts to an exercise in paradigm destruction. He encountered a conception of experience which did incorporate all three levels of the model, and he attempted to weaken its grip in a wide range of ways, realizing, in a highly original way, that the total package was subject to serious problems. I suspect that we are only just beginning to get the scale of his critical and constructive achievement in focus.[26]

[26] I wish to thank Dr McGinn for the invitation to contribute to this volume, but above all for the considerable help she has given me. This help has not left its mark on the actual chapter as much as it should have, but it has on my thinking. Thanks are also due to Professor Charles Travis, from whose remarks and papers I have learnt much, and also to Professor Grant Gillett, whose comments helped me greatly when I was writing. This chapter was written while on leave partly funded by an AHRC Research Leave Scheme grant, for which I am also very grateful.

REFERENCES

HACKER, P. M. S. (1990). *Wittgenstein: Meaning and Mind: Volume 3 of an Analytic Commentary on the Philosophical Investigations*, Part II: *Exegesis, 243–427*. Oxford: Blackwell.

KEMMERLING, ANDREAS (1991). 'The Visual Room', in R. L. Arrington and H.-J. Glock eds., *Wittgenstein's Philosophical Investigations, Text and Context*. London: Routledge.

McGINN, M. (1997). *Wittgenstein and the Philosophical Investigations*. London: Routledge.

PEARS, D. (2006). *Paradox and Platitude in Wittgenstein's Philosophy*. Oxford: Clarendon Press.

RHEES, RUSH (1993). 'The Language of Sense Data and Private Experience', in J. Klagge and A. Nordmann eds., *Philosophical Occasions 1912–1951*. Indianapolis: Hackett Publishing.

SLUGA, HANS (1996). 'Ludwig Wittgenstein: Life and Work. An Introduction', in H. Sluga and D. Stern eds., *The Cambridge Companion to Wittgenstein*. Cambridge: Cambridge University Press.

SNOWDON, PAUL (1992). 'How to interpret "direct perception"', in T. Crane ed., *The Contents of Experience*. Cambridge: Cambridge University Press.

WITTGENSTEIN, LUDWIG (1993). 'Notes for Lectures on "Private Experience" and "Sense Data"', in J. Klagge and A. Nordmann eds., *Philosophical Occasions 1912–1951*. Indianapolis: Hackett.

—— (1997). *Philosophical Investigations*, 2nd edn, ed. G. E. M. Anscombe and R. Rhees, trans. G. E. M. Anscombe. Oxford: Blackwell.

CHAPTER 19

....

PRIVACY

....

JOACHIM SCHULTE

THE following remarks are meant to clarify some aspects of Wittgenstein's use of the word 'private'. The relevant use can be traced back to manuscripts written as early as 1930 and 1931. These I shall leave out of account. Instead, I shall first outline ideas and tendencies connected with this use on the basis of passages written in 1935 or later. I shall then proceed to look at the notion of privacy in the light of certain metaphors that can be seen to inform Wittgenstein's discussion of the 'private-language argument(s)'.

1.

....

In some of Wittgenstein's writings the adjective 'private' is used in an all but inflationary way. By this I do not mean that the word occurs very frequently, which of course it does in some of his manuscripts, especially in those written around 1935. What I mean is that privacy is attributed to a fairly wild mixture of objects – if 'objects' is the word I want. To illustrate Wittgenstein's willingness to combine the adjective 'private' with all kinds of nouns, I shall here give a list of such nouns based on his 'Notes for Lectures on "Private Experience" and "Sense Data"': definition, experience, game of chess, impression, justification, language, language game, memory, personal experience, sensation, sense data, visual image.

Naturally, in speaking of Wittgenstein's 'willingness' to combine that adjective with all these nouns I do not want to claim that he himself wishes to assert that definitions, games of chess, etc. can rightly be called 'private'. In most of these cases it is quite clear that he mentions our, or philosophers', inclination to speak of the privacy of experiences or certain objects to expose and criticize it. Still, this form of criticism works by way of first rendering as intelligible as possible a position which is then shown to be open to all kinds of objections.

In his *Philosophical Investigations* Wittgenstein does very little to explain what he means by 'private'. It even remains unclear whether he uses the word in one more or less univocal sense or in more than one sense. Thus it is suggested by various authors who have written on this material that understanding Wittgenstein's text requires distinguishing between different senses of 'private'. Anthony Kenny, for example, claims that there are basically two such senses, and he goes so far as to say that it is Wittgenstein himself who

> distinguishes two senses of the word 'private'. The first sense of privacy has to do with knowledge and the second sense has to do with possession: in the first sense, something is private to me if only I can know about it, and in the second sense something is private to me if only I have it. (Kenny 1973, 185)

I am less sure than Kenny is that Wittgenstein really makes or implies such a distinction (see section 10, below). But if we wish to understand the point of Wittgenstein's use, or uses, of the word 'private', it is surely helpful to bear Kenny's claim in mind.

On the other hand, it is not as if Wittgenstein himself had never tried to clarify his use of the word. First of all, there are a number of remarks in some of his writings that can be read as supplying hints at how to interpret 'private' in a given context. Secondly, there is the occasional passage containing clues to the intended meaning of that word. One such passage can be found in a notebook which not only contains many occurrences of our word but also summarizes a good deal of what Wittgenstein wrote down in his 1935–6 lecture notes. Moreover, this manuscript anticipates a fair number of points made in *Investigations* §§243ff. At the same time, it gives an idea of the way Wittgenstein had to travel before he arrived at the relevant remarks as printed in the book. This notebook opens with reflections on the notion of privacy:

> Privacy of experiences. This privacy is superprivacy. *Something like* privacy. What seems to be the essential characteristic of privacy? Nobody but I can see it, feel it, hear it; nobody except myself knows what it's like. Nobody except I can get at it. Language game with the colour-chart. Let us imagine each man has a private chart (perhaps *besides* having a public one.) Imagine he points to green on his private chart when 'red' is said – why should we say he means by 'red' the colour we mean by 'green'? Privacy of feelings can mean: nobody can know them unless I show them, or: I can't really show them. Or: if I don't want to, I needn't give any sign of my feeling but even if I want to I can only show a sign and not the feeling. (PO, 447)[1]

Various points mentioned by Wittgenstein are noteworthy. (1) The general word singled out to stand in for a variety of terms is 'experiences'. If one looks back at the list given above, which was assembled on the basis of his earlier lecture notes, it is clear that items like justification, definition, and the game of chess are not covered by 'experiences', while impressions, sensations, and visual images are probably meant to fall under this heading. (2) The word 'super-privacy' recalls certain passages from the *Investigations* where Wittgenstein remarks on the role of what he calls 'philosophical superlatives':

---

[1] The notebook (MS 166) was very probably written sometime after 1935 and not much later than 1940. It bears the title 'Notes for the "Philosophical Lecture"'.

super-order and super-concept in §97, super-expression and super-fact in §192, and super-likeness in §389. This indicates that we may regard super-privacy, and hence certain forms of privacy, as another philosophical superlative. (3) Saying that the intended privacy of experiences is 'something like privacy' could be taken as a way of suggesting that it is not real, or ordinary, privacy but perhaps a kind of metaphorical privacy.

Wittgenstein then goes on to discuss the question of what characterizes privacy (in this special sense). (4) He points out that it signifies that no one except myself can draw on these experiences. In Kenny's terms, this would be a matter of knowledge – knowledge necessarily restricted to myself. To put it yet another way, this kind of privacy is a form of unsharable first-person access to certain mental items. (5) The example of the colour-chart is interesting but, perhaps, not entirely clear. As described by Wittgenstein, it is a chart which one can point to. It seems that this move is somehow meant to externalize the internal. But no person besides myself is supposed to look at this chart – and that turns it into a freewheeling cog in the machine (cf. PI §293: 'beetle in the box'). (6) The concluding remarks of the quoted passage can be taken to show that, in Wittgenstein's view, speaking of the privacy of mental occurrences (this time it is not *experiences*, but *feelings*) can mean different things. It may serve to bring out that I can, as it were, keep the lid on what is going on inside me. On the other hand, emphasizing privacy may also be a way of admitting defeat: I shall never succeed in fully getting across what I feel.[2] Whether I regard privacy as a chance or as a limitation may well depend on which of these two possible attitudes fits my present mood or attitude.

2.

So far we have chiefly, and in a fairly general way, talked about experiences or feelings, that is, about occurrences, processes, happenings. And as far as Wittgenstein's notes from the time around 1935 are concerned, the great majority of cases of privacy mentioned by him are cases of private experience. But what about *objects* – private objects? The main candidates for the position of private objects are sense data, at any rate sense data of the

---

[2] This aspect of the notion of privacy is forcefully brought out in the following passage from 'Notes for Lectures on "Private Experience" and "Sense Data"' (PO, 234): 'But doesn't the word "seeing red" mean to me a particular process /certain (private) experience/ or (mental) event, a *fact* in the realm of primary experience – which surely is utterly different from saying certain words?' What is also interesting about this passage is that (unwittingly?) it reverts to the terminology of primary (vs secondary) kinds of experiences much employed by Wittgenstein in his writings and discussions during the first years after his return to Cambridge in 1929. In that context, the world of primary experience was that corresponding to 'phenomenological' or 'primary' language, the language of verification, and hence the world of immediate acquaintance – of pictures on the screen as opposed to pictures on a strip of film, as he used to say around 1930. In 1935 this idea is expressed by the image of the 'real present experience's' having 'no neighbour'. Characteristically, this is now called a 'grammatical' feature (PO, 229).

kind discussed by Wittgenstein, that is, objects that I in the privacy of my mental cinema can study while no one else can observe what they do or present themselves as being. Of course, there are several ways of making sense of the idea of sense data, and Wittgenstein, who had had many discussions with Russell and Moore and various other Cambridge philosophers, was familiar with some of these ways. But it is clear that in his discussions of privacy his favourite target was a view that could be understood as construing sense data as inner objects corresponding to physical objects. One of his reasons for giving pride of place to this sort of conception must have been the fact that there is a palpable linguistic, or grammatical, temptation behind this sort of view. It is in this vein that he said in one of his last lectures before leaving Cambridge for Norway in 1936:

> Our craving is to make the *grammar* of the sense datum similar to the grammar of the physical body. That is why the term 'sense datum' was introduced – it being the 'private object' corresponding to the 'public object'. (PO, 357)[3]

The problem is that in talking about sense data we rely on linguistic means established in connection with ordinary physical objects while sense data are expected to support and lend philosophical respectability to physical objects. One way sense data are expected to support physical-object talk is through the process of learning the rudiments of one's mother tongue. This is believed to be a process that on the one hand involves public forms of teaching but on the other is dependent on effecting a connection between a private experience and a linguistic form of expression which is communicable in a generally accessible fashion. It is in this context that Wittgenstein writes (and we must remember that these are very sketchy notes for lectures):

> 'Our teaching /training/ connects the word "red" (or is meant to connect it) with a particular impression of his (a private impression, an impression in him). He then communicates this impression – indirectly, of course – through the medium of speech.'
>   Where is our idea of direct and indirect communication taken from?
>   How, if we said, as we sometimes might be inclined: 'We can only hope that this indirect way of communicating really succeeds.'
>   ...
>   'We teach him to make us see what he sees.' He seems in an indirect way to show us *the object* which he sees, the object which is before his mind's eye. 'We can't look at it, it is in him.' (PO, 220f.)

According to this picture, teaching a first language consists in establishing a connection between a word and an inner image that is not accessible to the teacher. So there is no way of being certain that the right kind of connection has been effected in the right way. Therefore all we can do is *hope* that this connection is the right one. If it is, there is a good

---

[3] For Wittgenstein's attitude towards sense data, see Schulte 1993, 85–94. There is an important connection between certain issues discussed in the context of examining the idea of sense data and Wittgenstein's remarks on 'the visual room' (PI §§398–400) as well as his more general discussion of questions of ownership introduced by these remarks. Many instructive references and quotations are given in Peter Hacker's commentary on PI §§398ff. See Hacker 1993.

chance that our 'indirect' way of communication will suffice to get across what is perceived. But it will always remain a dicey kind of business, simply because there is one stage in the process which is accessible to no one but the person who is supposed to do the reporting.

In this case, what is relevantly private is not so much a process of perceiving or inspecting but the *object* of inspection. And this seems to confront us with a much more serious kind of problem than the privacy of access (knowing, perceiving, inspecting, etc.). As soon as a thing is supposed to be private (in the sense of being inaccessible to everyone except the one person whose thing it is supposed to be), there seems to be no way of establishing identity.[4] As regards experiences, Wittgenstein says that we have no good reason for talking about *a* private experience – after all, we just do not know if there is one experience or a hundred. (PO, 243) In the case of objects – or alleged objects – this problem may turn out to be even more serious for the straightforward reason that the idea of an object is so evidently bound up with the idea of identifying, individuating, and counting objects. And if, in the face of an *ex hypothesi* impossibility of counting private objects, we insist on speaking of such objects, we are no doubt in a fix. (I am not suggesting that the problem is less serious in the case of occurrences or processes; only that it is more obvious in the case of – supposed – objects.)

3.

One of the things we want to understand is whether Wittgenstein's use of the adjective 'private' admits of an explanation that is in any way special and allows us to throw light on some of his remarks. In a number of cases there is an easy and reliable way of finding out about the intended meanings of Wittgenstein's words. This way consists in looking at the passages containing the relevant word to see whether the context offers synonyms or near-synonyms of that word which could then be used to elucidate it. Applying this method in the case of the word 'private', we shall find two synonyms or near-synonyms, viz. the words 'inner' and 'subjective'. There are several passages where these words are used to clarify the meaning of 'private' or where one of them is deleted and replaced by 'private'. A further instructive feature of some of these passages is that in them Wittgenstein makes essential use of the relevant opposites: 'public' in the case of 'inner' and 'objective' in the case of 'subjective'.

Most of these passages are interesting in their own right, and it is certainly useful to look at some of them. In a manuscript that, as it happens, served Wittgenstein as a kind of intermittent diary,[5] he gives various descriptions of a man who tries to report on inner

---

[4] Questions of identity play a great role in the discussion of the sameness of sensations mentioned at the end of section 6, below.

[5] This is MS 119 (see p. 122v), which Wittgenstein wrote between 24 September and 19 November 1937, that is, when he was living in Norway, working on what became the second part of the 'early version' of PI. A revised version of this part was printed as Part I of *Remarks on the Foundations of Mathematics*.

occurrences in a language known only to himself. This man, Wittgenstein observes, makes a 'basic mistake' which is often made in this area, and this mistake is enshrined in the idea that language has two kinds of sense – a public kind as well as a private one. In reality, Wittgenstein continues, a strictly private use would at best amount to emitting noises that accompany certain experiences. The crucial point is: 'a "private language" cannot be used to play a language game. After all, there are certain rules for the public use of the word "pain"; whereas we [who are tempted by the idea of a private use] imagine that the word is tied to a certain inner experience.' (MS 119, 122v–123r; cf. the points made in PI §§258–61.)

Another difficulty besetting the idea of a private use of words lies in the fact that he who aims at using 'signs' privately will somehow have to be able to *recognize* the occurrences or objects he wishes to refer to.[6] All the words we may be tempted to use in a private fashion gain their intelligibility from having an established public use. Once there is this public use, there is no basic difficulty in expressing feelings, experiences, sensations, etc. And there is another public element mentioned by Wittgenstein in this context. This is the fact that 'recognition' involves certain public criteria. If, on the other hand, one claims to recognize a private object, this seems to be 'the same as thinking that one recognizes it'.[7] At this point we understand that the public and the private do not mesh in a fruitful way.

> And this [Wittgenstein writes] as it were extinguishes language as if it had been switched off. We are completely in the dark. We become aware of the fact that the word 'red', for example, is a word only in our public way of using it and that language simply comes to an end as soon as we withdraw into privacy: the word 'red', for instance, will lose its use. It is nearly as if we wished to see the *real* colour by means of switching off all the lights around us. For these, we say, affect the colour, and hence I can never see the real natural coloration as long as outside light falls on it. Of course, this is a misunderstanding concerning the use of the words 'colour of an object'. (MS 119, 124r–v; 15 November 1937)

4.

As we have seen, the word 'inner' is sometimes used as an equivalent or near-equivalent of 'private', and the opposite 'public' indicates one relevant contrast that can be appealed to in order to sharpen our understanding of 'private'. The second near-synonym we

---

[6] That recognition poses a great problem if you want to proceed privately is mentioned in earlier manuscripts too, for instance in 'Notes for Lectures', PO, 238, where Wittgenstein describes the following exchange:

> 'Are you sure that you call "toothache" always the same private experience?'
> 'I recognise it as being the same'. And are you also recognising the meaning of the word the same, so you can be sure that 'recognising it to be the same' now means the same to you which it did before?

[7] MS 119, 124r; this and other translations from Wittgenstein's manuscripts are mine. The similarity between these words and the crucial formulations in PI §§202 and 258 is obvious.

mentioned was the word 'subjective'. There are manuscript passages where the word 'subjective' is deleted and replaced by 'private', and that is good evidence for holding that, while Wittgenstein regards these two words as nearly equivalent, there are certain contexts where he considers 'private' the more apposite expression. To mention just one passage where Wittgenstein exploits the near-equivalence of 'subjective' and 'private' (in the relevant sense), I want to draw attention to a sequence of remarks on subjective and objective understanding in manuscript 116 (pp. 116–18). Here, Wittgenstein points out that we are tempted to regard our capacity to associate pictures with words as a form of understanding these words. But this capacity, he says, does not tell us if we have understood a word correctly, that is, in the way it is commonly understood and used. At best, my ability to imagine a blue pot when I hear or read the words 'a blue pot' is a kind of *subjective* understanding. *Objective* understanding – e.g. by effecting a connection with the *right* image – is a different matter altogether. The way Wittgenstein spells out what is required for objective understanding is very instructive, also because it indicates what in his view is needed to be able to bring in a helpful notion of objectivity.

He begins his reflections by wondering whether the idea of subjective understanding could not be explained by saying that from a subjective point of view linguistic expressions are tools for private use; they do not count as means of communication with others. To this, Wittgenstein replies by saying that it is by no means obvious that it is legitimate to speak of 'tools' and 'language' in such a case. He illustrates his view by sketching one of several stories about Robinson Crusoe that can be found in his manuscripts.[8] If we observed Robinson doing all kinds of things by himself, we should quite naturally say that certain ways of employing symbols are private uses of such symbols. If, for example, he used a code to designate certain plants or types of event, it would be quite legitimate to conclude that he was playing language games with himself. One of our reasons for coming to this conclusion would be observable regularity in Robinson's behaviour. This case, however, is contrasted with the case of a man who on various occasions produces unfamiliar noises that as far as we can make out are not characterized by any form of regularity. Here, Wittgenstein suggests, it may happen that we respond to this situation by commenting: 'Well, this may be a purely private language; probably he imagines the same thing whenever he utters the same sound.' But this would of course be an unjustified extension of our willingness to credit people displaying a kind of behaviour superficially similar to that of language-users with the fully fledged ability to use symbols. And one reason for this unwarranted generosity resides in the following view, which many of us are tempted to accept: 'Once you know *what* a word refers to, you understand it and know all about its application.'

---

[8] Another fairly early passage involving Robinson Crusoe can be found in 'Notes for Lectures' (PO, 237): 'We can indeed imagine a Robinson [Crusoe] using a language for himself but then he must *behave* in a certain way or we shouldn't say that he plays language games with himself.' And on p. 247 he asks the following intriguing question: 'Imagine a Robinson [Crusoe] lying to himself. – Why is this difficult to imagine?'

Objectivity is one idea that Wittgenstein contrasts with privacy. And objectivity, he suggests, presupposes that the people concerned use a language in the minimal sense of making recognizably regular use of what we can conceive of as symbols. An alleged 'purely private' use of supposedly private symbols would not satisfy that condition. Therefore it could not be assessed as objective, and hence not as subjective either: the subjectivity from which this reflection took its start has turned out to be a kind of super-subjectivity – a philosophical superlative.

It is clear that languages or sign-systems used by Robinson Crusoe in a way which could helpfully be described as being used by him in playing language-games with himself are not private in the sense we are interested in. This becomes strikingly clear when one looks at a manuscript passage written in the summer of 1944, that is, at a time when Wittgenstein was working on the material we nowadays refer to as constituting great parts of the PI 'chapters' on rule-following and the private-language arguments. Here he notes that the 'private' language of which one may wish to say that Robinson uses it in talking to himself is one which an eavesdropper might understand: Robinson's behaviour could reveal what his words mean. In this manuscript, the very next remark is an early version of what became the second paragraph of PI §243: 'But couldn't one imagine a language in which a person wrote down or uttered his private sensations, his inner experiences for his personal use? Of course, this language would then be intelligible only to himself, since no one else could ever know what the words, the signs, of this language referred to.' (MS 124, 222) Naturally, reading these remarks in such close proximity in Wittgenstein's manuscript is striking, and the 'of course' in the second sentence of our quotation is absolutely arresting. But this is by no means the first occurrence of the idea of a private language in the relevant sense of 'private'.

In the lecture notes of 1935 one finds a short series of remarks dealing with the question of what might persuade us to believe that languageless creatures (like human infants) think certain kinds of thought which they may later claim to remember.[9] In this context Wittgenstein alludes to the passage from Augustine which came to form the beginning of PI §1. And he continues with the brief but remarkable question: 'Why shouldn't we consider the case that the child learns to think and always assume that it had a private language before it learnt ours?' In other words, Wittgenstein wonders why one should not start from a premise like the one attributed to Augustine (or, rather, an Augustine-like figure) who is said to hold a view according to which the child 'already had a language, only not this one. Or again: as if the child could already think, only not yet speak. And "think" would here mean something like "talk to itself"' (PI §32). In the lecture notes Wittgenstein rightly wonders what would become of our notions of teaching and learning under such an assumption. At any rate, this is an idea that middle-period Wittgenstein regarded as exemplifying a notion of privacy which clearly foreshadows what was to come in PI §§243ff.

---

[9] This question is also discussed in PI §342; cf. §344.

5.

What we need to get clearer about is Wittgenstein's use of the unexpected word 'private' in combinations such as 'private experience', 'private sensation', 'private image', 'private language', 'private explanation of a word', 'private impression of a picture', 'private picture', 'private showing (*Vorführung*)' (PI §§243–311, *passim*) and in its generalized form 'what is private (*das Private*)' (§274). The tone as well as the drift of these remarks suggest that there is a critical purpose behind Wittgenstein's use of that word. Even if this use does not serve to mount an attack on one specifiable view, most readers will get the impression that it is meant to point out a weakness inherent in a certain type of conception. In my opinion, this impression is entirely right; but there are at least two difficulties with this reading of the passages concerned. The first one is that it is not obvious how that type of conception is to be characterized on the basis of Wittgenstein's text. The second one is that the nature of the service that the word 'private' can, in Wittgenstein's view, be hoped to render is by no means self-evident.

So far, the second problem has received scant useful discussion that I am aware of. The simple reason for this state of affairs seems to be that readers are not sufficiently struck by Wittgenstein's unusual employment of that word. On the other front, however, a good deal of work has been done to characterize the target of Wittgenstein's critical remarks on privacy, and a number of authors have made attempts at identifying recognizable views that Wittgenstein may have had in mind. There surely is a fair amount of agreement in the literature about the outlines of the type of position criticized in the relevant part of the *Investigations*. But occasionally one hears dissenting voices. As a rough picture of the target position may help to gain a better understanding of what Wittgenstein was driving at with his curious use of the word 'private', and as arriving at such an understanding is my central aim in this chapter, I shall first try to give a brief account of what may safely be regarded as the standard view on this question. I shall proceed to discuss a few points raised by one dissenting voice, since this may help us get a clearer idea of what is at issue here. Against the background of this discussion and the material collected in the earlier sections of this chapter I shall then hazard a guess at what may have been Wittgenstein's point in choosing to draw our attention to privacy in the way he did.

As regards the standard perspective on what position could be regarded as a natural target of Wittgenstein's critical remarks, it will prove useful to look at Peter Hacker's succinct characterization of what he calls 'The traditional picture' that comes under scrutiny in that part of the *Investigations* which is generally held to contain the 'private-language argument(s)'. (Hacker 1993a, 17–36)[10] Here, Hacker emphasizes that the traditional

---

[10] In this chapter, most of the time I refrain from using the phrase 'private-language argument(s)' and simply refer to §§243–315. One reason for doing this is the fact that I do not directly deal with any of these arguments.

picture is associated with certain 'dualities' which can be seen to yield a number of contrasts (certain vs doubtful, corrigible vs incorrigible, etc.). In this chapter on privacy Hacker proceeds to distinguish three types of duality: an ontological, a metaphysical, and an epistemological one. The ontological duality involves a general distinction between a physical and a mental world. The metaphysical duality can be seen to rest on that first, ontological, one and carries with it a contrast between independent and essentially dependent or 'owned' entities. Whereas objects in the physical realm 'belong to the public domain, can be perceived by all who are appropriately situated, can often be owned, shared among several owners, or exist unowned', objects in the mental, or 'inner', realm are 'essentially owned,…essentially untransferable and unshareable. Each person's inner world is metaphysically private property'. (Hacker 1993a, 17) The third kind of duality is an epistemological one. This involves a contrast between public observability (and intersubjective checkability of observation statements), on the one hand, and privileged access to objects and occurrences in a subject's inalienable inner world, on the other.[11]

Hacker goes on to connect these dualities and their attendant contrasts with various doctrines defended by eminent philosophers of the past. This, he maintains, would go some way towards establishing the importance of Wittgenstein's criticisms of these notions, as the correctness of these criticisms would imply the more or less glaring falsity of those well-known doctrines – a consequence which would gain in importance to the extent these doctrines can be made out to continue to play a role in present-day philosophy. This is an aspect of Hacker's discussion that I shall leave aside. There is a connection he draws, however, which I find extremely instructive in the present context: he illustrates the dualities mentioned in his account by quoting from Frege's '*Der Gedanke*' ('Thoughts'), and these quotations can be used to highlight the metaphorical side of these questions, which is too often left out of account.

6.

....

Frege begins the relevant part of his discussion by pointing out that the world familiar to people who have never been troubled by philosophical thoughts is a world of physical objects – things that can be seen, touched, or otherwise perceived by our senses. But this 'external' world, Frege claims, is not the only one we may be familiar with: 'even an unphilosophical man soon finds it necessary to recognize an inner world distinct from the other world, a world of sense-impressions, of creatures of his imagination, of sensations, of feelings and moods, a world of inclinations, wishes and decisions' (66).[12] With

---

[11] Kenny uses the expression 'inalienable' to characterize the 'ownership' sense of 'private'; see his 1973, 185. (The epistemological sense of 'private' is distinguished by saying that what is epistemically private is 'incommunicable'.)

[12] The translations of this and the following passages from Frege are quoted in Hacker 1993a, 17–18. The page references given in brackets in the text are to the original publication, whose pagination is given in several editions of Frege's works.

the exception of decisions, the objects populating this world are summarily called 'Vorstellungen' ('ideas'). The next quotation, which is used to illustrate the second duality, is striking – and extremely useful in introducing a facet of privacy in a way which can be understood to give real bite to Wittgenstein's considerations. Frege writes: 'It seems absurd to us that a pain, a mood, a wish should go around the world without an owner [*Träger* = bearer] independently. A sensation is impossible without a sentient being. The inner world presupposes somebody whose inner world it is.' (67) And as Hacker points out, certain features of the notion of epistemological privacy can also be found in Frege, who describes our familiar material environment, the 'external' world, as a realm of potential error: 'I cannot doubt that I have a visual impression of green, but it is not so certain that I see a limeleaf. So...we find certainty in the inner world, while doubt never leaves us in our excursions into the external world.' (73)

The reason for quoting Frege does not lie in his being the most obvious target of Wittgenstein's remarks (he is not), nor in his being a particularly staunch and articulate defender of a notion of privacy that comes under attack in the relevant part of the *Investigations*. No, the reason is that the *terms* in which Frege describes what he, up to a point,[13] evidently regards as an absolutely standard view of the matter fit the expressions Wittgenstein uses in articulating his remarks in a particularly illuminating way. Some of the metaphors or images used by Frege in putting forward his distinctions and claims are similar or related to those used by Wittgenstein for his own purposes.

The parallels between Frege's and Wittgenstein's words that Hacker has pointed out are striking enough; and the mere fact that such similar words can be used to express such different ideas should give us pause. But the extraordinary thing is that there are yet further parallels – and they are all on the level of metaphor or image. Thus, in trying out what can be done with the notion that only my own ideas can be objects of reflection, Frege arrives at the image of the realm of our ideas as a stage that is set in our consciousness (70). A couple of pages later (72) he uses the image of the theatre to ask the even more pressing question whether experiences are possible without someone who has these experiences: what kind of spectacle would this be without a spectator? Can there be a pain without someone who has that pain? There can be no pain, he says, without the pain's being felt; and that in turn presupposes someone who feels it. This, however, shows that there must be something which is not an idea of mine and in spite of that an object of my thought: I am – my self is – a something of the relevant kind. For Frege, the whole point of rehearsing these notions is this: that an absolutely sharp distinction needs to be drawn between what belongs to the contents of my consciousness and what is an object of my thought. (The conclusion that Frege arrives at is the falsity of the claim that only what is part of the contents of my consciousness can be an object of reflection (72).)

---

[13] Frege regards his way of drawing distinctions between an external world of spatio-temporal objects and our inner world of ideas as absolutely standard. In his own view at any rate, the novelty of his approach resides in his claim that, besides the first two worlds mentioned by him, we have to recognize a 'third realm' of abstract entities – in particular, thoughts (69).

It is obvious that, in one form or another, all these images make an appearance in Wittgenstein's remarks. This does not show that Wittgenstein was thinking of Frege's work when he wrote down his remarks. What it does show is that these ideas were felt to be common ones: they were (and, perhaps, are) in the air, and Wittgenstein took them to be standard ideas that you would hit on easily enough if you thought along the lines Wittgenstein – or Frege, for that matter – found natural. Frege's very precise characterizations of these metaphors may help us see how natural these ideas are once you start reasoning a certain way. And we may add that it is exactly in this context that Frege claims that two people can, in their inner worlds, have similar but never identical sense impressions (75). The correctness of this way of putting it is just what Wittgenstein denies when, in this sort of context, he says that a criterion of identity (which would have to be forthcoming if we were dealing with numerical identity *as opposed to* qualitative sameness) simply is not available in the case of sensations and other mental occurrences (PI §253).[14]

7.

The three central metaphors neatly brought out by Frege were, following Hacker, introduced by describing three kinds of 'dualities' which can be seen to pervade many if not most philosophical discussions of what, broadly speaking, may be called psychological concepts. These central metaphors were: (1) there is an inner world of 'ideas' alongside the external world of physical objects; (2) ideas (sensations, images, etc.) are essentially owned – their existence presupposes the existence of a bearer to whom they can be ascribed; (3) the inner world is the world of certainty as opposed to the external world, which is a realm of potential error. Still following Hacker, we may want to claim that the total picture which emerges from these metaphors comes under attack in the *Investigations*. Parts of this claim have been challenged by the late Gordon Baker, who in the context of a paper aimed at sketching a novel way of approaching the private-language argument makes a number of observations that are very critical of the way the standard view tends to be introduced. While I think that the majority of Baker's observations in this part of his paper are mistaken, some of his remarks can be seen to indicate fruitful new directions for dealing with this material.

Baker agrees that the idea of characterizing the difference between outer and inner world in terms of degrees of certainty is misguided.[15] What he objects to are, first, a certain way of reading the dualities described and, second, the claim that the idea of an

---

[14] These questions are discussed at great length in Cook 1965.

[15] Baker 2001. Here I basically draw on sections 3.7 ('Anti-Cartesianism?') and 3.9 ('The inner world – a myth?'), 98–100, 102–4. On p. 103 Baker writes that 'we are inclined to go astray by representing these differences as differences in degree of certainty'.

inner world is completely useless or 'mere rubbish', as he puts it (102). Probably Baker is right in thinking that the dualities mentioned by Hacker are often simply read as features of a more general doctrine which it is supposedly fair to call 'Cartesian dualism' or just 'Cartesianism'. That this is probably so can, among other things, be seen from the fact that the phrase 'Cartesian privacy' (see Kenny 1966) has gained a certain currency as a label for a set of ideas criticized by Wittgenstein. Baker may well be right in holding that the Cartesianism believed to be the main target of Wittgenstein's criticisms has little to do with what the historical figure Descartes thought, but this question need not concern us here. And Baker is surely right in saying that 'Cartesianism' is not an exhaustive characterization of Wittgenstein's target. But his response to this insight seems to go in the wrong direction.

He responds by insisting that Cartesianism ought to be regarded as only one among several offenders – e.g. idealism, solipsism, introspectionism on the mentalist side and behaviourism on the other side. Baker focusses on behaviourism and claims that Wittgenstein's text contains objections, not only to various forms of mentalism, but also to behaviourism. What is clearly correct is that Wittgenstein explicitly said that his objections to mentalist ideas did not amount to advocating behaviourism. What he meant by that term remains indeterminate, however, except for his seeing it as a kind of reductivist attitude which regards the mind as a kind of appendix of the body.[16] As Baker notes, occasionally Wittgenstein compares behaviourism to finitism in the philosophy of mathematics, and this fact makes it additionally clear that Wittgenstein's reservations about behaviourism are basically a matter of his seeing it as an attitude involving a strong inclination towards reductivism.[17] Baker's attempts at locating objections to behaviourist doctrines in Wittgenstein's text are utterly unconvincing: the passages referred to are simply irrelevant to behaviourism. These manoeuvres also tend to conceal an important asymmetry. While it is a fact that the target of §§243–315 is a recognizable embodiment of more or less Cartesian forms of *mentalism*, it is also a fact that there are no similar figures which one might describe as proponents of physicalism, behaviourism, or materialism. This is significant, and the least it tells us is that Wittgenstein found it interesting to enter mentalists' minds to discover and expose what makes them tick whereas he felt no such curiosity in the case of behaviourists and their ilk.

[16] This is an attitude Wittgenstein explicitly deplores in remarks like the following where, quoting Nietzsche's *Zarathustra*, he writes: 'Am I saying something like, "and the soul itself is merely something about the body"? No. (I am not that hard up for categories.)' (RPP II §690). The remark was written in July 1948. The Nietzsche quotation is from memory; other versions can be found in manuscripts 115 and 152.

[17] RFM, 142: 'Finitism and behaviourism are quite similar trends. Both say, but surely, all we have here is....Both deny the existence of something, both with a view to escaping from confusion.' Cf. Baker 2001, 99. His claim that 'Wittgenstein thinks that each [behaviourism and mentalism] is as misconceived as the other' is as fanciful as his claim that in the passage quoted from the *Remarks on the Foundations of Mathematics* and in *Lectures on the Foundations of Mathematics* (LFM, 111), Wittgenstein 'sets about calling attention to basic defects in behaviourism'. The only defect Wittgenstein notes is the one mentioned above.

Baker's tendency to present behaviourism as a second offender besides the not-really-Cartesian Cartesianism attacked in §§243–315 prevents him from drawing fruitful conclusions from his own insights. At one point he writes that what Wittgenstein 'tries to do…is to undermine the foundations which support entrenched disputes among philosophers rather than to side with one or another party to the dispute' (2001, 99). The second part of this statement is a truly perceptive judgement, and a helpful one: Wittgenstein is not interested in discovering which philosophical doctrine of the relevant kind suits him best and defending it against competing views. What is also correct is the suggestion that Wittgenstein is keen on debunking or exploding what appears to be common ground between rival views. But that does not mean that he regards all these views as equally misguided or misleading; nor does it vindicate this sort of talk of 'foundations'. If it were correct to speak of foundations here, Wittgenstein would not want to undermine them. What he often aims to achieve is showing that alleged foundations are not real foundations; but this is a completely different activity from undermining existing foundations.

8.

There is another respect in which Baker disagrees with the standard view of Wittgenstein's target in §§243–315: he holds that the notion of an inner world is not simply discarded by Wittgenstein. Baker thinks that Wittgenstein treats this notion with a certain respect and even regards it as contributing valuable insights into the grammar of central psychological terms. Baker writes:

> At the root of Cartesian dualism lies the notion that each person has his own mental world, inner and private. Each of us has perfect knowledge of whatever is happening there, and nobody else can know anything at all about this. Experiences are essentially private: this idea of 'Cartesian privacy' entails a radical asymmetry between me and others.…Wittgenstein does not treat the picture of an inner world as mere rubbish. In his view this picture is deeply rooted in the soil of our thought, and it has a profound influence in virtue of clarifying some important aspects of the grammar of such words as 'pain', 'thought', 'intention', etc. (as well as masking other aspects from view). The idea that there is a whole world hidden behind perceptible human behaviour is not an isolated opinion, but rather an attitude that is interwoven with other ideas. (Baker 2001, 102)

No doubt it is a good strategy to regard Wittgenstein, even when he is clearly criticizing a certain position, as treating this position with respect. It seems quite unlikely, however, that Wittgenstein had any intention of handling the picture of an inner world with kid gloves. Below, I shall say more about his treatment of this picture, but it appears clear from the start that he finds hardly anything positive to say about it. In particular, Wittgenstein regards this sort of picture as ultimately unintelligible in the sense that we do not know how to apply it. Baker mentions PI §§423–4[18] as evidence for the view that in Wittgenstein's opinion that 'picture is far from worthless'. Well, surely the significance of these two short paragraphs is far from obvious, but does Baker really want to suggest that Wittgenstein, in claiming that he does not wish to dispute the 'validity' and 'correctness' of the picture concerned, is prepared to affirm that it is valid or correct? It is doubtless much more likely that his declaring himself at a loss how to apply the picture is meant to suggest that, unless we add an explanation, the picture cannot be assessed for correctness in the first place. *That* is why he does not dispute it – because judging its correctness presupposes that one knows how to make use of it.

The second point Baker makes in the passage quoted above is that, according to Wittgenstein, the picture of an inner world 'is deeply rooted in the soil of our thought'. This may be right – if it is meant in the sense of 'is a deeply rooted prejudice'. But Baker seems to suggest that the deep-rootedness of the picture makes it particularly apt to clarify the grammar of our psychological words. Again, Baker's references do not help; they are unconvincing or simply irrelevant. The only point one may want to consider is connected with Cartesianism's 'radical asymmetry between me and others'. Apparently Baker wants to say that this asymmetry is a kind of ancestor of the asymmetry between first- and third-person utterances described and exploited by Wittgenstein. 'In this way [Baker writes], there is something valuable to be salvaged from the idea of the epistemological asymmetry of mental states' (2001, 104). But is there any reason to regard the Cartesian asymmetry as an ancestor of – as a 'valuable' contribution to understanding – Wittgenstein's asymmetry? I do not think so – unless one wants to claim that every view that is successfully criticized has thereby 'valuably' contributed to the criticism. As far as I can see, there is nothing 'epistemological' in Wittgenstein's way of employing the asymmetry between first- and third-person utterances. On the other hand, many of the things he says in this context run directly counter to the spirit of all versions of the Cartesian project: to the extent that Wittgenstein's claim that I cannot properly be said to know that I am in pain can be made out to have a bearing on Cartesianism, it will be seen as a clear rejection of a central Cartesian thesis.

9.

On the whole, Baker's attempt to salvage Cartesian epistemological asymmetry under the protection of Wittgenstein's first/third-person umbrella is completely unsuccessful. What he is right about is, first, that Cartesian dualism is not the only way of thinking

---

[18] §423: '*Certainly* all these things happen in you. – And now all I ask is to understand the expression we use. – The picture is there. And I am not disputing its validity in any particular case. – Only I also want to understand the application of the picture.' §424: 'The picture is *there*; and I do not dispute its *correctness*. But *what* is its application? Think of the picture of blindness as a darkness in the soul or in the head of the blind man.'

attacked in §§243–315 and, second, that the positions attacked there have roots that go deeper than these doctrines themselves.[19] This second point is difficult to discuss, and I do not think that it helps much to say that those positions have roots in 'grammar' (or 'depth grammar', for that matter). I think it is more instructive, and truer to Wittgenstein's way of dealing with these questions, to stay on the level of the metaphors that Frege has so beautifully brought out. This is the level on which Wittgenstein operates most of the time in §§243–315. Of course, this is not the place to discuss a great variety of these metaphors, but I shall briefly try to point out a few examples, at the same time attempting to indicate Wittgenstein's peculiar take on these matters.

One of Wittgenstein's ways of bringing in and dealing with (rather than discussing) the notion of an inner world is presented in PI §§273–4. Clearly, these two remarks are not easy to understand, and I shall not try to say something about all the relevant aspects of what he may be wanting to convey here. At any rate, this is an English translation of these remarks:

> §273   What am I to say about the word 'red'? – that it means something 'confronting us all' and that everyone should really have another word, besides this one, to signify[20] his *own* sensation of red? Or is it like this: the word 'red' signifies something known to everyone; and in addition, for each person, it signifies something known only to him? (Or perhaps rather: it *refers* to something known only to him.)

> §274   Of course, saying that the word 'red' 'refers to' instead of 'signifies' something private does not help us in the least to grasp its function; but it is the more psychologically apt expression for a particular experience in doing philosophy. It is as if when I uttered the word I cast a sidelong glance at my own sensation,[21] as it were in order to say to myself: I know all right what I mean by it.

These remarks hint at several difficulties that a proponent of the image of an inner world (in brief: 'the proponent') will land himself in. Wittgenstein wonders how the proponent can talk about the use of certain words that he may need to explain his position. As the

---

[19]   To forestall misunderstandings it may be useful to clarify this observation. While it is true that Cartesian dualism is not the only recognizable target in §§243–315, it is also true that a loose description of it will fit quite a number of passages. I think it is safe to say that all the target positions are *mentalistic* ones. The fact that *dualistic* terms are often used by advocates of non-mentalistic positions may help to involve them too, at least to the extent they employ such terms to articulate their own views. But since solipsism (which in some of its theoretically possible versions need not be a dualist position) is evidently among the targets of Wittgenstein's remarks, dualism does not seem to be a common feature of all these targets.

[20]   Here as well as in other places I have modified the published translation. Anscombe, for reasons surely known to herself, has 'mean' for 'bezeichnen', which is here rendered as 'signify'. Where the English text has 'something "confronting us all"' Wittgenstein has the remarkably clumsy phrase 'etwas uns Allen Gegenüberstehendes'. As Peter Hacker has pointed out, this is a Fregean expression, cf. *Grundgesetze*, XVIII. The expression is also used in 'Thoughts', see e.g. 66 (original pagination). Cf. the parallels between Wittgenstein's words and Frege's formulations in his Husserl review and *Foundations of Arithmetic* pointed out by Hacker (1993) in his commentary on §273.

[21]   Anscombe translates 'the private sensation'. As Stuart Candlish has pointed out, this is not the only place where she has smuggled in an extra occurrence of the word 'private': in §380 'innere hinweisende Erklärung' becomes 'private ostensive definition'. Cf. Candlish 2004, 299.

proponent does not indulge in doubts about the existence of things in the external world, a word like 'red' will signify a feature of publicly accessible objects. But what about sensations of red? One possible answer is that the proponent needs an extra word to denote a sensation of his; this word would then be part of a private language – and in the context of the *Investigations* we have already seen that that is an absurd notion. Another possible response is that the word signifies two things at the same time: first, something known to us all and, second, something known only to the speaker himself. The parenthesis in §273 introduces the proponent's worry that it might be more appropriate to use the expression 'refer to' (rather than: 'signify'). The worry is probably due to his (correct) impression that 'signify' brings in public uses of language: it won't do to say, '"X" signifies one thing in the common language and another thing for me personally' – that would be a straightforward misuse of the word 'signify'. So he tries to wriggle out of this difficulty by talking about reference instead: we know, after all, that in certain situations words can have referents that are not fixed by what these words mean in the common language. Accordingly, there may be a second reference relation (besides the publicly checkable one) which is open to inspection by me – and no one else. But this shift in vocabulary (from 'signifies' to 'refers to') achieves only one thing: it brings out the way in which the proponent is driven to take certain steps if he wants to remain faithful to the picture of an inner world. The idea of casting a sidelong glance at one's own sensation is of course an absurdity – an absurdity you are saddled with if you insist on the picture of an inner world, and at the same time it is a joke Wittgenstein makes to get it across that this approach is hopeless.[22]

A similar move is made in PI §280. Here the situation is one in which a person makes a sketch of an imaginary scene. This sketch may then serve to tell other people what he had in mind, what he should like to get done, and which actions others are supposed to perform. But (one might want to say) for the person who made the sketch his picture fulfils an additional function: 'for him it is the picture of his image, as it can't be for anyone else. To him his private impression of the picture tells him what he has imagined, in a sense in which the picture cannot tell others.' Again, it is an object in the inner world which is expected to give us privileged information. But if words like 'information', 'sketch', 'depiction', etc. are meaningfully used in cases of the former kind, it is not clear how we are supposed to use them in a case like the second one.

The absurdity of the proponent's enterprise is epitomized in Wittgenstein's remark describing the famous case of the beetle in the box (PI §293, cf. §304). Here it is made clear that the picture of an inner world promotes the idea that there must be inner objects corresponding to our psychological words, and this notion is then reinforced by a conception which tends to construe as many words as possible after the model 'NAME – NAMED OBJECT'. It has been well said that 'the inner-object model, i.e., referentialism

---

[22] This does not in the least mean that we cannot talk about and describe sensations, feelings, impressions, etc. On the contrary, especially in his later remarks on the philosophy of psychology Wittgenstein takes great pains to show how we do it and how we manage to be successful in doing it. What is hopeless is the idea of an inner *world* populated by inner *objects*.

applied to sensation words' is at the root of many of the confusions pointed out in §§243–315.[23]

This is not the place to rehearse many of the cases described by Wittgenstein showing various ways in which the image of an inner world tempts us and leads us into confusion and absurdity, especially if it conspires with an ultra-referentialist view of the function of linguistic expressions. What I want to emphasize here is that this image – the idea of an inner world populated by inner objects amenable to certain forms of inspection and designation – constitutes part of what Wittgenstein means when he uses the word 'private'. The image is easily enriched by all the usual paraphernalia of inner stage performances, movie shows, acts of 'interviewing one's brains',[24] and so forth. In my view, Wittgenstein has decisively contributed to showing that this image is extremely misleading and prone to tempt us into saying all kinds of preposterous things. But how he did it and whether he was really as successful as I think he was are questions I shall not discuss here.

10.

What I want to bring out and discuss in the remainder of this chapter is that the idea of an inner world as well as all those notions connected with it form only *part* of what Wittgenstein is driving at when he uses the word 'private' in relevant contexts. What I have to say here is speculative and difficult to establish (I suppose it is also hard to refute). I want to introduce my observations by quoting a couple of later remarks (written in September 1946) which have been printed in slightly revised form in the collection *Remarks on the Philosophy of Psychology*. The first of these remarks begins with our familiar subject, my private world of inner occurrences:

> 'I had the same sensation three times': that describes a process in my private world. But how does someone else know what I mean? What I call 'same' in such a case? He relies upon it that I am using the word here in the same way as usual? But what in this case is the use that is *analogous* to the usual one? No, this difficulty is not an artificial one; he *really* does not know, cannot know, which objects are the same in this case. (RPP I §396)

In Wittgenstein's manuscript there is a schematic drawing attached to this entry, a drawing which may be familiar to readers of *Philosophical Grammar*.[25] What is probably the

---

[23] Schroeder 2006, 202, n. 27. There is one point, however, where I fail to understand Schroeder's otherwise perceptive account of the power of the arguments that can be derived from Wittgenstein's remarks. He says that for certain philosophers 'it is quite tempting to regard pain as private, in the sense that nobody who had not experienced pain himself could know what the word "pain" means – the inner-object model' (2006, 207). Surely this notion does not amount to anything deserving the title 'the inner-object model', nor does it exemplify an interesting sense of 'private', as far as I can see.

[24] This phrase seems to go back to Raymond Chandler.

[25] PG, 194. A similar remark, without the drawing, can be found in Z §248.

earliest version of this drawing can be found in a manuscript entry of July 1931 (MS 110, 286; 4 July 1931), where it is described as the sketch of a machine invented by Wittgenstein's father. The invention, however, was completely useless. The original drawing was supposed to be a design for the construction of a steam roller, but it is defective inasmuch as its various parts form a rigid system: the machine will not move. Wittgenstein was struck by the picture because he thought that it illustrated certain forms of philosophical error also exemplified by statements like 'These rules must not be violated' (added to a set of instructions) or 'This book must be read in this room' (inscription in a library book). In 1946 he associates the picture with the idea of a private world on which it is in some sense impossible to report because the notion of an analogous use is inapplicable. This much is familiar, of course. But the hint contained in the machine drawing may inspire us to develop the matter in a new way. In the manuscript, a few personal remarks follow the one quoted above. But then Wittgenstein goes back to the machine drawing and its context. He writes:

> 397. The example of the motor roller with the motor in the cylinder is actually far better and deeper than I have explained. For when someone showed me the construction I saw at once that it could not function, since one could roll the cylinder from outside even when the 'motor' was not running; but *this* I did not see, that it was a rigid construction and not a machine at all. And here there is a close analogy with the private ostensive definition. For here too there is, so to speak, a direct and an indirect way of gaining insight into the impossibility.

There is a direct and an indirect way of coming to see that private ostensive definitions are impossible. Let us assume that the way which takes its start from the implausibility of the image of an inner – private – world is the indirect way of grasping the impossibility of the envisaged form of privacy. What would be the *direct* way?

In a sense, the answer is simple: the direct way of coming to see the absurdity Wittgenstein wishes to point out is the insight that it is the idea of the private ownership of mental items itself which is preposterous and misleading. The real problem is not a theoretical one; it is there from the very start, deeply buried in our most elementary forms of thinking and talking about these matters.[26] As always in these matters, the sorts of difficulties exposed by Wittgenstein and other authors become noticeable only when people think about psychological concepts in a philosophical manner. In this area, however, a basic problem makes itself felt straightaway through the most unavoidable metaphors guiding our thought about our own mind and the minds of others. If I am in pain, then there is something – there is 'a something' which is 'important – and frightful' (PI §296). It would be foolish to deny that this is the way we think about it – if we *think* about it at all. And if we continue to think about it, we shall willy-nilly arrive at the conclusion that, since those somethings (sensations and feelings and so forth) are not out there in the external world, they must be in the internal world (Frege's first metaphor). But if we conceive of the inner world as *a world*, it might look as if all those mental items were

---

[26] This was one of Baker's valuable insights mentioned at the beginning of section 9, above.

'going around the world independently'. That would be obviously absurd, and therefore we have to acknowledge that all these items are essentially owned, that somehow it is a matter of logic that all these things belong to someone: 'The inner world presupposes somebody whose inner world it is' (Frege's second metaphor).

This is the decisive step, and by so insistently using the word 'private' in all kinds of unusual combinations Wittgenstein tries to make us see – see in as direct a way as possible – that this step encapsulates all the problems and nonsensical responses to them which he then goes on to point out. For, *of course*, introducing essential ownership or super-privacy (as he called it in a passage quoted above) does not remove the initial absurdity it was meant to eliminate. On the contrary, it compounds it. The very idea of privacy presupposes the possibility that what is privately owned by X could be owned by Y or Z or no one at all. If this possibility is excluded, it makes no sense to speak of privacy either. So, if we introduce the idea of privacy (or super-privacy, for that matter), we at the same time introduce the idea of an object that could be owned by more than one person or by no one at all. These two – privacy and object – are connected like the parts of Wittgenstein's father's machine: they form a rigid system, they do not move at all.

A particularly important consequence of this is that attempts at separating questions of ownership and questions of knowledge in Wittgenstein's treatment of privacy go against the drift of Wittgenstein's discussion (cf. the quotation from Kenny in section 1, above). By speaking of 'private' experiences, objects, etc. he wants to make us see that problems of ownership cannot be got rid of, whatever we do – as long as we continue to ask our philosophical questions within anything like the traditional framework.

Of course, once you see that the fault lies with the most basic step of all – the idea that there are mental items that are owned, essentially owned, by their 'bearers' (as Frege calls them) – you will notice that our whole philosophical way of talking about psychological phenomena is contaminated by this initial blockage caused by the systemic rigidity of what we mistakenly believed to be a prime mover. For example, the idea that we can 'ascribe' mental states to their subjects and, in particular, the widespread habit of talking about self-ascription vs other-ascription surely bear the stain of being derived from the original muddle.

There is little point in trying to produce a longer list of likely effects caused by the initial move: Wittgenstein's text abounds with examples. It is crucial to see that the idea of private ownership is the exact place where he locates the ultimate source of many unfortunate things we are tempted to say when philosophizing about the mind. Once you see this you will also notice that, within the system constituted by our three central metaphors and irremediably fettered by the idea of privacy, there is no solution which could be thought to get us out of this muddle. Putting it this way suggests a certain hopelessness. It is the same kind of hopelessness revealed by some philosophers who tried to show that, in certain areas anyway, human thought is bound to get itself into trouble if it applies its own faculties to itself.

Surprisingly, Wittgenstein offers us a 'solution': unsurprisingly, it amounts to getting rid of or escaping from the system. The solution is adumbrated in remarks like PI §281 ('only of a living human being and what resembles (behaves like) a living human being can one say: it has sensations; it sees; . . .'), §286 ('one does not comfort the hand, but the sufferer: one looks into his face'), §287 (on how one is 'filled with pity *for this man*'), §360 ('We only say of a human being and what is like one that it thinks', etc.), as well as a few scattered remarks in his later manuscripts on the philosophy of psychology. To all appearances these remarks contain the following sort of advice: in doing philosophy, avoid all ways of talking that might get you into the sort of trouble described in my book. One suspects that this kind of advice might amount to suggesting that you should opt out of philosophy as long as you have a chance; or else it might catch up with you.

References

BAKER, GORDON (2001). 'The Private Language Argument', in Stuart Shanker and David Kilfoyle eds., *Ludwig Wittgenstein: Critical Assessments of Leading Philosophers*, 2nd Series, Volume 3. London and New York: Routledge. (Originally published in *Language and Communication*, 18 (1998): 325–56.)

CANDLISH, STEWART (2004). 'Private Objects and Experimental Psychology', in Annalisa Coliva and Eva Picardi eds., *Wittgenstein Today*. Padua: Il Poligrafo.

COOK, JOHN W. (1965). 'Wittgenstein on Privacy', *Philosophical Review*, 74.3: 281–314.

FREGE, GOTTLOB (1980). *The Foundations of Arithmetic*. Evanston, IL: Northwestern University Press.

—— (1984). 'Thoughts', in B. McGuinness ed., *Collected Papers on Mathematics, Logic, and Philosophy*. Oxford: Basil Blackwell.

—— (2009). *Grundgesetze der Arithmetik: Begriffsschriftlich abgeleitet*, vols. 1 and 2. Paderborn: Mentis.

HACKER, P. M. S. (1993). *Wittgenstein: Meaning and Mind, Volume 3 of an Analytical Commentary on the Philosophical Investigations*, Part II: *Exegesis §§243–427*. Oxford: Blackwell.

—— (1993a). *Wittgenstein: Meaning and Mind, Volume 3 of an Analytical Commentary on the Philosophical Investigations*, Part I: *Essays*. Oxford: Blackwell.

KENNY, ANTHONY (1966). 'Cartesian Privacy', in G. Pitcher ed., *Wittgenstein: The Philosophical Investigations*. New York: Doubleday.

—— (1973). *Wittgenstein*. London: Allen Lane, The Penguin Press.

RHEES, RUSH ed. (1993). 'The Language of Sense Data and Private Experience', in *Philosophical Occasions 1912–1951*, ed. James Klagge and Alfred Nordmann. Indianapolis and Cambridge: Hackett.

SCHROEDER, SEVERIN (2006). *Wittgenstein*. Cambridge: Polity.

SCHULTE, JOACHIM (1993). *Experience and Expression: Wittgenstein's Philosophy of Psychology*. Oxford: Clarendon Press.

WITTGENSTEIN, LUDWIG (1967). *Zettel*, ed. G. E. M. Anscombe and G. H. von Wright, trans. G. E. M. Anscombe. Oxford: Basil Blackwell.

—— (1974). *Philosophical Grammar*, ed. R. Rhees, trans. A. Kenny. Oxford: Basil Blackwell.

—— (1976). *Lectures on the Foundations of Mathematics*, ed. Cora Diamond. Chicago: University of Chicago Press.

—— (1980). *Remarks on the Philosophy of Psychology*, vols. 1 and 2, ed. G. H. von Wright and H. Nyman, trans. C. G. Luckhardt and M. A. Aue. Oxford: Basil Blackwell.

WITTGENSTEIN, LUDWIG (1993). *Philosophical Occasions 1912–1951*, ed. James Klagge and Alfred Nordmann. Indianapolis and Cambridge: Hackett.

—— (1997). *Philosophical Investigations*, 2nd edn, ed. G. E. M. Anscombe and R. Rhees, trans. G. E. M. Anscombe. Oxford: Blackwell Publishers. [Certain difficulties of translation mentioned in the text have been taken care of in the 4th edition by P. M. S. Hacker and Joachim Schulte (Wiley-Blackwell, 2009), which contains a revised version of Anscombe's translation.]

—— (1998). *Remarks on the Foundations of Mathematics*, ed. G. E. M. Anscombe, R. Rhees, and G. H. von Wright, trans. G. E. M. Anscombe. Oxford: Basil Blackwell.

—— (2000). *Wittgenstein's Nachlass: The Bergen Electronic Edition*. Oxford: Oxford University Press.

CHAPTER 20

....

ACTION AND THE WILL

....

JOHN HYMAN

§611 to §632 and Part II, section 8 of Wittgenstein's *Philosophical Investigations* are concerned with action and the will.[1] In Peter Strawson's review of the *Investigations*, which appeared in *Mind* in 1954, he says of these remarks, 'rarely has a subject been treated so powerfully and suggestively in so few pages' (1954, 95). In some respects, I share Strawson's high opinion of this material, but I also believe that it is flawed, because Wittgenstein failed to challenge certain assumptions that shaped the philosophical tradition from which he was trying to break loose. I shall begin by describing the intellectual background to Wittgenstein's remarks; then I shall set out his arguments and conclusions; then I shall discuss the flaws.

THE INTELLECTUAL BACKGROUND

....

The main ideas we need to be acquainted with in order to understand Wittgenstein's remarks on this topic are, first, Schopenhauer's neo-Kantian theory of the will, which Wittgenstein seems to have fully accepted in 1916, and which still influenced his thinking in 1947, and second, the theory advanced in William James's *The Principles of Psychology*, which Wittgenstein encountered in the 1930s, and rejected root and branch (cf. Hacker 1996, ch. 5). Schopenhauer and James were in turn reacting, in very different ways, to the empiricist theory of the will, which received its classic exposition in Locke's *Essay Concerning Human Understanding*, with which we should therefore begin. Locke writes as follows:

This chapter is also published in *Grazer Philosophische Studien*, 82 (2011), 285–311.

[1] The other main places where remarks on this topic can be found are the 1914–16 notebooks, where he is still under the spell of Schopenhauer's idealist theory of the will, the *Brown Book*, where there are five pages on 'volition, deliberate and involuntary action' (150), and the 1947 typescript published as *Remarks on the Philosophy of Psychology*, volume 1 (some of these remarks also found their way into *Zettel*).

> All our voluntary Motions...are produced in us only by the free Action or Thought of our own Minds...
>
>   For example: My right Hand writes, whilst my left Hand is still: What causes rest in one, and motion in the other? Nothing but my Will, a Thought of my Mind. (Locke 1979, 4.10.19)[2]

Willing, Locke explains, is 'an act of the Mind, directing its thought to the production of any action, and thereby exerting its power to produce it' (ibid., 2.21.28). *Willing* is its proper name; but Locke concedes that it is hard to find the right words to describe it. At one point, he describes it as 'a thought or preference of the mind ordering, or, as it were, commanding the doing or not doing such or such a particular action' (ibid., 2.21.5). But he admits that the words *preferring, ordering,* and *commanding* do not capture the phenomenon precisely. He concludes that since willing is 'a very simple act, whosoever desires to understand what it is, will better find it by reflecting on his own mind, and observing what it does, when it *wills,* than by any variety of articulate sounds whatever' (ibid., 2.21.30). In other words, one should not try to *define* the act of will: one should simply discover it by introspection.

Schopenhauer has two objections to the empiricist theory of the will. First, he argues that an act of will cannot be 'something different from the action of the body, and the two connected by the bond of causality' (Schopenhauer 1966, 36)—like an internal order or command—for then we could choose whether or not to execute it or obey it, and the executive function would not belong to the will itself, but to whatever acted on this choice. Second, he claims that an act of will cannot be a Thought of my Mind—or, in Hume's phrase, an 'internal impression' (Hume 2000, 2.3.1)—because thoughts and impressions are mere phenomena. They are occurrences we can experience or be conscious of—for example, we can be conscious of a sensation or a wish. But in themselves they are quite passive and inert. Whereas the will is an active principle, if it is anything at all. Schopenhauer's own view was therefore that the act of will and the act willed—the action of the body, as he puts it—are identical:

> They are one and the same thing perceived and apprehended in a twofold manner. Thus what makes itself known to *inner* apprehension or perception (self-consciousness) as real *act of will,* exhibits itself at once in *outer* perception, in which the body stands out *objectively,* as the *action* of the body. (Schopenhauer 1966, 36)

In Wittgenstein's *Notebooks,* the same thoughts are repeated: 'The act of will is not the cause of the action but is the action itself' (NB, 87); 'Wishing is not acting. But willing is acting' (NB, 88); 'The act of will is not an experience' (NB, 89).

James was equally sceptical about the 'free Action or Thought of our own Minds' postulated by Locke. Instead, in *The Principles of Psychology,* he explains voluntary action by postulating sensations corresponding to each of the physical movements we are able to

---

[2] Was Wittgenstein aware of this passage? Z §586 includes the sentence: 'One's hand writes; it does not write because one wills, but one wills what it writes.' It is striking that he attributes writing to the hand.

perform. According to James, we are aware of the movements of our limbs and of various other parts of our bodies, without looking to see whether they occur, because these movements produce distinctive kinaesthetic feelings in our minds:

> Not only are our muscles supplied with afferent as well as efferent nerves, but the tendons, the ligaments, the articular surfaces, and the skin about the joints are all sensitive, and, being stretched and squeezed in ways characteristic of each particular movement, give us as many distinct feelings as there are movements possible to perform. (James 1950, 488)

James holds that while we are still infants involuntary movements produce these kinaesthetic feelings, and images of the feelings are stored in the memory. This process eventually equips us with 'a supply of ideas of the various movements that are possible'; and these ideas are the only mental antecedents of the voluntary movements they enable us to perform:

> We do not have a sensation or a thought and then have to *add* something dynamic to it to get a movement. Every pulse of feeling which we have is the correlate of some neural activity that is already on its way to instigate a movement.... The popular notion that [action] must result from some superadded 'will-force', is a very natural inference from those special cases in which we think of an act for an indefinite length of time without the action taking place. (Ibid., 526)[3]

The difference between willing and wishing, according to James, is simply that willing is desire accompanied by the knowledge that what is desired is within one's power, whereas wishing is desire unaccompanied by this knowledge.

PHILOSOPHICAL INVESTIGATIONS, PART I §§611–32 AND PART II SECTION 8

Wittgenstein's treatment of these theories in the *Philosophical Investigations* is more probing and less polemical than Ryle's famous attack on the Cartesian theory of the will in *The Concept of Mind*. But his conclusions are as radical as Ryle's, as we shall see. He begins with the following anti-Schopenhauerian remark:

> 'Willing too is merely an experience,' one would like to say (the 'will' too only 'idea').
> It comes when it comes, and I cannot bring it about. (§611)

Wittgenstein replies to this remark by challenging the idea that I cannot bring willing about. For on the one hand, we can use the phrases 'I can/cannot bring it about' to

---

[3] Russell agreed: 'Sensations and images,' he wrote, 'with their relations and causal laws, yield all that seems to be wanted for the analysis of the will, together with the fact that kinaesthetic images tend to cause the movements with which they are connected' (Russell 1921, 285f.).

distinguish between the kinds of change in my body that occur when I act, such as the motion of my arm when I raise it, and the kinds of change that simply happen to me, such as when the violent thudding of my heart subsides. But in this sense of the phrase, it is a mistake to think of willing as something that I either can or cannot bring about, because it is not an instance of either of these kinds of change. On the other hand, we can use the phrase 'bringing about' to mean exploiting a mechanism or a known causal connection to produce an effect. But in this sense, Wittgenstein cleverly points out, I *can* bring about willing. For example, I can bring about willing to swim by jumping in the water. It is true that I cannot *will* willing, 'that is, it makes no sense to speak of willing willing', simply because willing is not 'the name of an action; and so not the name of any voluntary action either' (§613). But the remark 'I cannot bring it about', which suggests that I am at the mercy of events, is a misleading way of making this grammatical point.

Why are we tempted to use this misleading form of words, that is, to say that we cannot bring about willing? Wittgenstein's puzzling answer is that it is because we want to think of willing itself as 'an immediate non-causal bringing-about' (§613; cf. Z §580). This is a baffling phrase, and probably a contradiction. (What is bringing about, if not causing?) But Wittgenstein probably meant it to capture the way Schopenhauer and his own earlier self had thought of willing: 'immediate' and 'non-causal' because there is supposed to be no gap between the 'real, immediate act of will' and the 'action of the body' for the 'bond of causality' to connect.[4] According to this way of thinking, Wittgenstein explains in a related manuscript remark,

> the causal nexus is constituted through a series of cog-wheels…whereas the nexus of the will corresponds, perhaps, to that between the inner and the outer or to that between the movement of a physical body and the movement of its appearance…(MS 11, 167)[5]

In any event, it is not difficult to see how, from the premise that I cannot will willing, one might infer that willing 'comes when it comes, and I cannot bring it about'. One only needs to add the premises that I can only bring something about if I can will it; and that whatever I cannot bring about comes when it comes. But what really interests Wittgenstein is that this train of thought seems to transmute the base metal of grammar—the simple grammatical truth that willing is not the name of an action, and so not the name of any voluntary action either—into the pure gold of metaphysics, viz. the doctrine that 'willing too is merely an experience', that is, a phenomenon I am powerless to control. His aim is not to defend the remark in the *Notebooks*: 'The act of will is not an experience' (NB, 89). It is to demystify the concept of voluntary action; and the result of this demystification, as we shall see, is that the act of willing as such vanishes altogether.

So far I have commented on §§611–13. §§614–16 are concerned with the two other remarks from the *Notebooks* I quoted earlier: 'The act of will is not the cause of the action but is the action itself' (NB, 87). 'Wishing is not acting. But willing is acting' (NB, 88).

---

[4] These are all Schopenhauer's phrases. See Schopenhauer 1966.

[5] The MS number follows the catalogue in von Wright 1982, 35ff.

§§614–616 do not challenge these remarks. Indeed they support the claim, which is implicit in them, that willing cannot be wishing, or presumably wanting either. For if it were, we would in effect make use of a kind of mental lever—the wish or the want—to make the motion of our limbs occur. But, Wittgenstein insists,

> When I raise my arm 'voluntarily' I do not use any instrument to bring the movement about. My wish is not such an instrument. (§614)

This train of thought leads to the self-consciously Schopenhauerian conclusion, placed in quotes:

> 'Willing, if it is not to be a sort of wishing, must be the action itself. It cannot be allowed to stop anywhere short of the action.' (§615)

And to this Wittgenstein replies that if it is the action, then it is so in the ordinary sense of the word. So willing is just speaking, writing, walking, etc., and imagining too, since this is also something we can do 'at will'; and also trying to speak, write, walk, imagine, etc. As I put it earlier, the act of willing as such vanishes, and we are left with the action it was postulated to explain. Wittgenstein's own answer to his famous question in §621— what is left over if I subtract the fact that my arm goes up from the fact that I raise my arm?—therefore seems to be: nothing. What is left over is not wishing or wanting; and, he will now argue, it is not trying to move my arm; it is not the kinaesthetic feelings James postulated; and it is not deciding to move my arm either. Voluntary action occurs in a characteristic context, as we shall see. But, as he puts it in *The Brown Book*, 'there is not one common difference between so-called voluntary acts and involuntary ones, viz. the presence or absence of one element, the "act of volition"' (BB, 151f.).[6]

Wittgenstein gives short shrift to the idea that willing should be equated with trying: 'When I raise my arm', he writes, 'I do not usually *try* to raise it' (§622; cf. RPP I §51). He takes James's theory more seriously and writes about it at greater length. As we have seen, James held that I am aware of the movements of my limbs when I walk and of my lips when I speak because these movements produce characteristic kinaesthetic feelings in my mind; and he held that my voluntary movements are caused by the images or ideas of kinaesthetic feelings stored in my memory. For example, when I raise my arm, the motion of my arm is caused by an idea of the feeling associated with this movement. No 'will-force' over and above the idea needs to occur. Hence, according to James's view, the occurrence of the idea, pure and simple, is what is left over if I subtract the fact that my arm goes up from the fact that I raise my arm.

Wittgenstein has much less sympathy for James than for his own earlier self, and his attack is radical and astute. He does not merely deny that voluntary movements are caused by memory images of kinaesthetic feelings: he rejects the very idea that

---

[6] One could also say that Wittgenstein meant the reader to understand that the question posed in §621 is misleading, to the extent that it makes us expect 'one element' to be left over when the subtraction is performed. I do not see a substantial difference between these ways of interpreting the remark.

kinaesthetic feelings 'advise me' (*belehren mich*) of the movement and position of my limbs. It is true, of course, that I can normally feel—i.e. I am normally aware of—how my limbs are disposed and how they are moving. But it does not follow that I am normally aware of feelings—'certain queer feelings in my muscles and joints', as Wittgenstein puts it in §624—which advise me of these things. And as a matter of fact, I am not normally aware of such feelings:

> I let my index finger make an easy pendulum movement of small amplitude. I either hardly feel it, or don't feel it at all. Perhaps a little in the tip of the finger, as a slight tension. (PI II, 185)

But if the idea that kinaesthetic feelings advise me of the movement and position of my limbs is not confirmed by experience, why does it seem plausible at all? Perhaps, as Wittgenstein writes in §598, 'When we do philosophy, we should like to hypostatize feelings where there are none. They explain our thoughts to us.' But he also suggests two reasons which bear more directly on the specific case.

First, philosophers have tended to confuse being aware of something and being aware of sensations or sense-impressions caused by something. This confusion, which sometimes trades under the name *indirect realism*, should be easier to expose in the case of a distance sense, because in this case there is a spatial (and sometimes a temporal) gap between the thing one is aware of and the sensation postulated by the philosopher, which should make it easier to see that being aware of the thing cannot be identified with being aware of the sensation. So Wittgenstein introduces an ingenious example, in which touch *is* a distance sense. If I press the end of a stick against a stone, he points out, it may be tempting to imagine that sensations of pressure in my fingers tell me that the stone is hard. But in fact what I feel is 'something hard and round there'; and not 'a pressure against the tips of my thumb, middle finger, and index finger ...' (§626).[7]

So one reason why we imagine that kinaesthetic feelings advise me of the movement and position of my limbs may be that we are confusing being aware of something and being aware of sensations or sense-impressions caused by something. The other reason is that we may postulate these feelings because there seems to be no other way of explaining how I know what my limbs are doing: 'But after all,' Wittgenstein imagines his interlocutor saying, 'you must feel it, otherwise you wouldn't know (without looking) how your finger was moving' (PI II, 185). To this he replies:

> But 'knowing' it only means: being able to describe it.—I may be able to tell the direction from which a sound comes only because it affects one ear more strongly than the other, but I don't feel this in my ears; yet it has its effect: I *know* the direction from which the sound comes; for instance, I look in that direction. (PI II, 185)

This remark is not convincing in detail. Knowing it does not only mean being able to describe it; and I can tell where a sound is coming from because of the phase difference

---

[7] The analogy between seeing something and feeling it with a stick was invented by the Stoics and used by Descartes, in his *Optics*, in both cases for very different purposes from Wittgenstein's. But it is unlikely that Wittgenstein knew this.

between my ears, in other words, because the sound reaches one ear slightly before it reaches the other one. But the substance of the remark is true: whatever physiological mechanism enables me to know where a sound is coming from, there is no need to postulate a sensation corresponding to the direction. Similarly whatever mechanism enables me to know how my finger is moving, there is no need to postulate a kinaesthetic sensation corresponding to the movement of my finger either. Pain, Wittgenstein points out, provides another analogy. I know that the itch is in my toe, but not because the itch has a toeish quality about it. And memory, he adds, provides yet another. I know I had toast for breakfast, but not because a feeling of pastness is associated with my thought of eating toast.

Finally, Wittgenstein considers the idea that willing to raise my arm is deciding to raise it:

> Examine the following description of a voluntary action: 'I form the decision to pull the bell at 5 o'clock, and when it strikes 5, my arm makes this movement.'—Is that the correct description, and not *this* one: '…and when it strikes 5, I raise my arm'?—One would like to supplement the first description: 'and see! my arm goes up when it strikes 5.' And this 'and see!' is precisely what doesn't belong here. I do *not* say 'See, my arm is going up!' when I raise it. (§627)

Wittgenstein's thought here is influenced by Schopenhauer again (see above, p. 452). It is, in effect, that if willing is deciding, the so-called act it is supposed to cause cannot be an act at all: it can only be a phenomenon I observe. Another gap—a temporal one this time— helps to underline the point; but the point is independent of the gap. If willing were 'something different from the action of the body, and the two connected by the bond of causality', then whether it was wishing, wanting, or deciding, a kinaesthetic feeling or a memory image of a kinaesthetic feeling, it could not make the motion of my arm qualify as my act.

At this point it seems fair to ask whether Wittgenstein has anything positive to say about how voluntary action should be defined. The answer is that he does, and what he says is bold and interesting; but it is not adequately developed or explored. First, he returns to an idea mentioned some half a dozen pages earlier where the topic is what he calls 'a false picture of the processes called "recognizing"'—a picture according to which one recognizes an object by comparing the impression of it with a memory image, and identifying the object in this way. There he writes:

> Asked 'Did you recognize your desk when you entered your room this morning?'—I should no doubt say 'Certainly!' And yet it would be misleading to say that an act of recognition had taken place. Of course the desk was not strange to me; I was not surprised to see it, as I should have been if another one had been standing there, or some unfamiliar kind of object. (§602)

Thus recognizing something need not involve an 'act of recognition' or a memory image of the object: it may involve no more than seeing the things in a familiar place, without feeling surprised. (It may also involve being able to confirm that this is the desk one would have expected to see had one thought about it, and similar things.)

Equally, Wittgenstein now suggests, voluntary action need not involve an 'act of volition' (to use his phrase from *The Brown Book* again) or a memory image of a kinaesthetic feeling: it too may involve no more than behaving in a familiar sort of way, without feeling surprised. Following on from the last sentence of §627—'I do *not* say "See, my arm is going up!" when I raise it.'—he makes the following suggestion:

So one might say: voluntary movement is marked by the absence of surprise.[8] (§628)

Then, pursuing this thought further, he suggests that I can anticipate or 'predict' my own voluntary movements without doing so 'on the grounds of observations of my behaviour' (§631).[9] For example, having decided to pull the bell at 5 o'clock, I can anticipate that I shall do so without depending on the kind of evidence that enables me to anticipate, say, the effect of taking an emetic drug.

It is doubtful whether either of these suggestions could be worked up into a definition of voluntary action (although Elizabeth Anscombe develops them fruitfully in her book *Intention*). Concerning the first, it is unclear whether Wittgenstein means that voluntary movement is invariably or normally marked by the absence of surprise, and whether he means to imply that involuntary movements are invariably or normally not marked in this way. Be that as it may, voluntary movement is not invariably marked by the absence of surprise. For example, a high-jumper may be surprised when she clears an exceptionally high bar, and I may be surprised when I succeed in wiggling my ears for the first time. Furthermore, we are not normally surprised by our involuntary movements and reactions. For example, I would not normally be surprised to find myself panting at the end of a strenuous run, and I am not surprised by the beating of my heart, or surprised when I blink or sneeze. Concerning the second idea, it is true that I can often anticipate my own voluntary movements without doing so 'on the grounds of observations of my behaviour', but the same is often true of involuntary reactions. For example, I may be able to predict that I will feel sad when my ailing friend or parent dies without relying on evidence of this kind.

It is therefore doubtful whether an analysis of voluntary action could be devised on the basis of these ideas. But what is significant about them is that Wittgenstein makes a complete break with the doctrine that voluntary action is action with a particular kind of cause, without embracing the mysterious idea that 'the nexus of the will corresponds...to that between the inner and the outer', or anything similar. Perhaps the most telling remark is §615. I quoted the first sentence above. Here is the remark in full:

'Willing, if it is not to be a sort of wishing, must be the action itself. It cannot be allowed to stop anywhere short of the action.' If it is the action, then it is so in the ordinary sense of the word; so it is speaking, writing, walking, lifting a thing, imagining something. But it is also trying, attempting, making an effort,—to speak, to write, to lift a thing, to imagine something etc. (§615)

---

[8] Aristotle's definition of pleasure (*Nicomachean Ethics*, 1153a14) as the unimpeded activity of a natural disposition discards the idea that pleasure is anything over and above the activity itself, and defines pleasure in terms of the absence of an impediment. Ryle's view, which is roughly that an activity enjoyed is one to which one gives one's full attention without any reluctance, is similar. See Ryle 1949, 108.

[9] §631 also implicitly contradicts TLP 5.1362: 'we could know them [*sc.* actions that still lie in the future] only if causality were an *inner* necessity like that of logical inference.'

The interlocutor here is surely Wittgenstein's earlier self, the author of the remarks in the *Notebooks* quoted above: 'The act of will is not the cause of the action but is the action itself' (NB, 87). 'Wishing is not acting. But willing is acting' (NB, 88). But Wittgenstein does not deny that what the interlocutor says is true. He merely points out what we are bound to acknowledge it implies, if we refuse to mystify the will.

Wittgenstein's conclusions flow naturally from this point. For if willing must be the action itself, then it cannot be what caused the action to occur, or an aspect of the action that is revealed to 'inner apprehension', whatever exactly this could mean. So perhaps it is the context of an act that makes it voluntary—'its character and its surroundings', as Wittgenstein puts it in a later remark (Z §587)—including, in most cases, the absence of surprise: 'Voluntary movements', he writes, 'are certain movements with their normal *surroundings* of intention, learning, trying, acting' (RPP I §776; cf. Z §577). For example, we regard the movements of a child playing with a doll as voluntary, not because we postulate invisible acts of will or images of kinaesthetic feelings preceding them and making them occur, but because we know that the child has learned how to make these movements, because the movements are coordinated and purposeful, because the child attends to what it is doing, is not alarmed or surprised or distressed by its own movements, and so on. If we feel the need to postulate a hidden cause, it is because we ignore these features of a movement and its context, which are for the most part in plain view.

Wittgenstein's critique of the theories he opposed is original and astute. But even if we set aside his failure to develop his ideas adequately and the obscurity of many of his remarks, there are also serious weaknesses in his treatment of this subject, because he fails to make a sufficiently radical break with the past. In particular, he makes three closely related mistakes, which have dominated philosophical thought about action and the will throughout the modern period. First, he confuses the voluntary/not voluntary distinction and the active/passive distinction. Second, he fails to distinguish between action and motion, for example, between raising something and the motion of the thing one raises. Finally, lying behind these two mistakes is—to use one of Wittgenstein's own phrases—a one-sided diet of examples, which in this case means that all of the actions he examines are movements of parts of the agent's body. Arms are raised and fingers are moved, but few other actions are mentioned, and then only in passing. I shall comment on the first two points in turn. What I have to say about the third will emerge as I go along.

The Voluntary/Not Voluntary Distinction and the Active/Passive Distinction

First, a terminological preliminary. The word 'involuntary' is normally defined in dictionaries as the contradictory of 'voluntary', but the actual use of the word is commonly confined to thoughts or changes in the body which a person is unable to control, such as 'an involuntary concurrence of ideas', 'the inuoluntarie running of vrine' or 'the involuntary closing of the eyelids when the surface of the eye is touched'. (All of these examples are taken from the OED's entry for 'involuntary'.[10]) Thus, in the actual use of these words, 'involuntary' and 'not voluntary' are not equivalent, and if something is not voluntary, we cannot assume that it must therefore be involuntary. For example, a man who is conscripted into the army is not a volunteer, but he does not join the army involuntarily, in this limited sense. We are now principally concerned with what is and what is not voluntary.

In reality, the voluntary/not voluntary distinction and the active/passive distinction cut across each other, since activity can be either voluntary or not voluntary, and the same is true of passivity. But philosophers have commonly ignored or failed to notice two of these possibilities. On the one hand, they have tended to think about the will exclusively in relation to action. They have not thought about it in relation to the feelings we experience or the conditions in which we place or find ourselves, or in relation to the occasions when we are acted upon. They have thought about voluntary activity, but they have ignored voluntary passivity, or even denied that it exists. On the other hand, activity and voluntary activity have commonly been equated, as if activity were always voluntary. So they have ignored activity that is not voluntary. The result is that the active/passive distinction and the voluntary/not voluntary distinction have appeared to coincide, and have commonly been confused. I shall discuss voluntary passivity and non-voluntary activity (sc. activity that is not voluntary) in turn.

It is a mistake to suppose that only activity can be voluntary. As it happens, the OED's entry for 'voluntary' begins with voluntary feeling and then proceeds to voluntary action; and if we turn to the entry for 'voluntarily', we find several quotations in which the word qualifies something passive, including the very first. Here are the first and the eighth:

> c1374 CHAUCER Boeth. III. pr. xii. (1868) 103 Ther may no man douten, that thei ne ben gouerned uoluntariely....1663 BP. PATRICK Parab. Pilgr. xiii. (1687) 87 At last he voluntarily, and without any compulsion but that of his Love, died upon a Cross.

The truth is that the distinction between what is and what is not voluntary applies to passivity and to inactivity in exactly the same way as it applies to activity. Children are sometimes picked up and carried voluntarily, they are sometimes kissed and tucked up in bed voluntarily, and they sometimes eat their green vegetables voluntarily. For their part, adults are sometimes voluntarily unemployed, sometimes undergo surgical procedures voluntarily, and sometimes die voluntarily, as Bishop Patrick says Christ did, and as the Italian poet and advocate of euthanasia Piergiorgio Welby did in 2006. There is no reason to deny that voluntariness can be attributed equally to all of these things; and

---

[10] The distinction between 'involuntary' and 'not voluntary' derives from Aristotle's distinction between actions that are performed unknowingly which we do not regret (*ouk hekousia*) and ones which we do regret (*akousia*), but this is not the way in which philosophers now use these terms. (*Nicomachean Ethics* III.1, 1110b18–12; see Broadie 1991, 126.)

there is no reason to think that it is a different attribute, depending on which of them we have in mind.

The idea that only actions can be voluntary—or only the things we do, as opposed to the things that happen to us or are done to us—is an unsupported dogma. In fact, conditions such as exile and poverty can be voluntary, despite not being things we do, because they may be the result of a choice and not of force or compulsion, or undue influence by others, and the same is true of the kisses we give and also of the kisses we receive. Roughly, voluntariness is about choice versus compulsion, and a child can sometimes choose whether to be kissed or carried, just as it can sometimes choose what to eat. Equally, a man may allow himself to fall in love with a woman, in the knowledge that he could avoid falling in love with her if he chose to, or allow himself to fall asleep in the knowledge that he could avoid falling asleep if he chose to; or he may fall in love willy nilly, or fall asleep despite trying to remain awake. In the first case, he falls in love or falls asleep voluntarily, in the second case not. But falling in love and falling asleep are not actions, any more than falling down the stairs.

Why has voluntary passivity been ignored? The most important reason is that the distinction between what is and what is not voluntary was regarded for three centuries as part of a story about the interaction between mind and body. The questions that exercised philosophers were not: what can the concept of voluntariness be applied to?, and how should it be defined? They were: what causes the kind of motion in our bodies that we regard as subject to our own direction and control?, and how does this kind of motion differ from blinking, sneezing, or the beating of the heart? Furthermore, the empiricist theory of the will reinforced the tendency to neglect voluntary passivity. For if a man falls asleep voluntarily or dies voluntarily on a cross, the cause is unlikely to be an 'internal impression' or a 'Thought of his Mind'. In fact it will probably be the same—tiredness in one case and asphyxiation in the other—whether he falls asleep or dies voluntarily or not. It was therefore hard to see that activity and passivity are equally capable of being voluntary, as long as the empiricist theory prevailed. However, it must be acknowledged that not only Wittgenstein, but also other trenchant critics of the theory, ignored voluntary passivity, or actually denied that it exists (Ryle 1949, 74; cf. Anscombe 2000 §49).

Finally, many philosophers today are interested in the concept of voluntariness because of its importance in ethics and the philosophy of law. In fact, the concept of voluntary passivity plays an important role in moral and legal reasoning, notably where consent is involved, e.g. in connection with the law of rape. Nevertheless, voluntary passivity has proved to be less salient than voluntary activity in this context, perhaps in the case of law because of what is called the 'act requirement', the doctrine that criminal liability requires an act.[11]

The other mistake that has encouraged philosophers to confuse the active/passive distinction and the voluntary/not voluntary distinction is the thought or assumption that action is always voluntary. This assumption was made by Hobbes, Locke, Hume, and

---

[11] On this topic, see Duff 2004.

Mill, and it remained dominant in philosophy during the first half of the twentieth century. It was also made by many nineteenth- and twentieth-century jurists.[12] By the nineteenth century, it commonly took the form of a definition. For example, Mill defines action as follows: 'What is an action? Not one thing, but a series of two things; the state of mind called a volition, followed by an effect' (Mill 1973, 1.3.5). And Austin (the nineteenth-century jurist, not the twentieth-century philosopher) offers the following definition: 'A voluntary movement of my body, or a movement which follows a volition, is an act' (quoted in White 1968, 5).

If we accept—as we certainly should—that action is not limited to animals capable of acting voluntarily, it is obvious that these definitions cannot be right (see Kenny 1975, 46; Alvarez and Hyman 1998, 243ff.). But even if we confine ourselves to human action they remain unconvincing. For some human actions are voluntary and some are not. It is debatable how much choice voluntariness requires. But if we are compelled to do something, and cannot choose whether to do it or not, then we do not do it voluntarily—whether the compulsion is physical, moral, psychological, or of some other kind. Do we pay our taxes voluntarily? Does a man who hands over his wallet do so voluntarily, if he is threatened with a gun? Does a prisoner reveal the names of his associates voluntarily, if he does so under torture? Perhaps we cannot answer these questions in general terms, and need to know more about each particular case. But it should be beyond dispute that some actions are not voluntary.

Again, we are bound to ask why philosophers failed to understand this for so long. And again the tendency of philosophers to regard the distinction between voluntary and not voluntary as part of a story about the interaction between mind and body played an important role. For it meant that when philosophers thought about action, they thought exclusively about human action and almost always about actions that consist in a human being moving part of his own body. This one-sided diet of examples reinforced the idea that all action is voluntary, because most of our actions that consist in moving parts of our own bodies *are* voluntary. For example, when we raise our arms or move our legs these actions are mostly voluntary. (Sleep is the main exception to this rule.[13]) The reason for this is that one of the principal factors that cancels voluntariness is ignorance, as Aristotle pointed out; and it is unusual for us to be unaware of the motion of our own limbs. (Again, sleep is the main exception.) Other kinds of action are quite different. For example, when I have a salad for lunch I may occasionally consume a bug. I choose to have the salad, but I do not consume the bug voluntarily, because I am unaware of

---

[12] See Williams 1978 and Dias 1970, 252. See also White 1985, 28ff. for examples and references.

[13] Wittgenstein comments on speaking in one's sleep in *The Brown Book*, and also on 'involuntary exclamations', such as 'Oh!' and 'Help!' His aim is to show that 'there is not one common difference between so-called voluntary acts and involuntary ones' (BB, 151). About speaking in one's sleep, he says, 'this is characterized by our doing it without being aware of it and not remembering having done it' (BB, 155). About the 'involuntary exclamations', he writes as follows: 'I agree that an act of volition preparatory to or accompanying these words is absent,—if by "act of volition" you refer to certain acts of intention, premeditation or effort. But then in many cases of voluntary speech I don't feel an effort, much that I say voluntarily is not premeditated, and I don't know of any acts of intention preceding it' (BB, 155).

consuming it, and would avoid doing so if I could. Since my arm-raisings are mostly voluntary, whereas my bug-consumings are not, it is much easier to equate action and voluntary action if our attention is exclusively directed towards actions of this kind.[14]

This is an important part of the reason why philosophers have believed or assumed that all action is voluntary. But an equally important part of the reason is that the doctrine that matter is inert was accepted by several influential philosophers in the seventeenth century—including Descartes, Malebranche, and Hobbes—and exerted an important influence on the way in which the relationship between action and voluntariness was understood. This comes out especially clearly in Locke's discussion about the origin of our idea of active power, as I shall briefly explain now.

According to Locke, the idea of power is indispensable in science, because it is, he says, 'a principal ingredient in our complex ideas of substances' (Locke 1979, 2.21.3). For example, the liability of gold to be melted in a fire and to be dissolved in *aqua regia* are no less essential to our idea of gold than its colour and weight. And even colour and weight, Locke claims, will also turn out to be powers, if we consider their nature carefully. But if all the materials of reasoning and knowledge—all of our ideas—are ultimately derived from experience, as Locke insists they are, what are the sources in experience of the idea of power?

Locke's answer depends on distinguishing between two complementary kinds of power: *active* powers are abilities to produce various kinds of change, whereas *passive* powers are liabilities to undergo various kinds of change. Action, which is the exercise of an active power, is the production of some kind of change; passion, which is the exercise of a passive power, is the undergoing of some kind of change. The origin of our idea of passive power is, Locke thinks, quite clear. The idea is produced in us by bodies, because we cannot avoid perceiving the changes that they undergo: 'and therefore with reason we look on them as liable to the same change'. But Locke claims that we cannot observe the *production* of a change in the same way. For example, when we see one ball strike another ball, and set it in motion, Locke says,

> [the first ball] only communicates the motion it had received from another, and loses in itself so much, as the other received; which gives us but a very obscure idea of an *active power* of moving in body, whilst we observe it only to transfer, but not produce any motion. (Locke 1979, 2.21.4)

Observing interactions between bodies cannot therefore be the source of our idea of active power. Rather, Locke claims,

> we have [this idea] only from reflection on what passes in ourselves, where we find by experience, that barely by willing it, barely by a thought of the mind, we can move the parts of our bodies, which were before at rest. (Ibid.)

---

[14] I ignore the doctrine, defended by Elizabeth Anscombe and Donald Davidson, that if someone performs one action by performing another action, for example crushes an ant by taking a step, these are one and the same action. This doctrine is criticized in Alvarez and Hyman 1998, 234f.

Thus, according to Locke, our idea of active power is drawn from the experience of producing motion voluntarily ourselves. Moreover, although Locke wanted to retain the idea that natural kinds of substance have characteristic active powers, it follows from these considerations that strictly speaking voluntary action is the only action there is. For when bodies interact, motion is communicated, but it is not produced; and action, Locke insists, is the production of motion, or some other kind of change. The mere transfer of motion does not amount to action. All real action must therefore be voluntary action, consciously effected by the mind.

Locke's argument is unconvincing, because the distinction between transferring and producing motion is specious. There is certainly a difference between producing and transferring people or goods. For example, manufacturers produce goods whereas exporters transport goods from one place to another; and parents produce children whereas bus-drivers transfer them from one place to another. Now if a bus-driver transfers children from a school to a playing-field, the same children who embark at the school disembark at the playing-field. Not just the same number of children, but the very same children. (That generally matters quite a lot to their parents.) But suppose one ball strikes another similar ball, sets it in motion, and decelerates appreciably itself. Has motion been transferred or produced? How are we to decide? We cannot ask whether the second ball acquires the very same motion—not merely the same *quantity* of motion but, as it were, the very same *package* of motion—that the first ball loses, because motion is not a substance that can be packaged and then either handed over or withheld.

But if, as Locke says, the first ball loses the same quantity of motion as the second ball gains, is this not a reason for denying that motion has been produced? It is not; but we need to be clear about why not. It is tempting to point out that when a cannon is fired, motion is not transferred from the powder to the ball. But it would be easy to reply on Locke's behalf that although he should have based his argument on the conservation of energy instead of motion, his basic point is sound. So this objection would not take us far. The real reason why the fact that the first ball loses approximately the same quantity of motion as the second ball gains should not encourage us to say that motion has been transferred rather than produced is that there is no reason why the production of motion—i.e. action—should be in breach of *whatever* conservation laws are enshrined in physics.[15]

This is the crux of the matter. Locke denies that the first ball produces motion in the second ball because it 'loses in itself so much, as the other received', in other words, because the interaction between the balls conserves the total quantity of motion. But it follows that he can only acknowledge that the production of motion—in other words, action—has occurred if the total quantity of motion is not conserved, but increased. An action must therefore be a breach of or an exception to the laws of nature. In other words,

[15] Interestingly, we distinguish between producing and transferring wealth in the way Locke wants to distinguish between producing and transferring motion. The rich man who leaves his money to his son merely transfers wealth from one person to another, but the entrepreneur (we say) actually creates wealth. The reason why we are able to think about wealth in this way is that there are no conservation laws in economics—something we all have reason to be grateful for most of the time.

it must be a *miracle*, an interference in the natural course of events by a being with the strictly *super*natural ability to inject motion into the natural world, rather than merely transferring it to something else.

Locke's conclusion, that we are acquainted with action by 'reflection on what passes in ourselves', is therefore unsustainable, since human beings do not have supernatural powers. If his argument were sound, it would really establish that miracles aside, action does not exist at all. Reflecting on Locke's argument from our present vantage-point, it is not difficult for us to see this, in particular because we understand that the conservation of energy—one of the great discoveries of nineteenth-century physics—applies to our voluntary behaviour no less than to the behaviour of billiard balls. Since we understand this, we can see that Locke's argument is really eliminativist in tendency. It does not confine action to the mind: it excludes it from the natural world altogether.

Thus in Locke's thought, and in the empiricist tradition stemming from Locke, the idea that all action is voluntary did not arise out of a theory of the will. It appears to have arisen from a combination of two things: first, the idea that matter is inert, never a source of motion or change in its own right; and second, a not yet fully naturalized conception of human beings. But as so often in philosophy, the idea long outlived the intellectual context in which it first arose, in this case because it was reinforced by the one-sided diet of examples I referred to earlier. It is therefore not surprising that we find the same focus of attention in Wittgenstein's writings on action and the will, from 1916 to 1947, with the same unfortunate results.

Like his predecessors, Wittgenstein is exclusively interested in the will in relation to action. Voluntary activity is the topic: voluntary inactivity and voluntary passivity are ignored in all of his writings, with the exception of the following remark from 1947 (RPP I §845):

> Can't rest be just as voluntary as motion? Can't abstention from movement be voluntary? What better argument against a feeling of innervation?

This remark, which is unique in Wittgenstein's writings, is specifically about Wilhelm Wundt's theory that voluntary actions are caused by feelings of innervation, which Wittgenstein was aware of because James opposed it in *The Principles of Psychology*. When one considers that the thought expressed here is just as good an argument against James and Russell, or indeed against Locke, as it is against Wundt, it is tantalizing to see Wittgenstein failing to develop it, or to consider how broad its implications are. It is also disappointing to see Wittgenstein noticing voluntary inactivity, but failing to notice, or at least to mention, voluntary passivity.

Also like his predecessors, Wittgenstein focuses on the distinction between the movements of parts of our bodies which we direct and control, such as the movements of our legs when we walk or our lips when we speak, and the ones which we do not control, such as coughing and sneezing (RPP I §806; cf. Z §579) or the beating of the heart (PI §612). He ignores the difference between taking a step or extending one's arm, which is normally voluntary, and crushing an ant underfoot or handing over one's wallet, which may not be. And he ignores the difference between a child eating ice-cream, which is normally voluntary, and a child eating green vegetables, which is often not. Thus a remark composed in 1947 (RPP I §763) reads as follows:

How do I know whether the child eats, drinks, walks, etc. voluntarily or not [*willkür-lich oder nicht willkürlich*]? Do I ask the child what it feels? No; eating, as anyone does eat, is voluntary.[16]

It would not be quite right to say that Wittgenstein assumes that action is always voluntary. Indeed a sentence in §613 implies the contrary: "'Willing' is not the name of an action; and so not the name of any voluntary action either.'[17] But he frequently confuses questions about voluntariness and questions about activity. That is surely why he says that 'eating, as anyone does eat, is voluntary'. This is far from being true, particularly in the case of children. But even when it is not voluntary, eating is active as opposed to passive, and therefore something that one does and not something that one undergoes.

So, once again like his predecessors, Wittgenstein confuses the voluntary/not voluntary distinction and the active/passive distinction. Some of the remarks in the *Investigations* are ostensibly about voluntariness—in particular, those which are directed against the theory that what makes an action voluntary is a special kind of mental cause, such as a kinaesthetic feeling. Others are clearly about action—for example, the famous question 'what is left over if I subtract the fact that my arm goes up from the fact that I raise my arm?' (§621), which has exactly the same meaning (and exactly the same answer) whether I raise my arm voluntarily or not. But there is no sign that Wittgenstein is aware of the difference between these topics. Only in 1947 does he begin to think about voluntariness as such. Now the focus of his attention broadens, he considers actions that do not merely consist in someone raising an arm or moving a finger (RPP I §§762ff., 902), he notices that inactivity as well as activity can be voluntary (§845), and he makes the connection between voluntariness and awareness (§§761, 844, 902). It is as if he has settled accounts with his earlier self in the *Investigations* and is now able to take a fresh look at the nature of action and the will.

ACTION AND MOTION

Wittgenstein's second major mistake was his failure to distinguish between action and motion, or to consider how they are related. For example, suppose I raise my arm. How are my action, my raising of my arm, and the motion of my arm related? Some

---

[16] The published translation (by Anscombe) reads, 'How do I know whether the child eats, drinks, walks, etc. voluntarily or involuntarily?' This is clearly not the correct translation of the German 'willkürlich oder nicht willkürlich', and it disguises the error. For of course the child who is made to eat his green vegetables, and does not do so voluntarily, does not eat them involuntarily either, in the sense explained above (p. 460)—that is, the movements of the child's mouth are under its physical control. It should also be noted that Wittgenstein's use of the word 'willkürlich' to mean 'voluntarily' (as opposed to 'willingly') is unidiomatic. He follows Schopenhauer's use of the word in *Die Welt als Wille und Vorstellung*.

[17] See also Z §577 and RPP I §902. In PI §614, the word 'voluntary' is in scare quotes, suggesting perhaps that the very concept may be tainted or unclear.

philosophers have claimed explicitly that they are identical. For example, when Donald Davidson considers the question of how actions should be located in space and time, he writes: 'if a man's arm goes up, the event takes place in the space-time zone occupied by the arm; but if a man raises his arm, doesn't the event fill the zone occupied by the whole man? Yet the events may be identical' (Davidson 1980, 124).

Wittgenstein does not make this claim explicitly; but like many of his predecessors, including Schopenhauer, he confuses action and motion. This comes out clearly in the passage in which he links voluntary action with the absence of surprise. I quoted this passage earlier, but it will be useful to have it before us again.

§627   Examine the following description of a voluntary action [*einer willkürlichen Handlung*]: 'I form the decision to pull the bell at 5 o'clock, and when it strikes 5, my arm makes this movement.'—Is that the correct description, and not *this* one: '...and when it strikes 5, I raise my arm'?—One would like to supplement the first description: 'and see! my arm goes up when it strikes 5.' And this 'and see!' is precisely what doesn't belong here. I do *not* say 'See, my arm is going up!' when I raise it.

§628   So one might say: voluntary movement [*die willkürliche Bewegung*] is marked by the absence of surprise.

In §627, Wittgenstein points out that we might describe a voluntary action (*eine willkürliche Handlung*) by saying 'I raise my arm', but not by saying 'My arm makes this movement' or 'See, my arm is going up!' (§627). And from this he infers, in §628: 'So one might say: voluntary movement [*die willkürliche Bewegung*] is marked by the absence of surprise.' Thus he appears to believe that the reason why I do not describe my action by saying 'See, my arm is going up!' is that I am not surprised, and that what is wrong with the description 'See, my arm is going up!', what prevents it from being a satisfactory description of a voluntary action, is the word 'See...!', the expression of surprise, rather than the phrase 'my arm is going up'. It does not occur to him that 'my arm is going up' describes the motion of my arm, and that the action and the motion—the *Handlung* and the *Bewegung*—are different things.

In the remarks that date from 1947, Wittgenstein still shifts back and forth between *Handlung* and *Bewegung*, without considering whether there is a difference between them (e.g. §§840, 901f.); and, as we might expect, he also misses the distinction between the action of moving a limb and the motion of the limb in the passage in *The Brown Book* which lies behind PI §§627–8. In this passage, he describes how one can press the back of one's hand against the wall, then step away from the wall and let one's arm rise 'of its own accord', commenting:

There is a difference between the voluntary act of getting out of bed and the involuntary rising of my arm. But there is not one common difference between so-called voluntary acts and involuntary ones. (BB, 151f.)

The difference Wittgenstein fails to notice is that getting out of bed is a case of action whereas 'the involuntary rising of my arm' is a case of motion. He may be right in saying that there is not one common difference between so-called voluntary acts and involuntary ones; but the difference between getting out of bed and the rising of my arm is the difference between action and motion, and not the difference between two kinds of act.

Commentators have uniformly failed to recognize the switch from *Handlung* to *Bewegung* in PI §§627–8.[18] But it is absolutely vital to see that these are different things, because if something is raised or lowered (or moved or affected in some other way) the raising or lowering of the thing is a case of action, whereas the motion of the thing raised or lowered is a case of passion. So if we fail to notice the difference between my raising of my arm (the *Handlung*) and my arm's going up (the *Bewegung*), we've missed the very distinction between activity and passivity that we were trying to explain. It is just the same if someone is killed: the killing is a case of action, whereas the dying is a case of passion. And it makes no difference what is raised or lowered or killed. If I raise my hand, my glass and the nail on my little finger in a single gesture, my raising of my hand and of the nail are no less certainly distinct from the motion of the hand and the nail than my raising of my glass is distinct from the motion of the glass, despite the fact that the hand and the nail are parts of my body whereas the glass is not. And if I commit suicide, this act is no less certainly distinct from my death than the killing is distinct from the death when one person kills another.

So, if I raise my arm, how is this action related to the upward motion of my arm? How is the *Handlung* related to the *Bewegung*? The answer is that the action, my raising of my arm, is, as Locke put it, the production of the motion, in other words, the causing of it, by the agent, namely me. Von Wright calls the *Handlung* an 'act' and the *Bewegung* its 'result'.[19] So, if we adopt this terminology, we can say that my act of raising my arm is my causing of the result of this action. (This is von Wright's own view, as we shall see.) Acting is not causing an action, as some philosophers in the 1950s and 1960s believed; it is causing an event—the event von Wright calls the action's result (see Taylor 1966, 115; Chisholm 1976). Hence the answer to Wittgenstein's question in §621—what is left over if I subtract the fact that my arm goes up from the fact that I raise my arm?—is not willing or wishing or wanting or trying; but it is not nothing either, or the absence of surprise. What is left over is the fact that I made it happen, the fact that I caused the motion of my arm to occur.

The other cases I mentioned are no different from raising my arm, in this respect. If I raise my glass, this action is my causing of the upward motion of my glass; and if A kills B, this action is A's causing of B's death. But notice that a causing is not the same thing as a cause. For example, we can trace our way back along the chain of causally connected events that led up to B's death—events occurring in B's body, in the space between A and B, and in A's body; but we shall not find A's killing of B anywhere along this chain of events. A's killing of B is (roughly speaking) the causal relation between A and one of these events, namely, B's death; A's pulling of the trigger is the causal

---

[18] For example, Hacker comments on §628, 'This concludes the discussion by citing one mark of voluntary action, which was intimated in the previous section. It is characteristic of voluntary actions that the agent is not surprised' (Hacker 1996, 610f.). In Anscombe's translation of RPP I, 'Handlung' is sometimes translated as 'action' and sometimes as 'movement' (e.g. §840).

[19] This is a quasi-technical use of the term 'result', but it is useful to mark the distinction in this way. See von Wright 1963, ch. 2.

relation between A and an earlier event in the chain, namely, the motion of the trigger; and so on.[20]

During the last three centuries, philosophers have generally failed to distinguish between my raising of my arm, which is an action, and the motion of my arm, which is a mere event. And when the action and the motion are not simply identified—as they are by most philosophers, including Wittgenstein—the action is held to be a combination of the motion and its cause (as we have seen it is by Mill) or else to be identifiable with the cause alone.[21] The most important exception is G. H. von Wright, who writes as follows:

> The notion of a human act is related to the notion of an event, *i.e.* a change in the world. What is the nature of this relationship? // It would not be right, I think, to call acts a kind or species of events. An act *is* not a change in the world. But many acts may quite appropriately be described as the bringing about or effecting ('at will') of a change. To act is, in a sense, to interfere with 'the course of nature'. (von Wright 1963, 35f.)

There was no need for von Wright to confine this observation to human acts, and the parenthetical phrase 'at will' is out of place, because while it is true that many acts are voluntary, it is equally true, as we have seen, that many are not. However, the principal idea expressed here is exactly right. An action is the bringing about or effecting—in other words, the causing—of an event. As I have already indicated, action cannot be described as interference in the course of nature, because it is part of the course of nature—unless it is miraculous, of course. But it can be described as interference in the course of events.

Returning to Wittgenstein, we can again ask how he could have missed this. How could he have confused the *Handlung* and the *Bewegung*, the act and its result, when the relation between these things is the key to understanding what action itself is? The answer is the same as it was last time. First, the distinction between act and result was missed in the philosophy Wittgenstein had read. Second, Wittgenstein's exclusive interest in actions that consist in human beings moving parts of their own bodies made the distinction between act and result less salient than it would otherwise have been. The reason for this is that the distinction is more obvious when the result is more remote from the agent. (This is another case where distance is an intellectual aid.) For example, it is harder to confuse my raising of a flag and the motion of the flag than it is to confuse my raising of my arm and the motion of my arm, because in the first case we can imagine the result without the action. We can cut the agent out of the picture, so to speak. But if the result is the motion of part of the agent's own body, we cannot do this; and if we imagine ourselves pointing to the action and pointing to its result, we are pointing towards roughly the same place.

---

[20] The reason for the parenthetical qualification is that there are more and less restrictive concepts of a relation. For example, if a relation is a way in which one thing can stand to another thing, or several things can stand to one another, then an action is not a relation, because acts are dynamic and not static. See Hyman 2001.

[21] The latter view is defended in Hornsby 1980.

CONCLUDING REMARKS

What conclusions should we draw about the treatment of action and the will in the *Philosophical Investigations*? On the one hand, it is seriously flawed. Wittgenstein fails to disentangle the active/passive distinction and the voluntary/not voluntary distinction; he fails to see that voluntariness is not only an attribute of activity, but of passivity as well; and he confuses action and motion. On the other hand, he discards the idealist mythology he had once accepted, although he retains Schopenhauer's claim that willing (unlike hoping, wanting, or deliberating) is not distinct from the act willed; and his criticism of James and Russell in Part II is radical and utterly convincing, in my view. Furthermore, there are signs in the remarks composed in 1947 that he is beginning to break fresh ground, although only glimpses of parts of a new picture can be found here: nothing is developed or sustained.

Finally, although the remarks in the *Investigations* are unsatisfactory, they are framed (so to speak) by the following remarks, which express a constant theme of Wittgenstein's writings about action and will, from *The Brown Book* onwards:

> There is not one common difference between so-called voluntary acts and involuntary ones, viz, the presence or absence of one element, the 'act of volition'. (BB, 151f.)

> Voluntary movements are certain movements with their normal *surroundings* of intention, learning, trying, acting. (RPP I §776)

Wittgenstein evidently agreed with Ryle's view, expressed in *The Concept of Mind*, that the theory of volitions is 'a causal hypothesis, adopted because it was wrongly supposed that the question, "What makes a bodily movement voluntary?" was a causal question' (Ryle 1949, 67). It is largely because of his subtle and resourceful defence of this idea that the destructive work in the *Investigations* and the positive ideas in the later writings, fragmentary as they are, together with Ryle's chapter on the will in *The Concept of Mind*, paved the way for the extraordinary renewal of the philosophy of action in the second half of the twentieth century.

REFERENCES

ALVAREZ, MARIA and HYMAN, JOHN (1998). 'Agents and their Actions', *Philosophy*, 73: 219–45.

ANSCOMBE, G. E. M. (2000). *Intention*, 2nd edn. Cambridge, MA: Harvard University Press.

ARISTOTLE (2000). *Nicomachean Ethics*, ed. R. Crisp. Cambridge: Cambridge University Press.

BROADIE, SARAH (1991). *Ethics with Aristotle*. Oxford: Oxford University Press.

CHISHOLM, R. M. (1976). 'The Agent as Cause', in *Action Theory*, ed. M. Brand and D. Walton. Dordrecht: D. Reidel.

DAVIDSON, DONALD (1980). *Essays on Actions and Events*. Oxford: Oxford University Press.

DIAS, R. W. M. (1970). *Jurisprudence*. London: Butterworths.

DUFF, A. (2004). 'Action, the Act Requirement and Criminal Liability', in J. Hyman and H. Steward eds., *Agency and Action*. Cambridge: Cambridge University Press.

HACKER, P. M. S. (1996). *Wittgenstein: Mind and Will*. Oxford: Basil Blackwell.

HORNSBY, J. (1980). *Actions*. London: Routledge & Kegan Paul.

HUME, DAVID (2000). *A Treatise of Human Nature*, ed. D. F. Norton and M. J. Norton. Oxford: Oxford University Press.

HYMAN, JOHN (2001). '-ings and -ers', *Ratio* (new series), 14: 298–317.

JAMES, WILLIAM (1950). *The Principles of Psychology*, vol. 2. New York: Dover.

KENNY, ANTHONY (1975). *Will, Freedom and Power*. Oxford: Basil Blackwell.

LOCKE, JOHN (1979). *An Essay Concerning Human Understanding*, ed. P. H. Nidditch. Oxford: Clarendon Press.

MILL, J. S. (1973). *A System of Logic, Ratiocinative and Deductive*, ed. J. M. Robson. Toronto: University of Toronto Press.

RUSSELL, BERTRAND (1921). *The Analysis of Mind*. London: George Allen & Unwin.

RYLE, GILBERT (1949). *The Concept of Mind*. London: Hutchinson,.

SCHOPENHAUER, ARTHUR (1966). *The World as Will and Representation*, vol. 2, trans. E. F. J. Payne. New York: Dover.

STRAWSON, P. F. (1954). 'Review of Wittgenstein's *Philosophical Investigations*', *Mind* 63: 70–99.

TAYLOR, R (1966). *Action and Purpose*. Englewood Cliffs, NJ: Prentice-Hall.

VON WRIGHT, G. H. (1963). *Norm and Action*. London: Routledge & Kegan Paul.

—— (1982). *Wittgenstein*. Oxford: Basil Blackwell.

WHITE, ALAN R. ed. (1967). *The Philosophy of Action*. Oxford: Oxford University Press.

—— ed. (1977). *The Philosophy of Action*. Oxford: Oxford University Press.

—— (1985). *Grounds of Liability*. Oxford: Clarendon Press.

WILLIAMS, GLANVILLE (1978). *Text Book of Criminal Law*. London: Stevens.

WITTGENSTEIN, LUDWIG (1958). *Philosophical Investigations*, ed. G. E. M. Anscombe and R. Rhees, trans. G. E. M. Anscombe, 2nd edn. Oxford: Basil Blackwell.

—— (1961). *Notebooks 1914–16*, ed. G. H. von Wright and G. E. M. Anscombe, trans. G. E. M. Anscombe. Oxford: Basil Blackwell.

—— (1961a). *Tractatus Logico-Philosophicus*, trans. D. Pears and B. F. McGuinness. London: Routledge & Kegan Paul.

—— (1967). *Zettel*, ed. G. E. M. Anscombe and G. H. von Wright, trans. G. E. M. Anscombe. Oxford: Basil Blackwell.

—— (1969). *The Blue and Brown Books*, 2nd edn. Oxford: Basil Blackwell.

—— (1980). *Remarks on the Philosophy of Psychology*, vol. 1, ed. G. E. M. Anscombe and G. H. von Wright, trans. G. E. M. Anscombe. Oxford: Basil Blackwell.

CHAPTER 21

WITTGENSTEIN ON CRITERIA AND THE PROBLEM OF OTHER MINDS

EDWARD WITHERSPOON

1. INTRODUCTION

IN the *Philosophical Investigations*, when Wittgenstein has reached a moment of perplexity about a concept like *understanding*, *meaning*, or *expecting*, he often tries to think his way out of it by asking, "What are the criteria of understanding?", "When do we say that someone has understood?", and similar questions. He explores the grammar of our concepts – especially the grammar of concepts that describe the mind – by looking at the grounds on which we apply them. Wittgenstein usually employs the term "criteria" for the grounds on which we apply a concept, so we may say that a major aim of Wittgenstein's philosophical enterprise is to understand and clarify the logic of psychological concepts through an examination of their criteria.

Criteria for psychological concepts are principally relevant to the application of mental state concepts to other people. (When I describe my own mental states, I normally do so without employing *grounds* at all.[1]) The fact that Wittgenstein is interested in how I apply psychological concepts to others means that his project runs up against the problem of other minds. A skeptic about other minds argues that I never have adequate justification for attributing mental state concepts to any being other than myself. The broad contours of philosophical dialectic thus suggest that Wittgenstein's discussion of criteria

---

[1] "What is the criterion for the redness of an image?...For myself, when it is my image: nothing" (PI §377).

For an account of our self-knowledge that discusses how hard it is to hold onto this insight when one starts philosophizing about first-person authority, see Finkelstein 2003.

ought to contain a response to skepticism about other minds. And this suggestion is borne out when we start to look in detail at Wittgenstein's remarks about criteria for mental states. His thinking is intimately responsive to such ideas as that other human beings may be pervasively and systematically hiding their thoughts, or may be constructed so as to manifest their thoughts in ways I cannot perceive, or may even be automata without thoughts or feelings at all. Wittgenstein does not wish to embrace any such skeptical scenario. It is not obvious how he earns the right to dismiss them, but his discussions typically invoke criteria. Consequently, the notion of a criterion has become a central topic for philosophers who wish to understand Wittgenstein's response to skepticism about other minds.

In this chapter, I will examine two very different interpretations of Wittgenstein on criteria; my assessment of the strengths and weaknesses of these interpretations will guide my own presentation of Wittgenstein's views about what criteria are and how they figure in a critique of skepticism. The first reader I will discuss is Rogers Albritton: he interprets criteria as conventions linking behavior with mental states. The second reader I will discuss, John McDowell, identifies the defects of that approach and offers a radically different way of thinking about criteria of mental concepts. According to McDowell's Wittgenstein, we don't need a convention to license inferences from a subject's behavior to her mental states, because in favorable circumstances we can cognitively grasp that someone else is in a particular mental state without making an inference from her behavior. According to McDowell, mode of knowing another's mind is tantamount to perceiving that the other exhibits the relevant criteria. I regard McDowell's emphasis on the possibility of non-inferential knowledge of others' mental states as a key step towards a satisfactory interpretation of Wittgenstein, but I will argue that his usage of the term "criterion" differs from Wittgenstein's. I will attempt to clarify what Wittgenstein means by the term "criterion" through a close reading of key passages in the *Investigations*. Once we understand Wittgenstein's conception of criteria, we will see that there is a real question whether criteria so conceived have anything helpful to offer against skepticism. In the final section of this essay, I will argue that Wittgenstein's remarks about criteria are indeed a crucial part of his critique of skepticism.

2. *THE BLUE BOOK* ON CRITERIA AND SYMPTOMS

Wittgenstein's earliest discussion of the concept of a criterion can be found in *The Blue Book*. The definition of "criterion" that Wittgenstein there propounds has set the stage for subsequent discussions of Wittgenstein and skepticism, so it provides a useful starting place for our inquiry.

In *The Blue Book*, Wittgenstein introduces the notion of a criterion as part of an examination of the grammar (the use) of the word "to know": to understand how we use the expression "to know" Wittgenstein thinks we should look at what we call "getting to know," and he provides, as an example, getting to know that someone has a toothache. And to study this he puts the question of how we learned to use the phrase "so-and-so has a toothache." He says that we were taught to apply it when a person exhibited "certain kinds of behaviour," for instance, clutching her cheek. He calls these "criteria" for telling when a person has a toothache. When we observe these criteria we can come to know that the person we are observing has a toothache. Wittgenstein also imagines another way in which we can come to know that someone else has a toothache. Suppose that I have discovered that whenever someone exhibits the criteria for having a toothache, she also has a red patch on her cheek, and vice versa. Then when I see a red patch on a subject's cheek, I can know that she has a toothache even if I do not observe the relevant criteria.

Wittgenstein then offers what seems to be a systematic articulation of this distinction between two routes to knowing something on the basis of observations:

> Let us introduce two antithetical terms in order to avoid certain elementary confusions: To the question "How do you know that so-and-so is the case?" we sometimes answer by giving "*criteria*" and sometimes by giving "*symptoms*". If medical science calls angina an inflammation caused by a particular bacillus, and we ask in a particular case "why do you say this man has got angina?" then the answer "I have found the bacillus so-and-so in his blood" gives us the criterion, or what we may call the defining criterion of angina. If on the other hand the answer was, "His throat is inflamed", this might give us a symptom of angina. I call "symptom" a phenomenon of which experience has taught us that it coincided, in some way or other, with the phenomenon which is our defining criterion. Then to say "A man has angina if this bacillus is found in him" is a tautology or it is a loose way of stating the definition of "angina". But to say, "A man has angina whenever he has an inflamed throat" is to make a hypothesis. (BB, 24)

Wittgenstein's distinction between "criteria" and "symptoms" is the difference between features that define a phenomenon (that make it the phenomenon it is) and features that are empirically correlated with a phenomenon. With this distinction comes a difference between knowing on the basis of criteria and knowing on the basis of symptoms – a difference that shows up when we imagine challenges to our knowledge-claims. If the basis for my claim that so-and-so has angina is a symptom, then if I am asked "How do you know that so-and-so has angina?" my answer will be to cite the empirical correlation. And a skeptic could pose a challenge as to whether I have an adequate basis for my generalization. But if my basis is the defining criterion, then I can answer the question "How do you know?" in a quite different way. I can point out that this is simply what we call "angina." The connection between the presence of the bacillus in the blood and my claim that he has angina is based on a convention within the medical community. If a philosopher of skeptical bent were moved to challenge this response, we would find that we have struck "rock bottom." To reject this answer would be to reject the convention that defines "angina" as "an infection by such-and-such bacillus," and this would be to cease speaking the language of the medical community. From the point of view of adherents of the convention, this would be to speak nonsense; from a metalinguistic point of view a challenge to this rock-bottom convention might be construed as a recommendation to adopt a different convention, that is, different criteria for applying the term "angina." But whatever we say about the skeptic's rejection of our convention (to call *this* "angina"), in neither case has the skeptic actually challenged the original claim "So-and-so has angina," for opting out of a way of speaking is not challenging a claim.

Without quite saying so, the structure of *The Blue Book* discussion leaves the impression that the defining criteria of toothache are a family of behaviors such as clutching one's cheek. If this is so, then skepticism about other minds can apparently be banished. For if I judge that a person is suffering toothache because I see her clutching her cheek and moaning, then if someone should ask "Do you *know* that she has toothache?" I could respond with a fully justified "yes." If a skeptic sought to challenge the legitimacy of my judgment, that would be tantamount to rejecting the language game that defines toothache in terms of the cheek-clutching behavior. So whenever my claims about someone else's thoughts or feelings are based on criteria they are immune to skeptical challenge.

But using behavior as the defining criterion of toothache puts us on the path to a form of behaviorism according to which the terms for feelings – and presumably also other states of mind – are stipulated to be synonymous with suitably specified ranges of behaviors. This is an unattractive program: it either leaves us without a term for the phenomenon that we initially wanted to capture with the term "toothache" or else denies the existence of such "subjective" phenomena. I will not address whether Wittgenstein in *The Blue and Brown Books* was sympathetic to behaviorism, for he is emphatic in the *Investigations* that he is no behaviorist, even as he seeks to understand the philosophical motivations for behaviorism.

3. ALBRITTON ON CRITERIA

Any reader of the *Philosophical Investigations* will notice both Wittgenstein's disavowal of behaviorism and his frequent appeals to criteria for the application of concepts like "reading," "intending," and "feeling pain." At the same time, the *Investigations* presents no obvious reason to alter *The Blue Book*'s emphasis on the conventional character of criteria. Hence it appears that Wittgenstein must be hypothesizing that there is a conventional relationship between behavioral criteria and inner states (construed in a non-behavioristic fashion). This is the thought that Rogers Albritton develops in his seminal essay entitled "On Wittgenstein's Use of the Term 'Criterion'".[2] Albritton regards the toothache itself as something inner, as not reducible to or definable in terms of behavior.[3] And the notion of a criterion for an inner state that Albritton finds in the

---

[2] Albritton 1966, originally published in 1959; reprinted with a postscript in 1966.

[3] Albritton writes: "But can what a man does or says be called his having a toothache, or referred to or described as that, or even referred to or described *by* saying that he has a toothache, under any circumstances, in a proper and literal sense of the words said? No" (Albritton 1966, 242).

Investigations is not, as in the *Blue Book*, a feature that defines or constitutes that state. Rather, criteria of a state are observable features that can justify one in judging that the state obtains:

> A criterion for a given thing's being so is something that can show the thing to be so and show by its absence that the thing is not so; it is something by which one may be *justified in saying* that the thing is so and by whose absence one may be justified in saying that the thing is not so. (Albritton 1966, 243–4)

The characterization of criteria as observable features that show something to be so imposes an interpretative challenge, for symptoms are also observable ways of knowing that something is so, and Wittgenstein in the *Investigations* continues to distinguish criteria from symptoms. According to Albritton's interpretation, the distinctive feature of criteria is that they, unlike symptoms, are necessarily connected to the state for which they are criteria. A criterion justifies us in saying that a thing is such-and-such "as a matter of 'logical' necessity. That is, on Wittgenstein's account of such necessity, its relation to the thing's being so is 'founded on a definition' or 'founded on convention' or is a matter of 'grammar' " (Albritton 1966, 244).

What does Albritton mean by this family of expressions for "logical" necessity? Continuing with Wittgenstein's example of toothache, Albritton has us imagine a man who "sits rocking miserably back and forth, holding his jaw, every now and then cautiously pushing at a loose tooth on that side with certain kinds of grimaces and sharp intakes of breath, and so on" (Albritton 1966, 245). Albritton observes that "Normally, I *would* be justified by this behavior in saying that the man had a toothache. A man who behaves in this manner, under normal circumstances, always or almost always does have a toothache" (Albritton 1966, 245).[4] And the justification that observing such behavior provides for my judgment that the man has a toothache does not depend on a theory or on causal connections; the justification rests on a convention, on grammar. According to Albritton's interpretation of Wittgenstein, the conventional character of the association of such behavior with having a toothache implies that it is a necessary truth that a "man who behaves in this manner, under normal circumstances, always or almost always does have a toothache" (Albritton 1966, 245), and this necessary truth entails that "anyone who is aware that the man is behaving in this manner, under these circumstances, is *justified in saying* that the man has a toothache, in the absence of any special reason to say something more guarded" (Albritton 1966, 246).

I wish to highlight several aspects of this interpretation of Wittgenstein which will serve as points of contrast with the interpretation I will propose. First, according to Albritton, Wittgenstein's notion of a criterion is meant to answer the question of whether a person or a thing is in a particular state or not. In the philosophically interesting case of

---

[4] The qualification "under normal circumstances" is meant to provide for cases in which there is reason to think that the individual clutching his jaw is rehearsing a part for a play, or providing a demonstration for a classroom lecture, etc.

others' inner states, the particular state in question cannot be directly observed: criteria are meant to provide the most definitive possible way of judging whether someone is in a particular inner state, but they do not provide a guarantee of the truth of that judgment.

Consequently, on Albritton's interpretation, criteria for an inner state are epistemologically prior to the state itself, in this sense: the way to know that someone is in the state in question is through knowing that the criteria for that state are satisfied.[5] Knowing that criteria are satisfied is philosophically unproblematic, whereas knowing that the corresponding state is present is problematic. So, for example, there is a problem whether we can know that a man has a toothache on a particular occasion, but there is no problem (or not the same kind of problem) as to whether he is behaving in some specified way or not.

Finally, criteria for a state may be logically distinct from the state itself. This may seem surprising, since the keystone of Albritton's interpretation is that it is a necessary truth that a man rocking back and forth and grimacing when his tooth is touched, etc., always or almost always is so behaving because he has a toothache. But the necessity Albritton finds in Wittgenstein's view here is a product of a convention that links each inner state to behavior specified in terms that make no reference to that inner state. The specification of the criteria of toothache, for example, does not employ the concept *toothache*; in principle, one could master the concepts employed in the specification of criteria and could determine in any case whether the criteria were satisfied, without any grasp of the concepts "toothache" or "pain." This feature of Albritton's interpretation is of a piece with his aim of providing an epistemologically unproblematic basis for judgments about epistemologically problematic phenomena.

Albritton seems to have hoped that the conception of criteria as conventions would refute skepticism. If it were the case that a certain range of behavior implied the presence of a certain state of mind, then we would have defeated the skeptic on his own terms. But Albritton sees that there is no such implication. No matter how detailed your specification of tooth-clutching, grimacing, and moaning behavior, it will always be possible for someone to mimic that behavior without in fact having a toothache. As we saw, *The Blue Book* may be read as maintaining that, as a matter of definition (or convention), whenever someone exhibits cheek-clutching behavior, he or she has a toothache. In order to avoid behaviorism and to accommodate the possibility of pretense, Albritton has to weaken that claim to the following: "A man who behaves in this manner, under normal circumstances, always, *or almost always* does have a toothache" (Albritton 1966, 245; emphasis added). Because a person's behavior does not entail her being in a particular inner state, observing that criteria are satisfied does not yield knowledge of the observed person's inner state. Observing that criteria are satisfied

---

[5] I here introduce the expression "criteria are satisfied." This locution and its cognates are not to be found in Wittgenstein, but they are a terminological convenience.

does *justify* the observer in claiming that the subject is in the corresponding inner state.[6]

In a remarkable "Postscript" to his original essay, Albritton explicitly faces these implications of the conception of criteria he attributes to Wittgenstein. This leads him to modify some of his earlier claims. Whereas the original essay argues that for Wittgenstein it is a necessary truth that a man who exhibits some range of specified behavior, in normal circumstances, always or almost always has a toothache, the "Postscript" asserts that "there are only contingent facts of those types" and that "Wittgenstein never meant to deny that." Albritton re-emphasizes that a person's behavior determines what others are justified in saying about her mental states: behavior that satisfies the criterion of having a toothache "may be taken to decide the question whether he has a toothache or not: he does." But criteria settle the question of what observers are justified in saying and judging; they do not settle the question of whether he has a toothache or not. And since observing that criteria are satisfied does not in general yield knowledge of others' minds, this position gains no leverage against skepticism.

The "Postscript" makes dramatically explicit a feature of criteria of inner states that I mentioned above: on Albritton's interpretation, there is no conceptual or logical connection between the behavior one exhibits and the inner state one is in. Albritton writes, "it seems conceivable that people with toothaches should cease to behave in any special way at all" (Albritton 1966, 248). Furthermore, "The concept [of toothache]...allows for unnerving contingencies...It allows us to imagine that behaving in such and such a way that was paradigmatic for having a toothache should come to have nothing to do with toothaches. It allows us to imagine a time when adults who say they have toothaches, and mean it, will *never* have toothaches" (Albritton 1966, 250).[7]

---

[6] Albritton writes: "What Wittgenstein calls a 'criterion' of having a toothache is a phenomenon by which, under certain circumstances, *one would be justified in saying* that a man had a toothache or *in saying*, should one have occasion to do so, that one knew he had a toothache. (It is therefore a phenomenon by which one *may know* that a man has a toothache, though sometimes, to be sure, one is justified in saying that one knows a thing and yet doesn't know it, because, as one may or may not discover, it isn't so)" (Albritton 1966, 244–5; emphasis in first sentence added).

[7] I cannot imagine how it could be that generally people said and meant that they had toothaches when they did not. I can imagine that people who spoke a language broadly similar to English could say "I have a toothache" when they did not have (what we now call) a toothache: the language we now speak could evolve so that the word "toothache" came to mean something else. But then the utterers of "I have a toothache" in that version of English would not be saying that they have a toothache. Albritton seems to be describing a linguistic community whose members systematically lie about having toothaches, and when I try to imagine that I don't see how we could keep a grip on what they mean by their words: in my view, the meaningfulness of an individual's lie is parasitic on the community members' generally telling the truth.

4. McDowell's Interpretation
of Wittgenstein on Criteria

Albritton's interpretation aims to counter skepticism about other minds by defining a criterion as a range of observable behavior that licenses an inference to the presence of an unobservable inner state. In the face of the possibility of pretense, however, he has to qualify the conclusion such inferences can justify: he concludes that someone exhibiting behavior that is criterial for having a toothache "always or *almost always*" has a toothache (Albritton 1966, 245; my emphasis). This is too weak a conclusion to defeat skepticism, and in the "Postscript" he effectively gives up on this anti-skeptical strategy.

John McDowell offers a general account of the failure of anti-skeptical gambits such as Albritton's, and he proposes a quite different way to think about the problem pretense raises for our knowledge of other minds. He begins his essay "Criteria, Defeasibility, and Knowledge" (McDowell 1998)[8] by identifying a set of features common to many interpretations of Wittgenstein.

> It is widely believed that in his later work Wittgenstein introduced a special use of the notion of a criterion. In this proprietary use, "criteria" are supposed to be a kind of evidence. Their status as evidence, unlike that of symptoms, is a matter of "convention" or "grammar" rather than empirical theory; but the support that a "criterion" yields for a claim is defeasible: that is, a state of information in which one is in possession of a "criterial" warrant for a claim can always be expanded into a state of information in which the claim would not be warranted at all. This special notion is thought to afford…a novel response to the traditional problem of other minds. (McDowell 1998, 369)

We are in a position to see that this characterization fits the notion of a criterion that Albritton attributes to Wittgenstein.[9] McDowell intends it to apply also to interpretations offered by W. G. Lycan, P. M. S. Hacker, Gordon Baker, and Crispin Wright.

McDowell raises a general epistemological concern that undermines the plausibility of the view these commentators ascribe to Wittgenstein. The "criterial" reading[10] holds that I may claim to know that someone else is in an inner state (e.g., that of having a toothache) when the observable "criteria" for that state are satisfied. However, the observable "criteria" (e.g., the grimacing, cheek-clutching behavior that Albritton

---

[8] Since McDowell endorses and defends the views he attributes to Wittgenstein in this essay, I will use phrases like "according to McDowell" and "according to McDowell's interpretation of Wittgenstein" interchangeably.

[9] With one proviso: in the "Postscript" Albritton withdraws the claim (implicit in the original essay) that the notion he finds in Wittgenstein will confound skepticism about other minds.

[10] In this section I will follow McDowell in putting scare quotes around the term "criteria" as it is employed in the interpretations that McDowell is criticizing.

alludes to) do not guarantee that the inner state is present, because of the possibility of pretense. (This is part of what is meant by saying that criteria are "defeasible.") Therefore, according to the "criterial" reading, I may claim to know that someone is in a particular inner state on grounds that are compatible with the person not being in that inner state. McDowell expresses his disquiet with such a position as follows:

> [T]he "criterial" view does envisage ascribing knowledge on the strength of some-thing compatible with the falsity of what is supposedly known. And it is a serious question whether we can understand how it can be knowledge that is properly so ascribed.... [S]ince "criteria" are defeasible, someone who experiences the satisfac-tion of "criteria" for the ascription of an "inner" state to another person is thereby in a position in which, for all he knows, the person may not be in that "inner" state. And the question is: if that is the best one can achieve, how is there room for anything recognizable as knowledge that the person is in the "inner" state?...The trouble is that if that is the best position achievable, then however being in it is supposed to relate to the claim to know that the person is in the "inner" state, it looks as if the claim can never be acceptable. (McDowell 1998, 372)

This statement of an inadequacy in the "criterial" reading is part of McDowell's argu-ment for an alternative view: according to McDowell, the fact that another person is in a particular "inner" state *can* come within the ambit of my experience. I can perceive that another person is suffering from a toothache; when I have such a perception it is *not* defeasible, and so it yields knowledge.

For Albritton (and for the other "criterial" theorists that McDowell discusses), "criteria" are epistemologically prior to the "inner" states for which they are criterial. I can tell whether someone is exhibiting the "criteria" of toothache without being able to tell whether that person actually has a toothache. McDowell rejects this epistemological priority of criteria over their corresponding "inner" states. He writes:

> I think we should understand criteria to be, in the first instance, ways of telling how things are, of the sort specified by "On the basis of what he says and does" or "By how things look"; and we should take it that knowledge that a criterion for a claim is actually satisfied – if we allow ourselves to speak in those terms as well – would be an exercise of the very capacity we speak of when we say that one can tell, on the basis of such-and-such criteria, whether things are as the claim would represent them as being. This flouts an idea we are prone to find natural, that a basis for a judgement must be something on which we have a firmer cognitive purchase than we do on the judgement itself; but although the idea can seem natural, it is an illu-sion to suppose it is compulsory. (McDowell 1998, 385)

Albritton's attempt to use criteria to defeat skepticism foundered on the possibility of pretense. It might seem that that possibility will vitiate or refute McDowell's position as well. For couldn't someone say she had a toothache, and act as though she did, when really she didn't? Wouldn't such a person satisfy the criteria for having a toothache with-out being in the corresponding inner state of actually having one?

McDowell responds to the possibility of pretense with what he calls a "disjunctive" conception of experience. In its most general terms, disjunctivism maintains that:

an appearance that such-and-such is the case can be *either* a mere appearance *or* the fact that such-and-such is the case making itself perceptually manifest to someone. (McDowell 1998, 386–7)

The disjunctive account of experience acknowledges our vulnerability to deception and pretense. In cases of deception, we are taken in by a mere appearance. But the disjunctive conception of experience conceives non-deceptive experience as the taking in of a manifest fact. This is the epistemological point most important to McDowell: in a non-deceptive case of perception, my experience takes in the fact itself, and not some intermediary (e.g., an appearance) that falls short of the fact. And among the facts that my experience encompasses is that someone else is giving expression to his "inner state." Through such experiences, I come to know others' minds.

How does disjunctivism apply to criteria and their corresponding inner states? For Albritton, if someone exhibits the behavior that is criterial for having a toothache, then we may justifiably assert that she has a toothache, even though she may not in fact have a toothache. For McDowell, if someone satisfies the criteria for having a toothache, then she has a toothache. Someone who is pretending to have a toothache does not satisfy the criteria for having a toothache; rather, she *causes it to appear* that she satisfies those criteria.[11]

For McDowell, criteria for states of mind are ways of knowing what state of mind another is in; when I know that another person satisfies the criteria for being in a particular inner state, then I know that the other is in that state. McDowell therefore agrees with "criterial" theorists in thinking that criteria tell me what state other people are in. McDowell disagrees with "criterial" theorists in believing that, in general, knowledge that someone satisfies criteria for being in an inner state is *not* obtainable independently of knowledge that the other is in that state; for McDowell, perceiving the satisfaction of criteria is perceiving that the other is in the relevant state.

McDowell's disjunctivism reflects an attitude towards skepticism quite different from that of Albritton and most other anti-skeptical thinkers. These thinkers start from the assumption that inner states are epistemologically problematic: what someone else is thinking or feeling is not available to me in any direct or quasi-perceptual form. Anything I might come to know about others' minds will have to be the product of inferences from information that is unproblematic, and that will amount to their bodily behavior (including verbal behavior).

McDowell, by contrast, seeks to purge philosophy of the assumption that knowledge of others' minds must be gained via an inference from their behavior, where that behavior is conceived in terms that make no reference to inner states. The disjunctive conception of experience allows him to say that, in favorable circumstances, what someone says and does expresses her mind, and that by experiencing what another person says and

---

[11] McDowell makes a correlative move in the parallel case of illusion about the external world. He considers a case in which we are under an illusion that it is raining: "[W]hen our 'sense-impressions' deceive us, the fact is not that criteria for rain are satisfied but that they *appear* to be satisfied" (McDowell 1998, 381).

does, I have a cognitive grasp on the fact that she is in the state those words and deeds express (McDowell 1998, 387). McDowell acknowledges that there may be cases of pretense in which I am taken in by someone else's words and deeds; but this does not, in his view, undermine the claim that in the favorable cases I do have direct cognitive access to the fact that the other is in a particular state of mind.

Albritton keeps criteria conceptually distinct from the states for which they are criterial. The criteria for toothache are described in ways that make no reference to toothaches, pains, or any other inner state. In McDowell's view, the attempt to frame criteria for inner states without reference to those states is a symptom of a suspect philosophical conception of human bodies, according to which our experience of others yields us (at best) information about physical objects which might or might not contain minds. The philosopher's task is accordingly to show that the physiological machines we encounter do after all contain minds. By contrast, Wittgenstein (on McDowell's interpretation) aims "to restore the concept of a human being to its proper place, not as something laboriously reconstituted, out of the fragments to which the sceptic reduces it, by a subtle epistemological and metaphysical construction, but as a seamless whole of whose unity we ought not to have allowed ourselves to lose sight in the first place" (McDowell 1998, 384).

McDowell's idea that there is a logical tie between criteria and the states for which they are criteria and his idea that we can have non-inferential knowledge of facts about others' mental states will be keystones of my interpretation of Wittgenstein on criteria. But the presence of criteria for an inner state does not, in my view, entail that the state is present. Illusions of external phenomena and dissimulations of inner states also, on my reading of Wittgenstein, present criteria for those phenomena and states. Criteria, as I see it, are not Wittgenstein's answer to the question, "How can I know what state another is in?" Rather, they answer the question, "How can one express an inner state?" The need for an answer to the latter question will become evident when we think through the implications of skepticism about other minds, and in particular when we see how such skepticism ends by denying us the conceptual resources to understand others' behavior as exhibiting minds at all.

5. CRITERIA IN THE *PHILOSOPHICAL INVESTIGATIONS*

I will develop my reading of Wittgenstein from the passage in the *Investigations* that most nearly echoes *The Blue Book* passage that distinguishes criteria from symptoms.[12]

---

[12] This is one of only two mentions of "symptoms" in the *Investigations*; the other, in §271, uses "symptoms" not in contrast with criteria but simply as a generic term for ways of telling whether someone is in pain.

§354   The fluctuation in grammar between criteria and symptoms makes it look as if there were nothing at all but symptoms. We say, for example: "Experience teaches that there is rain when the barometer falls, but it also teaches that there is rain when we have certain sensations of wet and cold, or such-and-such visual impressions." In defence of this one says that these sense-impressions can deceive us. But here one fails to reflect that the fact that the false appearance is precisely one of rain is founded on a definition.

§355   The point here is not that our sense-impressions can lie, but that we understand their language. (And this language like any other is founded on convention.)

This passage is unusual in the *Investigations*, in that Wittgenstein is talking about symptoms and criteria for a mundane phenomenon – rain – rather than those for a state of mind. I think he chooses this example so as to draw the distinction he cares about in a relatively unproblematic case.

We may notice at the outset that, although the notions of criteria and definition are at work in this passage, Wittgenstein's position here is radically different from his view in *The Blue Book*. In the earlier work, Wittgenstein was specifying (in his imaginary case) the defining criterion of angina: according to the *Blue Book*, if the criterion for angina (the particular bacillus in the blood) is present, then the patient *by definition* has angina, and if I find the bacillus in the patient's blood then I *know* that she has angina. We saw above, in §2, that this model of the relationship between criteria and the states for which they are criteria is not plausible as regards behavioral criteria for states of mind, because of the possibility of pretense. In this passage from the *Investigations*, the possibility of illusion (the analogue to pretense) is front and center: the criteria of rain to which Wittgenstein is alluding, and the sense in which they are "founded on a definition," are invoked in the case of illusion that Wittgenstein invites us to imagine. We will see the significance of this below.

Let's consider this passage from the beginning. Its point is to draw the distinction between criteria and symptoms, in the face of pressure to think that "there is nothing at all but symptoms." I won't yet explore the source of that pressure, but we can say what it would be for there to be nothing but symptoms: it would be for every indication of the presence of rain to be a feature that is empirically correlated with rain. As an instance of such empirical correlation Wittgenstein suggests the following: let us suppose that meteorologists have discovered that it rains every time the barometer falls so many units within such-and-such time span. Then observing such barometric readings would give me a way to know that it is raining. Acquiring this knowledge would not require that I perceive the rain. (I could have the barometer readings electronically transmitted into a windowless lab.) But gaining this knowledge would require my employing a causal, empirically confirmed hypothesis. And so this mode of coming to know about the weather is vulnerable to the possibility of disconfirmation: it could turn out that the correlation between barometric reading and rain sometimes fails to hold, in which case the readings would not after all yield knowledge of whether it is raining.

Even if we make the assumption that the connection between barometric reading and rain is perfectly confirmed, Wittgenstein wishes to distinguish this mode of coming to know that it is raining from another way. This is knowing about the rain through perceiving it, which Wittgenstein here describes as having "sensations of wet and cold and such-and-such visual impressions." This difference between criteria and symptoms is not a function of degree of subjective certainty (I may have absolute trust in the accuracy of the conclusions I reach from the barometer readings) or the objective reliability of these ways of coming to know (my senses might occasionally mislead me, while the judgments I based on the barometer readings might be always right). The difference is that, on a rainy day, when I look out the open door or walk out into the street, I am perceiving the rain, whereas when I look at the barometric readings, I am perceiving indicators or signs that it is raining. The knowledge that it is raining that I get from perceiving signs or symptoms is mediated by a causal hypothesis that justifies the inference that it is raining; the knowledge that I get from perceiving the rain is unmediated. Consequently, a belief gained through perceiving symptoms of rain is falsifiable in a way that a belief gained through perceiving rain is not.

In the wake of these remarks – and if we notice that in this section Wittgenstein seems to link criteria with *definitions* – we might try out the following definition of criteria: the criteria for a phenomenon specify what it is to be that phenomenon. So we might try to define rain in terms of "sensations of wet and cold" and "such-and-such visual impressions." But this won't do: rain is plainly something other than the sensations through which I perceive rain.

We might try a slightly different idea: define rain, not as the impressions themselves, but as *that which produces* "sensations of wet and cold" and "such-and-such visual impressions." But this definition also is unsatisfactory, for reasons manifest right in this passage. For Wittgenstein is willing to concede that "these sense-impressions may deceive us"; that is, we may have the sense-impressions of wet and cold and may have the visual impression of water falling from the heavens when it isn't raining. (Let's suppose for example a squadron of airplane pilots is training for fighting fires by dumping loads of water on my neighborhood.) Hence we cannot define rain as that which produces these (or any other) sense-impressions.

So what kind of definition does Wittgenstein have in mind when he speaks of criteria? Notice that he claims that, in a case of deceptive sense-impressions, "the fact that the false *appearance* is precisely one of rain is founded on a definition" (PI §354, my emphasis). Criteria (the visual impression of water falling from the sky, the feeling of countless drops of water soaking your hair and clothes) articulate the appearances that rain presents. That these appearances are *of rain* is "founded on a definition." The criteria tell us what we call "appearances of rain." This definition belongs to the "language" of sense-impressions.

As I read Wittgenstein, criteria of rain are the appearances that rain normally presents to normal observers in normal conditions. This passage discusses rain, but its context is one in which Wittgenstein is asking how we know what is going on in other people's (or in dogs'!) minds, so we may assume that what Wittgenstein says about criteria for rain may be extended to criteria for states of mind. Thus the criteria for a state of mind (e.g., anger) will be the appearances that that state of mind typically presents to observers. When I take in such appearances in a given case (impressions of water falling from clouds, or the angry utterances and gestures of my companion), either these appearances will be actual manifestations or genuine expressions of what they are appearances of (that is, the appearances will be actual rain or anger presenting itself to onlookers), or they will be "false appearances" that seem to present rain or anger but really do not. Whether I am caught in rain or in a downpour from a training run of fire-fighting airplanes, it still appears to me to be raining; whether my companion is genuinely angry or is feigning anger, he still appears to be angry. In both deceptive and non-deceptive cases I perceive criteria of rain or anger. (Hence, in the deceptive cases, the misleading appearance is "precisely one of rain" or precisely one of anger.)

These last remarks bring us back to the issue with which PI §354 begins, namely, the pressure to think that there is nothing at all but symptoms. Earlier I noted that knowledge gained through perceiving symptoms is mediated by a causal inference, whereas knowledge gained through perceiving criteria is not. But the fact that criteria of rain can be present even when rain is not might seem to entail that there is, after all, an inference involved in knowing on the basis of criteria. It would appear that in order to know that it is raining on the basis of criteria, I would start from perceiving the criteria of rain (some array of soggy appearances) and then, if there are no countervailing considerations, infer that those appearances are being produced by actual rain; if my conclusion should turn out to be true, then I will count as knowing that it is raining. Since criteria do not entail the presence of their corresponding states, it appears that they can be nothing more than especially well-confirmed correlates of the phenomena we wish to know about. Because, on this line of thought, criteria are essentially indicators of the phenomena of interest, and because the correlation between criterial appearances and rain is based on experience, just like the correlation between particular barometric readings and rain, it looks "as if there were nothing at all but symptoms."

We may provide two complementary responses to this line of thought. The first is to emphasize the possibility of direct cognitive access to phenomena. The line of thought we are considering argues that, since any appearance (including those that are criterial for the phenomenon in question) may be deceptive, the most that we ever have cognitive access to is appearances: the thing itself always lies behind a screen that might prove illusory. One of McDowell's chief insights is that the possibility of illusion does *not* entail that we can never have direct cognitive access to things themselves: the disjunctive conception of experience accommodates the possibility of illusion while maintaining the primacy of direct cognitive access to things themselves.

The second response to the pressure to think that all perception is the perception of symptoms rests on a logical priority of criteria over symptoms. This priority is brought out by the question Wittgenstein poses at the end of the following remark:

§376   When I say the ABC to myself, what is the criterion of my doing the same as someone else who silently repeats it to himself? It might be found that the same thing took place in my larynx and in his....But then did we learn the use of the words: "to say such-and-such to oneself" by someone's pointing to a process in the larynx or the brain? Is it not also perfectly possible that my image of the sound *a* and his correspond to different physiological processes? The question is: *How do we compare* images?

We now have two examples of contrasts between symptoms and criteria. A falling barometer is a symptom of rain, while sensations of wet and cold and certain visual impressions are *criteria* of rain. Saying the ABC to oneself has criteria (which Wittgenstein does not specify), and these are to be contrasted with symptoms of saying the ABC to oneself (which Wittgenstein speculates may be characteristic movements in the larynx).

Wittgenstein's question "How do we compare images?" points to the logical priority of criteria over symptoms. For the answer must be that to compare ideas, to determine whether another person has said the ABC to herself, I check to see whether she has exhibited criteria of saying the ABC to herself. What are these? Wittgenstein, as is typical of him, does not say. But certainly one criterion of having said the ABC to yourself is that you tell us that you did; a different criterion might be your silently moving your lips as though you were singing the ABC song while you alphabetize a pile of index cards with words written on them.[13] Any physiological investigation of what goes on in the brain or vocal cords of people who are saying the ABC to themselves must presuppose some way of telling when people are saying the ABC to themselves, and this, Wittgenstein thinks, will require criteria for saying the ABC to oneself. Once I can tell whether two people are both saying the ABC to themselves, I can investigate the causal correlates of their actions (for example, brain or vocal cord activity); but whatever I find out about the causal correlates (the symptoms) cannot force me to revise my original judgment based on criteria. Thus, suppose I find that there is some characteristic brain activity that normally occurs when someone is saying the ABC to herself. If I then encounter an experimental subject who says the ABC to himself (as judged by the usual criteria of doing so), but who lacks that characteristic brain activity, I will not judge that he therefore is not in fact saying the ABC to himself; instead, I will probably reject the claim that this particular brain activity is a perfectly reliable indicator, or symptom, of saying the ABC to oneself.[14]

This logical priority of criteria over symptoms has another aspect, which is that there is a tight conceptual tie between criteria and what they are criterial for. There is no such conceptual relation between symptoms and what they are symptoms of. Discovering that a falling barometer is a reliable indicator that it is raining – or discovering that what we took to be a reliable indicator of rain is not in fact reliable – does not alter our concept of rain. What we mean by the term "rain" is constant through these changes in our understanding of rain's causal properties. By contrast, were we to decide that the visual impression of water falling from the clouds is not an appearance of rain, this would alter our

---

[13] Compare PI §377: "What is the criterion for the redness of an image? For me, when it is someone else's image: what he says and does."

[14] The dialectic can be complicated here. Consider the contemporary notion that REM sleep is a criterion of dreaming. Prior to scientific research on sleep physiology, the only criterion of whether someone had dreamed was what he or she reported upon waking. But once researchers discovered that whenever a subject was woken during a period of REM sleep she would report that she was in the middle of a dream, they began to shift the criterion. Now we have no conceptual difficulty in accepting the proposition that a sleeper has many dreams (as evidenced by periods of REM sleep) that she is not aware of and does not remember. This is an example of the "fluctuation between criteria and symptoms"; but, as Wittgenstein points out, the fact that the way we draw the distinction between criteria and symptoms varies over time does not mean that we are not drawing a real distinction.

concept of rain beyond recognition. Similarly, were we to try to divorce our concept of pain from the behaviors that typically express it (such as wincing, groaning, protecting whatever part of the body is in pain), that would alter our concept of pain beyond recognition.

6. CRITERIA AND EXPRESSION

My assertion that there is a conceptual tie between criteria and the states for which they are criteria requires some elaboration and defense, as it is a thesis that both Albritton and skeptics would deny. Moreover, as I have noted, the version of the connection between criteria and their corresponding states that I find in Wittgenstein differs from McDowell's interpretation of criteria.

A conceptual tie between criteria and the state they are criterial for is easy to see in the case of rain. Since rain may be defined as liquid precipitation, rain necessarily presents the appearance of water falling from the clouds to any suitably situated, normal perceiver. It would be philosophically tidy if there were also a necessary connection between being in a state of mind and presenting certain appearances to any suitably situated, normal perceiver. But the conceptual tie takes a different form in the case of inner states and their criteria.

To describe this tie, I will use the term "expression" for criteria of inner states. This notion of *expression* is that which figures in the concept *facial expression*. Facial expressions are the most important members of a category I will call "natural expressions," which also encompasses posture, gait, and behaviors such as laughing, moaning, weeping, and clutching at one's cheek. It is a fact of human nature that we typically display our emotions and attitudes through such expressions. Moreover, we can perceive others' emotions through registering their expressions. This ability is to a large extent innate, and it becomes more refined in the normal course of human maturation with very little in the way of conscious tutelage.

In addition to natural expressions, we have an unlimited range of what I will call "artificial expressions": ways of expressing a state of mind that require language or conventions. Artificial expressions include assertions of belief, verbal expressions of desire, and statements of intention.[15]

When we learn and teach words for inner states, we rely on expressions. To learn how to apply the word "anger" we rely on the typical expressions of anger: we learn that

---

[15] Natural expressions differ from avowals of states of mind (such as assertions, statements of desire or intention, etc.) in that the latter are truth-evaluable, while the former are not. I can mislead you by putting on a mask of a smile when I am upset, but I cannot lie to you by smiling, as I can by saying "I'm perfectly content" when I am consciously upset. For my present purposes I am interested in the commonalities between different forms of expression. For an illuminating discussion of expression that respects both the similarities and differences between what I am calling natural and artificial expressions, see Finkelstein 2003, especially chapters four and five.

someone who scowls like *that* or who lashes out at a playmate or who yells angrily is angry. This is the basis for a conceptual connection: to know what anger is requires knowing that such behaviors are expressions of anger. This connection extends to artificial expressions too: someone who can apply the concept "believes that Lincoln was America's greatest president" must be able to recognize when someone's words or actions express that belief.

This thesis, that to possess the concept of a given inner state we must be able to recognize typical expressions of that state, rests on a more fundamental, and more controversial claim: in order for a thinker to possess an inner state, he or she must have some means to express it. This is what Wittgenstein is getting at when he writes: "An 'inner process' stands in need of outward criteria" (PI §580). This remark is sometimes taken as evidence that Wittgenstein embraces verificationism about mental states, where this means that in order to count as having something inner going on in you, you must exhibit some observable behavior. But Wittgenstein's point is not that *observers* stand in need of outward criteria in order to attribute an inner state to a subject, but rather that the "inner process" itself stands in need of outward criteria. And I take this to be a logical point about what it is to be an inner process or an inner state. The inner process is partly constituted by what would be the outward expression of it. If there is no possible outward expression of the inner state, then we lose our grip on there being anything inner at all. (This is, in my view, a lesson of the private language argument.) This interpretation explains why Wittgenstein puts "inner process" in scare quotes: ultimately, there is no mental state or process that is purely "inner."

This claim of a conceptual connection between inner states and outward expressions requires two qualifications. First, it is not the case that to possess the concept of a given inner state I must be able to recognize *any* possible expression of it; rather, I have to be able to recognize some range of typical expressions. Similarly, to be in a particular inner state I do not have to be capable of all possible expressions of it; rather, I have to be capable of some expression that some other person is capable of grasping. Second, the ability to recognize an expression as of a particular inner state is not foolproof. Even when I have mastered the concept of anger, I might think that some behavior is an expression of anger when really it isn't, and I might miss something that is a genuine expression of anger. My ability to employ the concept of an inner state, like my ability to employ any concept, is vulnerable to error.

McDowell and I both read Wittgenstein as claiming that there is a logical connection between criteria and the states for which they are criterial. But the connection McDowell finds differs from the one I have just described. According to McDowell, if the criteria for a given state are satisfied, then the state itself is present.[16] So if the state in question is not

---

[16] In this respect, McDowell retains an aspect of Albritton's interpretation, according to which the presence of criteria determines the presence of the corresponding state. McDowell's interpretation is a marked improvement over Albritton's, however, because he recognizes that telling that criteria for a claim are satisfied is "an exercise of the very capacity" for telling "whether things are as the claim would represent them as being" (McDowell 1998, 385). On McDowell's interpretation, therefore, criteria are not something epistemologically less problematic than the states for which they are criteria.

present (as in a case of pretended anger), the criteria for that state are not satisfied. As we saw, McDowell regards "pretending" as a case in which "one causes it to *appear* that criteria for something 'internal' are satisfied…; but the criteria are not really satisfied" (McDowell, 1998, 380). By contrast, as I read Wittgenstein's discussion of the criteria of rain at PI §354, the criteria of rain are appearances that rain presents, but that could also be presented by fire-fighting airplanes. So I would say that, in the case of someone pretending to be in pain, the criteria of pain are satisfied, but the inner state for which they are criteria is absent.

This disagreement hinges on precisely what question one thinks an appeal to criteria is supposed to answer. If one supposes, as McDowell does, that the question is something to the effect of "What grounds my judgment that another person is in a particular inner state?", then his account of criteria captures the answer Wittgenstein would want to give. If the question to which appeals to criteria are relevant is "What grounds my judgment that another's body is expressive of a mind?", then my account better captures what Wittgenstein would want to say. McDowell and I could agree that both questions are important for Wittgenstein. And we could agree about the shape of the answers Wittgenstein would offer. The difference would then be revealed as a relatively minor one regarding how one is to use the term "criterion."[17]

From what I have said so far about Wittgenstein's notion of criteria, it might seem that if I tell you that James is exhibiting criteria for anger, I haven't told you very much, since from what I've said you can (it seems) only infer that James may or may not be angry. And you knew that before I even opened my mouth. But of course telling you that James displays criteria of anger *is* telling you something – namely, that James is expressing anger, and so he appears to be angry. This carries implications about James. For if he appears to be angry, we can infer that either he is in fact angry, or he is in a state that is akin to anger (frustration perhaps) and is presenting appearances in common with expressions of anger, or he is feigning anger, or he is practicing for a play by acting angry. We could perhaps continue this list, but what all the items on it will have in common is that they are applications of the concept of anger. If James displays criteria of anger, then to describe him in such as way as to make his behavior intelligible we must invoke the concept of anger. Moreover, even if he is feigning or acting, he must do something concrete to feign or act: he must bellow, or make the veins on his neck stand out, or dash a teacup to pieces. Such behaviors are criteria of anger, and it is only through exhibiting them (or other criteria) that he can *feign* anger, and it is only through our competence with criteria of anger that we can recognize what he is doing as feigning *anger*. When James displays criteria of anger, then to explain or rationalize his behavior at the personal level, we must employ the concept of anger.

The conception of criteria that I have just sketched can be found in Stanley Cavell's *The Claim of Reason*. Here is a summary passage from that work that exhibits the affinities between our interpretations:

> But if the groan was in those circumstances a criterion of pain, an expression of pain, then pain is, and remains, at issue. And that means that only *certain* eventualities will

[17] This paragraph follows the suggested rapprochement between McDowell and Cavell on criteria that James Conant offers in his 2004, 127.

normally count as his not being in pain after all....Circumstances namely...in which we will say (he will be) feigning, rehearsing, hoaxing, etc. Why such circumstances? What differentiates such circumstances from those in which he is (said to be) clearing his throat, responding to a joke, etc.? Just that for "He's rehearsing" or "feigning," or "It's a hoax," etc. to satisfy us as explanations for his *not* being in pain (for it to "turn out" that he is not in pain) *what* he is feigning must be precisely *pain*, what he is rehearsing must be the part of a man *in pain*, the hoax depends on his simulating *pain*, etc. These circumstances are ones in appealing to which, in describing which, we *retain the concept* (here, of pain) whose application these criteria determine. And this means to me: In all such circumstances he has satisfied the criteria we use for applying the concept of pain to others. It is because of *that* satisfaction that we know that he is feigning pain (i.e., that it is pain he is feigning), and that he knows what to do to feign pain. Criteria are "criteria for something's being so," not in the sense that they tell us of a thing's existence, but of something like its identity, not of its *being* so, but of its being *so*. Criteria do not determine the certainty of statements, but the application of the concepts employed in statements. (Cavell 1979, 45)

7. CRITERIA AND SKEPTICISM

Wittgenstein's discussions of criteria, first in the *Blue Book* and then in the *Investigations*, generated intense philosophical interest because, to their early readers, they pointed the way to a novel solution of the problem of other minds. As we have seen, the response to skepticism that readers such as Albritton based on their interpretation of Wittgenstein on criteria turned out to be unsatisfactory. I have sketched an interpretation of Wittgenstein on criteria that is, I believe, closer to the text and spirit of Wittgenstein's later works. But now one may wonder what light if any this notion of criteria sheds on the problem of skepticism. For, as I read Wittgenstein, when an observer sees that someone is exhibiting criteria for a state of mind, the observer knows that the other is expressing that state of mind, but does not thereby know whether the expression is genuine or feigned. If this is what the perception of criteria comes to, it seems simply to restate the problem of other minds, not to solve it. Should we conclude that Wittgenstein's notion of criteria does not after all contribute to his critique of skepticism?

Appeals to criteria are indeed part of Wittgenstein's response to skepticism, but these appeals have a role in Wittgenstein's anti-skeptical dialectic very different from the role Albritton assigns them. Albritton thinks that appeals to criteria are to answer the question, "How can I know what mental state someone else is in?" I will argue that appeals to criteria instead answer the question, "How can I regard another human body as capable of housing a mind at all?"

The urgency of this latter question springs from pushing the skeptical attitude that generates the problem of other minds. The skeptic about other minds is impressed by the possibility of pretense. He argues that whatever outward behavior I use to ground my judgment about another's state of mind could be the result of pretense. Thus in any particular case, what I take in, the basis of my judgment about the other's state of mind, is compatible with her actually being in a very different state. This is true even when my judgment is correct: hence the other's mental state does not fall within the ambit of my perception, and it is a stroke of good fortune when my judgment turns out to be correct. The skeptic reaches the conclusion that what my experience encompasses is not the mental states of others, but only their behavior – behavior that is what it is regardless of the state of mind of the agent. Because behavior is epistemologically unproblematic (as compared to the agent's supposed mental states), and because the body is the source of behavior, we come to regard the body as epistemologically and metaphysically primary. The human body on this conception can, in principle, be fully described and fully understood without reference to a mind: the resources of natural science (neurophysiology, chemistry, physics, and allied disciplines) suffice to describe and explain the body and its behavior.

A traditional anti-skeptical philosopher starts from this conception of the human body and conceives his task as showing how we can be warranted in attributing mental states to such a body; this will amount to showing how we can infer a subject's mental states from his or her behavior. Albritton tried to use a notion of criteria to ground such an inference. His effort failed, and no other attempt will fare better, for reasons we will examine below.

This task is hard enough, but further reflection only deepens the skeptic problem. For when I conceive what another human being presents me with as mere behavior, not only do I have no basis for attributing one mental state rather than another to her, but I have no basis for attributing mental states to her at all. What I observe, the body described without reference to mental states, appears to be a complicated physiological machine. The body's behavior appears to be the causal effects of physiological stimulation, not a possible expression of a mind. From this point of view, the other appears to me as an automaton – very complicated, of course, but no more capable of harboring beliefs, desires, or emotions than a wind-up toy. Wittgenstein expresses this sense of the other as psychologically inert in this question:

> What gives us *so much as the idea* that living beings, things, can feel? (PI §283)

This question arises when, in a misguided effort to attain what purports to be metaphysical and epistemological rigor, we strip away mindedness from our conception of what we perceive when we look at another human being. In this mood, we cannot see how it is possible for bodily movement to even appear to express a state of mind. Because the center of Kant's philosophy is the attempt to answer such "how possible" questions (cf. "How is this association [of cause and effect] itself possible?"; Kant 1965, A113), I will call this moment of the skeptical dialectic, in which we face the question "How can it so much as seem that a body could express a mind?", a Kantian skeptical problem.[18]

We can better understand the Kantian skeptical problem about other minds, and Wittgenstein's response to it, by working through an analogous case. Consider

---

[18] My characterization of this problematic and the terminology of "Kantian" skepticism are drawn from Conant 2004.

Wittgenstein's discussion of signposts in the *Investigations*. We quite naturally think that a signpost carries a meaning (e.g., that taking the next highway exit will put you on the road to New York City), which is what we grasp when we see and understand the sign. But then a skeptic asks us to reflect on the possibility that we may misinterpret the sign (as can easily happen in a foreign country with unfamiliar sign conventions). This reminds us that any sign may be interpreted in various ways. So it seems obvious that what happens when we understand a sign is that we fasten on one out of this multiplicity of interpretations. We understand a sign *correctly* when we light on the *right* interpretation. The skeptic quite reasonably asks what guarantees that we have arrived at the correct interpretation. The guarantee cannot be the sign itself (since it stands in need of interpretation); and the interpretation I use cannot guarantee itself (since there is no such thing as a *superinterpretation* that prevents all possibility of mistake). If I cite the causal conditioning that leads me to turn in the direction the arrow points, that does not show why it is *correct* to take the next exit when you want to go to New York City (as opposed to its being what you are trained to do). The skeptic concludes that my conviction is groundless and that I don't have a good reason to think that the sign means that the next exit goes to New York City as opposed to any of the myriad of other things it might mean.

Then, since the challenges to my understanding of the sign are general – they have nothing to do with my particular infirmities or the limitations of my particular situation – every possible interpretation seems equally groundless. The sign therefore appears to be incapable of providing any guidance – *it* cannot answer the question, "How do I get to New York City from here?" – and we face the question of how it is possible for a sign to even *seem* to convey directions. At this moment of the dialectic, when we consider the sign itself, we see metal covered with a peculiar arrangement of paint. The sign seems to be an object that conveys nothing and provides no normative constraint on – but merely causal impetus for – the psychological process of interpretation. This line of thought leads Wittgenstein to remark, "Every sign *by itself* seems dead" (PI §432).

This conception of the sign is sustained by another tendency of modern philosophy. We assume that the meaningfulness of a sign must be located in the sign itself, and then we assume that the "sign itself" must be regarded in isolation from its use and must be described in purely physical terms (ink marks on paper, paint on metal). The assumption that the "sign itself" must be described in purely physical terms, as an arrangement of paint on metal, say, is in turn sustained by a deep-seated presupposition about the nature of reality: reality is all and only that which can be described in the vocabulary of physical science.[19]

Wittgenstein's response to the idea that the sign is a *dead* arrangement of marks on paper or of paint on metal, and so is incapable of conveying a meaning, is suggested in this exchange:

[19] The ontological pre-eminence assigned to physical science can be traced back at least to the entwined roots of modern philosophy and the scientific revolution of the seventeenth century. One of John McDowell's tasks in *Mind and World* is to respect the achievement of modern science while resisting the idea that our cognitive activity must be described within what he calls "the realm of [natural] law" (McDowell 1994, 71).

> How does it come about that this arrow → *points*? Doesn't it seem to carry in it something besides itself? – "No, not the dead line on paper; only the psychical thing, the meaning, can do that." – That is both true and false. The arrow points only in the application that a living being makes of it. (PI §454)

When Wittgenstein says that it is both true and false that only the meaning and not the dead line on paper can point, he is conceding that *if* we conceive the arrow as a dead line, as a mere arrangement of ink particles on paper, then it is true that it cannot carry information ("something besides itself"). But it is false that *only* a psychical thing, the meaning of the sign, can carry information. The arrow has an application within a practice; it is part of a custom belonging to living beings (cf. PI §§198, 202). When we are embedded in this practice, we grasp the meaning of the arrow itself without engaging in interpretation: "there is a way of grasping a rule which is *not* an *interpretation*, but which is exhibited in what we call 'obeying the rule' and 'going against it' in actual cases" (PI §201).

Wittgenstein's philosophical reminders show us, first, that if we conceive the sign in purely physical terms, we reach a Kantian skeptical problem, and, second, that there is no rational obligation to conceive the sign in those problem-inducing terms. We do not get a truer picture of what a sign is by seeing it only as an arrangement of paint on metal; on the contrary, the functional characteristics that make a sign what it is are invisible to such a view. The assumption that physics and chemistry can in principle fully describe everything is scientism, not science. Wittgenstein's remarks show how viewing the sign as a mere physical object, isolated from the context of human practices to which it belongs, falsifies and distorts our thinking about meaning and how we grasp it.

The argument that brings us from the possibility of pretense to the Kantian problem of how it is possible for a body to seem to express a mind has a structure analogous to the argument from the possibility of misinterpreting a sign to the Kantian problem of how it is possible for a sign to seem to convey a meaning. As we saw above, skepticism about other minds starts from the idea that I cannot tell what inner state someone else is in, because for all I know she might be pretending. Thinking through that problem yields the Kantian skeptical problem: it becomes puzzling how another human body can even seem to express a mind. In elaborating this problem, we think of the human body as a complex physiological machine, and this conception of the human body finds support from a scientific world view that grants ontological pre-eminence to the natural sciences.

Wittgenstein's response to this interwoven set of skeptical problems about other minds may be presented under two main headings. First, he wishes to chart the philosophical toll of this form of skepticism. Second, he wishes to show that the skeptic's arguments are not rationally compelling. He engages in a careful examination of the examples and assumptions that the skeptic starts with in order to expose 'the conjuring trick' that they contain (PI §308).

In considering the toll of skepticism, I suppose it is obvious that there is something problematic about conceiving of others as automatons. We naturally respond to other human beings as unities of body and mind, as Wittgenstein emphasizes in the discussions of the natural expressions of emotion and attitude that we touched on above. But the unnaturalness of conceiving of others as automatons need not dislodge the skeptic: he is aware that his conclusions cut against common sense and our natural responses to one another. His attitude is that we must reject common sense when it conflicts with the deliverances of rationally compelling argument.

The skeptic's willingness to reject our ordinary and primary modes of thinking about others is abetted by the philosophers who attempt to show that perceiving another's mere behavior (conceived as physiological happenings) can license inferences about a mind within the body.[20] This strategy seeks to put an interpretation on the movements of the body, so that we can say that the movement is significant – that it expresses feelings and attitudes and emotions. If successful, this strategy would yield an epistemologically and metaphysically hygienic reconstruction of the concept *human being* as a physiological body plus an interpretation of its movements.

In Wittgenstein's view, this strategy is no more successful than the strategy of reconstructing the meaning of a sign from dead paint on metal (the sign itself) plus an interpretation (a psychical thing that breathes life into the sign). Once the body is regarded as devoid of any natural significance, we have nothing that could ground the correctness of attributions of mental states to it. Many different interpretations could be assigned to an arrangement of paint on metal; likewise, many different mental states could be assigned to any bit of behavior, so long as the association of state and behavior respected causal regularities of the body's movements. And just as nothing can serve as a normative constraint on our choice of interpretations of a 'dead' sign, so nothing can serve as a normative constraint on our choice of an interpretation of a stretch of mere behavior. And if every assignment of meaning to an agent's behavior is equally ungrounded, we cannot coherently regard the behavior as meaningful.

The force of these Wittgensteinian arguments is that once we have conceived of the human body as a locus of mere behavior, as a physiological machine, there is no way to argue our way back to a conception of it as bearing meaning, as expressing a mind. The skeptic is therefore committed to thinking of others as physiological machines. Wittgenstein does not say that this is impossible, but he does highlight the difficulty of doing so:

> §420   But can't I imagine that the people around me are automata, lack consciousness, even though they behave in the same way as usual? – If I imagine it now – alone in my room – I see people with fixed looks (as in a trance) going about their business – the idea is perhaps a little uncanny. But just try to keep hold of this idea in the midst of your ordinary intercourse with others, in the street, say! Say to yourself, for example: "The children over there are mere automata; all their liveliness is mere automatism." And you will either find these words becoming quite meaningless;

---

[20] These philosophers may describe themselves as anti-skeptics, but because they accept the skeptic's fundamental doctrine that what we experience of others is *mere* behavior, they end up trying to remove the sting from a position that remains essentially skeptical. Albritton, in his original essay, is an example of such a philosopher.

or you will produce in yourself some kind of uncanny feeling, or something of the sort....

A determined skeptic might be willing to live with uncanniness as the price of rational rigor. But there is one more cost of his purported rigor. The skeptic's argument begins with the possibility of pretense. His argument ultimately leads to the conclusion that the only rationally legitimate conception of another is as a locus of behavior, as a complicated machine. If this correctly captures the dialectical arc to which the skeptic is committed, we have reached a paradox. For the skeptic's initial premise that another person could dissimulate her mental state plainly presupposes that the other *has* mental states to dissimulate. The conclusion of the argument is that we must conceive the other as a being without mental states. The conclusion therefore deprives us of the premise which led to it.

Again, a determined skeptic could find a way to live with this paradox. If the skeptical argument, rigorously pursued, ends in paradox, that may be because there is something defective in the very concept of a mental state; the skeptic could decide to retain his conception of what is given in his experience of others and simply eschew such troublesome concepts as *pretense* and *mental state.*

This is where the second strand of Wittgenstein's response to skepticism about other minds comes into play. Even if a skeptic should be willing to pay the philosophical price of his conclusions, there is no good reason to do so. In Wittgenstein's view, there is no rational obligation to accept the skeptic's arguments. Wittgenstein's basic argumentative strategy is to look for places in the skeptic's arguments in which he employs a false assumption, or changes the meaning of his terms, or commits some other fallacy. This strategy does not have a general form, as it must be adapted to each particular skeptical argument. And there is no guarantee that this strategy will always work. But Wittgenstein successfully employs it to neutralize several important skeptical arguments, and suggests a range of further applications.

To indicate the tenor of Wittgenstein's critique of skepticism, I will mention four examples of this strategy in operation.

(1) As we have seen, the skeptic argues that my experience of others cannot encompass their mental states, because whatever I perceive is compatible with the other's dissimulating. McDowell's articulation of disjunctivism has provided us with one response to this argument: in a good case, I do have a cognitive grasp of the other's state of mind, while in a bad case I take in a mere appearance, something less than the other's state of mind. This thesis accommodates the possibility that the other is deceiving me or that I am in some other way misperceiving the other, while insisting that when I am not misperceiving, I perceive the other's state of mind in a way that is *incompatible* with her dissimulating. The availability of disjunctivism neutralizes the skeptic's inference from the possibility of pretense to the conclusion that all I take in – in good and bad cases alike – is appearances or representations compatible with the falsity of what they present.

(2) The skeptical argument that a sign cannot carry a meaning rests on the claim that understanding a sign requires interpretation. Wittgenstein argues that this claim is false, and he does so without denying the fact that it is possible to misinterpret a sign. To make

this argument, Wittgenstein introduces clarity into the concept of interpretation (cf. PI §201). This lets us see that in some cases we understand a sign via an interpretation and in some cases we do not. (This difference is obscured when we oscillate between different meanings of the word "interpretation.")

(3) One argument for skepticism about other minds presupposes that any putative expression of a human body could be interpreted in multiple ways, and so is not *in itself* expressive. The claims I have made on Wittgenstein's behalf in (1) and (2) can be joined together in another Wittgensteinian response: just as someone embedded in the relevant practice can grasp the meaning of a sign immediately, without engaging in anything properly termed "interpretation," so also a normal perceiver can grasp another's mental states directly, without engaging in anything properly termed "interpretation." The capacity for such direct perception does not, on Wittgenstein's account, preclude the possibility that one will misperceive. But the availability of disjunctivism means that this possibility does not entail that my grasp of another's mental state is always mediated by an inference from something *less* than the mental state itself. (Criteria articulate the basis of my judgment that another person is cheerful, for example; but, in the cases we are considering, observing the presence of criteria is not epistemically prior to perceiving the other's inner state.)

Wittgenstein describes this perceptual ability as follows:

> "We *see* emotion." – As opposed to what? – We do not see facial contortions and make inferences from them (like a doctor framing a diagnosis) to joy, grief, boredom. We describe a face immediately as sad, radiant, bored, even when we are unable to give any other description to the features. – Grief, one would like to say, is personified in the face. (Z §225)

The faces and bodies of other people reveal their souls through displaying criteria of their states of mind.

(4) I will close with a sketch of how Wittgenstein could respond to a philosopher who continues to be impressed by the possibility of pretense and unimpressed by the possibility of cognitive openness to others' minds. To such a philosopher, Wittgenstein's idea that in encountering others we normally take in their states of mind will sound naïve or dogmatic. Such a philosopher may throw back at Wittgenstein the feature of criteria that I stressed in §6 above: the satisfaction of criteria determines what concepts must be employed in describing another, but does not confer certainty as to whether the other is actually in the corresponding state. Isn't that just a confession of our ignorance about what another is thinking or feeling that re-introduces the problem of skepticism?

It is true that someone's exhibiting criteria of anger does not entail that she is actually angry. But it does severely limit the range of acceptable explanations we can give for her behavior. How do we tell which of these remaining eventualities is actual? By employing essentially the same abilities by which we tell that she appears angry: that is, by looking at what she says and does, the context of her behavior (to see whether it is one where it makes sense that someone, or this particular person, would get angry), by considering the cultural norms that shape her behavior (to see whether the agent has, for example, received the kind of injury that members of her culture get angry about). In short, we find out whether she is really angry using tools on a par with those we used to judge that she appears to be angry. (How far we go in any particular case to confirm that the individual is *really* angry will be a function of what is at stake for us in determining this.)

The skeptic asks, "Are these techniques foolproof?" The answer to this must be "No." We are fallible perceivers with fallible cognitive techniques. The skeptic wishes to turn this admission into a ground for doubt: "Since your techniques are not foolproof, you might have made an error in this case, so you don't know what state this person is in." In Wittgenstein's view, this is a poor argument. If someone want to challenge my claim as to what someone else is thinking, the challenger needs to provide a ground for doubt. Raising a doubt doesn't come for free; challenging a knowledge claim has its conditions. To persuade me to retract my claim about another's state of mind, the challenger needs to provide some reason to think that the other is dissimulating or acting, some reason to think I may have misread her particular expression. The bare logical possibility of error is not sufficient. As Wittgenstein notes,

> But that is not to say that we are in doubt because it is possible for us to *imagine* a doubt. I can easily imagine someone always doubting before he opened his front door whether an abyss did not yawn behind it and making sure about it before he went through the door (and he might on some occasion prove to be right) – but that does not make me doubt in the same case. (PI §84)

8. CONCLUSION

The notion of a criterion highlights the expressive power of the human body. We encounter others as minded beings who express themselves through what they say and do and thereby allow us to know their minds. The perceptual capacity for obtaining such knowledge is fallible, like all human capacities. We sometimes misread others' expressions, and people sometimes lie about or dissimulate their states of mind. This is a fundamental feature of human relationships which does nothing to show that we can *never* know what another person is thinking or feeling.

The skeptic about other minds pushes this more radical conclusion. From the possibility of error and pretense he builds an argument that we cannot have the openness to one another that I just described. The short sketches of some of Wittgenstein's anti-skeptical moves that I have provided are preliminary schemas to suggest how one may resist skeptical arguments in an intellectually responsible way. Wittgenstein aims to recover the possibility of openness to one another – an openness that is partial, fallible, but genuine – from skeptical threat.[21]

[21] I am very grateful to Claire Baldwin, Jim Conant, David Finkelstein, and Marie McGinn for comments on earlier versions of this chapter. I also wish to thank the American Philosophical Society for a sabbatical enhancement grant that supported the writing of the first draft of this material.

References

ALBRITTON, ROGERS (1966). 'On Wittgenstein's Use of the Term "Criterion"', in George Pitcher ed., *Wittgenstein: The Philosophical Investigations*. Garden City, NY: Anchor Books. (Orig. printed in *Journal of Philosophy*, 56.22 (Oct 1959): 845–57.)

CAVELL, STANLEY (1979). *The Claim of Reason*. New York: Oxford University Press.

CONANT, JAMES (2004). 'The Varieties of Scepticism', in Denis McManus ed., *Wittgenstein and Scepticism*. New York: Routledge.

FINKELSTEIN, DAVID (2003). *Expression and the Inner*. Cambridge, MA: Harvard University Press.

KANT, IMMANUEL (1965). *Critique of Pure Reason*, trans. N. K. Smith. New York: St Martin's.

MCDOWELL, JOHN (1994). *Mind and World*. Cambridge, MA: Harvard University Press. (2nd edn, 1996.)

——(1998). 'Criteria, Defeasibility, and Knowledge', in *Meaning, Knowledge, and Reality*. Cambridge, MA: Harvard University Press.

WITTGENSTEIN, LUDWIG (1958). *Preliminary Studies for the "Philosophical Investigations", Generally Known as the Blue and Brown Books*. Oxford: Basil Blackwell.

——(1967). *Zettel*, ed. G. E. M. Anscombe and G. H. von Wright, trans. G. E. M. Anscombe. Oxford: Basil Blackwell.

——(1997). *Philosophical Investigations*, 2nd edn, ed. G. E. M. Anscombe and R. Rhees, trans. G. E. M. Anscombe. Oxford: Blackwell Publishers.

···

CHAPTER 22

WITTGENSTEIN ON THE EXPERIENCE OF MEANING AND SECONDARY USE

···

MICHEL TER HARK

1. INTRODUCTION

···

TYPICALLY, a person is said to understand the meaning of a particular sentence if he can replace it by, or translate it into, another. Asking students to produce a summary of a story in their own words, or to articulate their own views drawing on a sample of literature, is a way of finding out whether they understand the literature. But there are cases where understanding is not shown in how a person translates or paraphrases a sample of literature, or applies a mathematical formula. In poetry or rhetoric, understanding shows itself in seeing that a particular word is appropriate and that no synonym can replace it. Similarly, a person's understanding of a piece of music is shown in how he plays it, in his choosing the right tempo, in phrasing it in this way rather than that, and so on. This type of understanding is not confined to the aesthetic domain, though. It is shown in our reactions to puns, wordplay, in our choice of words to express deep feelings or of words one is reluctant to speak such as an adieu, a self-confession. In these cases, meaning seems to have a mental dimension, in that it is something we can experience.

Now it may be tempting to suppose that to experience the meaning of a familiar word is not limited to this scope of examples but that it is even fundamental to the understanding of (one's native) language as such. Consider how, for instance, G. E. Moore deals with our feelings of familiarity with words:

> It is quite plain, I think, that when we understand the meaning of a sentence, something else does happen in our minds *besides* the mere hearing of the words of which the sentence is composed. You can easily satisfy yourselves of this by contrasting

what happens when you hear a sentence, which you *do* understand, from what happens when you hear a sentence which you do *not* understand: for instance, when you hear words spoken in a foreign language, which you do not understand at all. Certainly in the first case, there occurs, besides the mere hearing of the words, another act of consciousness – an apprehension of their meaning, which is absent in the second case. (Moore 1953, 58–9)

A more accomplished writer on the mind, William James, even identified many unnamed states or qualities of states underlying both thought processes and the use of one's native language, what he calls 'fringes', 'intransitive states', or 'feelings of tendency'. For instance:

When I use the word *man* in two different sentences, I may have both times exactly the same sound upon my lips and the same picture in my mental eye, but I may mean, and at the very moment of uttering the word and imagining the picture, know that I mean, two entirely different things…This added consciousness is an absolutely positive sort of feeling transforming what would otherwise be mere noise or vision into something understood; and determining the sequel of my thinking, the later words and images, in a perfectly definite way. (James 1890/1950, vol. 1, 472)

Wittgenstein returned to the experience of meaning time and time again in his later writings on the philosophy of psychology.[1] In Part II of the *Philosophical Investigations*, experiencing the meaning of a word, or as it is also called, 'meaning-experience', is introduced in the chapter dominated by the discussion of seeing aspects. But it would be mistaken to think of his interest in the experience of meaning as entirely derivative from the interest in seeing aspects. On the contrary, Wittgenstein is concerned with the experience of meaning long before he begins to work on aspect perception in 1946. As his writings from the early 1930s bear out, the issue of experiencing the meaning of a word is especially urgent for him because of his view of meaning as use-in-the-language and of understanding in the sense of an ability.[2] The general moral of his discussions in the first part of the *Investigations* is that meaning and understanding do not refer to any simple item of experience at the moment of speaking. Experiencing the meaning of a word, however, seems to be a genuine phenomenon, a mental state that can be attained at a given time and, furthermore, we can recognize ourselves at that time as being in it. But how can meaning in the sense of use, i.e. the rule-guided application of words in time, be experienced in a moment? Indeed, how can a word have a meaning when it is not *used*?

---

[1] Long discussions of the experience of meaning occur in Wittgenstein's *Remarks on the Philosophy of Psychology* as well as *Last Writings on the Philosophy of Psychology*, vol. 1. Wittgenstein was well acquainted with especially James's *Principles of Psychology* and had a particular interest in the chapter on the stream of thought in which many examples are given of elusive experiences that are the 'soul' of our words or the feelings of direction underlying our speaking and thinking. See on the relation between James and Wittgenstein, ter Hark 1990 and Goodman 2002.

[2] Early discussions of the experience of meaning occur in the second part of the *Brown Book* (1958) and in *Philosophical Grammar* (1974) §§3–7 (pp. 41–5). See also Waismann 1965, 360ff. and Wittgenstein's 'Dictation for Schlick' published in Baker 2003, 20ff.

In the secondary literature, it has been noted that talking of experiences of meaning seems to be out of line with the approach to meaning and understanding so dominant in the first part of the *Philosophical Investigations*. Yet the apparent tension has not been resolved. In general, commentators have interpreted the remarks on experiencing meaning as supplementary to the account of meaning and understanding in Part I of the *Investigations*. Some have argued that the discussion of the experience of meaning is meant to fill a gap in the earlier account of meaning and rule-following. Rhees's Preface to the *Blue and Brown Books* has been the impetus to this view, which is further worked out by Kripke (1982) and Zemach (1995). On their view, the earlier account of language might provoke the question what the difference is between operating with signs in a rule-guided context and the automated use of language. Could there be a meaning-blind person, Rhees asks, who operated with words just as we do? If so, would we say that he is as much in command of our language as we are? Or is he missing something, something which we experience but which falls 'outside the use of language' and hence is beyond the reach of a logical investigation? (Rhees 1958, xiv) Others have argued that the discussion of the experience of meaning marks a shift of interest in new and still unexplored aspects and areas of language such as the quale of word-meanings (Goldstein 2004), the specific human attitude to language (Mulhall 2001), or aesthetics (Tilghman 1984; Hanfling 1991, 2002; Sibley 2001; Budd 2006).

In this chapter, I will show otherwise and establish, exegetically and argumentatively, that the discussion of the experience of meaning is not supplementary to the earlier account of meaning and understanding. It is not the case that Wittgenstein gradually came to see that the earlier account had left something out, i.e. the familiar feel of words to which Moore and James refer. Rather, the point of the discussion is to determine what it is that philosophers think that is left out in an account of language which emphasizes 'only' the use of signs. Put otherwise, what is under investigation here is the very concept of experience of which not only Moore and James but also Wittgenstein's commentators say that it has to be included in any account of language distinctive of human beings. To experience the meaning of words, our feelings of familiarity with them, therefore, is not the end of philosophical reflection, a sort of a Wittgensteinian discovery concerning the human attitude towards language (cf. Mulhall 2001), but rather the beginning.

More specifically, I argue that the aim of Wittgenstein's conceptual investigation is twofold. First of all it investigates the philosophical push to hypostasizing hard to get hold of experiences in order to explain and to accommodate *real* understanding. It is argued that such hypostasis takes for granted that 'experience' is here used as when we describe what we see on a display or what sound we hear coming from outside, and that at most there is only a gradual difference with these paradigmatic cases of experience. Secondly, investigating the specific circumstances in which meaning is experienced reveals that the 'missing link' is to be found not outside language, i.e. in elusive experiences, but in a secondary use of 'experience', a use which essentially depends upon language.

To recognize that this is what Wittgenstein's obscure remarks on meaning-experience are about, it is vital to consider the whole array of examples which he discusses. Thus

I will broaden the standard treatment of meaning-experience in the secondary literature to include such hard-to-get-hold-of phenomena as synaesthesia, 'déjà vu', 'momentary meanings' (*meinen*), feeling-of-unreality and physiognomic perception of linguistic items. Other concepts that either have been dealt with in the literature separately, e.g. 'secondary use', or have been completely ignored, e.g. 'illusion', 'inclination', and 'primitive reaction', turn out to be part of one and the same conceptual survey of meaning-experience. Indeed, by missing the connections between these latter concepts, even commentators who do consider secondary use in connection with the experience of meaning have failed to explain what sort of use is involved here, and how it relates to the primary use.

I begin in section 2 with a discussion of the philosophical push to hypostasizing experiences. A crucial role is played by Wittgenstein's discussion of 'meaning-blindness'. I identify a misunderstanding common to all parties in the debate about meaning-blindness: the idea that Wittgenstein introduces a meaning-blind person in order to get us to contemplate the effects of absent meaning-qualia. Both those who affirm and those who deny the existence of such meaning-qualia have failed to see what Wittgenstein is about in these remarks, and in fact take for granted that he is here using 'experience' in a primary sense. In section 3, I propose to interpret the notion of meaning-blindness as an object of comparison meant to throw light on the question what it is that an imaginary person suffering from this 'defect' would miss. Once this is clarified, it can be considered whether and in what sense we would call what they lack an experience. In section 4, I begin the description of the specific circumstances in which meaning is experienced, drawing on the analogy with the circumstances in which we speak of the dawning of visual or auditory aspects. The first analogy to be explored concerns Wittgenstein's idea of a special kind of illusion. The most important similarity between experiences of meaning and the seeing of aspects, however, is that in both cases a secondary use of language is involved. The final interpretation of secondary use holds centre stage in sections 5 and 6. In section 5, I first reject attempts to explain secondary use in terms of associative explanation. In section 6, I further explain what secondary use is by relating it to the concepts of inclination and primitive reaction.

2. Hypostasizing Experiences

Wittgenstein discusses a variety of experiences of meaning. One such variety concerns the physiognomic perception of linguistic items, like proper names: 'Goethe's signature intimates something Goethian to me. To that extent it is like a face, for I might say the same of his face' (RPP I §336; cf. PI II, 183), or specific feelings attached to specific words like the 'conditional feeling' tied to the word 'if' ('if-feeling') (PI II, 182), discussed also by James and Russell.[3] Another variety discussed widely by Wittgenstein, but largely left

---

[3] James 1890, vol. 1, 252; Russell 1921, 250.

unnoticed in the secondary literature, is synaesthetic experiences. Already in *The Brown Book*, Wittgenstein dealt with what is nowadays called 'colour-grapheme synaesthesia'; '"Listen to the five vowels a, e, i, o, u and arrange them in order of their darkness"' (BB, 136). Another frequent example is: '"For me the vowel *e* is yellow"' (PI II, 216).[4] Yet another category concerns subjective experiences of meaning a word, uttered in isolation and unrelated to practical purposes, in a particular way (e.g. the order 'Say "March!" and mean it as the name of the month!'), imaginative shifts in meaning the same word (for instance, 'When I said "bank", I first meant the bank where you can get money, but then the river bank'), as well as meanings of words suddenly occurring to one ('As I heard that word he occurred to me').[5] Echoing James's 'feelings of tendency', Wittgenstein speaks here sometimes of the experience of a 'germ' (cf. RPP I §777; LWPP I §843), but more generally he speaks of *meinen* while distinguishing this use of the term explicitly from 'intending' in a practical sense.[6] The term 'momentary meaning' is used in this article as a general name for these various cases of *meinen*. In addition to these cases, Wittgenstein also discusses related but more isolated phenomena such as the feeling of unreality and the déjà-vu experience (RPP I §125, 336).[7]

A description of a lack of meaning-experience that has in particular drawn the attention in the literature is 'meaning-blindness'. Towards the end of his extended discussion of aspect-seeing he raises the question whether there may be human beings lacking in the capacity to see something as something (PI II, 213). Then he notes: 'The importance of this concept lies in the connection between the concepts of "seeing an aspect" and "experiencing the meaning of a word". For we want to ask "What would you be missing if you did not *experience* the meaning of a word?"' (PI II, 214; cf. LWPP I, §783–4). Kripke (1982), Rhees (1958), and, more explicitly, Zemach (1995) argue that the concept of meaning-blindness is introduced for supplementary purposes in order to show that there is more to meaning than the use of a word. Meaning, Zemach says, 'has a certain

---

[4] See also LWPP I §§59, 362–3, 631, 799.

[5] See Z §1–53; LWPP I §90–138; PI II, 217–18. That certain uses of 'I meant' or 'I mean' are cases of meaning-experience, and hence of secondary use has been completely ignored by earlier commentators of these passages. See for instance Vesey 1968, Hunter 1973, Hacker 1996.

[6] See LWPP I §§ 65, 67. Wittgenstein explicitly distinguishes *meinen* and intention in a practical sense. *Meinen* is rather a kind of imaginative intending. Wittgenstein also says that the question how someone meant a word is a question of intention, which might be important in special cases, e.g. a law-court, but he adds: 'But could how he experienced a word – the word "bank" for instance – have been significant in the same way?' (PI II, 214). This distinction is even more explicit when he says 'Meaning is as little an experience as intending' (PI II, 217). A recent example of the confusion of *meinen* and intentions in the ordinary and practical sense of the word is Bouveresse, who claims that the target of Wittgenstein's discussion of meaning-experience is the idea of acts of intention that must always accompany words and which give them meaning. This overlooks two things. First, Wittgenstein has already subjected this view to scrutiny in the first part of the *Philosophical Investigations*, in particular §665f. Second, it fails to see that the issue in Part II is the specific relation between the use of the word 'intention' in particular games and the ordinary, practical use. Significantly, Bouveresse nowhere invokes the distinction between the primary and secondary use of words (Bouveresse 2007, 82).

[7] Synaesthetes often report precognitive experiences, déjà vu, and feelings of unreality. See Rich and Mattingley 2002; Rich, Bradshaw, and Mattingley 2005.

quale that "echoes" the word's use, matching the aspect under which we saw the things to which it applies. The shadow of its applicanda,…, lingers about the word and is felt as its special aroma' (Zemach 1995, 491). We need not be aware of this aroma in order to be able to apply a term, Zemach concedes, yet in some cases we do become aware of it and then meaning is directly experienced. Thus the meaning-blind person misses a genuine yet elusive quale. Others have claimed that the discussion of meaning-blindness is meant to show how small in importance and pertinence experiences of meaning are. On this view, experiences of meaning are sensations, impressions, and experiences that accompany the use of words and, as such, as Bouveresse claims, 'the thing that counts least', or they have argued, as Weiss (1995, 66), that such experiences are non-existent.

A striking feature of the preceding interpretations is that they all take the use of 'experience' for granted. Yet there is abundant evidence that the very issue for Wittgenstein is precisely what is meant by 'experience' here. In the preceding quote, he has italicized the word 'experience': 'For we want to ask, "what would you be missing if you did not *experience* the meaning of a word?".' Commentators have read the italics as just a sign of emphasis. Some, like Bouveresse (2007) and Weiss (1995), are then inclined to interpret the question as saying that the position it describes is false, i.e. there are no experiences of meaning *tout court*, whereas others, like Zemach and Kripke, take the correct answer to be 'an introspectively elusive yet pervasive experience', a condition that can be 'directly experienced'. Thus conceived, the question what the meaning-blind person misses would ask for the consequences of a certain sort of defect, analogous to colour-blindness or deafness, and the meaning-blind person would be blind for a peculiar sort of experience as the colour-blind person is blind for colours. This is the view Kripke apparently finds in Wittgenstein when he says that the meaning-blind person misses an experience which is introspectively more elusive than the feeling of headache (Kripke 1982, 48).[8]

By thus taking for granted the use of 'experience', commentators have argued either that there are experiences of meaning in addition to the (mere) use of words, or that there is not something besides the use of words. What they have failed to see is that Wittgenstein's objection is not to e.g. 'something besides', but to the logic or 'grammar' it suggests. To see this more clearly consider first a passage from James which may well have cued Wittgenstein's critical thoughts on the 'if-feeling' in section vi of Part II of the *Investigations*:

> When we read…is it true that there is nothing more in our minds than the words themselves as they pass? What then is the meaning of the words which we think we understand as we read? What makes that meaning different in one phrase from what it is in the other? 'Who?' 'When?' 'Where?' Is the difference of felt meaning in these interrogatives nothing more than their differences of sound? And is it not (just like the difference of sound itself) known and understood in an affection of consciousness correlative to it, though so impalpable to direct examination? (James 1890 vol. 1, 252)

---

[8] According to Kripke, Wittgenstein's descriptions are 'deeply introspective', and although he adds that 'introspection' is not used here in the traditional way, he fails to make clear in what other way.

> We ought to say a feeling of *and*, a feeling of *if*, a feeling of *but*, and a feeling of *by*, quite as readily as we say a feeling of *blue* or a feeling of *cold*. (Ibid., 245–6)

The path James takes toward getting a clear conception of experiences of meaning goes by way of introspection. If only we look attentively enough, James urges, we become acquainted with the referents of 'if', 'but', or 'and', and so can grasp the concept of experiencing the meaning of a word. Wittgenstein would object to the phrase 'quite as readily' in the preceding quote. This presumes not just that experiences of meaning can be compared with the various paradigmatic cases of experience, but rather that they must be so compared. For if using words would not make a difference to our experience, our understanding of language would not be different from the 'understanding' attributed to a mechanism operating with signs of various sorts. But this is already to be taken in by the grammar suggested by 'something besides'. Wittgenstein's aim, however, is to show that there is no paradox in rejecting this urge to hypostasize experiences and, at the same time, not espousing behaviourism or anti-realism.

The urge to hypostasize elusive experiences is a deep-seated intuition about the genesis of which Wittgenstein has much to say. In a series of scattered remarks he delves into what I call the psychological predicament of the philosopher (or scientist) determined to explain the nature of conscious experience. A particular motive for hypostasizing experiences arises when thinking about the exceptional, the unfamiliar. Thus Moore in fact concludes on the basis of his experience of a foreign language, i.e. the experience that the words have no meaning, the presence of experiences of meaning underlying the use of one's native language. This is an inference exactly like the inference from a feeling of unfamiliarity to the feeling of familiarity about which Wittgenstein says: 'But the existence of this feeling of strangeness does not give us a reason for saying that every object which we know well and which does not seem strange to us gives us a feeling of familiarity' (PI §596). To see more precisely how this argument applies to experiences of meaning and what is wrong with the inference, consider the following remark which I think is meant as an analogy:

> While I write, do I feel anything in my hand or in my wrist? Not generally. But still, wouldn't it feel different, if my hand were anaesthetized? Yes. And is that now a proof that I *nevertheless* do feel something when I move my hand in the normal way? No, I believe *not*. (RPP I §208)

By analogy, in normal linguistic intercourse we do not have if-feelings when making a conditional statement in the course of a discussion. Only in special situations the if-feeling may arise, e.g. when doing introspective philosophy or psychology. It was James's talent to make his readers aware of a variety of experiences of meaning, but what is perhaps his most effective example is a linguistic version of anaesthesia, i.e. the feeling that the meaning of a word may slip away when repeated several times. Thus Wittgenstein asks in another remark whether a word, as it is used in normal circumstances, does not perhaps feel as it does when it has lost its meaning through being often repeated: 'You certainly can't testify from your memory that the contrary is true. But one merely finds that *a priori* it can't be otherwise' (RPP I §194). The inference is no more than an a priori hypostasis of experiences caused by failing to see the special (mental) condition in which meaning-experiences are reported. This condition is like the one in which a person notices a certain aspect of a word familiar to him and which never occurred to him before. From this it seems to follow that he must have also been aware of a different aspect, i.e. an aspect under which he always, in normal conditions, understands these words.[9] For instance, because a certain linguistic joke, e.g. Wittgenstein's favourite example 'Weiche, Wotan, weiche', prompts a comic experience, it is concluded that when *Weiche* ('retreat') and *weiche* ('soft') are used in normal circumstances they must also be experienced in a specific way.[10] What one fails to see here, however, is that had one not 'discovered' the experiences in the special condition, one would never have thought that the words as used in normal conditions are experienced in a certain way. That is, when reading or saying 'if' in normal conditions one has no experiences whatsoever, despite the fact that in other circumstances one may 'experience' the word when looking at it closely and pronouncing it with a certain emphasis.[11]

Speaking of special experiences, acts of consciousness, underlying the command of one's native language is not only an a priori hypostasis but also a move which blurs the very distinction it is meant to explain. By assimilating the concept of experience as applied to the meaning of words to 'experience' as paradigmatically conceived, no understanding of the soulful use of language, of the familiar feel of words, is accomplished. The questionable presumption here is that in both the area of sound perception, i.e. hearing the phonetic differences between words, and the perception of word meanings, the same use of 'experience' is involved and that the difference between the areas is explained in terms of the content of experience. This presumed parallelism of 'experience' is precisely what Wittgenstein questions. His critique of meaning-experience therefore is entirely conceptual and the sought-for distinction can be found only by investigating how 'experience' is actually used in locutions such as 'hearing a word in a certain meaning', 'experiencing the chord as a conclusion', or in our use of and response to wordplay.

Indeed, even in passages where he seems most sceptical about meaning-experiences he neither denies nor affirms their existence but investigates 'experience' as we *picture* it. Pictured as an inner object which always accompanies our use of words, as James and Moore do, experiences of meaning turn out to be semantic epiphenomena. Thus, according to James, 'if', 'but', and 'and' are distinguished by specific feelings, yet is it not possible, Wittgenstein asks, that for some person 'if' and 'but' feel the same? 'Should we have the right to disbelieve him? We might think it strange' (PI II, 182). How strange comes out in a first draft of this remark. There Wittgenstein compares such a person with what I call a 'deviant synaesthete'. Consistency over time of synaesthetic colours elicited by

---

[9]   See RPP I §539 for a clear application of this argument to aspect-seeing.

[10]   Wittgenstein refers to this joke in RPP I §77. The words can be read as an instruction for Wotan to retreat and, on the other hand, as an answer to Wotan's question about whether one has a preference for hard- or soft-boiled eggs. See also Schulte 1993, 68.

[11]   But in this latter case the question has to be answered how the use of 'experience' relates to the use of this word in paradigmatic cases. See further below, sections 3, 4, and 6.

specific inducers, e.g. printed linguistic items, has been noted repeatedly among normal synaesthetes.[12] When Wittgenstein asks us to imagine people who associate one colour with *a, e, i,* and another with *o* and *u* (cf. LWPP I §362), therefore, he is really asking us something very strange. Indeed, such people 'differ from us to a far greater extent than those who associated no colours at all with vowels. One would almost like to call them colour blind' (LWPP I §363). And yet these different and very strong associations between specific feelings and specific words are no reason to assume that these people confuse words, i.e. that the person for whom 'but' and 'if' feel the same uses them interchangeably.[13]And if the person uses 'if' and 'but' as we do, 'shouldn't we think he understood them as we do?' (PI II, 182)

To conclude, to the extent that there are experiences of meaning in the Jamesian sense, there are also experiences associated with e.g. the tennis rackets, shoes, and shirts Roger Federer uses daily. But as much as Federer's experiences are irrelevant for the game of tennis, Jamesian experiences are unimportant epiphenomena when it comes to the use of language. This does not mean that talk of experiences of meaning is senseless; rather, it means that 'The if-feeling cannot be something which *accompanies* the word "if"' (PI II, 182). For, 'Otherwise it could accompany other things too' (LWPP I §369).

3. MEANING-BLINDNESS

I now proceed to the positive phase of Wittgenstein's discussion of the experience of meaning. Consider this explanatory shift from treating experiences of meaning as mental items always accompanying the use of words to relating them to the special circumstances of word use:

> 'If you didn't *experience* the meaning of the words, then how could you laugh at puns?' – We do laugh at such puns: and to that extent we could say (for instance) that we experience their meaning. (LWPP I §711)

Rather than assimilating experience of meaning to the paradigmatic use of 'experience', it is relativized to special circumstances of use. The proper question to ask therefore is: how is what is called an experience here related to how this word is used in other, more familiar contexts?

At this junction the relevance of the discussion of meaning-blindness comes in. Its point is not to ask for the causal consequences of a certain sort of defect, but rather to

---

[12] In a recent large-scale study, it was also found that there was a striking consistency in the colours induced by specific letters and digits across the sample as a whole, including synaesthetes and non-synaesthetes. For instance, it was found that the vowel *a* predominantly arouses the colours red and blue, and that *e* and *i* tend to be yellow and white (Rich, Bradshaw, and Mattingley 2005, 71).

[13] It is reported that synaesthetes typically do not confuse synaesthetic ('induced') colours with those of surfaces in the world, and that colour perception is normal as is colour naming (Rich and Mattingley 2002).

establish conceptual similarities and dissimilarities in order to explore the use of 'experience' here. It is meant to let us represent the experience of meaning without our being conceptually prejudiced by the paradigmatic sense. By asking us to imagine a person who lacks meaning-experiences, Wittgenstein urges us to think about the question what it is that such a person would lack and, when finally we come to know this, whether we are still inclined to call it an experience (like seeing colours or feeling a headache), and whether we can call it a form of blindness like any other. It is for this reason Wittgenstein has italicized the word 'experience' in the passage I have referred to just above.

Consider now the following descriptions of the 'defect' of meaning-blindness:

> Could one say that a meaning-blind man would reveal himself in this: One can have no success in saying to such a man: 'You must hear this word as…then you will say the sentence properly'. (RPP I §247)

For instance, it makes no sense to tell the meaning-blind person to pronounce 'weiche' in isolation and mean 'soft', or to say 'bank' in isolation and mean the riverbank. The incapacity of the meaning-blind person is like the incapacity of the aspect-blind person. As the latter cannot try to see the change of aspect when looking at an ambiguous drawing, the former cannot hear the change in 'weiche' when understood now as 'retreat', now as 'soft'. The meaning-blind person will be insensitive to the loss of meaning of a word when pronounced several times. He will not report that the word somehow sounds differently, feels differently, as the aspect-blind one will not report that 'it is as if the picture has changed and yet it has not changed'. It is important to note, however, that this incapacity does not imply that the meaning-blind person cannot consider a word under one interpretation rather than the other. Nor does it imply that he cannot first mean a word in this way and then suddenly realize that it has to be taken in another way. These are changes in interpretation rather than shifts of aspects. The occurrence of a (visual) aspect is logically related to a change of aspect. On the other hand, interpretations and shifts of interpretations of the same visual picture or the same word can exist without our noticing a change of aspect. As Wittgenstein puts it: 'I have always taken that for a bowl; now I see that it isn't one – without being conscious of any change of "aspect". I mean simply: I now see something different, now have a different visual impression' (RPP I §28). That is, when there is no change of aspect, the person simply treats his visual impressions, when seeing the picture first one way then another way, as two separate impressions. When an aspect dawns, however, it is the same figure which is seen now in this way, now in that way. The change of aspect, therefore, relates to a specific point in time, to a sudden and spontaneous transition of one aspect to another. This is also why we are inclined to speak of an experience. Likewise, a meaning-blind person need have no problems with understanding the expression 'I thought you meant the riverbank' as a response to someone's request to go to the bank. No experience of meaning is involved here, even though an interpretation of meaning is. On the other hand, he will not understand the expression 'I first thought you meant the riverbank, but then I realized you must be meaning the financial institute'. Here there is the acute experience of a transition of meaning a word in one way to meaning it in another way.

The intermediate conclusion is that, conceived as experiences in the primary sense, experiences of meaning are irrelevant for linguistic intercourse. Conceived by analogy with aspect-seeing, in particular change of aspect, experiences of meaning do play a role in (special) linguistic intercourse. In the remaining sections, I turn to a detailed consideration of Wittgenstein's description of experiences of meaning in the latter sense.

4. ILLUSION AND ASPECT-SEEING

Wittgenstein introduces his discussion of aspect-seeing by noting that there are two uses of 'to see', the one involving a straightforward description or copy of what one reports to see, the other noticing an aspect, such as a likeness between two faces (PI II, 193). He emphasizes that this is a categorical distinction. The same idea applies to experience of meaning. To say that one has just pronounced 'weiche' in the sense of 'soft' is a completely different use from informing another person that one has ordered soft eggs.[14] Closer examination of this use reveals that the reasons for this categorical distinction are similar to the case of aspect-seeing. The first reason to be explored is that of 'illusion'.[15] The illusory nature of aspect-seeing is that a change of aspect of what one sees is not a change in the perceived stimulus. Yet in a change of aspect everything appears different from what it was before the change, and one may even direct one's attention to a specific part of the perceived stimulus as if it is responsible for and hence characteristic of the changed experience, even though it is not. On the other hand, one may be inclined to argue that in aspect-seeing, e.g. seeing the face of a daughter in that of the mother, a visual impression is compared with a memorial image. But as Wittgenstein responds: 'Isn't it *as if* two pictures were getting compared here? But there aren't two pictures being compared; and if there were, one would still have to keep on recognizing one of them as the picture of the earlier face' (RPP I §1041).

What has been left unnoticed in the literature on meaning-experience is that Wittgenstein here too speaks of an 'as-if' experience, a 'typical kind of illusion' (RPP I §1055), of a 'mirage' ('Spiegelung') (LWPP I §69) and even of a dream (PI II 216). In a remark that is systematically overlooked, Wittgenstein draws a comparison between meaning-experiences and another 'typical kind of illusion', the feeling that a city lies in a certain direction (different from the actual direction):

> There is a special kind of illusion which throws light on these matters. – I go for a walk in the environs of a city with a friend. As we talk it comes out that I am imagining the city to lie on our right. Not only have I no conscious reason for this assumption, but some quite simple consideration was enough to make me realize

---

[14] That is, the use is different not the meaning. Cf. 'Suppose I hear one of Beethoven's works and I say "Beethoven!" – Does the word have a different meaning here than in the sentence "Beethoven was born in Bonn in 1770"?' (LWPP I §58). This point will be elaborated upon in section 6 below.

[15] The second reason is related to secondary use and is dealt with in section 6 below.

that the city lay rather to the left of us. I can at first give no answer to the question
why I imagine the city to lie in this direction. I had no reason. (PI II, 215; LWPP
I §69)

To speak here of a 'special kind of illusion' suggests a difference with straightforward
perceptual illusions. Perceptual illusions arise because experience distorts what there is.
They pass unnoticed except when they are strikingly inconsistent with what is accepted
as true. On the same walk the green hills in the distance may look purple and bluish.
Colours vary relative to the position of the percipient, the distance and media between
him and the object, the lighting, etc. In such a case one has conscious reasons for saying
that the hills are bluish and purple, because the hills look bluish to one. That the hills
look bluish has to do with the (changing) appearance of one's surroundings. The illusion
typically persists as long as one finds oneself at a certain distance of the hills. Such epistemic grounds are lacking, however, for saying that one is under the impression that the
city lies over there. It is not as if one saw (in the primary sense of seeing) the contours of
a city loom up in the distance and one stopped seeing the environment one saw before.
On the contrary, the appearance of the environment has not changed with respect to
colour, two- or three-dimensional shape, or the distance of any of its parts to one. That
one 'sees' the city on one's right has nothing to do with the (changing) appearance of the
surroundings. Moreover, one can easily switch one's attention back to the normal perception of the environment. By contrast, with perceptual illusions such as the Müller–
Lyer illusion or the Ponzo illusion, one cannot stop seeing the lines as unequal except by
measuring the horizontal bars. Here inappropriate knowledge was brought to bear on
the perceptual situation, producing errors. The 'illusion' that the city lies to one's right,
however, is different, for 'a quite simple consideration' is enough to realize that the city
lies to the left. In particular, no updating of one's beliefs, adding new beliefs and rejecting
old beliefs, is needed to realize that the city lies to the left. The illusion is typical, then,
because one feels as if the city lies to the right, and *at the same time*, one knows that it lies
to the left.

Now, about meaning-experiences Wittgenstein says:

And how can the word have stood for this thing – and not for that, when I pronounced it? And yet *that's* just what it looks like. (RPP I §687)

For instance, pronouncing 'weiche' in isolation may prompt a shift of meaning, first 'soft'
then 'retreat'. It is as if the same word has changed, as if it becomes a completely different
word when shifting between the two meanings. Indeed, as if *two* words are involved. As
with aspect-perception one may even be inclined to explain one's experience by saying
that in the case of 'soft' the 'ei' of 'weiche' sounds softer, and so on. That is, one is inclined
to attribute the change in experience to visible and audible features of the word itself.
But this is as unfounded as locating a change of aspect in a change of properties of the
stimulus. This may become clearer upon consideration of different examples. Consider
the tendency of some synaesthetes to 'gender' numbers. For instance, a subject may gender numbers: 1, 4, 6, 7, and 9 are male whereas 2, 3, 5, and 8 are female. Letters may all
have their genders too and the same goes for the months. In an unpublished remark,

Wittgenstein discusses this tendency to gender words and letters.[16] He notes that the letter *a* sounds differently when it is the ending of a masculine or a female word. Thus the *a* of *agricola* sounds differently from the *a* of *puella*. In the former case the *a* sounds aggressive, in the latter case it sounds soft. Now, one may want to account for this in terms of a difference in the actual sound of both endings. But it is evident that the masculine and female *a* do not sound differently. Moreover, in order to explain what one means to another person one does not refer to a change in the perceived stimulus, e.g. by saying 'Listen carefully when I say the words and you will hear that the *a* of *puella* sounds softer'. The subject therefore has no epistemic reason for this 'illusory experience' because nothing has changed – there is just this very same letter *a*. The ending *a* does not change in appearance, and the situation here is exactly like the preceding typical illusion: the change in experience has nothing to do with changes in the stimulus.

In other words, at the heart of the experience of meaning lies a paradox not unlike the one that characterizes seeing-as. With a change of aspect we feel that the ambiguous drawing is altogether different, as if it has altered before our very eyes; and yet we know that there has been no such change. Similarly, we know that a black-printed *e* is not yellow, that a proper name does not fit its bearer; and yet we are compelled to express ourselves in these ways. Before explaining how the notion of secondary use accounts for this paradox and thereby removes the philosophical puzzlement it produces, it is useful to look at an approach that is both historically and currently influential. This approach, shared by psychologists and neuroscientists, argues that experiences of meaning can be explained in terms of learning by association, and ultimately by the neurological hardware underlying such psychological processes. I will argue that by thus handing over the problem to science the paradox does not vanish.

5. ASSOCIATION

The use of a familiar word in a new situation seems like metaphor. Yet Wittgenstein explicitly denies that in secondary use metaphor is involved: 'If I say "For me the vowel *e* is yellow" I do not mean: "yellow" in a metaphorical sense, – for I could not express what I want to say in any other way than by means of the idea "yellow"' (PI II, 216). In denying that synaesthesia is metaphorical, Guttenplan has recently argued, Wittgenstein would be noting that metaphor requires something more than a purely associative link (Guttenplan 2005, 239). Consequently, the synaesthetic link between the vowel *e* and the predicate 'yellow' – and hence secondary use – is a matter of brute association (Guttenplan 2005, 237). In metaphor there is always the possibility of finding reasons or justifications for the relevant predications. But it makes no more sense to try to convince someone that the vowel *e* is yellow, or to take another example from Guttenplan, that the music is sad, 'then it does to try to convince someone by argument that, say, a standard

---

[16] MS 116, 326; TS 228, 170; TS 230, 152.

pillar box in normal lightning is red' (Guttenplan 2005, 239). What is interesting about Guttenplan's account is that he focuses specifically on synaesthesia. Yet he erroneously believes that the main issue for Wittgenstein is the nature of metaphor. To be sure, it is correct to say that there is no justification for the synaesthetic claim that the letter *e* is yellow, or that the music is sad. To the extent that metaphors presuppose the citing of reasons, synaesthesia is not metaphor. But what does Guttenplan's claim that synaesthesia is a matter of brute association tell us about this typical use of words? And what does it tell us about the relation of this use of words to the synaesthetic 'experience' – which after all can be particularly strong?

To these questions Guttenplan's treatment provides no answer, or better, the answer he gives confuses an explanation in terms of associative processes with a description of a use of words, and hence evades the philosophical issue. The difficulty of pinning down what meaning-experiences are, and hence what secondary use is, is intrinsically related to the ease with which a causal explanation is given. This is particularly well illustrated by what Guttenplan says about Wittgenstein's own causal hypothesis concerning the linkage between particular weekdays and the predicates 'fat' and 'lean': 'what he [Wittgenstein] says about "fat" would apply equally to synaesthesia: like a childhood association, a synaesthetic link is just an association. It is not something for which we can give a reason' (Guttenplan 2005, 239). Guttenplan fails to note two things. First, Wittgenstein offers this psychological explanation only to reject it as irrelevant for the philosophical issue at hand. Second, Guttenplan's view that when a metaphorical explanation fails the matter has to be handed over to psychological explanations rests on an explicit confusion of 'secondary use' and metaphor. As he explains: 'although we know that "fat" doesn't include Wednesday in its extension – it is not part of its "primary sense" – this is no reason to say that it has, as he puts it, a "secondary", metaphorical sense' (Guttenplan 2005, 239).

The tendency to overlook the conceptual level and switch to the psychological level, thereby failing to see what is irreducibly distinctive about the synaesthetic use of words, is not unique to Guttenplan, as is testified by a much earlier response by the Gestalt psychologist Wolfgang Köhler, echoed in recent scientific theories.[17] In discussing a range of synaesthetic examples he makes an interesting comment on the following lines from the German poet Morgenstern:

> Die Möwen sehen alle aus, als ob sie Emma hiessen.
> ('All seagulls look as though their name were Emma')

According to Wolfgang Köhler, Morgenstern was right: 'The sound of "Emma" as a name and the visual appearance of the bird appear to me similar' (Köhler 1947, 224). Köhler rejects the view that these and other 'synaesthetic' linkages are mere analogies from which nothing can be inferred about underlying facts. On the contrary, he defends the view that the analogies are all grounded in resemblances that exist between different realms of sense-experience. Significantly Köhler does not specify in which respects the

---

[17] See Ramachandran and Hubbard 2001.

sound of the name Emma and the appearance of the seagulls are similar. And what could the resemblance be here? It is obvious that the experience might be due to a childhood association between seeing seagulls walking lamely, unevenly, and the stiffness of women called Emma. Perhaps there is even an association between a particular Emma limping out of the house at the seaside and the gait impeded by stiffness of seagulls. But such associations are a far cry from noticing a resemblance between the sound of a name and a certain visual appearance. Indeed, there is no more similarity between Emma and the appearance of seagulls than between the name 'Beethoven' and the Ninth Symphony.[18] Hence Köhler, like Guttenplan, mistakenly believes that giving an associative explanation also amounts to having described this typical use of words.

In one passage, however, Guttenplan seems to show awareness of the distinction between causal explanation and description, but nevertheless fails to take the step towards acknowledging that this use of words requires an explanation of its own, irreducible to either metaphor or association. Discussing the example of 'sad music', he explains that a person may actually be cast down by the sounds of the music because of the synaesthetic and associative linkage, but he adds: 'this is certainly not what it means to claim that those sounds are sad. What the latter claim asserts is that certain sounds, like certain feelings, can be perfectly well described as sad. And synesthesia grounds the linkage between the sounds and the feelings that makes this sharing of a predicate intelligible' (Guttenplan 2005, 238). Guttenplan correctly notes that 'The music is sad' does not mean 'The music makes me sad.' But why is it perfectly intelligible to describe music as sad? It is intelligible either because of a rational connection or because of a causal connection. If the former, then it must be possible to give grounds or reasons for saying that music is sad. But this is precisely the view Guttenplan rejects. Hence the connection must be intelligible because it is (presumably) causally grounded. As the discussion of Köhler has shown, this leaves the usage of 'sad' or 'yellow' as applied to vowels as puzzling as before.

6. SECONDARY USE

Let me now turn to the passage in the *Investigations* where the distinction between the primary and secondary use of words is introduced explicitly:

> Given the two words 'fat' and 'lean' – would you rather be inclined to say that Wednesday was fat and Tuesday lean, or that Tuesday was fat and Wednesday lean? (I incline to choose the former.) Now have 'fat' and 'lean' some different meaning here from their usual one? They have a different use. So ought I really to have used different words? Certainly not that. I want to use *these* words (with their familiar meanings) *here*. (PI II, 216)

---

[18] See on this example LWPP I §69.

Here one might speak of a 'primary' and 'secondary' sense of a word. It is only if the word has the primary sense for you that you use it in the secondary. (Ibid.)

The secondary sense is not a 'metaphorical' sense. If I say 'For me the vowel *e* is yellow' I do not mean: 'yellow' in a metaphorical sense, – for I could not express what I want to say in any other way than by means of the idea 'yellow'. (Ibid.)

Commentators who defend a (quasi-)metaphorical interpretation of secondary use have deplored this pair of examples because it has led to the overlooking of examples that are clearly examples of the secondary use of words (especially in aesthetics) and that are not at all idiosyncratic.[19] But this falls short of seeing the purpose of the distinction. Its purpose is not to put hitherto neglected forms of speech on the map nor to argue that what has always been taken to be metaphor is actually secondary use. Rather, the idiosyncratic example is designed to evoke a certain response in us: 'fat' and 'lean' surely *must* have taken on a meaning different from the usual one! The person cannot be really meaning what he says. In this way the alleged incoherent use of 'fat' can be smoothed out because the person should have used a different word, one that suits this meaning more adequately. Wittgenstein's rejoinder is that the presumption that the word must have taken on a different meaning misrepresents the case at hand. That we are inclined to use *this* word, which we have learned for other purposes, in this new situation is the very phenomenon at issue. As he says elsewhere: 'It is a poor fit only if you take it the wrong way' (RPP II §574). By proposing to speak in this case of a secondary use of words, Wittgenstein wants to emphasize that we should be careful in interpreting a shift in the application of a word from the range of paradigms usable in teaching to objects that may seem of the wrong category for the subject of description as necessarily involving a change in what the word designates. Unlike cases of word ambiguity, a word used in a secondary sense cannot be explained by referring to *two* paradigms. Unlike figurative expressions that are dispensable – Wittgenstein's own example is 'cutting off someone's speech' (LWPP I §799) – a secondary use of words is not replaceable by a non-synonymous word.[20] The explanation of secondary use in terms of either word ambiguity or dispensable metaphor, therefore, leaves its inherent paradoxicality untouched.

According to Wittgenstein, the alleged need for a justificatory explanation which grounds the 'deviant' use of words in a change of meaning, or in pointing out similarities between the normal and the deviant use that a person need not even be aware of, results

---

[19] For instance Tilghman 1984; Fogelin 1976/1995.

[20] See PI II, 216; LWPP I §799. To the extent that words are taken over from another area, one might want to call secondary use metaphorical, but Wittgenstein emphatically says that the use itself is not metaphorical. Commentators who acknowledge this latter point, however, continue to speak of metaphor. Thus Hanfling (1991; 2002) speaks of 'irrational metaphor' and Budd (2006) of 'essential metaphor'. Hanfling comes closest to the idea that a secondary use of words is forced on us. However, he fails to understand 'irrational metaphor' as an expressive use of language presupposing and essentially making use of another, often descriptive, use of the same words. Budd too fails to take into account the specific nature of the 'language-game' involved when words are used in a secondary sense. Indeed, essential metaphors function as apt *descriptions* of experiences.

from a failure to recognize that what is in question here is a use of words (or a 'language-game') that is both the same as and different from the way they are used in their home-base.[21] Indeed, this is the message of Wittgenstein's most explicit statement of the analogy between seeing-as and experience of meaning: 'What he presents as an expression of his experience would otherwise be a perceptual report. (The strong similarity with the experience of meaning)' (LWPP I §176).[22] With synaesthetic experiences and other experiences of meaning, words that we have learned to use for a particular 'technique' are used as the expression (*Äusserung*) of experience. Only by noting how secondary use is both the same as and different from the primary use, we come to recognize that the 'deviant' use is not paradoxical, not a poor fit, and that it goes with the experience 'as the primitive expression of pain goes with pain' (RPP II §574). It is therefore worth taking into consideration Wittgenstein's general view of language-games with experiences and in particular the language-game with pain.

The leitmotiv of Wittgenstein's conception of language-games of psychological, and in particular experiential, concepts is that they are learnt as substitutes for 'primitive reactions', or, more generally, natural behaviour. Words for experiences of pain are not based on an inner practice of baptizing and recognizing experiences. Because of the presence of natural behaviour, parents dispose of a criterion to see whether the child follows the rules of e.g. 'pain' correctly, which is what 'learning' means. Thus the sentence 'I am in pain' modifies natural interaction patterns and 'primitive reactions'. It is in virtue of pain-language taking the place of natural behaviour that first-person *Äusserungen* of pain have meaning. But how do language-games with meaning-experiences get off the ground? For we have not learned to predicate colour concepts of vowels, nor to say that proper names fit their bearers. No one explained these expressions to us by referring to sensations, images, or thoughts; nor have they been learned as substitutes for natural behaviour.

At this point the importance of the remark, 'It is only if the word has the primary sense for you that you use it in the secondary', comes in. What is in question here is not just a matter of temporal precedence. Rather, what is in question is a logical dependency of one use of words upon another use. A secondary use of words relates to the primary use of these words as the verbal expression of pain relates to natural behaviour of pain. Were it not for this fact of nature, people would not have the concept of pain. Were it not for our pervasive awareness of the (primary) 'technique' of word use, of the linguistic and non-linguistic context in which words are used, people would not spontaneously use and understand words in a secondary sense. That can be seen most clearly by examining the question whether it makes sense to attribute experiences of meaning to young children. Thus we would be hesitant to say of a child that is just making single words and then joining them into short phrases that it can have the experience that a word loses its meaning

---

[21] The new use is not just an outgrowth or extension of the old use, but it is a new 'language-game'. Like seeing-as, secondary use involves a new language-game that is nevertheless intrinsically related to the language-game with the primary use of the relevant word(s). See RPP II §§245–6; LWPP I §69.

[22] This is also why he calls secondary use a 'new' use (cf. RPP I §126).

when repeated several times. To be sure, it may repeat a word several times but we only say of one that he has this experience of meaning if he has developed a feeling for words, as shown by, for instance, the ability to choose among synonymous words.[23] Secondary use therefore does not simply depend on the way the word is actually articulated and heard, nor on its visible appearance in print. Rather, what we have learned about the *use* of the word forces us to employ it in a secondary sense.[24] Indeed, if it was merely the appearance of the word we might as well have used another word which is similar in these respects. The experience could then not be an experience of meaning, since it is definitive of such experiences that the words we use are felt to be the only possible expression. Referring to the felt meaning of words also as an 'atmosphere', Wittgenstein writes in his late writings on the philosophy of psychology: 'The atmosphere of a word is its use' (LWPP II, 38). Using the word, e.g. 'fat', saying it in a certain tone of voice, and making certain gestures *is* what is called an experience in this context. There is not anything else which we call an experience. In particular, the situation is not to be conceptualized as if we first have to recognize and identify the weekdays as fat and then describe this experience by saying 'Wednesday is fat'. For asked what experience one refers to, one can only repeat the original expression, e.g. 'Wednesday is fat'. But if one cannot 'describe' the experience without repeating the same words, they are not what is called a description.[25] Hence their role is not to inform another person about something, i.e. an experience. Rather, they are aimed at inducing the other person to join the same expression (and hence the same experience).[26] As Wittgenstein says about the feeling of unreality: 'And how do I know that another has felt what I have? Because he uses the same words as I find appropriate' (RPP I §125). The other person knows what I am talking about not on epistemic grounds, but because we are in tune with the very verbal expression. A continuation of this use of words might be 'Yes, I should like to say what you say', but not a statement to the effect that there is something which we both describe by means of the same words.[27] Accordingly, the inclination to say such and such is not simply a (behaviouristic) reaction, but itself the psychological phenomenon or 'experience' that matters.

That one *has* to use the words one in fact uses, therefore, has to be explained in terms of the role of words *qua* primitive reaction. A person is precluded from expressing the same experience by means of other words not simply because they are appropriate – for they might be appropriate but still be descriptive – but because using another word

---

[23] See Wittgenstein's remark about how the familiar physiognomy of words is manifested: 'By the way we choose and value words' (PI II, 218).

[24] Cf. RPP II §370, where Wittgenstein makes this point as regards the use of 'to see' in cases of aspect seeing.

[25] For essential to description, according to Wittgenstein, is that the state of affairs described can be described in different ways and with different means.

[26] This is one of the features secondary use shares with metaphor. However, with secondary use we are *forced* to use the relevant word.

[27] Wittgenstein says that the point of the synaesthetic game is that we say 'e *is* yellow', and that if a person should say 'e corresponds to yellow', he would be as different from the other as someone for whom vowels and colours are not connected (cf. LWPP I §59).

would count as a different primitive reaction – and so as a different experience.[28] Consequently, what determines whether different tokens of a particular experience count as the same experience is whether the same words are used. If one person is inclined to use these words whereas another person is inclined to use other words, one cannot maintain that they have the same experience, only express it differently.

Synaesthetic expressions are bewildering uses of familiar words, yet they are the natural expression of the experience involved; there is no more direct expression. Wittgenstein's other examples of experiences of meaning, however, are not, or at any rate need not seem, so peculiar. In particular, the expressions 'momentary meaning' and 'to experience the meaning of a word itself' are a combination of familiar words that need not raise any suspicion. Indeed, to Moore and James this combination of familiar words does not seem to be incoherent at all. The meaning of a word *is* an experience, 'quite as readily' as red or pain. To commentators who credit Wittgenstein with a supplementary notion of meaning, the expression does not seem incoherent either. It only shows that 'meaning is use' falls short of accommodating our need for 'the soul' of words, and hence that it has to be supplemented by an experiential notion. But the very thing Wittgenstein points out here is that 'to experience the meaning of a word' is *not* a normal combination. It is as 'troublesome' a use of words as 'fat Wednesday' or '*e* is yellow'. Yet no action of revising this word use is required in order to account for the 'incoherence'. Rather, the *use* of this combination of familiar words needs thorough investigation (and this we fail to do precisely because it is so familiar). To this end Wittgenstein utilizes the distinction between the primary and secondary use of words.

Standardly employed, 'to mean' refers to the particular technique of using a word and particular intentions of a speaker in a specific context, e.g. 'What I mean by X is …', and now one points at an object, refers to a definition in a dictionary, etc. However, to say that a word is filled with its meaning, that one meant a word in a particular way before saying it, or saying an ambiguous word and meaning it in one way rather than the other, seems to suggests that one speaks of meaning as something that can be felt. Another reason for arguing that the word 'meaning' has taken on the sense of an experience here is that no hypothesis or inference seems to be involved. The person who has such experiences is certain and his expressions are as straight as his expressions of pain. On the other hand, no events or processes in the public world can be pointed at as that which our words – uttered in isolation – speak of. Accordingly, it is tempting to suppose that 'to mean' *means* a state of consciousness. Indeed, the grammar of the deviant uses themselves seems to support this interpretation. We say that we understand the music or the words *while* we

[28] To be sure, Wittgenstein suggests that there is an analogy between experience of meaning and the experience of the apt word (cf. LWPP I §62). In that case, however, the experience of finding the apt word is not to be construed as if there is an experience for which we find the apt word. This construal would drag into its train the apparatus of comparison, as well as metaphor, whereas for Wittgenstein one sees that a word is the apt word 'even before I know, and even when I never know, *why* it is appropriate' (RPP I §73).

hear it, that we meant the word at that particular time in the past so and so. Moreover, denying that we meant a word in a certain way in the past seems to imply that we meant or understood the word only later.[29]

What Wittgenstein questions, however, is not the legitimacy of saying that we understand the music or words while hearing it. Rather, what he questions is that the word 'meaning' has taken on a different meaning, e.g. an impalpable 'germ' (James) or an undefinable experience (Moore).[30] Moreover, what he rejects is that a supplement is needed to the idea that the meaning of a word is the way it gets used in the language in order to account for the familiar feel words may have. Again, unlike cases of word ambiguity, the word meaning cannot be explained by referring to *two* paradigms. If it could, one would owe someone else an explanation when saying e.g. 'This word means much to me', but one doesn't. Moreover, if two paradigms were involved, the whole problem would not have arisen. The fact of the matter is that we have not learned to use 'meaning' in two ways (LWPP I §79).[31] In the second place, we do not notice a similarity between meaning in the sense of use and momentary meanings, so that we extend the meaning of the former to include the latter (LWPP I §§64, 69). Like the preceding example of synaesthesia, what we have learned about the primary use of 'to mean', rather than its sound or the way it is written, makes us want to apply it in a new context. Therefore we *have* to use the word 'to mean' here.

And yet the tendency to interpret the shift in application of the word as involving a change of meaning of 'meaning' is very strong. In a series of remarks that are often overlooked, Wittgenstein makes clear that this tendency is based on an erroneous assimilation of momentary meanings to other uses of words (cf. PI II, 217–18). Consider for instance Wittgenstein's description of 'I meant' with reference to an ambiguous word. A particularly tempting idea is to suppose that the change of meaning is a process of transition of mental images or feelings of tendency. This raises the question as to the relationship between on the one hand the mental image, or whatever sort of experience, and, on the other hand, the particular words one uses. In particular the question is: does one *have* to use the words one in fact uses? The answer clearly is: no. The specific mental image I see before my mind's eye when experiencing 'bank' in the sense of, say, Barclays, does not require the expression 'I meant, e.g. Barclays', but could very well be described in other terms (cf. PI II, 175, 176). On the other hand, the shift between the experience of one meaning of 'bank' to another does require the explanation 'I meant...' (cf. LWPP I §63). This form of words, taken over from another language-game, therefore functions as an *Äusserung*, and like others of the kind it is not based on reading off what one was thinking from an experience. Rather, by *saying* 'I meant...' one is '*thereby* making the connection with that point of time' (LWPP I §96). The reference to a point of time in the

---

[29] 'And *that* I do *not* want to say' (LWPP I §844).

[30] In MS 116, 287, Wittgenstein explicitly compares the belief that germ-experiences are incomparable with sensorial images with the way Moore came to the conclusion that the word 'good' is undefinable.

[31] For instance, we have not learned to say: 'You said the word as if something different had suddenly occurred to you as you were saying it' (LWPP I §134).

past is not to be compared with memory statements but with statements to the effect that that one knows how to go on (cf. LWPP I §819). In particular, 'I meant' functions as a signal flagging the start of a further application of words. In this their role in the language is analogous to the use of words expressing the experience of seeing-as. 'I see this as a duck' signals one's ability to provide a context for what one says, hence to describe the perceptual situation *as if* e.g. a real duck were present. Similarly, 'I meant...' signals one's ability to go on, just as if one explains the meaning of words for practical purposes. Yet it is a new use, a secondary use of 'to mean'.

Contrary to what James and Moore, as well as Wittgenstein's commentators, assume, the feeling of familiarity with words of one's native language does not require experiences of meaning in addition to the bare use of language. This rejection of the urge to hypostasize, however, does not imply that Wittgenstein endorses behaviourism or anti-realism and that to speak of experiences of meaning rests only on our having the same inclinations. The expression 'to experience the meaning of a word' (or 'meaning-experience') is a secondary use of 'experience', i.e. one which presupposes and essentially makes use of language. By failing to see that this combination of familiar words hides a different use, i.e. a secondary use, philosophers of both camps are in the psychological predicament that they ask philosophical questions about our concepts in the grip of an unrealistic picture of what knowing about them would be.

REFERENCES

BAKER, G. ed. (2003). *The Voices of Wittgenstein: The Vienna Circle; Ludwig Wittgenstein and Friedrich Waismann.* London: Routledge.

BOUVERESSE, J. (2007). 'Wittgenstein on "Experiencing Meaning"', in D. Moyall-Sharrock ed., *Perspicuous Representations: Essays on Wittgenstein's Philosophy of Psychology.* Basingstoke: Palgrave Macmillan.

BUDD, M. (2006). 'The Characterization of Aesthetic Qualities by Essential Metaphors and Quasi-Metaphors', *The British Journal of Aesthetics*, 46: 133–43.

FOGELIN, R. J. (1976). *Wittgenstein.* London: Routledge. (Second edition 1995)

GOLDSTEIN, L. (2004). 'What does "Experiencing Meaning" Mean?', in D. Moyall-Sharrock ed., *The Third Wittgenstein: the Post-Investigation Works.* Aldershot: Ashgate.

GOODMAN, R. (2002). *Wittgenstein and William James.* Cambridge: Cambridge University Press.

GUTTENPLAN, S. (2005). *Objects of Metaphor.* Oxford: Clarendon Press.

HACKER, P. M. S. (1996). *Wittgenstein: Mind and Will, Volume 4 of an Analytical Commentary on the Philosophical Investigations.* Oxford: Basil Blackwell.

HANFLING, O. (1991). 'I Heard a Plaintive Melody', in A. Phillips Griffiths ed., *Wittgenstein Centenary Essays.* Cambridge: Cambridge University Press.

—— (2002). *Wittgenstein and the Human Form of Life.* London: Routledge.

HARK, M. R. M., ter (1990). *Beyond the Inner and the Outer.* Dordrecht: Kluwer Academic Publishers.

HUNTER, J. F. M. (1973). *Essays after Wittgenstein.* Toronto: Toronto University Press.

James, W. (1890/1950). *The Principles of Psychology*, 2 vols. New York: Dover Publications.

Köhler, W. (1947). *Gestalt Psychology*. New York: Liveright.

Kripke, S. (1982). *Wittgenstein on Rules and Private Language*. Oxford: Blackwell.

Moore, G. E. (1953). *Some Main Problems of Philosophy*. London: George Allen & Unwin.

Mulhall, S. (2001). 'Seeing Aspects', in H.-J. Glock ed., *Wittgenstein: A Critical Reader*. Oxford: Blackwell.

Ramachandran, V. S. and Hubbard, E. M. (2001). 'Synaesthesia – A Window Into Perception, Thought and Language', *Journal of Consciousness Studies*, 8: 3–24.

Rhees, R. (1958). 'Preface', in Wittgenstein 1958.

Rich, A. N., Bradshaw, J. L., and Mattingley, J. B. (2005). 'A Systematic, Large-scale Study of Synaesthesia: Implications for the Role of Early Experience in Lexical-Colour Synaesthesia', *Cognition*, 98: 53–84.

—— and Mattingley, J. B. (2002). 'Anomalous Perception in Synaesthesia: A Cognitive Neuroscience Perspective', *Nature Reviews Neuroscience*, 3: 43–52.

Russell, B. (1921). *The Analysis of Mind*. London: George Allen & Unwin.

Schulte, J. (1993). *Experience and Expression: Wittgenstein's Philosophy of Psychology*. Oxford: Clarendon Press.

Sibley, F. (2001). *Approach to Aesthetics: Collected Papers on Philosophical Aesthetics*. Oxford: Clarendon Press.

Tilghman, B. R. (1984). *But is it Art?* Oxford: Basil Blackwell.

Vesey, G. (1968). 'Wittgenstein on the Myth of Mental Processes', *Philosophical Review*, 77: 350–6.

Waismann, F. (1965). *Principles of Linguistic Philosophy*. London: Macmillan.

Weiss, T. (1995). 'Meinen, ein Erlebnis der besonderen Art', in E. von Savigny ed., *Wittgenstein über die Seele*. Berlin: Suhrkamp.

Wittgenstein, L. (1953). *Philosophical Investigations*. Oxford: Blackwell.

—— (1958). *The Blue and Brown Books*. Oxford: Blackwell.

—— (1967). *Zettel*. Oxford: Blackwell.

—— (1974). *Philosophical Grammar*. Oxford: Blackwell.

—— (1980) *Remarks on the Philosophy of Psychology*, Volumes 1 and 2. Oxford: Blackwell.

—— (1982). *Last Writings on the Philosophy of Psychology*, Volume 1. Oxford: Blackwell.

—— (1990). *Last Writings on the Philosophy of Psychology*, Volume 2. Oxford: Blackwell.

—— (2000). *Wittgenstein's Nachlass, The Bergen Electronic Edition*. Oxford: Oxford University Press.

Zemach, E. M. (1995). 'Meaning, the Experience of Meaning and the Meaning-Blind in Wittgenstein's Late Philosophy', *Monist*, 78.4: 480–95.

PART V

EPISTEMOLOGY

CHAPTER 23

WITTGENSTEIN ON SCEPTICISM

DUNCAN PRITCHARD

The difficulty is to realise the groundlessness of our believing.

(OC §166)

INTRODUCTION

THE problem of scepticism informs all of Wittgenstein's writing, from the remarks on solipsism in the *Tractatus*, to the claims about rule-following put forward in the *Philosophical Investigations*, and right up to his final notebooks dealing with G. E. Moore's (1925; 1939) famous commonsense response to scepticism, published as *On Certainty*. To survey all of Wittgenstein's work on scepticism would be the task of a book rather than a chapter, and so I won't be attempting this here. Instead, I will focus on Wittgenstein's remarks on scepticism in *On Certainty* since—in terms of the specific sceptical issue of our knowledge of the external world at any rate—it is these remarks that have had the most impact on contemporary treatments of scepticism.

Before I begin, I want to note an important caveat to my remarks on this text. *On Certainty* is not a book that Wittgenstein ever sanctioned for publication, but rather the edited product of his final notebooks. As such, it would be unwise to try to find a single cohesive set of theses emerging from the text, especially given the fragmentary and, in places, impressionistic nature of the remarks. I will certainly not be trying to offer a definitive interpretation here.

1. HINGE PROPOSITIONS AND THE STRUCTURE OF REASONS

I will begin by outlining what I take to be the leading idea about scepticism that Wittgenstein offers in *On Certainty*. There are two elements to the argument. The first part is quite explicitly expounded in the text and concerns a distinctive picture of the structure of reasons—i.e. what is able to count as a reason for what—which essentially incorporates the elusive Wittgensteinian notion of a 'hinge proposition'. The anti-sceptical force of this picture of the structure of reasons arises from the fact that it excludes the kind of fully general epistemic evaluation that is essential to the sceptical argument.

The second part of the argument is developed in a more implicit fashion, and for this reason its anti-sceptical import is often overlooked. It concerns the fact that the picture of the structure of reasons that Wittgenstein offers is the very picture that we ordinarily employ, at least when we are not in the grip of the alternative *philosophical* picture which the sceptic (and, following her, the *anti*-sceptic) employs. Moreover, and here is the crux of the point, the philosophical picture that the sceptic uses is *completely divorced* from the non-philosophical picture that we ordinarily employ. That is, the philosophical picture is not an extension or refinement of the ordinary picture, but a radical departure from it. As we will see, this feature of Wittgenstein's anti-sceptical view, which often goes unnoticed, has important dialectical implications.

The primary target of *On Certainty* is Moore's (1925; cf. Moore 1939) famous argument against scepticism. Moore responded to the sceptical challenge by enumerating some of the many things that he took himself to know; in particular, those propositions which he was most certain of, such as that he has two hands. The starting-point for *On Certainty* is the observation that there is something seriously amiss with Moore's assertions in this respect. As Wittgenstein puts the point:

> Now, can one enumerate what one knows (like Moore)? Straight off like that, I believe not.—For otherwise the expression 'I know' gets misused. (OC §6).

And later on he notes:

> We just do not see how very specialized the use of 'I know' is. (OC §11)

Even without bringing in Wittgenstein's critique of Moore in this regard, I think we can recognize that there is clearly something amiss with Moore's claims to know that which he is most certain of. For example, a familiar Gricean constraint on appropriate assertion is that the assertion be relevant to the conversational context. Given this constraint, however, how can asserting (what will be regarded as) the patently obvious be relevant to the conversational context? Is Moore really aiming to *inform* his audience of something, as one would normally do with a knowledge claim? That seems unlikely.

The Wittgensteinian critique of Moore's assertions goes beyond broadly Gricean complaints of this sort, however. Wittgenstein wants to claim that the impropriety of

Moore's assertions relates to the fact that he is in the grip of a faulty conception of the structure of reasons. Moore seems to suppose that he is entitled to make these assertions because he has such excellent epistemic support for his beliefs in the propositions claimed as known. Wittgenstein's contention, however, is that it is precisely *because* of the certainty that attaches to our beliefs in these propositions that we are unable to properly claim to know them.

Consider the following passage:

> One says 'I know' when one is ready to give compelling grounds. 'I know' relates to a possibility of demonstrating the truth....
>
> But if what he believes is of such a kind that the grounds that he can give are no surer than the assertion, then he cannot say that he knows what he believes. (OC §243)

In order to properly claim to know a proposition it is essential that one is able to offer compelling reasons in its favour; the sort of reasons which could 'demonstrate the truth' of what is asserted as known. On the face of it, this constraint on the propriety of claims to know would seem to be congenial to Moore, in that the kinds of proposition which Moore claims as known are those that he is most certain of and hence, one would think at any rate, are propositions his beliefs in which he has excellent epistemic support for. *Ceteris paribus*, then, it would seem that Moore is in an ideal position to put forward his claims to know. Wittgenstein, however, wants to invert this 'Moorean' picture of the structure of reasons, and this is where the second part of the quotation just given becomes important. Wittgenstein's claim is that whatever would count as a reason in favour of a claim to know must be more certain than the proposition claimed as known, since otherwise it would not be able to play this supporting role. But if the proposition claimed as known is something which one is most certain of, then it follows that there can be no more certain proposition which could be offered in its favour and stand as the required supporting reason. The propriety of Moore's claims to know are thus in doubt precisely *because* he is claiming to know that which he is most certain of.

One might wonder at this point why an appropriate claim to know should be supported by reasons which are *more* certain than that which is claimed as known. Why wouldn't it be enough that there is *something* compelling that one can say in favour of what one claims as known, even though what is claimed as known is more certain? A key part of the explanation for this is that Wittgenstein recognizes that claims to know are essentially tied to the practice of resolving doubts. Simply enumerating what one knows with no dialectical purpose in mind is incoherent on the Wittgensteinian picture; it just would not be clear what one was up to. Rather, one explicitly claims to know something because there is some contextually relevant challenge to what is claimed—a *doubt*, broadly speaking—which this claim to know is designed to meet. Consider the following passage:

> It is queer: if I say, without any special occasion, 'I know'—for example, 'I know that I am now sitting in a chair', this statement seems to me unjustified and presumptuous. But if I make the same statement where there is some need for it, then, although

I am not a jot more certain of its truth, it seems to me to be perfectly justified and everyday. (OC §553)

And it is clear that, for Wittgenstein, what would (at least ordinarily) count as a 'need' for such a claim to know would be some legitimate challenge being raised regarding what one claims as known. It is of course difficult to imagine (non-philosophical) contexts in which a challenge is raised regarding that which we are most certain of, such as that one is presently seated (we will return to this point), but we can easily think of cases where challenges are raised regarding those propositions which we are not most certain of. I may take myself to be seeing a goldfinch in my garden, and make a remark to this effect. And yet someone standing next to me might object to what I say by noting that goldfinches can look an awful lot like goldcrests from this viewpoint. In response I might say that *I know* that that's a goldfinch. In doing so, I would be representing myself as being in a position to offer reasons which are more certain than what is claimed as known, and which speak to the objection raised. Such reasons could include, for example, that I know from years of experience as an ornithologist that goldfinches have distinctive markings which are lacking in goldcrests, and which are clearly observable from this angle. If called upon to do so, I must be able to offer these grounds.[1]

Once one recognizes that claims to know play this dialectical function of resolving doubts (broadly conceived), then it becomes clear just why the supporting reasons had better be more certain than that which is claimed as known. It is only because it is more certain that the bird in question has the distinctive markings at issue than that it is a goldfinch that the former is able to function as an appropriate supporting reason for the latter. If it weren't more certain—if, for example, the markings in question were not clearly visible—then it would cease to be able to perform this supporting role.

So, for Wittgenstein, appropriate claims to know require compelling supporting reasons where, because of the dialectical role of a claim to know in resolving doubts, such compelling reasons must be more certain than the proposition which is claimed as known. Thus far, the Wittgensteinian picture of the structure of reasons is merely imposing constraints on when one can appropriately claim knowledge. It ought to be clear, however, that such a picture also has ramifications for doubt, in that it imposes constraints on when a doubt can be rationally entered. Wittgenstein tries to get us to see that just as claims to know need to be supported by specific grounds, grounds which are more certain than what is claimed as known, so too do doubts (e.g. OC §458).

Consider the following passage:

If a blind man were to ask me 'Have you got two hands?' I should not make sure by looking. If I were to have any doubt of it, then I don't know why I should trust my eyes. For why shouldn't I test my *eyes* by looking to find out whether I see my two hands? *What* is to be tested by *what*? (OC §125)

---

[1] This example is, of course, from Austin (1961). There are many common themes in Austin's and Wittgenstein's work on this score. I comment further on this below.

This passage neatly illustrates the point that the Wittgensteinian conception of the structure of reasons imposes a constraint on appropriate claims to know. Clearly, in this case
one could not appropriately claim to know that one has two hands as a means of resolving the issue in question, since there is nothing that one could cite in favour of such a
claim to know which is more certain than what is claimed as known. If, for example, one
is less certain that one's eyes are functioning properly than that one has two hands, then
how can what one sees be coherently cited as a reason in favour of one's having hands?
What is important for our purposes, however, is that this passage also illustrates how
this conception of the structure of reasons also imposes a constraint on what can count
as a reason for *doubting* (or otherwise challenging) a belief.

A blind man can rationally doubt whether I have two hands since he has specific
grounds available to him to make such doubt rational (i.e. he can't see how many hands
I have, and we may assume that he does not have knowledge of this subject matter via
another route, such as through my testimony). But imagine now an otherwise normal
situation in which someone who can see perfectly well that I have two hands nonetheless inquires as to how many hands I have, thereby expressing some doubt in this regard.
How could we make sense of such an assertion? More pertinently, what could possibly
suffice as an adequate response to this query? After all, one could not simply draw his
attention to your hands, since he can see your hands already. But if this does not satisfy
him, then what would?

Wittgenstein wants to disabuse us of a conception of doubt such that expressions of
doubt (like claims to know) are 'free'—i.e. can be entered into a conversational context
without motivation. In contrast, Wittgenstein reminds us that doubts do not function
like that, such that when they are entered without motivation they are incoherent
(e.g. OC §§154, 247, 372). Moreover, the picture that Wittgenstein offers of the structure
of reasons now becomes relevant to help us to see that certain doubts just could not of
their nature be grounded, and a doubt about whether or not one has hands—when one's
hands are in clear view—is a case in point. For now a reason needs to be offered to motivate the doubt and, crucially, such a reason must be more certain than what is doubted
since otherwise one would have more reason to doubt the reason for doubt than to doubt
what is doubted. In normal circumstances, however, what reason could there be for
doubting whether or not the person before you (in clear view) has two hands which was
not less certain than that she has two hands?

Wittgenstein's ultimate point about doubt goes beyond offering a mere constraint on
expressions of doubt, however, and extends to doubt itself, expressed or otherwise.
Imagine that I try to formulate a doubt myself about whether or not I have two hands.
Wittgenstein wants to maintain that such a non-expressed doubt just like an expressed
doubt, needs to be motivated if it is to have any content. It is unclear, however, what could
possibly motivate such a doubt, given that it concerns a proposition which I am opti-
mally certain about. For example, suppose that I try to motivate the doubt on the grounds
that I cannot at that moment see my hands. Presumably, however, I am less certain that
my eyesight is functioning correctly than that I have two hands. Accordingly, on the
Wittgensteinian picture of the structure of reasons the former cannot rationally be used

as a ground for doubt regarding the latter. This is because the lesser certainty of the ground for doubt will inevitably ensure that it is more rational to doubt the ground for doubt than to doubt the target proposition. That is, I've more reason to doubt what I see (in this case that I don't just now see my hands) than for doubting that I have two hands on the basis of what I (don't) see. Doubt of that which is most certain is thus necessarily groundless, and hence incoherent (e.g. OC §§4, 122–3).

Wittgenstein makes this point rather neatly in the quotation cited above with his remark about testing, where the target belief is 'tested' relative to the grounds offered against it. If I regard my having two hands as being more certain than that my eyesight is functioning properly, then I cannot rationally 'test' the former by appeal to the latter. If, for example, I were to look to see where my hands should be and not see them, then, given that I regard the reliability of my eyesight as being less certain than that I have two hands, this would be a reason to doubt my eyesight rather than a reason to doubt whether or not I have hands. In short, we 'test' claims relative to other, more certain, claims.

So Wittgenstein is offering a picture of the structure of reasons such that that which we are most certain of cannot be properly claimed as known or, for that matter, properly doubted. Such propositions are, as he describes them elsewhere, 'hinge propositions' (OC §§341–3): propositions which by their very nature 'lie apart from the route travelled by enquiry' (OC §88).[2] That I have two hands is clearly a hinge proposition for Wittgenstein, which is why Moore cannot properly claim to know it. He writes:

> My having two hands is, in normal circumstances, as certain as anything that I could produce in evidence for it.
> That is why I am not in a position to take the sight of my hand as evidence for it. (OC §250)

That is, in normal circumstances at least, there is nothing more certain than that I have two hands. If this is right, then, given the foregoing discussion about the structure of reasons, it follows that any claim to know that I have two hands cannot be coherently supported by reasons (and hence is inappropriate) and neither can it be rationally doubted.

It is worth noting that the examples that Wittgenstein offers of hinges are diverse in character. Aside from the specific 'Moorean' claim that one has hands, he cites, for instance, quite general claims about the world, such as that it has existed for a long time (e.g. OC §§182–92, 233, 262, 327, 411), along with elementary mathematical claims, such as that twelve times twelve equals one hundred and forty-four (e.g. OC §§447–8). Moreover, although hinges are *in a sense* indubitable, the indubitability in question here is rather different from that which is usually at issue in classical epistemology. For

---

[2] Although the 'hinge' metaphor is the dominant symbolism in the book, it is accompanied by various other metaphors, such as the following: that these propositions constitute the 'scaffolding' of our thoughts (OC §211); that they form the 'foundations of our language-games' (OC §§401–3); and also that they represent the implicit 'world-picture' from within which we inquire, the 'inherited background against which [we] distinguish between true and false' (OC §§94–5).

example, when Descartes treats the *cogito* as indubitable, and thus foundational, he has in mind a conception of indubitability whereby in doubting the proposition in question one ipso facto ensures its truth, so making rational doubt of this proposition impossible. The indubitability of the *cogito* is thus an indication of its truth. The kind of indubitability that Wittgenstein has in mind, however, is not of this sort. Instead, the claim is only that one can never offer the necessary rational support for such doubt. Clearly, that this is so in itself offers no indication of the truth of the target proposition.

A further issue regarding hinge propositions concerns what sense we can give to the idea that they are rationally grounded *at all*. While there is clearly a distinction that can be made between the reasons that one can legitimately cite in favour of a claim to know a proposition and the reasons that support one's belief in that proposition, it is not clear that on the Wittgensteinian picture of the structure of reasons such a distinction has any grip. The point is that while it is through an examination of our practices of claiming knowledge that this picture of the structure of reasons is revealed, the picture doesn't seem to only apply to reasons *qua* reasons offered in support of a claim to know (or in defence of a doubt). Suppose, for example, that one were to simply reflect on the epistemic standing of one's belief that one has two hands. Given the fact that one is unable to adduce any reason in support of this belief that is more certain than this belief, it now becomes an open question whether this belief is adequately rationally supported. Furthermore, it is not as if one can take the traditional route here of thinking of one's beliefs in hinge propositions as being somehow foundational—such that they do not require epistemic support from other beliefs in order to be rightly held—since these beliefs lack many of the features of foundational beliefs on the traditional picture. They are not, for example, self-evident or incorrigible, and while they are in a sense indubitable, as we have already seen they are not indubitable in the required manner.

Given that such beliefs do not appear to be appropriately rationally grounded, and given in addition that they do not seem to fulfil the usual classical foundationalist rubric for basic beliefs, we might well regard the epistemic standing of these beliefs as suspect. There are places in which Wittgenstein seems to encourage this thought, as when he writes that the 'difficulty is to realise the groundlessness of our believing' (OC §166). Indeed, that we hold hinge propositions as certain in the way that we do appears to reflect merely a kind of groundless *faith* on our part. But if my belief in something so basic as that I have two hands is not rational (and hence, it seems, not a case of knowledge), then it is hard to see how *any* belief could be rationally held (and thus that I could know anything). Thus far, then, the Wittgensteinian picture of the structure of reasons, rather than offering a route out of the sceptic's clutches, seems to actually *imply* scepticism. Scepticism of a sort at any rate, since the constraint imposed on rational doubt ensures that one could not follow through one's scepticism by rationally doubting one's beliefs. Instead, one is left with a kind of epistemic *angst* regarding one's epistemic position, albeit one that does not license rational doubt.

I take it that what motivates this sceptical line of thought, at least in part, is the idea that it is consistent with the conception of the structure of reasons that Wittgenstein offers, and of the role of hinges within that conception, that there could be an epistemic evaluation of our beliefs as a whole which found their epistemic standing wanting. It is precisely this possibility, however, that Wittgenstein wants to deny, and which he diagnoses as being part of the faulty conception of the structure of reasons that Moore buys into by enumerating what he is most certain of as claims to know. As the term 'hinge' itself indicates, our commitment to hinge propositions is essential to *any* epistemic evaluation—this commitment is the hinge on which any epistemic evaluation must turn. Wittgenstein is thus opposing a standard epistemological picture which would allow a wholesale epistemic assessment of our beliefs with a different philosophical picture which excludes such a possibility. Consider the following passage:

> the *questions* that we raise and our *doubts* depend upon the fact that some propositions are exempt from doubt, are as it were like hinges on which those turn.
>
> That is to say, it belongs to the logic of our scientific investigations that certain things are *in deed* not doubted.
>
> But it isn't that the situation is like this: We just *can't* investigate everything, and for that reason we are forced to rest content with assumption. If I want the door to turn, the hinges must stay put. (OC §§341–3)

As these remarks make clear, what Wittgenstein is suggesting is that it is not in any way *optional* that there be propositions which we believe and which play this hinge role of being devoid of rational support and yet nevertheless indubitable. (As Wittgenstein remarks elsewhere, certain doubts aren't 'doubts in our game', but he goes on to emphasize, in parentheses, that it is 'not as if we *chose* this game' (OC §317)). In short, the suggestion is that the very possibility that one belief can count as a reason for or against another belief presupposes that there are some beliefs which play the role of being exempt from needing epistemic support, and thus that it is not arbitrary that one believes hinge propositions. The hinge proposition idea is thus essential to ensuring that Wittgenstein's thesis as regards the structure of reasons does not lead directly to an epistemic *angst* akin to (but not equivalent to) scepticism, since it is only with this idea in play that one can avoid the conclusion that our commitment to hinge propositions is, from a purely epistemic point of view at least, entirely arbitrary—i.e. the conclusion that, strictly speaking, none of our beliefs is rationally held.

There is a further feature of the Wittgensteinian picture of the structure of reasons which is important here, and which is often missed. Much of what has been said about Wittgenstein's view of the structure of reasons thus far could equally apply to similar anti-sceptical remarks made by J. L. Austin regarding when it is appropriate to enter a doubt or a claim to know (see, especially, Austin 1961). Like Wittgenstein, Austin is also suspicious of the idea of a fully general epistemic evaluation and the theses that might be thought to go with such an idea, such as that there are no in-principle constraints on when a doubt can legitimately be entered or on when a claim to know can legitimately be made. Moreover, as in the case of Wittgenstein, Austin's suspicions are backed up by a subtle commentary on how we actually enter doubts and claims to know, a commentary which reveals that our ordinary epistemic practices themselves eschew the idea of a fully general epistemic evaluation. And if one can show that our ordinary epistemic practices exclude the kind of fully general epistemic evaluation that leads to the sceptical problem, then it would appear that one can thereby argue that the default position is the anti-sceptical view advocated by Austin rather than the alternative sceptical picture. Put simply, the sceptic is now exposed as being in the grip of a contentious philosophical theory, and if this is right then it seems that we can legitimately dismiss the sceptical conclusions as being simply the product of this faulty theory.

As Barry Stroud (1984, chapter 2) famously argued, however, the problem faced by this Austinian approach to the sceptical problem is that the anti-sceptical import of this observation is moot. The reason for this is that the sceptic does not need to claim that our ordinary epistemic practices license such epistemic evaluation in order to show that her doubts are not the product of a faulty theoretical picture. All she needs to do is maintain that the picture that she works with, while not the one we in fact use, is nevertheless a *purified* version of our everyday picture. The sceptic could argue, for example, that while it is true that we never undertake fully general epistemic evaluations in normal life, the reason for this is that such an evaluation would be impractical. The sceptical claim would thus be that in the context of an epistemologically 'pure' inquiry—i.e. one in which we set all practical limitations like time and opportunity cost to one side—we *would* seek a fully general epistemic evaluation. The sceptical claim, therefore, is that while there are good reasons why our ordinary epistemic practices do not lead to fully general epistemic evaluations, such practices nevertheless do legitimate such evaluations since it is only mere practical considerations which prevent the everyday epistemic practices from transforming themselves into the kinds of practices envisaged by the sceptic. Accordingly, the sceptic can maintain that she is not in the grip of a faulty theoretical picture at all, but simply working with a more refined version of our ordinary epistemic practices.

It is for this reason that I think it is important to the Wittgensteinian line not merely that it shows that our ordinary epistemic practices do not license the kind of fully general epistemic evaluations employed by the traditional epistemologist (both sceptic and anti-sceptic), but also that it highlights why such practices are in fact completely *disconnected* from the sceptical picture on which fully general epistemic evaluations are possible. And, indeed, this is exactly what Wittgenstein does in *On Certainty* with the picture that he offers of the structure of reasons with the notion of hinge propositions at its heart: it is precisely not a mere practical limitation on our practices that certain propositions are exempt from epistemic evaluation, but part of the very logic of an epistemic evaluation. Such, indeed, is the moral of the §§341–3 that we cited above.[3]

There are other arguments that Wittgenstein offers in order to motivate the idea that all epistemic evaluation must essentially presuppose commitment to hinges, many of which are direct consequences of the picture of the structure of reasons that he offers.

---

[3] It seems to me that many commentators have missed this aspect of the Wittgensteinian anti-sceptical thesis. One key exception, who has very much informed my reading of Wittgenstein here, is Michael Williams. See, especially, Williams (1991, *passim*). I discuss Williams' view further below.

For example, one argument that Wittgenstein puts forward in this respect proceeds by noting that these commitments are required in order for one to even make sense of the doubt in the first place—i.e. for the doubt to be meaningfully expressed. In essence, the claim is that given the certainty attached to hinges, to doubt them is to call the framework as a whole into question, and with it all that one believes. But if one does that, then one can no longer be confident of the meaning of one's words, and the ability to understand the doubt diminishes accordingly. As Wittgenstein remarks at one point:

> If you are not certain of any fact, you cannot be certain of the meaning of your words either.
> If you tried to doubt everything you would not get as far as doubting anything. The game of doubting itself presupposes certainty. (OC §§114–15; cf. §§514–15)

And elsewhere, 'A doubt that doubted everything would not be a doubt' (OC §450; cf. §§370; 490; 613).[4] Wittgenstein is thus again challenging the sceptical picture whereby a wholesale epistemic evaluation of our beliefs is even possible.

A related claim that Wittgenstein makes in this regard is that certain kinds of mistake are impossible. For example, he writes:

> If my friend were to imagine one day that he had been living for a long time past in such and such a place, etc. etc., I should not call this a mistake, but rather a mental disturbance, perhaps a transient one.
> Not every false belief of this sort is a mistake. (OC §§71–2; cf. §§54, 155–8)

The point behind these remarks concerns how accounting for a false belief as a mistake requires that one can place that belief within some rational structure. If the putative mistake is too extreme, however, then it cannot be so placed. Accordingly, we cannot offer *reasons* for the mistake, but can instead only look for *causes* (in this case that of a mental disturbance). Hence, the sceptic cannot coherently offer grounds for thinking that our beliefs as a whole may rest on a mistake, she can only at best suggest possible causes for such massive error.

2. Varieties of Non-epistemicism

A key issue facing the anti-sceptical import of the hinge proposition thesis concerns the epistemic standing of our beliefs in these propositions. As we noted above, it is hard to make sense of how such beliefs could be rationally grounded on the Wittgensteinian picture, and if they are not so grounded, then—at least given that such beliefs are not foundational in any classical sense—it would seem to follow that they cannot be cases of

---

[4] There are obvious affinities here with the anti-sceptical use of the principle of charity made by Davidson (1984; 1986).

knowledge either. But can we really make sense of the idea that, for example, I am unable to know that I have two hands (at least in normal circumstances)? In order to engage with this issue, we need to explore the notion of a hinge proposition further. There are three main anti-sceptical theses in the contemporary epistemological literature that are inspired by this picture of a hinge proposition. Each has a different take on the claim that hinges are unknown. I will consider them in turn, starting with the *non-epistemicist* view that simply takes at face value the claim that hinges are unknown, a thesis that would clearly demand quite a radical revision in our epistemological outlook.

This position can be developed in a number of ways, depending on the explanation one gives for why hinge propositions are unknowable. The most radical explanation for why hinge propositions are unknowable is that hinges are not in fact propositions at all. Call this the *non-propositional* reading.[5] One advantage that such a view has is that it ensures that our failure to know hinge propositions does not represent ignorance on our part, since there is *nothing*, strictly speaking, for us to be ignorant of. This feature of the view is obviously very important for its anti-sceptical credentials.

At least as regards certain propositions which might plausibly be classed as hinges, there is actually quite strong support for this reading. In particular, Wittgenstein's treatment of 'There are physical objects' (e.g. OC §35) seems to fit this reading. As Michael Williams (2003) has noted, the first sixty-five sections of *On Certainty* are focussed not on Moore's (1925) 'Defence of Common Sense', but rather on his 'Proof of an External World' (Moore 1939). Crucially, however, whereas the former paper is concerned with showing that we have knowledge of many of the everyday propositions that we think we know—such as that the earth has existed for many years—the latter paper is specifically concerned with the problem of idealism, and thus tries to prove that there are physical objects. As regards the statement that there are physical objects, however, Wittgenstein seems to want to hold that it does not succeed in saying anything at all. He refers to such a statement as 'nonsense' (OC §35), and goes on to explain why by saying that 'physical object' is a 'logical concept':

> 'A is a physical object' is a piece of instruction which we give only to someone who doesn't yet understand what 'A' means, or what 'physical object' means. Thus it is instruction about the use of words, and 'physical object' is a logical concept. (Like colour, quantity,...) And that is why no such proposition as: 'There are physical objects' can be formulated.
>   Yet we encounter such unsuccessful shots at every turn. (OC §36; cf. §§35 and 37)

The point being made here is that such a statement serves a purely grammatical role of showing how certain words can be used, and thus cannot play a fact-stating role.

Let us grant that a statement like 'There are physical objects' fails to express a proposition. The important question is what follows from this. In particular, it is far from clear that we should on this basis grant that hinge propositions are not, strictly speaking, propositions

---

[5] For some works which display a great deal of sympathy with the non-propositional construal of hinges, see Stroll (1994), Moyal-Sharrock (2004), and Phillips (2005).

at all. One reason for this arises out of the point that Williams makes concerning how the early sections of *On Certainty* seem to have a different focus to the rest of the remarks published as this text. Accordingly, one could regard Wittgenstein as offering a different treatment of the anti-idealist claims made by the Moore of 1939 in contrast to the 'commonsense' claims to know put forward by the Moore of 1925. Indeed, I think there is a great deal of merit in taking this interpretive line. After all, it is very much in the spirit of the more general Wittgensteinian approach to philosophical language to regard the theoretical statements made by philosophers—such as 'There are physical objects'—as suspect.

What Moore (1925) is at least *trying* to do with his claims to know, however, is not state some contentious philosophical thesis, but rather simply affirm common sense, so it is unclear why Wittgenstein's resistance to philosophical language should spill over to undermine the content of these claims. Of course, in saying this we need to remember that Moore is trying to make a philosophical point with his assertions, and part of the Wittgensteinian response to Moore is to (at least) argue that Moore cannot make the point that he wants to make in this way. It is beyond dispute, then, that what Moore is asserting is unclear, that it is in some way conversationally inappropriate, and that it is philosophically ineffective. One can grant this much, however, without thereby conceding that Moore fails to say anything at all.

A further problem facing anyone who adopts the non-propositional reading of *On Certainty* is that Wittgenstein clearly wants to hold that a statement like 'There are physical objects' is *always* contentless, and yet part of the point of the hinge proposition analogy is that what is at one time a hinge may not function as a hinge at another time. Consider these passages:

> The propositions describing this world picture [i.e. the hinges] might be part of a kind of mythology. And their role is like that of rules of a game; and the game can be learned purely practically, without learning any explicit rules.
>
> It might be imagined that some propositions, of the form of empirical propositions, were hardened and functioned as channels for such empirical propositions as were not hardened but fluid; and that this relation altered with time, in that fluid propositions hardened and hard ones became fluid.
>
> The mythology may change back into a state of flux, the river-bed of thoughts may shift. But I distinguish between the movements of the waters on the river-bed and the shift of the bed itself; though there is not a sharp division of the one from the other. (OC §§95–7)

Even putting to one side the fact that Wittgenstein here clearly regards the hinges as propositions, it is also obvious that he thinks it is of the very nature of a hinge proposition that at certain times that very same proposition may no longer function as a hinge. The plain unvarying contentlessness of a statement like 'There are physical objects' on the Wittgensteinian view thus seems to count decisively against its being a hinge.

A different source of support for the non-propositional reading of *On Certainty* comes from the way that Wittgenstein often associates hinge propositions with a kind of visceral conviction which he contrasts with a judgement. Consider the following passage:

> Giving grounds...comes to an end;—but the end is not certain propositions' strik-
> ing us immediately as true, i.e. it is not a kind of *seeing* on our part; it is our *acting*,
> which lies at the bottom of the language-game. (OC §204; cf. §§110, 148, 232, 342,
> 402)

Elsewhere, Wittgenstein characterizes the certainty that attaches to hinges as being 'something animal' (OC §§358–9). One might extract from these remarks the thought that what Wittgenstein is fundamentally interested in is our hinge-like convictions to act in certain ways, rather than in there being certain propositions which we are convinced of.

Still, if this is the account of hinge propositions that Wittgenstein has in mind, then it is at least odd that he refers to hinges as propositions throughout *On Certainty*. The proponent of the non-propositional view therefore has a fairly stiff exegetical task on her hands. A less radical form of non-epistemicism which avoids this difficulty holds that while hinges are indeed propositions, they are not fact-stating propositions but rather express norms. Call this the *non-factual* account of hinge propositions. Indeed, the 'riverbed' passages just quoted themselves provide strong support for this reading. After all, in talking of the hinges as 'rules of a game' (even despite being 'of the form of empirical propositions'), and also as 'channels' for ordinary empirical propositions, the conclusion might naturally be drawn that hinge propositions express norms rather than being fact-stating. But if they do not express facts, then it follows that they are not in the market for being known either, and hence we get an explanation of just why hinge propositions are unknowable.[6]

Taken at face value at least, there is certainly more mileage in this weaker non-epistemicist reading of *On Certainty*. While it avoids some of the more pressing problems that face the non-propositional account of hinge propositions, it retains the key advantage of that proposal that there is nothing, strictly speaking, that one is ignorant of when one fails to know a hinge proposition, since this would presuppose that there is something—a fact-stating proposition—which was in the market for knowledge in the first place. Nevertheless, such a view still needs to contend with the problem of explaining how a proposition like 'I have two hands' can be non-fact-stating, and this is no easy task.

This reading also has the advantage of avoiding two problems that afflict a third type of non-epistemicism.[7] This view is even weaker than the non-factual proposal in that it

---

[6] For what is perhaps the best attempt at running a non-epistemicist response to scepticism that is cast along these non-factualist lines, see Wright (1985), though note that Wright himself grants that such an approach will only work as regards certain kinds of sceptical problem. (We will consider how Wright approaches other types of scepticism below, since his work in this regard is also heavily influenced by *On Certainty*.) One can detect (varying degrees of) sympathy with this general approach to hinge propositions in a number of places. See, for example, McGinn (1989), Stroll (1994), Conant (1998) and Minar (2005).

[7] Albeit not a variety of non-epistemicism which, to my knowledge, has been explicitly defended in the literature (though I have heard this view presented in conversation on a number of occasions).

allows that hinge propositions do indeed express fact-stating propositions. It thereby avoids the problem of explaining how a proposition like 'I have two hands' can fail to be fact-stating. Nevertheless, it retains the core thesis of non-epistemicism that such propositions are unknowable. Call this view the *simple non-epistemic* account of hinge propositions.

One immediate problem that faces simple non-epistemicism is that there is now something that one is ignorant of when one fails to know a hinge proposition, i.e. the fact-stating proposition in question. The problem, however, is to explain how such a view is to be differentiated from scepticism. After all, the sceptic would surely agree that we are unable to know the most basic propositions which we believe.

One way of doing this, which would be very much in keeping with the approach to philosophical problems that Wittgenstein urges throughout his work, would be to argue that what Wittgenstein is trying to get us to recognize through his remarks in *On Certainty* is the illegitimacy of the philosophical context in which a problem like scepticism emerges. The import of this to the simple non-epistemicist reading of *On Certainty* is that the issue of the epistemic status of hinge propositions only arises in philosophical contexts.[8] Accordingly, if Wittgenstein's remarks in *On Certainty* enable us to see that such a context is somehow illegitimate, then this could be one way of reconciling us to the fact that hinge propositions are unknown. After all, if we (rightly) never enter the philosophical context, then we can feel no sense of loss at our lack of knowledge of these propositions.

For our purposes we can set to one side the issue of what motivates the claim that the philosophical context is illegitimate, since I think we can show that there is a fundamental problem facing simple non-epistemicism whatever thesis one puts forward in this respect. Moreover, it is also a problem which, as we will see, Wittgenstein himself alludes to.

The problem relates to the so-called closure principle for knowledge. We can formulate this principle, roughly, as follows:

The Closure Principle
If S knows that p, and S knows that p entails q, then S knows that q.[9]

---

[8] Of course, we might question the epistemic standing of these propositions in abnormal (though not philosophical) contexts—such as, in the case of 'I have hands', the context of a serious car accident—but in such abnormal contexts this proposition would no longer be functioning as a hinge. Relatedly, as we noted above, Wittgenstein seems open to the possibility that the class of hinge propositions might change over time, in which case a proposition which functioned as a hinge in normal circumstances today might be a normal empirical proposition at some point in the future, and so coherently subject to an epistemic evaluation. Again, though, we would not be epistemically evaluating this proposition *qua* hinge proposition.

[9] There are ways of refining the closure principle in order to deal with some fairly uninteresting counterexamples to the simple formulation offered here (such as cases in which one satisfies the antecedent but does not satisfy the consequent because one does not believe the entailed proposition, or believes it for unrelated, and poor, reasons). In order to keep matters simple, I will not engage with these issues here. For the most up-to-date discussion of the closure principle, see the exchange between Dretske (2005a; 2005b) and Hawthorne (2005).

So construed, the principle seems entirely uncontentious. For example, if I know that I am presently seated, and I know that if I am presently seated then I am not standing, then I also know that I am not presently standing. The principle only becomes contentious, however, once we feed in hinge propositions. After all, there are, it seems, non-hinge propositions which we know and which we know entail hinge propositions. If that is right, then it appears that we do know hinge propositions after all, contrary to what the simple non-epistemicist tells us.

For example, one proposition which Wittgenstein cites as being a hinge is that the earth has existed for a long time and has not recently come into existence (e.g. OC §§84ff.). Presumably, however, concrete historical claims are not hinges. One can discover, and coherently offer, reasons in support of one's discovery, that such-and-such happened at some point in the fairly distant past. Accordingly, one can know such concrete historical claims. But surely one also knows that these concrete historical claims entail that the earth has been around for a fairly long time and has not recently come into existence. With closure in play, then, it seems that we must know at least some hinges after all, in virtue of how they are entailed by other non-hinge propositions which we know.[10]

Wittgenstein alludes to this difficulty in the following passage:

> 'It is certain that after the battle of Austerlitz Napoleon....Well, in that case it's surely also certain that the earth existed then.' (OC §183; cf. §§182–92)

There would clearly be something amiss with anyone who reasoned in this way, and the obvious explanation of why is that it is an inference that takes one from a non-hinge proposition to a hinge proposition. It is hard to see, however, why such an inference should be problematic on the simple non-epistemicist view. One can know non-hinge propositions, and surely one can also know the entailments that exist from non-hinge propositions to (fact-stating) hinge propositions. Given the closure principle, then, one is committed to holding that hinge propositions can be known after all.

One option available to the simple non-epistemicist is, of course, to deny the closure principle. Motivating the denial of such a principle is far from easy, however, given how intuitive it is, and so this is not a dialectical option to be taken lightly.[11]

Moreover, notice that even if it is the case that it is only in the illegitimate philosophical context that the issue of the epistemic status of hinge propositions explicitly arises, this doesn't seem to help the proponent of simple non-epistemicism deal with this

---

[10] Note that this specific problem does not arise for the other two non-epistemicist readings of *On Certainty* for the simple reason that the relevant entailment cannot go through if the entailed 'proposition' is not a proposition (or at least not a fact-stating proposition). These non-epistemicist readings do face a related problem, however, which is to explain why a fact-stating proposition expressing a normal historical claim does not entail that the universe has been around for long enough to ensure that this historical claim could be true, such that there is a fact-stating proposition which expresses this hinge.

[11] That said, the principle has been denied, most notably by Dretske (1970) and Nozick (1981).

problem. Presumably, in a normal context one can know the non-hinge proposition, know the relevant entailment, and (on this basis) believe the hinge proposition, even if an occasion never arises which would bring one to assert either the entailment or the entailed proposition. Just so long as one meets these conditions, however, and the closure principle holds, then knowledge of the hinge proposition is inevitable.[12]

The moral we should draw from this problem is clear. If we are willing to go so far as to grant that the hinges are indeed fact-stating propositions—and if we want to retain the basic anti-sceptical thought that we are able to know lots of (non-hinge) propositions—then it is essential, given the highly intuitive closure principle, that we also regard hinge propositions as knowable. If one wishes to sustain a form of non-epistemicism, it is thus essential that one opts for either a version of the non-propositional account or a version of the non-factual account. Given the fairly major problems that affect the former, the latter seems the best option. In what follows, however, we will be considering two anti-sceptical views that are inspired by Wittgenstein's remarks on hinges and the structure of reasons in *On Certainty* but which allow, in contrast to non-epistemicism, that we *can* know these propositions.[13]

3. CONTEXTUALISM

The first *epistemicist* conception of hinges that we will consider is a view that I will call *contextualism*.[14] According to contextualism, the hinges are known just so long as one does not enter a context where such hinges are brought into question (which will usually

---

[12] One possible line of response to this problem that the proponent of simple non-epistemicism could offer is to claim that hinge propositions, while fact-stating propositions, are nevertheless not in the market for belief. Accordingly, the closure-based inference is blocked in virtue of the fact that the agent concerned is not able to even believe the entailed proposition, let alone know it. There may be some mileage in this manoeuvre since it is certainly true that on some accounts of belief it would be inappropriate to describe our pro-attitude to hinge propositions as being one of belief. Nevertheless, it is far from clear how this proposal helps the view since it remains that closure is being denied. Moreover, one would be left with the new problem of explaining how one could know a proposition, know that this proposition entailed a second proposition, and yet fail to even believe the entailed proposition. Such a state of affairs is itself mysterious.

[13] My discussion of non-epistemicism is inevitably a little glib, and leaves out a number of important considerations that are relevant to this topic (such as how best to understand the very notion of a proposition). Two further issues are also worthy of note. The first is the extent to which we can treat Wittgenstein as endorsing a radically context-sensitive approach to meaning, a thesis that would obviously be relevant in this regard. For discussion of such a view, see Travis (1989). The second is the issue of how best to understand the nonsense that results on the non-epistemicist view when one asserts (or doubts) a hinge. Is it, for example, just plain nonsense, or is it somehow philosophically significant nonsense (if such a thing is possible)? For more on this issue, see the exchange between Conant (1998) and McGinn (2002).

[14] It is important to remember that this view is very different from the kind of attributer contextualist views that are currently popular in the literature (e.g. DeRose 1995; Lewis 1996; Cohen 2000). For a comparative discussion of these two types of contextualism, see Pritchard (2002b).

be a philosophical context). Moreover, like weak non-epistemicism, this view also trades on a claim about the illegitimacy of the philosophical context in which the problem of scepticism arises. Although it is not offered as an interpretation of *On Certainty*—but merely as a position which is suggested by some themes in this text—Williams' (1991) inferential contextualism offers a good example of how such a view might run.

The starting point for Williams is the Wittgensteinian idea that all epistemic evaluation presupposes a groundless commitment to a set of hinge propositions—what Williams (1991, 121–5) calls 'methodological necessities'—where the hinges determine what counts as evidence for what. Williams notes that the standard sceptical response to this picture is to argue that while we may indeed take certain things for granted in normal everyday contexts, the true epistemic standing of our beliefs is exposed once we enter the philosophical context. In this context we abstract from the practical constraints that operate in normal contexts and instead consider the epistemic standings of our beliefs while taking nothing for granted (think, for example, of the method of doubt employed by Descartes in the *Meditations*). Relative to this context we discover, claims the sceptic, that we do not know any of the propositions which we thought we knew.

Williams' way of dealing with this sceptical response is ingenious. He argues that the force of sceptical arguments lies in the way that they seem not to depend on any theoretical claims at all, but rather simply fall out of common sense.[15] In contrast to this picture of sceptical doubt, Williams argues that the sceptic is in fact committed to a highly theoretical claim—what he calls 'epistemological realism'—to the effect that the propositions we believe have an epistemic standing simply in virtue of the kind of propositions they are. For example, if one were a classical foundationalist, then one would partition beliefs into different epistemic kinds (basic and non-basic) in terms of the sort of proposition believed (e.g. whether the proposition concerned the 'inner' realm of the mental, rather than being concerned with the 'outer' realm of the world). The kind of contextualism that Williams claims is inspired by *On Certainty* instead holds that

> the epistemic status of a given proposition is liable to shift with situational, disciplinary and other contextually variable factors: it is to hold that, independently of such influences, a proposition has no epistemic status whatsoever. (Williams 1991, 119)

Moreover, Williams argues that to suppose otherwise is to commit oneself to a highly theoretical and dubious claim. Thus scepticism does not fall out of common sense at all, but is rather a product of a contentious piece of epistemological theory. It can thus be rejected with impunity.

In particular, Williams' claim is that while the sceptic appears to have presented us with a context in which an epistemic evaluation takes place that is not relative to a set of hinges, in fact all they have presented us with is a context which takes as a hinge the theoretical commitment to epistemological realism. They have not then offered us a counterexample to the Wittgensteinian claim that all epistemic evaluation is relative to a

---

[15] As Stroud (1984, 82) famously puts it, scepticism falls out of 'platitudes' that 'we would all accept'.

set of hinges, but merely presented us with a context which has different hinges to those in operation in normal, non-philosophical, contexts.

Williams thus grants to the sceptic that it is true that in the sceptical context we do indeed know next to nothing, and thus that scepticism is in this sense correct. Nevertheless, that the sceptic can create a context in which we lack knowledge does not mean that we lack knowledge in *quotidian* contexts where our everyday hinge beliefs are not brought forward for epistemic evaluation. The crucial point here is that Williams claims that the sceptical context is just another hinge-relative context, and so the conclusions derived in that context must be understood in that light. As Williams puts the matter:

> The sceptic takes himself to have discovered, under the conditions of philosophical reflection, that knowledge of the world is impossible. But in fact, the most he has discovered is that knowledge of the world is *impossible under the conditions of philosophical reflection*. (Williams 1991, 130)

That is, the sceptical context is now just one context amongst others, with no theoretical ascendancy over other contexts and with unquestioned hinges of its own. That it is true, relative to the hinges of the sceptical context (such as the assumption that there is a context-invariant epistemic structure that can be discerned via philosophical reflection), that we know very little does not mean that in everyday contexts in which different hinges are in play we fail to know what we take ourselves to know, which is what the sceptic claims.

Unlike the non-epistemicist, however, Williams *does* claim that one can know the hinge propositions of one's context and, accordingly, he does not face the problem above that we saw was posed by the principle of closure for simple non-epistemicism. If I know that Napoleon won the battle of Austerlitz in 1805, and know that this entails that the earth did not spring into existence five minutes ago (replete with the apparent traces of a distant ancestry), then I also know that the earth did not spring into existence five minutes ago, even though commitment to such a claim is clearly part of the hinges of any normal context. What is crucial for Williams is that one cannot use the historical reasons that one might cite in favour of the former claim in order to motivate the latter claim, the hinge. In doing so, claims Williams, one is thereby no longer taking the relevant hinges for granted and so one enters a new context with different hinges and thus a different inferential structure. In particular, Williams argues that it is only in response to prompting by the sceptic that one would seek such a grounding for one's hinge beliefs, and so the context that one would enter would be the sceptical context. In this context, though, one lacks knowledge not only of the fact that the earth did not come into existence five minutes ago, but also of the historical fact in question. There is thus no single context in which both propositions are explicitly considered, and both known.

This is an elegant way of developing the Wittgensteinian line. It has affinities with some non-epistemicist views in that it in effect regards the philosophical context, with its claim to offer a fully general epistemic evaluation of our beliefs that does not presuppose any hinges, as essentially suspect. Crucially, though, in allowing us knowledge of hinge propositions, this view avoids the key problem posed for simple non-epistemicism by the closure principle, while also enabling us to clearly distinguish this anti-sceptical thesis from scepticism.

One potential problem that Williams' view faces concerns the odd status of the sceptical context. After all, Williams would surely agree that unless the hinges of one's context (the relevant ones at any rate) were true, then one could not gain knowledge via any inquiry conducted in that context. For instance, if the earth did indeed spring into existence five minutes ago, then I don't have any historical knowledge. The trouble is, the sceptical context employs a hinge proposition which Williams seems to be suggesting is a priori false. Accordingly, it seems that the sceptic does not 'discover' anything at all in the context of philosophical reflection, since to discover is to come to know, and the sceptic doesn't know even the truth of her scepticism. Thus the sceptic's context is not only illegitimate because of its use of a contentious theoretical hinge, but it is also a context in which nothing can be known.

In itself, this may seem to be more of an advantage to the view than a disadvantage, in that it further emphasizes the anti-sceptical credentials of the position. The problem emerges once one factors in that Williams wants his position to accommodate the prima facie pull which philosophers feel towards scepticism. That is, like all contextualists, he wants to offer a sense in which the sceptic is right, albeit not in the way that the sceptic supposes. Provided that we read his view correctly, however, it turns out there is no truth in scepticism at all, not even in the context inhabited by the sceptic.

Moreover, if this is right then it is hard to see why we should regard the view as a *contextualist* thesis at all. After all, if it is true that all epistemic evaluation takes places against a backdrop of a groundless commitment to hinges, and that scepticism presupposes a theoretical picture which is committed to a conflicting account of epistemic evaluation, then these two points alone will suffice to deal with the sceptical problem. We do not seem to need to appeal to contexts, much less to the idea that 'the epistemic status of a given proposition is liable to shift with situational, disciplinary and other contextually variable factors' (Williams 1991, 119).[16] In any case, it isn't at all clear that we can make sense of the thesis of epistemological realism as being a hinge, especially given that it is such a highly theoretical claim. Hinges, recall, are more akin to 'solidified' chunks of common sense, rather than contentious philosophical and theoretical theses.

A related problem facing Williams' position concerns the status of the context in which he conducts his own investigations into scepticism. If merely running through the 'Napoleon' inference described above suffices to take one into the sceptical context, then why aren't Williams' own reflections on knowledge conducted within such a context, and so (by his own lights) essentially pointless (since, recall, nothing can be discovered in this context)?

A final problem facing this position concerns how it can account for our knowledge of hinges given that such knowledge cannot be grounded in reasons. Since this problem

---

[16] Though, of course, one might have independent reasons for advancing a contextualism of this sort. Interestingly, there has been a recent upsurge of interest in the kind of subject contextualism that Williams advocates, prompted by two influential books by Hawthorne (2004) and Stanley (2005)—though, oddly, neither book so much as references Williams' version of subject contextualism—and in each case the view is motivated independently of the sceptical problem. It is because of the anti-sceptical irrelevance of the appeal to context that I have argued elsewhere that Williams' view is best read, *qua* anti-sceptical thesis, as a form of epistemic deflationism, since it aims to 'deflate' the epistemological project by showing that the idea of a fully general hinge-independent epistemic evaluation is impossible. See Pritchard (2004).

faces any epistemicist treatment of hinge propositions—i.e. any view which treats such propositions as knowable—we will examine this problem in the light of the second epistemicist thesis that we will be looking at here.

4. NEO-MOOREANISM(S)

The critical focus of *On Certainty* is, of course, Moore's remarks on scepticism. Given that Moore's central claim is that he knows the relevant hinge propositions, one might think that Wittgenstein's strong critical reaction entails that he regard us as being unable to know such propositions. As we have seen, there is some support in the text for this thesis, though the view faces some problems. Nevertheless, there are also grounds for caution on this score, since there are other passages which suggest a weaker reading according to which we can know these propositions, though not in any way that would license the sort of assertions that Moore makes. As Wittgenstein puts it at one point:

> Moore's mistake lies in this—countering the assertion that one cannot know that [a hinge], by saying 'I do know it'. (OC §521)

One influential version of this thesis—what I shall refer to as *neo-Mooreanism*—can be found in recent work by Crispin Wright (e.g. 1991; 2000; 2002; 2003a; 2003b; 2004a; 2004b; 2004c; cf. Davies 1998; 2000; 2003; 2004). Wright's idea is that what Wittgenstein is highlighting is that there are certain propositions belief in which is a prerequisite of engagement in any epistemic evaluation, and which therefore cannot be offered supporting grounds. Nevertheless, argues Wright, this does not mean that such beliefs are not epistemically supported (and so cannot be known), but only that the epistemic support that these beliefs enjoy cannot, as Wright puts it, be 'earned'. Instead, these beliefs enjoy epistemic support which is 'unearned', but which is positive epistemic support nonetheless.

Central to Wright's thesis is a distinction between the principle of closure and a related principle which he refers to as 'transmission'. We can roughly express the transmission principle as follows:

The Transmission Principle
If S knows that p on the basis of supporting grounds G, and S competently deduces q from p (thereby coming to believe q while retaining her knowledge that p), then G is sufficient to support S's knowledge that q.[17]

---

[17] One might need to complicate this principle in order to get it just right, but this version will do for our purposes here. For example, one might naturally hold that the inference will itself contribute epistemic support to one's belief in the entailed proposition, and hence that this should be included in the grounds which support that belief. What is important, however, is the idea that it is not just knowledge that transmits across known entailment in cases which satisfy the transmission principle, but also that the grounds which support the entailing proposition also transmit, even if they are necessarily accompanied by further grounds. In any case, in what follows I will set this problem of formulation, and others like it, to one side.

The key difference between the closure principle and the transmission principle is that while the former simply states that the known-to-be-entailed proposition is itself known, the latter specifies the manner in which this proposition is known. In particular, it specifies that the very same grounds which epistemically support knowledge of the entailing proposition will also support knowledge of the entailed proposition. This difference ensures that the transmission principle is more demanding than the closure principle.

We saw above that some of Wittgenstein's remarks on hinge propositions seem to have the result that closure must be rejected. This is because there are propositions which, it seems, we can know by Wittgenstein's lights but which are known to entail (fact-stating) hinge propositions, propositions which, on one reading of Wittgenstein at any rate, are unknowable. Wright's idea is that the distinction between closure and transmission can help us out here. What follows from Wittgenstein's claim that belief in hinge propositions cannot be epistemically supported is only that the transmission principle fails, since the grounds we have for belief in non-hinge propositions cannot 'transmit' across a known entailment to be grounds for belief in a hinge proposition. Nevertheless, that doesn't mean that closure fails, since it remains an option that hinge propositions are known so long as they are not known on the basis of grounds that we can coherently offer in favour of belief in these propositions (i.e. the epistemic standing of our belief in such propositions must be unearned).

Consider again the problematic inference that we considered above:

(1) Napoleon did X after the battle of Austerlitz.
(2) If Napoleon did X after the battle of Austerlitz, then the universe did not spring into existence five minutes ago replete with the apparent traces of a distant ancestry.
(C) The universe did not spring into existence five minutes ago replete with the apparent traces of a distant ancestry.

If closure holds, then if an agent knows (1) and (2), she will also know (C). There certainly does seem something wrong with this inference, however, and the Wittgensteinian explanation of what is wrong with it appears to fit very neatly. That is, if we grant that propositions of the sort that figure in (C) can function as hinges—such that they are the framework relative to which epistemic evaluations are conducted, and so cannot be subjected to an epistemic evaluation themselves—then it follows that there must be something wrong with an inference of this sort. After all, how can reasoning in this way provide one with supporting grounds for (C) given that a prior, and groundless, commitment to (C) must be in place in order for one to coherently offer grounds in favour of (1) in the first place? Recall our description of the Wittgensteinian conception of the structure of reasons. If (C) is a hinge proposition, then nothing is more certain than it, and so nothing can count as a supporting ground for it. Furthermore, (1), since it isn't a hinge proposition, is certainly less certain than (C). It would clearly be incoherent, then, for (1) to constitute one's supporting ground for (C).

This line of thinking naturally prompts one to wonder whether the principle of closure should be rejected in order to deal with the problem, but Wright's proposal offers an alternative strategy. Rather than holding that the problem here is that (C) is unknowable (at least *qua* hinge), one can instead maintain that the difficulty facing this inference is only that the grounds in favour of (1) do not transmit across the known entailment to offer support for (C). This claim, however, is consistent with the thought that (C) is nonetheless known, at least if we can make sense of an 'unearned' epistemic support for our belief in hinge propositions. But can we make sense of such support?

Here is the progression of argument in Wright's most recent article on this topic. First, we have the Wittgensteinian claim about the necessity of hinge propositions:

> To take it that one has acquired a warrant for a particular proposition by the appropriate exercise of certain appropriate cognitive capacities…always involves various kinds of presupposition….I take Wittgenstein's point…to be that this is essential: *one cannot but* take certain such things for granted. (Wright 2004c, 189).

On the face of it, of course, this conclusion is just as much a ground for scepticism as for any anti-sceptical thesis, since one might naturally conclude that from a purely epistemic point of view we lack adequate grounds in support of our beliefs (ultimately, our beliefs are groundlessly held). Wright's response to this charge is to argue, in effect, that what the Wittgensteinian thesis regarding the necessity of hinges highlights is that we are in the grip of a faulty conception of the epistemic landscape, and therefore aspiring to something that we should recognize as both unobtainable and incoherent. He writes:

> Since there is *no such thing* as a process of warrant for each of whose specific presuppositions warrant has already been earned, it should not be reckoned to be part of the proper concept of an acquired warrant that it somehow aspire to this—incoherent—ideal….
>
> This strategy of reply concedes that the best sceptical arguments have something to teach us—that the limits of justification they bring out are genuine and essential—but then replies that, just for that reason, cognitive achievement must be reckoned to take place *within such limits*. The attempt to surpass them would result not in an increase in rigour or solidity but merely in cognitive paralysis. (Wright 2004c, 190–1)

A quick reading of these passages might well give the reader the impression that what Wright is urging upon us here is a purely pragmatic response to the sceptical problem.[18] That is, that since the goal of earning a warrant for all of our beliefs, including our beliefs in hinges, is impossible, we should not allow all warrants to be earned. After all, to suppose otherwise would lead to 'cognitive paralysis'. One who is already swayed by sceptical arguments will not be persuaded by such a pragmatic line, however. It is hardly news to the sceptic that sceptical reasoning leads to cognitive paralysis.

---

[18]   Indeed, that was how I interpreted Wright's comments in this regard in Pritchard (2005b).

But such a purely pragmatic reading of Wright's anti-scepticism is too quick. In order to see this, suppose for a moment that one is a truth seeker who has come to recognize that there is no alternative but to groundlessly presuppose hinge propositions in one's inquiry. The choice, then, is between continuing one's inquiries and allowing the hinges to 'lie apart from the route travelled by enquiry' (OC §88), and ceasing to inquire at all. Given that the latter strategy would be *guaranteed* to prevent one from gaining true beliefs—and given that the former strategy is, *ex hypothesi*, the best strategy available for gaining true beliefs—wouldn't it be *rational* for such an agent to choose a hinge-directed inquiry over cognitive paralysis?[19] Moreover, and this is the crux of the point, since the goal here is explicitly the epistemic goal of gaining true beliefs, isn't the rationality in question here entirely *epistemic*?

This, I suggest, is the right way to read Wright's proposal: not as advocating a pragmatic response to scepticism, but rather as attempting to highlight that an anti-sceptical consequence of the picture of the structure of reasons offered by Wittgenstein is that it is epistemically rational to believe hinges even though we necessarily lack any direct epistemic support for them.[20]

Still, such a view faces a serious problem even on this construal, which is to explain in virtue of what the epistemic support for our hinge beliefs consists, given that it is not an epistemic support that comes through being appropriately grounded (this, recall, was the final problem facing Williams' contextualist thesis that we alluded to above). The reasoning that we just ran through—if successful at any rate—would certainly provide indirect support for our hinge beliefs by showing that such belief is epistemically rational, but this fact won't obviously be of any assistance to those mere mortals who lack the intellectual resources to run through the argument, and that is hardly satisfactory.[21]

Part of the problem that someone like Wright faces on this score is that he wishes to maintain this style of anti-scepticism whilst also holding on to his commitment to epistemic internalism (e.g. Wright 2004c, 205). Typically, epistemic internalists hold that a necessary condition of knowing a proposition is that one has adequate reflectively accessible supporting grounds in favour of one's belief in that proposition, and Wright would normally impose such a demand on knowledge. When it comes to (our everyday) belief in hinge propositions, however, he is forced to make an exception, and that has the problem of making his anti-sceptical strategy look ad hoc. After all, it is not as if our belief in hinge propositions could be thought to be self-justifying in any way—such beliefs are

---

[19] Of course, it is important to remember here that it is hardly a *decision* on our part to believe hinge propositions (recall that it is 'not as if we *chose* this game' (OC §317)). Such talk of 'choosing' a hinge-directed inquiry should thus be understood very loosely.

[20] Clearly, this approach requires some spelling out, which I haven't the space to attempt here. For a recent critical discussion of this 'epistemic rationality' reading of Wright's conception of hinge propositions, see Jenkins (2007). For an excellent critique of Wright's anti-sceptical view more generally, see McGinn (2008).

[21] Wright (2004c, 204–5) is in any case explicit that he does not want our unearned epistemic support for our hinge beliefs to be purely the preserve of the philosopher.

not self-evident, for example. What, then, from an internalist point of view, could possibly epistemically support such beliefs?

If one is willing to endorse some form of epistemic externalism, however, and consequently drops the requirement that knowledge always be supported by adequate reflectively accessible grounds, then this problem need not be decisive. An obvious example of an externalist theory of knowledge that could be relevant here is agent reliabilism, as defended by John Greco (e.g. 1999). On this view, knowledge is analysed as (roughly) true belief that arises out of the reliable operation of an agent's epistemic virtue, broadly conceived—that is, her intellectual virtues and cognitive faculties. Is one's belief in hinge propositions virtuous on this conception? For the person in the street, this question reduces to whether the strategy they unconsciously employ of taking the hinges for granted is indeed a reliable way of getting to the truth. If it is, then, since no reason has been presented for thinking that this strategy is problematic, one could certainly make the case that it is virtuous to believe hinge propositions.

One could claim, of course, that the virtuous person would always seek rational support for a belief before holding it, but there seems no obvious reason why we should build this demand into the notion of epistemic virtue, at least not unless we were already convinced by epistemic internalism. Moreover, the requirement to always seek grounds in favour of one's beliefs seems very unlike a virtue for the simple reason that a virtue, standardly conceived, lies between two viceful extremes. The epistemic virtue of being conscientious is surely intermediate between the epistemic vice of carelessness and the epistemic vice of being far too careful, such that one's inquiries become completely stymied.

The case of the agent who has confronted the sceptical problem raises a separate issue, however. That the conscientious person should not always actively seek epistemic support for her beliefs is one thing; that the conscientious person should not actively seek epistemic support for a belief which has *by her own lights* been called into question is quite another. Here, it seems, intellectual virtue demands that one remain agnostic where possible until further support is found. Nevertheless, the kind of 'epistemic rationality' interpretation of Wright's strategy outlined above could well suffice to ensure that such belief was again epistemically appropriate, so long, of course, as the reliability condition was also being met.

Epistemic externalism may thus have the resources to enable one both to allow that our beliefs in hinge propositions lack direct epistemic support in the form of reflectively accessible grounds and nevertheless hold that such beliefs can count as instances of knowledge. On the face of it, such an externalist response to the sceptical problem seems like a thousand miles away from what Wittgenstein was up to in *On Certainty*. That said, it is not obvious that such an approach is inconsistent with what Wittgenstein has to say there. After all, this approach grants the key Wittgensteinian point about the structure of reasons and the role that hinges have to play in that structure. Moreover, as noted above, Wittgenstein's primary focus is on Moore's *assertions* that he knows these hinge propositions, and our related practice of offering reasons for and against certain claims. The issue of whether or not Moore does indeed know these propositions is never fully resolved— what we are told is just that such knowledge (if it is possessed) is not grounded in reasons, and thus that a claim to know in this regard is inappropriate, possibly even incoherent.

Here, then, in essence, is the idea.[22] We take the Wittgensteinian conception of the structure of reasons as only imposing a constraint on both knowledge claims and doubts—i.e. this account of the structure of reasons entails both that we are unable to rationally doubt or properly claim to know hinge propositions. Both Moore's anti-sceptical assertions and the sceptic's doubts are thus undermined. Nevertheless, this claim about the propriety of certain assertions and the rationality of certain doubts is differentiated from the issue of whether we know hinge propositions, thus opening up logical space for an account of knowledge which allows knowledge to be possessed even in the absence of adequate reflectively accessible support grounds for the target belief.[23]

On the face of it, this line of argument may seem to trivialize Wittgenstein's remarks on scepticism, since it appears to radically constrain their import for the debate. I'm not convinced that this is so, however, at least once one spells out the idea adequately. After all, that we are unable to claim to know these propositions which we are most certain of clearly does require a radical revision in our conception of the epistemic landscape, especially since this constraint also impacts upon sceptical counterclaims. Moreover, the Wittgensteinian thesis that our practice of offering grounds presupposes a framework of ungrounded certainties is essential to giving this stance the motivation it requires, since it is only with this claim in play that we come to see that what the sceptic and the anti-sceptic are trying to achieve with their assertions is hopeless.

It would seem, then, that Wittgenstein's approach to scepticism has important ramifications for contemporary epistemology even if it is set within an externalist framework. Indeed, one might go further than this and plausibly argue that recognizing and incorporating the insights provided by Wittgenstein's treatment of scepticism in *On Certainty* is essential to the proper development of any externalist anti-sceptical epistemology.[24,25]

[22] I develop this style of neo-Mooreanism in more detail in a number of places. See especially Pritchard (2002a, §8; 2005a, part 1; 2007).

[23] Indeed, Wright's comments elsewhere indicate that he may be amenable to this approach, since he notes (Wright 2004c, 209–11) that his primary concern is with a notion of epistemic support which enables one to properly claim to have knowledge. Thus, he could be read as an internalist about the conditions under which one can properly claim knowledge while nevertheless being an externalist about knowledge who allows that knowledge is sometimes possessed even in the absence of adequate supporting reflectively accessible grounds.

[24] One lacuna in this chapter is the anti-sceptical writings of McDowell (e.g. 1995), which are in part inspired by Wittgenstein's remarks on scepticism. Discussing McDowell would take us too far afield, which is why I have not included his view here. For an unsympathetic reading of McDowell's anti-scepticism in the light of Wittgenstein's remarks in *On Certainty*, see Pritchard (2003), though note that in more recent work—especially Pritchard (2008)—I take a more sympathetic stance.

[25] An earlier version of this chapter was delivered at the 'Twentieth Century Philosophy: Scepticism' conference at the University of Manchester in May 2006. I am grateful to the audience that day, especially Marie McGinn and Michael Williams. I am in addition particularly grateful to Marie for the extremely helpful comments that she subsequently offered on a draft of this chapter. Thanks also to Peter Sullivan.

References

Austin, J. L. (1961). 'Other Minds', reprinted in his *Philosophical Papers*, ed. J. O. Urmson and G. J. Warnock. Oxford: Clarendon Press.

Cohen, S. (2000). 'Contextualism and Skepticism', *Philosophical Issues*, 10: 94–107.

Conant, J. (1998). 'Wittgenstein on Meaning and Use', *Philosophical Investigations*, 21: 222–50.

Davidson, D. (1984). 'The Method of Truth in Metaphysics' [1977], reprinted as essay 14 in *Inquiries into Truth and Interpretation*. Oxford: Clarendon Press.

—— (1986). 'A Coherence Theory of Truth and Knowledge' [1983], reprinted as chapter 16 in E. LePore ed., *Truth and Interpretation: Perspectives on the Philosophy of Donald Davidson*. Oxford: Blackwell.

Davies, M. (1998). 'Externalism, Architecturalism, and Epistemic Warrant', in C. J. G. Wright, B. C. Smith, and C. Macdonald eds., *Knowing Our Own Minds: Essays on Self-Knowledge*. Oxford: Oxford University Press.

—— (2000). 'Externalism and *A Priori* Knowledge', in P. Boghossian and C. Peacocke eds., *New Essays on the A Priori*. Oxford: Oxford University Press.

—— (2003). 'The Problem of Armchair Knowledge', in S. Nuccetelli ed., *New Essays on Semantic Externalism and Self-Knowledge*. Cambridge, MA: MIT Press.

—— (2004). 'Epistemic Entitlement, Warrant Transmission and Easy Knowledge', *Proceedings of the Aristotelian Society*, 78 (supp. vol.): 213–45.

DeRose, K. (1995). 'Solving the Skeptical Problem', *Philosophical Review*, 104: 1–52.

Dretske, F. (1970). 'Epistemic Operators', *The Journal of Philosophy*, 67: 1007–23.

—— (2005a). 'The Case Against Closure', in E. Sosa and M. Steup eds., *Contemporary Debates in Epistemology*. Oxford: Blackwell.

—— (2005b). 'Reply to Hawthorne', in E. Sosa and M. Steup eds., *Contemporary Debates in Epistemology*. Oxford: Blackwell.

Greco, J. (1999). 'Agent Reliabilism', *Philosophical Perspectives*, 13: 273–96.

Hawthorne, J. (2004). *Knowledge and Lotteries*. Oxford: Oxford University Press.

—— (2005). 'The Case for Closure', in E. Sosa and M. Steup eds., *Contemporary Debates in Epistemology*. Oxford: Blackwell.

Jenkins, C. (2007). 'Entitlement and Rationality', *Synthese*, 157: 25–45.

Lewis, D. (1996). 'Elusive Knowledge', *Australasian Journal of Philosophy*, 74: 549–67.

McDowell, J. (1995). 'Knowledge and the Internal', *Philosophy and Phenomenological Research*, 55: 877–93.

McGinn, M. (1989). *Sense and Certainty: A Dissolution of Scepticism*. Oxford: Blackwell.

—— (2002). 'What Kind of Senselessness is This? A Reply to Conant on Wittgenstein's Critique of Moore'. Unpublished.

—— (2008). 'Wittgenstein on Certainty', in J. Greco ed., *Oxford Handbook to Skepticism*. Oxford: Oxford University Press.

Minar, E. (2005). 'On Wittgenstein's Response to Scepticism: The Opening of *On Certainty*', in D. Moyal-Sharrock and W. H. Brenner eds., *Readings of Wittgenstein's On Certainty*. Basingstoke: Palgrave Macmillan.

Moore, G. E. (1925). 'A Defence of Common Sense', in J. H. Muirhead ed., *Contemporary British Philosophy* (2nd series). London: Allen and Unwin.

—— (1939). 'Proof of an External World', *Proceedings of the British Academy*, 25: 273–300.

MOYAL-SHARROCK, D. (2004). *Understanding Wittgenstein's On Certainty*. Basingstoke: Palgrave Macmillan.

NOZICK, R. (1981). *Philosophical Explanations*. Oxford: Oxford University Press.

PHILLIPS, D. Z. (2005). 'The Case of the Missing Propositions', in D. Moyal-Sharrock and W. H. Brenner eds., *Readings of Wittgenstein's On Certainty*. Basingstoke: Palgrave Macmillan.

PRITCHARD, D. H. (2002a). 'Recent Work on Radical Skepticism', *American Philosophical Quarterly*, 39: 215–57.

—— (2002b). 'Two Forms of Epistemological Contextualism', *Grazer Philosophische Studien*, 64: 97–134.

—— (2003). 'McDowell on Reasons, Externalism and Scepticism', *European Journal of Philosophy*, 11: 273–94.

—— (2004). 'Epistemic Deflationism', *The Southern Journal of Philosophy*, 42: 103–34.

—— (2005a). *Epistemic Luck*. Oxford: Oxford University Press.

—— (2005b). 'Wittgenstein's *On Certainty* and Contemporary Anti-Scepticism', in D. Moyal-Sharrock and W. H. Brenner eds., *Investigating On Certainty: Essays on Wittgenstein's Last Work*. Basingstoke: Palgrave Macmillan.

—— (2007). 'How to be a Neo-Moorean', in S. Goldberg ed., *Internalism and Externalism in Semantics and Epistemology*. Oxford: Oxford University Press.

—— (2008). 'McDowellian Neo-Mooreanism', in A. Haddock and F. Macpherson eds., *Disjunctivism: Perception, Action, Knowledge*. Oxford: Oxford University Press.

STANLEY, J. (2005). *Knowledge and Practical Interests*. Oxford: Oxford University Press.

STROLL, A. (1994). *Moore and Wittgenstein on Certainty*. Oxford: Oxford University Press.

STROUD, B. (1984). *The Significance of Philosophical Scepticism*. Oxford: Clarendon Press.

TRAVIS, C. (1989). *The Uses of Sense: Wittgenstein's Philosophy of Language*. Oxford: Oxford University Press.

WILLIAMS, M. (1991). *Unnatural Doubts: Epistemological Realism and the Basis of Scepticism*. Oxford: Blackwell.

—— (2003). 'Wittgenstein's Refutation of Idealism', in D. McManus ed., *Wittgenstein and Scepticism*. London: Routledge.

WITTGENSTEIN, L. (1969). *On Certainty*, ed. G. E. M. Anscombe and G. H. von Wright, trans. D. Paul and G. E. M. Anscombe. Oxford: Blackwell.

WRIGHT, C. (1985). 'Facts and Certainty', *Proceedings of the British Academy*, 71: 429–72.

—— (1991). 'Scepticism and Dreaming: Imploding the Demon', *Mind*, 397: 87–115.

—— (2000). 'Cogency and Question-Begging: Some Reflections on McKinsey's Paradox and Putnam's Proof', *Philosophical Issues*, 10: 140–63.

—— (2002). '(Anti-)Skeptics Simple and Subtle: G. E. Moore and John McDowell', *Philosophy and Phenomenological Research*, 65: 330–48.

—— (2003a). 'Some Reflections on the Acquisition of Warrant by Inference', in S. Nuccetelli ed., *New Essays on Semantic Externalism and Self-Knowledge*. Cambridge, MA: MIT Press.

—— (2003b). 'Wittgensteinian Certainties', in D. McManus ed., *Wittgenstein and Scepticism*. London: Routledge.

—— (2004a). 'Hinge Propositions and the Serenity Prayer', in W. Loffler and P. Weingartner eds., *Knowledge and Belief*. Vienna: Holder-Pickler-Tempsky.

—— (2004b). 'Scepticism, Certainty, Moore and Wittgenstein', in M. Kolbel and B. Weiss eds., *Wittgenstein's Lasting Significance*. London: Routledge.

—— (2004c). 'Warrant for Nothing (and Foundations for Free)?', *Proceedings of the Aristotelian Society*, 78 (supp. vol.): 167–212.

CHAPTER 24

....

WITTGENSTEIN AND MOORE

....

THOMAS BALDWIN

WITTGENSTEIN first encountered Moore when he came to Cambridge in autumn 1911. Moore had just been appointed a lecturer at Cambridge, and Wittgenstein soon let him know that he did not think much of his lectures. Nonetheless, and despite the fact that Moore was considerably older than Wittgenstein, they became friends and their relationship soon became one in which Wittgenstein was the teacher and Moore the pupil, as Moore recognized:

> When I did get to know him, I soon came to feel that he was much cleverer at philosophy than I was, and not only cleverer, but also much more profound, and with a much better insight into the sort of inquiry which was really important and best worth pursuing, and into the best method of pursuing such inquiries. (Moore 1942a, 33)

This early relationship culminated in Moore's visit to Norway in March 1914 during which Wittgenstein dictated his 'Notes on Logic' (Wittgenstein 1961) to Moore – though this was soon followed by a break in their relationship when Wittgenstein reacted angrily to Moore's letter informing him that under the University regulations the 'Notes on Logic' did not, as it stood, entitle Wittgenstein to the award of a Cambridge BA degree (Monk 1990, 103).

Their friendship was quickly resumed when Wittgenstein returned to Cambridge in 1929, and this time Moore was able to facilitate the award of a Cambridge degree to Wittgenstein – in this case the Ph.D. on the basis of the *Tractatus Logico-Philosophicus*.[1] Moore and Russell were Wittgenstein's 'examiners' and Moore famously wrote in his report: 'It is my personal opinion that Mr. Wittgenstein's thesis is a work of genius; but, be that as it may, it is certainly well up to the standard required for the Cambridge degree

---

[1] It was in fact Moore who had proposed this title for the English translation of *Logische-Philosophische Abhandlung*, thereby giving Wittgenstein's book the name by which it is now generally known.

of Doctor of Philosophy' (Monk 1990, 272). By this time Moore was editor of *Mind*, Professor of Philosophy at Cambridge, and widely respected as the leading British philosopher of the period. But although they met regularly for philosophical discussion and Wittgenstein greatly valued Moore's presence at his lectures, he did not engage much with Moore's philosophical position, presumably because he still judged Moore's general approach to philosophy to be unprofitable. He did, however, think that Moore had had some important insights whose value he (Moore) had not been able to exploit properly, and *On Certainty* shows Wittgenstein separating out Moore's mistakes from his insights concerning knowledge and certainty and then developing the latter.[2]

I *ON CERTAINTY* – THE TEXT

At the end of 1947 Wittgenstein left Cambridge, having resigned his professorship. He spent most of the next year and a half in Ireland before travelling to the USA in July 1949 to spend three months there as a guest of Norman Malcolm. Malcolm had recently published a paper 'Defending Common Sense' (Malcolm 1949) in which he took issue with Moore's defence of common sense, and he had just received a long letter from Moore rejecting Malcolm's criticisms (Moore 1993d). It is not surprising, therefore, that Malcolm's paper and Moore's response to it provided a ready topic for discussion between Malcolm and Wittgenstein; and one can see from the opening sections of *On Certainty* how Wittgenstein was stimulated to think in detail about these topics.

I will say more in the next section about the positions advanced by Moore and Malcolm which provide the context for the composition of *On Certainty*. Here I shall briefly describe the circumstances in which the text was composed. So far as is known, Wittgenstein did not write anything on the subject while he was staying with Malcolm. But soon after his return to Europe in autumn 1949 he travelled to Vienna to see his family and it seems likely that while he was there he wrote §§1–65, which now constitute the first part of *On Certainty*. In April 1950, having returned to England, he went to stay with Elizabeth Anscombe in Oxford and started a series of notebooks in which he set down what turned out to be his final philosophical reflections – on certainty, colour, 'the inner', and culture. Parts two, three, and four of *On Certainty* are the parts of these notebooks in which he discusses certainty. Towards the end, Wittgenstein noted the date on which he was writing, and as the published text of *On Certainty* indicates, part four begins 10 March 1951, by which time Wittgenstein had moved back to Cambridge. The last sections (§§670–6) have the date 27 April, just two days before his death.

---

[2] Another of Moore's insights which Wittgenstein identified and discussed concerns the absurdity of statements such as 'It's raining but I don't believe that it is'. Wittgenstein called this phenomenon 'Moore's Paradox' and discusses it in *Philosophical Investigations* II §x. For a recent survey of Moore's Paradox see Green and Williams (2007), esp. the editors' 'Introduction'.

The result is that the status of the text of *On Certainty* is quite unlike that of Wittgenstein's most famous works, *Tractatus Logico-Philosophicus* and *Philosophical Investigations*. *On Certainty* is an unrevised series of short paragraphs whose publication was neither planned nor overseen by Wittgenstein. Though the text itself comes straight from his notebooks, the title of the book and the numbering of the sections have been supplied by the editors. Thus in reading the book one is, so to speak, listening to Wittgenstein thinking aloud over a period of nearly two years on the topics of knowledge and certainty. Whatever the text lacks in overall structure and coherence is much more than made up for by the freshness of the thoughts presented here. It is a text which, more than any other, shows us directly the power and originality of Wittgenstein's philosophical imagination.

II MOORE AND MALCOLM

The first sentence of *On Certainty* is: 'If you do know that *here is one hand*, we'll grant you all the rest' (§1).[3] The allusion here is obvious: it is to Moore's famous 'proof' in his 1939 British Academy lecture 'Proof of an External World' (Moore 1993c) in which he maintained that simply by displaying his hand to his audience as an 'external thing' whose existence he certainly knew, he thereby proved to them the existence of the external world. Moore's proof is notoriously perplexing, and one task Wittgenstein undertakes is that of explaining why it fails even though what Moore says is, in a sense, true enough. Only a little bit further on in *On Certainty* (§6) Wittgenstein asks 'Now, can one enumerate what one knows (like Moore)? Straight off like that, I believe not.' Here the allusion is not to Moore's proof, but to his earlier 1925 paper 'A Defence of Common Sense' (Moore 1993b), in which Moore had listed a long list of common sense truisms 'every one of which (in my own opinion) I *know*, with certainty, to be true' (Moore 1993b, 106). One of these truisms is that 'the earth had existed for many years before my body was born', and Wittgenstein frequently uses this as an example of the things which Moore says he knows (e.g. §84ff.), but whose status, he thinks, Moore misunderstands and misrepresents.

It is therefore Moore's proof and Moore's defence which provide the initial dialectical context for Wittgenstein's accounts of knowledge and certainty. Indeed Moore is present throughout *On Certainty*, in two roles – as a rather eccentric character who likes to reassure others that he knows all sorts of things whose truth is obvious anyway, and as the famous philosopher whose attempts to use these odd claims to knowledge as a way of refuting sceptical philosophies has been a mistake. I will say much more later about Wittgenstein's critical response to Moore, but it is worth setting out briefly here some of the main themes of Moore's position, and then bringing in his debates with Malcolm, before concentrating thereafter on Wittgenstein's discussion.

---

[3] References such as this are to the numbered sections of *On Certainty*.

Moore first made a name for himself in philosophy as a critic of idealism,[4] and for him, as for Wittgenstein (see §24), scepticism was closely associated with idealism. So right from the start Moore was a critic of scepticism, particularly concerning knowledge of the external world, and his early response to philosophical sceptics of this kind was indeed to point to our normal certainty that we do have knowledge of this kind:

> But it seems to me a sufficient refutation of such views as these, simply to point to cases in which we do know such things. This, after all, you know, really is a finger: there is no doubt about it: I know it, and you all know it. (Moore 1922, 228)

By itself this affirmation of knowledge is just a denial of the sceptic's conclusion which fails to engage with the sceptic's argument. But Moore does have a little more to say, for the passage cited above continues:

> And I think we may safely challenge any philosopher to bring forward any argument in favour either of the proposition that we do not know it, or of the proposition that it is not true, which does not at some point, rest upon some premiss which is, beyond comparison, less certain than is the proposition which it is designed to attack. (Moore 1922, 228)

There is still a failure to engage with the details of sceptical arguments; but equally there is something right about Moore's challenge. For when the sceptical philosopher leaves his study, he too is content to speak with the vulgar and make the normal distinctions between what he knows and does not know. So even if Moore's 'refutation' is unpersuasive, it indicates something odd about the sceptical philosopher's position.

In writing 'A Defence of Common Sense' a few years later Moore was responding to an invitation to contribute a personal statement about his philosophical position for a collection of such statements by British philosophers.[5] This fact explains the style of the paper, in which Moore describes his 'Common Sense view of the world' by setting down a long list of 'truisms' which he takes himself to know with certainty and indeed takes to be common knowledge among 'very many' others. In setting out this position Moore is as critical of philosophical scepticism as ever, but he does not here employ a direct appeal to his readers' common sense knowledge to defend his position. Instead he argues that the sceptic's position is incoherent since the sceptic who asserts some general claims about the narrow limits of human knowledge commits himself thereby to knowledge of these limits (Moore 1993b, 117). This line of thought is disputable, but the thesis that assertion brings with it a claim to knowledge is an important one that recurs in *On Certainty*. A further point made by Moore is that one of the distinctive features of the common sense view of the world is that we do not know how we know the things which constitute it, such as that the earth has existed for many years before our birth:

> We are all, I think, in this strange position that we do *know* many things, with regard to which we *know* further that we must have had evidence for them, and yet we do

---

[4] As in his 1903 paper 'The Refutation of Idealism'; reprinted as Moore (1993a).

[5] The volume is *Contemporary British Philosophy*, second series, ed. J. Muirhead, London: Allen & Unwin, 1925.

not know *how* we know them, i.e. we do not know what the evidence was. (Moore 1993b, 118)

As we shall see, this is a line of thought which Wittgenstein takes much further in *On Certainty*.

It has seemed to many that in his 1939 'Proof of an External World' Moore reverted to the format of his earlier anti-sceptical argument, waving his hands at philosophical sceptics and challenging them to deny that he did know of their existence ('You might as well suggest that I do not know that I am now standing up and talking – that perhaps after all I'm not, and that it's not quite certain that I am!' Moore 1993c, 166–7). But in fact Moore limits himself here to offering a proof of the existence of an external world, and not a proof that he knows of the existence of an external world. The claim to knowledge comes in only because Moore takes it that to prove anything one needs to know the truth of the premises one asserts, in this case that he knows what he asserts when saying 'Here is one hand, and here is another'; and although, as the remark cited shows, Moore emphatically maintains that he does know this, he does not attempt to prove that he does. One result of this, however, is that the significance of Moore's proof is unclear: according to John Wisdom, Wittgenstein's ironic comment was that 'Those philosophers who have denied the existence of Matter have not wished to deny that under my trousers I wear pants' (Wisdom 1942, 431).

One person who did mistake Moore's intent in his proof, and interpreted him as maintaining that one could prove that one has knowledge of the external world just by holding up one of one's hands and declaring 'I know that this is a hand', was Norman Malcolm, who attributed this claim to Moore in his contribution to *The Philosophy of G. E. Moore* (Malcolm 1942). Malcolm went on to argue that although claims to knowledge cannot be empirically vindicated in this way, Moore's claim is 'a paradigm of absolute certainty' (Malcolm 1942, 354) and as such constitutes a refutation of sceptical doubt in virtue of the fact that it exemplifies the standard for our use of the language of knowledge and certainty. In his reply to Malcolm in the same volume, however, Moore made it clear that this had certainly not been his intention; and he further explained that it was his view that exemplary affirmations of first-person knowledge, however paradigmatic, do not provide by themselves a sufficient refutation of scepticism: 'further argument is called for' (Moore 1942b, 669). Just what this argument might be Moore does not here specify, but if one looks ahead to Moore's two final papers on this topic, 'Four Forms of Scepticism' (Moore 1959), and 'Certainty' (Moore 1993e), it seems that Moore took it that one needed to be able to bring forward evidence which would enable one to eliminate sceptical possibilities such as that one was dreaming. Notoriously, by the end of 'Certainty' (Moore 1993e, 194), Moore found himself unable to do this, and thus unable to refute scepticism, despite his lifelong anti-sceptical affirmations.

Meanwhile Malcolm, having appreciated that Moore's position was not that which he had initially taken it to be, shifted to the view that there was in fact something deeply wrong about Moore's position, in that it rested on claims to knowledge which, so far from being paradigmatic, in fact involve a 'misuse' of language of the kind which implies that these claims are 'without sense' (Malcolm 1949, 202). So in 'Defending Common Sense' Malcolm argues that first-person claims to knowledge only make sense where the person making the claim is able to explain how he knows what he does because he has carried out an investigation which resolves some substantive doubt. According to Malcolm, however, Moore's claims to knowledge (both in his 'Defence' and in his 'Proof') are presented by him as so completely uncontentious that his audience will have no doubts at all about them and will therefore be able to recognize their truth without any investigation. Malcolm uses an example which Wittgenstein later takes up, of Moore saying to him 'I know that that's a tree' when they were both sitting in front of a tree in Moore's garden in Cambridge. In this case, Malcolm maintains, there was no question at issue, no investigation to be undertaken, and nothing more certain than the presence before them of the tree which Moore could adduce as evidence for his claim that he then knew of the tree's presence. So, Malcolm concludes, Moore's claim was nonsense. To say this is not to say that it was false, and thus that the sceptic's denial of knowledge would be correct; for that too would be nonsense in the context in question.

Moore rejected Malcolm's criticism, arguing that there is a distinction between a pragmatic or conversational conception of what it would be senseless to say in a given context and a semantic conception of meaning or sense which is not dependent upon conversational context. Thus, discussing the case of him saying to Malcolm 'I know that's a tree' where Malcolm was beside him and could see the tree perfectly well, Moore remarks:

> It is perfectly possible that a person who uses [these words] senselessly, in the sense that he uses them where no sensible person would use them because, under those circumstances, they serve no useful purpose, should be using them *in their usual sense*, & that what he asserts by so using them should be *true*. (Moore 1993d, 215; my interpolation)[6]

As Malcolm subsequently observed (Malcolm 1977, 178), Moore's general distinction between the conversational and semantic is fair enough; but whether it deals with the case in hand remains questionable. As we shall see below, Wittgenstein argues that the context-dependence of claims to knowledge is not just a matter of conversational propriety.

This brief survey of the positions of Moore and Malcolm has been motivated by the assumption that these positions set the stage for Wittgenstein's *On Certainty*. But at this point a couple of qualifications should be introduced. First, although Malcolm says that it was through his discussions of these issues with Wittgenstein that Wittgenstein 'suddenly became absorbed in a subject matter that had not previously captured his attention' (Malcolm 1977, 172 fn. 9), this cannot be quite right. For there are some lecture notes from 1937 in which Wittgenstein sets out briefly several of the main themes of *On*

---

[6] Malcolm quotes Moore's letter to him in his helpful paper 'Moore and Wittgenstein on the Sense of "I know"' in which he describes Wittgenstein's visit to Ithaca and their conversations there; see Malcolm (1977), 174.

Certainty.[7] Hence the role of Malcolm's discussion was in fact to prompt the revival and development of some earlier ideas. Second, in the very first section of *On Certainty*, as well as alluding to Moore's 'Proof', Wittgenstein refers parenthetically to 'a curious remark by H. Newman'. This is likely to be a reference to J. H. Newman's *An Essay in aid of A Grammar of Assent* (Newman 1985) which it is known that Wittgenstein had read with interest. It is not obvious what remark Wittgenstein has in mind, but there is no doubt that some of Newman's reflections on 'certitude' resemble Wittgenstein's comments (Kienzler 2006). So there is here a possible further stimulus for Wittgenstein's reflections, though not one to displace the evident influence of Moore and Malcolm.

III *On Certainty*, Part One: §§1–65

As I have indicated, part one of *On Certainty* was written in rather different circumstances from the other parts. One can think of it as Wittgenstein's first attempt to make clear to himself what he thought about the issues he had been discussing with Malcolm a few months earlier, and three themes predominate: the nature of Moore's mistake, the way to understand Malcolm's claim that Moore's claims to knowledge have no sense, and the way the Moore–Malcolm debate relates to critical discussion of idealism and scepticism.

Moore's main mistake, Wittgenstein alleges, is that of thinking that we have the same kind of first-person authority with respect to first-person claims to knowledge as we have with respect to first-person avowals of belief or doubt (§6, §21; Wittgenstein later suggests that Moore thinks that 'I know' is comparable in this respect to 'I am in pain' – §178). Whether Moore was really guilty of this mistake is, I think, questionable;[8] but the important issue here is what the status of first-person claims to knowledge amounts to. For Wittgenstein these claims are generally an assurance that one is not making a mistake about the matter in hand (§15), and this leads him into a discussion of the way in which questions about the possibility of mistakes arise. The striking thesis which he advances is that mastery of a language-game includes a grasp of the circumstances under which these questions arise, and thus that their identification belongs to the 'logic' of the language-game (§56). So in learning to calculate we learn to recognize where mistakes are possible and, equally, where they do not occur, and this distinction is part of the logic of the concepts (§51). In drawing this distinction we do not follow a rule (§44); instead we apply a skill which we learned when we learned to calculate. This point applies generally: our understanding of where mistakes are possible in the case of observation is not a matter of our explicitly following a rule. Instead there is a range of cases, from observing a planet to observing one's hand: but the difference between them is not just a matter of the decreasing chance of a mistake – at some point a mistake is no longer conceivable (§54).

---

[7] This material is reprinted in PO; see esp. pp. 377–99.

[8] In effect this is what Moore denies in his reply to Malcolm; see Moore (1942b), 668.

Since this logic determines the limits of sense, it follows that where mistakes are not conceivable, doubt 'loses its sense' (§56); equally, it might seem, in these circumstances first-person claims to knowledge become logical propositions, so that neither 'I know' nor 'I do not know' makes sense – just as Malcolm had proposed concerning Moore's claims. Wittgenstein lays out this line of thought (§§57–8), but he does not clearly endorse it: it is presented only as a suggestion to be considered alongside the fact that one can hear Moore's claim to know about his hand as just the dismissal of any practical doubt about the matter (§19). But since he goes on to remark that the idealist is not interested in practical doubts and their resolution, his argument against Moore can be put as a dilemma. Where Moore's claim makes sense, it is because Moore is legitimately dismissing practical doubts concerning his hand's existence; but this is not the kind of consideration the idealist is concerned with when he doubts the existence of the external world (§20). The idealist's doubt is conceptual or logical; hence, on the face of it, the only kind of claim to knowledge which might be used in the course of a refutation of this doubt would be one whose status was similarly logical. But at this point, the thesis that no such claim to knowledge makes sense does undermine the thought that idealism could be refuted in this way; as Wittgenstein puts it '"I know" is here a *logical* insight. Only realism can't be proved by means of it' (§59).

How then is one to proceed in clarifying the errors made both by the sceptical idealist and the Moorean realist? In this first part of *On Certainty* Wittgenstein comments that all this talk of what makes sense or not, even if it is right, is not likely to be convincing, either to the idealist or to the realist. So 'a further investigation is needed in order to find the right point of attack for the critic' (§37).

IV *On Certainty*, Parts Two and Three: §§66–192, §§193–299

These next two parts of *On Certainty* belong together. They were both written while Wittgenstein was staying in Oxford, and since the division between them appears to be just the result of the fact that MS 174 ends at §192 while MS 175 begins with §193, it may well be that there was in fact no significant gap between their composition.[9] In these sections Wittgenstein commences his investigation by returning to the question of what it is to make a mistake or to have a significant doubt, and argues that both are possible only on condition that we have a background 'picture of the world' (§94) which is largely true and 'stands fast' (*feststeht*) for us (§112), and which is therefore exempt both from idealist criticism and from sceptical doubt. But, equally, it is not something whose truth we can legitimately claim to know, as the Moorean realist would like to maintain (§151), though towards the end of part three Wittgenstein expresses some uncertainty on this last point (§272, §288).

---

[9] See the 'Addendum to the "The Wittgenstein Papers"', PO, 509.

The first stage in this line of thought is an argument concerning the conditions for the possibility of mistakes and significant doubt. In the case of mistakes Wittgenstein argues that making a mistake is not simply a matter of being wrong about something; instead 'roughly: when someone makes a mistake, this can be fitted into what he knows aright' (§74). Notice the reference here to 'what he knows aright'; Wittgenstein soon expresses doubts about this and suggests that knowledge is not required – 'Suppose I replaced Moore's "I know" by "I am of the unshakeable conviction"?' (§86). I shall come back to this question, but Wittgenstein's main point is that mistakes are possible only against a background of beliefs which are not mistaken. An arithmetical mistake, for example, is recognizable as an attempt at a calculation only because some of the basic moves made in the course of the calculation are right (§217). The thesis which grounds this requirement is that although in attributing a mistake to someone we are attributing to them a belief whose falsehood counts against this very attribution, the presumption against this attribution is overturned where the belief is associated for the thinker with other more basic beliefs which are largely true and which show that the person understands what they are talking about: 'In order to make a mistake, a man must already judge in conformity with mankind' (§156) because 'if I make certain false statements, it becomes uncertain whether I understand them' (§81). So, Wittgenstein infers, 'The *truth* of certain empirical propositions belongs to our frame of reference' (§83).

In the case of doubt Wittgenstein's thesis is that 'Doubt comes *after* belief' (§160). In part this is a thesis about the temporal order in which we acquire these capacities: Wittgenstein the former school-teacher remarks that children learn by trusting both those who teach them (§159, §283) and the textbooks they use (§162, §263). But the deeper thesis here is conceptual, or logical: doubt requires grounds (§§122–3), and grounds are constituted by beliefs which are not in doubt. In part the argument for this thesis is like that used in connection with mistakes and concerns the content of what is doubted, the meaning of the statements by which doubts are expressed: 'I am not more certain of the meaning of my words than I am of certain judgments. Can I doubt that this colour is called "blue"?' (§126). But Wittgenstein also argues that where someone appears to doubt something for no reason, we lose our grip on what counts as a reason for them, and thus on whether their doubt is genuine (§231, §255). So, Wittgenstein infers, the philosophical sceptic's attempt at universal doubt is problematic: 'If you tried to doubt everything you would not get as far as doubting anything. The game of doubting itself presupposes certainty' (§115).

A philosophical sceptic may well object that this argument moves too quickly: for example it does not show what is unsatisfactory about the kind of sceptical argument which finally ensnared Moore by introducing the possibility that one is dreaming. We shall see in the next section that Wittgenstein returns to this issue in part four, so setting that aside now, I turn to Wittgenstein's account of the 'picture of the world' which is presupposed by the possibility of mistakes and doubts. Wittgenstein's first step is to appropriate for this role the common sense truisms of Moore's 'defence' (§§84–91, §234). Moore, as we saw above, maintains that these truisms have a 'strange' epistemological status, whereby although we do know them, we do not know how we know them. Wittgenstein questions whether we do know them at all and reinterprets their epistemological status as privileged starting points which we rely on in making sense of our experience:

§136   When Moore says he *knows* such and such, he is really enumerating a lot of empirical propositions which we affirm without special testing; propositions, that is, which have a peculiar logical role in the system of our empirical propositions.

This conception of their role is brilliantly captured by a metaphor in which they are compared to the banks of a river: they function likes the banks of a river in making possible the flow of water, that is, the verification and falsification of ordinary empirical propositions (§§96–7). Equally, though, sometimes the banks of the river themselves shift, i.e. some aspects of this common sense picture of the world are modified in the light of experience:

§99   And the bank of that river consists partly of hard rock, subject to no alteration or only to an imperceptible one, partly of sand, which now in one place now in another gets washed away, or deposited.

Thus although we are here dealing with an epistemological distinction between propositions whose truth 'stands fast' for us and others whose truth is an open question, we are not here dealing with a priori truths as traditionally conceived. Indeed Wittgenstein remarks that although our basic picture of the world has a special role within our web of belief, this role depends on the credibility of the whole system of beliefs that we thereby form (§142).

So far it is just Moore's defence that Wittgenstein has reinterpreted; what about his 'proof'? When Moore exhibited his hands to his audience he remarked he could not prove the truth of what he then asserted since there was nothing he could adduce as evidence for it which was more certain than the presence there of his hands. Wittgenstein agrees with Moore about this point (§250) but adds that it would be absurd to suppose that in this way one can prove the existence of an external world: such beliefs are 'part of the whole *picture* which forms the starting-point of belief for me' (§209). Thus, while rejecting Moore's proof as such, Wittgenstein takes from it a recognition of the special status of empirical judgements such as 'This is a hand' which we make without applying a rule (§140). Although we are not infallible with respect to these judgements, it is part of the logic of our language-games that there is a presumption that they are correct. So they do not need to be justified by an empirical theory about the reliability of experience: 'experience is not the ground for our game of judging' (§131). A similar point applies to judgements about the future: we have the practice of making inductive predictions, but in making them we do not reason from 'a universal law of induction' (§133):

§287   The squirrel does not infer by induction that it is going to need stores next winter as well. And no more do we need a law of induction to justify our actions or our predictions.

Thus although Moore's proof was misguided, his argument can be reinterpreted to indicate the fundamental role of ordinary practices for making judgements within our 'whole system of propositions'. These practices are not themselves part of our basic picture of the world, but they are the ungrounded ways in which we fill out this picture in the light of experience.

At this point the status of this picture of the world needs to be considered. As we have seen, in these sections of *On Certainty* Wittgenstein often suggests that with respect to these basic propositions Moorean claims to knowledge are inappropriate, largely because, as Moore himself acknowledged, there is nothing one can bring forward to justify one's claim to knowledge (§175). But towards the end of part three, he begins to express doubts on this issue. Having declared that he will be guided by the uses of 'I know' in 'normal linguistic exchange' (§260), he acknowledges that when Moore affirmed that his common sense view of the world was a matter of common knowledge, he was saying just the kind of thing we do say: 'And why shouldn't I say that I know all this? Isn't that what one does say?' (§288). The matter is then left open at the end of part three and Wittgenstein returns to it with a more sophisticated approach in part four of *On Certainty* which I discuss below.

Where Wittgenstein is unequivocal, however, is in his view that our picture of the world is one that stands fast for us (§151), and since that which stands fast for us is certain, this is the aspect of his position that the editors used in giving the book its title, *über Gewissheit (On Certainty)*. But there is a complication here: as well as *Gewissheit* and cognate terms Wittgenstein also uses the word *Sicherheit* and cognate terms (e.g. §§183–5). The translators do not note this difference, and in many contexts it is no doubt unimportant; but it may be significant where the issue of the relationship between knowledge and certainty is raised. When, towards the end of part three, Wittgenstein is reconsidering whether we do know Moore's truisms, he introduces the proposal *Ich weiß = Es ist mir als gewiß bekannt* (§272: 'I know = I am familiar with it as a certainty'), and here the etymological connection between *wissen* and *Gewissheit* makes this proposal a very natural one. But when at the start of part four (§308) he maintains '"Knowledge" and 'certainty' belong to different *categories*' he uses the term *Sicherheit*, and it seems to me that it is in fact *Sicherheit* which best expresses Wittgenstein's conception of the status of our fundamental picture of the world, as that which is *sicher*, or stands fast for us[10] – though I should add that *Sicherheit* could not sensibly be used in the book's title, since in ordinary German the word is used to mean security in general, and not just epistemic security, i.e. certainty.

What about the truth of our picture of the world? Initially Wittgenstein unequivocally affirms its truth (§§80–3); but then he appears to qualify this: it 'might be part of a kind of mythology' (§95); and he later comments, concerning the 'hypothesis' of the existence of the earth long before one's birth: 'is it certainly true? One may designate it as such – But does it certainly agree with reality, with the facts? – With this question you are already going round in a circle' (§191). I take it, however, that Wittgenstein is here just rejecting a correspondence conception of truth which commits one to a substantive conception (semantic and/or epistemological) of the 'agreement' between a statement and a fact, which he takes to be illusory (§199). It is consistent with this, then, to attribute to Wittgenstein a lightweight (deflationary) conception of truth of the kind affirmed in *Philosophical Investigations* §136. For what concerns Wittgenstein is not really the issue of truth but that of justification, or rather its absence: 'To be sure there is justification; but justification comes to an end' (§192) and the important, but difficult, task 'is to realize the groundlessness of our believing' (§166).

---

[10] In part four of *On Certainty* Wittgenstein almost always uses *Sicherheit* and cognate terms. One exception is in §415; but here he uses *Gewissheit* as well as *Sicherheit* to suggest a contrast which is lost in the translation.

As Wittgenstein recognizes, this thesis invites the anxiety that the objectivity of belief has been undermined (§108) because it suggests that we can have no good reason for ruling out alternative pictures of the world. He considers two main types of example: Roman Catholic beliefs, e.g. concerning the virgin birth of Jesus and transubstantiation (§239), which he regards as incredible; and also the beliefs of more or less imaginary tribes who believe such things as that people sometimes travel to the moon (§106).[11] For when we confront these tribes, he argues, we should not expect to be able to demonstrate to them that they are wrong. He illustrates this point with a nice tale about a meeting between the king of some tribe and Moore, who is here cast in the role of the missionary of the Church of Common Sense:

> Men have believed that they could make rain; why should not a king be brought up in the belief that the world began with him? And if Moore and this king were to meet and discuss, could Moore really prove his belief to be the right one? I do not say that Moore could not convert the king to his view, but it would be a conversion of a special kind; the king would be brought to look at the world in a special way. (§92)

Wittgenstein's response to this relativist anxiety is that even if our picture of the world is 'groundless' it is not 'a more or less arbitrary and doubtful point of departure for all our arguments' (§105); instead it is the context in which these arguments 'have their life', that is, in which all our reasonings function by directing us to beliefs which we cannot both endorse as rational and reflectively bracket as arbitrary. So although we have to acknowledge that there is an inescapable plurality of standards of rationality (§336), the internal logic of rational belief directs us away from a sceptical relativism to the conviction that the only reasons we can make sense of sustain our own system of beliefs. There is always scope for disagreement; but where someone appears to hold beliefs whose rationale conflicts with our fundamental picture of the world, we can only be amazed by them. For Wittgenstein the paradigm of this is the conflict between religious and secular views of the world; indeed one might say that for him even the secular view involves a groundless 'faith' (note that in the passage cited above from §92 Wittgenstein writes of Moore's 'conversion' of the king to his point of view). In radical disagreements it is not that the parties literally do not understand each other (Wittgenstein understood Catholic beliefs perfectly well); it is that they do not understand how each other could believe, or fail to believe, some fundamental propositions.

V ON CERTAINTY, PART FOUR: §§300–676

Part four is the longest part of *On Certainty*; indeed it comprises more than half of the text. It was written during the last two months of Wittgenstein's life, after he had left Oxford and was staying at Dr. Bevan's house in Cambridge. Although the early sections

---

[11] The belief that no one has ever been on the moon is a good case of a Moore-type proposition whose status has changed, from being a truism to an empirical falsehood: in this area, one might say, the banks of the river of belief have shifted.

of part four (§§300–425) continue the same manuscript book as part three (MS 175), the dates in the text show that there was a gap of nearly six months between the composition of the final section of part three (§299) and the start of part four. The remainder of part four is contained in two other manuscript books (§§426–637 in MS 176; §§638–76 in MS 177), but the consecutive dates in the text indicate that the change from one manuscript book to another has no significance.

To some extent Wittgenstein here repeats and refines lines of thought he has previously advanced, though there is no explicit reference back to earlier passages. Thus he again distinguishes between making a mistake and being wrong about something: to imagine that it somehow turns out that $12 \times 12 \neq 144$ is not to imagine that we have made a mistake about this – it is to imagine that our technique of calculation was fundamentally confused (§§303–4). In his previous discussion this point was related to our having a picture of the world which stands fast for us; and this is reiterated in a striking new metaphor:

> §341   That is to say, the *questions* that we raise and our *doubts* depend on the fact that some propositions are exempt from doubt, are as it were hinges on which those turn.

These hinge-propositions are the banks of the river of his previous metaphor (§97ff.): they stand fast for us precisely so that other propositions can turn, i.e. be called into question. As such, these propositions, he now says, 'form the foundation of all operating with thoughts (with language)' (§401), a remark which he clarifies by saying that they are not foundations in the same way as 'hypotheses which, if they turn out to be false, are replaced by others' (§402). Hypotheses of this kind are the fundamental postulates of a theoretical science, and Wittgenstein's hinge-propositions do not have this role. He then adds enigmatically a famous line from Goethe's *Faust*: "*Im Anfang war die Tat*" ("In the beginning was the deed"). The significance of this comment is best gathered from the passage in his 1937 lecture notes on 'Cause and Effect' in which he quotes the same line from Goethe:

> The origin and primitive form of the language game is a reaction; only from this can more complicated forms develop.
>   Language – I want to say – is a refinement. "*Im Anfang war die Tat.*"
>   First there must be firm, hard stone for building, and the blocks are laid rough-hewn one on another. *Afterwards* it is indeed important that the stone can be trimmed, that it's not *too* hard.
>   The primitive form of the language game is certainty (*Sicherheit*), not uncertainty. For uncertainty could never lead to action. (PO, 396–7)

Thus the foundational role (as 'firm hard stone') of the hinge-propositions is to be understood in terms of the conditions under which language-games are possible. Because these are practices in which language and behaviour are integrated for the achievement of goals such as building a house, the thoughts expressed in the language must facilitate these goals, and this brings a presumption of certainty; for 'uncertainty could never lead to action'. In part four of *On Certainty* this line of thought is connected with an allusion to our 'animal' being. He observes that our having a view of the world which is certain is not a matter of 'hastiness or superficiality' on our part; instead it is a 'form of life' (§358), and he continues: 'But that means I want to conceive it as something that lies beyond being justified or unjustified; as it were, as something animal' (§359). This last comment can be understood by reference to a later section:

> §475   I want to regard man here as an animal; as a primitive being to which one grants instinct but not ratiocination. As a creature in a primitive state. Any logic good enough for a primitive means of communication needs no apology from us. Language did not emerge from some kind of ratiocination.

So Wittgenstein's thought is that certainty is 'animal' in the sense that it is antecedent to 'ratiocination' (a slightly odd translation of the French word *raisonnement* which Wittgenstein uses). Reasoning brings with it evidence, criticism, argument, and justification; but these presuppose a background conception of the world which stands fast for us and is 'beyond being justified or unjustified.' This conception of the world is therefore characteristic of man 'as an animal' or 'as a primitive being'. The order of dependence here is both evolutionary, in a broad sense, and also logical: the basic abilities we need to attribute to ourselves include the capacity to have a view of the world which stands fast for us, for only with this in place does it make sense to attribute to ourselves a capacity for justification.

At this point I want to return to the issue of doubt and philosophical scepticism. Wittgenstein again insists that doubt requires grounds (§458), so that where what is doubted is such as to undermine its own grounds, doubt becomes not just unreasonable but empty (§454). As I mentioned in the previous section, however, it is not clear how this consideration shows what is unsatisfactory about sceptical arguments which invoke the possibility that one is dreaming in order to undermine confidence in knowledge of the external world. Wittgenstein does now address this challenge:

> §383   The argument 'I may be dreaming' is senseless for this reason: if I am dreaming, this remark is being dreamed as well – and indeed it is also being dreamed that these words have any meaning.

The thought here seems to be that the sceptic's suggestion that one might be dreaming can be dismissed on the grounds that the suggestion undermines itself, in that if it were true it would be meaningless, and thus that if it is not meaningless it must be false. This does not strike me as persuasive: let it be granted that if I am dreaming then my dream-remark 'I may be dreaming' has no meaning; it does not follow that in my dream the dream-remark may not appear to me to have a meaning. Hence the apparent meaningfulness to me now of the remark 'I may be dreaming' is no evidence for me that I am not now dreaming. In the very last section of *On Certainty* (§676) Wittgenstein returns to the issue and suggests that the possibility of dreams is no basis for sceptical doubt because 'I cannot seriously suppose that I am at this moment dreaming.' Again: the philosophical sceptic can grant Wittgenstein his premise; but he will object that it does not follow that while I am dreaming it cannot appear to me that I seriously suppose that I am dreaming. The issue, as ever with scepticism, is whether there is any evidence to distinguish deceptive from non-deceptive appearances. Wittgenstein's suggestion seems to be that the existence of meaning or 'serious supposition' provides such evidence; but as long as it is granted that there can be deceptive appearances of meaning or serious supposition, this line of thought is unconvincing.

There is more to be said here, but this is not the place to pursue the matter. Instead I want to go back to the line of thought which locates the certainty of our picture of the world in the conception of man as an animal; for this provides the basis of a different and, I think, more effective response to sceptical arguments. For Wittgenstein's conception of our basic certainties as part of our 'animal' nature implies that these are 'groundless' beliefs which we hold for no reason. Hence our assent to them need not be undermined by the sceptic's reasoning: although the sceptic suggests that we should withhold assent to them because they are called into question by the possibility he introduces, such as that we are dreaming (or whatever), the fact that these beliefs are pre-rational provides us with ever-renewed grounds to dismiss this possibility. This may sound at first like a dogmatic rejection of scepticism, but when Wittgenstein puts the point, he does so in a way which deflects this charge:

> §498   The queer thing is that even though I find it quite correct for someone to say 'Rubbish!' and so brush aside the attempt to confuse him with doubts at Bedrock, – nevertheless, I hold it to be incorrect if he seeks to defend himself (using, e.g., the words 'I know').

Our 'bedrock' certainties are not beliefs with a privileged epistemic status that resists sceptical argument; instead they are 'natural' dispositions, which makes them, given that they are held for no reason, inaccessible to the sceptic's rationalist argument.

So far I have been describing ways in which, in part four, Wittgenstein develops themes already present in the earlier sections of *On Certainty*. But there is one topic which belongs predominantly to part four, the topic of knowledge. At the end of part three Wittgenstein had wavered on the question as to whether Moore really knows the kinds of thing he claims to know; in part four he develops and delivers a new approach to this issue. The starting point is the thesis that '"Knowledge" and "certainty" belong to different *categories*. They are not two "mental states" like, say, "surmising" and "being certain"' (§308). So if being certain is a mental state, then knowledge is not; but what is it then? Wittgenstein's approach is to follow the maxim already affirmed of concentrating on normal uses of 'I know' (§260), which leads him to formulate several suggestions, of which the following is a representative selection:

> §330   So here the sentence 'I know...' expresses the readiness to believe certain things.
> §357   One might say: '"I know" expresses *comfortable* certainty, not the certainty that is still struggling.'
> §§379–80   I say with passion 'I *know* that this is a foot' – but what does it mean? I might go on: 'Nothing in the world will convince me of the opposite!' For me this fact is at the bottom of all knowledge. I shall give up other things but not this.

§424   I say 'I know p' either to assure people that I, too, know the truth p, or simply as an emphasis of |-p…

§§483–4   The correct use of the expression 'I know'.…In these cases, then, one says 'I know' and mentions how one knows, or at least can do so.

§561   'I know' and 'You can rely on it'. But one cannot always substitute the latter for the former.

It seems at first that there are too many different lines of thought here for there to be any determinate shape to Wittgenstein's reflections. But as the sections proceed one question becomes predominant, namely what the use of 'I know' and cognate terms adds to a language-game (§443, §564). Wittgenstein's answer to this is that suggested in §424 and §561 – 'Thus the purpose of the phrase "I know" might be to indicate where I can be relied on' (§575); but he goes on to add 'but where that's what it's doing, the usefulness of this sign must emerge from *experience*'. So my simply saying 'I know' is no guarantee of my reliability (it is not, so to speak, a performative speech-act comparable to promising); instead to use the phrase properly is to use it where I am in a position to know or have evidence which enables me to say how I know, as §§483–4 suggest. And if I then strongly emphasize my claim in the way described in §§379–80, it is likely to be because I want to insist to others that they should take my word for it because I am indeed in a position to know such a thing, and that nothing they or others can say will convince me otherwise.

Before we take this any further, however, some attention needs to be given to a different issue which Wittgenstein raises: 'isn't the use of the word "know" as a pre-eminently philosophical word altogether wrong? If "know" has this interest, why not "being certain"?' (§415). As he goes on to remark, the immediate response, namely that knowledge, unlike certainty (*Sicherheit*), implies truth, is not convincing, given that it is the account of certainty which, on the face of it, provides a robust response to the arguments of idealist and sceptics. Wittgenstein's response to his question comes towards the end of part four when he remarks 'And the concept of knowing is coupled with that of the language-game' (§560). This is followed by the comment which associates 'I know' with 'You can rely on it' (§561 – see above); and then by the injunction 'to imagine a language in which *our* concept "knowledge" does not exist' (§562), where, as the succeeding sections indicate, what Wittgenstein has in mind is a language in which 'know' and cognate terms are not overtly employed. Wittgenstein's discussion of this last hypothesis leads to the conclusion that much of our talk of knowledge is a way of making explicit who can be relied on as an informant or guide (§575). As §424 indicates, however, in making a simple assertion in the first place, we already represent ourselves as reliable informants, so that what use of the concept of knowledge achieves is to make explicit within a language a presumption that is there already, that 'the fact that I assert this gives to understand that I think I know it' (§588). As Wittgenstein observes, one common way in which this presumption is manifest is in the way in which it is appropriate to ask 'How do you know?' when someone makes a simple assertion, e.g. 'That's a zebra' (§588). Hence to go back to §560: the way in which the concept of knowing is coupled with that of the language-game is that insofar as a language-game involves assertions, as all normal ones do because of their involvement with action, a presumption of knowledge is inherent in the practice even if it is not overt in the language.

Once this point is taken, it is easy to see the importance of questions about knowledge. Equally, it is easy to see in general how ordinary claims to knowledge, understood as claims to epistemic authority, should then be assessed. For such claims to authority quite properly lead to questions about the possibility of mistakes and other grounds for doubt, and thus back to the considerations already explored concerning the status of our basic understanding of the world and ourselves. Although Wittgenstein was not in general a sceptic, nothing in his approach rules out challenges through such inquiries to putative kinds of knowledge, as his remark about the impossibility of knowledge of sensations indicates:

§504   Whether I *know* something depends on whether the evidence backs me up or contradicts me. For to say one knows one has a pain means nothing.

But the claims to knowledge that Wittgenstein is most concerned to assess in *On Certainty* are of course Moore's claims. Wittgenstein emphasizes two initial points here: first, Moore's assertions of knowledge, however emphatic, do not show that he does know – 'Moore's mistake lies in this – countering the assertion that one cannot know that, by saying "I do know it"' (§521). For 'whether I *know* something depends on whether the evidence backs me up or contradicts me' (§504). His second point, essentially that emphasized by Malcolm, is that what is odd about Moore's claims to knowledge is that they are typically made in a way which detaches them from the kind of context in which they would be unproblematic:

§347   'I know that that's a tree.' Why does it strike me as if I did not understand the sentence?…It is as if I could not focus my mind on any meaning….As soon as I think of an ordinary use of the sentence instead of a philosophical one, its meaning becomes clear and ordinary.

It is clear how this point applies to the common sense 'truisms' of Moore's defence; precisely because these are truisms, it is hard to see the point of a claim to knowledge here. With respect to the knowledge claims inherent in Moore's proof, however, ('I know that this is a hand', 'I know that that's a tree'), the issue is slightly different. Because Moore wants his proof to be unproblematic, he wants it to have premises whose assertion by him is minimally contentious; thus he picks premises such as 'Here's a hand/tree' whose truth will be obvious to his audience. By doing so, however, he lays himself open to Malcolm's complaint that because the truth of these premises is so obvious, his claim to know them is senseless. Moore's reply to this is that although *saying* 'I know…' in these cases is indeed very odd, it does not follow that it is incorrect. After all, the audience could rely on Moore on this matter although there was no reason for them to do so; and Wittgenstein makes an observation which counts in favour of Moore here, namely that a third person attribution of knowledge can be sensible in a situation where a first person claim sounds odd (§353); for in these Moorean cases, a third person attribution of knowledge does seem a good deal more sensible than the first person claim. So Moore's claim to know 'Here's a hand' (etc.) looks defensible. In fact, so far as I see, it was not essential to Moore's proof to rely on these extremely obvious truths; if premises whose truth is less obvious are required for him to substantiate the claims to knowledge implicit in his assertion of his premises, then Moore could acquiesce in that conclusion and pick a premise which is not immediately obvious to his audience (e.g. 'There are three misprints on this page', Moore 1993c, 167). His proof would still go through and its significance, whatever it is, would be unaffected by this change. But in the present context what is of interest here is not really Moore's proof at all; instead it is precisely the thesis that it makes sense to say that one knows such things as that 'that's a tree' or that 'this is a hand' for which one cannot adduce any evidence which is more certain than the claim one is making.

Thus what is at issue here is whether it is appropriate to apply the concept of knowledge to propositions which are either themselves truistic hinge-propositions which belong to our basic view of the world or matters of such immediate obviousness ('Here's a hand', '$12 \times 12 = 144$') that we cannot adduce in their favour any considerations which constitute evidence for them. The argument against saying this is that if, as proposed above, attributions of knowledge are not descriptions of a specially watertight mental state possessed by someone irrespective of their situation but, instead, claims to the effect that, concerning that which is said to be known, the audience should take the speaker's word for it in the current situation, then if what the speaker says is as obvious to the audience as it is to the speaker, there is no reason for them to rely on the speaker's word. On the other hand, given that assertion generally implies a claim to knowledge, it is not easy to see why this general principle should be qualified just because what is asserted is so obvious that the speaker cannot be mistaken about it. Indeed perhaps in some situations this fact itself is not obvious to the audience, and thus there is some reason for them to rely on the speaker's assertion even if they do not need to. More generally, if claims to knowledge are basically a form of assurance concerning the truth of what is asserted (§424), it should be sufficient to legitimate a claim to knowledge if there are possible situations in which an audience would have reason to rely on a speaker who cannot be mistaken about the matter in hand even if such assurance is not needed in the actual context of utterance because the truth of the matter is obvious there anyway. This is to take a claim to knowledge to be a claim to be in a position to know (§555), that is to be in a position in which one is able to offer assurance, even if none is in fact needed; and I think that this is where Wittgenstein is content to leave the matter when, in the last section in which he discusses the issue, he writes:

§622   But now it is also correct to use 'I know' in the contexts which Moore mentioned, at least *in particular circumstances*. (Indeed, I do not know what 'I know that I am a human being' means. But even that might be given a sense).

For each one of these sentences I can imagine circumstances that turn it into a move in one of our language-games, and by that it loses everything that is philosophically astonishing.

The final clause here is, however, crucial. If one thinks of knowledge as a specially watertight mental state, as, perhaps, Moore did, then even Moore's characteristic claims to this philosophically astonishing state should be resisted. But once claims to knowledge are brought down to earth by considering their role in our actual language-games, Moore's claims are no longer philosophically astonishing and there is no longer any reason to reject them.[12]

REFERENCES

GREEN, M. and WILLIAMS, J. N. (2007). *Moore's Paradox*. Oxford: Oxford University Press.

KIENZLER, W. (2006). 'Wittgenstein and John Henry Newman on Certainty', in M. Kober ed., *Deepening our Understanding of Wittgenstein*. Amtserdam: Rodopi.

MALCOLM, N. (1942). 'Moore and Ordinary Language', in Schilpp 1942.

—— (1949). 'Defending Common Sense', *Philosophical Review*, 58: 201–20.

—— (1977). 'Moore and Wittgenstein on the Sense of "I know"', in *Thought and Knowledge*. Ithaca, NY: Cornell University Press.

McGINN, M. (1989). *Sense and Certainty*. Oxford: Blackwell.

MONK, R. (1990). *Ludwig Wittgenstein: The Duty of Genius*. London: Jonathan Cape.

MOORE, G. E. (1922). 'Some Judgments of Perception', in *Philosophical Studies*. London: Routledge and Kegan Paul.

—— (1942a). 'An Autobiography', in Schilpp 1942.

—— (1942b). 'A Reply to my Critics', in Schilpp 1942.

—— (1959). 'Four Forms of Scepticism', in *Philosophical Papers*. London: George Allen and Unwin.

—— (1993a). 'A Refutation of Idealism', in *G. E. Moore: Selected Writings*, ed. T. Baldwin. London: Routledge.

—— (1993b). 'A Defence of Common Sense', in *G. E. Moore: Selected Writings*, ed. T. Baldwin. London: Routledge.

—— (1993c). 'Proof of an External World', in *G. E. Moore: Selected Writings*, ed. T. Baldwin. London: Routledge.

—— (1993d). 'Letter to Malcolm', in *G. E. Moore: Selected Writings*, ed. T. Baldwin. London: Routledge.

—— (1993e). 'Certainty', in *G. E. Moore: Selected Writings*, ed. T. Baldwin. London: Routledge.

NEWMAN, J. H. (1985). *An Essay in Aid of a Grammar of Assent*, ed. I. T. Ker. Oxford: Oxford University Press.

SCHILPP, P. A. (1942). *The Philosophy of G. E. Moore*. La Salle, IL: Open Court.

WISDOM, J. (1942). 'Moore's Technique', in Schilpp 1942.

---

[12] This conclusion conflicts with the widespread view that in *On Certainty* Wittgenstein holds that Moore's claims to knowledge are incorrect. My disagreement with those who have advanced this position, most notably McGinn (1989), is of course to be understood as combined with an appreciation of their discussions, from which I have learnt a great deal.

WITTGENSTEIN, L. (1961). 'Notes on Logic', in *Notebooks 1914-16*, ed. G. E. M. Anscombe and G. H. von Wright. Oxford: Blackwell.

—— (1969). *On Certainty*, ed. G. E. M. Anscombe and G. H. von Wright, trans. D. Paul and G. E. M. Anscombe. Oxford: Blackwell.

—— (1993). *Philosophical Occasions*, ed. J. Klagge and A. Nordmann. Indianapolis, IN: Hackett.

—— (1997). *Philosophical Investigations*, Second Edition, ed. G. E. M. Anscombe and R. Rhees, trans. G. E. M. Anscombe. Oxford: Blackwell.

CHAPTER 25

....

WITTGENSTEIN ON INTUITION, RULE-FOLLOWING, AND CERTAINTY: EXCHANGES WITH BROUWER AND RUSSELL

....

KIM VAN GENNIP

1. INTRODUCTION

....

The central theme of this chapter is the debate on perception or intuition between Russell and Wittgenstein as constructed largely from 'The Limits of Empiricism' (Russell 1937) and 'Cause and Effect: Intuitive Awareness' (Wittgenstein 1976).[1] In consulting several *Nachlass* items as written in 1935–6, I will show, first, that Wittgenstein puts forward a detailed criticism of Russell's account of perception, as Russell presents it in the context of a discussion on causation. This criticism is interesting in that it leads up to an account of knowledge and certainty that foreshadows the position known from *On Certainty*. In addition, I will show that a crucial element in Wittgenstein's critique of Russell is similar to his critique of Brouwer's intuitionist stance in mathematics, a criticism that Wittgenstein expressed in the early 1930s. The parallel in reasoning becomes visible when consulting the source text of 'Cause and Effect' and tracing relevant notes back to their first *Nachlass* sources. It is the principal

---

[1] The title 'Cause and Effect: Intuitive Awareness' derives from A heading that Wittgenstein wrote on page 100 of MS 119 A reprint was published in 1993 in PO, 370–406. All page references are to PO.

aim of this chapter to explain and comment on this connection, which has hitherto not been identified.

I will start with a brief historical introduction to the debate between Russell and Wittgenstein. We will see that the two men were not in close contact in the 1930s, but they knew of each other's philosophical ideas, and 'The Limits of Empiricism' heralds a new phase in their debate. Second, I will focus on Russell's paper and Wittgenstein's criticism of it. In order to find the basic propositions of our knowledge system, Russell presents an account of the relation between sense experience and knowledge that should produce propositions functioning as examples of our most immediate knowledge. As we will see, Wittgenstein disputed this account on all levels, thus showing his fundamental disagreement with Russell's epistemological endeavour. Finally, I will turn to Wittgenstein's reflections on intuition as found in 'Cause and Effect', the source text of 'Cause and Effect', and earlier *Nachlass* items. In doing so, a striking parallel emerges between Wittgenstein's critique of Brouwer's account of intuition on the one hand, and Russell's account of perception on the other. In both cases Wittgenstein draws attention to our actions.

2. Russell's Return to Philosophy in 1936, and Wittgenstein's Response

Russell and Wittgenstein met in 1911, and for a while, their personal and professional relation was one of respect and admiration. They started off as equals in their fascination for logic and mathematics. Due to differences in character and Wittgenstein's critical attitude towards Russell's work in epistemology and metaphysics, however, their friendship soon deteriorated. In the 1920s, when Wittgenstein had given up on academic philosophy and had returned to Austria, they were hardly in contact. They regained contact in 1929, when Wittgenstein returned to Cambridge, but their personal and philosophical relationship was never restored in the way it had started. Moreover, Wittgenstein proved to be very critical of Russell's popular and philosophical work, as written in the 1930s, and Russell found discussions with Wittgenstein becoming more and more tiresome.

Russell did not hold a university post in Cambridge in the 1930s, and he complied rather reluctantly with requests to read and/or discuss Wittgenstein's work. In 1930, Russell was asked to write a recommendation to the Trinity Council in order to obtain a grant for Wittgenstein. For this purpose, Wittgenstein had sent Russell TS 208,[2] a typescript that Russell studied and discussed with Wittgenstein. Also, in the academic year 1933–4, Wittgenstein dictated to a select group of students, and he sent a manuscript of

---

[2] Published as *Philosophical Remarks* in 1964.

this dictation, the so-called *Blue Book*, to Russell in 1935.[3] It is likely that Russell had read this typescript, as in a letter written later Wittgenstein noted that he is pleased that Russell is reading his work (CL, letter 160). Indirectly, Russell also learned of Wittgenstein's ideas as recorded in the so-called *Brown Book*. This book was again a dictation, made in the academic year 1934–5, and largely concerned with the philosophy of mathematics. Alice Ambrose, one of Wittgenstein's students, subsequently attempted to represent Wittgenstein's position in an article that was published in *Mind* in 1935.[4] Wittgenstein was deeply dissatisfied with this essay and he even tried to persuade Moore, then the editor of *Mind*, not to publish it – though without success. To Russell, Ambrose's article was a welcome stimulus that renewed his interest in theoretical philosophy, and in 1936 he formulated a critique of Ambrose in 'The Limits of Empiricism'. So, albeit indirectly, Wittgenstein's views functioned as a stimulus for Russell's renewed reflections on mathematics, knowledge, and perception in the late 1930s.[5]

In turn, Wittgenstein eagerly followed Russell's new step into the philosophical field, announcing his interest in a letter in which he expressed his hesitation to attend a meeting of the Moral Sciences Club, to which Russell was to deliver his lecture on the limits of empiricism on 28 November 1935.[6] Wittgenstein felt 'like someone who's intruding in a tea-party in which some people don't care to have him. If, on the other hand, you wished me to be there...then it would be as if the host wanted me to be at the tea-party, and in this case I would not care whether any of the guests objected' (CL, letter 160, 271–2).[7] In the same letter, Wittgenstein proposed to discuss Russell's paper the day after the meeting of the Moral Sciences Club. Eventually, Wittgenstein did not attend Russell's lecture, but he did see Russell at breakfast at Moore's place on the morning before the lecture.[8] It

[3] One of the four preserved letters from Wittgenstein to Russell written after 1929 mentions a manuscript which had been sent. See editor's note to letter 159 in CL, 269.

[4] Ambrose 1935. Wittgenstein addressed Ambrose's position in his Easter Term lectures in 1935. See AWL, 194–5.

[5] Russell only acknowledges the influence of the logical positivists in explaining his return to philosophical work. In a letter to Moore in February 1937, he writes: 'I have become very desirous of returning to purely philosophic work; in particular, I want to develop the ideas in my paper on "The Limits of Empiricism" & to investigate the relation of language to fact, as to which Carnap's ideas seem to me very inadequate' (Russell 1968, 214). In his *Autobiography* he mentions that 'the logical positivists, with whose general outlook I had a large measure of agreement, seemed to me on some points to be falling into errors which would lead away from empiricism into a new scholasticism' (Russell 1968, 194). 'The Limits of Empiricism', however, takes issue with Carnap, Ambrose, and Wittgenstein, so I think we may assume that Wittgenstein's views – or what Russell takes them to be – initially also provide an important stimulus for Russell's renewed interest in philosophy in 1935.

[6] On 6 April 1936 Russell read it to the Aristotelian Society, and it was subsequently published in their proceedings. Note that Russell wrote *another* article with the title 'The Limits of Empiricism', which is published in Russell 1948, 516–27. The purport of this later article differs considerably from that of the earlier one.

[7] Wittgenstein's hesitation is explained by the fact that he had stopped attending meetings after several members had objected to his dominant presence. See Monk 1990, 263; Rhees 1984, 16.

[8] See Moore 1929–1939, 5. A few weeks before Russell's visit to the MSC, Wittgenstein asked Moore not to invite Russell to stay when Russell was to present his paper. Wittgenstein's motives for this request are unclear, and Moore did not comply with it.

is unclear what was discussed at this meeting, but Wittgenstein's writings show that his interest was provoked: MS 150, a notebook written in 1935 or 1936, contains a critique of Russell's account of seeing. This notebook precedes MS 119, the main source text for 'Cause and Effect'.[9] I will discuss MS 150 and 'Cause and Effect' further on; in order to understand Wittgenstein's criticisms, however, I will first present a brief account of Russell's position.

2.1 'The Limits of Empiricism': isolation, classification, and causation

In line with Russell's central pursuit – from 1912 onwards – to understand the relation between knowledge and experience, 'The Limits of Empiricism' examines whether empiricism provides an adequate theory of knowledge so that it could be of service to the sciences. Russell observes four difficulties that adhere to pure empiricism. For my purpose it is not necessary to discuss all four problems that Russell identifies; I will only discuss the problem of the relation between knowledge and sense experience.

According to Russell, any understanding of the relation between knowledge and sense experience involves quasi-causal relations, which cannot be accounted for by the empiricist. His argument consists of two strands. First, in passing from sense experience to knowledge, two processes are important, namely noticing and classifying. For example, if someone plays the ten of spades in a card-game, others see and know that this card has been played. In passing from the 'sensible occurrence' or 'sense-datum' to knowledge, we first isolate the card from its visual background and we take into account only those features that mark it as the ten of spades, while ignoring other features – such as its size or weight. Thus we 'isolate' or 'notice' certain features at the expense of others, which are nevertheless there. Along with this noticing – which consists in stating less than we actually see – we also add something to what we see, namely that the card is a spade and that the card is a ten. This is what Russell calls 'classifying'. The result of this process of 'noticing' and 'classifying' is primitive sense-knowledge, which is logically necessary as a basis for other empirical knowledge. This primitive, propositional sense-knowledge is our most immediate knowledge, and it need not be verbal; I can look for example at my computer screen, isolate it from its surroundings, and classify it as a computer screen, but I need not say 'computer screen'. Russell thus avoids the implication that the difference between sense and knowledge is defined by words alone. Rather, noticing and classifying precede the use of words.

The second strand of Russell's argument connects to the transition from sense-knowledge to its propositional expression.[10] An account of this transition is needed, for

---

[9] MS 157b, a pocket notebook of 81 pages and written in February 1937, is the source text for the first five pages of MS 119 and so the first eight remarks of 'Cause and Effect'. Wittgenstein began MS 119 later in 1937.

[10] Russell speaks of 'verbal expression'; the context makes clear that he has propositional knowledge in mind.

if knowledge is to be a premise in philosophy or a basis for other empirical knowledge, it must be propositional. At this point, Russell presents a causal theory of perception and meaning. In his view, the process of the learning of language involves causal relations. For example, the presence of a cat causes the word 'cat' to be spoken, and if a child hears the word 'cat' this may cause the expectation of a cat. So this experience constitutes the learning of language, and the causal relations of the word 'cat' determine the meaning of the word 'cat'.[11] Besides the causal relations that Russell identifies in the process of the learning of language, he also identifies causal relations constituting the understanding of a language. These relations exist after the language has been learnt, and they are causal relations between words and what they mean. This type of causal relations, says Russell, can sometimes be perceived: 'the verbal premises of verbal empirical knowledge are sentences perceived to be caused by something perceived' (Russell 1937, 137). If these causal relations were not perceivable, Russell states, we would be unable to explain the connection between what we perceive and the words with which we describe it. Again, take the example of me seeing a cat and saying 'there is a cat'. According to Russell, my words express a piece of knowledge, but the question is how to understand 'express' here. In his view, there is a causal connection between the sensible appearance and my will to utter the appropriate word or words. Here, 'causal' means something other than 'invariable antecedent'; the causal relation must be one that can sometimes be perceived. Russell further qualifies this type of causal connection: as the sensible appearance is only part of the cause of the word (the sight of a cat will not cause the word 'cat' in a French speaker), Russell calls it a 'quasi-causal relation of producing'. There are cases in which such problems with language are absent. For example, if someone pinches me and I cry out, we indubitably perceive a connection between the pain and the cry. There are no terminological difficulties here, Russell adds.

To summarize the argument, the propositional premises that we need as the basis for our knowledge are the product of three processes: firstly, we isolate features of a sense-datum at the expense of other features; secondly, we classify just these features; and thirdly, a process of causation explains the step to a verbalization of the sensible fact, the result of which is premises such as 'this is a cat' and 'this is the ten of spades'. These sentences are examples of our most immediate knowledge. Russell concludes that the first two processes are relatively uncomplicated for an empiricist, but the third process is problematic. As mentioned, the conception of 'perceiving' a cause transcends the understanding of cause as 'invariable antecedent'. As such, it does not comply with an empiricist stance. Hume's lesson is that we can only rely on an enumeration of instances to prove a causal connection, which implies that causes are never directly perceived. This understanding of causation, however, says Russell, cannot explain the transition between

---

[11] Russell developed a causal theory of meaning in 1919, arguing that the connection between objects and our sense-data is established by causal relations, where objects are the causes of our sense-data: 'the relation of a word to its meaning is of the nature of a causal law governing our use of the word and our actions when we hear it used' (Russell 1921, 198). When *Analysis of Matter* was published in 1927, this theory had acquired a firm position in his thinking. See Eames 1969.

what is perceived and the words in which we describe it, and as such it cannot account for the possibility of empirical science. So in this respect empiricism fails to be an adequate theory of knowledge.

So far on Russell's account of the relation between experience and knowledge. I will now turn to Wittgenstein's response, starting with MS 150. As we will see, Wittgenstein questioned all three steps that Russell distinguished in his attempt to arrive at the propositional premises needed at the basis of our knowledge.

2.2 MS 150

MS 150 is a notebook of ninety-six pages in which Wittgenstein examines the notion of seeing. On page 62, Wittgenstein speaks of the notion of the 'purely visual' and mentions the notion of 'direct perception'. Although Russell's name is not mentioned explicitly, it is plausible that this explanation relates to 'The Limits of Empiricism', in which Russell spoke of the 'purely visual' as distinct from and opposed to the activity of classification: 'The additions to what is purely visual with which I am concerned at the moment are those involved in classification' (Russell 1937, 132). According to Russell, we first see a card in its most pure, visual form, and then we classify it as a 'spade' and/or a 'ten'. In this way, the process of seeing is an experience that starts from the purely visual and moves on to several subsequent levels. The experience of seeing thus consists of an element that is 'purely visible', and an interpretation of this element.

In MS 150 Wittgenstein writes: 'As if we had first the obvious pure seeing and then several other experiences were added....It is as though we saw a face first purely visual [sic.] then *in addition* to that as a face then *in addition* to that as a Chinese face and *in addition* to that as a well known one. No: we can imagine additional processes corresponding to each such case but these are not "directly perceived".'[12] Wittgenstein's idea is that when we see a face as for example a Chinese face, or as reminding us of someone, the change at hand is a change in attention, and not a change from the 'purely visual' to an act of classification, as Russell would have it. The *Philosophical Investigations* reads: 'I contemplate a face, and then suddenly notice its likeness to another. I *see* that it has not changed; and yet I see it differently. I call this experience "noticing an aspect"' (PI II, 193).[13] MS 150 does not speak of 'das Bemerken eines Aspekts'. Nevertheless, Wittgenstein attacks the idea of the 'purely visual' by focusing on the multifarious uses of the concept of seeing, emphasizing that it is misleading to say that the experience of seeing a face is a compound one, as Russell argues. In addition, Wittgenstein challenges Russell's suggestion that we need to attend to our own inner experiences if we want to understand what

---

[12] The first sentence is written in German: 'Als hätten wir zuerst das offenbar reine Sehen und dann träten verschiedene andere Erfahrungen hinzu' (MS 150, 62). The notebook contains remarks in both German and English.

[13] For an account of Wittgenstein's view on aspect-perception, see Budd 1989.

happens when we see a face or a card.[14] To clarify this point, MS 150 elaborately focuses on the process of reading. There is no room here to substantiate this point in great detail; the general purport of these remarks is that we should not focus on our own inner experiences to know what 'reading' means, but we need to focus on the use of the word. As we will see, this point becomes crucial in 'Cause and Effect', where Wittgenstein criticizes the idea that an inner experience or intuition provides an infallible link between a cause and its effect. I will turn to this text in the following.

2.3 'Cause and Effect'

As we have seen, Russell argued that we sometimes indubitably perceive a connection between a cause and its effect, for example when someone slaps me and I cry out. 'Cause and Effect' criticizes this idea of indubitability:

> Don't we recognise immediately that the pain is produced by the blow we have received? Isn't this the cause and can there be any doubt about it? But isn't it quite possible to suppose that in certain cases we are deceived about this? And later recognise the deception? It seems as though something hits us and at the same time we feel a pain. (Sometimes we think we are causing a sound by making a certain movement and then realise that it is quite independent of us). (CE, 373)

The idea of indubitability is a corollary of the view that we immediately see a causal relation between the blow and the pain. As the quotation shows, Wittgenstein's first response is to raise the possibility that we are mistaken about the causal relation. By giving the statement a proper place in the language-game, i.e. by clarifying how it is used in language, he intends to show that doubt is very much possible in a case such as this. It might simply *seem* like I feel a pain at the same time as something hits me. For example, I might be strolling around in the forest when a bird skims over my head, I then yell 'ouch', thinking that the animal has hurt me, only to realize later that it did not touch me at all. In other words, we might have an experience of the cause, but this experience does not show us the cause infallibly. Russell's statement, says Wittgenstein, misleads us into thinking both that we cannot possibly be mistaken about the causal connection, and that the connection between the pain and the cry is indubitable. This, however, is not the case.

Wittgenstein's second criticism of Russell's account of causation focuses on the idea that we 'perceive' a causal connection. Instead of speaking of 'perceiving', Wittgenstein

---

[14] In his lectures of 1938, Wittgenstein criticized Russell's notion of classification along similar lines. In 'classifying' something, we seem to put it in some sort of 'category table' in the mind. In Wittgenstein's view, this table comes to nothing at all, for we have no reason to suppose that this mind-table is ordered in this way, rather than in another; the word 'cat' might just as well have labelled another picture. In the end it is the result that matters, namely whether Russell calls a cat what we call a cat. See PO, 409.

prefers to speak of 'immediate awareness' or 'intuition'.[15] Wittgenstein wonders what intuition is:

> 'What do we know about intuition? What idea have we of it? It's presumably supposed to be a sort of seeing, recognition at a *single* glance'. (CE, 393)
>
> 'Russell said that before recognising something as a cause through repeated experience, we would have to recognise something as a cause by intuition'. (CE, 371)

In Wittgenstein's view, it is confusing to speak of intuition in the example of the relation between a pain and a cry or a slap and a cry, for here there is no such thing as 'being immediately aware' of the cause. Rather, we have an immediate *reaction* to the cause: 'We react to the cause. Calling something "the cause" is like pointing and saying: "He's to blame!"' (CE, 373) If someone stares at me rudely, I may feel uncomfortable and start moving nervously in my seat. I thus react to the cause of my uncomfortable feeling, and this reacting to the cause may be called 'immediate'.[16] Similarly, if someone throws a stone at me, I might pick up the stone and throw it back at him. Or, if someone touches me with a pole, I look along the pole towards the person, and this is a reaction to a cause, which consists in looking from one thing to another.[17] This, Wittgenstein adds, is what we instinctively do. So, where Russell speaks of being immediately aware of a causal connection, we are in fact dealing with a reaction against a cause, and this reaction may be called 'immediate'.

The crucial point is that, for Wittgenstein, speaking of 'intuition' or 'immediate awareness' gives the wrong impression. In his lectures of 1938, he explained that the expression 'intuition' or 'being immediately aware' makes you think that you are right about something, and that you can be shown to be right about it. However, the point is that there is no right or wrong about it. Wittgenstein acknowledged Russell's point that we do speak of cause and effect in cases where no experiments are made, but he opposed the idea that in these cases we are 'immediately aware' of the cause. We react to the cause, and the notion of 'immediate awareness' is out of place at the level of our reactions. Similarly, to speak of knowledge in these cases is equally misleading. In support of this idea, 'Cause and Effect' imagines a primitive or basic form of the language-game, such as a mother

---

[15] As Rhees noted in his preface to 'Cause and Effect', much of what Wittgenstein says of 'intuition' would apply to Russell's use of 'perceive' or 'see'. Russell does not use the term 'intuition' in his article, and speaks of 'immediate awareness' only once, in discussing the fourth problem of empiricism. (See Russell 1937, 146.) It is noteworthy that *The Problems of Philosophy* holds that intuitive knowledge is possible. In his later work, this notion plays a less prominent role, yet the account of immediate knowledge and indubitable perception in 'The Limits of Empiricism' is strongly reminiscent of the earlier account of intuitive knowledge.

[16] See Malcolm 1986, 150.

[17] This last phrase originates from CE, 390. The original German lines read: 'Ja, man kann sagen, es setzt voraus, dass er sich nach einer Ursache umschaut; dass er von dieser Erscheinung – auf eine *andere* schaut', which is falsely translated as 'that he does not attend to this phenomenon – but to *another* one'. The mistake here is 'does not', for Wittgenstein is not saying that *instead of* attending to this phenomenon one attends to another one, but that one starts looking for another phenomenon when confronted with the first one. So it is a matter of shifting one's view from the one to the other – and not ignoring the one to the benefit of the other.

responding to the cries of her newborn child. Imagine the mother ignoring the child when it cries, waking it up several times during the night, denying the baby food, etc. We would not call this behaviour the behaviour of doubt, but it would strike us as strange and perhaps crazy. The notion of the primitive form of the language-game is meant to illustrate the way in which our language-games are anchored in our actions and reactions. In its most primitive form, the language-game consists in a reaction to someone else, for example to someone's cries and gestures. The language-game has a 'biological function in our life', which means that the language-game is inextricably bound up with our biological make-up or natural history. Normally, human beings are responsive to the cries of their children and will do anything to remove the cause of their offsprings' pain and anxiety. We take care of our children, nurse and feed them and make sure they are safe against threats, and there is an enormous agreement here in our reactions. Features of doubt and conjecture only enter at a later level, when a child, for example, has learned to feign pain. At the primitive level of the language-game, doubt is absent.

To conclude, Wittgenstein's criticisms of Russell's account of indubitability and perception signify a fundamental disagreement in their outlook on epistemology in general. Where Russell seeks for empirical, propositional premises of our knowledge, assigning these premises the status of indubitability, Wittgenstein sees the basis of our knowledge not to be reflected in principles or propositions, but in our actions and reactions. These actions and reactions are at the basis of our language-game, and at this level epistemic concepts such as 'doubt' and 'knowledge' are not applicable. The basic form of the language-game, he adds, is certainty, and not uncertainty, for uncertainty could never lead to action. This account of certainty is prominent in *On Certainty*, where Wittgenstein again emphasizes that it is our acting which lies at the bottom of the language-game. Certainty is exhibited in our acting.[18]

Wittgenstein's and Russell's distinct approaches in epistemology should be seen in the context of their distinct views on the relation between language and the world. Both Winch (1987) and Rhees (1982) acknowledge this difference. Initially, Wittgenstein and Russell were on a similar path in seeking an account of this relation. As Winch explains:

> in the *Tractatus* the point of contact is located in the possibility of a direct 'comparison' between an elementary proposition and a *Sachverhalt*; and this possibility in its turn depends on the role of 'names' in the proposition whose meanings *are* their bearers; 'objects' which constitute 'the substance of the world'. (Winch 1987, 46)

Both Russell and Wittgenstein agreed on this point at that time. Wittgenstein later criticized this view, as he came to think that the attempt to explain the relation of language to reality – or of words to things – was confused. In his new perspective, the harmony between language and the world is not found in a correlation between names and objects, but it is found in intralinguistic connections, that is, in the grammar of our

---

[18] See e.g. OC §204. For a detailed account of the parallels between 'Cause and Effect' and *On Certainty*, see van Gennip 2008. An earlier, brief exposition is in ter Hark 1990, 52–61. Parallels are also noted by Malcolm (1986, 149–53) and Moyal-Sharrock (2004a, 123 n. 6; and 2004b, 10 n. 8).

language. Thus, Wittgenstein now opposes the idea that our ways of speaking should and could receive a justification from an extralinguistic insight into the relation between words and things. According to Rhees and Winch, 'The Limits of Empiricism' attempts to provide exactly such a justification. By means of a causal connection between words and objects, Russell seeks to establish a connection between sensible occurrences – cats, dogs, ploughs, and horses – and the verbal references to them. The idea that we need to establish such a connection is at the heart of Russell's epistemology, and the core of Russell's argument, says Winch, is that we understand the meaning of our words only because we see that they are caused by something extralinguistic. As Russell puts it, the presence of a cat causes the word 'cat' to be spoken: we may imagine someone seeing a cat, pointing at the animal, and saying 'there is a cat'. Winch and Rhees formulate a Wittgensteinian critique of this account of meaning. As they put it, Russell's example of the causal relation between a pain and a cry already presupposes the meaning of 'cause' – for how could one otherwise decide whether the word 'cause' fits this case? 'Cause and Effect' notes several times that words are 'public property'; that is, the perception of the cause is conceivable only within an established use of language. Rhees explains it as follows:

> If I am immediately aware of a causal relation between my words and what I see, this does not tell me or explain the *connection in language* between my words and what I see. This is a connection in 'the game I play with other people' – a connection which they can recognise as well as I can. (Rhees 1982, 32)

So the crucial point is that a private experience of a causal relation is not important in establishing the meaning of the word 'cause'. Rhees concludes that Russell's account suggests that there is something (that is, a private experience) that cannot be described, or at least not by the means we have at present. It is difficult to imagine what such description is or would be like.

Wittgenstein's criticism of Russell's causal theory of perception and meaning – which is limited to just a few remarks in MS 119 – is not new. In the early 1920s, Wittgenstein was already familiar with the purport of the theory, which was set forward in Russell's *The Analysis of Mind* (1921) and later defended by Ogden and Richards in *The Meaning of Meaning* (1922/1970).[19] Several notebooks written after 1929 contain

---

[19] Ogden aimed to connect Wittgenstein's *Tractatus* to a causal theory of meaning as developed by Russell. In a letter to Russell of 5 November 1921, Ogden wrote: 'I should very much like to know why all this account of signs and symbols [i.e. *Tractatus*' account] cannot best be understood in relation to a thoroughgoing causal theory' (LO, 3). Russell responded approvingly, and *The Meaning of Meaning* attempts to make the connection. In a letter to Ogden from March 1923 Wittgenstein wrote politely: 'I have however read in it [*The Meaning of Meaning*] and I think I ought to confess to you frankly that I believe you have not quite caught the problems which – for instance – I was at in my book (whether or not I have given the correct solution)' (LO, 69). To Russell, however, he was far from polite; Wittgenstein wrote to him saying that *The Meaning of Meaning* was a miserable and foolish book. Russell never replied to this letter.

substantial reasons for disputing the theory.[20] A causal theory of meaning as expressed by Ogden, Richards, and Russell, Wittgenstein argued, explains the relation between language and action externally; that is, the meaning of a sentence lies in its effect. However, says Wittgenstein, if we want to understand the meaning of a sentence, we are in need of internal or conceptual relations. Another criticism concerns the distinction between causes and grounds. Russell said that the cat is the cause of my saying 'here is a cat'. However, Wittgenstein objected, a cat could be the *ground* or reason of my saying 'there is a cat', but it is not the *cause* of it. This point against Russell is already made in 1931, in MS 110, and Wittgenstein continued to draw attention to the distinction between causes and grounds. One distinction is that reasons, unlike causes, play a justificatory role, while another distinction is that reasons come to an end, whereas the chain of causes can go on indefinitely. Russell fails to notice these distinctions.[21]

So, although Wittgenstein's criticism of Russell's causal theory of perception and meaning as expressed in MS 119/'Cause and Effect' is not new, his focus on the indubitability of a causal relation and the intuitive awareness of such connection is.

3. WITTGENSTEIN ON INTUITION

There is, however, more to Wittgenstein's remarks on intuition. I believe that his criticism of Russell gains depth if we follow trails on intuition in the *Nachlass* and see in what context they originally emerged. Originally, Wittgenstein examined intuition in the context of the philosophy of mathematics, examining the way in which rules govern our use of numbers and other mathematical expressions. Wittgenstein took issue with an intuitionist stance in mathematics as formulated by Luitzen Brouwer. As we will see, his critical analysis of intuitionism is strikingly similar to his critical analysis of Russell's account of perception. So the roots of Wittgenstein's criticism of Russell, and therefore the roots of Wittgenstein's account of knowledge and certainty, are found in his criticism of intuitionism in mathematics. I will elaborate on this point in the remainder of this chapter, starting with the remarks on intuition as written in 1937.

[20] For example in MS 107, published as *Philosophical Remarks*. Between 1919 and 1928 Wittgenstein wrote almost nothing, or he had these notebooks destroyed, so we do not know if Wittgenstein wrote on the causal theory of meaning before 1930. Several remarks on the causal theory of meaning as present in *Philosophical Remarks* are included in the *Investigations* (for example PI §169).

[21] Wittgenstein mentions Russell and Ogden in MS 110, 94. For an overview of the distinction between cause and ground, see Glock 1996, 74–6. *On Certainty* takes it up in relation to the concept of experience (OC, 130, 429). Experiences may be the cause of our judgements, but they are not the grounds of them. In Wittgenstein's criticism of Freud and Frazer this distinction also figures prominently. See LC, 41–52; and 'Remarks on Frazer's Golden Bough'.

3.1 Remarks on intuition in 1937: a 'sixth sense'

'Cause and Effect' contains seven entries on the notion of intuition (§§1, 2, 3, 25, 47, 48, and 50), and Wittgenstein makes two points here. Firstly, he tackles the idea that intuition is a kind of knowledge. CE §48 notes that: '"knowing the cause intuitively" means *somehow or other* knowing the cause, (experiencing it in a way different from the usual one)'. Wittgenstein adds that this experience as such is insufficient to substantiate a claim to knowledge. If I say 'I have the intuition that this is a cat' or 'I intuitively know that A caused B', it seems that I am right in saying this. However, it still has to be proved that I know what I say I know. That is, my knowing still has to prove its worth. I could just as well say that I have intuitive knowledge of, for example, human anatomy, but this assertion will surely not bring me a doctor's degree – only passing the appropriate examinations will. So intuition is not a sort of special knowing or knowledge that people sometimes have or experience, an experience that we accept as *being* a kind of knowledge that requires no further explanation or justification. We do not have a concept of this special knowing of the cause. Wittgenstein quotes Goethe's *Faust*: 'For where concepts [*Begriffe*] are lacking, we shall always find a word in good time' (CE, 393).[22] The point of this quote is to remind us that in order to find out what 'intuition' means, we have to look at the use of the word in the language-game. So a description of language-games with the word 'intuition' will show us what intuition is.

Secondly, Wittgenstein emphasizes that intuition is not some sort of natural capacity which some people have and others lack, and which as such gives us the right to say we know something. The idea that intuition is a natural capacity is closely connected to the thought that knowledge is a state of mind. Once we are in this state of mind, we are allegedly allowed to say that we know something. So, in order to determine whether I know something, I have to look inside myself to see what state I am in, and intuition, as a natural capacity that is at work in certain persons and not in others, may be one of the various causes that effects this state of mind. 'Cause and Effect' signifies that the view that knowledge is a state of mind leads to a misguided distinction between *real* knowledge and *derived* knowledge: real knowledge is supposedly knowledge of sense-data, and derived knowledge is supposedly knowledge of external facts. Wittgenstein wonders how we arrive at such a distinction between these kinds of knowledge. Suppose I say 'I know that someone else is in the room', and it turns out that there is nobody in the room. The question is whether I now have made a mistake in introspecting or identifying my state of mind: I took something for a knowing, when it was not a knowing. From this I may easily conclude that I cannot know *p*, or at least that this knowledge is not real knowledge, and the only real knowledge I have is knowledge of my own sense-data. In this case, the assumption goes, such a discrepancy cannot occur. To this line of reasoning Wittgenstein retorts that we do not look for a state of mind in order to find out what 'knowledge' means. In order for a claim to count as knowledge, we must have evidence that supports it, and mental states are of no interest here. Also, the idea that real knowledge is knowledge of sense-data suggests that we should use 'I know' in those

---

[22] 'Denn eben wo Begriffe fehlen, da stellt ein Wort zur rechten Zeit sich ein'. See Goethe 1990, part I, 1995.

cases where nobody uses it. Nobody says 'I know I am in pain' or 'I know I see something red'. Here, 'I know that *p*' means nothing: 'unless perhaps it means the same as "p", and the expression "I do not know that p" is nonsense' (CE, 391).

Wittgenstein unremittingly attacks the view from the early 1930s onwards. that we can only have knowledge of our own sense-data, sensations, or experiences This topic is beyond the scope of this chapter. (See PO, 200–88.)

It is interesting to see that although MS 119 contains only eight remarks on the concept of intuition – Rhees omits one entry from 'Cause and Effect', for no apparent reason – pages 82r–90v of MS 119 consider a concept that is synonymous with intuition, namely the concept of a 'sixth sense'. The question is whether intuition may be regarded as a sixth sense, that is, as a special sort of sense experience or sense perception.[23] These remarks are part of a longer discussion about the meaning of philosophical questions. One such question concerns the relation between bodies or objects, and sense perceptions. If I enter a dark house and I see something lying on the table, I may wonder if there is an object lying there. Sense perceptions are the criteria for deciding whether there *is* an object. However, a philosopher asks further if there is an object or body *behind* these sense perceptions. Wittgenstein (again) refers to Goethe's *Faust*, who speaks to 'Sorge': 'Unglückliche Geschöpfe…zu tausend Malen'.[24] This quote signifies a general sense of anxiety or a neurotic condition that, according to Wittgenstein, is exemplified in the puzzles of philosophy. (See McGuinness 2002, 454.) To ask whether there *really* is a body behind our sense perceptions is a philosophical construction. These sense experiences just *are* the criterion for the existence of the body. To get rid of the 'Sorge' in Goethe's sense is to get rid of philosophical questions in Wittgenstein's sense, and in order to eliminate such questions, we need a procedure to decide whether a question is meaningful or not. For that, we have to see whether we can *do* something with the question, in contrast to merely thinking it. In a similar vein, Wittgenstein wonders what substance there is to the thought of a sixth sense, answering that we have to look at what we say about this:

> How can I think of a new manner of sense experience/sense perception, something like a 'sixth sense'?…I do not even have access to this concept. To believe that my own general concepts can bring me further is to believe that a train could move beyond the rails that have been laid for it. (MS 119, 86r)[25]

---

[23] Intuition, in addition to the five senses of sight, touch, taste, hearing, and smell, is often regarded as an additional sensory or non-sensory sense or experience which attains knowledge or insight. There are several meanings of the term, where the most general would be 'immediate apprehension'. See *Encyclopedia of Philosophy*, 204–12. Descartes held that in searching for first principles, we 'intuit' or 'see' the truth of such principles (see Descartes 1993, especially 4th Meditation). According to Kant, true knowledge is based on intuition (see Kant 1998, A 50–51/B 74–75 and A 51–52/B 75–76).

[24] The correct lines of Goethe's *Faust* are: 'Unselige Gespenster! So behandelt ihr das menschliche Geschlecht zu tausend Malen' (Goethe 1990, 11490).

[25] 'Wie kann ich mir denn eine neue Art der [Sinneserfahrung/Sinneswahrnehmung], etwa einen "sechsten Sinn", denken?/ denn mit Sinn von einer neuen Art [Sinneserfahrung/Sinneswahrnehmung], etwa einem "sechsten Sinn", reden? Ich habe ja eben keinen Zugang zu diesem Begriff. Und zu glauben, meine eigenen allgemeinen Begriffe könnten mich weiterführen, das ist als meinte man eine Lokomotive könne weiter fahren als die Gleise die man für sie gelegt hat.'

We can think of a sixth sense or a new sense experience, but we cannot do anything with it or say anything about it. To think we can invent a use for it is to think that we can move beyond language.

The target of the remarks on a sixth sense in MS 119 is not always immediately evident. However, we enhance our understanding by tracing these notes back to their origin in earlier manuscripts of the 1930s. Here, Wittgenstein discusses the notion of a sixth sense in the context of following rules in mathematics, criticizing Brouwer's intuitionist stance in mathematics. For a good understanding of this criticism, some knowledge of Brouwer's position is necessary.

So, in the following I will discuss Brouwer's position and compare it to Wittgenstein's views. For this purpose, I will rely on Mathieu Marion's account of their relationship as presented in 'Wittgenstein and Brouwer'. It should be noted that my treatment is far from comprehensive; it is neither meant to evaluate Brouwer's position in the philosophy of mathematics, nor to examine the adequacy of Wittgenstein's criticism of this position.[26] Rather, my account intends to display the parallel between Russell's discussion of causation and Brouwer's discussion of following rules, and the similar defects that Wittgenstein finds in them. Furthermore, to fully appreciate these similar defects as analysed by Wittgenstein, we need an overview of the development of Wittgenstein's thoughts on intuition in the context of following rules. As we will see, in the early 1930s Wittgenstein's reflections on this theme changed several times, and in 1937 it reached a novel stage. At that point, the reflections on the philosophy of mathematics became entwined with reflections on the concepts of knowledge, doubt and certainty, and as such they connect to Russell's view on knowledge, perception, and causation. So, insight into these transformations of the 1930s is crucial for an adequate understanding of Wittgenstein's later criticism of Russell's account of causation. To grasp these changes, I will examine Stern's representation as presented in *Wittgenstein on Mind and Language*. As we will see, Stern's account is useful, but it is incomplete and contains a crucial mistake. Before attending to these points, let us start with the relation between Brouwer and Wittgenstein.

3.2 Remarks on intuition: *Nachlass* sources before 1937

Wittgenstein's reflections on intuition originate from 1929. In 1928, he attended a lecture by Brouwer in Vienna.[27] As the story goes, Wittgenstein was quite reluctantly dragged to this lecture, as he was not planning to return to his old job of philosopher. Friedrich

---

[26] Brouwer is not the only influence to be discerned when it comes to Wittgenstein's reflections on the role of intuition in mathematics. David Hilbert and Hermann Weyl are mentioned several times in the *Nachlass*. Shanker discusses Hilbert's view that certain mathematical truths are grasped intuitively; and he mentions Weyl's view that certain 'undecidable' mathematical propositions are grasped by intuition. (See Shanker 1987, esp. 228–31 and 93–5.) Shanker does not acknowledge the parallel between Wittgenstein's criticisms of Brouwer and Russell.

[27] On 10 March 1928 Brouwer gave a lecture in Vienna on 'Mathematics, Science and Language'. For recent studies on the relation between Brouwer and Wittgenstein, see McGuinness 1991; Hintikka 1994; Marion 1998; Marion 2003.

Waismann and Herbert Feigl finally managed to convince him to attend, and it seems that after Brouwer's lecture Wittgenstein's enthusiasm for philosophy was reawakened: 'Suddenly and very volubly Wittgenstein began talking philosophy – at great length. Perhaps this was the turning point, for ever since that time, 1929, when he moved to Cambridge University Wittgenstein was a philosopher again' (Feigl 1981, 92).[28]

In his account of the relation between Brouwer and Wittgenstein, Marion focuses on the connection between the remarks on logic and mathematics in the *Tractatus* and Brouwer's intuitionist views.[29] Marion challenges the view that Brouwer's lecture was the fundamental, or at least a notable, impetus for Wittgenstein's later philosophy.[30] According to Marion, it was the author of the *Tractatus* that listened to Brouwer, and Wittgenstein's enthusiastic reaction is best explained by his excitement on hearing someone propound rather similar views to those he had expressed in the *Tractatus*. This is not to say, however, that Wittgenstein entirely agreed with Brouwer's ideas, nor is it to claim that the *Tractatus* is a piece of proto-intuitionism. In his notebooks written from 1929 onwards, Wittgenstein repeatedly comments negatively on Brouwer's intuitionism, and these points of disagreement, says Marion, are the starting-point for Wittgenstein's later criticism of intuitionism in relation to following rules. Let us now consider Brouwer's views.

3.3 Connections and distinctions between Brouwer and the *Tractatus*: 1928–1929

In his lecture on 'Mathematics, Science and Language', Brouwer considers three modes of operation, namely mathematical contemplation, mathematical abstraction, and the imposition of the will by the means of sounds. The mode of mathematical contemplation arises in a 'temporal' and a 'causal' attitude. Brouwer describes the temporal attitude as the 'Ur-phenomenon' of the human intellect, which is to distinguish 'moments of life' into qualitatively different parts.[31] This phenomenon of distinguishing is referred to as

---

[28] Marion notes that Brouwer's views were not completely new to Wittgenstein in 1928; he had learned about them through Ramsey's paper on the foundations of mathematics, written in 1925. See Marion 2003, n. 6.

[29] Only few scholars focus on the relationship between Brouwer and Wittgenstein. See Wrigley 1989 and Sundholm 1994. For an account of Brouwer and intuitionism, see Dummett 2000. For historical overviews of the debate on the foundations of mathematics, see Mancosu 1998 and Ewald 1996.

[30] For this view, see Richardson 1976 and Hacker 1972, 98–105. Hacker withdraws this claim in the revised edition of 1986. Hintikka 1996 disputes that Brouwer's views were of great importance to Wittgenstein's later views.

[31] Van Stigt (1990 and 1998) discusses Brouwer's intuitionism in the context of Brouwer's views on life and philosophy. Intuitionism is 'a philosophical trend that places emphasis on the individual consciousness as the source and seat of all knowledge. Besides the faculty and activity of reasoning, it recognizes in the individual mind a definite faculty and act of direct apprehension, intuition, as the necessary foundation of all knowledge, both in grasping of first principles on which a system of deductive reasoning is built and as the critical link in every act of knowing between the knower and the object known' (Van Stigt 1998, 4). Shanker argues that Wittgenstein challenged such an epistemological approach to the philosophy of mathematics. See Shanker 1987.

the 'fundamental phenomenon of mathematical thinking', or the 'intuition' of the 'bare two-oneness or temporal twoness'. Brouwer's idea is that the natural numbers self-unfold from this twoness: one element of the twoness is subsequently thought of as a new twoness, with temporal threeness as the result, and so on. The natural numbers are thus generated by means of the self-unfolding of the Ur-phenomenon or the intuition of the bare two-oneness. Brouwer also speaks of the 'basal' or 'basic intuition of mathematics', and 'the first act of intuitionism'.

The *Tractatus* does not discuss the idea of a basic intuition, so at first sight Brouwer's ideas do not seem to correspond to those expressed in Wittgenstein's book. However, Marion argues that the *Tractatus*' theory of signs, which underlies the conception of logic and mathematics, does reveal similarities between Wittgenstein and Brouwer. In the *Tractatus*' theory of signs, the notion of 'operation' is pivotal. TLP 3.12 states that a proposition is the propositional sign in its projective relation to the world. Thus there are two components to the proposition: the propositional sign, which is a fact and perceptible by the senses (TLP 3.1, 3.11, 3.14); and the method of projection, which is the thinking of the sense of the proposition (TLP 3.11). The propositional sign is thus a 'physical' entity, and the method of projection is a 'phenomenological', that is an immediately given, entity.[32] Marion notes: 'it is crucial that one realizes here that the "perceiving", the "projecting", the "thinking", the "applying", etc. are all here *operations* by a (generic) user of (the system of) signs' (Marion 2003, 110).

This theory of signs, Marion adds, requires an agent that operates with these signs, and here we find the connection to Brouwer: Brouwer holds that the two stages of mathematical contemplation, that is, the causal and temporal attitude, are *acts* of the will. Similarly, the *Tractatus* contains a conception of phenomenological *acts*, and this conception, Marion argues, is close to Brouwer. Marion presents several points to substantiate this view. In the following, I will briefly mention two of these points, as they provide a good first impression of the convergences between Brouwer and Wittgenstein.

Firstly, both thinkers separate logic from mathematics. In Wittgenstein's view, mathematical equations are not, strictly speaking, propositions, but pseudo-propositions. Thus mathematical propositions express no thoughts (TLP 6.21). Consequently, if mathematical equations are not propositions, then we cannot say that they are true or false, as the calculus of truth-functions only applies to propositions. Wittgenstein thus divorces logic from mathematics, and this position, Marion argues, is partly compatible with Brouwer's view that theoretical logic describes the phenomena of language, whereas intuitionist mathematics is understood as a 'languageless activity of the mind'.

Secondly, Brouwer's idea that mathematics is a 'languageless activity of the mind' is similar to the *Tractatus*' distinction between saying and showing. The *Tractatus* argues that the correctness of a mathematical equation can be *perceived* or *seen*. If we consider '2+2=4', there is an internal relation between '2+2' and '4', and this relation can be seen. In addition, Wittgenstein states that it is characteristic of logical propositions that we can see that they are true. This emphasis on *seeing* is connected with the distinction

---

[32] See Hintikka 1996 for this 'phenomenological' conception of the *Tractatus*.

between 'saying' and 'showing'; TLP 4.121–4.1212 explains that the logical form of propositions shows itself. Thus Wittgenstein's equational conception of mathematics contains
an element that cannot be said but shows itself. Although Wittgenstein would not agree
with the idea that mathematics is an essentially languageless activity of the mind, Marion
suggests, this element that cannot be said can be deemed 'languageless', and as such it is
akin to Brouwer's idea of mathematics as a languageless activity of the mind.[33]

So much for the similarities between the *Tractatus* and Brouwer's views. As mentioned earlier, Wittgenstein was far from uncritical, so there is more to be considered.
Marion notes a crucial difference, one that most likely struck Wittgenstein in 1928, concerning the idea of intuition. The *Tractatus* reads:

> To the question whether we need intuition for the solution of mathematical prob-
> lems it must be answered that language itself here supplies the necessary intuition.
> (TLP 6.233)
> The process of calculation brings about just this intuition. Calculation is not an
> experiment. (TLP 6.2331)

For Wittgenstein, Marion explains, to rely on a basic intuition in calculation could only
be a mistake. Brouwer's understanding of the basic mathematical intuition might explain
how each individual number is attained, but the account leaves unclear how the very form
of finite sequences is reached. Put differently, Brouwer's account seems already to include
the notion of 'number' into the self-unfolding of the basal intuition. The *Tractatus* had
already provided a solution to this problem by stating that 'a number is an exponent of an
operation' (TLP 6.021). Thus the primary reason for Wittgenstein's negative stance
towards Brouwer is to be found in the *Tractatus*. Wittgenstein subsequently interprets
Brouwer as saying that a new intuition is needed to provide every new individual number
in a sequence. This interpretation of intuitionism provides the starting point for
Wittgenstein's reflections on the role of intuition in rule-following.[34] In MS 106, written in
1929, Wittgenstein writes that he is now better able to understand intuitionism, explaining it as the view that every application of a rule has its own individuality:

> Is it like this: I need a new intuition at each step in a proof? This is connected with
> the question of the individuality of each number. Something of the following sort:
> Supposing there to be a certain general rule, one containing a variable, I must rec-
> ognise each time afresh that this rule may be applied here. No act of foresight can
> absolve me from this act of insight. Since the form to which the rule is applied is in
> fact different at every step. (MS 106, 277; PR, 149)

---

[33] Another point that Marion discusses concerns Brouwer's and Wittgenstein's conception of proofs in
logic. Brouwer states that the proof of a judgement is the act of proving or grasping it, where as
Wittgenstein says that in logic, process and result are equivalent (TLP 6.1261). Marion substantiates this
parallel in 2001. For present purposes, it is not necessary to discuss this point in great detail. See Marion
2001.

[34] Marion notes that Wittgenstein's representation is a misinterpretation of Brouwer's Ur-intuition. As
I primarily focus on Wittgenstein's ideas, I will leave this controversy aside. For details, see Marion 2003,
115–16.

Marion concludes that the *Tractatus'* view on following rules in mathematics is close to Brouwer's intuitionist stance in mathematics, in the sense that both are 'phenomeno-logical'. That is, they assign a role to personal experience in the process of understanding and following a rule. A crucial difference, however, is that Wittgenstein believed that following a rule was merely a matter of repeating the intuition that is needed to grasp the requirement of the rule on one occasion. In other words, he believed that in order to understand what it is to follow a rule, he had merely to observe himself on one occasion while applying a rule.[35] In contrast to this view, the intuitionists claimed – at least in Wittgenstein's view – that a fresh intuition is needed for each new application.

This need for a fresh intuition inspired Wittgenstein to develop his account of rule-following and intuition in subsequent years. In the early 1930s, his views on the theme shifted, and up to 1937 his thoughts changed again and again. The *Nachlass* contains almost 120 remarks on intuition, entries that are sometimes literal copies of early remarks, but others are extensively revised in later years. For my purposes, it is of value to briefly consider these changes, as they culminate in an emphasis on actions. As such, they provide a starting-point for Wittgenstein's critique of Russell's account of causation.

3.4 From intuition to action: Wittgenstein's 1930 views on following rules

As the above quotation from MS 106 shows, in 1929 Wittgenstein stipulated an act of insight or intuition to grasp the relation between a rule and its application. In the 1930s, Wittgenstein's understanding of mathematics changed gradually, and these changes are well exemplified in his remarks on intuition. In *Wittgenstein on Mind and Language*, Stern provides a brief account of this development (Stern 1995, 110–20). As this account needs some corrections, I will examine it in the following.

First, Stern's account contains a mistake in arguing that Wittgenstein's appeal to insight in 1929 is a 'radical departure from the *Tractatus*, where he had unequivocally dismissed the role of intuition [*Anschauung*] in mathematics' (Stern 1995, 113).[36] As we have seen, however, the *Tractatus* held that the relation between '2+2' and '4' is *perceived* or *seen*, and mathematics thus involved some sort of 'mental' manipulation of signs.[37] So, at that time, Wittgenstein clearly had not unequivocally dismissed the role of

---

[35] See Hintikka 1989. This 'phenomenological' conception of rule-following is gradually rejected in the 1930s.

[36] In a footnote Stern refers the reader to another chapter and page in his book. This page, however, discusses a different topic and holds no arguments for a defence of the view as expressed later in the book on the 'act of insight'. (See Stern 1995, 113, n. 74.)

[37] 'Mental' is not to be interpreted as 'psychological'. As explained earlier, the *Tractatus'* terms of 'thinking', 'seeing', 'projecting', 'applying', etc. are operations by a generic user of the system of signs. In speaking of 'mentalism' in the *Tractatus*, one should thus be aware that 'mental' connects to the notion of the metaphysical subject, as mentioned in TLP 5.632, 5.633, and notably 5.641.

intuition in mathematics. Second, although Stern correctly points out that in 1929 Wittgenstein was unhappy with the idea of an act of insight, Stern does not explain why Wittgenstein would (want to) resort to an act of insight in 1929, while supposedly having dismissed any reliance on intuition in the *Tractatus*. Marion's account of the relation between Brouwer and Wittgenstein has put this dissatisfaction in its proper context by connecting it to the growing unease with the *Tractatus*' account of *seeing* internal relations. This unease is exemplified in TS 208, a typescript dictated in 1930 from MSS 105, 106, 107, and 108. To the remark quoted previously from MS 106 Wittgenstein now adds: 'act of decision, not insight'. (See PR, 171 n. 1.) This note recurs in several subsequent *Nachlass* items.[38]

As Stern indicates, this shift from insight to decision changed Wittgenstein's conception of rules and the relation between rules and their applications fundamentally. While he formerly believed that an additional element was needed to fully secure this connection, he now no longer believed that this element was needed, as it was both unnecessary and impossible: 'it was unnecessary because we do not need an unmoved mover in order to follow a rule; it was impossible because nothing could perform that task' (Stern 1995, 116).

Wittgenstein now realized that the appeal to an act of insight does not put an end to an infinite regress of interpretations of the rule. This danger of an infinite regress lies in assuming an intermediary – an intuition or an interpretation – between an action according to a rule, and the rule itself; any interpretation of a rule is to be applied, and the question is how we know that we apply this interpretation correctly. In Wittgenstein's view, no interpretation of a rule can determine what it is to accord with the rule, since every interpretation generates the same problem, that is, of how it should be applied.[39] Given that intuitionism stipulates an intuition to account for continuing with '12' after '6, 8, 10', its account of rule-following could be nothing but inadequate.

Finally, according to Stern, by replacing the act of insight by an act of decision Wittgenstein had fully set aside his former 'mental' understanding of mathematics. However, Stern fails to see that Wittgenstein's views on intuition and following rules were still about to change. In his classes of 1934–5 Wittgenstein expressed his dissatisfaction with the very notion of an 'act of decision':

> It is no act of insight, intuition, which makes us use the rule as we do at the particular point of the series. It would be less confusing to call it an act of decision, though this too is misleading, for nothing like an act of decision must take place, but possibly just an act of writing or speaking. And the mistake which we here and in a thousand similar cases are inclined to make is labelled by the word 'to make' as we have used it in the sentence 'It is no act of insight which makes us use the rule as we do', because there is an idea that 'something must make us' do what we do. And this again joins

---

[38] See for example MS 113, 104r; TS 213, 545. See PG, 301.

[39] PI §213 thus already crystallizes in the mid 1930s. See PI §§143–242. Kripke's controversial interpretation of these paragraphs has raised several criticisms. See Kripke 1982, and for a criticism Baker and Hacker 1984 and Stern 1994.

on to the confusion between cause and reason. *We need have no reason to follow the rule as we do.* The chain of reasons has an end. (BB, 143)

Instead of assuming an act of decision, Wittgenstein now focused on actions as such. This emphasis on actions in rule-following is connected to his changing conception of language.[40] In the mid 1930s, he began to see language as a motley collection of language-games, and the notion of language-games includes the background of training, instruction, and action in the process of learning language. Mathematics is subsequently no longer considered to be a collection of self-contained calculi, but mathematical language is a motley collection of language-games, and each game includes the background of the mathematical practice and actions. In August 1936 Wittgenstein writes:

It is not an act of insight that makes us apply the rule 'add 1' at every step, in such a way as we do apply it. One could rather speak of an act of decision. But that is also misleading, because no deliberating takes place, but we write something down or utter something. Here, as in a thousand other cases, we do not want to hold it true that the chain of grounds has an end. (MS 115, 131)[41]

So, the idea that we make a decision in applying a rule is misleading, says Wittgenstein, for it suggests an act of contemplation that precedes the act of 'adding 1' in each new case. Wittgenstein struggled against this inclination to fully rationalize our practices, not only in the context of mathematics. In an entry written in 1937 he wrote:

Why do I want to communicate also an intention to him, next to what I did? Not because the intention was something that also took place at that moment. Rather, because I want to communicate something about myself, something that transcends what happened at that moment. I show him my inner, when I tell him what I wanted to do. – Not however on the basis of self-observation, but rather via a reaction (one could also call it an intuition). (MS 116, 310)[42]

This last sentence is easily misunderstood. Wittgenstein is not saying that an intuition is the same as a reaction, but he is saying that intuition resembles a reaction in that intuition does not involve deliberation or contemplation. In June 1938, he even compares intuition to instinct (MS 121, 32v) in order to highlight that intuition is not an act of contemplation. So, a reaction or response to the order 'add 2' does not, as a rule, require contemplation. As the *Investigations* states: 'Following a rule is analogous to obeying an order. We are trained

---

[40] See Gerrard 1996 for an overview of the phases of Wittgenstein's thinking on mathematics.

[41] 'Es ist nicht ein Akt der Einsicht der uns die Regel "Addiere immer 1" bei jedem Schritt so anwenden läßt, wie wir sie eben anwenden. ... Eher noch könnte man von einem Akt der Entscheidung reden. Aber auch das [ist/wäre] irreführend, denn es findet kein Deliberieren statt, sondern [er schreibt etwas hin, oder spricht/wir schreiben (einfach) etwas hin, oder sprechen] etwas aus. – Wir wollen hier – wie in tausend andern Fällen – es nicht wahr haben, daß die Kette der Gründe zu einem Ende kommt.'

[42] 'Warum will ich ihm außer dem, was ich tat, auch noch eine Intention mitteilen? – Nicht weil die Intention auch etwas war was damals stattfand. Sondern weil ich etwas über mich mitteilen will, das über das hinausgeht, was damals geschah. Ich erschließe ihm mein Inneres, wenn ich sage was ich tun wollte. – Nicht aber auf Grund von Selbstbeobachtung, sondern durch eine Reaktion (man könnte es auch eine Intuition nennen).'

to do so; we react to an order in a particular way.' (PI §206) 'When I obey a rule, I do not choose. I obey the rule blindly.' (PI §219) That is, I act, and this action is not as a rule preceded by an act of deliberation. Wittgenstein's critical stance towards intuitionism in mathematics is again clearly stated in his lectures of 1939 on the foundations of mathematics:

> Intuitionism comes to saying that you can make a new rule at each point. It requires that we have an intuition at each step in calculation, at each application of a rule; for how can we tell how a rule which has been used for fourteen steps applies at the fifteenth? – And they go on to say that the series of cardinal numbers is known to us by a ground-intuition – that is, we know at each step what the operation of adding 1 will give. We might as well say that we need, not an intuition at each step, but a decision. – Actually, there is neither. You do not make a decision: you simply do a certain thing. It is a question of a certain practice. Intuitionism is all bosh – entirely. (LFM, 237)

The previous overview shows that Wittgenstein's understanding of rule-following in mathematics changed several times in the early 1930s, and in the second half of the 1930s he made a final step away from the Tractarian account by seeing the connection between a rule and an application not in an act of decision, but in an action as such. That is, whether someone has correctly understood the order 'add two' is exhibited in his continuing the series '1000, 1002, 1004...' with '1006, 1008, and 1010'. No intuition or act of decision is in play here. So this new understanding of rule-following, which abandons any reliance on 'mental' components, was not already in place in 1933, as Stern assumes, but only in the second half of the 1930s.

With the previous account on Wittgenstein's development on intuition and following rules in mathematics in place, we may now, in conclusion, return to Russell's account of perceiving a cause. As we have seen, Russell argued that in certain cases we indubitably see a relation between cause and effect. This 'seeing' thus functions as intermediary between cause and effect, and as such it supposedly establishes the connection between them. 'Cause and Effect' emphasized that it is of no use to assume an intermediary between cause and effect, as this 'seeing' or 'perceiving' does not put a halt to the question 'are you certain that this is the cause?' On Russell's account, we still need an understanding or interpretation of this 'seeing'. This 'seeing', Wittgenstein held, is liable to misinterpretation, and 'Cause and Effect' puts a halt to an infinite regress of interpretations by further explaining that our actions and reactions are at the basis of the language-game with cause and effect. The parallel between Wittgenstein's criticism of Brouwer's account of rule-following on the one hand, and his criticism of Russell's account of the relation between cause and effect on the other, is now obvious: in both cases, Wittgenstein criticizes the postulate of an intermediary, arguing instead that the seemingly unbridgeable gulfs between a rule and its application, and a cause and its effect, are chimeras.[43] Rather,

---

[43] Stern recognizes the close parallel between the demand for an act of insight to close the otherwise 'unbridgeable gulf' between a rule and its application, and the demand for a mental process to bring about the 'leap from the sign to what is signified' (see Stern 1995, 117). As Rhees and Winch have indicated,

the connection between a rule and its application, and between a cause and its effect, is exhibited in our actions and reactions. This parallel in reasoning has exhibited the close connection between Wittgenstein's reflections on rule-following in mathematics in the early 1930s and his reflections on causation in the second half of the 1930s.

4. CONCLUSION

It is widely acknowledged that many ideas in 'Cause and Effect' prefigure much of what is central to *On Certainty*. The core idea contained in both works is that certainty resides in our actions. I believe that the previous account of the parallel in Wittgenstein's criticism of Brouwer and Russell legitimizes the conclusion that the account of certainty as found in *On Certainty* has its precedent in the early 1930s, in reflections on rule-following in mathematics. In other words, the roots of Wittgenstein's account of certainty as expressed in 1949–51 are found in the early 1930s, in his critique of Brouwer's notion of intuition. The importance of Wittgenstein's reflections on mathematics in this respect is barely recognized. The fact that Rhees has decided not to include in 'Cause and Effect' the remarks on mathematics as found in the source text (MS 119) has hindered a clear understanding of this point. In addition to Rhees' suggestion (see CE §1 n. 1), I believe we should not only acknowledge Russell's influence on 'Cause and Effect', but also recognize Brouwer's influence, an influence that is thus still felt in *On Certainty*; in the last years of his life, Wittgenstein harks back to his earlier account of certainty as expressed in 'Cause and Effect', now in critical response to Moore's ideas on knowledge and certainty. For an adequate understanding of *On Certainty*, we should thus not only attend to Moore's ideas, but also to Wittgenstein's earlier responses to Brouwer and Russell.[44]

REFERENCES

AMBROSE, A. (1935). 'Finitism in Mathematics' (I), *Mind*, 44 (174): 186–203. (Revised version printed in *Essays in Analysis*, New York: Humanities Press, 1966.)

BAKER, G. P. and HACKER, P. M. S. (1984). *Scepticism, Rules and Language*. Oxford: Blackwell.

BROUWER, L. E. J. (1975). 'Mathematics, Science and Language', in *Collected Works*, vol. 1, ed. A. Heyting. Amsterdam: Elsevier. (Originally published in 1929.)

BUDD, M. (1989). *Wittgenstein's Philosophy of Psychology*. London: Routledge.

part of Russell's struggle in 'The Limits of Empiricism' is exactly to establish this leap between the sign and what is signified. Wittgenstein's criticisms of Brouwer and Russell, respectively, exactly exhibit this parallel.

[44] Part of the work on this chapter was done at the Wittgenstein Archives at the University of Bergen (WAB).

DESCARTES, R. (1993). *Meditations on First Philosophy*, ed. S. Tweyman. London and New York: Routledge; New York: Humanities Press.

DUMMETT, M. (2000). *Elements of Intuitionism*. Oxford: Clarendon Press.

EAMES, E. R. (1969). *Bertrand Russell's Theory of Knowledge*. London: George Allen & Unwin Ltd.

EWALD, W. ed. (1996). *From Kant to Hilbert: a Source Book in the Foundations of Mathematics*. Oxford: Clarendon Press.

FEIGL, H. (1981). 'The Wiener Kreis in America', in R. S. Cohen ed., *Inquiries and Provocations: Selected Writings 1929–1974*. Dordrecht: Reidel.

GENNIP, K. VAN (2008). *Wittgenstein's On Certainty in the Making: Studies into its historical and philosophical background*. PhD diss., University of Groningen, Netherlands.

GERRARD, S. (1996). 'A Philosophy of Mathematics between Two Camps', in H. Sluga and D. Stern eds., *The Cambridge Companion to Wittgenstein*. Cambridge: Cambridge University Press.

GOETHE, J. W. (1990). *Faust*, trans. and ed. W. Kaufmann. New York: Anchor Books.

GLOCK, H. J. (1996). *A Wittgenstein Dictionary*. Oxford: Blackwell (The Blackwell Philosopher Dictionaries).

HACKER, P. M. S. (1972). *Insight and Illusion*. Oxford: Oxford University Press.

HARK, M. ter (1990). *Beyond the Inner and the Outer: Wittgenstein's Philosophy of Psychology*. Dordrecht: Kluwer.

HINTIKKA, J. (1989). 'Rules, Games and Experiences: Wittgenstein's Discussion of Rule-following in the Light of His Development', *Revue Internationale de Philosophie*, 43: 279–97. (Reprinted in Hintikka 1996.)

—— ed. (1994). *Aspects of Metaphor*. Dordrecht: Kluwer.

—— (1996). *Ludwig Wittgenstein: Half-Truths and One-and-a-half-Truths*. Dordrecht: Kluwer.

KANT, I. (1998). *Critique of Pure Reason*, trans. and ed. P. Guyer and A. W. Wood. Cambridge: Cambridge University Press.

KRIPKE, S. A. (1982). *Wittgenstein on Rules and Private Language: An Elementary Exposition*. Oxford; Blackwell.

MALCOLM, N. (1986). 'Language as Expressive Behaviour', in *Nothing is Hidden: Wittgenstein's Criticism of his Early Thought*. Oxford: Blackwell.

MANCOSU, P. ed. (1998). *From Brouwer to Hilbert: The Debate on the Foundations of Mathematics in the 1920s*. New York and Oxford: Oxford University Press.

MARION, M. (1998). *Wittgenstein, Finitism, and the Foundations of Mathematics*. Oxford: Clarendon Press.

—— (2001). 'Qu'est-ce que l'inférence? Une relecture du *Tractatus-Logico Philosophicus*', *Archives de Philosophie*, 64: 545–67.

—— (2003). 'Wittgenstein and Brouwer', *Synthese*, 137: 103–27.

McGUINNESS, B. (1991). 'Wittgenstein's Beziehungen zum Schlick-Kreis', in P. Kruntorad, R. Haller, and W. Hochkeppel eds., *Jour fixe der Vernunft: Der Wiener Kreis und die Folgen*. Vienna: Holder–Pichler–Tempsky.

—— (2002). 'In the Shadow of Goethe: Wittgenstein's Intellectual Project', *European Review*, 10 (4): 447–57.

MONK, R. (1990). *Ludwig Wittgenstein: The Duty of Genius*. London: Vintage.

MOORE, G. E. (1929–1939). 'Wittgenstein. Extracts from Diaries', unpublished, Cambridge University Library, Add. 8330-1/5.

MOYAL-SHARROCK, D. (2004a). *Understanding Wittgenstein's On Certainty*. Basingstoke: Palgrave Macmillan.

—— ed. (2004b). *The Third Wittgenstein: The Post-Investigations Works*. Aldershot: Ashgate.

OGDEN, C. K. and RICHARDS, I. A. (1922/1970). *The Meaning of Meaning: A Study of the Influence of Language upon Thought and of the Science of Symbolism*. New York: Harcourt.

RHEES, R. (1982). 'Language and Reality', *The Gadfly*, 5 (2): 22–33.

—— (1984). 'The Language of Sense-data and Private Experience', *Philosophical Investigations*, 7 (1): 1–45. (Reprinted in PO.)

RICHARDSON, J. T. E. (1976). *The Grammar of Justification: An Interpretation of Wittgenstein's Philosophy of Language*. New York: St. Martin's Press.

RUSSELL, B. (1912). *The Problems of Philosophy*. Oxford: Oxford University Press.

—— (1921). *The Analysis of Mind*. London: George Allen & Unwin; New York: Macmillan.

—— (1927). *The Analysis of Matter*. London: Kegan Paul, Trench, Trubner; New York: Harcourt.

—— (1937). 'The Limits of Empiricism', *Proceedings of the Aristotelian Society*, 36: 131–50.

—— (1948). *Human Knowledge: Its Scope and Limits*. New York: Simon and Schuster.

—— (1968). *The Autobiography of Bertrand Russell*, vol. 2: *1914–1944*. London: George Allen & Unwin.

SHANKER, S. (1987). *Wittgenstein and the Turning-Point in the Philosophy of Mathematics*. London: Croom Helm.

STERN, D. G. (1994). 'Recent Work on Wittgenstein, 1980–1990', *Synthese*, 98: 415–58.

—— (1995). *Wittgenstein on Mind and Language*. Oxford: Oxford University Press.

STIGT, W. P. VAN (1990). *Brouwer's Intuitionism: Studies in the History and Philosophy of Mathematics*. Amsterdam: North-Holland.

—— (1998). 'Introduction', in Mancosu 1998.

SUNDHOLM, G. (1994). 'Existence, Proof and Truth-Making: A Perspective on the Intuitionistic Conception of Truth', *Topoi*, 13 (2): 117–26.

WINCH, P. (1987). 'Im Anfang war die Tat', in *Trying to Make Sense*. Oxford: Blackwell.

WITTGENSTEIN, L. (1958). *The Blue and Brown Books*. Oxford: Blackwell.

—— (1966). *Lectures and Conversations on Aesthetics, Psychology and Religious Belief*, from the notes of Y. Smythies, R. Rhees, and J. Taylor, ed. C. Barrett. Oxford: Blackwell.

—— (1973). *Letters to C. K. Ogden with Comments on the English Translation of the Tractatus Logico-Philosophicus*, ed. G. H. von Wright. Oxford: Blackwell.

—— (1974). *Philosophical Grammar*, ed. R. Rhees, trans. A. Kenny. Oxford: Blackwell.

—— (1975). *Philosophical Remarks*, ed. R. Rhees, trans. R. Hargreaves and R. White. Oxford: Blackwell.

—— (1976). 'Cause and Effect: Intuitive Awareness', *Philosophia*, 6 (3–4): 391–445. (Reprinted in PO.)

—— (1976). *Lectures on the Foundations of Mathematics, Cambridge 1939*, ed. Cora Diamond. Hassocks, Sussex: Harvester Press.

—— (1979). *Wittgenstein's Lectures: Cambridge, 1932–1935*, from the notes of A. Ambrose and M. Macdonald, ed. A. Ambrose. Oxford: Blackwell.

—— (1993). *Philosophical Occasions, 1912–1951*, ed. J. Klagge and A. Nordmann. Indianapolis and Cambridge: Hackett Publishing Company.

—— (1995). *Cambridge Letters: Correspondence with Russell, Keynes, Moore, Ramsey and Sraffa*, ed. B. McGuinness and G. H. von Wright. Oxford: Blackwell.

WITTGENSTEIN, L. (1998). *On Certainty*, ed. G. E. M. Anscombe and G. H. von Wright, trans. D. Paul and G. E. M. Anscombe. Oxford: Blackwell.

—— (1999). *Philosophical Investigations*, ed. G. E. M. Anscombe and R. Rhees. Oxford: Blackwell.

—— (2000). *Wittgenstein's Nachlass: The Bergen Electronic Edition*. Oxford: Oxford University Press.

—— (2005). *Tractatus Logico-Philosophicus*. London and New York: Routledge.

WRIGLEY, M. (1989). 'The Origins of Wittgenstein's Verificationism', *Synthese*, 78: 265–90.

PART VI

METHOD

CHAPTER 26

THE DEVELOPMENT OF WITTGENSTEIN'S PHILOSOPHY

OSKARI KUUSELA

WITTGENSTEIN writes in the Preface to the *Philosophical Investigations*:

> Four years ago I had occasion to re-read my first book (the *Tractatus Logico-Philosophicus*) and to explain its ideas to someone. It suddenly seemed to me that I should publish those old thoughts and the new ones together: that the latter could be seen in the right light only by contrast with and against the background of my old way of thinking.

In this passage Wittgenstein distinguishes between two aspects of the relation of his later work to his early philosophy, and between two senses in which knowledge of his early work can help in the interpretation of his later philosophy. On the one hand, he suggests that his later philosophy can 'be seen in the right light only ... against the background' of his 'old way of thinking'. Presumably this is so because the later work develops further certain ideas that were present already in the *Tractatus* and make Wittgenstein's philosophy a distinctive contribution to the tradition of philosophy. Thus a proper comprehension of the sense in which Wittgenstein's later work constitutes such a contribution, or a departure from the tradition, requires understanding how his early work constituted such a contribution or departure. On the other hand, to the extent that Wittgenstein in his later work moves beyond the *Tractatus*, the later thoughts can 'be seen in the right light only by contrast with' his early thought.

A key aspiration of this chapter is to maintain a balance between these two aspects of the relation of Wittgenstein's later work to his early work. I shall present the later Wittgenstein as developing a deeper understanding of certain central insights of his early philosophy which then, transformed, continue to be equally central to his later work. Thus the relation of the later Wittgenstein to his early philosophy is at the same time appreciative and critical. While the early work, according to him, contains something 'good and original' (MS 183, 31), he was also 'forced to recognize grave mistakes in what [he] wrote in that early book.' (PI, Preface; my interpolation) My focus will be on Wittgenstein's conception of philosophy and his method. But as I will explain, this has direct consequences, for example, for the interpretation of what he means when he says that in his early philosophy he did not understand the complexity of language (cf. PI §23). A proper grasp of the way in which Wittgenstein seeks to correct his early view of logic and language in his later philosophy requires understanding the development of his conception of philosophy and its methodology. Only thus is it possible, for instance, to avoid the mistake of portraying Wittgenstein's development in terms of a switch from one theory of language to another.

Correspondingly, I believe, it is the method of philosophy developed in Wittgenstein's early and later work that makes his philosophy a distinctive contribution to the tradition, or a departure from it. The *Tractatus*' method, as I will explain, constitutes a response to a fundamental confusion which philosophy in the traditional sense, according to Wittgenstein, is entangled in. His later methodological considerations, then, are a renewed attempt to deal with the same confusion and the problems it creates, but now he also takes into account how this confusion pervaded his early philosophy. In order, therefore, to understand the development of Wittgenstein's philosophy, we must begin with the *Tractatus*' method.

1. WITTGENSTEIN'S MAIN CONTENTION AND THE *TRACTATUS*' METHOD

Following the completion of the manuscript of the *Tractatus* Wittgenstein responds in a letter to Russell, who, having read the manuscript 'twice carefully' (CL, 124), presents him with a list of queries:

> – Now I'm afraid you haven't really got hold of my main contention,…The main point is the theory of what can be expressed (gesagt) by prop[osition]s – i.e. by language – (and, which comes to the same, what can be *thought*) and what can not be expressed by prop[osition]s, but only shown (gezeigt); which, I believe, is the cardinal problem of philosophy. (CL, 124)

Arguably, what Wittgenstein calls 'the cardinal problem of philosophy', and to which his theory of what can be expressed by language is intended as a solution, concerns the concept of necessity. The problem relates to an aspiration characteristic of the philosophical tradition to rise above the merely contingent and accidental and to achieve knowledge of what is necessary or essential. More specifically, the necessary or essential features of reality are considered in this connection as objects of true/false statements and the business of philosophy, correspondingly, as the assertion of necessary truths. This is where the cardinal problem – evidently, quite appropriately so called – lies. It is the question whether necessities can be the object of true/false statements at all, and in this sense, what can and cannot be said.[1]

In a stark contrast with the tradition, Wittgenstein maintains that necessities cannot be the object of statements, and that there is a 'confusion, very widespread among philosophers, between internal relations and proper (external) relations'. (TLP 4.122; cf. 4.126)[2] As he says, 'The holding of such internal properties and relations cannot…be asserted by propositions, but it shows itself in the propositions, which present the facts and treat the objects in question.' (TLP 4.122) Accordingly, when in the Preface Wittgenstein expresses his belief that the way philosophical problems are posed depends on misunderstanding the logic of language, he is presumably referring to this specific, widespread confusion among philosophers.

Here it is crucial, however, that although Wittgenstein calls his main contention 'the theory of what can be expressed by language', by such a theory he cannot be interpreted to mean a set of assertions intended to inform anybody about and to prescribe what can and cannot be expressed.[3] To begin with, this would contradict an explanation he gives to Russell in the very same letter in response to the latter's characterization of a theory of types as consisting of sentences of the form 'a…symbol must…'. (CL, 122) Wittgenstein writes: 'That's exactly what one can't say. You cannot prescribe to a symbol what it may be used to express. All that a symbol CAN express, it MAY express. This is a short answer but it is true!' (CL, 125) Notably, the same point is made also in the *Tractatus* where Wittgenstein writes: 'Logic must take care of itself.…Everything that is possible in logic is also permitted.…In a certain sense, we cannot make mistakes in logic.' (TLP 5.473) The philosophical significance of this point, characterized in the pre-*Tractatus* notebooks as 'an extremely profound and important insight' (MS 101, 13r/NB, 2), can be explained as follows.

There is a sense in which Wittgenstein is saying something quite uncontroversial and obvious. For, naturally, the possibility of meaningful statements does not depend on the work of philosophers and logicians. That languages as a matter of fact pre-date logicians shows this clearly enough. Accordingly, no theories are needed, in principle, to inform language users about what can and cannot be said, as if the capability to distinguish sense from nonsense (to recognize what is and is not a linguistic expression) were not already part of being a competent language user. Thus there is nothing for logicians, including Russell and Wittgenstein, to assert in the sense of informing and prescribing.

More specifically, insofar as logic's purpose would be to prescribe what can and cannot be said, apparently the principled, non-random way to do so would be by reference to

---

[1] For a discussion of what Wittgenstein means by 'the cardinal problem of philosophy' as well as further references to discussions of this term in Wittgenstein literature, see Kremer 2007. I shall not explicitly address the similarities and differences between my interpretation and those of others.

[2] Wittgenstein uses the term 'internal property' for necessary properties: 'A property is internal if it is unthinkable that its object does not possess it.' (TLP 4.123)

[3] This goes also for statements such as 4.122 whose status cannot ultimately be understood as that of a theoretical assertion.

the essence of language, i.e. by reference to the nature of the medium of expression itself. This brings to view how Wittgenstein's critique of the tradition of philosophy unfolds from his dictum that logic takes care of itself. It entails that it is not possible to make informative assertions (i.e. to provide knowledge or put forward true/false knowledge claims) about the necessary characteristics of language, nor about the necessary characteristics of anything else, insofar as a comprehension of such necessary features forms the basis for the correct application of the expressions in terms of which such assertions are made. That is, insofar as the correct application of a particular concept, for example, requires a comprehension of the criteria of identity of the object to which the concept is applied, i.e. knowledge of its essential/necessary characteristics, then in a certain sense language users already know everything a philosophical or logical theory of the essential/necessary features of this object might want to inform them about. Accordingly, the widespread confusion of philosophers can be described as the mistake of attempting to inform language users about something the knowledge of which is already presupposed by the possibility of trying to inform them about it. For this, in effect, is what treating necessary or essential characteristics as if they were on par with the accidental and contingent amounts to. Similarly, if Wittgenstein were trying to put forward theoretical assertions about what can and cannot be said, he would himself fall into the very confusion of which he seeks to convict others.

An alternative interpretation of what Wittgenstein means by 'theory' in the letter to Russell, and of the *Tractatus'* conception of the discipline of logic, can now be outlined as follows. Unlike a 'normative science', whose task is prescription, the task of logic is description. In accordance with this, Wittgenstein elaborates on the consequences of the dictum of 5.473 in a notebook: 'Logic takes care of itself; all we have to do is to look and see how it does it.' (MS 101, 39r/NB, 11; cf. 43) Thus, instead of attempting to prescribe or inform his reader about anything, the object of Wittgenstein's book and his theory is merely to *remind* the reader about something she already knows in the capacity of a language user.[4]

---

[4] Wittgenstein's comprehension of logic as a descriptive discipline is emphasized by McGinn (see 2006, 20ff.). That Wittgenstein only relies on his readers' 'ordinary logical capacity' in the *Tractatus*, and that its notion of nonsense is not a technical one, has been argued by the so-called resolute readers of the book. (See for example Conant 2002 , Diamond 1991 , and Kremer 2001.) Resolute readings stand in contrast with so-called ineffability interpretations. On the latter view, the readers' recognition of the nonsensicality of statements about necessities is based on their acceptance of Wittgenstein's theory of the essence of language, whereby a theory is a set of assertions based on argument and claimed to be true (although this truth is seen as ineffable). This leads to the paradox of the *Tractatus*: its nonsensicality is supposed to follow from its truth, but if it is nonsense it cannot be true. Accordingly, the problem with the ineffability interpretation is that it portrays Wittgenstein as falling prey to the widespread confusion of philosophers in such a straightforward way that it becomes hard to take his attempt at clarification quite seriously, or to see the *Tractatus* as a serious attempt at departure from the philosophical tradition. Currently, the foremost representative of the ineffability interpretation is Peter Hacker (1986; 2001, Chs. 4 and 5). Similarly, for example, according to Schroeder the notion of nonsense employed in the *Tractatus* is technical (2006, 110). The ineffability interpretation suggests a rather different account of the development of Wittgenstein's philosophy from that proposed here. But I shall not discuss this contrast explicitly.

A crucial point here is this: even though logic may take care of itself in principle, language users nevertheless (as a matter of empirical fact) have a tendency to get confused about logic. That is, although symbols might never fail to symbolize, individual speakers may sometimes so fail and, consequently, there is room for reminders and clarifications. The status of the statements of the *Tractatus* then is that of such clarifications. As Wittgenstein writes in remarks leading to the ones quoted above concerning the impossibility of stating anything (putting forward theories) about internal relations and properties:

> The object of philosophy is the logical clarification of thoughts.
> Philosophy is not a doctrine but an activity....
> Philosophy does not result in 'philosophical propositions' but in propositions becoming clear. (TLP 4.112)

But given this characterization of philosophy as a clarificatory activity, what more specifically should be understood by such an activity? At the end of his book Wittgenstein describes what he calls 'the only strictly correct method' by saying: 'To say nothing except what can be said, ... and then always when someone else wished to say something metaphysical, to demonstrate to him that he had given no meaning to certain signs in his propositions.' (TLP 6.53) This method is not the one actually employed in the *Tractatus*. For as Wittgenstein explains in the remark following the one just quoted, a criterion for understanding his book is the recognition of its propositions as nonsensical. An explanation for why Wittgenstein makes a point of distinguishing between these two methods is that the distinction is meant to indicate a division of labour. The strictly correct method is one which the *Tractatus* aims to introduce, and tries to make apparent that we should adopt it in philosophy. But in order to introduce the strictly correct method Wittgenstein makes use of the method that is not strictly correct. I will shortly explain why it is open for Wittgenstein to employ the not strictly correct method in introducing the correct one. Before that, however, I need to say something about the latter.

What Wittgenstein means by the strictly correct method is, arguably, a method of the logical analysis of language that involves the use of a particular kind of notation, a concept-script. In this notation logical distinctions that are easy to get confused about in the use of everyday language are readily detectable. Thus what is unclear can be rendered clear by translating expressions of everyday language into this notation, and philosophical confusions clarified this way. As Wittgenstein explains this idea of how to get rid of philosophy's 'fundamental confusions' (TLP 3.324): 'In order to escape such errors, we must employ a sign-language that excludes them....A symbolism that is governed by *logical* grammar – by logical syntax.' (TLP 3.325)

Logical analyses of the type just described would then exemplify the strictly correct method in the sense that when engaged in an analysis in terms of a concept-script one would not be making any statements about the necessary or essential features of reality or language. Rather than making statements, to provide logical analyses is to make what is necessary or essential more easily discernible by means of a transition from one mode of expression to another one.[5] Hence to philosophize in this manner is not to make any assertions about what cannot be said.[6]

It is a controversial question whether Wittgenstein actually introduces in the *Tractatus* a concept-script or merely discusses the philosophical significance of such a notation.[7] Nevertheless, my suggestion is that the *Tractatus'* notation for the truth-functional analysis of propositions and the (misleadingly so baptized) 'picture theory of propositions' are put forward as components of a concept-script, i.e. a scheme for a logical analysis of propositions. Wittgenstein, in other words, seeks to introduce in his book a conception of logical analysis according to which propositions are analysable into truth functions of elementary propositions which consist of simple names that stand for the simple objects of reality. Thus, rather than theoretical assertions about the essence of language, Wittgenstein's statements about, for example, the representational character of propositions constitute a part of his articulation of a scheme in terms of which language is to be analysed. In accordance with this, he elucidates the status of his conception of the essence of propositions by saying that it is the description of a logical constant, the only general primitive sign in logic. (TLP 5.47ff.)[8]

Naturally, in order to qualify as a successful tool of analysis, Wittgenstein's concept-script must reflect correctly the logic of language (or, as 3.325 formulates it, be governed by logical syntax; see above). Accordingly, the introduction of its principles already constitutes an exercise in logical clarification of language.[9] Here it is also important that, insofar as Wittgenstein's notation correctly reflects the essential characteristics of language, the statements in his book with the help of which the principles of his notation have been introduced

[5] The difference between making philosophical statements and clarification in terms of a concept-script can be explicated by reference to the distinction between asserting and translating: even though one may make statements about the correctness of translations, to translate is not to assert.

[6] Both the strictly correct method and the not strictly correct one are methods of reminding: of making clearer something that is already supposed to be known. This is a key characteristic that unites these methods.

[7] For instance, Ostrow 2002, 9 denies that he introduces a concept-script.

[8] Beyond this reference I shall not seek to provide any textual evidence from the *Tractatus* for this interpretation of the significance of the 'picture theory' (and so on). What speaks for this interpretation (as regards the issue of Wittgenstein's development in particular) is that it explains both how Wittgenstein could have maintained (by the time of the *Tractatus*) that he was not putting forward a theory of language (in the sense of making theoretical assertions) and how he was nevertheless tacitly committed to a theory of the essence of language. (I will return to this issue below.) Alternatively one might explain the point of the interpretation by saying: it explains how the *Tractatus* can be seen as clarifying the logic of language and articulating a conception of language, but not as involved in making theoretical assertions about language. (As I will explain, how Wittgenstein in effect ties himself to a theory of language has to do with the philosophical role he assigns to the concept-script or the *Tractatus'* conception of the methodology of philosophy.) See Kuusela 2006, 2008, and 2011 for more detailed discussions.

[9] Examples are his introduction of the principle that logical constants do not represent or that the kind of complete generality relevant to logic (associated with the notions of essence and necessity) is not expressed by propositions but by variables. (Cf. TLP 3.31ff., 4.0312.) These principles, incorporated in Wittgenstein's notation, constitute philosophical/logical clarifications of the employment of relevant expressions whose use, for example, Frege and Russell, according to him, did not construe correctly. For discussion of the *Tractatus'* clarifications of these issues, see McGinn 2006, Chs. 7 and 10.

are, indeed, nonsense, as Wittgenstein says about the propositions in his book (TLP 6.54). In this notation there simply is no room for propositions about necessities of the type the *Tractatus* seems to contain. But Wittgenstein's propositions are not assumed to be recognized as nonsense on the basis of a (paradoxically nonsensical) theory put forward by him. Rather, as explained, the reader is expected to be able to recognize their nonsensicality on the basis of her pre-theoretical comprehension of the logic of language, on which recognition of the legitimacy of Wittgenstein's notation and his method ultimately depends.

From the point of view of the present interpretation the not strictly correct method employed in the *Tractatus*, therefore, is, as it were, a method of gesturing (though not at ineffable truths). Wittgenstein's statements about the concept of necessity (or internal or formal properties and relations), for example, are attempts to talk about something that ultimately cannot be captured in terms of theoretical assertions. The purpose of these statements is to direct the reader's attention to the logical distinction between the expression of necessity and factual statements (true/false assertions) that she is already familiar with, but which is only obscurely delineated in the everyday language. If successful, Wittgenstein's statements lead the reader to the recognition that there is an important distinction to be drawn here which the tradition of philosophy ignores, and the *Tractatus*' statements only gesture at, ultimately collapsing into nonsense. Crucially, however, because Wittgenstein is not describing this distinction with the purpose of informing his reader about it, it is possible for him merely to hint at it. The situation differs radically from Wittgenstein's trying to make an informative true statement about the distinction, as such statements cannot at the same time both describe the relevant fact (inform about it) and be nonsensical.[10]

What it is to recognize a philosophical clarification as correct requires comment, however. Insofar as the task of philosophy is not to make true/false statements about its objects of investigation, the correctness of a philosophical clarification is not to be understood according to the model of the correctness of factual statements. The correctness of a philosophical clarification is not a matter of a logical model's correspondence with any logical or metaphysical facts, as it were. Rather, the criterion of correctness is the dissolution of relevant philosophical or logical problems. Thus, for example, the adoption of Wittgenstein's concept-script and the associated conception of language (assuming its correctness) constitutes the dissolution of problems relating to negation, the status of formal concepts, (justification of) inferential relations, and so on. But this is all: there is no ineffable metaphysics that explains why the problems disappear. Wittgenstein sums up this thought: 'we are in the possession of the right logical conception once we have a sign-language in which everything is all right'. (TLP 4.1213)

To conclude, my suggestion is that Wittgenstein's solution to the cardinal problem of philosophy consists in a methodological invention: the introduction of a method of

---

[10] According to this interpretation, to move beyond the *Tractatus*' statements (as the reader who understands Wittgenstein is expected to do – TLP 6.54) is to come to adopt, on the basis of Wittgenstein's clarifications, a particular approach to philosophy, not to adopt a paradoxically nonsensical theory about the logic of language.

analysis that respects the distinction between what can and cannot be said, and a set of logical tools. This invention is intimately connected with and ultimately inseparable from considerations relating to the logic of language. Such considerations, however, do not provide an independent justification for the method, but the idea of such a justification is nonsensical, involving a relapse to just that traditional mode of philosophizing Wittgenstein is trying to leave behind. Next, I will turn to certain central points of continuity between Wittgenstein's early and later thought.

2. CONTINUITIES: THE IDEA OF PHILOSOPHY AS CLARIFICATION

Wittgenstein writes (in 1948): 'Merely recognizing the philosophical problem as a logical one is progress. The proper attitude and the method accompany it.' (MS 137, 104b; LWPP I §256) Read in its context, this remark is most naturally interpreted as referring to the kind of progress Wittgenstein takes this approach to allow him to make with certain problems in the philosophy of mind. But it would not seem exaggerated to construe the remark as expressing a more general methodological point. In this sense, the *Tractatus* may be seen as constituting progress from Wittgenstein's later perspective when compared with more traditional approaches which are characterized by the aspiration to put forward theses, i.e. true/false assertions, about necessities. This is indicated by the fact that a number of ideas that separate the *Tractatus* from the tradition continue to be important also for the later Wittgenstein. My presentation of Wittgenstein's early thought above is designed to make it easy to notice such points of continuity to which I now turn.

A critical point which is central to the later philosophy and intimately connected with the 'widespread confusion' that the *Tractatus* sought to address is expressed thus: 'Philosophical investigations: conceptual investigations. The essential thing about metaphysics: that the difference between factual and conceptual investigations is not clear to it.' (RPP I §949/Z §458) Hence Wittgenstein evidently continues to hold on to the *Tractatus*' 'main contention' that necessities cannot be the object of factual statements. For the unclarity Wittgenstein sees as characteristic of metaphysics is the same both in his early and later philosophy: metaphysics approaches conceptual or logical questions as if they could be answered by means of factual statements (cf. BB 18, 35).

It is also important that philosophy can only be understood as a conceptual or logical investigation in Wittgenstein's sense insofar as it concerns something we already know. That is, only if logic or language 'takes care of itself' can philosophy be understood as clarification, i.e. as not being in the business of informing us about anything, for example, prescribing what we can or cannot say. Thus the idea of philosophy as helping us to grasp more clearly what we already knew remains equally central to Wittgenstein's later as it was to his early philosophy. He writes in the PI: 'The problems are solved, not by giving new information, but by arranging what we have always known. Philosophy is a battle against the bewitchment of our intelligence by means of language.' (PI §109) 'The work of the philosopher consists in assembling reminders.' (PI §127; cf. §89)

Similarly, in an apparently perfect agreement with the *Tractatus*' conception that the result of philosophy is not philosophical doctrines but clarity, and that philosophy dissolves rather than answers problems (TLP 4.003, 4.112), Wittgenstein characterizes the aim of his later philosophy as that of dissolving philosophical problems. He writes in the *Big Typescript* in the early 1930s:

> As I practice philosophy, its entire task consists in expressing myself in such a way that certain disquietudes . . . disappear. . . .
> If I am correct, philosophical problems must be completely solvable, in contrast to others. . . .
> The problems are solved in the actual sense of the word–like a lump of sugar in the water. (TS 213, 421/PO, 181, 183)

Corresponding characterizations are also found in the PI where he describes his investigation as one that 'eliminate[s] misunderstandings' (PI §91) or clears away misunderstandings concerning the use of words (PI §90). The aim of such an investigation is '*complete* clarity' which means that 'philosophical problems should *completely* disappear.' (PI §133) As in the early philosophy, the disappearance of problems is not thought to be the result of theoretical assertions or theses: 'And we may not advance any kind of theory. There must not be anything hypothetical in our considerations. We must do away with all explanation, and description alone must take its place.' (PI §109; cf. PI §128)

As regards Wittgenstein's development, it is remarkable how well the *Tractatus*' approach fits his later characterization that the task of philosophy consists in expressing oneself in such a way that problems disappear – or as he also says, that to solve philosophical problems is to change the mode of expression or thinking (MS 115, 36; MS 174, 6r).[11] Evidently, the method of dissolving philosophical problems by translating statements into a notation such as a concept-script provides us with a particular example of the possibly more manifold approach of attempting to find modes of expression that make problems disappear. Hence, although analyses in terms of logical calculi might not play a significant role in Wittgenstein's later philosophy, his later clarificatory remarks which suggest a change in the mode of expression should apparently be seen as having a similar status in the following sense. Neither analyses, as envisaged in the *Tractatus*, nor Wittgenstein's later remarks constitute true/false assertions about anything. Rather, in both cases particular modes of expression or presentation are articulated and put forward with the purpose of promoting conceptual clarity. (I will discuss differences between

---

[11] In the PI Wittgenstein writes about philosophical problems: '*Many* of them can be removed by substituting one form of expression for another one.' (PI §90; my italics) This may be taken as an indication of the later Wittgenstein's recognition that there is not only one (correct) method of philosophy, as if a philosophical problem were always to be dissolved through the transformation of a mode of expression. Rather, there are many methods (PI §133). I will return below to the issue of the plurality of methods in Wittgenstein's later philosophy, but for the moment will focus on the common ground between his early and later thought.

Wittgenstein's early and later conception of the status of philosophical statements below.) The character of such clarifications can be further elucidated as follows.

A highly interesting explanation of the kind of importance particular notations or modes of expression have for Wittgenstein is formulated as a comment on his regular interlocutor in the early 1930s, Frank Ramsey:

> R does not comprehend the value I place on a particular notation any more than the value I place on a particular word because he does not see that in it an entire way of looking at the object is expressed; the angle from which I now regard the thing. The notation is the last expression of a philosophical view. (MS 105, 10, 12; continuation of MS 106 on even pages)

This seems revealing in many respects with regard to questions that may arise about Wittgenstein's approach in the context of either his early or later philosophy. In particular the question might be raised: if Wittgenstein is merely concerned to introduce a method for the dissolution of philosophical problems, then are the results of his philosophy 'merely negative'? Does philosophy thus conceived not offer any 'positive philosophical insights'?[12] The quote may be read as explaining why an affirmative answer to these questions would be hasty.

The substitution of one mode of expression for another, to be sure, does not constitute a true/false statement about anything. But whether only statements can serve as vehicle for the expression of positive philosophical insights is not obvious, and this assumption cannot be taken for granted without begging relevant questions. To begin with, insofar as logical distinctions that are not perspicuous in one system of expression can be made perspicuous in another one, it seems that the articulation of an alternative mode of expression suited for the purpose (such as a concept-script) can indeed be philosophically significant. But looking at the issue from this angle, it would be odd to deny that a suggestion to exchange a particular mode of expression for another one, when it serves the purpose of the dissolution of philosophical problems, could not be seen as the expression of philosophical insight. (An example is the early Wittgenstein's dissolution of Russell's paradox through his clarification of the status of variables and his elucidation of how a function cannot take itself as an argument – TLP 3.33ff.; see McGinn 2006, 171ff. for discussion. Another example would be the later Wittgenstein's suggestion to substitute 'use' for 'meaning' in order to resolve philosophical problems relating to the concept of meaning.) More specifically, notations such as Wittgenstein's concept-script might be said to embody philosophical insights in the following sense.

As explained, one central purpose which the design of the notation introduced in the *Tractatus* serves is to render clear the distinction between the expressions of necessity

---

[12] For instance Anthony Kenny characterizes the dissolution of philosophical illusions as a negative task, complemented by the positive task of providing an overview of the workings of language (Kenny 2004, 175). But this distinction seems problematic. Instead one might say that problems are dissolved *by* providing an overview of the workings of language, i.e. making perspicuous the functioning of the relevant expressions. Accordingly, insofar as providing an overview is a positive task, so is the dissolution of a problem.

and statements regarding the contingent, and to enable us to avoid confusions concerning this distinction.[13] In this capacity the notation might be characterized as incorporating in itself insights into the logic of language: it gives clear expression to a logical distinction which everyday language obscures. Rather than being expressed in the form of statements, however, philosophical insights are here, so to say, built into the notation itself. This notation is the embodiment of a particular philosophical conception of language. Such a possibility of a philosophical conception being embodied in a notation rather than expressed in the form of true and false statements, I believe, is also what Wittgenstein is referring to in the above quote when he says that in a notation 'an entire way of looking at the object is expressed'. In this sense, what Wittgenstein offers by introducing his concept-script is not simply a programme for dissolving philosophical problems. The adoption of this notation is at the same time the adoption of a particular philosophical conception of language the expression of which is the notation.

Besides the conception of philosophy as the dissolution of problems, another (complementary) characterization of philosophy's task that Wittgenstein assumes throughout his career is the finding of 'the liberating word'.[14] He writes:

> Who philosophizes [earlier variant: the philosopher] strives to find the liberating word, that is, the word that finally permits us to grasp what up till now has intangibly weighed down our consciousness. (It is like when one has a hair on one's tongue; one feels it, but cannot grasp it, and therefore not get rid of it.) (TS 238, 11; cf. TS 213, 409/PO, 165)

Apparently, the notion of a liberating word is to be understood against the background of the conception that the task of philosophy is to find a mode of expression that makes problems disappear. What is liberating in the liberating word is that it releases one from certain philosophical problems and consequently – as Wittgenstein also characterizes the goal of philosophy – brings thoughts at peace (cf. MS 127, 41v/CV, 50; MS 115, 30). Moreover, just as a notation designed for philosophical purposes is to be seen as an expression of a philosophical view, so apparently is the liberating word. The liberating word is an expression of a conception which, in contrast to others, can render comprehensible what one has been trying to understand. As Wittgenstein says, it 'permits us to grasp what . . . intangibly weighed down our consciousness'. Importantly, however, as he explains, something can be recognized as a liberating word only with certain presuppositions or against a certain kind of background.

---

[13] In addition there are other logical distinctions Wittgenstein aims to clarify by introducing his notation. As the letter to Russell states, however, the distinction between necessary and contingent is a central concern for him.

[14] The expression 'liberating word' (erlösende Wort) occurs as early as in the pre-Tractatus notebooks (MS 102, 63r, 122r). Variants of the remark I am about to quote are frequent in manuscripts and typescripts throughout the 1930s. (In addition the term 'liberating word' occurs in a number of other contexts.) The remark quoted next makes its last appearance in TS 239, a typescript of the PI from 1942/3 where it is crossed out, and consequently does not appear in the final version of the PI. See MS 107, 114; TS 213, 409; MS 115, 30; TS 211, 218; MS 142, 109; TS 220, 83; TS 239, 84.

> The 'liberating word' is such only because it is, so to say, the final stone to a building; the last still missing link in the chain.
>
> For the one who does not have *these* assumptions it is not the liberating word. (MS 124, 218; cf. MS 179, 3v)

The liberating word can only have its liberating effect on a prepared mind, i.e. on someone in a position to recognize a solution as a solution. The liberating word, that is to say, is an expression of the core of the resolution of the problem, but the recognition of it as such requires that the problem be properly comprehended. For example, the last quote occurs in the context of a discussion of the concept of rule following and more specifically the question whether the notion of grasping something in a flash can be explained from the point of view of Wittgenstein's conception of meaning as use. Wittgenstein explains the case for himself with the help of an example: grasping something in a flash – for example the solution of a problem, or the development of a rule – is no more mysterious than noting down a long train of thought in a few strokes. It is the use made of such strokes that makes it a note of the train of thought, rather than some mysterious mental act. (Cf. MS 179, 1ff.; PI §197, 318, 319.) Here Wittgenstein's solution to the problem consists of description of a familiar case with which other cases are to be compared. But this comparison could hardly be illuminating without the background of a comprehension of difficulties with alternative mentalist conceptions of meaning and how the conception of meaning as use helps to resolve those problems.

What this brings to view is that the liberating word, although it may be the expression of a philosophical conception, does not constitute a self-standing philosophical doctrine. Rather, it marks the end point of a clarificatory process. In this connection it seems notable that in TS 238, as well as in the other draft versions of the PI where the remark on philosophy's task as the finding of a liberating word occurs, this remark is followed by another one that emphasizes the importance of accurate descriptions of problems. Problems need to be described in such a way that the person who has the problem really recognizes its description as the correct expression of the difficulty she feels. As Wittgenstein says, 'Only if he recognizes it as such, *is* it the correct expression.' (MS 142, 109; TS 220, 83; TS 238, 11) Accordingly, only against the background of an accurate description of a problem can someone be liberated and guided out of her problem. (See the context of the preceding quote.)

Thus the functioning of something as a liberating word, as Wittgenstein understands this in his later philosophy, seems to be something context- and, to an extent, person-specific. It is, of course, not excluded that what can solve a problem for one person can also solve the problem for another person. Nevertheless, there is, apparently, no guarantee that what can function as a liberating word for one person can liberate everybody else from their problems too. This depends on whether, and to what extent, the difficulty or difficulties that different people have in connection with an issue are the same.

But assuming that the preceding would be a correct characterization of Wittgenstein's later conception (the last quotes date from the 1940s), is there anything corresponding to it in his early philosophy? Wittgenstein begins the *Tractatus'* Preface by saying: 'Perhaps this book will be understood only by someone who has himself already had the thoughts that are expressed in it—or at least similar thoughts.—So it is not a textbook.' (TLP 3) Although these sentences are open to various interpretations, Wittgenstein evidently believes that a condition for understanding his book is an active engagement with the ideas presented in it. One has to think the matters through for oneself; passive reception of ideas is not a possible way of reading his book. Or, as one might say, only someone who works her way through the *Tractatus'* apparent theses and sees them collapse into nonsense fully understands the book and liberating word it offers. Thus, if one does not interpret the *Tractatus* as aiming to inform the reader about a theory of the limits of language, or as introducing a technical notion of nonsense, one can recognize a dialectical dimension in the book, not dissimilar to how Wittgenstein later characterizes the function of the liberating word.[15]

Nevertheless, by drawing parallels between Wittgenstein's early and later thought I do not wish to suggest that his comprehension of the continuous characteristics of his philosophy that I have mentioned remains invariable throughout his career. It is on the basis of certain broadly constant features that we can attribute to Wittgenstein a conception of philosophy as clarification, and contrast this with more traditional forms of philosophy. But this does not mean that his views on these matters did not develop significantly. It means that we must inspect his conception of philosophical clarification in more detail in order to understand how his views developed. For as Wittgenstein's later criticisms of the *Tractatus* show, even though he might later on still be in agreement with certain insights of the *Tractatus*, his comprehension of what it means to engage in philosophy as clarification was insufficient at best. Wittgenstein comments on the *Tractatus* in 1931:

> In my book I still proceeded dogmatically. Such a procedure is legitimate only if it is a matter of capturing the features of the physiognomy, as it were, of what is only just discernible – and that is my excuse. I saw something from far away and in a very indefinite manner, and I wanted to elicit from it as much as possible. (WVC, 184)

Next, I will turn to examine certain important differences between Wittgenstein's early and later views. The problem of dogmatism that comes up in the previous quote will constitute a focal point of this discussion.

3. DISCONTINUITIES: THE COMPLEXITY OF LANGUAGE AND THE PROBLEM OF DOGMATISM

Wittgenstein writes in a manuscript from 1936: 'Language is much more complex than logicians and the author of the Tract. Log. Phil. have imagined.' (MS 152, 47; cf. PI §23) According to a standard account of the development of Wittgenstein's view of language, he assumed in his early philosophy a simplified conception of language as a calculus

---

[15] For an interpretation of the *Tractatus* in the light of the notion of the liberating word, and as a dialectical undertaking, see Ostrow 2002, Ch. 4. But on the basis of my above discussion I would not agree with Ostrow's contention that Wittgenstein's aim in the *Tractatus* is to put an end to philosophy, or to liberate us from philosophy.

according to precise rules and took its use to be exhausted by true/false assertions. In his later philosophy he corrected this mistake, acknowledging the manifoldness of the uses of language: the existence of an innumerable variety of language-games.[16] Although there is something true in this account, it should raise suspicion that the kind of language use Wittgenstein envisages philosophers to be engaged in, i.e. clarification or logical analysis, goes here completely unmentioned, as if Wittgenstein – strangely – did not recognize it as an instance of language use at all (but see TLP 4.122). In effect, the standard account treats the *Tractatus* as if it were putting forward a theory of the nature of language rather than developing tools for its analysis. Problematically, however, this is to ignore what Wittgenstein claims to be most central to his early thought: his 'main contention' and, by implication, his methodological considerations (cf. section 1). I will approach the issue from a different angle, hoping to arrive at a deeper grasp of Wittgenstein's philosophical development. The question is: granted that the early Wittgenstein did not intend to put forward a theory of language, but thought of himself as engaged in the clarification of the logic of language, and sought to introduce a scheme for the logical analysis of language, how did he, in so doing, fail to do justice to the complexity of language?

An expression Wittgenstein uses frequently to describe the problem with the *Tractatus* is that the solution it offered to philosophical problems was not plain or homespun enough.[17] Even though the idea that there is a fundamental difference between philosophy and science was central to the *Tractatus*, its grasp of this difference was insufficient. Although philosophy was only supposed to clarify what we already know, philosophical clarification, as envisaged in the *Tractatus*, still appeared as if it involved discoveries. Wittgenstein writes:

> In my earlier book the solution to the problems is not yet presented nearly plainly [*hausbacken*] enough[;] it still makes it seem as though discoveries are needed to solve our problems and not enough has been done to bring everything in the form of grammatical truisms into an ordinary mode of expression. Everything gives too much the appearance of discoveries. (MS 109, 212, 213; see also MS 111, 132; my interpolation; translation based on translation in Rhees 2001, 154)

What Wittgenstein is objecting to is the impression created by the work of the clarification of logic undertaken in the *Tractatus* – its articulating a scheme for logical analysis – that something extraordinary had been brought to view. If the *Tractatus* is right, upon analysis every proposition can be revealed to be a truth function of elementary propositions which, in turn, are concatenations of simple names that stand for the simple objects of reality. But although Wittgenstein's laying out the logical structure of language in anticipation of such

---

[16] See for example Hacker 1986, 132; 2001, 23; Kenny 2006, 126ff.; Schulte 1992, 103, 104.

[17] The term Wittgenstein uses is *hausbacken*, literally home-baked (homespun). Later he substitutes 'trivial', 'ordinary', and 'humble' for this term (MS 142, 83, 84; MS 157a, 63r, v; cf. MS 110, 34; TS 211, 155; TS 213, 412; TS 220, 90; TS 239, 80; PI §94, 97). In the early 1930s the term *grob*, 'rough', is sometimes used as an alternative to *hausbacken* (MS 111, 132/MS 155, 21v, 22r). *Hausbacken* is contrasted with something sublime (MS 152, 96), extraordinary or unique (MS 117, 138), ideal (MS 114, 109), abstract (TS 213, 71v), something lying under the surface to be revealed by analysis (MS 157b, 8r, v).

analyses is merely supposed to clarify to us what we already know, all this certainly seems as if Wittgenstein had made a great discovery comparable to those of the sciences.

Behind this lie two connected, unexamined assumptions: (1) An ideal of ultimate clarity according to which to clarify a concept is to provide a definition that covers every possible case that falls under the concept, and settles all potentially unclear cases, so to say, in advance. As Wittgenstein remarks in the PI about the kind of questions the *Tractatus* sought to settle regarding language and proposition: 'We ask: "*What* is language?", "*What* is a proposition?" And the answer to these questions is to be given once for all; and independently of any future experience.' (PI §92; cf. 91, MS 157b, 7v, 8r) This assumption of ideal clarity is connected with and explainable in terms of: (2) A problematic conception of conceptual unity according to which all the cases that fall under a concept must possess a common characteristic, this characteristic being the criterion for their classification under the concept. Accordingly, the *Tractatus*' scheme for the analysis of propositions is based on the assumption that anything that qualifies as a proposition *must* possess what it calls 'the general propositional form', i.e. be a (re)presentation of a state of affairs (TLP 4.5). On the other hand, the fact that what we ordinarily call 'propositions' do not in any obvious sense seem to possess this formal characteristic is accounted for by reference to the misleading surface characteristics of language. The bond which secures the formal unity of the concept of proposition lies hidden under the surface of language (MS 183, 164).

The method of logical analysis, as envisaged in the *Tractatus*, therefore, involves in a certain sense a theory about what all propositions *must* be. Without realizing it, Wittgenstein was putting forward a theoretical claim about the nature of propositions that goes beyond what the discussion in the *Tractatus* could licence. He writes about this (in the pre-war drafts of the PI):

> We have a *theory*…of the proposition; of language, but it does not seem to us a theory. For it is characteristic of such a theory that it looks at a special, clearly intuitive case and says: '*That* shows how things are in every case. This case is the exemplar of *all* cases.' – 'Of course! It has to be like that' we say, and are satisfied. We have arrived at a form of expression that *enlightens us*. But it is as if we had now seen something lying *beneath* the surface.
>
> The tendency to generalize the case seems to have a strict justification in logic: here one seems *completely* justified in inferring: 'If *one* proposition is a picture, then any proposition must be a picture, for they must all be of the same nature.' For we are under the illusion that what is sublime, essential about our investigation consists in grasping *one* comprehensive essence. (TS 220, §93/MS 142, §§105, 106; modified from translation in Z §444; cf. PI §97)

As this remark explains, it is not that Wittgenstein consciously put forward a theoretical claim. But on the basis of the conception of conceptual unity which he assumed, it seemed legitimate to extend an insight derived from a certain example or examples he had contemplated to cover *all* propositions. What is regarded as an illuminating example, i.e. a particular case that seems to bring to view something essential about propositions, is here treated as if it opened up a window to the essence of all cases. The example seems to allow a clear perception of features barely visible in other cases, but which those other cases too *must* possess, insofar as they share the same essence. As Wittgenstein notes, if one proposition is a picture, then it seems we can say they all are, since they must share the same essential features, whereby philosophy's task then is to grasp this comprehensive essence (cf. MS 157a, 55v, 56r).

But if the conception of conceptual unity assumed here is problematic, then this employment of examples and the associated mode of inference are not justified. As Wittgenstein also remarks (in the late 1940s): 'The basic evil of Russell's logic, as also of mine in the *Tractatus*, is that what a proposition is is illustrated by a few commonplace examples, and then presupposed as understood in full generality.' (MS 130, 65; TS 229, 197; TS 245, 137/ RPP I, §38) More specifically, as Wittgenstein came to realize (by the early 1930s), conceptual unity need not be based on the possession of some single common feature or features by the cases that fall under the concept. What unites cases under a concept may be, as he says, a 'network of similarities'. (PI §66; cf. 65ff.) He writes about the conception that all members of a class delimited by a concept must have a feature/features in common:

> This notion is, in a way, *too primitive*. What a concept-word indicates is certainly a kinship between objects, but this kinship need not be the sharing of a common property or a constituent. It may connect the objects like the links of a chain, so that one is linked to another *by intermediary links*. Two neighbouring members may have common features and be *similar* to each other, while distant ones belong to the same family without any longer having anything in common. (MS 140, 31, 32/PG, 75)

A sense in which the *Tractatus* did not do justice to the complexity of language, then, is that its scheme for the logical analysis of language presupposed a simplistic conception of conceptual unity. The *Tractatus*' approach was based on the assumption that the concept of proposition can be given a general definition which was then made the centre of its scheme for logical analysis. Rather than putting forward a false statement about language, the *Tractatus*, therefore, failed to do justice to the complexity of language by imposing a simplified scheme of analysis on it, and assuming that every possible instance of meaningful language use is analysable by the means of this scheme. Notably, to introduce a notation or a scheme of analysis, such as Wittgenstein's concept-script, and to propose to use it for the purpose of clarification is not yet to make an assertion about anything. However, by making the programmatic statement that all philosophical problems can be dissolved by means of his concept-script – or as he states in the Preface, 'I am...of the opinion that the problems have in essentials been finally solved' – Wittgenstein came to claim in effect that all meaningful instances of language use *must* fit his model for meaningful language use. In this sense his relapse to a theoretical claim depends on assumptions relating to the task of philosophy (cf. the last sentence of the quote from TS 220).[18]

---

[18] By giving this account of how the *Tractatus* failed to do justice to the complexity of language, I do not wish to deny that there are problems in the details of its conception of language. Nevertheless, as regards the topic of the development of Wittgenstein's philosophy, the evolution of his conception of the method of philosophy, and the implications of this for his thought in general, seem more important than such details. For looking at the details of the *Tractatus*' conception of language we find ideas Wittgenstein *abandoned*, rather than modified or sought to improve upon, as in the case of his conception of the status of philosophical models, such as logical calculi. (I will return to this point below.)

The problem, therefore, is not that Wittgenstein was generalizing carelessly, as if making an illegitimate inductive judgement.[19] Rather, the problem is that he credited a certain logical model with the status of *the* ultimate means of clarification, thus coming to make a dogmatic claim about language.[20] Accordingly, the way Wittgenstein seeks to correct this mistake is not by substituting for the *Tractatus'* conception of propositions a different thesis about the nature of language, such as a thesis about language as a motley of language-games. Rather, his solution consists in the articulation of a novel conception of the role and status (employment) of philosophical models, such as logical calculi, simple language-games, definitions (or rules more generally), and so on. The problem of dogmatism, that is to say, can be avoided by adopting a different deployment of philosophical models. They are not to be put forward as something language use allegedly *must* fit, but to be used as what Wittgenstein calls 'an object of comparison'. In this capacity the models then 'are meant to throw light on the circumstances of our language by way of not only of similarities, but also of dissimilarities'. (PI §130; cf. MS 113, 45v; MS 115, 81)[21] He writes:

> For we can avoid injustice or emptiness in our assertions only by presenting the model as what it is, as an object of comparison—as, so to speak, a measuring-rod; not as a preconceived idea to which reality *must* correspond. (The dogmatism into which we fall so easily in doing philosophy.) (PI §131; cf. TS 220, 85; MS 142, 111; MS 157b, 15v, 16r)

In a certain sense it is then misleading to ask which conception of language the later Wittgenstein substitutes for the *Tractatus'* conception. According to the interpretation I am proposing, Wittgenstein does not have *a* conception of language in his later philosophy, but *many* conceptions employed as objects of comparison with the purpose of drawing attention to the different aspects of language. Examples of such conceptions are that of language as a rule-governed practice and language as a form of life, the former emphasizing the conventional and arbitrary aspect of language and the latter its non-conventional and non-arbitrary aspects. (Cf. PI §492.)

Here it is also important that whereas in the *Tractatus* Wittgenstein was committed to a single conception of language and a single (strictly correct) method, in his later philosophy there is no corresponding commitment to a particular conception of language or a method (cf. PI §133). For example, the method of clarification by tabulating grammatical rules for the use of language belongs together with the conception of

---

[19] The philosophical move at stake (as depicted in the quote from TS 220) is not appropriately described as generalization comparable to factual generalizations. When the transition from one example to all cases is thought of as licensed by the assumption that all cases *must* have a common essence, the role of the exemplary case is to illuminate (bring to view clearly) this common essence, not to function as the basis of a generalization.

[20] More precisely, we face a dilemma of dogmatism or emptiness. If the concept of a picture is interpreted loosely enough, anything counts as a picture (as the purpose of any tool can be explained to be to modify something – PI §14). Here the philosophical dogma becomes irrefutable, nothing qualifying as counter example to it. But this irrefutability is reached at the costly price of the dogma's emptiness. (Cf. TS 213, 188v; MS 116, 123; CV, 32, 33/MS 118 86v.)

[21] See Kuusela 2011, and 2008, Ch. 3, for a more detailed discussion.

language as a rule-governed practice. Similarly, the conception of language as a form of life is associated with particular methods such as quasi-ethnology and invented natural history. (Cf. MS 162, 67rff./CV, 45.) But rather than giving an absolute priority to a certain conception of language and a corresponding method, in his later philosophy Wittgenstein promotes a pluralism of conceptions and methods, the choice of method depending on its suitability for the particular clarificatory task at hand (cf. RC III §43).[22]

Similarly, examples in philosophy too are to be understood as objects of comparison. Thus Wittgenstein's critique of the *Tractatus'* use of examples by no means implies a rejection of the possibility of deriving philosophical illumination from examples, or of the possibility of employing a particular example to characterize other cases that fall under a concept. His point is only that theses about what all cases *must* be are not to be derived from such examples. Rather than constituting a basis for a claim about the characteristics that any case to be classified under a concept has to possess, the exemplary case is to be understood as a means of presentation. A case which exhibits clearly certain characteristics of interest can be used to draw attention to the presence or absence of those characteristics in other cases and thus used to create perspicuity. Importantly, deployed in this capacity of (so to say) a prototype with which other cases are compared, an example can still be used to bring to view something that applies very generally to the objects of investigation. Crucially, however, now the scope of the applicability of the example does not depend on a dogmatic assertion about the nature of *all* cases falling under a concept. Rather, Wittgenstein's procedure allows one to decide the applicability of the example case by case, when necessary. Accordingly, it is also important that when an example is deployed as an object of comparison, cases which do not match it do not constitute counter-examples, unlike in the case of a philosophical thesis about what all cases *must* be (MS 111, 119/CV, 21, 22; cf. TS 211, 72; MS 115, 56, 57; MS 183, 163).

This description of Wittgenstein's later method makes possible the following characterization of the problem with the *Tractatus*. As Wittgenstein later notes, it might be illuminating for certain purposes to compare propositions with pictures. This comparison highlights particular aspects of the concept of proposition or features of its grammar. (Cf. MS 110, 164, 216; MS 114, 68, 154; TS 213, 83; TS 220, 83; AWL, 108.) But in the *Tractatus* Wittgenstein did not recognize this characterization as a comparison. As he writes in a draft version of the PI: 'I had used a comparison; but through the grammatical illusion that a certain *one* thing, something *common* to all its objects, corresponds to a concept it did not seem like a comparison.' (TS 220 §92; cf. PI §104)

---

[22] This pluralism is to be distinguished from relativism: a conception whose status is that of an object of comparison is not a true/false claim. Thus, to allow for the possibility of the employment of incompatible conceptions is not the same as allowing for the possibility of incompatible truths. (For further discussion, see Kuusela 2008, Ch. 6 and Baker 2004.)

Rather than comprehending the comparison with pictures as the articulation of a particular mode of presentation, it seemed to Wittgenstein to reveal the hidden essence of propositions.[23] Thus, instead of confining himself to a plain or homespun employment of the conception as a comparison, Wittgenstein was drawn into theorizing about the ultimate nature of propositions (cf. MS 183, 164).[24] Consequently, by seeking to clarify the concept of proposition in such a theoretical manner, he turned it into a philosophical super-concept. In this role the concept of proposition was meant to be a central constituent of an ultimate philosophical conceptual order. Here the essence of proposition is understood at the same time as a characterization of the essence of language and thought, and, even more generally, of the essence of all representation. Moreover, insofar as it captures the essence of all representation, the concept of proposition is also taken to bring to view the essence of all reality to the extent that it is an object of representation. Thus the concept becomes a truly all-encompassing philosophical notion. (See TLP 5.4711; MS 152, 92, 93; PI §§92, 97.)

By contrast, the plain or homespun use of philosophical conceptions as objects of comparison explains the sense in which Wittgenstein abandons in his later philosophy any technical philosophical concepts. As he says: 'All considerations can be presented more plainly [hausbackener] than I did in earlier times. And therefore no new words need to be used in philosophy, but the old, ordinary words of language are sufficient.' (TS 213, 420/PO, 180; cf. MS 111, 133; MS 155, 21v; TS 211, 81) Naturally, the issue here is not words as such, but their special philosophical employment. However, insofar as philosophy merely employs its models (such as the conception of propositions as pictures) to make comparisons, and to illuminate specific aspects of concepts, the employment of the models does not constitute the articulation of philosophical super-concepts. Accordingly, for example, Wittgenstein speaks about a plain or homespun use of the notion of a simple as a mode of presentation, in contrast to its use as a sublime concept applied to refer to something extraordinary, an ultimate constituent of reality or representation, as in the Tractatus (MS 152, 96). In this way words are led back from their metaphysical employment to their everyday use (PI §116).

Similarly, the liberating word, as the articulation of a philosophical conception, is to be understood as something plain or homespun.

---

[23] McManus' (2006, Ch. 5) illuminating discussion of the 'picture theory' seems exegetically problematic in treating it as an analogy. That is, although McManus manages to make a truly homespun use of the theory which would, I believe, be welcomed by the later Wittgenstein, for the early Wittgenstein the conception was more than an analogy.

[24] In this sense the questions he was asking in the Tractatus took a particular form: they were to be answered once and for all by revealing the hidden essence of language. (See the quote from PI §92 above.) This contrasts with the later Wittgenstein's conception of philosophy as the clarification of particular problems, i.e. his not trying to answer a single big question, for example, regarding the essence of language. (See PI §133 and below.)

> Our difficulties can be dis/solved; & their dis/solution does not require new subtle
> discoveries, deeper reaching analyses or anything of the sort, but an ordering of
> right examples. (The liberating word.) (MS 115, 66; cf. MS 147, 9v)

Hence, for instance, the essence of proposition in a humble sense (or according to an
earlier variant homespun sense) is to be made perspicuous by ordering examples which
are used as objects of comparison to make perspicuous that variety of the cases to which
the concept of proposition is applied (MS 157b, 8r, v; PI §92). Here the role of an example
is not to show what all cases *really* are. Rather examples are used, as Wittgenstein says, as
centres of variation in relation to which other cases can be arranged perspicuously (MS
152, 16, 17; MS 115, 221). Accordingly, such orderings are not to be construed as constituting an ultimate philosophical order that contains the solution to all philosophical
unclarities relating to the concepts in question. Instead, their purpose is to serve the dissolution of particular (actual) philosophical problems (MS 156a, 19v, 20r; cf. PI §87). As
Wittgenstein writes in the PI, such an order is 'an order with a particular end in view; one
out of many possible orders; not *the* order'. (PI §132; cf. MS 142, 118; TS 220, 91)
Importantly, in the case of different problems it might be necessary to draw attention to
different aspects or features of the concepts, and thus different examples may emerge as
central in the case of different problems.

   Finally, these ideas relating to the employment of philosophical models also explain
what a plain or homespun use of logical models in Wittgenstein's sense would be. Calculi
such as the *Tractatus'* concept-script are not to be taken to be applicable *really* to ideal
examples lying hidden under the surface of language, and perhaps to be discovered only
at a later point. Insofar as they have an application they are to be applied to ordinary
instances of language use and employed to illuminate them. Wittgenstein writes:

> It is of the greatest significance that in the case of a logical calculus we always think
> about an example to which the calculus can be applied, & that we don't give examples
> saying they are not really the ideal ones which we don't have yet. This indicates a
> false conception. (Russell and I have in different ways worked under it. Compare
> what I say in the 'Tract. Log. Phil.' about elementary propositions and objects.) (MS
> 115, 55, 56; cf. MS 111, 118)

For instance, the notation of truth-functional analysis, insofar as it has an application
at all, is to be applied to propositions as we know them. It may be that the use of everyday language does not perfectly fit this model. As Wittgenstein notes, the notation of
truth functions only covers part of the grammar of logical connectives (TS 209, 35).
Nevertheless, such clarifications of particular aspects of the grammar of our expressions may be useful from the point of view of solving particular philosophical problems. (Cf. MS 115, 56ff.; cf. MS 111, 118ff.) Hence, importantly, as this possibility of a novel
employment of the truth-functional notation illustrates, central to Wittgenstein's development is the evolution of his comprehension of the status of philosophical models,
not a switch from one model to another or from one conception of language to another.
The old models too may still serve us well, if put into an undogmatic use as objects of
comparison.

4. CONCLUSION

Wittgenstein writes in the early 1930s:

> I might say: if the place I want to reach could only be climbed up to by a ladder, I would give up trying to get there. For the place to which I really have to go is one that I must actually be at already.
>
> Anything that can be reached with a ladder does not interest me. (MS 109, 207, 208/CV, 10)

The metaphor of the ladder leaves plenty of room for interpretation. In an apparently central sense, however, the *Tractatus'* ladder was meant to lead one to the adoption of a particular philosophical conception of language and a particular approach to philosophy. My discussion above is meant to explain why this no longer seems satisfactory to the later Wittgenstein. Rather than move beyond a plain homespun perspective to a position of ultimate clarity, a philosopher must learn to find his way in the labyrinth that is called 'language'. Or as Wittgenstein puts it in the late 1940s: 'When philosophizing one must descend into the old chaos and feel comfortable there.' (MS 136, 51a/CV, 74) More concretely, in not being able to resist the temptation to present our concepts and conceptual relations as more unified and neat than they are, the *Tractatus* came to compromise the idea of philosophy as clarification, that is, of only helping us to understand better what we already know. Accordingly, Wittgenstein's philosophical development can be seen as an attempt to achieve that goal which he saw as distinctive to philosophy from early on.[25]

REFERENCES

AMBROSE, ALICE, ed. (1979). *Wittgenstein's Lectures, Cambridge 1932–35.* Oxford: Basil Blackwell.

BAKER, GORDON (2004). 'The Grammar of Aspects and Aspects of Grammar', in K. Morris ed., *Wittgenstein's Method: Neglected Aspects.* Oxford: Blackwell.

CONANT, JAMES (2002). 'The Method of the *Tractatus*', in E. H. Reck ed., *From Frege to Wittgenstein: Perspectives on Early Analytic Philosophy.* Oxford and New York: Oxford University Press.

[25] I would like to thank the participants in the Philosophy Society meeting at the UEA, Norwich, 16 November 2006, the Wittgenstein Workshop at the University of Chicago on 16 February 2007, and the Unity of Wittgenstein's Philosophy conference in Odense, Denmark, June 2007 for questions and comments. I'm also grateful to the participants in the seminar 'The Unity of Wittgenstein's Philosophy', at the Department of Philosophy and the History of Science, University of Athens in 2006–2007, and especially my co-teacher and the organizer of the seminar Vasso Kindi, for the opportunity to discuss relevant matters. Marie McGinn's perceptive questions on an earlier draft helped me to improve the discussion, as did Mike Beaney's comments on a late version. This work is part of an Academy of Finland project no. 1212577.

DIAMOND, CORA (1991). *The Realistic Spirit*. Cambridge, MA: The MIT Press.

HACKER, P. M. S. (1986). *Insight and Illusion*. Revised edition. Oxford: Oxford University Press.

—— (2001). *Wittgenstein: Connections and Controversies*. Oxford: Oxford University Press.

KENNY, ANTHONY (2004). '"Philosophy States Only What Everyone Admits"', in E. Ammereller and E. Fischer eds., *Wittgenstein at Work: Method in the Philosophical Investigations*. London and New York: Routledge.

—— (2006). *Wittgenstein*. Revised edition. Oxford: Blackwell.

KREMER, MICHAEL (2001). 'The Purpose of Tractarian Nonsense', *Noûs*, 35: 39–73.

—— (2007). 'The Cardinal Problem of Philosophy', in Alice Crary ed., *Wittgenstein and Moral Life: Essays in Honor of Cora Diamond*. Cambridge, MA: The MIT Press.

KUUSELA, OSKARI (2006). 'Nonsense and Clarification in the *Tractatus* – Resolute and Ineffability Readings and the *Tractatus'* Failure', in Sami Pihlström ed., *Wittgenstein and the Method of Philosophy*. Acta Philosophica Fennica, Vol. 80. Helsinki: Philosophical Society of Finland.

—— (2008). *The Struggle against Dogmatism: Wittgenstein and the Concept of Philosophy*. Cambridge, MA: Harvard University Press.

—— (2011). 'The Dialectic of Interpretations: Reading Wittgenstein's *Tractatus*', in M. Lavery and R. Read eds., *Beyond the Tractatus Wars*. London: Routledge.

McGINN, MARIE (2006). *Elucidating the Tractatus: Wittgenstein's Early Philosophy of Logic and Language*. Oxford: Oxford University Press.

McMANUS, DENIS (2006). *The Enchantment of Words: Wittgenstein's Tractatus Logico-Philosophicus*. Oxford: Oxford University Press.

OSTROW, MATTHEW B. (2002). *Wittgenstein's Tractatus: A Dialectical Interpretation*. Cambridge and New York: Cambridge University Press.

RHEES, RUSH (2001). 'On Wittgenstein IX', *Philosophical Investigations*, 24: 153–62.

SCHROEDER, SEVERIN (2006). *Wittgenstein: The Way Out of the Fly-Bottle*. Cambridge: Polity.

SCHULTE, JOACHIM (1992). *Wittgenstein: An Introduction*. Albany: State University of New York Press.

WAISMANN, FRIEDRICH (1979). *Wittgenstein and the Vienna Circle: Conversations Recorded by Friedrich Waismann*, ed. B. McGuinness, trans. J. Schulte and B. McGuinness. Oxford: Blackwell.

WITTGENSTEIN, LUDWIG (1951). *Tractatus Logico-Philosophicus*, trans. C. K. Ogden. London: Routledge & Kegan Paul.

—— (1958). *Preliminary Studies for the "Philosophical Investigations", Generally Known as the Blue and Brown Books*. Oxford: Basil Blackwell.

—— (1961). *Tractatus Logico-Philosophicus*, trans. D. F. Pears and B. F. McGuinness. London: Routledge & Kegan Paul.

—— (1967). *Zettel*, ed. G. E. M. Anscombe and G. H. von Wright, trans. G. E. M. Anscombe. Oxford: Basil Blackwell.

—— (1974). *Philosophical Grammar*, ed. R. Rhees, trans. A. Kenny. Oxford: Basil Blackwell.

—— (1978). *Remarks on Colour*, ed. G. E. M. Anscombe, trans. L. McAlister and M. Schättle. Oxford: Blackwell.

—— (1980). *Remarks on the Philosophy of Psychology*, Vol. 1, ed. G. E. M. Anscombe and G. H. von Wright, trans. G. E. M. Anscombe. Oxford: Blackwell.

—— (1982). *Last Writings on the Philosophy of Psychology: Preliminary Studies for Part II of Philosophical Investigations*, Vol. I, ed. G. H. von Wright and H. Nyman, trans. C. G. Luckhardt and M. A. E. Aue. Oxford: Basil Blackwell.

—— (1993). *Philosophical Occasions 1912–1951*, ed. J. Klagge and A. Nordmann. Indianapolis: Hackett Publishing Company.

—— (1997a). *Philosophical Investigations*. Second edition, ed. G. E. M. Anscombe and R. Rhees, trans. G. E. M. Anscombe. Oxford: Blackwell Publishers.

—— (1997b). *Ludwig Wittgenstein: Cambridge Letters, Correspondence With Russell, Keynes, Moore, Ramsey and Straffa*, ed. B. McGuinness and G. H. von Wright. Oxford: Blackwell.

—— (1998a). *Notebooks 1914–1916*, ed. G. H. von Wright and G. E. M. Anscombe, trans. Anscombe. Oxford: Blackwell.

—— (1998b). *Culture and Value*, ed. G. H. von Wright in collaboration with H. Nyman, revised edition by A. Pichler., trans. P. Winch. Oxford: Blackwell.

—— (2000). *Wittgenstein's Nachlass: The Bergen Electronic Edition*. Oxford: Oxford University Press.

CHAPTER 27

WITTGENSTEIN'S METHODS

JAMES CONANT

THIS chapter comes in three parts. In the first part, I explore the question of the relation between the philosophies of the early and the later Wittgenstein as they are standardly distinguished, with the aim of raising some questions about whether that standard distinction might not obstruct our view of certain significant aspects of the development of Wittgenstein's thought. In the second part, drawing on the work of Marie McGinn and Warren Goldfarb, I distinguish two senses in which these two commentators have been moved to call upon the expression "piecemeal" in their respective attempts to characterize an important feature of Wittgenstein's conception of philosophical method. In the third part, I draw upon this distinction to help bring into focus a significant shift in Wittgenstein's conception of philosophical method which occurs fully within the so-called "later" period—a shift which has in no small part remained invisible due to the manner in which the opposition between an early and a later Wittgenstein has hitherto been conceived.

1. NORWAY, 1937, AND THE QUESTION OF WITTGENSTEIN'S *KEHRE*

Interpreters of Heidegger like to refer to a particular moment in the development of that philosopher's thought as "*die Kehre*". In colloquial German the expression means "the reversal" or "the turning" (if one is describing a motion performed) or even "the about-face" or "the hairpin turn" (if one is focusing instead on the shape of the path traversed by such a motion). Heidegger scholars tend to see their philosopher's version of such a hairpin turn occurring shortly after he completed his early masterwork *Being and Time*. They accordingly divide his corpus of writings into two fundamental categories: those which came before and those which came after *die Kehre*. There is some disagreement among Heidegger scholars about when exactly to date the event, but it is often placed in or around the year 1929. Commentators on Wittgenstein's work do not similarly unite in employing a common expression to refer to the pivotal juncture which they find in their philosopher's thought, but the parallel is otherwise striking: this community of commentators is no less prone to construct a narrative which imposes on the development of their philosopher's thought an equally abrupt segmentation into an earlier and a later phase. They, too, accordingly divide the corpus of their philosopher's writings into two categories of texts—those that are said to have been composed by "the early Wittgenstein" and those that are said to be composed by "the later Wittgenstein". Moreover, they also locate his *Kehre* in or around the year 1929. Beginning in or around that year, a new philosopher ("the later Wittgenstein") is thought to have been born and his primary mission in life is thought to have been that of prosecuting a merciless criticism of the ideas of the early Wittgenstein.

Once the habit of viewing a philosopher's work through the lens of such a radically bi-polar developmental narrative becomes thoroughly inculcated in a scholarly community, it tends to close off the possibility of a reader's so much as noticing forms of philosophical development from one text to the next which do not fit neatly into the entrenched narrative scheme. It thus becomes salutary, if possible, to loosen the grip of the scheme in question by considering and testing the plausibility of alternative developmental narratives. The simplest way to do this in the case of figures whose philosophical life stories have become tethered (as Heidegger's and Wittgenstein's have) to the organizing principle of a single epochal moment of *Kehre* is to uncover and spotlight equally decisive moments of discontinuity in their thought which are to be located substantially prior or subsequent to the supposedly epochal moment. One way to do this in the case of Wittgenstein would be to uncover a no less decisive development in his thought which occurred well before 1929, say, prior to his completion of the *Tractatus*.[1] Another would be to uncover a no less decisive development in his thought which occurred well after 1929, well after his initial return to the activity of regularly writing philosophy. This chapter will attempt a version of the latter strategy.

Wittgenstein spent most of the twenty-two years between 1929 (the year he returned to thinking mostly about philosophy and living mostly in Cambridge, England) and 1951 (the year of his death) trying to write the book that eventually would become published under the title *Philosophical Investigations*. Approximately one-third of the way through this period, in August of 1936, he withdrew to the tiny hut that he had built himself, in a remote location at the very end of the Sognefjord, in Skjolden, Norway, in order to be able to continue his work on the book in complete solitude. After an abortive start, he turned his attention in November 1936 to reworking material that essentially consisted of a draft of sections 1–189 of Part I of *Philosophical Investigations*. Roughly the first half of this material was reworked in the remaining two months of 1936 and (after a break to spend Christmas with his family in Austria) the second half of it was reworked in Skjolden between February and May of 1937. It was during these months

---

[1] Michael Kremer does an excellent job of making a case for a claim of just this form in his undeservedly neglected paper from 1997.

that sections 89 to 133 came to assume something close to the form in which they now appear in the final published version of *Philosophical Investigations*. What happened during this period in Norway?[2]

As already indicated, according to the standard narrative of Wittgenstein's philosophical development, *die Kehre*—the one really significant break in his philosophical development—comes in or around 1929. So, on this telling of the story, regardless of the precise terms in which one wants to account for the character of the philosophical shift in question, the period just before or during or shortly after 1929 *must* be the place to look if one wants to find the most significant shift in his conception of philosophy. With respect to questions pertaining to the development of at least the more fundamental aspects of his conception of philosophy, whatever happened in Norway in 1937, according to this narrative, must amount to something along the lines of a minor wrinkle. The following sort of wrinkle, for example, could be sanctioned and, indeed, is often advanced: During this period the later Wittgenstein turned his attention more closely to certain topics, thereby applying his already fully developed later conception of philosophy to hitherto comparatively unexplored philosophical issues, with the consequence that certain implications already latent in that conception (which he began to espouse in or around 1929) came to be further developed in connection with this or that particular philosophical topic.

A narrative along these lines, admittedly, still leaves lots of room for one to view what happened in Norway in 1937 to be of great consequence. Indeed, this would be an awkward thing to have to deny, in as much as it is there and then that Wittgenstein completed the first draft of the opening bit of the famous passages of the *Philosophical Investigations* now known as "the rule-following considerations". But what the standard narrative will not countenance is the idea that Wittgenstein's *conception of method in philosophy* underwent more than one *Kehre*, more than one revolution. It therefore precludes the possibility that his conception of philosophy itself could have undergone significant further metamorphosis while he was in Norway in 1937. One reason it does not countenance this possibility is that the standard narrative puts in place and operates with a particular sort of idea of what would and could count as a significant sort of development in Wittgenstein's conception of philosophy. This blinds it to certain possibilities.

This blindness is itself a symptom of the aforementioned ingrained tendency in the secondary literature to narrate the story of his development around a single organizing principle featuring a polar opposition between an early and a later Wittgenstein, where the philosophy of the latter is understood to be motivated largely out of a desire to vanquish the philosophy of the former; and a rather traditional picture of wherein the opposition of these philosophies must lie is assumed—namely, in their difference of philosophical doctrine. This much seems to me to be right about this standard telling of the story of Wittgenstein's development: if we want to understand the nature of a break between someone whom we want to call an "early" Wittgenstein and someone whom we want to

---

[2] For a helpful biographical account of this period of Wittgenstein's life, see Monk 1991.

call a "later" Wittgenstein, then we do need to understand the nature of the latter's criticism of the former. Only once we have properly understood the terms of that criticism will we be in a position to assess to what extent the criticism is properly classified as constituting a fundamental *Kehre*, and, if so, to what extent the *Kehre* in question is or is not the single most pronounced kink to be found in the overall arc of the philosopher's development. The tendency in the secondary literature, however, is to proceed in the opposite manner: to begin with a prior interpretative hypothesis which postulates the existence of a single fundamental *Kehre* as an indubitable fact (one that is perhaps claimed to have been independently established by various forms of testimonial evidence) and then to approach Wittgenstein's early and later writings with a correlatively structured interpretative assumption. The writings of "the early Wittgenstein" are read with an eye to uncovering the doctrines which one knows "the later Wittgenstein" to have been concerned to criticize and the later writings are read with an eye to singling out moments of self-criticism (of which there is no shortage in Wittgenstein) which are then uniformly construed as in every case constituting a criticism of "the" early Wittgenstein (as his identity is carved out by the standard account) which is delivered from the vantage of "the" later Wittgenstein (as his identity is carved out by the standard account). Such an approach to Wittgenstein's corpus naturally has a tendency to appear to confirm the a priori interpretative hypothesis which gave rise to the terms of its hermeneutic procedure in the first place.

The characteristic feature of the a priori interpretative hypothesis here at issue is its specification of the terms of Wittgenstein's supposed *Kehre* via certain philosophical doctrines—doctrines that are taken to be central to the teaching of the *Tractatus* and then subjected to criticism by the later Wittgenstein.[3] The doctrines that are usually seized upon and most highlighted in standard ways of telling this story (about what early Wittgenstein was for and later Wittgenstein was against) are ones that a circle of other readers of Wittgenstein, including myself, have argued are already fiercely under attack in the *Tractatus*.[4] This has led to others saying about such readers that their view must be that there are no significant differences between an early and a later Wittgenstein.[5] When these readers deny this, a situation then arises in which it becomes incumbent upon

---

[3] Kuusela 2008 is a notable exception to this tendency. Rather than being framed around the assumption that the crucial difference between an early and a later Wittgenstein lies in their respective philosophical doctrines, it takes its point of departure from the assumption that early and later Wittgenstein equally aspired to practice philosophy in a manner which eschewed all doctrine. The book then seeks to articulate the crucial differences between early and later Wittgenstein in terms of the details of the respective ways in which they sought to realize such an aspiration.

[4] These readers are sometimes known as resolute readers, to introduce a term which I will employ again below. To mention only some of the notable members of this circle: Silver Bronzo, Kevin Cahill, Alice Crary, Rob Deans, Cora Diamond, Piergiorgio Donatelli, Burton Dreben, Juliet Floyd, Warren Goldfarb, Logi Gunnarsson, Martin Gustafsson, Michael Kremer, Oskari Kuusela, Matt Ostrow, Rupert Read, Thomas Ricketts, and Ed Witherspoon. For an account of what makes a reading resolute, see Conant and Diamond 2004. For my own particular account of the relation between an early and a later Wittgenstein, see Conant 2007.

[5] See, for example, Stern 2005, especially p. 170.

them to offer an alternative picture of Wittgenstein's development. The challenge often comes in the form of an invitation to specify where and when, according to this alternative reading of Wittgenstein, *the* break between early and later Wittgenstein is now supposed to be located. This chapter will not contain an effort to meet a challenge posed in these terms. For the terms of the challenge themselves presuppose that the standard account of Wittgenstein's philosophical development is at least correct in its assumption that there is just one *Kehre* and thus that the fundamental point of disagreement between standard and non-standard accounts of these matters must be a function of how they answer the following two questions: (1) *Are* there significant differences between the early and the later Wittgenstein?, and (2) if so, *when* and *where* is the *Kehre* which separates them to be located?

Yet I find that the more closely I examine the actual contours of the trajectory traced by Wittgenstein's thought, the more nuanced and graduated the changes which that development undergoes come to appear to me to be. So, in answer to the question "What is *your* story of Wittgenstein's development?", I am inclined to say "Well, it's complicated." But that is hardly a satisfying answer.

As I don't think the aforementioned question ("Where and when did *the* break between early and later Wittgenstein come?") admits of a single answer (because I think the definite article should be replaced with an indefinite one), I am certainly not inclined to substitute the answer "Norway, 1937" for the usual answer of "Cambridge, 1929". I do think, however, that coming to see what can be said in favor of the former answer can serve as a useful corrective to the forms of blindness encouraged by an overly complacent acquiescence in the latter. It is in this spirit that the remainder of this chapter will present the outlines of a case in favor of the former answer, not in order to usher in a new dogma to the effect that the single moment of decisive discontinuity in Wittgenstein's philosophical development is henceforth to be reassigned from 1929 to 1937 and from Cambridge to Skjolden. Simply to substitute "1929" with "1937" and "Cambridge" with "Skjolden" would leave in place the idea that everything Wittgenstein wrote is to be assigned to either one of two correlated developmental phases, thereby underwriting a supposedly fundamental distinction between two categories of texts—the category of the texts that Wittgenstein wrote before the crucial moment dawned and the category of the texts that he wrote after that crucial moment dawned. And it is precisely this aspect of the standard narrative which I would most like to do away with.

In one respect, therefore, the goal in this chapter is a comparatively modest one—one of taking a small step towards loosening the standard narrative's stranglehold on our contemporary view of Wittgenstein's philosophy. The case for the alternative answer is presented with the thought that the attainment of a clear view of a second significant discontinuity will help to complicate our picture of the first. It therefore does not seek to propose its alternative candidate for an answer to the aforementioned question as a candidate for anything like the last word about how to tell the story of Wittgenstein's philosophical development. Rather, coming to see what can be said on behalf of the alternative candidate is meant to serve as an antidote to the standard narrative, precisely in the hope that the availability of this rather different answer might help to bring out certain aspects of the actual complexity of the development of Wittgenstein's philosophy—aspects which tend to go missing on the standard narrative.

In another respect, however, this chapter is not altogether free of a certain immodesty in its ambition. For it does seek to prepare the ground for a claim to the effect that the "break" in Wittgenstein's philosophy which comes around 1937 is no less significant than any which takes place in or around 1929. This is a strong claim. To say this, however, is not to deny that significant reasons for dissatisfaction with his early philosophy already began to come sharply into view for Wittgenstein in and around 1929. Nor is it to deny that there are other very significant revolutions that his thought undergoes, for example, in the period between 1913 and 1918, and, for example, again in the period between 1945 and 1951. Thus to claim the importance that I wish to for what happens in Norway in 1937 is not to suggest that this is actually where *the* real "break" happens. It is merely to suggest that a careful attention to the sort of criticism of his earlier conception of philosophy that Wittgenstein begins to initiate in 1937 can afford us a perspective from which we can begin to see much of what is partial and distorted in the standard narrative of Wittgenstein's philosophical development.

2. Two Senses of "Piecemeal"

In order to achieve this perspective, it will help first to distinguish between two different things that commentators have meant to say when they have said what seemingly amounts to the saying of a single sort of a thing about the character of Wittgenstein's approach to philosophy. In saying these two different things, in each case, commentators tend to use the same word—the word "piecemeal"—which helps to create a certain confusion that I would first like to undo.

Wittgenstein's approach to philosophical problems is a piecemeal one, we are told by the commentators whom I have in mind. But what does this mean? In the passages from McGinn and Goldfarb that I will cite below, we will encounter two different commentators explaining the sense in which the expression "piecemeal" does or does not properly apply to *early* Wittgenstein's conception of method in philosophy. In the former of these passages, Marie McGinn comments on the way in which early Wittgenstein strives not to treat each of the problems piecemeal; whereas, in the latter, Warren Goldfarb explicates the sense in which Wittgenstein's practice of philosophical clarification is only properly understood once it is recognized as essentially piecemeal in character. Thus, on a superficial reading, it might appear that one of these commentators is concerned to affirm something that the other is concerned to deny.

The apparent disagreement here might be summed up as follows: Goldfarb thinks early Wittgenstein's method is piecemeal (whatever that means); whereas McGinn denies this. I think the disagreement here is merely apparent. But, before I say why, I would like to examine more closely why each of these commentators is drawn to reach for the concept of the piecemeal in their respective attempts to characterize some aspect of early

Wittgenstein's philosophical procedure. This examination will reveal, first, that each of them has a hold of an important part of the truth of Wittgenstein's philosophy at this early point in its development, and, second, that it is not easy to keep these two parts of the truth about Wittgenstein's early philosophy sufficiently far apart—far enough apart so that one of these can vary independently of the other over the course of Wittgenstein's development.

McGinn's aim is to try to bring out what is at issue in remarks of Wittgenstein's, especially in his early *Notebooks*, in which he speaks of himself as grappling with "a single great problem". Here is one such remark:

> Don't get involved in partial problems, but always take flight to where there is a free view over the whole *single* great problem, even if this view is still not a clear one. (NB, 23)[6]

Let me say, first of all, that I agree with McGinn that the aspiration that is expressed here in the *Notebooks* is one that continues to shape the conception of philosophical method at work in the *Tractatus*. In fact, I wish to argue for an even stronger claim: namely, that this aspiration—for a single free view over the whole of philosophy—continues well into the period of work that people ordinarily think of as belonging to that of the "later" Wittgenstein. I will also be concerned to argue for two further related claims: (1) that Wittgenstein's eventual abandonment of this aspiration represents as significant a development in Wittgenstein's philosophical trajectory as any that is properly associated with the break between the *Tractatus* and those writings of Wittgenstein's which date from the first half of the 1930s; and (2) that it represents a shift in his thinking about the nature of philosophy whose momentousness becomes completely obscured on the standard telling of Wittgenstein's philosophical development.

Here is how McGinn summarizes what is at issue in the passage from the *Notebooks* in question:

> Wittgenstein here [in the above passage from NB, 23] instructs himself not to try to treat each of the problems piecemeal. (McGinn 2005, 100)

I will return to McGinn's point here in a moment. But before I do, let us complete our initial survey of the two different senses in which the expression "piecemeal" can be helpfully employed in the context of elucidating Wittgenstein's thought. Here is Goldfarb explaining the sense in which the *Tractatus* is committed to (to something one might want to call) "a piecemeal approach" to solving philosophical problems:

> The lesson is that "nonsense" cannot really be a general term of criticism. As a general term of criticism, it would have to be legitimized by a theory of language, and Wittgenstein is insistent that there is no such thing. ("Logic must take care of itself.")…Wittgenstein's talk of nonsense just is shorthand for a process of coming

---

[6] The following is a related passage: "The problem of negation, of disjunction, of true and false, are only reflections of the one great problem in the variously placed great and small mirrors of philosophy" (NB, 40).

to see how words fall apart when worked out from the inside. What Wittgenstein is urging is a case-by-case approach. The general rubric is nothing but synoptic for what emerges in each case. Here the commonality with his later thought is unmistakeable. (Goldfarb 1997, 71)

The sense of "piecemeal" that concerns McGinn—that is, the sense in which early Wittgenstein's approach to philosophical problems is anything but piecemeal—has to do with the unitary character of the method he employs, that is, with what makes it correct to speak of there being such a thing as *the* method of the *Tractatus*. The sense of "piecemeal" that concerns Goldfarb—that is, the sense in which early Wittgenstein's approach to philosophical problems of necessity requires a case-by-case approach—has to do with the application of "*the* method of the *Tractatus*" to individual philosophical problems, and with why such an application must of necessity be retail, rather than wholesale.

Let us first explore this latter sense of the term, in accordance with which early Wittgenstein's conception of philosophical method *can* properly be said to be piecemeal. This requires getting firmly into focus a critical difference between standard and (what have now become known as) resolute readings of the *Tractatus*. According to standard readers, what the author of that work, in section 6.54, aims to call upon his reader to do (when he says that she will understand him when she reaches the point where she is able to recognize his sentences as nonsensical) is something that requires the reader of the work first to grasp and then to apply to the sentences of the work a *theory* that has been advanced in the body of the work. In order to be able to give content to the idea that we are able to come to grasp the commitments of such a theory, a commentator must hold that there is a fairly substantial sense in which we can come to "understand" the sentences that "explain" the theory, despite the fact we are eventually called upon to recognize these very same sentences as nonsense. Resolute readers are committed to rejecting such a reading. Wittgenstein's declares that the kind of philosophy he seeks to practice in the *Tractatus* consists not in putting forward a theory, but rather in the exercise of a certain sort of activity—one of elucidation. A core commitment of a resolute reading lies in an insistence upon the thought that a proper understanding of the aim of the *Tractatus* depends upon taking Wittgenstein at his word here.

Peter Hacker is explicit about the fact that a standard reading of the Tractatus requires that one not take Wittgenstein at his word on this point:

> To understand Wittgenstein's brief remarks about philosophy in the *Tractatus*, it is essential to realize that its practice and its theory are at odds with each other. The official de jure account of philosophy is wholly different from the de facto practice in the book. (Hacker 1986, 12)

What would it be to take Wittgenstein's remarks about philosophy in the *Tractatus* at face value? According to resolute readers, to regard one of the sentences (which comprises the body of the book) as a *rung on the ladder* (that we are asked to climb up and then throw away) is to take it to belong to this aspect of the task that the author of the work has set us. The reader reaches a moment in which she understands the author (and what he is doing with one of his sentences) each time she moves from a state of appearing to herself to be able to understand one of these sentences to a state in which it becomes evident to her that her earlier "state of understanding" was only apparent. This point is reached not through the reader's coming to be convinced by an argument that forces her to believe *that* such-and-such is the case, say, by convincing her that the sentence fails to meet certain necessary conditions on sense. (Why should she ever believe the conclusion of such an argument, if she takes herself still to be able to understand the sentence in question? As long as she is able to do this, doesn't she have good reason to question the premises of the argument?) Rather, the point is reached, in each case, by her experience of the sentence (and the sort of understanding it can seem to support) undergoing a transformation. Each such moment of "understanding the author" involves, in this sense, *a change in the reader*. Her sense of the world as a whole, at each such moment, waxes or wanes, not by her coming to see *that p* (for some effable or ineffable, propositional or quasi-propositional *p*), but rather by her coming to see that there is nothing of the form '*that* _____' (of the sort she originally imagined) to believe. So a point of understanding the author is reached when she arrives at a moment in her relation to a given form of words when she is no longer able to sustain her original experience of "understanding the sentence". The task of thus overcoming each such particular appearance of sense (that each such rung on the ladder at first engenders in a reader) is an arduous one. The form of understanding that is at issue here for resolute readers can only be attained piecemeal, one set of sentences at a time.

Since they hold that the *Tractatus* has no general story about what makes something nonsense, resolute readers are obliged to hold that these moments of recognition that a reader is called upon (in section 6.54) to attain must come one step at a time, in the way that Goldfarb sketches in his account of the sense in which the Tractarian procedure of clarification is piecemeal. This is contrary to the spirit of most standard readings, according to which there can be a moment in a reader's assimilation of the doctrines of the book when the theory (once it has been fully digested by the reader) can be brought simultaneously to bear *wholesale* on all of the (putatively nonsensical) propositions that make up the work. According to such a reading of the *Tractatus*, once we have equipped ourselves with the right theory of language, we can determine where we have gone right and where we have gone wrong in philosophy, simply by applying the theory to each of the things we are drawn to say when speaking philosophically.

The foregoing distinction between two ways of uncovering of nonsense, retail and wholesale, has to be formulated carefully.[7] Otherwise it can easily lead to a distorted account of what is at issue between these two sorts of readers of the *Tractatus*. If one

---

[7] The following five paragraphs are indebted to comments by Cora Diamond on an earlier draft of this chapter. They are meant to constitute a response to her worry that one mischaracterizes what is involved in early Wittgenstein's conception of the practice of philosophy (as being essentially piecemeal in the Goldfarb sense) if one characterizes the form of interrogation of sentences thereby required as one which must necessarily proceed on a "sentence-by-sentence" basis.

were to claim that one can uncover nonsense only one sentence at a time according to resolute readers (with the unmasking of one sentence having no implications for one's view of any other), or, alternatively, if one were to claim that one could discover all of the (relevant) sentences of the *Tractatus* to be nonsense all at once according to standard readers (simply in virtue of having assimilated the correct theory of the limits of language, without having to do any further intellectual work), then, either way, one would have overstated matters. This way of putting the difference reduces it to a matter of the *quantity* of sentences which stand or fall through the exercise of a particular intellectual act: in the one case, only one sentence at a time; in the other case, a whole class of sentences at once. The opposition between the procedure of the piecemeal interrogation of sentences and that of the wholesale unmasking of sentences respectively envisaged by each of these sorts of readings is not properly framed through any such recourse to a merely quantitative unit of measure. What is true is that the resulting process of uncovering nonsense according to a resolute reader will be a far more arduous and gradual matter than it will be for a standard reader; but that is merely a secondary consequence of their real and deeper ground of difference. For the fundamental difference between these two readings lies not in their respective understandings of the quantity of exercises of the requisite intellectual capacity, but rather in their respective understandings of the *qualitative* nature of the capacity thus exercised.

For a standard reader, once a reader has fully grasped the theory advanced within the body of the work, the application of the theory to individual strings of words is essentially a mechanical matter, requiring only an inspection of the string in question in order to see if it accords with the dictates of the theory. Such an exercise of inspection, as standardly envisaged, requires neither any real imaginative effort nor any probing of the manner in which a particular speaker seeks to call upon the forms of words in question. This does not mean that in a single glance the devotee of such a theory will be able to take in that every nonsensical string is, indeed, nonsensical prior to having to inspect the strings in question. Such a discovery will take time and will require the examination of a great many individual linguistic strings. The verdict to be passed on each such string can, nonetheless, be said to be foreordained in the sense that it is a straightforward consequence of the theory. What is and what is not nonsense is a matter which has already been determined by the theory. What remains to be done, once the theory has been grasped, is simply the police work of applying its law and handing down its verdicts of guilt where appropriate. The subject, in each case, on whom such a verdict is passed is, in the first instance, the linguistic string itself. According to the standard reading, it is the linguistic strings themselves which are nonsense. The guilt of the speakers of such sentences is in this respect derivative: it is to be traced to their proclivity to call upon the services of such linguistic strings while philosophizing.

For a resolute reader, the envisaged method of clarification requires attempting to discover whether it is possible to discern a symbol in the sign in a manner which accords with the sort of (apparent) use to which a particular interlocutor wishes to put the sign in question. This requires both imaginative effort and a careful investigation into the manner in which the propositional signs in question admit of construal as propositional symbols. For a resolute reader, the charge of nonsense is directed not at the propositional sign itself, but rather at the character of the relation in which a particular speaker stands to a propositional sign. Such a charge is entered when a speaker imagines themselves to have conferred a method of symbolizing upon a sign while having failed to do so. According to the standard reading, what nonsense denotes (in its weighty sense as a term of criticism) is a logical characteristic of certain propositions: it inheres in the linguistic strings themselves. Whereas, according to resolute readers, the linguistic strings themselves are neither guilty nor innocent. They are at most the occasions for certain forms of confusion. What the term nonsense (in its weighty sense as a term of criticism) denotes instead is a form of illusion—one which is generated through an inability on the part of a speaker to command a clear view of what he is doing with his words.

This does not mean, however, that for resolute readers nonsense can only be revealed one sentence at a time. A discovery that certain forms of words are nonsense (i.e., that certain propositional signs to which one believed that one had attached a sense had not yet been given a sense) is a form of discovery which will tend to have a cascading effect, altering one's view of the standing of a great many other forms of words to which one was also previously attracted (revealing them, too, to be propositional signs upon which one had not yet conferred a method of symbolizing though one believed one had already done so). As a reader internalizes the lessons of the *Tractatus*, learning to employ its notational instruments for interrogating sentences, she will naturally encounter moments in which the sense of a whole family of cases of sentences will therefore come to be impugned together.

To take one example, such a reader may uncover a class of cases where there is a certain recurring kind of difference in symbol masked by a corresponding recurring kind of similarity of sign. She may then come to see that this whole family of cases (in which this sort of sign–symbol relation obtains) gives rise to a whole class of sentences which she had previously mistaken for sense. She can thereby come to see that constructions of this sort tend to conjure up for her a certain characteristic sort of illusion of sense. Once she sees through the manner in which this illusion is produced, the ensuing discovery can exert a pressure which ramifies throughout her relation to all sorts of related linguistic constructions. It is therefore perfectly open to a resolute reader to claim that the problems a reader uncovers in an especially clear example of a certain kind of sentence (one which exhibits a recurring characteristic sort of sign–symbol relation) are of such a sort that they can lead to the uncovering of nonsense in other cases: they can enable a reader of the work to come to see how the demands which she sought to place on a given sentence at one point in the text were also in play in the use to which she sought to put a great many other sentences elsewhere in the text. This means that the nature of the local awareness which a reader of the *Tractatus* is able to achieve of the incoherent nature of the demands she was prone to place on a particular sentence can be of such a sort that it can quite immediately lead to a more global awareness of the incoherent character of the demands which she is prone to place on a great many others.[8] This can allow her to discover that a whole class of sentences recurrently engenders philosophical perplexities of a certain characteristic sort for her. That a whole family of sentences can in this manner be seen to fall together, over the course of such a procedure of interrogation, does not render the procedure in question any less piecemeal in the Goldfarb sense. For what makes the procedure piecemeal rather than wholesale in the relevant sense is a function of the character of the method required, not merely of the quantity of sentences which stand or fall at any given point as a result of its application.

According to resolute readers, it is a central project of the *Tractatus* to criticize the standard reading's conception of the role that theory can play in philosophical clarification—the very conception that standard readers assume lies at the heart of the book. Equally controversially, according to resolute readers, this rejection of the understanding of the role of theory in philosophy not only marks an important point of *discontinuity* between Wittgenstein's thought and that of the philosophical tradition, but it also makes an important point of *continuity* between the thought of early and that of later Wittgenstein. We might sum up the alternative (so-called resolute) view of Wittgenstein in question here as follows: Wittgenstein, early and late, rejected a wholesale conception of how progress in philosophy is to be achieved—philosophical clarity must be won piecemeal, through a series of interrogative exercises which gradually refine one's capacity to distinguish sense from nonsense. It is thus not achieved through the application of a general philosophical account to a class of instances that fall under the categories catered for by the account, but rather through a procedure of philosophical clarification that requires successively examining and entering into a whole range of genuinely felt individual expressions of philosophical puzzlement.

The foregoing was an attempt to summarize (what we might call) the Goldfarb sense of "piecemeal"—the sense in which, according to resolute readers, Wittgenstein *is* committed to a piecemeal procedure in philosophy. Now what about (what we might call) the McGinn sense of "piecemeal"?

In the quotation from McGinn above, she comments on the passage about the 'single great problem' from the *Notebooks* by saying that Wittgenstein there "instructs himself not to try to treat each of the problems piecemeal". The first thing we need to see is that what McGinn takes early Wittgenstein to be there instructing himself not to do (in her use of the expression "treat each of the problems piecemeal") and what resolute readers (such as Goldfarb and myself) take early Wittgenstein to be committed to doing (in their use of the expression "treat each of the problems piecemeal")

---

[8] This is why climbing the ladder of the *Tractatus* involves ascending rungs. For the forms of discovery in which it issues constitute of a graduate series of phases of insight into the standing of whole classes of sentences. And this is why it is wrong to equate what is right in the Goldfarb conception (of the piecemeal character of the method of the *Tractatus*) with the idea that the interrogation of sentences must proceed on a sentence-by-sentence basis.

are *not* the same thing. The ambition touched on in the remark from the *Notebooks* (the ambition to attain a view of the problems of philosophy that allows them all simultaneously to come into view as aspects of "a whole *single* great problem") is an ambition that Wittgenstein takes himself to have realized by the time of completing the *Tractatus*. It is tied to the remark in the Preface of the *Tractatus* that "the problems have in essentials finally been solved". (TLP, Preface) The problems have in essentials been solved because *the* method of their (dis)solution has been found. The application of this method to the problems of philosophy (that require treatment by the method) is for early Wittgenstein, nonetheless, a piecemeal process in (what I have called) the Goldfarb sense—that is why the problems have been solved only in essentials, and not in their details. It is the latter distinction (between solving the problems in essentials vs. in their details) that mandates the early procedure of piecemeal interrogation of sentences that resolute readers insist upon. This is not to be confused with a more fundamental distinction in philosophical conception between the methodological monism of the early Wittgenstein (who seeks to present *the* method of clarification) and the methodological pluralism of a later Wittgenstein (who seeks to present an open-ended series of examples of methods—a series that can be continued in both unforeseen and unforeseeable ways—and that can be broken off at any point). A resolute reader who insists upon things being piecemeal in the sense that goes with the first of these distinctions need not hold that they are piecemeal in the sense that goes with the second of these distinctions (and therefore need not deny that there is an enormous difference in methodological conception between early and later Wittgenstein).[9] A resolute reader who fails carefully to distinguish these two senses (in which something about the early method can be said to be "piecemeal") runs the risk of falling into thinking that a bare commitment to resolution itself entails a remarkably severe claim regarding the extent of the continuity that can be found in Wittgenstein's philosophy.[10]

The expression 'piecemeal', therefore, employed in the Goldfarb sense, can be a useful locution for marking a profound continuity in Wittgenstein's thought that runs from the *Tractatus* to the end of his philosophical life. And the expression 'piecemeal', employed in the McGinn sense, can be a useful locution for marking a profound discontinuity in Wittgenstein's thought. At what point does this latter break in his conception of philosophy arise? This is the question I would now like to explore. The point of distinguishing the two different senses of 'piecemeal' above was to allow us to isolate and pose this question.

---

[9] The presence of the definite article in the title of an earlier paper of mine, "The Method of the *Tractatus*" (a paper which, incidentally, argues for the piecemeal character of any application of *the* method to particular philosophical problems) was intended to mark just this moment of discontinuity in the philosophical conceptions of the early and later Wittgenstein respectively. See my 2002.

[10] There are a number of resolute readers around nowadays who do seem to think something along these lines. Rob Deans, Phil Hutchinson, and Rupert Read all seem to be of such a view. See, for example, Read 2006; Read and Deans 2003; and Read and Hutchinson 2006.

3. FROM METHODOLOGICAL MONISM
TO METHODOLOGICAL PLURALISM

I believe that the correct answer to that question is 1937. To document that claim properly would require a level of scholarly detail considerably in excess of what can be made
to fit within the confines of a chapter in a volume of essays. I will therefore restrict myself
here to an attempt to sketch the larger framework within which such an investigation
would have to take place.[11]

I do think this much is clear: whenever exactly that break took place, it has been fully
accomplished in the final version of Part I of *Philosophical Investigations*. Of particular
interest in this connection is the entire stretch in *Philosophical Investigations* that runs
from §89 to §133. In almost every remark we have some effort on Wittgenstein's part to
bring his later methods of philosophy into relief by contrasting them with his earlier
conception of *the* method (cf. §133) of philosophy, and yet numerous local moments of
continuity surface within this overarching contrast. This contrast—between *the* (early)
method and the (later) method*s*—draws many of the other points of difference between
the early and later philosophies together and, in particular, the difference between the
Tractatus's point of view on the problems of philosophy (according to which they have
in essentials been solved) and the refusal of such a point of view in the *Investigations* (in
which the essentials can no longer be separated in such a manner from the details of
their treatment). The confidence expressed in the claim (in the Preface to the *Tractatus*)
that the problems of philosophy have in essentials been solved is tied to a confidence
that, at least in its essentials, *the basic outline* of the method for dissolving *all* such
problems has been put in place. (This, in turn, is tied to a confidence that there is something which is *the* logic of our language—the structure of which can be displayed in a
perspicuous notation.) The *Tractatus* aims to furnish this basic outline and demonstrate
its worth. Once it has successfully done so, it is now to become clear, in retrospect, that
the prior absence of a serviceable method had been the big problem for the early
philosophy—for the solution to all other problems had depended on the solution to this
one—and now that *it* has been resolved, they are in principle (if not yet in practice) also
resolved. This central (apparent) achievement of the early philosophy, in turn, becomes
a central target of the very late philosophy.

The entire stretch in *Philosophical Investigations* that runs from §89 to §133 can be
read as seeking to expose the latent preconceptions that allowed early Wittgenstein to

---

[11] The only work of secondary literature on Wittgenstein known to me where such spadework is
undertaken is by Joachim Schulte. He explores the topic of the relation between the respective conceptions of philosophical method to be found in the post-1929 and the post-1937 Wittgenstein in his 2002.
He, too, draws attention there to a contrast between there being *a* philosophical method (according to
the first of these Wittgensteins) and there being philosophical method*s* (according to the second, and
goes on to discuss how Wittgenstein rewrote a number of earlier passages in ways which reflect a preoccupation with his increasing awareness of the importance of such a contrast.

imagine that he had done this—that he had been able to survey *the* structure of the problems *as such* and attain a perspective on them from which there could appear to be one big problem that could admit of an overarching form of solution (at least in its essentials). Yet, at the same time, there is still on his later conception much of local value in his early conception of clarification that is to be recovered within this fundamental break with the early conception. Hence, even in the course of this markedly critical sequence of reflections on the relation between the early and later conceptions of philosophical method, a crisscrossing method of investigation is required—one that denies nothing of value and recoups each of the gains of the early philosophy, while laboring to identify each of the moments in which it oversteps or overreaches. The tendency is to think that this question of "the extent of the continuity and the discontinuity in Wittgenstein's philosophy", here at issue in his critique of his earlier self in these passages, has primarily to do with the relation between the author of the *Tractatus* and the author of the *Investigations*. But I think this would be quite mistaken. I will return to the mistake in question in a moment.

I need first to digress briefly in order to introduce some terminology. It will help here if we are able to operate provisionally with an alternative narrative scheme—one which remains simple enough to allow us to command a reasonably clear overview of the relevant aspects of the developmental landscape, while introducing enough additional complexity to allow a dimension neglected on the standard depiction of that landscape to begin to come sharply into view. The ensuing exercise may seem to involve us in substituting for our original simplistic narrative scheme another only very slightly less simplistic one. But that need be the case only if we cease to keep track of the purpose for which the scheme is introduced in the first place. The purpose for which it is introduced here is as a contrasting object of comparison for the purpose of an exercise which seeks to illuminate certain limitations in the currently entrenched scheme.

In what follows, I will accordingly distinguish between an early Wittgenstein who died in or around 1929, a middle Wittgenstein who was born in or around 1929 with his return to Cambridge but passed away sometime in the neighborhood of his extended sojourn in Norway in or around 1937, and a later Wittgenstein who was born in or around 1937 and who died in 1951. Partly in order that we not confuse these characters with the ones who figure (as "the early Wittgenstein" and "the later Wittgenstein") on a telling of the standard story, and partly in order to signal the artificiality of the resulting scheme, I propose to denominate the members of the triad induced by this alternative scheme with names which have capital letters, as if the terms in question designated the proper names of three distinct *personae dramatis*. When employing this threefold scheme, I shall accordingly henceforth speak of Early Wittgenstein, Middle Wittgenstein, and Later Wittgenstein. In introducing this alternative nomenclature, I do not mean to suggest that such a threefold manner of partitioning Wittgenstein's development is likely in the long run to prove any less interpretatively constricting than the merely twofold partition for which it is here being proposed as a temporary substitute. The point of the terminology is merely to furnish us with a perspicuous notation in which to formulate claims about forms of continuity and discontinuity in Wittgenstein's thought which go unnoticed in the standard account—for example, claims regarding the presence of certain commonalities in the thought of Early and Middle Wittgenstein which jointly constitute a central focus of critique in the work of Later Wittgenstein.

Now let us return to our discussion of the mistake in question which we left hanging above. The mistake here extends to the scope of the contrast between conceptions of philosophical method drawn in the last sentence of §133: "There is not *a* philosophical method, though there are indeed methods, like different therapies." (PI §133) I do not meant to suggest that it is incorrect to understand the contrast in play here to be one that marks a difference between the Tractarian methodological conception (the conception of *the* method) and that of §133 (the conception that there is not *one* philosophical method, though there are indeed methods). But one should not conclude on this ground that §133 contains no criticism by Later Wittgenstein of Middle Wittgenstein. For this idea of "the method" did not immediately die with Wittgenstein's return to full-time philosophizing in 1929. Not only its final sentence but, on Later Wittgenstein's mature understanding of it, the point of the whole of §133 is equally concerned to draw a contrast between the later methodological conception and the very emphatic views of Middle Wittgenstein. For, despite the far-reaching differences in their respective philosophies, there remains the following important similarity between Early and Middle Wittgenstein: each believes he has hit upon *the* method.

One of Middle Wittgenstein's favorite ways of putting this, in the context of discussing his "new" method, is to emphasize how philosophy can now become a matter of *skillful* practice. There can be skillful philosophers as there are skillful chemists, because "a new method" has been *discovered*, as happened when chemistry was developed out of alchemy: "The nimbus of philosophy has been lost. For we now have a method of doing philosophy…Compare the difference between alchemy and chemistry; chemistry has a method." (WL, 21) What matters above all now is not so much the truth or falsity of this or that specific philosophical result but rather this all-important fact: "a method had been found". (WL, 21) The contrast between there being a philosophical method (according to Middle Wittgenstein) and there being philosophical methods (according to Later Wittgenstein) represents an important difference in the respect in which the Later Wittgenstein comes to think that philosophy can and should aspire to a final and finished condition of maturity—to anything like the sort of finished state which is the mark of a once immature discipline's (say, alchemy's) having succeeded in transforming itself into a mature one, where a set of stable procedures for solving (or dissolving) problems holds sway. Chemistry successfully differentiated itself from the form it took in its infancy through having come to attain a condition in which the fundamental matters of controversy within the discipline were no longer ones of method. The mark of such a condition of maturity is that the practitioners of the discipline in question, at any given time, are properly able to rest content with a delimited number of antecedently fixed procedures for making progress within their field of inquiry. Both Early and Middle Wittgenstein sought, at least to this restricted degree, to usher in a sort of era of maturity for philosophy—an era in which philosophers would no longer need to wrangle with one another over questions of philosophical method.

It would be a mistake here to think that Middle Wittgenstein thought that philosophy should aspire to imitate the method (or methods) of science. That would be a misunderstanding of how Wittgenstein viewed philosophy, Early, Middle, or Late. Wittgenstein could not be clearer in any number of passages about the extent to which he thinks it is a constant temptation (to which philosophers repeatedly succumb) as well as a fateful error (with numerous far-reaching consequences) for philosophers to attempt to model the method of philosophy at all closely on that of science.[12] What Wittgenstein criticizes in such passages does not undercut the previous analogy, however. The target of those passages is the idea that the method of philosophy should simply be that of science. Wittgenstein nowhere seeks to criticize the very idea of method in philosophy. He craves method. The point of the earlier analogy between chemistry and philosophy, properly understood, therefore in no way contradicts the point of those of his passages which warn against the temptation to cast philosophy too closely in the image of science. Middle Wittgenstein's analogy between chemistry and philosophy will be misunderstood if one does not grasp the specific locus of the analogy, failing to appreciate that it is intended to apply only to the very idea of a shared method (and not to the particular character of the method thus shared). The point of application of the analogy has to do quite specifically with the transition within the history of a practice from a moment in which a method has not yet been found to one in which it has been found.

Middle Wittgenstein, like Early Wittgenstein, was attached to a conception of philosophical method which itself presupposed the possibility of a certain point of view on the problems of philosophy—a point of view from which one could take in the entire logical space within which such problems could be located as instances of a single sort of structure. As Early Wittgenstein's conception of a single logical space gradually gave way to Middle Wittgenstein's conception of a plurality of grammars, Middle Wittgenstein vastly complicated Early Wittgenstein's conception of how the structure in question ought to be characterized. Nevertheless, Middle Wittgenstein continued to yearn for the possibility of a synoptic overview of the various possible forms of difficulty that characterize philosophical problems—an overview which was synoptic not only in the sense that it permitted one to get into view what was necessary in order to solve a particular problem, but one which was synoptic in a far more radical sense. What was sought was an overview in which one could classify the different forms of philosophical confusion and situate them within a grid of possible forms of confusion. As Early Wittgenstein's conception of logic gradually gives way to Middle Wittgenstein's conception of grammar, the nature of the grid in question becomes increasingly intricate and multidimensional (thereby containing the seeds of the eventual destruction at Later Wittgenstein's hands of the very idea that grammar is properly to be characterized in terms of the sort of rules which can be laid down over language like a grid). Yet his

---

[12] A particularly famous example of such a passage is the following: "Philosophers constantly see the method of science before their eyes, and are irresistibly tempted to ask and answer questions in the way science does. This tendency is the real source of metaphysics and leads the philosopher into complete darkness" (BB, 18).

early aspiration to equip the philosophical practitioner with the requisite tools to tackle any sort of difficulty which might come along continues to exercise the philosophical imagination of the Middle Wittgenstein.

To see the point at issue here more clearly, it might help to vary the analogy and to compare stages in a possible history of philosophy with stages in a possible history of medicine, rather than with stages in the actual history of chemistry. The reader must take the invitation *cum grano salis* if I invite her to imagine a fantastic future state of affairs in which the science of medicine has attained the sort of maturity that Wittgenstein postulates the science of chemistry has attained—a state in which medical science has found "the" method, so that we can now speak of the method of medicine. (This assumes, with Middle Wittgenstein, that it makes sense to speak of the method of chemistry.[13]) Attaining such a form of maturity is consistent with the following possibility: the art of medicine might well persist as a form of craft that cannot itself be reduced to a form of science, even if that craft's instruments of cure rest on a unitary form of scientific method. It may help to bring out the important point here, if we make the example even more fanciful. Let us imagine not only that medicine has attained the form of a science characterized by a single uniform method but that it is has succeeded in fully analyzing the etiology of every possible form of human ailment and discovered a correlative form of successful treatment for each and every such ailment. In one sense of the term, in this fanciful future state, medicine has become a completed science of the possible forms of disease and their possible forms of cure. Having attained this state, then, at least in one sense of the term, medicine has come to an end: there is no longer any reason to fund pure research in medicine. Yet even in this utopian state of completion (*qua* branch of scientific inquiry into the structure of the natural world), medicine *qua* craft of the diagnosis and treatment of individual ailments may well continue to involve the exercise of many of the very forms of phronesis currently possessed by the best physicians. Regardless of how systematic the pure science of medicine has become, the practice of the art of medicine may continue to remain piecemeal in the Goldfarb sense.

What makes this comparatively fanciful analogy more fitting for the purpose of this chapter than the one drawn from the history of chemistry is the way in which it permits us to incorporate a parallel to the distinction between the two different dimensions along

---

[13] I am inclined to think that the less one knows about the real workings of science (and thus the less clear one is about what one means when speaking of "the method of a science"), the more one is apt to be able to go in for such a thought-experiment. (For a critique of such ideas of scientific method, see James Bryant Conant 1951.) I am therefore of the view that the thought-experiment here deployed is not merely fanciful, but actually involves a mistaken conception of the nature of science (and not merely of medical science). I do not think, however, that its ineliminable basis in fantasy need detract from the capacity of the thought-experiment to illuminate the point at issue here. It only means that a non-fantastic analogy which permitted one to make the same point would take considerably more care to construct and would, in all likelihood, be considerably more *recherché*. (It might involve, say, an elaboration of a moment in the history of a branch of mathematics in which a certain loosely related family of heuristics for solving an apparent motley of problems gave way, through the appropriate sort of discovery, to a general theory enabling one to identify all members of the family as problems of a common form.)

which one can enter a claim about the piecemeal character of Wittgenstein's method in philosophy. This allows us to accord the proper significance, in our handling of the analogy, to the complexity in the way in which these two dimensions then can be seen to come apart in the conceptions of method with which Early Wittgenstein and Middle Wittgenstein operate. For Early Wittgenstein, for example, the provision of a proper *Begriffsschrift* is the sort of thing which would afford an inventory of all of the possible forms of philosophical confusion, and the tools for clarification it affords would provide a complete toolkit for the treatment of those forms of confusion. Yet its exhaustiveness in these respects would not eliminate the need for a form of elucidatory craft when it came to the clarification of individually felt philosophical problems.

Thus the author of the *Tractatus* can claim to have attained an overview of all of the forms of possible philosophical confusion while not needing to deny that the successful discernment of their proper modes of treatment remains a delicate matter. The question as to which form or forms of treatment (which particular—or which particular combination of—forms of notation of the sort which the *Tractatus* introduces for the clarification of philosophical problems[14]) ought to be brought to bear and will prove genuinely of help with this or that felt confusion is one which may not admit of an easy answer—and, moreover, one which cannot be answered simply by surveying the structure of logical space. The answer to such a question requires entering oneself, at least provisionally, into the realm of confusion and allowing oneself to come to appreciate what it is like to experience this or that particular confusion from the inside—to allow oneself to imagine that a particular proposition occupies a position in logical space when it does not.[15] Early Wittgenstein is already of the view that such a form of discernment will require more than that one merely be armed with a perspicuous logical notation. It will require considerable elucidatory experience, delicacy of judgment, and philosophical craft.[16] Similarly, even once the appropriately effective elucidatory tools have been identified, their application to a particular form of confusion, for Early Wittgenstein, may remain in yet a further respect still a piecemeal matter in the Goldfarb sense. For if one is suffering from a genuinely gripping philosophical perplexity, then the application of these tools will, in all likelihood, yield forms of relief and freedom from perplexity which can only come in turns and degrees, through a series of graduated steps over the course of a sustained elucidatory process, such that the overall procedure (which aims to make the problems completely disappear) might require considerable deftness, patience, and art on the part of its practitioner.

To employ a dangerous (because potentially misleading) analogy: just as even in the utopian world of the fanciful thought-experiment the discovery of all possible medical

---

[14] Such as the Scheffer-stroke notation for logical connectives, the truth-table notation for representing propositions, the *Klammerausdruck* notation for generality, the N-operator notation for the general form of the proposition, etc.

[15] For further discussion of this issue and the sort of exercise of imagination which it requires, see Diamond 1991.

[16] The difference in this respect between Early Wittgenstein's and Carnap's respective conceptions of the role of logical notation in philosophical elucidation is explored in Conant 2001.

vaccines and cures for all possible forms of disease would not eliminate the need for the art of medicine, since even the medical practitioner armed with a complete medical toolkit would still require experience, judgment, and medical craft properly to diagnose, treat, and heal any particular form of illness (so that the true office of medicine to heal the sick must remain a forever piecemeal and unfinished task); so, too, for the author of the *Tractatus*, even after *the* method of philosophy has been discovered (and thus, in this sense, the problems have been in their essentials solved), still the work of philosophical elucidation—the true office of philosophy—must remain a forever piecemeal and unfinished task (one which, with respect to its application in detail, must go on indefinitely without ever reaching a final resting place). The danger of this analogy lies in its comparison of a philosophical problem with an illness.[17] Like any analogy, it will be misunderstood if one construes it as involving an identification of the items on the left and right hand side of the analogy (philosophy and illness are the same thing) or a subsumption of the concept of the one item wholly under the concept of the other (philosophy is an illness).

The emphasis in the preceding paragraph is on the manner in which the conception of philosophical method already for Early Wittgenstein is piecemeal in the Goldfarb sense. As I have already indicated, I am of the view that this aspect of his conception of philosophical method remains one of the most striking continuities in his philosophy, as we move from Early to Middle to Later Wittgenstein.[18] The point of the specific similarity between Early and Middle Wittgenstein mentioned above lay elsewhere and had to do with the way in which both of these Wittgensteins operated with a conception of philosophical method which was, at least in aspiration, radically anti-piecemeal in the McGinn sense. It is this dimension of the methodological aspiration of the *Tractatus* which remains very much alive in Middle Wittgenstein. So much so that I have made bold to suggest that its abandonment might constitute the most significant *Kehre* in the transition from Middle to Later Wittgenstein.[19] It is the difference between these two philosophers, thus delineated, to which the concluding pages of this chapter will especially seek to draw attention.

The Middle Wittgenstein is still a philosopher who aspires to be able to say in the preface to his completed work that the problems have at least in essentials been solved—they have in essentials been solved in so far as one is able to claim that the central problem of *the* method of philosophy has been solved. The details of clearing up hosts of individual philosophical confusions will, of course, have to be left to the generations of practitioners who inherit the method. But the crucial contribution has been made, in as much as the various possible ways in which they are to be cleared up have been delineated in advance and bequeathed to posterity. If such an advance is accomplished, then we may

---

[17] The comparison is Wittgenstein's own: "The philosopher's treatment of a question is like the treatment of an illness" (PI §255).

[18] Needless to say, it necessarily cannot come into view on standard accounts of wherein the differences between Early and Later Wittgenstein lie.

[19] If one permits oneself such a conception of a second 1937 *Kehre*, and combines this with an attachment to the first 1929 *Kehre*, while retaining the usual terminology for talking about such matters, then it becomes natural to speak of there being an early Later Wittgenstein and a later Later Wittgenstein.

speak of the history of philosophy as containing a kink, as Middle Wittgenstein some-times does. This is also why it makes sense to speak of philosophy, in the light of the discovery of a method, as now having been reduced to a form of skill or craft. The funda-mental fantasy which underlies Wittgenstein's conception of the sort of change which he, still throughout this middle period, hopes to introduce into the history of philosophy might be put as follows: no fundamental form of originality will any longer be required on the part of the philosophical practitioner in order for him to be able to make genuine progress with philosophical problems.

This is not to deny that there are countless significant differences between Early Wittgenstein and Middle Wittgenstein in this region of their thought. Here is one: The formulation of the problem of method has itself now become a much messier business for Middle Wittgenstein than Early Wittgenstein had ever imagined it might become. For the problems of philosophy no longer rest for Middle Wittgenstein on a misunder-standing of something we can call *the* logic of our language, where it is crucial to the point of the definite article here that there is just that one logical space. (That is the point of the spatial metaphor, after all; as Kant almost says: all parts of space must be parts of *one* space.[20]) For only a manifold with such a character can admit of a single overarching form of delimitation from within language. This was to have been effected through the provision of a perspicuous logical notation—one which is able to highlight the nodes through which that manifold is articulated and through which it allows for its more determinate possible local forms of logical multiplicity. Early Wittgenstein's conception of *the* logic of our language gives way to Middle Wittgenstein's conception of grammars, where the emphasis on the plural now becomes essential to the conception. Starting in the middle period, an interest prevails in mapping the contours of alternative logical terrains which cannot be accommodated within a single space.

This transition from a definite article ("the" logic of our language) in Early Wittgenstein to a plurality ("grammars") in Middle Wittgenstein presages and prepares the ground for a subsequent transition, yet again from a definite article ("the" method) in Middle Wittgenstein to a further plurality ("methods") in Later Wittgenstein. The second transition, however, does not follow immediately upon the heels of the first. Middle Wittgenstein seeks to find a middle ground: a way to fit a newfound pluralism in his conception of the object and medium of philosophical investigation (logic/gram-mar) with a continuing attachment to a unitary conception of how to proceed (*the* method) in philosophy. A number of the tensions in the thought of Middle Wittgenstein arise directly from the awkwardness of this fit. It is through his increasing appreciation of the character of these tensions that Later Wittgenstein comes to arrive at the shift in his conception of philosophy which forms the central topic of this chapter. One might

[20] Or, as he actually says: "First...if we speak of diverse spaces, we mean thereby only parts of one and the same unique space. Secondly, these parts cannot precede the one all-embracing space, as being, as it were, constituents out of which it can be composed; on the contrary, they can be thought only as *in* it. Space is essentially one; the manifold in it, and therefore the general concept of spaces, depends solely on [the introduction of] limitations." (Kant 1963, 69)

formulate the negative aspect of the insight which underlies the shift here in question as follows: the relinquishing of the first of these definite articles (*the* logic of our language) requires the correlative abandonment of the second of these definite articles (*the* method of philosophy). One can also formulate the point here at issue in more positive terms as follows: an open-ended, infinitely extendable conception of a family of possible forms of grammar comes to be seen to require a correlatively open-ended, infinitely extendable conception of a family of possible forms of philosophical method. That the one requires the other, however, takes time and work for Middle Wittgenstein to come to appreciate.

If the foregoing is correct, then it would be a mistake to think that, for example, a passage such as §133 (in its denial that there is "*a* philosophical method") is primarily concerned to draw a contrast along the standard lines between the "early" view (where early = *Tractatus*) and the "later" view (where later = after 1929). It is worth noting in this connection that the predecessor version of §133 in *The Big Typescript* is missing the last sentence (about there not being *a* philosophical method, but rather different methods).[21] Yet much of §133 as we find it in the *Investigations* is already in *The Big Typescript*. In its latter incarnation, the entire passage, however, becomes incorporated into a single extended meditation. It can now be read as revolving around a concern to mark a contrast which echoes various related contrasts drawn in the preceding stretch of sections in the book (such as that between the logic of language and a family of grammars). In this way, the section as a whole becomes inscribed into what emerges throughout these sections as part of a single overarching contrast between the author's earlier (i.e., in some cases, *both* Early and Middle Wittgenstein's) attachment to certain forms of philosophical monism and his later conception of the place of a plurality not only in his understanding of what philosophy investigates but also in his understanding of how the investigation ought to be prosecuted.

That we find many of the same sentences in both versions of a passage such as this one is consistent with the possibility that Wittgenstein has come to understand (and wants us

---

[21] See BT, 316. The first recorded version of the last sentence of §133 actually dates from February 23, 1938. On these grounds, Wolfgang Kienzler has proposed to me, not without some irony, I take it, that my thesis should actually be that it is this very day which constitutes the date of Wittgenstein's second *Kehre*. The jest does help to underscore an important point which it is perhaps worth making as explicit as possible: it would be a misunderstanding of the relevant claim at issue here (regarding the manner in which Wittgenstein begins to rethink his views with regard to method during his sojourn in Norway) to take that claim to turn on the truth of any specific thesis regarding precisely when the first occurrence of the verbatim version of some particular remark to be found in the final version of the *Philosophical Investigations* happens to fall within a proposed timeframe—so that the entire proposal might be overturned simply by showing that some particular remark falls slightly outside that timeframe, say, with its first formulation coming as early as January 1936 or as late as sometime in 1938 or whatever. The claim in question has to do with a pattern of movement which is to be discerned in Wittgenstein's thought and is thus to be assessed through a careful investigation of the overall character of the manner in which Wittgenstein begins to revise his earlier remarks about the nature of philosophy—a process which, according to this claim, first begins to take on the aspect of a concerted and systematic revision of his earlier views during the period of the proposed timeframe.

to understand) the import of some of the sentences about the nature of philosophy (which have been allowed to stand in the final version of the *Investigations* while their context has been altered from that of *The Big Typescript*) now in a different way than he would have had us understand them prior to his emendations of the sections about the nature of philosophy in *The Big Typescript*. This means that one cannot assess the extent of the continuity in Wittgenstein's conception of philosophy simply by pointing to passages which happen to occur both at an earlier and a later point in his writing. What matters is whether the overall context in which those passages occur encourages and supports the same understanding of their significance. It is frequently the case that Wittgenstein continues to retain a sentence which purports to sum up some aspect of his thinking about a particular topic of philosophy while resituating it in a larger context which profoundly transforms its earlier significance.[22] The form of inquiry in which one must engage in order to assess the presence and the degree of a development in his thought with regard to a topic as fundamental as this one (namely, the topic: what is philosophy?) is thus necessarily exceedingly delicate and difficult.

I hope to have managed to say enough in the preceding pages to allow the reader at least simply to recognize that we here stand at the threshold of a broader inquiry. In order to see how the point just made about §133 represents only the tip of a larger iceberg of forms of revision in Wittgenstein's texts—forms of revision that themselves are symptomatic of a sea-change in his conception of philosophical method—what one would need to do is to investigate the detailed ways in which the entire stretch in *Philosophical Investigations* which runs from §89 to §133 involves a careful rewriting of the chapter "Philosophy" in *The Big Typescript*. Such an investigation will reveal that that chapter was rewritten, bit by bit, in a manner which gradually began to purge it of its commitment to the idea that the method has been found once and for all (so that the problems of philosophy had been revealed to be of such a sort that the essentials of their solution allowed for a sort of discovery which could be separated from the messy details of their treatment). This meant purging many individual passages of his writing of the manner in which they were stamped by Middle Wittgenstein's continuing aspiration to be able to find a way to put philosophy on an absolutely solid footing—a footing which would leave much work for subsequent individual practitioners of the subject to do while, nonetheless, having altered the internal character of philosophy forever. For the nimbus of philosophy would have been lost once and for all: philosophy would have been reduced to a craft of applying a now fully available set of tools. It is this conception of what he seeks, in seeking *the* method of philosophy, that Wittgenstein finally came to abandon in Norway in 1937.

On Later Wittgenstein's conception, the treatment of philosophical problems can no longer be separated in this way from a continuing exploration of the fundamental character

---

[22] This is a point which can be demonstrated with respect to a great many of the sentences which continue to resurface in Wittgenstein's writing as we move from the early, through the middle, to the later period. I make such a case at more length in connection with the sentences which figure on what I call "the third list" in Conant 2007.

of philosophy itself—which is to say that philosophy can never lose its nimbus while remaining philosophy. The forms of creativity required for the discovery of fruitful methods in philosophy and the forms of creativity required for the fruitful application of such methods to particular problems of philosophy are recognized by Later Wittgenstein as two aspects of a single task, each of which requires an unending cultivation of the other. This means that the most that philosophy can hope to achieve is to bring us moments of peace—moments in which we are able to break off philosophizing—because this or that philosophical perplexity has been made to completely disappear. For Later Wittgenstein, this means not only that the task of philosophical elucidation can never come to an end (as was already the case for Early Wittgenstein) because it is piecemeal in the Goldfarb sense, but also that we can never settle on a final and definitive answer to the question "What is philosophy?" (as Early and Middle Wittgenstein both thought we could), for the task has come to be recognized as one which is piecemeal also in the McGinn sense.

A careful examination of the relevant differences between §89 to §133 of *Philosophical Investigations* and the chapter "Philosophy" in *The Big Typescript* nicely brings out one aspect of the way in which the break with the *Tractatus* was a graduated one—one which was distributed over widely dispersed junctures in his philosophical development. Here, if we look closely, we can see two crucial steps coming one after the other. Middle Wittgenstein (who still thought there was one method) thought that Early Wittgenstein had been confused (in thinking that it was possible to survey the space of *all* possible problems *at once* through a single medium of representation). So we get the transition from Early Wittgenstein to Middle Wittgenstein which comes with the shift from the logic of our language to a plurality of logical grammars. Yet, at a later stage, we encounter Later Wittgenstein (who thinks there can only be methods) charging Middle Wittgenstein with having failed to be fully resolute in his criticisms of Early Wittgenstein (i.e., with having unwittingly preserved an essential feature of the metaphysics of the *Tractatus*). For Later Wittgenstein comes to believe that a full thinking through of the consequences of Early Wittgenstein's conception of the unity of language has implications for how the unity of philosophy is, in turn, to be conceived—implications which Middle Wittgenstein was loath to draw.[23]

If we have these two distinct moments of transition in Wittgenstein's thought clearly in view, along with a vivid sense of the difficulty which he experienced in negotiating each of them, then it will allow us to appreciate how, as a matter of historical fact, the process of purging *himself* of the unwitting metaphysical commitments of the *Tractatus* is one that unfolded for Wittgenstein, over the course of his own philosophical development, in (what we might call) a "piecemeal" manner—in yet a third application of that term to Wittgenstein's philosophy. In this third application of the term, what is at

---

[23] One consequence of this transition to the thought of the Later Wittgenstein is that the question of the *unity* of philosophy becomes much more vexed—though no more vexed than the question of the unity of language (or thought) had already become for Middle Wittgenstein. A proper discussion of this topic would require another chapter—one which explored Later Wittgenstein's conception of unity or essence, hence his conception of the sort of unity which characterizes (what he calls) a *family* of cases.

issue is not some particular aspect of Wittgenstein's conception of philosophical method, but rather the shifts that the various aspects of that conception undergo over time. The suggestion which I have sought to render plausible in this paper is that a proper and careful charting of such a *Kehre* in Wittgenstein's "later" philosophy would constitute a difficult but worthwhile task—one which has been largely neglected, thereby allowing the significance of the corresponding shift in his conception of philosophy to go hitherto largely unnoticed.[24]

REFERENCES

CONANT, JAMES (2001). 'Two Conceptions of *Die Überwindung der Metaphysik*', in Timothy McCarthy and Sean C. Stidd eds., *Wittgenstein in America*. Oxford: Oxford University Press.

—— (2002). 'The Method of the *Tractatus*', in Erich H. Reck ed., *From Frege to Wittgenstein: Perspectives in Early Analytic Philosophy*. Oxford: Oxford University Press.

—— (2007). 'Mild Mono-Wittgensteinianism', in Alice Crary ed., *Wittgenstein and the Moral Life: Essays in Honor of Cora Diamond*. Cambridge, MA: MIT Press.

—— and DIAMOND, CORA (2004). 'On Reading the *Tractatus* Resolutely', in Max Kölbel and Bernhard Weiss eds., *The Lasting Significance of Wittgenstein's Philosophy*. London: Routledge.

CONANT, JAMES BRYANT (1951). *Science and Common Sense*. New Haven, CT: Yale University Press.

DIAMOND, CORA (1991). 'Ethics, Imagination, and the Method of the *Tractatus*', in R. Heinrich and H. Vetter eds., *Bilder der Philosophie*. Vienna: Oldenbourg. (Reprinted in Alice Crary and Rupert Read eds., *The New Wittgenstein*. London: Routledge, 2000.)

GOLDFARB, WARREN (1997). 'Metaphysics and Nonsense: On Cora Diamond's *The Realistic Spirit*', *Journal of Philosophical Research*, 22: 57–73.

HACKER, P. M. S. (1986). *Insight and Illusion*, 2nd edition. Oxford: Oxford University Press.

KANT, IMMANUEL (1963). *Critique of Pure Reason*, trans. Norman Kemp Smith. Oxford: Clarendon Press.

KREMER, MICHAEL (1997). 'Contextualism and Holism in the Early Wittgenstein: from *Prototractatus* to *Tractatus*', *Philosophical Topics*, 25.2: 87–120.

KUUSELA, OSKARI (2008). *The Struggle against Dogmatism: Wittgenstein and the Concept of Philosophy*. Cambridge, MA: Harvard University Press.

McGINN, MARIE (2005). 'Wittgenstein's Early Philosophy and the Idea of "The Single Great Problem"', in Alois Pichler and Simo Säätelä eds., *Wittgenstein: The Philosopher and his Works*. Working Papers from the Wittgenstein Archives at the University of Bergen, No. 17.

MONK, RAY (1991). *Ludwig Wittgenstein: The Duty of Genius*. London: Penguin.

READ, RUPERT (2006). 'A No-Theory? Against Hutto on Wittgenstein', *Philosophical Investigations*, 29.1: 73–81.

—— and DEANS, ROB (2003). 'Nothing is Shown', *Philosophical Investigations*, 26.3: 239–68.

---

[24] I am indebted to conversations about these issues with Cora Diamond, Wolfgang Kienzler, Michael Kremer, Oskari Kuusela, and John McDowell, as well as to comments by Cora Diamond and Michael Kremer on an earlier draft of this chapter.

—— and HUTCHINSON, PHIL (2006). 'An Elucidatory Interpretation of Wittgenstein's *Tractatus: A Critique of Daniel D. Hutto's and Marie McGinn's Reading of Tractatus 6.54*', *International Journal of Philosophical Studies*, 14.1: 1–29.

SCHULTE, JOACHIM (2002). 'Wittgenstein's "Method"', in Rudolf Haller and Klaus Puhl eds., *Wittgenstein and the Future of Philosophy*. Vienna: OBV & HPT.

STERN, DAVID (2005). 'How Many Wittgensteins?', in Alois Pichler and Simo Säätelä eds., *Wittgenstein: The Philosopher and his Works*. Working Papers from the Wittgenstein Archives at the University of Bergen, No. 17.

WITTGENSTEIN, LUDWIG (1953). *Philosophical Investigations*. Oxford: Blackwell.

—— (1961). *Notebooks, 1914–1916*. Oxford: Blackwell.

—— (1965). *The Blue and the Brown Books*. Oxford: Blackwell.

—— (1980). *Wittgenstein's Lectures: Cambridge, 1930–1932*, ed. Desmond Lee. Totowa, NJ: Rowman and Littlefield.

—— (1981). *Tractatus Logico-Philosophicus*, trans. C. K. Ogden. London: Routledge.

—— (2005). *The Big Typescript*, trans. C. G. Luckhardt and M. A. E. Aue. Oxford: Blackwell.

CHAPTER 28

GRAMMAR IN THE *PHILOSOPHICAL INVESTIGATIONS*

MARIE MCGINN

INTRODUCTION

WITTGENSTEIN describes the kind of investigation he is engaged in in the *Philosophical Investigations* as 'a grammatical one' (PI §90). He speaks of looking for 'grammatical differences' (PI II, 185) and of 'the rules of grammar' (PI §497); and he makes a distinction between the 'surface grammar' of a word and its 'depth grammar' (PI §664). He traces the misunderstandings which he holds to lie at the root of philosophical problems and paradoxes to 'grammatical illusions' (PI §110), and to the creation of 'grammatical fictions' (PI §307). It is clear that he places the concept of grammar and of grammatical investigation at the heart of his understanding of the aims and methods of his later philosophy. Understanding what he means by the terms 'grammar', 'depth grammar', and 'grammatical investigation' is therefore fundamental to an understanding of the *Investigations*. 'What is Wittgenstein's conception of grammar, depth grammar, and grammatical investigation?' is one of the most important questions to ask when approaching the task of understanding his later work.

One issue raised by this question is how Wittgenstein's conception of grammar and grammatical investigation relates to the traditional understanding of the notion of grammar. It is clear that Wittgenstein does not use the term 'grammar' in a way which implies a clear separation between syntax (grammar) and semantics (meaning). The conception of grammar associated with the traditional grammatical categories—sentence, noun, noun phrase, adjective, transitive and intransitive verbs, adverb, and so on—and their permitted concatenations is one that abstracts from the meaning of words. Wittgenstein, by contrast, 'want[s] to say the place of a word in grammar is its meaning' (PG, 59). This linking together of grammar and semantics is not, however, unique to Wittgenstein. There is a conception of what might be called 'philosophical grammar', which is concerned with the general semantic types that are correlated with the syntactic categories of traditional grammar, and with their potential for combination in significant sentences. The aim of such a grammar might be to identify the basic types of logico-semantic elements which comprise our conceptual scheme, and their modes of combination. Its vocabulary will be overtly ontological, rather than syntactic: spatio-temporal particular, property of a spatio-temporal particular, event, property of an event, state, disposition, state of affairs, and so on. Philosophical grammar, like traditional grammar, is concerned with an understanding of the function of different kinds of linguistic expression within well-formed sentences.

If this shows that Wittgenstein's use of the word 'grammar' is not egregious, it does little to illuminate either the aims of his grammatical investigation or the form it takes. It is not merely that the concepts of traditional semantic categories are largely absent from his work, but even when he employs a traditional semantic distinction—for example, the distinction between dispositions and states—the *making* of such distinctions does not appear to be his whole, or even his primary, concern. It would clearly be a mistake to suppose that Wittgenstein's conception of a grammatical investigation implies that his aim is to provide an orderly classification of kinds of expression into distinct semantic categories. One of the main difficulties in understanding Wittgenstein's emphasis on the concept of grammar is the apparent lack of system, or concern to identify categories of grammatical classification, which characterizes his later work: 'In giving all these examples I am not aiming at some kind of completeness, ... They are only meant to enable the reader to shift for himself when he encounters conceptual difficulties' (PI II, 206). How can a work which aims to make 'our grammar' 'perspicuous', or to achieve '*a clear view* of the use of our words' (PI §122), be apparently so uninterested either in making use of traditional grammatical concepts, or in articulating precise semantic distinctions, or in achieving what could properly be regarded as a genuine overview of the structure of our thought?

The first thing to say here is that, although Wittgenstein describes his investigation as 'a grammatical one', he never claims that his concern is with the grammatical description as such, or suggests that the aim of his philosophy is to provide a comprehensive grammar for our language. It is clear that Wittgenstein is not claiming that traditional metaphysics should be replaced by a form of philosophical enquiry whose aim is to identify the basic semantic or conceptual categories which characterize our conceptual scheme. His concern is with grammar—with the way words function—but his aim is not to provide a systematic grammar for our language. At PI §132, Wittgenstein remarks that 'we want to establish an order in our knowledge of the use of language', but he makes it clear that this order is merely 'an order with a particular end in view; one of many possible orders; not *the* order'. At PI §133, he makes clear the end he has in view: 'that the philosophical problems should *completely* disappear'.

Insofar as his concern is with 'the use of words' (PI §90), Wittgenstein describes his investigation as 'a grammatical one' (PI §90), but it is clear that his investigation does not share the traditional grammarian's concern with a systematic classification of semantic categories, or with a comprehensive description of the structure of a natural language. Wittgenstein's grammatical investigation is concerned with 'looking into the workings of language'—the topic of traditional grammars—but his investigation is distinctive insofar as it 'gets its light, that is to say its purpose, from the philosophical problems' (PI §109). This suggests that we should not see his concern with grammar as undertaken with a particular preconception of the grammatical distinctions—the differences in the uses of words—which are relevant for his enquiry. Rather, he is concerned to clarify those aspects of employing expressions which will help us to resolve the particular philosophical problems and paradoxes which are the focus of his enquiry. If this is so, then it seems that we cannot hope to understand the significance of Wittgenstein's grammatical investigations, or the nature of the grammatical distinctions he is concerned with, in abstraction from the problems to which his investigation is a response. If we want to understand the purpose of Wittgenstein's grammatical investigation, the significance of his concept of depth grammar, and the nature of the grammatical distinctions he is concerned to clarify, then we need to have a clear view of the problems from which his investigation 'gets its light'.

IDENTIFYING THE PROBLEMS

One of the fundamental differences between the *Tractatus* and the *Investigations* lies in how Wittgenstein conceives his philosophical task, and the approach he takes to achieving it. The early philosophy is dominated by a particular set of problems, which together express a preconceived idea of language as a precise calculus, or system of representation, whose essence is logic. The problems he is concerned with include the nature and status of the propositions of logic, the nature of truth and falsity, the nature of negation, and the logical constants generally, and the nature of inference. Wittgenstein is, moreover, convinced that, at bottom, each of these problems is an aspect of what he calls in the *Notebooks* 'a single great problem'. He instructs himself not to try to treat each of these problems piecemeal: 'Don't get involved in partial problems, but always take flight to where there is a free view over the whole *single* great problem, even if the view is not a clear one' (NB, 23). And he identifies this 'single great problem' as follows: 'My whole task consists in explaining the nature of the proposition' (NB, 39). The question is: how does a proposition represent a possible state of affairs? At PI §133, Wittgenstein expresses his outright rejection of the idea of 'the single great problem': 'Problems are solved (difficulties eliminated), not a *single* problem'. The idea of a 'single great problem' is now associated with '[t]he dogmatism into which we fall so easily in doing philosophy' (PI §131), and with what Wittgenstein describes as our tendency to picture logic as 'something sublime' (PI §89). Understanding what the latter idea amounts to is, I want to argue, one route to identifying at least a large class of philosophical problems with which the *Philosophical Investigations* is centrally concerned, and which may therefore be regarded as giving Wittgenstein's grammatical investigation 'its light'.

Wittgenstein first introduces the idea of 'subliming' in the *Investigations* in connection with Russell's claim that the word 'this' is 'the only *genuine* name'. He describes the idea that 'this' is the only genuine name as a 'queer conception' which 'springs from a tendency to sublime the logic of our language' (PI §38). He responds to this 'queer conception' as follows:

> The proper answer to it is: we call very different things 'names'; the word 'name' is used to characterize many different kinds of use of a word. Related to one another in many different ways....(PI §38)

This suggests that at least part of what is involved in what Wittgenstein calls 'subliming' is our tendency to over-generalize, or to take one paradigmatic case as a model for all cases. Thus we sublime the logic of our language when we assume that there is a common essence to everything we call a 'name' or a 'proposition', and that it is the task of philosophy to make this common essence clear. There is certainly something correct in this suggestion. However, it does not fully capture Wittgenstein's sense of what is 'queer' in Russell's conception of a genuine name, for the sentence from PI §38, quoted above, continues:

> —but the kind of use 'this' has is not among them.

It is not, therefore, that Russell has focused on a paradigm case and taken what are merely features of the paradigm for the essence of names. Rather, his 'queer' conception of naming, which springs from a tendency to sublime the logic of our language, has led him to take as a paradigm of a name something which, according to Wittgenstein, we should not ordinarily call a name at all. Wittgenstein acknowledges that the word 'this' often occupies the same position in a sentence as a name. However, he does not think that this is enough to show that the word 'this' functions in the way that a name does. The word 'this' is connected with names, in that names are characteristically defined by means of the demonstrative expression—'This is N', or 'This is called "N"'—but we do not use the word 'this' in the way that we use a name: we do not, for example, also give the definition 'This is called "this"' (PI §38). However, the issue is not merely one of whether Russell has classified the word 'this' correctly. The question is why Russell takes something which we would not ordinarily, outside of philosophy, even think of as a name to be the only *genuine* name. As we've just seen, Wittgenstein believes that Russell's view has its source in 'a tendency to sublime the logic of our language', and he now goes on to connect this tendency with 'the conception of naming as, so to speak, an occult process', 'as a *queer* connexion of a word with an object', or with our thinking 'naming to be some remarkable act of mind, as it were a baptism of an object' (PI §38).

Wittgenstein sees the same process of 'subliming' at work in the following thought:

> 'Thought must be something unique'. When we say, and *mean*, that such-and-such is the case, we—and our meaning—do not stop anywhere short of the fact; but we mean: *this-is-so*. (PI §95)

Meaning, like naming, is seen as a remarkable act of mind. It seems to belong to the nature of a thought that it has a meaning; a thought is not a matter of certain signs coming before the mind, but of my *thinking* something, representing something to myself. A physical sign—a word or a sentence—can be interpreted or used in indefinitely many ways, but a thought or a proposition cannot be interpreted; a thought has the meaning it has. Thus we picture a thought as a remarkable act of mind which accomplishes what no physical sign can accomplish: it is a unique representation of a state of affairs; an uninterpretable propositional content; we mean *this-is-so*. Wittgenstein expresses this idea in the *Tractatus* as follows:

> We use the perceptible sign of a proposition (spoken or written) as a projection of a possible situation.
> The method of projection is to think the sense of the proposition. (TLP 3.11)

Wittgenstein connects this picture of thought as a remarkable act of mind with the conception of logic which provides the framework for the investigation of the nature of a proposition in the *Tractatus*, which he describes in PI §97:

> Thought is surrounded by a halo.—Its essence, logic, presents an order, in fact the a priori order of the world: that is, the order of *possibilities*, which must be common to both world and thought. But this order, it seems, must be *utterly simple*. It is *prior* to all experience, must run through all experience; no empirical cloudiness or uncertainty can be allowed to affect it—It must rather be of purest crystal.

Thus he sees a connection between the subliming of thought and the idea that there is an essence of representation common to all propositions. The idea of logic as the essence of representation goes along with the tendency to think that 'something extraordinary, something unique, must be achieved by propositions', 'as if a proposition *did* something queer' (PI §93). Logic concerns everything that is essential to the representation of states of affairs in thought; it is everything that is essential to our method of projecting the propositional sign onto reality. This conception of logic goes along with our being 'under the illusion that what is peculiar, profound, essential, in our investigation, resides in its trying to grasp the incomparable essence of language' (PI §97), that is, of representation as such.

From this brief outline, we can see that Wittgenstein takes our tendency to sublime the logic of our language to cover at least all of the following:

(1) To think of naming as the directing of the mind onto an object.
(2) To think of a thought or proposition as a unique representation of a state of affairs, which consists in a thinker's projecting a propositional sign onto reality.
(3) To think that sense—that is to say, a thought—is in its nature determinate.
(4) To think that there are rules of projection by means of which the mind transforms mere signs into symbols which have a determinate sense.
(5) To think of logic as the essence of representation, as everything that is essential to a thought's being about reality.

All of these tendencies are manifest in Wittgenstein's early work. Many of the philosophical problems and paradoxes which Wittgenstein addresses in the *Investigations* have their roots in this sublimed picture of how we use language to represent states of affairs. His grammatical investigations are repeatedly directed at resolving the problems and paradoxes—in particular, those associated with the concepts of understanding and grasping a rule—that it gives rise to; it is ultimately this picture which gives his grammatical investigation its light. In order to resolve the paradoxes, we need to 'attain greater clarity about the concepts of understanding, meaning, and thinking' (PI §81), and it is to this central task that the bulk of the remarks in the *Investigations* are addressed.

However, as we noted earlier, Wittgenstein associates the sublimed picture of the logic of our language with the idea of 'a single great problem', or with the assumption that the questions, 'What *is* language?', 'What *is* a proposition?' can be answered 'once and for all; independently of any future experience' (PI §92). Thus, part of what is involved in resisting our tendency to sublime the logic of our language is recognizing that '[p]roblems are solved (difficulties eliminated), not a *single* problem' (PI §133). The aim is not to replace one conception of the essence of thought, or essence of language, with another. The whole idea of a grammatical investigation is that it is opposed to any attempt to say, once and for all, what the essence of a proposition is; the idea is that we should instead 'look into the workings of language' if we want to recognize how the concepts of understanding, meaning, and thinking actually function. And this is something that we do in a piecemeal way, in response to the problems and paradoxes to which our tendency to sublime the logic of our language gives rise. Wittgenstein connects this piecemeal approach to the problems with the idea that '[t]here is not *a* philosophical method, though there are indeed methods, like different therapies' (PI §133). What unifies these different methods, or therapies, is the overall pragmatic aim of clearing misunderstandings away.

Thus it becomes clear that Wittgenstein's interest in the use of words is quite different from that of the traditional grammarian. The aspects of the use of words that we need to clarify are not determined by the interests of traditional grammar, but by the problems with which Wittgenstein is concerned, namely, those that arise from our tendency to picture understanding, thinking, and meaning as remarkable acts of mind. He wants to create an order in our knowledge of the use of language that resolves the problems, but this order is created piecemeal, unsystematically, in response to each problem as it arises. The fact that the order he intends to create involves, not *one* philosophical method, but a variety of methods suggests that it would be a mistake to try to say, once and for all, what form his grammatical investigations take. The lack of system, the absence of any concern with either a comprehensive grammar for our language or with a unified characterization of the method of grammatical enquiry, belongs to the nature of the enquiry that Wittgenstein intends to undertake. The order that he creates in response to any particular problem takes its significance from the philosophical problem it helps to resolve.

Thus, instead of saying what he means by 'grammar', or what the method of 'grammatical investigation' is, Wittgenstein begins the *Investigations* with two examples of a grammatical enquiry into the use of the words in two simple language-games, which he presents in response to a tendency to sublime the logic of language. It could be argued that one of the intended roles of the grammatical investigation of these primitive languages is to serve as a model of the sort of investigation Wittgenstein wants us to undertake when we set about 'looking into the workings of language'. The examples introduce a range of methods for creating an order in our knowledge of the use of words, which Wittgenstein goes on to employ in the investigation of our language, and thus they serve to illustrate the way he wants us to investigate the use of expressions as a means to overcoming the problems and paradoxes to which our tendency to sublimation gives rise. In the next section I look at what these examples, taken as models of Wittgenstein's philosophical method, show us about his conception of grammatical investigation.

A Simple Model of a Grammatical Investigation

The following picture of the essence of language, which Wittgenstein derives from the passage from Augustine's *Confessions*, is a clear example of subliming:

> Every word has meaning. This meaning is correlated with the word. It is the object for which the word stands. (PI §1)

In response to this tendency to sublime, Wittgenstein presents an example in which we 'can command a clear view of the aim and functioning of the words' (PI §5):

> Now think of the following use of language: I send someone shopping. I give him a slip marked 'five red apples'. He takes the slip to the shopkeeper, who opens the drawer marked 'apples'; then he looks up the word 'red' in a table and finds a colour sample opposite it; then he says the series of cardinal numbers—I assume that he knows them by heart—up to the word 'five' and for each number he takes an apple of the same colour as the sample out of the drawer.—It is in this and similar ways that one operates with words. (PI §1)

The suggestion is that at least one role of this example is to present the kind of approach that Wittgenstein intends to take to the task of understanding how the expressions 'to think', 'to mean', 'to understand', and so on function. The example presents us with a scene in which language is employed in the context of a task with a clear practical goal. There is clearly no suggestion that any claim concerning the essence of language is to be derived from the example. The significance of the example is rather that it turns our attention away from a concern with the question of what words signify, or of what occurs in the mind of someone who employs them, and redirects it towards a concern with how the shopkeeper *operates* with words. The use of language is primitive, in the sense that each word in the sentence is associated with a distinct way of acting, and the purpose of using the words is a clear one. However, this does not prevent the example's serving to illustrate Wittgenstein's distinctive approach to the task of clarifying the difference between kinds of expression, or between different parts of speech, by looking at how speakers operate with words in their life with language. The suggestion is that he intends to attain clarity about how the concepts of understanding, meaning, and thinking function by following the kind of approach exemplified in the investigation of this simple language-game: the aim is to see how we actually operate with these words in our life with language. It is in this way, the suggestion is, that we can overcome the problems and paradoxes that surround the sublimed picture of understanding, meaning, and thinking as remarkable acts of mind. The methods we use in this endeavour will be various, but each of them is intended to help us see an order in how we operate with words, one which will remove these problems completely.

PI §1 is also used to introduce a second important theme in Wittgenstein's response to our tendency to picture understanding, meaning, and thinking as remarkable acts of mind:

> 'But how does he know where and how he is to look up the word "red" and what he is to do with the word "five"?'—Well, I assume that he *acts* as I have described. Explanations come to an end somewhere.

This is a theme Wittgenstein returns to again and again throughout the *Investigations*: as a result of their training, speakers acquire the capacity to employ the expressions of their language independently, without hesitation, and without guidance from a rule. Even the laborious techniques employed by the shopkeeper are ones that depend, in the end, upon his having, as a result of his training, the capacity to employ these techniques, without further guidance, independently, in new cases, in ways that are in accord with an established practice. Wittgenstein repeatedly draws attention to the way in which our developing a life with language is grounded in natural reactions, primitive responses, and innate forms of expression; and to the fact that speaking a language is a form of life, in which there is something that is called 'obeying an order' or 'rebelling against it', 'following a rule' or 'going against it', in particular cases. The turn towards a concern with how speakers operate with words is made within the framework of what might be called a 'naturalistic' approach to the task of understanding the workings of language: 'Commanding, questioning, recounting, chatting, are as much a part of our natural history as walking, eating, drinking, playing' (PI §25). His grammatical investigations are also, at least in part, 'remarks on the natural history of human beings' (PI §415).

Thus Wittgenstein's grammatical investigation of how we operate with words wants us to look at what happens, in particular cases, when someone is given an order and obeys it, infers one proposition from another, suddenly understands a word or the principle of a series, expects an explosion, remembers that he meant NN, and so on. He wants us to look at the circumstances in which we learn to use expressions, and at 'the primitive reaction with which [a] language-game begins' (PI II, 218). He does not attempt to explain our capacity to take part in the linguistic practices which characterize our form of life, but aims merely to achieve a clear view of them. In this way, he aims to overcome our tendency to imagine that understanding, meaning, thinking are remarkable acts of mind, resolve the problems and paradoxes this tendency gives rise to, and get us to see that there is nothing occult about these processes. If we look at the sort of training we receive, and at how, as a result of this training, we operate with the words 'understand', 'mean', 'think'—at the kind of employment these words have in our life with language—then we will no longer be tempted to say 'A proposition is a queer thing'. We will at last be able to see 'that nothing out of the ordinary is involved' (PI §94). There is no suggestion that this description of how we operate with words—of how we employ words in our life with language—describes the only possible order that can be discerned in our knowledge of the use of language, but it describes the order, the aspect of our knowledge of the use of expressions, which interests Wittgenstein. For it is this order, he believes, that will clear away the misunderstandings arising out of our tendency to sublime the logic of our language, or to picture understanding, meaning, and thinking as remarkable acts of mind.

These points are reinforced in the extended discussion of the language of the builders (PI §§2, 8). Wittgenstein places particular emphasis on our looking at how '[t]he children are brought up to perform *these* actions, to use *these* words as they do so, and to react in *this* way to the words of others' (PI §6). Thus we are directed to look at differences in the kind of instruction or training that a child receives with different kinds of words. We're also asked to reflect on the criteria by which we judge whether a child has understood a word he is being taught to use. There is no suggestion that these reflections are intended to function as hypotheses which explain the way in which expressions function; rather the descriptions are used to help us to see the way speakers operate with words in a new light. This dual approach becomes central to Wittgenstein's method for investigating how the words 'to think', 'to mean', 'to understand', 'to intend', and so on function. The interest is in coming to command a clear view of the use of these words and the idea is that focusing on the circumstances in which we teach a child these particular linguistic techniques, and on the criteria by which we judge that he has mastered them, will help us to see more clearly how we actually operate with these expressions, and thus to overcome our tendency to imagine that they are used to describe remarkable acts of mind. These are not the only methods Wittgenstein employs in his grammatical investigation, but they once again serve to show the distinctive nature of Wittgenstein's concern with the way words function: it is the role expressions play in our lives that he aims to command a clear view of.

Perspicuous Representation and Depth Grammar

At PI §664, Wittgenstein makes a distinction between 'surface grammar' and 'depth grammar':

> In the use of words one might distinguish 'surface grammar' from depth grammar'. What immediately impresses itself upon us about the use of a word is the way it is used in the construction of the sentence, the part of its use—one might say—that can be taken in by the ear.

It seems reasonable to suppose that both traditional grammar and philosophical grammar are concerned with what Wittgenstein here describes as 'surface grammar': the part the expression plays in the construction of sentences. These grammars focus on the construction of grammatical strings, or with the rules of concatenation of grammatical elements which result in well-formed sentences of the language. Wittgenstein makes it clear that his interest, by contrast, is with 'depth grammar':

> And now compare the depth grammar, say of the word 'to mean', with what its surface grammar would lead us to suspect. No wonder we find it difficult to know our way about.

Wittgenstein leaves the contrast between surface grammar and depth grammar, tantalizingly, at that. However, if we take the examples of PI §§1 and 6 as models of the approach that Wittgenstein intends us to take to attaining greater clarity about the concepts of understanding, meaning, and thinking, then the contrast he intends is clear. His concern is not with the construction of well-formed sentences, but with the way words are employed in our life with language, with the ways in which we *operate* with words. 'Depth grammar' is, on this reading, concerned with aspects of use that both traditional grammar and philosophical grammar ignore: the circumstances in which we use expressions, the circumstances in which we are trained to use them, the way in which their use is integrated with other activities, and so on. This understanding of the distinction between 'surface grammar' and 'depth grammar' is one that has been defended by Gordon Baker. He writes as follows:

> This interpretation has the great advantage that the term 'depth' can be given a straightforward explanation. It would here connote not hiddenness, but rather exploration of *new dimensions* different from any investigation of the principles of sentence-construction ('surface grammar'). The model for contrasting depth grammar and surface grammar is the distinction between solid and plane geometry. On this reading, Wittgenstein had the clear intention to encourage us to look in new directions for the purpose of dissolving philosophical confusions. (Baker 2006, 84)

This does not, of course, preclude Wittgenstein's having an interest in aspects of surface grammar—for example, in whether a psychological concept stands for a disposition or an occurrent state, something which is reflected, for example, in how it interacts with temporal concepts in the construction of well-formed sentences—but it recognizes that this is not his sole, or even his primary, interest. It is not where he thinks the resolution of the problems arising from our tendency to sublime the logic of our language lies.

This interpretation of Wittgenstein's distinction between surface grammar and depth grammar contrasts with one put forward by Peter Hacker. Hacker takes surface grammar to be the 'obvious syntactic features of the sentence and the words of which it is composed' (Hacker 1996a, 708); by contrast, depth grammar is 'what demands description of, and reminders of, the overall use of [an] expression' (Hacker 1996a, 709). Surface grammar is what is described by the limited range of grammatical distinctions that we ordinarily employ. Expressions which belong to the same surface grammatical category are differentiated at the level of depth grammar, that is, when the whole intricate network of rules for their use in well-formed sentences is properly attended to. For example, the words 'saying' and 'meaning' appear to belong to a single surface-grammatical category, namely, the category of *action-verb*. However, attention to the depth grammar of these expressions—for example, to the fact that it makes sense to say 'I intend to say...tomorrow', but not 'I intend to mean...tomorrow'; that it makes sense to say 'I decided to say...', but not 'I decided to mean....'; that one can say, but not mean, something quickly, elegantly, or gladly; and so on—shows that they have quite different combinatorial possibilities, and thus occupy quite different places in our conceptual scheme. On this interpretation, the concept of depth grammar does not introduce a new dimension of concern, but rather calls for the accumulation of hitherto neglected details about possibilities for sentence construction, which, on the alternative understanding of depth grammar suggested above, still count as surface.

These contrasting interpretations yield quite different understandings of Wittgenstein's notion of a 'perspicuous representation'. Hacker holds that the problems of philosophy arise when similarities in surface grammar (obvious syntactic features) prompt philosophers to assimilate expressions which have quite different depth grammars (possibilities for use in well-formed sentences). This assimilation leads to philosophical confusion when the depth grammar of one expression is projected, inappropriately, onto the other. For example, the similarity in surface form of the verbs 'to say' and 'to mean' leads the philosopher to picture meaning as a peculiar mental activity, in which a connection between a name and an object is made by the mind at the time an expression is uttered. The confusions arising out of the assimilation are resolved through the perspicuous arrangement of the 'familiar rules for the use of expressions [which makes] the [depth] grammar of the relevant expressions surveyable' (Hacker 1996b, 107). Thus, 'by a careful description of the grammatical reticulations of...philosophically confusing expressions...we...attain a perspicuous representation of the field of interconnected concepts that is the locus of our problems' (Hacker 1996b, 107).

Such a perspicuous tabulation of the rules for the use of expressions 'enables us to see differences between concepts which are obscured by the misleadingly similar [surface] grammatical forms of expressions, the use of which is fundamentally different, and connections between concepts and sentences in use which superficially appear to be quite different' (Hacker 1996b, 107–8). The idea is that through the clear arrangement of all the grammatical rules for the use of the word 'to mean', and their juxtaposition with the rules for the use of the word 'to say', we can see how philosophical theories of what meaning consists in 'transgress the bounds of sense', or how they misconstrue sentences which give rules for the use of the word 'to mean' as statements of fact, which, so understood, are not false but nonsense. Not only that, but the method of perspicuous representation 'gives philosophy, for the first time in its history, a well founded title to criticize other disciplines, if and when they transgress the bounds of sense' (Hacker 1996b, 123). Hacker's interpretation of the nature and aims of a perspicuous representation leads to the idea that '[t]he task of philosophy is...to audit the account books of *sense*', and to 'unmask...scientific mythology (which is to be distinguished from scientific error)' (Hacker 1996b, 123); philosophy is 'the tribunal of science; it adjudicates not the truth of scientific theorizing, but the sense of scientific propositions' (Hacker 1996b, 123). Once we attain a perspicuous representation of the rules for the use of expressions, we can 'restrain [science] within the bounds of sense, ..., [and] restrain scientists and philoso-phers who have been beguiled by their myth-making from metaphysical nonsense' (Hacker 1996b, 123).

As Baker notes, on this interpretation, '[t]he adjective "perspicuous" in the phrase "a perspicuous representation" is used attributively. It ascribes a property to a particular arrangement of grammatical rules, namely that they can be taken in at a glance' (Baker 2006, 28). He contrasts this understanding of the phrase with his own interpretation of it as follows:

> The adjective 'perspicuous' in the phrase 'a perspicuous representation' is *not* used attributively. Whether a representation is perspicuous is not an intrinsic feature of it (e.g. whether it can be taken in at a glance or easily reproduced from memory), but rather a characterization of its role or function. It is a representation which *makes perspicuous* what is represented. (Baker 2006, 42)

There is no longer the implication that a perspicuous representation takes the form of a tabulation of rules for the use of expressions. The aim of a perspicuous representation is relative to the particular problems that concern us; the purpose is to make clear some aspect of the use of a particular expression, and the aspects we're concerned with are determined by the problems. This leaves open the possibility that a perspicuous repre-sentation is concerned with a dimension of use that is not captured in the notion of rules for the construction of well-formed sentences, but focuses on how speakers operate with words, understood in a way which gives the distinction between surface grammar and depth grammar its point: the circumstances in which we use expressions, the circum-stances in which we are trained to use them, the way in which their use is integrated with other activities, and so on. The methods by which we make these aspects clear are vari-ous, and there is no suggestion that they result in a definitive mapping of interconnec-tions of concepts in our conceptual scheme. The criterion of success in giving a perspicuous representation is that the specific problems which prompt our grammatical investigation completely disappear; there is no suggestion that what is achieved is a systematic representation of rules for the use of words in well-formed sentences, which could serve as norms against which the utterances of others may be deemed to 'trans-gress the bounds of sense'.

Clarifying Understanding, Meaning, and Thinking

What difference does each of these interpretations make for how we read the grammatical investigations that make up the *Philosophical Investigations*? Both interpretations see Wittgenstein as aiming to clarify the use of the concepts of understanding, meaning, and thinking. And both recognize that the task of clarification is undertaken in response to the temptation to assume that these concepts stand for states or processes occurring in the mind of the subject. This leads, no doubt, to important points of agreement between the two interpretations, both in respect of how to understand the overall significance of Wittgenstein's investigations, and in respect of the interpretation of the details of particular remarks. However, despite important points of agreement, there are also important differences to be discerned which, although they may, at least in part, be a question of emphasis, nevertheless reflect a fundamentally different conception of the kind of grammatical investigation Wittgenstein undertakes in response to what puzzles us about understanding, thinking, and meaning. Hacker holds that puzzlement is resolved by the description of grammatical conventions, or by the articulation of intra-grammatical connections between expressions, which can then be used to justify the dismissal of philosophical propositions as nonsense. The alternative interpretation has both a wider view of what is involved in coming to command a clear view of our actual employment of an expression, one which calls on us to attend to our life with language, and a different conception of Wittgenstein's aim. Thus the primary focus of the investigation is on the way in which our use of these expressions is woven in with other activities, on the way in which we are taught to operate with them in the course of our everyday lives, on how we judge that someone has mastered the technique of employing them, and so on. The aim of the investigation is that we come to see how we operate with the words 'to understand', 'to mean', and 'to think', and in coming to see this, to recognize that 'nothing out of the ordinary is involved': '[t]his role is what we need to understand to resolve the philosophical paradoxes' (PI §182). Once we see this role clearly, the idea is, the problems and paradoxes will 'completely disappear'; there is no longer the suggestion that the aim is to articulate rules which could function as a tribunal, or be used to restrain others 'within the bounds of sense'.

The following example may be taken as a model of Hacker's conception of how a grammatical investigation works. Hacker argues that the question how thought can be of something in reality, or how an expectation can be of what is not yet the case, is misleading. At its root is the confusion that thinking and expecting are peculiar mental states or processes. It is this picture which prompts us to ask how these states and processes can perform the feat of catching reality in their net. How is it that the thought that p is made true by the fact that p? In the *Tractatus*, Hacker holds, Wittgenstein is in the grip of this picture and sets out to show that the relation between a thought and the fact that makes it true depends upon a metaphysical connection between thought and the world, between language and reality. 'With the collapse of the metaphysics of the *Tractatus*,' he argues, 'Wittgenstein had to start afresh. Now his task was to give a "flat" description of the ... grammatical network, in order to demythologize the mysteries of intentionality and representation which the *Tractatus* had tried to explain' (Hacker 1996a, 34). Thus, in the *Investigations*, Wittgenstein recognizes, for example, that the proposition that the thought that p is made true by the fact that p, '[f]ar from expressing a substantive if, strictly speaking, ineffable relationship,...expresses a grammatical rule, viz. that "the thought that p"="the thought that is made true by the fact that p"'; it 'merely articulates an *intra-grammatical* connection of expressions'; '[i]t gives a rule for the use of signs' (Hacker 1996a, 33).

Philosophical problems arise when we conceive of the internal relation between a thought and the fact that makes it true as a relation between thought and reality, 'rather than as a link between concepts within the grammatical network' (Hacker 1996a, 35). It is this mistaken conception which sends us in fruitless search of a mythological representational content that consists in a metaphysical relation between thought and reality, which determines the identity of a thought, and which the subject of the thought must be incapable of misinterpreting. The idea is that we happily relinquish this fruitless search when we realize that '[w]hat we naturally, but misleadingly, think of as "the connection between language and reality" is made by definitions of words, explanations of what a word means', and that '[t]hese belong to the grammar of the language and are part of the symbolism' (Hacker 1996a, 38). In the same way, what individuates A's thought as the thought that p, rather than the thought that q, lies in the verbal expression of the thought: 'Trivially, if A thinks that p, the verbal expression of his thought is the sentence "p", and he can be said to be thinking *of* (and the thought he has can be said to be *about*) whatever the constituent expressions of "p" refer to or signify' (Hacker 1996a, 41). When someone says that he thinks that p, there is no process of recognizing that he has a thought with a certain content. For there is no such thing as—that is, it makes no sense to say—one is *perceiving* a thought. Thus it makes no sense to say that a thinker may have misinterpreted his thought, but this is not because his thought does not need interpreting, rather there is nothing to interpret; misinterpretation is excluded by grammar, that is to say, by the rules for the use of expressions.

On this interpretation, Wittgenstein's grammatical investigations are seen as essentially concerned with the description of the intricate network of grammatical connections between expressions which are held to constitute 'the grammar of our language'. Thus we describe the grammar of the words 'know' and 'think' by noting that it makes no sense to say that one knows what one thinks, unless one means that one has made up one's mind about what one thinks; that it makes no sense to say that someone is mistaken about what he thinks; that it makes no sense to raise the question, 'How do you know?'; and so on. On Hacker's view, it is by means of a perspicuous arrangement of these familiar facts about how we use expressions in sentences, about what we do and do not say, about the connections between one well-formed sentence and another, and so on, that Wittgenstein is held to overcome the mythology of thoughts as mental states with a representational content. For the way the word 'to think' is used—its place in the network of expressions which constitutes our system of representation—shows that 'I think that p' does not have the role of a report of an inner process, which only the person speaking has access to, and about which he may be said to be infallible. Thus it can now be seen, on the one hand, that in Wittgenstein's remarks on thoughts in the *Tractatus*, and in his attempts to explain how thoughts represent reality, '[t]he bounds of sense have been violated again and again' (Hacker 1996a, 18–19). For both the remarks and the theory of representation assume that having a thought is a matter of something's occurring in an inner realm, whereas a grammatical investigation of the role of the word 'to think' in our conceptual network shows that this is not how the expression is used. On the other hand, the question that Wittgenstein allegedly tried to answer in *Tractatus*, by means of a theory of representation, is now recognized as thoroughly confused; the connection between thought and reality, which the theory tries to explain, is now seen to be grammatical: a matter of the transitions between expressions that are licensed by rules for the use of expressions, or by the grammar of our language.

It is not so much that I want to dispute the grammatical facts that Hacker marshals, or even their significance for overcoming the picture of thought as a remarkable act of mind. Rather, it seems to me a question of how the mere accumulation of alleged facts about conceptual connections, or about what we do or do not say, *could* on its own dissolve the confusions which arise when we feel compelled to say: 'When we say, and *mean*, that such-and-such is the case, we—and our meaning—do not stop anywhere short of the fact; but we mean: *this-is-so*' (PI §95). For it may still strike us, even in the face of all these alleged linguistic data, that thought achieves something that a mere sign, written or spoken, can never achieve. For a sign can always be interpreted in many different ways, but a thought has the meaning it has. Thus, when I have a thought, it seems that it cannot be a matter of mere physical signs coming before my mind, for I think *this-is-so*: 'We want to say: "When we mean something, it's like going up to something, it's not having a dead picture (of any kind)"' (PI §455). It is just not clear how the power of this idea could be removed merely by observations about how we use the word 'think' in sentences, or about the transitions between sentences that are licensed by grammar. Nor is it clear how pointing out that the words with which I express my thought are not mere signs, that they have a meaning insofar as they have a use in our language, helps us out of the difficulty. For the use of the words is something extended in time, whereas when I say the words and mean something by them, it seems that the meaning is present in that very act of thinking: 'True, the essential properties of the negation sign become apparent only gradually, as it's being used, but I *think* the negation all at once' (BT 177).

The problem is that the idea that in having a thought I represent something to myself as the case—I think *this-is-so*—seems to us a mere truism, which could not possibly be at odds with the use of the word 'think' in well-formed sentences. If this is the picture that lies at the root of philosophical paradoxes which surround the idea of thought as a remarkable act of mind, as something which achieves what no mere sentence could achieve, then it seems that liberation from it must be sought in a dimension other than 'the way [the word] is used in the construction of the sentence', for what we need to get clear about is what thinking really consists in, what this process which we call 'thinking' amounts to. The idea is that, given that this is our problem, we need to look at an aspect of our use of words which is not captured in the idea of how the word is used in the construction of sentences. We need to look in another dimension, the one which is invoked by the interpretation of the distinction between surface grammar and depth grammar that I want to recommend, and which sees Wittgenstein's grammatical investigations as having a focus which is quite other than that suggested by Hacker's picture of a concern to tabulate an intricate network of grammatical rules that are alleged to fix a word's place in the symbolism. The idea is that we need to become clear about how we operate with these expressions, about what is involved in learning to operate with them, about the way their use in well-formed sentences is woven into our life with language, and so on.

On this interpretation, the grammatical investigation Wittgenstein undertakes aims not merely to show us that the idea of an uninterpretable thought-content is indeed a grammatical chimera, but also to help us get clear about what the processes we call 'thinking' ('meaning', 'intending', 'expecting', and so on) consist in, and to show us that 'nothing out of the ordinary is involved' (PI §94).

At PI §430, Wittgenstein gives clear expression to the temptation to picture thought as a remarkable act of mind:

> 'Put a ruler against this body; it doesn't say that the body is of such-and-such a length. Rather is it in itself—I should like to say—dead, and achieves nothing of what thought achieves.'

The ruler is a physical object; in itself it says nothing; placing it alongside an object in itself means nothing. It is, by contrast, in the nature of a thought that it has a meaning; a thought is not a matter of mere, dead signs coming before the mind, but of my *thinking* something, representing something to myself. The physical object, the physical sign, can be interpreted or used in indefinitely many ways, but a thought cannot be interpreted; a thought has the meaning it has. Thus we are tempted to separate out the dead sign and the remarkable act of mind which accomplishes what no physical sign can accomplish: the representation of a state of affairs.

Wittgenstein presents the following comparison with the move we are tempted to make:

> It is as if we had imagined that the essential thing about a living man was the outward form. Then we made a lump of wood in the form, and were abashed to see the stupid block, which hadn't even any similarity to a living being. (PI §430)

The suggestion is that we picture thought as a remarkable act of mind, which achieves what no physical sign achieves, in part because we are looking at the physical sign in the wrong way. The comparison suggests that the aspect we're neglecting is a dynamic one, for the aspect of a living human being that the lump of wood shaped like a man neglects is the ways of acting and responding which characterize a living human being. The suggestion is that in seeing the ruler as a dead sign we have neglected the practice of measuring, and the role that measuring plays in our lives. When we see the act of placing a ruler alongside an object in the context of a practice of measuring, and the activities into which this practice is woven, then what measuring the length of a body by means of a ruler amounts to no longer seems mysterious. Seeing how we operate with the ruler in the countless practical activities into which taking measurements is woven, we no longer feel tempted to say that 'it achieves nothing of what thought achieves'. Wittgenstein's thought is that an essential step in overcoming the picture of thought as a remarkable act of mind is to remind ourselves of how we operate with signs; thinking will not seem an extraordinary achievement when we see it under the aspect of learning to do things with signs; we will no longer be tempted to think that thought achieves something that cannot be achieved outside the mind. It is not simply that the words that come before a speaker's mind have a use in a symbolism which determines their meaning, but by focusing on the way a speaker operates with words, the sense that thinking is a remarkable act of mind can be overcome.

At PI §431, Wittgenstein continues to explore our tendency to think that the thought, or the act of understanding, achieves something that mere words cannot achieve:

> When we give an order, it can look as if the ultimate thing sought by the order had to remain unexpressed, as there is always a gulf between an order and its execution.

When we give an order, the signs we utter can be interpreted in indefinitely many ways, but the order itself is surely something determinate. It seems to us that our words, insofar as they are interpretable, necessarily fail to express the order as we imagine it. Even if we 'try to supplement the order by means of further signs', the person receiving the order still cannot know just what it is that I intend him to do: 'How does he know at all what use he is to make of the signs I give him, whatever they are?' (PI §433). The order exists as a determinate order only in the realm of the understanding, and it is '[a]s if the signs were precariously trying to produce understanding in us' (PI §433); the sign 'tries to portray, but cannot do it' (PI §434).

Wittgenstein responds to this tendency to imagine that thought—the order as I understand it—achieves something that mere words cannot achieve by asking a question:

> But if we now understand [the signs], by what token do we understand?

This directs our attention to our ordinary criteria for someone's having understood an order that he is given. We have been tempted to picture understanding as the uninterpretable thought which the uttered signs cannot express, but if we think of our criteria for someone's understanding an order, then we can see that it is, for the most part at least, that he *acts* in such-and-such a way. If we are inclined to puzzle over the question, '"How do sentences manage to represent?"' (PI §435), then this is because we neglect our life with language, and picture representing as something that only an uninterpretable thought, or act of understanding, can achieve. However, when we try to catch hold of this uninterpretable thought, it eludes us, for all we can produce are further signs: 'Here is it easy to get into that dead-end in philosophy, where one believes that the difficulty of the task consists in our having to describe phenomena that are hard to get hold of' (PI §436). When we look at how speakers actually operate with signs in the context of the activities into which their use is woven—for example, at a particular case of what we call giving and obeying an order, and the criteria by which we judge that it has been understood, obeyed, disobeyed, rebelled against, and so on—then all is clear and open to view, and the sense of a thought, or understanding, as something incommunicable, lying in the background, disappears. This is not so much a matter of the careful or perspicuous description of 'the grammatical reticulations of…philosophically confusing expressions', but of careful attention to the way in which the use of signs is woven into speakers' life with language.

It is against the background of a recognition of the connection between learning to think and learning to operate with signs that Wittgenstein raises the question how we learn to use the words 'to think', 'to say something to oneself', 'I calculated in my head', 'I'm reading to myself', 'I meant NN', 'I wasn't just saying that, I meant it', 'For a moment I was going to…', and so on. Wittgenstein's exploration of these examples goes well beyond anything that might be described as the tabulation of rules for the use of a particular expression in well-formed sentences. For example, he asks us to reflect on how we teach someone to read to himself or to calculate in his head, how we judge that he can do these things, and how the pupil knows that he is doing what is required of him, what goes on when he does these things, and so on. The aim is not merely to get us to recognize what we do or do not say, but to get us to see the role that the relevant expressions play in our life with language, the way in which learning these expressions is woven in with our acquiring certain characteristic abilities, and with a propensity to give spontaneous expression to our thoughts, feelings, and intentions.

Certain themes recur in these remarks, in particular a concern with the circumstances in which we learn to use these expressions, an emphasis on the importance of the primitive responses and natural reactions which provide the roots of our linguistic techniques, the concern with getting us to see one language-game as a complication of one that we have already learned, and with getting us to see a natural order in the development of our life with language. And in all of this, the theme of first-person/third-person asymmetry is of fundamental importance, not merely because it is a defining feature of psychological concepts, but because recognizing the distinctive nature of the first-person present indicative use of the relevant expressions is essential to our overcoming the temptation to picture thinking, expecting, intending, and so on as remarkable acts of mind.

Thus one of the principal themes of Wittgenstein's remarks is that we learn to use the words 'I think…', 'I meant…', 'I understand…' and so on, in the context of acquiring the capacity to operate with signs, in which developing the ability to speak independently and confidently *for myself* is essential. This is reflected in the fact that no question of justifying, or of saying how we know, comes in. If I reflect on what goes on when I have a lightning-like thought, suddenly see the solution to a problem, or grasp the principle of a mathematical series, what I describe may be a few words or images, or just a sudden feeling that I can give fluent expression to what I think, say what the solution to the problem is, or continue the series independently. In certain circumstances, the certainty that I can go on with the series, express my thought, or solve the problem, will be 'well founded' or justified. But Wittgenstein wants us to recognize that the circumstances which justify my confidence have nothing to do with anything occurring at the time. Rather, it is facts about my past training and performance, and my capacity to use signs in calculating, describing, inferring, and so on, which justify my use of the words 'Now I understand', 'Now I can go on'. There will also be cases in which nothing can be said to justify my certainty, but 'it will be justified by success' (PI §320). A child learns to use the words 'Now I understand', 'Now I know how to go on', not by having his attention drawn to something 'occurring in his mind', or to an empirical connection between his feeling of confidence and his ability to go on. Rather, he learns to use them in the context of his developing autonomous, confident responses that are in harmony with our practice of judging, describing, calculating, and inferring, and so on. Thus the use of these words, Wittgenstein suggests, might be compared with an exclamation, 'an instinctive sound, a glad start' (PI §323).

In the same way, Wittgenstein wants us to see that a child's learning to use the words 'I said to myself...', 'I did the calculation in my head', 'I'm reading to myself', and so on, has nothing to do with his being taught to observe or describe processes occurring in him. Only a child who has already learned to speak, to calculate, or to read is in a position to develop the capacities which provide the context for his learning to use these expressions. We teach the child to do something, and he learns to use these words spontaneously, in the context of developing these abilities, in ways that fit in, in certain characteristic ways, with other things he has already learned to say and do. In the context of developing these abilities, the child learns to say, straight off and without hesitation, that he has done a calculation in his head, imagined a certain colour, said such-and-such to himself, and so on, and, in normal circumstances, this is a criterion of his having done so. There is no question of the correctness or incorrectness of what he says, other than that of his utterance's being sincere, or truthful. This is how we learn to use these words, how we learn to operate with them. Thus Wittgenstein works against the idea that the first-person use of these expressions functions as a report of states or processes occurring in an inner realm, not merely by describing their role in our network of concepts, but by clarifying what is involved in learning to use them, the criteria by which we judge that their use has been grasped, and the way in which their use is woven in with other things we say and do. His aim is to get us to see how distinctive the first-person present indicative use of these words is, the way in which it is woven in with our developing capacities for autonomous participation in the practices which characterize our form of life. It is in this way that we come to see that the way we learn to operate with these words has nothing to do with describing processes occurring in an inner realm.

At PI §410, Wittgenstein makes a connection between his grammatical observations about the distinctive nature of the first-person present indicative use of psychological concepts and a grammatical observation about the use of the word 'I': ' "I" is not the name of a person'. Wittgenstein does not, of course, deny that 'I' occupies the same place in a sentence as a name, or the logical link between 'I am thinking of Vienna' and 'MM is thinking of Vienna', but he suggests that these connections should not blind us to the difference in the way we operate with the words 'I' and 'MM'. The sentence 'MM is thinking of Vienna' involves an identifying reference to a person and the predication of a property, on the basis of criteria, to the person identified. Nothing comparable is involved when I use the words 'I am thinking of Vienna': there is no step of identifying a subject of predication; there is no step of recognizing, on the basis of criteria, that a predicate applies. I simply speak for myself in giving expression to the subject of my thought. It is clear that Wittgenstein makes a connection between the non-referring role of 'I' and the idea that the first-person present indicative use of psychological concepts is not, in general, to be understood on the model of description of a process which occurs in the mind and justifies my use of the words I utter. He tries to show that our acquisition of the distinctive human capacities of judging, calculating, inferring, and so on—capacities which provide the context for our learning to use the expressions 'I think...', 'I imagine...', 'I said to myself...'—goes hand in hand with our acquiring the ability to operate with the word 'I' in the distinctive way he describes.

Wittgenstein's aim is to show that the temptation to picture mental states as possessing special representational powers—a power to fly beyond themselves in a way that words alone can never do—arises when we neglect our life with language. He continually works to overcome this temptation by directing our attention to the way we are trained to operate with signs, to the contexts in which we are trained to use them, to the way in which their use is woven in with other activities, and so on; in this way we gradually come to see that 'everything lies open to view' and that 'nothing out of the ordinary is involved'. It is in this context that the grammatical observations about rules for the use of expressions—in the sense which counts as their surface grammar—are made. For example, it is a rule of (surface) grammar that my expectation or wish is fulfilled by an event which can be described, with appropriate changes of tense, in the same words as those I use in the expression of my expectation or wish. One of Wittgenstein's central concerns is to get us to recognize that the link between, for example, an expectation and an event which 'fulfils' or 'satisfies' it is 'made "in language"' (PI §445). However, these grammatical observations are no longer seen as aiming at a surveyable representation of all the rules for the use of expressions in well-formed sentences, which will provide us with a tribunal against which the words of philosophers can be judged as sense or nonsense. Rather, they have the status of rules which we formulate in order to draw attention to an aspect of our use of words, and are to be seen within the context of Wittgenstein's wider concern: to come to see clearly how we learn to operate with words, and to recognize that everything we need to understand what thinking, meaning, understanding, intending, and so on amount to is there to be seen in our life with language.

It is, on this interpretation of the nature of Wittgenstein's grammatical investigation, the clarified view of how we learn to operate with words that releases us from the picture of thinking, meaning, intending, understanding as remarkable acts of mind, and from the paradoxes and puzzles that it generates. Instead of picturing meaning NN as an occult process of mental pointing, we achieve a clarified view of a speaker's capacity to say what he is thinking of, and of the criteria by which we judge, in particular cases, when a particular name's coming to mind amounts to a speaker's meaning NN. Instead of picturing a wish as something which, in some mysterious way, anticipates what fulfils it, we achieve a clarified view of the circumstances in which someone learns to say 'I wish...', of the contexts in which we use these words, and of the way the words that give expression to the wish are woven in with our wider practice. Instead of trying to say in a primitive way what the difference between a prediction and the expression of an intention is, we achieve a clarified view of the kind of training we receive with fundamentally different techniques, and of the distinctive capacities for voluntary action which form the context for a statement about the future which constitutes the expression of an intention. It isn't, or isn't merely, a matter of what it makes sense to say, but of seeing that what we need to understand what thinking is, what understanding is, what intending is, what wishing is, and so on is a clarified view of the capacity to operate with words that speakers acquire through the sort of training that human beings receive with language. It is Wittgenstein's concern with this aspect of the workings of our language which makes his grammatical investigations distinctive. It accounts, in part, for his concern with looking at particular cases, with the primitive roots of our language-games, with the kind of training that forms the background to our use of expressions, and to the distinctive nature of the first-person present indicative use of psychological concepts.

References

BAKER, G. (2006). *Wittgenstein's Method: Neglected Aspects.* Oxford: Blackwell.

HACKER, P. M. S. (1996a). *Wittgenstein: Mind and Will, Volume 4 of an Analytical Commentary on the Philosophical Investigations.* Oxford: Blackwell.

—— (1996b). *Wittgenstein's Place in Twentieth Century Analytic Philosophy.* Oxford: Blackwell.

WITTGENSTEIN, L. (1971). *Tractatus Logico-Philosophicus,* trans. D. F. Pears and B. F. McGuinness. London: Routledge and Kegan Paul.

—— (1974). *Philosophical Grammar,* ed. R. Rhees, trans. A. Kenny. Oxford: Blackwell.

—— (1979). *Notebooks 1914–1916,* 2nd edition, ed. G. H. von Wright and G. E. M. Anscombe, trans. G. E. M. Anscombe. Oxford: Blackwell.

—— (1998). *Philosophical Investigations,* 2nd edition, trans. G. E. M. Anscombe. Oxford: Blackwell.

—— (2005). *The Big Typescript: TS 213,* ed. and trans. G. Luckhardt and M. A. E. Aue. Oxford: Blackwell.

CHAPTER 29

WITTGENSTEIN'S USE OF EXAMPLES

BETH SAVICKEY

As Wittgenstein moves from the *Tractatus* to the *Philosophical Investigations* he dramatically alters his use of examples. His early work, almost entirely devoid of examples, gives way to later writings that could be described (with little exaggeration) as nothing but examples. The *Tractatus* becomes an important example in the later writings, which Wittgenstein characterizes as the description of 'a field of varying examples by means of centers of variation' (WLPP, 142).[1] The dramatic shift in Wittgenstein's use of examples expresses a new understanding of language, and enacts a new method of philosophical investigation. The use of examples becomes an important method of conceptual imagination.

There are approximately three dozen examples in the *Notebooks* and *Tractatus*. These include examples of propositions and examples of systems of representation. In the *Notebooks*, examples of propositions include: 'this chair is brown,' 'this watch is shiny,' 'this book is lying on the table,' 'all men are mortal,' and 'Socrates is a man' (NB, 5, 61, 67, 69).[2] The *Tractatus* contains the following three examples: 'Green is green,' 'There are 2 objects which ...,' and 'All men are mortal' (TLP 3.323, 4.1272, 6.1232). According to Wittgenstein, these examples are not ideal:

> A proposition like 'this chair is brown' seems to say something enormously complicated, for if we wanted to express this proposition in such a way that nobody could raise objections to it on grounds of ambiguity, it would have to be infinitely long. (NB, 5)

> To anyone [who] sees clearly, it is obvious that a proposition like 'This watch is lying on the table' contains a lot of indefiniteness, in spite of its being completely clear and simple in outward appearance. So we see that this simplicity is only constructed. (NB, 69)

---

[1] In the preface to the *Investigations* Wittgenstein writes that his later thoughts could be seen in the right light only by contrast with and against the background of his old way of thinking (PI x). For further references to the *Tractatus* in the *Investigations* see PI §§23, 46, 65, 81, 89–109, 114, 134, and 136. (For further discussion see below.)

[2] Also see NB, 37, 60, 64, 66, 68–70.

In these early writings, Wittgenstein seeks the general form of propositions and language, and particular examples fall out of consideration as irrelevant (PI §65; see also §§114, 136). 'We don't have any examples before our minds when we use Fx and all the other variable form-signs' (NB, 65):

> We portray the thing, the relation, the property, by means of variables and so show that we do not derive these ideas from particular cases that occur to us, but possess them somehow *a priori*.

The second set of examples illustrates systems of representation using drawings and imaginary scenes. Wittgenstein uses a picture depicting two fighting figures to exemplify how a proposition can be true or false (NB, 7). He presents an example of taking black and white balls out of an urn to exemplify knowledge of natural laws (NB, 28; TLP 5.154); he uses puzzle-pictures to exemplify seeing situations (NB, 28; TLP 5.5423); and he describes two railway trains that must not stand on the rails in such-and-such a way to exemplify the representation of negative facts by means of models (NB, 30; TLP 4.463). He also describes covering a white surface (of irregular black spots) with a suitably fine square network to exemplify how Newtonian mechanics brings the description of the world into a unitary form (NB, 35; TLP 6.341); he uses two theories of heat to exemplify the significance of description in physics (NB, 37); and he uses the points of a visual field to exemplify the 'simple' (NB, 45). He uses a drawing to (negatively) exemplify the form of a visual field (NB, 80; TLP 5.6331) and the act of drawing a square in a mirror to exemplify acts of the will (NB, 87). In addition to the examples found in both the *Notebooks* and *Tractatus* (indicated above), the *Tractatus* also refers to a propositional sign composed of spatial objects (such as tables, chairs, and books) to exemplify propositional essence (TLP 3.1431); a gramophone record, a musical idea, written notes, and sound-waves to exemplify the internal relation of depiction that holds between language and the world (TLP 4.014); the drawing of a cube to exemplify the perception of a complex (TLP 5.5423); the simultaneous presence of two colours at the same place in the visual field to exemplify logical impossibility (TLP 6.3751); and facial features and various shades of blue to exemplify internal properties (TLP 4.1221 and TLP 4.123).[3]

Wittgenstein is critical of this use of examples in lectures and writings from the early 1930s to the late 1940s. In 1932, he notes that both he and Russell were at fault for not giving examples of atomic propositions or of individuals. 'We both in different ways pushed the question of examples aside' (AWL, 11). This is evident not only in the paucity of examples found in the early writings (and the limited role they play) but in the fact

---

[3] Variations on these examples are found throughout the later writings (where they are often used to challenge or refute the points being made in the early works). See, for example, *The Blue and Brown Books* and the *Investigations*. One exception to these two sets of examples is found in the *Notebooks*, where Wittgenstein asks us 'to imagine a man who could use none of his limbs and hence could, in the ordinary sense, not exercise his *will*. He could, however, think and *want* and communicate his thoughts to someone else, and could therefore do good or evil through the other man. Then it is clear that ethics would have validity for him, too, and that he in the *ethical sense* is the bearer of a *will*' (NB, 76–7). This example is unique in the early writings. In the later writings, Wittgenstein frequently asks us to imagine such scenes.

that examples are dismissed, not as a result of logical investigation, but as a requirement.[4] This leads to several difficulties in the early writings. In 1946–7, Wittgenstein writes that 'the basic evil' of Russell's logic (as also of his own in the *Tractatus*) is that the nature of a proposition is illustrated by a few commonplace examples, and then presupposed as understood in full generality (RPP I §38). This proves too simple a portrayal of language. (For further discussion, see below.) Further, if logic is an exact calculus operating according to precise rules, it must be able to account for all linguistic phenomena. Wittgenstein acknowledges that this too proves problematic:

> I believe our main reason for feeling [that logic was hell] was the following fact: that every time some new linguistic phenomenon occurred to us, it could retrospectively show that our previous explanation was unworkable. (We felt that language could always make new, and impossible, demands; and that this made all explanation futile.) (CV, 30)

In the transitional writings of the *Big Typescript*, Wittgenstein begins to articulate a new understanding of examples:

> It is of the utmost importance that for a logical calculus we always think of an example to which the calculus is actually applied, and not of examples of which we say: 'These really aren't the ideal ones – we don't have those yet'. That is the sign of a totally false view.[5] If I can use the calculus at all then this is also the ideal use and *the* use that is at issue. For on the one hand we're embarrassed to acknowledge our example as the proper one because we recognize a complication in it to which the calculus doesn't apply. But it *is* the archetype for the calculus and the latter is derived from it, and this is no mistake, no imperfection in the calculus. The mistake lies in promising its use in the nebulous future. (BT, 203)

He takes this criticism further (in the *Investigations*) when he challenges the idea of the calculus itself: 'In philosophy we often *compare* the use of words with games and calculi which have fixed rules, but cannot say that someone who is using language must be playing such a game' (PI §81).

Wittgenstein comes to recognize that the *Tractatus* not only presents a picture theory of meaning, but is itself only a particular picture of language: 'We predicate of the thing what lies in the method of representing it. Impressed by the possibility of a comparison, we think we are perceiving a state of affairs of the highest generality' (PI §104).

> (*Tractatus Logico-Philosophicus*, 4.5): 'The general form of propositions is: This is how things are.' – That is the kind of proposition that one repeats to oneself countless times. One thinks that one is tracing the outline of the thing's nature over and over again, and one is merely tracing round the frame through which we look at it. (PI §114)

---

[4] 'The crystalline purity of logic was, of course, not a *result of investigation*, it was a requirement' (PI §107). Also see PI §108.

[5] In MS 115, 55–6 this sentence is followed by: '(Russell and I have in different ways laboured under it. Compare what I say in the *Tractatus* about elementary propositions and objects.)' (BT, footnote 102) For Wittgenstein's refutation of the view that the examples we use are not ideal see PI §§81, 98, 100, 103, 105, 106.

> A *picture* held us captive. And we could not get outside it, for it lay in our language and language seemed to repeat it to us inexorably. (PI §115)

In the later writings, the focus shifts from logic to grammar. This is evident in remarks concerning 'essence'. In the *Tractatus*, the essence of language is logic, while in the *Investigations* 'essence is expressed by grammar' (PI §371).[6] Logic and grammar are not synonymous or interchangeable. They play different roles in Wittgenstein's investigations and alter his philosophical method:

> This finds expression in questions as to the *essence* of language, of propositions, of thought. – For if we too in these investigations are trying to understand the essence of language – its function, its structure, – yet *this* is not what those questions have in view. For they see in the essence, not something that already lies open to view and that becomes surveyable by a rearrangement, but something that lies *beneath* the surface. Something that lies within, which we can see when we look *into* the thing, and which an analysis digs out.
> 'The essence is hidden *from us*': this is the form our problem now assumes. We ask: '*What is* language?', '*What is* a proposition?' And the answer to these questions is to be given once for all; and independent of any future experience. (PI §92)

In the *Tractatus*, logic is the essence of language *and* thought. It presents 'an order, in fact the *a priori* order of the world: that is, the order of *possibilities*, which must be common to both world and thought' (PI §97). In the *Investigations*, this preconceived idea of logic is removed by turning the examination around: 'One might say: the axis of reference of our examination must be rotated, but about the fixed point of our real need…We are talking about the spatial and temporal phenomenon of language, not about some non-spatial, non-temporal chimera' (PI §108).

Essence is expressed by grammar and lies open to view through a rearrangement:

> When I talk about language (words, sentences, etc.) I must speak the language of every day. Is this language somehow too coarse and material for what we want to say? Then how is another one to be constructed? – And how strange that we should be able to do anything at all with the one we have!
> In giving explanations I already have to use language full-blown (not some sort of preparatory, provisional one); this by itself shews that I can adduce only exterior facts about language.
> Yes, but then how can these explanations satisfy us? – Well, your very questions were framed in this language; they had to be expressed in this language, if there was anything to ask!
> And your scruples are misunderstandings. (PI §120)

As Wittgenstein moves from the early to the later writings, he begins to understand and acknowledge 'the infinite variety of functions of words in propositions'. In *The Blue Book*, he writes that 'it is curious to compare what we see in our examples with the simple and rigid rules which logicians give for the construction of propositions' (BB, 83). And in the

---

[6] I prefer this translation to 'essence is expressed in grammar' because this makes it appear as if grammar lay beneath the surface or was hidden. For further discussion see below.

Investigations, he notes that 'it is interesting to compare the multiplicity of the tools in language and of the ways they are used, the multiplicity of kinds of word and sentence, with what logicians have said about the structure of language. (Including the author of the *Tractatus Logico-Philosophicus*.)' (PI §23)[7] Wittgenstein challenges the simple examples of propositions found in his earlier writings as well as the idea of a logical calculus.

By contrast with, and against the background of, his old way of thinking, he introduces a new method of philosophical investigation that involves the use of examples (and is itself demonstrated by example) (PI §133). The number of examples found in the later writings increases exponentially. In contrast to the few dozen examples found in the early works, the later writings contain *thousands* of examples. Examples no longer play a secondary (or supporting) role in the investigations, but assume a primary (or leading) role. The *Tractatus* (with its list of numbered propositions) is understood as complete without them.[8] In the later writings, examples are omnipresent. If they were discarded, there would be no text. According to the *Tractatus*, philosophical problems are posed because the logic of our language is misunderstood. In the later writings, 'concepts lead us to make investigations; are the expression of our interest, and direct our interest' (PI §570). Wittgenstein shifts from logical to conceptual investigation:

> (We felt that language could always make new, and impossible, demands; and that this made all explanation futile.)
> But this is the difficulty Socrates gets into in trying to give the definition of a concept. Again and again a use of the word emerges that seems not to be compatible with the concept that other uses have led us to form. We say: but that *isn't* how it is! – it *is* like that though! and all we can do is keep repeating these antitheses. (CV, 30)

The concept of 'pain' is one such example. It plays an important role in our lives, and raises philosophical questions about language, behaviour, the expression of sensation, and personal identity.[9] (It will be used as an example throughout this chapter.)

Wittgenstein describes concepts as forming enormous families with various resemblances:

> One of our main philosophical troubles, which constantly recurs, is that we have such a family. We want to get clear about the use of a word, and so we hunt for something common to the instances the word applies to, even when there is hardly anything in common…In the *Theaetetus*, Socrates fails to produce a definition of 'knowledge' because there is no definition giving what is common to all instances of

---

[7] Wittgenstein writes of the 'bad influence of Aristotelian logic. The logic of language is immeasurably more complicated than it looks' (LWPP II, 44).

[8] This movement is similar to the treatment of the propositions of the *Tractatus* itself, which are to be transcended once the meaning of the text becomes clear. In the penultimate remark Wittgenstein writes, 'My propositions are elucidatory in the following way: anyone who understands me eventually recognizes them as nonsensical, when he has used them – as steps – to climb up beyond them. (He must, so to speak, throw away the ladder after he has climbed up it.) / He must transcend these propositions, and then he will see the world aright' (TLP 6.54).

[9] Wittgenstein investigates this concept from his earliest writings in *Philosophical Remarks* to his last writings in *On Certainty*.

knowledge. Because the word 'knowledge' is used in all sorts of ways, any definition given will fail to apply to some cases…The method of giving a definition of a word and then proceeding to other instances of its application which have very little in common is a mistaken method. We *can* show links, which some cases have with others, but that is all. Furthermore, giving examples of usage is not a second-best method of giving the meaning of a word. (AWL, 96)[10]

In other words, 'we are unable clearly to circumscribe the concepts we use; not because we don't know their real definition, but because there is no real "definition" to them' (BB, 25).[11] Instead, Wittgenstein describes concepts as 'limitless' within the bustle of human life (RPP II §625).[12] They are constantly fluctuating and not for use on a single occasion (Z §568). 'We, in our conceptual world, keep on seeing the same, recurring with variations. That is how our concepts take it' (RPP II §672).[13] Thus, to give the definition of a word and then proceed to other instances of its application that have very little in common is a mistaken method. Wittgenstein seeks a method that is open-ended and will allow for the investigation of concepts while all is in flux.

Concepts are also learnt through example and practice: 'If a person has not yet got the *concepts*, I shall teach him to use the words by means of *examples* and by *practice*. – And when I do this I do not communicate less to him than I know myself' (PI §208). We learn the *concept* 'pain' when we learn language (PI §384). It is for this reason that Wittgenstein repeatedly asks, 'How did we *learn* the meaning of this word…? From what sort of examples?' (PI §77) He is not asking for an explanation, but for the description of numerous and diverse examples and practices (BB, 14). 'As children we learn concepts and what one does with them simultaneously' (LWPP II, 43). Wittgenstein acknowledges that the concept of pain is tangled: 'The way in which we learn to use the word, and therefore the way in which it is used, is…complicated and difficult to describe' (LWPP II, 30). The *role* of words in our language is much more complicated than we are tempted to think, and it is this role that we need to understand in order to resolve philosophical problems. 'Hence definitions usually fail to resolve them, and so, *a fortiori*, does the assertion that a

[10] Wittgenstein sometimes refers to this tendency as a craving for generality, or as a contemptuous attitude toward the particular case (BB, 17–18). He also connects this search with the idea that a general concept is a common property of its particular instances, and other primitive, too simple, ideas of the structure of language. It is comparable to the idea that properties are ingredients of the things that possess them. Wittgenstein notes that 'Russell and Frege take concepts as, as it were, properties of things' (Z 704).

[11] Wittgenstein challenges us to make a radical break with the idea that language always functions in one way, always serves the same purpose, 'to convey thoughts – which may be about houses, pains, good and evil, or anything else you please' (PI §304). Also see §§317, 449, and the discussion of naming sensations below.

[12] 'The formation of a concept has, for example, the character of limitlessness, where experience provides no sharp boundary lines' (RPP II §636). He also describes concepts as 'unbounded' and 'without fixed edges' (PI §§68–71, 84).

[13] This limitlessness, or indefiniteness, is connected with the various repetitions of concepts, and 'it is the very concept "bustle" that brings about this indefiniteness. For a bustle comes about only through constant repetition. And there is no starting point for "constant repetition"' (RPP II §626). Indefiniteness no longer poses a problem for Wittgenstein.

word is "indefinable"' (PI §182). According to Wittgenstein, 'the concept of pain is characterized by its particular function in our life' (Z §532). He writes that we must 'think about the purpose of words. What does language have to do with pain?' (RPP II §655; also see the discussion of PI §§244–5 below.)

Wittgenstein challenges the idea that definitions are more *fundamental* or *applicable* than examples:

> The word 'proposition' is explained in the way 'game' and 'sense' are, by grouping examples. The examples give a clear enough idea. A person who has drawn the line by a definition might be held to have a clearer idea. And if you like you can give a definition; but as a usual thing one does not…Logicians seem to have given a clear-cut definition, whereas I have explained the idea of a proposition only by giving examples. How does what I have done compare with the clear-cut idea which the logicians talk about? The logical calculus is clear-cut enough, but it is not fundamental and it is not very applicable. For a definition would apply to some things fairly well and to others less and less well. (AWL, 68)

He questions not only the accuracy and relevance of definitions for conceptual investigation, but their ability to clarify. Referring to the definitions of propositions given in logic books (including his own), he writes:

> Most definitions of a proposition,…as what is true or false, or as the expression of a thought, are futile. For we do not understand the terms of the definition. If one wants to explain what a proposition is, one thing one might do is to give examples, by means of which it might be said one could get a general idea. (AWL, 77)

We sometimes demand definitions, not for the sake of their content, but their form.[14] Wittgenstein describes this requirement as architectural: 'The definition [is] a kind of ornamental coping that supports nothing' (PI §217). He notes that we do not think of definitions while using language, and that when we are asked to give definitions we are, in most cases, unable to do so (BB, 25).

Take, for example, the concept of pain. 'Pain' is often defined as 'a private (inner) sensation'. Wittgenstein suggests that this definition does not offer clarification, because we do not understand the terms of the definition itself. He investigates the concepts of 'private', 'inner', and 'sensation':

> How do words *refer* to sensations? – There doesn't seem to be any problem here; don't we talk about sensations every day, and give them names? But how is the connexion between the name and the thing named set up? This question is the same as: how does a human being learn the meaning of the names of sensations? – of the word 'pain' for example. Here is one possibility: words are connected with the primitive, the natural, expressions of the sensation and used in their place. A child has hurt himself and he cries; and then adults talk to him and teach him exclamations and, later, sentences. They teach the child new pain-behaviour.

---

[14] For example, when we define a proposition as what is true or false, or as the expression of a thought.

'So, you are saying that the word "pain" really means crying?' – On the contrary: the verbal expression of pain replaces crying and does not describe it. (PI §244)

For how can I go so far as to try to use language to get between pain and its expression? (PI §245)

Wittgenstein also questions how words refer to sensations in a series of playful examples involving the phrase 'It'll stop soon'. He creates a scene in which someone says 'It'll stop soon' while feeling pain and, simultaneously, hearing a nearby piano being tuned (PI §§666, 682). He asks whether the phrase refers to the pain or to the piano-tuning. He then alters the scene so that the individual uses the phrase while *simulating* pain, and then while *lying* (PI §§667–8). If the phrase has meaning in all three examples, the variations demonstrate that meaning is not based on *reference*, since pain is absent in two out of three of the examples.[15] Wittgenstein also investigates whether sensations are *private*:

In what sense are my sensations *private*? – Well, only I can know whether I am really in pain; another person can only surmise it. – In one way this is wrong, and in another nonsense. If we are using the word 'to know' as it is normally used (and how else are we to use it?), then other people very often know when I am in pain. – Yes, but all the same not with the certainty with which I know it myself! – It can't be said of me at all (except perhaps as a joke) that I *know* I am in pain. What is it supposed to mean – except that I *am* in pain? (PI §246)[16]

Wittgenstein's examples challenge the definition of 'pain' as a 'private (inner) sensation' and demonstrate that we often do not understand the terms themselves. Instead, he suggests that we give examples.

As early as 1934, philosophers begin to label Wittgenstein's new method 'the description of meaning by exemplification'. Although this label affirms the emphasis placed on examples in the later writings, Wittgenstein is quick to qualify and clarify his method:

The question has been raised how far my method is the same as what is called description of meaning by exemplification. That sounds as if I had invented a method, a means of giving a meaning [that] is *just as good* as definition. The point of examining the way a word is used is not at all to provide another method of giving its meaning. When we ask on what occasions people use a word, what they say about it, what they are right to substitute for it, and in reply try to describe its use, we do so only insofar as it seems helpful in getting rid of certain philosophical troubles. (AWL, 96–7)

It is not the function of examples to show the essence of a word through a veil of inessential features:

The examples [are] not descriptions of an outside letting us guess at an inside which for some reason or other could not be shown in its nakedness. We are tempted to think that our examples are *indirect* means for producing a certain image or idea in

---

[15] For further discussion see the beetle-in-a-box example below.

[16] For detailed discussion see below. Wittgenstein also investigates the concept of the 'inner' at PI §§256, 305, 580, and pp. 167–8.

a person's mind, – that they *hint* at something which they cannot show…Our method is *purely descriptive*; the descriptions we give are not hints at explanations. (BB, 125)[17]

This remark highlights several themes that are expressed throughout the later writings. To approach examples as hints at explanations, or as indirect means of producing a certain image or idea in a person's mind, is similar to approaching the meaning of a word (or the expression of sensation) on the model of object (whether mental or physical) and designation. It is to claim that everyone has their own *exemplar*.[18] Thus Wittgenstein's *use* of examples changes as his understanding of concepts and language-use change.[19] His examples do not hint at something they cannot show. However, it is important to understand what they *show* us:

> One gives examples and intends them to be taken in a particular way – I do not, however, mean by this that he is supposed to see in those examples that common thing which I – for some reason – was unable to express; but that he is now *to employ* those examples in a particular way. Here giving examples is not an indirect means of explaining – in default of a better. For any general definition can be misunderstood too. (PI §71)

Examples exhibit the *application* or *use* of words. They are the materials with which Wittgenstein works. 'Whether it is another person or ourselves that we have to answer – we shall give examples' (PI §135). In other words, examples are points of departure for further activities (PG, 273). Wittgenstein's examples attempt to persuade us to *action*.[20]

Examples enable Wittgenstein to describe concepts by putting words into motion. To provide an example is to invent a surrounding in which the *use* of a word becomes a *move* in a game.

> Logicians use examples which no one would ever think of using in any other connection. Whoever says 'Socrates is a man'? I am not criticizing this because it does not occur in practical life. What I am criticizing is the fact that logicians do not give these examples any life. We must invent a surrounding for our examples. We might use 'man' as a predicate if we wanted to distinguish whether someone dressed as a woman was a man or woman. We thus would have invented a surrounding for the word, a game in which its use is a move. It does not matter whether in practice the word has a place in a game, but what matters is that we have a game, that a life is given for it. (AWL, 124)

For Wittgenstein, examples are *dynamic*. In the *Big Typescript*, he emphasizes the importance of thinking of an example to which a calculus applies. In the later writings, he ceases to speak of a logical calculus, but continues to speak of language-*use* and the

---

[17] 'Examples are decent signs, not rubbish or hocus-pocus' (PG, 273). Also see PI §§75, 210.
[18] For further discussion see PI §§272, 293.
[19] Burnyeat makes a similar point (Burnyeat 1977, 398).
[20] 'How much I am doing is changing the style of thinking and how much I'm doing is persuading people to change their style of thinking' (LC, 28). He describes his teaching as an attempt to persuade us to look at things differently (LC, 27).

importance of examples. He also uses the term 'language-game' to describe primitive examples of language. 'Here the term "language-*game*" is meant to bring into prominence the fact that the *speaking* of language is part of an activity, or a form of life' (PI §23). He reminds us that we are investigating the spatial and temporal phenomena of language. In other words, concepts such as pain are embedded in life and described by showing the actions of a variety of human beings as they are all mixed up together (RPP II §150).[21] 'Not what *one* man is doing *now*, but the whole hurly-burly, is the background against which we see an action, and it determines our judgment, our concepts, and our reactions' (RPP II §629; Z §567). Concepts stand *in the middle* of our lives (LWPP II §72).

Wittgenstein's examples are, in many ways, similar to theatre pieces or improvisational exercises. We are asked to imagine different scenes, and they can be played out in a variety of ways (and often involve variations of gesture, tone of voice, facial expression, and physical movement).[22] The *Investigations* can be read as a script – one in which we enact, embody, or voice the examples we encounter. To borrow a phrase from Apollinaire, if we look at these examples carefully they will 'burst into drama' (Apollinaire 1949, 23). In response to the claim that the expression of pain involves identifying who is in pain (drawing attention to a particular person, or distinguishing between oneself and others), Wittgenstein asks us to imagine the following:

> 'But surely what you want to do with the words "I am ...." is to distinguish yourself and other people.' – Can this be said in every case? Even when I merely groan? And even if I do 'want to distinguish' between myself and other people – do I want to distinguish between the person L.W. and the person N.N.? (PI §406)

> It would be possible to imagine someone groaning out: 'Someone is in pain – I don't know who!' and our then hurrying to help him, the one who groaned. (PI §407)[23]

This scene challenges simple claims about identity and calls for further detailed investigation. Wittgenstein continues by introducing an elaborate and unusual scene in which 'knowing whether I or someone else is in pain' becomes a possible move in a game:

> Imagine several people standing in a ring, and me among them. One of us, sometimes this one, sometimes that, is connected to the poles of an electrical machine without our being able to see this. I observe the faces of the others and try to see which of us has just been electrified. – Then I say: 'Now I *know* who it is: for it's myself'. In this sense I could also say: 'Now I know who is feeling the shocks; it is myself'. This would be a rather queer way of speaking. – But if I make the supposition that I can

---

[21] Concepts are *in their element* in language and life (RPP II §184). They are also widely manifested and have complicated relationships (RPP II §220). Also see LWPP I, 581; PI II ix, 170; RPP II §§16, 132, and 372.

[22] 'One may also say: "He made *this* face" or "His face altered like *this*" imitating it – and again one can't describe it in any other way. (There are just many more language-games than are dreamt of in the philosophy of Carnap and others.)' (RPP I §920) Plato's dialogues are another form of dramatic philosophy.

[23] 'To say "I have pain" is no more a statement *about* a particular person than moaning is' (BB, 67). For further discussion see BB, 67–9.

feel the shock even when someone else is electrified, then the expression 'Now I know who...' becomes quite unsuitable. It does not belong to this game. (PI §409)[24]

The highly unusual details of this scene allow us to put these words into motion, and to compare and contrast them with our previous (mis-)conceptions. We can also imagine this scene as humorous or menacing (etc.), thereby reminding ourselves of the complex role of words in our lives.

Wittgenstein also uses specific theatre examples throughout his later writings:[25]

'When I imagine that someone who is laughing is really in pain I don't imagine any pain-behaviour, for I see just the opposite. So *what* do I imagine?' – I have already said what. And I do not necessarily imagine *my* being in pain. – 'But then what is the process of imagining it?' – Where (outside philosophy) do we use the words 'I can imagine his being in pain' or 'I imagine that...' or 'imagine that...'?

We say, for example, to someone who has to play a theatrical part: 'Here you must imagine that this man is in pain and is concealing it' – and now we give him no directions, do not tell him what he is *actually* to do. For this reason the suggested analysis is not to the point either. – We now watch the actor who is imagining this situation. (PI §393)

When we play out these examples, we become participants (not merely spectators) in the investigation. And once we are participants, these examples aid us in developing our own creativity and conceptual imagination.[26] Wittgenstein demonstrates numerous different techniques and practices for investigating concepts.[27] He repeatedly asks, 'Where does this concept take us?' and 'How can this concept be followed through consistently?' (RPP II §579) In other words, can we imagine further applications? To imagine further applications is to fill in the blank spaces between the remarks in Wittgenstein's texts. It is not to provide missing information, but to add imaginatively to the variations already recorded. Wittgenstein asks us to imagine examples more than a thousand times in his collected works. As Cerbone notes, 'in requesting that one imagine an alteration in

---

[24] For a related discussion of 'what distinguishes *his* toothache from *mine*' (and other similar concepts) see PR, 90–95. Also see BB, 61–2 for an example in which all human bodies look alike and different sets of characteristics seem to change their habitation among these bodies.

[25] He suggests that 'the contexts of a sentence are best portrayed in a play. Therefore the best example for a sentence with a particular meaning is a quotation from a play' (LWPP I §38). He also refers to *acting* and *play-acting* (PI, 161 and 186). For further theatre examples and references see Z §9; PI §§257, 642; RPP II §§321, 537, 630; and LWPP I §850. For further discussion see Schalkwyk 2005.

[26] Wittgenstein notes the resemblance between philosophical and aesthetic investigations. See CV, 25; PI §§104, 401. Binkley writes that Wittgenstein 'demonstrates methods by exemplifying them...he is trying to teach an art by demonstrating how it is done' (Binkley 1973, 39).

[27] For example, asking on what occasions people use a word, what they say about it, and what they are right to substitute for it (AWL, 97); examining how a word is taught and learned (AWL, 156); investigating how a word is used in ordinary life (AWL, 156); describing how a proposition can be verified and what can be done with it (AWL, 19); and showing what a proposition follows from and what follows from it (AWL, 19).

concepts there is not some one thing to be imagined...one can imagine variants'
(Cerbone 1993, 175).

Wittgenstein writes that in his early work he illustrates the nature of a proposition
with a few commonplace examples and then presupposes it as understood in full generality (RPP II §38). He characterizes this as 'the basic evil' of his earlier writings. In the
1930s, he acknowledges that his way of speaking is now always in terms of *specific*
examples (AWL, 20). As he moves from the *Tractatus* to the *Investigations*, he shifts from
talk of 'the world' to 'this table' or 'that tree'.[28] He acknowledges that this is an important
philosophical change:

> Here we come up against the great question that lies behind all these consider-
> ations. – For someone might object against me: 'You take the easy way out! You talk
> about all sorts of language-games, but have nowhere said what the essence of a lan-
> guage-game, and hence of language, is: what is common to all these activities, and
> what makes them into language or parts of language. So you let yourself off the very
> part of the investigation that once gave you yourself most headache, the part about
> the *general form of propositions* and of language.'
>
> And this is true. – Instead of producing something common to all that we call
> language, I am saying that these phenomena have no one thing in common which
> makes us use the same word for all, – but that they are *related* to one another in
> many different ways. And it is because of this relationship or these relationships,
> that we call them all 'language'. I will try to explain this. (PI §65)

He encourages students to give examples rather than talk in abstract terms (Drury 1973,
38). And based on his experiences as an elementary school teacher (during the decade
between his early and later writings) he suggests that it is possible to learn through an
interesting though difficult *specific* case (even if other standard examples are easier to
comprehend). Again, particular cases, or detailed, specific examples enable us to investigate concepts by providing systems of application.

> The idea that in order to get clear about the meaning of a general term one had to
> find the common element in all its applications has shackled philosophical investi-
> gations; for it has not only led to no result, but also made the philosopher dismiss as
> irrelevant the concrete cases, which alone could have helped him to understand the
> usage of the general term. (BB, 19)

Even when Wittgenstein appears to be making general claims about human beings (or
human nature) he is always drawing attention to specific examples and concepts. He
notes, for example, that classifying colours, measuring time, playing games, are *specific*:
'I'll show you a thing which we humans do' (WLPP, 142).[29]

---

[28] In his *Remarks on Frazer's Golden Bough* he asks, 'When I began in my earlier book to talk about the
"world" (and not about this tree or table), was I trying to do anything except conjure up something of a
higher order by my words?' (RFGB, vi)

[29] 'There's something specific' may equal 'I'll show you something – an activity we humans do' (WLPP,
264).

This specificity is evident in examples involving animals.[30] Instead of comparing and contrasting human beings with animals in general, Wittgenstein refers (variously) to dogs, cats, parrots, fish, orang-utans, crocodiles, flies, and grasshoppers. The humour and eclecticism of this list betrays its methodological purpose. These examples do not present factual claims about dogs, cats, crocodiles, flies, or grasshoppers but examine the concepts of speaking, teaching, thinking, hoping and fearing, and feeling joy, sorrow, or pain.[31] For example, he asks us to imagine the following scene:

> Look at a stone and imagine it having sensations. – One says to oneself: How could one so much as get the idea of ascribing a *sensation* to a *thing*? One might as well ascribe it to a number! – And now look at a wriggling fly and at once these difficulties vanish and pain seems able to get a foothold here, where before everything was, so to speak, too smooth for it. (PI §284)

He acknowledges that even the example of a fly is complicated, for we are sometimes uncertain whether (lower) animals feel pain: 'The uncertainty whether a fly feels pain is philosophical' (RPP II §659). In other words, we do not always know whether we are being cruel.[32] Wittgenstein also uses examples of animals to investigate pain and pretence. Not every creature that expresses fear, joy, or pain can feign them (LWPP I §859). He suggests that a dog can't pretend to be in pain because his life is too simple (LWPP I §§862, 870). Wittgenstein does not deny that a dog can be taught to feign certain pain-behaviours, but he denies that they occur in a context that would make such behaviour true pretence: 'A clever dog might perhaps be taught to give a kind of whine of pain but it would never get as far as conscious imitation' (Z §389).[33]

In the earlier writings, Wittgenstein is embarrassed to acknowledge examples that introduce complications (which he is unable to account for in his calculus). In the later writings, he uses specific examples to introduce complications into his investigations. Even simple examples prove complex and difficult.[34] 'Show what it's like when one is in pain. – Show what it's like when one pretends that one is in pain. In a play one can see both portrayed.

---

[30] Wittgenstein refers to animals during a discussion of 'spirit' and 'the will' in his *Notebooks*. Although referring to the spirit of the snake, lion, elephant, fly, and wasp, he makes a general claim about 'psychophysical parallelism' and asks whether 'this is the solution of the puzzle why men have always believed that there was *one* spirit common to the whole world' (NB, 85). Thus, although he refers to specific animals in his early writings, he does so to make a general claim.

[31] See BB, 90, 157; PI §§344, 346, 650; RPP II §§16, 23–4, 29 192, 308–10, 659; Z §§103, 117, 129; LWPP I §§859, 862, 870. Wittgenstein is not doing natural science or natural history (PI, 195).

[32] 'If I doubt whether a spider feels pain, it is not because I don't know what to expect' (Z §564). Wittgenstein challenges us to 'look at the problem of uncertainty as to whether someone else is feeling pain in light of the question whether an insect feels pain' (RPP II §661). As objects of comparison, these examples involve two different kinds of uncertainty.

[33] 'Why can't a dog simulate pain? Is he too honest? Could one teach a dog to simulate pain? Perhaps it is possible to teach him to howl on particular occasions as if he were in pain, even when he is not. But the surroundings which are necessary for this behaviour to be real simulation are missing' (PI §250).

[34] See PI §§403–10, 617; BB, 7–8, 150–54; RPP II §109. Wittgenstein also develops standard philosophical examples in greater detail in order to demonstrate their complexity, and remind us that their application is not always clearly before our eyes.

But now the difference!' (LWPP II §26)[35] Wittgenstein takes the philosophical preoccupation with pretence and complicates it. However, it is the complication that offers clarification, for portraying pain (or the pretence of pain) in a play forces us to imagine a scene differently than we would if we were doing philosophy alone in a room. We are compelled to imagine a scene (perhaps with others) and to 'look around' rather than within. Both the concept of pain *and* the concept of pretence are complicated by this example.

> So we always want to say: We know what 'pain' means (namely *this*), and so the difficulty only consists in simply not being able to determine this in someone else with certainty. What we don't see is that the *concept* 'pain' is only beginning to be investigated. The same is true of pretence. (LWPP II, 43)

Pretence, or simulating pain, 'doesn't consist merely in giving expressions of pain when one has no pain. There must be a motive present for the simulation, hence a situation which is not quite simple to describe' (RPP I §824).[36]

> If you consider the reasons someone might have for stifling pain, or simulating it, you will come up with countless ones. Now why is there this multiplicity? Life is very complicated. There are a great many possibilities. (RPP II §639)

Not all behaviour can be simulation or dissimulation under all circumstances (LWPP I §§252–3). According to Wittgenstein, 'it takes a very specific context for something to be an expression of pain; but the pretence of pain requires an even more far-reaching particular context' (LWPP I §861).[37] In other words, 'pretending is not as simple a concept as being in pain' (LWPP II, 81). Wittgenstein describes pretence as a pattern within the weave of life. It is repeated in an infinite number of variations (LWPP I §862). The complex variations of pretence challenge simple distinctions between the inner and the outer:

> 'In the inner there is either pain or pretence. On the outside there are signs (behaviour), which don't mean either one with complete certainty.'
>   But that's not the way it is. In an extremely complicated way the outer signs sometimes mean unambiguously, sometimes without certainty; pain, pretence and several other things. (LWPP II, 59)

The inner/outer distinction is itself misleading. In drawing attention to the complexity of pain and pretence, Wittgenstein shifts our focus: 'It is not the relationship of the inner to the outer that explains the uncertainty of the evidence, but rather the other way around' (LWPP II, 68).

Several insights come from these imaginative variations. Juxtaposing different examples of pain and pretence highlights their multiplicity and complexity (effectively challenging

---

[35] Also see PI, 153; LWPP I §§262–4, 268–71, 859ff.

[36] Wittgenstein notes that pretence is only one quite special case of someone expressing pain and not feeling it. A particular drug might produce a similar case (RPP I §137). Also see RPP II §612.

[37] Wittgenstein also writes that 'after all, from a person's behaviour you can draw conclusions not only about his pain but also about his pretence' (LWPP I §901). He also notes that 'a child has to learn all sorts of things before he can pretend' (LWPP I §868). Also see LWPP I §§239, 242, 867–72, 912.

our generalizations and abstractions). Further, these examples provide concrete cases that help clarify the concepts themselves. The more examples we investigate and imagine, the less problematic the possibility of pretence becomes: '"He can also simulate pain" – that is to say: he can behave as if he had pains without having them. Certainly; and such a proposition underlines a particular picture; but is the employment of "He has pain" influenced by this?' (RPP I §143; also see LWPP I §§871–2) Consider the following example:

> I can perhaps even imagine (though it is not easy) that each of the people whom I see in the street is in frightful pain, but is artfully concealing it. And it is important that I have to imagine an artful concealment here. That I do not simply say to myself: 'Well, his soul is in pain: but what has that to do with his body?' or 'After all it need not shew in his body!' – And if I imagine this – what do I do; what do I say to myself; how do I look at the people? Perhaps I look at one and think: 'It must be difficult to laugh when one is in such pain', and much else of the same kind. I as it were play a part, *act* as if the others were in pain. When I do this I am said for example to be imagining…(PI §391)

All of these cases *complicate* the employment of propositions involving pain. They do not invalidate them. '"Feigning" poses no problem with the concept of pain. It makes it more complicated' (LWPP I §876).[38] In Wittgenstein's field of varying examples, 'any other example is not a contradiction, it is only a contribution' (WLPP, 142). Unlike standard examples (that result in the amendment or dismissal of particular philosophical positions), Wittgenstein's examples aim to render our concepts clear to us in all of their variations. There is nothing to amend or dismiss, for he offers clarification of our concepts (or our lives in language).[39] At the end of the *Investigations* we are left – not with nothing – but with everything. (See PI §124 and AWL, 97.)

> How could you explain the meaning of 'simulating pain,' 'acting as if in pain'? (Of course the question is: *To whom?*) *Should you act it out?* And why could such an exhibition be so easily misunderstood? One is inclined to say: 'Just live among us for a while and then you'll come to understand'. (RPP II §630)

To complicate matters further, Wittgenstein introduces the possibility of pretending to pretend. This does not lead to an infinite regress, but to a more subtle and complex investigation of our concepts:

> Uncertainty: whether a man really has this feeling, or is merely putting up an appearance of it. But of course it is also uncertain whether he is not merely putting up an appearance of pretending. This pretence is merely rarer and does not have grounds that are so easily understood. – But what does this uncertainty consist in? Am I

---

[38] See RPP I §§143, 570; LWPP I §§81, 874–6, 946; LWPP II, 36–7, 59e. As demonstrated in these and other examples, Wittgenstein emphasizes the importance of finding and inventing intermediate cases (PI §122).

[39] 'On all questions we discuss I have no opinions; and if I had, and it disagreed with one of your opinions, I would at once give it up for the sake of argument because it would be of no importance for our discussion. We constantly move in a realm where we all have the same opinions. All I can give you is a method; and I cannot teach you any new truths' (AWL, 97).

really always in some uncertainty whether someone is really angry, sad, glad, etc., etc? No…(RPP I §137)[40]

This remark is not a dismissal of questions concerning pretence and pain, but an acknowledgement of their complexity. Inherent in Wittgenstein's use of examples is an acknowledgement that there is no short answer to a philosophical question. This may appear ironic, or counter-intuitive, given the repeated accusation that Wittgenstein himself dismisses philosophical questions in a hasty or simplistic manner.[41] However, he cautions against such responses:

> Philosophers should not attempt to present the idealistic or solipsistic position, for example, as though they were absurd – by pointing out to a person who puts forward these positions that he does not really wonder whether the beef is real or whether it is an idea in his mind, whether his wife is real or whether only he is real. Of course he does not, and it is not a proper objection. (AWL, 108–9)

Wittgenstein advises students not to try to avoid philosophical problems but to present them as they arise with most power. He encourages them to use their imaginations:

> You must allow yourself to be dragged into the mire, and get out of it. Philosophy can be said to consist of three activities: to see the commonsense answer, to get yourself so deeply into the problem that the commonsense answer is unbearable, and to get from that situation back to the commonsense answer. But the common-sense answer in itself is no solution; everyone knows it. One must not in philosophy attempt to short-circuit problems. (AWL, 109)

Philosophical *movement* is of fundamental importance. 'If we are in the mire, a specially chosen example may immediately pull us out' (AWL, 109).

Wittgenstein's examples call for *a play of the imagination*. This is perhaps most evident in his use of fictitious examples:

> Laughing cattle, eyes that see despite being attached to the ends of tree branches, people who feel pain in the mouths of other people, cheese that shrinks or grows spontaneously, and tribes of men who do not dream: This is the world of Wittgenstein. (Peach 2004, 299)[42]

He notes that 'nothing is more important for teaching us to understand the concepts we have than constructing fictitious ones' (CV, 74; LWPP I §19). Fictitious examples function as *objects of comparison*. (Also see PI §130.) They draw attention to certain aspects of our language-use and exhibit characteristic features of the use of words; some by

---

[40] See PI §§249–50, p. 166; LWPP I §§252, 253, 859–62, 866–76, 861, 863, 946; RPP I §§137, 149–50, 610, 612, 613, 692, 718, 824.

[41] Beginning with Russell, this criticism pervades the secondary literature.

[42] To note but a few additional examples: PI §§2, 84, 142, 157, 200, 282, 283, 312, 350, 390, and 409.

showing these features in exaggeration, others by showing transitions, and still others showing the trailing off of such features (BB, 125).[43] Wittgenstein writes:

> I should like you to say: 'Yes, it's true, that can be imagined, that may even have happened!' But was I trying to draw your attention to the fact that you are able to imagine this? I wanted to put this picture before your eyes, and your *acceptance* of this picture consists in your being inclined to regard a given case differently; that is, to compare it with *this* series of pictures. I have changed your *way of seeing*. (Z §461)

Examples are presented as objects of comparison, not as preconceived ideas to which reality must correspond (PI §131). For example, in response to the interlocutor's insistence that Wittgenstein admit that there is a difference between pain-behaviour accompanied by pain and pain-behaviour without pain, Wittgenstein asks 'What greater difference could there be?' But when this difference is described in terms of a private exhibition of pain, Wittgenstein claims that this is illusory (PI §311). The interlocutor asserts, 'In the case of pain I believe that I can give myself a private exhibition of the difference. But I can give anyone an exhibition of the difference between a broken and an unbroken tooth' (PI §311). Wittgenstein responds, 'I can exhibit the visual sensation to myself as little or as well as the sensation of pain' (PI §312). He continues:

> Let us imagine the following: The surfaces of the things around us (stones, plants, etc.) have patches and regions which produce pain in our skin when we touch them. (Perhaps through the chemical composition of these surfaces. But we need not know that.) In this case we should speak of pain-patches on the leaf of a particular plant just as at present we speak of red patches. I am supposing that it is useful to us to notice these patches and their shapes; that we can infer important properties of the objects from them. (PI §312)

In this fictitious example, Wittgenstein creates a scene in which we speak of pain patches just as we speak of red patches (thus giving meaning to the expression 'the exhibition of pain'). The interlocutor distinguishes between private and public exhibitions of pain, while Wittgenstein introduces pain patches that have no reference to a bearer. (Wittgenstein notes that the importance of these patches involves the inferences we draw concerning the properties of the objects themselves.) Thus Wittgenstein challenges the original dichotomy drawn between private and public exhibitions of pain.

In order to challenge the philosophical distinction that is often drawn between private and public (or first- and third-person) perspectives, Wittgenstein uses examples to *shift* perspectives. This movement occurs within extended investigations, and in response to particular philosophical pictures or puzzles. If we do not recognize this grammatical *movement*, we will misread examples as philosophical claims.

> What gives us *so much as the idea* that beings, things, can feel?
> Is it that my education has led me to it by drawing my attention to feelings in myself, and now I transfer the idea to objects outside myself? That I recognize that

---

[43] Wittgenstein connects aspect-seeing and the use of imagination throughout his writings. See, for example, PI, 177, 179.

there is something there (in me) which I can call 'pain' without getting into conflict with the way other people use this word? – I do not transfer my idea to stones, plants, etc.

Couldn't I imagine having frightful pains and turning to stone while they lasted? Well, how do I know, if I shut my eyes, whether I have not turned into a stone? And if that has happened, in what sense will *the stone* have the pains? In what sense will they be ascribable to the stone? And why need the pain have a bearer at all here?!

And can one say of the stone that it has a soul and *that* is what has the pain? What has a soul, or pain, to do with a stone?

Only of what behaves like a human being can one say that it *has* pains.

For one has to say it of a body, or, if you like of a soul which some body *has*. And how can a body *have* a soul? (PI §283)[44]

What originally appears to be an empirical investigation proves to be conceptual. In response to the claim that one does not transfer ideas about one's own pain to stones or plants, Wittgenstein asks us to imagine being in frightful pain and *turning to stone*. The question is no longer whether objects outside us feel pain, but whether *we* feel pain if turned to stone.[45] It is a conceptual investigation: what has pain to do with a stone? In the above example, Wittgenstein shifts from stones and other people to a first-person perspective. On other occasions, he does just the opposite. He suggests that 'the examples that philosophers give in the first person should be investigated in the third' (LWPP II, 44). In other words, 'forget, forget that you have these experiences yourself!' (Z §179; also see RPP II §445.) (The shift is grammatical not experiential.) Wittgenstein does not privilege or dismiss one grammatical perspective over another, but reminds us that they coexist: '[A child] learns the use of the expression "to be in pain" in all of its persons, tenses, and numbers' (LWPP I §874). Further:

> It is a help here to remember that it is a primitive reaction to tend, to treat, the part that hurts when someone else is in pain; and not merely when oneself is – and so to pay attention to other people's pain-behaviour, as one does *not* pay attention to one's own pain-behaviour. (Z §540)

If we miss the grammatical movement inherent in these remarks, Wittgenstein will appear to be a behaviourist in disguise: '"Aren't you really a behaviourist in disguise? Aren't you at bottom really saying that everything except human behaviour is a fiction?" – If I do speak of a fiction, then it is of a *grammatical* fiction' (PI §307).

> 'But doesn't what you say come to this: that there is no pain, for example, without *pain-behaviour*?' – It comes to this: only of a living human being and what resembles (behaves like) a living human being can one say: it has sensations; it sees; is blind; hears; is deaf; is conscious or unconscious. (PI §281)

---

[44] Similarly, 'the kernel of our proposition that that which has pains or sees or thinks is of a mental nature is only that the word "I", in "I have pains" does not denote a particular body, for we can't substitute for "I" a description of a body' (BB, 74). Wittgenstein asks, 'isn't it absurd to say of a body that it has pain?' (PI §286)

[45] In related remarks, Wittgenstein investigates whether machines can feel pain, and compares machines with physical bodies (PG, 64 and PI §359). Also see PI §288.

This is a grammatical, not an empirical, remark.

Wittgenstein's use of *fictitious* examples is consistent with the claim that he is not doing natural history or natural science (PI, 195). Within the philosophical tradition, fiction is often contrasted with truth. The use of fictitious examples signals an important shift from questions of truth to questions of meaning.[46] Wittgenstein suggests that the philosopher's task is one of imagining possibilities. (See RPP II §639 and Z §452.) His investigations are not directed towards phenomena, but towards the '*possibilities*' of phenomena (PI §90):

> What kind of investigation are we carrying out? Am I investigating the probability of the cases that I give as examples, or am I investigating their actuality? No, I am just citing what is possible and am therefore giving grammatical examples. (P §187)

He asks, 'Is scientific progress useful to philosophy?' 'Certainly,' he answers, 'The realities that are discovered lighten the philosopher's task, imagining possibilities' (LWPP I §807).[47] In the *Tractatus*, science is the paradigm of meaningful discourse and logic involves 'possible states of affairs'. In the *Investigations*, Wittgenstein continues to direct his attention towards the *possibilities* of phenomena, but scientific discovery is understood as one possibility among others.

Wittgenstein's fictitious examples are described as interesting, unusual, extraordinary, bizarre, fascinating, queer, astonishing, unnatural, puzzling, mysterious, nonsensical, and absurd. In other words, the emergence of new and different examples (which once caused grief) is now employed as a method of investigation. These examples expand our imagination:

> In philosophy one feels *forced* to look at a concept in a certain way. What I do is to suggest or invent other ways of looking at it. I suggest possibilities of which you had not previously thought. You thought there was one possibility, or only two at most. *I made you see that it was absurd to expect the concept to conform to those narrow possibilities.* (Wittgenstein as quoted in Malcolm 1984, 43; emphasis added)

Our expectations, rather than Wittgenstein's examples, are absurd. He attempts to show us that there are countless different kinds of uses of words or expressions – kinds of uses of which we had not dreamt (Malcolm 1984, 43). In a striking passage he notes:

> The uses of words can differ from each other in the way beauty differs from a chair. They are incomparable in the way in which some things we buy are incomparable, such as a sofa and permission to sit in the theatre. When we talk of words and their meanings we tend to compare them with money and the things it buys rather than

---

[46] He writes, 'this method is basically the transition from the question of truth to the question of meaning' (PR in Nedo 1993, 7).

[47] A variation of LWPP I §807 reads: 'Realities are so many possibilities for the philosopher'. Wittgenstein also writes, 'I may find scientific questions interesting, but they never really grip me. Only *conceptual* and *aesthetic* questions do that. At bottom I am indifferent to the solution of scientific problems; but not the other sort' (CV, 79).

with money and the uses it has. A thing we buy with money is not the same as the use of the money. (AWL, 46)[48]

He writes that 'a main source of philosophical disease [is] an unbalanced diet: one nourishes one's thinking with only one kind of example' (PI §593). Thus he does not select food for his pupils with the aim of flattering their taste, but with the aim of changing it (CV, 17). '[Wittgenstein also] suggests that we go from the unusual to the ordinary rather than, as many have hitherto supposed, from the ordinary to the unusual' (Bartley 1974, 79). It is for this reason that he often uses anomalies. 'Why is it important to depict anomalies accurately? If someone can't do this, that shows that he isn't quite at home yet among the concepts' (RPP II §606; CV, 72). The purpose of anomalies is not to give an example of the use of a word, and then proceed to other instances of its application that have very little in common. Anomalies are not presented as counter-examples (although they often challenge our preconceptions and generalizations). Rather, the belief that a picture forces a particular application on us sometimes consists of the fact that only one case and no other occurred to us (PI §140).[49]

Another purpose of Wittgenstein's fictitious examples is to shock: 'Our method is not merely to enumerate actual usages of words, but rather deliberately to invent new ones, some of them because of their absurd appearance' (BB, 28). Malcolm recounts how Wittgenstein would often grin at what he imagined during his lectures, but that if any member of the class were to chuckle, he would exclaim in reproof 'No, no; I'm serious!' (Malcolm 1984, 28)

> What if something *really unheard-of* happened? – If I, say, saw houses gradually turning into steam without any obvious cause, if the cattle in the fields stood on their heads and laughed and spoke comprehensible words; if trees gradually changed into men and men into trees. Now, was I right when I said before all these things happened 'I know that that's a house?' etc., or simply, 'That's a house', etc. (OC §513)[50]

Wittgenstein refers to the absurd *appearance* of such examples (not to their *absurdity*). Whether or not a particular example is absurd (and what it would mean to make such a claim) is often part of the conceptual investigation and open to question. Scholars debate the 'possibility' or 'impossibility' of Wittgenstein's examples in general and, more often than not, attempt to demarcate the difference between sense and nonsense.[51] Almost invariably, Wittgenstein's fictitious examples are understood as a

---

[48] Variations of this remark are found at AWL, 30 and PG, 63. To paraphrase Wittgenstein, when commentators claim that 'meaning is use' they have so far said nothing whatever unless they have described or exhibited that use (PI §13).

[49] See PI §§115, 173, 349, 352, 374, 402, 422–4, 518, 520, and their corresponding investigations.

[50] Also see OC §§413, 430, 441, 450, 460, and 461. Wittgenstein writes that he has no grounds for the opinion that cats do not grow on trees or that he has a father and a mother (OC §282).

[51] See, for example, Cook 1985; Malcolm 1989, 1990; Scheer 1990; and Peach 2004. Wittgenstein himself attempts to demarcate the difference between sense and nonsense in the *Tractatus*. For further discussion see Peach 2004.

means of highlighting very general facts of nature (or 'scaffolding facts'). According to Broyles, 'fantasy can be employed in promoting an awareness of scaffolding facts. Indeed, fantasy is required if we are to supply the contrast in bringing these facts before the mind, for this contrast involves what is not possible, but only fanciful' (Broyles 1974, 296). Cerbone writes that Wittgenstein's imaginary scenarios are best read as devices to aid in recovering the naturalness and familiarity of our concepts (Cerbone 1993, 159, 178).

Wittgenstein anticipates and challenges these readings:

> If the formation of concepts can be explained by facts of nature, should we not be interested, not in grammar, but rather in that in nature which is the basis of grammar? – Our interest certainly includes the correspondence between concepts and very general facts of nature … But our interest does not fall back upon these possible causes of the formation of concepts; we are not doing natural science; nor yet natural history – since we can also invent fictitious natural history for our purposes. (PI, 195)

This passage does not suggest that we discover (or remember) very general facts of nature by using fictitious examples, but that fictitious examples could *replace* natural history or natural science for our purposes. Wittgenstein is not suggesting that if we cannot imagine something otherwise, it must be true. Rather, he draws attention to the difference between empirical and grammatical propositions:

> What does it mean when we say: 'I can't imagine the opposite of this' or 'What would it be like, if it were otherwise?' – For example, when someone has said that my images are private, or that only I myself can know whether I am feeling pain, and similar things.
>
> Of course, here 'I can't imagine the opposite' doesn't mean: my powers of imagination are unequal to the task. These words are a defence against something whose form makes it look like an empirical proposition, but which is really a grammatical one.
>
> But why do we say: 'I can't imagine the opposite?' Why not: 'I can't imagine the thing itself'? (PI §251)

Consider the following example in which very general facts of nature are changed:

> 'What would it be like if human beings shewed no outward signs of pain (did not groan, grimace, etc.)? Then it would be impossible to teach a child the use of the word "tooth-ache".' – Well, let's assume the child is a genius and himself invents a name for the sensation! – But then, of course, he couldn't make himself understood when he used the word. – So does he understand the name, without being able to explain its meaning to anyone? – But what does it mean to say that he has 'named his pain'? – How has he done this naming of pain?! And whatever he did, what was its purpose? – When one says 'He gave a name to his sensation' one forgets that a great deal of stage-setting in the language is presupposed if the mere act of naming is to make sense. And when we speak of someone's having given a name to pain, what is presupposed is the existence of the grammar of the word 'pain'; it shews the post where the new word is stationed. (PI §257)

The interlocutor presents a case in which very general facts of nature are changed, but the concept of pain remains. This appears to confirm the naturalness and familiarity of our concepts (presenting an interpretation similar to those of Broyles, Cerbone, and others). However, Wittgenstein develops the example further and investigates how the concept of pain changes. In response to an example in which human beings show no outward signs of pain (and the subsequent assertion that it would be impossible to teach a child the use of the word 'toothache'). Wittgenstein imagines a child who invents a name for his sensation. (It is the mirror image of the interlocutor's example and conclusion, for the interlocutor imagines a case in which human beings have a sensation but do not have any natural expression for it (PI §256).) Inherent in Wittgenstein's example is the claim that the child 'names his pain'. This demonstrates that there is a great deal of stage-setting presupposed in both examples (involving the grammar of the word 'pain'). Wittgenstein demonstrates that the interlocutor's example does not go far enough. It is not merely that we cannot teach the use of the word 'toothache' without outward signs of pain, but that without the natural expression of pain the concept itself changes. This example is further played out in a case involving an individual who keeps a diary noting the recurrence of a particular sensation (PI §§258–70).

Wittgenstein encourages us to imagine general facts of nature different from what we are used to, not to *affirm* what we already know, but to challenge philosophical complacency. He does not use fictitious examples to affirm facts, common sense, or the *status quo*. Rather, he continues to move in the realm of conceptual possibilities.

> I am not saying: if such-and-such facts of nature were different people would have different concepts (in the sense of a hypothesis). But: if anyone believes that certain concepts are absolutely the correct ones, and that having different ones would mean not realizing something that we realize – then let him imagine certain very general facts of nature to be different from what we are used to, and the formation of concepts different from the usual ones will become intelligible to him. (PI, 195)[52]

Consider the possibility of having pain in another person's body:

> In order to see that it is conceivable that one person should have pain in another person's body, one must examine what sort of facts we call criteria for a pain being in a certain place. It is easy to imagine the following case: When I see my hands I am not always aware of their connection with the rest of my body. That is to say, I often see my hand moving but don't see the arm which connects it to my torso…Therefore the hand may, for all I know, be connected to the body of a man standing beside me (or, of course, not to a human body at all)…What I wish to say is that the act of pointing determines the place of pain. (BB, 49–50)

> An innumerable variety of cases can be thought of in which we should say that someone has pains in another person's body; or, say, in a piece of furniture, or in an empty spot. (BB, 50–51)

---

[52] Wittgenstein also introduces examples where tribes have different concepts of pain. See Z §§380, 383, 389; RPP I §§149–50, 662; and LWPP I §203.

According to Wittgenstein, we can conceive of *innumerable* cases.[53]

Ordinary, everyday examples play a role similar to that of fictitious examples in the later writings. Wittgenstein does not *appeal* to ordinary, everyday examples in order to counter wonder or puzzlement, but asks us to be puzzled or disturbed by the ordinary and the everyday.[54] Ordinary, everyday examples also call for a play of the imagination. Although drawn from everyday life, there is nothing ordinary or obvious about their use. On first reading, these remarks may strike us as extraordinary or counter-intuitive. (See, for example, PI §251 and p. 190.) We may even have difficulty *imagining* or playing out these examples. Wittgenstein acknowledges that 'what we say will be easy, but to know why we say it will be very difficult' (AWL, 77). He describes his remarks as 'trivial' (in the sense that we already know what he describes) but adds that 'what is not trivial is seeing them all together' (AWL, 44). What are *given* are the examples themselves, but we must find ourselves in relation to them. Like fictitious examples, his ordinary, everyday examples are conceptual. There is nothing hypothetical about them.[55] 'It is the essence of philosophy not to depend on experience' (AWL, 97). He explains:

> Don't take it as a matter of course, but as a remarkable fact, that pictures and fictitious narratives give us pleasure, occupy our minds.
>
> ('Don't take it as a matter of course' means: find it surprising, as you do some things which disturb you. Then the puzzling aspect of the latter will disappear, by your accepting this fact as you do the other.) (PI §524)

Even when Wittgenstein appears to be appealing to ordinary, everyday examples, he is challenging us to expand our imagination. He writes, 'If I see someone writhing in pain with evident cause I do not think: all the same, his feelings are hidden from me' (PI, 190). He does not write, '*When* I see someone...' but '*If* I see someone...' The example challenges us to imagine someone writhing in pain with evident cause and, by implication, to imagine an even more complex context in which we might think that someone's feelings were hidden from us in such a situation. This is an interesting example because there is a point at which imagining this scene shifts from doubts about the pain of others to doubts about our own humanity. '"I can only guess at someone else's feelings" – does that really make sense when you see him badly wounded, for instance, and in dreadful pain?' (LWPP I §964) Further:

> 'I can never *know* what is going on in him; *he* always knows': When one thinks philosophically, one would like to say that. But what situation does this statement correspond to? Every day we hear one man saying of another that he is in pain, is sad, is merry, etc., without a trace of doubt, and we relatively seldom hear that he does not know what is going on in the other. In this way, then, the uncertainty is not

---

[53] He also investigates whether we would speak of feeling the same pain if sharing a body (BB, 54–5). Also see BB, 67; LWPP II, 92–5; PI §253; and RC, 127.

[54] Wittgenstein writes, for example, that 'we find certain things about seeing puzzling, because we do not find the whole business of seeing puzzling enough' (PI, 181).

[55] 'There must not be anything hypothetical in our considerations. We must do away with all *explanation*, and description alone must take its place' (PI §109).

so bad. And it also happens that one says 'I know that you felt like this then, even if you won't admit it now'. (RPP I §138)

Contrary to the picture 'he knows – I don't know', which makes our lack of knowledge appear in an irritating light, Wittgenstein reminds us that we often hear people saying of one another that they are in pain, and that occasions of uncertainty are not only rare but 'not so bad' (RPP I §139). By imagining everyday examples, we shift the significance and implications of these philosophical claims.

Wittgenstein anticipates that his remarks may be dismissed as irrelevant to philosophical concerns and responds:

> Some will say that my talk about the concept of knowledge is irrelevant, since this concept as understood by philosophers, while indeed it does not agree with the concept as it is used in everyday speech, still is an important and interesting one, created by a kind of sublimation from the ordinary, rather uninteresting one. But the philosophical concept was derived from the ordinary one through all sorts of misunderstandings, and it strengthens these misunderstandings. It is in no way interesting, except as a warning. (RPP II §289)

Thus Wittgenstein also uses examples drawn from philosophy itself. Like other everyday examples, our philosophical acts provide detailed cases with which to work (and remind us that doing philosophy is itself an activity – not to be abstracted or sublimated). Once again, Wittgenstein sets words into motion. He repeatedly describes cases in which we stare ahead or attempt to look inside ourselves. He describes acts of philosophical confusion in which we 'attempt to take sidelong glances at private sensations'. (See PI §§274, 316, 412, 413, 420, 428, 607, 608.) He also investigates the use of words 'that doubtless only occurs in doing philosophy' (PI §§38 and 174). When Wittgenstein writes that 'what *we* do is to bring words back from their metaphysical to their everyday use' he is not denying or dismissing the metaphysical use of words without investigation, but asking us to imagine our philosophical acts in all of their complexity and detail (PI §116). The result is that these acts often prove otiose, and our language idle (PI §88): 'You think that after all you must be weaving a piece of cloth: because you are sitting at a loom – even if it is empty – and going through the motion of weaving' (PI §414; also see PI §§38, 132). This remark follows an investigation of introspection, in which Wittgenstein notes that what William James showed was not the meaning of the word 'self' but the state of the philosopher's attention when he says the word 'self' to himself and tries to analyse its meaning. Wittgenstein suggests that a good deal can be learned from this (PI §413). He also challenges us to try, in real cases, to doubt someone else's fear or pain, or to imagine children as mere automata (PI §303):

> But can't I imagine that the people around me are automata, lack consciousness, even though they behave in the same way as usual? – If I imagine it now – alone in my room – I see people with fixed looks (as in a trance) going about their business – the idea is perhaps a little uncanny. But just try to keep hold of this idea in the midst of your ordinary intercourse with others, in the street, say! Say to yourself, for example: 'The children over there are mere automata; all their liveliness is mere automatism.'

And you will either find these words becoming quite meaningless; or you will produce in yourself some kind of uncanny feeling, or something of the sort.

Seeing a living human being as an automaton is analogous to seeing one figure as a limited case or variant of another; the cross-pieces of a window as a swastika, for example. (PI §420)

These philosophical acts (and Wittgenstein's subsequent challenges) constitute everyday examples that are meant to be compared, contrasted, developed, and enacted as part of our ongoing grammatical investigations. The request to try, in real cases, to imagine something *specific* forces us to develop our conceptual imagination by attending to all the details that escape notice.[56] Wittgenstein does not attempt to *return* us to ordinary, everyday life for we never left, and it was in ordinary, everyday life that our philosophical puzzlement began.

Further, 'being unable – when we surrender ourselves to philosophical thought – to help saying such-and-such; being irresistibly inclined to say it – does not mean being forced into an *assumption*, or having an immediate perception or knowledge of a state of affairs' (PI §299). Philosophy can also involve false imagination (RPP II §417).

> People who make metaphysical assertions such as 'Only the present is real' pretend to make a picture, as opposed to some other picture. I deny that they have done this. But how can I prove it? I cannot say 'This is not a picture of anything, it is unthinkable' unless I assume that they and I have the same limitations on picturing. If I indicate a picture which the words suggest and they agree, then I can tell them they are misled, that the imagery in which they move does not lead them to such expressions. It cannot be denied that they have made a picture, but we can say they have been misled. We can say 'it makes no sense in this system and I believe this is the system you are using'. If they reply by introducing a new system, then I have to acquiesce. (AWL, 27)

In the opening of the *Investigations*, Wittgenstein suggests that the words of Augustine give us a particular picture of the essence of human language (PI §1). He illustrates this picture with the example of the builders. If we recognize this picture as our own, he can demonstrate that we are misled – that *the imagery in which we move* does not lead us to make such claims or use such expressions. And while we *may* acknowledge this picture as an apt description of our way of thinking, Wittgenstein always leaves open the possibility of new and different responses.[57]

---

[56] 'The aspects of things that are most important for us are hidden because of their simplicity and familiarity. (One is unable to notice something because it is always before one's eyes.) The real foundations of his enquiry do not strike a man at all. Unless *that* fact has at some time struck him. – And this means we fail to be struck by what, once seen, is most striking and most powerful' (PI §129).

[57] While Wittgenstein never claims that something is 'unthinkable' or 'impossible to imagine', he sometimes demonstrates that we have not *yet* been able to think or imagine what we claim. In response to Augustine, he asks us to imagine an example for which Augustine is *right* (PI §§1–47). In such cases, we imagine an example in order to *give* a sense to a problematic expression or claim. For an example involving the concept of pain, see the discussion of the beetle-in-a-box below.

The later writings are filled with examples of false imagination. For instance, Wittgenstein investigates the claim that we imagine someone else's pain on the model of our own:

> If one has to imagine someone else's pain on the model of one's own, this is none too easy a thing to do: for I have to imagine pain which I *do not feel* on the model of the pain which I *do feel*. That is, what I have to do is not simply to make a transition in imagination from one place of pain to another. As, from pain in the hand to pain in the arm. For I am not to imagine that I feel pain in some region of his body. (Which would also be possible.)
>
> Pain-behaviour may point to a painful place – but the subject of pain is the person who gives it expression. (PI §302)[58]

In response to the interlocutor's insistence that there must be *something* accompanying a cry of pain, Wittgenstein introduces the following example: 'Of course, if water boils in a pot, steam comes out of the pot and also pictured steam comes out of the pictured pot. But what if one insisted on saying that there must also be something boiling in the picture of the pot?' (PI §297; also see PI §161 and 419.) When Wittgenstein speaks of false imagination he is not trivializing or dismissing philosophical problems or philosophy itself. These examples involve important concepts, and are among the most difficult in his writings. (Also see PI §§39, 46, 55, 216, 246, and 299.) Nor is he claiming that philosophy is itself the result of false imagination. Rather, he recognizes that when imagining conceptual possibilities we may make false moves or find ourselves unable to go on:

> 'I know.... only from my *own* case' – what kind of proposition is this meant to be at all? An experiential one? No. – A grammatical one?
>
> Suppose someone does say about himself that he knows what pain is only from his own pain. – Not that people really say that, or are even prepared to say it. But *if* everybody said it — it might be a kind of exclamation. And even if it gives no information, still it is a picture, and why should we not want to call up such a picture? Imagine an allegorical painting taking the place of those words.
>
> When we look into ourselves as we do philosophy, we often get to see just such a picture. A full-blown pictorial representation of our grammar. Not facts; but as it were illustrated turns of speech. (PI §295)

Wittgenstein develops the idea of full-blown pictorial representations of our grammar (and illustrated turns of speech) in examples that 'replace every process of imagining by a process of looking at an object or by painting, drawing or modeling; and every process of speaking to oneself by speaking aloud or by writing' (BB, 4, 41–2). He frequently presents examples in which he replaces visual images with painted pictures, and processes of thinking with acts of looking at real objects (AWL, 27; BB 4, 53). We find such examples throughout his later writings: 'understanding' is replaced by 'rendering out loud what is written or printed', and also 'writing from dictation, writing out something printed, or playing from a score' (PI §156); 'a visual room' is replaced by 'a picture

---

[58] Also see PI §§286 and 350–51. PI §448 provides an example of false imagination that relates to the absence (rather than the presence) of pain.

of an imaginary landscape' (PI §398); and 'thinking something real' is replaced by 'painting something real' (PI §518).[59] In his lectures, he replaces 'having a self' with 'having a shilling', and it is this technique that he uses in his famous beetle-in-a-box example (AWL, 61–2):

> If I say of myself that it is only from my own case that I know what the word 'pain' means – must I not say the same of other people too? And how can I generalize the *one* case so irresponsibly?
>
> Now someone tells me that *he* knows what pain is only from his own case! — Suppose everyone had a box with something in it: we call it a 'beetle'. No one can look into anyone else's box, and everyone says he knows what a beetle is only by looking at *his* beetle. – Here it would be quite possible for everyone to have something different in his box. One might even imagine such a thing constantly changing. – But suppose the word 'beetle' had a use in these people's language? – If so it would not be used as the name of a thing. The thing in the box has no place in the language-game at all; not even as a *something*: for the box might even be empty. – No, one can 'divide through' by the thing in the box; it cancels out, whatever it is.
>
> That is to say: if we construe the grammar of the expression of sensation on the model of 'object and designation' the object drops out of consideration as irrelevant. (PI §293; also see §§257; Z §641; RPP II §47)

In this example, a beetle-in-a-box is substituted for a pain-in-the-body and the logic of Wittgenstein's argument becomes clear. The example shifts our focus and demonstrates that the inner/outer distinction is itself a form of false imagination. Wittgenstein's use of Jastrow's duck-rabbit picture (and other optical illusions) is an extended application of this technique. And using theatre examples, he turns 'accompanying, conscious processes' into theatrical 'asides' and monologues.[60] This technique also reminds us that imagination does not involve producing a certain image or idea in a person's mind (hinting at something it cannot show) for Wittgenstein's imaginative examples are *purely descriptive* (BB, 125).

One technique that Wittgenstein uses to reveal false imagination is to present examples that do not initially puzzle us, and develop them until they become puzzling. By illustrating how we come to be puzzled, he effectively demonstrates how to extricate ourselves from a particular problem. 'My method is to take a parallel case where one is not initially puzzled and get the same puzzle about it as in cases where one is puzzled' (AWL, 58).

> This queer situation can be cleared up somewhat by looking at an example; in fact a kind of parable illustrating the difficulty we are in, and also showing the way out of this sort of difficulty. (BB, 45)

---

[59] See, for examples, PI §§1, 47, 120, 319, and 634. For a detailed discussion of PI §§156–85 see Savickey 1999.

[60] 'One ought to ask, not what images are or what happens when one imagines anything…I am only saying that this question is not to be decided – neither for the person who does the imagining, nor for anyone else – by pointing; nor yet by a description of any process. The first question also asks for a word to be explained; but it makes us expect a wrong kind of answer' (PI §370). Wittgenstein repeatedly tells us to *look* and learn from the use of a word. Similarly, he admonishes us not to think but to look (PI §§340 and 66). See BB, 35; PI §§243, 450, 642; RPP II §604; and LWPP II §72.

We see such movement throughout his later writings. (See, for example, PI §§47–65 and 156–85.) Wittgenstein's parallel cases and examples also serve to destroy the uniqueness of the case at hand.

> The particular peace of mind that occurs when we place other similar cases next to a case that we thought was unique, occurs again and again in our investigations when we show that a word doesn't have just one meaning (or just two) but is used in five or six different ways (meanings). (P, 175)

He anticipates that we may not recognize the usefulness of these examples: 'You may question whether my constantly giving examples and speaking in parables is profitable. My reason is that parallel cases change our outlook because they destroy the uniqueness of the case at hand' (AWL, 50). Destroying uniqueness is not synonymous with finding something common to all. Rather, it lessens our obsession or 'mental cramp'. Wittgenstein explains:

> This is not a problem but a mental cramp. That this is so appears on asking when this problem strikes us…The characteristic thing about all philosophical problems is that they arise in a peculiar way. As a way out, I can only give you examples, which if you think about them you will find the cramp relaxes…to relieve the mental cramp it is not enough to get rid of it: you must also see why you had it. (AWL, 90)

Once again, Wittgenstein's examples challenge us to change our style of thinking in order to resolve philosophical difficulties.

Wittgenstein's examples present new possibilities, and encourage new ways of looking at things. They alter the form, content, and tone of both philosophical investigation and criticism. Inherent in the use of examples is the insight that definitions, explanations, and theories are not only inadequate for the investigation of concepts, but gratuitous or superfluous (Z §614). Instead of giving examples, 'one is tempted again and again to talk more than still makes sense. To continue talking where one should stop' (RPP II §402). Wittgenstein's advice is not to stop doing philosophy, but to stop seeking definitions or giving explanations: 'Isn't this explanation enough? Isn't it too much?' (RPP II §519; PI, 179)

> Here the temptation is overwhelmingly to say something further, when everything has already been described – Whence this pressure? What analogy, what wrong interpretation produces it? (Z §313)

> Here we come up against a remarkable and characteristic phenomenon in philosophical investigation: the difficulty – I might say – is not that of finding the solution but rather that of recognizing as the solution something that looks as if it were only a preliminary to it. 'We have already said everything. – Not anything that follows from this, no, this is the solution!'
>
> This is connected, I believe, with our wrongly expecting an explanation, whereas the solution of the difficulty is a description, if we give it the right place in our considerations. If we dwell upon it, and do not try to get beyond it.
>
> The difficulty here is: to stop. (Z §314)

To give the right place to description in our considerations is to take examples seriously and investigate them in detail. Examples offer clarification of our concepts in all of their variations. This is Wittgenstein's real discovery. The difficulty is not that of finding the solution, but of recognizing Wittgenstein's use of examples *as* the solution, not as something preliminary to it. The difficulty here is: to stop.[61]

REFERENCES

AMBROSE, ALICE ed. (1982). *Wittgenstein's Lectures: Cambridge 1932–35*. Oxford: Basil Blackwell.

APOLLINAIRE, G. (1949). *The Cubist Painters: Aesthetic Meditations 1913*, trans. L. Abel. New York: George Wittenborn, Inc.

BARTLEY, W. W., III (1974). *Wittgenstein*. London: Quartet Books.

BINKLEY, T. (1973). *Wittgenstein's Language*. The Hague: Martinus Nijhoff.

BROYLES, J. (1974). 'An Observation on Wittgenstein's Use of Fantasy', *Metaphilosophy*, 5(4): 291–7.

BURNYEAT, M. F. (1977). 'Examples in Epistemology: Socrates, Theaetetus and G. E. Moore', *Philosophy*, 52: 381–98.

CERBONE, D. (1993). 'Don't Look But Think: Imaginary Scenarios in Wittgenstein's Later Philosophy', *Inquiry*, 37(2): 159–83.

COOK, J. (1985). 'The Metaphysics of Wittgenstein's *On Certainty*', *Philosophical Investigations*, 8(2): 81–119.

DRURY, MAURICE O'C. (1973). *The Danger of Words*. London: Routledge and Kegan Paul.

GEACH, P. T. ed. (1988). *Wittgenstein's Lectures on the Philosophy of Psychology 1946–47*. London: Harvester Wheatsheaf.

MALCOLM, N. (1984). *Ludwig Wittgenstein: A Memoir with a Biographical Sketch by Georg Henrik von Wright*. Oxford: Oxford University Press.

—— (1989). 'Turning to Stone', *Philosophical Investigations*, 12(2): 101–11.

—— (1990). 'Reply to Scheer', *Philosophical Investigations*, 13(2): 165–8.

NEDO, M. (1993). *Ludwig Wittgenstein: Wiener Ausgabe*. New York: Springer-Verlag.

PEACH, A. (2004). 'The Origins of Wittgenstein's Imaginary Scenarios', *Philosophical Investigations*, 27(4): 299–37.

SAVICKEY, B. (1999). *Wittgenstein's Art of Investigation*. London and New York: Routledge.

SCHALKWYK, D. (2005). 'Wittgenstein's "imperfect garden": the ladders and labyrinths of philosophy as *Dichtung*', in J. Gibson and W. Huemer eds., *The Literary Wittgenstein*. London and New York: Routledge.

SCHEER, R. K. (1990). 'What if Something Really Unheard-of Happened?' *Philosophical Investigations*, 13(2): 154–64.

WITTGENSTEIN, L. (1953/2001). *Philosophical Investigations*, 3rd edition, trans. G. E. M. Anscombe. Oxford: Basil Blackwell.

—— (1961). *Notebooks 1914–1916*, 2nd edition, ed. G. H. von Wright and G. E. M. Anscombe, trans. G. E. M. Anscombe. Oxford: Basil Blackwell.

---

[61] My thanks to Marie McGinn for encouraging me to give examples, and for providing helpful comments on an earlier version of this chapter.

—— (1961). *Tractatus Logico-Philosophicus*, trans. D. F. Pears and B. F. McGuinness. London: Routledge and Kegan Paul.

—— (1969). *The Blue and Brown Books: Preliminary Studies for the Philosophical Investigations.* Oxford: Basil Blackwell.

—— (1975). *Philosophical Remarks*, ed. R. Rhees, trans R. Hargreaves and R. White. Oxford: Basil Blackwell.

—— (1978). *Lectures and Conversations on Aesthetics, Psychology and Religious Belief*, ed. Cyril Barrett. Oxford: Basil Blackwell.

—— (1978). *Remarks on Colour*, ed. G. E. M. Anscombe, trans. L. McAlister and M. Schättle. Oxford: Blackwell.

—— (1979). *On Certainty*, ed. G. E. M. Anscombe and G. H. von Wright, trans. D. Paul and G. E. M. Anscombe. Oxford: Basil Blackwell.

—— (1979). *Remarks on Frazer's Golden Bough*, ed. Rush Rhees. Retford: The Brynmill Press. (Reprinted in PO.)

—— (1980). *Culture and Value*, ed. G. H. von Wright and H. Nyman, trans. P. Winch. Oxford: Basil Blackwell.

—— (1980). *Remarks on the Philosophy of Psychology*, vol. 1, ed. G. E. M. Anscombe and G. H. von Wright, trans. G. E. M. Anscombe. Oxford: Basil Blackwell.

—— (1980). *Remarks on the Philosophy of Psychology*, vol. 2, ed. G. H. von Wright and H. Nyman, trans C. G. Luckhardt and M. A. Aue. Oxford: Basil Blackwell.

—— (1981). *Zettel*, 2nd edition, ed. G. E. M. Anscombe and G. H. von Wright, trans. G. E. M. Anscombe. Oxford: Basil Blackwell.

—— (1982). *Last Writings on the Philosophy of Psychology*, vols. 1 and 2, ed. G. H. von Wright and H. Nyman, trans. C. G. Luckhardt and M. A. E. Aue. Oxford: Basil Blackwell.

—— (1984). *Philosophical Grammar*, ed. R. Rhees, trans. A. Kenny, Oxford: Basil Blackwell.

—— (1993). *Philosophical Occasions 1912–1951*, ed. J. Klagge and A. Nordman. Cambridge: Hackett Publishing Company.

—— (2000). *Wittgenstein's Nachlass: The Bergen Electronic Edition.* Oxford: Oxford University Press.

—— (2005). *The Big Typescript: TS 213*, ed. and trans. C. G. Luckhardt and M. A. E. Aue, Oxford: Basil Blackwell.

....

CHAPTER 30

ASPECT PERCEPTION AND PHILOSOPHICAL DIFFICULTY

....

AVNER BAZ

INTRODUCTION

I want in this chapter to trace a new line of thought through, or actually *to*, Wittgenstein's writings on aspect perception, and to stay away as much as possible from old controversies. My point of bearing will be the second part of the *Brown Book*. I believe it has not previously been noted that this is where Wittgenstein's first *sustained* engagement with the topic of aspect perception takes place. This fact might well have been of a merely biographical interest. I shall try to show, however, that the trail of philosophical reflection that apparently naturally leads Wittgenstein in *The Brown Book* from questions concerning how we ought to conceive of our various mental states (and processes)—i.e., from what is arguably one of the underlying overall concerns of the first part of the *Investigations*—to the topic of aspect perception, is in fact *philosophically* interesting. It is also different from what previous attempts to relate the remarks on aspects to the first part of the *Investigations* would have made one expect.

Before I set out, however, I would like to briefly put my cards on the table. First, I do not take Wittgenstein's numerous remarks on aspect perception to be anything like the first part of the *Investigations* when it comes to how far each one of them individually, and the way in which they may, or ought to, fall together, were thought through by him. In fact, I see no reason to suppose that Wittgenstein ever came as far as to form an idea of how his remarks on aspects, or some selection of them, may fall together to form some sort of a unified whole. The first part of the *Investigations*, as I understand it, was extremely carefully designed, over many years, to make its *reader* work; in the remarks on aspects, on the other hand, we see Wittgenstein himself at work, making his way. I suppose all this is quite uncontroversial; and it might also seem merely external to the work of Wittgenstein's remarks, whatever it may be. I would not have felt the need to remark upon it here were it not for the prevailing tendency among readers of

Wittgenstein's remarks on aspects to look for a comprehensive, unified, and complete account of them, and to look for it under the presumption that Wittgenstein himself had such an account on offer.

Second, and more specifically, I see no reason to think of section xi of the second part of the *Investigations* as constituting some sort of a philosophically unified whole. The circumstances of its composition and the way in which it made its way into what became the *Philosophical Investigations* no more justify thinking about it in that way than does the form it ended up taking.[1] Once again I would not have felt the need to make this remark if it were not for the tendency among readers to claim support for their interpretations from the particular composition of section xi and from the particular order in which its remarks are arranged. I do not say that the composition and order of the remarks in section xi are entirely arbitrary, for evidently they are not: some remarks clearly rely upon or even make reference to previous remarks (much more so in the first half or so of section xi than in the second half). At some point, however, interpretive moves that take the form of 'from his discussion of A Wittgenstein moves to discuss B, and it is *therefore* clear that his intention was to connect A to B, and to do so in this or that way' strike me as unwarranted.

Third, even if Wittgenstein had worked twenty more years on his remarks on aspects and had managed to come to the point at which some particular selected set of them more or less satisfied him and seemed to him to fall together more or less satisfyingly (perhaps together with the remarks currently comprising the first part of the *Investigations*), I doubt very much that those remarks would have presented us with Wittgenstein's 'views' on aspect perception and on perception more generally.[2] If Wittgenstein had anything that might aptly be described as 'philosophical views', they pertained to the nature of philosophical difficulty, to what lies at its roots, and to the method, or methods, of philosophical response called for by difficulty of this nature. As for the seeing of aspects, or for perception more generally, or, for that matter, for naming, or understanding, or meaning, or reading, or following a rule, and so on, I think that an important point of departure for Wittgenstein's work was that he found literally incredible the dominating conception of philosophy, according to which it ought to enable us to form correct views about these sorts of phenomena—the sort of views that one person could teach another, who until then had been holding incorrect views. That we repeatedly and seemingly inevitably come to expect just that of philosophy is something to which Wittgenstein's work is everywhere responsive.

Fourth, when it comes to perception, or to what Western philosophy at least since Kant has called 'experience' (*Erfahrung*), there is a further reason for resisting the

---

[1] I take this on the authority of Michael Nedo from the Wittgenstein Archive in Cambridge.

[2] For the idea that Wittgenstein had 'views' about aspect perception which can be 'formulated' and 'justified', see Mulhall 2000, 246. I do not mean to make a fuss about some particular choice of words; and of course 'view' can be used in any number of different ways, to mean any number of different things. The point is rather to contest a prevailing conception of what one ought to look for in Wittgenstein's remarks on aspects (as well as on other topics), and of what understanding these remarks requires.

temptation to attribute a unified and comprehensive view of it to Wittgenstein. In contrast to virtually any other treatment of perception in the tradition of Western philosophy, Wittgenstein's remarks are everywhere attuned to the richness and complexity of all that may fall under the concept of 'perception'. Here, as in other areas of philosophical reflection, one of Wittgenstein's chief aims was to teach us differences. 'There are here hugely many interrelated phenomena and possible concepts', he says in the course of his investigation of aspect perception (PI II, 199). The following is only a sample of all of the 'concepts of experience' (*Erfahrungsbegriffe*) that come up for consideration in the *Investigations* (many of them in section xi of part two of that text): 'a feeling (*Gefühl*) of familiarity (unfamiliarity)', 'a feeling of naturalness (unnaturalness)', 'finding something conspicuous (inconspicuous)', 'seeing' (and, or versus, '*seeing*'), 'seeing a property of the object' (as opposed to 'seeing an aspect'), 'being struck', 'noticing', 'interpreting', 'knowing (merely knowing) what one sees', 'seeing something as something', 'treating something as something (*behandeln als*)', 'regarding something as something (*betrachten als*)', 'taking something as (or for) something (*halten für*)', 'conceiving (*auffassen*) something in one way or another (as opposed to *seeing* it as this or that)', 'having what one sees come alive for one', 'seeing something three-dimensionally', 'being conscious (aware) (*Bewußtsein*) (of something)', 'looking without being aware (of something)', 'thinking (of what one sees/looks at)', 'recognizing', 'seeing something without recognizing it', 'imagining', 'feeling (as in 'one *feels* the softness of the depicted material')', 'knowing one's way about (with a drawing, say)', 'concerning one's self with what one sees', 'paying attention', 'being blind to an expression'...And consider further that the criteria that inform the application of each one of these terms are themselves complex and context-dependent. It is not obvious that one ought to lose one's appetite for a philosophical theory of perception upon consideration of the richness and complexity of the forms that the human relation to the world can take. It does, however, seem to me rather difficult to consider seriously the richness, complexity, and context-sensitivity of our concepts of experience and not become rather suspicious of the (purportedly) comprehensive, unified, and complete theories of perception (or experience) that Western philosophy has so far produced.[3]

Fifth, and relatedly, I do not take, and I do not take Wittgenstein to have taken, the experience he calls 'the dawning of an aspect' to be a manifestation of some *one* underlying, basic, relation that we have to the things of our world. It has been argued on Wittgenstein's behalf that the experience of aspect dawning is somehow a manifestation of some such basic relation, that it is that relation which constitutes Wittgenstein's true interest in his numerous remarks on aspect perception, and that that relation is what he refers to by 'continuous seeing (of an aspect)'. (See Mulhall 1990 and 2001, 153–82. See also Johnston 1994.) Elsewhere I have argued (see Baz 2000, 2010), first, that there is a very important sense in which aspects, as Wittgenstein thinks of them, can (conceptually) '*only* dawn, but not remain' (RPP I §1021); and, second, that in the one place in which Wittgenstein speaks of the 'continuous seeing' of an aspect, he is talking about a

---

[3] With the sole exception, perhaps, of the one presented in Merleau-Ponty 2002.

rather special and very local phenomenon—the case, namely, in which someone looks at an object that *others* know to be ambiguous (which is not our relation to most objects in our world), 'sees it under' one of its two or more 'aspects', and *fails to realize* that there are other 'aspects under which the object can be seen'[4]—a phenomenon which is not at all at the centre of Wittgenstein's concern, but rather is one that he feels he 'must distinguish' from what concerns him (Baz 2000, 112–14). I therefore propose, though I will not in this chapter argue for this proposal, that we take Wittgenstein at his word when he tells us that he is interested in the concept of 'the *dawning* of an aspect' and in *its* relation to other concepts of experience (PI II, 193).

Sixth, and finally, I do not take, and I do not take Wittgenstein to have taken, the experience of aspect dawning to present us with an apparent paradox, or indeed with anything like some particular *obvious* problem (or apparent obvious problem) that calls in some obvious way for a philosophical solution (or dissolution).[5] What we do have is an experience, or a set of variously related types of experience, which is *indeed* striking—the striking experience of being struck, if you will. As *such*, it may well be given *causal* explanations. There is nothing wrong with such explanations, but Wittgenstein clearly thinks that there are certain types of difficulty that would remain intact, however good our causal explanation of some particular type of experience may be. (See PI II, 193.)

The striking experience of aspect dawning may invoke any number of *conceptual* difficulties and unclarities; and Wittgenstein was very much concerned with those. But *conceptually* speaking, 'Everything has changed and yet nothing has changed', or 'I see that it has not changed; and yet I see it differently', is no more paradoxical or apparently paradoxical in the case of aspect perception than it would be if said by someone who has had a revelation, or by someone who has undergone successful therapy, or by someone who simply has had a mood swing. Similarly, 'Now it's a duck (or a rabbit, or a face)' is no more paradoxical when used to express the dawning of an aspect than 'Now it is clear' would be if we said it of a mathematical formula that had just been explained to us (while knowing, of course, that the formula itself has not changed). Our typical ways of giving voice to the dawning of an aspect are no more paradoxical, or apparently paradoxical, than 'war is war' (or Mary Poppins' characteristic 'Oh well, if we must, we must') would be tautological, or apparently tautological, when used significantly (see PI II, 221). In all such cases, if we could only become clear on what Wittgenstein calls 'the application (*Anwendung*) or use (*Gebrauch*)' of the words—that is, on the circumstances under which they would (normally) be uttered, on the point they would (normally) have when uttered, on the significance and possible consequences of uttering them under various

---

[4] I use quotation marks here so as not to pre-judge what exactly 'seeing' and 'aspect' come to in this case.

[5] The idea that there is an 'inherent paradoxality' which for Wittgenstein 'defines' the dawning of an aspect is the point of departure for Mulhall's interpretation (see, for example, 2001, 154). Now of course, Mulhall will ultimately wish to show us how this inherent paradoxality can be 'dissolved' (by reminding ourselves of our basic and typical relation to pictures and possibly also to all of the other objects of our world). I take issue both with the details of Mulhall's 'dissolution of the paradox' as well as with its general thrust in Baz 2010. For Mulhall's response, see Mulhall 2010.

circumstances, on what proper (and improper) responses to them would be under various circumstances, on the significance and possible consequences of different kinds of response, on the conditions that must be in place if they are to be meant in one way or another etc.—there would, *conceptually speaking*, be nothing further to find out, or discover, about what is referred to, or what is expressed, by means of those words.[6] This is not to say that attaining conceptual clarity with respect to the seemingly thoroughly familiar phenomena of our world is easy. In the case of aspect perception, for example, the pursuit of clarity ended up requiring hundreds of remarks, and many years of work on Wittgenstein's part that never resulted in anything like a satisfying conclusion.[7]

Background

I said that the second part of the *Brown Book* contains Wittgenstein's first sustained engagement with the topic of aspect perception, or seeing something as something. And indeed, here we encounter for the first time the picture puzzle wherein mere dashes come to be seen as a face, the schematic drawing of a cube which can be seen as a cube but also as the plane figure of a square and two rhombuses, a square with two diagonals which can be seen as a swastika, a line of four dots that can be seen as two pairs of dots side by side with each other or as two interlocking pairs, W which can be seen as an upside down M, and other more or less similar cases, of the sort that also come up in section xi and elsewhere in Wittgenstein's later writings. What leads Wittgenstein to the topic of aspect perception, or seeing something as something? Neither the idea that his philosophy aims at re-presenting us with 'aspects of things that are most important to us [but which] are hidden because of their simplicity and familiarity' (PI §129);[8] nor the attempt to solve 'the paradox of rule-following' by proposing the seeing of aspects as 'a way of grasping a rule which is *not* an *interpretation*' (PI §201);[9] nor his realization of the limitations of his 'idea' that 'the meaning of a word is its use in the language' (PI §43), or that 'essence is expressed by grammar' (PI §371).[10] And he certainly does not come to speak of aspects as a way of revealing something general about human perception as such. Rather, Wittgenstein comes to the topic of aspect perception in an attempt to say

[6] Here I find myself in thorough agreement with Marie McGinn (1997). See, for example, p. 179.

[7] Witness Wittgenstein's saying to Maurice Drury, not long before his death and after many years of thinking about aspect perception: 'Now try and say what is involved in seeing something as something; it is not easy. These thoughts I am now having are as hard as granite' (quoted in Monk 1990, 537). He, apparently, did not find that the remarks composing section xi, or indeed all of the remarks he had written up to that point, had laid to rest all that may be puzzling and difficult to see clearly about aspect perception.

[8] A line of approach to the remarks on aspects that was first proposed by Debra Aidun (1982), explored later at much greater length by Judith Genova (1995), and received a quite insightful and contemporary twist in Affeldt 2010.

[9] A line of interpretation pushed by Eddy Zemach in his 1992 and 1995.

[10] In line with Rush Rhees' preface to the *Blue and Brown Books*.

something about the nature and source of a certain type of difficulty that arises when we 'do philosophy'.

To summarize the second part of the *Brown Book* would be impossible. Not only does Wittgenstein attack his target from various directions and in different ways, and not only does each line of attack open up new difficulties and possible confusions, but it is also the case that the target itself has several dimensions and sometimes seems to shift in mid-argument. In reading this text one sees what Wittgenstein means when he says in the preface to the *Investigations* that it used to be his ambition to present his thoughts in such a way that they would 'proceed from one subject to another in a natural order and without breaks'; for this ambition is clearly manifested in the *Brown Book*. But one can also see why Wittgenstein ultimately came to the conclusion that his ambition resulted in a 'crippling' of his thoughts, and why he decided to give it up.

One theme that comes up again and again in *The Brown Book*, however, just as it comes up again and again in the *Investigations*, is how we ought to conceive of our mental states and processes—states and processes as varied as recognizing, understanding, reading, being guided, finding a similarity, thinking, wishing, expecting, believing, knowing, deriving, and following a rule. There is a tendency 'in philosophy' to which Wittgenstein is responding to think that any particular sort of mental state (or process)—the state of recognizing something, for example—is the particular sort of 'object' that it is in virtue of a particular *something* which all 'objects' of this sort have in common and which *makes us* call them what we call them. So the philosophical position to which Wittgenstein is responding takes the general form of insisting that there must be (a) *something* in which Φing consists (where 'Φing' stands for recognizing, understanding, reading, etc.). (See BB, 86, 99, 144.)

To this tendency to look for that something in which Φing consists, Wittgenstein responds in a variety of ways, not all of which are directly relevant to the purposes of this paper. Two central moves, familiar from the *Investigations*, are the invitation to 'look and see' that there is in fact no one thing (in the *Brown Book* mostly spoken of in terms of 'an experience') which is common to all of the cases of Φing (see BB, 156), and the introduction of the idea of 'family resemblance' as an alternative to the prevailing picture of how all of the things (and 'things') to which some particular word (or concept) applies relate to one another (see BB, 87–8, 125).

The above moves are not specific to Wittgenstein's treatment of mental state concepts. In the case of these concepts, there is the further move of suggesting that what guides and informs our application of the concepts (our use of the words) are 'outward'—that is, publicly accessible and assessable—criteria. This move is still not fully developed in the *Brown Book* (and, in fact, the word 'criteria' is nowhere used in that text, though it is used a few times in the *Blue Book*); but it is certainly present there, together with one of the strongest sources of resistance to it—namely, the idea that the mental state cannot *consist* in the presence of criteria, for it is conceptually possible for any set of criteria for Φing to be present while Φing itself is absent (see BB, 144, 149). In response to this objection Wittgenstein invokes the example of the 'friendly face' (BB, 145)—a beautiful example, to my mind, which did not make it to the *Investigations* (but see PI §583–4). The example is meant to remind us that it may be perfectly correct to say of certain eyes that they are friendly, and even to say that they are what makes the face friendly, even though those very same eyes, or eyes perfectly (descriptively) identical to them, could feature in a face that was not at all friendly, and even though in such a face they would *not be* (aptly describable as) friendly. And the lesson of the example is that some particular feature (or set of features) may, under suitable circumstances, perfectly legitimately, and correctly, be taken as a criterion of, say, understanding, even though it is possible for that same feature (or set of features) to be present where understanding is absent. And just as in the case of the eyes what makes the difference is not something essentially hidden but rather the rest of the face (and possibly other features of their environment), in the case of criteria what makes the difference is what Wittgenstein calls the 'circumstances' (or sometimes, in the *Investigations*, the 'context') in which they are present. And this in effect suggests that the criteria for someone's '*merely appearing* to understand' (or 'saying something *without* believing it', etc.) are no less public, outward, than those for someone's 'understanding' (or 'believing what she says', etc.) (see BB, 144–5).

This attempt to effect a transformation in the way that we think of our various mental states takes another form in what may most generally be described as a distinction that Wittgenstein draws between '*What happens* when one Φs (recognizes, understands, reads, etc.)' and 'What Φing *is* (what "Φing" means)'. The general idea is that we confuse the two, or confusedly look for the latter in the former: we attend to instances of Φing in an attempt to find out what Φing is (what 'Φing' means); but the only thing we may reasonably expect to find in this way is, at best, things that happen when one Φs. And then we are bound to be disappointed, for even if we did (rather implausibly) find something that happens whenever one, say, understands, what would justify taking *it* to be that in which understanding consists? 'Even supposing that I had found something that happened in all those cases of understanding,—why should *it* be the understanding?' (PI §153).

The reader may begin to wonder at this point how all of this connects with the seeing of aspects. And the answer is that it connects in at least two ways. First, seeing an aspect is itself a mental state; and here too there is the tendency, as we shall see, to attend closely to *the experience* in an attempt to find out what seeing an aspect is—what it consists in. And this tendency, as we shall see, may lead to philosophical difficulties. More immediately, however, Wittgenstein's discussion of the tendency, in philosophy, to attend closely to an instance of Φing in order to find out what Φing is provides the background for his engagement with the seeing of aspects in the *Brown Book*.

'A QUITE PARTICULAR'

In both the *Brown Book* and the *Investigations* Wittgenstein comes to attend to what he calls 'the grammar (or use)' of the expression '(a quite) particular (peculiar, certain, *bestimmt*)' (BB, 135, and note attached to PI §165). And it is in the course of his investigation of the grammar of that expression that he comes, in the *Brown Book*, to the topic of aspect perception. Wittgenstein's reason for attending to the grammar of this expression is that he finds that 'in philosophy' the expression is often used to give voice to a kind of experience that involves what Wittgenstein calls 'an illusion (or delusion)'.[11]

I said above that according to Wittgenstein there is a tendency 'in philosophy' to attend to an instance of Φing in order to find out what Φing is, or what it consists in. I believe that Wittgenstein is quite right about this. (Just think, for example, of G. E. Moore waving an envelope in front of his audience and inviting them to attend to what happens when they see it, in order to find out what seeing something consists in.) Now, when 'in philosophy' we attend in this way to an instance of Φing (mostly an *enacted*, or *imagined* instance of Φing), we tend, according to Wittgenstein, to come out with utterances like 'the name of the color comes *in a particular* way (when I *name* the color of the object, as opposed to merely uttering the word while looking at the object)' (BB, 149, see also 150), or 'In reading the spoken words come in *a particular* way' (BB, 167), or 'reading is *a quite particular process*' (PI §165), or 'being guided is surely *a particular* experience' (PI §173).

As we've already seen, one thing that Wittgenstein says about this type of philosophical moment is that we should 'look and see' and 'ask ourselves' whether the experience to which we attend in such moments is always present whenever one Φs. He goes further than this, however, and suggests that the experience we attend to in such moments is not only not common to all of the cases of Φing, but is actually one that *we create* by attending in the way that we do to an (enacted) instance of Φing. For example, the experience of 'homely feeling' that we might wish to claim as characteristic of moments in which we encounter a word that we understand may in fact be 'an experience rather characteristic for the particular situation…of philosophizing about "understanding"' (BB, 157). Similarly, 'what is *particular* about the way "red" comes [when we name the colour of a red object] is that it comes while you're philosophizing about it' (BB, 159, see also 160, 167, and 177).

This very same idea—that what we find when we attend to an instance of Φing in order to find what Φing consists in is really something that we create by this very (specific form of) attending—returns in the *Investigations* (cf. PI §170, 175), with the additional suggestion that what we experience in such moments results from our looking at the case through 'the medium' of the very concept that we are trying to clarify for ourselves or some related concept (see PI §§176–7). I find thought-provoking the suggestion that we affect what we find when we attend philosophically to an instance of Φing, by looking at 'what happens' through the medium of our concept of 'Φing' or some related concept. For one thing, it seems to connect with the topic of 'experiencing the meaning of a word' that comes up in section xi: the medium of the concept of 'Φing', as Wittgenstein thinks about it in this connection, may plausibly be thought of, it seems to me, as the experienced meaning (physiognomy) of 'Φing'. I note this connection without expanding, partly as a way of further indicating the complex ways in which Wittgenstein's topics of investigation intertwine, but partly also in order to alert those interested in the notion of 'experiencing the meaning of the word' to the possibility that here too a kind of illusion might be in play that results from our attending to *the word* in a rather atypical and artificial way (see, in this connection, PI II, 215).

---

[11] In the *Brown Book*, Wittgenstein seems to be using these two terms interchangeably.

Still on our way to aspect perception, let us go back to '(a quite) particular' and to the idea that 'in philosophy' this expression often betokens a particular kind of illusion. Wittgenstein attempts to explicate the nature of the illusion (or delusion) he is talking about by distinguishing between the 'transitive' and 'intransitive' uses of 'particular (peculiar, certain)' (BB, 158). In the transitive use we talk, for example, of the particular expression of a face, or of the particular way in which someone enters a room, where the expression or way we speak of is separable from the particular object that we perceive (the face, the person walking into the room), in the sense that we can describe it, or otherwise specify or identify it as this or that expression (or way of entering the room), which can be shared by other faces (or persons). So we may say, for example, 'She has a quite particular way of walking into a room, namely ...', and now we give a description.

In the intransitive use of the term, on the other hand, we again may talk about the particular expression of a face, or the particular way in which someone enters a room, but here the expression, or way, is inseparable from the particular instance we speak of, in the sense that we could *try* to specify what expression, or way, we are talking about, but ultimately we find that no such specification satisfies us (BB, 162); and what we rather find we want to do is simply point to the face, or to the person walking into the room, and let the expression, or way, identify itself, as it were, as the *particular* expression, or way, that it is. I will come back to this Heideggerian idea of letting something present itself in the final section of this chapter.

The 'delusion' Wittgenstein is talking about results from confusing the intransitive and the transitive uses of 'a quite particular' and taking ourselves to have *identified* the expression (or way, etc.) just by attending to it. This has an interesting connection to the topic of 'private language' in the *Investigations*; for the mistake we make in such moments, according to Wittgenstein, is to think that we could, so to speak, identify a *nameable* something—a possible name-bearer—to which we could now give any name that we would like (say, 'expression A'), 'without at the same time committing ourselves about its [the name's] use, and in fact without any intention of using it at all' (BB, 159, see also 172–3).

The moments in which we attend, in the course of 'doing philosophy', to an instance of Φing in order to find out what Φing consists in, are, according to Wittgenstein, moments in which we are likely to fall into the above illusion: We take ourselves to have *identified*, individuated, some particular experience that occurs whenever one recognizes something, or reads, or follows a rule, etc., whereas in fact we are only 'laying an emphasis' on the particular instance to which we attend, *by* attending to it in the particular way that we do (see BB, 160).

Of course, we *need not* merely attend to what happens to or in us in such moments. We *could* try to identify, by describing, the particular experience to which we attend when we look for the essence of Φing. But what is likely to happen if we succeeded is one of two things (or some combination of them). Either we would find that it is utterly implausible to suppose that 'the experience' of, say, understanding, *as we have described it*, is present whenever one understands something; or we would find that we have merely managed to push elsewhere the bump in the rug, not to eliminate it. The latter would occur if we tried, for example, to explicate the notion of 'naming' in terms of 'finding a similarity' (between all of the things to which some particular name applies). Wittgenstein would then invite us to 'look and see' and 'ask ourselves' what is similar between all of the cases of 'finding a similarity' (BB, 132). Or if we tried to explicate the notion of 'reading' in terms of 'being guided' (by the signs), Wittgenstein would invite us to consider all of the different possible cases of being guided and to acknowledge that there is no particular feature that is common to all of those cases and which makes them (or makes us call them) cases of being guided (PI §172).[12] And so we find ourselves in a philosophical bind: the attempt to identify 'transitively' the particular something in which Φing consists leads us to a something all right, but a something which cannot plausibly be taken to be that in which Φing consists. The attempt to identify that something 'intransitively' by means of what is essentially 'a private ostensive definition', on the other hand, does not amount to so much as an *identification* of anything in which Φing might consist.

And here, finally, is how I understand Wittgenstein's way of connecting all of the above with aspect perception. We spoke of the 'illusion' or 'delusion' of attending to something and taking oneself to have managed to identify something in or about it—something which one takes to be separable from the particular thing in which it is manifested, but which is not in fact thus separable, in the sense that it has not (yet) been identified in a way that would enable one to re-identify it correctly or incorrectly in other things and on other occasions. And here it might seem that seeing an aspect—seeing something as something—is precisely *not* an example of *that*; for in the case of the aspect it seems that we do have two things—namely, the object and the particular aspect, or aspects, under which it can be seen. Consider, however, how you might specify the aspect you see—how you might say, or describe, *what you see* when a particular aspect strikes you. Take the duck-rabbit, for example. What do you see when you see, not merely the duck-rabbit (which may be described and thereby identified geometrically), but, say, *the rabbit aspect*? The obvious answer would seem to be 'a picture-rabbit' (or maybe 'a rabbit') (PI II, 194). Now, if you were asked what *that* (i.e. a picture-rabbit, or a rabbit) was, you could point to non-schematic pictures of rabbits, or to real rabbits, etc. (ibid.). But note the important sense in which pointing to a non-ambiguous rabbit, whether flesh and blood or depicted, as a way of specifying what you saw, would be misleading: it would suggest that you were somehow *mistaking* the duck-rabbit for a non-ambiguous rabbit, whereas this is clearly *not* what happens (BB, 164). What you see, when you see the rabbit aspect, is, well, *this*. And now one would like simply to point to the duck-rabbit, perhaps with the addition of hints to help the other see the rabbit aspect, if for some reason she has not yet been able to see it.

Similarly, when you look at a picture-puzzle and suddenly see a face where before you saw mere dashes, there is a sense in which it would be quite misleading to point to

---

[12] And if we wanted to insist that there was in fact a common feature to all of the instances of 'being guided', and proposed that it was, say, a certain *carefulness* with which we attended to what guided us (PI §173), or a certain kind of *deliberation* with which we were following the signs (PI §174), then we would find ourselves running once again into the above two difficulties.

anything other than the picture-puzzle as a way of specifying what you saw.[13] Seeing something as something is importantly not a case of seeing two independently describable things (BB, 169). In this respect, the aspect is like the expression of the face or someone's way of entering a room (insofar, of course, as those cannot (fully) be described and thereby identified)—it too is inseparable from the object in which it is manifested. It is this similarity between aspects, on the one hand, and what we find when we attend to instances of Φing in order to discover what Φing consists in, on the other hand, that leads Wittgenstein to the topic of aspect perception in the *Brown Book* (see BB, 163–4 and 168–9).

Aspect Perception, Aspect–Blindness, and Philosophical Difficulty

Here we could have ended; but I wanted to propose two possible directions for future thinking that proceed from what I have said so far.

I spoke of Wittgenstein's attempt to transform the way in which we think of our various mental states; and I said that the attempt involved drawing a distinction between, on the one hand, the various things that happen when one Φs and, on the other hand, what Φing is, or what 'Φing' means or refers to. In section xi the distinction between what happens when one Φs and what Φing is comes up a couple of times in connection with phenomena other than the seeing of aspects. Thus Wittgenstein talks of 'important phenomena of talking' that are missing when one talks without thinking, but warns us against supposing that those phenomena are the thinking (PI II, 218); or he talks about whatever might be going on 'in our consciousness' when a word is on the tip of our tongue, and warns us against supposing that *that* is what is meant by 'The word is on the tip of my tongue' (PI II, 219).

But now, the seeing of an aspect is itself a mental state. And here too we may suppose that there is no better way of clarifying the nature of that state for ourselves than enacting an instance of it and attending to what happens while we are 'in it' (see BB, 164). We may ask, for example, what happens when the likeness of one face to another strikes us, and any number of phenomena would then suggest themselves to us as 'the phenomena of being struck' (PI II, 211). But is any of these phenomena, or some particular subset of

---

[13] In the two cases I discuss, there may be another way of describing what one sees. One could try to describe the *particular* rabbit one sees—its expression, perhaps, if one finds that it has a ('transitively') particular one. One could similarly try to characterize the face one has seen in the picture-puzzle—its features, expression, etc. It is important for Wittgenstein's purposes in the *Brown Book* that the examples he uses would not be taken as allowing for this option, I think, which is perhaps why he does not use the duck-rabbit, and focuses rather on the square with diagonals that can be seen as a swastika and on the schematic cube which can be seen three-dimensionally. There is nothing *specific* about the (three-dimensional) cube one sees in the drawing; and the only non-misleading way of characterizing the *specific* swastika that one sees the square with diagonals *as* would make it descriptively identical to a square with diagonals.

them, what being struck is? Wittgenstein's answer to this question is 'No' (ibid.). Earlier we mentioned some of his general reasons for giving that answer; but let me try to motivate it in the specific case of aspect perception.

Take the 'aspect-blind'—the person defined by Wittgenstein as someone 'lacking in the capacity to see something *as something*' (PI II, 213). In my experience, the general tendency among readers of Wittgenstein's remarks on aspects is to take it to be quite clear what aspect-blindness is—what 'aspect-blindness' means.[14] Wittgenstein, on the other hand, goes on to say, immediately after introducing the term, that we should 'next consider what might be meant [by "aspect-blindness"]' (ibid.), suggesting that what is, or might be, meant by that term may turn out not to be clear at all.

Who, or what, is the aspect-blind? What is it, more specifically, that he cannot see, or have? Here we may be inclined to enact for ourselves an instance of the experience of aspect dawning, focus our attention on the experience—on what happens when we have it—and say 'Why, clearly, *this* is what the aspect-blind cannot see (or have)!' To see that this answer to our question ought not to satisfy us, consider our friend the 'aspect denier'. He says:

> Call me an aspect-blind, if you want, but I think that you have gotten yourself altogether confused by speaking of what you call 'aspects' in terms of a particular type of *visual* experience, and by describing the dawning of an aspect as a moment in which *what you see* changes. You take yourself to have identified some clear and definite advantage that you supposedly have over those that you call 'aspect-blind', but I think that the advantage is illusory, and is, at any rate, not a matter of one person having and the other lacking the capacity to have some *particular kind of visual experience* or to *see* some particular kind of 'object of sight'. It seems to me rather more plausible to think of the difference between you self-titled 'aspect-perceivers' and people like myself as a difference in manner of speaking; and mine seems to me better, in that it does not encourage false, or at any rate unduly complicated, pictures, and theories, of what you call 'aspect perception' and 'aspect dawning'.
>
> No one would deny that many things in our world, maybe even all of them, are such that they may serve different purposes, naturally or conventionally mean different things, or in any other way come to have different significances *for us*. Accordingly, those things may occasion different modes of engagement on our part: we may come to take them in different ways, regard or handle them in different ways, and feel different things in relation to them, depending on the circumstances under which we encounter them.
>
> Now, many of Wittgenstein's examples rely on our ability to imaginatively place ourselves variously with respect to some given object; and this is helped by the fact that many of the examples feature very schematic drawings that are encountered in the artificial context of psychological or philosophical inquiry—apart from any of the specific circumstances in which objects normally are encountered in the course of everyday life. So now, take the duck-rabbit, for example—a schematic drawing cleverly made in such a way that most people would quite easily be able to see

---

[14] For a refreshing recent move in the opposite direction—in the case of '*meaning*-blindness'—though one very different from the one I attempt in what follows, see Minar 2010.

(or brought to see)—and 'see' *not* in the sense of 'having some particular visual experience', but in the sense of 'come to (propositionally) know through the sense of sight'—that it could equally well be (in the sense of *serve as*) a schematic picture of a duck and a schematic picture of a rabbit. I can easily see these two 'aspects' of the drawing myself—I mean, see that the drawing 'has' them. And in focusing my attention on one of the two things this drawing could have been (the two different things it could serve as) I can enact in myself various kinds of sensations, emotions, feelings, images, etc. My ability to do this is not essentially different or more mysterious than my ability to imagine my front door opening to an abyss, and thereby to enact in myself various experiences associated with *that*.

And so, I *see* the duck-rabbit, and I *see* (in the sense of 'coming to (propositionally) know through the sense of sight') *that* it could serve to schematically depict either a duck or a rabbit. Beyond this, there is nothing to *see*—nothing particularly *visual* to be had—in or about the duck-rabbit. The two 'visual achievements' that *can* be had, on the other hand, can be had by any normal person with normal eyesight; and to think of the person you call 'aspect-blind' as unable to do *these* two things would be to think of him as suffering from a handicap *far* worse than that of merely 'being unable to see something as something', whatever exactly *that* may mean.

What could we say in response to this? Shall we say, 'But what about the flipping back and forth, and the totality of the change? Look, *now* it's a duck, and *now* it's a rabbit!'? Or shall we say, 'But look, *everything* changes when the rabbit-aspect replaces the duck-aspect; we see that the drawing has not changed, and yet see it *altogether* differently!'? I think it ought to be clear that these kinds of response will not impress our aspect-denier (or aspect-redescriber). Nothing that we can say about *our experience* and what it is like would be taken by him as a reason to think that he was missing something in his account.

We might think: 'But of course he cannot see what is missing in his account. That is precisely because he is an aspect-blind. He cannot, by hypothesis, have *this* type of experience (and now we enact the experience for ourselves and focus our attention on it as we say "*this*"); and this is precisely why nothing would convince him that he was missing something. Until he has had an aspect dawn on him, he is bound to misunderstand our various ways of expressing ourselves when an aspect dawns on us, and there can be no way for us to show him that he really does misunderstand. But let him just once *experience* the dawning of an aspect, and he will never thereafter deny the existence of this type of experience.' I think it ought to be clear that this response too will not do: our aspect-denier is going to insist that he is not denying anything real, that he knows exactly what experience we talk about and has fully accounted for it, and that he simply refuses to join us in speaking of that experience in misleading and confusing ways that make it appear mysterious.

Let me emphasize that the question under dispute is not whether aspect-dawning may aptly be described as a type of *experience*. The question is rather *what sort* of an experience it is, or how we should *conceive* of it. And my aim, in invoking the aspect-denier, has only been to show the futility of trying to answer *this* question by means of attending to what happens in or to us when we enjoy this type of experience.

A more promising line of response to the aspect-denier, it seems to me, would require shifting the focus away from the duck-rabbit and the other schematic drawings. This would anyway be an advisable move, for there is something importantly artificial and therefore impoverished in those examples of 'aspect-dawning'. The simplicity of those examples makes them useful for certain purposes; but one has got to keep in mind that none of the concepts that are under investigation in Wittgenstein's remarks has its 'original home' in artificial encounters of the sort that we have with these schematic drawings, which is why we are almost bound to mislead ourselves in important respects if we take these encounters as paradigmatic instances of the seeing of aspects.

Essential to the aspect-denier's account is the fact that each of the schematic drawings is such that, in a suitable context, it *could* just have *been*, could just have served as, a schematic drawing of whatever aspect it could be seen under. Thus the duck-rabbit could have served as a schematic drawing of a duck, or a rabbit; and similarly, the triangle that can be seen as triangular hole, as a solid, as an overturned object which is meant to stand on the shorter side of the right angle, etc. (PI II, 200) could have actually served as a representation of any of those things. This is something that Wittgenstein recognizes when he considers the proposal that 'the aspects in a change of aspects are those ones which the figure might sometimes have *permanently* in a picture' (PI II, 201). And so, in the case of these schematic drawings there are possible 'interpretations' of the drawing, and the different aspects under which it can be seen *correspond* to its possible interpretations (see PI II, 193). The availability of such interpretations is essential to the aspect-denier's account; for his proposal is that we attend at will to different such interpretations, and thereby enact in ourselves different experiences that are associated with the different interpretations and which we misleadingly think of as *visual*.

Consider, however, the example that Wittgenstein uses to introduce the concept of 'aspect dawning': being struck by the similarity between two faces. This case is different from that of the duck-rabbit in several important respects.[15] The difference that is important for our present purposes is that here the aspect that dawns does not normally correspond to a possible interpretation of the object, or to something that, in a suitable context, that object could just have *been*. There is normally, in other words, no *fact* about the object which may simply be *known* and on our knowledge of which the various experiences invoked in the aspect-denier's account could be parasitic. It is, of course, *possible* for one face just to be similar to another—as a matter of empirical fact that can empirically be established; but this is not normally the case when the similarity of one face to another dawns on us. On the contrary, it is precisely typical of those moments that there is no such empirically establishable fact, and that the perceiver *acknowledges* that the similarity she sees is not such that it could empirically be established: if the other could

---

[15] One of which is that here the object is not ambiguous in the way that the duck-rabbit (or even the triangle) is, and the aspect that dawns cannot plausibly be thought of as competing with, and as having replaced, something else that may sensibly be called 'an aspect'. This has important implications for the prevailing tendency to propose, on behalf of Wittgenstein, that our normal (and continuous) relation to what we see is that of seeing it under some aspect or another.

not see it, or even denied its presence, there would be no way of proving her wrong (though we sometimes feel, and say, that there is something to which she is blind).[16]

But now, how do I know all this? How do I know that aspects need not, and in fact normally do not, correspond to a possible interpretation of the object, or to an empirically establishable fact about it? Not, I wish to propose, by attending to instances of aspect perception and asking myself what happens, but rather by attending to what Wittgenstein would call 'the language-game of seeing aspects': the circumstances under which aspects would normally be seen, the ways in which the seeing of an aspect normally would be expressed, the intersubjective significance of giving voice to the seeing of an aspect, and so on.

The crucial move in the aspect-denier's 'conjuring trick' (PI §308) is to encourage us to focus on *what happens* when an aspect is seen (and on examples whose artificiality pretty much ensures that there would be nothing else for us to focus on), and to suppose that *that* is what one would need to know in order to know what the dawning of an aspect is and what the aspect-blind would, by definition, be incapable of seeing, or having. Again, I am not saying that it is wrong to think of the aspect-blind as lacking in the capacity to enjoy a particular kind of *experience*; I am saying, rather, that it is philosophically unhelpful and even dangerous to try to answer the question of *what* sort of experience it is by attending to instances of it and asking ourselves what happens.

It is better—philosophically less confusing—to think of the aspect-blind as failing to cotton on to, failing to see and appreciate the *point* of, a language-game in which we 'say what we see', not in order to *inform* the other, who typically sees the object as clearly as we do (PI II, 193), of some empirical fact about that object, and not merely in order to let the other know what experiences the sight of the object happens to invoke *in us*, but rather in order to *invite* the other to see something in or about the object—something that strikes us as there to be seen, even though we normally acknowledge that there is no way for us to establish its presence. *Pace* the aspect-denier, the concept of 'seeing' does force itself on us here; but what seeing comes to in this case is not to be discovered by focusing on an enacted or remembered instance of aspect perception, nor by consulting our ideas of what 'seeing' *must* mean. Rather, it is to be found by reminding ourselves of how 'seeing' is used when it is used to express, and speak of, the seeing of an aspect.

Aspect Perception and Things that Speak to Us

So as not to end this chapter on a 'negative', 'merely' therapeutic, note, let me very briefly indicate one further line of thinking. I spoke above of the 'illusion' or 'delusion' that Wittgenstein detects in those moments in which we attend to instances of Φing in order to find out what Φing is, and of how he connects it with our failure to distinguish between the transitive and intransitive use of *'ein ganz bestimmt'*. These are the moments, Wittgenstein

---

[16] This is what led me, in Baz 2000, to liken the seeing of an aspect to the seeing of beauty, especially as characterized by Kant in his *Critique of the Power of Judgment*.

tells us, in which we wish simply to point to what we see and let it, or whatever in or about it that strikes us, articulate itself, as it were—speak for itself (see BB, 174–5 and 177).

The illusion that Wittgenstein is talking about is a matter of taking ourselves to have *already* successfully identified that which struck us about the object, merely by focusing our attention on 'it'. It is important for Wittgenstein that we do not (yet) have a nameable something if there is no way of distinguishing between correct and incorrect identifications of it; and this is not something that can be achieved by sheer acts of attention, or by what Wittgenstein calls 'an "inward" act of pointing' (BB, 174).

I want to end this chapter by emphasizing that there is nothing inherently or necessarily confused in those moments in which we seem to see something about an object that on the one hand impresses us, or strikes us as worth attending to, but on the other hand is such that no attempt at describing or articulating it satisfies us. (Compare Kant's 'aesthetic idea'—the intuition to which 'no determinate thought would be adequate'.[17]) I see no reason to suppose, and nothing said in this chapter was meant to imply, that Wittgenstein wanted to dismiss as illusory or deny the significance of these moments. There is nothing necessarily confused about 'Words can't exactly describe it' (BB, 162), as long as we do not take ourselves to have already identified the 'it' which words cannot exactly describe, but rather acknowledge, precisely, that there is something about the object which we have not yet been able, and maybe never will be able, to identify in a way that would satisfy us and enable us to conceive of it apart from its particular manifestation in a particular object.

When Wittgenstein speaks of the 'illusion [that] possesses us [when in] repeating a tune to ourselves and letting it make its full impression on us, we say "This tune says *something*", and it is as though [we] had to find *what* it says' (ibid.), it is important to remember that the illusion he speaks of is only a matter of our taking ourselves to have already identified the something which the tune says. *That* we are drawn to the tune, and find ourselves *wanting* to 'say what it says', or to say that 'it says something', does not *need* to involve any kind of illusion—not as long as we see these moments, and their significance, for what they are.[18,19]

---

[17] Kant 2000, academy page number 314.

[18] Wittgenstein says in this connection that he once looked with a friend at beds of pansies, and both he and his friend were impressed by each bed in turn. His friend then said: 'What a variety of colour patterns, and each says something', and Wittgenstein adds that this is what he himself wished to say, without dismissing as illusory that moment and that way of expressing oneself (BB, 178). And compare things that he is reported by a student to have said in a lecture given a few years after the composition of the *Brown Book*:

> One of the most interesting points which the question of not being able to describe is connected with, [is that] the impression which a certain verse or bar in music gives you is indescribable. 'I don't know what it is…Look at this transition….What is it?…' I think you would say it gives you experiences which can't be described. First of all it is, of course, not true that whenever we hear a piece of music or a line of poetry which impresses us greatly, we say: 'This is indescribable'. But it is true that again and again we do feel inclined to say: 'I can't describe my experience'. I have in mind a case that saying one is incapable of describing *comes from* [my emphasis] being intrigued and *wanting* [Wittgenstein's emphasis] to describe, asking oneself: 'What is this? What's he doing, wanting to do here?—Gosh, If I could only say what he's doing here.' (LC, 37)

[19] In writing this chapter I was very helpfully challenged, provoked, and informed by Dan Dennett. I am grateful to a Tufts Bernstein Faculty Fellowship that enabled and encouraged us to converse on the

REFERENCES

AFFELDT, STEVEN (2010). 'On the Difficulty of Seeing Aspects and the "Therapeutic" Reading of Wittgenstein', in William Day and Victor Krebs eds., *Seeing Wittgenstein Anew*. Cambridge: Cambridge University Press.

AIDUN, DEBRA (1982). 'Wittgenstein's Philosophical Method and Aspect-Seeing', *Philosophical Investigations*, 5: 106–15.

BAZ, AVNER (2000). 'What's the Point of Seeing Aspects?', *Philosophical Investigations*, 23(2): 97–121.

—— (2010). 'On Learning from Wittgenstein; or What Does it Take to *See* the Grammar of Seeing Aspects?', in William Day and Victor Krebs eds., *Seeing Wittgenstein Anew*. Cambridge: Cambridge University Press.

GENOVA, JUDITH (1995). *Wittgenstein: A Way of Seeing*. London: Routledge.

JOHNSTON, PAUL (1994). *Rethinking the Inner*. London: Routledge.

KANT, IMMANUEL (2000). *Critique of the Power of Judgment*, ed. Paul Guyer and Eric Mathews. Cambridge: Cambridge University Press.

McGINN, MARIE (1997). *Wittgenstein and the Philosophical Investigations*. London: Routledge.

MERLEAU-PONTY, MAURICE (2002). *Phenomenology of Perception*. London: Routledge.

MINAR, EDWARD (2010). 'The Philosophical Significance of Meaning Blindness', in William Day and Victor Krebs eds., *Seeing Wittgenstein Anew*. Cambridge: Cambridge University Press.

MONK, RAY (1990). *The Duty of Genius*. London: Vintage.

MULHALL, STEPHEN (1990). *On Being in the World*. London: Routledge.

—— (2000). 'Seeing Aspect', in Hans-Johann Glock ed., *Wittgenstein: A Critical Reader*. Oxford: Blackwell.

—— (2001). *Inheritance and Originality*. Oxford University Press.

—— (2010). 'The Work of Wittgenstein's Words: A Reply to Baz', in William Day and Victor Krebs eds., *Seeing Wittgenstein Anew*. Cambridge: Cambridge University Press.

WITTGENSTEIN, LUDWIG (1958). *Preliminary Studies for the 'Philosophical Investigations', Generally Known as the Blue and Brown Books*. Oxford: Basil Blackwell.

—— (1980). *Remarks on the Philosophy of Psychology*, Vol. 1, ed. G. E. M. Anscombe and G. H. von Wright, trans. G. E. M. Anscombe. Oxford: Blackwell.

—— (1983). *Lectures and Conversations on Aesthetics, Psychology and Religious Belief*, ed. Cyril Barrett. Oxford: Basil Blackwell.

—— (1997). *Philosophical Investigations*, 2nd edition, ed. G. E. M. Anscombe and R. Rhees, trans. G. E. M. Anscombe. Oxford: Blackwell Publishers.

ZEMACH, EDDY (1992). *The Reality of Meaning and the Meaning of 'Reality'*. Providence, RI: Brown University Press.

—— (1995). 'Meaning, the Experience of Meaning and the Meaning-Blind in Wittgenstein's Late Philosophy', *The Monist*, 78 (4): 480–95.

subject of aspect perception. The impact of those conversations on my thinking shows itself at many points in this chapter, and especially in my invocation of the aspect-denier, whose 'voice' is very much Dennett's. Needless to say, there is much in this chapter with which Dennett does not (fully) agree. I would also like to thank Christian Wenzel for a set of details and very helpful comments.

CHAPTER 31

WRITING PHILOSOPHY
AS POETRY: LITERARY
FORM IN WITTGENSTEIN

MARJORIE PERLOFF

"His disposition," Bertrand Russell wrote of the young Wittgenstein in 1912, "is that of an artist, intuitive and moody" (cited in Monk 1990, 43). A similar judgment was made some fifteen years later by Rudolf Carnap in Vienna:

> His point of view and his attitude toward people and problems...were much more similar to those of a creative artist than to those of a scientist; one might almost say similar to those of a religious prophet or a seer. When he started to formulate his view on some specific philosophical problem, we often felt the internal struggle that occurred in him at that very moment, a struggle by which he tried to penetrate from darkness to light under an intense and painful strain....When finally, sometimes after a prolonged and arduous effort, his answer came forth, his statement stood before us like a newly created piece of art or a divine revelation. (Monk 1990, 244)

And Wittgenstein himself, hoping, in 1919, to persuade Ludwig von Ficker, the editor of the literary journal *Der Brenner*, to publish his controversial *Tractatus Logico-Philosophicus*, remarked, "The work is strictly philosophical and at the same time literary" (Monk 1990, 177).

What is it that makes Wittgenstein's philosophical writing also—or perhaps even primarily—*literary*? "What is it," asks Terry Eagleton in the introduction to his own screenplay about the philosopher, "about this man, whose philosophy can be taxing and technical enough, which so fascinates the *artistic* imagination?" (Eagleton 1993, 5) The appeal is especially remarkable, given that Wittgenstein's writing, in the *Tractatus*, as well as in the *Philosophical Investigations* and the various posthumously published collections of notes and lectures, is known primarily in English translation—translation that for those of us who are native Austrian German-speakers often seems to distort what are in the original colloquial speech patterns and conversational rhythms. This is especially true of Wittgenstein's most obviously "poetic" work, *Culture and Value*, a collection of aphorisms and meditations on literary, religious, and anthropological topics, assembled from the philosopher's notes by G. H. von Wright in 1977. In the translator's note to the 1998 edition, Peter Winch admits that his original translation (1980) was problematic enough to warrant extensive revision[1] (Winch 1998, xviii–xix). But even this new version is characterized by translations like the following:

> Die Tragödie besteht darin daß sich der Baum nicht biegt sondern bricht.
> You get tragedy where the tree, instead of bending, breaks. (CV, 3)

More accurately, this would read, "Tragedy occurs when the tree doesn't bend, but breaks." Or again,

> Die Religion ist sozusagen der tiefste ruhige Meeresgrund, der ruhig bleibt, wie hoch auch die Wellen oben gehen.
> Religion is as it were the calm sea bottom at its deepest, remaining calm, however high the waves rise on the surface. (CV, 61)

But "sozusagen" literally means "so to speak," not the coy "as it were," and the "Meeresgrund" would not today be designated as the "sea bottom" but rather as the ocean floor, the stillness at whose deepest point is compared by Wittgenstein to the unshakability of true faith, impervious as that faith is to the passing religious fashions (the waves) of everyday life.

Elizabeth (G. E. M.) Anscombe, the translator of the *Investigations* and much of the later work, is more faithful to the original but similarly misleading when it comes to Wittgenstein's vernacular phrasing.[2] The adjective "herrlich," as in "Ist das Wetter heute nicht herrlich?" ("Isn't the weather beautiful today?") for example, is regularly rendered by the rather prissy "glorious." "Reigenspiele" is oddly translated as "games like ring-a-ring o' roses," a name that overspecifies, since there are many other circle games (e.g. "A tisket, a tasket") (PI §§21, 32). Or again, the proposition "Es ist uns, als müßten wir die Erscheinungen *durchschauen*" (PI §90), "We feel as if we had to *see through* outward appearances"—a common enough state of mind—becomes the more abstract "We feel as if we had to *penetrate* phenomena."

Even in such ungainly translation, however, Wittgenstein's writing has impressed its readers as decidedly "poetic." But in what sense? In a well-known journal entry of 1934, reproduced in *Culture and Value*, Wittgenstein remarks:

> Ich glaube meine Stellung zur Philosophie dadurch zusammengefaßt zu haben indem ich sagte: Philosophie dürfte man eigentlich nur *dichten*.
>
> I think I summed up my position vis-à-vis philosophy when I said: philosophy should really be written *only* as one would write poetry. (CV, 28)

---

[1] I have used my own translations of remarks from *Culture and Value* and *Philosophical Investigations*.
[2] Having chosen Anscombe as the official translator of the *Philosophical Investigations*, Wittgenstein arranged for her to spend some time in Vienna to improve her Oxford-acquired German. Wittgenstein's own last stay in Vienna (December 1949–March 1950), on the occasion of his sister Hermine's death, coincided with Anscombe's, and they evidently met two or three times a week, but he was himself so ill he may not have paid much attention to the actual translation process (see Monk 1990, 562).

These words, so difficult to render in English,[3] accord with the frequent links made in *Culture and Value* between philosophy and aesthetics, for example, "The strange resemblance between a philosophical investigation (perhaps especially in mathematics) and an aesthetic one (e.g., what's wrong with this dress, what it should look like, etc... " (CV, 29). But *how* the two are related, how philosophy is to be written *only* as poetry: this remains a puzzle, not just for Wittgenstein's reader, but for the philosopher himself. Indeed, no sooner has he made the statement above than Wittgenstein adds somewhat sheepishly, "With these words, I was also acknowledging myself to be someone who cannot quite do what he would like to do" (CV, 28). And a few years later: "I *squander* untold effort to make an arrangement of my thoughts that may have no value whatever" (CV, 33).

This is not just false modesty. In its first "poetic" forays, Wittgenstein's writing has a predilection for aphorisms—terse and often gnomic utterances—modeled, it has been suggested, on those of Schopenhauer (see for example Glock 2000), and, more immediately, on the maxims of Heraclitus. In Guy Davenport's words:

> "The limits of my language are the limits of my world." "The most beautiful order of the world is still a random gathering of things insignificant in themselves." Which is Heraclitus, which Wittgenstein? "The philosopher," says one of the *Zettel*, "is not a citizen of any community of ideas. That is what makes him a philosopher." And: "What about the sentence—*Wie ist es mit dem Satz*—'One cannot step in the same river twice'?" That Heraclitean perception has always been admired for its hidden second meaning. *One* cannot step....it is not only the flux of the river that makes the statement true. But is it true? No, Wittgenstein would smile (or glare), but it is wise and interesting. It can be examined. It is harmonious and poetic. (Davenport 1981, 334)[4]

But unlike Heraclitus, Wittgenstein embedded his philosophical aphorisms into a network of "dry" logical and mathematical propositions of the sort "If p follows from q, the sense of 'p' is contained in that of 'q'" (TLP 5.123). How to reconcile these two seemingly unlike modes of discourse? This was the problem the young Wittgenstein posed for himself, as we can see in the *Notebooks 1914–1916*, composed during the First World War, sometimes in the midst of battle. On 6 July 1916, for example, Wittgenstein confided in his diary, "Colossal strain this last month. Have thought a lot about all sorts of things, but oddly enough, can't make the connection with my mathematical train of

---

[3] Wittgenstein's proposition, as I have noted elsewhere (Perloff 2004, 53 n. 12) is all but untranslatable, because there is no precise English equivalent of the German verb *dichten*—a verb that means to create poetry but also, in the wider sense, to produce something fictional, as in Goethe's *Dichtung und Wahrheit*, where fiction is opposed to truth. My own earlier translation: "Philosophy ought really to be written as a *form of poetry*" (Perloff 1996, xviii and *passim*) is not quite accurate, since there is no reference to *form of writing* here. Peter Winch, whose first edition of CV renders Wittgenstein's sentence as "Philosophy ought really to be written only as a *poetic composition*," revises it for the 1998 edition to read "Really one should write philosophy only as one *writes a poem*." The word "poem" is misleading—Wittgenstein did not, after all, write poems—and perhaps the most accurate translation is David Schalkwyk's: "Philosophy should be written only as one would write poetry" (2004, 56). Or, to be even more colloquial, one can follow David Antin's "One should really only do philosophy as poetry" (1998, 161).

[4] The reference is to Wittgenstein's 1933 note: "The man who said that one cannot step into the same river twice said something wrong; one can step into the same river twice" (PO, 167).

thought" (GT, 68).[5] The very next day, however, he notes, "But the connection will be made! What cannot be said, *can* be not said" (GT, 69). And a few weeks later, "Yes, my work has expanded from the foundations of logic to the nature of the world" (NB, 79).

How does such expansion work? In §4.46 and its sequelae in the *Tractatus*, Wittgenstein concerns himself with *tautology*: "the tautology [e.g., either it rains or it does not rain] has no truth-conditions, for it is unconditionally true" (TLP 4.461). Again (§6.12), "The fact that the propositions of logic are tautologies *shows* the formal—logical—properties of language, of the world." Now consider the implications of the role of tautology in logic for a discussion of the word *happy* (*glücklich*). In the *Notebooks*, the word first appears in the entry of 8 July 1916 as part of a meditation on belief in God:

> I am either happy or unhappy, that's all. It can be said: good or evil do not exist.
> He who is happy must have no fear. Not even of death.
> Only someone who lives not in time but in the present is happy. (NB, 74)

The first sentence above is a tautology, although of a seemingly different kind from the mathematical and logical tautologies Wittgenstein has been discussing in earlier sections. And now tautology gives way to judgment: to be happy is to have no fear of death, in other words to live in the present, not the future. And so, after insisting that "Death is not an event in life. It is not a fact of the world," Wittgenstein posits:

> In order to live happily I must be in agreement with the world.
> And that is what "being happy" *means*....
> > The fear of death is the best sign of a false, i.e. a bad, life.
> > When my conscience upsets my equilibrium, then I am not in agreement with something. But what is this? Is it *the world*?
> > > Certainly it is right to say: Conscience is the voice of God.
> > > For example: it makes me unhappy to think that I have offended this or that man.
> > Is that my conscience?
> > Can one say: "Act according to your conscience whatever it may be"? (NB, 75)

But the meaning of "conscience" turns out to be as elusive as that of "happiness." Indeed, the final line of this sequence suggests that all one can say is "Lebe glücklich" (Be happy!). And this bit of non-advice leads, in its turn, to the formulation of 29 July 1916, that "the world of the happy is a *different* world from the world of the unhappy"—a return to the tautological mode of 8 July 1916 that is picked up verbatim in *Tractatus* 6.43.

The discourse now turns to good and evil and once again the issue of the will, but at the end of this section (NB, 78), we read yet again:

> The world of the happy is a different world from that of the unhappy.
> The world of the happy is *a happy world*.
> Can there then be a world that is neither happy nor unhappy?

---

[5] My translation: there is not yet an English translation of the *Geheime Tagebücher*. The methodological importance of this and subsequent passages in the GT was first noted by Antin (1998, 154–5).

Can one transcend tautology? In his next entry (30 July 1916), Wittgenstein writes:

> Again and again I come back to this! Simply the happy life is good, the unhappy bad. And if I *now* ask myself: But why should I be *happy*, then this of itself seems to me to be a tautological question; the happy life seems to be justified, of itself, it seems that it *is* the only right life. (NB, 78)

There seems, indeed, to be no further *explanation* of the happy life—only its assertion:

> But one could say: the happy life seems in some sense to be more *harmonious* than the unhappy. But in what sense?
>   What is the objective sign of the happy, harmonious life? Here it is again clear that no such sign, one that can be described, can exist.
>   This sign cannot be a physical, but only a metaphysical, a transcendental one. (NB, 78)

There we have it. In circling round and round the word *happy*, the text cannot reach conclusion. When, some entries later (29 October 1916), Wittgenstein declares, "For there is certainly something in the conception that the end of art is the beautiful. And the beautiful *is* what makes happy" (NB, 86), we have not really gotten anywhere, for *beauty*, as he well knows, is just as elusive as *happiness*—it is here called "transcendent," which is to say, indefinable. "What cannot be said, *can* be not said."

The *Notebook* entries on "happy" were made over a three-month period, and the reader may well wonder why variations on the original distinction between "happy" and "unhappy" are made again and again, both here and in the *Tractatus*. But repetition with slight permutation—a form of repetition reminiscent of Gertrude Stein or Samuel Beckett rather than of Plato or Heraclitus—is the key to Wittgenstein's method here.[6] Only by beginning again and again, to use Stein's phrase, by reformulating a particular notion until it gradually manifests or reveals itself, can philosophy make any sort of progress. And "progress" is too strong a word here, for, as Wittgenstein puts it in a 1930 Lecture, "Philosophical analysis does not tell us anything new about thought (and if it did it would not interest us)." Rather, "Philosophy is the attempt to be rid of a particular kind of puzzlement" (WL, 35, 1). In this case, it is only by circling round the proposition "The world of the happy is a happy world" that we begin to understand that happiness, man's most persistent goal, cannot be defined or even specified. Nor is definition or specification necessary. When, for example, we read the famous opening sentence of Tolstoy's *Anna Karenina*—"Happy families are all alike. Each unhappy family is unhappy in its own way"—we don't stop to ask what Tolstoy means by the words "happy" and "unhappy." We know very well what is at stake; we also know that this novel is not going to be about happy families.

But what makes a sentence like "The world of the happy is a happy world" an instance of *Dichtung*? In a 1931 entry in *Culture and Value*, we read:

---

[6] I discuss in Perloff 2002 Lyn Hejinian's Wittgensteinian long poem "Happily" (Hejinian 2000), which plays further variations on the word *happy* and its cognates and shows how this kind of conceptual poetry works.

Die Grenze der Sprache zeigt sich in der Unmöglichkeit die Tatsache zu beschreiben, die einem Satz entspricht (seine Ubersetzung ist) ohne eben den Satz zu wiederholen.

The limit of language manifests itself in the impossibility of describing the reality that corresponds to (is the translation of) a sentence without simply repeating the sentence. (CV, 13)

And in *Zettel*, we read, "Knowledge is actually not *translated* into words when it is expressed. The words are not a translation of something else that was there before they were" (Z §191).[7]

Poeticity, these statements suggest, depends upon the conviction that "language is not *contiguous* to anything else. We cannot speak of the use of language as opposed to anything else" (WL, 112). For if one *begins* with the actual words spoken or written, word choice and grammar are seen to be everything. The variations on the proposition "The world of the happy is a *different* world from the world of the unhappy" are essential, not because they say anything "new"—they don't—but because the very act of repetition and qualification, repetition and variation brings home to the reader, as to the philosopher-poet himself, the impossibility of defining happiness, even as its central function in our lives is clearly demonstrated.

Indeed, unlike traditional aphorisms, Wittgenstein's short propositions don't really "say" anything. Or, to put it another way, what they "say" is enigmatic. "Death is not an event in life," (TLP 6.4311), for example, is an arresting aphorism but not because it is true. For death (someone else's) could certainly be an event in my life. And even the specter of my own death determines how I live, what I do. Wittgenstein's sentences are thus characterized, not by their metaphorical force or their use of the rhetorical figures like antithesis and parallelism, but by what I would call their *opaque literalism*. The sentences say just what they say—no difficult words to look up!—but they remain mysterious, endlessly puzzling, enigmatic. In what context and to whom is it meaningful to say "The world of the happy is a happy world"? Isn't it rather like saying, to quote a famous little poem, "So much depends / upon / a red wheel / barrow / glazed with rain / water / beside the white/ chickens"? And how do we move from one proposition to the next, the decimal system of the *Tractatus* constituting, as David Antin has so convincingly demonstrated (Antin 1998, 151–6), a framework that defies the very logic it claims to put forward?

No Gaps in Grammar

In Wittgenstein's later writings, the propositional – aphoristic mode of the *Notebooks* and the *Tractatus* gives way to a rather different style. To begin with a representative passage, consider the famous analogy, early in the *Investigations*, between the language-game and the game of chess (PI §§30–1):

---

[7] In German, this reads, "Das Wissen wird eben nicht in Worte *übersetzt*, wenn es sich äußert. Die Worte sind keine Übersetzung eines Andern, welches vor ihnen da war."

[End of §30.] One must already know something (or do something with it) in order to be able to ask its name. But what must one know?

31.   When you show someone the king in a game of chess and say, "This is the king", you are not explaining to him how the piece is used—unless he already knows the rules of the game, except for this last identification: the shape of the king. It is possible that he learned the rules of the game without ever having been shown an actual chess piece. The form of the piece here corresponds to the sound or the physical appearance of a word.

But it is also possible that someone has learned the game without ever having learned or formulated the rules. Perhaps first he learned by watching quite simple board games and advanced to increasingly complicated ones. Here again one could give him the explanation "This is the king"—if, for example, one were showing him chess pieces of an unfamiliar design. But again, this explanation teaches him the use of the chess piece only because, as we might say, the place for it had already been prepared. Or even: we might say explanation only teaches him the use of the piece, when its place has been prepared. And in this case, it happens, not because the person to whom we give the explanation already knows the rules, but because, from another perspective, he already has command of the game....

Consider this further case: I am explaining chess to someone and begin by pointing to a chess piece and saying "This is the king. It can move like this, etc. etc." In this case, we'll say that the words, "This is the king" (or this one is called "king") only provide a definition if the learner already "knows what a piece in a board game is." That is, if he has already played other games or watched other people playing "with understanding"—and so on. Again, only then would he be able to ask the relevant question, "What is this called?"—that is, this piece in a game.

We can say: only someone who already knows how to do something with it can meaningfully ask for its name.

And we can also imagine a situation in which the person questioned answers, "You choose the name", and so the questioner would have to take the responsibility for the whole thing.

In this passage, the terse and enigmatic propositions of the *Tractatus* are replaced by what looks like a much more casual, free-wheeling discourse. Its central figure is the analogy between a given word and a chess piece: just as the meaning of the various chess figures—king, queen, pawn—depends entirely on their *use* in the game itself, so, Wittgenstein asserts in §43, *contra* the Augustinian theory of language as pointing system where "Every word in the language signifies something" (PI §13), that "*the meaning of a word is its use in the language.*"

Commentary on Wittgenstein's passage often refers to the "chess metaphor" in the *Investigations*, but it is important to note that here and elsewhere, Wittgenstein's figures are not full-fledged metaphors or even similes. Metaphor is by definition a figure of transference in which *a* can be *substituted* for *b*. In Shakespeare's sonnet #73, for example, we read:

> That time of year thou mayst in me behold
> Where yellow leaves, or none, or few, do hang
> Upon the boughs that shake against the cold,
> Bare, ruin'd choirs where late the sweet birds sang.

Here the identity of old age and the autumn of the year is complete; the metaphor, moreover, doubles over in line 4 as the bare branches "where late the sweet birds sang" become the "bare, ruin'd choirs" of medieval churches—perhaps the Gothic vaults of monasteries destroyed during the Reformation. The choristers (sweet birds) no longer sing in the empty church stalls (the tree branches).

Wittgenstein's figures of speech, on the other hand, always begin with the assumption that the analogy between *a* and *b* is only that—an analogy, useful for exemplifying one's points in a philosophical discussion. The chess piece called the king cannot be substituted for a particular word or phrase in a discussion of language: we all know, in other words, that language is not *really* chess. Or consider the following locutions in *Culture and Value*:

> A new word is like fresh seed thrown on the ground of the discussion. (CV, 4)

> Compare the solution of philosophical problems to the gift in the fairytale that magically appears in the enchanted castle and when one looks at it outside in daylight, it is nothing but an ordinary piece of iron (or something similar). (CV, 13–14)

> Talent is a spring from which fresh water is constantly flowing. But this spring loses its value if it is not used in the right way. (CV, 20)

> The idea is worn out by now & no longer usable....in the way silver paper, once crumpled, can never quite be smoothed out again. Nearly all my ideas are a bit crumpled. (CV, 24)

> Language sets everyone the same traps; it is an immense network of well kept wrong turnings....So what I should do is erect signposts at all the junctions where there are wrong turnings, to help people past the danger points. (CV, 25)

> My thinking, like everyone's, has sticking to it the shrivelled husks of my earlier dead thoughts. (CV, 27)

Such proverbial statements, as Wittgenstein students have long remarked, are characterized by their homely, everyday wisdom, their common sense. Old ideas can't be recycled any more than silver foil can be smoothed out again; outmoded thoughts are like shriveled husks; seemingly brilliant solutions to philosophical problems are like those fairy tale gifts that emerge in the harsh light of day as pieces of junk. Wittgenstein knows very well that the items compared are discrete, that words and phrases function only in specific language-games.

Now let us return to the chess passage in §31. Here, as throughout the *Investigations*, the author presents himself dialogically—as someone having a conversation with someone else. Typically, he begins with a question: here, at the end of §30, "But what does one have to know?" Question, exclamation, interruption, interpellation: even when, as in the *Investigations*, there is a written text, not a series of lecture notes recorded by others, Wittgenstein "does" philosophy by setting up everyday dialogues or interviews, as enigmatic as they are childlike. In the chess discussion, for example, Wittgenstein begins by positing that the explanatory sentence "This is the king" makes no sense unless the player already knows the rules of the game. But there are other possibilities. The interlocutor might have learned chess by watching, first simple board games and then more difficult ones. "This is the king" might refer to an unusual chess piece, one that doesn't have the usual shape of the king. Or again, the sentence "This is the king" may be spoken by a master of the game to explain what move he is about to make. Or a non-native speaker who knows how to play chess may ask what this particular piece is called in the foreign country he is visiting.

Is it all common sense? Yes and no. Each example appeals to our actual practices, to our reference to how we do things in everyday life. But precisely because we are so familiar with these practices, it is difficult to understand what they mean. It seems as if the exempla in §31 work up to the authoritative generalization in the penultimate sentence, "*We can say: only someone who already knows how to do something with a given piece can meaningfully ask for its name*"—a generalization that actually repeats the final proposition of §30 cited above, "One must already know something (or do something with it) in order to be able to ask its name." Has the interim passage with its chess examples then made no difference in understanding, especially given that the final sentence—

> And we can also imagine a situation in which the person questioned answers, "You choose the name", and so the questioner would have to take the responsibility for the whole thing

—far from providing closure, opens up the debate for further possibilities?

Consider what happens in §32:

> Someone coming into a foreign country will sometimes learn the language of the natives from ostensive definitions that they give him; and he will often have to *guess* the meaning of these definitions; and will guess sometimes right, sometimes wrong.
>
>   And now, I think, we can say: Augustine describes the learning of human language as if the child came into a foreign country and did not understand the language of that country; that is, as if the child already had a language, only not this one. Or again: as if the child could already *think*, only not yet speak. And "think" would here mean something like "talk to oneself."

The continuity between §31 and §32 is at first elusive. Just when we think we understand that the word "king" in chess is meaningless unless we know how to play the game, Wittgenstein shifts ground and attacks the Augustinian theory of language as pointing system from a different angle. The new analogy—wonderfully absurd—is between a stranger in a foreign country and a child communicating within its own not-yet-learned language system. Is the child's "thought" then like the foreigner's native language, prior to the "new" language to be learned? The posited analogy is patently absurd, for what could that prior language possibly look and sound like? How does one talk to oneself without talking? As Wittgenstein puts it frequently, does a young child hope before it has learned the word "hope"?

Analogies thus provide sometimes positive, sometimes negative, reinforcement: in either case, they lead us to *revise* our previous understanding of this or that fixed notion. It is this *processive*, self-corrective, and even self-canceling nature of Wittgenstein's propositions—their deployment of language as "a labyrinth of paths" (PI §82), their use of countless examples, anecdotes, narratives, and analogies—that gives the text its poetic edge. For the "naturalness" of its talk, its colloquial, everyday language and story-telling is everywhere held in tension with a set of larger assumptions that are as fixed and formally perfect as is the architectural design of the severely modern house Wittgenstein designed for his sister in Vienna. However much the individual exempla in the text are open for discussion and debate, the unstated axiom governing them is that "language is not contiguous to anything else," and that accordingly, the meaning of a word is its use in the language. And the text enacts that theorem, presented as a non-theorem, at every turn. *Showing*, not *telling*, is the mode.

Here the testimony of Wittgenstein's Cambridge students is apposite. "His lectures," Norman Malcolm recalls, "were given without preparation and without notes. He told me once he had tried to lecture from notes but was disgusted with the result; the thoughts that came out were 'stale,' or, as he put it to another friend, the words looked like 'corpses' when he began to read them" (Malcolm 1984, 23). Two other Cambridge students describe the performance as follows:

> At first one didn't see where all the talking was leading. One didn't see, or saw only very vaguely, the point of the numerous examples. And then, sometimes one did, suddenly. All at once, sometimes, the solution to one's problems became clear and everything fell into place. In these exciting moments one realized something of what mathematicians mean when they speak of the beauty of an elegant proof. The solution, once seen, seemed so simple and obvious, such an inevitable and simple key to unlock so many doors so long battered against in vain. One wondered how one could fail to see it. But if one tried to explain to someone else who had not seen it one couldn't get it across without going through the whole long story. (Gasking and Jackson 1967, 50)[8]

In a literary context, the "exciting moments" described here are known as epiphanies. Suddenly, in such Wordsworthian "spots of time," the object of contemplation becomes radiant, and we *see* into the life of things. Consider Wittgenstein's late notebook entries published under the title *On Certainty* (*Über Gewissheit*).[9] The basic subject of this little book is what one knows and how one knows it: the paragraphs numbered 300–676, written in the last months of Wittgenstein's life, try to define the point when doubt becomes senseless—a question that is answerable only by referring it to actual practice. And here Wittgenstein's examples are especially imaginative:

> 332. Suppose that someone, without wanting to *philosophize*, were to say, "I don't know if I have ever been on the moon; I don't *remember* ever having been there". (Why would this person be so alien from us?)

---

[8] I owe my knowledge of this and related passages to David Antin (1998, 160). Antin's own "talk pieces" are later instances of this Wittgensteinian paradigm.

[9] The selection of notes and their numbering was made posthumously by the editors, not the author.

In the first place: how would he know that he was on the moon? How does he picture it to himself? Compare: "I don't know if I was ever in the village of X." But I couldn't say this either if X were in Turkey, because I know that I have never been to Turkey.

333. I ask someone, "Have you ever been to China?" He answers, "I don't know." Here one would surely say, "You don't *know*? Do you have any reason to believe that perhaps you have ever been there? Have you for example ever been near the Chinese border? Or were your parents there at the time you were about to be born?"— Normally, Europeans do know whether they have been to China or not.

334. In other words; the reasonable person doubts such a thing only under such-and-such circumstances…

341. …the questions that we raise and our doubts depend on the fact that some propositions are exempt from doubt, like the hinges on which these turn.…

343. But it isn't that we just *can't* investigate everything and are therefore forced to be satisfied with assumptions. If I want the door to move, the hinges must be intact.

344. My life consists in that there are certain things I am content to accept.

Here is the negative capability of the late Wittgenstein—the capacity, in Keats's words, "of being in uncertainties, Mysteries, doubts without any irritable reaching after fact & reason"[10]—a mental state closely allied to the moment of poetry. Of course, Wittgenstein suggests, one can always demand specification of a proposition to the point where there could be certainty, as in "$2 \times 2 = 4$," but, even in this case, "the spoken or written sentence '$2 \times 2 = 4$' might in Chinese have a different meaning or be pure nonsense" (OC §10). Not what a statement *is* but what one does with it is what matters. So, to use the hinge analogy above, if you want the door to move, the hinges must work. In everyday life we know quite well whether or not we have been to China or on the moon, just as we know that we have two hands and two feet without looking at them to check out the truth. "Ordinary language is alright" (BB, 28).

But Wittgenstein's "ordinary language" is of course extraordinary. In the passage above (§§332–43) and throughout *On Certainty*, persuasion depends on the poet-philosopher's astonishing rhetorical skill. Examples must be short and concrete; they must speak to the interlocutor's everyday experience, using conversational speech patterns, reinforced by vivid analogies like that of words turned to corpses or worn-out ideas like crumpled silver foil. The exempla must meet the test of common sense; indeed, they must be so literal that they make us laugh. Even in our own age of moon exploration, the response "I don't know" to the question, "Have you ever been on the moon?" is absurd. Indeed, the absurdity of many of Wittgenstein's propositions shows their affinity to the joke, the riddle, or the tall tale, as these variants appear in the language-game itself: "Imagine a language-game 'When I call you, come in through the door'. In an ordinary case, it will be impossible to doubt that there really is a door"

---

[10] Keats 1982, 43.

(OC §391). A child, presented with such a possibility, would either laugh or put forward an alternate game—for example, "Let's pretend none of the things in this room exist." And therein would lie a different language-game, a different poetic act.

THE RIGHT TEMPO

In the much-cited Preface to the *Philosophical Investigations*, Wittgenstein describes the method whereby he ordered the "*remarks*, short paragraphs, of which there is sometimes a fairly long chain about the same subject" into the larger structure of the book:

> After several unsuccessful attempts to weld my results together into such a whole, I realized I should never succeed. The best that I could write would never be more than philosophical remarks; my thoughts were soon crippled if I tried to force them on in any single direction against their natural inclination.—And this was of course connected with the very nature of the investigation. Namely, it forces us to travel over a wide range of thoughts, criss-cross [*kreuz und quer*], in all directions....Thus this book is really only an album. (PI, Preface)

An album is most typically a medley, a commonplace book or loose collection of disparate items, collaged together *kreuz und quer*, without much thought of the controlling structure. But despite this disclaimer, Wittgenstein's "remarks" are the result of much more intensive *dichten* than is usually thought. Etymologically, the verb *dichten* comes from the adjective *dicht* (thick, dense, packed): *dichten* originally meant "to make airtight, watertight; to seal the cracks (in a window, roof, etc.)"—in other words, something like the Zen phrase "to thicken the plot."

Poets, indeed fiction-makers of all stripes, are those that make thick or dense, that pack it in. Again and again, in *Culture and Value* and related texts, Wittgenstein talks of the need for *slow* reading:

> Sometimes a sentence can be understood only if it is read at the *right* tempo. My sentences are all to be read *slowly*. (CV, 65)

> Thoughts rise to the surface slowly, like bubbles. (CV, 72)

> Of the sentences that I write down here, only the occasional one represents a step forward; the others are like the snip of the barber's scissors, which must be kept in motion so as to make a cut with them at the right moment. (CV, 76)

> Raisins may be the best part of a cake; but a bag of raisins is no better than a cake; and he who is in a position to give us a bag full of raisins, cannot necessarily bake a cake with them, let alone do something better.
>   I am thinking of [Karl] Kraus & his aphorisms, but of myself too & my philosophical remarks.
>   A cake is not, as it were, thinned out raisins.(CV, 76)

The last remark here is especially telling. Aphorisms, so central to the *Tractatus* and earlier work, cannot *in themselves* make a poetic–philosophical discourse. If they remain discrete, like so many separate raisins in a bag, they fail to cohere into a fully formed "cake." But coherence, in this instance, is not a matter of linearity, of logical or temporal movement from a to b to c. For Wittgenstein, the *criss-crossing* of threads must be *dicht*—thick and dense—and, as in the case of lyric poetry, only *slow reading* can unpack the meanings in question.

"My sentences must be read *slowly.*" The necessity, in an information age, of slowing down the reading process, was central to the thinking of many of Wittgenstein's contemporaries—for example, the Russian avant-gardists Velimir Khlebnikov and Alexeii Kruchenykh: the term *ostranenie* (estrangement, defamiliarization) was always associated with slowing down the reading (or viewing) process in art. Duchamp's concept of the *delay*, as in calling his *Large Glass* (*The Bride Stripped Bare by her Bachelors, Even*) a "delay in glass," is another instance. To say "Philosophy must be written only as one would write poetry" is to be aware of the need for density and resonance—rather than logic and sequential argument—in the verbal construct.

One of Wittgenstein's most intriguing works in this regard is the "Remarks on Frazer's *Golden Bough*" (1936), first edited and published in 1967 by Rush Rhees.[11] On the surface, this seems to be a rather loosely organized set of scattered "remarks": it begins "One must start out with error and convert it into truth," and then contains the isolated lyric line, "I must plunge into the water of doubt again and again" (PO, 119). Again and again is the key here: in what follows, Wittgenstein repeats, questions, challenges, exclaims, circling round and round the issue of Frazer's misunderstanding of "primitive" religious practices in *The Golden Bough*. "One would like to say: This and that incident have taken place; laugh if you can" (PO, 123). Or, "What a narrow spiritual life on Frazer's part! As a result: how impossible it was for him to conceive of a life different from that of the England of his time!" (PO, 125). And even more scathingly, "Why shouldn't it be possible for a person to regard his name as sacred? It is certainly, on the one hand, the most important instrument which is given to him, and, on the other, like a piece of jewelry hung around his neck at birth" (PO, 126–7).

Only after pages of such "criss-cross" emotional commentary does Wittgenstein zero in on what is his central case: that if the vegetation ceremonies of the peoples in question are understood, not as opinions or beliefs, but as *practices*, their behavior will emerge as not so "primitive" after all:

> I read among many similar examples, of a Rain-King in Africa to whom the people pray for rain *when the rainy period comes*. But surely that means that they do not really believe that he can make it rain, otherwise they would do it in the dry periods

---

[11] In *Philosophical Occasions*. In their head note, the editors point out that the first bilingual book edition of this text (Retford: Brynmilll, 1979) left out a considerable number of the remarks; "the extant editions disagree about what to include and what to leave out of Wittgenstein's remarks" (PO, 116). There is, then, no definitive text of this essay.

of the year in which the land is "a parched and arid desert." For if one assumes that the people formerly instituted this office of Rain-King out of stupidity, it is neverthe-less certainly clear that they had previously experienced that the rains begin in March, and then they would have had the Rain-King function for the other part of the year. Or again, toward morning, when the sun is about to rise, rites of daybreak are celebrated, but not during the night, when they simply burn lamps. (PO, 137)

And the essay now multiplies examples of similar misunderstandings on Frazer's part, culminating in the assertion, "If they [the primitive people Frazer talks of] were to write it down, their knowledge of nature would not differ *fundamentally* from ours. Only their *magic* is different" (PO, 141).

"Remarks on Frazer's *Golden Bough*" was, of course, not intended for publication, at least not in the present form, and so our expectations of it are different from those we have of the *Investigations*. But when we remember that even the latter, his most "fin-ished" work, was undergoing continual change between the time of its "completion" and Wittgenstein's death in 1951,[12] we can see that the formal constraints are quite similar. To insure that the reader will absorb them "slowly," Wittgenstein's sentences are paratactic and metonymic; they circle around a "point," at first quietly, even casually, then with increasing deliberation, until the "meaning" of this or that argument suddenly crystal-lizes. From the gnomic aphorisms of the *Tractatus* to the "common-sense" analogies that multiply and spill over into the next paragraph in the *Investigations* and *On Certainty*, Wittgenstein's writings enact their central motive: words and phrases can be understood only in their particular context, their use. Not *what* one says but *how* one says it is the key to doing philosophy. And that, of course, is what makes it poetry as well.

REFERENCES

ANTIN, DAVID (1998). "Wittgenstein among the Poets," *Modernism/Modernity*, 5(1): 149–66.

DAVENPORT, GUY (1981). "Wittgenstein," in *The Geography of the Imagination*. San Francisco: North Point Press.

EAGLETON, TERRY (1993). *Wittgenstein: The Terry Eagleton Script: The Derek Jarman Film*. London: Film Institute.

GASKING, D. A. T. and JACKSON, A. C. (1967). "Wittgenstein as a Teacher," in K. T. Fann ed., *Ludwig Wittgenstein: The Man and his Philosophy*. New Jersey: Humanities Press.

GLOCK, HANS-JOHANN (2000). "Schopenhauer and Wittgenstein," in Christopher Janaway ed., *The Cambridge Companion to Schopenhauer*. Cambridge: Cambridge University Press.

HEJINIAN, LYN (2000). *Happily*. Sausalito: Post-Apollo Press.

KEATS, JOHN (1982). "Letter to George and Tom Keats, 21, 27 December 1817," in Robert Gittings ed., *Letters of John Keats*. Oxford: Oxford University Press.

LEE, DESMOND ed. (1980). *Wittgenstein's Lectures Cambridge, 1930–32: From the Notes of John King and Desmond Lee*. Chicago: University of Chicago Press.

---

[12] See especially *Last Writings on the Philosophy of Psychology*, vols. 1 and 2. In these volumes, Part II of the *Investigations* is heavily revised and expanded.

MALCOLM, NORMAN (1984). *Ludwig Wittgenstein: A Memoir*, 2nd edn. Oxford: Oxford University Press.

MONK, RAY (1990). *Ludwig Wittgenstein: The Duty of Genius*. New York: Macmillan.

PERLOFF, MARJORIE (1996). *Wittgenstein's Ladder: Poetic Language and the Strangeness of the Ordinary*. Chicago: University of Chicago Press.

—— (2002). *21st-Century Modernism*. Oxford: Blackwell.

—— (2004). "'But Isn't the *Same* at Least the Same?' Wittgenstein and the Question of Poetic Translatability," in John Gibson and Wolfgang Huemer eds., *The Literary Wittgenstein*. New York: Routledge.

SCHALKWYK, DAVID (2004). "Wittgenstein's 'Imperfect Garden': the Ladders and Labyrinths of Philosophy as *Dichtung*," in John Gibson and Wolfgang Huemer eds., *The Literary Wittgenstein*. New York: Routledge.

WINCH, PETER (1998). "Note by Translator," in Ludwig Wittgenstein, *Vermischte Bemerkungen: Eine Auswahl aus dem Nachlaß / Culture and Value: A Selection from the Posthumous Remains*, rev. edn, ed. G. H. von Wright and Alois Pichler. Oxford: Blackwell.

WITTGENSTEIN, LUDWIG (1961). *Tractatus Logico-Philosophicus*, trans. D. F. Pears and B. F. McGuinness. London: Routledge.

—— (1965). *The Blue and Brown Books: Preliminary Studies for the "Philosophical Investigations"*, 2nd edn. New York: Harper & Row.

—— (1967). *Zettel*, ed. G. E. M. Anscombe and G. H. von Wright, trans. Anscombe. Berkeley: University of California Press.

—— (1972). *On Certainty*, ed. G. E. M. Anscombe and G. H. von Wright. New York: Harper & Row.

—— (1979). *Notebooks 1914–1916*, 2nd edn, ed. G. H. von Wright and G. E. M. Anscombe. trans. Anscombe. Chicago: University of Chicago Press.

—— (1982). *Last Writings on the Philosophy of Psychology*, vol. 1, ed. G. H. von Wright and Heikki Nyman. Oxford: Blackwell.

—— (1991). *Geheime Tagebücher 1914–1916*, ed. Wilhelm Baum. Vienna: Turia and Kant.

—— (1992). *Last Writings on the Philosophy of Psychology*, vol. 2, ed. G. H. von Wright and Heikki Nyman. Oxford: Blackwell.

—— (1993). *Philosophical Occasions 1912–1951*, ed. James C. Klagge and Alfred Nordmann. Indianapolis and Cambridge: Hackett.

—— (1997). *Philosophische Untersuchungen/Philosophical Investigations*, 2nd edn, trans. G. E. M. Anscombe. Oxford: Blackwell.

CHAPTER 32

....

WITTGENSTEIN AND THE MORAL DIMENSION OF PHILOSOPHICAL PROBLEMS

....

JOEL BACKSTRÖM

WITTGENSTEIN's so-called *Big Typescript* from the early 1930s includes a famous chapter on 'Philosophy'. Most of it describes philosophy as concerned in different ways with clearing up misunderstandings concerning *language*, but all this is framed by the curious heading: 'DIFFICULTY OF PHILOSOPHY NOT THE INTELLECTUAL DIFFICULTY OF THE SCIENCES, BUT THE DIFFICULTY OF A CHANGE OF ATTITUDE. RESISTANCES OF THE WILL MUST BE OVERCOME' (PO, 161).[1]

This chapter attempts to understand what Wittgenstein might have had in mind here. How did he see the character of the philosophical problems he was dealing with, in particular the connection between them, language trouble, and the broadly speaking moral – existential difficulties apparently referred to in the opening statement. And how are *we*, quite apart from any concern with Wittgenstein-exegesis, to understand this? These questions seem both very important and much neglected. Generally sympathetic readers of Wittgenstein still tend to treat philosophical problems, in practice if not in their official methodological pronouncements, as though they were what Wittgenstein claims they are not: essentially intellectual difficulties, and this is true even of those who emphasize (rightly I think) the 'therapeutic' character of his philosophical activity, the way he doesn't argue for particular answers to philosophical question but rather aims to *change us*, i.e. change the way we approach the matter in hand so that the very questions disappear or are transformed.

That philosophical difficulties concern our ways of *thinking* is clear, but the point is that we tend to have an all too intellectualistic conception of thinking and its difficulties – just as we have, if I may say so, an all too linguistic conception of language. This, in turn, is connected

---

[1] When quoting from Wittgenstein's writings, I have on a few occasions made slight modifications to published translations, without making special note of this. Translations of quotes from manuscript sources written in German, as well as from *Denkbewegungen*, are mine.

with a failure to see how deeply embedded we are in conventional, socially conditioned modes of thinking and response; how difficult it is for us to think for ourselves, to come to anything like self-knowledge, that age-old, self-declared aim of philosophy; indeed, how uncomfortable, even terrifying, is the prospect of doing so. Wittgenstein, I suggest, found the peculiar difficulty of philosophy to lie somewhere in these regions.

1. THE MORAL DIMENSION: A SUBMERGED THEME

My opening quote from the *Big Typescript* is no isolated occurrence. Throughout Wittgenstein's writings and recorded conversations, early and late, we find striking remarks which seem either to intimate or directly claim that philosophical difficulties have a moral – or existential, or whatever exactly we want to call it – dimension. Wittgenstein famously said of the *Tractatus* that the 'point' of the book was 'ethical' (Luckhardt 1979, 94). This is not said in the book itself, however, and in the *Philosophical Investigations* there are hardly any remarks that seem, on the face of them, to be concerned with an 'ethical' dimension. On the whole, the moral – existential theme in Wittgenstein's writings seems both strangely persistent and strangely anomalous, like a subterranean stream which suddenly bursts forth in an explicit and forceful remark, only to apparently disappear again. Thus, in 1931 Wittgenstein wrote in pencil in a notebook 'A confession must be part of the new life' (MS 154, 1r); as Rush Rhees notes, there is 'Just the one sentence. Then he goes on to discuss the philosophy of mathematics' (1981, 191).

One possible reaction to such remarks is represented by Joachim Schulte, who claims that while 'the *man* Ludwig Wittgenstein' no doubt had strong ethical views, the scattered remarks in his philosophical manuscripts bearing on 'ethical, religious, and other "dimensions"...did not normally form part of what he was basically writing about in [these] manuscripts' (1986, 69, text of fn 2). It seems to me, however, that Schulte begs the question by assuming a separation of the remarks into those that do and do not form part of the philosophical discussion. Even if, as von Wright tells us, Wittgenstein himself frequently 'hinted at such a separation – by the use of brackets or in other ways' (CV, Preface), the salient point is that these remarks crop up in the midst of discussions of *apparently* quite unrelated questions, and were often left standing as Wittgenstein worked over his texts. Surely this raises the question what Wittgenstein *was* 'basically writing about' in his philosophical manuscripts.

More importantly, any easy separation of the ethical from the philosophical in Wittgenstein's work seems positively precluded by remarks where he explicitly characterizes philosophical work itself *as* ethical. Thus he writes that he is inclined to think that 'every philosophical problem really springs from a character defect' (MS 158, 6r), and Rhees reports him saying that 'character is more important than intellect, if you are going to do philosophy' (2001, 161). These claims, which may at first seem bizarre, become more intelligible when connected to Wittgenstein's claim that

> What makes a subject hard to understand – if it's something significant and important – is not that before you can understand it you need to be specially trained in abstruse matters, but the contrast between understanding the subject and what most people *want* to see. Because of this the very things which are most obvious may become the hardest of all to understand. What has to be overcome is not a difficulty of the intellect but of the will. (CV, 17; cf. PO, 161)

If this is so, it will be most important to push on with philosophical questions precisely when one feels a *resistance* in oneself against doing so, when the question doesn't feel intellectually thrilling any more, nor yet merely frustrating, but actually starts to hurt. As Wittgenstein writes, 'You can't think decently if you don't want to hurt yourself' (Malcolm 2001, 94). And again: 'Anyone who is unwilling to descend into himself, because it is too painful, will naturally remain superficial in his writing, too' (MS 120, 72v). To be sure, it is not clear how precisely these claims should be understood, but certainly there is something important to try to understand here.

It is crucial to realize that reflection on the possible intertwining of philosophical problems and moral difficulties will not only challenge standard conceptions of philosophy, but also of morality. Thus, *if* moral difficulties were simply, as is often thought, about living up to certain social norms by 'doing the right thing', they could hardly be importantly related to philosophical confusions. Things appear in a different light, however, if we think instead of the difficulties facing a person struggling with their vanity or cowardice, for example – to name moral difficulties that preoccupied Wittgenstein, and that he saw as closely connected.[2] Such difficulties concern the spirit in which one reacts and relates to oneself and others, and so will show in one's thinking as much as in one's actions. The difficulty, furthermore, is not *knowing* what's right, as though there would be a question whether e.g. vanity is a bad thing, but rather *acknowledging* and *fighting* the vanity in oneself – which, in one's vanity, one precisely does not *want* to do (cf. CV, 58). It is a struggle to know and change oneself, 'a working on oneself…On how one sees things. (And what one expects of them)' – to quote Wittgenstein's well-known characterization of *philosophical* work (CV, 16).

In fact, a moral dimension seems implied in simply taking seriously the time-honoured notion that the aim of philosophy is to *know ourselves* in our thinking. Let me explain. In the printed Foreword to *Philosophical Remarks*, Wittgenstein says that 'the book is written in good will, and in so far as it is not so written, but out of vanity, etc., the author would wish to see it condemned'. It might seem natural to object that the book may surely contain worthwhile arguments and observations, even if their author was led to make them out of vanity, or other questionable motives. This is correct insofar as you or I as readers of the book may find a good use for such arguments. The point, however, is that we had better make sure that the use *we* make of them is not itself motivated by vanity or other morally problematic modes of response, for insofar as it is thus motivated, this means that *our* aim is not to get clear about our own thinking. Rather, we want to reassure, flatter, shock, or otherwise impress others

---

[2] The best document of this struggle is perhaps the notebooks published as *Denkbewegungen* (DB).

and ourselves in ways that flatter our vanity, systematically making the moves in our thinking demanded by this aim while avoiding thoughts that threaten it – including, of course, the thought that this *is* what we are doing. Exchanging truth for the rhetorically effective and plausibly arguable, our arguments thus become 'just a clever game', as Wittgenstein says (CV, 19), a pointless exercise from the point of view of self-knowledge and real understanding.

This shows, I believe, something of the sense of Wittgenstein's insistence that character is more fundamental than intellect in philosophy. When he exclaims 'But how can I be a logician before I'm a human being!' (CL, 58), the point is not that it matters little how one thinks as long as one is a decent person, but rather that one's moral difficulties, the ways in which one tends to distort one's relation to others, and to oneself *in* that relation, will manifest themselves in one's thinking, too. This is not to reject every distinction between the personal and the philosophical, between ourselves and our philosophizing, but to question the assumption that it is clear how, or indeed that, such distinctions can be drawn.[3]

2. PHILOSOPHICAL NONSENSE AND ITS MOTIVES

Wittgenstein always stresses the 'depth' of philosophical problems (e.g. PI §111). Through his patient work of reflection and questioning of philosophical preconceptions and prejudices, he reveals how difficult it is, not just to free oneself from their grip but to realize that one is *in* their grip. In treating philosophical problems as though they could, in general, be resolved by arguments or conceptual analysis as traditionally understood, i.e. as though the difficulty were essentially intellectual, we fail to realize *how* deep-seated and intractable these problems are. I suggest that the same intellectualism is found in the idea often attributed to Wittgenstein – mistakenly, I believe – that we can resolve philosophical perplexity simply by offering reminders of how words are used in everyday contexts, and by showing how, on closer examination, the apparent sense of philosophical claims breaks down. That this was not Wittgenstein's view emerges, for instance, from two passages in the early pages of *On Certainty*. The first reads:

> I know that a sick man is lying here? Nonsense! I am sitting at his bedside, I am looking attentively into his face. – So I don't know, then, that there is a sick man lying here? Neither the question nor the assertion makes sense. Any more than the assertion 'I am here', which I might yet use at any moment, if suitable occasion presented itself.... [I]t is only in use that the proposition has its sense. And 'I know that there's a sick man lying here', used in an *unsuitable* situation, seems not to be nonsense but rather seems matter-of-course, only because one can fairly easily imagine

---

[3] For more on this topic, in relation to Wittgenstein, see e.g. Rhees 1981, Monk 2001, and Conant 2001, 2002.

a situation to fit it, and one thinks that the words 'I know that...' are always in place where there is no doubt, and hence even where the expression of doubt would be unintelligible. (OC §10)

This passage is a perfect short summary and illustration of Wittgenstein's preferred line of attack against philosophical claims and positions which rely on a 'subliming' (PI §38) of our concepts (in this case the concept of knowing something); his attempt to 'bring words back from their metaphysical to their everyday use' by asking how they are 'actually used in...the language which is [their] original home' (PI §116). Briefly stated, the idea is to bring out how the apparent sense of metaphysical claims depends on unhinging our words from any concrete – practical, scientific, moral, religious, or other – application, thus allowing them to express an apparently profounder sense than they otherwise do precisely *because* we refuse them any concrete application, and so any clear sense. This is the point of Wittgenstein's remark that philosophical confusions 'arise when language is like an engine idling, not when it is doing work' (PI §132). The point I want to emphasize here, however, is that even supposing one can show all this to be so in a particular case, Wittgenstein does not consider that to be the end of the matter. Thus he writes, a few pages further on in *On Certainty*:

But is it an adequate answer to the scepticism of the idealist, or the assurances of the realist, to say that 'There are physical objects' is nonsense? For them after all it is not nonsense. It would, however, be an answer to say: this assertion, or its opposite is a misfiring attempt to express what can't be expressed like that. And that it does misfire can be shown; but that isn't the end of the matter. We need to realize that what presents itself to us as the first expression of a difficulty, or of its solution, may as yet not be correctly expressed at all. Just as one who has a just censure of a picture to make will often at first offer the censure where it does not belong, and an *investigation* is needed in order to find the right point of attack for the critic. (OC §37)

What does Wittgenstein have in mind here? Perhaps something like this: showing that the apparently clear sense of a philosophical claim comes undone will, as such, merely produce frustration in the person wanting to make the claim. For insofar as the *motivation* behind the claim is not brought out into the open, it will remain effective even after the incoherence of the claim in which it sought expression has been exposed (supposing there *was* any such incoherence, of course), and so the person who made the claim – who, alas, may be oneself – will not be convinced, but feel cleverly talked into or fraudulently argued out of something. While one has proved unable to defend one's claim or even state it coherently, *what one tried to say* has not been addressed. But this, Wittgenstein insists, is what needs to be addressed: 'Getting hold of the difficulty *deep down* is what is hard. Because if it is grasped near the surface it simply remains the difficulty it was. It has to be pulled out by the roots...' (CV, 48); we must get a hold of 'the *source* of [the] puzzlement' (BB, 59), the apparent problem, in other words, which prompted the philosophical claim as its apparent solution.

Whether one's words make sense, and the extent and ways in which they may fail to make sense, cannot be decided independently of understanding what one wanted to say, what one was motivated by or took oneself to be aiming at in saying it. In thinking about what we say, we are, or should be, trying to understand ourselves and each other, not trying to determine whether the *sentences* as such are 'in order' according to some external, and therefore arbitrary, rule. This is what 'it is only *in use* that the proposition has its sense' *means*: there are no simply given standards or limits of sense – whether these be supposed 'standards of philosophical reasoning' or of 'ordinary use' – but rather the sense is where *we* manage to make, and find, it. Therefore Wittgenstein has no objection as such to the seemingly most bizarre claims and idiosyncratic uses of words in philosophy; he simply wants to know what the person advancing a claim wants to *do* with it: '[W]hat follows from it and from what does it follow? From what experiences can we establish it? Or from none at all? What is its role?…I'm ready to go along with anything, but at least I must know this much' (VW, 73; cf. PI §374; Z §§272, 275).

This is not to say, of course, that sense can be made by an act of will. Sense is not made or changed by fiat, nor by merely wishing, however intensely, that one could make things out to be a certain way, nor by helping oneself to the associations and general feel of one's words, 'as if [their] sense were an atmosphere accompanying [them], which [they] carried over into every kind of application' (PI §117). The question in philosophizing is whether we really *can* make it clear to ourselves what we want to say, and this includes acknowledging and owning our motives and aims in claiming, denying, or assuming things. Insofar as we find that we cannot make clear sense of our claims, that we ourselves are unwilling or unable to fully and lucidly *mean* them, that we are thus undermining the sense of our own words, what we need to do is to understand what *tempted* us nonetheless in these claims.[4]

What I'm suggesting is that, if we are to understand why we come out with philosophical vagueness and nonsense, what is at stake in our doing so, we need to find some kind of intelligible *motivation* – which need not mean a simple, clear-cut motive – that connects our words with what we want, fear, are attracted or repelled by. Note that this shouldn't be conceived of as a search for hidden psychological *causes*. Whatever interest such a search might have, Wittgenstein rightly insists that 'what is hidden…is of no interest' in philosophy (PI §126). Faced with an inclination of thought, the philosophical task is not to explain it but to *acknowledge* its existence and character; 'Whatever the explanation, – the inclination is there' (PI II, 216). Now while finding the cause of a belief – e.g. your believing it's cold outside because I told you so – does not, as such, change our understanding of what is believed, seeing a motive, perhaps a wish or fear, at work in

---

[4] The disagreement between 'therapeutic' and more 'orthodox' (or 'elucidatory') readers of Wittgenstein turns in important part on whether, in criticizing metaphysical claims, we can appeal to somehow given standards of sense, nonsense, and contradiction or whether, as therapeutic readers insist, all we can show is that the person making the claim is somehow involved in *self*-contradiction. I think the therapeutic reading is basically right on this point, but that still leaves crucially important matters open, especially the question of the moral dimension of philosophy and philosophical 'therapy', that I think therapeutic readers haven't addressed satisfactorily. For representative therapeutic readings, see Baker 2004, Crary and Read 2000, Kuusela 2008, and (*avant la lettre*) Bouwsma 1995 and Wisdom 1965; 'orthodox' responses include Glock 1991 and Hacker 2000 and 2007.

inclining one to a belief may give a *further characterization* of the belief in the sense of showing what one is being drawn to in it, the light in which one sees it. So the need to bring out intelligible motives for our tendencies to misunderstand things, or to understand them only in a particular way, in philosophical discussions, is the need to understand *what* attracts and repels us in various philosophical views.

3. Philosophical Problems and Language

It may seem, however, that there is no need to look for motivations at work in creating philosophical prejudice and confusion. For has not Wittgenstein himself made it very plain that what misleads us in philosophy is language itself, more precisely the misleading 'surface grammar' of the expressions of our language (PI §664)? As he notes, 'our ordinary forms of language easily make us overlook' certain important distinctions (PI §108); 'certain analogies between the forms of expression in different regions of language' mislead us (PI §90) – as when the fact that one can be said to *have* an intention leads us to think that it must be something like a mental 'object' that one then *has*; furthermore, similes 'absorbed into the forms of our language' produce apparent contradictions which confuse us (PI §112), as when we say that 'time flows' even though flowing is a process *in* time. When Wittgenstein says that philosophy is 'a battle against the bewitchment of our intelligence by means of language' (PI §109), is this not the kind of thing he has in mind?

Certainly. That is not the end of the matter, however, for there are questions to ask about *why* we should be misled by the surface forms of our language. Is that just a matter of carelessness or stupidity? Or is it perhaps due to our poor skill in *describing* the everyday use of concepts we master, so that what we need in order to avoid philosophical confusions is a kind of professional training in grammatical description? No doubt we are inept at such description, as Wittgenstein notes (cf. Z §§111–21), but if that were the whole explanation of our troubles, the difficulty of philosophy would after all be no different, in principle, from 'the intellectual difficulty of the sciences', to be conquered by more skill and diligence. This would not only contradict Wittgenstein's stated view of the matter, but also leave it quite unexplained why we are inclined to raise or be struck by philosophical questions in the first place, rather than just staying with the ordinary language games we know how to play, or why philosophical puzzles are felt to be deep and important rather than just curious or absurd. It would also make the *emotional charge* of many philosophical debates quite unintelligible. This is, again, something Wittgenstein insists on; as he observes, giving up a philosophical idea can be 'as difficult as holding back tears or containing an explosion of anger' (PO, 160). Now while our reasons may be very unclear, and we often do not *want* to know them, we don't cry or get angry for *no* reason.

And indeed, Wittgenstein does not merely say that philosophical problems are 'solved…by looking into the workings of our language', but that this is to be done 'in such a way as to make us recognize those workings: *in despite of* an urge to misunderstand them' (PI §109). This suggests that the important thing is not the mere fact that we are misled by the forms of our language, but that we have a kind of craving to mislead ourselves about the sense of our own words. This may sound strange, but in fact we try to do precisely that in countless everyday situations; just think of how easily we trick ourselves into believing that the untruth we spoke was no lie and that we have nothing to feel guilty about. The attempt to present the sense of what we say as different from what it is, to conjure up a sense that isn't there, that isn't supported by anything more substantial than a wish, or again by an anxious denial of the actual sense of our words, is not a specialty confined to philosophizing. On the level of general attitudes, this can be exemplified by *sentimentality*, which might be characterized as a habit of fantasizing a sense one doesn't have the courage or humility to give oneself to, while *cynicism* is a denial of, an attempt to harden oneself against, a sense that is there; the sentimental person pretends she cares, the cynic pretends she doesn't.[5]

When Wittgenstein says that the 'roots' of philosophical problems are 'as deep in us as the forms of our language and their significance is as great as the importance of our language' (PI §111), he does not think of anything merely linguistic; how could *that* be deep? Actually, I would say that the central aim of Wittgenstein's discussions of language is to get us to see that the question 'What *is* the importance of our language?' is one that we have no idea how even to begin answering. His discussions are set to undermine the idea that there is a well-defined 'thing' called 'language' – whether understood in terms of logico-linguistic structure, or more pragmatically as a 'tool of communication', or in some other way – which could be prised apart and inspected in isolation from the life of its speakers.

We can of course speak of language in ways which pick out only certain limited features, but then we shall not be speaking of language in the sense that interests philosophers, which is connected with puzzles about how words can *mean* anything at all, how language, thought, and world are related, and so on. It is about language in this sense that Wittgenstein says: 'to imagine a language means to imagine a form of life' (PI §19). Thus what we say and think about the weight or measure of things gets its sense from our practices of weighing and measuring (cf. PI §§ 240–2), and what we say and think about closeness and distance between people gets its sense from the way we move, touch, caress, kiss, but also avoid or refuse contact with others – and here issues of e.g. desire, love, shame, (self-)disgust are in play. Our words and verbal thoughts get their sense, as also their *charge* and *difficulty*, from reactions that are not essentially verbal, although these are in turn formed by the way we come to articulate them in language.

But if this is true, the point of insisting – as Wittgenstein certainly does – that philosophical problems arise from our difficulties with *language* seems to become

---

[5] For some remarks about the role of fantasy (as opposed to imagination) in creating philosophical *and* moral confusion, see 'Realism and the Realistic Spirit' in Diamond 1991.

unclear. With language as opposed to what? Perhaps there is indeed a lack of clarity in Wittgenstein's thinking on this point; perhaps he goes on insisting on his early idea that philosophy is 'critique of language' (TLP 4.0031) even where his own thinking has made such insistence obsolete. On the other hand, maybe Wittgenstein does not want us to *contrast* language with life at all – a move I have claimed would in fact be senseless by his own lights. Focusing on *language* as the source of philosophical problems may still have point in at least two respects (I will add a third later). First, because such problems are connected with 'our way of expressing ourselves' (CV, 48), of framing our philosophical questions – about e.g. time or the mind – rather than being somehow just 'out there', rooted in 'the very nature' of time or the mind. As Wittgenstein says 'The philosophical puzzle seems insoluble if we are frank with ourselves, and *is* insoluble. That is until we change our question' (MS 149, 56). The task, then, is to change the question, to free ourselves from the grip of the 'picture' that is intimated by our very way of expressing the supposed problem (cf. PI §115) – and this includes the task, noted above, of making clear *what* tempts us in various pictures/ forms of expression.

Secondly, insisting on language underlines that philosophical confusions are not isolated misunderstandings or mistakes in this or that *particular claim*, due to simple mishaps of reasoning or lack of intellectual acumen, say. Rather, as Wittgenstein says, philosophical problems are connected with 'general, deeply rooted, tendencies of [our] thinking' (BB, 30) which cannot be pinned down to this or that idea, opinion, or argument. Indeed, he writes:

> People are deeply imbedded in philosophical...confusions. And to free them from these *presupposes* pulling them out of the immensely manifold connections they are caught up in. One must so to speak regroup their entire language. (PO, 185)

The view of philosophical problems and language that is emerging from our discussion goes against two ideas common in the secondary literature – ideas which themselves, moreover, seem opposed. One is that our philosophical confusions are not continuous with confusions in our everyday lives and language, but somehow begin only when we start philosophizing. The other idea pictures language itself as a kind of quasi-agent which 'itself has the power to draw us into' misunderstandings (McGinn 1997, 21), the claim being that Wittgenstein saw 'the ultimate source of...metaphysics...as lying in language itself, in so much as language itself lures us, tempts us, tricks us into confusing conceptual and factual matters' and into various other misunderstandings (Hilmy 1987, 226). The former notion makes everyday language out to be completely innocent of our philosophical confusions, while the latter seems to blame this confusion on language, which is thus represented alternatively as a maiden pure as snow or a deviously irresistible temptress. The apparent conflict between these two ideas might be dissolved, however, by suggesting that language indeed constantly misleads us, but does so *only when we start philosophizing*, and in any case both ideas seem to presuppose the same picture of something called 'language itself' that we stand over against, either misunderstanding or being misled by it.[6] Against this, I would say that the very notion of 'language itself' is one that Wittgenstein undermines; all we are left with is the fact that *we* make ourselves clear or, as the case may be, confuse ourselves *in language*, in speaking and reflecting. We live speaking, and our problems in speaking are problems in living.[7]

The claim that confusions appear only when we start philosophizing might, however, seem not to depend on any pictures of 'language itself', but simply to register the plain fact that, as Wittgenstein says, 'We don't encounter philosophical problems at all in practical life' (PO, 189). Every day, we deal as a matter of course with things which strike us as mysterious or impossible when we try to grasp them philosophically. As Augustine noted, while I can easily tell you what time it is, I can hardly begin to tell you *what time is* (cf. PI §89). We should remember, however, that everyday language comprises much more than the straightforwardly *practical* uses of language, such as those involved in telling the time or making schedules. Thus we also talk about how time should be used or related to – e.g. we tell someone not to waste their time or to be patient – and about our experience of time, for instance feeling stressed or bored. Here we cannot say that everything runs along smoothly in terms of meaning, as we can in the practical case, where by definition we have only practical problems. Wasting one's time or feeling bored may be characterized precisely as *problems with meaning* – problems, therefore, that tend to arouse conflicting responses in different people ('*I'm* not the one wasting my time!') and within individuals; to be bored *is* a state of internal tension, not knowing what to do with oneself.

It seems to me that, insofar as we can even imagine the life of people who were *only* engaged in narrowly practical tasks, who gave no thought to anything else and never experienced problems of meaning (cf. the builders in PI §2), we could not imagine them ever starting to philosophize. To put the same point differently: if there were a clear demarcation line between 'just living' and reflecting on life, there would *be* nothing to reflect on. Philosophy does not come into being as if out of nowhere, but is rather an outgrowth, continuation, and reflection in sophisticated, intellectual idiom, of the musings and wonderings, the disquiets, yearnings, and refusals that go on in everyday life – an outgrowth also of our everyday wishes to declare, with a quasi-metaphysical emphasis, 'how things *really* are (and will always be)', as revealed e.g. in the use of proverbs to reassure oneself that what just happened confirms what we have always known.

Now the main focus of Wittgenstein's interest is not on the sophisticated arguments of developed philosophical theories, but rather on revealing those 'first steps' in our reasoning that usually 'altogether escape notice', but by which we surreptitiously commit ourselves to 'a particular way of looking at the matter' (PI §308). Warren Goldfarb has

---

[6] Commentators move easily between the two ideas. Thus Hilmy, whose statement of the devious temptress view of language I quoted, in a later text (1995, 238) insists that language itself is not to blame for our misunderstandings.

[7] Wittgenstein does on occasion speak of language as though it were a kind of agent, e.g. he says that 'our language seduces us into asking the same questions over and over' (PO, 185). What I'm arguing is that such claims either contradict Wittgenstein's considered view, or else must be read as figurative speech, and in a way which doesn't contrast 'our language' with 'our life'.

called this the 'proto-philosophical level' of unnoticed preconceptions, pictures, and analogies, 'which then functions to establish what questions are to be asked and answered by philosophical theorizing' (1997, 78). As I understand it, Wittgenstein's view is that the confusions in our philosophizing are connected through these 'proto-philosophical' pictures etc. with widely ramified confusions and difficulties in our lives. What else could he mean by saying, to revert to the quotes above, that freeing someone from philosophical confusion 'presupposes pulling them out of the immensely manifold connections they are caught up in'? And what could be meant by a 'general, deeply rooted, tendency of a person's thinking' that would *only* appear in their philosophizing?

4. LOVE AND EVASION

How, then, might philosophical confusions be intertwined with difficulties in everyday life – elaborate variations on common themes, as it were? Well, suppose one is confused about *love*, for example. This might not sound like a typically Wittgensteinian theme, although there are, as it happens, some striking and quite radical remarks about love in Wittgenstein (see CV, 33, 46, 58). In any case, we do not learn from Wittgenstein by discussing only those particular problems he happened to write about, but by bringing what we have learnt from his way of engaging with the problems that troubled him to bear on our own.

Questions and doubts about love might arise in response to troubles in a particular relationship; a joyless marriage, perhaps, which gives rise to a creeping feeling that the commitment and affection one imagined to be the core of love are there, and yet the most essential thing seems to be missing. Then one may ask, 'Is this love? Do I love my spouse? Does (s)he love me? What is love, really?' – the personal intertwined with the general and philosophical. In fact, it seems that if these questions were *only* about this one relationship, about how the spouses do and do not in fact get along, it would not be a question about *love* at all, but rather about some kind of psychological adjustment, a matter of mere strategy or technique – whereas love, while it is certainly all about one's relation to those one loves, at the same time concerns the sense and meaning one can find in life.

Or is love about that? Perhaps it is just a matter of hormones, or of historically changing conceptions and socially sanctioned ideals, as in the idea of romantic love – or maybe it's about self-affirmation or comfort for loneliness? Or perhaps about all these things? Is there no truth about love; does everyone answer according to their inclination or ideology? *Who is to say?* Can we decide what love is by appeal to some generally agreed upon criteria given in 'our everyday use of the word', as a view of philosophy often, but I believe falsely, attributed to Wittgenstein would seem to imply? What would these criteria be? Cannot all the views I sketch above be found in more or less inchoate or elaborate, momentary or tenacious, forms in our everyday conversations about love? Do they not go into characterizing our life with the concept 'love'?

And yet this is not to say that they are all somehow 'in order'. At any rate, if you're struggling to make sense of your relationships, you don't see it that way; if you did, there would be no struggle. You are rather struggling to see love aright in the absence of any external standard of what is right – and this is connected to the fact, of which you in your reflections are acutely aware, that we can *deceive ourselves* about love, come to see that our understanding has been sentimental or cynical, for example.

Now might not an important reason for the appeal of conventional ideas about love, on which specifically philosophical accounts then elaborate, be precisely that they allow us to deceive ourselves by conventionalizing, impersonalizing our personal problems with love? More specifically, might we not latch onto such conventional ideas in order to *protect* ourselves against what we feel is something overwhelming, perhaps both too terrifying *and* too wonderful, about love; in order to make love *manageable* ('Love is just...'), to *justify* our cowardice in the face of the pain and joy of love, our refusals of those we claim to love ('No one can help their feelings', 'No one can demand that I should...', and so on)? And could not the 'craving for generality' that Wittgenstein speaks of as a main source or form of philosophical confusion (BB, 17–18) often be seen as a desire to *fix* the meaning of challenging notions such as love, to declare a *limit* to what e.g. love is and can be, to its demands and possibilities (consider again the reassuring function of proverbs, noted above)? Furthermore, might not the *allegedly* Wittgensteinian idea that our mere competence as native speakers allows us to describe 'the' grammar of 'love' and other concepts, and thus to fix what it means to love, be one more idea we grasp for to protect ourselves from the challenge of love?

I don't mean these as rhetorical questions. I think they are very real – and important for understanding the peculiar difficulty of philosophical thinking. It will no doubt be said that love, being such an emotionally charged and personal matter, is a special case: if we puzzle over concepts such as 'mind', 'body', or 'language', for instance, then there *are* common and stable standards of use we may refer to. Perhaps. Note, however, that the objection tacitly presupposes a particular, quite conventional and limited, understanding of love and of what it means for something to be a personal matter; otherwise one could not assert so confidently that these 'other' matters are not personal and can be kept separate from love. But may not a change in one's understanding of love change one's understanding of body and mind also – of what it may mean to know another's mind, or to know one's own body, for instance? Do we not sometimes speak of, and *speak*, a 'language of love' – and are we sure that this can be treated as only a marginal case that will not alter our conception of what *language* may be?

Furthermore, might not the focus of most philosophy of language on questions of truth, reference, rule-following, and so on be unsettled – which doesn't mean simply replaced – if we approach language rather with our difficulties with love (broadly understood) in mind? Then, we would have to give a more central place to the kind of facts that Wittgenstein points to in noting that words can be 'charged with...desire', that they can be 'wrung from us – like a cry', or again that 'Words can be *hard* to say: such, for example, as are used to effect a renunciation, or to confess a weakness' (PI §546). Such existentially charged aspects of language can hardly be clarified with the help of concepts like rule-following or language-games, useful as Wittgenstein has shown them to be, throughout the *Philosophical Investigations*, in combating *particular* kinds of misunderstanding of how language works. It might be said that words can be e.g. 'charged with desire' only once we *have* a language in which words have specific meanings, and this must be accounted for in terms of rule-following and so on. That is no doubt true, but might one not with equal justification say that there would be no language at all if people didn't feel a need and desire to address each other, to reach out to each other in language, and that this fundamental aspect cannot be accounted for in the terms philosophers of language usually operate with, but rather seems to open the kind of perspective sketched here.

This is not a plea for doing philosophy of language one way rather than the other, however. Rather, I want to suggest that the kinds of topic we feel drawn to in philosophy and the way we address them may be significantly tied up with questions we feel *uneasy* about. Topics and approaches (e.g. traditional approaches in philosophy of language) may interest us and appeal to us as fundamental precisely because they allow us to marginalize and avoid questioning certain other things (e.g. love), in the same way as one might engage a person in discussion not because one finds *him* so interesting, but rather because someone else, whom one doesn't want to talk to, enters the room. Naturally, I don't claim that our interests in philosophy are always thus defensively motivated, nor do I mean to insinuate anything about where such motivations are likely to be found; philosophy of language is a random example, and one can clearly think about love, too, in all sorts of defensive ways. The two points I wanted to make are simply that we should not unthinkingly assume that philosophy can be neatly divided into discrete topics, and that we should pay attention to the dubious *function* interests which appear simply and thoroughly intellectual may have in our thinking and our lives. What that function is in concrete cases, what *actually* motivates our thinking, is clearly a question each one of us must pose to him- or herself.

5. Philosophy as Critique of its Times

I spoke above about *conventional* notions of love, and a further point of Wittgenstein's insistence that philosophical problems are difficulties with our *language* is, I take it, precisely to underline the communal, cultural, and historical dimensions of our life and troubles with concepts, the way in which our puzzles and blind-spots tend to be more than mere private idiosyncrasies. Wittgenstein writes – in the context, we should note, of discussing quite abstruse matters in the philosophy of mathematics – that '[t]he sickness of a time is cured by an alteration in the mode of life of human beings, and it was possible for the sickness of philosophical problems to get cured only through a changed mode of thought and of life' (RFM II §23). As this quote reminds us, there are changes from one generation or epoch to the next in how we move and speak and think together, changes in intellectual preoccupations, styles, and fashions, and corresponding changes in typical philosophical confusions; such broad changes give the concepts of 'generation' or 'epoch' their sense. Wittgenstein emphasizes the power over our thinking, philosophical and otherwise, of such communal shifts in interest. He remarks on his criticism of particular philosophical ideas: 'At present we are combating a trend. But this trend will die out, superseded by others, and then the way we are arguing against it will no longer be understood; people will not see why all this needed saying' (CV, 43).

Alas, imbibing and expressing the trends, the collective spirit, around us is what we do by default, as it were, insofar as we do not struggle for clarity. Philosophy, as Wittgenstein practises it, is precisely this struggle for clarity, and so a struggle against the domination of collective conceptions and identifications – and here we should note that *individualism* in its various forms is one of the most powerful *collective* conceptions of our times; we all of us tend to think of ourselves in the same way, as autonomous individuals. What I take Wittgenstein to be suggesting is that the unnoticed or seemingly innocuous moves we make at the 'proto-philosophical level' (Goldfarb) express, and help sustain and form, a cultural – collective climate of opinion. This suggestion has been succinctly formulated by Stanley Cavell:

> What directly falls under [Wittgenstein's] criticism are not the results of philosophical argument but those unnoticed turns of mind, casts of phrase, which comprise what intellectual historians call 'climates of opinion', or 'cultural style', and which, unnoticed and therefore unassessed, defend conclusions from direct access – fragments, as it were, of our critical super-egos which one generation passes to the next along with, perhaps as the price of, its positive and permanent achievements: such fragments as 'To be clear about our meaning we must define our terms'…'Language is merely conventional'…'Moral judgments express approval or disapproval'…'Knowledge is increased only by reasoning or by collecting evidence', 'Taste is relative, and people might like, or get pleasure from anything'. (Cavell 1979, 175)

The items on Cavell's short ad hoc list of ideas that contribute to making up our current cultural climate – all of which seem to me indeed influential and worth reflecting on, and all of which are criticized by Wittgenstein – do not necessarily pull in the same direction; there is no suggestion here that the cultural climate must be a homogeneous thing. We should also note that such general ideas do not only or primarily figure in explicit statements about e.g. taste or knowledge; they do that, too, but more importantly they are revealed in the implicit presuppositions that determine what appears to us remarkable and unremarkable, in the spontaneous direction, structure, and feel – and also in the instinctive patterns of evasion – of our conversations, inquiries, and stories. In short: they permeate our lives and our language. This gives sense to Wittgenstein's remark that '[a]n entire mythology is laid down in our language' (PO, 199).

Now the very fact that one can become aware of the sway held over one's thinking by climates of opinion shows that their dominance is not absolute, for *insofar* as we are indeed quite *dominated* by them they do not appear as such; rather we simply see the world as it looks from inside them. We can become aware of their existence only from a point outside them. This, however, need not be conceived of as a complete and once-and-for-all displacement of one perspective by another; the situation is, at least often, rather one of internal conflict, of feeling dissatisfaction with prevalent ways of thinking which at the same time one feels drawn to. When Wittgenstein says that in his philosophical activity he is 'engaged in a struggle with language' (CV, 11), I believe he means the struggle to become clear about such feelings of dissatisfaction: not just to suffer them inarticulately, nor to try to suppress them so as not to come into conflict with one's times, but rather to confront them and think them through. Thus he says that what he develops are 'thoughts and doubts of the kind' we, as well-adjusted members of society, will be 'horrified' by, since we have 'always been trained to avoid indulging' in them and to regard them as 'contemptible'; Wittgenstein tries – like Freud, whom he in fact mentions in this passage – to bring to light precisely those 'problems that education represses without solving'; he says to those repressed doubts: 'you are quite correct, go on asking, demand clarification!' (PG, 381–2).

As G. H. von Wright aptly says, Wittgenstein's attitude to language is 'a fighting, but not a reformist attitude' (1982, 209); he nowhere suggests that our confusions could be remedied by constructing an ideal language, or through some other kind of language reform. Such reforms can be introduced for special purposes, practical, scientific, political, and so on, but, as Wittgenstein emphasizes, 'that will only be in very definite and small areas, and it presupposes that most concepts remain unaltered' (LWPP II, 43). 'Could a legislator abolish the concept of pain?' he asks – rhetorically, we realize, pain being one of those 'basic concepts [that] are interwoven so closely with what is most fundamental in our way of living that they are therefore unassailable' (ibid., 43–4). That is, if we actually try to imagine a human life lacking all the myriad ways of acting and reacting, of perceiving, feeling, and thinking, in which pain comes to expression or is related to, we will soon realize that we don't know what to imagine.

Yet, as our earlier discussion of love indicated, the fact that a concept is 'unassailable' in the sense of being impossible to isolate or imagine absent, nowise implies that our grasp of the concept, of what e.g. love and pain are, is somehow simply given. On the contrary, the tensions, the troubles and conflicts of our lives can be connected to our attempts to articulate and live with such fundamentals as love and pain (I'm not suggesting we could draw up an official list of 'the' fundamentals; the point is simply that particular conflicts etc. may sometimes be helpfully described as manifesting more fundamental issues). And such articulations are not unassailable; they can be criticized. We have an instance of such criticism in Wittgenstein's claim that 'the concept of "the beautiful"' has done 'a lot of mischief' in connection with how we relate to music and many other things, insofar as it expresses a refusal to 'countenance what is distorted, frightful' in human life (CV, 55).

I would say that this judgement is not, or at least it could be developed in a way which showed it not to be, an expression of mere preference or opinion. Nonetheless, it does not presuppose any absolute standard, as though Wittgenstein would have to be able to say what 'the right way' of relating to e.g. music is, on pain of lacking a standard for his criticism. Rather, in our criticisms we react to how we see others reacting and/or realize that we ourselves have been reacting, and we do so from a perspective that, while having no intrinsic claim to be truer than the one we criticize, may nonetheless reveal, to us and to others who were dominated by the perspective we criticize, something we were blind to – or in the case of music rather deaf to, for the requirement that music be 'beautiful' may make one instinctively close one's ears to music that is not; one will hear in it nothing but noise and barbarity. As Wittgenstein notes, to find a new concept, to enter into a 'new way of speaking' is no mere movement of the intellect, but may amount to discovering 'a new sensation' (PI §400).

Wittgenstein is not, then, only trying to teach us 'to pass from [pieces] of disguised nonsense to something that is patent nonsense' (PI §464) by showing how, in making philosophical claims, we often imagine we are making perfect sense when we don't. Just as importantly, he wants to enliven us to possibilities of sense – wonderful, terrible, comical, as the case may be – that are there in our own reactions, but that we haven't acknowledged, and therefore fail to develop. He is always telling himself, and us: don't say that things *must* be like this or *cannot* be like that, but *look and see* what they are like (cf. PI §66). If we do, unexpected facts and possibilities come into view. As Wittgenstein once remarked, 'You'd be surprised!' would make a good motto for the *Investigations* (Drury 1984, 157).

Is the kind of criticism of our self-understanding or lack of it that I have outlined philosophical? Well, if thoughtful scrutiny of our conceptual habits is not philosophy, I don't know what to call it. And while Wittgenstein undermines philosophical pretensions to establish a position as it were outside language, outside life, from which a kind of super-criticism of our actual concepts and forms of life could be launched (cf. PI §97) – a criticism that would therefore as it were be made by no one – he does not rule out the kind of situated criticism I have outlined, where 'situated' does *not* imply 'moderate'. On the contrary, he insists on its necessity if we are to get clear about the roots of our own thinking.

6. COURAGE WITHOUT HEROISM

To make the moral – existential aspect of these remarks about philosophy as a critique of its times more explicit, I want to quote at greater length a passage from Wittgenstein quoted in part above:

> People are deeply imbedded in philosophical...confusions. And to free them from these *presupposes* pulling them out of the immensely manifold connections they are caught up in. One must so to speak regroup their entire language. – But this language...developed as it did because people had – and have – the *inclination to think* in this way. Therefore pulling them out only works with those who live in an instinctive state of *rebellion* against //dissatisfaction with// language. Not with those who following all of their instincts live with the *herd* that has created this language as its proper expression. (PO, 185)

This passage with its Nietzschean-sounding reference to 'the herd' is sure to provoke – but we should ask ourselves *why* it does. If we feel it is 'arrogantly elitist', may that not reveal that we have identified precisely with what might indeed be called the herd? For are we not then thinking something like: 'Who is Wittgenstein to suggest that *we*, common decent people, would somehow be living in collective confusion! Does he think he knows something we don't? Does he think he's somehow better than we are?' I believe this kind of reaction – instinctively identifying oneself as 'one of us', taking offence at the mere suggestion that there might be something wrong with what 'we' do, and implying that *no individual* can be in a position to criticize 'us', the collective – is precisely what Wittgenstein means by 'the herd'. It is not a sociological concept, but denotes an attitude which is just as widespread among social elites as among other people. And if I'm dominated by the 'herd-attitude' I have, indeed, placed myself beyond the reach of philosophical clarification, since I indignantly reject any suggestion that I *need* to get clear about anything; projecting this refusal of self-scrutiny onto others, I take a *question* addressed to me as a *claim* by the other to 'know better'.

But it is precisely as a question to us that I think we should hear Wittgenstein's remark about the herd. It is not a claim about who belongs to the herd – Wittgenstein knows nothing about you or me, so how could he make any claims about us? – but a call to each one of us to consider what our attitude is. You may ask what right Wittgenstein has to ask us this; is it not arrogant for him to do so? I would say: philosophy has nothing to do with questions about 'right' or 'arrogance'. Philosophy is not polite conversation, and the only philosophical questions to ask about what someone says are such as: what does it mean? Is it illuminating and true? Does it point to – or again try to evade or conceal – something important?

I hope the herd-quote has managed to bring vividly into focus the violence and anxiety of the reactions called forth by, and hence the personal challenge involved in, any confrontation with collective identifications as soon as we move away from the level of general statements about 'the times' to something that *actually provokes us*, the people whose concrete patterns of thought and life give the times their shape.

It is against this background, I think, that we should read Wittgenstein's frequent remarks on the necessity for courage in thinking: 'What I do think essential is carrying out the work of clarification with COURAGE: otherwise it becomes just a clever game' (CV, 19; cf. CV, 52). These are certainly among those remarks it seems hard to make sense of if one shies away from a moral – existential interpretation of the character of philosophical difficulties. To reflect on one's inclinations to use words this misleading way or that may be difficult and demanding in all kinds of ways, but as such it hardly takes *courage*. When might it take courage to acknowledge, even to oneself, thoughts or inclinations one finds in oneself? To put it differently: when might it seem dangerous to do so? It seems that the answer, at least a good part of it, is: when it threatens isolation from or confrontation with others – or, to be more exact, threatens a confrontation with others that raises for oneself the unsettling question of who one is in relation to them: 'Who am I to think *this*, feel *that*, when everyone else thinks or feels differently?'

Note two things. First, cowardice is not only or primarily manifested – neither in life generally nor, certainly, *in thinking* – in running away from a danger one acutely faces, but rather in manoeuvres of evasion which allow one to keep out of danger's way without overt humiliation. Secondly, the question '*Who am I* to think *this*...?' does not automatically arise whenever one has a thought which is in some sense radical and critical, for one way in which one's thinking may *fit* the current climate of opinion is precisely by raising what to those at home in that climate seem pertinent and hard questions, but which rather than challenging its defining assumptions facilitate interesting new developments within it, and therefore appear simultaneously *comfortable* (at bottom, nothing needs to change) and *exhilarating* (yet new lines of advance and topics of debate have been opened). When a thought starts to feel dangerous, frightening, we have crossed into a different dimension; it is only then that the challenge of thinking for oneself really makes itself felt.

To think for oneself has always been the heroic ideal of philosophy, but we rarely give much thought to what this really means. Here, if ever, we should heed Wittgenstein's injunction to 'describe in practical details and dispassionately what a reality looks like which corresponds to the general world-description of philosophers', to take 'the general (vague) talk of philosophers seriously and make a practical application of it' (MS 130, 51). If we reflect on what it is like to be considered by colleagues and friends a dangerous fanatic, a 'difficult' character always raising awkward questions, or a vulgar and disgusting person, then the deceptive air of heroism quickly evaporates, and we are left with a nasty and terrifying prospect. But that is the prospect that thinking for oneself threatens, and that is why it takes courage – a courage without heroism, insofar as heroism itself is a thoroughly social notion, concerned with cutting a heroic appearance in the eyes of others and/or oneself, whereas the difficulty here is precisely to retain or gain a sense of oneself in relation to others in the *absence* of any social validation and affirmation of the appearance one makes. Wittgenstein singles out as the most tenacious aspect of his own cowardice the 'fear of appearing ridiculous' (DB, 58–9); it seems to me that our concept of the heroic would self-destruct, as it were, if we took as its paradigm the courage to appear ridiculous.

7. The Challenge
of the Non-hypothetical

Wittgenstein's remark that 'the philosopher' is not 'a citizen of any community of ideas' (Z §455) means, in concrete terms, that in philosophizing one must free oneself from the vain fear of appearing ridiculous – or irrelevant, incomprehensible, and so on – in the eyes of this or that community with its normative ideas. In philosophy, there are no given norms of reasonableness, propriety, or relevance to appeal to. Although we always *start out* from some such norms, in the end each one of us can 'only step forth as an individual and speak in the first person' – to quote Wittgenstein's words about ethical speech in the 'absolute' sense where one is also not concerned with registering communal norms of propriety or decency (Waismann 1965, 13).

The claim here is not that philosophizing could or should take place in a kind of social vacuum, where private insight would somehow go its own way with no regard for community with others even in thought. No, the point is precisely that philosophizing means raising *questions* about the character of the community we have, and the community we might have, and so by definition opening up a space which is not simply of or in any given community. The aim of philosophizing is thus not to stand alone – quite the contrary. If thoughts that go against the collective grain merely made their authors 'stand alone', we might pity them, or leave them alone, but we would not feel threatened by them. Insofar as we do feel threatened, it's because their thoughts *come all too close*, provoking questions in us about our *own* relation to important matters. What provokes us is the sense that what they say puts what *we* do into question, somehow revealing it as different from what we supposed or pretended it to be.

Mere differences of opinion or preference do not create such provocation: you may dislike and oppose my opinion, but if you view it as merely an opinion this means that you will not feel provoked by it; the private fact about me that I hold this opinion does not as such concern you. External facts, including those discovered by science, more or less probable hypotheses, explanations, and theories, and such propositions as can be proved by logic and reasoning, all likewise fail to provoke personally. To be sure, it may be very disagreeable to have to acknowledge certain facts or to admit that a piece of reasoning seems to entail an unwanted conclusion. Nonetheless, such apparent truths remain external to us and to that extent hypothetical, insofar as we may come to find a flaw in the reasoning or a decisive fact that had been overlooked, which allows us after all to dismiss, without further ado, the disagreeable conclusion.

With regard to moral – existential insights *and* philosophical insights as Wittgenstein conceives of them, things are different. Wittgenstein insists that in philosophy we must 'treat as irrelevant every question of opinion' (MS 155, 40r); that there 'must not be anything hypothetical in our considerations'; that we are not advancing debatable claims, but 'arranging what we have always known' (PI §109) in a reflection which 'simply puts everything before us, and neither explains nor deduces anything' (PI §126) – where this thing we had always known may, to repeat, be something we did not *want* to see, something we were deceiving ourselves about. Furthermore, Wittgenstein insists that 'we do not draw conclusions' in philosophy; '"But it must be like this!" is not a philosophical proposition' (PI §599).

All this sounds absurd, given the standard view of philosophy as concerned precisely with proving things and arguing for conclusions, but it makes perfect sense if philosophy is indeed a struggle with basically moral rather than intellectual difficulties. To become clear about what one has done in a moral sense is not to be convinced by argument. 'I must have hurt him' is not the expression of moral insight, but a reconstruction of what happened from an external standpoint; you might e.g. conclude from my hurt look that the words you meant quite innocently in fact hurt me. It is different if you exclaim, in remorse, 'Oh God, how I hurt him!' Here, you do not draw a conclusion based on arguments or evidence, you 'simply put everything before yourself', not trying to explain anything, or explain it away. This you may sometimes do in response to what someone else says, but then she will not have told you what you 'should' or 'must' think about things; rather what she said has made you see for yourself how things are with you.

This is what Wittgenstein gives as his aim in philosophy, too. 'I ought', he says, 'to be no more than a mirror, in which my reader can see his own thinking with all its deformities so that, helped in this way, he can put it right' (CV, 18); his aim is to place things 'right in front of our eyes, not covered by any veil' (CV, 6).

If philosophy were a primarily intellectual pursuit like the sciences, this last quote would be mere metaphysics of the kind whose empty pretensions to arrive at 'naked reality' – as opposed to some particular conceptualization or other of reality – Wittgenstein is always exposing. In moral – existential terms, it makes another kind of sense to speak this way, however. For we know what it means to come to see that we have been deceiving ourselves, have allowed ourselves to be blinded by prejudice or cynicism or sentimentality, and so on: to realize such things *is* to tear away a veil with which we had ourselves covered the reality of our life. The challenge of philosophy, Wittgenstein seems to suggest, is to tear away such veils, thus exposing our own unacknowledged and disowned attitudes to the world and ourselves.

This is not to deny that there is a sense in which moral and philosophical insight is never final, and tearing away one veil may just reveal others behind it. Thus, to truly struggle with one's vanity involves an ever deepening insight into how it hides even in apparently quite innocent and laudable reactions, and one's understanding of a philosophical insight may similarly, as Wittgenstein points out, undergo infinite displacements or deepening – without on that account becoming hypothetical. For 'every new problem which arises may put in question the *position* which our previous partial results are to occupy in the final picture' (BB, 44), and we may come to see that we mistook, distorted, or banalized the *point* of a philosophical remark, failed to see *where* it really works (cf. DB, 94).

What needs special emphasis here, however, is the way in which such deepening philosophical understanding is tied to a deepening or opening up of one's life, and thus to a personal, moral-existential challenge. To return to the case of love, the desire to fix the meaning of love that I spoke of above arises, I would say, as an attempt to protect oneself against the insight that love is a task and a struggle; that a crucial aspect of love is that we can *learn*, as we can also deceive ourselves, about love; that we may be, and most certainly will be, *changed* by our struggles with love; that this change in us is also a change in our concepts, or in our conception of our concepts (I think it can be put either way), and that such changes are not separable from how far we *dare to go in loving*. As Wittgenstein says, speaking of how someone might come to understand and embrace Christian concepts like redemption or hell, or again love in the Christian sense:

> A different way of living will bring quite different pictures to the fore, make quite different pictures *necessary*. In the way need teaches one to pray. That is not to say that living differently will necessarily change one's *opinions*. But if one lives differently, one will speak differently. With a new life one learns new language-games. (DB, 75)

If the new way of living brings new concepts, conversely understanding concepts such as love differently may challenge one's current way of living and loving – for some possibilities are such that the mere recognition of them will itself work as a kind of criticism of actuality, e.g. by making it impossible for one to hold on to the comfortable notion that there is no alternative to one's current way of life. This concrete moral challenge that conceptual reflection may bring is a crucial aspect, it seems to me, of the peculiar difficulty of philosophical thinking. Criticisms of our general ideas and conceptual habits are effective – in other words hit home, and therefore provoke us – precisely to the extent that they manage to point not just to 'different possibilities' in general, but to ways in which our current ideas and habits are built on and reveal *refusals* on our part to countenance certain realities or real possibilities (e.g. the reality of the 'distorted and frightful' in human life). Such refusals – we may also speak of repression here – are not 'hidden', but on the contrary revealed in the way we talk and think, especially in the ambiguities and lacunae where we cease to make, because we don't want to make or can't stand making, clear sense. A main business of philosophy, I take Wittgenstein to be suggesting, is precisely to bring out in concrete, provocative detail where and how this happens.[8]

8. The Constant Difficulty

Before ending, I must explicitly address the peculiar, as it were second-order, difficulty that seriously discussing this view of philosophical difficulties implies. In general, it can be stated by saying that it is characteristic of the kind of difficulty we have been discussing – the kind, that is, having to do with our not *wanting* to see how things are (cf. PO, 161) – that if the difficulty is indeed present, if one is, in one's philosophizing, trying to avoid or distort certain matters, then this fact will itself tend to make one reject a correct diagnosis of one's difficulty; one will instinctively feel that it is, for instance, outrageous or unconvincing or in some other way false, or one may react as Wittgenstein says Ramsey reacted to the fundamental philosophical questions he disliked, by getting 'in part disquieted and in part bored', while looking for some way to declare the whole matter 'trivial' (CV, 17). This is precisely what gives moral struggles their characteristic difficulty: understanding and change are blocked not by simple misunderstanding but by a refusal to see the character of our own motivation and involvement in situations; thus the envious person doesn't see her envy, but only how 'unfair' it is that others are so 'undeservedly' successful. A 'refusal to see', I said, but of course it is the refusal of self-deception or repression, and thus a refusal to see which refuses to see itself, too, and is thus subjectively experienced as a real blindness.

---

[8] A fruitful analogy between Wittgensteinian philosophy and Freudian psychoanalysis, one that hasn't so far been developed in the literature on their relation, might be worked out in terms of such a tracing of the patterns of repression in our language. In Backström 2007 I investigate a number of such patterns in our use of moral concepts.

The problem is twofold: how can one ever get others to see that they are deceiving themselves; how can we ever hope to get any answer other than 'No!' to a question whether this or that motive might not be what is driving allegiance or resistance to certain philosophical ideas – since either it isn't the motive, or if it is, it will be denied? Secondly, and more importantly still: how can one discover such self-deception in oneself? For as Wittgenstein notes, or confesses: 'Nothing is so difficult as not deceiving oneself' (CV, 34), and '[w]hen you bump against the limits of your own honesty it is as though your thoughts get into a whirlpool, an infinite regress: You can *say* what you like, it takes you no further' (CV, 8).

It seems clear that there can be no general method for tackling these problems. What we can do, however, is to remind ourselves that we *do* sometimes see through our own self-deceptions, and sometimes others can help us do so. This may seem mysterious, but it is surely no more mysterious than the fact that we can manage to deceive ourselves in the first place. Other than this, I think all we can do is reflect on these matters, keep them in mind as we discuss philosophical questions, while reminding ourselves constantly, in the spirit of Wittgenstein, that winning arguments and proving others wrong is quite useless. The promise of philosophy is rather that one may come to prove *oneself* wrong, to see through one's own illusions.

References

Backström, Joel (2007). *The Fear of Openness: An Essay on Friendship and the Roots of Morality*. Åbo: Åbo Akademi University Press.

Baker, Gordon P. (2004). *Wittgenstein's Method: Neglected Aspects*, ed. Katherine Morris. Oxford: Blackwell.

Bouwsma, O. K. (1995). *Bouwsma's Notes on Wittgenstein's Philosophy, 1965–1975*. Lewiston/Queenston/Lampeter: The Edwin Mellen Press.

Cavell, Stanley (1979). *The Claim of Reason: Wittgenstein, Skepticism, Morality, and Tragedy*. Oxford: Oxford University Press.

Conant, James (2001). 'Philosophical and Biography', in James C. Klagge ed., *Wittgenstein: Biography and Philosophy*. Cambridge: Cambridge University Press.

——(2002). 'On Going the Bloody *Hard* Way in Philosophy', in John H. Whittaker ed., *The Possibilities of Sense*. Basingstoke: Palgrave.

Crary, Alice and Read, Rupert eds. (2000). *The New Wittgenstein*. London and New York: Routledge.

Diamond, Cora (1991). *The Realistic Spirit: Wittgenstein, Philosophy and the Mind*. Cambridge, MA: MIT Press.

Drury, M. O'C. (1984). 'Some Notes on Conversations with Wittgenstein' and 'Conversations with Wittgenstein', in Rush Rhees ed., *Recollections of Wittgenstein*. Oxford: Oxford University Press.

Glock, H.-J. (1991). 'Philosophical Investigations section 128: "theses in philosophy" and undogmatic procedure', in R. Arrington and H.-J. Glock eds., *Wittgenstein's Philosophical Investigations: Text and Context*. London: Routledge.

Goldfarb, Warren (1997). 'Wittgenstein on Fixity of Meaning', in William W. Tait ed., *Early Analytic Philosophy: Frege, Russell, Wittgenstein*. Chicago: Open Court.

HACKER, P. M. S. (2000). 'Was He Trying to Whistle It?', in Crary and Read 2000.

—— (2007). 'Gordon Baker's Late Interpretation of Wittgenstein', in G. Kahane, E. Kanterian, and O. Kuusela eds., *Wittgenstein and His Interpreters*. Oxford: Blackwell.

HILMY, S. STEPHEN (1987). *The Later Wittgenstein: The Emergence of a New Philosophical Method*. Oxford: Blackwell.

——(1995). 'Wittgenstein on Language, Mind and Mythology', in R. Egidi ed., *Wittgenstein: Mind and Language*. Dordrecht: Kluwer.

KUUSELA, OSKARI (2008). *The Struggle Against Dogmatism: Wittgenstein and the Concept of Philosophy*. Cambridge, MA: Harvard University Press.

LUCKHARDT, C. G. ed. (1979). *Wittgenstein: Sources and Perspectives*. Hassocks, Sussex: Harvester.

MALCOLM, NORMAN (2001). *Ludwig Wittgenstein: A Memoir*. Oxford: Clarendon Press.

McGINN, MARIE (1997). *Routledge Philosophy Guidebook to Wittgenstein and the Philosophical Investigations*. London: Routledge.

MONK, RAY (2001). 'Philosophical Biography: The Very Idea', in James C. Klagge ed., *Wittgenstein: Biography and Philosophy*. Cambridge: Cambridge University Press.

RHEES, RUSH (1981). 'Postscript', in R. Rhees ed., *Ludwig Wittgenstein: Personal Recollections*. Oxford: Basil Blackwell.

——(2001). 'On Wittgenstein', *Philosophical Investigations*, 24(2): 153–62.

SCHULTE, JOACHIM (1986). 'Wittgenstein and Conservatism', in S. G. Shanker ed., *Ludwig Wittgenstein: Critical Assessments*, Vol. 4. London: Croom Helm.

WAISMANN, FRIEDRICH (1965). 'Notes on Talks with Wittgenstein', *Philosophical Review*, 74: 12–16.

WISDOM, JOHN (1965). *Paradox and Discovery*. Oxford: Blackwell.

WITTGENSTEIN, LUDWIG (1958). *Philosophical Investigations*, trans. G. E. M. Anscombe. Oxford: Basil Blackwell.

——(1958). *Preliminary Studies for the "Philosophical Investigations", Generally Known as the Blue and Brown Books*. Oxford: Basil Blackwell.

——(1961). *Tractatus logico-philosophicus*, trans. D. F. Pears and B. F. McGuinness. London: Routledge & Kegan Paul.

——(1975). *Philosophical Remarks*, ed. R. Rhees, trans. R. Hargreaves and R. White. Oxford: Blackwell.

——(1980). *Culture and Value*, ed. G. H. von Wright, trans. Peter Winch. Chicago: University of Chicago Press.

——(1989). *Zettel*, ed. G. E. M. Anscombe and G. H. von Wright, trans. G. E. M. Anscombe. Oxford: Basil Blackwell.

——(1992). *Last Writings on the Philosophy of Psychology*, vol. 2, ed. G. H. von Wright and H. Nyman, trans. C. G. Luckhardt and M. A. E. Aue. Oxford: Basil Blackwell.

——(1993). *On Certainty*, ed. G. E. M. Anscombe and G. H. von Wright, trans. G. E. M. Anscombe and D. Paul. Oxford: Blackwell.

——(1995). *Ludwig Wittgenstein, Cambridge Letters: Correspondence with Russell, Keynes, Moore, Ramsey and Sraffa*, ed. B. McGuiness and G. H. von Wright. Oxford: Basil Blackwell.

——(1997). *Denkbewegungen: Tagebücher 1930–1932, 1936–1937*. Part 1: *Normalisierte Fassung*, ed. Ilse Somavilla. Innsbruck: Haymon-Verlag.

——(1998). *Remarks on the Foundations of Mathematics*, ed. G. E. M. Anscombe, R. Rhees, and G. H. von Wright, trans. G. E. M. Anscombe. Oxford: Basil Blackwell.

WITTGENSTEIN, LUDWIG (1999). *Philosophical Occasions*. Indianapolis: Hackett Publishing Company.

——(2000). *Wittgenstein's Nachlass: The Bergen Electronic Edition*. Oxford: Oxford University Press.

——with FRIEDRICH WAISMANN (2003). *The Voices of Wittgenstein: The Vienna Circle*, ed. Gordon Baker. London and New York: Routledge.

WRIGHT, G. H. VON (1982). *Wittgenstein*. Oxford: Basil Blackwell.

PART VII

RELIGION, AESTHETICS, ETHICS

CHAPTER 33

WITTGENSTEIN ON RELIGIOUS BELIEF

STEPHEN MULHALL

THIS chapter is based on three (I hope uncontroversial) assumptions. The first is that Wittgenstein's impact in the philosophy of religion has been more a function of the work of those inspired by him than of his own writings on this topic (which are exiguous and fragmentary in the extreme[1]). To be sure, there is still much to be learnt from Wittgenstein's own remarks; and some recent work on them has been particularly helpful in the difficult task of discerning the coherent and powerful philosophical perspective that might underlie their apparent lack of systematicity.[2] But the slim, multiply mediated, and exceptionally tentative nature of the relevant textual evidence makes it all but impossible to establish interpretative conclusions with any real confidence; and insofar as any such conclusions have been established, I have discussed the central themes of the position that emerges, and defended them against both obvious and sophisticated misunderstandings, elsewhere.[3] Accordingly, I felt that it would be more useful in the present context to focus on those writers inspired by Wittgenstein whose work has certainly been the primary means of determining his contemporary resonance in this philosophical field.

My second assumption is that these Wittgensteinian philosophers of religion took their primary inspiration from Wittgenstein's later approach to philosophy in general, as manifest in the *Philosophical Investigations*, rather than from his specific writings on

[1] They include brief remarks in the *Tractatus Logico-Philosophicus*, and the 'Lecture on Religious Belief'; some material in *Lectures and Conversations on Aesthetics, Psychology and Religious Belief*, which are in fact a collation of notes taken by those attending the lectures; and scattered passages in *Culture and Value*.

[2] I think here particularly of Cora Diamond's 2005 essay 'Wittgenstein on Religious Belief: The Gulfs Between Us'.

[3] In my essay 'Wittgenstein and the Philosophy of Religion' (2001), in particular, I discuss such matters as Wittgenstein's governing sense of the key differences between religious and empirical beliefs, his understanding of what it is for God's existence to be eternal, and his presentation of religious faith as akin to a passionate commitment to a system of reference; and I identify a number of misinterpretations of these claims by his critics.

religion (most of which were not published until after much canonically Wittgensteinian work in the field had been done[4]). And my third assumption is that such Wittgensteinian philosophy of religion has been burdened virtually from its outset by the fateful charge of fideism. This charge originated with Kai Nielsen (1967), who argued that assumptions common to a range of Wittgensteinian authors entailed an unacceptable immunization of religious belief against rational criticism (just as theological fideists hold that religious belief is grounded on faith rather than reason). Repeated and fervent attempts on the part of those authors to rebut the charge have never succeeded in removing it from this intellectual scene.

Consequently, Wittgenstein's influence on the field thus far has been determined by two opposed models of his approach: the first might be called 'The Fideist Wittgenstein' (as specified by Nielsen), and the second 'The Canonical Wittgenstein' (as actually advanced by those canonical authors that Nielsen – mistakenly, in their view – regarded as fideists). The extent to which Wittgensteinian philosophy of religion risks remaining trapped in the vice created by this oppositional structure, as if fated to battles over the rights and wrongs of its own history, and to the endless reiteration of points never apparently appreciated by those to whom they are made – what one might call the predominance of heat over light in these struggles – is evident in the recent collection entitled *Wittgensteinian Fideism?*[5] This chapter cannot therefore avoid engaging with the issue of fideism; but it will also attempt to unsettle its dominance by exploring Cora Diamond's development and application of a third perspective, one we might call 'The Realistic Wittgenstein' (after the title of her collection *The Realistic Spirit*). For this gives us a way of seeing both the fideistic and the canonical versions of Wittgensteinian philosophy of religion as based on a questionable reading of the later Wittgenstein, and so as failing to open up a genuinely Wittgensteinian approach to philosophical questions concerning the phenomena of religious belief.

1. The Fideist Wittgenstein: Grammar as Veil

Nielsen specifies the unacceptable core of Wittgensteinian fideism as follows:

> There is no Archimedean point in terms of which a philosopher (or for that matter anyone else) can relevantly criticize whole modes of discourse or, what comes to the same thing, ways of life, for each mode of discourse has its own specific criteria of rationality/irrationality, intelligibility/unintelligibility and reality/unreality. (Nielsen and Phillips 2005, 22)

---

[4] Uncontroversial members of this canon include Winch 1958; Malcolm 1960 ('Anselm's Ontological Arguments'); and Phillips 1965.
[5] Nielsen and Phillips 2005.

Nielsen emphasizes that this unacceptable conclusion results from attempts by Wittgensteinian philosophers to elaborate certain, possibly insightful, strands of Wittgenstein's thought in ways that Wittgenstein himself might not have endorsed; but he also asserts that these elaborations are perfectly natural developments of claims that Wittgenstein did make, and that the conclusion they license is patently absurd. The strands of thought he has in mind are as follows: (i) to imagine a language is to imagine a form of life (see e.g. PI §19); (ii) what must be accepted – the given – are forms of life (see e.g. PI II, 226); (iii) ordinary language is in order as it stands (see e.g. PI §98, citing TLP 5.5563); (iv) philosophy must in no way interfere with the actual use of language, but can in the end only describe it (see e.g. PI §124). One can hardly deny that Wittgenstein makes these claims, or something like them. The key question is: to what extent does a proper understanding of them license a species of fideism in the philosophy of religion?

It is worth emphasizing that these four claims are not restricted to the field of religion; their range of reference is perfectly general, including all aspects of our ordinary lives with words. At the same time, they are primarily addressed to philosophers: they form part of Wittgenstein's various attempts to articulate his sense of what philosophy – with its particular cares and commitments – can and cannot do with respect to our ordinary lives with words. Two points follow immediately. First, if the consequence of applying these claims with respect to religious belief is a species of fideism, then a parallel conclusion must follow from their application to any other mode of discourse. If Wittgenstein is a fideist about religion, that will be because he adopts what amounts to a fideist stance with respect to human language and forms of life in general – a substitution of faith for reason. Second, Nielsen's assumption (expressed in the first bracketed clause of the above quotation from his essay) that the apparent restrictions Wittgenstein places upon the critical activities of philosophers must also apply more generally is potentially misleading. That assumption is trivially true if it means that the 'restrictions' apply not just to those who profess to be academic philosophers, but to anyone with a genuinely philosophical interest in our language and forms of life; but it is false if it means that those 'restrictions' apply to everyone, regardless of whether their critical interest in our language and forms of life is genuinely philosophical.

What does Wittgenstein take to be distinctive of a philosophical interest in things? What is the typical character of a philosophical question or problem? According to the discussion of philosophical method in sections 89–133 of the *Investigations* (from which two of Nielsen's four claims are taken), a philosopher is interested in the essence of things; she is driven by an urge to comprehend not the facts of nature but rather the basis or essence of everything empirical – the space of possibilities within which what happens to be the case locates itself. A philosophical question is thus one to which the acquisition of further empirical knowledge is irrelevant: the philosopher does not seek new knowledge in order to alleviate ignorance; she seeks understanding in order to relieve a sense of confusion about what she already knows. And whereas traditional philosophers tend to conceive of the essence of things as hidden from view, hence as having to be revealed, say by penetrating the veil of mere appearance, Wittgenstein suggests instead that essence finds expression in grammar – in the kinds of statement that we make about the relevant phenomenon. In short, our philosophical inquiries into essence can and must take the form of grammatical investigations; the essence of things can be rendered surveyable simply by a rearrangement of what any speaker always already knows – how to use words, what to say when.

Wittgenstein's view seems to be that the kinds of statement that we make about a phenomenon, and the kinds of statement that we do not make, make manifest the kind of phenomenon it is; if we clarify the criteria we employ for counting something as a phenomenon of the relevant kind, we thereby clarify that without which such a phenomenon would not be the kind of thing it is. What we judge that it does (not) make sense to say about something makes manifest its essential possibilities, the kinds of features it must possess if it is to count as the kind of thing it is, as well as those features it may possess (and the kinds of variation of feature to which it might intelligibly be subject) without ceasing to count as that kind of thing. To know this is, in effect, to grasp our concept of that thing; and what more might there be to knowing the essence of a thing than that?

But might not the essence of the thing nevertheless differ from our concept of it, so that its true, underlying nature is not manifest in, but rather hidden by, the grammar of our discourse about it? If so, grammar is simply one more veil of appearance that philosophical inquiry must, in principle, be willing to penetrate. But to conceive of grammar as an (at least potentially) concealing veil involves conceiving of it as a false or otherwise misleading representation of what is really the case; and that in turn involves conceiving of it as being in the business of representation (as if modes of discourse were theories). But if a grammatical investigation displays what it makes sense to say about something (what it is for any talk about something to count as, to be, talk about that kind of thing), then the grammar thereby made manifest is not itself a kind of talk about that thing, and so cannot be saying anything false or otherwise misleading about it – any more than it can be saying something true.

Grammar, one might say, articulates a logical space of possibilities within which something of the relevant kind will occupy some particular location or other; it articulates the terms in which that kind of thing can intelligibly be represented (truly or falsely). But if one regards those terms as themselves representations of something, one is attempting to conceive of a mode of discourse as if it were a particular discursive act – to think of this logical space as itself the occupant of a particular location in a larger space of possibilities, as if grammar itself were a deployment of grammar, and clarifications of meaning were descriptions of reality. It amounts to viewing the distinction between sense and nonsense as if it were a species of the distinction between truth and falsehood.

This is one way of recounting the grammar of Wittgenstein's concept of grammar, as understood by the canonical Wittgensteinian philosophers Nielsen targets. And the point of recalling it is not to demonstrate that the highly controversial conception of philosophy it engenders is right, but to clarify what the consequences of adopting it really are. First, Wittgenstein's methodological advice is directed primarily to those with a distinctively philosophical interest in the essence of things, and a distinctively philosophical tendency to imagine that our modes of discourse with respect to those things stands in need of a certain kind of rational justification (because they presupposed a mode of correspondence to reality that they might not possess). It is only to those in the grip of such a picture of grammar as a kind of representation that Wittgenstein's methodological remarks are worth making.

Second, although those remarks appear to restrict philosophy to the task of describing grammar (as opposed to explaining, hypothesizing, or theorizing about an essence of things that grammar might veil), they do not in fact impose a restriction of any kind. For if, as Wittgenstein claims, evaluations in terms of truth or falsity are not amongst the kinds of things we say about articulations of grammar, then there is no intelligibly specifiable task of the kind philosophers take themselves to be envisaging when they suggest that grammar might veil essence from our sight, and so nothing that we are prevented from doing, or even from attempting to do, when observing Wittgenstein's methodological advice. That advice is, strictly speaking, not a recommendation or a command, but a reminder – a reminder that what we are tempted to picture as a limitation (beyond which there is something specific that we cannot do) is in fact a limit (beyond which nothing, neither a possible task nor an impossible task, has thus far been specified). One might say: there is no larger philosophical space of the relevant kind within which Wittgenstein's conception of the subject locates itself, and hence no alternative conception to which one might oppose it. Accordingly, a criterion for properly understanding his remarks is the realization that they are in a certain sense self-subverting – that their apparently prohibitive intention is in fact nothing of the kind, and that they leave everything precisely as it was for those who wish to criticize any given mode of discourse or form of life.

In the specific case of religious practices and ways of life, it is not just that one can wield the full range of internally acknowledged ways of criticizing specific elements, as well as specific versions, of that way of life (modes of criticism embodied in such notions as 'superstition' and 'heresy'). There is also a wide range of what one might call external modes of criticism, including ones that question the legitimacy of religious ways of life as such. Nothing Wittgenstein claims about the grammar of 'grammar' prohibits someone from finding religious belief to encourage immorality, political and social discrimination, cultural primitivism, and barbarism, to name but a few of the more familiar objections to which religions are heir.

Nietzsche is a particularly significant reference point here, since his critical perspective is one that, on the conception of philosophy I have outlined, must be recognized as a mode of philosophical criticism of religion. His genealogical analysis of Christianity is an attempt to characterize the essence of that mode of religious belief – where essence here is understood exactly as Wittgenstein proposes: as a matter of the function or structure of the phenomenon under consideration, taken not as a doctrinal system on which a set of practices is founded but as a mode of speaking, thinking, and living – a way of making sense of things as a whole. When Nietzsche characterizes that form of human life as inherently ascetic, hence as a sado-masochistic mode of life-denial, he aims to provide a criticism of the point or purpose of the Christian religious enterprise as such (together with its secular variants and offshoots). And nothing Wittgenstein says about the essentially descriptive nature of philosophy provides any reason for believing that religious forms of life, taken as a whole, cannot coherently be criticized in such terms.

Nielsen's critical characterization of Wittgensteinian philosophy of religion as fideistic implies that it regards religious forms of life as founded on faith rather than reason, hence immune to any kind of rational criticism, because their intelligibility depends on criteria internal to those forms of life, and essentially distinct from those governing other modes of discourse. In fact, Wittgenstein's general philosophical principles (if they deserve so grand a title) suggest only that one apparently coherent kind of rational evaluation of modes of discourse is really empty; there is no obvious sense to be made of such criticism at the level of forms of life taken as a whole. But if there is no conceptual space for such exercises of reason, then there is no space that might be occupied by faith as opposed to reason, either in general or in the specific case of religious forms of life. And since 'external' critiques of the kinds mentioned above plainly make sense both to religious believers and to others, we have no reason to believe that the intelligibility or the rationality of religious belief must be settled in terms determined by religious believers, and essentially distinct from the terms appropriate to other forms of life. Nietzsche's criticism, for example, aims rather to subvert the terms of religious self-understanding, as well as the central concepts of modern, non-religious ethics.

What *is* (trivially) required of such 'external' critiques is that they be comprehensible as critiques of the particular forms of religious life that they purport to target: in other words, we must be able to make sense of them as criticisms of this specific phenomenon. But whether any such critique does so cannot be settled a priori – as if grammar determines in advance which forms of criticism of religion are licit and which are not. It can only be settled in our actual judgements, from case to case, of actually constructed criticism; and as the case of Nietzsche shows, such cases might as easily compel us to revise our hitherto-settled overall sense of what religion can and does mean as they might confirm it.

2. The Canonical Wittgenstein: Grammar, Coherence, and Sense

It certainly seems hard to deny that, if we wish critically to evaluate a given phenomenon, we must first clarify what is to count as an instance of it; before questions about the value of something arise, questions about the meanings of the terms in which we grasp it should be settled. It is, however, central to the work of many canonical Wittgensteinian philosophers of religion that this trivial condition for pertinence is systematically violated by much of the writing in their discipline – that many philosophers do not attend to the ways in which religious believers actually employ their distinctive discursive terms, and so fail to appreciate the actual significance of religious discourse in its human *Heimat*. In short, they fail to treat religious words in the context of the language-games that are their original homes (PI §116).

A famous instance of Wittgensteinian work in this spirit is Norman Malcolm's essay 'Anselm's Ontological Arguments'. Malcolm distinguishes two different ontological arguments in Anselm's *Proslogion*: one which presupposes that existence is a perfection; and another which presupposes that necessary existence is a perfection. Malcolm concurs with the general opinion that Kant's critique decisively refutes the first of these arguments, but he denies that it refutes the second; for whereas it seems evident that 'existence' cannot be regarded (logically or grammatically speaking) as greater or more perfect than 'non-existence', the same is not true of 'necessary existence' when compared with 'contingent existence'. On the contrary: Malcolm claims that there are straight-forward grammatical connections in ordinary language between the ideas of contingent existence, dependency, limitation, and imperfection, and hence between the idea of a perfect being – that than which nothing greater can be conceived – and non-contingent or necessary existence.

A being whose existence is contingent is one that might not have existed; hence its actual existence must have an explanation – it must in some way be dependent upon the existence and/or actions of something else. A computer that requires a mains electricity source if it is to function can intelligibly be said to be less great or more limited, hence less perfect, than one that does not; hence any being whose existence is dependent upon something outside itself could not intelligibly be said to be a perfect being, for it would then be possible to imagine something greater or more perfect than it (namely, something which lacked that dependency or limitation). Since the Christian tradition conceives of God precisely as 'that than which nothing greater can be conceived', it follows that God's existence must be non-dependent, non-contingent – that is, necessary. But unless the very idea of a necessarily existent being is incoherent, then its existence cannot be an open (that is, a contingent) question: its non-existence is simply inconceivable.

On Malcolm's view, this idea of God's necessary existence must be accurately articulated before the question of its coherence can be assessed. It certainly cannot be adequately captured in the following formulation, so popular with Kantians: if God exists, then he exists necessarily. For the antecedent clause takes away what the consequent clause appears to allow, presenting what it acknowledges is a necessity as if it were really a contingency; it amounts to a form of words which subverts its apparent sense, and thus necessarily fails to be about what it professes to be about. Insofar as it conceives of its subject-matter as something whose existence is a contingent matter, then whatever it purports to pick out cannot be whatever the concept 'God' picks out.

In Wittgensteinian terms, one might say that such a formulation embodies an incoherent attempt to speak simultaneously from within and without the relevant religious language-game; its internal invocation of necessity attempts to acknowledge the actual meaning of the religious believer's words, but its overarching commitment to contingency in fact gives expression to an outsider's incomprehension of that meaning. In terms closer to Anselm's: insofar as the atheist's denial of God's existence (whether in his heart or in public) takes a form which implies that what he claims does not exist might conceivably have done so, then what he denies is not and cannot be what the believer affirms when she says that God exists. Such an atheism is fated to miss its target; it is not false, but inherently foolish – the expression of a conceptual confusion.

But can the very idea of necessary existence, and so of God's necessary existence, be coherent? Must not all genuinely existential propositions be synthetic or contingent? Malcolm counters this suspicion by means of a comparison between the proposition 'God necessarily exists' and the Euclidean theorem 'There is an infinite number of prime numbers'. For if we can say that the latter asserts the existence of something *in some sense*, then we can surely say the same of the former. What we need to understand in each case is the particular sense of the proposition, more specifically the differences between such ways of talking of existence and the ways in which we talk of it in empirical contexts (which might themselves be various, e.g. 'There is a low pressure area over the Great Lakes' as opposed to 'He still has a pain in his abdomen'). A good way of appreciating these differences, Malcolm suggests, is to clarify the differences in the ways in which each proposition might be supported. In short, '[t]here are as many kinds of existential propositions as there are kinds of subjects of discourse' (Malcolm 1960, 153).

Malcolm uses his comparison between Anselm and Euclid to establish two further points: the general intelligibility of properties that are necessary rather than contingent; and the internal relation between grasping the sense of a proposition that concerns existence and grasping that and how that proposition might be demonstrated. With respect to the latter, Malcolm imagines once again a Kantian who argues that whenever I think of a being as supremely or perfectly real, even as the supreme reality, the question surely remains whether it exists or not; then he asks whether we would say the same in response to Euclid's demonstration of the existence of an infinity of primes. In the face of a proof of this theorem, it would surely not remain an open question whether or not there is an infinity of primes. But if so, then why can we not say that, once Anselm has demonstrated the necessary existence of a being a greater than which cannot be conceived, no question can then remain as to whether it exists or not? If we understand the kind of proof with which Euclid presents us, then we understand the sense in which there is an infinity of primes; and likewise, insofar as we understand the proof with which Anselm presents us, we likewise understand the sense in which there is a God – the sense in which he exists necessarily.

Nevertheless, to clarify the specifically religious sense of the idea of necessary existence, we must ultimately depart from our comparison with mathematics, and focus on its distinctively religious employment. Here, Malcolm cites Psalm 90: 'before the mountains were brought forth, or ever thou hadst formed the earth and the world, even from everlasting to everlasting, thou art God'. He comments:

> Here is expressed the idea of the necessary existence and eternity of God, an idea that is essential to the Jewish and Christian religions. In those complex systems of thought, those 'language-games', God has the status of a necessary being. Who can doubt that? Here we must say with Wittgenstein, 'This language-game is played!' I believe we may rightly take the existence of those religious systems of thought in which God figures as a necessary being to be a disproof of the dogma...that no existential proposition can be necessary. (Malcolm 1960, 156)

Suppose, then, we accept the coherence of the notion of God's necessary existence. Malcolm accepts that questions would remain about its significance – its point or purpose. As he puts it, how can the concept have any meaning for anyone? Why should human beings even form such a concept, let alone participate in the forms of religious life surrounding it? If we cannot answer such questions, Malcolm thinks, then our admittedly coherent concept of God as a necessary being will nonetheless appear to be an 'arbitrary and absurd construction' (Malcolm 1960, 161). His own answer to both questions is the following: the concept arises from recognizable experiential phenomena of human life, certain kinds of psychological (more precisely, emotional) responses to its vicissitudes. His primary example is that of guilt – a guilt so great that one is sure that nothing one could do oneself, nor any forgiveness offered by another human being, would remove it: a guilt greater than which cannot be conceived. 'Out of such a storm in the soul, I am suggesting, there arises the conception of a forgiving mercy that is limitless, beyond all measure' (Malcolm 1960, 160).

What, then, should we conclude about the relation of Anselm's argument to religious belief? Does it show that believing in God is rationally required of us? The whole thrust of Malcolm's paper thus far has been to suggest that Anselm's argument is indeed a deductively valid proof of God's (necessary) existence; but in its final paragraph, he declares that he

> can imagine an atheist going through the argument, becoming convinced of its validity, acutely defending it against objections, yet remaining an atheist. The only effect it could have on the fool of the Psalm would be that he stopped saying in his heart 'There is no God', because he would now realize that this is something he cannot meaningfully say or think. It is hardly to be expected that a demonstrative argument should, in addition, produce in him a living faith. (Malcolm 1960, 161)

The religious value of the argument is thus, in the first instance, negative – it may remove some misplaced scruples about faith; but it would be unreasonable to require that recognizing Anselm's demonstration as valid must produce a conversion. Indeed, Malcolm suggests, Anselm's argument 'can be thoroughly understood only by one who has a view of that human "form of life" that gives rise to the idea of an infinitely great being, who views it from the *inside* not just from the outside and who has, therefore, at least some inclination to *partake* in that religious form of life' (Malcolm 1960, 162). The relevant inclination here derives, Malcolm says, from the emotions – the very human phenomena that prompt the construction and inform the deployment of the concept that the proof aims to support. And Malcolm concludes by asserting that this inclination is not an effect of Anselm's argument, but is rather presupposed in the fullest understanding of it.

This final paragraph certainly serves sharply to differentiate the proper functioning of Anselm's proof from that of Euclid's, and so presumably the notion of proof in religious contexts from the same notion in mathematical contexts. For someone who grasped the deductive validity of Euclid's demonstration of his theorem about prime numbers could hardly reject its existential implications throughout number theory and beyond; whereas Malcolm appears to accept such a diremption in the religious case. But by concluding his paper on this note, Malcolm also brings to the surface a number of issues central to the critique of Wittgensteinian philosophy of religion as fideist. At the very least, such a paragraph makes it easier to see why Wittgensteinian work in this area might elicit that kind of critical response.

First, this concluding differentiation of mathematical from religious proofs is of a piece with Malcolm's insistence on the need to distinguish religious senses of terms from their sense in other contexts; and such emphasis on the logical distinctness of various modes of discourse lies at the root of someone like Nielsen's sense that Wittgensteinians picture our life with language as falling apart (at least analytically) into self-sufficient linguistic compartments or sub-systems. Moreover, Malcolm's distinction between appreciating Anselm's argument as a piece of logic, and appreciating its fullest or deepest religious significance, looks like an instance of a more general distinction between the deliverances of reason and the deliverances of faith; and then the core dogma of fideism will seem certainly to be in the offing (particularly when Malcolm explicitly links his line of thought with Kierkegaard's claim that 'There is only one proof of the truth of Christianity and that…is from the emotions'). For what at first seems to be an exposition of a deductively valid rational argument for religious belief turns out in the end to articulate a chain of reasoning that can only be properly understood, let alone endorsed, from the perspective of faith.

Malcolm invites further trouble by associating his first distinction with another – that between viewing religion from the outside and viewing it from the inside – and linking the latter with the perspective of a participant in religious forms of life. It is not hard to see why Nielsen might read this as an invitation to conclude that the significance of religious concepts can only be grasped by religious believers. And Malcolm's earlier comparison of the concept of God with the concept of a material object might further suggest that the religious believer's position is as little open to the prospect of substantial criticism as is our conviction in the existence of an external world. Since Wittgensteinians notoriously see no sense in expressions of scepticism of the latter kind, why should they be any more open to the possibility that the concept of God might be subject to thoroughgoing sceptical critique?

I have already argued (in the previous section) against the validity of the last inference; and the other apparent difficulties for Malcolm's position can, in fact, be significantly eased. First, his insistence on the variety of kinds of existential proposition is in fact counterbalanced (however infrequently) by an acknowledgement of logical connections between the relevant modes of discourse, insofar as each has its place in the unifying context of the human form of life. After all, Malcolm does insist that the religious idea of divine perfection has its grammatical counterpart, and perhaps even its origins, in empirical contexts, when the various dependencies and limitations of material objects and instruments are under evaluation. And his concluding attempt to show that religious concepts are not only coherent but also possessed of sense and point depends precisely upon underlining their relation to elements in the common fabric of human experience.

Second, Malcolm's pivotal distinction between appreciating the logical validity of the argument and appreciating its religious significance is *not* a distinction between no understanding and genuine understanding: it is a distinction between one level of understanding and another, deeper or fuller, level. The atheist who grasps the validity of Anselm's argument does indeed grasp one aspect of the grammar of the concept of God as it is employed in the Judaeo-Christian tradition, and hence must (on Malcolm's understanding of the significance of grammar) to that extent grasp the meaning of that concept. What he lacks is the deepest or fullest understanding of it – a grasp of what he calls 'the *sense* of the concept' (Malcolm 1960, 161), by which I take him to mean the point or purpose of using it, which in turn he associates with an appreciation of the view of human life that it serves to articulate. And Malcolm never says that this deeper understanding is available only to participants in religious forms of life; he claims rather that only those who have at least some inclination to partake in such forms of life can attain it. One might well have such an inclination without ever acting upon it: one might not only understand that some human beings can suffer guilt of a kind greater than which cannot be conceived, but actually suffer it oneself, without coming to believe that there is a source of forgiveness commensurate with it. If so, then, in principle, both levels or aspects of a genuine understanding of religious concepts, proofs, and practices are attainable by those who are not practising believers, hence by at least one subset or category of atheists.

Even if one is inclined to accept these defences, however, difficulties remain – and ones to be taken seriously from a Wittgensteinian perspective. In the first place, if it is so important to a deeper understanding of Anselm's argument and the concept it supports to appreciate the specific sense, the distinctive point or purpose, of their religious uses, then Malcolm's article does little to encourage that deeper understanding. I don't just mean that his invocation of unforgivable guilt and despair are merely gestures towards an account of the point of religious concepts (although they are, as Malcolm recognizes); one cannot, after all, do everything in one journal article. I also mean that Malcolm's way of elucidating Anselm's argument about God by comparing it with other, non-religious modes of discourse on existence and necessity appears, on closer examination, to tell us far more about what religious discourse is not than about what it is.

For example, Malcolm repeatedly emphasizes that the religious sense of claims about God's existence should be distinguished from empirical existential claims; but his account of Anselm's argument attempts to clarify the grammatical link in religious discourse between God's perfection and his necessary existence primarily by invoking a chain of grammatical links (between imperfection, dependence, and limitation, on the one hand, and perfection, independence, and absence of limitation on the other) which have their home in empirical contexts. In illustrating these links, I talked of computers, whereas Malcolm talks of dishes and engines, but all concern beings of a kind with which God must be contrasted rather than compared. A less limited or dependent empirical object might well be said to be more perfect or greater than its more limited counterparts, but it could never entirely lack the very possibility of limitation, which is internal to Anselm's characterization of God. In other words, the relevant comparisons succeed only in establishing what we cannot say about God (namely that his existence is contingent), and so only in giving a negative or exclusionary sense to talk of God's existence as necessary. Such propositions, one might say, ward off mistaken or irreligious talk of God as if he were a being amongst beings; but they do not tell us what genuinely religious talk of God – talk that is properly directed to its target – might amount to.

Similarly, although Malcolm points to mathematical talk of necessary existence primarily as a way of blocking the suggestion that religious talk of necessary existence is illegitimate because *any* talk of necessary existence is illegitimate, it is far from clear that he properly acknowledges that such talk of necessity has a different sense in these two different contexts. Invoking Psalm 90 certainly allows him to point out that religious believers connect the idea of God's necessary existence with the idea that he is eternal; but his only specification of what God's eternity might amount to consists in pointing out that the notion excludes all sentences implying that God has duration, even endless duration (Malcolm 1960, 148). Once again, this appears to tell us what cannot legitimately be said of God, rather than what can; and in addition, it fails to distinguish God in this respect from numbers, in relation to which talk of duration is surely equally excluded.

In fact, Psalm 90 could give us further help here, since it relates the necessity of God's existence not only to the idea of eternity, but also to that of creation *ex nihilo*, and all in a context of praise and worship (not a set of connections in which numbers would obviously be at home, although they adumbrate a possibility worth bearing in mind when accounting for the quasi-devotional attitudes of mystically inclined mathematicians and philosophers to these perfect, timeless entities). But Malcolm makes nothing of this; and even if he did, a genuinely useful grammatical explanation of the distinctively religious sense of necessary existence cannot boil down to citing a religious text in which some of these distinguishing grammatical connections are made – as if that kind of austere philosophical practice were what the Wittgensteinian phrase 'this language-game is played' were meant to license. What we need to understand is not just the fact that these connections are made but how and why they are made, which means understanding how and why the game is played.

This raises another difficulty. For Malcolm's sharp distinction between viewing Anselm's argument as a piece of logic and as the expression of a religious view of the world strongly suggests that he sees an equivalently sharp distinction between the grammar of a religious concept and its sense – between its logical structure and its point or purpose. But this seems deeply puzzling from a Wittgensteinian point of view: if meaning is manifest in use, then how could one, even in principle, grasp the grammar of a concept without grasping the point or purpose of using it? It is as if Malcolm imagines that we might be said to have successfully clarified the grammar of a concept even if it continues to appear to us to be an utterly arbitrary and absurd construction; but if it does so appear to us, then how can we be said to have appreciated its use, its mode of employment, at all?

Furthermore, when Malcolm suggests that grasping a concept's point or purpose as opposed to its grammar depends upon access to a certain range of emotions, he conjures up a picture of the human forms of life with that concept as having two analytically distinct elements: a logical or grammatical shell or skeleton, and a body of human emotional responses. It is a curiously positivist vision of logical form married to emotional matter, as if experiential content alone could perform the necessary conjuring trick with these dry grammatical bones. Perhaps, philosophically speaking, we do have to accept forms of life as given; but it is not obvious that we have to accept this particular picture of what a form of life with language amounts to.[6]

3. THE REALISTIC WITTGENSTEIN: GRAMMAR AND 'GRAMMAR'

Of course, certain strands in the religious traditions on which Malcolm draws might see one of these 'failings' as a potential strength. For from the perspective of apophatic or negative theology, the fact that Malcolm's account of Anselm ultimately presents it as a way of specifying how we must not talk about God would simply reflect the fact that any attempts positively to characterize God's nature are doomed to failure. It cannot be a weakness of his Anselmian grammatical clarifications of God-talk that they restrict themselves to identifying ways in which our words fail to hit their target if all of our words are fated to do so – if all that we can know of God is what he is not. And Malcolm's apparently contradictory tendency to employ notions at home in non-theological contexts to clarify the grammar of religious terms need not be seen as subverting this apophatic insight. Indeed, Denys Turner has identified forms of religious thinking that see apophatic theology as inextricably related to its affirmative or cataphatic counterpart, because they see all religious language as necessarily subject to the twin pressures of affirmation and negation (Turner 1995; 2004).

Insofar as God is the source of all that is, possessing in his being all the perfections he causes, then everything in creation is a potential source of imagery for the divine, and the more of it we activate in religious language the better, since only thus can we acknowledge God's superabundant variety. And yet, using language in all these ways simultaneously will inevitably lead to us speaking contradictorily about God (as male and female, light and darkness, weakness and strength); and nothing we say about him can conceivably capture his nature anyway. But that transcendence of God is best acknowledged precisely by following out the consequences of attributing contradictory attributes to him; for if he is both male and female, and we know that no person can be both male and female, we thereby appreciate that our idea of him as a personal God is itself a misrepresentation – a necessarily unsuccessful attempt to delineate that which is beyond delineation.

In short, the best way to appreciate the transcendence of God to human language is not to fall into silence, avoiding even the assertion that nothing is assertible of him, or to attempt some inconceivable synthesis of affirmation and negation; it is, rather, endlessly to employ that language in relation to him, and endlessly to experience its inevitable

---

[6] This, for example, is the point at which Iris Murdoch dissents from what she sees as Malcolm's otherwise attractive approach: see Murdoch 1992, ch. 13.

collapse upon itself. Theological language is thus essentially self-subverting language; the repeated collapse of its affirmations into complete disorder *is* its mode of order – it is, one might say, the only way these language-games should be played.

Turner identifies a species of this self-subversion in Aquinas' treatment of the cosmological argument for God's existence. On the one hand, he accepts that the cosmological question, 'Why is there anything rather than nothing?', is crucially different from its intraworldly model 'Why is there this rather than that?' It is in the nature of the former question that we lack terms for answering it of the kind we use in answering the latter, i.e. specific elements of the universe; and whilst the 'rather than' relation presupposes an overarching categorical unity in relation to which a more specific difference is posited (as the category of colour is presupposed when we ask 'Why red rather than green?'), it is hard to see the corresponding categorical context when we attempt to relate 'everything' and 'nothing' in this way. For that 'nothing' must not be thought of as a something of however peculiar a kind: the Christian notion of creation *ex nihilo* does not point to a uniquely peculiar kind of antecedent condition for making, but rather negates the very idea of an antecedent condition. It says 'there is a making here, but no "out of"'; and that amounts to registering that the religious notion of creation is not to be thought of as anything like our everyday, empirical notion of creation.

On the other hand, Aquinas also sees a certain continuity with our everyday modes of employing such language. After all, human beings naturally tend to ask the cosmological question: they have found it natural to extend the familiar grammatical form of causal questioning in this direction, and in retaining that form, they find themselves committed simultaneously to seeking an answer to it that must have the character of a cause, whilst acknowledging that it cannot be any kind of causal process, any kind of making of something out of something else. In other words, they find themselves inclined to pose a question whose terms are self-cancelling, to extend the notion of causation in such a way as to lose control over any understanding of the causality that any answer to it presupposes. One might say: insofar as it retains its causal shape, the question is asked cataphatically; but God is necessarily given in answer to it only apophatically (in the knowledge that we lack any understanding of *how* God is the answer to that question).

Thus Turner's Aquinas presents the cosmological proof as an instance of the necessary self-subversion of religious language. Of course, Aquinas rejects the ontological proof on the grounds that it lacks this self-cancelling virtue; but Malcolm's reading of Anselm's version of the argument (with its cataphatic moment inextricably generating an apophatic realization that the sense in which God exists is one that differs absolutely from any of our familiar ways of talking of existence, whether as contingent or as necessary) rather suggests that even the ontological proof might be recruitable to the Thomist ranks – as one more instance of the way in which we naturally extend the fundamental logical shapes of human reason to the limits of intelligibility so as to point towards the mystery underlying the world's comprehensibility.

But doesn't such an interpretation of religious language run counter to the Wittgensteinian grain? Does it not amount to saying that the distinctive grammar of religious language is its lack of grammar – that to speak religiously is to use words in such a way as to void them of sense? This is certainly the basic assumption behind such recent work in the field as that of Bede Rundle (e.g. 2004); but the work of Cora Diamond suggests another possibility, another way of understanding the Wittgensteinian recommendation that grammatical investigations are a matter of looking to see how language is actually employed – a task that can as easily be hindered by preconceptions about what it is for words to have a grammar as by preconceptions about what particular grammar a given word may possess. In 'Riddles and Anselm's Riddle',[7] Diamond specifically contests Malcolm's reading of Anselm by exploiting another aspect of the general connection he makes between religious discourse and mathematics, namely Wittgenstein's conception of mathematical conjectures as akin to riddles.

Suppose I ask: 'What has four legs in the morning, two at noon, and three in the evening?' To solve this riddle, you need to know more than what that form of words describes; you need to know *how* it describes it – to see how a human being might be seen as fitting that description, how those words might be seen as a description of human existence. If so, then until we have the solution to the riddle, together with an understanding of how it counts as a solution to it, to that extent we lack an understanding of the riddle-phrase that the question employs, and so lack an understanding of the question.

And yet we can seek the solution to such riddles. How? We might think that this is because we can at least judge that any solution will have to meet certain conditions. It seems clear in advance, for example, that if something has four legs, it must have more than two legs; but since human beings do not typically have more than two legs, that would imply that, whatever the solution to our riddle might turn out to be, it can't be a human being. This shows that we no more understand the further conditions we might impose on a solution to our riddle than we understand the riddle itself: part of grasping its solution *as a solution* will be grasping how it can be said to meet these ancillary conditions, and so those conditions can't be said to control what will count as a solution. But it also shows that our imaginative engagement with the riddle is controlled by *something* – by existing patterns of use in our language, on the basis of which the riddle-phrase has been constructed.

In the case of this riddle, there are existing patterns of employing number words, of describing animal anatomy and its supplements, and of measuring time; and familiar ways of extending those patterns – for example, comparing different ways of measuring time (measuring the course of a life in terms of the progress of a day). Finding a solution to the Sphinx's riddle is a matter of finding a way to see something as inviting us to project all those patterns onto it in an appropriate way; but what we need in order to answer it is not something of which we have been given a determinate description, but something that it will strike us as right to call by the riddle-phrase. The familiarity of the phrase's construction, and of its grammatical connections with other phrases, is what orients our seeking, and gives the phrase whatever meaning we wish to say that it has at

---

[7] In Diamond 1991.

this pre-solution stage, but without allowing us simply to read off what we will be prepared to count as its solution, or indeed whether there is one.

Diamond notes that Wittgenstein compares a mathematical conjecture that lacks a proof to a riddle for which we have not found a solution. By fixing its place in the system of mathematical propositions, a proof gives the conjecture a determinate meaning it hitherto lacked, although the task of seeking a proof of it is given such orientation as it has, and so the conjecture has whatever meaning we may wish to say that it has for us prior to the construction of that proof, on the basis of our familiarity with other mathematical concepts and procedures on analogy with which the conjecture has been constructed. But we may conclude that nothing will count as an application of the relevant phrase – say as 'the rational number p/q which when squared gives 2'. This phrase puts together meaningful mathematical concepts on analogy with meaningful mathematical propositions; but if by following out these and other analogies we can show that any such p cannot be odd, and cannot be even either, then we may abandon the idea that the original phrase is meaningful, because the only alternative would be to have a system in which we would call something a cardinal number even though it was neither odd nor even. A *reductio* proof of this kind can do its work without assuming that the phrase to which it relates makes sense; we play at using a phrase of that shape as an assumption, and establish further conditions on that to which it may be held to apply, and then conclude that we are not willing to accept that anything could meet all those conditions – at which point we stop playing with the possibility that the phrase makes any mathematical sense. We conclude, in other words, that the promise of a necessary connection articulated by the 'conditions' we 'established' is unfulfilled.

Diamond suggests that Anselm's ontological argument is a working out of just such promissory connections. The riddle-phrase 'that than which nothing greater can be conceived' (hereafter TTWNGCBC) is itself constructed on the basis of a familiar model (great, greater, greatest, greatest conceivable); and Anselm draws upon existing linguistic connections between lacking something, being limited, being dependent, coming into existence, and having a beginning in order to establish that if we were to call anything TTWNGCBC, then it would be something that had no beginning. The point is not that, on the basis of our understanding of TTWNGCBC, we know that it has no beginning, as if we were simply reminding ourselves of a language-game we know how to play; we are simply forging the outer shell of a necessary connection in a language we do not yet know how to speak. In contemplating TTWNGCBC, we are entertaining familiar words combined in a familiar pattern, and we don't rule out the possibility of a new language-game in which that word-shape has a place and in which we might find ourselves at home; but if that possibility were realized, it would be the articulation of a logical space, not a discovery within such a space.

Anselm's emphasis on the difference between existence in the understanding and existence in reality can then be seen as a misleading way of distinguishing between ideas that we can, and those that we cannot, conceive of being the result of human inventive capacities. He wants to emphasize that our conception of what is possible might itself be shown up by reality, that reality might show us not only that something is the case that we imagined was not the case, but that something beyond what we had ever taken to be possible, something beyond anything we could imagine as possible, was actual. If so, then TTWNGCBC could not possibly be identified with anything we can imagine to be a product of the human imagination; for we can think of something greater than that – namely something that could not conceivably have been conceived by us, something in the light of which the products of our religious imagination appear as a queer collection of bloodless abstractions, sentimental projections, and so on, something that reveals a logical space where none had seemed to exist.

Now, if anything we were willing to count as TTWNGCBC must be something that we cannot imagine having merely imagined, it must also be such that, if we were ever to encounter it, we could not imagine it never having existed. For if we could, then we could separate the idea of it from its actuality, could make sense of the possibility of making sense of it as a mere possibility to which nothing actual happened to correspond; and if so, then we could conceive of something greater than it – namely, something whose actuality is a condition for the possibility of conceiving it, something without which it is inconceivable that we could possess a language of any kind for it. Hence, anything we were willing to count as TTWNGCBC would have to be something whose non-existence could not be conceived, something whose conceivability is itself conceivable only on condition of its actuality.

In the case of ordinary riddles, and mathematical proofs, Diamond argues that it is only when we discover that there is a solution to the riddle, and how it counts as a solution to that riddle, that we fully understand the question the riddle poses; before this, the relevant phrases or propositions have only promissory meaning. But in the case of TTWNGCBC, Anselm has established that every statement we can make about it has, and can only have, a promissory meaning; the full transparency to us of that language is ruled out, because if it were to have a meaning we could fully grasp now, then we could conceive of something greater than whatever those words describe (namely, something whose nature exceeds the grasp of any concepts of which we can even conceive). And of course that form of words ('something whose nature exceeds the grasp of any concept of which we can even conceive') is no more fully transparent to us than any other form of words to which it is 'grammatically' linked, via the outer shell of a 'necessary connection'. All are 'allusions' to a 'language' we cannot even conceive of speaking before actually finding ourselves in a position to speak it – a language given to us by the being to whom it applies, and whose revelation of himself will effect the radical conversion of all our existing concepts of him.[8]

---

[8] One might regard this line of thought as Diamond's way of reading the following passage from *Culture and Value*:

> God's essence is supposed to guarantee his existence – what this really means is that here what is at issue is not the existence of something.
>
> For could one not equally say that the essence of colour guarantees its existence? As opposed, say, to the white elephant. For it really only means: I cannot explain what 'colour' is, what the word 'colour' means, without the help of a colour sample. So in this case there is no such thing as explaining 'what it *would be like* if colours *were to* exist'.
>
> And now we might say: There could be a description of what it would be like if there were Gods on Olympus – but not: 'what it would be like if there were God'. And this determines the concept 'God' more precisely. (CV, 94)

Accordingly, in the sense in which Wittgenstein normally claims that words have a grammar, these words do not; they are grammatically distinctive in that they have no grammar, but only a 'grammar'. On Diamond's view, that is what a close attention to the way we employ such words will reveal. She is not denying that we do talk of God in the context of honest, transparent language-games, whose grammar tells us what kind of thing is being spoken of; but she is claiming that whatever we are talking about in such games is not a possible solution to the riddle posed by the phrase TTWNGCBC – for that is a form of words which does not tell us the kind of thing to which it refers, but rather stands in need of a determination of meaning, one which must come not from us but from whatever it turns out to apply to. Since ordinary riddle-phrases can be given meaning by us, insofar as we can find a way of meaning them, Diamond talks of riddle-phrases such as TTWNGCBC as embodying a great riddle (alluding thereby to Wittgenstein's Tractarian invocation of the 'question' of the meaning of life, which he tells us will remain even were we to arrive at answers to all our articulable, grammatically coherent questions, and to which he tells us there is no conceivable solution, only a dissolution of the question *qua* question).

Hence those who claim that there is a solution to the great riddle cannot mean that they grasp *how* that solution is a solution to the riddle (since they would then be able to translate the riddle-phrase into an honest bit of language, something ruled out by the phrase itself). They can only mean that they know *that* something is the solution, without knowing how – rather as if I were to take someone's word that they have a proof of a mathematical proposition, even if I don't know what it is. This, Diamond claims, is Anselm's position with respect to the fool of the Psalm: Anselm thinks that the fool cannot rule out TTWNGCBC as a word-shape which might be given a use, whereas for Anselm itself it is already the shape of a truth he has been given. If the fool were to rule it out, he would be purporting to judge something that leaves him without the linguistic footing for any judgement of his own about it.

By the same token, however, it would be as foolish to judge of such a being that something greater cannot be conceived as that it can; God cannot conceivably come up to scratch in this respect any more than he can fail to. The only demonstration that such-and-such is TTWNGCBC is one that cannot be separated from the apparent authority of the being in question (for example, the resurrected Jesus, who shows what would otherwise have remained invisible – that the Messianic passages of the Old Testament refer to him). In other words, even the bare identification of something as TTWNGCBC is a truth of faith, or it is nothing. If the fool were to deny any such identification, then to Anselm he is like someone who, groping for a solution to the Sphinx's riddle, thinks 'it certainly can't be a man'. The fool simply doesn't understand his own words, and his atheistic belief depends upon that failure of understanding. From the fool's own point of view, however, TTWNGCBC is either at home in a language-game, or it remains a (non-great) riddle devoid of any solution (since none in his view has been authoritatively identified, let alone shown be to a solution), or it is a mere form of words. And no argument on Anselm's part can show any of these responses to be incoherent.

Diamond's conclusion thus sounds remarkably like Malcolm's distinction between proofs and faith; but she reaches it by rejecting his reading of both Anselm and Wittgenstein. She recognizes that much philosophical confusion is caused by taking words away from the ordinary contexts of their use, and so acknowledges that it might sometimes be philosophically useful to emphasize that and how certain language-games are played. But she also emphasizes that nothing in Wittgenstein's work supports the idea that if a form of words has a place in some activity, then that form of words cannot be expressive of deep confusion; Wittgenstein certainly knows that set theory is 'played', for example, but this does not prevent him from claiming that mathematics is riddled with its 'pernicious idioms'. Hence we cannot show that people who wish to think of the God of the Old Testament as a genocidal maniac are conceptually or philosophically confused simply because language-games are played in which such things cannot be said of God (because he is conceived of as perfect). Indeed, Anselm might well countenance the possibility of our coming to say of that game, and of religious forms of life as a whole, that they are 'judged and condemned by TTWNGCBC'.

There are two fundamental points of disagreement here. First, where Malcolm sees a coherent expression with a grammar, Diamond sees a riddle-phrase – not only words seeking a sense, and so a grammar, but words for which sense can only come from without. From Diamond's perspective, one could charitably say that this is why Malcolm is tempted to distinguish the logical coherence of Anselm's concept of God from its point or purpose, whilst simultaneously and incoherently trying to suggest that the gap is bridged by the emotional content of a form of life; his hollowed-out notion of grammar as mere logical form dimly registers the fact that it is internal to the significance of these words that they have only a 'grammar'.

Second, whereas Malcolm is inclined to assume that the thinking and seeking expressed in such terminology as TTWNGCBC belongs exclusively to those who play religious language-games, and hence participate in religious forms of life, Diamond thinks that such language has a life of its own – that it belongs to anyone; the *Heimat* of such questions is our life with language, not any particular language-game. For the tendency to ask them does not depend on any form of life more specific than that of speaking; it is as much something primitive or given as our responses to other people – no more and no less than natural to us speakers (which of course means that for some people it does not come naturally at all). Such questions arise from our ability and willingness to play with linguistic analogies, to find certain means of extending our ways with words to be natural and worth pursuing, to catch our imaginations in such a way as to hold open the possibility of a possibility of sense before we have established any technique of use corresponding to it.

This is where Diamond's reading of Anselm and Turner's reading of apophatic theology meet. For both wish to emphasize that the great riddle-questions arise naturally for all, as part of the natural condition of those burdened with speech or reason, and that the cataphatic or grammatical uses of religious concepts within religious language-games can be severed from their apophatic or 'grammatical' uses only at the cost of hollowing out their true religious significance. The reading of Wittgenstein on which Diamond's work is based thus puts imagination and inclination rather than rule-governed techniques at the heart of his vision of language. For Diamond, our love of riddles exemplifies the interplay of what comes naturally with our capacity for imaginative play; our ways of responding to mathematical conjectures manifest its centrality to the *Heimat* of reason; and Anselm's way with TTWNGCBC shows how, at its fullest extent, that interplay can acknowledge its own limits – by acknowledging the possibility that reality might utterly overturn our best efforts to imagine what might lie beyond our wildest imaginings.

References

DIAMOND, CORA (1991). *The Realistic Spirit*. Cambridge, MA: MIT Press.
—— (2005). 'Wittgenstein on Religious Belief: The Gulfs Between Us', in D. Z. Phillips and M. von der Ruhr eds., *Religion and Wittgenstein's Legacy*. Aldershot: Ashgate.
MALCOLM, NORMAN (1960). 'Anselm's Ontological Arguments', *Philosophical Review*, 69: 41–62. (Reprinted in *Knowledge and Certainty*. Englewood Cliffs, NJ: Prentice-Hall, 1963.)
MULHALL, STEPHEN (2001). 'Wittgenstein and the Philosophy of Religion', in D. Z. Phillips and T. Tessin eds., *Philosophy of Religion in the 21st Century*. Basingstoke: Palgrave.
MURDOCH, IRIS (1992). *Metaphysics as a Guide to Morals*. London: Chatto and Windus.
NIELSEN, KAI (1967). 'Wittgensteinian Fideism', *Philosophy*, 42: 191–209.
—— and PHILLIPS, D. Z. eds. (2005). *Wittgensteinian Fideism*. London: SCM Press.
PHILLIPS, D. Z. (1965). *The Concept of Prayer*. London: Routledge.
RUNDLE, BEDE (2004). *Why There is Something rather than Nothing*. Oxford: Oxford University Press.
TURNER, DENYS (1995). *The Darkness of God*. Cambridge: Cambridge University Press.
—— (2004). *Faith, Reason and the Existence of God*. Cambridge: Cambridge University Press.
WINCH, PETER (1958). *The Idea of a Social Science*. London: Routledge.
WITTGENSTEIN, LUDWIG (1922). *Tractatus Logico-Philosophicus*, trans. C. K. Ogden. London: Routledge & Kegan Paul.
—— (1953). *Philosophical Investigations*, trans. G. E. M. Anscombe. Oxford: Blackwell.
—— (1965). 'A Lecture on Ethics', *Philosophical Review*, 74: 3–26.
—— (1966). *Lectures and Conversations on Aesthetics, Psychology and Religious Belief*. Berkeley: University of California Press.
—— (1977). *Culture and Value*, trans. P. Winch. Oxford: Blackwell.

CHAPTER 34

WITTGENSTEIN ON AESTHETICS

MALCOLM BUDD

1.

WITTGENSTEIN had a deep and enduring interest in at least two of the major art forms, literature and music; practised, if only briefly, two others, architecture and sculpture;[1] was an artistic benefactor, leaving part of the fortune he inherited from his father, all of which he gave away, to be distributed to Austrian artists who needed financial support; and towards the end of his life acknowledged aesthetic along with conceptual questions as the only ones that really gripped him (CV, 91 (1949)). But in his first masterpiece his conception of the nature of propositions precluded him from saying anything about art, and art makes only a rare intrusion into his second. In truth, art did not lie at the centre of his philosophical concerns. Nevertheless, it is precisely because he held the finest art in such high esteem, assigning to it an absolute value, that it eludes the net of language as articulated in the *Tractatus*, and he confessed that because it was impossible for him to say in *Philosophical Investigations* one word about all that music had meant in his life, it would be difficult for him to be understood.

This chapter was previously published as Chapter 13 of Malcolm Budd, *Aesthetic Essays* (Oxford: Oxford University Press, 2008).

[1] Wittgenstein is also assumed to have written the poem he gave to Hofrat Ludwig Hänsel, which is appended to the notes taken from his writings as published in the revised edition of *Culture and Value*. If this composition, which suffers from a number of defects, really is by Wittgenstein, it provides some confirmation of his own opinion that he would be unable to write a poem (CV, 67 (1947)). According to Paul Engelmann, 'Wittgenstein certainly never wrote a poem in his life', EL, 89).

2.

The *Tractatus* has only a single gnomic remark about aesthetics: 'Ethics and aesthetics are one' (6.421).[2] One, but not the only, meaning of this is clear. Both ethics and aesthetics are concerned with judgements, not of relative but of absolute value. But absolute value lies outside the world (of facts), so that it cannot be expressed in propositions. Accordingly, ethics and aesthetics are in this sense one: neither can be put into words. Hence the silence of the *Tractatus* about aesthetics.

It follows that Wittgenstein's early aesthetics, insofar as it can be recovered, must be pieced together from a handful of somewhat scattered remarks that he wrote in the second half of 1916 and which are recorded in the *Notebooks 1914–16* (which, happily, are not so strictly governed by the self-denying ordinance more or less observed in the *Tractatus*). But these remarks are expressed either in an oracular manner, and so stand in need of interpretation, or in a tentative, questioning form, in which case, if they are to be of use, they must be taken as definite indications of Wittgenstein's thoughts. Some of the pieces required to build a picture of Wittgenstein's aesthetics fit fairly easily together; some that are needed to complete the picture are missing. So any reconstruction must be in some respects conjectural. It is clear that the roots of his aesthetics lie in that of Schopenhauer, for whom the aesthetic attitude was one of pure will-less contemplation in which the subject's entire consciousness is filled by a single perceptual image, so that the object contemplated becomes for the duration of the contemplation the subject's whole world; Schopenhauer quotes Spinoza's 'Mens aeterna est, quaternus res sub aeternitatis specie concipit' in support of his idea that in aesthetic contemplation a person becomes timeless. However, Wittgenstein's aesthetics diverges from Schopenhauer's in important respects.

According to the *Notebooks*, the connection between art and ethics is that 'The work of art is the object seen *sub specie aeternitatis*; and the good life is the world seen *sub specie aeternitatis*' (7 October 1916). Focussing exclusively on art, what this means is that the work of art is the object seen from the point of view of one who is living eternally (in the sense of timelessly) in that she is living in the present (NB, 8 July 1916; TLP 6.4311). More precisely, the work of art is the representation of the object as the object is seen from the point of view of such a person. The point of view of one living in the present is such that the perceived object is seen without concern for what might happen in the world: it is seen as by one for whom life is unproblematic, one who, being in agreement with the world, experiencing neither fear nor hope (NB, 14 July 1916), is living a good, a happy life, one whose world is happy (NB, 8 July 1916). Accordingly, 'the essence of the artistic way of looking at things [is] that it looks at the world with a happy eye' (NB, 20 October 1916). Correlatively – since 'Art is a kind of expression. Good art is complete expression.' (NB, 19 September 1916), and 'There is certainly something in the conception

---

[2] This derives from NB, 24 July 1916.

that the end of art is the beautiful. / And the beautiful *is* what makes happy.' (NB, 21 October 1916) – the imaginative adoption of this point of view in the engagement with a beautiful work of art, one in which the artist has completely expressed the manner in which the represented object has been seen, renders one happy.

This is an incomplete picture for more than one reason. Most importantly, it omits the unusual form of mysticism that formed the foundation of Wittgenstein's attitude to human life. To fill this gap it is necessary to add a number of ideas. The first is that, in contemplating an object the object becomes one's world, each thing, as a world, being equally significant (NB, 8 October 1916). The second is that for a person who experiences wonder at the existence of the world, the experience is one of absolute value (LE, 41). The third is that what is mystical is *that* the world exists (TLP §6.44). The fourth is that 'aesthetically ['künstlerische', literally 'artistically'] the miracle is that the world exists' (NB, 20 October 1916). The fifth is that to view the world *sub specie aeternitatis* is to view the world as a limited whole, the feeling of which is the mystical feeling (TLP 6.45). The final idea is that things that cannot be put into words *make themselves manifest* and are what is mystical (TLP 6.522). From these, sympathetically interpreted, it is possible to derive the conclusion that in the appreciation of a work of art, which involves the contemplation of the object as represented by the artist, the object as represented being for the duration of the contemplation one's world, one undergoes an experience of wonder at the existence of the object, an experience encouraged by the artist, a mystical experience of intrinsic, absolute value in which the wonderfulness of the object (as represented) – something that cannot be expressed in propositions – is made manifest to one.[3] And this involves the idea that although the most important aspect of human life, the ethical, cannot be put into words, it makes itself manifest in good art, as, for example, Uhland's poem 'Count Eberhard's Hawthorn', which Paul Engelmann, who described it as being rare in not attempting to express the inexpressible, and so achieving it, sent to Wittgenstein and which Wittgenstein responded to by writing:

> The poem by Uhland is really magnificent. And this is how it is: if only you do not try to utter what is unutterable then *nothing* gets lost. But the unutterable will be – unutterably – *contained* in what has been uttered! (Engelmann 1967, 7)

Assuming that this is a fairly accurate sketch of Wittgenstein's early aesthetic, and abstaining from any direct criticism of the mysticism of which it is an expression, whatever merits it might have as an account of a certain kind of experience of contemplating an object – one that can also be obtained from a beautiful artistic representation of the object – as a philosophy of art it suffers from a number of manifest weaknesses, of which I shall mention three. First, as it stands it is applicable only to those art forms, such as representational painting, fiction, and poetry, in which works can properly be thought of as representing objects – objects that, as represented, are available for contemplation.

---

[3] For a greatly more detailed construction of Wittgenstein's early aesthetics along these lines, enriched by both an outline of Wittgenstein's early ethics and an account of those aspects of his early aesthetics that he rejected in his mature thought, see R. K. Elliott's outstanding 1993.

Second, it appears blind to the many valuable works of art that, in the sense at issue, can be said to present an object for contemplation, but which are not experienced as beautiful, before which one does not undergo an experience of wonder at the existence of the object, which are not seen from the point of view of one who is, even temporarily, living in the present, and which do not render one happy (in Wittgenstein's or any other sense of the word). Third, it fails to do justice to the way in which the manner of representation of the object figures in the aesthetic appreciation of a work of art. For it assigns to the manner of representation only an enabling function – the function of enabling the spectator or reader to duplicate the way in which the artist viewed the object with wonder – rather than recognizing it as itself a constituent of the work's aesthetic appeal.

3.

If we turn to Wittgenstein's later thoughts about art, although there is no extended treatment of aesthetics in his own writings, the resources are not so meagre. In addition to remarks scattered across his published writings, there are notes, more or less reliable, more or less fragmentary, of what he is supposed to have said about aesthetics in various informal 'lectures' that he gave in Cambridge in 1932–3 and in the summer of 1938, taken by some of those who attended his classes. The lecture notes confirm that he had strong opinions about aesthetics; it should be remembered, however, that many of the recorded thoughts were not considered and carefully articulated opinions but spontaneous remarks.

4.

In his lectures Wittgenstein makes a number of claims about the concept of beauty, some of which appear also in his published writings. In the first place, he distinguishes two uses of the word 'beautiful', the first as an expression of approval, the second as giving an item a character, comparable to describing a melody as 'youthful' or a piece of music as 'springy', 'pompous', 'stately', or 'melancholy'. One claim is that such adjectives as 'beautiful' and 'lovely', used as words of approval, play little role in real life when aesthetic judgements are made or in aesthetic controversies – except by those who cannot express themselves well and who use them as interjections. But this claim is of little importance, being compatible with the fundamental status in aesthetic or artistic appreciation of the idea of aesthetic or artistic value, which has often been designated, rightly or wrongly, as beauty. A second claim is that 'beautiful' does not mean the same as 'agreeable'. It does not, Wittgenstein argues, since, for example, we might choose not to attend a performance of a particular work precisely because we cannot stand its greatness and we might prefer one work to another that we think is much finer. Here, it is clear, the notion of beauty is going proxy for that of artistic value and this second claim, understood in this way, is now widely recognized. A third, which might best be considered as a conjunction of propositions, can be expressed like this: the word 'beautiful' is a 'family resemblance term', being applied to its instances in virtue, not of something common and peculiar to them, but of 'a complicated network of similarities overlapping and criss-crossing'; it has different meanings when applied to things of different kinds: the beauty of a face is something different from the beauty of a chair or a flower or the binding of a book; the fact that more can be said about whether the arrangement of flowers in a bed is beautiful than about whether the smell of lilac is beautiful shows that 'beautiful' differs in meaning in the two cases.

Now it is unsurprising to find Wittgenstein applying one of the leading ideas of his later thought to the concept of beauty, denying that beautiful things fall under the concept of beauty in virtue of having a property common to and distinctive of them. But it might be thought that this is not tantamount to asserting that it has a multiplicity of meanings. However, Wittgenstein was in fact happy to present his insight in this fashion, as his representing the word 'good', as used in ethics or aesthetics, as having 'a family of meanings' shows (PI §77). Moreover, for any family resemblance term in our language, it would be possible for there to be a language in which the range of the term in our language is divided up amongst a number of terms in the foreign language, and yet for it to be possible, on a certain occasion, in application to particular things, for us to lose nothing of the sense of what we want to say in using our term by using instead the more specialized word (see CV, 27–8); and Wittgenstein himself, with the idea of family resemblances in mind, advocated approaching the melodies of different composers 'by applying the principle: every species of tree is a "tree" in a different sense of the word' (CV, 54). But it might well be better to express the reason why the beauty of one kind of thing (a person's eyes, say) is very different from the beauty of another kind (a Gothic church, for example) is because 'beautiful', like 'good', is often used as an attributive rather than a predicative adjective, needing to be taken together with the substantive it qualifies, so that what makes an instance of one kind of thing beautiful (as something of that kind) differs from what makes an instance of another kind a beautiful thing of that kind.[4]

In aesthetic judgements, about music or poetry or clothes, for example, the words used are not such aesthetic adjectives as 'beautiful' but, Wittgenstein maintains, words akin to 'right' and 'wrong', 'correct' and 'incorrect'. A certain kind of sensitive, discriminating person who is adept at distinguishing what is correct from what is incorrect in a particular area, who experiences aspects of objects within that domain as in accordance with or as transgressing the rules (of harmony and counterpoint, or of the measurements of a coat, for example), or as close to or distant from an ideal, is said to appreciate items of that

---

[4] Alice Ambrose's notes of Wittgenstein's lectures 1932–3 represent Wittgenstein as saying 'The words "beautiful" and "ugly" are bound up with the words they modify, and when applied to a face are not the same as when applied to flowers and trees' (AWL, 35), which might perhaps be interpreted as in a rough way making the point that 'beautiful' is often used as an attributive adjective.

kind. This normative element in the appreciation of a work of art or non-artistic artefact is misrepresented if artistic or aesthetic appreciation is thought of as merely a matter of what gives pleasure to the listener, reader, or viewer. In fact, Wittgenstein maintains, it is impossible to describe properly what aesthetic appreciation consists in; it can be made sense of only by locating it in the cultural context to which it belongs and from which it derives its distinctive shape; different cultures determine different forms of artistic and aesthetic appreciation; the character and scope of appreciation vary from person to person; and any description of a culture that illuminates the nature of aesthetic judgements within that culture will be a description of a complicated set of activities from which the words used to express those judgements draw their life.[5]

Wittgenstein has been criticized for making a grasp of rules an integral element of the notion of aesthetic appreciation.[6] For although aesthetic judgement and artistic criticism are certainly directed towards the evaluation of an object or work of art and the identification of its merits or demerits, the reasons available for judgements of these kinds are not restricted to what agrees with or flouts a rule, or – to take up the other element Wittgenstein acknowledges – in what way or to what degree something is distant from or near to an ideal. Moreover, there are no established rules that many poor or mediocre works of art violate or to which many fine works conform. But, as far as rules are concerned, Wittgenstein's view appears to be no more than that a knowledge of rules is essential in certain areas for the formation and refinement of aesthetic appreciation, not that criticism is confined to or in the main consists of appreciation of rule-following or rule-transgression. It is true, however, that the idea of something's being correct or incorrect has little relevance to what is usually understood by aesthetic appreciation, and unless the notion of an ideal is understood to cover every aesthetic merit, the elements explicitly acknowledged in Wittgenstein's account of aesthetic judgement fail to recognize the variety of resources available to the critic in praising or criticizing a work. Wittgenstein excludes 'the *tremendous* things in Art' from the domain of appreciation, for in these cases it is not a matter of finding them correct. But since, as I have already indicated, the notion of correctness lacks an important place in the ordinary notion of aesthetic appreciation, the fact that the 'entirely different things' that come into play with the tremendous are not specified need not concern us.

This is underlined by the fact that Wittgenstein's account of aesthetic judgement outlined above is restricted to a single kind of aesthetic judgement, one that explicitly evaluates the object judged, deeming it admirable, wonderful, well done, defective, lacking in some desirable quality, or whatever. But the language of criticism encompasses more than one sort of aesthetic judgement, and this range is implicitly recognized by Wittgenstein in his remark 'It is possible – and this is important – to say a *great deal* about a fine aesthetic difference' (LWPP I §688; PI II, 219; see also RPP I §357) and is manifest in his concern with the enhancement of the understanding of art through appropriate characterization of a work, a topic I consider later. However, what can be

---

[5] Michael Tanner's highly sympathetic and intelligent 1966 contains the best elucidation of this view.
[6] See, for example, Osborne 1966.

said here is that, at least as far as the individual appeal of a work is concerned, if not the work's artistic value, Wittgenstein held that if you get another to perceive a work as having the same aesthetic character as you do but it does not appeal to them, then that is the end of the discussion; and he pointed to a parallel with a discussion in a court of law, where, reaching agreement on the circumstances of some action, you hope that what you say will appeal to the judge. (See AWL, 39 and MWL, 106.)

5.

Although Wittgenstein on one occasion practised architecture, assuming control of the project to design a house in Vienna for his sister Gretl, applying himself to the task with characteristic fanatical zeal, he believed that he possessed only artistic taste, understanding, and good manners, rather than creative power, and thought of his architectural work as merely the rendering of an old style into a language appropriate to the modern world. Nevertheless, in light of his strong feelings about architecture it is disappointing to find virtually nothing in his published writings about architectural aesthetics. In fact, there is little more than these remarks:

> Remember the impression made by good architecture, that it expresses a thought. One would like to respond to it too with a gesture. (CV, 26)

> Architecture is a *gesture*. Not every purposive movement of the human body is a gesture. Just as little as every functional building is architecture. (CV, 49)

> Architecture glorifies something [its purpose] (because it endures). Hence there can be no architecture where there is nothing to glorify.[7] (CV, 74)

The principal thought is that a building is properly thought of as architecture only if it is a gesture, and good architecture, through its endurance, glorifies the function of the building – as palace, church, or house, for example – and inclines one to respond to it with a gesture of one's own (a response that I seem to be immune to). Wittgenstein does not explain his characterization of architecture as being a gesture and there is no indication of what the connection might be between architecture's being a gesture and good architecture's glorifying something. If we leave aside the idea of glorification, two linked questions arise. The first is what exactly the characterization of a work of architecture as a gesture comes to: can a building be communicative or expressive in the sense that a gesture is, and, if so, how large a range of psychological states can buildings encompass? The second is whether this characterization, properly understood, is an appropriate indication of the kind of aesthetic significance architecture possesses.

Perhaps it will be thought that to pose these questions is to take too seriously an isolated remark or two from writings that Wittgenstein had no intention of publishing. But this is

---

[7] I have chosen one of Wittgenstein's formulations and inserted the words in square brackets from another of the variations he rings on this theme.

not so. For Wittgenstein's notion of a gesture informs his thoughts about another art – one that was especially dear to him. Wittgenstein had an exceptionally good musical memory and an acute ear, and frequently – 'every day & often' (CV, 32) – heard music in his imagination; he played the clarinet very well and was unusually adept at whistling music, sometimes performing complete works. Music was, perhaps, his favourite art, and he regarded it as being in a certain sense 'the most sophisticated art of all' (CV, 11). So it is unsurprising that by far the greatest number of remarks on aesthetics in his published writings are on music; and he is fond of representing a musical theme that impresses him as being a gesture. To understand Wittgenstein's aesthetics of music it is necessary to understand this characterization, and a correct interpretation of it will make clear whether the idea of architecture as being a gesture identifies architecture's principal aesthetic character.

6.

The main issue that occupies Wittgenstein is: what is it to listen to or to play a piece of music with understanding?

As in the familiar case of understanding language, Wittgenstein argues that it is wrong to think of understanding a piece of music – one you are playing or are merely listening to – as consisting in a process of some kind accompanying the playing or listening: no accompanying process is either necessary or sufficient for understanding.[8] But he goes further and likens understanding a sentence to understanding a theme in music:

> Understanding a sentence is much more akin to understanding a theme in music than one may think. What I mean is that understanding a sentence lies nearer than one thinks to what is ordinarily called understanding a musical theme. (PI §527)[9]

To see more clearly what this comes to it is necessary to look at Wittgenstein's thoughts about understanding and failing to understand a musical theme.

What Wittgenstein writes about understanding a picture applies equally to understanding music:

> Here too there is understanding and failure to understand. And here too these expressions may mean various kinds of thing. (PI §526)

The principal form of lack of understanding is, of course, not hearing (or playing) the music correctly. Wittgenstein rightly emphasizes the importance of phrasing, 'which can refer to hearing as well as to playing' (PI II, 202), and other phenomena that are akin to perceiving an aspect, such as 'the reinterpretation of a chord in music, when we hear it as a modulation first into this, then into that key' (PI §536), or understanding a Gregorian mode, where coming to understand it is a matter of hearing

---

[8] See, for example, RPP II §§466–9, 497, 502–4 (= Z §§162–5, 159, 171–3).
[9] The previous version of this at BB, 167 elaborates a little. The entire PI §527 puts together two passages, edited, from BB, 167, 166.

something new, in the same sense as that in which suddenly seeing grouping or seeing a flat pattern three-dimensionally is seeing something new (PR §224).[10] A rather different case that Wittgenstein mentions is that of hearing a movement of a Bruckner symphony not as so many little bits, which are always falling short, but as an organic whole (LWPP I §677). All these cases (which could be added to indefinitely) are ones where music can be *heard* in different ways. It is therefore unsurprising that Wittgenstein should write:

> The understanding of a theme is neither sensation nor a sum of sensations. Nevertheless it is correct to call it an experience inasmuch as *this* concept of understanding has some kinship with other concepts of experience. You say 'I experienced that passage quite differently this time'. (RPP II §469 = Z §165)

A rather different case that Wittgenstein mentions is that of hearing a repeat or transition as correct or necessary. In *Remarks on the Foundations of Mathematics* there is the isolated enigmatic sentence 'The *exact* correspondence of a correct (convincing) transition in music and mathematics' (RFM III §63), which, happily, is illuminated by a much later remark:

> Take a theme like that of Haydn's (St. Antony Chorale), take the part of one of Brahms's variations corresponding to the first part of the theme, and set the task of constructing the second part of the variation in the style of its first part. That is a problem of the same kind as mathematical problems are. If the solution is found, say as Brahms gives it, then one has no doubt; – that is the solution. (RFM VII §11)

In *Philosophical Grammar* Wittgenstein distinguishes two kinds of musical understanding: (a) intransitive (or autonomous) understanding, as in understanding a melody in the sense of being able to follow the melody as a melody (PG I §§37, 34), and (b) understanding a piece of music in the sense of understanding why it should be played in a certain manner, the understanding consisting in the ability to translate what is understood into another 'medium' or 'expression' (PG I §§4, 37). Wittgenstein does not there explain what is meant by such a translation, but this becomes clear if we now consider another form of musical understanding, one to which Wittgenstein frequently returned, that of understanding what a musical phrase or theme 'says' or expresses, that is, what its character is, and this, for Wittgenstein, is equivalent to making sense of the impression the music makes on one, or, as he sometimes puts it, the special 'feeling' that a musical phrase gives us (PI II, 182).[11] In fact, Wittgenstein passes freely between this issue and that of understanding how a theme should be played and why it should be played in this manner, and it is easy to see why: if a theme has a certain character then it should be played in such a manner that brings out or respects that character, and if it should be played in a certain manner this is precisely because of the character it possesses. The lack of understanding that Wittgenstein is

---

[10] Hence Wittgenstein's characterization of lack of a 'musical ear' as being *akin* to aspect-blindness (PI II, 214).

[11] The treatment that Wittgenstein accords this issue of understanding a theme's character he also applies to certain other examples of musical understanding – understanding the necessity for the repeat of a theme or part of one (CV, 59), or the necessity with which one theme follows another (CV, 65), for example.

concerned with is manifested when, being struck by the character of a theme, one finds that one does not know how to describe it. It is also manifested when one does not know how a theme should be played or feels unable to explain why it should be played in a certain manner. It is in response to this difficulty that a crucial aspect of Wittgenstein's thoughts about the aesthetics of music emerges – his emphasis on the importance of comparisons, an emphasis that is given additional significance when it is generalized across the arts in his opposition to the relevance of experimental psychology to aesthetics. For, Wittgenstein maintains, it is often the case that there is no better way, and sometimes there is no other way, of characterizing or making clear a theme's expression – 'A theme has a facial expression just as much as a face does'[12] (RPP I §434, CV, 59) – than by drawing a comparison between the theme and something else; and a person's understanding of a theme's character may consist in the ability to produce an apt comparison.

7.

The comparisons one finds in Wittgenstein's writings are more or less restricted to comparisons of music with the same small set of linguistic, more specifically vocal, *actions*:

> Here it's as if a conclusion were being drawn, here as if something were being confirmed, *this* is like an answer [reply] to what was said before. (Z §175)

> Why is just *this* the pattern of variation in loudness and tempo [of a certain musical theme]?…I should not be able to say [what it is all about]. In order to 'explain' I could only compare it with something else which has the same rhythm (I mean the same pattern). (One says 'Don't you see, this is as if a conclusion were being drawn' or 'This is as it were a parenthesis', etc. How does one justify such comparisons? – There are very different kinds of justification here. (PI §527)

But this gives a false impression of Wittgenstein's conception of the range of possible apt comparisons. For, as he notes:

> There is a strongly musical element in verbal language. (A sigh, the intonation of voice in a question, in an announcement, in longing; all the innumerable *gestures* made with the voice.) (Z §161; cf. RPP I §888)

And this, it seems clear, implies Wittgenstein's readiness to extend the range of appropriate examples to all aspects of the voice that can be mirrored in music. He himself refers to music 'that corresponds to the expression of bitter irony in speech' (CV, 63).[13]

---

[12] Hence Wittgenstein's suggestion that following a musical phrase with understanding is comparable to observing a face and drinking in the expression on the face (CV, 58), and his other suggestion that just as suddenly understanding the expression on a face might consist in finding the word that sums it up, so suddenly understanding a musical theme might consist in finding a verbal counterpart of the theme (BB, 166–7).

[13] See also CV, 93. Wittgenstein is referring to the fugato in the first movement of Beethoven's ninth symphony.

Moreover, he mentions at least one kind of comparison that is not with a linguistic act – the entry of a new character in a story or a poem (CV, 65). Furthermore, the following passage might perhaps be interpreted to license comparisons with more or less anything:

> Does the theme point to nothing beyond itself? Oh yes! But that means: – The impression it makes on me is connected with things in its surroundings – e.g. with the existence of our language & of its intonation, but that means with the whole field of our language games.
>
> If I say e.g.: It is as if a conclusion were being drawn here, or, as if here something were being confirmed, or, as if *this* were the answer to what went before – then the way I understand it clearly presupposes familiarity with conclusions, confirmations, replies, etc. (See CV, 59 and the near identical RPP I §§433 and Z §175)

Even if this interpretation should be resisted, there is nothing in Wittgenstein's writings that rules out comparisons with many kinds of phenomena other than vocal actions or expressive aspects of the voice.[14] He himself, referring to Labor's playing, writes:

> What was it about this playing that was so reminiscent of speaking? And how remarkable that this similarity with speaking is not something we find incidental, but an important and big matter! – We should like to call music, & certainly *some* music, a language; but no doubt not *some* music. (CV, 71)[15]

And if not all music is highly reminiscent of speech, as it certainly is not – Wittgenstein writes that 'Bach's music is more like language than Mozart's & Haydn's' (CV, 40) – comparisons with speech will not always be an appropriate way of inducing understanding. Sometimes comparisons with silent thought processes will be more apt. Furthermore, although music is, like speech, an audible phenomenon, it is, simply in virtue of its character as a process, open to characterization other than by reference to speech, and it is clear that comparisons with many kinds of non-linguistic phenomena – all the various modes of motion, fusion and fission, transformations, rising and falling, decline and regrowth, waxing and waning, outbursts of energy, feelings and emotions themselves (rather than their expressions in behaviour), to list but a few – are often more suitable than comparisons with anything specifically linguistic.

Now the ordinary idea of a gesture covers a variety of meaningful bodily actions – actions that express a psychological state or attitude, convey a greeting, request, assent, or rejection, indicate an object, or are used as a device to impress, to intimidate, to enforce, or to persuade – bound together by the fact that the meaning they possess is not

---

[14] Wittgenstein used to recite with a shudder of awe Mörike's description of music: 'Coming as from remotest starry worlds, the sounds fall from the mouth of silver trombones, icy cold, cutting through marrow and soul; fall through the blueness of the night' (EL, 86).

[15] This might be thought to be incompatible with Wittgenstein's remark 'Understanding a musical phrase may also be called understanding a *language*' (RPP II §503 = Z §172). But the point of Wittgenstein's remark is not that music is a language (or a set of languages) in the sense in which the English language is one, but that, like the understanding of a sentence, the understanding of a musical theme requires familiarity with and understanding of much more of the same kind.

determined by a vocabulary and syntactical conventions (as the meaning of sign language is). But it will have been noticed that Wittgenstein operates with a rather unusual notion of a gesture, for under the head of gestures he includes, not just expressive movements of the body, but all characteristics of the voice that, considered in abstraction from any thought-content that an utterance may possess, are indications of either the kind of vocal action performed or the psychological state of the speaker. Accordingly, Wittgenstein uses 'gesture' and 'expression' more or less interchangeably, indicating that the item referred to has, in this wide sense, an expressive character, as when, speaking of a door that is slightly too large, he is reported as saying that 'it hasn't the right expression – it doesn't make the right gesture' (LC, 31). And this use of the term 'gesture' renders Wittgenstein's characterization of architecture as a gesture relatively uninteresting, for its application to architecture is intended, not to imply that architecture's aesthetic character should be thought of in terms of kinds of linguistic actions, but only to indicate that the physiognomic perception of buildings, an oft-remarked phenomenon, is of prime importance in the aesthetic appreciation of architecture – a standard position (although one not above criticism).

Wittgenstein also characterizes music for which a gesture is an apt comparison as itself a gesture:

> there *is* a paradigm outside the theme: namely the rhythm of our language, of our thinking and feeling. And the theme is also in its turn a *new* bit of our language, it is incorporated in it; we learn a new *gesture*.
> The theme and the language are in reciprocal action. (RPP I §§435–6)

> This musical phrase is a gesture for me. It creeps into my life. I make it my own. (CV, 83–4)

And although Wittgenstein does not elaborate, this must mean that by imagining, whistling, or playing a musical phrase, the character of which he finds expressive, he uses the phrase as an expression of that character.

Wittgenstein does not explain the connection between, on the one hand, a theme's being a gesture[16] and, on the other hand, its character or the manner in which it should be played being explicable by a comparison. But the explanation is obvious: if a theme can itself be thought of as a gesture, then its character or the manner in which it should be played can be elucidated by comparing it with a gesture that has a similar expressive character. A musical theme which, as such, lacks a thought-content cannot be a question; but it may nevertheless have the character of a question (a questioning character), and if it does, then bringing this to a person's consciousness endows them with the requisite understanding.

---

[16] Wittgenstein nowhere maintains that every theme is a gesture or that a piece of music consists of a succession of gestures (although see CV, 84). Roger Scruton (1997) has placed the notion of gesture at the heart of his aesthetics of music but has developed it in a way which would not have gained Wittgenstein's approval, for he represents the very experience of music – of hearing sounds as music – as essentially involving the imagination of a bodily action, something that Wittgenstein never countenanced.

8.

The elucidation of an object's character by means of comparisons plays a significant role in Wittgenstein's opposition to the relevance of psychological experiments or causal investigations to aesthetics.

Wittgenstein identifies aesthetic reactions that manifest admiration, distaste, or dissatisfaction, for example, as being of prime importance in aesthetics. The crucial feature of such aesthetic reactions is that they are 'directed', that is, intentional, having some item or some feature of an item as their object. Although not wrong, it is, he claims, misleading to think of an expression of discontent, such as 'The door is too low', as an expression of discomfort combined with knowledge of the cause of the discomfort, or to take the question 'What's wrong with this picture?' as announcing a certain discomfort and seeking its cause. For although the word 'cause' is sometimes used to refer to the object of a reaction, it also has other uses in which what is caused does not have an object it is directed to, which is its cause, and it is likely to suggest an analogy with such a use, as, for example, when what is being referred to is a pain and its cause, so that an expression of discontent is thought of as an expression of an 'undirected' discomfort combined with knowledge of (or belief about) its cause. Such an expression of aesthetic discontent as 'The door is too low' is not a conjecture but a criticism. It is clear that psychological experiments designed to determine which musical or pictorial arrangement produces the more pleasing effect on a particular person or a set of people are irrelevant to aesthetics, for aesthetics is concerned, not with whether people like a work, but with what reason there may be for a work to be as it is or whether the work would be better if it were different in a particular way. More importantly, Wittgenstein maintains that a psychological investigation of an aesthetic reaction aimed at determining its cause is of no interest to aesthetics, for aesthetics is concerned with the reasons for a person's admiration, satisfaction, or discontent, and these reasons, which will be given by characterizations of the object of the reaction, will be correctly identified only if they command the assent of the person. In close connection with this, Wittgenstein maintains that the sort of explanation one wants when one is puzzled about an aesthetic impression – puzzled about the effect a work has upon one, as he sometimes puts it – is not a causal explanation (corroborated by experience, psychological experiments, etc.). Rather, the puzzlement can be dissolved only in another kind of way – by certain kinds of comparison:

> The sort of explanation one is looking for when one is puzzled by an aesthetic impression is not a causal explanation…(LC, 21)

> The puzzles which arise in aesthetics, which are puzzles arising from the effects the arts have, are not puzzles about how these things are caused. (LC, 28)

> As far as one can see the puzzlement I am talking about can be cured only by peculiar kinds of comparisons…(LC, 20)

It has been thought that Wittgenstein moves directly from the fact that an aesthetic reaction is intentional to the conclusion that no investigation aimed at discovering the cause of the reaction is necessary to discover what it is directed to and that no causal investigation could show the subject's identification of its object to be mistaken – the subject's belief about the reaction's object has no causal implications and the subject cannot but be aware of what its object actually is.[17] But this fails to do justice to Wittgenstein, and it does not engage with Wittgenstein's principal concern, which is aesthetic puzzlement. Now Wittgenstein was well aware that the object of an aesthetic reaction can also be, in the sense at issue, its cause:

> The cause, in the sense of the object it is directed to is also the cause in other senses. When you remove it, the discomfort ceases and what not. (LC, 15)

Moreover, one case that Wittgenstein mentions – looking at a picture and saying 'What's wrong with this?' – makes clear that an aesthetic reaction can be directed to an object in such a manner that it leaves room for an uncertainty on the subject's part that could be removed by identifying the cause of dissatisfaction: the intentional object of the person's reaction is, for the subject at the time, nothing more specific than the picture, the subject being unaware of what feature of the picture mars it for him or her. Cases of this kind can be multiplied indefinitely. Most importantly, there are different kinds of aesthetic puzzlement, in some of which the puzzle is amenable to causal investigation and the puzzled subject might easily come to embrace a false solution to the puzzle. Wittgenstein's examples are something of a medley; and it is necessary to identify the real focus of his concern.

The principal forms of aesthetic puzzlement that Wittgenstein seems to have had in mind are ones which concern what it is about a work of art that makes it so impressive, or impressive in a particular way – where this means, not what elements of it are responsible for its being impressive, but what its impressiveness consists in, i.e. how it should be characterized; or what is wrong with a certain work or a performance of it – where this means what character has been given to it and why that is misplaced; or why a work has just the distribution of features that it does – where this means what character this distribution gives it and why it has been given this character. In such cases, what is needed to remove the puzzlement is, Wittgenstein claims, some means of focussing attention on the character of the work in such a manner as to enable us to perceive the work as having this character. One way in which this can be achieved is by placing side by side with the work other items that possess the character or by indicating an analogy between the work and something else, as with Wittgenstein's favourite kind of example, the comparison of the particular pattern of variation in loudness and tempo in a musical theme with various speech acts. Such an explanation, if accepted, is persuasive, rather than diagnostic, effecting a clarification or change in the perception of the work, the subject's formerly inchoate impression becoming definite; it differs from the causal diagnosis of a

---

[17] If Wittgenstein had made this move it would have been vulnerable to the arguments brought against it by Frank Cioffi in his excellent 1976.

pain in the stomach, where the sufferer's acceptance of the diagnosis is unnecessary and leaves the pain unchanged. This makes it clear that the principal concern of Wittgenstein's interest in aesthetic puzzlement is the enhancement of artistic appreciation: the kind of explanation that dissolves the puzzlement must further the understanding and appreciation of the work of art. This explains his emphasis on comparisons, the requirement that the puzzled subject should agree with a proposed solution to his problem, if the proposed solution is to remove the puzzlement, and the resultant transformation of the subject's impression.

9.

Wittgenstein's emphasis on the possibility of musical understanding being effected through the drawing of a comparison between a piece of music and a speech act or succession of speech acts (or 'gestures' of the voice) leaves a number of issues untouched or unresolved. He was, of course, well aware that someone's understanding of a piece of music can be transformed by means of an explanatory comparison even though the person has not been given compelling reasons for accepting the explanation, that is, for the aptness of the comparison, its suitability to indicate, by analogy, the music's character (CV, 79). He certainly believed that there are right and wrong ways in which a piece of music can be understood, and the appropriateness of any suggested comparison will be determined by what is a correct understanding of the piece. It is regrettable that although he asserts that there are different kinds of justification for explanatory comparisons (PI §527), he nowhere indicates any of them, and he does not engage with the issue of the intersubjective validity of a description of the aesthetic character of a work of art. It is clear that for him a comparison that effects the understanding of the character of a piece of music explains how the piece 'fits into the world of our thoughts and feelings' (CV, 65; see also RPP I §§34–6, 433–6), which is certainly a desirable aim. But although he regarded the similarity of (some) music with speech as being 'a big and important matter' (CV, 71), he did not elucidate its importance; and there is no suggestion as to what the importance might be of similarities with other kinds of phenomena for the vast body of impressive music the character of which is not illuminated by comparison with vocal actions.

   In an insightful paper Jerrold Levinson (2003), taking inspiration from some of Wittgenstein's remarks, in particular from Wittgenstein's emphasis on comparisons with speech acts, has explored the possibility of construing music, not just as revealing thought processes in the composer, but as itself, like speech, a vehicle of thought, thought embodied by the music. Now similarities between music and speech acts of the kind that Wittgenstein specifies in his comparisons license only that pieces of music that sustain such comparisons have the *audible appearance* of speech acts, acts which express thoughts. Levinson, who at one point clearly recognizes this limitation, makes a powerful case for the presence and importance of thinking in music, which goes a certain way towards vindicating Wittgenstein's conviction; but the strength of his argument is weakened, happily only minimally, by his flirtation with the view that just as the thought expressed by a stretch of discourse cannot be rendered into music, so the thought expressed by a musical passage cannot be rendered into words – a view that effectively equivocates on the notion of thought by severing the essential connection between the idea of thought and the content of a propositional attitude (something that can be doubted, believed, known).

10.

Wittgenstein's elucidation of his claim, quoted above, that 'The puzzles which arise in aesthetics, which are puzzles arising from the effects the arts have, are not puzzles about how these things are caused' (LC, 28), reveals that it is in fact directed at a certain conception of the aim of art, which in an unacceptable manner locates the value of a work in its effects. In his published writings Wittgenstein's greatest aesthetic concern is to enforce the autonomy of artistic value, and in particular musical value, against views that deny works of art a distinctive value. His principal target is those theories or tendencies of thought that fail to recognize the true character of artistic value by succumbing to a certain temptation. This temptation – one that Tolstoy fell victim to, as Wittgenstein was well aware (CV, 67) – arises in reflection upon the nature of art and consists in misrepresenting the appreciation of a work of art. Appreciation is construed as an effect of engaging with the work, but not as the perceptual or perceptual-cum-imaginative experience of the work itself, the 'impression' of the work. Rather, the experience of the work itself is thought of as inducing some other experience, rewarding if we find the work valuable, unrewarding if we do not, which is then conceived of in abstraction from the work that gives rise to it: it is not internally related to the work, and so in principle it could be produced by quite a different cause. The result is that the value of a work of art is thought of as residing in its effects, and these effects are thought of as possessing a nature independent of the work that causes them. So the value of a work of art stands to the work in much the same relation that the value of a medicine stands to the medicine: just as the valuable results of the medicine can be fully characterized without mentioning the nature of the medicine that causes them, so the value of a work of art is located in an independently specifiable effect. But, as Wittgenstein insisted, this is certainly a misrepresentation of artistic value. For the experience of a work of art does not play a merely instrumental role in artistic appreciation. On the contrary, to appreciate the value of a work is to experience it with understanding – to read, listen to, imagine, look at, perform the work itself. When we admire a work without reservation, it is not replaceable for us by another that creates the same effect, for we admire the work itself, so that its value does not consist in its performing a function that another work could perform just as well. Wittgenstein emphasizes the autonomy of artistic value many times and in a variety of ways, usually with reference to music. For example:

There is a tendency to talk about the 'effect of a work of art' – feelings, images, etc. Then it is natural to ask: 'Why do you hear this minuet?', and there is a tendency to answer: 'To get this and that effect.' And doesn't the minuet matter? – hearing *this*: would another have done as well? (LC, 29)

If I admire a minuet I can't say: 'Take another. It does the same thing.' What do you mean? It *is* not the same. (LC, 34)

There is *much* that could be learned from Tolstoy's false theorizing that the work of art conveys 'a feeling'. – And you really might call it, if not the expression of a feeling, an expression of feeling, or a felt expression. And you might say too that people who understand it to that extent 'resonate' with it, respond to it. You might say: The work of art does not seek to convey *something else*, just itself. As, if I pay someone a visit, I don't wish simply to produce such & such feelings in him, but above all to pay him a visit, & naturally I also want to be well received. (CV, 67)

It has sometimes been said that what music conveys to us are feelings of joyfulness, melancholy, triumph, etc., etc. and what repels us in this account is that it seems to say that music is an instrument for producing in us sequences of feelings. And from this one might gather that any other means of producing such feelings would do for us instead of music. – To such an account we are tempted to reply 'Music conveys to us *itself*!' (BB, 178)

11.

At this point it is instructive to consider the distinction Wittgenstein draws in *The Brown Book* (BB, 158f.) between a transitive and an intransitive use of the word 'particular'. It is used transitively when it is used as 'preliminary to a specification, description or comparison', intransitively when it is used 'as what one might describe as an emphasis', where this covers two kinds of emphasis; on the one hand, using it to mean something like 'striking' or 'uncommon'; on the other, as an expression of our state of attention when it is focussed on the phenomenon to which we are referring. And Wittgenstein identifies a common illusion generated by such a double usage of a word, one that is liable to arise when we are contemplating something and giving ourselves up to the character of the object, allowing it to make its full impression on us. The illusion comes about because it seems to us as if we are attempting to describe the object, despite the fact that no description will satisfy us, the reason being that really we are using the word in the intransitive manner, as an emphasis of the second kind, our confusion leading us to express ourselves by means of a reflexive construction, something of the form 'This has *this* character', indicating the object in question both times, as it were comparing the object with itself. Wittgenstein illustrates this with an example of the particular expression on a pictured face, and later writes:

The same strange illusion which we are under when we seem to seek the something which a face expresses whereas, in reality, we are giving ourselves up to the features before us – that same illusion possesses us even more strongly if repeating a tune to ourselves and letting it make its full impression on us, we say 'This tune says *something*', and it is as though I had to find *what* it says. And yet I know that it doesn't say anything such that I might express in words or pictures what it says. And if, recognizing this, I resign myself to saying 'It just expresses a musical thought', this would mean no more than saying 'It expresses itself'. (BB, 166)

And to say 'It expresses itself' would be to use 'express' intransitively, saying nothing about the music's character but being as it were hypnotized by it.

Now Wittgenstein rightly asserts that:

When a theme, a phrase, suddenly says something to you, you don't have to be able to explain it to yourself. Suddenly *this* gesture too is accessible to you. (RPP I §660; cf. Z §158)

But the inability to describe the impression a theme (line of poetry, or whatever) makes on you, can, as Wittgenstein remarks, result in a reaction closely related to that of the intransitive pronouncement, namely the claim that the impression is indescribable. Of course, Wittgenstein does not concede this claim, for it might well be the case that some description is forthcoming which is accepted as fitting the impression perfectly. But he is more concerned to expose the inadequacy of an idea that might underlie the belief that the impression is indescribable, namely, that we lack the vocabulary or technique necessary for describing it,[18] and another idea, that the impression is separable from the theme, which he undermines with a wry question:

'The impression (made by this melody) is completely indescribable.' – That means: a description is no use (for my purpose); you have to hear the melody.

If art serves 'to arouse feelings', is, perhaps, perceiving it with the senses included amongst these feelings? (CV, 42)[19]

12.

It has been argued that Wittgenstein regards the intransitive notion of expression as being fundamental in aesthetics and does not allow that (some) music can properly be thought of as, in the transitive sense, the expression of a feeling (Scruton 2004). But this is wide of the mark and betrays a lack of understanding of the transitive/intransitive distinction. The intransitive notion of expression, as Wittgenstein explains it, could not play a significant role in aesthetics, especially in connection with understanding the character of a piece of music; and for it to be illegitimate to apply the transitive notion to music it would have to be always false that a piece expresses a specifiable feeling. But, of course, Wittgenstein is happy to acknowledge that there is no impropriety in thinking of

[18] See LC 37–40; PI §610.
[19] See also PI II, 182–3 and LWPP I §§373, 376, 380–2.

a piece of music as being an expression of a feeling (in the transitive sense); on the contrary, it is frequently correct to characterize it by reference to the feeling it expresses (LWPP I §774). At the same time he wishes to enforce a point of a familiar kind, which can be illustrated best by a passage near the end of *The Brown Book* (BB, 184). Here Wittgenstein discusses an experience that, he writes, he would call a feeling of pastness, and which he roughly describes by saying that it is the feeling of 'long, long ago', these words and the tone in which they are said being a 'gesture' of pastness, this feeling being specified further as that corresponding to the tune 'Wie aus weiter Ferne' from Schumann's *Davids Bündler Tänze*. This tune, played with the right expression, is, he writes, 'the most elaborate and exact expression of a feeling of pastness which I can imagine.' He then raises this question:

> [S]hould I say that hearing this tune played with this expression is in itself that particular experience of pastness, or should I say that hearing the tune causes the feeling of pastness to arise and that this feeling accompanies the tune? I.e., can I separate what I call this experience of pastness from the experience of hearing the tune? (BB, 184)

It is clear that Wittgenstein denies the separability. His point is that to experience the tune as the expression of the feeling is not to hear the music and to undergo a separable feeling. It is, rather, to hear the tune in a certain manner, as having a certain aesthetic character, comparable – in respect of the inseparability of the experience of pastness from the experience of the music – with hearing a musical phrase as if it were asking a question or drawing a conclusion (PI II, 182–3).

13.

In his later philosophy Wittgenstein's thoughts about aesthetics appear to have been focussed almost exclusively upon art, issues in the aesthetic appreciation of nature not appearing to engage him. But one late remark (1947), the interpretation of which is uncertain, appears to indicate that our aesthetic response to nature's most wonderful products played a fundamental role in his thought about art:

> The miracles of nature.
>   We might say: art *discloses* ['zeigt' = 'shows', 'displays'] the miracles of nature to us.
> It is based on the *concept* of the miracles of nature. (The blossom, just opening out.
> What is *marvellous* about it?) We say: 'Look, how it's opening out!' (CV, 64)

This is not a mere recrudescence of Wittgenstein's early aesthetic, for which the exclusive contemplation of any object whatsoever – Wittgenstein's example is a stove (NB, 8 October 1916) – is, for the right person, an experience of wonder. Here the emphasis is on *natural* things and, specifically, those that are most likely to induce wonder, whether or not we live in the present; and the claim is that art is based, not on the miracles of nature, but on the concept of them. The concept of the miracles of nature is the concept of those natural objects (crystals) or phenomena (the opening of blossom) that are best suited to arouse wonder in human beings. If Wittgenstein's claim were that the *concept* of art is based on the concept of the miracles of nature, it would, whatever its merits or defects, be easy to interpret it as an assertion about the logical priority of the two concepts. But that is not his claim. If 'art' is understood to cover all the main art forms, so that every art is supposed to be based on the concept of wonder-inducing natural things, I believe that there is no way in which the claim can be interpreted so as to render it both interesting and viable.[20]

References

Ambrose, Alice, ed. (1979). *Wittgenstein's Lectures, Cambridge 1932–35*. Oxford: Basil Blackwell.

Cioffi, Frank (1976). 'Aesthetic Explanation and Aesthetic Perplexity', *Acta Philosophica Fennica*, 28(1–3): 417–49.

Elliott, R. K. (1993). 'Wittgenstein's Speculative Aesthetics in its Ethical Context', in Robin Barrow and Patricia White eds., *Beyond Liberal Education: Essays in Honour of Paul H. Hirst.* London: Routledge.

Engelmann, Paul (1967). *Letters from Ludwig Wittgenstein – With A Memoir*, trans. L. Furtmüller, ed. B. F. McGuinness. Oxford: Basil Blackwell.

Levinson, Jerrold (2003). 'Musical Thinking', *Midwest Studies in Philosophy*, 27: 59–68.

Moore, G. E. (1993). 'Wittgenstein's Lectures in 1930–33', in *Philosophical Occasions 1912–1951*, ed. J. Klagge and A. Nordmann. Indianapolis: Hackett.

Osborne, H. (1966). 'Wittgenstein on Aesthetics', *The British Journal of Aesthetics*, 6(4): 385–90.

Scruton, Roger (1997). *The Aesthetics of Music*. Oxford: Clarendon Press.

—— (2004). 'Wittgenstein and the Understanding of Music', *The British Journal of Aesthetics*, 44(1): 1–9.

Tanner, Michael (1966). 'Wittgenstein and Aesthetics', *The Oxford Review*, 3: 14–24.

Wittgenstein, Ludwig (1958). *Preliminary Studies for the "Philosophical Investigations", Generally Known as the Blue and Brown Books*. Oxford: Basil Blackwell.

—— (1961). *Tractatus Logico-Philosophicus*, trans. D. F. Pears and B. F. McGuinness. London: Routledge & Kegan Paul.

—— (1961). *Notebooks 1914–1916*, ed. G. E. M. Anscombe and G. H. von Wright, trans. G. E. M. Anscombe. Oxford: Basil Blackwell.

—— (1966). *Lectures and Conversations on Aesthetics, Psychology and Religious Belief.* Berkeley: University of California Press.

—— (1967). *Zettel*, ed. G. E. M. Anscombe and G. H. von Wright, trans. G. E. M. Anscombe. Oxford: Basil Blackwell.

—— (1974). *Philosophical Grammar*, ed. R. Rhees, trans. A. Kenny. Oxford: Basil Blackwell.

---

[20] I here diverge from R. K. Elliott (see fn. 3), who interprets Wittgenstein's 1947 remark as filling a gap in his early aesthetic, construing 'miracles of nature' to include, not specifically products of nature, but anything whatsoever, as long as it is seen from the right point of view.

—— (1975). *Philosophical Remarks*, ed. R. Rhees, trans. R. Hargreaves and R. White. Oxford: Basil Blackwell.

—— (1980). *Remarks on the Philosophy of Psychology*, Vol. 1, ed. G. E. M. Anscombe and G. H. von Wright, trans. G. E. M. Anscombe. Oxford: Blackwell.

—— (1980). *Remarks on the Philosophy of Psychology*, Vol. 2, ed. G. H. von Wright and Heikki Nyman, trans. C. G. Luckhardt and M. A. E. Aue. Oxford: Blackwell.

—— (1982). *Last Writings in the Philosophy of Psychology, Preliminary Studies for Part II of Philosophical Investigations*, vol. 1, ed. G. H. von Wright and H. Nyman, trans. C. G. Luckhardt and M. A. E. Aue. Oxford: Basil Blackwell.

—— (1993). 'A Lecture on Ethics', in *Philosophical Occasions 1912–1951*, ed. J. Klagge and A. Nordmann. Indianapolis: Hackett.

—— (1997). *Philosophical Investigations*, 2nd edn, ed. G. E. M. Anscombe and R. Rhees, trans. G. E. M. Anscombe. Oxford: Blackwell.

—— (1998). *Culture and Value*, rev. edn, ed. G. H. von Wright in collaboration with H. Nyman, rev. edn by A. Pichler, trans. P. Winch. Oxford: Blackwell.

—— (1998). *Remarks on the Foundations of Mathematics*, ed. G. E. M. Anscombe, R. Rhees, and G. H. von Wright, trans. G. E. M. Anscombe. Oxford: Basil Blackwell.

....

CHAPTER 35

WITTGENSTEIN AND ETHICS

....

ANNE-MARIE S. CHRISTENSEN

But an ethical sentence is a personal action

(Wittgenstein, MS 183, 76)

1. THE CRITIC OF MORAL PHILOSOPHY AND WITTGENSTEIN'S CONCEPTION OF ETHICS

....

It is often noted that Wittgenstein's remarks on ethics are both sparse and sporadic. Moreover, Wittgenstein is very critical of philosophers' attempts at discussing ethics, especially all attempts at developing forms of ethical theory. He expressed these reservations several times throughout his life, most notably in a conversation with the Vienna Circle. Here, Wittgenstein condemns all the 'claptrap about ethics', which he defines as talk of 'whether intuitive knowledge exists, whether values exist, whether the good is definable' (WVC, 68–9). In a later conversation, he says that, in ethics, he would reject any attempt at providing an explanation, 'not because the explanation was false, but because it was an *explanation*. If I were told anything that was a *theory*, I would say, No, no! That does not interest me. Even if the theory was true, it would not interest me – it would not be *that* I was looking for. What is ethical cannot be taught' (WVC, 116–17). Any investigation of Wittgenstein's view of ethics thus has to start by giving up the assumption that Wittgenstein will offer us a theory of ethics, a theory that may explain whether or how ethics does or does not exist. This in turns raises the question of what we might then expect from a 'Wittgensteinian ethics'. An alternative idea would be that he provides us with normative guidance or that he presents a picture of the worthwhile, the right way of living. However, in a manuscript from 1930, Wittgenstein rejects this possibility when he dismisses the need for, and even intelligibility of, a general answer to ethical questions:

> If anyone should think he has solved the problem of life & feels like telling himself everything is quite easy now, he need only tell himself, in order to *see that he is wrong*, that there was a time when this 'solution' had not been discovered; but it must have been

possible to live *then* too & the solution which has now been discovered appears *in relation to how things were then* like an accident. (CV, 6; MS 108, 207, 29 June 1930)[1]

In the remark, Wittgenstein talks of 'the problem of life', and as he uses this phrase interchangeably with ethics (and religion, see below) elsewhere, we find two implications for our investigation of ethics. First, Wittgenstein points out that any form of discovery in ethics is discredited simply by the fact that people have managed to live and act well at a time before any such 'solution' was discovered. Secondly, Wittgenstein thereby shows us that whatever is required in order to live well cannot be *specific* knowledge; ethical problems are not theoretical questions – this is the reason why 'What is ethical cannot be taught'.[2] Wittgenstein's general lesson is that ethics does not present us with something that we need to explain, a puzzle we need to solve. Here we find the right interpretative background for one of the most cryptic remarks in the *Tractatus*: 'The solution of the problem of life is seen in the vanishing of that problem' (TLP 6.521). The answer to a theoretical problem provides us with something new, new information for example, or with a theory that bridges a former gap in our understanding, but is seems vital for Wittgenstein to stress that ethical problems are different, and that neither philosophical nor theoretical answers will help us here.

This insistence on the irrelevance of theory to ethics could lead us to assume that Wittgenstein argues against all philosophical investigations of ethics – an assumption that would cause trouble for the interpreter of his remarks on ethics (and, for example, cut this chapter rather short). Some commentators have argued in favour of this conclusion (especially Richter 1996), but there are convincing reasons to resist it. What we find Wittgenstein opposing is a *particular* form of moral philosophy with a particular purpose, namely that of building a moral theory, and this accords with his general view of the goal of philosophical activity as 'elucidations', 'clarification', or 'a perspicuous representation of our use of language' (TLP 4.112; BT sec. 86; see also TLP 6.54 and PI §122). In his critique of moral philosophy, Wittgenstein does not express reservations about the possibility of reflecting on ordinary ethical discussions or of elucidating ethically significant uses of words, and the claim that he has no such reservations finds support in that fact that Wittgenstein's own remarks on ethics are not restricted to the critique of moral philosophy. The remarks quoted above do not exclude the possibility of doing intelligible, philosophical work in ethics; rather, they serve as a caution regarding what we should expect to achieve by doing such work. Wittgenstein is trying to make us see 'the contrast between the understanding of the subject and what most people *want* to see' (BT sec. 86). Therefore, an investigation of Wittgenstein's remarks on ethics does not present a theory of ethics; rather, it clarifies what it is we do when we use words with an ethical point and elucidates the characteristic features of such a use.

If we leave the critique of moral philosophy and move on to an overview of the rest of Wittgenstein's remarks on ethics, this reveals that they have a common, but somewhat

---

[1] We find the same reservations about the idea of significant discoveries within ethics in a footnote to the preface of *Critique of Practical Reason* (Kant 1949: 123, footnote).

[2] Wittgenstein makes a parallel claim concerning his own philosophical method in the introduction to the *Tractatus* and in 4.112, where he states that 'Philosophy is not a body of doctrine [*keine Lehre*] but an activity'.

untraditional conception of ethics. According to Wittgenstein, ethics concerns a set of general questions such as the questions of the 'purpose of life' (NB, 72, 11 June 1916), the 'sense of the world' (TLP 6.41) or the 'problem you see in life' (CV, 31; MS 118: 20r, 27 August 1937; cf. NB, 74, 6 July 1916 and Rhees 1965: 21); questions that are related to questions in aesthetics (TLP 6.421; NB, 77 and 83; and PI §77) and religion (TLP 6.432; NB, 72–9; and LE, 12). Wittgenstein ties together these different ways of describing ethics in his 'Lecture on Ethics' when he says that ethics is 'the enquiry into what is valuable, or, into what is really important…into the meaning of life, or into what makes life worth living, or into the right way of living' (LE, 5). This conception of ethics is, of course, extremely general, but at the very least it shows that Wittgenstein sees ethics as being connected to a subject's conception of her life or of the world in which this life is situated. Moreover, in a central remark from 1946, Wittgenstein develops his conception by connecting it to our general attitude towards the world. Here Wittgenstein says, 'If life becomes hard to bear we think of improvements [a change of situation]. But the most important & effective improvement, in our own attitude [*Verhaltens*], hardly occurs to us, & we can decide on this only with the utmost difficulty' (CV, 60; MS 132: 136, 7 October 1946). Ethics is not just a particular view of the world, but an active perspective or attitude that structures this view in a particular way, because it concerns the world as a place in which one has to live. Cora Diamond captures the ubiquitous character of this conception when she notes that to the early Wittgenstein, 'ethics has no particular subject matter; rather, an ethical spirit, an attitude to the world and life, can penetrate any thought or talk' (Diamond 2000: 153; cf. Edwards 1982).

The quoted remark from 1946 shows us that this notion of ethics as an attitude is not restricted to Wittgenstein's early remarks.[3] In the quote, Wittgenstein points to the fact that when we experience ethical problems, we will often be inclined to think that our only chance to solve them is to transform the circumstances in which they arise. In contrast, Wittgenstein is trying to make us aware that problems of life do not arise from such circumstances considered in isolation, but from the way in which these circumstances figure in our life, and this is why he urges us to pay attention to our own attitudes. What Wittgenstein means by 'attitude' is not, however, obvious. First, we could be misled by the word into thinking that such an attitude is easily adopted or abandoned, e.g. as the result of deliberation, or, at least, that we can easily do so if we realize the need for such change, but this does not seem to be Wittgenstein's view. Even if he stresses the possibility of changing the way we relate to life, it not only 'hardly occurs to us'; we also have difficulties in making such a change, and thus the attitude Wittgenstein is characterizing forms a stable set of reactions that may stubbornly resist reflection. Another important qualification concerns the translation of the original German version, where Wittgenstein writes 'Verhaltens'. In German, this word means both 'to have an attitude towards' in the specific sense of relating to or having a relationship with something or someone, and also simply 'behaviour'; that is, Wittgenstein is commenting on 'attitude' in a sense that is necessarily relational and that is intimately related to action. Our ethical attitude, our 'Verhaltens', is not just a particular view of the world; it encompasses our entire way of relating to and acting in particular circumstances.

---

[3] The picture of ethics as an attitude towards the world reappears in a number of recorded discussions (see for example Rhees 1965: 22 and Bouwsma 1986: 40).

This clarification of the remark from 1946 draws out two important aspects of Wittgenstein's view of ethics. First, any ethical attitude involves the requirement that you strive for an initial understanding of what it is you are relating to, because if you do not have such an understanding as your starting point, you will simply be having a relationship with something *else*. As Wittgenstein cautions us, 'don't apologize for anything, don't obscure anything, look & tell how it really is – but you must see something that sheds a new light on the facts' (CV, 45; MS 123: 112, 1 June 1941). Secondly, if having an attitude towards the world concerns action, then it involves an idea of what the world means to you; it is seeing it as a meaningful context of your life, your plans, actions, relationships, etc. When you relate ethically to the situations in which you find yourself, you see them as presenting possibilities, necessities, demands, etc. In this sense, the relationship is something that concerns *you* as an active, living person, and this is the reason why you may relate to situations in ways that makes life 'hard to bear'. What Wittgenstein implies is that the very fact of being a subject requires that you reflect on whether you relate to the circumstances of your life in a constructive way – a requirement that is fundamentally ethical. When he notes how you may find life problematic and still not be able to notice important issues or make significant changes, he does not think we fail to live up to some concrete, ethical ideal: rather, we reveal inconsistencies in the way we ourselves view our place in the world.

Wittgenstein thus insists on the controversial claim that we cannot account for an ethical problem by looking at a situation in isolation, because the problem is in fact the result of a discrepancy or tension between a particular subject's expectations of that situation and the way in which things actually are or turn out to be. The ethically significant change therefore concerns whether the subject changes the way she relates towards the situation or the people involved, e.g. by moving from acceptance to rejection or from being involved in something to withdrawing. This interpretation of Wittgenstein's remark is the only one that explains why he thinks that any attempt to improve the situation is, in a certain sense, ethically irrelevant. To flesh out Wittgenstein's point, we note that if a situation presents you with something you find unacceptable, unjust, or cruel, then the specifically *ethical* problem only arises if you, despite this view, do not voice your opinion and do nothing to change it. It does not raise an *ethical* problem if you notice injustice and fight it – even though it may, of course, raise all sorts of other problems – because this kind of consistency in attitude and action is what living ethically is.

Wittgenstein's noncommittal starting point means that he is working from a view of philosophical ethics that seems foreign when compared to the majority of contemporary philosophical descriptions of ethics. To him, philosophy does not decide which ethical principles we ought to approve of or what kind of people we ought to be. Instead, it concerns the very possibility of having normative attitudes towards our lives and the circumstances in which they unfold; that is, the possibility of relating to the world in a way that establishes distinctions between what we find important and unimportant, valuable and neutral, right and wrong. This also means that Wittgenstein places ethics within what might be the most important, but also one of the most debated questions in philosophy, namely that of the meaning of life. What we should keep in mind is that he is not trying to answer this question; instead, he is simply showing us how it arises, namely in any attempt to live a human life. In the following, I will attempt to spell out this conception of ethics in detail, but the effort to do so will reveal that there are significant differences between the way it is characterized in the *Tractatus* and in the later remarks.

2. ETHICS IN THE *TRACTATUS*

If we turn to Wittgenstein's remarks on ethics in the *Tractatus*, one central difference immediately appears: here, Wittgenstein does not allow for ethical sentences, a claim that later simply seems to disappear. It is thus of some importance to explain why Wittgenstein introduces the idea of the ineffability of ethics, why he subsequently abandons it, and how he manages to maintain a common notion of ethics over the course of this considerable change. In the *Tractatus*, the remarks on ethics are made in the very last part of the book, following sections on logic, mathematics, and natural science. The question of ethics is introduced in 6.4:

> All propositions are of equal value.
> The sense of the world must lie outside the world. In the world everything is as it is, and everything happens as it does happen: *in* it no value exists – and if it did, it would have no value....
> And so it is impossible for there to be propositions of ethics.
> Propositions can express nothing of what is higher.
> It is clear that ethics cannot be put into words.
> Ethics is transcendental.
> (Ethics and aesthetics are one and the same.) (TLP 6.4–6.421)

Taken alone, these remarks seem enigmatic at best, and this section of the *Tractatus* has also been subject to a vast number of interpretations. Those interpretations have substantial differences, often because they involve incompatible readings of the work as a whole, but most of them are still based on the assumption that if there are no ethical sentences, then all talk of ethics will result in nonsense.[4] This is not, however, what we find

---

[4] It is possible to group many of the interpretations of ethics in the *Tractatus* roughly within one of three groups, according to the way in which they respond to Wittgenstein's claim that 'It is clear that ethics cannot be put into words'. The first group of commentators takes for granted that the claim about the ineffability of ethics springs from a theory of language allegedly presented in the *Tractatus*, and they consider the section on ethics to be an example of plain inconsistency on Wittgenstein's part (see for example Russell 1921/1961: xxi). The problem with this response is that it does not provide us with any insight into what Wittgenstein himself thought he was doing in writing these paragraphs. A second group, now often referred to as the metaphysical interpreters, tries to answer this question by drawing in Wittgenstein's concept of showing and claiming that according to Wittgenstein, we, when working on ethics, use some nonsensical utterances to point to truths about the world (see for example Anscombe 1959: 162–3; Hacker 2000: 381–2; Hacker 1986; and McGuinness 1966). Against this, Cora Diamond and James Conant (amongst others) have forcefully argued that the early Wittgenstein does not allow any room for a view of illuminating nonsense, offering an alternative, so-called resolute, reading (see for example Diamond 1991b, Conant 2000, 2005, Conant and Diamond 2004 and Mulhall 2007).

in the quote. At the very end of the *Tractatus*, Wittgenstein stresses that his own elucidations are nonsensical (6.54), but he does not say the same of ethics, and his warning thus concerns the philosophical treatment of ethics, not statements with an ethical perspective. Moreover, the way in which Wittgenstein characterizes ethics has much stronger affinities with his characterization of logic than of philosophy, just as the brevity of the remarks on ethics indicates that they draw on what Wittgenstein believes he has achieved with the rest of the work.

We thus have to work out the connection between the treatment of logic and ethics, and in order to do so we need to make a short digression on the treatment of logic in the *Tractatus*. Here Wittgenstein presents logic as the necessary condition for representation and thus for language. Logic is what is presupposed in any meaningful representation, and that is, within a Tractarian framework, any meaningful sentence. However, as we are relying on the whole of logic in any particular instance of language use, we cannot represent logic. 'Propositions cannot represent logical form'; instead they '*show* the logical form of reality' (TLP 4.12; see also 4.0312, 4.121, and 4.1212). Logic has no subject matter and does not express any general truths; instead it is a way of showing what is essential to the activity that language is. As Wittgenstein writes, 'Logic is not a body of doctrine, but a mirror-image of the world. Logic is transcendental' (TLP 6.13). Logic is thus taken to be the norms or rules that structure the activity of representation, and therefore logic cannot itself be represented by this activity; it is only shown as its condition. Moreover, as logic does not represent anything, it does not require the existence of anything in particular; instead it connects to the very fact that something exists, something that we can represent in language. 'Logic is *prior* to every experience – that anything *is so*' (TLP 5.552). In this way, logic reveals the necessary connection between the representation and the represented, between the notions of language and world.

We can now return to the question of how the account of logic connects to remarks on ethics in the *Tractatus*. First, Wittgenstein describes ethics in a way that is very similar to his description of logic. As we have already seen, ethics, like logic, does not represent; there are no 'propositions of ethics', just as ethics, again like logic, is said to be 'transcendental' (TLP 6.42 and 6.421), and in the following sections Wittgenstein develops the similarities. He connects ethics to the concept of the mystical and notes that it is 'not *how* things are in the world that is mystical, but *that* it exists' (6.44), just as he notes that ethics as part of what cannot be put into words '*shows itself*' (TLP 6.522).[5] Wittgenstein thus rejects the view of ethics as a representational activity in a way that is similar to his rejection of logic as a representational activity. The remark that '*in* [the world] no value exists' (TLP 6.41) makes it clear that the ethical character of utterances does not spring from their reference to reality, but the fact that Wittgenstein talks of value as not 'in' but 'outside' ('ausserhalb') the world may tempt us to think of value as being established by reference to something that exists in a sphere beyond the world.[6] Nevertheless, such a

---

[5] A more literal translation of the German wording than the expression '[things that] *make themselves manifest*' that we find in the translation of Pears and McGuinness.

[6] This interpretation is a vital argument for the metaphysical reading of ethics in the *Tractatus*.

reading would be at odds with the insight of the *Tractatus* that we have just identified, namely that the very possibility of representation links the concepts of language and world in a way that makes it impossible to talk – or think – of an 'outside' to the world (or to language). We should therefore resist the temptation to think of value as being placed beyond or outside language. Ethics does not come about by talking about anything in particular, in the world or somehow beyond it.

We are assured in this resistance by the fact that ethics is not described as *transcendent*, that is, as being beyond the realm of the real, but as *transcendental*, that is, as a part of what conditions our experience of the real.[7] In the notebooks written during his work on the *Tractatus*, Wittgenstein renders explicit this similarity between logic and ethics when he states that, 'Ethics does not treat of the world. Ethics must be a condition of the world, like logic' (NB, 77, 24 July 1916).[8] However, if ethics is a condition of the world, it must show, not in nonsensical utterances that say nothing of the world, but in our ability to represent the world in meaningful propositions. Wittgenstein is not saying that the non-representational character of ethics dooms us to utter nonsense or simply to keep silent on ethical matters. Instead, he simply insists that we cannot say *what* ethics is, and offers us the possibility that ethics 'shows itself' in what we do say about something else, namely the world. In order to understand this idea, we can turn to a remark made by Wittgenstein in a letter to his friend, Paul Engelmann, where he comments on a poem by Ludwig Uhland. Wittgenstein writes, 'this is how it is: if only you do not try to utter what is unutterable then *nothing* gets lost. But the unutterable will be – unutterably – *contained* in what has been uttered' (Engelmann 1967: 7). Wittgenstein here develops the idea that what we say by meaningful sentences shows something else besides the structure of logic. Moreover, this 'else' is shown in a way where – notably – 'nothing gets lost', and if nothing gets lost then Wittgenstein is not talking about something that is indicated, hinted at, or implied. Instead, he draws a picture in which ethics is a dimension of the things we say, a correlate to meaningful speech.

This does, however, leave us with the problem of accounting for the distinctively 'ethical dimension' of ordinary sentences, and this is linked to another question, namely how to spell out the idea that ethics is a condition of the 'sense of the world' (TLP 6.41). Ethics cannot be a condition for the very possibility of meaningful sentences, because the only condition of representation as such is, as we have just seen, logic. If we return to the text of the *Tractatus*, we see that, in the section following the introduction of ethics, Wittgenstein goes on to talk about action and how, in a particular act, we can both abide

---

[7] A use of words that accords with Kant's definition of the transcendental in his *Critique of Pure Reason*. Kant writes: 'I apply the term *transcendental* to all knowledge which is not so much occupied with objects as with the mode of our knowledge of objects, so far as this mode of knowledge is possible *a priori*' (Kant 1991: A11/B25, see also A294/B350–A296/B352).

[8] There is, however, a substantial difference between the *Notebooks* and the *Tractatus* which calls for caution, namely that Wittgenstein is more inclined to offer substantial ethical recommendations in the former than in the latter, for example the emphasis on the Schopenhauer-inspired idea of 'the life of knowledge' as the only way to ward off 'the misery of the world' (NB, 81, 13 August 1916). We should note that Wittgenstein has carefully removed all such normative recommendations from the final version of the *Tractatus*.

by *and* break any ethical law with which we are presented. Wittgenstein further notes that we cannot account for this difference in terms of consequences, as these have no value like other facts. Even so, he still concludes that, 'there must be something right about the question we posed. There must indeed be some kind of ethical reward and punishment, but they must reside in the action itself' (TLP 6.422). Summing up the part that focuses exclusively on ethics, Wittgenstein turns his attention to the will and notes that even if it seems to be of central interest in ethics, 'the will as a phenomenon is of interest only to psychology', just as it is 'impossible to speak' of the will insofar as it is the bearer of the ethical (TLP 6.423).[9] In this way Wittgenstein continues to stress that ethics and value have nothing to do with facts, but he also establishes a connection between ethics and the subject considered as will, as the ability to act – the subject seen as agent.

This again connects to the investigation of logic. Marie McGinn convincingly argues that the section on solipsism in 5.6–5.641 is an integrated part of this investigation – one which develops Wittgenstein's insight that 'world' and 'logic' are mutually dependent or correlated notions. The critical target of the section is Russell's view of the subject as a particular form of fact, because Wittgenstein thinks this view of the subject leads us to think that we need to account for the relationship between this peculiar fact and the facts that we encounter in experience. This view is, however, just another attempt to look at the relationship between language and world 'from sideways on', as McDowell has notoriously phrased it – an attempt to investigate whether the propositions in the language of the subject, *my* propositions, actually describe an independently available reality. Such an investigation would square badly with the realization that the notions of language and world are interdependent, and its mistaken character shows in the fact that we have no clear conception of a world that is not, at least in principle, understandable for a subject. The 'truth' that Wittgenstein finds 'in solipsism' (TLP 5.62) is that 'the world is essentially thinkable', and that 'the idea of a projection of language onto reality contains the idea of the subject who makes the projection; wherever there is representation of the world in propositions, there is a subject who is in a position to say "I think…"' (McGinn 2006: 273). When Wittgenstein emphasizes that language is an activity, he calls our attention to the fact that it necessarily involves a *subject* (e.g. TLP 2.1). The subject is not an independent entity able to enter into relationships with other facts in the world; the subject 'does not belong to the world: rather it is a limit of the world' (TLP 5.632). The world and the subject, like the world and language, are correlate notions, and this notion of the subject is, according to Wittgenstein, the only sense in which the subject becomes philosophically interesting (TLP 5.641).

We thus cannot speak of representation of the world without including an idea of the subject. Wittgenstein makes this connection in 5.641, when he writes that what 'brings the self into philosophy is the fact that "the world is my world"'. In the remarks on ethics, he further develops this conception of the subject to involve the idea of a will, that is, the

---

[9] This is a more literal translation of the German 'Träger des Ethischen' than the phrase 'subject of ethical attributes' found in Pears and McGuiness' translation. Moreover, the alternative translation fits an entry in the *Notebooks* where Wittgenstein remarks, 'I will call will first and foremost the bearer of good and evil' (NB, 76, 21 July 1916).

possibility for action. 'Good and evil only enter through the *subject*' (NB, 79, 2 August 1916), as Wittgenstein says in the *Notebooks*, and here he also elucidates the connection between subject and will by considering an example of a paralysed man who is unable to act in any straightforward sense. Nonetheless, Wittgenstein notes that as long as this man is able to 'think and *want* and communicate his thoughts', he is still '*in the ethical sense*…the bearer of a will*' (NB, 76–7, 21 July 1916). That is, the very concept of a rational subject, a subject that can represent the world in language, involves the possibility of will; as McDowell accurately phrases it, 'we cannot make sense of a creature acquiring reason unless it has genuinely alternative possibilities of action, over which its thought can play' (McDowell 1998d: 170). Moreover, for a range of 'possibilities of action' to be genuine alternative options, we must be able to distinguish between these options *as actions*, but if we look at the world as a neutral set of facts, it makes no difference whether I do this or that, because my possible actions would simply be 'accidental' (TLP 6.41). Any talk of genuine alternative possibilities of action requires a viewpoint from which these possibilities are substantially different; that is, the viewpoint of the subject. An action is not just something that happens; instead, we use the word 'action' for an event that is connected to a will. The reason why Wittgenstein does not elaborate on this point is that he does not consider it a substantial discovery of what 'actions' are, for example one which would explain whether they are caused or not; he is simply elucidating how we use the word 'action', which is to talk of events that we relate to in a certain way. Ethics, 'the ethical reward and punishment', arises from this relation between the subject and her actions, and in this way 'they must reside in the action itself' (TLP 6.422).

We can explore this point by looking at an example discussed by Wittgenstein in a conversation recorded by Rush Rhees, where Rhees suggests that they talk about a man 'who has come to the conclusion that he must either leave his wife or abandon his work within cancer research' (Rhees 1965: 22). Wittgenstein notes that the man may adopt a number of possible attitudes towards the two options; he may connect them in different ways to his future actions and the effects of his choices, just as other people may present the man with such possible attitudes. As Wittgenstein remarks, 'Suppose I am his friend, and I say to him "Look, you've taken this girl out of her home, and now, by God, you must stick to her." This would be taking up an ethical attitude' (ibid.). The ethical attitude thus involves a comprehensive view of the situation at hand, and presents the debated action as part of a meaningful whole; if Wittgenstein had instead observed that 'your wife is a strong and independent woman', the ethical perspective of his remark would have been completely different. In conclusion, Wittgenstein remarks, 'Whatever [the man] finally does, the way things then turn out may affect his attitude. He may say, "Well, thank God I left her: it was better all around." Or maybe, "Thank God I stuck to her." Or he may not be able to say "thank God" at all, but just the opposite. I want to say that this is the solution of an ethical problem' (Rhees 1965: 23). The ethical problem arises from the man's inability to find a coherent and ethically valid understanding of his actions, both past and future, and the circumstances upon which they both depend and influence. Moreover, the ethical problem disappears when he finally reaches an understanding of the sense, or value, or importance (positively or negatively) of what he did and the effect it had, in this case notably on the life of his wife. If we want to find out what ethical attitude the man has adopted, the true answer will show in what he does and says and in the facts he later chooses to accentuate.

Ethics, in the example and in the *Tractatus*, is, then, a structure established by the way we act and the way we relate to these actions, and to Wittgenstein it does not represent a particular normative view of right and wrong, but simply the possibility of having such a normative view. What we have seen is that if language is possible, it necessarily involves a world and a subject (that represents the possibility of projection), and the introduction of the subject necessarily involves the problem of ethics, because our understanding of a subject involves notions of thinking, willing, and action that are only possible against the background of some normative structure. This normative structure is ethics. What Wittgenstein does not say and *what he does not think can be said* is what ethics *is*, and here we find the key to an understanding of the description of the *Tractatus* that Wittgenstein presents in a letter to a potential publisher, Ludwig von Ficker. Wittgenstein writes, 'The book's point is an ethical one....My work consists of two parts: the one presented here plus all that I have *not* written. And it is precisely this second part that is the important one....In short, I believe that where *many* others today are just *gassing*, I have managed in my book to put everything firmly into place by being silent about it' (Engelmann 1967: 143). The ethical point of the *Tractatus* lies in the realization that philosophy can only show the reality of ethics, not contribute to it, and by insisting on a second, unwritten part of the *Tractatus*, Wittgenstein marks his refusal to add to such contributions. In the *Tractatus*, he is simply pointing out that ethics shows as a universal perspective on the world that is present in the actions and specific utterances of a particular person, a point we will return to in the following. However, if this is all he does, we may ask why Wittgenstein uses such enigmatic concepts as the 'mystical' (TLP 6.45) and the 'higher' (TLP 6.42 and 6.432) to describe ethics. The answer is because in a certain sense it *is*. Ethics is the very possibility of seeing a particular purpose or meaning in what we say or do; that is, it raises the contentious, but also vital, question of 'the meaning of life'.

3. ETHICAL NORMATIVITY

In the early remarks, Wittgenstein thinks that ethics shows as a condition of the world tied to the life of the subject, but he does not provide us with any concrete description of the form of ethical normativity. In the later remarks he does, however, contribute to such a description, and we can attribute this change to a general change in his view of language. Even if, in the *Tractatus*, Wittgenstein sees philosophy as an activity of 'logical clarification' (TLP 4.112), he still holds particular methodological commitments that do not follow from this view, such as the idea that we can reach a complete and final analysis of language. As Cora Diamond notes, the *Tractatus* 'is metaphysical in holding that the logical relations of our thoughts to each other can be shown, completely shown, in the analysis of our propositions' (Diamond 1991a: 18, see also Kuusela 2005). This idealized view of language as representation makes Wittgenstein assume that what we achieve by such an analysis is a complete and general set of conditions of language, namely the correlated notions of logic, world, and subject. Moreover, as the thinking subject correlates with the ethical dimension of reality, he is led to think that this dimension is present in everything the subject says and does. In the later writings, however, Wittgenstein gives up the idea of a unified set of conditions for all instances of language use; he now investigates ethics as one possible perspective amongst others, a particular way of using and addressing language, and this marks an important difference between the early and the later remarks. What does not change is Wittgenstein's view of ethics as the subject's relationship with the world, as well as his idea that all forms of language use may have an ethical point, at least in principle.

The idea of ethics as a particular form of language use allows us to substantiate our sketch of Wittgenstein's view of ethics by relating it to his general reflections on linguistic and epistemic normativity in the *Philosophical Investigations* and *On Certainty*. In §§138–242 of the *Philosophical Investigations*, Wittgenstein investigates a range of normatively structured activities such as reading, identifying a cube, or developing a series of numbers in order to provide a clearer view of the workings of language. His investigations show that the normative structure of these activities depends on a wide range of elements, amongst others the particular circumstances surrounding the rule, the fact that the rule is embedded in a web of shared human practices, our individual ability to apply a rule and assess particular applications of it, as well as a certain level of regularity, that is, agreement in the judgements reached. Wittgenstein thus describes recurring elements in normative activity, but he also stresses that we cannot give any general account of the role of each individual element; this question only makes sense in relation to particular instances of rule-following.[10] Moreover, Wittgenstein cautions us that we cannot expect to be able to reduce or eliminate the different standards on which we rely in normative behaviour to something more fundamental that would enable us to explain or eliminate their essentially normative character. He provides this caution by critically investigating possible 'explanations' of our normative abilities, such as those offered by theories of dispositions and Platonism (see PI §§147–50, §§185–98, and §§219–22, respectively, and §§220–39 for a general account of such 'mythological' descriptions).

The investigations confirm the insight of the *Tractatus* that we cannot explain language by reference to something outside or independent of it. What Wittgenstein now rejects is the Tractarian picture of a uniform and universal set of conditions of language that settles the question of how language works 'once and for all; and independently of any future experience' (PI §92). In the *Philosophical Investigations*, Wittgenstein warns us that we can only describe the numerous and diverse conditions of language with a particular problem or purpose in view – a warning that also concerns any investigation of

---

[10] We find Wittgenstein's dismissal of general accounts of the conditions of language in this remark about the use of moral concepts. Wittgenstein writes, 'We learn the meaning, the use of words in particular circumstances...Do I here have to state all of the circumstances? Does it not suffice that I say: "These concepts do not work here any longer"? (Just as we cannot use the moral concepts of a being that has created the hippopotamus and the crocodile)' (MS 136: 47b, 1948; my translation).

ethical normativity. When, in the later remarks, Wittgenstein shows us how the normativity of language depends on individual abilities to 'do the same again' as well as on the existence of actual human practices, we should not be led into seeing this as a challenge to the objectivity of language; rather, he is showing us how linguistic objectivity does not necessarily take the form we expect. In John McDowell's words, we do not find a 'fantastic super-rigid machine' at the heart of linguistic normativity that guarantees the possibility of correct use; instead we need to accept how this use depends on our 'sharing routes of interests and feeling' (McDowell 1998c: 242 and 1998a: 60 respectively; the last sentence is a quote from Cavell 2002: 52). We only see this as threatening to linguistic objectivity if we take it for granted that genuine objectivity must be understandable independently of anything distinctively human.[11] What Wittgenstein shows us is that this conception of objectivity is an illusion, and what we have to accept is that in all cases, 'Following a rule is a human activity' (RFM VI, §29).

Even if the investigation of ethics benefits from a comparison with Wittgenstein's investigation of rule-following, we should still be aware that there are at least three important differences between the two forms of normativity. The first is that the rules investigated in the *Philosophical Investigations* do not involve descriptive elements and therefore constitute a borderline case of 'pure' normative imperative. It is unnecessary to check anything in reality to know what '2+2' is, because knowing this is what knowing the rule +2 means.[12] By contrast, most ethical utterances include some descriptive elements; our understanding of 'X is cruel' or 'Y acted with great compassion' involves some relevant descriptions of cruel and compassionate actions.

One way to bring out the significance of this difference is to look at Wittgenstein's discussion of reason-giving in aesthetics, because the reasons offered here display a structural similarity to those offered in ethics. In a lecture recorded by Moore, Wittgenstein notes that we find 'the same sort of "reasons"' that we use in discussions on aesthetics, 'not only in Ethics, but in also in Philosophy' (MWL, 278). Later, Wittgenstein characterizes the particular nature of such reasons by saying that they are 'of the nature of further descriptions', and that all we do in aesthetics is 'to draw your attention to a thing' and to 'place things side by side' (ibid., 312; see also Lovibond 2002: 39–42). In the 'Lectures on Aesthetics', Wittgenstein shows how our primary purpose in offering aesthetic reasons is not to provide other people with new knowledge of a particular case or to explain to them the necessity of certain ways of acting; rather, we accentuate certain features of that case as the ones relevant or important to the discussion. Moreover, we do so in order to change people's attitude towards the situation discussed, and, certainly as a part of that, change what they find is right to do in that particular case. This means that our descriptions make sense only when regarded in conjunction with what we do in a

[11] A primary concern of McDowell's hugely influential work on Wittgenstein-inspired ethics is to show that overly demanding and empty conceptions of objectivity and rationality block our understanding of their role in ethics (see especially McDowell 1998b and 1998d).

[12] It is, however, possible to think of certain ethical utterances as purely normative in a similar way; one might e.g. consider how uttering the sentence 'Murder is wrong' in most cases would not amount to an assertion, but simply to a reminder of what murder is.

particular situation or the way we act towards a particular object described. 'How do I show my approval of a suit?' as Wittgenstein asks and answers, 'Chiefly by wearing it again and again' (LC I, §13; see also §36).

It is easy to find an example with a similar structure in ethics. Let us imagine a case where a person is trying to make her friend do volunteer work in a youth club in a poor area. She might say 'It's the generous (or right, or good) thing to do', but she may also offer reasons such as 'These kids have a lot of energy, they just don't know what to do with it', 'You have a lot of experience with underprivileged kids', or 'You have plenty of time now when our children have moved on their own'. Even though these sentences superficially look like descriptions, the pleading person is not trying to persuade her friend by presenting her with new information, because for these facts to work as reasons, they have to be mutually agreed upon. Instead, she is trying to present particular facts of the case as important or valuable, that is, present descriptions with a certain *point*. Consequently, we cannot separate the factual and the evaluative dimension of the reasons she offers, because even if the meaning of her sentences appears, in principle, to be completely descriptive, any understanding of them must incorporate both their descriptive content *and* her particular purpose in offering them. In the same way, we cannot understand the ethical meaning of the sentence 'Look, you've taken this girl out of her home, and now, by God, you've got to stick to her' independently of its context and the particular point of presenting it. In general, we can only understand the use of reasons in ethics if we look at them placed within a context that provides them with a particular point.

The second difference between the rules investigated in *Philosophical Investigations* and ethics concerns the level of agreement that we can expect within different practices. Here we find a contrast between the almost uniform agreement involved in activities such as reading or doing mathematics and the notorious possibility of disagreement in ethics – a difference that is, of course, only a matter of degree, because all instances of language use only have meaning within particular circumstances. When we learn a word, we can never just mindlessly go on to apply it. The investigations of the *Philosophical Investigations* remind us that concepts are 'context specific and dependent on the reach of the speaker's understanding and imagination', as Stephen Mulhall phrases it, going on to state that 'any concept must be flexibly inflexible in these ways: its normativity is of a kind that enables or rather constitutes individual freedom of judgement, because its grammatical schematism is such that our projections of words are at once deeply controlled and ineliminably creative' (Mulhall 2002: 315). The different degrees of agreement that we find in mathematical and ethical practices do not arise because our use of mathematical concepts is completely controlled while our use of ethical concepts unfolds without restrictions; rather, it is a result of the different degrees of variation we allow in different practices, and this in turn depends on why we engage in them, on their point. We could paraphrase a remark from *Philosophical Investigations* and say that the kind of agreement is the kind of language-game (cf. PI II, 191). The point of learning basic mathematics is, amongst other things, to have a common practice that we use for example when we deal with the world, meaning that when we learn to do mathematics, we also learn not to value any possibilities of disagreement (cf. PI §240 and Diamond 1991a: 28). By contrast, we do not consider agreement a goal in itself in ethics, and this difference in purpose affects our ethical concepts. When parents teach a child to use an evaluative word like 'good', they may consider it a sign of understanding if the child starts to use the word about objects that differs substantially from the ones that were used in the teaching – even if the parents themselves do not consider these objects good. In ethics, we accept wide limits for the creative use, not just of moral concepts, but of concepts in general.

Within a Wittgensteinian framework, we can see how this tolerance springs from our understanding of the purpose of ethics, namely to express individual attitudes to the world. Moreover, such attitudes consist not only of norms and rules, but also of all the ethical assumptions that I normally simply do not challenge in ethical reflection. In this respect, the normativity involved in ethical activity is more akin to the epistemic normativity that Wittgenstein investigates in *On Certainty*, structured around certain hinges – propositional or otherwise – that are not themselves open to questioning, but work as the background against which a person will discuss ethical problems. In this way, we can describe an ethical attitude as a form of personal worldview. The assumption or norms of such a worldview need not be fundamentally different from the ones that I am willing to discuss, and they are, in principle, not immune to ethical questioning; rather, their status as part of my worldview shows in my reluctance, if not outright refusal, to discuss their ethical validity in actual cases. Moreover, the elements of the worldview are normative, not because I provide a par-ticular form of justification for them, but because I act as if they constitute the necessary condition for right ethical judgement (cf. OC §94–5 and §162). As Wittgenstein writes in *On Certainty*, 'Giving grounds, however,…comes to an end; – but the end is not a kind of *seeing* on our part; it is our *acting*, which lies at the bottom of the language-game' (OC §204). Moreover, the way we react in ethical discussions is analogous to the way we react in discus-sions of knowledge: in both cases we are inclined to meet worldviews that differ substan-tially from our own with confusion or outright denial. We find an example of such a reaction in G. E. M. Anscombe's categorical claim that it 'shows a corrupt mind' if someone 'really thinks, *in advance*, that it is open to question whether such an action as procuring the judi-cial execution of the innocent should be quite excluded from consideration' (Anscombe 1958: 17). The difference is that we do not expect the same degree of agreement in ethical as in epistemological questions, and this seems inevitable, as long as we, in ethics, accept that other people may differ from us in terms of what they find important or valuable. This leads us to the third difference between linguistic and epistemological normativity on the one hand and ethical normativity on the other: the essentially personal character of ethics.

4. Ethics is Personal

The investigations of the *Philosophical Investigations* and *On Certainty* provide us with a context in which to place Wittgenstein's specific descriptions of ethical language use, but they do not help us elucidate the defining characteristic of ethics in Wittgenstein's view: the fact that it is essentially personal. The question is what the personal character of ethics involves. In the *Tractatus*, ethics arises from our concept of a subject as someone who has to act and live, from the very possibility of a subjective perspective, but elsewhere Wittgenstein makes the further claim that ethics connects to the perspective of a *particular* person. In a conversation with the Vienna Circle, Wittgenstein remarks, 'at the end of my lecture on ethics I spoke in the first person: I think this is something very essential. Here is nothing to be stated anymore; all I can do is to step forth and speak in the first person' (WVC, 117). And in the discussions with Rush Rhees, he notes that ethical sentences express what a person considers to be of fundamental importance to her life. 'Well, suppose I say Christian ethics is the right one. Then I am making a judgement of value. It amounts to adopting Christian ethics. It is not like saying that one of these physical theories must be the right one. The way in which reality corresponds – or conflicts – with a physical theory has no counterpart here' (Rhees 1965: 24). We cannot determine whether an ethical view of the world is right or wrong by trying to determine whether it describes the world correctly, because the only way to show that you think this particular way of living is the right one is to adopt this view.

As ethics is the activity of establishing a framework for a meaningful life, it therefore requires a personal commitment to certain ways of living. Thus Wittgenstein insists that ethical questions essentially connect to the practice of an individual. Around the time of 'A Lecture on Ethics', he made the following entry in his diary:

> But an ethical sentence is a personal action. Not a statement of fact. Like an exclamation of admiration. Just consider how the justification of the 'ethical sentence' only tries to trace the sentence back to another, which makes an impression on you. If, in the end, you have no aversion against this and no admiration for that, then there is nothing to deserve the name of justification. (MS 183: 76, 5 June 1931, my translation)

Ethics originates in actions of the individual person, and what counts as ethical for her is what shows in her actions and attitudes, for example in the way she prizes some things and condemns others. This does not mean that we cannot find instances of uniformity in ethics or that a person's ethical convictions cannot be influenced by others or by what happens in her life (cf. CV, 95). What it does mean, however, is that we only understand an utterance as having an ethical dimension by relating it to the life from which it springs. The 'ethical sentence' of which Wittgenstein talks is part of what establishes our ethical worldview, and if we were to ask what gives these rules their status in that person's life, he simply answers that they get their status because they are the ones she actually lives by, the ones that make 'an impression on her' and therefore guide her practical involvement with the world or other people. We can say that such sentences are a form of constitutive rules in ethics, but we should also notice that the establishment of such ethical rules is not something that happens before or independently of actual instances of ethical language use, as the constitutive rules of chess are established before and independently of actual games of chess.[13] Instead, the constitutive rules are inherent to a person's moral

---

[13] The idea that ethical statements express such constitutive rules is fundamental in Wisnewski 2007. He argues that ethical inquiry is possible as clarifications of such rules, and then goes on to re-read the ethics of Immanuel Kant and John Stuart Mill as examples of such clarifications.

practice. Ethical justification thus takes place within the framework provided by the life of an individual person, and as this framework is upheld by – or simply *is* – what this person considers ethically valuable, it cannot itself be justified (MS 183: 119 and CV, 23; cf. Kremer 2001: 51–6).

In noting this personal character of ethics, Wittgenstein is not, however, implying that ethical statements spring from some mystical, private, ethical faculty or feeling, or that they are essentially *private*.[14] It may prove difficult for us to understand the rules that constitute the ethical outlook of others, but this is not surprising, because it simply means that it may prove difficult for us to understand the way they act and live. However, if we reach such an understanding of other people's normative commitments, we are able to have perfectly meaningful conversation about ethically relevant features of our lives. Wittgenstein's view of ethics does, however, imply that we cannot determine questions of ethical significance independently of what people actually refer to when discussing ethical questions. When we look at a particular system of ethics, Wittgenstein tells us, 'the real reasons are the reasons that are given. These *are* the reasons for or against an action. "Reason" doesn't always mean the same thing; and in ethics we have to keep from assuming that reasons must really be of a different sort from what they are seen to be' (Rhees 1965: 26). To Wittgenstein, ethics involves everything that actually has significance for people, and the inclusiveness of his view of ethics becomes apparent when Rhees mentions a slogan by Herman Göring, '*Recht ist das, was uns gefällt*', and Wittgenstein remarks that 'even that is a kind of ethics. It is helpful in silencing objections to a certain attitude' (Rhees 1965: 25).[15] The essentially personal side of ethics means that ethics concerns everything that people actually find ethically relevant or absolutely good, and what this is may vary immensely from person to person. In this way, Wittgenstein again criticizes the idea that ethics is a particular area of life or the world that we talk *about* (cf. LE, 12, Diamond 1996 and 1997).[16]

Wittgenstein thus seems to accept a radically relativistic view of ethics, where there are – at least in principle – just as many ethical positions as there are people. This ready acceptance of the possibility of relativism appears to challenge the objective and imperative character of ethics, especially as Wittgenstein at the same time refuses to provide a shared foundation from which we may evaluate the value of different ethical viewpoints. In the discussion with Rhees, Wittgenstein notes how the fear of relativity fuels many philosophical attempts to develop an ethical theory in order to secure or justify the

---

[14] Kelly argues, I think mistakenly, that both the early and the later remarks on ethics involve the idea that ethics is essentially private, because ethics is placed 'outside any shared constitutive framework' (Kelly 1995: 585).

[15] Wittgenstein continues by saying that even positions like Göring's should be included in 'the anthropological study of ethical discussions that we may have to conduct' (ibid.), which could indicate that he thought about making such a philosophical investigation himself.

[16] As accurately phrased by Cora Diamond, Wittgenstein does not consider ethics to be 'a subject matter alongside others'. Diamond remarks: 'It is not that trees are a subject for *botany*, and human character a subject for *ethics*, but rather that human character in many circumstances, and trees in somewhat rarer circumstances, can be so described as to be morally interesting' (Diamond 1997: 83).

objectivity of ethics, but Wittgenstein finds this fear misguided.[17] We can identify different ethical attitudes and still hold on to the idea that each of them involves a claim to objectivity – in fact, they all do, because this is what makes them ethical. 'If you say there are various systems of ethics you are not saying that they are all equally right. That means nothing. Just that it would have no meaning to say that each man was right from his own standpoint. That could only mean that each judges as he does' (Rhees 1965: 24). In philosophical investigations of ethics, we do not establish the content of ethical sentences or evaluate their possible validity; instead, we describe the particular form of such sentences. We need to distinguish the role of ethical sentences, which is to advance claims of objective value, from the existence of actual ethical disagreement – something that will also allow us to see that the imperative character of ethics is independent of such disagreement. In the diary entry quoted earlier, Wittgenstein contributes to such a philosophical description of ethics when he writes, 'An ethical sentence says "You must do that!" or "That is good!" but not "People say that this is good"' (MS 183: 76, 5 June 1931, my translation). Ethics is, in principle, independent of what most people would do or think is right in a particular situation; the defining feature of an ethical sentence is that it presents an imperative demand, and this means that if we want to participate in ethical discourse, we must accept the possibility of such imperatives. We find another contribution to the description of the characteristic shape of ethical expressions in 'A Lecture on Ethics', where Wittgenstein distinguishes between a relative and an absolute use of value concepts, noting that to use language ethically is to use it to make categorically imperative statements, to make 'absolute judgements of value' (LE, 5). If you disagree with a particular ethical utterance, you may either contest it by presenting an alternative utterance or challenge the very attempt to put forward such imperative statements. However, like any other ethical attitude, the last possibility amounts to a personal action, not a theoretical insight into the truth of relativism.[18]

5. Ethics in the Later Remarks

The later Wittgenstein thus views ethics as an attitude or a way of relating to the world, a set of constitutive rules that governs our interaction with the world. Furthermore, he allows that we can consider any attitude ethical, as long as the person holding it actually ascribes to it an objective and imperative character – even an attitude as radical – and seemingly unethical – as that of Göring's reference to power. This could make it seem as if ethics to Wittgenstein is unrestrained and freely chosen, but we find a very important

---

[17] Wittgenstein's example of this attempt is Plato. 'Plato wanted…to achieve objectivity and avoid relativity. He thought relativity must be avoided by all costs, since it would destroy the *imperative* in morality' (Rhees 1965: 23).

[18] Johnston 1999 uses this insight to criticize a number of influential contemporary moral philosophers.

restriction on this view in a number of remarks from the 1940s. Here, Wittgenstein identifies an element that is of *special* importance for our ethical attitude, because it works as a condition for what we accept as ethical, namely our relationship to the other person. We find an example of Wittgenstein's novel interest in the relationship with the other person in a longer remark from 1949, where he introduces a more traditional picture of ethics during a discussion of the conditions for calling something an ethical teaching.

> Suppose someone were taught: There is a being who, if you do this & that, live in such & such a way, will take you after your death to a place of eternal torment; most people end up there, a few get to a place of eternal joy. – This being has picked out in advance those who are to get to the good place; &, since only those who have lived a certain sort of life get to the place of torment, he also picked out in advance those who are to lead that sort of life....
>
> Teaching this could not be an ethical training. And if you wanted to train someone ethically & yet teach him like this, you would have to teach the doctrine *after* the ethical training, and represent it as a sort of incomprehensible mystery. (CV, 92–3; MS 138: 13b, 2 February 1949)

From this quote, it is clear that Wittgenstein now considers freedom and the possibility of forming one's own life a necessary condition for ethics, and when he rejects the possibility of calling the proposed teaching ethical, he further supplements this notion of positive freedom with an idea of justice. '"He has chosen them, in his goodness, & you he will punish" really makes no sense', as Wittgenstein puts it, and continues, 'The two halves belong to different kinds of perspective. The second half is ethical & the first is not. And taken together with the first the second is absurd' (CV, 93; MS 138: 14a, 2 February 1949). In this way, Wittgenstein introduces limitations on what it makes sense to call *ethical* – not just any way of relating to the world will fall into this category.[19] Another change is that in the remark, Wittgenstein talks of ethical training and thus assumes that we want to pass on our ethical views, which indicates that he sees ethics as a phenomenon that essentially concerns human relations. We find the same emphasis on the need to share ethical views with others in a remark from Wittgenstein's journal from 1937, where he notes that the ethical justification of an action "must appeal to the man" to whom I want to make it understandable' (MS 183: 119, my translation). Wittgenstein here holds on to the idea that ethics must be of personal importance, but he also investigates how, under these conditions, we are able to justify our ethical view to others; that is, he presents it as an essential part of the ethical that we discuss and give reasons for our particular ethical view of the world. In this way, Wittgenstein now emphasizes both that in ethics we try to make the other person grasp the intelligibility of particular ways of acting and the importance of the other person as a partner in our quest for ethical intelligibility.

---

[19] Wittgenstein makes the same point in a conversation with O. K. Bouwsma, remarking, 'Not everything is an ethical principle. How is an ethical principle identified? ... A principle is ethical by virtue of its surroundings ... there are limits surely to what is an "ethical" principle' (Bouwsma 1986: 5–6).

The other person does, however, play an even more crucial role in Wittgenstein's later remarks, because he also focuses on our relationship with the other person as the fundamental source of ethics. This comes out in one of the more dramatic remarks, where Wittgenstein says, 'A cry of distress cannot be greater than that of *one* human being. Or again *no* distress can be greater than what a single person can suffer. Hence one human being can be in infinite distress & so need infinite help.' Later in the remark, Wittgenstein turns the perspective around and continues, 'Someone to whom it is given in such distress to open his heart instead of contracting it, absorbs the remedy into his heart' (CV, 52–3; MS 128: 49, around 1944). Wittgenstein thus presents two different perspectives on human suffering. First, he presents the distress or suffering of human beings as the greatest and the most terrible form of distress, and he thereby presents the other person as a source of ethical responsibility. A need for 'infinite help' is one that we have to respond to, and even if we refuse to help, this can be said to count as a response. Our relationship with the other is presented as ethically relevant from the very outset. Secondly, Wittgenstein changes the perspective and notes that a suffering person also faces a responsibility, namely to resist the temptation to isolate herself in her own suffering, for example by indulging in self-pity; she must strive instead to see the potential help of others – the potential 'remedy'. Taken together, these two perspectives represent a change of emphasis in Wittgenstein's ethics, because he now emphasizes that the attempt to come to terms with the circumstances of my life is an attempt to come to terms with my life in the presence of the other. Indirectly, Wittgenstein here counters an accusation often raised in connection with his early view of ethics, that is, that its personal character and exclusive focus on the individual's attempt to make sense of the world results in a form of ethical egoism. Against this, Wittgenstein now insists that ethical reflection must start from our dependence on and our obligation towards other people; it must acknowledge the responsibilities that the very existence of other human beings entails.

As we have already seen, Wittgenstein often refers to God in his attempt to spell out this demand. However, we find the most striking example of this connection between ethics and the idea of God in another of Wittgenstein's journals:

> To know oneself is horrible, because one simultaneously recognizes the living demand, &, that one does not satisfy it. But there is no better means to get to know oneself than seeing the perfect one. Thus the perfect one must arouse in people a storm of outrage; unless they want to humiliate themselves through and through….What do you want to call the perfect one? Is he a human being? – Yes, in a certain sense he is of course human being. But in another sense he is yet something *completely different*. What do you want to call him? don't you have to call him 'God'? For what would correspond to this idea, if not that? But formerly you saw God perhaps in the creation, that is, in the world; & now you see him, in another sense, in a human being.
>
> Now at one time you say: 'God created the world' & at another: 'This human being is – God.' But you don't mean that this human being created the world, & yet there is a unity here. (PPO, 221–3, 15 March 1937)

Wittgenstein reflects on the attempt to achieve a true understanding of one's own self and notes that such self-understanding will lead one to see the 'living demand', an expression that is fundamentally ambiguous. On the one hand, it seems to imply that there is an ethical demand inherent in one's very life – an interpretation which finds support in the original notes that reveal how Wittgenstein considered writing the 'essential demand' instead. We have seen how this demand takes a number of different forms through Wittgenstein's writing, for example as a demand arising from our relationship to the world, from the existence of other people, and now from the attempt to achieve self-knowledge. On the other hand, the expression 'living demand' often refers to Jesus Christ, and this reference seems relevant too, as Christ in Wittgenstein's writings represents someone who lives *in* truth, that is, who lives a life that exemplifies his values. Moreover, the two different connotations both seem to be at play when Wittgenstein develops the idea of 'the perfect one', the one that may be said to be human as well as divine.

In our attempt to improve ourselves, we thus meet both an ethical and a religious picture of perfection, and in both cases these pictures of perfection present themselves through the example of the other, whether the other human being or Christ. What is unusual is that the two play almost the same role, and that what starts out as an ethical investigation almost forces Wittgenstein to draw on religious vocabulary. His point is that ethics and religion in this particular connection show us two sides of the same coin: that we are fundamentally fallible creatures. The attempt 'To know oneself' reveals ethical standards that one will never be able to live up to, because the other person represents a possibility of perfection that exceeds one's own. The reason why the other 'in a certain sense…of course' is a human being and in another sense is God is that other people may show us the possibility of perfection in their different actualizations of life, but it is only the one that lives perfectly, as did Christ, that can show us the unlimited character of the standard that we face. In this way, the notion of the 'living demand' reaches beyond any idea of reasonability, and this is why it appears in an interplay between the ethical and the religious vocabularies. The living demand tells me that I always have reason to improve.

Throughout Wittgenstein's writings, he thus rejects the idea that ethics provides explicit standards in favour of the suggestion that the key to living ethically resides in the very aspiration to do so. Importantly, however, we may pursue this aspiration only through the acceptance of our own inadequacy: as we measure ourselves against an absolute standard, we will always fail. This is the reason why any clear perception of 'the perfect one' – whether that is experienced through the other human being or God – will always raise a 'storm of outrage' in us: a natural reaction for anyone met with such a preposterous demand. There is also, however, a significant difference between Wittgenstein's early and later descriptions of the absolute character of ethics. In the early thinking, it is mirrored in the ineffability of ethics, in the fact that talk of ethics is 'to run against the boundaries of language', 'the running against the walls of our cage' (LE, 12). In the later remarks, however, Wittgenstein describes our experience of the absolute as an experience of something that *faces* us: an experience of the other as unlimited need or unlimited perfection. Here, then, our relationship to other people represents a precondition for any true understanding of ethics as well as of ourselves. One might see a parallel

KUUSELA, O. (2005). 'From Metaphysics and Philosophical Theses to Grammar. Wittgenstein's Turn', *Philosophical Investigations*, 28: 95–133.

LOVIBOND, S. (2002). *Ethical Formation*. Cambridge, MA: Harvard University Press.

MCDOWELL, J. (1998a). 'Virtue and Reason', in *Mind, Value and Reality*. Cambridge, MA: Harvard University Press.

—— (1998b). 'Non-Cognitivism and Rule-Following', in *Mind, Value and Reality*. Cambridge, MA: Harvard University Press.

—— (1998c). 'Wittgenstein on Following a Rule', in *Mind, Value, and Reality*, Cambridge, MA: Harvard University Press.

—— (1998d). 'Two Sorts of Naturalism', in *Mind, Value and Reality*. Cambridge, MA: Harvard University Press.

MCGINN, M. (2006). *Elucidating the Tractatus*. Oxford: Clarendon Press.

MCGUINNESS, B. (1966). 'The Mysticism of the Tractatus', *The Philosophical Review*, 75 (3): 305–28.

MOORE, G. E. (1959). 'Wittgenstein's Lectures in 1930–33', in *Philosophical Papers*. London: Allen and Unwin.

MULHALL, S. (2002). 'Ethics in the Light of Wittgenstein', *Philosophical Papers*, 31 (3): 293–321.

—— (2007). 'Words, Waxing and Waning: Ethics in/and/of the Tractatus Logico-Philosophicus', in G. Kahane, E. Kanterian, and O. Kuusela eds., *Wittgenstein and his Interpreters. Essays in Memory of Gordon Baker*. Oxford: Blackwell.

RHEES, R. (1965). 'Some Developments in Wittgenstein's View of Ethics', *Philosophical Review*, 74 (1): 17–26.

RICHTER, D. (1996). 'Nothing to be said: Wittgenstein and Wittgensteinian Ethics', *The Southern Journal of Philosophy*, 34 (2): 243–56.

RUSSELL, B. (1921/1961). 'Introduction', in L. Wittgenstein, *Tractatus Logico-Philosophicus*, trans. D. F. Pears and B. F. McGuinness. London: Routledge.

WAISMANN, FRIEDRICH (1979). *Wittgenstein and the Vienna Circle*, recorded by F. Waismann. Oxford: Blackwell.

WISNEWSKI, J. J. (2007). *Wittgenstein and Ethical Inquiry: A Defense of Ethics as Clarification*. New York: Continuum.

WITTGENSTEIN, LUDWIG (1921/1961). *Tractatus Logico-Philosophicus*, trans. D. F. Pears and B. F. McGuinness. London: Routledge.

—— (1953/2001). *Philosophical Investigations*, trans. G. E. M. Anscombe. Oxford: Blackwell.

—— (1965). 'A Lecture on Ethics', *Philosophical Review*, 74 (1): 3–12.

—— (1966). *Lectures and Conversations*, ed. C. Barrett. Oxford: Blackwell.

—— (1969/2003). *On Certainty*, ed. G. H. von Wright and G. E. M. Anscombe. Oxford: Blackwell.

—— (1978). *Remarks on the Foundations of Mathematics*, trans. G. E. M. Anscombe. third rev. edn. Oxford: Basil Blackwell.

—— (1984). *Notebooks, 1914–1916*, ed. G. H. von Wright and G. E. M. Anscombe. Oxford: Blackwell.

—— (1998). *Culture and Value*, ed. G. H. von Wright, revised second edition with English translation. Oxford: Blackwell.

—— (2003). *Private and Public Occasions*, ed. J. C. Klagge and A. Nordmann. Lanham, MD: Rowman & Littlefield.

—— (2000). 'The Big Typescript'. Vienna: Springer.

—— (2000). *Wittgenstein's Nachlass: The Bergen Electronic Edition*. Oxford: Oxford University Press.

INDEX

Printed and bound by CPI Group (UK) Ltd, Croydon, CR0 4YY